293156

KT-425-196

Lecture Notes
in Business Information Processing   66

Michael zur Muehlen
Jianwen Su (Eds.)

Business Process Management Workshops

BPM 2010 International Workshops
and Education Track
Hoboken, NJ, USA, September 13-15, 2010
Revised Selected Papers

 Springer

Volume Editors

Michael zur Muehlen
Stevens Institute of Technology
Howe School of Technology Management
07030 Hoboken, NJ, USA
E-mail: mzurmuehlen@stevens.edu

Jianwen Su
University of California
Department of Computer Science
93106-5110 Santa Barbara, CA, USA
E-mail: su@cs.ucsb.edu

ISSN 1865-1348   e-ISSN 1865-1356
ISBN 978-3-642-20510-1   ISBN 978-3-642-20511-8 (eBook)
DOI 10.1007/978-3-642-20511-8
Springer Heidelberg Dordrecht London New York

Library of Congress Control Number: 2011924904

ACM Computing Classification (1998): J.1, H.4, D.2

Typesetting: Camera-ready by author, data conversion by Scientific Publishing Services, Chennai, India

Printed on acid-free paper

Springer is part of Springer Science+Business Media (www.springer.com)

Preface

Business process management (BPM) is an established research domain for computer science, information systems, and management scholars. The record number and wide scope of submissions to the eighth installation of the International Conference on Business Process Management was an indication of the vibrancy of the area and the varied interests of BPM researchers. It is tradition that topical workshops accompany the main BPM conference in order to allow groups to coalesce around new research topics, to present emerging research issues, or focus in depth on a particular area of research. BPM 2010 was accompanied by nine workshops – some new, some well established with the stature of mini-conferences. In addition, a dedicated track for education papers complemented the main research program. The workshops and education track attracted 143 submissions, out of which the respective Program Committees chose 66 papers for presentation – a healthy acceptance ratio of 46% that rivals some mainstream information systems conferences. The workshops were organized by an illustrious group of BPM scholars with a global reach. We were particularly excited by the first BPM workshop organized by the South American research community – the First International Workshop on Reuse in BPM.

The following workshops of the BPM 2010 conference were held on September 13, 2010 on the campus of Stevens Institute of Technology in Hoboken, NJ:

- 6th International Workshop on Business Process Design
- 6th International Workshop on Business Process Intelligence
- 4th International Workshop on Event-Driven Business Process Management
- Third Workshop on Business Process Management and Social Software
- First International Workshop on Traceability and Compliance of Semi-Structured Processes
- First International Workshop on Reuse in Business Process Management
- First International Workshop "Process in the Large"
- First International Workshop on Business Process Management and Sustainability
- First International Workshop on Cross-Enterprise Collaboration, People, and Work

The special track on Advances in Business Process Education was held on Wednesday, September 15, 2010.

We would like to express our sincere gratitude to the Organizing Committees of each workshop for arranging entertaining, high-quality programs that were well received by all attendees. We are grateful to the service of the countless reviewers that supported the Workshop Chairs and provided meaningful feedback to the authors. Several workshops had invited keynote presentations that framed the presented research papers and we would like to thank the keynote speakers for their contribution to the workshop program. We would like to thank Ralf

Gerstner, Christine Reiss and Viktoria Meyer at Springer for their support in
the publication of this LNBIP volume. Finally, our most heartfelt thanks go to
Chelsea Shupe, who spent countless hours collecting, assembling, and format-
ting the proceedings before you – her initiative made the production of this book
possible. Thank you.

February 2011   Michael zur Muehlen
                                                                    Jianwen Su

BPM 2010 Organization

General Chair

Michael zur Muehlen
Howe School of Technology Management
Stevens Institute of Technology
Castle Point on Hudson
Hoboken NJ 07030
USA

Program Chairs

Rick Hull	IBM Research, USA
Stefan Tai	Universität Karlsruhe, Germany
Jan Mendling	Humboldt-Universität Berlin, Germany

Education Chairs

Yvonne Antonucci	Widener University, USA
Catherine Usoff	Bentley University, USA
Wasana Bandara	Queensland University of Technology, Australia

Industry Chair

Michael Rosemann	Queensland University of Technology, Australia

Workshop Chair

Jianwen Su	University of California, Santa Barbara, USA

Doctoral Consortium Chair

Ted Stohr	Stevens Institute of Technology, USA

Demo Chair

Marcello La Rosa	Queensland University of Technology, Australia

Publicity Chair

Marta Indulska	The University of Queensland, Austalia

Table of Contents

BPD Workshop

BPI Workshop

rBPM Workshop

BPMS2 Workshop

SusBPM Workshop

IW-PL Workshop

CEC-PAW Workshop

TC4SP Workshop

edBPM Workshop

Education Track

6th International Workshop on Business Process Design (BPD 2010)

Workshop Organization

Workshop Organizers

Marta Indulska
UQ Business School
The University of Queensland
St Lucia, QLD 4072
Australia

Selma LimamMansar
Information Systems Program
Carnegie Mellon University
Qatar Campus,
PO BOX 24866, Doha
Qatar

Michael Rosemann
Business Process Management Research Group
Queensland University of Technology
Level 5 / 126 Margaret Street, Brisbane Qld 4000
Australia

Program Committee

HyerimBae (Pusan National University, South Korea)
JyotiBhat (Infosys, India)
Jan vomBrocke (University Liechtenstein)
Jorge Cardoso (SAP Research, Dresden)
Lilia Gzara (Grenoble Institute of Technology, France)
Paul Harmon (BPTrends, USA)
Stefan Jablonski (University of Bayreuth, Germany)
Mathias Kirchmer (Accenture, USA)
Agnes Koschmider (University of Karlsruhe, Germany)
Peter Kueng (Credit Suisse, Switzerland)
Marcello La Rosa (Queensland University of Technology, Australia)
Jan Mendling (Humboldt University Berlin, Germany)
Jan Recker (Queensland University of Technology, Australia)
HajoReijers (Eindhoven University of Technology, The Netherlands)
Stefanie Rinderle-Ma (University of Ulm, Germany)
ShaziaSadiq (The University of Queensland, Australia)
Roger Tregear (Leonardo Consulting, Australia)
Kees van Hee (Eindhoven University of Technology, The Netherlands)
Andreas Wombacher (University of Twente, The Netherlands)
Michael zur Muehlen (Stevens Institute of Technology, USA)

Interactive Business Modeling with BusinessMapper and Dependency Modeling Language (DML)

Sebastian Reinisch, Robert Mertens, Aliasghar Esteghlal,
Frank Ruwolt, and Martin Jähne

Fraunhofer IAIS,
Schloss Birlinghoven, 53754 Sankt Augustin, Germany
name.surname@iais.fraunhofer.de

Abstract. This paper introduces DML, a dependency modeling language for analyzing and developing business process models in a front-loading context. Front-loading describes an approach for up front analysis of problems and effects that come with the development and introduction of new products and accompanying processes into an existing portfolio. The paper also describes BusinessMapper, a graphical editing tool for DML that enables users to interactively model interrelations and interactions between business processes on an abstracted level. By employing run time evaluation mechanisms, BusinessMapper makes the effects of new processes or other entities in the model instantly evident to the user. Users can thus interactively adjust parameters to fit new products and their accompanying processes into existing process landscapes.

Keywords: Front-Loading, Business Modeling, Process Modeling, Dependency Modeling, Process Design Methods, Process Design Tools.

1 Introduction

The introduction of new products and processes is often associated with the risk of unexpectedly high costs or development lead times. One approach to reduce this risk is the implementation of flexible production IT systems that accommodates for changes in the product portfolio and in the processes supported [2]. Another successful approach that aims to reduce this risk is front-loading [1]. This approach involves modelling and testing at very early stages of development in order to identify problems and unforeseen interrelations. If a better overview is gained at these early stages of a project, actions can be taken to avoid problems at later stages of that project. Especially in early stages of a project, however, definitions are often largely unclear and even the aims of a project are not yet agreed upon by all those involved, at least not on the necessary level of detail. One explanation for this can be, that those who shape a project at its very beginning are mostly experts. And experts do not primarily rely on hard definitions, they heavily rely on visual representations, creativity and experience [3]. Mind maps provide this kind of visual representation [4] and are widely accepted in business settings throughout Europe. In fact, the authors have observed an extensive use of mind maps in early project definition phases in a

M. zur Muehlen and J. Su (Eds.): BPM 2010 Workshops, LNBIP 66, pp. 5–15, 2011.

major telecommunications company. Mind maps can even be used to improve communication among experts from different areas since they can to a certain extend be used to visualize ontological relations though not completely [5]. However, contemporary mind maps leave out one important aspect of front-loading. In order to become familiar with new situations, experts often explore dynamic models that allow anticipating the effects of adjustments and modifications [3]. With a static mind map, this sort of trial and error problem solving approach is not supported. Therefore, the approach described in this paper incorporates a dynamic modelling language with a classical mind map representation. This modelling language called DML (Dependency Modeling Language) is designed specifically to model dependencies between the nodes of a mind map-like structure on an algorithmic level. With this technique, nodes of a mind map can be semantically linked to other nodes of that mind map. This makes it possible to use the mind map as a dynamic visual model that can be changed at a mouse click. And these changes do not only occur on a node value level but also in terms of the model's very structure, depending on whether the user chooses to alter a node statement or the map itself. Hence, the approach described in this paper combines the flexibility of a mind map representation with expressiveness of a mathematical model. This makes it an ideal tool for front-loading modelling in a context where most environment variables still have to be explored - like most complex business situations.

The remainder of the paper is organized as follows: Section 2 briefly discusses related work in the intersection of the fields of business process simulation and mind maps. Section 3 discusses DML, while section 4 describes the basics of the user interface. In section 5, an example application scenario is presented. The paper concludes with a summary and an outlook on further work in section 6.

2   Related Work

In recent years the technique of mind mapping and its application has become tremendously popular in the fields of education, engineering and business. Particularly the use of computer-based mind mapping tools offers enormous advantages in business settings, as shown by Joanne M. Tucker et al. [6]. In their paper, the authors examine mind mapping techniques comparing several mind-mapping software applications. They concentrate on advantages and disadvantages of creating maps manually versus using mind mapping-software. They found having real time collaboration, like teamwork or other interaction between parties in building a mind map, may make it worth the expense of using such software. As an example they state that "creating *mind maps of business processes within the supply chain requires interaction and communication between businesses the ability of software to allow sharing and editing of mind maps become more relevant.*". This flexibility makes software based mind mapping suitable especially for business purposes, for instance strategic planning, problem solving or event planning. Besides supporting communication and collaboration, mind mapping is a *"powerful analytical tool for case teaching, especially in Executive MBA programs, where students are required to gather, interpret, and communicate large quantities of complex information."* as found by Anthony J. Mento et al. [7]. The authors highlight in their work some specific applications of the mind mapping technique based on their work in executive education and in management development consulting. In addition to being beneficial in team-building processes and being extremely flexible, mind-mapping supports learning based on one's work experiences which *"is one of the building block for establishing a learning organization"* as they conclude. Due to the benefits mentioned above, mind-mapping can be used for front-loading in business processes. For instance in [8] the mind mapping approach is used for informal modelling in the primary steps of process building. The authors use mind maps to add information about concepts and relations *"enabling business users to manipulate the ontology without any detailed technical knowledge in building ontology with higher semantic expressiveness."* In the context of business simulation Peter J. A. Reusch et al. [9] found mind maps to be the *"core module that collects information about the preparation, the execution and the evaluation of the simulation"* making it a strong tool for general project planning. Especially in early phases where expertise is lacking, mind maps can be useful for structural analysis and object role analysis. In the author's overview paper [9] they also raise the important issue of how mind maps and topic maps can be used for better integration, in particular, of business games and simulations in an overall modelling and controlling concept. As they point out, mind map files are often stored XML-based which provides the opportunity to link the information with other tools and be used by further applications. This makes the integration in simulation and business games very easy, as they conclude.

The works cited in this section show that mind maps are very well suited to the task of front-loading. However, current mind map based approaches that tackle the problem of defining a process or product landscape lack a means of handling the dynamic aspects that come with front-loading. In this context, anticipating effects of adjustments and modifications is indispensable. The next sections show how these dynamic aspects can be integrated in a mind map based model. The very next section starts by introducing the dynamic modelling language DML.

3   DML

The complexity of a business largely depends on interrelations of business elements and processes. Hence it is particularly important to acquire knowledge about existing dependencies and - in case of newly developed products - about dependencies and impacts generated by these products and their introduction into an existing portfolio.

In comparison to the software construction domain, where dependencies can be extracted from existing source code [10], the modelling and analysis of dependencies in a business context is harder because of unclear aims and definitions during development and planning the introduction of new products. Therefore sophisticated tools are needed.

The Dependency Modeling Language (DML) supports the modelling and analysis of aspect-based business models. Such a model contains qualitative and quantitative dependencies between elements/aspects of the modelled business, which are represented as nodes in a mind map-like structure.

Qualitative dependencies show that aspects somehow depend on other aspects but leave out the details. Quantitative dependencies describe relationships between business aspects in a mathematically precise way.

DML statements are an essential part of the business model. They represent attributes of aspects and combine common data types (like decimal numbers or boolean values), arithmetic operations (e.g. addition, multiplication, relational operators) and variables. By using variables it is possible to point to nodes within the hierarchical model. DML differentiates between two types of variables - qualified and partially qualified variables. Qualified variables refer to exactly one node of the hierarchical structure. In contrast, a partially qualified variable refers to a set of nodes, e.g. to the set of all subordinate aspects belonging to a given node. It is a combination of a qualified variable, which points to the topmost (given) node, followed by an expression using wildcard-symbols (like "*" or "?") to define filter attributes. Partially qualified variables get especially important when applying built-in arithmetic functions. These functions are comparable to functions in common spreadsheet applications. They allow different calculations like averaging over a set of attributes or calculating the maximum values of different aspects.

Additionally, the combination of relational operators and conditional statements allows a great amount of flexibility within the set of arithmetic expressions.

Figure 1 shows a simple model of a company producing and selling just one product. The model contains some basic facts about this company and its product, organized in a mind map – like structure.

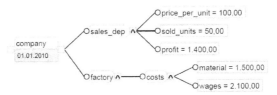

Fig. 1. Simple example using qualified and partially qualified variables

The summarized costs of production are 3.600 € (material and wages), the number of sold units is 50 €, and the sales price of the product is 100 €.

To calculate the profit, the sales department created a new attribute which contains the following DML statement:

*profit = (sales_dep.price_per_unit * sales_dep.sold_units) - sum(factory_costs.*)*

At first, this simple model contains dependencies, e.g. between the company and its two departments (production and sales). These qualitative dependencies basically show that there is a relationship between the company and its departments. The statement used to calculate the profit comprises quantitative dependencies between the two business aspects production and sales.

Second, it makes use of variables. The model contains two qualified variables (sales_dep.sold_units and sales_dep.price_per_unit) to point at particular nodes within the DML statement. The partially qualified variable (factory.costs.*) is used as an argument of a function to calculate the sum of multiple nodes.

The expressiveness of DML syntax is based on a definition in EBNF (Extended Backus Naur-Form). By using EBNF, the DML syntax can be easily expanded, e.g. by adding new arithmetic functions.

The following table shows the basic EBNF definition of DML:

Table 1. EBNF definition of DML

simplified EBNF productions of DML	
arithmeticOperator	= "+" | "-" | "*" | "/";
boolOperator	= "<" | ">" | "<=" | ">=" | "<>" | "=";
digitWoZero	= "1" | "2" | ... | "8" | "9";
digit	= "0" | digitWoZero;
decimalNumber	= "0" | "0."(digit)+ | digitWoZero(digit)* "."(digit)+ | digit-WoZero(digit)*;
char	= "a" | ... | "z" | "A" | ... | "Z";
identifier	= (char | digit) (char | digit | "_")* (char | digit)*;
qualVariable	= identifier ("."identifier)*;
identifierwWilcard	= (char | digit | "*" | "?") (char | digit | "*" | "?" | "_")* (char | digit | "*" | "?")*;
partQualVariable	= qualVariable".*."identifierwWilcard) | qualVari-able"."identifierwWilcard);
funcArgument	= decimalNumber | qualVariable | partQualVariable;
listOfFuncArg	= funcArgument(","funcArgument)*;
function	= "max(" listOfFuncArg ")" | "avg(" listOfFuncArg ")" | "sum(" listOfFuncArg ")" | ... ; /* plus additional functions*/
boolExp	= (decimalNumber | qualVariable | expression) boolOperator (decimalNumber | qualVariable | expression);
expression	= (decimalNumber | qualVariable | expression) arithmeticOper-ator (decimalNumber | qualVariable | expression);
conditionalFunction	= "if(" boolExp "," expression "," expression ")";
dmlStatement	= attributName "=" expression operator expression;

Based on this definition, an interpreter can be constructed, which automatically parses the given expressions and calculates their results.

An additional major task of a DML interpreter is to support analysing the model in different ways. It helps gathering information about the complexity of introducing new products, e.g. to identify processes which will be influenced by the new product. Furthermore it supports users to acquire knowledge about dependencies between the domains of the business. By evaluating quantitative dependencies it is possible to calculate indicators for an estimation of costs or the risk of changes in the existing portfolio of products and processes. The hierarchical model provides the possibility to evaluate local impacts as well as global effects of changes caused by the introduction of new products. This helps in identifying causal chains within the model, which would otherwise be hard to discover due to the complexity of business interrelations.

In summary, DML combines well know techniques like arithmetic expressions similar to widely-used spreadsheet applications and the simplicity of modelling dependencies with help of a hierarchical, mind map - like structure. That makes DML an easy to use, yet powerful and flexible modelling language.

4   The Graphical Editing Tool: BusinessMapper

As mentioned before experts rely on visual representations and make vigorously use of graphical modelling tools when shaping a project. Based on this insight we started developing a graphical editing tool called "BusinessMapper". BusinessMapper combines common approaches of graphical modelling tools paired with the simple application of arithmetic functions. According to the model built by the user and its current parameters, any kind of dependencies between aspects will be dynamically visualized during runtime. In the following subsections, the integration of DML in BusinessMapper will be illustrated.

4.1   Node Types

BusinessMapper currently supports three different node types that represent different modelling components. The kind of node is determined automatically by its content.

Default Nodes. Newly created nodes are always initially default nodes. Their content may consist of characters (also space characters), ciphers and underscores. As the name implies, these nodes do not exhibit any special properties.

DML Nodes. A DML-node inscription has the form of an attribute name followed by a DML-expression. An example for such an inscription could be:

*sales = products.product_1.costs * products.product_1.disposal*

To make editing of DML-nodes easier, the user could revert to some support-functions. For instance a calculation may have multiple nodes with long paths. The user needs not to enter a node's path manually. If the node is already in editing-mode, just clicking with the mouse button on another node inserts its complete path into the currently edited DML-expression. If [SHIFT] is pressed during this process, the path will be extended by the character sequence ".*". Thus partially qualified variables can be used much easier.

If a DML-node contains a calculation formula, its result will be displayed after editing mode has been left. The DML-node will then contain the attribute name and the result of the DML-expression. If the DML-expression is incorrect, there is no result and the expression itself will be displayed in red. The status bar will offer additional information in this case, to help the user identify the error in the formula.

Link Nodes. This kind of node is used to describe qualitative dependencies. A qualitative variable has a point-notation-syntax. For example: products. product_1.cost. The support-function used for DML-nodes can be used here too: clicking with the mouse button on another node puts in the complete path. If a path inside of a Link-node cannot be resolved, the node is coloured red to indicate the failure. In this case the status bar will offer failure-information.

4.2 Calculating with DML/Functions

DML-expressions consist of different calculation-statements. Standard operators such as "+, -, /, *, (,)" are allowed. Calculations inside DML-nodes are not constrained to ciphers, but also offer the use of links to other attributes described by other DML-nodes. To facilitate working with this tool, a set of predefined functions are provided:

sum(expression)/sumtree(expression): Addition of all attribute values inside the expression; *sub(expression)/subtree(expression)*: Subtraction of all attribute values inside the expression; *mult(expression)/multtree(expression)*: Multiplication of all attribute values inside the expression; *avg(expression) /avgtree(expression)*: Average over all attribute values; *min(expression)/mintree(expression)*: Calculates the minimum value; *max(expression)/maxtree(expression)*: Calculates the maximum value

There is a difference between functions with the add-on "tree" and the ones without: if the user takes a function without "tree", calculations will only implicate attributes inside of that map-branch. If functions with "tree" add-on are used, calculations will also follow Link-nodes to resolve any partially qualitative variables and take them into account. Nesting of functions is also available. All attributes used inside of an expression must be separated by a comma.

4.3 Displaying Node-Dependencies and Extracting Dependencies

Initially the user does not see any dependencies of a selected node. This can be configured in the context menu. There are two checkboxes "display incoming nodes" and "display outgoing nodes" for enabling/disabling. If enabled, the user will see all incoming dependencies (other nodes) marked as yellow. Outgoing dependencies are marked by a grey background.

Fig. 2. Simple example using qualified and partially qualified variables

Figure 2 shows an example map with the currently focused node "total". As explained above, all dependencies are marked with the corresponding colour. In this case: "total" may lead to "receipts = 3.554.185,65". This node is an outgoing dependency. Contrariwise "total" itself is dependent on "Books", so "Books" is an incoming dependency.

To set the point of view on dependencies the user has the possibility the extract an incoming or outgoing dependency to a newly created map. On such a new map the previously selected node now presents the root of the map and its dependencies (previously grey or yellow marked in the other map) are represented as child nodes.

5   Showcase "Bookstore"

In figure 3 a "Bookstore" is modelled exemplarily. The node "Bookstore" symbolizes the root (Root-Node) of the map. Only issues that are important for the intended purpose are shown.

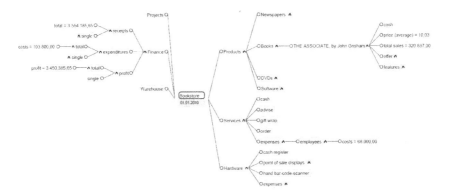

Fig. 3. Bookstore model in BusinessMapper

5.1   Global and Local Modelling

Nodes of highly comprehensive nature are attached immediately to the root. For instance "Products" is such a node. Those nodes may have many of child nodes and could be seen as global or main aspects in a map. On the other hand, the further a node is away from the root, the more local are its effects. I.e. the node "total sales" under "Books/The Associate, by John Grisham" represents a value only belonging to that type of book.

5.2   Calculations

The main aspect node "Finance" has three child nodes. One of them is "receipts" which calculates miscellaneous scopes of receipts. As discussed in earlier sections calculations can be realized in "DML-nodes". The node "total = 3.554.185,65" is the result of the total receipts in the Bookstore. One possible formula to calculate that value is:

total = sum(finance.receipts.single.*.*receipts*)

If we follow the formula, we can see that all single receipts have been taken into account. To assure that all receipts are implicated, wildcards (*-symbol) are used. In this formula, all leaf-nodes that contain the word "receipts", below the node "single", were comprised. Calculations below the node "expenditures" or "profit" operates analogically.

5.3 Linking Nodes

Underneath the main aspect "Products" is, among others, the branch "Books". In figure 4 the book "The Associate, by John Grisham" has been modelled exemplarily.

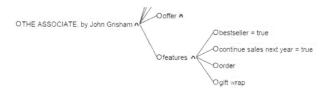

Fig. 4. The book "The Associate, by John Grisham" and its features

Underneath "features" different nodes are modeled. Among some information providing nodes, i.e. "bestseller = true", there are also two links to services. These Link-Nodes describe which services are provided, especially relating to that book. I.e. this book can be ordered and wrapped as gift. Maybe another book, which is not a bestseller, would not provide those features.

Fig. 5. Provided services

Both services were modelled as Link-Nodes and were picked out of a services repository. In figure 5 the main aspect "Service" handles all services and presents that repository. If a service is needed in the map, it must not be shaped as a usual node somewhere else. A Link-node should be created, pointing to the desired service, as done in figure 5.

6   Conclusion

In this paper we presented DML, a dependency modelling language and a graphical editing tool for DML called "BusinessMapper". DML is designed to support the modelling and analysis of aspect-based business models. It comprises concepts like arithmetic expressions similar to well-known spreadsheet applications or the use of variables to reference attributes within the model. The definition of DML in EBNF makes it easily expandable and capable of being analyzed and evaluated automatically. The graphical editor is a powerful tool which supports aspect-based modeling. While fully supporting DML, it enables the users to interactively model interrelations and interactions between business processes and entities. It empowers users to create hierarchically structured business models similar to the widely used concept of mind maps.The given example shows the combination of an expressive visual representation of a business model and the use of concepts like arithmetic expressions, variables and links within the model. This combination results in a powerful tool which is flexible and easy to use. A main feature of BusinessMapper is the possibility to simulate adjustments and modifications of the model. That is how experts can become familiar with new situations and anticipate the impact on the current business or a future project like the introduction of a new product. The use of conditions and arithmetic algorithms supports the simulation of dynamically changing parameters. This allows for interactive modelling and testing of processes and fitting them into an existing business landscape.

The tool has been successfully tested in various usability studies within the field of telecommunication companies. BusinessMapper was used in the early beginning of huge development projects to describe the dependencies and interrelations between different work packages and levels of aspects, like technical infrastructure, IT and products. The tool also has been used as project management software during the whole project life cycle and mainly to show the interrelations between different projects and to forecast a realistic timeline of the project. In another project the tool was used to accompany and evaluate a vendor selection based on specific customer requirements and different releases. In all the usability studies BusinessMapper could show its value to the management in the process of decision making or in the discovery of so far unidentified dependencies. The wide range of projects shows the flexibility and usability of BusinessMapper. All these usability studies were very successful and at the moment we aim to release BusinessMapper as a commercial software product.

References

1. Thomke, S., Fujimoto, T.: Front-Loading Problem-Solving: Implications for Development Performance and Capability. In: Proc. PICMET 1999, Portland International Conference on Technology and Innovation Management, vol. 2, pp. 234–240 (1999)
2. Steffens, T., Mertens, R., Andres, S.: A exible high-performance service-oriented production system for Triple Play telecommunication products. In: Proceedings of Informatik 2008 - Beherrschbare Systeme Dank Informatik, vol. 133, pp. 152–157 (2008)
3. Hunt, A.: Pragmatic Thinking and Learning: Refactor Your Wetware (Pragmatic Programmers). Pragmatic Bookshelf (Paperback). Raleigh, North Carolina, Dallas, Texas, USA (2008)
4. Buzan, T.: The Ultimate Book of Mind Maps. Harper Thorsons, London (2006)
5. Sarker, B.K., Wallace, P., Gill, W.: Some Observations on Mind Map and Ontology Building Tools for Knowledge Management,
   http://www.acm.org/ubiquity/volume_9/pf/v9i9_sarker.pdf
6. Tucker, J.M., Armstrong, G., Massad, V.J.: Mind Maps and Mind Mapping Software. In: Proceedings of Applied Business Research Conference 2009, Oahu, HI (2009),
   http://www.cluteinstitute.com/Programs/Hawaii_2009/Article119.pdf
7. Mento, A.J., Jones, R.M.: Mind mapping in executive education: applications and outcomes. Journal of Management Development 18, 390–407 (1999)

8. Lavbic, D., Krisper, M.: Rapid Ontology Development Model Based on Business Rules Management Approach for the use in Business Applications. Doctoral Consortium Paper, University of Ljubljana, Slovenia (2008),
   `http://www.lavbic.net/delo-in-raziskovanje/`
   `(2008,ICEIS)iceis-2008.pdf`
9. Reusch, P.J.A., Bozguney, E., Reusch, P.: Integrated Tool Sets for Business Games and Simulation. In: IDAACS 2007, 4th IEEE Workshop on Intelligent Data Acquisition and Advanced Computing Systems, pp. 485–489 (2007)
10. Sangal, N., Jordan, E., Sinha, V., Jackson, D.: Using dependency models to manage complex software architecture. In: OOPSLA 2005: Proceedings of ACM SIGPLAN Conference on Object Oriented Programming, Systems, Languages, and Applications, vol. 40(10), pp. 167–176. ACM Press, New York (2005)

Corporate Culture in Line with Business Process Orientation and Its Impact on Organizational Performance

Markus Kohlbacher[1], Stefan Gruenwald[2], and Ernst Kreuzer[2]

[1] Campus 02 University of Applied Sciences
markus.kohlbacher@processorientation.com
[2] Campus 02 University of Applied Sciences
{stefan.gruenwald,ernst.kreuzer}@campus02.at

Abstract. Business process orientation can be interpreted as the organizational approach making business processes the platform for organizational structure, strategic planning, and information technology. While
recent research focused on the question whether process-oriented organizational design impacts firm performance, there is a lack of studies
measuring the construct of process orientation by means of whether the
process approach is actually *lived* in the organization. This paper empirically explores the relationship between a corporate culture in line with
business process orientation and firm performance in industrial settings.
The empirical evidence indicates that firms which actually live the process approach are outperforming other firms in terms of financial firm
performance, delivery time, and delivery reliability.

Keywords: business process orientation, corporate culture, firm performance.

1 Introduction

A central question in strategic management research is: How do firms achieve
sustainable competitive advantage? According to the resource-based view (RBV)
of the firm, organizations in the same industry perform differently because they
possess different resources and capabilities [1], [2]. Organizational processes have
emerged as critical building blocks in these difficult-to-imitate capabilities [3],
[4]. At the same time, a focus on organizational processes has increased in managerial practice [5]. Business process orientation means focusing on business
processes ranging from customer to customer instead of placing emphasis on
functional and hierarchical structures [6]. Several authors (e.g. [7], [8]) argue
that a lot of the existing literature of the process-oriented organization has been
in the popular press and lacks research or an empirical focus. Many case studies
refer to a positive relationship between process orientation and organizational
performance, but a solid empirical verification of this central guideline has not
happened yet [9]. Business process orientation is not a unidimensional construct

M. zur Muehlen and J. Su (Eds.): BPM 2010 Workshops, LNBIP 66, pp. 16–24, 2011.

[8]. Several dimensions shape the construct, e.g. definition of business processes [10], management commitment towards the process approach [11], [12], the process owner role [13], process performance measurement [11], [14], and information technology as an enabler or implementer of process orientation [15]. In particular, process orientation is a matter of enterprise culture [11], [6], [15]. The real problems when implementing the process approach are of a cultural nature [10]. The cultural fit is an important issue since people and processes must combine to produce output [16]. We consider a corporate culture in line with the process approach as strong indicator for process orientation and will focus our analysis on this specific dimension of the process orientation construct. We focus on the question whether there is a positive relationship between a culture in line with the process approach (`POCulture`) and financial performance, delivery speed and delivery reliability. The study uses a sample of 132 Austrian firms operating in metal and machinery industry. The quality of the collected data is considered to be very high since we collected the data by conducting personal interviews. The paper will begin by developing the hypotheses about the impact of a lived process approach on firm performance. Next, research design is specified and operationalization of the variables is carried out, followed by a presentation of the empirical findings. The paper concludes with a discussion of the results, implications, and issues for further research.

2 Theory and Hypotheses

Process orientation introduces transparency in the organization [17]. By discovering and analyzing an organization's business processes, non-value adding activities are easily detected. The elimination of non-value adding activities therefore should lead to cost reductions which in turn should lead to improved financial performance. Several authors state that process orientation leads to better financial performance [11], [18]. Case study research projects also report a positive contribution of process orientation on financial performance [19], [20]. The literature therefore suggests that process orientation leads to better financial performance.

Hypothesis 1. *A corporate culture in line with the process approach is related positively to financial firm performance.*

As already mentioned above, time-consuming but non-value adding activities are easily detected by analyzing an organization's business processes. The elimination of non-value adding activities therefore should lead to speed improvements. Several authors argue that process orientation leads to throughput time reductions [11], [21], [18]. Also, case study research report that process orientation led to throughput speed improvements [22], [23], [24], [25], [26], [20]. This leads us to hypothesize that:

Hypothesis 2. *A corporate culture in line with the process approach is related positively to delivery speed.*

Delivery reliability, defined as the extent to which an organization delivers its orders on time, is in many businesses an order-qualifier instead of an order-winning criterion. If a company continues to not deliver on time, customers will stop considering the company as a potential supplier [27]. Customers have become so demanding that if their suppliers do not deliver on time, they may go elsewhere. The trend towards on time deliveries has reached practically all industries [28]. The delivery reliability of a supplier is often related to various manufacturing performance measures on the customers' side and therefore it is reasonable that customers will demand high delivery reliability from their suppliers [29]. Management unfamilarity with business process design and absence of institutional knowledge of process designs causes process variation [30]. Business processes with high variation may cause insufficient delivery reliability [18]. In line with these thoughts, several case study research projects report a positive effect of process orientation on delivery reliability [31], [22]. The last hypothesis of this paper is therefore formulated as:

Hypothesis 3. *A corporate culture in line with the process approach is related positively to delivery reliability.*

3   Research Design

3.1   Operationalizing Corporate Culture in Line with the Process Approach

For operationalizing the `POCulture` construct, we used existing models and studies which already measured business process orientation: the Process and Enterprise Maturity Model (PEMM) by Hammer [11], and the models by McCormack and Johnson [32], Reijers [6], Vera and Kuntz [9], and Willaert et al. [15]. From these models, we derived five characteristics of an organization which actually lives the process approach. A statement was formulated for each of the five items. Each statement had to be rated by the respondents using a six point Likert scale ranging from full disagreement to full agreement.

Existence of inter-departmental teamwork. A process-oriented organization needs a culture which values teamwork, since business processes cutting across functions must be operated by people in a team [11]. Teams are playing an important role in process management, since e.g. a large process like order fulfillment still requires working together across geographical boundaries [33]. A precondition for successful process management is introducing empowered teams [10]. This indicator was derived from the models by [11], [32], [9], [15] and captures whether teamwork between different departments can be taken for granted in the organization.

Customer-focused attitude of employees. It is often argued that organizations emphasizing functions and hierarchy are failing to focus on the customer [10], [18], [34]. By contrast, in a process-oriented organization, each business process has a clearly defined customer who receives the result of the process [35]. This indicator is derived from the models by [11], [6], and [15] and captures whether the organization's employees understand that the purpose of their work is to fulfil the needs of the internal/external customers.

Employees' accountability for enterprise results. Only organizations whose culture values personal accountability will find it possible to move forward with their degree of process orientation [11]. This indicator is derived from the model by [11] and captures whether the organization's employees feel accountable for enterprise results.

Use of process language. Process orientation is a construct which becomes "real" by communication and interaction, i.e. the construct becomes real if it is communicated by means of a language. By communicating about business processes and their design, process orientation becomes a reality [36]. This indicator is derived from the models by [32] and [6] and captures whether employees on all levels of the organization are speaking about business processes, customers, teams, process performance indicators, etc.

Knowledge of process workers about how their process is executed. Process performers must have appropriate knowledge about the business process they are working for, otherwise they won't be able to implement the process design [11]. This indicator is derived from the model by [11] and captures whether the organization's employees can describe the design of the process they work for. Furthermore the indicator captures whether the employees know how their work affects subsequent work, customers and process performance.

3.2 Operationalizing Firm Performance

Financial performance was measured by return on sales (ROS); the data was gathered by inspecting the official financial statements of the firms in our sample. Delivery speed and delivery reliability were measured by perceptual ratings. Perceptual ratings rely on the interviewee's judgment and allow him/her to give an answer without giving specific numerical information. Interviewees are more willing to answer a subjective question than to queries about numerical data [37]. Respondents were asked to evaluate delivery speed (as compared to their major competitors) and delivery reliability using six point Likert scales. The end-points of the scales were selected such that high rating reflects high performance.

We use several control variables in our model where financial performance is the dependent variable of interest. Market share is positively associated with financial performance [38] and is therefore included as a control variable. Respondents were asked to rate the market share of their company in comparison to their major competitors using a six point Likert scale (if the company was operating in various industries, respondents were asked to estimate a weighted mean of the different market shares resulting in a single rating representing the firm's average market share). Firm size, measured by the natural logarithm of number of employees, is associated with economies of scale and, hence, is expected to have a positive association with firm performance [39]. Capital structure has been argued to affect firm performance. In particular, debt can produce tradeoffs such as reductions in long-term expenditures (e.g. R&D). Such reductions can be harmful to the firm over time [40]. Capital structure is therefore also used as a control variable and is measured by the ratio of liabilities to total assets.

3.3   Sample and Data Collection

The population of this study is defined as Austrian corporations operating in metal and machinery industry with at least 50 employees. For practical reasons, the metal and machinery industry was chosen since these industries include a sufficient large number of organizations in Austria. Firms were selected randomly and telephone interviews were used for data collection. All telephone interviews were personally conducted by the researchers. On average, an interview took about 15 minutes. For every firm one executive (CEO, CIO or quality manager) was interviewed. This is a clear difference to studies which are using a mail survey method for data collection. Data quality of this study is expected to be high since respondents are personally identified and interviewed assuring that the interviewee has the knowledge to truthfully answer the questions. A total of 200 organizations were contacted. Out of them, 152 organizations were willing to give an interview. However, only 132 firms remained in the sample as some respondents did not have the knowledge to truthfully answer the questions.

4   Analysis and Results

Before one can proceed with testing the hypotheses, one has to ensure that the POCulture construct is unidimensional, reliable, and valid. Unidimensionality of POCulture was assessed by a principal components analysis. All items loaded on one single factor (all loadings on this factor were 0.724 or greater). Adequate construct reliability was checked by using Cronbach alpha (Cronbach's alpha accounted for 0.814). Construct validity was assessed by the criteria that none of the items loaded greater than 0.50 on more than one factor reported by the factor analysis. Having assessed undimensionality, reliability, and validity, the construct measure was calculated by computing the equally-weighted average of the item scores.

We used regression analyses to investigate the relationships between culture in line with the process approach (as the independent variable) and firm performance variables (as the dependent variables). In order to examine if the results are affected by multicollinearity, the variance inflation factors (VIFs) and the tolerance values were examined [41]. For all regression models, the VIFs were well below the threshold value of 10 or greater, which is indicative of multicollinearity (none of the VIFs were above 1.589), and the tolerance values were well above the suggested 0.10 or less threshold, which is indicative of multicollinearity (for all models, the tolerance values were 0.629 or greater). In addition, normality and homoscedasticity violations were assessed by applying the Kolmogorov-Smirnov test and by visually inspecting normal probability and residual plots. The plots and the tests did not indicate deviations from normality nor from homoscedasticity.

The results of the regression analyses are reported in Table 1. The control variables debt, market share, and firm size were included in the regression analysis where ROS was the dependent variable (Model 1). With Hypothesis 1, we consider the effect of corporate culture in line with the process approach on financial firm performance (ROS). As we show in Table 1, Model 1, a corporate culture in line with the process approach positively affects financial firm performance (b=0.223, p<0.10). The model also shows that debt has a significant negative impact on profitability (b=-0358, p<0.01). This finding is in line with the results of other studies (e.g. [42]), which also found a negative impact of debt on financial firm performance. Hypothesis 2 deals with the relationship between corporate culture in line with the process approach and delivery speed. As Model 2 shows, POCulture relates positively to delivery speed (b=0.282, p<0.01), in support of Hypothesis 2. In Hypothesis 3, we assess the impact of POCulture on delivery reliability. As we show in Model 3, POCulture relates positively to delivery reliability (b=0.318, p<0.001), supporting Hypothesis 3. In summary, the findings provide support for all our hypotheses. The empirical evidence therefore indicates that firms which actually live the process approach are outperforming other firms in terms of profitability, delivery speed, and delivery reliability.

Table 1. Impact of Corporate Culture in Line with the Process Approach on Firm Performance

	Model 1	Model 2	Model 3
Dependent variable	ROS	Delivery speed	Delivery reliability
POCulture	0.223[+]	0.282**	0.318***
	(1.870)	(3.025)	(3.662)
Debt	-0.358**	–	–
	(-3.051)		
Market share	0.178	–	–
	(1.489)		
Firm size	0.191	–	–
	(1.643)		
R^2	0.263	0.079	0.101
F	4.994**	9.150**	13.412***
n	61	108	121

Standardized regression coefficients are reported. t-values in parenthesis; [+]p<0.10, *p<0.05, **p<0.01, ***p<0.001; all tests are two tailed.

5   Conclusions

Most previous empirical studies which investigated the impact of process orientation treated process orientation as a unidimensional measure. However, we believe that process orientation is a multidimensional construct and focused our analysis on whether the process approach is actually lived within the organization. Therefore, we focused on the cultural dimension of the construct. The findings of our study indicate that a corporate culture in line with the process approach is positively associated with profitability, delivery speed and delivery reliability. Our work therefore extends the existing process management literature by providing new empirical insights into the impact of process orientation on organizational performance.

There are several important limitations to this study. First, the sample in this work only included Austrian manufacturing firms. Generalizability of the findings to other industries or other countries is open to scrutiny. A second important limitation of this work is the small number of cases in certain regression models. Such a small number of cases is not appropriate for a clear demonstration of causal effects. Third, as is common with most organizational studies, this work relies on survey data, which leaves open the possibility of self-serving bias in the data. Finally, future works should survey two or more key informants at each company to increase the accuracy of the survey information.

There are a number of avenues for further research. First, the dynamics of process orientation could be investigated through a longitudinal study of process orientation efforts and their outcomes. Second, this study could be applied to other industries (particularly interesting would be service industries) and/or other countries. One could e.g. carry out a cross-industry study which investigates the effects of process orientation in highly versus in less competitive industries. Third, financial performance was assessed by the widely used financial performance ratio return on sales, indicating short run performance. One might wonder whether the findings also hold in the long run, e.g., with organizational survival as the dependent variable.

References

1. Barney, J.B.: Strategic factor markets: expectations, luck, and business strategy. Management Science 32(10), 1231–1241 (1986)
2. Peteraf, M.A.: The cornerstones of competitive advantage: a resource-based view. Strategic Management Journal 14(3), 179–191 (1993)
3. Teece, D.J., Pisano, G., Shuen, A.: Dynamic capabilities and strategic management. Strategic Management Journal 18(7), 509–533 (1997)
4. Eisenhardt, K.M., Martin, J.A.: Dynamic capabilities: what are they? Strategic Management Journal 21(10-11), 1105–1121 (2000)
5. Benner, M.J., Veloso, F.M.: Iso 9000 practices and financial performance: a technology coherence perspective. Journal of Operations Management 26(5), 611–629 (2008)
6. Reijers, H.A.: Implementing BPM systems: the role of process orientation. Business Process Management Journal 12(4), 389–409 (2006)
7. Sussan, A.P., Johnson, W.C.: Strategic capabilities of business processes: looking for competitive advantage. Competitiveness Review 13(2), 46–52 (2003)
8. Kohlbacher, M.: The effects of process orientation: a literature review. Business Process Management Journal 16(1), 135–152 (2010)
9. Vera, A., Kuntz, L.: Process-based organization design and hospital efficiency. Health Care Management Review 32(1), 55–65 (2007)
10. Hinterhuber, H.H.: Business process management: the european approach. Business Change & Re-engineering 2(4), 63–73 (1995)

11. Hammer, M.: The process audit. Harvard Business Review 85(4), 111–123 (2007)
12. Trkman, P.: The critical success factors of business process management. International Journal of Information Management 30(2), 125–134 (2010)
13. Hammer, M., Stanton, S.: How process enterprises really work. Harvard Business Review 77(6), 108–118 (1999)
14. Bosilj-Vuksic, V., Milanovic, L., Skrinjar, R., Indihar-Stemberger, M.: Organizational performance measures for business process management: A performance measurement guideline. In: Tenth International Conference on Computer Modeling and Simulation, pp. 94–99 (2008)
15. Willaert, P., Van den Bergh, J., Willems, J., Deschoolmeester, D.: The process-oriented organisation: A holistic view developing a framework for business process orientation maturity. In: Alonso, G., Dadam, P., Rosemann, M. (eds.) BPM 2007. LNCS, vol. 4714, pp. 1–15. Springer, Heidelberg (2007)
16. Armistead, C., Machin, S.: Implications of business process management for operations management. International Journal of Operations & Production Management 17(9), 886–898 (1997)
17. Kohlbacher, M.: The perceived effects of business process management. In: Science and Technology for Humanity (TIC-STH), 2009 IEEE Toronto International Conference, pp. 399–402. IEEE, Los Alamitos (2009)
18. Schmelzer, H.J., Sesselmann, W.: Geschäftsprozessmanagement in der Praxis, 5th edn. Carl Hanser, München (2006)
19. Bulitta, C.: Geschäftsprozessmanagement bei Siemens Medical Solutions, Geschäftsgebiet AX. In: Schmelzer, H.J., Sesselmann, W. (eds.) Geschäftsprozessmanagement in der Praxis, 5th edn., Hanser, München and Wien, pp. 475–489 (2006)
20. Wahlich, S.M.: Prozessorientierte Organisation bei Vaillant Hepworth. In: Ellringmann, H., Schmelzer, H.J. (eds.) Geschäftsprozessmanagement inside, Hanser, München, pp. 1–40 (2004)
21. Hirzel, M.: Erfolgsfaktor Prozessmanagement. In: Hirzel, M., Kühn, F., Gaida, I. (eds.) Prozessmanagement in der Praxis, 2nd edn., pp. 11–22. Gabler, Wiesbaden (2008)
22. Hertz, S., Johansson, J.K., de Jager, F.: Customer-oriented cost cutting: process management at Volvo. Supply Chain Management: An International Journal 6(3), 128–141 (2001)
23. Küng, P., Hagen, C.: The fruits of business process management: an experience report from a swiss bank. Business Process Management Journal 13(4), 477–487 (2007)
24. Mittermaier, G., Braun, M.: Geschäftsprozessmanagement bei Infineon. In: Ellringmann, H., Schmelzer, H.J. (eds.) Geschäftsprozessmanagement inside, Hanser, München, pp. 1–40 (2004)
25. Ongaro, E.: Process management in the public sector. the experience of one-stop shops in italy. The International Journal of Public Sector Management 17(1), 81–107 (2004)
26. Setti, C., Stückl, R.: Geschäftsprozessmanagement bei OSRAM. In: Schmelzer, H.J., Sesselmann, W. (eds.) Geschäftsprozessmanagement in der Praxis, 5th edn., Hanser, München and Wien, pp. 461–474 (2006)
27. Hill, T.: Manufacturing Strategy. Palgrave, New York (2000)
28. Kumar, A., Sharman, G.: We love your product, but where is it? The McKinsey Quarterly (1), 24–44 (1992)

29. Sarmiento, R., Byrne, M., Contreras, L.R., Rich, N.: Delivery reliability, manufacturing capabilities and new models of manufacturing efficiency. Journal of Manufacturing Technology Management 18(4), 367–386 (2007)
30. Frei, F.X., Kalakota, R., Leone, A.J., Marx, L.M.: Process variation as a determinant of bank performance: evidence from the retail banking study. Management Science 45(9), 1210–1220 (1999)
31. Bocionek, S.: Einführung des Geschäftsprozessmanagements in der Siemens Health Services Corp., USA. In: Schmelzer, H.J., Sesselmann, W. (eds.) Geschäftsprozessmanagement in der Praxis, 5th edn., Hanser, München and Wien, pp. 443–460 (2006)
32. McCormack, K.P., Johnson, W.C.: Business Process Orientation. In: Gaining the E-Business Competitive Advantage. St. Lucie Press, Boca Raton (2001)
33. Armistead, C., Rowland, P.: The role of people in processes. In: Armistead, C., Rowland, P. (eds.) Managing Business Processes: BPR and beyond, pp. 61–71. John Wiley & Sons, Chichester (1996)
34. Gulati, R.: Abschied vom Silodenken. Harvard Business Manager (12), 90–106 (2007)
35. Schantin, D.: Makromodellierung von Geschäftsprozessen. Deutscher Universitätsverlag, Wiesbaden (2004)
36. Gaitanides, M.: Prozessorganisation, 2nd edn. Vahlen, München (2007)
37. Ahire, S.L., Golhar, D.Y.: Quality management in large vs small firms. Journal of Small Business Management (April 1996)
38. Capon, N., Farley, J.U., Hoenig, S.: Determinants of financial performance: A meta-analysis. Management Science 36(10), 1143–1159 (1990)
39. Hitt, M.A., Hoskisson, R.E., Kim, H.: International diversification: effects on innovation and firm performance in product-diversified firms. The Academy of Management Journal 40(4), 767–798 (1997)
40. Hitt, M.A., Smart, D.L.: Debt: a disciplining force for managers or a debilitating force for organizations? Journal of Management Inquiry 3(2), 144–152 (1994)
41. Hair, J.F., Black, W.C., Babin, B.J., Anderson, R.E., Tatham, R.L.: Multivariate Data Analysis, 6th edn. Pearson Prentice Hall, Upper Saddle River (2006)
42. Chari, M.D.R., Devaraj, S., David, P.: The impact of information technology investments and diversification strategies on firm performance. Management Science 54(1), 224–234 (2008)

Agent Assignment for Process Management: Goal Modeling for Continuous Resource Management

Ramzan Talib, Bernhard Volz, and Stefan Jablonski

University of Bayreuth, Applied Informatics IV,
D-95440 Bayreuth, Germany
{Ramzan.Talib,Bernhard.Volz,Stefan.Jablonski}@uni-bayreuth.de

Abstract. Workflow Management Systems (WfMS) support modeling and execution of business processes, but they lack to define a criteria that can be used to determine how successfully certain processes are being performed by authorized agents. As a consequence, agents go on and on with their work even they have a poor success history and thus cause a process to become inefficient. Therefore, this paper introduces means for including goal modeling into workflow modeling, enabling a WfMS not only to support performance evaluation mechanisms but also to select those agents for a certain task who will most likely be performing best.

Keywords: Process Inefficiencies Diagnosis, Process Improvement, Resource Management, Agent Assignments, Goals Modeling, Continuous Resource Management, Performance Evaluation, Process Design.

1 Introduction

Workflow Management Systems (WfMS) have been widely used to support the modeling and execution of business processes. One of the crucial functions of a WfMS is assigning tasks to users (i.e. human agents) in order to execute them. The assignment of tasks relies on an authorization model which expresses the eligibilities of agents. In order to determine agents who are eligible to perform a specific task, they are firstly classified according to their capabilities and skills into roles. A process in the model is then assigned to a role instead to a specific agent during the design phase. For example consider garment production processes of a textile industry where a **Cutting Process** is assigned to *cutters* (role; group of users capable to cut fabric for specific garment) and **Sewing Process** is assigned to s*ewers* (role; group of users capable to sew garment). Secondly, when a process step (e.g. **Cutting Process**) is executed its associated role (e.g. *cutter*) is taken and all agents assigned to that role are informed about the task to perform.

In almost all WfMS, it is simply assumed that the staff members who are capable performing a certain task and are assigned to a process will execute the process 'successfully'. But currently, WfMS do not have any mechanism to determine 'how successfully' certain processes are actually being performed by an authorized agent [3-5]. In fact, no definition is given that would say what 'successful' means. As a result, agents simply continue with their work even if some of them have poor success

M. zur Muehlen and J. Su (Eds.): BPM 2010 Workshops, LNBIP 66, pp. 25–36, 2011.

history. This situation is unsatisfactory as it has a negative impact on the overall business performance [1] and also contradicts the philosophy of continuous resource management [2] i.e. only successful agents should remain enacting processes.

In contrast, a competitive business environment requires the assignment of task specific goals to agents. Goals are measurable targets that an organization sets up to be achieved by authorized agents [6]. The achievement of a goal is essential for authorized agents to continue with forthcoming process executions and also for the overall business process performance. For example, consider a goal like "cutting fault in each quarter should be less than 2%" which defines a 'success criteria' for **cutters** against which they can be evaluated.

Therefore, there is an eminent need to first define task specific goals within the model of a workflow. Basing on that definition, a WfMS can be built that supports performance evaluation mechanisms. Finally, the result of the evaluation mechanisms can then be reflected within an organizational model so that only successful agents will be selected for the forthcoming process executions, thus eliminating one reason for inefficient processes – the assignment of merely qualified instead of excellent staff – not only during runtime but also during the design phase of a process when goals are specified.

This paper makes two contributions: First, it utilizes a process modeling environment to extend traditional business process modeling with goal modeling. Second, it demonstrates how goal modeling can be utilized in different phases of the workflow life cycle in order to support continuous resource management and to improve business process performance.

The paper is structured into six sections. Related work is presented in Section 2. Section 3 outlines the extension of process modeling with a goal modeling approach. Section 4 explains the configuration of goal modeling in the different phases of the workflow life cycle in order to support continuous resource management. We outline our experiences and experiments in Section 5. Section 6 concludes the paper and gives an outlook regarding future research.

2   Related Work

This section details about the state of the art of WfMS resource management that deals with the definition of organizational models in terms of organizational entities (i.e. user, role, group, department) and their assignment to processes (i.e. assignment strategies).

In [2, 8-10], organizational models are proposed that define organizational structures as entities with relationships among them and organizational population as instantiation of the organizational structure in terms of users and the roles they play or the groups they belong to. In [8], Bussler developed an abstract meta-model for specifying an organizational structure. It is more general than [2, 9, 10] since it does not impose any restriction on the organization being modeled ([2, 9, 10] presume limited organizational entities and relationships).

WfMS traditionally use roles as means for abstracting from the assignment of a concrete agent and his or her skills; but, as [8-11] point out, the role concept alone is not sufficient to cope with the requirements of task assignment within real world workflow applications. Some examples where this can be easily seen were presented by Bussler in [8]: assignment of a task to an agent that is somehow related to another agent (e.g. ManagerOf(clerk)), the same agent as the previous task, etc. As a solution, Bussler presents a Policy Language and Policy Resolution Framework for the specification and execution of generic task assignments in a WfMS.

The work of Bussler was expanded by HP-Lab [9] and Cao et al. [10]. HP-Lab proposed an SQL-like policy language called Resource Query Language (RQL) [9] that is able to specify three types of policies: *requirement, qualification* and *substitution* policies. These policies deal with organizational constraints like *role delegation* (e.g. if a user is not available, WfMS should be able to locate alternate users to avoid excessive delay), *binding of roles* (e.g. customer complaint should be handled by a person who sold the product) and *separation of duties* (e.g. user should not approve his own bill). This work is further extended by Cao et al. [10] in which they define the Task Assignment Policy Language (TAPL) for handling similar constraints (*role delegation, role binding* and *separation of duties*). TAPL adds some new features with respect to RQL such as WHERE, WHEN and WITH clauses in *require, substitute* and *reject* policies to represent complicate conditions for resource allocation. Further, they also developed more policy search algorithms and enforcement methods. The downside of all these approaches is a missing support for enforcing the assignment of successful agents to processes.

In [11], Kumar et al. pointed out that role based assignments are critical when suitable workers are not available. This becomes crucial especially when a process has to be executed before reaching a certain deadline. Processes then need to be assigned to a lesser qualified staff. They observed that there is a tradeoff between the urgency of a task and the suitability of agents. To manage this tradeoff they propose an *agent suitability metrics* and a *process urgency metrics*. Values in these metrics are between 0 (lowest) and 1 (highest). These metrics are then applied during enactment and – in general – they represent an assignment methodology along with a simulation model. The assignment methodology dynamically creates a balance between a qualified agent and accomplishment of work. In comparison to our work these metrics do not incorporate the success history of an agent because they are firstly static and secondly defined only during design time (i.e. updating the assignment strategy or rules is not part of the methodology).

State of the art workflow resource allocation patterns are presented in [3-5]. These patterns capture different ways in which resources are utilized to perform a task independent of any workflow technology. It is pointed out that existing modeling notations such as Business Process Management Notations (BPMN) and Unified Modeling Language (UML) 2.0 Activity Diagrams do not support history based resource allocation mechanisms (Pattern 9: R-HBA) [7]. Also, existing WfMSs such as Staffware Process Suite version 9 (TIBCO), WebSphere MQ Workflow 3.4 (IBM), FLOWer 3 (Pallas Athena) and COSA 4.2 (TRANSFLOW) do not directly support history based resource allocation ([3], [4], [5]) i.e. neither the history of 'business success' is evaluated nor it is used for future task assignments. For example, it would be very beneficial to allocate a heart bypass task to the surgeon who has 'successfully' completed such tasks over the past three months.

Only Oracle BPEL Process Manager V.10.1.2 and iPlanet 6.0 (SUN) partially supports history based resource allocation mechanisms (Pattern 9: R-HBA). They evaluate history just on the basis of 'more executions; more experience' and or 'quick execution time' without focusing on business 'success criteria'. For example, the *heart bypass task* doesn't need to be allocated to a surgeon who quickly or mostly completes this surgery – instead needs to be allocated to a surgeon who 'successfully' completes this operation.

After a profound analysis of current workflow resource management technologies and workflow modeling notations along with experiences taken from collaboration with industry partners in medical [18] and textile industry [27], it reveals that history constraint need to be defined in terms of a measurable goal in the process model. Putting a goal definition into a workflow model allows for continuous evaluation of assignments. Results of a performance evaluation which then can take place continuously could be fed back into the process and the organizational model in order to leverage from this knowledge in future assignment decisions and to improve the efficiency of a process.

3   Extension of Goal Construct in Process Modeling Compositions

3.1 Conceptual Foundation

Our proposed solution is based on the Perspective Oriented Process Modeling (POPM) framework [21]. It covers all facets of process based applications and structures issues in a modularized manner. Integrated Process Manager (i>PM, [20]) is a graphical process modeling tool built to support POPM and is implemented on top of a flexible meta-model [18].

The idea behind POPM is that a modeling construct consists of several building blocks, which are called perspectives. Modeling constructs are then defined through a composition of several of these blocks; an example for such a modeling construct is a 'process step' – a fundamental construct for modeling processes. For a basic process modeling language, five main perspectives are utmost important, namely Functional, Data, Operational, Behavioral and Organizational perspectives.

The **Functional** perspective defines the skeleton of the process. It identifies a process step and defines its purpose. A process step can either be atomic or it can be composite, i.e. it serves as a container for other elements and thus establishes a hierarchy. The **Data** perspective defines input and output data of a process. It relates data of the process to external data models. Additionally, it defines business objects, their structure and flow between the steps of a process and maps them to external data models. The **Operational** perspective describes tools, (programs, systems, etc.) that are available for the execution of a process. The **Behavioral** perspective determines the control flow, i.e. the order in which the single steps of a process are being scheduled for execution by a WfMS. Last but not least the **Organizational** perspective determines agents who are eligible to perform a certain process. A significant difference to other process modeling approaches is the ability to easily adapt this list of perspectives. Even though the above mentioned perspectives are considered to establish a foundation every process based application will need, perspectives may be added or removed freely.

Thus, POPM can be extended to support **Goal Modeling** by introducing a new perspective. This extensibility is especially important for competitive business environments: an environment where performance and quality is no longer a luxury – rather is of utmost importance in order to survive and remain competitive with the global market.

Figure 1 shows a screenshot of the i>PM modeling environment which is focusing on a process step from a garment production process, called **Cutting Process**. Within the POPM modeling tool each step of a process is depicted as a rectangle; the **Functional** perspective is represented within that rectangle in a text box. Small text at the lower left corner of the process step represents the **Organizational** perspective; here the role "Cutter" was assigned to the step. The **Goal** perspective is described by the small text at the lower right corner ("Cutter Goal"). **Data and Data Flow** are described by small boxes (data) that are placed on the black arrows (data flow) which connect two steps of a process; a data flow arrow always starts at the producer side of a data item and ends at the consumer side. The execution order of a process is, when this is not specified by data dependencies, defined with the help of the **Behavioral** perspective represented by grey arrows. A text just above the upper left corner of a process step denotes information about the **Operational** perspective.

3.2 Goal Modeling

Goal modeling is concerned with the description of goals in a systematic way that defines 'what success is' and 'how to measure it' [6]. When a goal is aligned with the process it establishes a 'success criteria' for authorized agents against which they are evaluated. A goal can be aligned either with the elementary process or a complex process. When a goal is aligned with a complex process it establishes the 'success criteria' (which is a measure for the efficiency of a process) for the collaborative work of all the employees part of a department, team or group involved in the complex process. It also helps to evaluate how successfully department heads, teams or groups in-charge are managing their subordinates?

A goal need to be measurable and must be assigned to either a simple or a complex process. For example "cutting fault in each quarter should be less than 2%" is a measurable goal for a **Cutting Process** because it can be easily determined up to what extend this goal was achieved. Harrington [14] stated "Measurement is the key. If you cannot measure it, you cannot control it. If you cannot control it, you cannot manage it. If you cannot manage it, you cannot improve it.". In contrast, "improve cutting faults" is not a measurable goal – it is more an utterance of an intension.

Some of the modeling languages like Non Functional Requirements (NFR) [22], Extended Enterprise Modeling Language (EEML) [23] and User Requirements Notation (URN) [24] support goal modeling [15, 16]. They model goals as a "purpose" or and "intension" and therefore cannot directly support performance evaluation mechanisms. Also, well known modeling notations like the Business Process Management Notation (BPMN), Event-driven Process Chain (EPC), Yet Another Workflow Language (YAWL) and Integrated Definition Method 3 (IDEF 3) currently do not support goal modeling [17].

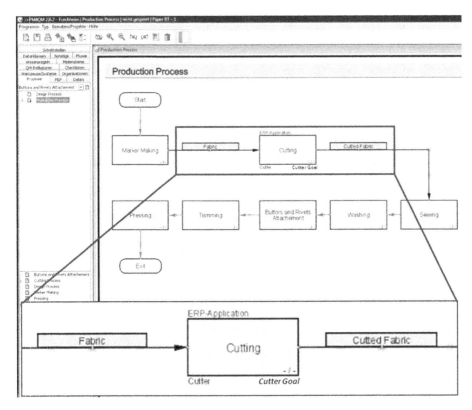

Fig. 1. i > PM Modeling Environment

Most of the existing Business Intelligence (BI) frameworks like IBM WebSphere, Global 360 enterprise BPM suite, Tibco iProcess Suite, and EMC BPM suites use Key Performance Indicators (KPIs) in their monitoring model for tracing business process performance and efficiency. Their monitoring models only issue alerts when KPI values deviate from predefined target values but do not allow for pro-active feedback. KPIs in general are good for measuring the current performance but they are unable to detect the causes of the problem because they usually only look at one factor – the outcome of a process – but do not establish a link between the outcome and an agent that is producing it. Thus, a KPI alone does not allow for correcting an assignment and thus does not allow for increasing the overall efficiency.

Therefore, we propose that goal modeling has to include not just one but – in an optimal case – all perspectives of a process model in order to support continuous resource management. Who will identify different perspectives of process (those, which influence the achievement of specific goal) and how goal is defined into process model, will be discussed in detail in Section 4 aligned with different phases of workflow lifecycle.

A goal definition consists of two parts: a *Context Definition* and a *Measurement Definition*. Within our new process improvement strategy, goals are defined using their Measurement Definitions along with their Context Definition. This initiative is motivated by the fact that any information taken out of process context lessens its value, i.e. when information is taken out of context, the results are, at best, limited, if not downright misleading. Therefore, goal modeling on the process layer along with its context as well as its measurement definition enables performance evaluation mechanism to act on processes for resource management — instead of having an adjunct performance evaluation mechanism (like BI tools) that do not support actions on the process layer.

The *Context Definition* describes the information about different perspectives of a process that influence the achievement of a specific goal, i.e. application data used during process execution and agents who execute the process. It is the Context Definition that establishes a basis for the application of data mining algorithms in order to evaluate the performance. Therefore, performance evaluation mechanism can evaluate with data mining techniques 'who' is performing 'how well' and under 'what certain conditions' goals are being achieved by 'whom' and up to 'what certain success level'. Such evaluation is possible when a context is provided and only then performance evaluation can support actions for continuous resource management.

Fig. 2. Goal Measurement Definition

The *Measurement Definition* in contrast adds a formula after which a measure for the defined goal is computed. As shown in Figure 2, this description includes *goal name*, *goal description*, *goal metric* (data used to measure the goal), *data source* (e.g. FaultTable), *data type*, and a *goal query* which is needed for retrieving required data. It also includes the specification of different groups. Each group is specified in terms of *group name*, *start value*, *end value*, and *priority* as shown in Figure 2 (lower part). These groups are used to describe:

- What are different success levels?
- How to identify a certain success level using goal metric values?
- How to rank the superiority of different success levels i.e. which group is better than others?

Based on the current goal metric value, a performance evaluation mechanism determines a particular group. For example, when the goal metric value (FabricFaultPercentage) is less than 2 (%) this corresponds with the group "Good". Next, for this identified group (i.e. "Good"), a performance evaluation mechanism determines its "priority" utilizing its concern group specification. The priority of that particular group determine the rank of its 'success' among different success levels – the higher the value of the group priority, the better the level of its business success.

These priorities are essential because performance evaluation mechanism cannot rank different levels of goal achievement simply from interpreting the words like "Good", "Average" or "Poor". Also, these priorities guide performance evaluation mechanisms to perform certain actions that are required for continuous resource management. For example, it could revoke the authorization of a person who achieved a goal having lowest priority (e.g. -100 for 'Poor' group). On the whole these priorities are used by performance evaluation mechanism to determine the superiority of certain 'success level' so that it can perform corresponding action that is ultimately required for continuous resource management.

Therefore precise description of goal *Context Definition* along with *Measurement Definition* enables performance evaluation mechanism to evaluate how successfully certain processes are being performed by their authorized agents and under what particular conditions.

4   Goal Modeling for Continuous Resource Management

This section explains how goal modeling is integrated into the standard workflow lifecycle [2, 28]. We will show that continuous resource management means to consider goal modeling not as an add-on to the normal lifecycle but as an integral part of it thus influencing every phase of the lifecycle.

The workflow lifecycle starts with the **Requirements Analysis** phase. Additional to the normal function of this phase, a *Process Engineer* is asked to identify goals which should be reached and that will be later on used within the performance evaluation. This identification is informal, i.e. it will not output a concrete measurement. As a process engineer usually is not deeply concerned with business plans, metrics and company strategies, a *Business Expert* will assist him within that task.

Within the **Process Design** phase, the *Process Engineer* is asked to make the former informal specification formal in the sense that it is aligned with processes, data, organizations, etc. Even most of the parameters of the Measurement Definition and Context Definition (see Section 3) are set, some are still open – e.g. *data source* (table) and *goal query* cannot be specified yet since this is information related to the execution environment. Completing this information is part of the next phase.

During the **Process Implementation** phase, Process Engineers interact with *Data Experts* in order to fill the open gaps in the Context and Measurement Definition.

Since data of the process log (artifacts of a workflow event log) and the application data store (e.g. fabric FaultTable) need to be queried, a Data Expert can be asked to integrate both sources at least into a common view. For the details of such integration we refer the interested reader to [19].

During the **Process Execution** phase, individual instances of a process model are enacted in a real business environment. Artifacts of the single process instances are stored within the process log and application data stores. In order to perform an evaluation, the integrated data store must be updated on a regular basis either automatically or manually.

The **Process Evaluation** phase completes the workflow lifecycle. In this phase, single workflow instances are evaluated from an ex-post perspective in order to draw conclusions for better assignments. The results of this evaluation could then be used in another round of the lifecycle providing extend information to people concerned with the design of a process. The evaluation phase, with respect to our approach, comprises three steps, namely Data Extraction, Performance Analysis and Feedback.

Within the first step **Data Extraction** data which are needed for computing involved metrics are extracted. Relevant sources and queries are specified within the *goal query* and *data source* fields of the goal definition.

It is then the task of the **Performance Analysis** step to compute values for metrics and determine a result of how well agents performed. Further, factors which have an impact on the overall performance are being determined. Especially in the latter computation methods known from the field of data mining are helpful ([12], [13]). The result of a performance evaluation mechanism can then be fed back (step **Feedback**) into the organizational database, i.e. profiles of agents are updated.

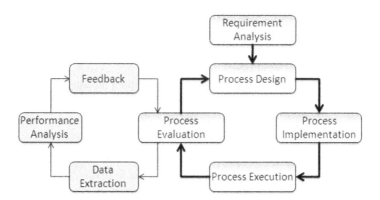

Fig. 3. Workflow Lifecycle Integrated with Performance Evaluation Mechanism

Therefore, by integrating the method of performance evaluation into the process lifecycle (Figure 3) and also by defining 'what is success' and 'how to measure it' into the process model, performance evaluation mechanisms are enabled to perform actions on the basis of performance analysis. Thus modeling goals in the process layer shows promising support for improving the efficiency of process instances performance and also for allowing more sophisticated continuous resource management.

5 Experiences and Experiments

Our approach is as follow. We define a goal along with its context into process models that defines 'what success is' and 'how to measure it'. It fills the gap of process modeling environments that lack to define 'success criteria' for a process (execution).

Our process models are developed in the i>PM process modeling environment; they also encompass goal definitions. Processes are executed by the ProcessNavigator [25]. The ProcessNavigator is a process execution infrastructure based on a BPEL workflow engine [26]. During process execution, the ProcessNavigator presents tasks to their authorized agents in order to execute them. The ProcessNavigator maintains a process log (in a relational database). This process log – when integrated with the process application data – provides an 'information source' for a performance evaluation mechanism.

As an example implementation of a performance evaluation mechanism, we chose agent performance evaluation methods defined in [12, 13] that apply techniques from data mining. These performance evaluation methods were tested by our textile industry partner [27] successfully. This field test has convincingly demonstrated that static assignment methodologies can greatly be improved towards continuous resource management especially when goals are defined into process model and performance evaluation mechanism supports actions on the process layer. For example, it can update agent expertise profiles into organizational databases when certain agents are not performing well i.e. not achieving a defined goal.

This field test is not perfect and yet complete since some implementations are still on the way. For example, we are developing more performance evaluation methods and then integrate them into a complete Agent Performance Evaluation Framework. So that this framework can utilize goal context definition to automatically select and trigger appropriate method that can then determine 'who' is performing 'how well' and under 'what certain conditions' goals are being achieved by 'whom' and up to 'what certain success level'. This framework can then update these finding into organizational database (semi)automatically.

6 Conclusion and Outlook

The aim of this paper was to introduce a goal construct to define 'success criteria' that can be used to determine how successfully certain processes are being performed by their authorized agents. We demonstrated that goal modeling, when integrated into the process layer, supports continuous resource management. Also, the suitability of goal modeling in process model is illuminated along with its configurations that are required in different phases of a workflow lifecycle. An exemplary implementation in the i>PM modeling environment is verifying its feasibility.

Our next step in this research is to develop a performance evaluation mechanism – a complete framework. This framework aims to utilize 'workflow execution history as a data source' and 'goal definition as a success criteria' to evaluate agent performance. It then needs to update agent expertise profiles into organizational database in order to support continuous resource management. Also legal aspects of our method must be investigated since personal performance measurement must not violate personal rights.

References

1. Moore, C.: Common Mistakes in Workflow Implementations. Giga Information Group, Cambridge (2002)
2. zur Muehlen, M.: Organizational Management in Workflow Applications. Informational Technology and Management Journal 5(3), 271–291 (2004)
3. Russell, N., ter Hofstede, A., Edmond, D., van der Aalst, W.: Workflow resource patterns. Technical Report WP 127, Eindhoven Univ. of Technology (2004)
4. Russell, N., von der Aalst, W.: Evaluation of the BPEL$People and WS-Human Task Extension to WS-BPEL 2.0 using the Workflow Resource Patterns. BPMN Center Report BPMN-07-10 (2007)
5. Russell, N., van der Aalst, W.M.P., ter Hofstede, A.H.M., Edmond, D.: Workflow Resource Patterns: Identification, Representation and Tool Support. In: Pastor, Ó., Falcão e Cunha, J. (eds.) CAiSE 2005. LNCS, vol. 3520, pp. 216–232. Springer, Heidelberg (2005)
6. Shaheen, A., Mahbob, A.: Prioritization of Key Performance Indcators: An Integration of Analytical Hierarchical Process and Goal Setting. International Journal of Productivity and Performance Management 56(3), 226–240 (2007), doi:10.1108/17410400731437
7. Wohed, P., von der Aalst, W., DoDumas, M., ter Hofstede, A., Russell, N.: On the suitability of BPMN for business process modelling. In: Dustdar, S., Fiadeiro, J.L., Sheth, A.P. (eds.) BPM 2006. LNCS, vol. 4102, pp. 161–176. Springer, Heidelberg (2006)
8. Bussler, C., Jablonski, S.: Policy Resolution for Workflow Management Systems. In: The Proceeding of the 28th Hawai International Conference on System Sciences, p. 831. IEEE Computer Society, Los Alamitos (1995)
9. Yan-Nong, H., Ning-Chien, S.: Policies in Resource Manager of Workflow Systems: Modeling, Enforcement and Management, HPL-98-156 (1998), http://www.hpl.hp.com/techreports/98/HPL-98-156.pdf
10. Cao, J., Chen, J., Zhao, H., Li, M.: A Policy-based Authorization Model for Workflow Enabled Dynamic Process Management. Journal of Network and Computer Applications 32, 412–422 (2009)
11. Kumar, A., von der Aalst, W., Verbeek, E.: Dynamic Work Distribution in Workflow Management Systems: How to Balance Quality and Performance. Journal of Management Information Systems 18(3), 157–193 (2002)
12. Jablonski, S., Talib, R.: Agent Assignment for Process Management: Pattern Based Agent Performance Evaluation. In: Cao, L., Gorodetsky, V., Liu, J., Weiss, G., Yu, P.S. (eds.) ADMI 2009. LNCS, vol. 5680, pp. 155–169. Springer, Heidelberg (2009)
13. Jablonski, S., Talib, R.: Agent Assignment for Process Management: Agent Performance Evaluation. In: FIT 2009, ACM Digital Library, Abbottabad, Pakistan (2009) (in press) ISBN 978-1-60558-642-7
14. Harrington, J.: Business Process Improvement – The Breakthrough Strategy for Total Quality, Productivity, and Competitiveness. McGraw-Hill, New York (1991)
15. Pourshahid, A., Chen, P., Amyot, D., Weiss, M., Forster, A.J.: Business Process Monitoring and Alignment: An Approach Based on User Requirement Notation and Business Intelligence Tools. In: 10th Workshop on Requirements Engineering (WER 2007), Toronto, Canada, pp. 80–91 (2007)

16. Pourshahid, A., Chen, P., Amyot, D., Peyton, L., Weiss, M., et al.: Towards an Integrated User Requirements Notation Framework and Tool for Business Process Management. In: 3rd International MCeTech Conference on e-Technologies, pp. 3–15. IEEE Computer Society, Montreal (2008)

17. Pourshahid, A.: A URN-Based Methodology for Business Process Monitoring. Thesis submitted to the Faculty of Graduation and Post-doctorial Studies, University of Ottawa, Ontario, Canada (2008)

18. Jablonski, S., Volz, B.: A Meta Modeling Framework for Domain Specific Process Management. In: 1st IEEE Int'l Workshop on Semantics for Business Process Management (SemBPM 2008) in Conjunction with the 32nd Annual IEEE Int'l Computer Software and Applications Conference (COMPSAC 2008), Turku, Finland (July 2008)

19. Radeschutz, S., Mitschang, B., Leymann, F.: Matching of Process Data and Operational Data for a Deep Business Process Analysis. In: Enterprise Interoperability III, Part II, pp. 171–182. Springer, London (2008) ISBN 978-1-848000-220-3

20. ProDatO Integration Technology GmbH: Handbuch iPM Integrated Process Manager. Softwaredocumentation (in German), Erlangen, Germany (2005),
http://www.prodato.de

21. Jablonski, S., Bussler, C.: Workflow Management – Modeling Concepts, Architecture and Implementation. Int. Thomson Computer Press, London (1996)

22. Mylopoulos, J., Chung, L., Yu, E.: From Object-Oriented to Goal-Oriented Requirements Analysis. Communications of the ACM (January 1999)

23. Jhon, K.: Extended Enterprise Modeling Language. [Report]. - [s.l.] Norwegian Unviersity of Science and Technology, EEML 2005 (2005)

24. User Requirements Notation (URN), http://www.usecasemaps.org

25. Faerber, M., Meerkamm, S., Jablonski, S.: The ProcessNavigator – Flexible Process Execution for Product Development Projects. In: International Conference on Engineering Design (ICED 2009), Standford (CA), USA, August 24-27 (2009)

26. Business Process Execution Language (BPEL), http://www.bpelsource.com

27. Kohinoor Weaving Mills Limited, http://www.kohinoorweaving.com

28. zur Muehlen, M.: Workflow-based Process Controlling: Foundation, Design, and Implementation of Workflow-driven Process Information Systems. Logos, Berlin (2004)

Measuring the Understandability of Business Process Models - Are We Asking the Right Questions?

Ralf Laue[1] and Andreas Gadatsch[2]

[1] Chair of Applied Telematics / e-Business
Computer Science Faculty, University of Leipzig, Germany
laue@ebus.informatik.uni-leipzig.de
[2] Bonn-Rhine-Sieg University of Applied Sciences, Germany
andreas.gadatsch@fh-bonn-rhein-sieg.de

Abstract. In this paper, we show how experiments on the understandability of business process models can depend on the exact wording used in the experiments' questionnaires. For this purpose, we partially replicated a published experiment. We asked a group of students a number of questions on relations between tasks in a business process model. Alternatively, we used a set of modified questions which were aimed to ask for exactly the same relations. The result was that there was a significant difference in the number of correct answers between the two systems to construct a question. We argue that a non-negligible part of the wrong answers given in the experiment did not result from problems to understand the model, but rather from problems to understand the question. It follows that it is dangerous to draw conclusions from such an experiment until enough effort has been taken to select appropriate questions.

1 Introduction

Understandability of a model is regarded as an important quality criterion [1–3]. This quality criterion becomes even more important if the purpose of the model is to be used in the area of business process design, where the aim of the model is to develop a collective understanding of business processes and to support the discussion between domain experts and process analysts.

In the past years, several authors have published studies on different aspects of the understandability of business process models (BPM). A common experimental setup for such studies is to ask the participants of an experiment questions on the content of one or more models.

Up to now, there are no accepted guidelines on how to construct such questions on BPM understandability. A survey of the related literature leads to the conclusion that often understandability questions are constructed in a rather non-systematic way. Most of the papers describing the experiments do not attach much importance to the selection of the questions.

This way, the research on BPM understandability does not yet reach the high standard that has been achieved in other research areas that deal with

M. zur Muehlen and J. Su (Eds.): BPM 2010 Workshops, LNBIP 66, pp. 37–48, 2011.

questionnaires (for example psychology). It is known from literature on constructing surveys in social sciences [4] that details like the order of questions and the exact wording in a question can have a significant influence on the results of a study.

In this paper, we discuss the great influence that the questions about the models in BPM understandability experiments can have on the results of the experiment and hence on the quality of the experimental results.

The classical criteria for the quality of an experiment are objectivity, reliability and validity (see e.g. [5]). **Objectivity** addresses the question whether the experiment is independent of the persons involved in conducting the experiment and independent of the analysis of the experimental results. **Reliability** determines whether the results can be regarded as consistent over time. This definition is strongly connected with the requirement that an experiment should be replicable. **Validity** concerns the question whether a measurement in an experiment truly measures the concept it is intended to measure.

In this paper, we will discuss the point that current experiments on BPM understandability often do not meet the criterion of validity. We will discuss the question to what extent a questionnaire on properties of a given process model actually measures "model comprehensibility".

In Sect. 2, we will provide a survey on empirical research on BPM understandability. For the purpose of our paper, we replicated a part of a published experiment. The questions that have been used in this experiment are discussed in Sect. 3. In Sect. 4, we introduce an alternative set of questions. The answers given for both systems of questions are presented in Sect. 5 and discussed in Sect. 6. In Sect. 7, we conclude by discussing some guidelines on how to select questions for measuring model understandability.

2 Published Work on Measuring BPM Understandability

In the published work on measuring the difficulty to understand a BPM, we find three different methods to measure model understandability:

At first, some authors (for example [6]) ask the participants of their study to rank the perceived difficulty/complexity of a BPM. Second, in some experiments (for example [7]), the participants actually have to work with the model, for example by making changes.

The focus of this article lies on a third type of measuring method where participants of an experiment have to answer questions on a BPM. The papers that follow such a measuring approach are summarized in Tab. 1. The column "Questions available?" refers to the availability of the full set of questions used in experiment - either as a part of the paper or as additional material published elsewhere.

The extent to which the selection of questions is discussed varies between the papers mentioned in Tab. 1. [14] refers to cognitive theories about learning [17] in order to explain why counting the percentage of correct answers to questions about the model can be regarded as a valid measure for understandability. However, there is little discussion about the question *which* questions are appropriate

Table 1. Empirical Work on Complexity and Understandability of BPM

Paper	Questions available?	Type of Questions
Rolón et al. [8]	yes	questions on order between activities and possibility to execute activities in parallel
Sarshar et al. [9]	yes	8 questions on nodes that have to be executed directly before/after another node is executed; 2 questions on properties of all possible executions
García et al. [10]	no	uncategorized yes/no-questions on the model
Lara Proano [11]	yes	categorized questions on concurrency, exclusiveness, recurrence and reachability
Reijers and Mendling [12]	no	model-specific questions, validated by the original creators of the models who confirmed that the questions were a proper way to test the understanding of the models
Mendling et al. [13]	no	8 questions on order, concurrency, exclusiveness and repetition of tasks
Recker and Dreiling [14]	no	multiple-choice questions where participants were asked to recall basic features of the BPM, no further details have been published
Mendling and Strembeck [15]	no	8 questions on order, concurrency, exclusiveness and repetition of tasks
Vanderfeesten et al. [16]	no	8 questions on order, concurrency, exclusiveness and repetition of tasks
Rittgen [3]	no	6 questions per model, two example questions were given in the paper

to find out how good a model has been understood: In [8], [9], [10], [14] and [3], no rationale for the selection of questions is given.

[13] explains very shortly that the questions aim to test the understanding of the four properties order, concurrency, exclusiveness and repetition of tasks. Two example questions are given in full text.

More information about the types of questions used in the experiment are provided in [11]. In [11], the questions are grouped into questions related to concurrency (*Can task A and task B be executed in parallel?*), exclusiveness (*Can task A and task B both be executed for the same execution of the model?*), recurrence (*Can task A be executed more than once?*) and reachability (*Can/must task A be executed before/after execution of task B?*).

Reijers and Mendling [12] are the only authors among those mentioned in Tab. 1 who spent a remarkable effort to justify the suitability of the questions used in their experiment. Their questions have been validated by the original creators of the models who confirmed that the questions were a proper way to test the understanding of the models. Furthermore, Reijers and Mendling ran a pre-test in order to test whether their questions give raise to misunderstandings.

Against this background, Melcher and Seese [18, 19] criticize the current state-of-the-art in generating understandability questions. In particular, they analyze the questions asked in [13, 15, 16], for which they come to the conclusion that "the small number of asked questions and the non-systematic selection of these questions could cause that only especially easy or difficult process parts are examined by the questions." In [20], Melcher et al. discuss the challenge to raise the quality of experiments for measuring BPM understandability. They investigate the hypothesis that different aspects of structural process understandability have to be considered by asking different types of questions. Also, the authors attempt to find out how many questions should be asked in order to come to a reliable statement about the difficulty to understand a given aspect of interrelationship between tasks in a BPM. They make the claim that "the asked questions should be selected at random as to minimize the risk of choosing particularly easy or difficult questions."

Melcher et al. [20] can take credit for the first discussion of the number and types of understandability questions that should be asked in BPM understandability experiments. This discussion is related to the quality criterion of *Reliability* (see Sec. 1).

However, another issue which is related to the quality criterion of *Validity* has not been addressed – the understandability of the questionnaire items (i.e. the questions that aim to measure understandability). This is an important issue, because a failure to answer a question about a BPM can stem from difficulties in understanding the model or from difficulties in understanding the question.

In this paper, we will show that neglecting this aspect in the setting of an experiment can make the whole experiment worthless. For this purpose, we will replicate a part of a published experiment using two alternative sets of questions. At first, in the following section we will recapitulate the original questions that have been used in the original experiment.

3   Understandability Questions Used by Melcher et al.

3.1   Definitions

For the purpose of the experiment published in [20], the following definitions (which we quote literally from the original paper) have been made:

Definition 1 (Activity Period). *An activity period of task t is the period between a point in time when t becomes executable and the next point in time when the actual execution of t terminates.*

Definition 2 (Concurrency). *For the questions about task concurrency, the relations $c_{\not\parallel}$, $c_{\exists}$, $c_{\forall}$ with the following meanings are used:*

$(t_1, t_2) \in c_{\not\parallel} \Leftrightarrow$ There is no process instance for which the activity periods of tasks t_1 and t_2 overlap.

$(t_1, t_2) \in c_{\exists} \Leftrightarrow$ There is a process instance for which the activity periods of tasks t_1 and t_2 overlap at least once (Several executions of t_1 and t_2 per process instance are possible!). – But there also exists a process instance for which this does not hold.

$(t_1, t_2) \in c_{\forall} \Leftrightarrow$ For each process instance, the activity periods of tasks t_1 and t_2 overlap at least once.

Definition 3 (Exclusiveness). *For the questions about task exclusiveness, the relations $e_{\sharp}$, $e_{\exists}$, $e_{\forall}$ with the following meanings are used.*

$(t_1, t_2) \in e_{\sharp} \Leftrightarrow$ There is no process instance, for which tasks t_1 and t_2 are both executed.

$(t_1, t_2) \in e_{\exists} \Leftrightarrow$ There is a process instance, for which tasks t_1 and t_2 are both executed. - But there also exists a process instance for which this does not hold.

$(t_1, t_2) \in e_{\forall} \Leftrightarrow$ For each process instance, the tasks t_1 and t_2 are both executed.

Definition 4 (Order). *For the questions about task order, the relations $o_{\sharp}$, $o_{\exists}$, $o_{\forall}$ with the following meanings are used.*

$(t_1, t_2) \in o_{\sharp} \Leftrightarrow$ There is no process instance for which an activity period of task t_1 ends before an activity period of task t_2 starts.

$(t_1, t_2) \in o_{\exists} \Leftrightarrow$ There is a process instance for which an activity period of task t_1 ends before an activity period of task t_2 starts. - But there also exists a process instance for which this does not hold.

$(t_1, t_2) \in o_{\forall} \Leftrightarrow$ For each process instance, an activity period of task t_1 ends before an activity period of task t_2 starts.

Definition 5 (Repetition). *For the questions about task repetition, the relations $r_{=1}$, $r_?$, r_* and r_+ with the following meanings are used.*

$t \in r_{=1} \Leftrightarrow$ For each process instance, task t is executed exactly once.

$t \in r_? \Leftrightarrow$ For each process instance, task t is executed not once or exactly once. Both cases really occur.

$t \in r_* \Leftrightarrow$ For each process instance, task t is executed not once, exactly once or more than once. There exists a process instance for which t is executed not once and another one for which t is executed more than once.

$t \in r_+ \Leftrightarrow$ For each process instance, task t is executed at least once. There exists a process instance for which t is executed more than once.

3.2   Experimental Setting

The participants of the experiment described in [20] was given the model shown in Fig. 1. It uses a notation which is similar to Event-Driven Process Chains: AND-splits and -joins (used to model parallel execution) are depicted as $\wedge$. XOR-splits and -joins (used to model an exclusive choice) are depicted as $\otimes$.

The questions asked had to be answered in accordance to the above definitions. For example, for answering the *Order* relationship between tasks F and G, the participants had to chose exactly one of the following answers (alternatively, they also had the possibility to skip the question):

(a) There is no process instance for which an activity period of task F ends before an activity period of task G starts.
(b) There is a process instance for which an activity period of task F ends before an activity period of task G starts. - But there also exists a process instance for which this does not hold.
(c) For each process instance, an activity period of task F ends before an activity period of task G starts.

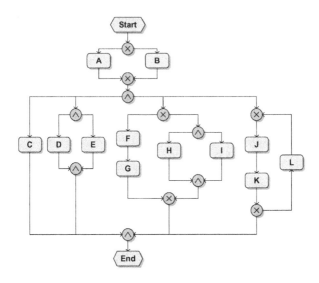

Fig. 1. Model used for the experiment in [20]

3.3   Problems Observed with Answering the Questions

The above question about the *Order* relationship between tasks F and G was the question for which the largest number of wrong answers was given in [20]: Only 6% of the participants gave the correct answer. The large number of wrong answers is not surprising: The focus of the question lies on the order between F and G, and it is very easy to see that F precedes G. (c) seems to be the obvious answer. However, the intended answer was (b), because due to the XOR-split it can happen that F and G are not processed at all. It seems to be reasonable to argue that such a question does not really ask for the *Order* relationship between tasks F and G but rather for the *Repetition* property of F and G.

Similarly, the question about the *Concurrency* relationship between tasks H and I has been answered correctly by only 39% of the participants. Because H and I are located directly after the AND-split, the obvious answer seems to be that the activity periods always overlap. However, the intended answer was that there are also process instances for which this is not the case, namely those for which the AND-control block with H and I is not executed (and there is no activity period for H and I).

Both questions described above have in common that it seems as the failure to answer the question does not result from difficulties in understanding the model but rather from difficulties in *understanding the question.*

Ultimately, the purpose of experiments on BPM understandability can be nothing else than to come to a hypothesis on how such models can be understood by those people who actually work with them. However, it is not reasonable to assume that those people care about subtle details like the difference between "a task becoming executable" and "a task actually being executed" in Def. 1.

In practice, a question like "Can it happen that D and J are executed at the same time?" would be relevant. Of course, the answer is "Yes – it can happen, although it does not have to happen", because business process notations like EPC and BPMN do not include information about the actual start and end time of a task. From a practical point of view, the question whether E and K can be executed at the same time should be answered in the same way as the above question on D and J. However, in the experiment described in [20], the intended answer was that the activity periods of D and J always overlap (because the tasks "become executable"), but the activity periods of E and K can overlap (but do not have to). While the first question was answered correctly by 80% of the participants, the second one was answered correctly by 70% of the participants. Once again, it is reasonable to suppose that the reason for the larger percentage of wrong answers comes from difficulties to understand the question instead of difficulties to understand the model.

4   An Alternative Set of Questions

In order to research to which extent the questions can have an influence on the correctness of the answers, we developed an alternative set of questions. These questions deal with the same aspects *Concurrency*, *Exclusiveness* and *Order*. We did not develop alternative questions for the aspect *Repetition*, because the questions on this aspect in [20] did not give rise to misunderstandings in such a way the other questions did.

The wording of our questions is aimed to be in agreement with the informal understanding of those aspects. As it was the case with the questions described in the previous sections, our questions can be represented in a way that one out of two or three possible alternatives has to be selected.

Our questions on *Concurrency* have the form:
"The execution times of task t_1 and task t_2 can overlap"
(a) right, (b) wrong
Our questions on *Exclusiveness* have the form:
(a) In each process instance for which task t_1 is executed, task t_2 will always be executed as well at some point of time.
(b) If t_1 is executed for a process instance, task t_2 will never be executed as well in this process instance.
(c) If t_1 is executed for a process instance, it can happen that task t_2 will be executed as well, but it can also happen that t_2 will not be executed.
Our questions on *Order* have the form:
"When the execution of task t_1 begins, it is always guaranteed that the execution of tasks t_2 (if t_2 has been executed at all) has already been finished."
(a) right, (b) wrong

Additionally, we added two new types of questions that deal with the logical dependency between two tasks which is not yet fully reflected by the questions on *Order*. The first type of questions deals with the "forward dependency" (called *Response* in the catalog of specification patterns by Dwyer at al. [21]):

"If task t_1 is executed, task t_2 will always be executed as well later."
(a) right, (b) wrong

The second type of questions deals with the "backward dependency" (called *Precedence* in [21]):

"If task t_1 is executed, task t_2 must always have been executed before."
(a) right, (b) wrong

As it can be seen from the questions above, we avoid the misunderstandings that could happen with the questions discussed in Sect. 3.

5   Experimental Evaluation

To partially replicate the experiment described in [20], we used the same BPM (Fig. 1) that has been used in the original study. The model was given to 22 business administration students at the Bonn-Rhine-Sieg University of Applied Sciences. The students took a course on business process modeling and were familiar with the basics of reading a BPM. Each student had to answer 118 questions on the model, i.e. we have collected 2596 answers in total.

The pairs of tasks that occur in our questions have not been selected at random. Instead, we selected those pairs of tasks for which the most wrong answers have been given in [20].

For describing the design of our questionnaire, we refer to the questions from [20] (see Sect. 3) as Style 1-questions and to our alternative set of questions (see Sect. 4) as Style 2-questions.

The students have been arranged into two groups. The order of the items in the questionnaires was different for both groups in order to eliminate order and learning effects:

Questions for group A:
- 15 *Order* questions (Style 1)
- 8 *Exclusivity* questions (Style 2)
- 15 *Order* questions (Style 2)
- 11 *Concurrency* questions (Style 2)
- 8 *Exclusivity* questions (Style 1)
- 11 *Concurrency* questions (Style 1)
- 6 *Response* questions
- 6 *Precedence* questions

Questions for group B:
- 15 *Order* questions (Style 2)
- 8 *Exclusivity* questions (Style 1)
- 15 *Order* questions (Style 1)
- 11 *Concurrency* questions (Style 1)
- 8 *Exclusivity* questions (Style 2)
- 11 *Concurrency* questions (Style 2)
- 6 *Response* questions
- 6 *Precedence* questions

The questions on Concurrency, Exclusivity and Order have been arranged such that if group A had to answer a Style 1-question for a pair of tasks, group B had to answer the corresponding Style 2-question for the same pair of tasks and vice versa. The results of our experiment are shown in Tab. 2

In addition to the answers documented in Tab. 2, 75% of the answers to the Style-2 questions on Response and 85% of the answers to the Style-2 questions on Precedence were correct. Both have no direct counterpart in the catalog of Style-1 questions but are very similar to the questions on *Order*.

The numbers of correct and wrong answers to the questions on Order, Exclusivity, and Response are summarized in the contingency table Tab. 3.

Table 2. Numbers of questions answered correctly

Aspect	Style 1 Questions	Style 2 Questions
Concurrency	59%	72%
Exclusivity	80%	79%
Order	39%	90%
Average	55%	76%

Table 3. Contingency Table

	Style 1	Style 2
correct answers	414	628
wrong answers	334	120

Pearson's χ^2-test shows that the differences between Style-1 answers and Style-2 answers are significant at a level of significance of $1/1000$.

6   Discussion

The results of our experiment give raise to the assumption that a reasonable part of the wrong answers to the *Concurrency* and *Order* questions in the original experiment resulted from problems to understand the questions, i.e. the original experiment can be criticized as not fulfilling the quality criterion of *Validity*. The result highlights the importance of a careful examination of the questions in BPM understandability experiments.

The selection of questions (selecting those questions for which the most wrong answers have been given in [20]) can be criticized as a problem in our experimental design. One can expect that those Style 1 questions are the most difficult to answer. In the same way, for the Style 2 questions other pairs of tasks might exist for which the Style 2 questions can become more difficult to answer. However, it is not the purpose of our paper to test a hypothesis like "Style 2 questions are easier to answer than Style 1 questions." What we want to prove is to which extent the exact wording of the questions influences the number of correct answers, without giving preferences to any style.

In the same way, it is possible to argue that the larger percentage of correct answers in the Style-2 questions mainly stems from the fact that for *Order* and *Concurrency* we provided only two instead of three alternative answers. Once again, we stress that we do not want to compare the question systems. The main purpose of this paper is to demonstrate to which extent the measuring of BPM understandability can be influenced by the experimental setup.

To illustrate this point, let's assume that we want to test the hypothesis "XOR-control blocks are more difficult to understand than AND-control blocks". An experiment could be designed in the following way:

One group of participants has to answer questions on the model shown in Fig. 1. Another group has to answer questions on another model which is Fig. 1 modified such that the XOR-control block containing task A and task B has been replaced by an AND-control block with the same tasks. By using Style 1-questions, it is not unlikely that the hypothesis will be confirmed. As discussed in Sect. 3.3, the presence of the XOR-block will lead to wrong answers about the Order aspect when one of the tasks A or B is involved. For example, the obvious answer for the Order relation between A and C seems to be $o_\forall$, while the intended answer would be o_3. However, by using Style 2-questions, the hypothesis will most likely not be confirmed, i.e. by modifying the questions we would come to the opposite conclusion about our research hypothesis.

The example shows that modifying the wording of a question can have a critical impact on the results of the study. This is even more true if we take into account the small number of questionnaire items used in published BPM understandability experiments (which is itself already a threat to validity). For example, Sarshar et al. [9] asked only *four* questions on OR-splits/joins in *only one* model in order to confirm their hypothesis "OR-connectors were significantly less comprehended than AND-connectors and XOR-connectors".

7   Conclusion

The main purpose of this paper was to create awareness on the difficulties that can arise from taking not enough care to select the questions for understandability experiments. Discussing the guidelines for creating such experiments is out of the scope of our paper. The interested reader can find a lot of excellent information on this topic in general books about survey design [4, 22, 23]. Guidelines for the evaluation of model comprehensibility can be found at [24] and [25].

However, we do not want to conclude without mentioning the main consequences that should be drawn from the discussion in this paper:

1. **Make every effort that your questions are easy to understand**
    In particular, we have to keep in mind which aspects are really relevant for the understandability of a BPM in practice. Technical terms like "activation period" that require the knowledge of additional definitions should be avoided. In a business environment, BPM have to be understood in a rather ad-hoc way without referring to formal definitions.
2. **Pre-test the questionnaire**
    Before starting an experiment, the questionnaire should be tested with a small number of participants. If possible, these persons should belong to the same group of persons that will be included in the experiment. This step can help to realize which difficulties in understanding a question can arise.
3. **Select an appropriate number of questions**
    Surprisingly, none of the papers shown in Tab. 1 discusses how many questions should be asked in order to measure BPM understandability in a suitable way. It seems that time restrictions were the dominant force that led to questionnaires with as few as 6 questions. However, it is crucial to make sure that the number and the types of questions are large enough to ensure that the result will be meaningful, i.e. in order to guarantee that the experimental setup meets the quality criterion of *Reliability*. Suggestions on selecting an appropriate number of questions can be found in [20].
4. **Select the questions in accordance with your research hypothesis**
    The general recommendation (given in [20]) that the understandability questions should be generated at random does not have to apply for all experiments. Instead, the questions should be generated with respect to the

research hypothesis. This is a direct conclusion from the quality criterion *Validity*. A good example is described in [12] where the effect of modularity on the understandability to a BPM has been examined. It turned out that there were two types of questions in the experiment: local questions for which the answer could be found within a single subprocess of a modular BPM and global questions for which this was not the case. A good balance between local and global questions was important for getting a meaningful result in a paper that deals with modularity. Such dependencies should be taken into account in order to make the experiment valid.

We are convinced that by adhering to the three principles "ask understandable questions, ask enough questions, ask the right questions", it will be possible to raise the standard of future experiments on BPM understandability.

Acknowledgement

We would like to thank Joachim Melcher, one of the authors of [20], for providing details about the experimental setup. Also, we thank Kathrin Figl for her valueable comments on a previous version of this paper.

References

1. Lindland, O.I., Sindre, G., Sølvberg, A.: Understanding quality in conceptual modeling. IEEE Softw. 11, 42–49 (1994)
2. Becker, J., Rosemann, M., Uthmann, C.v.: Guidelines of business process modeling. In: Business Process Management, Models, Techniques, and Empirical Studies, pp. 30–49. Springer, London (2000)
3. Rittgen, P.: Quality and perceived usefulness of process models. In: SAC 2010: Proceedings of the 2010 ACM Symposium on Applied Computing, pp. 65–72. ACM, New York (2010)
4. Schuman, H., Presser, S.: Questions and Answers in Attitude Surveys. Academic Press, San Diego (1981)
5. Carmines, E., Zeller, R.: Reliability and Validity Assessment. Sage Univ. papers, Thousand Oaks (1979)
6. Cardoso, J.: Process control-flow complexity metric: An empirical validation. In: IEEE International Conference on Services Computing, pp. 167–173 (2006)
7. Holschke, O., Rake, J., Levina, O.: Granularity as a cognitive factor in the effectiveness of business process model reuse. In: Dayal, U., Eder, J., Koehler, J., Reijers, H.A. (eds.) BPM 2009. LNCS, vol. 5701, pp. 245–260. Springer, Heidelberg (2009)
8. Aguilar, E.R., Sanchez, L., Carballeira, F.G., Ruiz, F., Piattini, M., Caivano, D., Visaggio, G.: Prediction models for BPMN usability and maintainability. In: 2009 IEEE Conference on Commerce and Enterprise Computing, pp. 383–390 (2009)
9. Sarshar, K., Loos, P.: Comparing the control-flow of EPC and petri net from the end-user perspective. In: van der Aalst, W.M.P., Benatallah, B., Casati, F., Curbera, F. (eds.) BPM 2005. LNCS, vol. 3649, pp. 434–439. Springer, Heidelberg (2005)

10. Canfora, G., García, F., Piattini, M., Ruiz, F., Visaggio, C.A.: A family of experiments to validate metrics for software process models. J. Syst. Softw. 77, 113–129 (2005)
11. Lara Proano, M.D.: Visual layout for drawing understandable process models. Master's thesis, Technische Universiteit Eindhoven (2008)
12. Reijers, H., Mendling, J.: Modularity in process models: Review and effects. In: Dumas, M., Reichert, M., Shan, M.-C. (eds.) BPM 2008. LNCS, vol. 5240, pp. 20–35. Springer, Heidelberg (2008)
13. Mendling, J., Reijers, H.A., Cardoso, J.: What makes process models understandable? In: Alonso, G., Dadam, P., Rosemann, M. (eds.) BPM 2007. LNCS, vol. 4714, pp. 48–63. Springer, Heidelberg (2007)
14. Recker, J., Dreiling, A.: Does it matter which process modelling language we teach or use? In: 18th Australasian Conference on Information Systems (2007)
15. Mendling, J., Strembeck, M.: Influence factors of understanding business process models. In: 11th International Conference, Business Information Systems, BIS 2008, Innsbruck, Austria, pp. 142–153. Springer, Heidelberg (2008)
16. Vanderfeesten, I.T.P., Reijers, H.A., Mendling, J., van der Aalst, W.M.P., Cardoso, J.: On a quest for good process models: The cross-connectivity metric. In: Bellahsène, Z., Léonard, M. (eds.) CAiSE 2008. LNCS, vol. 5074, pp. 480–494. Springer, Heidelberg (2008)
17. Mayer, R.: Models for understanding. Rev. of Educational Research 59, 43 (1989)
18. Melcher, J., Seese, D.: Process measurement: Insights from software measurement on measuring process complexity, quality and performance. Technical report, Universität Karlsruhe, TH (2008)
19. Melcher, J., Seese, D.: Towards validating prediction systems for process understandability: Measuring process understandability. In: 10th International Symposium on Symbolic and Numeric Algorithms for Scientific Computing, pp. 564–571. IEEE Computer Society, Los Alamitos (2008)
20. Melcher, J., Mendling, J., Reijers, H.A., Seese, D.: On measuring the understandability of process models. In: Revised Papers of the BPM 2009 International Workshops. LNBIP, vol. 43, pp. 465–476. Springer, Ulm (2010)
21. Dwyer, M.B., Avrunin, G.S., Corbett, J.C.: Patterns in property specifications for finite-state verification. In: Proc. of the 21st International Conference on Software Engineering, pp. 411–420. IEEE Computer Society Press, Los Alamitos (1999)
22. Sudman, S., Bradburn, N.M.: Asking Questions: A Practical Guide to Questionnaire Design. Jossey-Bass, San Francisco (1982)
23. Converse, J.M., Presser, S.: Survey Questions: Handcrafting the Standardized Questionnaire. Sage Publications, Thousand Oaks (1986)
24. Aranda, J., Ernst, N., Horkoff, J., Easterbrook, S.M.: A framework for empirical evaluation of model comprehensibility. In: International Workshop on Modeling in Software Engineering, MiSE 2007 (2007)
25. Patig, S.: A practical guide to testing the understandability of notations. In: Fifth Asia-Pacific Conference on Conceptual Modelling (APCCM 2008). CRPIT, vol. 79, pp. 49–58. Australian Computer Society (2008)

What You See And Do Is What You Get: A Human-Centric Design Approach to Human-Centric Process

Gal Shachor, Yoav Rubin, Nili Guy (Ifergan), Yael Dubinsky, Maya Barnea,
Samuel Kallner, and Ariel Landau

IBM Research – Haifa
Mount Carmel, Haifa 31905
{shachor,yoav,ifergan,dubinsky,mayab,kallner,ariel}@il.ibm.com

Abstract. Designing human-centric processes is complex. It involves the definition of interactions between humans and machines, interactions between machines and machines, information transfer, and scenarios based on decisions taken by both humans and machines. Traditionally, designing such processes is performed by design experts who define the processes in a way that mimics a bird's eye view of it, usually expressed by a graph composed of nodes and arrows. In this work, we suggest a design approach based on the way that a process is perceived by the users who participate in it. We present a novel approach termed "What You See And Do Is What You Get" that enables defining an entire human-centric process with a lowered expertise entry bar for process designers. Further, we present a model-driven, web-based tool that realizes the presented design approach and enables fast development of applications that support human-centric processes.

Keywords: Human-centric process, process design, WYSIWYG, What You See And Do Is What You Get (WYSADIWYG).

1 Introduction

In an integration-driven, service-oriented architecture (SOA), process activities apply automated logic to data by invoking services to perform the various tasks of the process [30]. When humans play a role in such processes, process activities are provided to model the human tasks and provide a service interface to "invoke" the human actors [20] [22]. To an extent, many integration-driven processes aim to replace humans with computer systems.

Increasingly, however, businesses are employing more Human-Centric Processes (HCPs) [18]. We define the main goal of HCPs as facilitating the collaborative flow of work between humans. An HCP differs from the common service and/or integration oriented process in that it applies human judgment to information contained in data, documents, or surfaced via the user interface (UI). As such, the vast majority of activities in the HCP focuses on coordinating decision-making and other work done by humans. The activities in the process interact with human actors; presenting them with UIs (such as web forms), collecting the resulting information and decisions, and inviting the next human actor to participate in the business process.

M. zur Muehlen and J. Su (Eds.): BPM 2010 Workshops, LNBIP 66, pp. 49–60, 2011.

Clearly, HCPs also include activities that communicate with SOA-based services (very few processes are just integration, or just human-centric [27]), but these activities are not common since human actors perform the majority of decisions and work.

Workflows involving humans have unique characteristics, such as the tendency to revisit past activities [19]. In this work we focus on the design experience and development aspects of HCPs and illustrate some of their characteristics.

1.1 Traditional HCP Development

A typical, standards–based, business process management (BPM) environment takes a service-oriented design approach. In such an environment, HCPs are composed of the following main elements:

- Workflow model – orchestrates the execution of services. Traditionally, workflow models are executed using Business Process Execution Language (BPEL) [21] and are composed of activities that interact with services, which, in the case of HCP, are human interaction services.
- User interaction services – communicate with human actors by leveraging a human task service facade. These services are traditionally implemented using forms-based UI and are exposed to the process using the BPEL4People [20] and WS-Human Task [22] standards.
- Web Service Description Language (WSDL) [31] and XML schema-based service and data type definitions – instantiate process variables and communicate with services.

Traditionally, developers first design the workflow part of the HCP using a diagram-based workflow design tool that outputs a workflow execution language such as BPEL [24]. Then, a separate tool is used to construct the UI that will be exposed to the human actors. Lastly, the UI and the flow are integrated and tested.

1.2 Challenges

It is important to understand that the challenges that make developing service-oriented processes a time-consuming and error-prone task (e.g., service integration and transactional integrity) are considerably different from the challenges associated with developing HCPs.

Since most activities in an HCP simply interact with users, there is less emphasis on working with a large number of radically different services. Moreover, while for many integration processes a substantial effort is invested in codifying the business, integration, and compensation logic into the workflow, human-centric flows exhibit simpler patterns [19] since many of the decisions are driven by human judgment (Has the user approved? Rejected? Requested more information?). In fact, human-centric process can be modeled using radically fewer Business Process Model and Notation (BPMN) [32] activities [18]. As a result, most service integration challenges are of lesser importance for HCPs.

On the other hand, HCP developers need to address UI and human interaction related challenges. These challenges may vary; including addressing various usability concerns and human-oriented tuning [28], encoding presentation logic into the UI (e.g., role- and context-based presentation), adhering to branding and regulatory requirements (e.g., accessibility and language support), and digitally signing electronic documents in a legally acceptable manner and archiving those signings for later inspection. As a result of these challenges, developing an HCP involves a great deal of UI and UX focused effort to the point that this effort overshadows all other development tasks.

Last but not least, HCPs are much more prone to agility, even after the process is deployed. Since HCPs are very visible to business users, and in many cases greatly impact their productivity, there is greater exposure to change requests. Users are always on the lookout for better ways of getting things done; for example, requesting additional input fields in their UIs (that now need to be saved and propagated to other interfaces). It should be noted that while users often express their requests by pointing at the UI (the only part of the HCP that is exposed to the user), such changes need to propagate into the workflow, type systems, etc.

Clearly, there is a rebalance in HCP development between UI modeling and other development efforts that is not addressed today by conventional process design tools. In a similar vein, the need for agility, even when triggered from the UI, cuts through the various technologies and needs to be addressed. Specifically, the situation today where one wants to change the UI (e.g., by adding a button) and then drive this change all the way to the flow (e.g., by adding a branch) may require not just different tools, but different skills and developer roles.

In light of the above, we propose a novel, integrated approach for HCP design that leverages the concept of "What You See Is What You Get" (WYSIWYG) to greatly reduce the effort in constructing HCPs and link the design of the user interface with that of the process. Based on this approach, we developed a model-driven, web-based tool that targets the usage and support of ad-hoc tasks with matching workflow applications to easily create fully fledged business processes. The tool, named Freedom, targets process designers, without any prior assumptions regarding their development skills (thus including end users), and lets them quickly develop ad-hoc HCPs in a fraction of the time it takes to develop an HCP with traditional tooling.

The paper is structured as follows. In Sections 2 and 3 we present our design approach and the tool that actualizes it, respectively. In Section 4 we relate to existing work, and in Section 5 we conclude.

2   Design Approach

It is well understood that the gap between the mental model of a development environment designer and the mental model of that environment's user has a major effect on the way that the usage experience of that environment is perceived by the environment's user (such an effect may be reflected by the affordance of various design actions). In the interplay between the designer and the user, the environment designer's key task is to minimize this gap, while it is up to the environment user to bridge the remaining gap, if any, between the previously described mental models.

When the created artifact is a business process, the gap, as it is found today in the state-of-the-art technologies, is still often unbridgeable by non-expert users, as none of these technologies seems to be widely adopted by less technically savvy people.

In this spirit, we have designed and implemented a business process design environment that follows the "What You See Is What You Get" (WYSIWYG) concept and extends it beyond static visual design and layout, all the way to capturing the dynamic changes of a process, and allowing the classic WYSIWYG concept to evolve to the novel design concept of "What You See *And Do* Is What You Get" (WYS*ADI*WYG).

Providing a WYSADIWYG development environment that produces an HCP and targets less skilled users requires delivering novel solutions to a set of already answered design issues. Obviously, the main issue is how to design the process. Whilst traditional HCP design is done via a bird's eye view of the process, the WYSADIWYG approach focuses on how the process is perceived by the process user. This radical shift of design focus can be thought of as the essence of the WYSADIWYG design approach. Still, it is up to the design environment to ultimately derive a process, and this is achieved by requesting the process designer to provide answers to the question of "What happens now?" in specific places during the interaction of the process user with the process. These questions allow the environment to build a process, behind the scenes.

The process design environment presents questions to the process designer by implicitly expecting her to walk through the process, as would be done eventually by the process user. At any stage where there is a possibility for the system to perform an action, the process designer is presented with an appropriate UI tool (such as dialog or property configuration panel) that represents the "What happens now?" question.

To provide such a design experience, the process itself is built of a set of interconnected phases. Each phase displays a WYSIWYG UI component to the process user. In our implementation, this UI component is a web form, and a phase change is invoked by clicking one of the Submit buttons that are part of the form.

Following on from the definition above, we recognize two main situations in which there is a control transfer. These situations are *Phase-Entry*, which occurs upon entering a phase; and *Phase-Exit*, which occurs upon leaving a phase. For each such control transfer, an ad hoc UI metaphor that simulates this situation is created to provide the process designer with a WYSADIWYG-based design environment (enacted by the process user clicking the Submit button or displaying the web form).

A Phase-Entry situation is when control shifts from the system to the process user. This is done by displaying the form and making it available for the process user to use. The process designer needs to configure how each form field can be used by the process user when the form is displayed. Ultimately, the process designer defines this via a minimal number of clicks in the field properties, as shown in Figure 1A. Each field can be configured as visible or hidden, and if visible, whether it is editable or not. These settings are presented to the process designer immediately, as shown in Figure 1B (from top to bottom, the fields are visible and editable, visible and non-editable – grayed out, hidden).

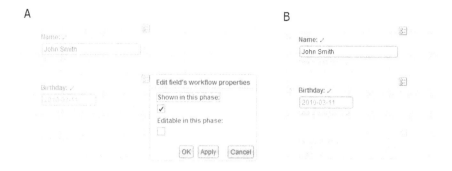

Fig. 1. Phase-Entry configuration for a specific field

A Phase-Exit situation is when control shifts back from the process user to the system, and it is up to the process designer to configure the system's reaction. The first thing to configure for the Phase-Exit situation is whether to display a message to the process user or to redirect to another web page. The second possible configuration is to define for the system a set of services and actions to run through, such as sending e-mail notifications, performing various logging and auditing operations, or invoking an available program or service. The process designer is able to orchestrate the behavior of the system upon leaving the phase by selecting which steps are taken and configuring each such step. Figure 2 reflects the configuration for a Submit button in a specific phase.

Fig. 2. Phase-Exit properties pane

From the process designer's point of view, exiting a phase is initiated when the process user submits the form by clicking one of its action buttons. Therefore, when the process designer clicks such a button (and the set of buttons can be managed as part of the design of the form), the design environment is updated and presents the process designer with all she needs to configure what happens in this situation, as well as connecting to the next phase (even creating it if it does not exist).

The set of phases is presented to the process designer at any given point, and she can toggle between the different phases and view how each phase is perceived by the human actor by presenting the relevant web form. When the process designer selects an action button in a form, all the activities that will be invoked when the process user clicks this button are presented too.

3   Freedom – An Exemplary Tool

Freedom is a model-driven, web-based, WYSADIWYG development environment that is optimized for users without programming and application development as part of their skill arsenal. This environment targets the usage and support of ad-hoc tasks with matching workflow applications to easily create fully fledged business processes.

3.1   Realizing WYSADIWYG

Freedom serves as an integrated development environment (IDE) that allows the development, consumption and execution of several interconnected tools. To this end, Freedom provides the following elements:

- A model definition and execution runtime platform. The model represents an information set that accepts the "no redundancy" policy that is required to construct situational enterprise applications with support for UI, human-centric workflow, service calls, scripting, and security. The various Freedom-based tools produce the model and use Freedom to actualize it as an application.
- Mechanisms to manage, define, consume and execute application templates. Application templates are developed by programmers and provide all the means required to design and generate an application that covers a single, yet broad, goal. Each application template is composed of a UI editor component that the user employs to develop the application, and an application generation component that emits a Freedom model.
- A web-based application development and management shell alongside a default WYSADIWYG tool for creating form-driven, database-dependent workflow applications.

3.2   Forms: The Default Freedom WYSADIWYG Tool

Forms are central to HCPs. The human actors are required to complete their tasks by reviewing and submitting forms. Freedom bridges the gap between workflows, forms, and business users by providing a friendly, WYSADIWYG, form-driven, workflow development environment, as presented in Figure 3.

The portion of the UI that is visible to the user is focused on the goal; that is, the form and the workflow. There is no place where the user can define Submit buttons, data models, or mappings in a database. The user simply designs the fields on the set of forms that constitute the application from the user's point of view. It is the responsibility of the form editor and the Freedom shell to deduce the required details automatically.

Fig. 3. Form development and design UI

Figure 4 presents the workflow environment as realized by doubling down on WYSADIWYG and UI design. The transition between flow states is designed by determining the next phase for each button. The form look can be adjusted for each phase of the flow. Figure 4 presents the views visible to the developer creating a workflow, with a Start phase and an Approved phase. Each phase is described by a tab with a phase-adjusted form and thus enables maximal visualization of the flow as presented to the end user. Button properties determine the next phase, whether creating a new phase or choosing a pre-existing phase. Moreover, for each button, for each phase, the developer can select actions to be performed when moving to the next phase (e.g., the message to display, or who to notify on phase change).

Fig. 4. Workflow development and design UI

3.3 Evaluating Freedom

To evaluate our approach we conducted a face-to-face user experiment with seven participants who had no prior knowledge of business process creation.

After a five-minute introduction to the Freedom tool, the participants were asked to create a business process for the first few steps of the following scenario.

The scenario involves a user who wishes to set up a purchase-request system as part of her role in the organization. The system should allow the requestor to initiate a request to purchase an item. The request flows to various people in the organization for handling in the following order: the requestor's manager for approval, a finance department person for financial approval, and a purchasing person for supplier selection and ordering. When the item arrives, a person on the loading dock updates the item, stating it has been received. When the requestor has the item in hand she checks the item and verifies that indeed what was requested was received. Accordingly, the purchase request goes through seven states: Start, Requested, Mgmt-approved, finance-approved, Ordered, Received, and End. We note that the scenario is simplified to keep the focus on the workflow and its implementation using our approach and tool.

The steps were

1. Creating a purchase request
2. Asking for approval from the requester's manager
3. Upon manager's approval, requesting approval from finance
4. Upon approval from finance, creating the order

The participants were given fifteen minutes to complete the task. This was followed by a short questionnaire, which included statements relating to the simplicity of generating a workflow using Freedom.

The chosen experimental methodology was not comparative but focused on the design approach at hand due to the nature of the experiment and its goals. The experiment itself was designed to see whether the WYSADIWYG approach can open the BPM door for users with no prior knowledge of BPM. Hence, a comparative approach, which requires performing a similar task on state-of-the-art HCP BPM Suites (e.g., Lombardi [34], Questetra [33]), would require deep training of the participants, thus harming the experiment's precondition of "no prior knowledge of BPM".

In our experiment, all the participants were able to complete the task and produce a running workflow within fifteen minutes. Table 1 depicts the distribution of answers to three related questions over the seven participants. Overall, there was a strong agreement about the intuitiveness of creating a workflow and the simplicity of testing the workflow. A weaker yet consistent agreement was around the lack of complexity in transitioning between phases. These results and the fact that users with such profiles were able to complete the task within a very short time frame indicate that WYSADIWYG is a promising design approach for such HCP workflows.

Table 1. Post-experiment questionnaire results

		Strongly Disagree	Disagree	Agree	Strongly Agree
1.	Creating a workflow using Freedom is intuitive	0	0	1	6
2.	Describing a transition between phases is complex	0	7	0	0
3.	Testing the workflow is simple	0	0	0	7

4 Related Work

The need for improved design and runtime experience of user interaction in business process is reflected by recent work in this area. For example, standards bodies are busy defining the lower level runtime and language components for integrating HCP into service-oriented flows (e.g., BPEL4People and WS-HumanTask [20][22]); however, task execution, rendering, and definition of user interface elements are out of their scope. In [18], the authors describe two different patterns for inclusion of humans in a business process. Specifically, they conclude that many integration-driven processes even try to take the "Automator" approach and replace humans with computer systems. Increasingly, however, a "Facilitator" process emerges and facilitates the collaboration between humans. Next, the authors show how a BPMN diagram can change "Facilitator" processes significantly.

Several research efforts leverage existing BPM modeling techniques and supplement them with UI and task modeling. For example, in [9], the authors extend the standard process modeling language, BPMN, with DIAMODL [26], a dataflow-oriented visual modeling language, for task and UI modeling. A complementary effort in [11] teaches a model-driven approach to keep BPMN and DIAMODL synchronized so that separate tools can be used to model the various process aspects.

In [4], the authors extend BPEL with new activities that describe user involvement and interfaces. Unlike existing standards such as BPEL4People, the authors explicitly define how to integrate and render user interfaces by extending the BPEL specification and adding to it the ability to embed actual Xml User interface Language (XUL) [35] markup in it.

In [7], the authors introduce an integrated framework for process modeling process-oriented systems called Process with User interface and Data modeling Integration (PUDI). PUDI leverages Form-Oriented Analysis [5] for user interface modeling and the submit-response type of interaction, and Unified Modeling Language (UML) to supplement BPMN with data modeling. In PUDI, Form-Oriented artifacts are modeled using BPMN (e.g., formcharts).

Finally, in [14] and [15], the business process models are used to create low fidelity starting points or prototypes for the user interfaces to be used in the process.

In contrast to the above-mentioned research, the main contribution presented in this article is around a radically different development experience for human-centric interaction in BPM. As such, the specific workflow technology used for execution or modeling is of lesser importance.

Another interesting and important advancement that can be spotted is the increasing importance of processes in the situated software [13] domain that is driving a large number of unorthodox workflow definition approaches, which can be studied.

In [3], the authors teach architecture that allows business users to become more active participants in the composition of business process. Using the Collaborative Task Manager prototype, a process definition was embedded in the existing end users' working environment (groupware), and process models were inferred from the captured activities. In [16], the authors introduce the concept of "artful processes" as alternative to "formalized processes" for those cases where formalizing a process is too expensive or is simply not a viable approach due to the high rate of change and customization required per specific process instance. The authors then suggest the use of activity-based computing to better support business users who need to define and use those "artful processes".

A more recent effort we studied is app2you [1][2], where the researchers provide a hosted tool for the creation of Do-It-Yourself (DIY), customized, hosted, database-driven web applications. The general approach behind app2you is very similar to the one taken in Freedom: in general, app2you introduces the concept of page-centric design, where the user is presented with a web-based, WYSIWYG- and wizard-based development tool that allows visual creation of an application with very little attention to low-level details. The application's owner (who develops the application) builds the application's UI. The app2you design facility infers low-level details such as database tables and control logic. The owner can also introduce simple operations such as routing and construct rules that allow building a simple "in-application" process involving several users (essentially, the implicit process modeling with hypertext, discussed in [25]).

Freedom differs from app2you in several ways: to start with, Freedom allows more control over the process definition; specifically, one can implicitly model the state machine inside forms, connect to backend services, perform branches, etc. Another point of difference is around the use of WYSADIWYG, as opposed to WYSIWYG and wizards. We consider the use of WYSADIWYG essential to support users who are looking to create a complex workflow involving multiple approval steps, visibility rules, service access, and notifications, all without sacrificing usability.

5 Conclusion

In this work we present an intuitive approach for designing human-centric processes. Using this approach, we answer the need to provide a simple yet powerful method to develop HCPs, by focusing on the way that the process is perceived by the process user when she uses it. This was done by expanding the "What You See Is What You Get" concept to "What You See *And Do* Is What You Get" thus greatly reducing the effort in constructing HCPs and linking the design of the user interface with that of the process.

Furthermore, we have developed the Freedom tool based on that design approach, and verified that it does answer the requirement of elaborated simplicity without a loss of functionality. The Freedom tool itself is a model-driven, web-based tool that targets process designers without any prior assumptions regarding their development skills (thus including end users) and lets them quickly develop ad-hoc HCPs in a fraction of the time it takes to develop an HCP using traditional tooling.

In future work we intend to continue developing the Freedom tool to support more features, e.g., the ability to track HCPs along their timeline and organization goals. These features will be developed and evaluated based on a design approach that places the perspective of the process users at its center, while ensuring that the skills entry barrier for process designers is as low as possible.

Acknowledgements

We thank Anne Lustig-Picus for proof reading; Pablo Srabstein, Xiao Xi Liu, and Ksenya Kveler for their contributions in implementing the Freedom tool; and Asaf Adi for cooperating with us in developing the approach and the tool.

References

[1] Bhatia, G., Fu, Y., Kowalczykowski, K., Ong, K.W., Zhao, K.K., Deutsch, A., Papakonstantinou, Y.: FORWARD: Design Specification Techniques for Do-It-Yourself Application Platforms. In: WebDB 2009 (2009)

[2] Kowalczykowski, K., Ong, K.W., Zhao, K.K., Deutsch, A., Papakonstantinou, Y., Petropoulos, M.: Do-It-Yourself custom forms-driven workflow applications. In: CIDR 2009 (2009)

[3] Stoitsev, T., Scheidl, S., Flentge, F., Mühlhäuser, M.: From Personal Task Management to End-User Driven Business Process Modeling. In: Dumas, M., Reichert, M., Shan, M.-C. (eds.) BPM 2008. LNCS, vol. 5240, pp. 84–99. Springer, Heidelberg (2008)

[4] Lee, J., Lin, Y.-Y., Ma, S.-P., Wang, Y.-C., Lee, S.-J.: Integrating Service Composition Flow with User Interactions, sose. In: 2008 IEEE International Symposium on Service-Oriented System Engineering, pp. 103–108 (2008)

[5] Form-Oriented Analysis A New Methodology to Model Form-Based Applications. Dirk Draheim, Gerald Weber. Springer, Heidelberg (2005)

[6] Balbo, S., Draheim, D., Lutteroth, C., Weber, G.: Appropriateness of user interfaces to tasks. In: TAMODIA 2005, pp. 111–118 (2005)

[7] Auer, D., Geist, V., Draheim, D.: Extending BPMN with Submit/Response-Style User Interaction Modeling. In: CEC 2009, pp. 368–374 (2009)

[8] Blom, S., Book, M., Gruhn, V.: Executable Semantics of Recursively Nestable Dialog Flow Specifications for Web Applications. In: Schwabe, D., Curbera, F., Dantzig, P. (eds.) Proc. 8th Intl. Conference on Web Engineering (ICWE 2008), Yorktown Heights, NY, USA, July 14-18, pp. 135–147. IEEE Computer Society, Los Alamitos (2008)

[9] Trætteberg, H., Krogstie, J.: Enhancing the Usability of BPM-Solutions by Combining Process and User-Interface Modelling. In: PoEM 2008, pp. 86–97 (2008)

[10] Trætteberg, H.: UI Design without a Task Modeling Language - Using BPMN and Diamodl for Task Modeling and Dialog Design. In: TAMODIA/HCSE 2008, pp. 110–117 (2008)

[11] Dividino, R.Q., Bicer, V., Voigt, K., Cardoso, J.: Integrating business process and user interface models using a model-driven approach. In: ISCIS 2009, pp. 492–497 (2009)

[12] Boyer, J.M., Wiecha, C., Akolkar, R.P.: A REST protocol and composite format for interactive web documents. In: ACM Symposium on Document Engineering 2009, pp. 139–148 (2009)
[13] Situated Software: Concepts, Motivation, Technology, and the Future
[14] Sousa, K.S., Filho, H.M., Vanderdonckt, J., Rogier, E., Vandermeulen, J.: User interface derivation from business processes: a model-driven approach for organizational engineering. In: SAC 2008, pp. 553–560 (2008)
[15] Sukaviriya, N., Sinha, V., Ramachandra, T., Mani, S., Stolze, M.: User-Centered Design and Business Process Modeling: Cross Road in Rapid Prototyping Tools. INTERACT (1), 165–178 (2007)
[16] Hill, C., Yates, R., Jones, C., Kogan, S.L.: Beyond predictable workflows: Enhancing productivity in artful business processes. IBM Systems Journal 45(4), 663–682 (2006)
[17] Hollingsworth, D.: Workflow Management Coalition. The Workflow Reference Model (1994)
[18] Fischer, L. (ed.): BPM & Workflow Handbook, SPOTLIGHT ON HUMAN-CENTRIC BPM. Published in association with the Workflow Management Coalition, WfMC (2008)
[19] Takayama, Y., Ghiglione, E., Wilson, S., Dalziel, J.: Human Collaborative Workflow and Business Process and Services Computing, BPSC 2007, pp. 152–168 (2007)
[20] IBM, SAP: WS-BPEL Extension for People – BPEL4People. A Joint White Paper by IBM and SAP (2005), http://www-128.ibm.com/developerworks/webservices/library/specification/ws-bpel4people/
[21] Jordan, D., Evdemon, J., et al.: Web Services Business Process Execution Language Version 2.0, http://docs.oasis-open.org/wsbpel/2.0/wsbpel-v2.0.html
[22] Ings, D., et al.: Web Services – Human Task (WS-HumanTask) Specification Version 1.1, http://docs.oasis-open.org/bpel4people/ws-humantask-1.1.html
[23] The Forrester Wave[TM]: Human-Centric Business Process Management Suites, Q1 (2006)
[24] 2007 Human-Centric Business Process Management with WebSphere Process Server V6. IBM Corp. (2007)
[25] Brambilla, M., Ceri, S., Fraternali, P., Manolescu, I.: Process modeling in Web applications. ACM Trans. Softw. Eng. Methodol. 15(4), 360–409 (2006)
[26] Diamodl home page, http://www.idi.ntnu.no/~hal/research/diamodl
[27] Forester - The Importance of Matching BPM Tools to The Process, September 4 (2009), http://www.forrester.com/rb/Research/importance_of_matching_bpm_tools_to_process/q/id/55220/t/2
[28] A Human-Oriented Tuning of Workflow Management Systems
[29] Weske, M.: Business Process Management: Concepts, Languages, Architectures (2007)
[30] Zimmermann, O., Grundler, J., Tai, S., Leymann, F.: Architectural Decisions and Patterns for Transactional Workflows in SOA. In: Krämer, B.J., Lin, K.-J., Narasimhan, P. (eds.) ICSOC 2007. LNCS, vol. 4749, pp. 81–93. Springer, Heidelberg (2007)
[31] Christensen, E., Curbera, F., et al.: Web Services Description Language (2001), http://www.w3.org/TR/wsdl
[32] White, S.A., et al.: Business Process Model and Notation (2009), http://www.omg.org/spec/BPMN/1.2/PDF/
[33] Questetra, http://www.questetra.com/
[34] Lombardi, http://www.lombardisoftware.com/
[35] XML User Interface Language, https://developer.mozilla.org/En/XUL

An Exploratory Study of IT-Enabled Collaborative Process Modeling

Christopher Hahn[1], Jan Recker[2], and Jan Mendling[1]

[1] Humboldt University, Unter den Linden 6,
10099 Berlin, Germany
[2] Queensland University of Technology 126 Margaret Street,
Brisbane QLD 4000, Australia
hanchris@cms.hu-berlin.de, j.recker@qut.edu.au,
jan.mendling@wiwi.hu-berlin.de

Abstract. Process modeling is an important design practice in intra- as well as inter-organizational process improvement projects. Inter-organizational process modeling often requires collaboration support for distributed participants. We present the results of a preliminary exploratory of study of process modeling on basis of collaborative technology. We examine a group of process modelers that rely on a collaborative modeling editor to complete two process modeling tasks in distributed settings. We examine how the participants learn to appropriate the technology, the key phases and tasks of collaborative process modeling, the breakdowns encountered and workarounds employed by the participants. With our study, we provide a first understanding of the IT-enabled process of process modeling, and detail a set of guidelines and implications for the research and design of collaborative process modeling.

Keywords: process modeling, collaboration, distributed modeling, collaborative technology.

1 Introduction

Information Technology has enhanced many work practices within large and small organizations. Specifically, the introduction of collaborative technology has provided organizational staff with the opportunity to engage in remote forms of collaboration, first by email, then via attachments in email, chatting, from text to multimedia forms involving audio and video, and, recently, to fully collaborative virtual environments [1].

Collaborative technologies have found widespread use by analysts in decision making [2], requirements engineering [3] and even complex design work [4]. Following this work, our interest in this paper is to examine how collaborative technology can be applied to process modeling – the design of graphical blueprints of inter- or intra-organizational business process for the act of process performance measurement, organizational re-design or workflow automation.

Process modeling is typically performed using process modeling grammars [5], semi-formal notations that provide graphical elements to map out business processes

M. zur Muehlen and J. Su (Eds.): BPM 2010 Workshops, LNBIP 66, pp. 61–72, 2011.

in terms of the tasks that have to be performed, the actors that are involved in the execution of these tasks, relevant data and sources (papers, forms, systems and technology) of the data, and the business rule logic that describes the logical and temporal order in which tasks are to be performed [5]. While a variety of tools are available to create and analyze these models of business processes, studies and anecdotal evidence alike still report challenges in the process of process modeling, most notably in the phases of *eliciting* business process information from relevant stakeholders, and *formalizing* them in process model [6]. Some authors have argued that this challenge is due to a lack of support for the process of process modeling, i.e., support for the collaboration between business analysts and domain experts in the development of process models [7].

This challenge is exacerbated further in globalized setups of organizations and projects in which cross-organizational processes need to be designed. This is because in these contexts, required modeling stakeholders (e.g., analysts, project managers and domain experts) are often geographically dispersed and need to engage in the process modeling effort from remote locations. Yet, while such remote collaborative process modeling could, theoretically, benefit from collaborative technology as in use in other organizational tasks (e.g., project management [8]), to date, tool solutions have only recently begun to explore potential support features for collaborative process modeling [e.g., 9]. Still, the effect the emerging collaborative technology has on the process or outcome of process modeling is yet to be understood.

In this paper, therefore, we examine collaborative process modeling using a novel research prototype for collaborative process modeling on basis of the Google Wave technology (http://wave.google.com). Specifically, we examine in two settings how a group of process modelers working in a distributed setting are appropriating the collaborative process modeling technology, and how the process of collaborative process modeling is carried out.

The sections that follow first describe related work in the areas of process modeling, collaboration and collaborative technology. We then discuss the setup of our empirical study and how we collected and analyzed data. In section 4 we discuss the findings from our exploratory study. We discuss the emerging implications for research and technology design. Then, we conclude the paper with a review of contributions, limitations and an outlook to future work.

2   Related Work

2.1   The Process of Process Modeling

To be able to gauge the potential positive and negative consequences of collaborative technology on process modeling in distributed environments, an understanding of the process and product of process modeling is required first. In the context of this article we understand process modeling as an act of facilitating a shared understanding and to increase knowledge about a business process domain [10].

Several studies have examined the process of modeling in terms of its key phases or stages [7] and the main involved roles [11]. Specifically, it was found that process modeling often is not conducted in a linear fashion but is a rather repetitive and cyclic task that is going back and forth, thereby re-defining the problem, re-setting the borders or re-iterating and revising the artifact. Rittgen [12] has proposed a set of negotiation models to understand the patterns of human interactions in the process of process modeling. He [13] also studied differences in the final product (i.e., the model/ script) with collaborative tool support. Ssebuggwawo et al. [14] examined collaborative modeling by looking for rules, goals and interactions proposing the notion of Modeling Games. All of the above work used setups where participants were locally attendant and therefore be able to communicate directly.

We argue that the characteristics of collaboration (distributed participants around the globe) pose different requirements to the modeling process and its tool support. Furthermore the findings of recently mentioned work do not give implications for collaboration technology design.

2.2 Collaboration and Collaborative Technology

Collaboration and collaborative technology has already been applied and examined in related areas such as design or learning. For example, Susman et al. [15] synthesized and extended existing theories on the appropriation of collaborative technologies in new product development by "recognizing misalignments between technology, task, organization and the group." Marjanovic [16] validated an interactive methodology for learning and teaching in a synchronous electronic collaborative environment emphasizing the necessity of understanding collaborative processes in order to design better methodologies.

Our interest in this study is to look how collaborative technology can be used for process modeling and what effects are observable from this technology appropriation. We selected the research prototype *Gravity* as a possible collaboration technology. Gravity is a collaborative modeling editor on the basis of Google Wave. It enables to communicate (chatting) and to model in real time thereby largely supporting BPMN in its version 1.0, albeit some grammar constructs are missing, such as pools and swim lanes. Furthermore, it automatically keeps a history log that can be viewed later again and therefore supports data collection and analysis in a research setting.

3   Research Design

3.1 Study Overview

We decided not to offer a priori hypotheses and instead opted for an exploratory study design. Consequently, our objective was to observe the practices employed in the collaborative modeling environment without having expectations about the efficacy of such a setup (e.g., in terms of accuracy, efficiency or other criteria).

To be able to collect sufficient data whilst maintaining control over potentially confounding external factors, we selected a quasi-experimental design [17].

Our explorative study is structured with the help of the framework for evaluating conceptual modeling techniques (CMT) proposed by Gemino and Wand [18]. This framework is based on two main dimensions. The first dimension comprises factors that affect the conceptual modeling technique whereas the second consists of affected factors (i.e. outcomes).

The first affecting factor is *content to be delivered*, which refers to the type of information contained within the cases. We selected two cases to be modeled each describing a different domain, but both being described in a process-oriented way. The participants did not receive the complete description but instead only partial information, which each represented the knowledge of a specific role has in the process (domain experts, e.g., a clerk, an administrative office, a line manager). For example, our second case described a purchase order process in a company and the partial information given to one participant refers to the role of the requester. In total, all relevant information was given to the participants but it required them to communicate in order to assemble the case.

The second affecting factor, *presentation of content*, includes the following dimensions:

- The choice of grammar constructs to consider: We include all BPMN constructs that are available in the selected collaborative modeling technology (SAP Gravity).
- The nature of comparison (within or between grammars): Since this study does not aim to compare different grammars it denotes an intra-grammar comparison (always BPMN) [19].
- Rules regarding the use of the grammar and how it is applied: We do not change the grammar rules, instead all BPMN rules should be applied (if possible).
- The way the script is presented (text, graphics, narrated, animated, etc.): Each participant was distributed using Wave & Gravity for Collaboration support which offers textual representation (Google Wave) as well as graphical features (SAP Gravity).

The third affecting dimension describes the *characteristics of the persons participating in the communication*. Gemino and Wand [18] suggest to classify the participants´ experience with respect to conceptual modeling and domain knowledge. Our participants varied alongside both dimensions to be able to examine effects stemming from different levels of domain or modeling knowledge. Still, we did not capture explicitly the experience levels of the participants in this study, but we will in our overarching research project.

The last dimension to be considered is the task itself, which usually is either model creation ('writing') or model viewing ('interpretation'). In our research we will focus on the act of model creation, thereby complementing the active stream of research investigating process model interpretation [e.g., 20].

The dimension of affected variables comprises observable outcomes of the tasks that can be used as the source of dependent measures in empirical comparisons. *Focus of observation* points to what has been measured, either the process or the product of using a CMT. Our interest is on the process of process modeling. The *criterion for comparison* refers to the measurement criteria that have been applied. These criteria can either be effectiveness or efficiency focused in nature [18]. The criteria we choose are focused on understanding the process of creating the model, both in terms of effectiveness and efficiency of the modeling process. Our measurements include the formation of requirements specification and elicitation actions performed, observable modeling actions, modeling phases and milestones, as well as the number and type of communication breakdowns across these stages.

In summation, our study design provides an opportunity to obtain a deeper understanding of the process of collaborative process modeling, and the actions taken within. This understanding, in turn, can lead to design guidelines for the development of technology-based support instruments to support process modeling, as well as the development of normative guidelines (checklists, instructions etc.) for the conduct of process modeling projects in collaborative settings. Of course, due to the limitations of this research setup in terms of ecological validity, our study will also set the stage for a large study using repeated field setting.

3.2 Setup

The four selected participants are Business Process Management researchers, each with a slightly different background. Specifically, there are two PhD students in information systems with extensive experience in process modeling, one PhD student in computer science with less experience in process modeling and one senior researcher with background in conceptual modeling but not process modeling. Participation was voluntary, with the only incentive offered being free food during the experiment. The workplaces were distributed across several research offices. Each participant was assigned an individual workstation.

The instructions are constrained to the goal of collaboratively modeling the described cases using only Gravity for communication. The objective of the modeling was to collaboratively produce an accurate and understandable BPMN process of the given process.

3.3 Materials

A case description (provided in disassembled form to the participants) was sent out ten minutes before the experiment officially started via e-mail. Case 1 described a mail distribution process, the description of which we separated according to the involved roles (mail processing unit, registry and cashier). The second case described a procurement process, again separated according the involved roles (requester, approver, purchase department clerk, clerk at goods receipt department and financial department clerk).

During the modeling sessions, participants were monitored to enforce silence (i.e., no active verbal communication) throughout the study, to simulate a geographically distributed setup. The modeling tool provided chatting but not VoIP functionality albeit, admittedly, such functionality could have been used through other software (e.g., Skype). Participants were given two hours in total to solve both cases. Due to technical difficulties with the tool prototype, both cases could not be modeled completely. This breakdown brings forward a limitation pertaining to the scope of study (e.g., we could not collect data on model validation activities conducted), but otherwise did not affect the data collection. After the second case, a focus group with the research team and the participants was conducted, to gather data about impressions, feedback and thoughts. The focus group meeting was audio-recorded, and notes were taken during the session.

3.4 Measurement

In order to measure the effectiveness of the modeling process we use the notion of breakdowns [21], which observed difficulties that occur during problem-solving processes [22]. We apply this notion to the process of process modeling using a categorization based on three steps of the semiotic ladder [23], following Rittgen's [12] classification of modeling as a language act on basis of Stamper's [23] theory of signs. Although Stamper [23] proposed four ladder steps, we will constrain our categorization on the originally used stages in semiotics [24], viz., syntax, semantics and pragmatics.

Specifically, we will summarize breakdowns related to the organization of the modeling session (e.g. setting the agenda), tool features requests (e.g. video conferencing) and tool deficiencies (e.g. errors) as pragmatic breakdowns. The semantic level will comprise breakdowns associated to the elicitation of the problem domain (e.g. defining the sequence) and mapping the domain to notation constructs (e.g. classifying activities). Impediments in applying the grammar of the notation are classified as syntactic breakdowns (e.g. restrictions for the usage of sequence flows in BPMN).

4 Results and Discussion

4.1 Findings

Process of Modeling – Case Comparison
In this section we will present similarities and differences found at comparing the process of process modeling employed by the participants for each case. For visualization purposes, we adapted BPMN diagrams to conceptualize these processes. In particular, we abstracted observable activities (BPMN symbol: activity) and status notifications (BPMN symbol: Signal Event). Furthermore, all breakdowns identified in the process are depicted as error event symbols. Annotations are provided to capture evidence from the observed actions and communications. The applied color codification scheme on activities indicates their occurrence in both cases as follows:

- white – found in both cases and at the same position
- grey – found in both cases but different position
- black – uniquely found in one case

Figure 1 depicts the process of modeling for the first case. In the beginning the participants agreed on the task and pasted the given case information pieces to make them available to all. We noticed that, during this case data collection phase, someone directly started to model. Subsequently the participants agreed to paste all case descriptions and defined their interdependencies as well as the respective sequence. Then they started modeling, concurrently the session suffered from several breakdowns. The agenda had to be revised, as one participant noticed a missing part and offered to model this part of the case. Additionally, lessons learnt were raised as they noticed issues ("We should have discussed the modeling approach first"). The participants were not able to complete the model because of a steadily reoccurring error of the modeling prototype. Therefore no final verification or validation activities could be observed. Still, we observed "on the fly" attempts to verify and validate the model, e.g., to connect two modeled parts ("Sort Mail should be connected to Register Mail"). In total 9 breakdowns (7 pragmatic, 1 semantic, 1 syntactic) were observed during case 1.

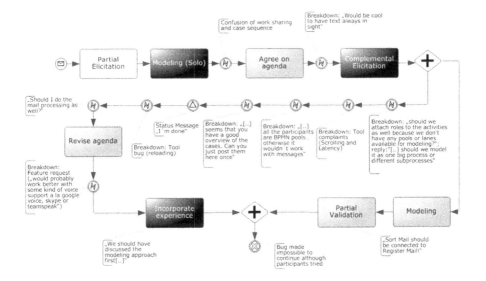

Fig. 1. Process of Modeling for Case 1

Figure 2 depicts the process of modeling for the second case. Similar to case 1 the participants started with a partial elicitation which in this situation means they pasted all relevant case information but did not agree on their sequence. In contrast to the first case, the participants structured the modeling session by agreeing on individually modeling exactly the role each participant received, which points to a learning effect carried over from the first case.

During this process, the participants discovered problems due to insufficient modeling space, which, in turn caused interferences to the modeling process and forced them to adapt the agenda. This breakdown became more cumbersome as the size of the "individual" models rose.

Similar to case one, the given process scenario could not be modeled completely due to re-occurring prototype functionality issues. Hence, we were not able to observe final verification or validation activities or discussions although, again, interactions indicated a partial validation (e.g. missing connection of the "individual" models: "someone has to consolidate the models"). In case 2 we found 3 breakdowns that are all on the pragmatic level.

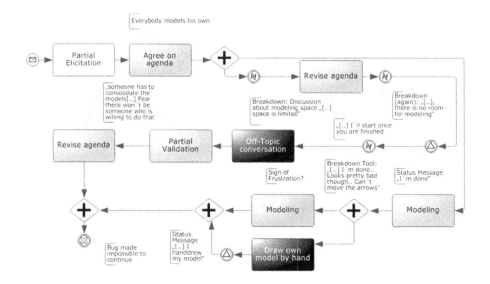

Fig. 2. Process of Modeling for Case 2

Comparing both cases we found one activity at the same position in both cases (partial elicitation), and a further four activities (agree on agenda, modeling, revise agenda, partial validation) that occurred in both cases albeit in a different order. This finding would suggest that these activities appear essential (but non-exhaustive) for a collaborative modeling session. The activity 'complementary elicitation' was only observed in case 1, as in case 2 no sequence has been defined. A possible reason is the chosen modeling approach in case 2 that did not require a sequence definition upfront. Therefore, we would expect this activity to be done at the end of the session if it has not been interrupted. Similarly, the same holds for a final validation. The immediate individual modeling activity observed at the beginning of case 1 could possibly be ascribed to his/her curiosity of how the tool works. The "incorporate experience" activity in case 1 could reflect a familiarization effect with the new environment (group, tool, collaboration etc.). Both residual activities ("off-topic conversation" and "draw own model by hand") in case 2 are considered as effects (i.e. frustration and workaround) of a breakdown.

The comparison of the number of breakdowns in each process shows that there are a lot more breakdowns during the first case (case 1: 9, case 2: 3). Possible explanations are learning effects associated with the attempt of technology appropriation. Furthermore, due to the subsequent accomplishment of both cases participants may have regarded mentioning of similar problems as needless. The elaboration and categorization of breakdowns will follow in the next section.

Breakdowns
We now discuss the number and types of breakdowns identified during both modeling cases. We group the observed breakdowns according to the categorization proposed in

section three and provide quote examples in order to show evidence. In total, we classified the 12 observed breakdowns into 5 breakdowns types on a pragmatic (P), 1 on a semantic (SE) and 1 on a syntactic (SY) level.

- **P.1 Information Elicitation:** information representation (i.e., case description to all participants) was requested to be visible at all times ("Would be cool to have text always in sight", "[..] can you just post them here once"; observed in case 1)
- **P.2 Organization/ Agenda Setting:** participants did not know what to do (next) or how to share work ("We should have discussed modeling approach first", "Should I copy my text?", "Should I do the mail processing as well?"; observed in case 1)
- **P.3 Tool Feature Request:** support for a more natural communication was requested as a result of dissatisfaction ("[..] would probably work better with some kind of voice support[..]"; focus group interview; observed in case 1)
- **P.4 Tool Deficiency:** handling issues prevented participants from what they wanted to do (e.g. scrolling), Latency, Errors (e.g. steady reloading) ("[..] I can't scroll[..]", "[..] system keeps reload all the time"; observed in both cases)
- **P.5 Tool Feature Request:** insufficient modeling space resulted in conflicts at concurrent modeling ("[..] there is no room for modeling"; observed in case 2)
- **SE.1 Process Decomposition:** participants struggled in structuring the process model appropriately beforehand ("should we model it as one big process or different sub-processes based on different roles?"; observed in case 1)
- **SY.1 Construct Grammar Rules:** participants needed to recapitulate grammar rules as an effect of missing constructs ("[..] all participants are BPMN pools.. otherwise it wouldn´t work with messages"; observed in case 1)

It was clearly observable that the participants tried to better organize the session in case 2 (how to proceed and who does what). A re-organization became necessary through additionally discovered tool limitations. Other breakdowns have not occurred or not been articulated again. Especially on the syntactic and semantic level, this might be either because it has been already cleared in the case 1 or the process description for case 2 does not demand for this thinking.

The dominance of breakdowns on the pragmatic level poses an important question: Does collaboration technology supporting process modeling require more features for organizational guidance? Due to the fact that both cases had to be aborted and we included tool issues in this category, we will neither support nor decline this hypothesis but instead note it as an interesting avenue for future study.

4.2   Discussion

In the last section we learned about activities and breakdowns occurring in collaboration technology supported process modeling. In our exploratory study, we observed two main findings. First, we identified similar activities present in both cases and derived possible explanations for differences. Second, we found that participants learned to appropriate the working environment provided by the technology, and adapted the modeling process such that the modeling could be carried out within the framework of conditions set by the tool.

Implications for Future Research

Our findings have important implications for future research on process modeling.

Notably, we observed not only breakdowns but also breakdown workarounds employed by the participants in the collaborative modeling process. These actions indicate a familiarization process by the participants during their continued technology use. Future studies should study how this familiarization process is enacted in the context of collaborative modeling, and how it affects both the process and product of modeling.

Secondly, in our study we examined the process of process modeling on the basis of collaborative technology. A complementary stream of research could build upon our conceptualization of the IT-enabled modeling process to study the emergent implications on the outcome of the modeling process, i.e., the quality of the model produced. Such work could build on existing work on different quality measures of process models, e.g., soundness [25], understandability [20] or re-use [26].

Implications for Technology Design

Our findings further provide information for the design of collaborative technology. Specifically, we believe that the breakdowns we identified can be used to inform a design agenda to (re-) develop or address features that can assist to prevent or overcome those breakdowns.

P.1. (Information Elicitation) suggests the importance of a feature that allows the textual description of the domain to be displayed throughout the modeling activities.

P.2. (Organization/ Agenda Setting) was mainly overcome with the help of chat. While an initial discussion needs to be done to agree on the agenda, other mechanisms seem more appropriate to guide und support participants (e.g. keep track of work packages, their status as well as completion notifications). The request for organizational guiding is supported by the observed status messages during both cases and the focus group.

P.3. (Tool Feature Request (Natural Communication)) addresses the need for faster communication. In both cases, instant messaging functionality was provided as the only communication feature. Prominent weaknesses are the slow communication pace and "complexity" of several ways to reply in Google Wave which was communicated during the experiment and the focus group. Nevertheless, the chat (especially the collaborative messaging) can be used to support communication. A possible scenario would be to take notes during brainstorming or elicitation that are visible to all participants and afterwards provide these into the Dialogue Document within the tool.

P.4. (Tool Deficiencies) need to be addressed by the tool vendor as they lead to frustration among participants.

P.5. (Tool Feature Request (Modeling Space)) requires a greater modeling panel to avoid conflicts in modeling activities. The possibility to collaboratively edit a model on the same panel seemed to create a greater visibility which is supported by on the fly validation and verification activities in both cases.

SE.1. (Process Decomposition) suggests for specific modeling guidelines or rules that help the participants to structure their model. A possible implementation can be performed through, for instance, a checklist or FAQ using emerging knowledge on process model understandability [20].

SY.1. (Construct Grammar Rules) suggests for a syntactical check during the modeling. Although the research prototype of Gravity does not offer this feature, there are several other (single) modeling environments available providing such functionality.

In summary, we proposed requirements for collaborative support in process modeling addressing various aspects. In particular, a technology must provide support to modeling (P.1., P.5., SE.1., SY.1.), communication (P.3.) and coordination (P.2.).

5   Conclusion

In this paper we reported on an exploratory study of distributed process modeling with collaborative technology. Through a quasi-experimental setup we obtained preliminary insights about activities and breakdowns in collaborative process modeling, and identified a number of technology features that support various stages of the collaborative modeling exercise.

Our research bears some limitations. Specifically, this paper reports on an exploratory examination of 4 people modeling 2 cases. Therefore, we are well aware that our study is preliminary in nature. Still, we believe that our initial findings already inform an emerging body of knowledge and will also be useful to use in our work that follows. In moving forward from our study, we aim to replicate our experimental studies with larger cohorts of users. In doing so, we will incorporate the experiences gathered in this study resulting in adjusted setup.

References

1. Benford, S., Greenhalgh, C., Rodden, T., Pycock, J.: Collaborative Virtual Environments. Communications of the ACM 44, 79–85 (2001)
2. Kiesler, S., Sproull, L.S.: Group Decision Making and Communication Technology. Organizational Behavior and Human Decision Processes 52, 96–123 (1992)
3. Brouse, P.L., Fields, N.A., Palmer, J.D.: A Multimedia Computer Supported Cooperative Work Environment for. Requirements Engineering. In: Proceedings of the International Conference on Systems, Man and Cybernetics, pp. 954–959. IEEE, Chicago (1992)
4. Davis, A., Murphy, J., Owens, D., Khazanchi, D., Zigurs, I.: Avatars, People, and Virtual Worlds: Foundations for Research in Metaverses. Journal of the Association for Information Systems 10, 90–117 (2009)
5. Recker, J., Rosemann, M., Indulska, M., Green, P.: Business Process Modeling: A Comparative Analysis. Journal of the Association for Information Systems 10, 333–363 (2009)
6. Koschmider, A., Song, M., Reijers, H.A.: Social Software for Business Process Modeling. Journal of Information Technology 25 (2010) (in press)
7. Frederiks, P.J.M., van der Weide, T.P.: Information Modeling: The Process and the Required Competencies of Its Participants. Data & Knowledge Engineering 58, 4–20 (2006)
8. Lee-Kelly, L.: Locus of Control and Attitudes to Working in Virtual Teams. International Journal of Project Management 24, 234–243 (2006)
9. Brown, R., Recker, J.: Improving the Traversal of Large Hierarchical Process Repositories. In: Schepers, H., Davern, M.J. (eds.) Proceedings of the 20th Australasian Conference on Information Systems, pp. 144–153. Association for Information Systems, Melbourne (2009)

10. Recker, J.: Continued Use of Process Modeling Grammars: The Impact of Individual Difference Factors. European Journal of Information Systems 19, 76–92 (2010)
11. Stirna, J., Persson, A., Sandkuhl, K.: Participative Enterprise Modeling: Experiences and Recommendations. In: Krogstie, J., Opdahl, A.L., Sindre, G. (eds.) CAiSE 2007 and WES 2007. LNCS, vol. 4495, pp. 546–560. Springer, Heidelberg (2007)
12. Rittgen, P.: Negotiating Models. In: Krogstie, J., Opdahl, A.L., Sindre, G. (eds.) CAiSE 2007 and WES 2007. LNCS, vol. 4495, pp. 561–573. Springer, Heidelberg (2007)
13. Rittgen, P.: Collaborative Modeling - A Design Science Approach. In: Proceedings of the 42nd Hawaii International Conference on System Sciences, pp. 1–10. IEEE, Waikoloa (2009)
14. Ssebuggwawo, D., Hoppenbrouwers, S.J.B.A., Proper, E.: Interactions, Goals and Rules in a Collaborative Modelling Session. In: Persson, A., Stirna, J. (eds.) PoEM 2009. Lecture Notes in Business Information Processing, vol. 39, pp. 54–68. Springer, Heidelberg (2009)
15. Susman, G.I., Gray, B.L., Perry, J., Blair, C.E.: Recognition and Reconciliation of Differences in Interpretation of Misalignments When Collaborative Technologies Are Introduced into New Product Development. Journal of Engineering and Technology Management 20, 141–159 (2003)
16. Marjanovic, O.: Learning and Teaching in a Synchronous Collaborative Environment. Journal of Computer Assisted Learning 15, 129–138 (1999)
17. Cook, T.D., Campbell, D.T.: Quasi-Experimentation: Design and Analysis Issues. Houghton Mifflin, Boston (1979)
18. Gemino, A., Wand, Y.: A Framework for Empirical Evaluation of Conceptual Modeling Techniques. Requirements Engineering 9, 248–260 (2004)
19. Gemino, A., Wand, Y.: Evaluating Modeling Techniques based on Models of Learning. Communications of the ACM 46, 79–84 (2003)
20. Mendling, J., Reijers, H., van der Aalst, W.M.P.: Seven Process Modeling Guidelines (7PMG). Information and Software Technology 52, 127–136 (2010)
21. Guindon, R., Krasner, H., Curtis, B.: Breakdowns and Processes During the Early Activities of Software Design by Professionals. In: Olson, G.M., Sheppard, S., Soloway, E. (eds.) Empirical Studies of Programmers: Second Workshop, pp. 65–82. Ablex Publishing, Norwood (1987)
22. Vessey, I., Conger, S.A.: Requirements Specification: Learning Object, Process, and Data Methodologies. Communications of the ACM 37, 102–113 (1994)
23. Stamper, R.K.: The Semiotic Framework for Information Systems Research. In: Nissen, H.-E., Klein, H.K., Hirschheim, R. (eds.) Information Systems Research: Contemporary Approaches and Emergent Traditions, pp. 515–528. North Holland, Amsterdam (1991)
24. Morris, C.W.: Writings on the General Theory of Signs. Mouton de Gruyter, The Hague (1971)
25. Verbeek, H.M.V., van der Aalst, W.M.P., ter Hofstede, A.H.M.: Verifying Workflows with Cancellation Regions and OR-joins: An Approach Based on Relaxed Soundness and Invariants. The Computer Journal 50, 294–314 (2007)
26. Irwin, G.: The Role of Similarity in the Reuse of Object-Oriented Analysis Models. Journal of Management Information Systems 19, 219–248 (2002)

Business Process Compliance Tracking Using Key Performance Indicators

Azalia Shamsaei, Alireza Pourshahid, and Daniel Amyot

SITE, University of Ottawa, 800 King Edward,
Ottawa, ON, K1N 6N5, Canada
{asham092,apour024,damyot}@site.uottawa.ca

Abstract. Compliance of business processes with authoritative rules is significantly important to avoid financial penalties, efficiency problems, and reputation damages. However, finding the right measures to evaluate and track
compliance is very challenging. We propose a novel method to model the context and measure compliance using the User Requirements Notation (URN). We
mainly use Key Performance Indicator (KPI) extensions of URN to measure the
level of compliance to rules. Such KPIs have been used in the past to measure
the satisfaction level of goals and the performance of business processes. Yet,
they have never been used for measuring compliance. Our method highlights
the non-compliant policies and rules on a quadrant map based on their importance and compliance levels. Furthermore, we suggest a new method for importance calculation in this context. We use a human resource policy example to
illustrate our method.

Keywords: Business Processes, Goal Modeling, Legal Compliance, Key Performance Indicator, Rules, User Requirements Notation.

1 Introduction

Compliance management is a critical activity in any organization. Every year, organizations invest time and money to ensure their processes comply with different regulations and policies. There are four different categories of *authoritative rules* [5] by
which a business process can be governed. Each of these categories may be considered voluntarily or imposed to an organization. The first category is internal policies
used in organizations to give better direction to business processes. Regulations and
laws imposed by governments represent the second category. Violating rules from
this category can cause important consequences, including financial penalties, loss of
reputation, and lawsuits. The third category is composed of Service Level Agreements
(SLA) used between organizations to ensure promised services are provided according to expectations. The last category of authoritative rules is that of standards.

With so many rules to follow, large organizations have a difficult time keeping
track of compliance levels of different processes as well as of the organization as a
whole. Some will only assess their compliance level based on the audits they pass or
fail, an approach that is usually not very proactive and that may lead to some of the
consequences mentioned earlier. One challenge is that it is next to impossible to

M. zur Muehlen and J. Su (Eds.): BPM 2010 Workshops, LNBIP 66, pp. 73–84, 2011.

comply with all imposed rules given limited resources and rules that may conflict. Another is to keep the compliance level under continuous scrutiny to make sure the next important audit will pass.

In this paper, we propose a method enabling organizations to calculate their compliance level and discover business processes that violate authoritative rules. We use organization business goal, process and authoritative rule models as the input of our method. This method builds on the *User Requirements Notation* (URN), which is the first international standard to combine and integrate goal modeling (with URN's Goal-oriented Requirement Language — GRL) and scenario/process modeling (with URN's Use Case Map notation — UCM) [7,15]. URN models are graphical and can be created, managed and analyzed with jUCMNav [9], a free, Eclipse-based open source tool. The method outputs the compliance levels as well as target processes that require improvement. It takes advantage of an extension to URN used to model *Key Performance Indicators* (KPIs), which have been recently introduced for performance management [13], to calculate the compliance level of organizations. In addition, we define an algorithm that calculates the importance of low-level rules based on high-level goals and propagate the result to business processes and rules.

Related work in this area will be discussed in section 2, followed by an overview of our method in section 3. A case study from the human resource sector is elaborated in section 4 to illustrate our method and its benefits. Finally, the conclusion and future work will be discussed in section 5.

2   Related Work

Namiri and Stojanovic [12] have proposed a formal framework for managing business process compliance for enterprises. First, the accounts with a major impact on the enterprise's bottom-line are selected. Then, all relevant business processes are identified. Finally a set of controls is defined and tested regularly to protect the processes against identified risks. In addition, the framework suggests a set of properties to check the completeness of the compliance management system. These are essentially static constraints on the set of accounts, processes, controls, risks, and their relationships. This framework mainly focuses on compliance from a financial point of view for some of the business processes. We believe compliance monitoring should allow for all business processes and non-financial goals and constraints to be considered.

Kharbili and Stein [10] have proposed a policy-based semantic framework for enterprise compliance management. This framework defines a three-layer architecture and the transformations between these layers. The first layer uses semantic policies and rules to formalize regulations. In the second layer, these policies are transformed into business rules utilized in business process models. Finally, the business rules are transformed to operational rules used in automated business processes.

As suggested by Kharbili and Stein, a comprehensive compliance management framework should be integrated with business processes and support different levels of policy and rule definitions. Furthermore, according to zur Muehlen *et al.* [16], a combination of formal business process modeling and rule modeling language is required for proper documentation and modeling of compliance in an organization. Governatori *et al.* [4] go further by providing a heavily formalized, logic-based representation of rules and business processes where semantic annotations and model checking are used to detect statically violations of obligations. Furthermore, Lu *et al.* [11] have also proposed a logic-based approach to evaluate compliance distance degrees (values between 0 and 1) between business processes and control objectives/rules. The end result of this method can be utilized by process designers to improve the compliance degree, but the complexity of the method may be an impediment for regular business users.

Although our proposed method does not provide the level of formalization and automated transformations of the above frameworks, the use of URN allows business users to model not only polices, rules, and processes but also other types of business and stakeholder goals. Hence, our approach supports business analysts in having a holistic view of the context. Furthermore, finding the source of problems and tracking compliance issues continuously becomes more systematic and better supported. Logic-based approaches have their own advantages and can perhaps be used to provide the theoretical background for the development of tools for compliance, but we believe that URN with KPIs adds a complementary and appropriate level of formalization in a business context, especially for end users. This combination is also more pragmatic for applications to actual running processes, not just to analysis of models.

Note that URN has already been used in the context of compliance. Ghanavati *et al.* [2,3] have proposed a URN-based requirements management framework for compliance management involving healthcare organization/legal goals (in GRL) and business processes (in UCM) linked to policies and legal documents. With this framework, they defined and analyzed different types of traceability and compliance links between organization models and regulation models. Although the modeling notation used in this framework is the same as in our proposed method, we not only establish traceability links between organization and regulation models but also *measure* the level of compliance of business processes against policies/regulations, with KPIs. Furthermore, we suggest a new method to calculate the relative importance of rules in this context.

3   Method Overview

The main objective of this method is to provide a modeling approach and guidelines enabling organizations to measure the current compliance level of their processes, track down and address compliance problems, and also evaluate the impact of changes on the overall compliance level of the organization. In order to meet this objective, the method requires the following inputs:

- The policy/regulation model, including sub-policies, rules and key performance indicators modeled with standard GRL extended with KPIs.
- The organization goal model (in GRL) and business process model (UCM).
- The importance level of high-level business goals.

The GRL policy/regulation model shows the high-level policies, their decomposition into sub-policies, and ultimately the operational rules stating how the processes can be compliant with the policies (see Fig. 6 and Fig. 7). Furthermore, we connect a set of KPIs that measure the level of compliance for the rules. Each rule can have one or more KPIs to measure its compliance level. The KPIs are defined by the analysts who know both the business and the policies. Obviously, there may be situations where the required measures do not exist in current corporate data sources. Although this may seem to be a problem, this is usually a short-term one as such situation helps organizations detect inadequacies in their data sources and improve them to address their requirements for measuring compliance.

We also use business goals and business process models in our approach to make the analysis more accurate, based on facts, and provide better outcomes. The main usage of the business goal model is to specify the importance of the related business processes to each rule and policy and to illustrate the business context for the analysts. Measuring the importance of rules allows us to identify the most important problems that need to be fixed first. This is detailed further in section 4.2.

The expected outcomes of our method are:

- Compliance level measures for policies and rules.
- Location of policies/rules applied to the organization on a quadrant according to their compliance level and importance.
- Tracking compliance changes after business process or policy modifications.

As illustrated in Fig. 1, our method is iterative and consists of four main steps.

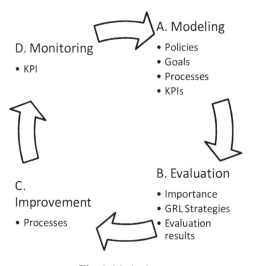

Fig. 1. Method steps

Step A. In the modeling step we:

1. Model the organization's business processes and business goals.
2. Associate processes to organization goals using URN links to define the importance level of processes as well as of the rules and policies applied to the processes.
3. Model policies, sub-policies and rules.
4. Associate rules to existing organization processes using URN links, to show where the rules are used in the organization.
5. Define key performance indicators for each rule.

Step B. In the evaluation step we:

1. Add GRL strategies (initial set of satisfaction values to some nodes in the goal model) and define values for the *target*, *threshold*, and *worst* attributes of KPIs. The values of KPIs' *evaluation* attributes come from external data sources. GRL's KPI construct maps the evaluation value to a satisfaction level (on a scale from -100 to 100, by linear interpolation considering the target, threshold, and worst values) that can then be propagated to other elements in the goal model according to the goal evaluation algorithms presented in [1].

2. Define the importance level of high-level business goals and calculate the importance of process and rules accordingly. The importance of the rules should be calculated considering both the importance of related business goals and the policies/regulations that the rule is part of. At this point, we have only considered business goal importance related to a rule and the algorithm result is added to the model manually (see section 4.2), but in the future we plan to provide an automatic algorithm propagation to make this effort easier.

3. Evaluate the compliance (i.e., the satisfaction level of policies)

    I. Illustrate policies on a quadrant diagram according to their compliance level (satisfaction level) and importance value.
    II. Highlight the critical rules with low satisfaction levels and track down the associated processes using the URN traceability links defined in step A.

Step C. In the improvement step, we change processes to address the problems highlighted in the quadrant diagram. We also evaluate whether our modifications to fix one problem affect negatively the compliance against other rules/policies. This is done again with GRL strategies, where we can simulate many what-if situations.

Step D. In the monitoring step, we monitor the compliance KPIs to observe whether the expected changes actually happen. If the results are not the ones expected, we take corrective actions, otherwise we can move on to improve other necessary processes.

4 Human Resource Case Study

In our case study, we focus on a human resource policy described in [6]. This particular policy is divided into three groups totaling 36 sub-policies. The main policy we focus on is the hiring policy. In the rest of this section, we go through the steps of the method presented in section 3 (except the monitoring step due to space limitation) and explain them in more detail in the context of the case study.

4.1 Step A: Modeling

In this first step, we concentrate on providing the inputs required for performing the analysis. These inputs include the business process model (see Fig. 2, Fig. 3, and Fig. 4) in UCM, the organization goal model (see Fig. 5), and the policy model (see Fig. 6 and Fig. 7) in GRL.

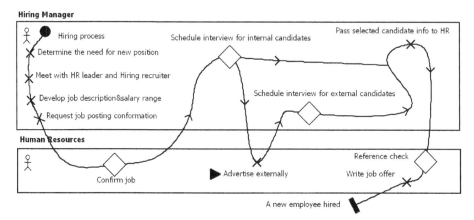

Fig. 2. Hiring process (UCM)

UCM models (see Fig. 2) consist of causal sequences of responsibilities that can be allocated to components. A scenario path is triggered by a start point (●, e.g., Hiring process) and results in an end point (▮, e.g., A new employee hired). Responsibilities (✗, e.g. Determine the need for new position) can be defined along the way to represent actions or tasks performed during the process. UCM supports both concurrent (─┼─) and guarded alternative (─⌐) paths. Furthermore, stubs (◇, e.g., Confirm job) contain sub-maps used to organize complex processes in hiearchies of sub-processes (e.g. Fig. 3 and Fig. 4). Finally, actors (▭, e.g., Hiring Manager) can be used to separate different parts of a process based on organizational units or roles.

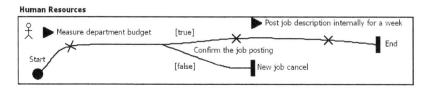

Fig. 3. Confirm job sub-process (UCM)

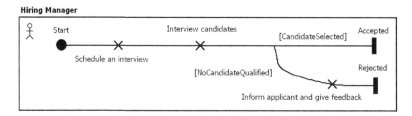

Fig. 4. Schedule interview for internal candidate sub-process (UCM)

In the hiring process case study, a Hiring Manager determines the need for a new job position and discusses the job description and salary with Human Resources. It is Human Resources' responsibility to confirm a new job while considering the department's budget. Upon successful confirmation, Human Resources post the job internally for a week and the Hiring Manager schedules an interview with successful internal candidates. If no internal candidate is qualified for a job then interviews will be scheduled for external candidates until a successful candidate is found.

In the next step, we model the organization's high-level goals. GRL models (Fig. 5 to Fig. 7) consist of *intentional elements* such as softgoals (⬭, e.g., Successful business), goals (⬭, e.g., HR Policies) and KPIs (⬭). Intentional elements can be assigned to stakeholders through actors (⬭). In addition, intentional elements can be connected to each other using different types of links, including AND/OR decomposition (not used here) and weighted contribution links (→). The latter indicate the positive or negative impact of intentional elements on each other (with a quantitative scale from 100 to -100), which is used for evaluations and analysis. The model elements explained above are the subset or URN used in this paper. Both UCM and GRL have more model elements used in other contexts (see [7] for a complete list).

Fig. 5 illustrates the parts of the organization goals we are interested in. This model is useful for analysts to know the context and better prioritize the processes and rules according to the organization goals. The high-level goal Successful Business is part of our method for calculating the importance level.

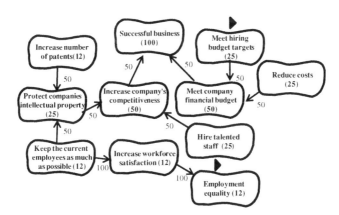

Fig. 5. Organization's high-level business goal model

Policies and regulations can be modeled in a similar way. For example, we have modeled 5 sub-policies for HR Policy with GRL (Fig. 6). We assume that all sub-policies have an equal impact on HR Policy, and hence the contribution links have a weight of 20. We continue modeling sub-policies until we reach the rule level. Due to space limitation, we only indicate sub-policies, rules and key performance indicators for the Hiring sub-process. Fig. 6 shows HR Policies (at the top) and sub-policies for the Hiring Policy (at the bottom). Fig. 7 models rules and key performance indicators for the job posting policy. We have assigned an identifier to each rule (R1 to R4) for reference in the rest of the paper.

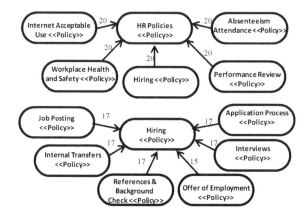

Fig. 6. Sub-policies for Human Resources (top) and Hiring (bottom)

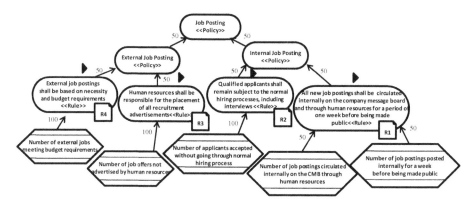

Fig. 7. Rules and key performance indicators for Job Posting

Table 1. Mapping rules to business processes

Business Process	Rule
Determine whether the department can afford hiring employees	R4
Post job description internally for a week	R1
Advertise externally	R3
Schedule an interview for internal candidates	R2

We then map rules to business processes with *URN links* (whose presence is indicated by a black triangle). Table 1 shows the traceability links between business processes and rules in our case study. These links allow us to highlight the processes that need to be modified in the improvement step, if any. Furthermore, they allow us to indentify the importance of rules based on their associated business processes.

4.2 Step B: Evaluation

In this step, we define the GRL *strategies* used to evaluate the satisfaction level of policies. Each GRL strategy initializes the KPI value sets [13]. Table 2 shows the values for a sample strategy we have used in this scenario. The evaluation values can be entered manually like other value sets (which is useful for the analysis of what-if situations) or automatically obtained from a data source such as a Business Intelligence system. These strategies are used to evaluate the satisfaction level of the other intentional elements (i.e., rules and policies) using the standard quantitative evaluation method supported by GRL and jUCMNav [1].

Table 2. List of key performance indicators for rules

Rule	Key Performance Indicator	Target	Threshold	Worst	Evaluation
R1	Number of job postings circulated internally on the CMB through human resources	10	10	0	10
	Number of job postings posted internally for a week before being made public	10	10	0	5
R2	Number of applicants accepted without going through normal hiring process	0	0	10	6
R3	Number of job offers not advertised by human resources	0	2	10	1
R4	Number of external jobs meeting budget requirements	10	10	0	8

In addition to the satisfaction value, the *importance* value (to the containing actor/stakeholder) is also calculated using a new algorithm for GRL intentional elements in this step. As illustrated in Fig. 5, Successful business is the highest goal in the organization model has an importance value of 100. The algorithm will calculate the importance for other intentional goal using their contribution links' values. Importance values are propagated down from high-level goals to business processes and rules according to the following formula:

Importance Value= (Parent Importance Value)*(Proportion of Contribution Level)

For instance, the importance value of R4 is propagated down all the way from the highest level goal of the business (see Fig. 5). Success business's importance value is 100 and it is connected to Meet company financial budget through a contribution link with a contribution level of 50. Therefore, the importance value of company financial budget becomes 50. Subsequently, the importance value of Meet hiring budget target (the goal linked to the process to which R4 is applied) becomes 25. This value is propagated to business processes and rules through URN links.

Using these two values, the rules will be laid out on a quadrant as shown in Fig. 8. A similar quadrant diagram was used before for performance monitoring [14]. However, using the quadrant in the context of policy monitoring is another application explored here. This quadrant allows us to *identify what is the most important rule that the organization is not compliant with*. This will allow the people in charge to more easily prioritize the improvement candidates for the next step.

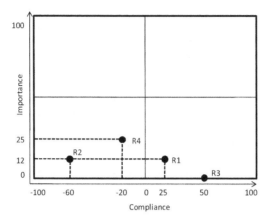

Fig. 8. Importance and compliance of rules on a quadrant diagram

4.3 Step C: Improvement

As shown in Fig. 8, the compliance levels of R2, R4, R1 and R3 have the highest to lowest levels of non-compliance, in that order. In terms of importance levels, R4 is the most important rule while R3 is the least important. Rule R2 has the highest level of non-compliance and its importance is in the same quadrant area as R4. Even if there is a slight different between their importance levels, since R2 has the highest non-compliance value, it takes priority over R4. Therefore, we should try to improve the process associated to R2 in order to get the highest impact on our global compliance level.

As the KPIs related to R2 indicate, out of ten internal applicants in a year, six were employed without being interviewed first. We suggest here two modifications to this business process model to better enforce the rules and increase the compliance:

- Human Resources shall be involved in scheduling and performing interviews.
- Interviewers shall fill out the job candidate evaluation form while performing interviews.

By adding these two steps to the business process, the number of candidates hired without interviews will be reduced. When comparing the new process with the previous one, this time not only the hiring manager will be part of interview process but also will human resource personnel. Furthermore, each employee should have a job candidate evaluation form that will be filled out by interviewer team during interview.

Before making any concrete change to the processes, we also estimate its cost to the organization. A human resource manager working in Canada earns an average salary of $83,859 [8]. We have assumed there are five one-hour interviews per job. Hence, the total cost of a human resource manager participating in 10 interviews would be about $2966 (assuming 49 weeks * 37.5 hours/week of work, plus 30% of overhead). Although the suggested modification will improve the compliance of the current business process, it also clearly increases its cost. However, in this case, the cost is not really that high and it is worthwhile to increase the chances of hiring an external talented candidate (who could be productive well over the additional cost during his/her career) by adding the extra suggested steps to the business process.

5   Conclusions and Future Work

Today's organizations cannot comply fully with all the various rules imposed on them, and hence they should comply with the rules that affect their business the most. In this paper, we defined a method that enables compliance tracking for business processes using key performance indicators. Organization goals and processes are modeled using the same lightweight language (URN) as policies and rules. This method helps finding how well authoritative rules are satisfied based on the importance and compliance values for the rules. The importance values are propagated down from high-level business goals to business processes and rules. Also, the non-compliant business processes are highlighted for further analysis and actions. In addition, our method is not limited to one aspect of the organization (e.g., financial). Although this is not apparent from our small example, the goals of all the organization's stakeholders can be considered during the analysis using GRL actors. These capabilities are quite powerful and allow one to have a holistic view of the organization.

Although our method is based on URN capabilities, other process (e.g., BPMN or YAWL) and goal modeling languages (e.g., *i** or TROPOS) could also be used to address the same issue. However, at this point we are not aware of any other language that provides the same level of support for modeling and analyzing goals and processes in an integrated manner, especially when KPIs need to be considered.

This method also suffers from several limitations that require further investigation. As we mentioned earlier, the importance value of each rule is based on the business goal importance set by the organization's managers. We may not have a business goal for all rules. We should be able to set the importance from the policy/regulation side as well. This is very important in the context of regulations. Furthermore, this example only has one business process per rule, which makes improvements very localized. In more complex situations, multiple rules may apply to a particular process, and hence a change to improve the satisfaction of one rule may have side effects on the satisfaction of the other rules. This will require i) making assumptions about the impact on the KPIs (to simulate whether the change can lead to a globally better set of satisfactions, and this can be done with jUCMNav), and ii) monitoring the situation to make sure the desired effect is really happening (step D of the method).

Acknowledgments. This research was supported by NSERC's Business Intelligence Network.

References

1. Amyot, D., Ghanavati, S., Horkoff, J., Mussbacher, G., Peyton, L., Yu, E.: Evaluating Goal Models within the Goal-oriented Requirement Language. International Journal of Intelligent Systems 25(8), 841–877 (2010)
2. Ghanavati, S., Amyot, D., Peyton, L.: Towards a Framework for Tracking Legal Compliance in Healthcare. In: Krogstie, J., Opdahl, A.L., Sindre, G. (eds.) CAiSE 2007 and WES 2007. LNCS, vol. 4495, pp. 218–232. Springer, Heidelberg (2007)

 3. Ghanavati, S., Siena, A., Perini, A., Amyot, D., Peyton, L., Susi, A.: A Legal Perspective on Business: Modeling the Impact of Law. In: 4th Intl. MCeTech Conf. on eTechnologies. LNBIP, vol. 26, pp. 267–278. Springer, Heidelberg (2009)
 4. Governatori, G., Hoffmann, J., Sadiq, S., Weber, I.: Detecting Regulatory Compliance for Business Process Models through Semantic Annotations. In: Business Process Management Workshops (BPM 2008). LNCS, vol. 17, pp. 5–17. Springer, Heidelberg (2009)
 5. Hamou-Lhadj, A.K., Hamou-Lhadj, A.W.: Towards a compliance support framework for global software companies. In: 11th IASTED Int. Conf. on Software Engineering and Applications, pp. 31–36. ACTA Press, Anaheim (2007)
 6. HRdownloads Website (2010), `http://www.hrdownloads.com/`
 7. International Telecommunication Union: Recommendation Z.151 (11/08), User Requirements Notation (URN) – Language definition,
    `http://www.itu.int/rec/T-REC-Z.151/en`
 8. Job Canada, `http://www.jobcanada.org/salary.html` (last accessed April 15, 2010)
 9. jUCMNav, Version 4.2.1, University of Ottawa (2010),
    `http://softwareengineering.ca/jucmnav`
10. Kharbili, M.E., Stein, S.: Policy-Based Semantic Compliance Checking for Business Process Management. In: MobIS Workshops 2008. CEUR Workshop Proceedings, vol. 420, pp. 178–192 (2008)
11. Lu, R., Sadiq, S., Governatori, G.: Measurement of Compliance Distance in Business Processes. Information Systems Management 25(4), 344–355 (2008)
12. Namiri, K., Stojanovic, N.: Towards A Formal Framework for Business Process Compliance. In: Multikonferenz Wirtschaftsinformatik (MKWI 2008). GITO-Verlag, Berlin (2008)
13. Pourshahid, A., Amyot, D., Chen, P., Weiss, M., Forster, A.J.: Business Process Monitoring and Alignment: An Approach Based on the User Requirements Notation and Business Intelligence Tools. In: 10th Workshop on Requirements Eng. (WER 2007), pp. 80–91 (2007)
14. Pourshahid, A., Chen, P., Amyot, D., Forster, A.J., Ghanavati, S., Peyton, L., Weiss, M.: Business Process Management with the User Requirements Notation. Electronic Commerce Research 9(4), 269–316 (2009)
15. Weiss, M., Amyot, D.: Business process modeling with URN. International Journal of E-Business Research 1(3), 63–90 (2005)
16. zur Muehlen, M., Indulska, M., Kamp, G.: Business Process and Business Rule Modeling Languages for Compliance Management: A Representational Analysis. In: ER (Tutorials, Posters, Panels & Industrial Contributions) 2007. ACM Int. Conf. Proceeding Series, vol. 334, pp. 127–132. Australian CS, Darlinghurst (2007)

Temporal Specification of Business Processes through Project Planning Tools

Camilo Flores and Marcos Sepúlveda

Computer Science Department
School of Engineering
Pontificia Universidad Católica de Chile
Vicuña Mackenna 4860, Macul, Santiago, Chile
`ciflores@uc.cl, marcos@ing.puc.cl`
`http://dcc.ing.puc.cl`

Abstract. Business Process Management has gained importance within organizations due to the need to streamline their operations. Nevertheless, despite the existence of process modeling standards such as BPMN, nowadays it is difficult to specify complex temporal constraints and relationships among tasks of a given process, which prevents the specification and subsequent automation of processes where these restrictions are relevant. To solve the exposed difficulty, we have resorted to the project planning and management field, developing a BPMN equivalency of all temporal constraints and relationships that can be specified in a standard project planning tool: Microsoft Project. This not only enables a simple interface for specifying complex temporal restrictions in business processes, but also defines an execution semantic for the models developed in the field of project planning, allowing their later automation through process execution engines.

Keywords: Process design methods and methodologies, Process design tools, Notations and methods, BPMN, Project planning.

1 Introduction

Business Process Management has gained importance within organizations due to the need to streamline their operations. An important aspect of this discipline is the process modeling or design stage [1]. In this stage, the modeler specifies through a language, which is usually graphic, the desired characteristics and behaviors of the process, suchas precedence or parallelism between tasks, definition of the actors who execute them, among others. To this end, several graphical notations have been developed, e.g., UML, IDEF, EPC and BPMN. Some of them can represent the "time dimension" of processes to a certain extend; for example, BPMN provides the time event. Nevertheless, despite the possibility to represent the "temporal dimension", nowadays it is difficult to specify complex temporal constraints and relationships among tasks of a given process in a simple way, which in practice prevents the specification of processes where these restrictions are relevant [2]. This is a problem

M. zur Muehlen and J. Su (Eds.): BPM 2010 Workshops, LNBIP 66, pp. 85–96, 2011.

because failing to include this information turns out in higher process execution costs, either by loss of productivity, lack of coordination in the process execution, or missed deadlines committed with the client.

On the other hand, in the project planning field, Gantt charts have long been used as an effective mean to specify thecoordination and execution of projects. These charts allow the description of all sorts of temporal constraints and relationships among tasks, graphically and with great ease [3]. Nevertheless, Gantt charts do not specify what to do when, due to contingencies in the execution, a temporal constraint or a temporal relationship is violated. In these cases, the course of action is left to the project coordinator's discretion due there is no behavior specified. This in turn is one of the strengths of BPMN, since models which are specified in this notation have a defined execution semantic [4], leaving no room for interpretation and even allowing the automation of processes through execution engines.

In this work, we propose equivalencies between the concepts defined in a widely used project planning tool –Microsoft Project–, according to the formalization proposed in [5], and constructs proposed in BPMN. This not only allows the definition of a unique interpretation of Gantt charts, leaving no room for the coordinator's discretion during the execution, but also allows to easily specify processes with complex temporal constraints and relationships in many planning tools, as models developed in these are interoperable [6].

This article is organized as follows: in section 2 we present a comparison of the ability to represent the "time dimension" between BPMN and Gantt charts through a simple example case, while in section 3 we present the equivalences proposed in BPMN. Finally, in section 4 we show the implications of our proposal and future research.

2   Comparison of the Ability to Represent the Time Dimension between BPMN and Project Planning Tools

Time is very important in every activity, since it is not possible to control it and once it has elapsed, it is not possible to recover. This is very important in business processes, especially when it is necessary to meet deadlines, achieve optimal coordination between tasks, or when the nature of some tasks requires certain synchronization in their execution. However, few process-oriented notations have emphasized this temporal coordination. Only recently new initiatives have arisen that include the "time dimension", such as the incorporation of the time event in the first specification of BPMN [7]. Despite this effort, it is difficult to specify temporal constraints or relationships between tasksin BPMN, due to its inability to visually represent a temporal execution order.This causes to beextremely difficult to specify or deduce the execution timing (at least the expected one) of a given process instance.

Following, we will observe this problem through a simple example case.

2.1   Example Case

The main process that runs a company dedicated to the innovation in the IT area is the organization of conferences throughout the year. A coordinator leads the organization of the event, who must delegate responsibilities to different actors that participate in the process. The first activity is to define the topic of the conference. Subsequently, invitations are sent to potential attendees to the event; then, they are expected to confirm their presence. In parallel, it is necessary to reserve the hotel's room, which must be done not before 10 days prior to the event day. At least 24 hours before the event, the coordinator must confirm the number of participant to the hotel. Another important activity is to print the material to be distributed at the conference, which must be printed at least one day before the conference. Finally, on the day of the event, attendees are received only up to 30 minutes after the conference has started.

The lunch break is scheduled at 13:00 pm and it is programmed to last 1 hour. When the conference finishes, parking tickets are given to guests; tickets must be validatednot before 30 minutes prior to the end of the event, considering that each ticket allows 60 minutes to leave the parking lot.

It is important to note that conference dates during the year are immutable: no matter how late the activities that precede it are; in many cases it is necessary to abort or to start the next activity to meet the event deadline. The implicit assumption is that the loss of quality for not completing a task is less important than the loss of credibility due to the cancellation or delay of the event.

2.1.1 Example Case in BPMN
The BPMN model that represents the process is outlined in Figure 1:

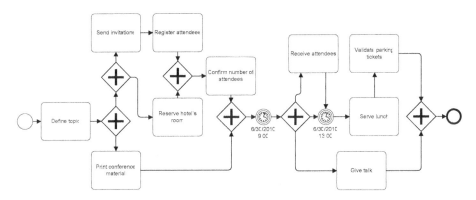

Fig. 1. Proposed BPMN model for the example process

This model defines precedence relationships between tasks, specifying which of them can run in parallel. Finally, we include time events to indicate that the conference start on 6/30/2010 at 9:00 and that lunch is on the same day at 13:00. Although this model can help to coordinate its execution, does not specify important aspects such as:

— How long can take certain activities without delaying the entire process. For example, it would be useful to know how long can the *"Receive Attendees"* taskbe executed, or when it should be started to meet the conference's deadline.

- When to close the registration and confirm attendees without delaying the entire process. This task should end as late as possible in order to maximize the number of attendees.
- How to coordinate the *"Receive Attendees"* and *"Validate Parking Tickets"* tasks with the *"Give Talk"* task, since they are mutually dependent.

2.1.2 Example Case in a Gantt Chart

We also model the example case using a Gantt chart (Figure 2), taking advantage of its features that allow a simple representation of temporal restrictions. We specify information about the duration of the tasks (which a priori is neither interesting nor obvious to include in a BPMN model), precedence relationships among some tasks, and the actual date of the event.

	❶	Task Name	Duration	Start	Finish	Predecessors
1		Define topic	1 day?	Tue 6/15/10	Tue 6/15/10	
2		Send invitations	1 day?	Wed 6/16/10	Wed 6/16/10	1
3		Print conference material	4 days?	Wed 6/16/10	Mon 6/21/10	1
4		Register attendees	5 days	Thu 6/17/10	Wed 6/23/10	1,2
5		Reserve hotel's room	1 hour?	Wed 6/16/10	Wed 6/16/10	7SS-10 days
6		Confirm number of attendees	2 hours?	Mon 6/28/10	Tue 6/29/10	4
7	📅	Give talk	6 hours	Wed 6/30/10	Wed 6/30/10	3FS+1 day,6FS+1 day
8		Receive attendees	1 hour?	Wed 6/30/10	Wed 6/30/10	7SF+30 mins
9	📅	Serve lunch	1 hour	Wed 6/30/10	Wed 6/30/10	
10		Validate tickets	30 mins?	Wed 6/30/10	Wed 6/30/10	7FF

Fig. 2. Proposed Gantt chart for the example process. Relationships between tasks are specified in the "Predecessors" column, linking their Start (S), Finish (F) or a combination of both.

It is possible to observe that given the nature of the Gantt chart, it is easy to specify temporal constraints and relationships among tasks. Also it allows deriving useful information that would help to coordinate the process execution, such as:

- Given the constraints and estimated task durations, it is possible to know how much in advance it is required to start tasks to meet the conference's deadline. Since the conference is scheduled on 6/30/2010 at 8:30, MS Project calculated that the first activity - *"Define topic"* - should be started on 6/15/2010.
- The constraints Start No Earlier Than (SNET) and Start No Later Than (SNLT) can be used to specify temporal boundaries in which tasks should be executed.
- Through As Late As Possible (ALAP) behavior, MS Project calculates the start date of *"Confirm Number of Attendees"* task, in order to maximize the number of attendees at the conference without delaying the process.

However, as a deficiency, the presented Gantt chart does not provide information to enable the process execution. For example, there is no information that allows deciding what to do if the *"Print conference material"* task takes more than 4 days. This is an aspect that differs greatly from the proposed BPMN model. As BPMN has a specification of its execution semantic, there is no room for interpretation; in the proposed BPMN model, it is necessary to wait for the completion of all precedent tasks in order to continue with the next one, no matter how long they take.

2.2   Usage and Goals of Process Modeling Notations

It was possible to observe in the example case that the process designer and the process coordinator use the process modeling notations in different ways. This agrees with Eder and Panagos [8], who recognized at least two instances in which a process execution support system (and implicitly the notation for specifying the model) should allow the inclusion or delivery of information:

1. Design/build-time: When the modeler is specifying the required process design, needsto represent the temporal dimension and check the feasibility of executing the proposed plan.
2. Run-time: Having specified the design, the system must meet the temporal constraints and relationships specified at design timeas well as make changes to the planning according to contingencies in the process execution.

The specification of a business process through a project planning tool such as MS Project, meets the requirements needed at design time, unlike BPMN. However, at runtime the roles are inverted, making interesting to take advantage of the approach of each notation through a mechanism that allows specifying the temporal restrictions of a business process using a project planning tool, and then automatically obtain its equivalence in BPMN, so as to get an unequivocal specification of its execution. The aim is to generate a BPMN model executable by a coordinating agent based on a Gantt chart planning, allowing the specification of the process's temporal dimension and the specification of its execution, even in those cases where contingencies force to make a diversion from the plans made.

3   Specification of Temporal Constraints and Relationships in BPMN 1.2 through MS Project

In this section we present the conceptual model that supports the equivalence between the two notations. To accomplish this, the following considerations should be taken into account:

- Although many similarities can be found between process and project models, it is important to notice that their interpretation differs greatly in their repeatability: while project plans are made for being executed once, process models are made for being executed many times. As a consequence, it is not possible to specify alternate paths in project plans, resulting in the impossibility to specify processes with conditional paths using project planning tools. However, planning tools can be used to specify the so-called process "happy path"; afterwards, standard BPMN tools can be used to specify conditional paths or other behaviors.
- Since Gantt charts do not specify what to do when a contingency takes place, it is necessary to define a heuristic to follow in these cases. There are different alternatives for this heuristic (i.e. different a-priori coordination decisions) and its

selection will affect the resulting Gantt chart-BPMN equivalence. In this work, we use a heuristic that achieves the minimization of the difference between the plan made and the actual process execution.

3.1 Process Orchestration Approach

The notations and languages for specifying processes can be divided into two types: those oriented to task's orchestration and those oriented to task's choreography. The orchestration-oriented notations center their description on the participant's point of view, including general information that allows the coordination of the involved parties. On the other hand, the goal of choreography-oriented notations is enabling collaboration, providing information to all participants, so as they can perform the tasks entrusted to them without central coordination [9]. Hence, both Gantt chart and BPMN models can be seen as specifications for process orchestration: they include information from the point of view of the process owner that can be used by a coordinating agent to run the process and coordinate activities with the various parties involved. In BPMN, this is called the representation of "public processes" that can be translated into a process orchestration language, such as WS-BPEL, allowing automation through process execution engines [10][11]. In Gantt charts, the equivalent is the reading and control of a project by a human agent, the "project coordinator", who is responsible for guiding its execution.

Taking in consideration the process orchestration approach, we use the semantic defined by Gagné and Trudel for project planning tools [5] as well as an exploration of additional concepts through the research of XML schema files generated by MS Project and online documentation [12]. Following, we will introduce the proposed equivalencies for all temporary constructs found according to the orchestration paradigm, the execution semantics defined in the BPMN 2.0 draft [4].

3.1.1 Task

The fundamental concept to define equivalences between BPMN and MS Project is the task concept. According to the process orchestration approach, it is important to notice that the actual execution of the work cannot be controlled by the coordinator. Therefore, the coordinator gets control only for delegating the responsibility of execution of a given task to a task performer. We will denote by A_s, the time when the coordinator delegates the responsibility of execution of task "A", and by A_e, the time when the task finishes. Additionally, since the real end may not coincide with the one specified in the model, we willmake a distinction between the real task completion time $A_e(real)$, defined as the time when the performer communicates tasks' completion, and the planned completion time $A_e(scheduled)$. The difference between them can be either due toan underestimation of the actual task duration ($A_e(scheduled)<A_e(real)$) or conversely, by an overestimation of its duration.

To join the proposed orchestrated process executionmodel with the semantic defined for the execution of BPMN, we distinguish two cases: (1) when the duration of the task is not limited and the performer is expected to communicate the task completion, and (2) when the coordinator must control the task completion and may revoke the task execution responsibility from the performer.

3.1.2 Task Duration

MS Project allows the specification of the estimated duration of tasks. Two types of durations can be defined: estimated and fixed. The proposed equivalent BPMN representations are shown in Table 1.

- Estimated duration: It is used to represent the duration of the task when there is no certainty. It is assumed that at runtime tasks finish as soon as possible, i.e., when the task performer informs the coordinator that the task has been completed. This is the default behavior of tasks in BPMN.
- Fixed duration: The modeler has the intention to specify the duration of the task. This intention may be different depending on which parameter is set fixed in the equation above:

  o Fixed units: The task will be completed as soon as possible, according to the restriction of resources available for its execution. In our proposal, it will be assumed that there is no specific restriction on the duration of the task, so it will be ended as soon as possible, as in the estimated durationcase.
  o Fixed work: The task will be completed as soon as possible; the units can be adjusted to complete the work. The equivalency is the same as on the previous case.
  o Fixed duration: The modeler has the intention to define a given duration for the task. Unlike the above cases, we establish a special execution semantic, in which the coordinator will revoke the execution responsibility from the task performer to ensure the task duration will be exactly as specified.

Table 1. BPMN equivalencies for different task duration types

Estimated duration (fixed units and fixed work)	Fixed duration

3.1.3 Inflexible Temporal Constraints

As defined in [5], inflexible time constraints have precedence over any other restriction or relationship between tasks. The proposed BPMN equivalencies are shown in Table 2 and detailed below:

- Must Start On (MSON): The coordinator should offer this task to the corresponding performer at the specified date, regardless of what happen with other related tasks. This is represented by placing the task in a parallel sequence flow with the other tasks, thus ensuring its execution in the specified time. It is important to remark that the use of dates in time events makes processes that can be executed only once. To avoid this, the project start date could be used as a reference and, by calculating the difference between this date and the specified in the time event, the duration of the time interval can be obtained.

- Must Finish On (MFON): We define the coordinator-driven completion time of a task as the instant when the coordinator will revoke the execution responsibility from the performer. This is specified in BPMN through a time event attached to the task. On the specified date (a point in time, not a time interval as in the case of fixed duration) the taskis finished and the process flow continues.

Table 2. Proposed BPMN equivalencies for inflexible temporal constraints

Must Start On	Must Finish On

3.1.4 Task Temporal Behaviors

This kind of temporal constraint defines the "temporal behavior" of tasks. Two possibilities arise: tasks can be executed as soon as the sequence flow arrives (ASAP) or it can be needed to delay their execution as much as possible without delaying the entire process (ALAP). The corresponding BPMN equivalencies are shown in Table 3.

Table 3. BPMN equivalencies for tasktemporal behaviors

As Soon As Possible	As Late As Possible

3.1.5 Flexible Temporal Constraints

Flexible temporal constrains define limits within which the task must be performed. The proposed BPMN equivalencies are shown in Table 4.

- Finish No Later Than (FNLT): This constraint establishes a deadline for the execution of the task. The defined BPMN equivalence is very similar to the one defined for MFON inflexible temporal constraint but includes the possibility of finishing the task before the established deadline.
- Start No Later Than (SNLT): It specifies that regardless the execution of other tasks, this task should start not later than the specified date. It is important to

mention that asignal event is added to coordinate the start of the execution of the taskwith the completion of its predecessor tasks, maintaining the default ASAP behavior.

- Finish No Earlier Than (FNET): It specifies that the task must finish after the specified date. However, since the coordinator has no real influence on the end of the task, it can only be specified the date after which the process flow is transferred the next task, by adding a time event.
- Start No Earlier Than (SNET): In this case, the task should start no earlier than the specified date, which is easily specified using the time event in BPMN.

Table 4. BPMN equivalencies for bounded execution constraints

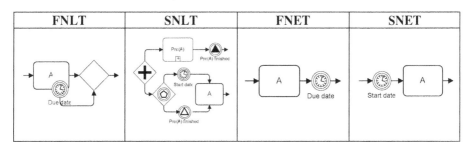

FNLT	SNLT	FNET	SNET

3.1.6 Temporal Relationships between Tasks

Temporal relationships are specified between two tasks (A and B), in order to coordinate their starting and finishing times, or a combination of both. Notice that MS Project can associate a displacement parameter (Δ) between these times, which can be positive or negative. It is important to notice that these relations are used in MS Project to calculate the start date of the dependent task (B) based on the estimated start or completion time of independent task (A). Also, in the absence of a relationship between two tasks, we define its equivalence in BPMN as both being in parallel flows, allowing any temporal execution order between them. The proposed BPMN equivalencies are shown in Table 5.

- Finish to Start (FS): B cannot begin before A ends. In the event that Δ is negative, we will use the estimated duration of A since it is not possible to know a priori its real completion time.
- Start to Start (SS): B cannot begin before A starts. This case is simple since the starting times of both tasks are under the total control of the coordinator. A time event is enough to cause the time lags defined by Δ, except when is negative.
- Finish to Finish (FF): B cannot finish until A has finished. In this case, since the real execution of the task cannot be controlled by the coordinator, we use the interrupting semantic defined by an interrupting event attached to the task.
- Start to Finish (SF): B cannot finish until A is started. As MS Project uses this relationship to calculate the estimated start date of the dependant task (B), we use the MSON equivalency with a calculated start date.

Table 5. Proposed BPMN equivalencies for temporal relationships between tasks

4   Conclusions

In this article, we exposed the weakness of BPMN to represent the temporal dimension of processes in comparison to the possibilities offered by project planning tools, as well as the weakness of the latter to guide the process execution when a contingency forces to divert from the initial planning. Given this situation, we proposed an equivalence between the concepts involved in a project planning tool -Microsoft Project- and BPMN constructs, in order to achieve an easy way to specify business processes that incorporate complex temporal constrains and relationships. This equivalence was made considering both notations as specifications for process orchestration, in which a coordinator assigns the execution of tasks to performers, analogously as a coordinator does in a project through a Gantt chart, or a process automation engine based on a BPMN diagram.

The proposal opens up interesting research opportunities. In first place it would be interesting to develop a concrete implementation of the submitted proposal. Currently we are implementing an application that receives an XML file exported from MS Project and generates a XPDL file, which canlater be opened with available BPMN editors.

Another interesting research line is related to the different heuristics that can be used to specify the equivalency Gantt chart-BPMN. Our proposal is based on the heuristic of minimizing the time difference between the actual and planned task completion. However, it is possible to define other behaviors based on different heuristics, for example, to ensure the complete execution of all tasks.

Finally, it may be interesting to investigate how to adapt the proposal for its inclusion in the process analysis phase, for example, making the derivation of temporal constraints and relationships of a process based on real executions of it.

References

1. van der Aalst, W.M.P., ter Hofstede, A.H.M., Weske, M.: Business process management: A survey. In: van der Aalst, W.M.P., ter Hofstede, A.H.M., Weske, M. (eds.) BPM 2003. LNCS, vol. 2678, pp. 1–12. Springer, Heidelberg (2003)
2. Gagné, D., Trudel, A.: Time-BPMN. In: Proceedings of 1st International Workshop on BPMN (2009)
3. Wilson, J.: Gantt charts: A centenary appreciation. European Journal of Operational Research 149(2), 430–437 (2003)
4. Object Management Group: Business Process Modeling Notation Beta 1 for Version 2.0, `http://www.omg.org/spec/BPMN/2.0/`
5. Gagné, D., Trudel, A.: The Temporal Perspective: Expressing Temporal Constraints and Dependencies. In: Process Models in BPM and Workflow Handbook (2008)
6. Cheng, J., Law, K.H.: Using Process Specification Language for Project Information. In: 3rd International Conference on Concurrent Engineering in Construction, Berkeley, CA, pp. 63–74 (2002)
7. BPMI.org, OMG: Business Process Modeling Notation Specification, Final Adopted Specification. Object Management Group (2006)
8. Eder, J., Paganos, E.: Managing Time in Workflow Systems. In: Fischer, L. (ed.) Workflow Handbook 2001, Future Strategies Inc. (2001)
9. Peltz, C.: Web Services Orchestration and Choreography. IEEE Computer 36 (2003)
10. Recker, J., Mendling, J.: On the Translation between BPMN and BPEL:Conceptual Mismatch between Process Modeling Languages. In: Proceedings of Workshops and Doctoral Consortium for the 18th International Conference on Advanced Information Systems Engineering (2006)
11. Ouyang, C., Dumas, M., ter Hofstede, A.H.M., van der Aalst, W.M.P.: From BPMN process models to BPEL Web services. In: Proceedings of the 4th International Conference on Web Services (ICWS 2006), pp. 285–292 (2006)
12. Microsoft Corp. MS Project Developer documentation, `http://msdn.microsoft.com/en-us/library/ bb251741%28v=office.12%29.aspx`

Appendix

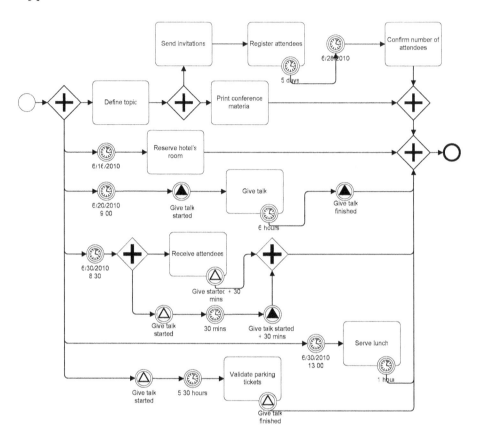

Fig. 3. Resultant BPMN model of the example case using the proposed Gantt-BPMN equivalencies

Supporting Context-Aware Process Design: Learnings from a Design Science Study

Karsten Ploesser[1,2], Jan Recker[1], and Michael Rosemann[1]

[1] SAP Research CEC Brisbane, South
Brisbane QLD 4101, Australia
[2] Queensland University of Technology,
Brisbane QLD 4000, Australia
`karsten.ploesser@sap.com`,
`{j.recker,m.rosemann}@qut.edu.au`

Abstract. Recent studies have started to explore context-awareness as a driver in the design of adaptable business processes. The emerging challenge of identifying and considering contextual drivers in the environment of a business process are well understood, however, typical methods and models for business process design do not yet consider this context. In this paper, we describe our work on the design of a method framework and appropriate models to enable a context-aware process design approach. We report on our ongoing work with an Australian insurance provider and describe the design science we employed to develop innovative and useful artifacts as part of a context-aware method framework. We discuss the utility of these artifacts in an application in the claims handling process at the case organization.

Keywords: process design, design science, context-awareness.

1 Introduction

Recent studies have explored 'context-awareness' [1] as a new paradigm in designing and managing business processes. This paradigm is grounded in the observation that business processes are coupled with elements in their external context (e.g., weather patterns, commodity prices, or industrial actions). For example, an Australian agency handling disaster claims had to apologise to victims of the Victorian bushfire in 2009 after automated letters were sent out, demanding that they provide identification, despite the fact that many of them had lost all proof of identification in the inferno [2]. In another example, a German bank lost €300 million in an automated swap transaction with its business partner, Lehman Brothers, on the day the American investment bank announced bankruptcy [3]. As a result of coupling, processes need to rapidly adapt if their context changes.

However, there is a lack of concrete artifacts to support the 'context-aware' manager in adapting processes to a changing context. Typical methods of process design do not yet consider context but instead focus on optimizing internal process variables such as throughput, quality, and/or time. As we will show, this internally focused viewpoint creates several challenges in practice.

M. zur Muehlen and J. Su (Eds.): BPM 2010 Workshops, LNBIP 66, pp. 97–104, 2011.

This paper reports on the design and application of artifacts to support context-aware process design decisions. Based on a case study with an Australian insurance provider, we explore limitations of traditional approaches and derive two key requirements for design artifacts. We ground our design work in the theory of complex systems, describe the nature and type of our initial design artifacts, and conclude by demonstrating the application of the artifacts to a scenario in the case study.

2 Motivating Example

Consider in the following our case study work with an Australian insurance company [4]. Since 2008, the insurer has been exposed to a string of natural disasters while investment returns have been diminishing in the global financial crisis. The constant pressure on its claims organization and claims handling & fulfillment processes has had an adverse effect on the insurer's profitability.

For each loss incurred and reported, the insurer needs to balance grade of service, indemnity cost, and claims handling expenses. Under normal circumstances, the 'claims process system' (i.e., the organizational and technical components of the claims organization) is calibrated to handle losses as efficient and effective as possible. This is achieved by a set of controls (e.g., what proofs are requested from the insured, which policy limits are to be applied, etc.) and according processes (e.g., 'no-touch', 'light-touch', and 'case-managed').

However, the claims process system is not static but needs to be recalibrated for each different 'context' in which losses are incurred (e.g., global financial crisis, Victorian bushfires, Sydney sandstorms, Queensland floods, etc.). This has two reasons. Firstly, disasters require the insurer to handle different volumes in different time-frames (e.g., numerous moderate losses in the weeks following a storm, few major losses over months after bushfires). Secondly, each disaster exposes the insurer to different types of leakage (i.e., inflated payouts) or opportunistic fraud (e.g., the risk of fraud differs between rural and urban areas).

In the case interviews, respondents provided a narrative of decisions taken to adapt the process in different contexts and recurring issues they observed. In the interest of brevity, we refer the reader to our extensive case analysis [4], and summarize key findings in Table 1.

Table 1. Process management gaps observed in case study

Case study finding	Illustration
Context-driven process change creates flow-on effects	A decision to increase capacity and processing rate in one process step in a storm incident led to significant bottlenecks and an increased error rate in subsequent steps.
Market swiftly adapts to context-driven process changes	The market responded to a decision to loosen process controls in a flooding incident with an increase in opportunistic fraud

3   Background and Related Work

Business process design is generally associated with moving from a current state (AS-IS) to an improved state (TO-BE) of process operations. This has often been accompanied by the introduction of Enterprise Resource Planning (ERP) systems into functional areas such as procurement, human resources, etc. The ERP approach to process improvement is founded on 'best practices', i.e., the reduction of a complex problem such as general ledger to a simple, repeatable, standardized set of transactions that can be supported in an IS. Accordingly, much of the focus of process design has been on optimizing internal process variables such as throughput, process cost, or quality.

We suggest that the ERP approach to process improvement and its underlying conceptualization of the firm are materializations of 'closed-system' thinking [5]. Closed-system thinking assumes that the performance of a system can be explained by reducing it to its finite parts, which are studied in isolation from one another and the environment. Such systems are 'linear', i.e., changing one part has no effect on the performance of other parts or the system environment.

However, a growing debate in the management and IS disciplines [cf. 6] conceptualizes firms as 'open systems', 'open' because they exchange resources with their environment and 'systems' because they consist of interconnected parts. Open systems are tightly coupled with their environment [7].

According to 'open-system' thinking, both environment and system 'co-evolve' through constant interaction [6]. This implies that the performance of a core process cannot be explained solely by the performance of its parts. Instead, it emerges from the interactions between these parts and the external environment. Such systems are 'non-linear', i.e., changes to one part affect others.

In this paper, we argue that the process management gaps observed in section 2 can be overcome by conceptualizing business processes as non-linear systems. In our earlier work [1, 4] we have shown how this conceptualization enables managers to extend their viewpoint of business processes, and to develop a more comprehensive understanding of important design and change drivers.

However, to act upon this understanding, managers and analysts need to be supported through a set of design artifacts that build upon the theoretical premise of context-awareness. In the following, we describe the design science process we executed to build such artifacts.

4   Design Approach

We follow the design science (DS) paradigm of IS research [8]. DS postulates that artifact design needs to demonstrate both *relevance* of the artifact proposed and *rigor* in its inception. Relevance of our artifact will be evaluated in the application to the process scenario described in section 2, and is detailed in section 5. To ensure rigor of our design process, we follow the guidelines proposed by Gregor and Jones [9], which inform the search process [8] outlined in section 5.

Following the classification of Gregor et al. [9], the *purpose and scope* of our design work is to support process managers in making process changes in accordance to changing context parameters. This choice is motivated by the findings of our case study work presented in section 2 and the *theoretical construct* of 'tight coupling' and 'co-evolution'. Through the application of the artifact, process managers should have the ability to analyze the feedback structure of a non-linear system and identify suitable, context-aware process adaptation strategies. The artifact should perform at least as well as extant process management frameworks (*artifact mutability*).

The following sections outline guidelines for context-aware process adaptation (*principles of implementation*) and provide an *instantiation* by applying the framework to the process scenario in section 2.

5   Designing the Framework

Two key challenges arise in the design of an artifact for context-driven process improvement. According to the case study findings presented in section 2, such an artifact needs to support managers and business analysts in understanding a) the coupling between external and internal process variables and b) the effect of changes to internal variables on external variables.

We draw from the theory of complex systems [7] to ground these findings in the concepts 'tight coupling' and 'co-evolution'. Tight coupling emerges from the interconnectedness of system components, i.e., the elements inside or outside the organization that participate in or influence the process. Co-evolution emerges from the constant interaction of these components, i.e., processes are shaped by, and also shape, their environment [6]. Table 2 summarizes this discussion and proposes two requirements for artifact design.

Table 2. Properties of a context-aware process management method

Case study finding	Theoretical construct	Artifact requirement
Context-driven process change creates flow-on effects	Tight coupling	Capability to describe the coupling of system components and environment
Market swiftly adapts to context-driven process changes	Co-evolution	Capability to identify the wider implications of adapting a business process to context change

Research in the representation of non-linear behavior in organizations and business processes as "knowledge for action" [10] has traditionally been treated in different research streams. System dynamics modeling [7], for example, represents the structure and dynamics of complex systems as highly aggregate variables in *continuous* interaction. The typical representation approach used by process analysts, process modeling [11], on the other hand, abstracts from real world processes by focusing on *discrete* events (e.g., 'order to cash').

In the following, we seek to integrate both approaches by defining them as different perspectives, or 'viewpoints', onto a common problem. We suggest that a solution to this problem, i.e., nonlinearity in business processes, needs to consider both the high-level feedback structure of the system as well as the individual actions undertaken by the system (i.e., core processes) to convert inputs into outputs.

We commence by modeling the 'macro-level' viewpoint of the system, i.e., a 'causally closed' model of system variables and their interactions. This has traditionally been the domain of system dynamics modeling. There is a comprehensive body of literature [c.f. 7, 12] on issues dealing with the identification, creation, and communication of such models. The purpose of such a model is to provide management with an overview of the principal process variables and external 'risk' in business processes [13].

The next step in model creation consists of defining the global observable behavior of the system, i.e. the 'core process' that converts inputs received by the system into outputs. Issues dealing with the identification, modeling, and communication of processes have been exhaustively researched [cf. 11]. The purpose of this model is to provide a detailed specification of the firm's value chain, i.e., the revenue- or cost-generating activities in the core process. We refer to this viewpoint as the 'meso-level' viewpoint of the process system.

Ultimately, both specifications need to be assembled into an overall model. The purpose of this model is to analyze a) how process activities are affected by system variables and b) how process activities affect system variables. This model can be used, e.g., to simulate different process variants in a given process context. To facilitate such application, in Fig. 1, we introduce an extended business process meta-model that integrates the concepts of both viewpoints.

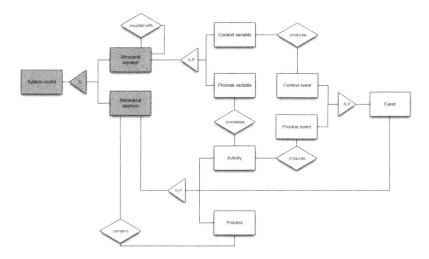

Fig. 1. Extended business process meta-model based on Rosemann et al. [1]

6 Applying the Framework

In the following, we apply the concepts developed in section 5 to a core problem observed in the insurance case study introduced earlier. We use Sterman's [12] stock & flow notation to model the structural features of the system under observation. Natural disasters trigger spikes in claims volume that require the insurer to handle more claims in less time. In response to this situation, the insurer developed a stream-lined lodgment system that allows the fast capture of loss information. In a linear system (Fig. 2), this should lead to an increase in the overall processing rate achieved by the insurer.

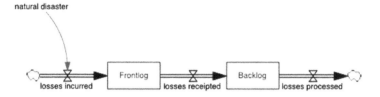

Fig. 2. Linear model of process chain

However, the relationship between claims volume and settled claims in a disaster is not linear. The system is tightly coupled and any change in one component can gener-ate flow-on effects on other components. In the insurance case study, the increased lodgment rate did not result in a linear increase in the overall processing rate. Instead, the overall processing rate fell below expectations. This called for an explanation.

Fig. 3 extends Fig. 2 by feedback loops. These feedback loops were reported by re-spondents in the case interviews, and show how pressure slowly builds up after a disas-ter as a result of a spike in volume and heightened attention. The streamlined lodgment system, once activated, requires the claims handler in the 'frontend' to spend less time in handling a call and to capture less information about the loss cause. However, the time gained is lost later in the 'backend' of the process. Claims handlers now spend increasing time in recovering the missing information and handling return calls from disgruntled customers. This ultimately slows the overall processing capacity.

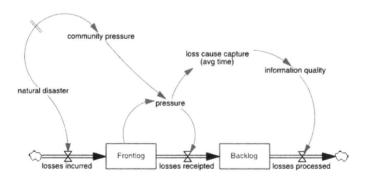

Fig. 3. Non-linear model of process chain

Next, we model the process activities from the time the first notice of loss is re-ceived (the 'frontlog') to the time the claim is passed to the 'backend' for settlement (the 'backlog'). We then integrate the feedback structure modeled in the previous step. The purpose of this exercise is to trace the flow of information and identify those activities that contribute to the problem. Fig. 4 shows the activities conducted by claims handlers in the 'frontend' of the process following BPMN notation [14]. Note that the concept of system variable is mapped to the concept of 'data store' according to version 2.0 of BPMN.

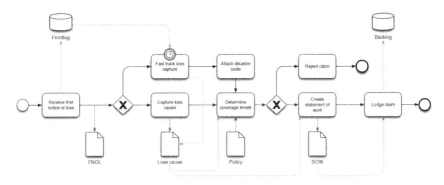

Fig. 4. Integrating feedback structure and process model

7 Discussion

In section 6, we introduced a process scenario in which tight coupling of process components with the environment generates nonlinear behavior. We showed how traditional approach to process modeling and improvement that focus on internal process variables are insufficient to explain this problem. Furthermore, we demonstrated how the application of the two modeling viewpoints introduced in section 5 enables us to capture the feedback between *external* and *internal* process variables and thus gain an enhanced understanding of the behavior of the system.

Our work makes an original contribution to the scholarly discussion in process modeling by extending its reach to the domain of context-driven business processes and context-awareness. The two viewpoints introduced in section 5 serves as explanatory devices to describe the coupling between context and process and to explain the resulting behavior. Furthermore, the work makes an early attempt to integrate two modeling approaches that have to date been treated in different research streams, system dynamics and discrete-event/process modeling.

We acknowledge two limitations of our research. On the one hand, the typical limitations of case study [15] as well as design science research [8] apply. We have sought to increase generalisability of our findings by applying the framework to a second case in a different industry. On the other hand, a more rigorous field testing of the artifacts is required. We are in the process of setting up a test infrastructure with the insurer.

8 Conclusion

In this paper, we have suggested that organizational processes are social systems that are tightly coupled and co-evolve with their environment. Drawing on examples from an insurance case study, we furthermore suggested that such systems show nonlinear behavior emerging from the interaction between external (weather patterns, community attitudes) and internal process variables (grade of service, throughput, cost). However, traditional approaches to process design focus mostly on optimizing internal variables but ignore external ones.

In an attempt to rectify this issue, we introduced a process design framework covering two viewpoints, the 'macro-level' feedback structure of the system and the 'meso-level' processes. In our future work, we will extend the framework to a holistic portfolio of decision-support tools to assist management with making informed decisions about process designs and process changes in accordance to relevant contextual factors. Our framework extensions specifically will address *impact measurement*, and *change implementation* strategies.

References

1. Rosemann, M., Recker, J., Flender, C.: Contextualisation of business processes. International Journal of Business Process Integration and Management 3, 47–60 (2008)
2. Maher, S.: Centrelink will apologise to victims. The Australian, Sydney (2009)
3. Moore, M.S.: German bank under fire for strange Lehman deal. Spiegel Online, Hamburg, Germany (2008)
4. Ploesser, K., Recker, J., Rosemann, M.: Building a methodology for context-aware business processes: Insights from an exploratory case study. In: Johnson, R., de Villiers, C. (eds.) Proceedings of the 18th European Conference on Information Systems, Pretoria, South Africa (2010)
5. Ackoff, R.L.: Science in the systems age: Beyond IE, OR, and MS. Operations Research 21, 661–671 (1973)
6. Merali, Y.: Complexity and information systems: The emergent domain. Journal of Information Technology 21, 216–228 (2006)
7. Forrester, J.: System dynamics, systems thinking, and soft OR. System Dynamics Review 10, 245–256 (1994)
8. Hevner, A., March, S., Park, J., Ram, S.: Design science in information systems research. MIS Quarterly 28, 75–106 (2004)
9. Gregor, S., Jones, D.: The anatomy of a design theory. Journal of the Association for Information Systems 8, 312–335 (2007)
10. Krogstie, J., Sindre, G., Jørgensen, H.: Process models representing knowledge for action: a revised quality framework. European Journal of Information Systems 15, 91–102 (2006)
11. Indulska, M., Recker, J., Rosemann, M., Green, P.: Business process modeling: Current issues and future challenges. In: van Eck, P., Gordijn, J., Wieringa, R. (eds.) CAiSE 2009. LNCS, vol. 5565, pp. 501–514. Springer, Heidelberg (2009)
12. Sterman, J.: Business dynamics: systems thinking and modeling for a complex world. Irwin/McGraw-Hill, Boston (2000)
13. zur Muehlen, M., Rosemann, M.: Integrating risks in business process models. In: Proceedings of the 16th Australasian Conference on Information Systems, Manly, Sydney, Australia (2005)
14. Object Management Group: Business Process Model and Notation, v2.0 Beta 1. Needham, MA (2010)
15. Lee, A.S.: A Scientific Methodology for MIS Case Studies. MIS Quarterly 13, 32–50 (1989)

6th International Workshop on Business Process Intelligence (BPD 2010)

6th International Workshop on Business Process Intelligence (BPD 2010)

Workshop Organization

Workshop Organizers

MaluCastellanos
Intelligent Enterprise Technologies Lab
Hewlett-Packard Laboratories
1501 Page Mill Rd, CA 94304
USA

Boudewijn van Dongen
Department of Mathematics and Computer Science
Eindhoven University of Technology
P.O. Box 513
5600 MB, Eindhoven
The Netherlands

Diego R. Ferreira
IST – Technical University of Lisbon
Avenida Prof. Dr. Cavaco Silva
2744-016 Porto Salvo
Portugal

Barbara Weber (Corresponding Organizer)
InstitutfürInformatik
Universität Innsbruck
Technikerstraße 21a
6020 Innsbruck
Austria

Workshop Program Committee

Wil van der Aalst, Eindhoven University of Technology, The Netherlands
Ana Karla Alves de Medeiros, Capgemini Consulting, The Netherlands
Gerardo Canfora, University of Sannio, Italy
MaluCastellanos, HP, USA
Peter Dadam, University of Ulm, Germany
Boudewijn van Dongen, Eindhoven University of Technology, The Netherlands
Diogo R. Ferreira, Technical University of Lisbon, Portugal
WalidGaloul, DERI Galway, Ireland
Gianluigi Greco, University of Calabria, Italy
Daniela Grigori, France
AntonellaGuzzo, University of Calabria, Italy
Joachim Herbst, DaimlerChrysler Research and Technology, Germany
Jun-Jang Jeng, IBM Research, USA

Mining Context-Dependent and Interactive Business Process Maps Using Execution Patterns

Jiafei Li[1,2], R.P. Jagadeesh Chandra Bose[2,3], and Wil M.P. van der Aalst[2]

[1] College of Computer Science and Technology,
Jilin University, China 130012
`jiafei@jlu.edu.cn`, `l.j.f.Li@tue.nl`
[2] Eindhoven University of Technology, The Netherlands
`j.c.b.rantham.prabhakara@tue.nl`, `w.m.p.v.d.aalst@tue.nl`
[3] Philips Healthcare, Veenpluis 5-6, Best, The Netherlands

Abstract. Process mining techniques attempt to extract non-trivial knowledge and interesting insights from event logs. Process models can be seen as the "maps" describing the operational processes of organizations. Unfortunately, traditional process discovery algorithms have problems dealing with less-structured processes. Furthermore, existing discovery algorithms do not consider the analyst's context of analysis. As a result, the current models (i.e., "maps") are difficult to comprehend or even misleading. To address this problem, we propose a two-phase approach based on common execution patterns. First, the user selects relevant and context-dependent patterns. These patterns are used to obtain an event log at a higher abstraction level. Subsequently, the transformed log is used to create a hierarchical process map. The approach has been implemented in the context of ProM. Using a real-life log of a housing agency we demonstrate that we can use this approach to create maps that (i) *depict desired traits*, (ii) *eliminate irrelevant details*, (iii) *reduce complexity*, and (iv) *improve comprehensibility*.

1 Introduction

Process mining aims at extracting process-related information from event logs. Process mining techniques can deliver valuable, factual insights into how processes are being executed in real life. The majority of research in process mining so far has focussed on process discovery (both from a control-flow and organizational perspective). Process models can be seen as the "maps" describing the operational processes of organizations. Unfortunately, *accurate and interactive business process maps* are missing. Either there are no good maps or maps (if available) are static and/or outdated [1].

Process mining techniques can be used to generate process maps [2,3,4]. We have applied our process mining tool ProM in more than 100 organizations and our experiences show that processes tend to be less structured than expected.

M. zur Muehlen and J. Su (Eds.): BPM 2010 Workshops, LNBIP 66, pp. 109–121, 2011.

Traditional process discovery algorithms have problems dealing with such unstructured processes and generate spaghetti-like process models that are hard to comprehend. The granularity at which the events are logged is typically different from the desired granularity. Analysts and end users prefer a higher level of abstraction without being confronted with lower level events stored in raw event logs.

Analogous to cartography, process mining techniques should allow for various context-dependent views on the process maps. For example, the perspective of analysis may be different depending on someone's role and expertise e.g., a manager may be interested in a high level view, while a specialist may be interested in a detailed analysis of some process fragment. Process discovery techniques should facilitate the extraction of process maps eliciting the respective desired traits and hiding the irrelevant ones for various users. Furthermore, these techniques should uncover comprehensible models by providing a hierarchical view with a facility to seamlessly zoom in or zoom out the process maps. There is an imperative need for *techniques that automatically generate understandable and context-dependent business process maps* [1].

In this paper, we propose a *two-phase approach to mine interactive and context-dependent business process maps based on common execution patterns.* The *first phase* comprises the pre-processing of a log with desired traits and at a desired level of granularity. This paper will show one means to realize this by uncovering common execution patterns in the log, selecting context-dependent patterns, and defining abstractions over these patterns. Pattern selection and the mapping with abstractions can be interactively performed by the user. Event logs are then pre-processed (transformed) with these abstractions. In the *second phase*, the transformed log is used for process discovery. Any discovery algorithm with an ability to zoom-in/out the sub-processes defined by the abstractions can be used. This paper presents an adapted version of the Fuzzy Miner [3] and shows that it can provide such hierarchical view of process maps. The two-phase approach presented in this paper has been implemented in ProM 6.0[1]. Figure 1 highlights the difference between the traditional approach to do process discovery and the two-phase approach. Note that the process model (map) mined using the two-phase approach is simpler and that this approach enables the abstraction of activities based on functionality and provides a seamless zooming into the sub-processes captured in the abstractions.

The remainder of the paper is organized as follows. Our two-phase approach to mining process maps is introduced in Section 2. Section 3 presentes pattern definitions and pattern metrics while Section 4 proposes one approach to form abstractions based on patterns. In Section 5, we detail our two-step approach and describe an adaptation of Fuzzy Miner to discover process maps. Section 6 presents a case study of a real-life log from a rental agency. Related work is discussed in Section 7. Section 8 concludes the paper.

---

[1] ProM 6.0 is not officially released yet, but nightly builds, including the reported functionality are available from www.processmining.org

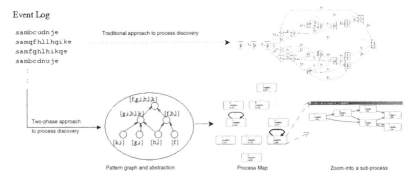

Fig. 1. Traditional approach vs. two-phase approach

2   Two-Phase Approach to Mine Process Maps

We use the following notations in this paper. Let Σ denote the set of activities. $|\Sigma|$ is the number of activities. Σ^+ is the set of all non-empty finite sequences of activities from Σ. We denote traces by bold face lower case letters $\mathbf{t}_1$, $\mathbf{t}_2$ etc. A trace $\mathbf{t}$ is an element of Σ^+. $\mathbf{t}(i)$ denotes the ith activity in the trace. For $i < j$, $\mathbf{t}(i,j)$ denotes the subsequence from the ith position to the jth position in the trace $\mathbf{t}$. An event log $\mathcal{L}$ corresponds to a bag (i.e., a multiset) of traces.

Phase-1: Preprocessing Log. In this phase, the log is simplified based on the desired traits of the context of analysis. A mapping $\mathcal{M} \subseteq 2^{\Sigma} \times \mathcal{A}$ is defined between the *original alphabet* of the event log Σ, and an *abstract alphabet* $\mathcal{A}$. An example mapping is $\mathcal{M} = \{(\{a, b\}, x), (\{b, c, d\}, y), (\{e\}, z), (\{d\}, z)\}$. This mapping is analogous to the grouping and tagging of streets as a town/city in cartography and to the selection of a desired perspective of viewing maps (restaurant maps vs. fuel station maps). The analyst can define this mapping based on domain knowledge or can be assisted by uncovering common execution patterns and relationships between them in the log. These common execution patterns typically capture a sub-process/functionality. Analysts would like to capture such subprocess behavior in its totality as an *abstract activity* in a mined process model with a facility to zoom in/out the subprocess if needed. The mapping is defined over the sets of activities manifested as patterns. We present techniques that assist in automatically uncovering such patterns and relationships between activities in Section 3.

$\mathcal{D} = \bigcup_{(A,\mathbf{a}) \in \mathcal{M}} A$ denotes the set of activities in Σ for which a mapping is defined. The original event log $\mathcal{L}$, is transformed into an *abstract log* $\mathcal{L}'$. Each trace $\mathbf{t} \in \mathcal{L}$ is transformed into a corresponding trace $\mathbf{t}' \in \mathcal{L}'$. In each trace $\mathbf{t}$, the manifestation of each pattern captured by $(A, \mathbf{a}) \in \mathcal{M}$ is replaced with its *abstract activity*, $\mathbf{a}$, in the transformed trace. The activities in $\Sigma \setminus \mathcal{D}$ being not involved in the definition of mapping indicate activities that are insignificant from the context of analysis and are filtered from $\mathbf{t}$ during this transformation. In Section 5, we describe the transformation of log in detail.

Phase-2: Mining Maps. The second phase is to mine a process model on the abstract log. The mapping defined in Phase-1 induces a hierarchy over the abstract activities. Upon zooming into an abstract activity, a process model depicting the subprocess captured by this abstract activity is shown. The patterns replaced by the abstract activity are used to create this sub-process model. We adapted Fuzzy Miner for this phase and the details are presented in Section 5. Note that this is a generic approach that can be iterated over any number of times with the event log for iteration $i + 1$ being the output event log of iteration i.

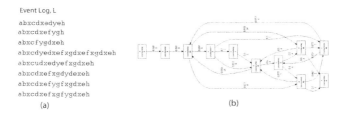

Event Log, L

    abxcdxedyeh
    abxcdxefygh
    abxcfygdxeh
    abxcdyedxefxgdxefxgdxeh
    abxcudxedyefxgdxeh
    abxcdxefxgdydexeh
    abxcdxefygfxgdxeh
    abxcdxefxgfygdxeh

        (a)   (b)

Fig. 2. (a) An example log (b) process models discovered using Heuristic miner

We use a running example log depicted in Figure 2(a) to illustrate the approach. This log contains 8 process instances with 11 event classes. Figure 2(b) depicts the model mined using traditional process discovery techniques. It is imperative to find that both these models are not easy to understand. In the following sections, we will present our two-phase approach in more detail using this example.

3   Pattern Definitions and Pattern Metrics

In this section, we adapt the pattern definitions proposed in [5] and focus on defining metrics over these patterns. We consider only the *maximal repeat* patterns for the discussion in this paper. However, other patterns such as *tandem arrays* capturing the manifestation of loop constructs proposed in [5] can also be used. These patterns are later used to define the mapping $\mathcal{M}$ between activities and abstractions.

3.1   Pattern Definitions

Definition 1 (Maximal Repeat). *A maximal pair in a sequence, s, is a pair of identical sub-sequences α and β such that the symbol to the immediate left/right of α is different from the symbol to the immediate left/right of β. In other words, extending α and β on either side would destroy the equality of the two strings. A maximal pair is denoted by the triple (i, j, α) where i and j correspond to the starting positions of α and β in s with $i \neq j$. A maximal repeat in a sequence, s, is defined as a subsequence α that occurs in a maximal pair in s.*

Maximal repeats capture execution patterns (sequence of activities) common within a trace and/or across a set of traces in an event log. Such patterns might be evidence of common functionality (often abstracted as a sub-process). In order to find these commonalities across multiple traces in the entire event log, we first construct a single sequence, say, $\mathbf{s}$, which is obtained by the concatenation of traces in the event log with a distinct delimiter between the traces. Maximal repeats are then discovered over this concatenated sequence $\mathbf{s}$. Maximal repeats can be efficiently discovered in linear time using suffix trees for strings [6]. Let $\mathcal{P_L}$ be the set of all patterns in log $\mathcal{L}$. In this paper, $\mathcal{P_L}$ includes all maximal repeats and $\{\mathbf{a} \mid \mathbf{a} \in \Sigma\}$. A *base pattern* is a pattern that does not contain any other pattern within it. The pattern abxc is a base pattern while abxcdxe is not because the latter pattern contains the pattern x within it. Let $\mathcal{P}_\mathcal{L}^b$ be the set of all base patterns in $\mathcal{P_L}$.

Consider the trace $\mathbf{t}_6 = $ abxcdxefxgdyedxeh in the log of Figure 2(a). The maximal pairs in $\mathbf{t}_6$ are $(3, 6, \mathbf{x})$, $(5, 11, \mathbf{d})$, $(7, 13, \mathbf{e})$ and $(5, 14, \mathbf{dxe})$. There are a total of 39 maximal repeats in the example log (e.g., abxc, abxcd, abxcdxe, dxe, fxg, dye, fyg, dyedxe, dxedye, h). $\mathcal{P}_\mathcal{L}^b = \{$a, b, c, u, x, d, g, f, h, e, y, gf, gd, ef, ed, eh, fxg, dye, fyg, dxe, fxgd, abxc, gdxe, dxeh, dxef, efxg, efxgd, abxcd, gdxeh,fygdxeh$\}$.

Definition 2 (Pattern Alphabet). *The pattern alphabet $\Gamma(p)$, of a pattern, $p \in \mathcal{P_L}$, is the set of activities that appear in p.*

Definition 3 (Equivalence Class of Pattern Alphabet). *The equivalence class of a pattern alphabet PA, is defined as $[PA] = \{p \mid p$ is a pattern and $\Gamma(p) = PA\}$*

For example, for the patterns fxg, dyedxe and dxedye, the pattern alphabets correspond to {f,x,g}, {d,x,y,e}, and {d,x,y,e} respectively. The equivalence class of the pattern alphabet {d,x,y,e} is {dyedxe,dxedye}. Equivalence classes of pattern alphabets capture variations of patterns e.g., due to parallelism.

3.2   Pattern Metrics

Pattern metrics such as the frequency of occurrence, significance etc. need to be estimated. A careful consideration needs to be done when estimating the frequency of a pattern. It is due to the fact that certain regions in a trace can contribute to more than one pattern (in the case of overlapping patterns) and might result in misleading frequency counts. For example, consider the trace $\mathbf{t}$ = abxcdxedfxgdxeh and the pattern alphabet equivalence classes [{a,b,x,c}] = {abxc}, [{a,b,x,c,d}] = {abxcd}, and [{d,x,e}] = {dxe,dxed}. Now, *what should be the pattern (alphabet) counts?*. If we consider each of the patterns separately, the pattern, frequency-count pairs are (abxc, 1), (abxcd, 1), (dxe, 2) and (dxed, 1). If we define the pattern alphabet count to be the sum of counts of the patterns captured in its equivalence class, then the pattern alphabet, frequency-count pairs are ($\{$a, b, x, c$\}$, 1), ($\{$a, b, x, c, d$\}$, 1), and ($\{$d, x, e$\}$, 3). It is imperative to see that certain regions in the trace are contributing to more

than one pattern (alphabet). The activities in the subsequence $\mathbf{t}(5,7)$ contributed
to two patterns viz., dxe and dxed. Similarly, the activities in the subsequence
$\mathbf{t}(1,4)$ contributed to two patterns viz., abxc and abxcd.

We identify three distinct methods of dealing with overlaps and counting pattern occurrences. The above method of computing pattern (alphabet) counts is
referred to as *Overlapping Alphabet Count (OAC)*. The significance computed using overlapping alphabet counts may be misleading. A more accurate method of
computing pattern frequencies is to consider non-overlapping pattern counts. We
distinguish two variations here: (i) considering non-overlap counts for each alphabet separately (local) and (ii) considering non-overlap counts across all alphabets
(global) in the event log. These two metrics are referred to as *Non-Overlapping
Alphabet Count (NOAC)* and *Non-Overlapping Global Alphabet Count (NO-
GAC)* respectively. Conflicts arise when more than one pattern can potentially
contribute to the count at a region in a trace. One can assign preference to say
shorter (longer) patterns to resolve such conflicts. The *NOAC* (with preference
to shorter patterns) for the above example is $(\{a, b, x, c\}, 1)$, $(\{a, b, x, c, d\}, 1)$,
and $(\{d, x, e\}, 2)$. Note that the conflict at position 5 in $\mathbf{t}$ for pattern alphabet
$\{d,x,e\}$ is resolved in favor of the pattern dxe thereby making $\mathbf{t}(5,7)$ contribute
to only one pattern. The *NOGAC* across all alphabets (with preference to longer
patterns) is $(\{a, b, x, c\}, 0)$, $(\{a, b, x, c, d\}, 1)$, and $(\{d, x, e\}, 1)$. A position/sub-
sequence in a trace can contribute to more than one pattern alphabet when
considering *NOAC* for each alphabet separately (e.g., index 1 in $\mathbf{t}$) while in
NOGAC, a position contributes to at most one pattern alphabet.

In order to assess the significance of a pattern alphabet PA, we define a metric
Conservedness $(CON_{PA}) = \frac{NOAC}{\mu} * (1 - \frac{\sigma}{\mu}) * 100\%$ where μ and σ are the mean
and standard deviation of the frequencies of activities in PA. *Conservedness*
measures the degree to which the individual activities involved in the pattern
alphabet manifest as the patterns defined by the alphabet. For example, consider the non-overlap alphabet count of three pattern alphabets $(\{d, x, e\}, 100)$,
$(\{d, x, e, f\}, 60)$, and $(\{d, x, e, h\}, 40)$. Let the frequency of activities be $(d, 100)$,
$(x, 100)$, $(e, 100)$, $(f, 60)$, and $(h, 40)$. Conservedness value of the pattern alphabets $\{d,x,e\}$, $\{d,x,e,f\}$, and $\{d,x,e,h\}$ is 100%, 51% and 30% respectively. The
formal definitions of the above pattern metrics are presented in [7].

4   Abstractions Based on Patterns

4.1   Pattern Graph

Relationships exist between patterns (alphabets). For example, consider the patterns dxefxg, dxe, and fxg. It could be the case that dxe and fxg are sub-
functionalities used also in a larger context dxefxg. One can try to define a
partial order capturing the relationships on the pattern alphabets. For example,
subsumption can be used as the cover relation. A pattern alphabet PA_i is defined
to cover another pattern alphabet PA_j if $PA_j \subset PA_i$ and there is no PA_k such
that $PA_j \subset PA_k \subset PA_i$. A *pattern graph* $G = (V, E)$, is a Hasse diagram defined
over the partial order on the pattern alphabets, where $V = \{PA_1, PA_2, \ldots, PA_n\}$

represents the set of pattern alphabets and E denotes the set of edges (PA_i, PA_j) defined by the cover relation. One can choose either $\mathcal{P}_{\mathcal{L}}$ or $\mathcal{P}_{\mathcal{L}}^b$ to define V. Figure 3(a) depicts a pattern graph on some of the pattern alphabets identified for the example log. We considered pattern alphabets defined by $\mathcal{P}_{\mathcal{L}}^b$ with a conservedness value above 17% to generate this graph.

4.2   Pattern Selection

Nodes in a pattern graph form the basis for abstraction. An analyst can select the pattern nodes based on domain knowledge or by using the pattern metrics defined in Section 3. We provide two types of node selection modes for abstraction.

Single Node Mode: All manifestations of patterns under the equivalence class of this node's pattern alphabet are represented by the same abstract activity in the transformed log.

Sub-graph Mode: All manifestations of patterns under the equivalence classes of the pattern alphabets defined by the *induced subgraph* at the selected node are substituted by the abstract activity of the selected node during transformation.

It could be the case that a pattern graph contains a large number of nodes. We recommend to first filter the nodes in the pattern graph before considering them for abstractions. All the metrics defined in Section 3.2 can be used to prune the graph. For example, consider the pattern alphabets {a,b,x,c} and {a,b,x,c,d} in Figure 3(a). The $NOGAC$ of {a,b,x,c,d} with preference to shorter patterns (ignoring individual activity patterns) is zero. Similarly, the $NOGAC$ of {d,x,e, f}, {d,x,e,h}, {g,d,x,e,h}, {g,d,x,e}, {e,h}, {e,d}, {e,f}, {g,d} and {g,f} are all zero. This indicates that manifestations of all patterns under the equivalence class of these pattern alphabets in the log are overlapping with some other pattern. For example, the equivalence class of the pattern alphabet {e,d} is {ed}. There are two manifestations of the pattern ed in $\mathcal{L}$ (in traces abxcdxedyeh and abxcudxedyefxgdxeh). However, both of these manifestations overlap with dxe and dye in the example log; thus making the $NOGAC$ of {e,d} as 0.

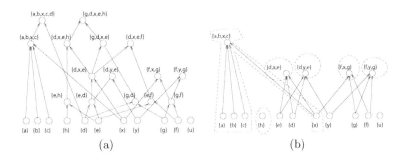

(a)   (b)

Fig. 3. (a) Pattern graph (b) pattern graph with abstractions for the example log

We recommend to consider nodes capturing longer patterns with a high conservedness value and significant $NOAC$ and $NOGAC$ to be used under sub-graph mode for abstractions. However, for two pattern alphabet nodes PA_i and PA_j such that $(PA_i, PA_j) \in E$ (i.e., $PA_i \subset PA_j$), if $CON_{PA_i} > CON_{PA_j}$ then, we recommend to consider PA_i under sub-graph mode instead of PA_j though PA_i captures shorter patterns. For example, consider the pattern alphabets {d,x,e}, {d,x,e,f}, {d,x,e,h} and {g,d,x,e}. The conservedness value for these alphabets are $52\%, 22\%, 21\%, 22\%$ respectively. It could be seen that the pattern dxe (defined by the alphabet {d,x,e}) occurs in different contexts in $\mathcal{L}$. The different contexts are captured by the other three alphabets and are reflected with the relatively low conservedness values for these three alphabets. We recommend to consider {d,x,e} as a node for abstraction instead of the other three. Coincidentally in this example the $NOGAC$ (with preference to shorter patterns) for the three larger alphabets is also zero.

If nodes in the sub-graph of a pattern node PA_i are covered by one or more nodes PA_j that are not in the sub-graph of PA_i then we recommend to consider PA_i under single-node mode for abstraction (assuming PA_i is selected). For example, the node {d,x,e} is recommended to be considered under single-node mode because the nodes {d} and {e} in the sub-graph of {d,x,e} is also covered by another node {d,y,e}. Note that these are just recommendations and an analyst can make exceptions if it makes sense according to the context of analysis. Using these guidelines we use the abstractions as defined in Figure 3(b). Here {a,b,x,c} is used in the sub-graph mode while {d,x,e}, {d,y,e}, {f,x,g}, {f,y,g} and {h} are chosen under single-node mode. Certain nodes not pertaining to the context of analysis can also be filtered out (e.g., {u}). Let us define the mapping $\mathcal{M}$ as {({a,b,x,c},A1), ({a},A1), ({b},A1), ({c},A1), ({x},A1), ({d,x,e},A2), ({f,x,g},A3), ({d,y,e},A4), ({f,y,g},A5), ({h},A6)} on the abstractions chosen for the example log.

5   Process Discovery Based on Patterns

5.1   Transformation of Log

Algorithm 1 presents the details of transforming the log based on the patterns. The *basic idea* is to first replace the continuous and intermittent manifestation of each pattern alphabet chosen for abstraction with its abstract activity and make the corresponding low level manifestations part of the sub-log corresponding to the abstract activity. The sub-log of an abstract activity can be used to zoom in the detailed behavior. The intermittent manifestation here refers to the situation where the execution of the subsequence corresponding to a pattern is interrupted by other activities. For instance, let dye be a pattern, the manifestation of dye in the trace abxcdxefxgdydexeh is intermittent because dye is interrupted by d.

Steps 9-12 in the algorithm deal with the intermittent manifestation of a pattern and substitutes it with the abstract activity. Algorithm 1 will transform

```
 1: Let 𝓜 be the mapping chosen by the user. 𝒜 = ∪₍ₚₐ,ₐ₎∈𝓜{a} defines the set of defined
    abstractions. 𝒮𝒫 = ∪₍ₚₐ,ₐ₎∈𝓜[PA] denotes the set of all patterns for which
    abstractions are defined. Let f : 𝒮𝒫 → 𝒜 be the function defining the abstraction for
    each pattern. Let l : 𝒜 → 𝒮ℒ be the function defining the sub-log for each abstraction.
    Let ℒ′ be the transformed log of ℒ. Initialize ℒ′ = {} and l(a) = {} for all a ∈ 𝒜
 2: for all t ∈ ℒ do
 3:     Let t′ be an empty trace. Set j = 1.
 4:     while j ≤ |t| do
 5:         Let LDₓ be the list of patterns in 𝒮𝒫 starting with t(j) ordered in descending
            order of their length
 6:         for every pattern α ∈ LDₓ do
 7:             if there exists a continuous manifestation of a pattern α at index j in t then
 8:                 l(f(α)) = l(f(α)) ⊎ {t(j, j + |α|)};Append f(α) to t′;Set j = j + |α| − 1;exit for
 9:             else if there exists an intermittent manifestation of α at index j in t then
10:                 Re-adjust the intermittent manifestation in t.
11:                 l(f(α)) = l(f(α)) ⊎ {α}; Append f(α) to t′; Set j = j + |α| − 1; exit for
12:             end if
13:         end for
14:         Set j = j + 1
15:     end while
16:     ℒ′ = ℒ′ ⊎ {t′}
17: end for
```

Algorithm 1. Single-phase pattern-based log transformation

the trace abxcdxefxgdydexeh in our example log to A1A2A3A4A2A6. In this way, one can cope with situations where a common functionality is interrupted by other activities in concurrency.

5.2 Adapting Fuzzy Miner to Discover Maps

ProM's *Fuzzy Miner* [3] is inspired by cartography to provide business process maps. However, the existing miner has some limitations. It (i) cannot customize maps from a defined context (city maps vs. highway maps) (ii) introduces the risk of aggregating unrelated activities together in a cluster (a street in Eindhoven is clustered along with streets in Amsterdam) and (iii) provides two level hierarchy instead of a multi-level hierarchical view of the process map.

We adapted Fuzzy Miner to support the discovery of process maps. The pattern selection techniques presented in Section 4 facilitate customization from an user's context and getting meaningful abstract activities. By using the sub-log of each abstract activity, we implemented the functionality of zooming in/out the abstract activity and showing the detailed sub-process captured by it. Furthermore, by combining with the existing functions in the Fuzzy Miner of zooming in/out the cluster nodes, a three-level view of the process map is provided.

To illustrate this two-phase approach, let us transform the log as described in Algorithm 1 using the mapping 𝓜. The transformed log is shown in Figure 4(a). Figure 4(b) depicts the process map mined by the adapted Fuzzy miner, while Figure 4(c) shows the sub-process maps when zooming in the abstract activities A2 and A3. It is evident from Figure 2 and Figure 4 that our two-phase approach helps in presenting more accurate and more readable models.

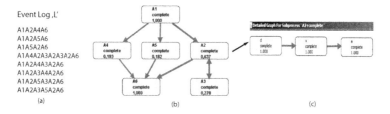

Fig. 4. (a) Transformed Log (b) process map mined from the transformed log using adapted Fuzzy miner (c) sub-process maps when zooming in on A2 and A3

6   Case Study and Discussion

We applied the techniques proposed in this paper on a real life log of a rental agency where the cases corresponded to cancellation of a current rental agreement and subsequent registration of a new rental agreement. This log was provided by a large Dutch agency that rents houses and apartments and contains 210 cases, 6100 events and 74 event classes. Figure 5(a) depicts the process model mined using heuristic miner. This process model included two types of cancelation as highlighted by two rectangles in Figure 5(a). The unselected region corresponds to common functionality used by both of them. The resulting model is difficult to comprehend.

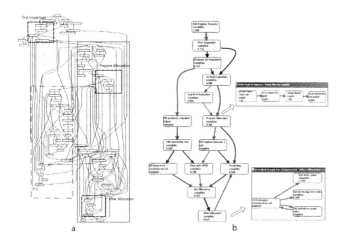

Fig. 5. (a) Heuristic net mined on the whole log (b) process map and zoomed-in sub-processes mined from transformed log based on interactive and context-dependent abstractions

In this study, we assume that the analyst wants to focus on the type of cancellation process defined by the solid rectangle and we identify the patterns from the analyst's point of view. The primary steps involve the registration of a request, multiple inspections of the rented house, determining (future) tenants, (re-)allocation and archiving of the case. We first identified the common execution patterns in this log and chose 17 abstract activities (some involve pattern alphabets and some involve individual activities) concerned with the above primary steps. We used these seventeen abstractions to do the first phase of log transformation. Then, to make the result process map more comprehensible, we performed a second iteration of pattern identification. This visualized in a process map consisting of 14 abstract activities as shown in Figure 5(b). Three of these activities are given in Table 1 which shows the three pattern alphabets used in defining abstractions. Pattern alphabets capturing a functionality from a domain point of view are chosen as candidate nodes (under sub-graph mode) for abstractions. A meaningful name is defined for every candidate abstraction. Those pattern alphabets with a significant $NOAC$ as well as a high CON value have priority to be selected for abstractions as can be seen in Table 1. Figure 5(b) also presents the sub-process when zooming in the abstract activities of **Prepare Allocation** and **After Allocation**. Each sub-process subsumes the manifestation of patterns captured in the sub-log defined by the abstraction.

Table 1. Three of the pattern alphabets chosen for abstraction

No.	Abstraction Name	Pattern Alphabet	$NOAC$	$CON(\%)$
1	First Inspection	[050 Plans appointment 1st Inspection,060 Edit confirmation letter / Tenancy form, 070 Is 1st inspection performed?,100 Ready report 1st Insp. / Make-Calculation For]	80	66
2	Prepare Allocation	[500 Rate / Modify vacancy type,540 Are there bonuses / costs awarded?, 510 Is completion form signed?530 Edit command]	145	93
3	1st Final Inspection	[120 Plans final inspections,400 Is final inspection performed?, 440 Are there new or repaired defects?]	53	61

Comparing with the cancellation process mainly defined by the solid rectangle in Figure 5(a), it is apparent that the process map discovered by our two-step approach is more comprehensible and captures the main steps of this specific type of rental cancellation process. This resulting process map not only facilitates the analyst to get an overview of the whole process, but also makes it easy to seamlessly zoom-in each abstract activity to observe the detailed sub-process. This shows that using our two-step approach indeed leads to better understandable process maps without sacrificing precision.

7   Related Work

Several approaches based on trace clustering [8,9,10] have been proposed in literature. Trace clustering enables the partitioning of the event log based on coherency of cases. Process models mined from each of the resulting clusters are expected to be simpler than that of the one mined from the entire event log.

Greco *et al.* [10] augmented trace clustering with an approach to mine hierarchies of process models that collectively represent the process at different levels of granularity and abstraction. This approach tries to analyze the mined process models (post-processing) for identifying activities that can be abstracted. However, for large complex logs, the mined process models (even after clustering) can be quite spaghetti-like. In contrast, the approach proposed in this paper analyzes the raw traces and defines abstraction (pre-processing) and has the ability to zoom-in hierarchically into the abstract entities. Furthermore, the user has flexibility and control when selecting the abstractions/activities of interest based on his/her context of analysis.

Taking cartography as a metaphor, Günther and Aalst [3] have proposed the fuzzy mining approach to implement process simplification. Less significant activities/edges are either removed or clustered together in the model. However, this approach poses a danger of clustering activities/edges having no domain significance. Polyvyanyy *et al.* [11] have proposed a slider approach for enabling flexible control over various process model abstraction criteria. Approaches such as [11,3] look at abstraction from the point of retaining highly significant information and discarding less significant ones in the process model where the notion of significance is defined over the (relative-)frequency of occurrence of an entity and not based on the context. In contrast, the approach proposed in this paper looks at abstraction from a functionality/subprocess point of view which performs filtering of activities based on the context of analysis. Our approach can be used as a preprocessing step for the logs and can be seamlessly integrated with other approaches for abstraction [10,3] as well as with classical approaches for process discovery such as the heuristic approach in [4].

8   Conclusions and Future Work

This paper presented a two-phase approach to mining business process maps that comprises the pre-processing of a log based on desired traits and at a desired level of granularity as a first step and discovering the maps with seamless zoom-in facility as the second step. We discussed one means of realizing this two-phase approach by exploiting the common execution patterns in the event log. Metrics assessing the significance of these patterns and ways of selecting these patterns for abstractions were presented. Our initial results on a few real-life logs show encouraging results. Concurrency in process models adds complexity to the discovery of patterns. As future work, we focus on more real-life applications and improving the robustness of the approach in the context of concurrency.

Acknowledgments. This work is supported in part by the NNSF (No.60873149) and the 863 project (No.2006AA10Z245) of China, and in part by EIT, NWO-EW, and STW. R.P.J.C. Bose and W.M.P. van der Aalst are grateful to Philips Healthcare for funding the research in Process Mining.

References

1. van der Aalst, W.M.P.: Challenges in Business Process Mining. Applied Stochastic Models in Business and Industry (to appear)
2. van der Aalst, W.M.P.: Using process mining to generate accurate and interactive business process maps. In: BIS (Workshops). LNBIP, vol. 37, pp. 1–14. Springer, Heidelberg (2009)
3. Günther, C.W., van der Aalst, W.M.P.: Fuzzy Mining – Adaptive Process Simplification Based on Multi-perspective Metrics. In: Alonso, G., Dadam, P., Rosemann, M. (eds.) BPM 2007. LNCS, vol. 4714, pp. 328–343. Springer, Heidelberg (2007)
4. Weijters, A., van der Aalst, W.M.P.: Rediscovering workflow models from event-based data using little thumb. Integrated Computer-Aided Engineering 10(2), 151–162 (2003)
5. Jagadeesh Chandra Bose, R.P., van der Aalst, W.M.P.: Abstractions in Process Mining: A Taxonomy of Patterns. In: Dayal, U., Eder, J., Koehler, J., Reijers, H.A. (eds.) BPM 2009. LNCS, vol. 5701, pp. 159–175. Springer, Heidelberg (2009)
6. Gusfield, D.: Algorithms on Strings, Trees, and Sequences: Computer Science and Computational Biology. Cambridge University Press, Cambridge (1997)
7. Li, J., Bose, R.J.C., van der Aalst, W.M.: Mining Context-Dependent and Interactive Business Process Maps using Execution Patterns. Technical report, University of Technology, Eindhoven (2010),
   http://www.win.tue.nl/~jcbose/MiningBusinessProcessMaps.pdf
8. Bose, R.P.J.C., van der Aalst, W.M.P.: Context Aware Trace Clustering: Towards Improving Process Mining Results. In: Proceedings of the SIAM International Conference on Data Mining (SDM), pp. 401–412 (2009)
9. Bose, R.P.J.C., van der Aalst, W.M.P.: Trace Clustering Based on Conserved Patterns: Towards Achieving Better Process Models. In: Business Process Management Workshops. LNBIP, vol. 43, pp. 170–181. Springer, Heidelberg (2009)
10. Greco, G., Guzzo, A., Pontieri, L.: Mining Taxonomies of Process Models. Data Knowl. Eng. 67(1), 74–102 (2008)
11. Polyvyanyy, A., Smirnov, S., Weske, M.: Process Model Abstraction: A Slider Approach. In: Enterprise Distributed Object Computing, pp. 325–331 (2008)

Towards Robust Conformance Checking

A. Adriansyah, B.F. van Dongen, and W.M.P. van der Aalst

Department of Mathematics and Computer Science
Eindhoven University of Technology
P.O. Box 513, 5600 MB Eindhoven, The Netherlands
{a.adriansyah,b.f.v.dongen,w.m.p.v.d.aalst}@tue.nl

Summary. The growing complexity of processes in many organizations stimulates the adoption of business process management (BPM) techniques. Process models typically lie at the basis of these techniques and generally, the assumption is made that the operational business processes as they are taking place in practice conform to these models. However, recent experience has shown that this often isn't the case. Therefore, the problem of checking to what extent the operational process conforms to the process model is increasingly important.

In this paper, we present a robust approach to get insights into the conformance of an operational process to a given process model. We use logs that carry information about which activities have being performed, in which order and we compare these logs to an abstract model. We do not only provide several different conformance metrics, but we show an efficient implementation for the calculation of these metrics.

Our approach has been implemented in the ProM framework[1], evaluated using simulated event logs and compared against an existing conformance technique based on Petri nets.

Keywords: Process mining, conformance, process analysis.

1 Introduction

The growing complexity of business processes has triggered a wide usage of process models. The emergence of many systems that base their functions around process models such as BPM (Business Process Management), BAM (Business Activity Monitoring), and BPI (Business Process Intelligence) shows how important process models are to organizations. Models are not only used as instruments to describe existing processes. They have become an integral part of process optimization, monitoring, and even auditing [14].

Unfortunately, process models do not always conform to reality. Even in automated processes, deviations can occur [10]. In some other cases, it is desirable to have models that allow for flexibility [8]. Hence, before performing any sort of process analysis based on process models, it is important to know in advance to what extent the models *conform* to reality.

---

[1] See http://www.processmining.org

M. zur Muehlen and J. Su (Eds.): BPM 2010 Workshops, LNBIP 66, pp. 122–133, 2011.
© Springer-Verlag Berlin Heidelberg 2011

Conformance checking techniques evaluate the relation between process models and reality presented in form of *event logs*. Given a process model and an event log, the following orthogonal dimensions of conformance can be measured [11]:

Fitness: is the observed behavior captured by the model?

Precision: does the model only allow for behavior that happens in reality?

Generalization: does the model allow for more behavior than encountered in reality?

Structure: does the model have a minimal structure to describe its behavior?

Many existing conformance checking techniques require process models in the form of Petri nets (e.g. [2, 7, 11]). Given a Petri net and an event log, various conformance metrics are calculated by replaying the log in the net. However, there are at least two drawbacks of Petri net-based conformance checking techniques. First, their metrics are often based on notions that only exist in Petri nets such as tokens and "invisible" transitions and second, Petri-net-based conformance checking techniques may produce "false negative" results. Thus, without in depth knowledge about the language and the algorithm used, it is difficult to utilize the metrics for further analysis.

In Figure 1, we show the result of applying conformance checking technique in [11] to a Petri net and an event log. The event log was obtained by simulating the net, hence it conforms fully to the model. The positive number in each place indicates the number of remaining tokens after replay and negative number indicates missing tokens. The existence of missing and remaining tokens leads to a fitness value less than 100%, although it should be 100% [9]. In this case, the false negative is caused by the invisible transitions that model an OR-split [9].

In [3], problems of Petri-net-based conformance checking are solved by using fuzzy models that have very relaxed semantics. For these fuzzy models, conformance calculations are again made by replaying the log in the model. However, the problem with this conformance is that it is difficult to perform further analysis given a conformance value, because the semantics of fuzzy models are too relaxed.

In this paper, we propose a new way of looking at conformance in the context of event logs. In Section 2, we introduce a model with semantics, such that these

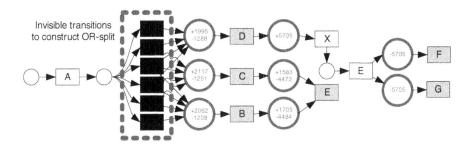

Fig. 1. False negative fitness indication in Petri-net based conformance checker

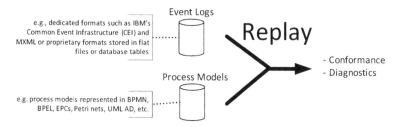

Fig. 2. Common approach to analyze conformance of process models to logs

semantics are more relaxed than Petri net semantics, but stricter than fuzzy-model semantics. Then, in Section 3, we show how several conformance metrics can be defined for these models. Section 4 shows, for one of these metrics, how to compute one of the metrics for a given log and model and in Section 5, we show some experiments. Section 6 concludes the paper.

2   Preliminaries

Conformance is measured by replaying event logs in process models (see Figure 2). With the existence of various process modeling languages, each with its own semantics, replaying event logs is a unique problem for each process modeling language. Hence, rather than developing a replay algorithm for each existing process modeling language, we use a modeling language that provides an abstraction of existing languages, while maintaining some notion of semantics.

Based on existing process modeling languages (e.g. BPMN[2], EPC [13], YAWL [5], Heuristic nest [16], Fuzzy models [3], and Petri nets), we propose an extension of *flexible models* [9] to be a process modeling language that captures the essential aspects of existing languages in the control-flow dimension by focusing on activities and their synchronization and/or enabling alternatives.

Before introducing our flexible model, we first introduce some basic graph notation for directed graphs.

Definition 2.1. (Successor/Predecessor nodes in a directed graph) Let $G = (N, E)$ with $E \subseteq N \times N$ be a directed graph. For $n \in N$, we say *successor nodes* of node n as $n \overset{G}{\bullet} = \{n' \in N \mid (n, n') \in E\}$ and *predecessor nodes* of node n as $\bullet n = \{n' \in N \mid (n', n) \in E\}$. We omit the superscript G if the context is clear.

Definition 2.2. (Path in a directed graph) Let $G = (N, E)$ be a directed graph. For $n, n' \in N$, there exists a path from n to n' if and only if there is a sequence of edges $\langle (n_1, n_2), (n_2, n_3), ..., (n_{x-1}, n_x) \rangle$ with $x > 1$ where $n_1 = n \wedge n_x = n' \wedge \forall_{1 \leq i < x} (n_i, n_{i+1}) \in E$ holds. By $n \rightsquigarrow n'$ we denote that a path from n to n' exists.

Definition 2.3. (Acyclic graph) Let $G = (N, E)$ be a directed graph. We say that G is an acyclic graph if $\forall_{n \in N} \nexists n \rightsquigarrow n$ holds

---

[2] Business Process Model and Notation http://www.bpmn.org/

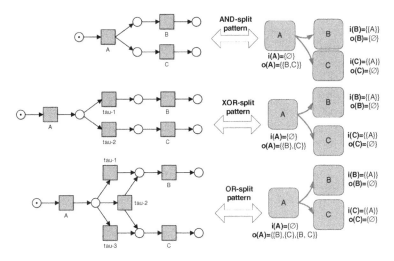

Fig. 3. Petri nets with invisible transitions labeled *tau* (left) and their possible flexible model counterparts (right)

2.1   Flexible Models

A flexible model is a (potentially cyclic) directed graph consisting of tasks and edges. A task represents an activity in a process. For each task, possible sets of predecessors tasks (indicated by i or ι), and sets of successors tasks (o) are enumerated. An activity in the business process may be represented by more than one task (i.e. *duplicate tasks* are permitted). Using input and output sets of tasks, flexible models can express either strict or relaxed semantics.

The idea of our work is to model processes as flexible models and measure the conformance of an event log and the flexible model. In Figure 3, we illustrate how a flexible model can express patterns that are often needed to model processes in reality, using Petri net as its counterpart. Note that the often-needed OR-split construct can be modeled using flexible model in a straightforward way.

The formal definition of Flexible Model is given as follows:

Definition 2.4. (Flexible Model)
Let A be a set of activities. A flexible model M_A over A is a tuple (T, F, ι, o, β), where:

- T is a finite set of tasks,
- $F \subseteq (T \times T)$ is a set of directed edges connecting tasks,
- $\iota : T \to \mathcal{P}(\mathcal{P}(T))$ is a function, such that for $t \in T$ and $s \in \iota(t)$, s is a synchronization alternative for t. We require that $\iota(t) \neq \emptyset$ and $\bigcup_{s \in \iota(t)} = {}^\bullet t$.
- $o : T \to \mathcal{P}(\mathcal{P}(T))$ is a function, such that for $t \in T$ and $s \in o(t)$, s is an enabling alternative of t. We require that $o(t) \neq \emptyset$ and $\bigcup_{s \in o(t)} = t^\bullet$.
- $\beta : T \to A$ is a surjective function mapping tasks to activities, i.e. each activity appears as at least one task in the model.

It is important to realize that flexible models can be obtained using several approaches, e.g. by discovering them directly from event log, by converting existing process models, or by modeling them manually. In this paper, we assume that such model already exists for a given event log.

Flexible models are intended to be models with a formal semantics. However, we do not provide execution semantics. Instead, we later provide semantics only in the context of a case, i.e. for a given sequence of task executions, we can say whether or not this sequence is a (partial) execution of a flexible model. Therefore, we formally introduce the notion of a partial and full instance of a flexible model.

Definition 2.5. (Partial instance of flexible model) Let A be a set of activities and $M_A = (T, F, \iota, o, \beta)$ be a flexible model over A. Let $I = (N, R, \lambda)$ be a tuple where N is a set of unique task instances, $R \subseteq N \times N$ is a set of edges such that (N, R) is an acyclic graph, and $\lambda : N \to T$ is a function mapping the elements of N to their corresponding tasks. We say I is a partial instance of M_A if and only if the following holds:

- $\forall_{(n,n') \in R} (\lambda(n), \lambda(n')) \in F$,
- $\forall_{n \in N} \forall_{n_1, n_2 \in n\bullet} n_1 \neq n_2 \implies \lambda(n_1) \neq \lambda(n_2)$
- $\forall_{n \in N} \forall_{n_1, n_2 \in \bullet n} n_1 \neq n_2 \implies \lambda(n_1) \neq \lambda(n_2)$
- $\forall_{n \in N} \exists_{s \in o(\lambda(n))} \lambda(n\bullet) \subseteq s$, and
- $\forall_{n \in N} \exists_{s \in \iota(\lambda(n))} \lambda(\bullet n) \subseteq s$

A partial instance of a flexible model is a partial order of task instances, such that the edges respect the existence of edges in the original flexible model. Furthermore, the input and output sets as defined in the flexible model are partly respected. Once all input and output sets are fully respected, we say that an instance is complete.

Definition 2.6. (Complete instance of flexible model) Let A be a set of activities and $M_A = (T, F, \iota, o, \beta)$ be a flexible model over A. Let $I = (N, R, \lambda)$ be a partial instance of M_A. We say I is a complete instance of M_A if and only if the following holds:

- $\forall_{n \in N} \exists_{s \in o(\lambda(n))} \lambda(n\bullet) = s$, and
- $\forall_{n \in N} \exists_{s \in \iota(\lambda(n))} \lambda(\bullet n) = s$

2.2 Event Logs

As described in Figure 2, we also need event logs in order to check for conformance. An event log records which activities have been performed in a business process. Hence, we formalize log-related terms as follows:

Definition 2.7. (Event logs)
Let A be a set of activities. An event log over A is defined as $L_A = (E, C, \alpha, \gamma, \succ)$, where:

- E is a finite set of events,
- C is a finite set of cases,

- $\alpha : E \to A$ is a function relating each event to an activity,
- $\gamma : E \to C$ is a surjective function relating each event to a case.
- $\succ \subseteq E \times E$ imposes a total ordering on the events in E. The ordering is typically based on timestamps of events.

Definition 2.8. (Case events)
Let A be a set of activities and $L_A = (E, C, \alpha, \gamma, \succ)$ be an event log over A. Let $c \in C$ be a case identifier. With E_c, we denote the events of case c, i.e. $E_c = \{e \in E \mid \gamma(e) = c\}$. As $\succ$ imposes a total ordering on E, it also imposes a total ordering on E_c.

In the following section, we show how several conformance metrics can be defined for the combination of an event log and a flexible model.

3   Conformance in Flexible Model

A flexible model as defined in Definition 2.4 is not executable. Given a task in a flexible model, we cannot provide insights into which tasks can be executed next such that in the end, a complete instance of this flexible model will be constructed. However, this is not the goal of flexible models. Instead, we aim at deciding if and to what extent a given event log can be replayed in a flexible model, i.e. for a *given* execution, we need to say whether or not this execution conforms to the flexible model.

In this paper, we focus on conformance between a model and a log that refer to the same set of activities. Through standard filtering techniques, a log can always be pre-processed to meet this requirement for a flexible model.

For a log and a flexible model, we need to define a match between a partial instance and a case, i.e. for a given case, we need to define a *class of* partial instances that this case can correspond to. At this point, we do not provide insights into constructing instances. However, in Section 4, we show how to obtain an element of the class of partial instances that matches a case and minimizes a specific conformance metric.

Definition 3.1. (Matching case and flexible model instance)
Let A be a set of activities, let $L_A = (E, C, \alpha, \gamma, \succ)$ be an event log over A and let $M_A = (T, F, \iota, o, \beta)$ be a flexible model over A. Let $c \in C$ be a case and let $I = (N, R, \lambda)$ be a partial instance of M_A.
  We say that c and I match if and only if:

- $E_c = N$, i.e. each event is a node in the partial instance,
- $\forall_{e,e' \in E_c} \ (e \succ e') \Rightarrow (e \not\rightsquigarrow e')$, i.e. the ordering of events in the log is respected in the instance, and
- $\forall_{e \in E_c} \lambda(e) \in \{t \in T \mid \beta(t) = \alpha(e)\}$, i.e. each event is mapped to a task that corresponds to the activity represented by this event.

We use I_c to denote an arbitrary instance I matching c and we use $\Im_c$ to denote the (possibly infinite) set of all instances matching c.

In order to reason about matching instances for a case, we show that at least one matching instance always exists, i.e. $\Im_c \neq \emptyset$.

Lemma 3.2. (Matching partial instance exists for any case)
Let A be a set of activities, let $L_A = (E, C, \alpha, \gamma, \succ)$ be an event log over A and let $M_A = (T, F, \iota, o, \beta)$ be a flexible model over A. Let $c \in C$ be a case and let $I = (E_c, \emptyset, \lambda)$ be a partial instance of M_A. We show that I matches c (i.e. $I \in \Im_c$ for any λ that satisfies $\forall_{e \in E_c} \lambda(e) \in \{t \in T \mid \beta(t) = \alpha(e)\}$.

Proof. It is trivial to see that I follows definition 2.6. Furthermore, since there are no edges, we know that for all $e, e' \in E_c$ holds that $e \not\rightarrow e'$. Since $N = E_c$ and $\forall_{e \in E_c} \lambda(e) \in \{t \in T \mid \beta(t) = \alpha(e)\}$, we know that I is a matching partial flexible model instance, hence $I \in \Im_c$.   □

As stated before, in a partial instance of a flexible model, there can be instances of tasks for which the input conditions are not completely satisfied. If such an instance matches a case, then there are events in the log that correspond to these task instances. We call these events *unsatisfied*.

Definition 3.3. (Unsatisfied events) Let A be a set of activities, let $L_A = (E, C, \alpha, \gamma, \succ)$ be an event log over A and let $M_A = (T, F, \iota, o, \beta)$ be a flexible model over A. Let $c \in C$ be a case and let $I_c = (E_c, R, \lambda)$ be a partial instance of M_A matching c.

We say that $e \in E_c$ is an unsatisfied event if and only if $\lambda(\overset{I_c}{\bullet} e) \notin \iota(\lambda(e))$. We denote the set of unsatisfied events by $E_{I_c}^{us}$.

Similar to unsatisfied events, we define *unhandled events*.

Definition 3.4. (Unhandled events) Let A be a set of activities, let $L_A = (E, C, \alpha, \gamma, \succ)$ be an event log over A and let $M_A = (T, F, \iota, o, \beta)$ be a flexible model over A. Let $c \in C$ be a case and let $I_c = (E_c, R, \lambda)$ be a partial instance of M_A matching c.

We say that $e \in E_c$ is an unhandled event if and only if $\lambda(e \overset{I_c}{\bullet}) \notin o(\lambda(e))$. We denote the set of unhandled events by $E_{I_c}^{uh}$.

Using the notion of unhandled and unsatisfied events, we define several conformance metrics.

3.1 Conformance Metrics

Given a flexible model and a log, we can always obtain a matching instance for each case in the model. In this section, we define several metrics to express the conformance between a case and a matching instance. In Section 4, we use these metrics to construct a matching instance that maximizes conformance for each case.

Definition 3.5. (Single case fitness metrics) Let A be a set of activities, let $L_A = (E, C, \alpha, \gamma, \succ)$ be an event log over A and let $M_A = (T, F, \iota, o, \beta)$ be a flexible model over A. Let $c \in C$ be a case. We define two fitness metrics for matching instances as follow:

Case absolute fitness , $f_c^{abs} : \Im_c \to \{0, 1\}$, is a function that returns 1 only if there are no unsatisfied events in the case.
$$f_c^{abs}(I_c) = \begin{cases} 0 \text{ if } |E_{I_c}^{us}| > 0 \text{ holds, else} \\ 1 \text{ if previous condition doesn't hold} \end{cases}$$
Task ratio fitness , $f_c^{rat}(I_c) : \Im_c \to [0, 1]$, is a function that indicate the ratio between unsatisfied events and total number of events in a case.
$$f_c^{rat}(I_c) = 1 - \frac{|E_{I_c}^{us}|}{|E_c|}$$

The *absolute* fitness metric states that a case is only fitting a flexible model instance if this instance does not have unsatisfied events. On the other hand, *task ratio* fitness provides the percentage of events that are unsatisfied. We extend these two fitness metrics to the level of flexible models as follows.

Definition 3.6. (Fitness metrics) Let A be a set of activities, let $L_A = (E, C, \alpha, \gamma, \succ)$ be an event log over A and let $M_A = (T, F, \iota, o, \beta)$ be a flexible model over A.

Our fitness metrics are defined as follow:

Absolute fitness $f^{abs} \in [0, 1]$ indicates the average maximal absolute fitness.
$$f^{abs} = \frac{\sum_{c \in C} \max_{I_c \in \Im_c} f_c^{abs}(I_c)}{|C|},$$
Task ratio fitness $f^{rat} \in [0, 1]$ indicates the average maximal task ratio fitness.
$$f^{rat} = \frac{\sum_{c \in C} \max_{I_c \in \Im_c} f_c^{rat}(I_c)}{|C|},$$
Event fitness $f^{evt} \in [0, 1]$ indicates the maximal ratio of events in the log that can be satisfied by some instance.
$$f^{evt} = \frac{\sum_{c \in C} \max_{I_c \in \Im_c} f_c^{rat}(I_c) \cdot |E_c|}{|E|}$$

So far, we defined several fitness metrics that can be computed only when for each case in the log, we can obtain a matching (partial) instance of the flexible model that maximizes any of our two case-based fitness functions. Therefore, in the following section, we present an algorithm that constructs a partial model instance that maximizes the fitness metrics we defined.

4   Constructing Matching Partial Model Instance

Given a flexible model and an event log over a set of activities, our fitness values depend on a matching (partial) model instance for each case in the log. From Definition 3.6, it is clear that for each case, we need to construct a partial model instance that maximizes the value of the case based fitness metrics defined in Definition 3.5. In this section, we introduce an algorithm that achieves this.

As an illustration, consider the flexible model and events of a case as shown in Figure 4. More than one matching partial model instance can be generated from the model, each of which has a different fitness value for the task ratio fitness f^{rat}. Since the model can capture the behavior of the case as shown by instance 1, the fitness value should be 1. Hence, an instance with task ratio fitness 1 should be selected as the basis for fitness calculation.

Let **A** = {X,Y,Z} be a set of activities and let
L_A = (**E**,**C**,α,γ,>) be an event log over **A** where **E**
= {x,y,z}, **C** = {c}. Each event is mapped to case
c by **γ** and mapped to its uppercase activity by
α. Let **M_A** be a flexible model over **A**.

Flexible Model   M_A

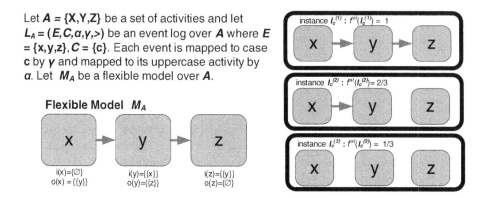

Fig. 4. Matching partial instances given a case and a flexible model

From Definition 3.5, it can easily be concluded that maximum fitness will be achieved if the number of unsatisfied events of a case in an instance is minimal. According to Definition 2.5, all predecessor/successor relations between task instances should honor the same relation between tasks in the original model. However, from Definition 3.3, we can see that only the predecessor relation matters for the fitness metrics we defined. Therefore, the selection of predecessors of task instances is important to minimize the number of unsatisfied events.

Given a case in an event log and a flexible model, we have shown that the set of matching partial instances for that case is non-empty (Lemma 4). Furthermore it is easy to see that the number of matching partial instances is finite (in fact, it is at most exponential in the number of events in the case). Although in theory this implies that we could iterate all instances to find one maximizing fitness, this would be infeasible for real-life event logs. Therefore, we introduce a search algorithm, based on the A* algorithm [4], that guarantees us to find an instance that minimizes the number of unsatisfied events and hence maximizes the case-based fitness metric.

The A* algorithm was developed to find the shortest path from a *source* node to a *target* node in a weighted directed graph. Given a directed graph $G = (N, E)$ where N is a set of nodes and $E : N \times N$ is a set of directed arcs, A* heuristic relies on cost function $f(n) = g(n) + h(n)$, where $n \in N$ is a node in the graph. Function $g(n)$ returns the total cost so far to reach n from a source node n_{src}, and heuristic function $h(n)$ returns estimation cost from node n to target node n_{trg}. Function h should not return a value that overestimates the cost to reach the goal, and cost function f should exhibit incremental monotonicity [12]. If functions with such properties are used, the algorithm has been proven to be complete and optimal (i.e. return path from n_{src} to n_{trg} with the minimum value of $f(n)$)[1, 12].

The A* algorithm can be used in the construction of matching partial instances which maximize a case's fitness value. The sketch of the approach is given as follows. We start our search from the matching partial instance that always exists, i.e. a matching partial instance that contains no edges, but only the events as nodes. Then, we consider all events one by one, in the order provided by the log. For each event, we try to satisfy one of the synchronization alternatives defined in the flexible model (i.e. we need to consider all tasks in the flexible model that refer to the same activity as the event). In order to satisfy a synchronization alternative, we add edges from earlier events to the event under investigation, while maintaining the restrictions on the enabling alternatives provided by the flexible model. If no synchronization alternative can be satisfied, we do not add any edges.

Obviously the algorithm sketched above could be used to generate all matching partial instances. However, we use the A* algorithm to limit our search in the following way. First, we define the target function f as the *number of events in the case plus the number of unsatisfied events so far*. As the number of events in the case is fixed, minimizing this will also minimize the number of unsatisfied events. Furthermore, function g represents the number of events considered so-far (the depth of the search tree) plus the number of unsatisfied events so far and h provides the number of events still to consider.

During our search, no edges are ever added *to* an earlier event. Therefore, once an event was unsatisfied, it will never be satisfied later. Hence, function f is strictly increasing as the search progresses and the A* algorithm is guaranteed to find a matching partial instance with minimal number of unsatisfied events.

5   Experiments

We implemented our calculation approach with A* heuristic in the ProM framework. In addition to conformance values such as the fitness metrics presented in this paper, other useful information obtained from replaying the log in the model is projected onto the original flexible model [15].

Using our implementation, we compared the results of our approach to an existing Petri net based approach proposed in [11] that is also the basis for [7]. The goal of this experiment is to show that our approach returns the right fitness values, where Petri net based approach does not.

To perform our experiment, five event logs were generated from various Petri nets, each with OR-split or OR-join constructs, duplicate transitions, or loop constructs. For modeling the nets and generating logs, we used CPN Tools [6]. The conformance of each log is measured against both the original Petri net and a flexible model that is the counterpart of that Petri net. Each log has a size reasonable for simulating real-life data (≥ 5000 cases).

The experiments results are shown in Table 1. As shown in the table (columns 4,5 and 6), our conformance metrics return 1 for all logs. This is expected, as the models were used to generate the log. When the same logs are checked against the Petri nets the fitness is less than 1, due to the inability of existing algorithms to handle the chosen constructs (e.g. it detects false negatives).

Table 1. Experiment results

Log ID	# Case	# Evts	f^{abs}	f^{rat}	f^{evt}	Petri net based.
OrSJn1	5000	18556	1	1	1	0.77
OrSJn2	10000	37153	1	1	1	0.77
OrS1	5000	26323	1	1	1	0.89
OrS2	10000	52762	1	1	1	0.89
Loop	10000	115384	1	1	1	0.89

6   Conclusion and Future Work

In this paper, we provide a robust method for calculating conformance between a log and a process model. First, we introduced flexible models that provide an abstraction of many languages and allow for the modeling of complex control flow constructs, such as OR-split/joins and multiple tasks that represent the same activity. We provided semantics for these models, but without specifying how to execute them. Instead, we showed that in the context of a case that has been recorded in the log, we can construct instances of the model that maximize certain conformance metrics. Finally, using experiments on simulated data (comparable in size to real-life data sets), we have shown that our approach calculates fitness correctly in the presence of complex constructs, where existing approaches do not.

The work presented in this paper provides a solid basis for robust conformance checking. Since our flexible models do not have executable semantics, we do not rely on state-space exploration (which is required in Petri-net based conformance checking).

In the future, we plan to extend this work by defining metrics that do not only capture the unsatisfied events, but also the unhandled events. Furthermore, we aim at developing metrics related to other aspects of conformance, such as appropriateness. Next to that, there is also a need to identify the "skipping" of activities, i.e. by identifying which tasks were executed but not logged.

Finally, to make our work applicable in real-life settings, we aim to investigate possible approaches to obtain flexible models, both using mining and by conversion from other models.

References

1. Dechter, R., Pearl, J.: Generalized Best-first Search Strategies and the Optimality of A*. Journal of the ACM (JACM) 32(3), 505–536 (1985)
2. Goedertier, S., Martens, D., Vanthienen, J., Baesens, B.: Robust Process Discovery with Artificial Negative Events. The Journal of Machine Learning Research 10, 1305–1340 (2009)
3. Gunther, C.W.: Process Mining in Flexible Environments. PhD thesis, Eindhoven University of Technology, Eindhoven (2009)

4. Hart, P.E., Nilsson, N.J., Raphael, B.: A Formal Basis for the Heuristic Determination of Minimum Cost Paths in Graphs. IEEE Trans. Syst. Sci. and Cybernetics SSC-4(2), 100–107 (1968)
5. Hofstede, A.H.M., van der Aalst, W.M.P., Adams, M., Russell, N.: Modern Business Process Automation. Springer, Heidelberg (2010)
6. Kurt, J., Kristensen, L.M., Wells, L.: Coloured Petri Nets and CPN Tools for modelling and validation of concurrent systems. International Journal on Software Tools for Technology Transfer (STTT) 9(3-4), 213–254 (2007)
7. Muñoz-Gama, J., Carmona, J.: A fresh look at precision in process conformance. In: Hull, R., Mendling, J., Tai, S. (eds.) BPM 2010. LNCS, vol. 6336, pp. 211–226. Springer, Heidelberg (2010)
8. Pesic, M.: Constraint-Based Workflow Management Systems: Shifting Control to Users. PhD thesis, Eindhoven University of Technology, Eindhoven (2008)
9. Rozinat, A.: Process Mining: Conformance and Extension. PhD thesis, Eindhoven University of Technology, Eindhoven (2010)
10. Rozinat, A., de Jong, I.S.M., Gunther, C.W., van der Aalst, W.M.P.: Conformance Analysis of ASML's Test Process. In: Sadiq, S., Indulska, M., zur Muehlen, M., Dubois, E., Johannesson, P. (eds.) Proceedings of the Second International Workshop on Governance, Risk and Compliance (GRCIS 2009), vol. 459, pp. 1–15 (2009), CEUR-WS.org
11. Rozinat, A., de Medeiros, A.K.A., Günther, C.W., Weijters, A.J.M.M.T., van der Aalst, W.M.P.: The Need for a Process Mining Evaluation Framework in Research and Practice. In: ter Hofstede, A.H.M., Benatallah, B., Paik, H.-Y. (eds.) BPM Workshops 2007. LNCS, vol. 4928, pp. 84–89. Springer, Heidelberg (2008)
12. Russel, S., Norvig, P.: Artificial Intelligence: A Modern Approach, 1st edn. Prentice Hall, Englewood Cliffs (1995)
13. van der Aalst, W.M.P.: Formalization and Verification of Event-driven Process Chains. Information and Software Technology 41(10), 639–650 (1999)
14. van der Aalst, W.M.P., van Hee, K.M., van der Werf, J.M., Verdonk, M.: Auditing 2.0: Using Process Mining to Support Tomorrow's Auditor. Computer 43, 90–93 (2010)
15. van Dongen, B.F., Adriansyah, A.: Process Mining: Fuzzy Clustering and Performance Visualization. In: Business Process Management Workshops, vol. 43, pp. 158–169. Springer, Heidelberg (2009)
16. Weijters, A.J.M.M., van der Aalst, W.M.P., Alves de Medeiros, A.K.: Process Mining with the Heuristics Miner-algorithm. Technical report, Eindhoven University of Technology, Eindhoven, BETA Working Paper Series, WP 166 (2006)

User Assistance during Process Execution - An Experimental Evaluation of Recommendation Strategies

Christian Haisjackl and Barbara Weber

Department of Computer Science, University of Innsbruck, Austria
{Christian.Haisjackl,Barbara.Weber}@uibk.ac.at

Summary. In today's changing business environment, flexible Process-aware Information Systems (PAISs) are required to allow companies to rapidly adjust their business processes to changes in the environment. However, increasing flexibility poses additional challenges to the users of flexible PAISs and thus requires intelligent user assistance. To address this challenge we have previously proposed a recommendation service for supporting users during process execution by providing recommendations on possible next steps. Recommendations are generated based on similar past process executions considering the performance goal of the supported process. This paper follows up on this work and suggests additional strategies for generating recommendations. In addition, as major contribution of this paper, we investigate how effectively the recommendation strategies work for different processes and logs of different quality.

1 Introduction

In today's fast changing business environment, flexible Process-aware Information Systems (PAISs) are required to allow companies to rapidly adjust their business processes to changes in the environment [1]. Several proposals on how to deal with this challenge have been made (e.g., [2,3,4,5]) relaxing the strict separation of build-time and run-time. By closely interweaving modeling and execution the above mentioned approaches all provide more maneuvering room for the end-users [4]. In particular, users are empowered to defer decisions regarding the exact control-flow to run-time, when more information is available.

With this increase of flexibility, however, additional challenges are imposed to the users of flexible PAISs. A recently performed experiment at the University of Innsbruck shows that with increased flexibility users with little experience have greater difficulties during process execution, which in the worst case may result in process instances that cannot be properly completed [6]. This trade-off between flexibility and support is also described in [7].

To address the above mentioned challenges and to assist users during process execution, we previously presented an approach for intelligent user assistance in flexible PAISs [8]. In particular, we proposed a recommendation service (including an implementation in ProM) which exploits the information available in

M. zur Muehlen and J. Su (Eds.): BPM 2010 Workshops, LNBIP 66, pp. 134–145, 2011.

event logs to guide users during process execution. The recommendation service provides information to users of a flexible PAIS on how to best proceed with a particular process instance depending on the execution state of that instance to best achieve a certain performance goal (e.g., minimizing cycle time, or maximizing profit). The paper also proposed several simple strategies for calculating recommendations. In this paper, we extend the recommendation strategies introduced in [8] with additional ones. In addition, as major contribution of this paper, an experimental evaluation of the recommendation strategies is conducted and the impact of log quality on recommendation quality is investigated.

The results of our experiment show that even though there is no single recommendation strategy which is always outperforming all the others, log-based recommendations are effective and mostly outperform randomly created process instances. Our data further points to the importance of log quality for obtaining recommendations of high quality.

The remainder of this paper is structured as follows. In Section 2 an overview of the recommendation service is provided. Then, Section 3 introduces different miners for finding similar traces and Section 4 elaborates on different recommendation strategies for generating recommendations. In Section 5, we describe the experiment for evaluating the described recommendation strategies. Finally, we discuss related work in Section 6 and provide conclusions in Section 7.

2   Overview of the Recommendation Service

This section gives an overview of the recommendation service and explains how users are supported during process execution (cf. Fig. 1). For a formalization of the recommendation service see [8]. At any point during process execution the user of a flexible PAIS can ask the recommendation service for support on how to proceed with the execution of a particular process instance (1). The recommendation client then sends the user request containing information about the activities which have already been executed by the users for that particular process instance (i.e., *partial trace*) and all *enabled activities* (i.e., all activities the user is able to execute in the next step for this particular process instance) to the recommendation engine (2). The recommendation request is then passed to the pre-configured *recommendation strategy* (3), which determines the algorithm to be used for calculating recommendations. The strategy then consults one of the *miners* (4) to search the log for traces similar to the partial trace (5). The miner compares the *partial trace* with the traces in the event log (i.e., the *log traces*) and determines how well they fit the partial trace. In addition, for each log trace a *weight* (i.e., a number between zero and one) is calculated reflecting the degree of fit with the partial trace. In addition, the miner provides a *result bag* (with the mining results) which is then passed on, together with the weights, to the strategy for further evaluation. (6). Based on the obtained results the strategy evaluates each of the *enabled activities* (i.e., possible activities to be executed next) in respect to the *performance goal* (e.g., minimizing cycle time, maximizing customer satisfaction) and ranks them accordingly. The resulting

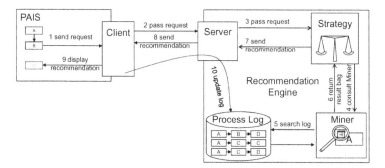

Fig. 1. Overview of the Recommendation Service

list of recommendations is then sent to the server (7) and passed on to the the client (8), which returns the recommendations to the PAIS for displaying them to the user (9). After the process instance is completed, the PAIS sends the information about the recently executed process instance to the recommendation engine to update the log and to allow for learning (10).

3   Finding Similar Log Traces through Miners

This section introduces different miners for finding similar log traces. In [8], we have already introduced the Prefix Miner, the Set Miner and the MultiSet Miner. This paper adds the Partial Trace Miner, and the Chunk Miner. Each of the miners iterates over the *log* to calculate the result bag for a given *partial trace* (cf. Algorithm 1). Depending on the chosen miner the calculation of the result bag slightly differs (cf. Fig. 2) and is detailed in the following.

Algorithm 1 calculateResultBagFor(logTrace, partialTrace)
1: Bag resultBag = new Bag ()
2: **for each** logTrace in log **do** resultBag.add(calculateResultFor (logTrace, partialTrace))
3: **return** resultBag

- **Prefix Miner:** The Prefix Miner considers the exact ordering of activities when comparing the partial trace with a log trace (cf. Fig. 2A). If the partial trace is a prefix of the log trace (Line 2), the log trace obtains a weight of one (Line 3) and the result trace is obtained by removing the partial trace from the log trace (Line 4), otherwise an empty result is returned to the miner (Line 1 + 7). Finally, a resultMap including a result trace and its weight is returned to the miner (Line 5 + 7). *Example: Fig. 2A shows an example of the Prefix Miner. Given the partial trace <A,B,C>, Log Trace 1 obtains a weight of 1 (since the partial trace is a prefix of the log trace) and result trace <U,V>. Log Trace 2, in turn, results in an empty result map since it does not match the partial trace.*
- **Set Miner:** In contrast to the Prefix Miner, the Set Miner does not consider the ordering of activities in the log when calculating fitness, but only the presence / absence of activities (cf. Fig. 2B). Thereby, the weight is calculated by dividing the number of distinct matching activities by the number of distinct activities in

	Partial Trace	Algorithm 2 calculateResultFor(logTrace, partialTrace)
A) Prefix Miner	(A) (B) (C) Log Trace 1: resultMap = {(<U,V>, 1)} (A) (B) (C) (U) (V) Log Trace 2: resultMap = {} (A) (F) (C) (X) (Y)	1: Map resultMap = new Map () 2: **if** logTrace.startsWith(partialTrace) **then** 3: weight = 1 4: Trace resultTrace = logTrace.remove(partialTrace) 5: resultMap.put(resultTrace, weight) 6: **end if** 7 **return** resultMap

B) Set Miner	Partial Trace
	 (A) (B) (C)
	 Log Trace 1: resultMap = {({A,B,C,U,V}, 1)}
	 (B) (C) (A) (U) (V)
	 Log Trace 2: resultMap = {({A,C,F,X,Y}, 2/3)}
	 (A) (F) (C) (X) (Y)
	 Log Trace 3: resultMap = {({A,U}, 1/3)}
	 (A) (A) (A) (U)
		Algorithm 3 calculateResultFor(logTrace, partialTrace)
		 1: Map resultMap = new Map ()
		 2: Set resultSet = getDistinctActivities(logTrace)
		 3: numberDistinctMatchingActivities =
		   getDistinctMatchingActivities(logTrace, partialTrace)
		 4: int weight = numberDistinctMatchingActivities /
		   countDistinctActivities(partialTrace)
		 5: resultMap.put(resultSet, weight)
		 6: **return** resultMap

C) MultiSet Miner	Partial Trace
	 (A) (B) (C) (A)
	 Log Trace 1: resultMap = {({X},1)}
	 (A) (A) (C) (B) (X)
	 Log Trace 2: resultMap= {({A,Y},1)}
	 (A) (A) (A) (B) (C) (Y)
	 Log Trace 3: resultMap= {({Z},3/4)}
	 (A) (B) (C) (Z)
		Algorithm 4 calculateResultFor(logTrace, partialTrace)
		 1: Map resultMap = new Map ()
		 2: Set resultSet = calculateComplement(logTrace, partialTrace)
		 3: numberMatchingActivities =
		   getMatchingActivities(logTrace, partialTrace)
		 4: int weight = numberMatchingActivities /
		   countActivities(partialTrace)
		 5: resultMap.put(resultSet, weight)
		 6: **return** resultMap

D) Partial Trace Miner	Partial Trace with horizon=2 (A) (B) (Z) (Y) Log Trace 1: resultMap = {(<X,Z,Y,A>,1), (<A>,1)} (Z) (Y) (X) (Z) (Y) (A) Log Trace 2: resultMap = {(<B>,1)} (C) (D) (Z) (Y) (B)	Algorithm 5 calculateResultFor(logTrace, partialTrace) 1: Map resultMap = new Map () 2: searchTrace = getLastNEntries(partialTrace, horizon) 3: **if** logTrace.contains(searchTrace) **then** 4: **for each** occurenceOf(searchTrace) **do** 5: resultMap.put(activitiesSuccSearchTrace(logTrace, 1)) 6: **end if** 7: **return** resultMap
E) Chunk Miner	Partial Trace; Chunk Size =2 (A) (B) (Z) (Y) Log Trace 1: resultMap = {(<X,B,Z,Y>, 1), (<Y>,1)} (A) (B) (X) (B) (Z) (Y) Log Trace 2: resultMap = {(<B>,1)} (C) (D) (Z) (Y) (B)	Algorithm 6 calculateResultFor(logTrace, partialTrace) 1: Map resultMap = new Map () 2: searchChunks = chopInChunksOfSize(partialTrace, chunkSize) 3: **for each** chunk in searchChunks **do** 4: **for each** occurenceOf(chunk) **do** 5: resultMap.put(activitiesSuccChunk(logTrace, 1)) 6: **return** resultMap

Fig. 2. Miners for Finding Similar Log Traces

the partial trace (Line 3-4). In addition, all distinct activities of the log trace are added to the result set (Line 2). *Example: Fig. 2B illustrates the Set Miner for a partial trace <A,B,C>. Log Trace 1 obtains a weight of 1, because all activities in the partial trace can also be found in the log trace. Log Trace 2 obtains a weight of 2/3 and Log Trace 3 a weight of 1/3. The result set for Trace 1, for example, is {A,B,C,U,V}. The result set for Trace 3, in turn, is {A,U}.*

• **MultiSet Miner:** Like the Set Miner, the MultiSet Miner does not consider the ordering of activities in the log. However, it takes the number of occurrences of an activity in a log trace into account. Thus, the weight is calculated by dividing the number of matching activities by the number of activities in the partial trace (Line 3-4). In addition, all activities from the log trace minus the activities from the partial trace are added to the result set (Line 2). *Example: Fig. 2C shows an example of the MultiSet Miner. Given a partial trace <A,B,C,A>, Log Trace 1 and 2 obtain a weight of 1 (i.e., all activities from the partial trace* *occur exactly as often in the log traces). The result set of Log Trace 1 only contains activity X; all other activities are already part of the partial trace. For Log Trace 2 the result set contains activities A and Y; A occurs more frequently in the log trace than in the partial trace and Y has not been executed yet. The result set for Log Trace 3 contains activity Z, but only with a weight of 3/4 because A has been executed in the partial trace once more than in the log trace.*

- **Partial Trace Miner:** Like the Prefix Miner, the Partial Trace Miner takes the ordering of activities into consideration (cf. Fig. 2D). However, instead of comparing the entire partial trace with the log traces, it only considers the last n activities of the partial trace (denoted as horizon) (Line 2). All activities succeeding the found search trace(s) are considered as result traces (Line 3-6). *Example: Given a partial trace <A,B,Z,Y> and a horizon of two, both Log Trace 1 and Log Trace 2 obtain a weight of one (i.e., the last two activities of the partial trace are contained in both log traces). For Log Trace 1 two result traces are obtained, <X,Z,Y,A> for the first match and <A> for the second match. The result trace for Log Trace 2 is <B>.*

- **Chunk Miner:** Like the Partial Trace Miner, the Chunk Miner does not compare the entire partial trace with the log traces (cf. Fig. 2E). Instead the partial trace is divided into chunks of size n (i.e., sliding window of size n), each of which is then compared with the log trace (Line 2). All activities succeeding any of the found chunks are considered as result traces (Line 3-5). *Example: Fig. 2E shows an example of the Chunk Miner. Given a partial trace <A,B,Z,Y> and a chunk size of two, the trace is divided into chunks <A,B>, <B,Z>, <Z,Y>, which are then compared with the log traces. Both Log Trace 1 and Log Trace 2 obtain a weight of 1 (i.e., at least one chunk is contained in both log traces). Result traces for Log Trace 1 are <X,B,Z,Y> and <Y>, while Log Trace 2 results in trace <B>.*

4   Strategies for Generating Recommendations

The miners introduced in the previous section are responsible for weighting log traces according to their fit with the partial trace and provide a result bag containing the mining results (cf. Algorithm 1) which is then taken by the strategies as input for generating recommendations. In particular, based on this information the strategies evaluate all *enabled activities* (i.e., possible next activities) in respect to the *performance goal* (e.g., minimize cycle time, minimizing error rates or maximizing customer satisfaction). For this, the strategies calculate for each activity a so-called *do value* representing the *expected target value* (e.g., cycle time) a user obtains when executing that particular activity. In addition, a *don't value* representing the expected target value after executing any other activity is calculated. For predicting the expected target value for executing or not executing a particular activity the strategies use historic data from the event log. In particular, a *target function* is applied to all log traces calculating their *target values* (e.g., cycle time for executing the trace). This information is then combined with the weighting information provided by the miners to calculate the do and don't values. The difference of do and don't values is then used by the strategies to provide a sorting of the enabled activities. If the performance goal is to minimize (maximize) a certain target value (e.g., cycle time, error rate) recommendations are sorted by increasing (decreasing) order.

In [8], we have introduced the Randomized Strategy, the Prefix Strategy, the Set Strategy and the MultiSet Strategy. This paper adds the Partial Trace Strategy and the Chunk Strategy. The following describes them briefly.

• **Randomized Strategy:** The Randomized Strategy randomly picks one of the possible next tasks and recommends this task for execution. This strategy can be used to create random traces and is used as baseline for the experiments.

A) Prefix/Partial Trace/Chunk Strategy

Possible Next Activities	Result Trace	Weight	Target Value
A	A B	1	10
B	A B	1	50
C	B C	1	40
	C E A	1	20
	D A	1	30

Act	Do Value	Don't Value	Diff.
A	(1*10 + 1*50) / 2 = 30	(1*40 + 1*20) / 2 = 30	0
B	(1*40) / 1 = 40	(1*10 + 1*50 + 1*20) / 3 = 26,67	13,33
C	(1*20) / 1 = 20	(1*10 + 1*50 + 1*40) / 3 = 33,33	-13,33

B) Set/MultiSet Strategy

Possible Next Activities	Result Set	Weight	Target Value
A	A B C	1	10
B	A D G	1/2	30
C	A B G	1	50
	D C B	1/2	40
	C E G	0	20

Act	Do Value	Don't Value	Diff.
A	(1*10 + 1/2*30 + 1*50) / (5/2) = 30	(1/2*40 + 0*20) / (1/2) = 40	-10
B	(1*10+1*50+1/2* 40) / (5/2) = 32	(1/2*30 + 0*20) / (1/2) = 30	-2
C	(1*10+1/2 *40+ 0*20) / (3/2) = 20	(1/2*30 + 1*50) /(3/2) = 43,33	-23,33

Fig. 3. Examples of Strategies

• **Prefix Strategy, Partial Trace Strategy, Chunk Strategy:** All these strategies use the same method for calculating the do and don't values and only differ in terms of the used miner. They all consider the first task of each result trace (from the result bag) for calculating the do and don't values. Traces which do not contain an enabled activity at position one of the result trace are discarded. For each enabled activity the do value is then calculated as the weighted average of target values of all traces where the respective activity can be found at position one. The don't value, in turn, is the weighted average of target values of all traces having another enabled activity at position one in the result trace. *Example: Fig. 3A shows 5 traces as returned by the Prefix/Partial Trace/Chunk Miner, as well as the enabled activities (i.e., activities A,B,C). For the calculation of do and don't values Trace 5 is discarded, since it does not contain an enabled activity at position one. Activity A in Fig. 3A, for example, obtains a do value of 30 (i.e., weighted average Traces 1-2) and a don't value of 30 (i.e., weighted average Traces 3-4).*

• **Set Strategy, MultiSet Strategy:** Unlike the Prefix Strategy, the Set Strategy and MultiSet Strategy consider all activities of each result set in the result bag for calculating the do and don't values. Results sets which do not contain any of the enabled activities are discarded. For each possible next activity the do value is calculated as the weighted average of target values of all result sets containing that particular activity. The don't value, in turn, is the weighted average of target values of all result sets which do not contain that particular activity (but any other enabled activity). *Example: Fig. 3B shows five traces as returned from the Set/MultiSet Miner including their weights. The possible next tasks are activities* A,B,C. *Activity* A, *for example, obtains a do value of 30 (i.e., weighted average Traces 1-3) and a don't value of 40 (i.e., Trace 4).*

5   Evaluation

To evaluate the effectiveness of the suggested recommendation strategies, an experiment has been conducted. The design of the experiment is explained in Section 5.1. Section 5.2 discusses the major results of our experiment.

5.1   Experimental Design

This section introduces the experiment goal, its objects, independent variables and the considered response variable.

Experiment Goal: The main goal of our experiment is to investigate how effectively the recommendation strategies described in Section 4 work depending on the business process and on the log quality.

Object: The strategies were tested using six distinct processes.[1]

• *Process A* consists of five mandatory activities A,B,C,D,E, which can be executed in any order. If Activity B is executed exactly before Activity C the cycle time will be 35 (due to reduced set-up times), otherwise it is 50. This process model has already been used in [8] and can thus serve as a reference.

• *Process B* is relatively well structured and consists of a parallel branching at the beginning, which is followed by an exclusive branching where one activity from the set {G,H,I} has to be executed. The cycle time will be 60 if G is executed, 50 if H is executed and 35 if I is executed.

• *Process C* comprises ten activities from which exactly three have to be executed, whereby each activity can only be chosen once. If activities A, B and C (in any order) are executed in one process instance the cycle time will be 35. For all other cases the cycle time will be 50.

• *Process D* offers, similar to Process C, a pool of ten activities from which exactly three distinct activities have to be executed. Activities A, B and C have a cycle time of 10, all other activities have a cycle time of 20. Depending on which activities are executed, the cycle time will thus be 30, 40, 50 or 60.

• *Process E* provides a pool of 14 activities, which all can be executed at most once. Half of them have a cycle time of 10, the other half has a cycle time of 20. Exactly six of these activities must be executed, resulting in a cycle time of either 60, 70, 80, 90, 100, 110 or 120.

• *Process F* comprises activities A,B,C,D,E,F. First, a sequence <A,B,C> is executed, followed either by a loop consisting of a sequence <D,C> (which can be executed up to three times) or activity E. Finally, activity F is performed. Whenever D is executed the cycle time is reduced by 20 (due to reduced set-up times of activity E) resulting in cycle times of 40, 60, 80 and 100.

---

[1] Due to limited space a graphical representation of the used processes is omitted, but can be obtained from http://barbaraweber.org/images/processes.pdf

Independent Variables: In our experiment we consider the recommendation strategy and the log quality as independent variables. For variable *recommendation strategy* we consider all strategies described in Section 4. Variable *log quality*, in turn, represents how well the instances in the log fulfill the performance goal (i.e., minimizing cycle time). In detail, we define log quality as the number of instances in the log (which is used as learning material for the recommendation strategies) falling into a particular cycle time category. For example, Process B has three different cycle time categories (i.e., 35, 50 and 60). Thus, a log with log quality [0;15;15], for example, contains 15 instances of cycle time category 2 (50) and 15 instances of category 3 (60). The considered factor levels for variable log quality are calculated according to Algorithm 7 (cf. Fig. 4A), considering the number of cycle time categories of each process and a log size of 30 process instances. Fig. 4B illustrates the obtained factor levels for Process B.

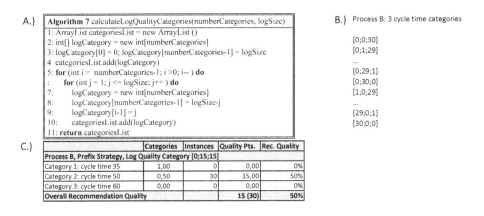

Fig. 4. Calculating Factor Levels of Log Quality

Response Variable: The response variable in our experiment is the *recommendation quality* of our recommendation strategies when applied to a given process using a log of a given quality. Thereby, recommendation quality measures how well the recommendations fulfill the performance goal. For each process and log quality we count how many process instances were obtained for each cycle time category when applying a particular recommendation strategy. As illustrated in Fig. 4C, for example, the application of the Prefix Strategy for Process B and a log quality of [0;15;15] (i.e., log with 15 instances of cycle time 50 and 15 instances of cycle time 60) resulted 0 times in cycle time 35 and 30 times in cycle time 50 and 0 times in cycle time 60. Depending on the cycle time, different weights are assigned as follows: the best cycle time is weighted with 1 and the worst one with 0. The remaining cycle times obtain values in between. By multiplying the number of process instances with the respective weights, quality points are calculated for each strategy. Since for every combination of process, log quality and strategy 30 process instances are created, a particular strategy can obtain at most 30 quality points for a particular combination. The recommendation quality is then measured as the sum of quality points divided by the maximum number of quality points, for example, 50% in Fig. 4C.

5.2 Experimental Results

This section summarizes major results and illustrates how effectively our recommendation strategies work depending on the log quality (cf. Fig. 5).

• *Process A:* Regarding Process A, the Prefix Strategy obtained a recommendation quality of 100% (except for category [0;30]) and consistently outperformed all other strategies. This shows that the abstractions used by the other strategies are less appropriate for Process A indicating that they disregard information relevant for that particular process.

• *Process B:* Process B causes little problems for any of the recommendation strategies (i.e., all strategies led to a recommendation quality corresponding to the best process instance in the log).

• *Process C:* For Process C, the Prefix Strategy, the Set Strategy and the MultiSet Strategy turned out to be well suited and delivered a recommendation quality of 100% (except for category [0;30]).

• *Process D:* For Process D, the Prefix, Set and MultiSet Strategies showed a good recommendation performance. Again, the Prefix Strategy obtained, for all log categories, a recommendation quality corresponding to the best process instance in the log. The Set Strategy and the MultiSet Strategy, in turn, could even outperform the best process instance in the log for 30 and 32 categories respectively. For additional 44 and 46 categories the recommendation quality corresponds to the log quality. However, for 15 categories both strategies obtained a recommendation quality below the best process instances in the log. The biggest deterioration in quality can be observed for categories [0;30;0;0] and [0;0;30;0] (cf. Fig. 5D2). In these two cases the log only contains process instances with the same cycle time, leading to the same do and don't values for all activities and thus to a random selection.

• *Process E:* Regarding Process E, the Set Strategy and the MultiSet Strategy are particularly well suited and delivered for 114 out of 181 categories a recommendation quality better than the best process instance in the log. For additional 60 categories, these strategies obtained a recommendation quality corresponding to the best process instance in the log. Again, like illustrated in Fig. 5E2, a deterioration in quality can be observed whenever the log contains process instances all belonging to the same cycle time category.

• *Process F:* Finally, regarding Process F the Chunk Strategy showed the best performance[2]. For all categories except [0;0;0;0], [30;0;0;0] and [0;30;0;0], the Chunk Strategy obtained a recommendation quality of 100% and outperformed for 59 out of 91 categories the best process instances in the log (cf. Fig. 5F1). The outliers for categories [30;0;0;0] and [0;30;0;0] can be explained by looking at both the characteristics of Process F and the do and don't value calculation. After having executed activity C there is a choice between performing activity D or E. However, since the log contains for categories [30;0;0;0]

---

[2] Note that we used a chunk size of two in the experiment.

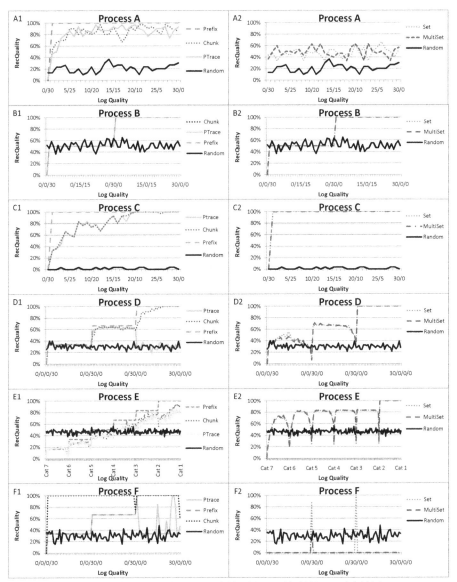

Cat 1: 0/0/0/0/0/0/30; Cat 2: 0/0/0/0/0/30/0; Cat 3: 0/0/0/0/30/0/0; Cat 4: 0/0/0/30/0/0/0; Cat 5: 0/0/30/0/0/0/0; Cat 6: 0/30/0/0/0/0/0;
Cat 7: 30/0/0/0/0/0/0

Fig. 5. Experimental Results

and [0;30;0;0] 30 process instances with the same traces, all comprising both activity D and E, the same difference of do and don't values is obtained for both activities. Thus, one of these activities is chosen on a random basis.

For Process F both the Set Strategy and the MultiSet Strategy performed very badly, leading to a recommendation quality of 0% for amost all categories. The poor performance of these two strategies can again be explained by the way how do and don't values are calculated. When it comes to selecting between activities D or E, activity E is preferred (as it is mandatory and thus has an undefined don't value, while D only appears in some of the traces). For categories [0;30;0;0] and [0;0;30;0] two peaks can be observed (cf. Fig. 5F2). For these two special cases, the same difference of do and don't values is obtained for both activities D and E and a random selection is performed.

• *Summary:* Since no strategy is always outperforming all other strategies, these findings have important implications for the selection of an appropriate recommendation strategy. A consistently good performance is delivered by the Prefix Strategy which provides a recommendation quality of 100% whenever at least one trace in the log has the optimal target value. Consequently, it is the best choice whenever logs of high quality are available. However, a downside of the Prefix Strategy is that this strategy never provides recommendations which are better than the best process instance in the log. In contrast, the Set Strategy and the MultiSet Strategy have the potential to outperform the best process instances in the log (e.g., Process D and E). As a drawback of these strategies, however, it has to be considered that they are only suitable for selected processes (e.g., not Process F) and have troubles when all process instances of the log belong to a single cycle time category (cf. outliers in Fig. 5D2 and Fig. 5E2). In the majority of cases, both the Partial Trace Strategy and the Chunk Strategy are outperformed by the Prefix Strategy. However, the Chunk Strategy might bear some potential for processes comprising loops (e.g., Process F).

6   Related Work

The need for user support in flexible systems has been recognized by the research community and several proposals have been made to tackle this issue. Related work in the context of adaptive PAISs aims at facilitating structural process adaptations through change reuse [9,10]. While the focus of this work is on user support in exceptional situations, our recommendation service assists users during process execution by providing recommendations on what enabled activity to best execute next. In the context of late binding and late modeling basic support for the reuse of previously defined strategies is offered [11,12]. Similar to our approach, [13] suggests the usage of recommendations to guide users during process execution to meet performance goals of the process best (e.g., lowest cost, shortest remaining cycle time). Unlike our approach, the recommendations are not based on a log, but on a product data model and are thus tailored towards product based workflows. Related to our work is also the approach described in [14] which aims at predicting the completion time of a particular process instance. In contrast to this work, our recommendation service aims at predicting which steps should be executed to achieve certain performance goals best.

7   Conclusion

The increasing flexibility of existing PAISs goes along with an increasing need for user assistance and support. To address this challenge we have previously proposed a recommendation service for assisting users during process execution to best meet the processes' performance goals [8]. This paper extends this work by proposing additional recommendation strategies for calculating recommendations on how to best proceed with a partially executed process instance. To evaluate how effectively the strategies work and to investigate the impact of log quality on recommendation quality we conducted an experiment. Our results indicate that there is no single recommendation strategy which always outperforms all the others. Therefore, depending on the process characteristics a suitable strategy has to be chosen. In addition, our experiments show that traces created using the described recommendation strategies mostly outperform randomly created logs. Moreover, our data also points to the importance of log quality for obtaining high quality recommendations. Future work aims at further experiments based on both real-life scenarios and simulated experiments to obtain more insights into the performance of our recommendation strategies.

References

1. van der Aalst, W., Jablonski, S.: Dealing with Workflow Change: Identification of Issues an Solutions. IJCSES 15(5), 267–276 (2000)
2. Reichert, M., Dadam, P.: ADEPT$_{flex}$ – Supporting Dynamic Changes of Workflows Without Losing Control. JIIS 10(2), 93–129 (1998)
3. Sadiq, S., Sadiq, W., Orlowska, M.: A Framework for Constraint Specification and Validation in Flexible Workflows. Information Systems 30(5), 349–378 (2005)
4. Pesic, M., Schonenberg, M., Sidorova, N., van der Aalst, W.: Constraint-Based Workflow Models: Change Made Easy. In: CoopIS 2007, pp. 77–94 (2007)
5. van der Aalst, W., Weske, M., Grünbauer, D.: Case Handling: A New Paradigm for Business Process Support. DKE 53(2), 129–162 (2005)
6. Zugal, S.: Agile versus Plan-Driven Approaches to Planning - A Controlled Experiment. Master's thesis, University of Innsbruck (October 2008)
7. Dongen, B., Aalst, W.: A meta model for process mining data. In: Proc. CAiSE WORKSHOPS, pp. 309–320 (2005)
8. Schonenberg, H., Weber, B., van Dongen, B., van der Aalst, W.: Supporting flexible processes through recommendations based on history. In: Dumas, M., Reichert, M., Shan, M.-C. (eds.) BPM 2008. LNCS, vol. 5240, pp. 51–66. Springer, Heidelberg (2008)
9. Weber, B., Reichert, M., Wild, W., Rinderle-Ma, S.: Providing Integrated Life Cycle Support in Process-Aware Information Systems. IJCIS 18(1), 115–165 (2009)
10. Minor, M., Tartakovski, A., Schmalen, D., Bergmann, R.: Agile Workflow Technology and Case-Based Change Reuse for Long-Term Processes. International Journal of Intelligent Information Technologies 1(4), 80–98 (2008)
11. Adams, M., ter Hofstede, A., Edmond, D., van der Aalst, W.: A Service-Oriented Implementation of Dynamic Flexibility in Workflows. In: Coopis 2006 (2006)
12. Lu, R., Sadiq, S.K.: Managing process variants as an information resource. In: Dustdar, S., Fiadeiro, J.L., Sheth, A.P. (eds.) BPM 2006. LNCS, vol. 4102, pp. 426–431. Springer, Heidelberg (2006)
13. Vanderfeesten, I., Reijers, H., van der Aalst., W.: Product based workflow support: A recommendation service for dynamic workflow execution. Technical Report BPM-08-03, BPMcenter.org (2008)
14. van der Aalst, W.M.P., Schonenberg, M., Song, M.: Time prediction based on process mining. Technical Report BPM-09-04, BPMcenter.org (2009)

Run-Time Auditing for Business Processes Data Using Constraints

María Teresa Gómez-López and Rafael M. Gasca

Departamento de Lenguajes y Sistemas Informáticos,
Universidad de Sevilla, Spain
{maytegomez,gasca}@us.es
http://www.lsi.us.es/~quivir

Abstract. Business processes involve data that can be modified or up-dated by various activities. These data must satisfy the business rules associated to the process. These data are normally stored in a relational database, and hence the database has to be analyzed to determine whether the business rules can be satisfied.

This paper presents a framework including a run-time auditing layer where the correctness of a database can be analyzed at different check-points of a business process according to the data flow. It provides an early detection of incorrect action on stored data. Furthermore, in order to manage the current business rules, the use of the constraint programming paradigm is proposed and the enlargement of the Constraint Database Management Systems to support business rules.

Keywords: Reasoning related to business processes, business rules, Constraint Programming.

1 Introduction

Organizations currently need to manage a great deal of data. This data must be conveniently gathered, transformed and stored according to a business data model. The evaluation of the correctness of data is very important since none of the activities of a process can work correctly using incorrect data.

For the design of a whole business process management (BPM) [1], it is necessary to design the database, the model of activities, and the causal and temporal relationships between them. Business rules can help to complete this information, since they can be used to validate business data [2]. In [3] there is a depth analysis about the integration of rule and process modelling and the shortcomings of the existing solutions. Our work is based on [4], although we propose to separate the evaluation into an independent layer that checks the business rules oriented to databases as a contract that describes the behaviour of the activities in different moments of the business process instance and only for involved data.

This paper takes a new data-oriented view of business rules engines, when there is greatest number of requirements, vast amount of data and rules. It

M. zur Muehlen and J. Su (Eds.): BPM 2010 Workshops, LNBIP 66, pp. 146–157, 2011.

makes necessary to search new solutions and to define higher expressiveness for business rules. Due to the complexity of business rules and data relations, it has become necessary to create a new way to represent, store and validate business rules in function of data stored in a relational database. This paper is based on to validate *Business Data Objects*, that are defined by the set of data stored in a relational database that are updated in a business process instance. This Business Data Object is changed for the different tasks of the process, passing through different *Business Object States*. Based on these ideas, the contributions of this paper are:

- **To define a business rules language based on Constraints.** When we mention the world *Constraint* in this paper, we are talking about the constraint programming paradigm, a way to represent the correct values of a set of variables related by equations and inequations. To the best of our knowledge, no constraint satisfaction problems have been used to represent and validate business rules. Current business rules engines use the *if ... then* format to represent business rules. However by using constraints the information is represented at a more abstract level, since languages based on constraints include and improve all the capacity of representation of current rules engines, such us Drools, Fair Isaac Blaze Advisor, ILOG JRules and Jess.
- **To redefine a repository to store business rules.** If business rules are stored and well structured in a database, it will be easier to support continuous evolution of the rules in accordance with business demands, and to select which rules can be validated at any moment. To this end, we propose the use of Constraint Databases.
- **To propose a run-time auditing framework to check the conformity of the persistent data managed and data flow in a business process.** Not all the business rules are activated in the whole business process [5]. We propose a framework where it is possible to validate a set of data from a database depending on the data flow.

The combination of Constraint Databases and an audit layer permits the determination of unsatisfiable rules as soon as possible. Auditing the stored information and data flow is very important since data are normally introduced by hand. Hence, this type of population of databases produces numerous errors and inconsistent information that fluctuate. When a software activity works incorrectly, for the same input it will produce the same output, but this axiom is not true for human tasks.

This paper is organized as follows: Section 2 gives a motivating example where constraints can be used to validate relational databases. Section 3 presents the most interesting aspects related to Business Rules and the new orientation to constraints. Section 4 explains how business rules can be stored in an efficient way. Section 5 sets out the proposed framework. Section 6 presents an extension of the constraint language for aggregate operators, and shows an example of it. Finally, conclusions and future work are presented.

2   Motivating Example of Business Process and Business Rules

The use of business rules represented as constraints has been applied to a real business process where the goal is to negotiate the collaboration projects between private companies and research groups. The persistent layer of the business process is formed of a database with 86 tables, 900 fields within these tables, more than 112.200.000 tuples, 224 triggers and 107 integrity constraints. A total of 25 employees belonging to 6 separate departments modify the stored information. In this case, the audit layer must analyze 23 states. The business process for the example is shown in Figure 1. In the given example, 270 business rules have been created where 435 variables are involved.

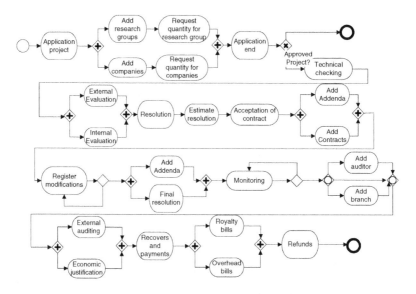

Fig. 1. Example of a real business process

This process is formed of a set of tasks which are related through various sets of business rules. Each task is in charge of a state of the project. Business rules are not described in a global way, since each task modifies certain data of a relational database and it will be necessary to evaluate different business rules.

3   Business Rules by Constraints

Business rules represent a natural step in the application of computer technology aimed at enhancing productivity in the workplace. When administrators of a business process want to change some functionality of the business, they have to wait for the reprogramming of the system. The adoption of business rules adds another tier to systems that automate business processes. Compared to traditional systems, this approach presents major advantages, as analyzed in depth in [6], and includes: A lower cost incurred in the modification of business logic; a shorter development time; externalization of the rules and ease of sharing among multiple applications; faster changes and with less risk.

If the expressiveness of business rules is improved, the above mentioned characteristics are also improved. For this reason, we propose the use of constraints instance of the *if ... then* axiom. The constraints proposed for the definition of business rules can be expressed as a Boolean combination with and/or operators of numerical equations and inequations for Integer, Natural and Float domains.

The use of constraints to represent business rules extends their formal semantics, since more knowledge can be represented and the description is less limited than when decision trees or a set of facts are employed. The use of constraints enables Integrity Rules, Derivation Rules, Reaction Rules and Production Rules to be represented, and the evaluation of whether a set of data is correct for an organization policy. For example, after the *Resolution* task of Figure 1, it is necessary to check that: whether the summation of hardware cost, software cost and human cost is equal to the total cost of the project, then the human cost is less or equal than 10% of the software cost; and whether the summation of these three values is smaller than the total cost, then the human cost has to be less or equal than 15% of the hardware cost. These business rules can be expressed with the constraints: $(hardCost + softCost + humanCost = totalCost \wedge humanCost \leq hardCost * 0.10) \vee (hardCost + softCost + humanCost < totalCost \wedge humanCost \leq hardCost * 0.15)$ where hardCost[1..100], softCost[1..150], humanCost[1..100], totalCost[5..250] for Float domain.

By using constraints to represent business rules, it is possible to validate tuples with business rules that are not explicitly described. Some examples of the inferred business rules for the above constraints can be:

- $hardCost \leq totalCost, softCost \leq totalCost, humanCost \leq totalCost$
- $humanCost \leq totalCost * 0.10$
- if $hardCost = 10$ then $totalCost[12..161] \wedge humanCost = 1$

By using constraints and depending on the instantiation of the variables, it is possible to evaluate a tuple even if some values are not still instantiated (stored in the database), that it is equivalent to say that the value of the variable in the tuple is *null*. Hence, it permits an early detection of errors, before the whole tuple of values of variables is fixed. In order to infer these unknown values, a Constraint Satisfaction Problem (CSP) can be created.

The CSPs represent a reasoning framework consisting of variables, domains and constraints. Formally, it is defined as a triple $<X, D, C>$ where $X = \{x_1, x_2, ..., x_n\}$ is a finite set of variables, $D = \{d(x_1), d(x_2), ..., d(x_n)\}$ is a set of domains of the values of the variables, and $C = \{C_1, C_2, ..., C_m\}$ is a set of constraints. A constraint $C_i = (V_i, R_i)$ specifies the possible values of the variables in V simultaneously to satisfy R [7]. When an objective function f has to be optimized (maximized or minimized), then a Constraint Optimization Problem (COP) is used, which is a CSP and an objective function f.

By using the constraint programming paradigm, when the values of variables related to a business rule are determined in various tasks of a business process, it is not necessary to wait until all the variables are instantiated to determine whether the business rules are satisfiable. Through solving the CSP, the possible values for the variables will be found, although they are not stored in the database and cannot be inferred using only classic business rule management.

4   Database Management and Business Rules

Most computer applications read and update data from databases. Therefore, data (the stored representation of facts in databases) is a fundamental component of information technology. Improvements in the integration of data in business processes are necessary, since it is common that not all information is transferred by means of data flow, but is modified via a database.

Business data is data that is directly used in business operations and would be used even in the absence of computerized systems. Metadata is additional data that describes what these computerized systems contain and how they work. Metadata also describes the business data, such as definitions of business terms. In order to define the equivalence between the business rules layer and data persistence layer, the BOM (Business Object Model) was introduced [8], although not the relation between persistence layer and business layer was defined.

In order to add business rules to a business process related to its data, it is necessary to add semantic information to business rules to support database correctness.

Current architectures contain no data flow integrity and audit trail since all business logics are hard-coded. This means that business processes cannot be easily related to any which involves complete data flow traceability.

The data model and the database are not the same thing, and the data model cannot simply be derived from the database by automated reverse engineering, something that is often postulated as a solution where no data model exists. For instance, the database contains only physical column names, but the rules engine will inevitably need the names of these columns. Hence, each business rule has to be transformed into a query evaluation over real tables and columns with a condition. The relation between business rules variables and database fields has to be stored. We propose the use of a system based on a wrapper over a database management system to store it and to transform business rules into query evaluations. We propose supporting the relation between business rules and persistence data through the use of Constraint Databases. These constraints can be associated to different moments of business process, in order to avoid the evaluation of all business rules, and the whole database.

4.1   Constraint Database Management System

When a great deal of business rules have to be handled, the use of a database is a mandatory decision, especially when not all the business rules are established for the whole business process. The storage of business rules also implies storing all the details related to its variables, the domain of variables and data persistence relationships. These types of information and business rules expressed by constraints can be supported by Constraint Database Management Systems (CDBMS).

Constraint Databases (CDBs) were initially developed in 1990 with a paper by Kanellakis, Kuper and Revesz [9]. The basic idea behind the CDB model is to generalize the notion of a tuple in a relational database to a conjunction of constraints, since a tuple in relational algebra can be represented as an equality constraint between an attribute of the database and a constant. In real business process, a great quantity of business rules must be defined, hence a repository is necessary in order to evaluate them as soon as possible, and to render updating easy and efficient [10].

The CDB used in this paper is based on Labelled Object-Relational Constraint Database Architecture (LORCDB Architecture) [11] with an extension to represent data business object and database model relations. LORCDB Architecture stores numerical constraints as objects indexed by the variables contained within, hence, when a CDB is created, three auxiliary tables are also automatically created (*Constraints*, *Variables* and *Constraints/Variables*) which relate each constraint with its variables (Figure 2). The table *Variables* stores the names of the variables, their identification and their type (Integer, Natural or Float), and for business rules, two new fields have been included in the *Variables* table (*Table* and *Field*) to store the relation between metadata and persistence data layer. This design enables to update the business rules according to the persistence layer modifying the value in the tables of the CDBs.

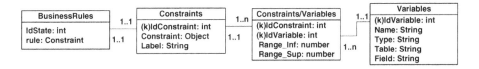

Fig. 2. CDB tables to index business rules with constraints and variables

5   Run-Time Auditing Framework

In order to permit the validation of business data in different states, and to represent and store business rules using constraints, we propose an extension of the classic Process Aware Information System (PAIS) framework [6].

Increasingly, business rules are also considered as a critical component of BPM solutions, due to the need to ensure flexibility. Some analysts believe the combination of business rules technology with BMP offers an agile approach to workflow and enterprise integration. The definition of an auditor of business data objects into separated layers enables the updating of processes or rules. In this context, the notion of PAIS provides a guiding framework to understand and deliberate on the above developments [12], [13]. In general, a PAIS architecture

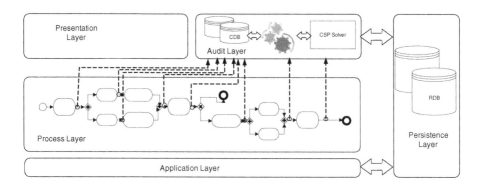

Fig. 3. Framework for Run-time Auditing

can be viewed as a 4-tier system as presented in [6], where from top to bottom the layers are: Presentation Layer, Process Layer, Application Layer and Persistency Layer. As a fundamental characteristic, PAIS provides the means to separate process logic from application code. We propose a new framework shown in Figure 3, where a new layer is added to validate the business data objects, and where the persistence layer can also be accessed from the Audit Layer in order to facilitate database auditing. This framework enables the relational database to be audited according to an associated set of business rules and according to the data flow.

Audit and business process layers are two parallel and "independent" systems. They are independent since they can be executed in separate machines, for different applications, and at the same time. This independence is breaking from the point of view of data flow information, since the Auditor uses data flow information of the process layer to detect the non-satisfiable business rules.

The Audit layer is called from the process layer, and depends on the business state or activity and the data flow instances of each moment. In order to determine how the communication between these layers is done, it is necessary to describe the Audit Layer in a deeper way.

Audit Layer
The function of the Audit layer is to capture the identification of the state to determine which business rules have to be analyzed, and the data flow values to delimit the tuples of the database. The behaviour of the auditor enables the determination of whether a business data object satisfies a set of rules from several points of view. The use of the audit layer implies:

- For reasons of complexity in time, it is neither possible nor necessary to analyze all the tuples of the database. In the different instances of the business process, only a set of tuples is modified. For example, if a business process is in charge of updating the information related to a project, then it is only necessary to analyze the tuples where this project is involved. This information is transferred to the Audit layer by means of the data flow. As presented in

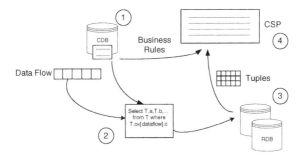

Fig. 4. Audit Layer Procedure

Section 4.1, the constraints, variables and fields of the relational database are indexed, hence a query can be created using the data flow (query condition parameters) and business rules variables.
– We propose that business rules are related to a temporal aspect [14], which means that business rules depend on the state of the business object, hence the auditor has to be informed about which business object state to evaluate. This information is used by the auditor to establish which set of rules stored in the Constraint Database has to be analyzed and combined with the tuples of the relational database to build a CSP.

Audit Layer Procedure Steps:
The steps (represented in Figure 4) to audit the data of a relational database, which depend on the data flow values and the business rules stored in the CDB, are to:

1. Select the business rules related to the state from the CDB, thereby obtaining the tables and field of relational database that are involved in the audit process.
2. Build a query where the attributes of the "projection" are the related attributes obtained in the previous step, and the condition (where) is defined by the values of the data flow.
3. Obtain the tuples that have to be evaluated, by executing the query of the previous step in the relational database.
4. Create and solve the CSPs for each tuple obtained from Step 3 and the business rules obtained from Step 1.

Applying the process to the example presented in Section 3, where the table of the database that has to be validated is presented in Table 1, the steps for the procedure become:

1. The constraints obtained to create the CSP are:
   Float var hardCost[1..100], softCost[1..150], humanCost[1..100], totalCost[5..250]
   (hardCost + softCost + humanCost = totalCost ∧ humanCost ≤ hardCost ∗0.10) ∨ (hardCost + softCost + humanCost < humanCost ∧ humanCost ≤ hardCost∗0.15)

2. Using the table *Variables* of the CDB to know that the fields of the variables *hardCost, softCost, humanCost, totalCost* are respectively F_{haC}, F_{sC}, F_{huC} and F_{tC}, then the following query is created:

> `Select` $T.F_{haC}$, $T.F_{sC}$, $T.F_{huC}$, $T.F_{tC}$ `from` T `where` $T.ID=[dataflow]$

and where it is supposed that the data flow has the value for identification equal to 430, and there is no condition about *year*.
3. The result of this step is the four first tuples of Table 1.
4. Each obtained tuple is evaluated by building a CSP. For the example of Table 1, the business rules are satisfiable for the first and fourth tuples. In this example, it is known that the third tuple is not satisfiable although not all its values are instantiated.

Table 1. Example of tuples to evaluate

ID	Year	haC	sC	huC	tC
430	2007	20	8	1	29
430	2008	20	7	1	15
430	2009	100	150	null	null
430	2010	100	null	4	null
431	...	...	...	...	...

6   Extending Constraint Business Rule Language with Aggregate Operators

The use of constraints to represent business rules can be extended with aggregate operators. Although other proposals exist which are oriented towards the definition of a monitoring language [15], they are not related to monitoring data flow to audit database information depending on business rules. We propose the addition of new types of business rules that can be defined over a set of tuples of relational databases: Minimum($min(v)$), Maximum($max(v)$), Count($count(v)$), Summation($sum(v)$) or Average($avg(v)$), where v represents any variable involved in a business rule.

Going back to the example of Table 1, it is possible to define a business rule where the summation of *hardCost* for an ID has to be equal to the summation of *softCost* for the same ID.

We have adapted the existing operators in SQL, using them to represent business rules: sum, avg, min, max and count. For each type, the creation of the model is:

– **Sum(v):** The summation will obtain the n tuples that satisfy the condition of the query. With the variables involved in the rule, and with the domain of v, the following CSP is built where i and j represent the domain of v stored in the CDB:

```
Integer var v₁[i..j], v₂[i..j], ..., vₙ[i..j]
v₁ + v₂ + ... vₙ = ...
```

- **Min(v) and Max(v):** The minimum or maximum summation value of a variable will obtain the n tuples that satisfy the condition of the query. With the variables involved in the rule, and with the domain of v, the following COP is built where n_i represents each one of the values obtained in the tuple for variable v:

```
Integer var v[i..j]
v = n₁ ∨ v = n₂ ∨ ... ∨ v = nₙ
Max(v)(orMin(v))
v = ...
```

If some value of v is *null* for the selected tuples, the constraint $v = n_1 \lor v = n_2 \lor \ldots \lor v = n_n$ will not be included, since the non-instantiated field can take any value of the domain.
- **Count(v):** In this case, the SQL evaluation itself of the Count operator is used. The obtained value will be included in the business rules for the CSP.

Example of business rules with aggregate operators
As an illustration of our proposal, we show an example of business rules expressing by constraints for the "Acceptation of Contract" task of the business process shown in Figure 1.

```
sum(incentive) ≤ demanded
sum(incentive) = sum(potentialIncentive)*IncentivePercentage
sum(demandPerYear) = demanded
sum(incentivePerYear) = incentive
FinalFund = FundPercentage*demanded
max(incentive) < FundPercentage*demanded
FundPercentage + RefundPercentage = 1
count(incentivePerYear) ≤ demanded/min(demandPerYear)
```

The CSP will be composed of any undetermined number of variables that will be established at the evaluation time, where the set of related tuples is known. Supposing that i tuples of *incentive*, j tuples of *potentialIncentive*, k tuples of *demandPerYear* and m tuples of *incentivePerYear* have been obtained, and the maximum value of incentive is described by the variable $incentive_i$, the minimum incentive per year $incentivePerYear_m$, and the number of years with incentive is m, then the following CSP is built:

```
Float incentive₁[domain₁], ..., incentiveᵢ[domainᵢ]
Float potentialIncentive₁[domain₁]
...
Float potentialIncentiveⱼ[domainⱼ]
Float demandPerYear₁[domain₁], ..., demandPerYearₖ[domainₖ]
Float incentivePerYear₁[domain₁]
...
Float incentivePerYearₘ[domainₘ], demanded[domain]
Float incentive[domain], FinalFund[domain]
Float FundPercentage[domain], ReFundPercentage[domain]
incentive₁ +...+ incentiveᵢ ≤ demanded
incentive₁ +...+incentiveᵢ = (potentialIncentive₁+
   ...+ potentialIncentiveⱼ)*IncentivePercentage
demandPerYear₁ +...+demandPerYearₖ = demanded
incentivePerYear₁ +...+ incentivePerYearₘ = incentive
FinalFund = FundPercentage*demanded
incentiveᵢ < FundPercentage*demand
FundPercentage + RefundPercentage = 1
m ≤ demanded/incentivePerYearₘ
```

Finally, we must highlight that the CSPs cannot be pre-built and/or precompiled, since although the business rules are stored in the CDB, the number of variables and the final representation of the constraints for aggregate functions remain unknown until the time of evaluation.

7   Conclusions and Future Work

In this paper, the necessity to describe a methodology to audit stored relational data in a business process is presented. In order to describe the business rules related to the stored data, the constraint programming paradigm has been proposed. These constraints can be associated to different states of a business process, in order to prevent the unnecessary evaluation of all business rules, and the whole database.

A framework is proposed where an audit layer has been included. The combined use of CDBs and the audit layer enables early detection of incorrect data in business processes, by creating and solving CSPs and COPs in run-time.

There are significant research lines that can be analyzed in further depth, such as: what actions can be taken when an inconsistency is detected; how would it be possible to automatically located the rules better to improve the early detection of errors; and how the business rules expressed by constraints can help in company decision making, proposing correct or promising values.

Acknowledgment

This work has been partially funded by the Junta de Andalucía by means of la Consejería de Innovación, Ciencia y Empresa (P08-TIC-04095) and by the

Ministry of Science and Technology of Spain (TIN2009-13714) and the European Regional Development Fund (ERDF/FEDER).

References

1. van der Aalst, W.M.P., ter Hofstede, A.H.M., Weske, M.: Business Process Management: A Survey. In: van der Aalst, W.M.P., ter Hofstede, A.H.M., Weske, M. (eds.) BPM 2003. LNCS, vol. 2678, pp. 1–12. Springer, Heidelberg (2003)
2. Chesani, F., Mello, P., Montali, M., Riguzzi, F., Sebastianis, M., Storari, S.: Checking compliance of execution traces to business rules. In: Business Process Management Workshops, pp. 134–145 (2008)
3. zur Muehlen, M., Indulska, M.: Modeling languages for business processes and business rules: A representational analysis. Inf. Syst. 35(4), 379–390 (2010)
4. Meng, J.: Achieving dynamic inter-organizational workflow management by integrating business processes, e-services, events, and rules. PhD thesis, Gainesville, FL, USA, Chair-Su, Stanley Y. and Chair-Helal, Abdelsalam (2002)
5. McDermid, D.C.: Integrated Business Process Management: Using State-Based Business Rules to Communicate between Disparate Stakeholders. In: van der Aalst, W.M.P., ter Hofstede, A.H.M., Weske, M. (eds.) BPM 2003. LNCS, vol. 2678, pp. 58–71. Springer, Heidelberg (2003)
6. Weber, B., Sadiq, S.W., Reichert, M.: Beyond rigidity - dynamic process lifecycle support. Computer Science - R&D 23(2), 47–65 (2009)
7. Dechter, R.: Constraint Processing. The Morgan Kaufmann Series in Artificial Intelligence. Morgan Kaufmann, San Francisco (2003)
8. Heumann, J.: Introduction to business modeling using the unified modeling language (uml). In: Rational Edge (2001)
9. Kuper, G.M., Kanellakis, P.C., Revesz, P.Z.: Constraint query languages. In: Symposium on Principles of Database Systems, pp. 299–313 (1990)
10. Chisholm, M.: How to Build a Business Rules Engine: Extending Application Functionality through Metadata Engineering. The Morgan Kaufmann Series in Data Management Systems. Morgan Kaufmann Publishers Inc., San Francisco (2003)
11. López, M.T.G., Ceballos, R., Gasca, R.M., Valle, C.D.: Developing a labelled object-relational constraint database architecture for the projection operator. Data Knowl. Eng. 68(1), 146–172 (2009)
12. Ma, H.: Process-aware information systems: Bridging people and software through process technology: Book reviews. J. Am. Soc. Inf. Sci. Technol. 58(3), 455–456 (2007)
13. Weske, M.: Business Process Management: Concepts, Languages, Architectures. Springer-Verlag New York, Inc., Secaucus (2007)
14. Walzer, K., Breddin, T., Groch, M.: Relative temporal constraints in the rete algorithm for complex event detection. In: DEBS 2008: Proceedings of the Second International Conference on Distributed Event-based Systems, pp. 147–155. ACM, New York (2008)
15. Beeri, C., Eyal, A., Milo, T., Pilberg, A.: Monitoring business processes with queries. In: VLDB 2007: Proceedings of the 33rd International Conference on Very Large Data Bases, pp. 603–614. VLDB Endowment (2007)

A Critical Evaluation Study of Model-Log Metrics in Process Discovery

Jochen De Weerdt[1], Manu De Backer[1,2,3], Jan Vanthienen[1], and Bart Baesens[1]

[1] Department of Decision Sciences and Information Management, Katholieke
Universiteit Leuven, Naamsestraat 69, B-3000 Leuven, Belgium
Jochen.DeWeerdt@econ.kuleuven.be
[2] Department of HABE, Hogeschool Gent, Universiteit Gent,
Voskenslaan 2, B-9000 Ghent, Belgium
[3] Department of Management Information Systems, University of Antwerp,
Prinsstraat 13, B-2000 Antwerp, Belgium

Abstract. The development of a well-defined evaluation framework for
process discovery techniques is definitely one of the most important challenges within this subdomain of process mining. Any researcher in the
field will acknowledge that such a framework is vital. With this paper,
we aim to provide a tangible analysis of the currently available model-log
evaluation metrics for mined control-flow models. Also, we will indicate
strengths and weaknesses of the existing metrics and propose a number
of opportunities for future research.

Keywords: process discovery, evaluation metrics, machine learning.

1 Introduction

The topic of process mining is relatively new and can be situated at the intersection of the fields of Business Process Management (BPM) and data mining
[1]. It is inherently related to data mining and to the more general domain of
knowledge discovery in databases (KDD) since the nature of its objectives is
extracting useful information from large data repositories. Likewise, process discovery is strongly associated with BPM because of its purpose of gaining insight
into business processes. As a result, process mining fits flawlessly into the BPM
life cycle framework [2]. It should be noted that business process mining comprises process discovery because process mining describes a family of a-posteriori
analysis techniques for extracting knowledge from event logs while process discovery only deals with extracting control-flow models. However, most of the
attention in the process mining literature has been given to process discovery
techniques.

Processes occur in a more or less structured fashion, containing structures
such as or-joins, or-splits, and-joins, and-splits, and loops. The learning task for
any process discovery technique can be formulated as follows: given an event log
that contains the events about a finite number of process instances, find a model

M. zur Muehlen and J. Su (Eds.): BPM 2010 Workshops, LNBIP 66, pp. 158–169, 2011.
© Springer-Verlag Berlin Heidelberg 2011

that correctly summarizes the behavior in the event log, striking the right balance between generality (allowing enough behavior) and specificity (not allowing too much behavior). One important complexity for process mining techniques is that there are no natural negative cases available in an event log. In most KDD applications, negative instances are generally available. Due to the situation of learning from positive instances only, the straightforward application of traditional data mining techniques is non-trivial.

What is more, not only the development of process mining techniques is challenging, also the definition of appropriate metrics is a complex encounter. The quantification of accuracy as well as the trade-off between generality and precision is difficult. Desirably, a process discovery metric should measure only one dimension of a mined process model in reference with its event log. This is because in case a metric captures multiple dimensions, the metric quickly becomes incomprehensible.

We acknowledge the existence of a discussion in current literature concerning the absence of a "perfect model". However, we think that the availability of proficient metrics remains vital. As such, we will evaluate existing model-log evaluation metrics for mined control-flow models. Furthermore, we will discuss strengths and weaknesses of the existing metrics and propose a number of opportunities for future research.

In order to realize our goal of elucidating and assessing currently available process discovery metrics, this paper is structured as follows. In section 2, we will provide an overview of existing process discovery metrics. In section 3, a number of key metrics will be clarified in a simplified example. Furthermore, the metrics will also be illustrated and assessed within a more comprehensive Driver's License example. Finally, section 4 outlines the conclusions and some important opportunities for future research.

2   Overview of Process Discovery Metrics

When evaluating the quality of mined process models, appropriate metrics need to be at hand. However, the quality of process models can be evaluated along different perspectives and by using different methods [3]. One method is to compare the traces in the event log and the model mined from this event log (model-log metrics). Another approach is to compare an apriori model with the discovered model, but then an apriori model needs to be available (model-model metrics). In this paper, we will only consider model-log metrics. These metrics can be applied in any setting, whether a predefined process model exists or not.

2.1   Available Model-Log Metrics and Their Dimensions

Existing model-log metrics evaluate mined process models along four important dimensions, as illustrated in table 1. It can be seen that most evaluation metrics reflect the recall dimension. However, good recall is certainly not the only dimension a model should score well on. Also very important for comprehensible and useful models is a good balance between precision and generality.

Table 1. Overview of process mining evaluation metrics: model-log metrics

Name	Symbol	Author	Available in ProM	Range	Model input type	Recall	Specificity	Precision	Generality
Parsing Measure	PM	Weijters et al. [4]	✓	[0,1]	Heuristic net	✓			
Soundness		Greco et al. [5]		[0,1]	Workflow schema				✓
Completeness		"		[0,1]	Workflow schema	✓			
Fitness	f	Rozinat and Van der Aalst [6]	✓	[0,1]	Petri net	✓			
Behavioral Appropriateness	a_B	"	✓	[0,1]	Petri net			✓	
Advanced Behavioral Appropriateness	a'_B	"	✓	[0,1]	Petri net			✓	
Structural Appropriateness	a_S	"	✓	[0,1]	Petri net				✓
Advanced Structural Appropriateness	a'_S	"	✓	[0,1]	Petri net				✓
Completeness	$PF_{complete}$	Alves de Medeiros et al. [7]	✓	[-∞,1]	Heuristic net	✓			
Behavioral Recall	r^p_B	Goedertier et al. [8]		[0,1]	Petri net	✓			
Behavioral Specificity	s^n_B	"		[0,1]	Petri net		✓		

The recall dimension. Recall or sensitivity is a very important aspect. This dimension reflects how much behavior present in the event log is captured by the model. For every process discovery algorithm, it is of utmost importance to render models with good recall because representing the control-flow behavior in an event log is the major objective of any technique. Hence, it is definitely satisfying that a number of researchers have proposed different measures to capture recall.

- The *parsing measure (PM)* was proposed by Weijters et al. [4]. It quantifies the percentage of traces in the log that can be replayed by the discovered process model. It should be noted that *PM* is a coarse-grained metric. A single missing arc in a Petri net can result in parsing failure for all traces.
- A very similar metric is *completeness* as defined by Greco et al. [5]. This is the percentage of traces in the event log that are compliant with the workflow schema or process model. Completeness always ranges between 0 and 1.
- *Fitness (f)* is a metric that is obtained by trying whether each trace in the event log can be reproduced by the generative model. This procedure is called sequence replay [6]. During replay, the transitions in the Petri net will produce and consume tokens to reflect the state transitions. Consequently,

the fitness measure punishes for tokens that must additionally be created in the marked Petri net and also for tokens that remain after replay.

- *Completeness (PF$_{complete}$)* proposed by Alves de Medeiros et al. [9] is very similar to the fitness metric, but it additionally exploits trace frequencies in order to take into account the severity of missing and remaining tokens.
- *Behavioral recall (r$_B^p$)* as defined by Goedertier et al. [8] is the percentage of correctly classified positive events in the event log. During sequence replay, it is verified whether every positive event can be parsed by the model. Note that this measure originates from a process discovery technique that makes use of inducing artificial negative events in order to mine control-flow models. By verifying the parsing of positive events, recall can be quantified.

The specificity dimension. Specificity is the counterpart of recall. It captures the percentage of correctly classified negative cases. Of course, in process discovery, negative events or negative traces are typically not available. However, Goedertier et al. [8] propose a technique that generates artificial negative events. These artificial negative events can be used to define a state-of-the-art specificity metric. The availability of both recall and specificity metrics allows for the definition of an approved accuracy measure for process discovery models.

- *Behavioral specificity (s$_B^n$)* is the percentage of correctly classified negative instances during sequence replay. Negative events can be generated with the technique developed by Goedertier et al. However, the definition of the metric does not exclude the use of negative events stemming from other techniques.

The precision and generality dimensions. The trade-off between precision and generality is a major challenge in process discovery. Although models should be precise, generalizing beyond observed behavior is also a necessity. This is because assuming that all behavior is included in an event log is a much too strong completeness assumption. So, process discovery algorithms should be able to balance between underfitting (overly general models) and overfitting (overly precise models). Therefore, superior precision and generality metrics should be at hand. The following list enumerates the currently available measures.

- *Soundness* (Greco et al. [5]) is the first of three precision metrics. Soundness is the percentage of traces compliant with the process model that have been registered in the log. Calculating soundness is not straightforward because enumerating all possible paths in a process model is hard. Even for smaller process models, it might be impossible to determine all the traces that are compliant with a process model.
- The first of four appropriateness measures defined by Rozinat and Van der Aalst [6] is the simple *behavioral appropriateness (a$_B$)*. This simple approach measures the amount of possible behavior to determine a mean number of enabled transitions during log replay. Because this metric is not independent of structural properties, it is advised to use the advanced behavioral appropriateness.

– *Advanced behavioral appropriateness* (a'_B) allows to compare the behavior
  that is specified by the model with the behavior that is actually needed to
  describe the behavior in the event log. Therefore, this metric makes use of
  an analysis of "follows" and "precedes" relations, both in the model and the
  event log. Comparing the variability of these relations allows the definition
  of a precision metric that penalizes extra behavior.

Balancing between precision and generality also involves metrics that quantify
generality. The structural and advanced structural appropriateness measures are
the only currently available model-log metrics that quantify generality.

– *Structural appropriateness* (a_S) is based on the number of different task
  labels in relation to the graph size of the model. As identified by Rozinat
  and Van der Aalst [6], this metric's applicability is limited because it is only
  based on the graph size of the model.
– *Advanced structural appropriateness* (a'_S) is a generality metric that evaluates two specific design guidelines for expressing behavioral patterns. This
  measure will punish for both alternative duplicate tasks and redundant invisible tasks. Note that these guidelines are definitely not the only behavioral preferences of control-flow models. However, a'_S is the only metric that
  quantifies generality in some way. Ideally, a process model does not contain
  redundant invisible tasks nor alternative duplicate tasks. Accordingly, this
  measure will punish for models that simply enumerate all traces in the event
  log and for models that entail to much irrelevant invisible tasks.

2.2 Discussion

So far, we have discussed a number of process discovery evaluation metrics.
Four important dimensions were identified along which process models should
be judged: recall, specificity, precision and generality. Many evaluation metrics
have already been proposed in literature. However, existing model-log metrics
might insufficiently capture all of the underlying dimensions. For example, the
currently available precision and generality measures are insufficiently capable
of capturing all the complexities related to the trade-off between underfitting
and overfitting.

3 Illustration of Key Metrics in Process Discovery

In this section, we will illustrate the most important currently available process
mining metrics and show how they capture the different dimensions discussed in
the previous section. We have selected five metrics: fitness, advanced behavioral
appropriateness, advanced structural appropriateness, behavioral recall and behavioral specificity, so that the four identified dimensions are covered by at least
one metric. Although the other metrics definitely have value, they do not add
to this analysis because most of them are very comparable to one of the metrics
selected. Furthermore, metrics like soundness and both simple appropriateness
measures suffer from different shortcomings and are therefore left out.

3.1   A Simplified Example to Elucidate the Most Important Metrics

The event log of this simplified example contains 50 traces "ABCDA" and 50 traces "ACBDA". Accordingly, the best model representing the traces in the log is model 1(a). Table 2 shows that this model scores 1 on every metric and thus can be considered excellent along all evaluation dimensions.

Table 2. Model-log metrics for a simple artificial event log and four different models

Metric	Fitness	Adv. Behavioral Appropriateness	Adv. Structural Appropriateness	Behavioral Recall	Behavioral Specificity
Symbol (dimension)	f (recall)	a'_B (precision)	a'_S (generality)	r^p_B (recall)	s^n_B (specificity)
Best Model	1	1	1	1	1
Incomplete Model	0.92	1	1	0.90	0.89
Flower Model	1	0.17	1	1	0
Explicit Model	1	1	0.40	1	1

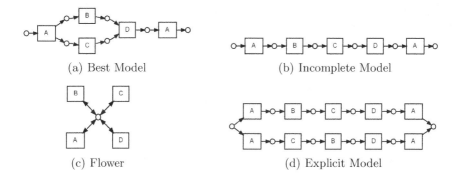

(a) Best Model   (b) Incomplete Model

(c) Flower   (d) Explicit Model

Fig. 1. Different control-flow models for the simple event log

The other models in figure 1 are in one way or the other erroneous. The incomplete model does not recall all traces in the log, the flower model allows too much behavior and the explicit model is only a mere enumeration of the traces in the log. We will now elucidate how different metrics are able to identify the dimension(s) along which a mined process model misses the mark.

Fitness. Model 1(b) is not able to capture all the behavior that is present in the event log. Thus, metrics quantifying the recall dimension should indicate this problem. The fitness measure (f) is a particularly useful metric to do so. With 50 traces (n_i) for each of the grouped traces, both the number of missing tokens (m_i) and the number of remaining tokens (r_i) amounts to 1 for the second grouped trace ("ACBDA") and 0 for the first grouped trace ("ABCDA"). Furthermore each of the traces requires 6 tokens to be consumed (c_i) / produced (p_i) in order to be replayed. Accordingly, the fitness of the incomplete model sums up to 0.92. Note that i is an index running over the number of different grouped traces (k), which is two in this simplified case.

- Fitness: $f = \frac{1}{2}\left(1 - \frac{\sum_{i=1}^{k} n_i m_i}{\sum_{i=1}^{k} n_i c_i}\right) + \frac{1}{2}\left(1 - \frac{\sum_{i=1}^{k} n_i r_i}{\sum_{i=1}^{k} n_i p_i}\right)$

$= \frac{1}{2}\left(1 - \frac{50*0+50*1}{50*6+50*6}\right) + \frac{1}{2}\left(1 - \frac{50*0+50*1}{50*6+50*6}\right) = 0.92$

The other models in figure 3 are able to reproduce all the behavior in the event log. Accordingly, this is also demonstrated by the fitness measure. During sequence replay, there are no missing tokens nor remaining tokens for any of the other models and thus the fitness evaluates to 1. Notice that a fitness value of 0.92 for the incomplete model is an unattractive high value for a model that only parses half of the traces correctly.

Advanced behavioral appropriateness. The flower model (1(c)) is a generic model that allows any sequence of activities. Because it overgeneralizes, it is useless for any process intelligence activity. Nevertheless, the flower model captures all the behavior in the event log perfectly, so the model is not penalized by a recall-metric. The advanced behavioral appropriateness does punish the flower model for its overly general representation.

- Adv. behavioral appropriateness: $a'_B = \frac{|S^l_F \cap S^m_F|}{2.|S^m_F|} + \frac{|S^l_P \cap S^m_P|}{2.|S^m_P|} = \frac{2}{2*12} + \frac{2}{2*12} = 0.17$

The advanced behavioral appropriateness for the simplified example flower model is found by calculating the elements in the "sometimes follows" and "sometimes precedes" relations in the model (S^m_F and S^m_P) and in the log (S^l_F and S^l_P) [6]. The calculation for the follows relations is illustrated in figure 2.[1] According to ProM, there are a total of 12 sometimes follows relations and 12 sometimes precedes relations in the model. However, the model and the log have only 2 sometimes follows and 2 sometimes precedes relations in common. Therefore, a'_B adds up to 0.17.

↗	A	B	C	D
A	A_F	S_F	S_F	S_F
B	S_F	A_F	S_F	S_F
C	S_F	S_F	A_F	S_F
D	S_F	S_F	S_F	A_F

↗	A	B	C	D
A	S_F	S_F	S_F	S_F
B	S_F	S_F	S_F	S_F
C	S_F	S_F	S_F	S_F
D	S_F	S_F	S_F	S_F

(a) Model relations: calculated manually (r) and by ProM (l)

↗	A	B	C	D
A	A_F	A_F	A_F	A_F
B	A_F	N_F	S_F	A_F
C	A_F	S_F	N_F	A_F
D	A_F	N_F	N_F	N_F

(b) Log relations

Fig. 2. Follows relations for the flower model (1(c)) and for the simplified event log

For perfectly precise models, a'_B will equal 1. This is illustrated in table 2 as the other three models are not overgeneralizing and their a'_B evaluates to

---

[1] For clarity, we make abstraction of the artificial Start and End activities.

1 accordingly. For models 1(a) and 1(d), the sometimes follows and sometimes precedes relations in the model and the log are exactly the same. For model 1(b), the relations are not completely identical, but the model is in fact more restrictive with respect to the relations in the log, so the generality measure evaluates to 1. This signifies correctly that the model is not underfitting. Other metrics should signpost the incompleteness of the model.

An important remark should be made concerning the calculation of a'_B. The calculation involves a state space analysis which can be computationally very demanding. Furthermore, the calculation seems approximate because a manual analysis of the metric for the flower model results in a total of 16 sometimes follows and sometimes precedes relations. Apparently, (A,A), (B,B), (C,C) and (D,D) relations are categorized as always follows/precedes (see figure 2(a)), despite the fact that the flower model allows more variability for these relations. As such, a'_B, as obtained from ProM, slightly underestimates the overgenerality of the flower model.

Advanced structural appropriateness. Another problem in process discovery are overly precise models or overfitting models. Figure 1(d) shows an explicit model that is a mere enumeration of the traces in the log. Again, such a model is undesired and should be punished by a generality measure. Advanced structural appropriateness is the only currently available metric that allows to quantify some kind of generality. Because model 1(d) contains six alternative duplicate tasks (T_{DA}) and no redundant invisible tasks (T_{IR}), a'_S evaluates to 0.4 (note that $|T|$ denotes the total number of tasks). These alternative duplicate tasks are activities B, C and D, occurring once in each of the branches of the explicit process model. They are alternative duplicate tasks because they never happen together in one execution sequence.

- Structural appropriateness: $a'_S = \frac{|T|-(|T_{DA}|+|T_{IR}|)}{|T|} = \frac{10-(6+0)}{10} = 0.40$

Artificially generated negative event metrics. In [8], Goedertier et al. propose two state-of-the-art metrics originating from a process discovery technique called AGNEs (Artificially Generated Negative Events). This technique involves the induction of negative events in the event log in order to allow the application of advanced machine learning techniques (Inductive Logic Programming) for control-flow discovery (see also [10]). The availability of both positive and artificial negative events allows the definition of behavioral recall r^p_B and behavioral specificity s^n_B, metrics that are grounded in traditional data mining theory. According to their definition, they are able to penalize inaccurate process models.

The induction procedure generates artificial negative events as displayed in table 3. A total of 28 negative events are induced in the event log. In order to calculate the metrics, a confusion matrix can be constructed. The confusion matrix for the incomplete process model (1(b)) is shown in table 4.

Behavioral recall and behavioral specificity for the incomplete model are calculated according to the following formulae.

- Behavioral recall: $r_B^p = \dfrac{\sum_{i=1}^{k} n_i\, TP_i}{\sum_{i=1}^{k} n_i\, TP_i + \sum_{i=1}^{k} n_i\, FN_i}$

$$= \frac{50*5+50*4}{(50*5+50*4)+(50*0+50*1)} = \frac{9}{10} = 0.90$$

- Behavioral specificity: $s_B^n = \dfrac{\sum_{i=1}^{k} n_i\, TN_i}{\sum_{i=1}^{k} n_i\, TN_i + \sum_{i=1}^{k} n_i\, FP_i}$

$$= \frac{50*14+50*11}{(50*14+50*11)+(50*0+50*3)} = \frac{25}{28} = 0.89$$

Table 3. Artificially generated negative events for the simplified event log

	Trace 1					Trace 2				
Positive events	A	B	C	D	A	A	C	B	D	A
Artificially	B^n	A^n	A^n	A^n	B^n	B^n	A^n	A^n	A^n	B^n
generated	C^n	D^n	B^n	B^n	C^n	C^n	D^n	C^n	B^n	$\mathbf{C^n}$
negative events	D^n		D^n	C^n	D^n	D^n		$\mathbf{D^n}$	$\mathbf{C^n}$	D^n

Table 4. Confusion matrix for the negative event metrics

	true pos.	true neg.	total
pred. pos.	9	3	12
pred. neg.	1	25	26
total	10	28	

From this simplified model, it can be concluded that within process discovery research, different evaluation dimensions are covered by existing model-log metrics. However, it cannot be determined whether these metrics are sufficient in order to capture all the complexities of assessing process discovery models. Therefore, we also evaluate the presented metrics within a more extended example.

3.2   Further Insights Using an Extended Driver's License Example

We apply the evaluation metrics to a more extended example by using a modified version of a Driver's License (from [7]) event log. This event log and the according models contain more complex control-flow constructs such as a loop and non-free choice constructs. As such, this experiment will allow us to verify whether the available metrics can distinguish between worse and better models in a more complex setting. Figure 3 shows the results of four state-of-the-art process discovery techniques. By examining these results, some further elements in the analysis of existing process discovery metrics can be highlighted.

First of all, it can be seen that the fitness metric (f) reveals that every technique, except for the α-algorithm [11], discovers models with perfect recall. This can also be concluded from the behavioral recall metric (r_B^p). Although both metrics seem to measure the same dimension, an important remark should be made. The interpretation of the fitness measure requires some attention: although it accounts for recall as it punishes for the number of missing tokens

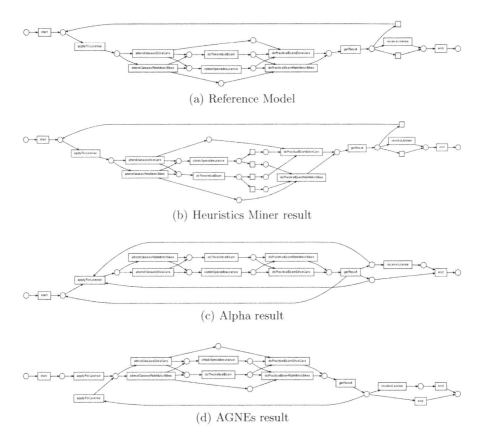

(a) Reference Model

(b) Heuristics Miner result

(c) Alpha result

(d) AGNEs result

Fig. 3. Different control-flow models for the simple event log

that had to be created, it also punishes for the number of tokens that remain in the Petri net after log replay. The latter can be considered extra behavior. Therefore, the fitness metric also has a specificity semantics attached to it. As mentioned previously, metrics desirably measure only one dimension in order to remain comprehensible.

Secondly, some observations concerning the advanced behavioral appropriateness (a'_B) are discussed. As for the flower model in the simplified example, the state space analysis for calculating this metric was calculated swiftly. However, for this Driver's License example, the more or less exhaustive simulation of all the behavior in the model was unable to be completed within an acceptable time period. Furthermore, it is also suspicious that a'_B does not evaluate to 1 for the reference model. It is definitely counterintuitive that the reference model is judged not to be completely precise with respect to the event log. Nevertheless, a'_B is capable of identifying the non-detection of the non-free choice construct.

Finally, we notice that it is not obvious which model is to be preferred. Models score differently along distinct dimensions, but there are no rules that define how these dimensions should be put together. Are there dimensions that are more

Table 5. Model-log metrics for the extended Driver's License example

Metric	Fitness	Adv. Behavioral Appropriate-ness	Adv. Structural Appropriate-ness	Behavioral Recall	Behavioral Specificity
Symbol *(dimension)*	f *(recall)*	a'_B *(precision)*	a'_S *(generality)*	r^p_B *(recall)*	s^n_B *(specificity)*
Reference Model	1	0.927	1	1	0.985
Heuristics Model	1	0.874	1	1	0.985
Alpha Model	0.921	1	1	0.917	0.983
AGNEs Model	1	0.906	0.846	1	0.985
Flower Model	1	0.500	1	1	0

important than others? How can this be included in the analysis phase? How should differences along one and multiple dimensions be assessed? We think that these questions bring about the necessity for a more rigorous and comprehensive evaluation framework for discovered process models.

4   Conclusion

With this paper, we discussed currently available process discovery metrics, which can be categorized along four important dimensions: recall, specificity, precision and generality. The analysis was restricted to model-log metrics because these metrics can be applied at all time, even when a predefined model is unavailable. Although the explicit illustration of some key metrics is very insightful, the analysis of strengths and weaknesses of the existent metrics is indispensable. We identified the following shortcomings with respect to the currently available process mining metrics.

- Metrics should be *one-dimensional*. The fitness (f) metric for example does not fulfil this requirement. Metrics that are multi-dimensional in nature will quickly become incomprehensible.
- The currently available precision and generality measures suffer from computational inefficiency. The advanced behavioral and structural appropriateness metrics require an *exhaustive simulation* of the mined process model. This state space analysis procedure is only *approximate* and this causes difficulties with respect to benchmarking new or existing process discovery algorithms. Even though conceptually proficient, the imprecise calculation of the metrics brings about the necessity of new precision and generality measures. Although not trivial, it is crucial that the trade-off between precision and generality is adequately quantified. This is because this trade-off is a key determinant of model comprehensibility. Accordingly, the definition of new, insightful metrics is definitely a challenge for future research.
- Process discovery metrics developed in the light of *machine learning* theory are definitely of added value. Behavioral recall and behavioral specificity are valuable measures, but their integration with the ProM-framework should allow researchers to exploit these state-of-the-art recall and specificity metrics.

Finally, this analysis demonstrates that, within process discovery, a more rigorous and comprehensive evaluation framework is definitely needed. Although this need has been formulated previously [12], such a framework is still missing. We think that this paper is a new, valuable impetus hereto. It can be concluded that in any process discovery analysis, combining different metrics is indispensable, as metrics preferably measure only one aspect of a mined process model and models will always have to be judged along multiple dimensions. In future research, we will actively contribute to the further development of an evaluation framework.

Notes and Comments. We would like to thank the Flemish Research Council for financial support under Odysseus grant B.0915.09. Furthermore, we would like to thank the team of prof. Van der Aalst for their comments and valuable input.

References

1. Tan, P.N., Steinbach, M., Kumar, V.: Introduction to Data Mining. Addison-Wesley, Reading (2005)
2. Weske, M.: Business Process Management: Concepts, Languages, Architectures. Springer, Heidelberg (2007)
3. Rozinat, A., Veloso, M., van der Aalst, W.M.P.: Using hidden markov models to evaluate the quality of discovered process models. BPM Center Report BPM-08-10 (2008)
4. Weijters, A.J.M.M., van der Aalst, W.M.P., Alves de Medeiros, A.K.: Process mining with the heuristicsminer algorithm. BETA Working Paper Series 166. Eindhoven University of Technology (2006)
5. Greco, G., Guzzo, A., Pontieri, L., Saccà, D.: Discovering expressive process models by clustering log traces. IEEE Trans. Knowl. Data Eng. 18(8), 1010–1027 (2006)
6. Rozinat, A., van der Aalst, W.M.P.: Conformance checking of processes based on monitoring real behavior. Information Systems 33(1), 64–95 (2008)
7. Alves de Medeiros, A.K.: Genetic Process Mining. PhD thesis, TU Eindhoven (2006)
8. Goedertier, S., Martens, D., Vanthienen, J., Baesens, B.: Robust process discovery with artificial negative events. Journal of Machine Learning Research 10, 1305–1340 (2009)
9. Alves de Medeiros, A.K., Weijters, A.J.M.M., van der Aalst, W.M.P.: Genetic process mining: an experimental evaluation. Data Mining and Knowledge Discovery 14(2), 245–304 (2007)
10. Ferreira, H., Ferreira, D.: An integrated life cycle for workflow management based on learning and planning. International Journal of Cooperative Information Systems 15(4), 485–505 (2006)
11. van der Aalst, W.M.P., Weijters, A.J.M.M., Maruster, L.: Workflow mining: Discovering process models from event logs. IEEE Trans. Knowl. Data Eng. 16(9), 1128–1142 (2004)
12. Rozinat, A., de Medeiros, A.K.A., Günther, C.W., Weijters, A.J.M.M., van der Aalst, W.M.P.: The need for a process mining evaluation framework in research and practice. In: Business Process Management Workshops, pp. 84–89 (2007)

BPAF: A Standard for the Interchange of Process Analytics Data

Michael zur Muehlen[1] and Keith D. Swenson[2]

[1] Stevens Institute of Technology, Howe School of Technology Management,
Castle Point on Hudson, Hoboken, NJ 07030 USA
Michael.zurMuehlen@stevens.edu
[2] Fujitsu America Inc., 1250 E. Arques Avenue, Sunnyvale, CA
KSwenson@us.fujitsu.com

Abstract. During the initialization and execution of a process instance, multiple events occur which may be of interest to a business, including events that relate to the instantiation and completion of process activities, internal process engine operations and other system and application functions. Process mining and other analytical techniques often involve extracting this process history data from a process execution environment and submitting the data to the process analytics environment for processing. We present the Business Process Analytics Format, an XML-based interchange format for process audit events that combines an extensible state model with a robust XML representation, is able to accommodate multiple event originators and can map to the popular MXML format used in process mining applications.

Keywords: BPAF, Process Analytics, MXML, Workflow Audit Trail.

1 Introduction

Business Process Management Systems support technical and human processes through the coordination of tasks, the governing of data exchanges, and the orchestration application and service invocations. These functions are governed by a formal process model, which in the majority of systems serves as the blueprint for individual process instances.[1] During the initialization and execution of a process instance, multiple events occur which may be of interest to a business, including events that relate to the instantiation and completion of process activities, internal process engine operations and other system and application functions [4]. Process mining and other analytical techniques often involve extracting this process history data from a process execution environment and submitting the data to the process analytics environment for processing. Many commercial BPMS provide analytics environments that are tightly coupled to their internal persistency mechanisms for process history. Such tight coupling makes for the effective design of product-specific dashboards, but

---

[1] We acknowledge the existence of systems that do not follow this type-instance dichotomy, but for the purposes of the subject matter discussed in this paper the distinction between design- and run-time does not limit the applicability of the BPAF format.

M. zur Muehlen and J. Su (Eds.): BPM 2010 Workshops, LNBIP 66, pp. 170–181, 2011.
© Springer-Verlag Berlin Heidelberg 2011

limits the integration of history data with third-party analytics tools, such as the ProM process mining suite [8]. In addition, the integration of process history data with events that are recorded outside the scope of a BPMS promises richer insights into corporate events, as the analyst is able to extend the scope of his work beyond the boundaries of a BPMS-supported process.

For the purpose of discussion, we will call the process execution environment a "process server" and the analytics environment as an "analytics server". Readers should understand that while this invokes the image of two separate unique machines communicating, other configurations are not excluded. These "servers" might both be on the same machine, they might be themselves distributed services over many machine, they might be simple programs executed under the command of a user, or any combination of these.

The remainder of this paper is structured as follows: In the next section we provide a brief overview of the history and development of process history event formats. In section three we describe the design considerations behind the Business Process Analytics Format (BPAF). In section four we detail the structure of a BPAF event. We conclude this paper with an outlook on potential next steps in the evolution of standardized process history data.

2   A Brief History of Process Audit Event Formats

The availability of process execution logs within BPMS environments can be traced back to the first commercial workflow systems of the late 1980s and early 1990s. Initially thought of as a way to enable troubleshooting and recovery of process instances in case of server failures, the use of process log files for analytics purposes was first highlighted by McLellan in 1996 [4]. But the overhead generated by the constant logging of event information frequently overwhelmed available computing capacity, even in mainframe environments. For example, the IBM FlowMark workflow system was capable of recording up to five different event types for each process activity instance. In scenarios where large-scale throughput was required, such as transactional workflows in the financial industry, operators had to reduce the amount of audit information recorded by switching from a verbose logging format to a condensed format that did not record every event type and omitted certain parameters for each event record.

The first attempt at standardizing process audit events came from the Workflow Management Coalition (WfMC) in 1996, when the Common Workflow Audit Data format was proposed. A revision of this CWAD format was published in 1999 [9]. Members of the WfMC had realized that over time organizations were likely to have more than one BPMS as part of their IT infrastructure and were proposing standards to ease the management and integration of these different systems. The purpose of CWAD was to allow for the aggregation of audit trail information from different data sources (i.e., different workflow systems that might execute parts of an overall process). CWAD specified the data structure for audit events using proprietary data types. Each audit event consisted of a prefix, a suffix, and an interchangeable body, depending on the type of event that was recorded. While some event types were predefined, naming conventions were specified so that different vendors could create extensions to the default events. The events defined in the CWAD specification go beyond the process- and activity-based events that are the basis for process monitoring, mining and analytics applications. They include the invocation of system API functions, such as the receipt of a request for a process instance attribute value (*WMReceivedRequestGetProcessInstanceAttribute*).

CWAD never found much acceptance in commercial systems. One reason was the still significant performance degradation that workflow management systems of the late 1990s experienced through the logging of audit data. The other reason was that by the time the CWAD specification was ratified, XML had become the predominant format for data exchange between Information Systems and vendors showed little interest in implementing a specification that was not XML-based. Because CWAD was not based on XML it contained a large number of proprietary type definitions (e.g. for timestamps) that an XML-based standard would simply inherit from the default XML types. Since CWAD did not specify how audit events should be serialized it is theoretically possible to create an XML representation of CWAD events, but the technical advantages of XML such as built-in common datatypes would be lost in the process.

When the interest in process mining grew in the academic community, a shared format for audit trail information for these types of applications was proposed by van der Aalst et al. [7][2]. This Mining XML Format (MXML) became the import format of choice for the popular ProM framework, and several converters for proprietary commercial formats (e.g. Staffware, Pallas Athena) are available. MXML is based on a core data structure for process events, and allows for the addition of arbitrary data structures at the event, process instance, process (model) and log level. The event types supported by MXML are based on the lifecycle of a process (or activity) instance, and focus on the transitions between lifecycle states, e.g., suspend or resume. MXML has demonstrated usefulness as part of the ProM framework but has two shortcomings. One is the limited support for structured extensions. For instance, if a system wants record the business owner of a process instance it can record this information at the instance level or the individual event level, and can use any data structure. The other is the limited number of state changes that are part of the underlying lifecycle model. For instance, the state model does not distinguish between between a graceful abort (where running activities and subprocesses are allowed to finish) and a forced terminate (where any child activities and subprocesses will be terminated as well).

As part of the EU-funded SUPER project, a semantic extension to the MXML format was proposed [1]. The SA-MXML format links MXML entries with ontologies to allow for semantic reasoning over audit trails, but does not address the two limitations listed above.

More recently, a successor format for MXML has been proposed in OpenXES [3]. The OpenXES format is designed as an open event log standard that can accommodate arbitrary event types and offers defined extension mechanisms, e.g. for different lifecycle models or event log attributes.

MXML, SA-MXML and OpenXES have in common that they are oriented toward the collection of log events in a coherent trace. For this purpose, the underlying XML schemas allow for the roll-up of atomic events into instances, models, and logs. CWAD on the other hand focuses on individual events, and treats the aggregation of these events as out of scope.

3 BPAF Design Considerations

One lesson learned from the standardization of CWAD was that a mere syntactical standardization of the event format is not sufficient for the integration of audit trail data from different systems. A shared state model for processes and activities is necessary to standardize event types that can be recorded. The Wf-XML specification for the loosely coupled integration of independent processes was built on such a state machine, and its applicability for process monitoring has been demonstrated in the *Africa* prototype [11]. While the Wf-XML state model represents a good starting point for a universal state machine for process and activity events, it is limited due to its focus on machine-to-machine interaction at the process level. In Wf-XML the states of a process instance are defined so that a client can invoke state transitions through predefined messages [5], but it does not include states for activities, and user interaction with these activities. Suitable sources for these states are the state models that are part of the BPEL extensions for human interaction, BPEL4People [6] and WS-HumanTask [6]. In basing parts of the BPAF state model on these two standards we enable BPMS that implement BPEL4People and WS-HumanTask to create a simplified mapping between their internal state machines and the states represented in the BPAF model.

3.1 The BPAF State Model

BPAF is based on one unified state machine for both activities and processes. One reason for this unification is the recognition that a process in one system may correspond to an activity in another system, i.e. there may be more than one level of processes. The other reason is that in some systems elementary activities can spawn sub-processes of their own, e.g. in BPMS that support the dynamic modification of process instances or ad-hoc diversions from a predefined process model.

At the highest level BPAF distinguishes between the two states *Open* and *Closed*. A process (or activity) is in the state *Open* if it can traverse though the state model through internal or external impulses. A process (or activity) is *Closed* if it has reached a terminal state that it will not exit on its own. It is theoretically possible that an administrator might take a terminated process instance and reopen it, but this would constitute a manual intervention. Each state is divided into a number of sub-states. The design consideration behind the sub-states was that different BPMS may expose a different level of fidelity with regard to the events that can be observed. It is possible that one system records events that represent state changes in another system without access to the internal workings of this system. Take for instance a web service that is invoked by a service activity within a BPMS. The BPMS might record the service as *Open* when the service is invoked, and *Closed* when the service returns a result to the calling activity. It might even record whether the service invocation was successful from a business perspective (*Closed.Completed.Success*) or whether it did not deliver the desired results (*Closed.Completed.Failed*).

Figure 1 shows the BPAF state model. Note that the transitions shown in figure 1 are the most typical transitions in a BPMS context, but manual interventions and different system implementations may lead to additional transitions not depicted in the model.

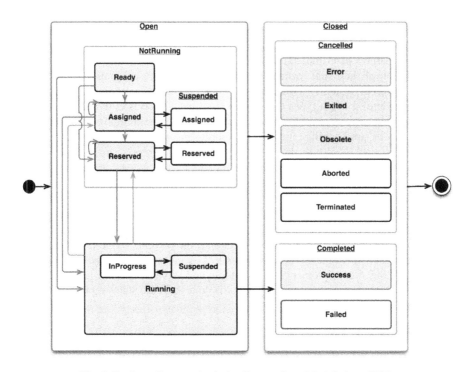

Fig. 1. Business Process Analytics Format State Model (from [10])

The *Open* state is divided into the two sub-states *Running* and *NotRunning*. A process in the state *Running* is actively progressing toward its objective and is consuming resources, while a process in the state *NotRunning* can be scheduled for execution, but does not progress toward its objectives. The state *NotRunning* is further divided into the sub-states *Ready*, *Assigned*, and *Reserved*, as well as *Suspended* (and its sub-states *Assigned* and *Reserved*). These states accommodate the behavior of a BPMS with human activities that are handled through a worklist. An activity that is ready for execution may be placed on the worklists of suitable performers (*Open.NotRunning.Assigned*), and one of these performers chooses to work on the activity instance (*Open.NotRunning.Reserved*). During this time the activity instance may be barred from execution, i.e. it is moved to the *Open.NotRunning.Suspended* sub-state. Transitions between these states accommodate events such as the reassignment of activity instances (*Assigned* to *Assigned*) or the delegation of an activity from one performer to another (*Reserved* to *Reserved*).

The *Closed* state is divided into the sub-states *Cancelled* and *Completed*. The *Completed* state represents that natural end of processing for a process or activity instance. It is further divided into successful and unsuccessful completions (*Success* and *Failed*). For example, a sales process may not lead to the signing of a contract. While the process was executed successfully, it was not successful from a business perspective. The distinction between *Success* and *Failed* allows for the quick aggregation of activity and process instances based on the different exit points that may be defined at the model level.

The *Cancelled* state summarizes all completions of process and activity instances that were premature or forced. It is divided into sub-states that detail the cause for the cancellation. These might be a forcible abort or termination, the obsolescence of a process or activity (e.g. in case of a timeout), an error condition or the manual exit from an activity instance.

BPAF assumes at the most basic level that a system will record *Open* and *Closed* states, but a system can choose to implement any number of sub-states, and may choose to extend the state model with sub-states of its own. If an analytics system is presented with a BPAF event that is based on an extended state model it can reduce the extended state until it arrives at a state it recognizes. For example, the extended state *Closed.Completed.Failure* would be reduced to *Closed.Completed* by an analytics system that does not understand the extended state model.

3.2 Sample Transitions through the BPAF Model

In this section we provide two sample transitions through the BPAF models – one for an automated activity that might be implemented through a web service, the other for a manual activity that might be part of a human workflow.

The simplest example of a BPAF transition is an automated activity that does not involve queuing for a scarce resource. Such an automated activity will typically begin in the state *open.running.inProgress* and when successfully completed it will enter the *closed.completed.success* state. If the data handled by the activity needs to be recorded (for example to enable roll-back), BPAF provides an extension mechanism that can be used for this purpose – this is described in section 4.

A human activity that involves distribution through a role-based worklist and selection by an individual performer will begin in the state *open.notRunning.Assigned*, indicating that the corresponding work item has been placed on a worklist. If the assignment involves pre-processing as part of the activity (e.g. determination of the correct role based on process instance data) the activity might initialize in the *open.notRunning.Ready* state and transition to *open.notRunning.Assigned* once the correct role has been determined and the activity has been placed on the appropriate worklist. As soon as an individual performer selects the workitem for processing it will either transition into the state *open.notRunning.Reserved* if the performer can build up a private queue of workitems, or into the state *open.running.inProgress*, if the BPMS automatically starts activity instances upon selection by performers (a feature found in most commercial BPMS). If the performer interrups processing of the activity it will transition to *open.running.suspended*. If a manager (or the performer) decides to reassign the activity instance to another performer, the instance will move back to the state *open.notRunning.Reserved* and progress to *open.running.inProgress* once the new performer starts working on it.

If the performer completes the activity instance, it will move to the state *closed.completed* (with success or failure substates if those can be determined), but if the execution is forcefully ended by the BPMS the activity instance will move to the *closed.cancelled* state and one of its substates, if the cause for cancellation can be determined. For example, if a processing time Quality of Service agreement is violated the activity instance might move to *closed.cancelled.obsolete*. Figure 2 shows how these boundary states relate to a process representation in BPMN.

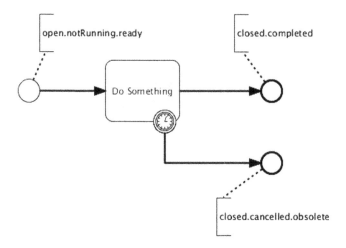

Fig. 2. Boundary States of an Activity

3.3 Mapping to MXML

Contrary to MXML the BPAF event model is based on the state that a process or activity instance enters at a particular point in time, not on the transition in the lifecycle model. To construct the transition information recorded by MXML an analytics system must look at the current event and the immediately preceding event that relates to the same object (i.e. activity instance or process instance). As a result, there is a 1:N mapping of MXML transitions to BPAF transitions, because the BPAF state model allows different transitions into the same state. For example, a manual activity may transition through the states *Ready* → *Assigned* → *Reserved* → *Running*, while an automated activity would move directly from *Ready* → *Running*. This means that the transition Reserved to Running and Ready to Running would both map to the MXML event start. Table 1 illustrates the mapping of BPAF state transitions to MXML events. It is evident that audit events in the BPAF format can easily be transformed into the MXML format.

Table 1. Mapping between MXML transitions and BPAF transitions

MXML Event	BPAF source state	BPAF target state
schedule	NULL	Open.NotRunning.Ready
assign	Open.NotRunning.Ready	Open.NotRunning.Assigned
	Open.NotRunning.Assigned	Open.NotRunning.Reserved
	Open.NotRunning.Ready	Open.NotRunning.Reserved
withdraw	Open.NotRunning.Assigned	Open.NotRunning.Ready
	Open.NotRunning.Reserved	Open.NotRunning.Ready
reassign	Open.NotRunning.Ready	Open.NotRunning.Assigned
reassign	Open.NotRunning.Assigned	Open.NotRunning.Assigned
start	Open.NotRunning	Open.Running
suspend	Open.Running	Open.Running.Suspended
resume	Open.Running.Suspended	Open.Running
pi_abort	Open	Closed.Cancelled.Aborted
	Open	Closed.Cancelled.Terminated
ate_abort	Open	Closed.Cancelled.Aborted
	Open	Closed.Cancelled.Terminated
complete	Open	Closed.Completed
autoskip	Open	Closed.Cancelled
manualskip	Open	Closed.Cancelled.Exited
unknown	N/A	N/A

4 BPAF Event Format

The BPAF event format is described as an XML Schema. Each event has a unique identifier, as there could be concurrent events with the same timestamp. In particular when events from different sources are to be integrated the ability to distinguish between the different events is critical. Each event contains references to a process definition (i.e. the underlying process model) and a process instance, as well as the state that the process or activity instance entered. Additionally, the names of process and activities can be recorded. This element is useful when audit events are aggregated over longer periods of time. Since modifications to process and activity definitions will typically result in different process and activity IDs, the availability of names simplifies the correlation of similar processes and activities, even if the underlying models have changed.

Optional elements of the BPAF schema are elements related to activities (if the system distinguishes between activities and processes), the preceding state of the process or activity instance (in order to ease the identification of transitions) and an extension mechanism for arbitrary data elements. This extension mechanism will typically be used to record key attributes of a process instance in order to provide a link to business data, or it can be used to link an event to an originator, such as the performer of the current activity. While the availability of an activity performer ID is a common requirement for the analysis of process logs (e.g. for the analysis of social

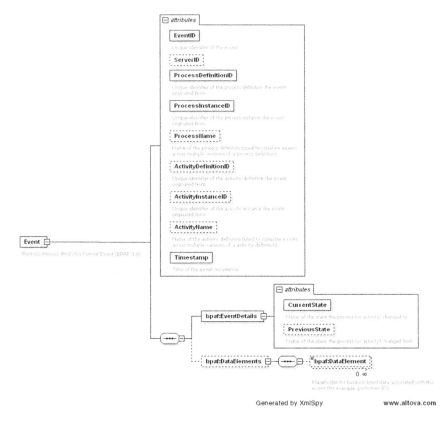

Fig. 2. BPAF XML Schema (from [10])

networks based on process log data), privacy laws and/or union agreements may pro-
hibit the recording of personally identifiable information in an automated log file, thus
the BPAF standard recommends how this information can be recorded as part of the
extended elements, but does not mandate it.

5   Summary and Future Directions

This paper introduced the Business Process Analytics Format, illustrated the design
rationale behind its features, and discussed its relationship to the popular MXML format. BPAF was built on the lessons learned from the WfMC CWAD format and takes
into account the developments of Wf-XML, BPEL4People and WS-HumanTask.

The purpose of BPAF is to enable data interoperability between the events generated by BPMS and different process analytics platforms. These platforms range
from Process Mining applications to monitoring dashboards, Business Intelligence
systems, simulation platforms and Complex Event Processing systems. We do not
assume a single process server and a single analytics server. In practice there is
often a many-to-many relationship: Analytics servers need to consolidate events
from multiple process servers, while a process server may need to fan-out events to

multiple analytics servers. Full interoperability among these tools requires a single common format for the representation of events. A standard format is important for long term archival of case histories, and for making those histories readily accessible. We need interoperability not only at a given instant of time, but over long spans of time as well.

Events might be extracted from a process server that includes months or years of historical event data to be processed in a single batch job. Alternately, the process server may be delivering information about an event to the analytics server in near-real-time as a stream. Both batch mode and stream mode should be supportable through the analytics format. Although BPAF focuses on individual events, it is designed to allow for the easy aggregation of information to the process level. However, it does not contain the aggregation structures present in MXML. This, and the proposed OpenXES format are areas of possible convergence between BPAF and the formats in use in the Process Mining community.

References

1. de Medeiros, A.K.A., Pedrinaci, C., van der Aalst, W.M.P., Domingue, J., Song, M., Rozinat, A., Norton, B., Cabral, L.: An Outlook on Semantic Business Process Mining and Monitoring. In: Chung, S., Herrero, P. (eds.) OTM-WS 2007, Part II. LNCS, vol. 4806, pp. 1244–1255. Springer, Heidelberg (2007)
2. van Dongen, B.F., van der Aalst, W.M.P.: A Meta Model for Process Mining Data. In: Proceedings of the CAiSE 2005 Workshops (EMOI-INTEROP Workshop), vol. 2, pp. 309–320 (2005)
3. Guenther, C.: OpenXES Development Guide, 1.0 RC5 (2009)
4. McLellan, M.: Workflow Metrics - One of the great benefits of workflow management. In: Oesterle, H., Vogler, P. (eds.) Praxis des Workflow-Management, pp. 301–318. Vieweg, Braunschweig (1996)
5. Mendling, J., zur Muehlen, M., Pierce, A.: Standards for Workflow Definition and Execution. In: Dumas, M., van der Aalst, W.M.P., ter Hofstede, A.H.M. (eds.) Process-Aware Information Systems. Bridging People and Software Through Process Technology, pp. 281–316. John Wiley & Sons, Hoboken (2005)
6. OASIS: WS-BPEL Extension for People (BPEL4People) Specification Version 1.1. 1.1 Working Draft, oasis-open.org (2008)
7. van der Aalst, W.M.P., de Beer, H.T., van Dongen, B.F.: Process mining and verification of properties: An approach based on temporal logic. In: Chung, S. (ed.) OTM 2005. LNCS, vol. 3760, pp. 130–147. Springer, Heidelberg (2005)
8. Van Dongen, B.F., De Medeiros, A.K.A., Verbeek, H.M.W., Weijters, A., van der Aalst, W.M.P.: The proM framework: A new era in process mining tool support. In: Ciardo, G., Darondeau, P. (eds.) ICATPN 2005. LNCS, vol. 3536, pp. 444–454. Springer, Heidelberg (2005)
9. WfMC: Audit Data Specification. Version 2, Document Number WFMC-TC-1015 (1999)
10. WfMC: Business Process Analytics Format - Draft Specification. Document Number TC-1015. Version 1.0, WfMC (2009)
11. zur Muehlen, M., Klein, F.: AFRICA: Workflow Interoperability based on XML-messages. In: CAiSE 2000 International Workshop on Infrastructures for Dynamic Business-to-Business Service Outsourcing, Stockholm, Sweden (2000)

Appendix: BPAF XSD

```xml
<?xml version="1.0" encoding="UTF-8"?>
<xs:schema xmlns:bpaf="http://www.wfmc.org/2009/BPAF2.0"
xmlns:xs="http://www.w3.org/2001/XMLSchema" targetName-
space="http://www.wfmc.org/2009/BPAF2.0" elementFormDefault="qualified"
attributeFormDefault="unqualified">
    <xs:element name="Event">
      <xs:complexType>
        <xs:sequence>
          <xs:element name="EventDetails">
            <xs:complexType>
              <xs:attribute name="CurrentState" type="bpaf:State"
use="required">
              </xs:attribute>
              <xs:attribute name="PreviousState" type="bpaf:State">
              </xs:attribute>
            </xs:complexType>
          </xs:element>
          <xs:element name="DataElements" minOccurs="0">
            <xs:complexType>
              <xs:sequence>
                <xs:element name="DataElement" minOccurs="0" maxOc-
curs="unbounded">
                </xs:element>
              </xs:sequence>
            </xs:complexType>
          </xs:element>
        </xs:sequence>
        <xs:attribute name="EventID" type="bpaf:ID" use="required">
        </xs:attribute>
        <xs:attribute name="ServerID" type="xs:NMTOKEN"/>
        <xs:attribute name="ProcessDefinitionID" type="xs:NMTOKEN"
use="required">
        </xs:attribute>
        <xs:attribute name="ProcessInstanceID" type="xs:NMTOKEN"
use="required">
        </xs:attribute>
        <xs:attribute name="ProcessName" type="xs:string">
        </xs:attribute>
        <xs:attribute name="ActivityDefinitionID" type="xs:NMTOKEN">
        </xs:attribute>
        <xs:attribute name="ActivityInstanceID" type="xs:NMTOKEN">
        </xs:attribute>
        <xs:attribute name="ActivityName" type="xs:string">
        </xs:attribute>
        <xs:attribute name="Timestamp" type="xs:dateTime"
use="required">
        </xs:attribute>
      </xs:complexType>
    </xs:element>
    <xs:simpleType name="State">
      <xs:list>
        <xs:simpleType>
          <xs:restriction base="xs:string">
            <xs:enumeration value="Open"/>
            <xs:enumeration value="Open.NotRunning"/>
            <xs:enumeration value="Open.NotRunning.Ready"/>
            <xs:enumeration value="Open.NotRunning.Assigned"/>
```

```
            <xs:enumeration value="Open.NotRunning.Reserved"/>
            <xs:enumeration value="Open.NotRunning.Suspended"/>
            <xs:enumeration value="Open.NotRunning.Suspended.Assigned"/>
            <xs:enumeration value="Open.NotRunning.Suspended.Reserved"/>
            <xs:enumeration
value="Open.NotRunning.Suspended.InProgress"/>
            <xs:enumeration value="Open.Running"/>
            <xs:enumeration value="Closed"/>
            <xs:enumeration value="Closed.Completed"/>
            <xs:enumeration value="Closed.Completed.Success"/>
            <xs:enumeration value="Closed.Completed.Failed"/>
            <xs:enumeration value="Closed.Cancelled"/>
            <xs:enumeration value="Closed.Cancelled.Exited"/>
            <xs:enumeration value="Closed.Cancelled.Error"/>
            <xs:enumeration value="Closed.Cancelled.Obsolete"/>
            <xs:enumeration value="Closed.Cancelled.Aborted"/>
            <xs:enumeration value="Closed.Cancelled.Terminated"/>
          </xs:restriction>
        </xs:simpleType>
      </xs:list>
    </xs:simpleType>
    <xs:simpleType name="ID">
      <xs:restriction base="xs:NMTOKEN"/>
    </xs:simpleType>
</xs:schema>
```

Revising Process Models through Inductive Learning

Fabrizio Maria Maggi[1], Domenico Corapi[2] Alessandra Russo[2],
Emil Lupu[2], and Giuseppe Visaggio[3]

[1] Department of Mathematics and Computer Science,
Eindhoven University of Technology, P.O. Box 513, 5600 MB
Eindhoven, The Netherlands
f.m.maggi@tue.nl
[2] Department of Computing, Imperial College London,
180 Queen's Gate, SW7 2AZ
London, UK
{d.corapi,a.russo,e.c.lupu}@imperial.ac.uk
[3] Department of Computer Science,
University of Bari, Via Orabona 4, 70126
Bari, Italy
visaggio@di.uniba.it

Abstract. Discovering the Business Process (BP) model underpinning existing practices through analysis of event logs, allows users to understand, analyse and modify the process. But, to be useful, the BP model must be kept in line with practice throughout its lifetime, as changes occur to the business objectives, technologies and quality programs. Current techniques require users to manually revise the BP to account for discrepancies between the practice and the model, which is a laborious, costly and error prone task. We propose an automated approach for resolving such discrepancies by minimally revising a BP model to bring it in line with the activities corresponding to its executions, based on a non-monotonic inductive learning system. We discuss our implementation of this approach and demonstrate its application to a case-study. We further contrast our approach with existing BP discovery techniques to show that *BP revision* offers significant advantages over *BP discovery* in practical use.

Keywords: Information systems, processes, inductive learning, maintenance of process models.

1 Introduction

In numerous applications a Business Process (BP) model must be uncovered from existing procedures and practices. The effort required to acquire and adapt models has been estimated to amount to around 60% of the total development time [8]. Thus, a variety of techniques have been proposed for mining process models from event logs of executed activities as recorded by information systems [14]. Event logs typically contain rich information about events occurred

M. zur Muehlen and J. Su (Eds.): BPM 2010 Workshops, LNBIP 66, pp. 182–193, 2011.

during the process execution. Process mining approaches have shown that this information can be used to construct models of the underlying BP (i.e. *process discovery*) [15].

However, once uncovered, the model must remain a faithful representation of the reality even in the face of changes to the underlying procedures and practices. This requires users either to *re-discover* the process or to identify *discrepancies* and *revise* the BP model to address them. The first option may not be optimal in real applications because the techniques employed so far may re-discover models that differ significantly from those previously learnt, and any analysis performed on those models needs to be redone entirely. The second option, has led to *conformance testing* approaches that can identify and evaluate the discrepancies between existing models and actual process executions [11]. But when discrepancies are detected, the analyst has to manually apply changes to the process model to reconcile the model with the actual execution. This can be a difficult, costly and error prone task that relies mainly on the effort and expertise of the analyst. The task is even harder for models where different processes must cooperate within the frame of a set of constraints [13].

In this paper, we propose an approach for automated *revision* of process models. It takes as input a set of event logs corresponding to the actual execution of the tasks (and thus considered positive examples of the actual process), and an existing process model (either specified by an expert or learnt in a previous iteration). Our approach then minimally revises the existing process model to account for the discrepancies between the model and the logs. This has the advantage of giving users a model which is "close" to the one they have previously used, thus enabling them to re-use the analysis and reasoning previously conducted, whilst highlighting the changes necessary to account for the new log entries. Our work builds on AGNEs (Artificially Generated Negative Events) [7], a logic based approach for discovering business process, from which we reuse the logical formalisation of the process and the method for generating the training data. The latter includes generating from the logs negative examples that account for executions *not* present in the logs. Our main contribution in this paper consists in a novel framework for the revision of process models based on non-monotonic inductive logic programming (NMILP). Whenever discrepancies are detected between the current model and the logs, an inductive learning system is used to compute *changes* and automatically suggest revised models that would resolve the detected inconsistencies. The implementation of the learning system guarantees *minimal changes* to the existing model, and in particular that all aspects of the model unaffected by the discrepancies will be preserved in the revised model. This would not necessarily be the case if the model was simply re-discovered from the event logs.

We present and employ in an exemplifying case study a new NMILP system called *TAL* [3], that compared to AGNEs (where a hill-climbing search is performed) introduces an explicit semantics for negation and a different search method, based on a thorough exploration of the space of the solution. In essence, our solution trades efficiency for soundness and in turn enables effective learning with less training data. With respect to traditional process discovery techniques we inherit all the advantages of AGNEs such as a richer representation language that enables learning more complex process models (e. g. time-varying properties and history-dependent conditions) [5,6,7].

This paper is organized as follows. Section 2 describes the main features of our proposed approach. Section 3 details the revision algorithm. Section 4 provides an illustrative case study on a real application domain. A summary and some remarks about future work conclude the paper.

2   Approach

Starting from an event log and an existing BP model (encoded as a Petri net) that is not in line with the log, our approach provides a systematic and automated way for learning minimal revisions to the model so that the revised Petri net fits the logs. More formally, a process revision task can be defined as follows:

Definition 1 (Process model revision task)
Given an event log W of execution instances of a BP and an existing Petri net P modelling the BP, the process model revision is the task of finding a Petri net P' that minimally revises P according to W.

What is considered "minimal" and the metrics which define the level of conformance of P' wrt W characterise the task and will be defined in more detail in Section 3.

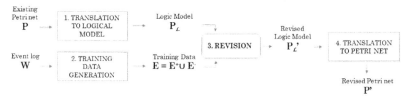

Fig. 1. Approach

The proposed approach is divided in four phases (see Fig. 1). In the first step the existing Petri net P is automatically translated into a logic program $P_{\mathcal{L}}$. In the second phase a training data set $E = E^+ \cup E^-$ (with positive and negative examples) is generated from the event log W. Whilst positive examples are naturally derived from the log, the negative examples are artificially generated. $P_{\mathcal{L}}$ and E are then used in the third phase by an Inductive Logic Programming (ILP) system to compute the revision task. The output of this revision task is a logic program $P'_{\mathcal{L}}$ that minimally revises $P_{\mathcal{L}}$. This is then translated, in the fourth phase, back into a Petri net, P', that represents the revised BP model.

Note that the proposed approach is meant to be applied under human supervision. In particular, the analyst can lock, through an explicit language bias, parts of the model he/she considers to be correct and can explore alternative revisions. In this way every final choice on changes to be applied on the business process is ultimately delegated to the developer.

The formalisation of Petri nets into logic programs and the generation of training data follow the approach described in [7]. Though we provide, for completeness of our presentation, a brief description of these two steps we refer the reader to [7] for further details.

Before presenting the individual phases in detail, we briefly summarise the notations and terminology used throughout the paper.

2.1   Notation and Terminology

Given a logic-based alphabet consisting of variables, constants and predicates, an *atom* is an expression of the form $p(t_1, .., t_n)$, where p is a predicate and t_i are terms (variable or constants) in the alphabet. A *negated atom* is an expression of the form $\neg p(t_1, .., t_n)$, where $\neg$ (or equivalently "not") is the Prolog negation-as-failure (NAF) operator [1] and $p(t_1, .., t_n)$ is an atom. A *literal* is either an atom or a negated atom; we will refer to it as *positive* and *negative* literal respectively. A set $\{l_1, ..., l_m\}$ of literals is a *clause*, which is also denoted, in logic programming, as the rule

$$h \leftarrow b_1, ..., b_n$$

where h is positive literal, called the *head* of the clause, and $b_1, ..., b_n$ is a conjunction of literals, called *body* of the clause. Each b_i is also referred to as *condition* or *antecedent* of the rule. The intuitive meaning of a clause is "if all the conditions are true then the head must be true". Using Prolog convention [12], predicates, terms and functions are denoted with initial lower case letter, whereas variables are written with an initial capital letter. Clauses can be of two types, *definite* and *normal*. The former are clauses whose body literals are all positive, the latter as clauses whose conditions can be either positive or negative literals. Clauses with a single literal (the head) are called *facts*, whereas clauses with a body and an empty head are called *goals*. A *normal logic program* is thus a finite set of normal clauses $\{c_1, ..., c_n\}$ assumed to be in conjunction with each other. In the remainder of the paper the symbol $\models$ denotes the notion of entailment over stable model semantics for normal logic programs [4] (equivalent to logical entailment for definite programs).

2.2   Logical Translation of a Petri Net

The first phase of our approach translates automatically a Petri net into a normal logic program. The formalisation is based on a predicate ns ("no-sequel") defined as follows:

$$
\begin{aligned}
ns(&AT1, AT2, BId, Now) \leftarrow \\
&event(AT1, BId, completed, AgentId, Parameters, T1), T1 < Now, \\
&\neg eventFromTill(AT2, BId, completed, T1, Now))
\end{aligned}
\tag{1}
$$

$$
\begin{aligned}
eventFromTill(&AT, BId, ET, From, Till) \leftarrow \\
&event(AT, BId, ET, AgentId, Parameters, T), From < T, T < Till
\end{aligned}
\tag{2}
$$

where the predicate *event* is defined through the logical formalization of a state transition (as explained in the next section).

Informally the predicate $ns(AT1, AT2, BId, Now)$ is true if at the time point Now, in the process instance BId, activity $AT1$ has happened but since $AT1$ has happened $AT2$ has not happened yet.

Using the ns predicate any Petri net can be translated into a normal logic program, by expressing each Petri net *transition* in terms of the preconditions under which the transition can take place [7].

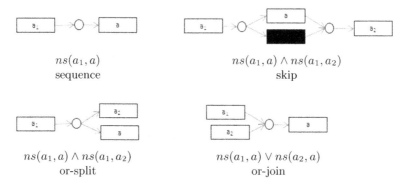

Fig. 2. Formalization of Petri net constructs

In the rest of the paper, we consider only the completion of activities (i.e. events of type *completed*) and we abbreviate the predicate $ns(AT1, AT2, BId, Now)$ to $ns(AT1, AT2)$, whenever there is no ambiguity about the process instance id and the time.

Figure 2 shows the patterns used to map basic constructs of a Petri net in terms of ns predicate as preconditions for the activity a. The rules defining the preconditions for a certain activity a in the logic program $P_{\mathcal{L}}$ are of the type

$$class(a, BId, T, completed) \leftarrow ns(...), ..., ns(...)$$

2.3   Training Data Generation

In the encoding of an event log into logic programs each state transition is represented using the predicate $event(AT, BId, ET, AgentId, Par, TS)$ where AT represents the activity name, BId is the unique id of the corresponding process instance, ET denotes the event type, $AgentId$ the agent who has performed the state transition, Par a lists of additional parameters and TS is the time point at which the state transition has happened. In the rest of the paper only the activity name, the process instance id and the time point are used in the revision. However, other arguments can be used to revise richer models than the ones considered here.

To allow the process models revision through supervised multi-relational learning, negative information is also required. A *negative example* defines state transitions that cannot take place. Our training data set generation uses the algorithm proposed in [7] for extracting negative information from given event logs. Briefly, given a process instance t_i in an event log and $e_{(i,k)}$ state transition in the position k of the process instance t_i, the algorithm checks the occurrence of any other state transition, ϵ, in the position k. If there exists a process instance t_j: $\forall l, l < k, similar(e_{(i,l)}, e_{(j,l)})$ and $similar(e_{(j,k)}, \epsilon)$ (two state transitions are similar if they have the same activity type and the same event type) then the state transition ϵ is not added as negative information (because this behaviour is present in the event log). If such transition t_j does not exist, then ϵ is added as a negative state transition at position k. For further details we refer the reader to [7] where this algorithm is extensively discussed.

3 Revision

The revision phase takes as input the logic program representation of an existing Petri net and the training set data and generates as output a new logic program that covers all the positive examples and none of the negative examples. Using the terminology introduced in [7] we derive models with $TP = 1$ and $TN = 1$ (respectively true positive rate and true negative rate, i.e. the ratio of the number of positive/negative examples correctly classified by the model over the total number of positive/negative examples). The algorithm uses an underlying non-monotonic ILP system to find, as inductive solutions, prescriptive syntactic changes to be made to the original model. The computation of such changes is performed within a search space defined by a *language bias*, given as input to the underlying learning system, which defines the syntactic form of the possible changes that can be learned. In contrast to the hill climbing learning approaches used in AGNEs, our learning system explores the entire search space, and therefore it always finds a solution, if one exists.

Let us now define our generic notion of revision through learning.

Definition 2 (Revision through learning)
Given a revisable set T of rules, a background knowledge B (not revisable), a set E of positive and negative examples and a language bias L, revision through learning is the task of finding a set of minimal changes, within the scope of L, that when applied to T gives a revised set T′ of rules that, together with the background knowledge B, covers all the positive examples and none of the negative one.

The key notion in the above definition is that of *minimal change*. In general, a revision system avoids the computation of new models that are "unrelated" to the revisable part of the original model. Therefore, whenever an initial (even if not correct) model exists, either because provided by an expert or available from previous revisions, minimal revision is, in general, preferable to rediscovery. Our revision algorithm uses a measure of minimality similar to that proposed in [16], and defined in terms of *number of revision operations* required to transform one model into another. The atomic revision operations covered by the language bias of our system include deletion of a condition in an existing rule, addition of a condition in an existing rule, addition of a new rule, and deletion of an existing rule. The number of revision operations needed to transform a model T into a new model T' is then given by the number of atomic revision operations made to the model T to obtain T'. We denote this number as $f(T, T')$. Thus, given a model T, T' is a revised model of T which satisfies the minimality criteria if there is no another model T'' such that $f(T, T'') < f(T, T')$. In our approach, computing a *minimally revised* Petri net P' from a given Petri net P, corresponds to computing a logic program T' that can be obtained from the logic program T representing P, by means of a minimal number of atomic revision operations.

Note that the learning system used can be configured to handle different notions of minimality, defined as a cost function of the logic revision thus allowing, for instance, different "weights" for different revision operations applied on the original model.

The background knowledge is used to define any concept that can be used in the target rules and the extensional knowledge supporting the learning. The instantiation of the inputs of the learning is made clear in the reminder of the paper.

3.1   Revision Algorithm

Our revision algorithm takes as input a logic program T representation of a Petri net model (as revisable model), a background knowledge B, a set E of examples and a language bias L. It then produces as output a revised logic program T' using three main computation steps [2].

At first, during the *pre-processing* phase, all the rules in the given revisable program are transformed into defeasible rules. This step intuitively changes the meaning of the rules from "the head of a rule is true if all the conditions are true" to "the head of a rule is true if all the conditions are true and the exception to the rule is not true". Defining an exception for a revised rule is equivalent to add conditions to it.

The second step of the algorithm is the *learning* phase. This takes the transformed revisable program generated by the pre-processing phase and computes the revision in terms of conditions that can be added and/or deleted from the transformed rules to cover all the given positive examples and none of the negative ones. This phase uses a prototype non-monotonic learning systems called TAL (*Top-directed Abductive Learning*) [3]. The system performs a top down search starting from the most general set of hypothesis rules within the scope of the given language bias. In a top-down fashion (where the top goal is the given set of examples) it identifies and keeps track of the general rules of an hypothesis theory that together with the background knowledge are needed to derive the examples.

The third phase is a *post-processing* phase. This takes the output of the learning system and automatically generated the revised program T' by re-factoring the original rules together with the new learned rules.

4   Case Study

To validate the proposed approach a well known "driver's license" case study [9], [7] has been used. We report in this section the main results, we discuss them and exemplify the revision step for one of the activities.

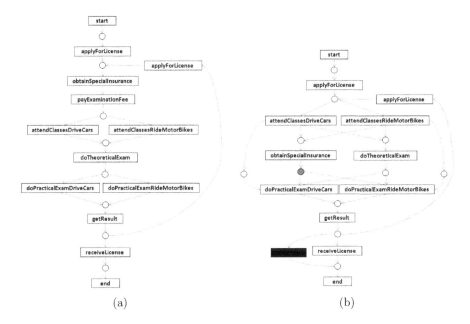

Fig. 3. (a) Existing Petri net   (b) Petri Net after the revision process

An event log W (containing 50 process instances) is generated simulating the execution of the *actual* process through CPN Tools [10]. We use artificial traces produced by a simulation rather than real-life logs because real-life event logs usually contain imperfections. On the contrary, by using simulation we can have more control about the properties of the event log to validate the approach under different conditions. The *actual* process is described by the Petri net shown in Fig. 3(b). This Petri net contains a loop, a duplicate task (*applyForLicense*), an invisible task (to skip *receiveLicense* at the end of the process) and it is a non-free-choice Petri net because, for instance, the grey *place* in Fig. 3(b) is in the *preset*[1] of more than one transition (*doPracticalExamDriveCars* and *doPracticalExamRideMotorBikes*) but it is not the only place in the preset of *doPracticalExamDriveCars* neither in the preset of *doPracticalExamRideMotorBikes*.

The Petri net P, shown in Fig. 3(a), describes a currently available model of the process. The structure of this Petri net is similar to the Petri net representing the actual process. However here the non-free-choice constructs and

---

[1] A preset of a transition x is the set of the places y such that there is an arc from y to x.

the invisible task are missing. These constructs should be identified in the revised Petri net. Moreover in P the activities $obtainSpecialInsurance$ and $payExaminationFee$ are performed before attending the courses. In the revised Petri net $obtainSpecialInsurance$ should be performed after attending the courses and the activity $payExaminationFee$ should be deleted.

1. Translation to logical model. The first step of our approach is to formalise P as a logical model $P_{\mathcal{L}}$ using the predicate ns. $P_{\mathcal{L}}$ is obtained using the patterns shown in Fig. 2 and is shown schematically in Fig. 4(a).

activity		precondition
a	start	true
b	applyForLicense	ns(a,b)
b	applyForLicense	(ns(j,b) ∧ ns(j,k) ∧ ns(j,l)) ∧ occursLessThan(b,3)
c	obtainSpecialInsurance	ns(e,c) ∨ ns(f,c)
e	attendClassesDriveCars	ns(b,e) ∧ ns(b,f)
f	attendClassesRideMotorBikes	ns(b,e) ∧ ns(b,f)
g	doTheoreticalExam	ns(e,g) ∨ ns(f,g)
h	doPracticalExamDriveCars	(ns(g,h) ∧ ns(g,i)) ∧ (ns(c,h) ∧ ns(c,i)) ∧ ns(e,h)
i	doPracticalExamRideMotorBikes	(ns(g,h) ∧ ns(g,i)) ∧ (ns(c,h) ∧ ns(c,i)) ∧ ns(f,i)
j	getResult	ns(h,j) ∨ ns(i,j)
k	receiveLicense	ns(j,b) ∧ ns(j,k) ∧ ns(j,l)
l	end	ns(k,l) ∨ (ns(j,b) ∧ ns(j,k) ∧ ns(j,l))

activity		precondition
a	start	true
b	applyForLicense	ns(a,b)
b	applyForLicense	(ns(j,b) ∧ ns(j,k)) ∧ occursLessThan(b,3)
c	obtainSpecialInsurance	ns(b,c)
d	payExaminationFee	ns(c,d)
e	attendClassesDriveCars	ns(d,e) ∧ ns(d,f)
f	attendClassesRideMotorBikes	ns(d,e) ∧ ns(d,f)
g	doTheoreticalExam	ns(e,g) ∨ ns(f,g)
h	doPracticalExamDriveCars	ns(g,h) ∨ ns(g,i)
i	doPracticalExamRideMotorBikes	ns(g,h) ∧ ns(g,i)
j	getResult	ns(h,j) ∨ ns(i,j)
k	receiveLicense	ns(j,b) ∧ ns(j,k)
l	end	ns(k,l)

(a)   (b)

Fig. 4. (a) Obsolete model   (b) Revised model

Note that $occursLessThan(b, 3)$ specifies that the activity b ($applyForLicense$) cannot be executed more than three times in a process instance.

2. Training data generation. In the second step the training data set $E = E^+ \cup E^-$ is generated from W. In particular, approximately 600 positive examples are extracted from the event log. Starting from the positive examples AGNEs algorithm allows to generate the negative ones. In our experiment we use an injection probability $\pi = 0.2$. This means that we consider only 20% of the whole set of the generated negative examples. Approximately 100 negative examples are generated. For instance for the activity c ($obtainSpecialInsurance$) positive and negative examples have the form: $class(c, 1, 4, completed)$, $class(c, 1, 9, completed)$, ... $not\ class(c, 15, 11, completed)$. $class(act, t_1, t_2, completed)$ means that the activity act can be *completed* in the process instance t_1 at the time point t_2, since this is what happens in the log. In contrast, negative examples show the behaviours which cannot take place.

3. Revision. Starting from $P_{\mathcal{L}}$ and E the revision algorithm is executed on each activity x singularly. As previously stated, the iterative deepening implementation of TAL first checks if a solution with no revision exists, i. e. whether $B \cup P_{\mathcal{L}} \models E_x$, where E_x is the subset of E that refers to the activity x and B contains rules (1) and (2) and the definition of the $occursLessThan$ predicate.

This holds only for the $doTheoreticalExam$ and $getResult$ activities. For all other activities a revision is learned. The result of the revision is the definition reported in given in Figure 4(b). The preconditions of the activities are reported in terms of the ns predicate and the or-split patterns are enclosed in brackets. Note that adding or deleting or-split is considered as a single atomic revision. We illustrate the partial results of the revision process for the activity $obtainSpecialInsurance$.

Example 1. Revision for the activity c ($obtainSpecialInsurance$). P_c refers to the rules in $P_\mathcal{L}$ referred to the activity c.

3.1. Revision: pre-processing. In this phase, all the rules in $P_\mathcal{L}$ are rewritten using the *meta-predicates try* and *exception*. This transformation sets the learning task to compute exceptions cases for rules in $P_\mathcal{L}$ and instances of body literals that can be deleted.

$$\tilde{P}_c = \begin{cases} class(c, BId, T, completed) \leftarrow \\ \quad try(1, 1, ns(b, c)), \\ \quad \neg exception(1, class(c, BId, T, completed)) \end{cases}$$

3.2. Revision: learning. The learning phase takes as input the transformed (revisable) program $\tilde{T}$, the (unrevisable) background knowledge B, the extended language bias $\tilde{P}_\mathcal{L}$ and a set E of examples. It computes an inductive solution H containing information about deletions, exceptions and new rules (whenever the given language bias $L \neq \emptyset$) such that $B \cup \tilde{P}_\mathcal{L} \cup H \models E$ (ensured by the soundness of the ILP system deployed in our revision approach).

$$H = \begin{cases} class(c, BId, T, completed) \leftarrow \\ \quad ns(e, c) \\ class(c, BId, T, completed) \leftarrow \\ \quad ns(f, c) \\ exception(1, class(c, BId, T, completed)) \end{cases}$$

3.3. Revision: post-processing. The last phase constructs the revised theory $P_\mathcal{L}'$ from the output of the learning phase. This is an automatic re-factoring process that takes the revisable program $\tilde{P}_\mathcal{L}$ given to the learning system and the generated hypothesis H and transform them into an equivalent program $P_\mathcal{L}'$ that represented the revised Petri net model. The transformation satisfies the property that $B \cup \tilde{P}_\mathcal{L} \cup H$ is equivalent to $B \cup P_\mathcal{L}'$.

$$P_c' = \begin{cases} class(c, BId, T, completed) \leftarrow \\ \quad ns(e, c) \\ class(c, BId, T, completed) \leftarrow \\ \quad ns(f, c) \end{cases}$$

The learning phase generates an exception that has the effect of deleting the entire existing rule ($ns(b,c)$). Two new rules are learned defining an or-join ($ns(e,c) \lor ns(f,c)$).

4. Translation to Petri net. The final outcome of the learning is mapped into a model which is identical to the actual model shown in Figure 3(b). The revision algorithm is able to tranform the free choice Petri net P in the non-free choice

Petri net P'. Moreover the preconditions of the *end* activity, reveal the presence of an invisible task. In general the presented revision algorithm is able to handle all common constructs in a Petri net.

5 Conclusion

The approach proposed in this paper presents various advantages with respect to the existing techniques for mining process models from event logs. The main one is that it is able to learn incrementally from event logs whilst preserving as much as possible of the previously learnt model. By using our *revision through learning* approach, we have shown that minimally revised process models can be learnt through an automated process.

Moreover we provide a uniform methodology and tool support for both the tasks of extraction (i.e. mining) of process models as well as revision of an existing model.

Although not shown in this paper due to space limitations, our approach can also be used in the presence of incomplete or noisy data. In particular we are extending our learning system through a probabilistic approach aimed at handling noise in the event logs. The outcomes in this case will be a revised model that is a "best fit" to the given data.

In the near future we want to further experiment our methodology using process models with different peculiarities. In fact, the generality of the declarative representation of the business process model used as input to our learning system can be appropriately extended to allow notions of time, composite events, as well as any additional feature expressible in first-order logic. Through further experimentations we want to show that it is possible to extract and revise models with some, any or all such characteristics using the same underlying learning system.

References

1. Clark, K.L.: Negation as failure. In: Logic and Data Bases, pp. 293–322 (1977)
2. Corapi, D., Ray, O., Russo, A., Bandara, A., Lupu, E.: Learning rules from user behaviour. In: Artificial Intelligence Applications and Innovations III, vol. 296, pp. 459–468 (2009)
3. Corapi, D., Russo, A., Lupu, E.: Inductive logic programming as abductive search. In: ICLP (Technical Communications), pp. 54–63 (2010)
4. Gelfond, M., Lifschitz, V.: The stable model semantics for logic programming. In: Kowalski, R., Bowen, K. (eds.) Logic Programming, pp. 1070–1080. MIT Press, Cambridge (1988)
5. Goedertier, S., Martens, D., Baesens, B., Haesen, R., Vanthienen, J.: Process Mining as First-Order Classification Learning on Logs with Negative Events. In: ter Hofstede, A.H.M., Benatallah, B., Paik, H.-Y. (eds.) BPM Workshops 2007. LNCS, vol. 4928, pp. 42–53. Springer, Heidelberg (2008)
6. Goedertier, S., Martens, D., Baesens, B., Haesen, R., Vanthienen, J.: A new approach for discovering business process models from event logs, vol. 716

7. Goedertier, S., Martens, D., Vanthienen, J., Baesens, B.: Robust process discovery with artificial negative events. Journal of Machine Learning Research 10, 1305–1340 (2009)
8. Hammori, M., Herbst, J., Kleiner, N.: Interactive workflow mining: requirements, concepts and implementation. Data Knowl. Eng. 56(1), 41–63 (2006)
9. Medeiros, A.K., Weijters, A.J., Aalst, W.M.: Genetic process mining: an experimental evaluation. Data Min. Knowl. Discov. 14(2), 245–304 (2007)
10. Alves De Medeiros, A.K., Günther, C.W.: Process mining: Using cpn tools to create test logs for mining algorithms. In: Proceedings of the Sixth Workshop and Tutorial on Practical Use of Coloured Petri Nets and the CPN Tools, pp. 177–190 (2005)
11. Rozinat, A., van der Aalst, W.M.P.: Conformance Testing: Measuring the Fit and Appropriateness of Event Logs and Process Models. In: Bussler, C., et al. (eds.) BPM 2005. LNCS, vol. 3812, pp. 163–176. Springer, Heidelberg (2006)
12. Shapiro, L., Sterling, E.Y.: The Art of PROLOG: Advanced Programming Techniques. The MIT Press, Cambridge (1994)
13. van der Aalst, W., Dumas, M., Ouyang, C., Rozinat, A., Verbeek, H.M.W.: Choreography conformance checking: An approach based on bpel and petri nets. In: Leymann, F., Reisig, W., Thatte, S.R., van der Aalst, W. (eds.) The Role of Business Processes in Service Oriented Architectures, Dagstuhl, Germany. Dagstuhl Seminar Proceedings, vol. 6291. Internationales Begegnungs- und Forschungszentrum für Informatik (IBFI), Schloss Dagstuhl (2006)
14. van der Aalst, W.M.P., van Dongen, B.F., Herbst, J., Maruster, L., Schimm, G., Weijters, A.J.M.M.: Workflow mining: A survey of issues and approaches. Data Knowl. Eng. 47(2), 237–267 (2003)
15. van Dongen, B.F., Alves de Medeiros, A.K., Wen, L.: Process mining: Overview and outlook of petri net discovery algorithms. T. Petri Nets and Other Models of Concurrency 2, 225–242 (2009)
16. Wogulis, J., Pazzani, M.: A methodology for evaluating theory revision systems: Results with Audrey II. In: 13th IJCAI, pp. 1128–1134 (1993)

Improving the Diagnosability of Business Process Management Systems Using Test Points

D. Borrego, Maria Teresa Gómez-López, R.M. Gasca, and R. Ceballos

Dept. de Lenguajes y Sistemas Informáticos, Universidad de Sevilla, Sevilla, Spain
{dianabn,maytegomez,gasca,ceball}@us.es

Abstract. The management and automation of business processes have become an essential task within IT organizations, where the diagnosis is a very important issue, since it enables fault isolation in a business process. The diagnosis process uses a set of test points (observations) and a model in order to explain a wrong behavior. In this work, an algorithm to allocate test points is presented, where the key idea is to improve the diagnosability, getting a better computational complexity for isolating faults in the activities of business processes.

Keywords: Process tracing and monitoring, constraint programming, fault diagnosis, fault isolation, test points.

1 Introduction

A business process (BP) is composed of activities which are logically related to achieve a goal. BP management includes concepts, methods and techniques to support the design, administration, configuration, enactment and analysis of BPs [1]. A BP instance is a concrete case in the operational process for a model. If a BP is monitored, some errors can be detected. The diagnosis process detects which tasks are responsible of the incorrect behavior for a business instance.

Fault diagnosis determines why a BP correctly designed does not work as it is expected. Its aim is to identify the reason of an unexpected behavior. The computation is based on observations, which come from the public information existing in the BP, which can be measured by means of test points allocated in certain places of the BP model. In [2] the diagnosis is performed according to the topology of the BP and the relation with the public information monitored.

Test points are control points where it is possible to know data that are available at a moment of the execution. The aim of this work is to improve the diagnosability of a BP by means of the allocation of test points.

The paper is structured as follows: Section 2 raises the allocation of test points in BPs, including three different objectives to achieve. Section 3 shows some experimental results. And finally, conclusions and future work are presented.

2 Allocation of Test Points in a Business Process

The aim of this paper is to apply techniques to allocate test points in BPs.

M. zur Muehlen and J. Su (Eds.): BPM 2010 Workshops, LNBIP 66, pp. 194–200, 2011.

Definition 1. *Cluster of activities: Being the private information the non-observable information exchanged between the activities, a set of activities T is a Cluster, (i) if it does not exist common private information of any activity of the cluster with any activity outside the cluster, and (ii) if for all $Q \subset T$ then Q is not a cluster of activities.*

Definition 2. *The Diagnosability level is the quotient of the number of faults which can be distinguished each other and the number of all possible faults. Being $nAct$ the number of activities in a BP, the possible faults are initially 2^{nAct} - 1.*

The test points make possible the separation of the activities into different clusters. Also, as it is explained in [4], the computational complexity in the clusters separately is lower than in the whole BP, since the number of possible diagnoses is minor. If all the information within the BP is private, only one fault can be distinguished: the $nAct$ activities fail or not. When some test points are allocated and m clusters are obtained, the number of faults that can be distinguished, according to Definition 2, are 2^m - 1.

The proposed algorithm can be configured to achieve three objectives related to diagnosability, presented in next sections. Since the BPs are going to be modelled as CSPs, the transformation into a graph is detailed in the following.

2.1   Improving the Diagnosability by Using Constraint Programming

A CSP consists of $\langle X, D, C \rangle$ where X is a set of n variables $x_1, x_2, ..., x_n$ whose values are taken from finite, discrete domains $D_1, D_2, ..., D_n$ respectively, and C is a set of constraints on their values [3].

A BP can be considered as a directed graph. Its nodes and edges give rise to variables in a CSP (with their domains D):

Variables:
$nAct$: number of activities
$nCon$: number of edges
$clusterOfAct_i$: set of $nAct$ variables representing the cluster where each activity i is contained ($D : \{0..nAct - 1\}$)
$testPoint_j$: set of $nCon$ variables holding the possible new test points in the BP, with possible values *true* (which implies that there must be a test point in a determined connection) and *false* (the opposite)
$nTestPoints$: number of allocated test points ($D : \{0..nCon\}$)
$nClusters$: number of obtained clusters ($D : \{1..nAct\}$)

Each edge gives rise to a constraint within the CSP. As an example, being the connection between two activities A and B the n-th possible test point of the set $testPoint_j$, the constraint added to the CSP would be:

`if`($testPoint_n$ = `false`) $\Rightarrow clusterOfAct_A = clusterOfAct_B$

That constraint means that if the connection between A and B does not count on a test point, they are necessarily in the same cluster. The opposite statement cannot be asserted, since the existing of the test point cannot imply that A and B are in different clusters since it is possible that they are connected through another path in the graph.

2.2   Objective 1: To Maximize the Number of Clusters Allocating a Fixed Number of Test Points

In order to achieve this objective, the number of test points must be limited to a value t in the CSP. Likewise, the goal is included: taking all the combinations of pairs of values in the set $clusterOfAct_i$, the number of different pairs of values must be maximized, so that the maximum number of activities are placed in different clusters, maximizing the number of clusters obtained.

Being $pairs_{i,j}$ a variable that indicates if each pair of activities i and j are in a different cluster (value 1) or in the same one (value 0).

Constraints: $nTestPoints = t, t \in \{1, \ldots, nCon\}$
$\qquad\qquad \forall i, j \in \{1, \ldots, nAct\} \ (clusterOfAct_i \neq clusterOfAct_j) \leftrightarrow pairs_{i,j} = 1$
Goal: $maximize(\sum_{i=1}^{nAct-1} \sum_{j=i+i}^{nAct} pairs_{i,j})$

The temporal complexity to solve the CSP is exponential for the number of connections. When the BP has a large number of activities, the time needed to solve the CSP makes this solution inappropriate. In order to avoid this problem, the greedy algorithm presented in [4] is used. That algorithm applies the Floyd's algorithm to find the bottlenecks of the BP, which are the most important connections to allocate test points. They are used to select the connections where will be better to allocate test points. Those connections will be the only ones taken into account in the solution of the CSP, improving the computational complexity, although the optimal solution is not guaranteed.

2.3   Objective 2: To Allocate the Minimum Number of Test Points in Order to Obtain a Fixed Number of Clusters

New constraints are added to the initial CSP to establish the number of clusters in a value $numClusters$. The goal is to minimize the number of values equal to $true$ in the set $testPoint_j$. This CSP does not present computational problems.

Constraint: $nClusters = numClusters, numClusters \in \{1, \ldots, nAct\}$
Goal: $minimize(nTestPoints)$

2.4   Objective 3: To Minimize the Number of Test Points to Allocate in Order to Obtain Clusters with a Maximum Number of Activities

The initial CSP needs new constraints to limit the number of activities that belong to each cluster to the value $maxNumAct$, and constraints to keep the CSP solver from finding out equivalent solutions (reducing the computational complexity, since it gets a huge search space reduction). The goal is to minimize the number of test points to allocate, including the following constraints.

The temporal complexity is exponential, so that it is necessary to add some kind of bound to reduce the search space of the variables. In order to get a bound, a new greedy method is used whose solution may not be the optimal solution, but it provides a very useful bound for the number of test points in a linear time that reduces drastically the domain of the variables $clusterOfAct_i$.

Constraints: $clusterOfAct_1 = 0$
$\forall i \in \{0, \ldots, nClusters - 1\}\ occurrences(i, clusterOfAct) \leq maxNumAct$
$\forall i \in \{0, \ldots, nAct - 1\}clusterOfAct_i \leq max(clusterOfAct_j) + 1, j \in \{1, \ldots, i - 1\}$
Goal: $minimize(nTestPoints)$

The greedy algorithm is based on the topology of the BPs, using the different control flow patterns existing in the BP model. Since frequently there is a set of branches that form a split and are synchronized by means of a join, it is possible to analyze the processes in a deep way. The splits and joins will enable to divide a BP in different levels. This is, when a single thread of execution splits into branches, and those branches later converge in a join, the activities in those branches are in an inferior level than the activities in the main thread.

Figure 1 shows an example where the BP counts on nine activities. The splits and joins make that the BP has three levels (L1, L2 and L3).

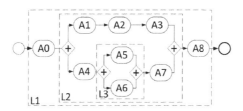

Fig. 1. Business process with three levels

Based on this idea of levels, the greedy algorithm is made up of several steps:

Step 1: Transformation of the BP into a graph and labelling the nodes.
The labels of the edges are used to describe if there is a test point in this place. Likewise, each nodes counts on the name of the activity which it is representing, and their labels depend on the levels where they are located: the splits are matched to their corresponding joins, assigning labels from upper to lower levels. The label of the main level (the whole BP) is the string "1". In the rest of levels it is formed by the label of its upper level, concatenating the number of the new level. The numbers in a label indicate the levels where the node is located. At the same time, a tree with the hierarchy of levels is built. Each node of this tree stores the label of a level and the nodes of the graph which are previous and subsequent to that level.

Following with the example in Fig. 1, the different labels assigned to its nodes are shown in Fig. 2(a) and the tree of levels in Fig. 2(b). Level "1" does not have previous and subsequent node, since that level represents the whole BP.

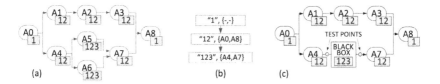

(a)   (b)   (c)

Fig. 2. (a) Graph with labels in the nodes, (b) tree of levels and (c) reduced graph

Step 2: Allocating the test points. Using the tree of levels, this task performs (based on Algorithm 1) a recursive process to allocate the test points. The sentences marked with numbers (1, 2, 3) in the algorithm are detailed in the following.

Algorithm 1. Recursive algorithm to allocate test points

---

if there are more activities in this level than the maximum per cluster **then**
    if the level is a leaf of the tree of levels **then**
        (1) allocate test points in the input and outputs of the level in the graph
        (2) allocate test points in the activities of this level in the graph
    else
        for all child c in the tree **do**
            recursive call: run this algorithm over activities in level c
            if any test point was allocated in level c **then**
                (3) reduce the graph
            end if
        end for
        (1) allocate test points in the input and outputs of the level
        (2) allocate test points in the activities of this level
    end if
else if this level has exactly the maximum activities per cluster **then**
    (1) allocate test points in the input and outputs of the level
end if

- (1) Allocate test points in the input and outputs of a level: the idea is to isolate the activities of a level from the rest of the activities in the BP. This sentence entails the fact of allocating test points after the previous node and before the subsequent node of the level. For example, if it is necessary to isolate the level "12" of Fig. 2(a), a test point is allocated in the input of the level (output of $A0$) and two in the outputs of the level (outputs of $A3$ and $A7$).
- (2) Allocate test points in a level: either because the level is a leaf or because it has already been isolated, this sentence entails the moment of allocating test points in the activities of a level using the exhaustive CSP explained at the beginning of this subsection.

– (3) Reduction of the graph: once the test points have been allocated in a level, this level must be considered as a *black box* in upper levels. Therefore the graph must be reduced in order to allocate the test points in the whole BP without taking into account the activities of that level.

In Fig. 2(c) the level "123" has been isolated by means of the test points allocated on it. This level is replaced by a *black box* delimited by test points.

3 Experimental Results

In this section, the temporal complexity of the exhaustive and greedy methods for Objectives 1 and 3 are compared. We present the execution time applied to some BPs with different number of activities (from 5 to 50), which are benchmarks that have been generated to check the Objectives 1 and 3.

Figure 3(a) shows the execution time for the Objective 1. In the chart, the execution time of the exhaustive algorithm and the one that uses the greedy method can be compared. The exhaustive method presents an exponential execution time, whereas the greedy method is polynomial.

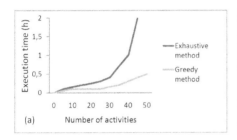
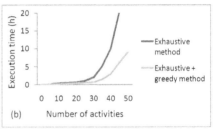

Fig. 3. Execution time for objectives 1 and 3

Likewise, Fig. 3(b) depicts the difference between the execution time spent by the exhaustive and the greedy method for Objective 3. It is possible to see the difference between the exponential execution time for the exhaustive method and the polynomial complexity when the greedy algorithm is used to establish a bound in the number of test points.

4 Conclusions and Future Work

The aim of this work is to improve the diagnosability through applying techniques of allocation of test points, improving the computational complexity of isolating faults in the diagnosis process.

As future work, it is interesting to perform the diagnosis once the test points have been allocated, since they give us additional information that is useful to achieve a more efficient and precise process to find out the minimal diagnosis.

Acknowledgements

This work has been partially funded by Junta de Andalucía by means la Consejería de Innovación, Ciencia y Empresa (P08-TIC-04095) and by the Ministry of Science and Technology of Spain (TIN2009-13714) and the European Regional Development Fund (ERDF/FEDER).

References

1. Weske, M.: Business Process Management. Concepts, Languages, Architectures. Springer, Berlin (2007)
2. Borrego, D., Gasca, R.M., Gómez-López, M.T., Barba, I.: Choreography Analysis for Diagnosing Faulty Activities in Business-to-Business Collaboration. In: 20th International Workshop on Principles of Diagnosis (DX 2009), Stockholm, Sweden (2009)
3. Rossi, F., van Beek, P., Walsh, T.: Handbook of Constraint Programming. Elsevier, Amsterdam (2006) ISBN 978-0-444-52726-4
4. Ceballos, R., Cejudo, V., Gasca, R.M., Del Valle, C.: A topological-based method for allocating sensors by using CSP techniques. In: Marín, R., Onaindía, E., Bugarín, A., Santos, J. (eds.) CAEPIA 2005. LNCS (LNAI), vol. 4177, pp. 62–68. Springer, Heidelberg (2006)

Toward Obtaining Event Logs from Legacy Code

Ricardo Pérez-Castillo[1], Barbara Weber[2],
Ignacio García-Rodríguez de Guzmán[1], and Mario Piattini[1]

[1] Alarcos Research Group, University of Castilla-La Mancha
Paseo de la Universidad, 4 13071, Ciudad Real, Spain
{ricardo.pdelcastillo,ignacio.grodriguez,
mario.piattini}and@uclm.es
[2] University of Innsbruck
Technikerstraße 21a, 6020 Innsbruck, Austria
barbara.weber@uibk.ac.at

Abstract. Information systems are ageing over time and become legacy information systems which often embed business knowledge that is not present in any other artifact. This embedded knowledge must be preserved to align the modernized versions of the legacy systems with the current business processes of an organization. Process mining is a powerful tool to discover and preserve business knowledge. Most process mining techniques and tools use event logs, registered during execution of process-aware information systems, as the key source of knowledge. Unfortunately, the majority of traditional information systems is not process-aware and does not have any built-in logging mechanisms. Thus, this paper defines the main challenges to be addressed as well as a preliminary solution to obtain event logs from traditional systems. The solution consists of a technique that statically analyzes the source code and modifies it in a non-invasive way. Finally, the modified source code enables the event log registration at runtime based on dynamic source code analysis.

1 Introduction

Business processes have become a key asset in organizations, since processes allow them to know and control their daily performance, and to improve their competitiveness [2]. Thereby, information systems automate most of the business processes of an organization [14]. However, due to uncontrolled maintenance information systems are ageing over time and become legacy information systems (LIS) [11]. They gradually embed meaningful business knowledge that is not present in any other asset of the organization [7]. When maintainability of LISs diminishes below acceptable limits, they must be replaced by improved versions [8]. To ensure that the new system is aligned with the organization's business processes, the embedded business knowledge needs to be preserved [5]. The business knowledge preservation requires an in-depth understanding of how the information systems currently support the organization's business processes. This problem motivates the use of process mining, which became a powerful tool to understand what is really going on in an organization by observing the information systems [12].

Usually, event logs are obtained from Process-Aware Information Systems (PAIS) [3], i.e., whose nature facilitates the registration of events throughout process

M. zur Muehlen and J. Su (Eds.): BPM 2010 Workshops, LNBIP 66, pp. 201–207, 2011.

execution. Indeed, most process mining techniques and tools are developed for this kind of information systems [2]. In addition to PAIS, there is a vast amount of traditional systems that also support the business processes of an organization, and could thus benefit from process mining. Nevertheless, non process-aware systems imply five key challenges for obtain meaningful event logs. This paper proposes a technique for addressing these challenges and for obtaining process event logs from traditional (non process-aware) information systems. The technique is based on both static and dynamic analysis of the source code of the systems. Firstly, the static analysis syntactically analyzes the source code and injects pieces of source code in a non-invasive way in specific parts of the system. Secondly, the dynamic analysis of the modified source code makes it possible to write an event log file in MXML format during system execution. The proposed technique is further supported by specific information provided by business experts and system analysts who know the system.

The remainder of this paper is organized as follows. Section 2 introduces the main challenges for obtaining event logs from traditional information systems. Section 3 presents the proposed technique to tackle these challenges. Section 4 discusses related work and finally, Section 5 provides a conclusion and discusses future work.

2   Process-Awareness Challenges

Challenge 1 - Missing Process-Awareness. The first challenge is to know what business activities are executed. While PAISs manage processes (i.e. a sequence of activities with a common business goal using explicit process descriptions) [14], LIS are a set of methods, functions or procedures (*callable units* in general) where processes are only implicitly described. LIS can be seen as a graph where the nodes are the different callable units, and the arcs are the calls between callable units, i.e., the call graph represents the control flow of a LIS. To address this challenge *Zou et al.* [15] proposed the *"a callable unit / a business activity"* approach, which considers each callable unit as a candidate business activity in a process mining context. This approach provides a good starting point, but ignores other important challenges such as, for example, the different granularity of callable units and activities (Challenge 1) and the mixture of business- and technical-related callable units (Challenge 3).

Challenge 2 - Granularity. The different granularity of business activities and callable units in LIS constitutes an important challenge. In [12], each callable unit in a LIS is considered as an activity to be registered in an event log. However, LISs typically contain thousands of callable units many of which are very fine-grained, not directly supporting any business activity. To avoid that the mined processes get bloated with unnecessary details, too fine-grained callable units should not be considered in the event log. In this sense, different solutions can be implemented to discard fine-grained callable units. On the one hand, source code metrics (such as the lines of source code or cyclomatic complexity metric) could be used to determine if a callable unit is a coarse- or fine-grained unit. On the other hand, heuristics (like discarding *getter* and *setter* methods, or discarding units when call hierarchies reach a specific depth) could offer a good alternative with minimal computational costs.

Challenge 3 - Discarding Technical Code. Challenge 3 is caused by the fact that LISs typically contain several callable units, which cannot be considered as business activities. Callable units can be grouped into two domains: (i) the *problem domain* contains the callable units related to the business entities and functionalities of the LIS (i.e., these units implement the business processes of the organization) and (ii) the *solution domain* contains the callable units related to the technical nature of the platform used in the LIS and aids the callable units of the previous group. Since callable units belonging to the solution domain do not constitute business activities, they should not be considered in the event log. Therefore, callable units in charge of auxiliary or technical functions that are not related to any use case of the system could be discarded. However, due to the delocalization and interleaving problems [10], the problem and solution domain groups are not always disjoint sets (i.e., the technical and business code are usually mixed), thus requiring that system analysts provide the information about whether a callable unit belongs to the problem or solution domain.

Challenge 4 - Process Scope. Another challenge is to establish the scope of a business process (i.e., to identify where a process instance starts and ends). While the start and end points of a business process are explicitly defined in PAISs, LS lack any explicit information about the supported processes. Unfortunately, the information where a process starts and ends cannot be automatically derived from the source code, but must be provided by business experts (who know the business processes of the organization as well as their start and end activities) and system analysts (who know what callable units in the source code support the start and end activities).

Challenge 5 - Process Instance Scope. The lack of process-awareness in LIS causes another fundamental challenge which is due to the fact that a business process is typically not only executed once, but multiple instances are executed concurrently. If a particular business activity is executed (i.e., callable unit is invoked), this particular event has to be correctly linked to one of the running process instances. Correlating an activity with a data set, which uniquely identifies the process instance it belongs to, poses significant challenges. In particular, it has to be established which objects can be used for uniquely identifying a process instance (i.e., what the correlation data is). If correlation objects have been identified, the location of these objects in each callable unit has to be determined (i.e., the argument or variable in each callable unit that contains the correlation data). This requires the input of business experts and systems analysts who know the LIS and the process it supports. Unfortunately, however, there are some units where the selected correlation data is not present. For this reason, traceability mechanisms throughout callable units are needed to have the correlation data available at any place of the legacy source code.

3 A Preliminary Solution

This paper proposes a technique to obtain event logs from non process-aware systems based on a combination of static and dynamic analysis of source code addressing the discussed challenges. Our proposal presents a generic technique, although it is specially designed for object-oriented systems. The *static analysis* is the key stage of the technique, where special sentences for writing events during system execution are injected in the code. Due to the missing process-awareness of LISs this stage poses several challenges (cf. Section 2). While challenges C1 and C2 can be addressed in a fully automated manner (Task 5 and 6 in Fig. 1), challenges C3, C4 and C5 require input from business experts and system analysts (Task 1 - 4 in Fig. 1).

In Task 1, to deal with the process scope challenge (Challenge 4) business experts establish the start and end business activities of the business processes to be discovered. In parallel, system analysts examine in Task 2 the legacy source code and filter the directories, files or set of callable units that support business activities (i.e., they select the callable units belonging to the problem domain), thereby reducing potential noise in the event log due to technical source code (Challenge C3). Task 3 is the mapping between start/end business activities and the callable units supporting them, which is again supported by system analysts (Challenge C4).

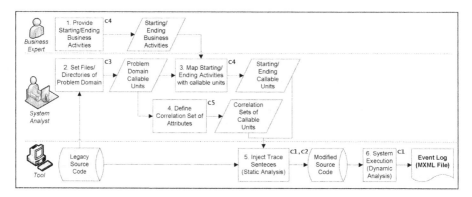

Fig. 1. The overall process carried out by means of the proposed technique

In Task 4 system analysts establish the correlation data set for each callable unit which is uniquely identifying a process instance (Challenge C5). For this, the correlation data is mapped to parameters of each callable unit. This information is then used during run-time to correlate the executed activities with the proper process instance. After that, Task 5 consists of the syntactic analysis of the source code. A parser automatically analyzes and injects on the fly the special sentences writing the event long during system execution. During the static analysis, the source code is broken down into callable units (Challenge 1). All callable units not belonging to the problem domain subgroup selected by the system analyst in Task 3 (Challenge 3) and all fine-grained callable units (e.g., *setter*, *getter*, *constructor*, *toString* and *equals* callable units) are then discarded (Challenge C2). Finally, in each of the filtered callable units, two sentences are injected at the beginning and the end of each respective unit (one with a *start* event type, and the second one represents the *complete* event for the same business activity). Moreover, the correlation data defined for the unit as well as information whether or not the unit represents a start or end activity are included in the sentences. When the modified code is executed, the injected sentences invoke a function, which writes the respective event in the log.

The *dynamic analysis* is performed after the static analysis, thus the modified source code can be released to production again. The new code allows to write event log files according to the MXML (Mining XML) format, which is used by the process mining tool *ProM* [13]. When the control flow of the information system reaches an injected sentence, a new event is added to the event log. The events are written by means of a function, which searches the adequate process of the event log where the event must be written using an *Xpath* expression. If the process is null, then a new process is created. After that, the function examines the correlation data to determine to which process instance the event has to be added. If the correlation data is empty, then the function takes the correlation data of the previously executed callable unit to add the event to the correct process instance. This solution is based on simple heuristics and allows correlating events and process instances when no correlation data is available for the respective event. Moreover, in order to add the event to the correct process instance, the function again uses an *Xpath* expression taking the correlation data into account. If the expression does not find a process instance for the correlation data (i.e., because the event belongs to a start activity), the function creates a new process instance for the correlation data. Finally, when the function has determined the correct process instance, it adds the event to that instance. The event, represented as an *AuditTrailEntry* element in an MXML file, is created with (i) the name of the executed callable unit that represent the *WorkflowModelElement*; (ii) the event type that is also a parameter of the function; (iii) the user of the system that executed the callable unit (or the user of the session if the system is a web application), which represents the *originator* element; and finally (iv) the system date and time when the callable unit was executed to represent the *timestamp* element.

4 Related Work

There are some works related to business processes recovery from non process-aware information systems. *Zou et al* [15] developed a framework to recover workflows from LISs. This framework statically analyzes the source code and applies a set of heuristic rules to discover business knowledge from source code. *Pérez-Castillo et al* [9] make another proposal based on static analysis that uses a set of business patterns to discover business processes from source code. Both approaches solely rely on static analysis, which has the disadvantage that activities cannot be linked correctly to process instances, since the required correlation data is only known at runtime. Thus, other solutions based on dynamic analysis have been suggested. *Cai et al.* [1] propose an approach that combines requirement reacquisition with dynamic analysis. Firstly, a set of use cases is recovered by means of interviewing the system's users. Secondly, the system is dynamically traced based on these use cases to recover business processes. In all these works, the technique for recovering event logs is restricted to a specific mining algorithm. In contrast, our solution proposes a technique based on dynamic analysis (combined with static analysis) to obtain MXML event logs from traditional information systems that is not restricted to a specific process mining algorithm. Similar to our approach the work of *Ingvaldsen et al.* [6] aims at obtaining logs in MXML format from ERP systems. Thereby, they consider the SAP transaction data to obtain event logs. In contrast, our approach aims at traditional information systems without any built-in logging features. In addition, *Günther et al.* [4] provide a generic import framework for obtaining MXML event logs from different PAISs.

5 Conclusions and Future Work

This paper presents a novel technique based on static and dynamic analysis of source code to obtain event logs from non process-aware systems. Thereby, the obtained event log can be used to discover business processes in the same way than an event log obtained from any PAIS. Thus, all the research and development efforts carried out in the process mining field may be exploited for traditional information systems. Achieving this goal is very ambitious since at least five key challenges must be addressed: (i) missing process-awareness, (ii) granularity, (iii) discarding technical code, (iv) process scope and (v) process instance scope.

In a first step, the proposed technique applies static analysis for injecting special sentences in the source code. In a second step, the modified source code is executed, and an event log is written during system execution. In principle, the static analysis of the system has to be performed only once, and then the modified source code can be dynamically analyzed several times to obtain different event logs. However, the feedback obtained by business experts and systems analysts, after the first static and dynamic analysis, can be used to incrementally refine the next static analysis for improving the results obtained during dynamic analysis.

Our work in progress focuses on the improvement of the proposed technique. A traceability mechanism will be implemented taking the call hierarchies into account to deal with lost and scattered correlation data. In addition, to accurately detect the strengths and weakness of the proposal it be validated by means of a case study.

Acknowledgement

This work was supported by the FPU Spanish Program; by the R+D projects ALTAMIRA (PII2I09-0106-2463), INGENIO (PAC08-0154-9262), and PEGASO/ MAGO (TIN2009-13718-C02-01), and by the University of Innsbruck.

References

[1] Cai, Z., Yang, X., Wang, W.: Business Process Recovery for System Maintenance - An Empirical Approach. In: ICSM 2009, pp. 399–402. IEEE Computer Society, Los Alamitos (2009)

[2] Castellanos, M., de Medeiros, K.A., Mendling, J., Weber, B., Weijters, A.J.M.M.: Business Process Intelligence. In: Handbook of Research on Business Process Modeling, pp. 456–480. Idea Group Inc., USA (2009)

[3] Dumas, M., van der Aalst, W., Ter Hofstede, A.: Process-aware Information Systems: Bridging People and Software Through Process Technology. John Wiley & Sons, Inc., Chichester (2005)

[4] Günther, C.W., van der Aalst, W.M.P.: A Generic Import Framework for Process Event Logs. In: Eder, J., Dustdar, S. (eds.) BPM Workshops 2006. LNCS, vol. 4103, pp. 81–92. Springer, Heidelberg (2006)

[5] van der Heuvel, W.-J.: Aligning Modern Business Processes and Legacy Systems: A Component-Based Perspective (Cooperative Information Systems). The MIT Press, Cambridge (2006)

[6] Ingvaldsen, J.E., Gulla, J.A.: Preprocessing Support for Large Scale Process Mining of SAP Transactions. In: ter Hofstede, A.H.M., Benatallah, B., Paik, H.-Y. (eds.) BPM Workshops 2007. LNCS, vol. 4928, pp. 30–41. Springer, Heidelberg (2008)

[7] Mens, T.: Introduction and Roadmap: History and Challenges of Software Evolution. In: Software Evolution, vol. 1, pp. 1–11. Springer, Heidelberg (2008)

[8] Newcomb, P.: Architecture-Driven Modernization (ADM). In: WCRE 2005, p. 237 (2005)

[9] Pérez-Castillo, R., García-Rodríguez de Guzmán, I., Ávila-García, O., Piattini, M.: MARBLE: A Modernization Approach for Recovering Business Processes from Legacy Systems. In: REM 2009, pp. 17–20 (2009)

[10] Ratiu, D.: Reverse Engineering Domain Models from Source Code. In: REM 2009, pp. 13–16 (2009)

[11] Ulrich, W.M.: Legacy Systems: Transformation Strategies, vol. 448. Prentice Hall, Englewood Cliffs (2002)

[12] van der Aalst, W., Weijters, A.J.M.M.: Process Mining. In: Process-aware Information Systems: Bridging People and Software Through Process Technology, pp. 235–255. John Wiley & Sons, Inc., Chichester (2005)

[13] van der Aalst, W.M.P., van Dongenm, B.F., Günther, C., Rozinat, A., Verbeek, H.M.W., Weijters, A.J.M.M.: ProM: the process mining toolkit. In: BPM 2009, pp. 1–4 (2009)

[14] Weske, M.: Business Process Management: Concepts, Languages, Architectures, Leipzig, Alemania, vol. 368. Springer, Heidelberg (2007)

[15] Zou, Y., Hung, M.: An Approach for Extracting Workflows from E-Commerce Applications. In: ICPC 2006, pp. 127–136. IEEE Computer Society, Los Alamitos (2006)

Dimensions of Business Process Intelligence

Markus Linden[1], Carsten Felden[2], and Peter Chamoni[1]

[1] University of Duisburg-Essen, Mercator School of Management
Department of Technology and Operations Management
Chair of Information Systems and Operations Research
Lotharstraße 63, 47057 Duisburg, Germany
[2] University for Mining and Technology of Freiberg
Faculty of Business Administration
Chair of Information Systems and Information Management
Lessingstraße 45, 09599 Freiberg, Germany
{Markus.Linden,Peter.Chamoni}@uni-due.de,
Carsten.Felden@bwl.tu-freiberg.de

Abstract. Some approaches to support decision making in the context of busi-ness process management exist since a couple of years. Most of them are not systemized. This fact leads to the necessity of a classification of this broad area. The paper´s objective is to evaluate and differentiate approaches of Business Process Intelligence (BPI) within the last decade. The results of this analysis are a morphological box and a definition to clarify potentials of Business Process Intelligence. The definition integrates the most frequently used characteristics as well as different understandings of BPI and it indicates a holistic view on the dimensions of this area. Additionally, the literature-based propositions regard-ing current shifts provide the author´s perspective to the field of BPI and point out a guideline for further research.

Keywords: Business Process Intelligence, Process-centric Business Intelli-gence, Operational Business Intelligence, Process Mining.

1 Introduction

This paper contributes to the fields of Business Intelligence (BI) and Business Process Management (BPM) in providing a classification of different understandings and po-tentials of process-oriented BI. In general, the term BI was defined and published by DRESNER [14] in 1989. From his point of view, BI describes a set of concepts and methods to improve business decision making by using fact-based support systems. Since the year 2000, the area of BI focuses more and more on decision support by analyzing business processes. For demonstrating this development and the upcoming dimensions, the methodology of this paper is a literature review, which focuses on in-ternational scientific and practical papers from the year 2000 until 2010. Hereby, the main characteristics of the terms Operational Business Intelligence (OpBI), Process Mining (PM), Business Process Intelligence (BPI) etc. are identified. Based on the

M. zur Muehlen and J. Su (Eds.): BPM 2010 Workshops, LNBIP 66, pp. 208–213, 2011.

analysis of different definitions and descriptions in these papers, similarities and potentials are extracted and filtered. This process leads to a morphological box, which contains characteristics and types in the area of BPI.

2 Definitions and Concepts of Process Analyses

Several approaches referring to process analyses models are discussed in the literature of Business Intelligence and Business Process Management (cf. Table 1):

Table 1. Extract of definitions in the area of Business Process Intelligence

CASTELLANOS / WEIJTERS [3]	Broadly speaking we can say that BPI is the application of business intelligence to business processes so as to improve different aspects of how such processes are being conducted.
GENRICH / KOKKONEN / MOORMANN / ZUR MUEHLEN / TREGEAR / MENDLING / WEBER [5]	BPI builds on techniques such as data mining and statistical analysis that were developed or inspired by business intelligence techniques such as data mining or statistical analysis, and adapts them to the requirements of business process management.
GRIGORI / CASATI / CASTELLANOS / DAYAL / SAYAL / SHAN [7]	Business Process Intelligence (BPI) relates to a set of integrated tools that supports business and IT users in managing process execution quality.
HALL [8]	Recently, Business Process Intelligence (BPI) has emerged as another term for using Operational BI to inform business process management decisions.
HARMON [9]	We will use Business Process Intelligence (BPI) to refer to the products being offered by the BI and Data Warehouse and Packaged Application vendors who seek to drive executive dashboards with data from processes.
HOSNY [10]	BPI refers to the application of various measurement and analysis techniques in the area of business process management. The goal of BPI is to provide a better understanding and a more appropriate support of a company´s processes at design time and the way they are handled at runtime.
INGVALDSEN / GULLA [11]	Ingvaldsen and Gulla present the need to combine data from external sources, such as the department and employee involved in a process with actual process logs to achieve better knowledge discovery results.
KANNAN [12]	More than Sales Intelligence or Financial Intelligence, Business Process Intelligence provides you with objective measurement of your various activities within the company.
PÉREZ / MÖLLER [13]	The management of business process and thus the concept of business process management (BPM) are central and one of the techniques is process intelligence (BPI).
ROWE [16]	The business process intelligence derived from this analysis can then be used to optimize different elements of the predictive enterprise and enable all components to react to changes in the external business environment.
VAN DER AALST / REIJERS / WEIJTERS / VAN DONGEN / ALVES DE MEDEIROS / SONG / VERBEEK [17]	Business process mining, or process mining for short, aims at the automatic construction of models explaining the behavior observed in the event log. For example, based on some event log, one can construct a process model expressed in terms of a Petri net.
VANTHIENEN / MARTENS / GOEDERTIER / BAESENS [18]	Business Process Intelligence (BPI) is a concept that can be described as the application of Business Intelligence (BI) techniques (such as performance management, OLAP analysis, data mining, etc.) in BPM in order to understand and improve the company´s processes.

For instance, Operational Business Intelligence focuses on the analyses of business processes and their connection with analytical information. BAUER and SCHMID [1] differentiate between classical Business Intelligence and Operational Business Intelligence regarding process status and process result. A decision support regarding analytical information can only be made reactively, which means that latencies mostly exceed reaction time. Because of its focus on process execution and control, OpBI is directly related to existing approaches like Business Activity Monitoring (BAM) as well as Business Performance Management.

The term *Business Process Intelligence* appeared almost at the same time like OpBI. This dilution has been supported by software vendors, who used BPI as a signal word for management dashboards in order to stimulate their business [9]. As a result, the boundaries between these terms are considered to be indeterminate. That is why BPI and OpBI are often used as synonyms especially in the Anglo-Saxon area [8].

CASTELLANOS and WEIJTERS [3] point out the confusion of ideas and the different aspects of BPI and their relation. According to them, BPI aims at the improvement of processes, which focus on process identification, process analyses, process simulation and static and dynamic process improvement. HOSNY [10] states, that the aim of BPI is a better understanding and support of business processes at the time of construction and during the runtime of a process. According to KANNAN [12], BPI represents an objective measure of different activities within a company that gives an indication of current efficiency and bottlenecks of business processes.

PEREZ and MOELLER also come up with a distinction consisting of many degrees of freedom. According to them, Business Process Management offers the central concept, while BPI is just a method which reflects this concept [13]. In terms of the usage of BPI, GRIGORI et al. [7] point out a selection of tools. These tools support companies´ IT and include the domains *analyses, prediction, control* and *improvement of business processes*. On the one hand, those methods are supposed to allow an integrated approach regarding networks and electronic business platforms. On the other hand, they are supposed to identify, analyze and forecast a process, in order to improve the whole process [6, 9]. These analyses are executed by using data mining methods and statistical proceedings. According to GENRICH et al. [5], the methods have to be assimilated to specific demands of Business Process Management.

3   Classifying the Characteristics of Business Process Intelligence

This section presents the identified characteristics within the literature review. Thus, the morphological box (cf. Table 2) classifies the above mentioned distinctions. Morphological boxes are used in the literature to arrange and visualize concept characteristics [15]. Task and process oriented descriptions were taken and mapped to each other to identify the characteristics and the range of different types to structure the term *Business Process Intelligence*. So, the highlighted cells within the morphological box are the most frequently used characteristics and their types in the field of BPI research. Therefore, the types show the broad area and the various understanding of BPI, which can lead to the integrated definition given on the following page. In this context, the Business Process Management steps *process identification, process implementation, process control* and *process improvement* [2] constitute as a core of

BPI. Against this background, BPI focuses on process design and process redesign with a business orientation. For this purpose, ratios are used to implement measurements, structure analyses and efficiency of business processes. This leads to a process improvement beyond IT and organizational boundaries. Therefore, automated techniques find conspicuous events and determine potentials regarding core and supporting processes.

Table 2. Extended Morphological Box of Business Process Intelligence [4]

Characteristics	Types			
Focus	Process Design	Process Redesign	Process Control	
Direction	Business		Technology	
Management Level	Operative	Tactical	Strategic	
Data Level	Instance Level	Model Level	Meta Model Level	Meta Meta Model Level
Process Phase	Identification / Definition / Modelling	Implementation / Execution	Monitoring / Controlling	Continuous Improvement
Kind of Process	Business Process		Technical Process	
Time Relevance	Real Time		Historical	
Range of Users	Small	Middle	Broad	
Technology	Business Activity Monitoring	Service-orientated Architecture	Complex Event Processing	Process Warehouse
Information Sources	Internal Data		External Data	
Kind of Information	Unstructured Data		Structured Data	
Type of Process	Support Process	Core Process	Management Process	
Process Execution	Manual Process	Semi-automated Process	Automated Process	
Process Structure	Unstructured Process		Structured Process	
Decision Intensity	Low	Middle	High	

In the context of BPI, simulations and what-if-analyses investigate processes, generate guidance and support decisions made by the tactical and strategic management. The tactical and the strategic management level receive process information, because the information does not only describe indicators for the creation of value but also an addition to a periodic description of business performance. Accordingly, the user group stays functional focused and small, especially in contrast to operative process control. Due to this, BPI works as well as classical Business Intelligence. This relies on the inspection of historical data. According to the time relevance, a Process Warehouse (PWH) plays an important role, because process logs which have to be analyzed are stored within a PWH. The Process Warehouse receives structured and unstructured data from internal and external data sources. In this context, an application of Process Mining [19] is necessary, concentrating on the identification of process structures. Thus, the result of such analyses and simulations is an improvement of whole process landscapes and not of single processes. The following definition can be stated on the basis of this systematization and the existing distinctions in the academic literature.

Business Process Intelligence (BPI) is the analytical process of identifying, defining, modelling and improving value creating business processes in order to support the tactical and strategic management.

In conclusion, Business Process Intelligence is understood as a generic term, which includes areas like the shown data analysis and brings it on a holistic level.

4   Conclusion

This position paper provides a framework of guidance implications in favor of Business Process Intelligence. It is the aim of BPI to advice analytical activities and the dynamic assimilation of business processes. In this sense, a strategic and tactical integration of Business Process Management and Business Intelligence offers innovative concepts for supporting management´s decisions. The fundament for these propositions is the literature review of the last decade and the analysis of the main characteristics of the terms Business Process Intelligence, Operational Business Intelligence, Process Mining etc. These characteristics are systematized in a morphological box, which indicates a holistic view of the different dimensions in this area.

Finally, it can be constituted, that the future activities will focus on the integration of external data (e.g. involving dynamic market changes) and its impact on the dependencies and alignment of whole process landscapes of a company.

References

1. Bauer, A., Schmid, T.: Was macht Operational BI aus? BI-Spektrum 4(1), 13–14 (2009)
2. Bucher, T., Dinter, B.: Anwendungsfälle der Nutzung analytischer Informationen im operativen Kontext. In: Bichler, M., Hess, T., Krcmar, H., Lechner, U., Matthes, F., Picot, A., Speitkamp, B., Wolf, P. (eds.) Multikonferenz Wirtschaftsinformatik 2008 (MKWI 2008), München, pp. 1–13. GITO, Berlin (2008)
3. Castellanos, M., Weijters, T.: Preface (BPI 2005). In: Bussler, C.J., Haller, A. (eds.) BPM 2005. LNCS, vol. 3812, pp. 159–161. Springer, Heidelberg (2006)
4. Felden, C., Chamoni, P., Linden, M.: From Process Execution towards a Business Process Intelligence. In: Abramowicz, W., Tolksdorf, R. (eds.) BIS 2010. LNBIP, vol. 47, pp. 195–206. Springer, Heidelberg (2010)
5. Genrich, M., Kokkonen, A., Moormann, J., zur Muehlen, M., Tregear, R., Mendling, J., Weber, B.: Challenges for Business Process Intelligence: Discussions at the BPI Workshop 2007. In: ter Hofstede, A.H.M., Benatallah, B., Paik, H.-Y. (eds.) BPM Workshops 2007. LNCS, vol. 4928, pp. 5–10. Springer, Heidelberg (2008)
6. Gluchowski, P., Gabriel, R., Dittmar, C.: Management Support Systeme und Business Intelligence: Computergestützte Informationssysteme für Führungskräfte und Entscheidungsträger. Springer, Heidelberg (2008)
7. Grigori, D., Casati, F., Castellanos, M., Dayal, U., Sayal, M., Shan, M.C.: Business Process Intelligence. Comput. Ind. 53, 321–343 (2004)
8. Hall, C.: Business Process Intelligence. Business Process Trends 2(6), 1–11 (2004)
9. Harmon, P.: Business Performance Management: The Other BPM. Business Process Trends 2(7), 1–12 (2004)
10. Hosny, H.: Business Process Intelligence. In: ATIT 2009, Cairo (2009)

11. Ingvaldsen, J.E., Gulla, J.A.: Model-Based Business Process Mining. Inf. Syst. Manage. 23, 19–31 (2006)
12. Kannan, N.: BPI: What is it and how does it help (2008),
    `http://www.businessprocesstrends.com/deliver_file.cfm?`
    `fileType=publication&fileName=07%2D05%20%` (11-12-2009)
13. Pérez, M., Möller, C.: The Predictive Aspect of Business Process Intelligence: Lessons Learned on Bridging IT and Business. In: Ter Hofstede, A., Benatallah, B., Paik, H. (eds.) BPM Workshops 2007. LNCS, vol. 4928, pp. 11–16. Springer, Heidelberg (2008)
14. Power, D.J.: A Brief History of Decision Support Systems (2010),
    `http://dssresources.com/history/dsshistory.html` (8-7-2010)
15. Ritchey, T.: Modeling Complex Socio-Technical Systems using Morphological Analysis,
    `http://www.swemorph.com/it-art.html` (5-2-2010)
16. Rowe, A.: From Business Process Management to Business Process Intelligence. DM Review 46 (2007)
17. van der Aalst, W.M.P., Reijers, H.A., Weijters, A.J.M.M., van Dongen, B.F., Alves de Medeiros, A.K., Song, M., Verbeek, H.M.W.: Business Process Mining: An Industrial Application. Information Systems 32, 713–732 (2007)
18. Vanthienen, J., Martens, D., Goedertier, S., Baesens, B.: Placing Process Intelligence within the Business Intelligence Framework. In: Proceedings of EIS 2008 (2008)
19. Weijters, A.J.M.M., van der Aalst, W.M.P.: Process Mining: Discovering Workflow Models from Event-Based Data. In: Kröse, B., de Rijke, M., Schreiber, G., van Someren, M. (eds.) Proceedings of the 13th Belgium-Netherlands Conference on Artificial Intelligence, pp. 283–290. BNVKI, Maastricht (2001)

PLG: A Framework for the Generation of Business Process Models and Their Execution Logs

Andrea Burattin and Alessandro Sperduti

Department of Pure and Applied Mathematics
University of Padua, Italy
{burattin,sperduti}@math.unipd.it

Abstract. Evaluating process mining algorithms would require the availability of a suite of real-world business processes and their execution logs, which hardly are available. In this paper we propose an approach for the random generation of business processes and their execution logs. The proposed approach is based on the generation of process descriptions via a stochastic context-free grammar whose definition is based on well-known process patterns. An algorithm for the generation of execution instances is also proposed. The implemented tools are publicly available.

Keywords: process mining; business processes; log generation; Petri net; benchmark dataset.

1 Introduction

Process mining aims to discover the structure and relations among activities starting from business process logs. An important issue concerning the design of process mining algorithms is their evaluation: how well the reconstructed process model matches the actual process? This evaluation requires the availability of an as-large-as-possible suite of business processes logs and the corresponding original models (necessary for the comparison with the mined ones). In Fig. 1 we give a visual representation of such evaluation "cycle".

Unfortunately, it is often the case that just few (partial) log files are available, while no clear definition of the business process that generated the log is available. This is because many companies (the owners of "real" processes and logs) are reluctant to make public their own private data. Of course, the lack of extended process mining benchmarks is a serious obstacle for the development of new and more effective process mining algorithms. A way around this problem is to try to generate "realistic" business process models together with their execution logs.

In this paper, we present a new tool, the "Processes Logs Generator" (or PLG), developed for the specific purpose of generating benchmarks. It allows to: *i)* generate a random (hopefully "realistic") business process (according to some specific user-defined parameters); *ii)* "execute" the generated process and register each executed activity.

M. zur Muehlen and J. Su (Eds.): BPM 2010 Workshops, LNBIP 66, pp. 214–219, 2011.
© Springer-Verlag Berlin Heidelberg 2011

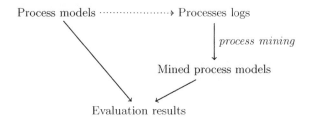

Fig. 1. The evaluation "cycle" for process mining algorithms

The idea of generating process models for evaluating process mining algorithms is very recent. In [5][1] van Hee & Liu presented an approach to generate Petri nets representing processes. Specifically, they suggested to use a top-down approach, based on a stepwise refinement of Workflow nets [8], to generate all possible process models belonging to a particular class of Workflow networks (Jackson nets). A related approach is presented in [1], where the authors proposed to generate Petri nets according to a different set of refinement rules. In both cases, the proposed approaches do not address the problem of generating traces from the developed Petri nets.

2   The Process Generation Phase

In this section the procedure for the generation of a business process is presented together with a description of the model we used.

Since our final aim is to ease the generation of business process models by the user, we decided to adopt a very general formalism for our process model description. Petri net [6] models are unambiguous and in-depth studied tools for process modelling, however controlling the generation of a complex process model via refinement of a Petri net may not be so easy for an inexperienced user. For this reason, we decided to model our processes via dependency graphs. A dependency graph is defined as a graph $G = (V, E, a_{start} \in V, a_{end} \in V)$ where V is the set of vertices and E is the set of edges. The two vertices a_{start} and a_{end} are used to represent the "start" and the "end" activities of the process model. Each vertex represents an activity of the process (with its possible attributes, such as author, duration, . . .), while an edge $e \in E$ going from activity a_1 to a_2 represents a dependency relationship between the two activities.

In order to proceed with the presentation of our proposal, we need to introduce some definitions. Let's consider $v \in V$. The set of incoming activities for v is defined as $in(v) = \{v_i \mid (v_i, v) \in E\}$; its set of exiting (or outgoing) activities as $out(v) = \{v_i \mid (v, v_i) \in E\}$; the value of the fan-in of v is defined as $\overrightarrow{} \deg(v) = |in(v)|$ (i.e. the number of edges entering in v), while its fan-out is defined as $\deg^{\rightarrow}(v) = |out(v)|$ (i.e. the number of edges exiting from v).

In order to be able to correctly represent parallel execution (AND) and mutual exclusion (XOR) we introduce functions $\mathcal{T}_{out} : V \to \{\text{AND}, \text{XOR}\}$ and

---

[1] We discovered this work through the IEEE CIS Task Force on Process Mining.

$\mathcal{T}_{in} : V \rightarrow \{\text{AND}, \text{XOR}\}$ which have the following meaning. For every vertex (i.e. activity) a with $\deg^{\rightarrow}(a) > 1$, $\mathcal{T}_{out}(a) = \text{AND}$ specifies that the flow has to jointly follow all the outgoing edges, while $\mathcal{T}_{out}(a) = \text{XOR}$ specifies that the flow has to follow only one of the outgoing edges. The meaning of $\mathcal{T}_{in}$ is analogous but it is referred to the type of the incoming edge (the type of join).

The strategy we adopt for the generation of a process is based on the recursive composition of basic patterns. The basic patterns we consider are (they correspond to the first patterns described in [7]): *i)* the direct succession of two workflows; *ii)* the execution of more workflows in parallel; *iii)* the mutual exclusion choice between some workflows; *iv)* the repetition of a workflows after another workflow has been executed (as for "preparing" the repetition).

The idea is to use these basic patterns for the generation of the process via a grammar whose productions are the patterns. Formally, we consider a context-free grammar $G_{Process} = \{V, \Sigma, R, P\}$, where $V = \{P, G, G', G_{\leftarrow P}, G_\wedge, G_\otimes, A\}$ is the set of non-terminal symbols, $\Sigma = \{;, (,), \leftarrow P, \wedge, \otimes, a_{start}, a_{end}, a, b, c, \dots\}$ is the set of all terminals (their "interpretation" is described in details in [3]), and R is the set of productions:

$$
\begin{aligned}
P &\rightarrow a_{start} \; ; \; G \; ; \; a_{end} \\
G &\rightarrow G' \mid G_{\leftarrow P} \\
G' &\rightarrow A \mid (G; G) \mid (A; G_\wedge; A) \mid (A; G_\otimes; A) \\
A &\rightarrow a \mid b \mid c \mid \dots
\end{aligned}
\qquad
\begin{aligned}
G_{\leftarrow P} &\rightarrow (G' \leftarrow P \; G) \\
G_\wedge &\rightarrow G \wedge G \mid G \wedge G_\wedge \\
G_\otimes &\rightarrow G \otimes G \mid G \otimes G_\otimes
\end{aligned}
$$

P is the starting symbol. Using the above grammar, a process is described by a string derived from P. It must contain a starting and a finishing activity and, in between, there is a sub-graph G. A sub-graph can be either a "single sub-graph" or a "repetition of a sub-graph". Let's start from the first case: a sub-graph G' can be a single activity A; the sequential execution of two sub-graphs $(G; G)$; or the execution of some activities in "AND" $(A; G_\wedge; A)$ or "XOR" $(A; G_\otimes; A)$ relation. It is important to note that the generation of parallel and mutual exclusion edges is "well structured", in the sense that there is always a "split activity" and a "join activity" that starts and ends the edges. The repetition of a sub-graph $(G' \leftarrow P \; G)$ is described as follows: each time we want to repeat the "main" sub-graph G', we have to perform another sub-graph G; the idea is that G (that can just be a single activity) corresponds to the "roll-back" activities required in order to prepare the system to repeat G'. The structure of $G_\wedge$ and $G_\otimes$ is simple and it expresses the parallel execution or the choice between at least 2 sub-graphs. Finally, A is the set of alphabetic identifiers for the activities (actually, this describes only the generation of the activity name, but the implemented tool "decorates" it with other attributes, such as a unique identifier, the originator, ...).

In order to allow the control on the complexity of the generated processes, we added a probability to each production. This addition required the introduction of user defined parameters to control the probability of occurrence into the generated process of a specific pattern. Besides that, for both the parallel pattern and the mutual exclusion pattern, our framework requires the user to specify the maximum number of edges ($m_\wedge$ and $m_\otimes$) and the probability distribution that calculates the number of branches to be generated. The system will generate, for each AND-XOR split/join, a number of forks between 2 and $m_\wedge$ or $m_\otimes$, according to the given probability distribution.

In the current implementation, the system supports the following probability distributions: uniform distribution; standard normal (Gaussian) distribution and beta distribution (with α and β as parameters). These distributions generate values between 0 and 1 that are scaled into the correct interval ($2 \dots m_\wedge$ or $2 \dots m_\otimes$). The resulting values indicate the number of branches to be generated.

3   The Execution of a Process Model

The procedure used to record the execution of the input activity and its successors (via a recursive invocation of the procedure) is reported in Algorithm 1. The two input parameters represent the current activity to be recorded and a stack containing stopping activities (i.e., activities for which the execution of the procedure has to stop), respectively. The last parameter is used when there is an AND split: an instance of the procedure is called for every edge but it must stop when the AND join is reached because, from there on, only one instance of the procedure can continue. The first time, this procedure is called with: ActivityTracer($a, \emptyset$) where a is the starting activity of the process.

This algorithm is explained in details in [3]; it has to record the execution of an activity and then call itself on the following activity, considering all the possible cases ($\deg^{\rightarrow}(a) = 0$, $\deg^{\rightarrow}(a) = 1$ or $\deg^{\rightarrow}(a) > 1$). The function RecordActivity(a) is the one that writes the activity logs when executing the process; it can also introduce noise and information on the duration of the activity itself.

4   The Implemented Tool

The whole procedure has been implemented in a tool[2] developed in Java language. The implementation is formed by two main components: a library (PLGLib) with all the functions currently implemented and a visual tool, for the generation of one process. The idea is to have a library that can be easily imported into other projects and that can be used for the batch generation of processes. In order to have a deep control on the generated processes we added another parameter (with respect to the probabilities described in Section 2): the maximum "depth". With this, the user can control the maximum number of non-terminals to generate. Suppose the user sets it to the value d; once the grammar has nested d instances of G', then the only non-terminal that can be generated is A. With this parameter there is the possibility to limit the maximum "depth" of the final process.

---

[2] Available, at `http://www.processmining.it/sw/plg`

Algorithm 1. for the execution of an activity and its successors

---

ActivityTracer(a, s)

Input: a: the current activity

         s: a stack (last-in-first-out queue) of activities

1 **if** $s = \emptyset$ *or* $top(s) \neq a$ **then**

2   RecordActivity(a)

3   **if** $\deg^{\rightarrow}(a) = 1$ **then**

4   ActivityTracer($out(a), s$)   `// recursive call`

5   **else if** $\deg^{\rightarrow}(a) > 1$ **then**

6   **if** $\mathcal{T}_{out}(a) = XOR$ **then**

7            $a_1 \leftarrow random(out(a))$ `// random outgoing activity`

8   ActivityTracer(a_1, s)   `// recursive call`

9   **else if** $\mathcal{T}_{out}(a) = AND$ **then**

10          $a_j \leftarrow join(a)$ `// join of the current split`

11          $push(s, a_j)$

12   **foreach** $a_i \in out(a)$ **do**

13   ActivityTracer(a_i, s)   `// recursive call`

14   **end**

15          $pop(s)$

16   ActivityTracer(a_j, s)   `// recursive call`

17   **end**

18   **end**

19 **end**

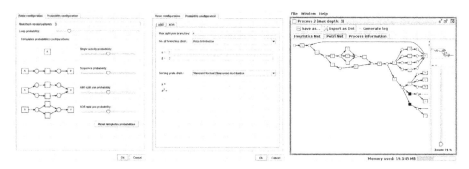

Fig. 2. Three screenshots of the implemented application. From left to right: two configuration panels and the process presentation window.

The tool uses many libraries from ProM [4]. For storing the execution logs we use MXML. In the visual interface, we also implemented the calculation of two metrics for the new generated process, described in [2] (Extended Cardoso metric and the Extended cyclomatic one).

In Fig. 2 three screenshots of the GUI are shown. They give an idea of how the proposed tool allows to drive the creation of random processes, to configure all the parameters, and to visualize the obtained process as a Petri net.

5   Conclusions and Future Works

In this paper, we have proposed an approach for the generation of random business processes in order to ease the evaluation of process mining algorithms. The proposed approach is based on the generation of process descriptions via a (stochastic) context-free grammar whose definition is based on well-known process patterns; each production of this grammar is associated with a probability and the system generates the processes according to these values.

The work presented in this paper can be considered a first step to address the problem of random generation of business processes, and much more work has to be done before reaching a complete and satisfactory solution. Concerning the generation of processes, the next goal to be achieved is the characterization of the space of the processes generated by our approach. Another open issue is on how much the generated processes can be considered "realistic": while using process patterns for their generation increases the probability to generate a realistic process, it would be nice to have control on this issue.

Acknowledgements

This work was supported by SIAV S.p.A. We thank Prof. Dr. Ir. W.M.P. van der Aalst, Prof. Dr. K.M. van Hee and Liu Zheng for their important suggestions.

References

1. Bergmann, G., Horváth, A., Ráth, I., Varró, D.: A Benchmark Evaluation of Incremental Pattern Matching in Graph Transformation. In: Ehrig, H., Heckel, R., Rozenberg, G., Taentzer, G. (eds.) ICGT 2008. LNCS, vol. 5214, pp. 396–410. Springer, Heidelberg (2008)
2. Bisgaard Lassen, K., van Der Aalst, W.M.P.: Complexity Metrics for Workflow Nets. Information and Software Technology 51(3), 610–626 (2009)
3. Burattin, A., Sperduti, A.: PLG: a Process Log Generator (2010), http://www.processmining.it/publications
4. van Dongen, B.F., de Medeiros, A.K.A., Verbeek, H.M.W., Weijters, A.J.M.M., van der Aalst, W.M.P.: The proM framework: A new era in process mining tool support. In: Ciardo, G., Darondeau, P. (eds.) ICATPN 2005. LNCS, vol. 3536, pp. 444–454. Springer, Heidelberg (2005)
5. van Hee, K.M., Liu, Z.: Generating Benchmarks by Random Stepwise Refinement of Petri Nets. In: Proceedings of Workshop APNOC/SUMo (2010)
6. Peterson, J.L.: Petri Nets. ACM Computing Surveys (CSUR) 9(3), 223–252 (1977)
7. Russell, N., Ter Hofstede, A.H.M., van Der Aalst, W.M.P., Mulyar, N.: Workflow control-flow patterns: A revised view. BPM Center Report BPM-06-22, BPMcenter.org (2006)
8. van Der Aalst, W.M.P., van Hee, K.M.: Workflow management: models, methods, and systems. The MIT press, Cambridge (2004)

1st International Workshop on Reuse in Business Process Management (rBPM 2010)

Introduction to the First International Workshop on Reuse in Business Process Management (rBPM 2010)

Marcelo Fantinato[1], Maria Beatriz Felgar de Toledo[2],
Itana Maria de Souza Gimenes[3], Lucinéia Heloisa Thom[4], and Cirano Iochpe[4]

[1] School of Arts, Sciences and Humanities - University of São Paulo - Brazil
m.fantinato@usp.br
http://www.each.usp.br/fantinato
[2] Institute of Computing - University of Campinas - Brazil
beatriz@ic.unicamp.br
http://www.ic.unicamp.br/~beatriz
[3] Department of Informatics - State University of Maringá - Brazil
itana@din.uem.br
http://www.din.uem.br/~itana
[4] Institute of Informatics - Federal University of Rio Grande do Sul - Brazil
{lucineia,ciochpe}@inf.ufrgs.br
http://www.inf.ufrgs.br/~[lucineia,ciochpe]

Abstract. The main objective of the rBPM workshop was to provide a forum to be discussed systematic reuse techiniques applied to BPM domain. Already in its first edition, the workshop could be considered as having achieved great results. Technical papers of very good quality have been submitted, of which 9 full papers and 2 work in progress papers were accepted (with a 46% of acceptance rate), bringing together researchers of high quality during the workshop day. Moreover, a keynote given by Professor Dr Manfred Reichert from University of Ulm in Germany was an important contribution for all the workshop attenders to improve their knowledge regarding "Reuse in the Business Process Lifecycle: Challenges, Methods, Technologies".

Keywords: reuse, BPM, SOA.

1 Aims and Scope

The current complexity inherent in the corporative world demands a great dynamism from the IT infrastructure in order to provide technical solutions for conducting business. Business Process Management (BPM), including its service-oriented foundation, has been providing important technological support to improve organization competitiveness. In order to increase dynamism and competitiveness, BPM can benefit from reuse approaches and techniques at several stages of business process life cycle.

M. zur Muehlen and J. Su (Eds.): BPM 2010 Workshops, LNBIP 66, pp. 223–225, 2011.
© Springer-Verlag Berlin Heidelberg 2011

The **First International Workshop on Reuse in Business Process Management** was dedicated to explore any type of reuse in the Business Process Management domain. Therefore, it was a forum to discuss systematic reuse applied to BPM at its various levels:

1. the basic service-oriented foundation level - including issues such as service development, description, publication, discovery and selection;
2. the service composition level - encompassing service negotiation and service aggregation;
3. the management and monitoring upper level - including business process modeling, execution, monitoring, and contract establishment and enactment; and,
4. the Quality of Service and Semantics orthogonal level.

Moreover, the impact of reuse on business- and service-oriented engineering as well as how it can help in the design of more high-quality process models were very important topics to be discussed in this workshop.

Different existing reuse approaches and techniques can be extended to be applied to this fairly new domain, including: software product line or software product families; variability descriptors; design patterns such as feature modeling; aspect-orientation; and component-based development. In addition, completely new approaches and techniques can be proposed. Their use must also be discussed, preferably under experimentation as well as results analysis.

2 Workshop Co-organizers

- Dr. Marcelo Fantinato (University of São Paulo, Brazil)
- Dr. Maria Beatriz Felgar de Toledo (University of Campinas, Brazil)
- Dr. Itana Maria de Souza Gimenes (State University of Maringá, Brazil)
- Dr. Lucinéia Heloisa Thom (Federal University of Rio Grande do Sul, Brazil)
- Dr. Cirano Iochpe (Federal University of Rio Grande do Sul, Brazil)

3 Programm Committee

- Akhil Kumar (Penn State University, USA)
- Antonio Ruiz-Cortés (University of Seville, Spain)
- Alessandro F. Garcia (Pontifical Catholic University of Rio de Janeiro, Brazil)
- Barbara Weber (University of Innsbruck, Austria)
- Bertram Ludäscher (University of California at Davis, USA)
- Christoph Bussler (Saba Software, Inc., USA)
- Daniel A. Menasce (George Mason University, USA)
- Dennis Smith (Carnegie Mellon University, USA)
- Fernanda A. Baião (Federal University of Rio de Janeiro State, Brazil)
- Flávia M. Santoro (Federal University of Rio de Janeiro State, Brazil)
- Hajo Reijers (Eindhoven University of Technology, The Netherlands)
- Heiko Ludwig (IBM's TJ Watson Research Center, USA)

- Jaejoon Lee (Lancaster University, UK)
- Jan Bosch (Intuit, Inc., USA)
- Jan Mendling (University of Berlin, Germany)
- João Porto de Albuquerque (University of São Paulo, Brazil)
- José Palazzo M. de Oliveira (Federal University of Rio Grande do Sul, Brazil)
- Luciano A. Digiampietri (University of São Paulo, Brazil)
- M. Brian Blake (University of Notre Dame, USA)
- Manfred Reichert (University of Ulm, Germany)
- Masao J. Matsumoto (Kyushu Sangyo University, Japan)
- Miriam A. M. Capretz (The University of Western Ontario, Canada)
- Peter Green (The University of Queensland, Australia)
- Renata de M. Galante (Federal University of Rio Grande do Sul, Brazil)
- Sergiu Dascalu (University of Nevada, USA)
- Stefanie Rinderle-Ma (University of Ulm, Germany)
- Tammo van Lessen (University of Stuttgart, Germany)
- Wil M. P. van der Aalst (Eindhoven Univ. of Technology, The Netherlands)

4   Additional Reviewers

- André Kalsing
- Diego Garcia
- Elder Cirilo
- Gleison Nascimento
- Ingrid Nunes
- Manuel Resinas
- Maria Leitner

A Framework for Modeling and Enabling Reuse of Best Practice IT Processes

Hamid R. Motahari-Nezhad, Sven Graupner, and Claudio Bartolini

Hewlett Packard Laboratories,
Palo Alto, CA, United States
{hamid.motahari,sven.graupner,claudio.bartolini}@hp.com

Abstract. Best practices frameworks such as ITIL provide a generic description of best practice processes that are intended to be followed by people. These processes are refined into more concrete steps before they are actionable. The refinement often is specific to the organization where the process is adopted, as well as people who are enacting the process. Modeling best practice processes is challenging. On one hand, these processes need a high-level, abstract representation. Current process modeling languages are too rigid for modeling them. On the other hand, automation of the enactment of these processes among people requires formal models. In this paper, we propose a framework for modeling best practice processes at three levels: user-level, formal process model level and machine representation level to support the collaborative and ad-hoc refinement of process models as well as the automation of their enactments. We also propose an approach to learn from the past enactments of processes to enable reuse of organizational domain knowledge.

Keywords: Best Practice Processes, Process Modeling, Process Reuse, ITIL.

1 Introduction

Best practice frameworks such as ITIL (IT Infrastructure Library)[1] [1] describe a general set of guidelines and processes for IT management. In particular, ITIL is a best practices framework for IT Service Management (ITSM). ITIL V3 covers the lifecycle of offering ITSM as a service including phases of service strategy, design, transitions, operation and continual service improvement. Each lifecycle phase describes a number of specific processes such as supplier management (part of service design) and incident management (part of service operation). These descriptions are intended to be followed by people in organizations with respective work domains. In order to allow variation and flexibility of organizations, best practices frameworks provide their descriptions at a rather high and generic level. We refer to these processes as *descriptive processes* as opposed to *prescriptive processes* which are processes specified using existing business process languages.

The prescriptive processes are often enacted with workflows (they may involve human interaction, as well). Descriptive processes are interpreted, refined and enacted

---

[1] www.itil-officialsite.com

M. zur Muehlen and J. Su (Eds.): BPM 2010 Workshops, LNBIP 66, pp. 226–231, 2011.

by people. They are often used in *collaborative*, *ad-hoc* and *agile* work environments where the exact process steps become known as the work progresses among the people but may not completely be known ahead of time.

Currently, there are two main categories of tools supporting best practice processes in ITIL. On one hand, there are enterprise-grade tools that support the whole service lifecycle with processes (such as HP Service Manager[2]). Those tools encode a specific interpretation of the processes from best practices in internally coded logic. They impose rigid processes onto the organization and do not support flexibility and the ad-hoc nature of such process. They do not capture people interactions in the context of process enactment. On the other hand, there are productivity and office automation tools that are used among people through which processes are enacted. This category of tools usually has no explicit support for processes definition and hence has no visibility into its execution. A major issue in both approaches is *information loss* and the inability to reuse organizational domain knowledge on how people refine descriptive processes and enact them.

In this paper we focus on the problem of providing a modeling framework that addresses the following challenges: first, how to model descriptive processes supporting people to define, refine and enact processes in a collaborative and ad-hoc manner, and second, given the fact that descriptions from the best practice process provide only informal high-level guidelines, how to capture the knowledge of how people refine and enact those processes. Learning and representing process enactments enables the reuse of organizational domain knowledge.

The work in this paper complements our previous work, the IT Support Conversation Manager (ITSCM) [2]. ITSCM supports people in the context of ITIL incident management process while they define, refine and enact the incident management processes in a collaborative, flexible and ad-hoc manner. A conversation is a container for the interactions of people and process steps. ITSCM allows monitoring and tracing how people perform their job. This paper describes the ITSCM's multi-level framework for modeling descriptive processes. The framework consists of a user level, a formal process model level and a machine representation level. The paper also outlines an approach for learning the organizational knowledge on refinement and enactment of descriptive processes by people to enable reuse.

The paper is structured as follows. Section 2 presents the lifecycle of descriptive processes. Section 3 presents the modeling framework for descriptive processes. Section 4 presents the progress for learning refined process templates from previous process enactment instances. Section 5 discusses related work and open challenges.

2   Lifecycle of Descriptive Processes

The concrete form of a descriptive process from best practice frameworks is often influenced by two considerations: organization adaptation, for accommodating the specifics of the organization that is adopting the framework, and people who are following the process. Fig. 1 shows the lifecycle of best practice processes for an

---

[2] www.managementsoftware.hp.com

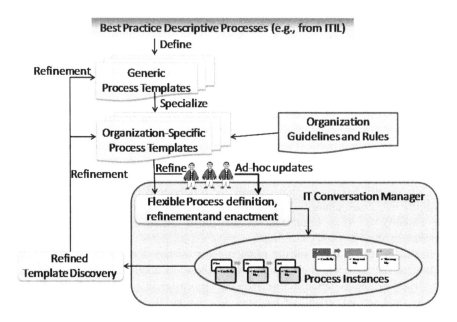

Fig. 1. The proposed lifecycle of best practice processes in organizations

organization. In particular, we envision creating process templates for descriptive processes. Process templates translate general textual guidelines into a structured form, which can be used by people to instantiate the process.

The current approach for creating process templates for descriptive processes is manual. It is performed by domain experts via reading the textual descriptions of the best practice processes. In order to support domain experts, we have introduced a framework that identifies the set of important concepts for people-intensive processes in [3]. Experts can use this framework as a guideline for extracting concepts and their relationships. Further research is required to enable the fully automated extraction of these process-related concepts and their relationships from the textual description in best practice processes.

In some organizations, generic process templates may be adapted to create organization-specific process templates, which then can be more specific compared to the generic process templates. People working within a best practice framework may choose to use one of the generic or one of the organization-specific templates to start a conversation (e.g., for handling an IT incident). They may also start a new conversation specifying the process in an-hoc manner. In our framework, there is no distinction between a process definition and a process instance, as processes are running as soon as they are partially defined by people in a conversation. A process definition may not exist in advance at the required level of details, and so the concrete definition emerges as the result of a collaboration among people performing a specific task (e.g., handling the incident) during the process enactment.

The concrete best practice processes live in the process instance repository, which is a repository containing all past enactments of processes. In the case of ITSCM, the repository contains the set of past conversations. Therefore, identifying how best practice processes are enacted in an organization requires the understanding of process instances in this repository. In this work, we propose to learn the process model from past process instances using a reverse engineering approach similar to process mining methods [4]. The inferred process model can be used to create new organization-specific process templates or to update existing templates. This approach does not only enable the understanding of concrete enactments of best practice processes in an organization, it also fosters reuse of organizational domain knowledge that is captured from people during past process enactments.

3 Modeling Framework for Descriptive Processes

We propose a three-level framework for descriptive processes to support people in the flexible and collaborative definition of descriptive processes, as well as to provide automated support for the enactment of these processes. The framework consists of the user level, the formal process model level and the machine representation level.

The user level. At the user level we define a set of concepts and corresponding relationships for best practice processes. Our observation shows that knowledge workers usually do not work based on formal or graphical process models. Using existing graphical modeling languages often leads to over-specification of process models. A qualitative user study [5] shows that a semi-formal modeling approach is preferred by users for modeling reference models such as ITIL processes. We, therefore, intentionally do not introduce an explicit process model with a graphical notation. We capture a descriptive process in terms of a set of concepts and associated relationships called the *process concept model*. It defines the key high-level concepts of "Process", "Task", "Item" (process resources, documents and artifacts), "Actor", "Role", and "Event". Each concept can also include a set of properties. The set of relationships includes the generic "has" and "is-a" relationships with more process-centric concepts such as "assigned-to", "receives" (inputs), "produces" (outputs), "depends-on" (tasks relationships) and "reacts-to" (events). Note that the process concept model can grow beyond the built-in concepts. For instance, users can add new tasks that are not part of the built-in processes. Users can introduce new concepts and relationships and choose to add them to a conversation-specific or to the central library of concepts. The enriched process models can include relationships between various processes in a best practice framework as well as pointers to service lifecycle phase(s) to which the process belong (refer to [3] for more details).

The formal process model level. The process concept model is still abstract and therefore not actionable. In order to provide automation support for enactment, we construct a corresponding process model based on dependency graphs from the process concept model. The process model is constructed considering the "depends-on" relationship between tasks in the process concept model. We also provide update operations on the model, such as add, delete, update (see [2,3] for details about this layer). Operations allow ad-hoc updates of the process model based on changes in the process concept model. The resulting process model is used by an enactment engine in ITSCM to provide functionality such as sending notifications, sending reminders and enabling the tracking of progresses.

The machine representation model. We choose to store the process model with the process instances as RDF graphs (see [2] for an example of a process description using RDF). Our process concept graph and the formal process model based on dependency graphs are RDF graph models as well. The process model and process instances can be updated by adding, removing or updating the concepts and relationships in the RDF graphs. The main motivation for choosing RDF is that the process graph in RDF is extensible, and it also allows incorporating information and relationships in the process that are not necessarily related to the process enactment, but are needed to link the process to the containing project, customer information and service such as the phase of the service within which the process is enacted, etc. RDF graphs also allow applying a variety of reasoning and querying techniques on process instances such as SPARQL. At the implementation level, we use the Jena toolkit (http://jena.sourceforge.net/) which includes a variety of model stores for the repository as well as libraries for query and inference (refer to [2,3] for examples and details on this layer).

4   Learning Refined Process Templates from Process Instances

Process instances are enriched process models in our framework. They include a detailed formal process model. This process model is often refined and customized for a specific enactment. Therefore, it can include process tasks and concepts that are not part of the built-in set of concepts in the process template. For each type of process (e.g., incident management process) we want to infer the common (frequent) process template refinements from a set of past process instances. Refinements that occurred during enactment can be applied on various aspects of the process including roles that performed a process step, the actual process flows that updated the process structure or conditions that led to a particular step. The process instances are also a good source for extracting statistical information on the enactment of processes such as how long it takes to enact a process step or the process itself, in average, or how many people are involved, etc.

In particular, the refinement of process templates includes two steps of analyzing process instance traces (which are RDF graphs), and updating the process templates. In the analysis step, we learn a process model which is annotated with conditions that lead to a particular step (by looking at the attributes of previous steps), and statistical information on how many instances contain a particular step, whether this step is new or a built-in process step. Then, we define the following operations to update the original process template.

Adding and removing steps: If a certain number of instances (above a user-defined threshold) include a new step that is not included in the template, the method suggests to add the activity to the process template in the same order that has been observed in instances. If a certain step of the template has not been used in many process instances (above a threshold), it suggests removing the step from the template.

The step refinement: this operation suggests updating the details of the step in the template based on the analysis of the enactment information of the step. In particular, the runtime information of the process activity is updated including the involved roles, average enactment time, number of instance of the template that include this activity, etc. In addition, if a step is refined into more concrete steps, the concrete sub-steps are extracted and their frequency is computed. This information is included in the template to enable their reuse.

Refine Structure: this operation analyzes the process instance and identifies cases where the order of activities is different compared to that of the template. In such cases, it adds metadata to the activities in process templates providing alternative ordering of activities and the frequency of such re-ordering in the realizations.

5 Discussion and Related Work

The existing work on process mining [4] focuses on learning a process model from the set of process instances. In that context, a process instance is often a sequence of steps. In the context of descriptive processes, the process instances are richer (in our case they are represented as RDF graphs) with complex relationships. In addition, we need to learn not only the process model in terms of the graph but also information such as conditions or explanations (from textual descriptions in conversations) which lead to choosing a specific process steps. The next set of challenges is related to applying the refinement information on the original template. One issue is that not always the execution of a descriptive process agrees with the definition in the template in terms of the process structure. We have taken a first step in updating the templates as described above by annotating the template, and providing alternative enactment orders during enactments. However, more research is needed on strategies to update the template to avoid making the templates complex but rather easy to understand for people and to reuse.

References

1. Hendriks, L., Carr, M.: ITIL: Best Practice in IT Service Management. In: Van Bon, J. (Hrsg.) The Guide to IT Service Management, Band 1, London u. a., pp. 131–150 (2002)
2. Motahari-Nezhad, H.R., et al.: IT Support Conversation Manager: A Conversation-Centered Approach and Tool for IT Incident Management. In: Proc. of EDOC (2010) (to appear)
3. Graupner, S., et al.: Making Processes from Best Practice Frameworks Actionable. In: DDBP 2009: Second International Workshop on Dynamic and Declarative Business Processes, Auckland, New Zealand, September 1 (2009)
4. van der Aalst, W., et al.: Workflow mining: a survey of issues and approaches. DKE Journal 47(2), 237–267 (2003)
5. Taylor, C., Probst, C.: Business Process Reference Model Languages: Experiences from BPI Projects. In: Proceedings of INFORMATIK (2003)
6. Orbus Software, The iServer ITIL Solution,
   http://www.orbussoftware.com/business-process-analysis/
   products/itil-solution/

Managing Process Assets in a Global IT Service Delivery Environment

Melissa Buco[1], Hani Jamjoom[1], Tom Parsons[2], and Scott Schorno[3]

[1] IBM Research, Hawthorne, NY, USA
[2] IBM GTS, Research Triangle Park, NC, USA
[3] IBM GTS, Fishkill, NY, USA

Abstract. At IBM, we recognize that our processes are our business. This is especially true in the area of IT Delivery where we have long been focused on the management and reuse of process assets. The current economic climate and advances in technology are rapidly driving IT Delivery to a truly global model. This transition greatly expands the scope of the process assets which need to be managed at a global level to include even the lowest level processes for service delivery. Customers, many of whom are also global, expect consistent quality and reasonable cost, regardless of from where services are delivered. The global management and reuse of IT Delivery process assets at all levels is no longer a desired objective but rather a business imperative. In this paper, we describe a system we are developing to manage, govern, and evolve process assets on a global scale by leveraging expertise of the entire IT Delivery community. We describe the history of the effort, the business drivers, the challenges and solutions we have devised, as well as future work.

Keywords: crowd computing, IT service delivery, business process management, governance, service quality.

1 Introduction

There are any number of industry standards, such as, ITIL [2] and ISO9000 [1], which apply to IT Service Delivery. It is the responsibility of an organization's management to define the high level processes in conformance with the appropriate industry standards. Although these processes are essential for the overall operation, the vast majority of the daily work performed by an IT service delivery organization happens at much lower levels. For example, the Change Management process governs much of what is done by the delivery personnel. However, the average system administrator is more concerned with the procedure for provisioning a new database server or work instructions for executing specific tasks needed to fix a particular problem or for installing a particular product on a given operating system (see Fig 1). The extremely large number and dynamicity of services offered, the diversity of customers, the heterogeneity of the customers' IT environments, and the global distribution of delivery personnel make managing these process assets and driving standardization to

M. zur Muehlen and J. Su (Eds.): BPM 2010 Workshops, LNBIP 66, pp. 232–237, 2011.

best practices a challenging problem of considerable scope. Moreover, the need for some level of customization to address customer specific business needs must also be taken into account.

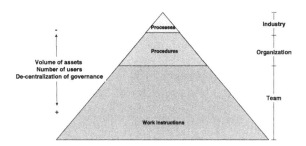

Fig. 1. Process levels

History and Related Work. At IBM, the enterprise level IT Service Delivery processes have been managed and continually improved for many years at a global level. However, lower level process assets have historically been created in a variety of formats and types of repositories by each delivery location. This has made standardization which is essential for driving down cost challenging.

Several years ago a group in IBM Research began a work on a system called *Cyano* [7] as part of a broader effort to capture, socialize, and evolve lean [3] best practice procedures executed by the IT delivery teams and links these procedures to the enterprise level processes. The resulting system captured approximately 600 procedures with a global user community of 13,000 users and more than 65,000 user annotations such as process variations and suggestions for improvement. Cyano was a Web based application that enabled the capture, display, and annotation of best practice assets. These assets were shown as flowchart diagrams together with a text description. Cyano provided a single interface into global process components such as: enterprise processes, procedures, tools, and variances. Cyano was limited to supporting process and procedures assets only.

Within the past year, Cyano has evolved into a business process management system (bpms)and been established as the strategic repository for process assets in IT Delivery. In bpms, there is an increased focus on content quality, standardization, and governance. The scope of the effort has also been expanded to address the lowest level process assets, that is, work instructions and other supporting documents which can be customer specific. It is at this low level where the bulk of process assets exist, where most of the delivery team operates, and therefore where the greatest impact of standardization and reuse can be achieved.

The lowest level process assets, such as, instructions for performing specific tasks have long been captured in various local repositories in various formats and levels of detail by teams delivering services to specific accounts. Efforts to standardize across teams for areas of interest, e.g. Unix and Intel, have had limited success. This is largely due to the effort required to develop standards across many groups.

Business process management is a broad area in enterprise operation and management. A number of commercial systems have been used heavily for various purpose, such as IBM MQSeries for workflow and message management, SAP or Oracle for process and data management. Many research efforts have been focusing on framework design and process integration, transformation, and verification. Examples of such research include process transformation and integration [6,5], and verification framework for web service [9,8].

One work on this area is by Yang et al. [10] in which they propose a social network framework for Web 2.0 application. Our work has a different focus, namely, on leveraging social network and data mining for IT Delivery processes.

Benefits. As a global repository for processes, bpms is an essential component in eliminating variability and driving standardization of processes. Less variability equates to improved reliability, service level attainment, and reduced costs of service delivery. The use of consistently documented processes in bpms is also expected to reduce human error. Moreover, bpms will facilitate training which is important in an industry with a large number of sub-contracted resources and a high rate of turnover.

Having assets in a common repository with an assessment and review process will facilitate the identification of best practices and reduce the total number of processes needed. In some cases, bpms will also enable the identification of "gaps" or deficiencies in existing processes. Additionally, bpms will be useful in transforming to best practices during the on boarding new customers.

The remainder of this paper is organized as follows: in Section 2 we discuss the design of bpms, in particular, the role of crowd computing and the importance of governance,linking of process assets, and continual improvement; in Section 3 we discuss future work; in Section 4 we summarize this work in progress.

2   Bpms Design

Bpms and its predecessor Cyano were designed to be both scalable and extensible solutions for managing process assets. Some of the key design points were the involvement of the community by using crowd computing technologies, the need for governance to maintain consistency and quality, the ability to link and categorize assets to facilitate navigation and profile user interests, and the importance of continual improvement to maintain the vitality of the content.

Crowd Computing. When we began work on Cyano, it was evident that community involvement was a critical success factor to be able to capture and evolve assets at the procedure level. As we move to a global delivery organization, the value of standardization at the work instruction level in term of cost and quality becomes increasingly clear. The size of this effort is considerable - two to three orders of magnitude greater that the Cyano effort. Therefore, the need for community participation is absolutely essential. Certainly, management support and incentives for community participation will be required.

The adoption of social computing technologies by enterprises has not been very far reaching to date. For the Cyano project, it was an ideal fit. The ability to leverage the wisdom of the crowd, that is, the expertise of the subject matter experts across the delivery organization, was exactly what was needed in order to capture the best practice procedure being used in the field. In addition to providing a global environment in which users could record process assets, Cyano also provided a means of registering usage and any process variations, suggesting improvements, and commenting on usability. The expanded scope of bpms has increased its audience and heightened the usefulness of and necessity for community involvement.

Governance. In most social computing applications, governance is not a major concern. However, with bpms, we had an overriding need for standardization, high quality, and consistency. Our goal has been to involve the community while making sure at the same time to incorporate their input in a consistent and controlled manner in order to enhance the quality and usefulness of the community's input.

One community involvement technique is to use folksonomy[4]. A folksonomy is a social networking tagging or indexing classification system derived from collaboration which allows users to suggest new category values as a way to improve the users ability to navigate the system. We chose to allow bpms users to propose new categories which are reviewed prior to becoming visible to the community in order to ensure the validity and usefulness of the category. In this way we can eliminate having different spellings and abbreviations for the the same category.

The bpms approach is to encourage community participation while controlling the overall quality of the assets stored in the system. To achieve this, each asset in bpms has a designated owner or group of owners. The owner is encouraged to leverage user feedback on the asset for the purpose of continual asset improvement. Users enrich the asset through the use of annotations. Annotations can be applied against the asset as a whole or just parts of the asset. In bpms, an annotation is the adding of commentary or explanatory notes, such as references, tools, and variations, to a process artifact. An annotation can be entered for a specific account or a group of accounts (known in bpms as an Account Group). Examples of bpms annotations include: Overview, Policy, Reference (includes URL), Tool, and Variation. All general users can author annotations, but general users can not edit or delete the annotations of other users. A general user is allowed to edit or delete annotations he or she authors.

The editing and deleting of other users annotations is restricted to a set of bpms power users. In IT Delivery, the responsibility of "Power User" is assigned to process leaders responsible for their bpms content. Power Users can also link and unlink assets to other assets or categories. General users are not allowed to manage asset links.

Bpms assets can be created using business modeling tools such as WebSphere Business Modeler (WBM) and Rational Method Composer (RMC). Assets can also be created and stored in bpms as attachments to a bpms web form using tools such as Microsoft Word, Power Point, and Visio. Assets can also be created directly using a Rich Text style editor built into a Web form. This powerful bpms capability allow assets to be created using a variety of authoring tools which minimizes concerns regarding asset migration to bpms. General users are allowed to author work instructions, while only power users are allowed to author procedures or processes in bpms.

Linking of Assets. Our experience with Cyano has shown that the ability of our users to locate the process assets readily is crucial. Toward achieving that end, we have found the linking the process assets to one another and to a variety of hierarchical categories greatly enhances the users' ability to define their scope of interest and locate assets of interest. For example, users link process assets to the owning organization, geography and accounts where used, delivery catalog entry for which applied, etc. The user can then specify his/her interests in terms of the same categories to scope the set of process assets to be shown. Bpms has the ability to easily define new categories and even content types to meet the needs of the community. In addition, process assets are linked to reflect the natural hierarchy of work instructions supporting procedures or other work instructions, procedures linking to processes or other procedures.

Continuous Improvement. Continuous improvement is a well recognized requirement in the business of IT Delivery. We understand that the usefulness of bpms to the delivery community is directly related to the vitality and relevance of the process assets it contains. Feedback of the usefulness of the assets, suggestions for improvement, ratings, usage counts, registering process variations, and linkage between related processes can all be used by asset owners to evolve the assets and drive standardization. Our goal is to record all process assets in use by the organization and continually update these and maintain the minimal set needed to support the business.

3   Future Work

There are many areas which we plan to explore in our future work on the bpms project. In this section, we will address a subset of areas which we considered particularly important.

Incenting Participation. A system such as bpms relies on community participation. How to incent users to participate is an ongoing issue but especially at start up. In the case of the Cyano, users were mandated to record their procedures in Cyano. Simple incentive such as a top contributors' list have proved popular. Clearly, the value of the system and of participation by community members has to be recognized and encouraged by management for the system to succeed.

Linking Process Assets to the Execution Environment(s). An eventual goal of bpms is to link process assets to the environment(s) in which these assets are executed. For example, if a user is assigned a task in a particular execution tool, we plan to present the user with the appropriate set of process assets (e.g. procedures, work instructionm and other supporting documents) needed to complete the task. This capability relies on having a well categorized process assets and an API for obtaining assets from the bpms system

Tooling to Help Manage Feedback. As the size of the bpms repository grows, there is potential for an asset owner to receive more feedback that can easily be handled. To address this situation, we are exploring tooling which will assist the owner with identifying those ideas which are common and have reached a level of maturity to warrant action.

4   Conclusion

Managing a large scale process asset repository for a large community of users presents a number of challenges in terms of usability, governance, and vitality. However, we believe for a large scale global IT Delivery organization such a repository is a necessity. The effort to create and maintain the repository is considerable but the return in terms of reduced cost and increased quality is also considerable and a critical success factor in today's economy.

References

1. http://www.iso.org/iso/home.htm
2. http://www.itil-officialsite.com/home/home.asp
3. http://www.lean.org/whatslean/
4. http://www.useyourweb.com/blog/?p=62
5. Chituc, C.-M., Toscano, C., Azevedo, A.L.: Collaborative business processes integration and management - lessons learned from industry. In: IEEE SCC, pp. 451–457 (2007)
6. Fujiwara, K., Ramachandran, B., Koide, A., Benayon, J.: Business process transformation wizard: a bridge between business analysts and business process transformation technology. In: IEEE SCC, pp. 83–90 (2007)
7. Jamjoom, H., Qu, H., Buco, M.J., Hernandez, M., Saha, D., Naghshineh, M.: Crowdsourcing and service delivery. IBM Systems Journal (2009)
8. Luo, N., Yan, J., Liu, M.: Towards efficient verification for process composition of semantic web services. In: IEEE SCC, pp. 220–227 (2007)
9. Moser, S., Martens, A., Gorlach, K., Amme, W., Godlinski, A.: Advanced verification of distributed ws-bpel business processes incorporating cssa-based data flow analysis. In: IEEE SCC, pp. 98–105 (2007)
10. Yang, S.J.H., Zhang, J., Chen, I.Y.L.: Web 2.0 services for identifying communities of practice through social networks. In: IEEE SCC, pp. 130–137 (2007)

Business Process Model Retrieval Based on Graph Indexing Method

Daniel Felipe Rivas[1], David S. Corchuelo[1], Cristhian Figueroa[1],
Juan Carlos Corrales[1], and Rosalba Giugno[2]

[1] Telematics Engieneering Group (GIT), University of Cauca,
5th Street 4 – 70 Popayán, Colombia
{drivas,dacorchuelo,cfigmart,jcorral}@unicauca.edu.co
[2] Department of Mathematics and Computer Science, University of Catania,
viale A. Doria 6, 95125 Catania, Italy
giugno@dmi.unict.it

Abstract. Nowadays, business process reuse is very important and necessary inside large organizations that continually increase their process collections. Therefore, an efficient system to manage and search for concrete and relevant processes is necessary. Here we overcome to this problem proposing business process model retrieval based on a Graph Indexing Method. It takes into account a measure similarity between two graphs and provides a ranking of business process retrieved.

Keywords: Business process, graph indexing, similarity measure.

1 Introduction

Many organizations with different degree of Business Process Management (BPM) maturity have a considerable amount of business process models. Manage process collections inside an organization is a difficult task and demand many efforts to business analysts who need to expend time and knowledge taking important decisions. BPMS software allows internal operations inside organizations to be agile and efficient. This information is stored in business process repositories and consequently, tools to reuse relevant processes or similar processes to the given one are needed. An example is introduced in [32] which use a repository containing about 500 process models to be consumed by local councils from Netherlands government. However, this number is small compared with thousands of processes that could have a multinational company.

In this sense, an efficient system to manage and search for concrete and relevant processes is necessary. This approach proposes business process model retrieval based on a Graph Indexing Method taking into account measuring similarity between two graphs and finally shows to user a ranking of business process retrieved.

The paper is organized as follows: Section 2 presents Related Work. Section 3 describes Business Process Model Background. Section 4 focuses on the Reference Architecture. Section 5 describes Ranking Process and section 6 concludes the paper and draws future directions.

M. zur Muehlen and J. Su (Eds.): BPM 2010 Workshops, LNBIP 66, pp. 238–250, 2011.
© Springer-Verlag Berlin Heidelberg 2011

2 Related Work

There are several research projects addressing the main idea of storing business process models across different storage and retrieval techniques. For example, in [1] is described BPL (Business Process Library) which can store information related to process in relational databases, also it allows semantic queries through process ontologies. In [2], is shown ebXML (Electronic Business using eXtensible Markup Language) Registry/Repository from OASIS (Organization for the Advancement of Structured Information Standards), this one stores any data types such as Web services descriptions, documents and XML data; queries are made through XML or SQL languages. In [3] is described IBM BPEL Repository which can store BPEL and XML documents; in this case querying XML files as objects EMF (Eclipse Modelling Framework) are allowed. Other business process model repositories such as IPM[4], RepoX[5], BPMN Repository[6], Oryx[7], BP-Suite[8] can be found in [9]. Here the authors describe additional and detailed information about these repositories and also indicate a framework to manage large collections of business process. It also analyzes and compares 16 business process repositories according with their data, functionality and management features and takes into account storing, retrieval, integration and indexing aspects. Comparison results throw indexing techniques to retrieve process are few, only five use as common index a process models classification in terms of their available business functions.

The business process models used in this paper are represented by graphs, thus process retrieval is changed to a graph retrieval based on graphs indexing techniques. Some related works of graph searching and mining are described in [10-14] where given a graph database and a query graph; it can find all graphs which contain that query. In [15] is explained a recent work where the author propose an integration of previous concepts. They introduce an efficient support for querying business process model repository. Given a process fragment (a model query), it finds all process models in the repository containing this fragment. These results are filtered through the use of indexes obtaining a set of candidate process models. Then, is applied an adaptation of Ullman's subgraph isomorphism check on a subset of the models in the repository. Here, Petri Nets are used as uniform representation of business process. In our case, the main differences with the above approach are the use of Business Process Modeling Ontology (BPMO) [16] as modeling language and we also use a process retrieval based on graphs indexing technique called GraphBlast[11] which applies a subgraph isomorphism algorithm denominated VF2[27]. This algorithm is more efficient in matching time than Ullman's algorithm as is described in [27]. In addition, we rank all relevant process according to previous defined criteria. Finally, in this paper we introduce an extension of the previous research presented in [24] explaining the indexing method and ranking applied to business processes.

3 Business Process Model Background

We reviewed some business process modeling techniques and we considered the most widely adopted business process modeling languages in industrial and academic contexts. The results throw that was found from abstract process modeling such as: EPC[17], BPMN[18], to executable process modeling such as: WF Nets[19], YAWL[20], BPEL[21]. Each of them have some features covered by the organizational, functional, behavioral and informational perspectives, as it is described in [22] and also they have advantages and disadvantages over other ones. For example BPMN is very rich graphically respect to the control flow but is weak in organizational context, EPC is well represented in functional and behavioral perspectives, but organizational and informational perspectives are partly supported. WF Nets as extension of Petri Nets are semantically well defined but they do not support organizational and informational perspectives at all. YAWL is an academic effort to make a well defined notation in complex business process but is not widely adopted by industry and few semantics are implemented. Finally, BPEL is oriented to web services orchestration and composition.

According to previous information we decided to use the Business Process Modeling Ontology (BPMO) which includes most features from the above languages. This modeling language attempts being a common translation and source for industry notations, as well as, try to provide a common representation through BPMN notation without being as low level as WF Nets. BPMO preserves and builds on the organizational and domain modeling capabilities of EPC language, rather than concentrating only on behavior. It attempts to establish a formal connection to both an underlying behavioral semantics and to executable processes via ontology based reasoning [23]. BPMO is also a language that allows modeling business process at semantic level and provides support to various BPM activities, from modeling and querying to execution and analysis.

Through BPMO we modeled some business process (BP models) through WSML (Web Service Modeling Language), and then we transformed them to formal models represented by graphs. Mainly, our efforts are focused on behavioral perspective, taking into account the Data Flow and Control Flow elements described by different connectors such as tasks, messages and gateways defined by BPMO 1.4 version [16]. In section 4.2, we introduce more detailed information about transformation process between a BP Model and its graphs representation. Then, we present the reference architecture.

4 Reference Architecture

In [24], we described the reference architecture which has five general layers: Presentation Layer, BP Parser, BP Management Layer, Repository Management Layer and Storage Layer. The aim of the present work is to extend information related to some of these Layers in order to complement previous research efforts. Next we describe the architectural layers.

4.1 Presentation Layer

The reference architecture is defined by the modular description presented in [9]. This layer is a Web application composed by a CMS (Content Management System) and

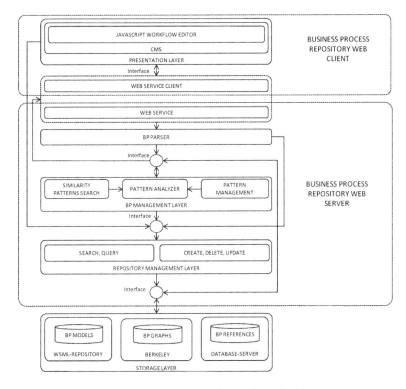

Fig. 1. Business Process Model Repository Architecture

provides functionalities such as content Web administrator and user account management. Through a Workflow JavaScript Editor, user can upload business process models to server, throw queries on process stored and visualize obtained results with a good usability degree, and also allowing access to business process repository services published on server as web services.

4.2 BP Parser

The BP Parser module receives as input a process modeled in BPMO which contains a set of tasks, messages and execution flows. It is transformed to the output graph representation (BP graph) which shows tasks and events as simple nodes, gateways as AND (Split, Join); OR (Split, Join); XOR (Split, Join) nodes, together with all their nested tasks and events. In addition, control flow connectors are represented as edges, and block patterns (WHILE and REPEAT) are represented as gateways. Next, Table 1 describes some connector types defined by the BPMO 1.4 version, as well as their corresponding graph representations used for our approach.

Table 1. BPMO Elements represented as Events, Tasks and Gateways and their corresponding graph representation

BPMO Element		Graph Label	Graph Representation
Events		**Events**	
Start	Start	Events are taken as nodes type Event node represented by label (E)	E
End	End		
Timer	Timer		(Start, End, Timer, Error, SendMessage, ReceiveMessage) Events
Error	Error		
Send/Receive Message	Send Message Receive Message		
Tasks		**Tasks**	
ManualTask	(Manual/Goal/ WebService) Task	Tasks are taken as nodes type Task node represented by label (T)	T
GoalTask			(Manual, Goal, WebService) Tasks
WebServiceTask			
Gateways		**Gateways**	
DeferredChoice	Deferred Choice	Gateways are taken as nodes type AND, OR, XOR Split;Join. Represented by labels (ANDS, ANDJ, ORS, ORJ, XORS, XORJ)	XORS
ExclusiveChoice	Exclusive Choice		
InterleavedParallelRouting	Interleaved routing		(DeferredChoice, ExclusiveChoice, InterleavedParallelRouting, Multiple Instantiation) Gateways
MultipleInstantiation	Multiple Instantiation		
Discriminator	Discriminator	Nodes type XOR Split. Represented by Labels (XORS)	XORJ
SimpleMerge	Simple Merge		(Discriminator, SimpleMerge) Gateway
ParallelSplit	Parallel Split	Nodes type AND Split. Represented by Labels (ANDS)	ANDS
			ParallelSplit Gateway
MultipleMergeSynchronise	Multi Merge Synch	Nodes type AND Join. Represented by Labels (ANDJ)	ANDJ
Synchronisation	Synchronize		(MultipleMergeSynchronise, Synchronisation) Gateways
Multimerge	Multi Merge	Nodes type OR Join. Represented by Labels (ORJ)	ORJ
			Multimerge Gateway
MultipleChoice	Multiple Choice	Nodes type OR Split. Represented by Labels (ORS)	ORS
			MultipleChoice Gateway

Next, we present a process metamodel using an UML class diagram, which is based on the approach introduced in [25]. The metamodel shows an abstract representation of concepts related to BPMO tasks, events, and gateways connectors and their interactions (Fig. 2). A *ProcessModel* contain a *ProcessGraph* which is a directed graph composed by *Nodes* and *Edges*. Nodes can be *Function* or *Connector* types, while Edges can be *SequenceFlow* or *MessageFlow* types where the last ones represent the links between Nodes. *Connector* nodes are all process model elements which are used to control flow, and these could have many In/Out Edges. *Connector* nodes can be *OR, XOR, AND* (Split, Join) and *Wait* indicates the flow state. *Split* elements have one *In* Edge and multiple *Out* Edges. *Join* elements have multiple *In* Edges and one *Out* Edge and *Wait* elements could have multiple *In/Out* Edges. Function nodes are relevant from business perspective; they have at least one *In* Edge and one *Out* Edge and are classified in *Task* and *Event* Nodes. *Task* node is a process element which performs activities as part of a process, for example *Configure equipment activity* or *Translate information activity*. *Task* nodes are also classified as *Manual, WebService* or *Goal* tasks. Finally, *Events* are used to show the *Start* or *End* of a process, also to present dispatch and reception messaging between different processes, or to signal if it is necessary to wait while a task is being executed.

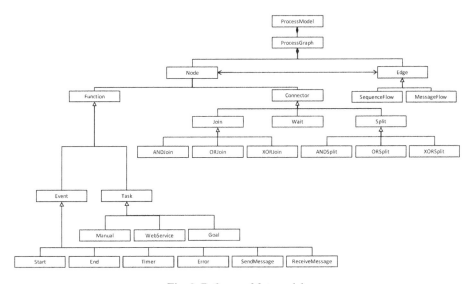

Fig. 2. Reference Metamodel

4.3   BP Management Layer

This layer is composed by the modules: management, analysis and similarity search of patterns. Bellow, we describe each one of them.

4.3.1   Pattern Management
This module contains a set of predefined patterns and it captures aspects related to control flow dependencies between connector elements. Table 2 shows six basic patterns out of

eleven that we implemented, described in BPMO language and their graphs representation, these patterns are defined in [26] and can be changed according to user needs.

Table 2. Reference patterns modeled at **(a)** BPMO and **(b)** Graphs representation

4.3.2 Pattern Analyzer

This module takes a predefined number of patterns, in order to make an exact detection of which set of patterns a Query Graph includes. This detection is done by a subgraph algorithm called VF2[27], this algorithm is used to achieve a better performance searching on large graphs. Below is described the concept related to substructures detection and the indexing method applied:

Substructures detection

Consider two graphs $\mathbf{G}$ and $\mathbf{G}'$; a graph isomorphism between $\mathbf{G}$ and $\mathbf{G}'$ is a bijective mapping $\mathbf{f} : \mathbf{V} \longrightarrow \mathbf{V}'$ such that $\alpha(\mathbf{v}) = \alpha'\big(\mathbf{f}(\mathbf{v})\big) \forall \mathbf{v} \in \mathbf{V}$. For any edge $\mathbf{e} = (\mathbf{u}, \mathbf{v}) \in \mathbf{E}$ exists an edge $\mathbf{e}' = \big(\mathbf{f}(\mathbf{u}), \mathbf{f}(\mathbf{v})\big) \in \mathbf{E}'$ such that $\beta(\mathbf{e}) = \beta'(\mathbf{e}')$ and for any edge $\mathbf{e}' = (\mathbf{u}', \mathbf{v}') \in \mathbf{E}'$ exists an edge $\mathbf{e} = \big(\mathbf{f}^{-1}(\mathbf{u}'), \mathbf{f}^{-1}(\mathbf{v}')\big) \in \mathbf{E}$ such that $\beta(\mathbf{e}) = \beta'(\mathbf{e}')$. If $\mathbf{f} : \mathbf{V} \longrightarrow \mathbf{V}'$ is an isomorphism between graphs $\mathbf{G}$ and $\mathbf{G}'$, and $\mathbf{G}'$ is a subgraph of another graph $\mathbf{G}''$, i.e. $\mathbf{G} \subset \mathbf{G}''$, then $\mathbf{f}$ is called a subgraph isomorphism from $\mathbf{G}$ to $\mathbf{G}'$.

Indexing Method

We use the LNE (List of Nodes and Edges ids format) technique to describe process exact querying[10] and GraphBlast as graph indexing algorithm. A LNE format is composed by a collection of graph specifications stored in a file. GraphBlast uses a graph representation based on nodes which has an identification number (*node-id*) and an identification label (*node-label*) (Fig. 3). It defines an *id-path* of length *n* (i.e. list of *n+1 node-ids*) with an unlabeled edge between any two consecutive nodes, and a *label-path* of length *n* as a list of *n+1* (*node labels*) [11]. For example, a label-path is: EANDS, and an id-path would be: (0, 1). For each graph and for each node, it founds all paths that start in this node and have length from one to a predefined size using a variable named *lp*, (*lp*=4 as default, but it can vary). Index construction is made through a set of *id-paths* and *id-labels* using a hash table, whose keys are the hash values of the label-paths. In our case we use the label-path to define and describe a graph pattern that will be sought within each graph of the BP Graphs database (Fig. 3b), it means that *h(TTXORJT)* label-path describes a predefined graph pattern contained in the Pattern Management module (these patterns can vary according to patterns predefinition). Then, index construction is made by the number of occurrences of this label-path within each graph. The hash table is defined as a *fingerprint* of the database and is composed by a matrix where rows are labeled with label-paths and each column is associated to a graph stored in Database.

All information related to graph representation and index construction is stored in Berkeley DB[28]. (Fig. 3a) shows a collection of id-paths of all the paths representing a label sequence into a label-path-set; collections that are stored in Berkeley DB Tables.

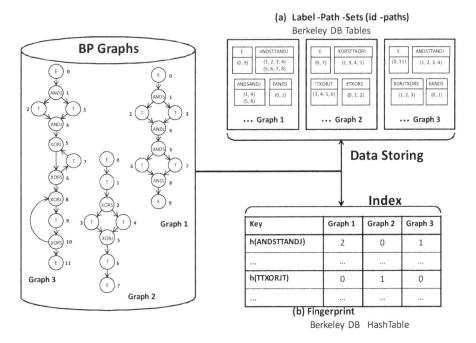

Fig. 3. Data Storing and Index creation on Berkeley BD Tables and DB Hash Table

4.3.3 Similarity Pattern Search

This module makes an inexact subgraph detection using GLIDE (Graph LInear DEscriptor) language [10]. The expressions in Glide, called graph regular expressions, allow the description of portions of graphs, and approximate query, and let make various approximate queries identifying different locations of the control flow patterns inside BP Graph analyzed. Below in Fig.4 (a) are described two patterns in Glide. These representations depict the BP graphs of Fig.4 (b) respectively, where nodes are expressed only with their labels (*AND_Split, AND_Join, XOR_Join, XOR_Split, Task, GoalTask and WebServiceTask*) and are joined by a '/' character representing the edges (e.g. *XOR_Split/GoalTask*, it means two nodes joined by an edge). The branches are grouped using nested parentheses (e.g. *XOR_Split (*/AND_Split...)*, parentheses mean a branch starting in *XOR_Split* node) and cycles can be viewed as a cutting edge and a label with an integer number (e.g. *AND_Split%1*, it means a cycle starting in *AND_Split* node and go back itself). The nodes of cutting edges are represented by their labels, followed by the characters '%', '/' and the integer number.

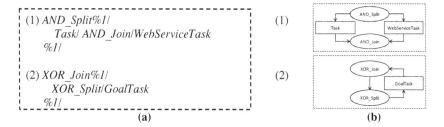

Fig. 4. Two patterns described in (a) GLIDE language (b) Graph representation

Glide also allows inexact queries using wildcards such as: '.' matches any single node, '*' matches any sequence of nodes, '?' matches at most one node,'+' matches any sequence of one or more nodes [11]. In Fig. 5, an inexact query is presented, where there is at least one route between the patterns (2) and (1) which is expressed through the character '*'.

```
XOR_Join%1/
   XOR_Split(
      */AND_Split%2/
         Task/AND_Join/WebServiceTask%2/
   )
./GoalTask %1/
```

Fig. 5. An inexact query described in GLIDE language

Depending of the exact querying (LNE format) or inexact querying (GLIDE format) applied over the Query process, pattern detection is applied almost in the same way. Moreover, it stores the number and type of identified patterns. This information can be utilized to rank process as well is described in section five.

4.4 Repository Management Layer

This layer contains drivers required to enable the creation, read, update and delete (CRUD) in each one of the repositories. In BP models (WSML documents) were used the WSMO and WSMO4J APIs. In BP Graphs was used GraphBlast, and for RDBMS were used drivers such as JDBC.

4.5 Storage Layer

This layer contains three repositories. The first one known as ORDI [29] is responsible for storing WSML documents, this works together with WSMO and WSMO4J APIs. The second one called Berkeley DB stores the BP Graphs and is directly related to GraphBlast. And the third one uses a relational database which contains the WSML documents location routes, and relates every document to every BP graph represented in order to make agile the delivery of similarity results to user, this consideration was taken into account from the recommendations described in [30]. In addition, is stored all data concerning to patterns detection of a given BP model, such as the number and type of identified patterns.

5   Ranking Process

Taking into account the number of identified patterns, we make a ranking where user can observe the results of all retrieved process. It is possible that similar process exist in these results, so it is necessary to use a pattern similarity measure between Query (Q) graphs and Target (T) graphs to define the order in which results will be presented. This ranking process is based on the approach defined in [31].

Ranking process of target graphs takes the number of patterns (P_Q and P_T) in the target graphs that were found by Pattern Analyzer or the Similarity Pattern Search modules and thus build the similarity measure defined as $Sim_{pattern}(Q,T)$. If two target graphs have the same number of patterns to the query graph, then the one matching of subgraph with more patterns will be preferred. The similarity function is:

$$Sim_{Pattern}(Q,T) = \frac{|P_Q \cap P_T|}{|P_Q|}$$

If still appear similar results, a second similarity measure is defined, based on the number of different sequences between the patterns found in two graphs:

$$Sim_{SeqPattern}(Q,T) = \frac{1}{1 + |P_{seq}(Q)| + |P_{seq}(T)| - 2|P_{seq}(Q) \cap P_{seq}(T)|}$$

In the same way of $Sim_{Pattern}$, if two target graphs have the same number of patterns but they are matched to subgraphs with different number of pattern sequences, the one that matches a subgraph with more pattern sequences will be preferred. In this similarity function the P_{seq} parameter represents the number of consecutive patterns ($P_{seq}(Q)$ for query graph and $P_{seq}(T)$ for target graph) and $P_{seq}(Q) \cap P_{seq}(T)$ represents the mapped sequences into query graph with respect to the target graph. For instance, if we select $P_{seq}(Q) = 3$ (tri sequence), then the function will consider all sequences of three consecutive patterns of the query and target graph and their intersection. Thus, $tri_{Pattern}(Q)$, $tri_{Pattern}(T)$ and $|tri_{Pattern}(Q) \cap tri_{Pattern}(T)|$ will be calculated.

Finally, a third similarity measure appears in the case that before similarity measures can not define an adequate ranking. In this measure, the user gives a cost to some patterns or pattern sequences found after querying process and he decides by himself the relevant results according to needs.

6 Conclusions

This paper introduces a method of storing and retrieving business process models supported in a formal representation based on graphs. Besides, it pretends to extend and confirm previous working research with the architecture proposed. It shows some patterns implemented and described in BPMO. The problem of processes recovering was reduced to a subgraph isomorphism detection problem using as a pattern detection technique called GraphBlast in which LNE was used as query language for exact querying and GLIDE as query language for approximate querying. The processing time for each graph is a polynomial function on the number of nodes in the graph and its degree depends on the path length defined as lp. In future work we would make some evaluation tests about efficiency retrieval and we could exploit all semantics capabilities disposed in BPMO adding semantic discovery through applying ontological concepts.

References

[1] Kaczmarek, M., Konstantinov, M.: D3.4 Business Process Library Final Prototype. IP-SUPER Project, Information Society Technologies (2008)
[2] Dugac, A., Laceli, G., Kabak, Y., Unal, S.: Exploiting ebXML registry semantic constructs for handling archetype metadata in healthcare informatics. In: IJMSO 2006, vol. 1(2) (2006)
[3] Kaczmarek, M., Konstantinov, M.: D3.4 Business Process Library Final Prototype. IP-SUPER Project, Information Society Technologies (2008)
[4] Choi, I., Jung, H., Song, M., Eyu, Y.: Ipm-epdl: an xml-based executable process definition language. Computers in Industry 56(1), 85–104 (2005)
[5] Song, M., Miller, J.A., Arpinar, I.B.: RepoX: An XML Repository for Workflow Designs and Specifications. Technical Report UGA-CS-LSDIS-TR-01-012, University of Georgia, USA (2001)
[6] Theling, T., Zwicker, J., Loos, P., Vanderhaeghen, D.: An architecture for collaborative scenarios applying a common bpmn-repository. In: Kutvonen, L., Alonistioti, N. (eds.) DAIS 2005. LNCS, vol. 3543, pp. 169–180. Springer, Heidelberg (2005)
[7] Decker, G., Overdick, H., Weske, M.: Oryx – An Open Modeling Platform for the BPM Community. In: Dumas, M., Reichert, M., Shan, M.-C. (eds.) BPM 2008. LNCS, vol. 5240, pp. 382–385. Springer, Heidelberg (2008)

[8] Beeri, C., Eyal, A., Milo, T., Pilberg, A.: Bp-mon: Query-based monitoring of bpel business processes. SIGMOD Record 37(1), 21–24 (2008)

[9] Yan, Z., Dijkman, R.M., Grefen, P.W.P.J.: Business process model repositories - framework and survey. BETA publicatie: working papers 292, p. 26, Internal Report (2009)

[10] Giugno, R., Shasha, D.: GraphGrep: A Fast and Universal Method for Querying Graphs. In: ICPR 2002 (2002)

[11] Ferro, A., Giugno, R., Mongiovì, M., Pulvirenti, A., Skripin, D., Shasha, D.: GraphBlast: multi-feature graphs database searching. In: NETTAB 2007 Workshop: Posters (2007)

[12] Zhu, F., Yan, X., Han, J., Yu, P.S.: gPrune: A constraint pushing framework for graph pattern mining. In: Zhou, Z.-H., Li, H., Yang, Q. (eds.) PAKDD 2007. LNCS (LNAI), vol. 4426, pp. 388–400. Springer, Heidelberg (2007)

[13] Srinivasa, S., Singh, M.H.: GRACE: A Graph Database System. In: COMAD 2005b (2005)

[14] Yan, X., Han, J., Yu, P.S.: Graph Indexing: A Frequent Structure-based Approach. In: ACM SIGMOD 2004 (2004)

[15] Jin, T., Wang, J., Wu, N., La Rosa, M., ter Hofstede, A.H.M.: Efficient and Accurate Retrieval of Business Process Models through Indexing. QUT ePrints Techinical Report #31996, Queensland University of Technology (2010)

[16] Cabral, L., Norton, B., Domingue, J.: The Business Process Modelling Ontology. In: 4th International Workshop SBPM 2009 (2009)

[17] Keller, G., Nüttgens, M., Scheer, A.-W.: Semantische Processmodellierung auf der Grundlage Ereignisgesteuerter Processketten (EPK). Veröffentlichungen des Instituts für Wirtschaftsinformatik, University of Saarland, Saarbrücken, Germany (1992)

[18] OMG. Business Process Modeling Notation. V 2.0. FTF Beta 1 for Version 2.0 (2009)

[19] van der Aalst, W.M.P.: Verification of Workflow Nets. In: Azéma, P., Balbo, G. (eds.) ICATPN 1997. LNCS, vol. 1248, pp. 407–426. Springer, Heidelberg (1997)

[20] van der Aalst, W.M.P., ter Hofstede, A.H.M.: YAWL: yet another workflow language. Information Systems 30(4), 245–275 (2005)

[21] Andrews, T., Curbera, F., Dholakia, H., Goland, Y., Klein, J., Leymann, F., Liu, K., Roller, D., Smith, D., Thatte, S., Trickovic, I., Weerawarana, S.: Business process execution language for web services, version 1.1. In: Standards proposal by BEA Systems, International Business Machines Corporation, and Microsoft Corporation (2003)

[22] List, B., Korherr, B.: An evaluation of conceptual business process modelling languages. In: Proceedings of the 2006 ACM Symposium on Applied Computing, SAC 2006, pp. 1532–1539. ACM, New York (2006)

[23] Norton, B., Cabral, L., Nitzsche, J.: Ontology-Based Translation of Business Process Models. In: Proceedings of the 2009 Fourth International Conference on Internet and Web Applications and Services, ICIW, pp. 481–486. IEEE Computer Society, Washington, DC (2009)

[24] Rivas, D.F., Corchuelo, D.S., Figueroa, C.N., et al.: Business Process Repository based on Control Flow Patterns. In: Euro-American Conference on Telematics and Information Systems EATIS, Panama (2010)

[25] La Rosa, M., Reijers, H.A., van der Aalst, W.M.P., Dijkman, R.M., Mendling, J., Dumas, M., Garcia-Banuelos, L.: APROMORE: An Advanced Process Model Repository. QUT ePrints Techinical Report #27448, Queensland University of Technology (2009)

[26] Russell, N., ter Hofstede, A.H.M., van der Aalst, W.M.P., Mulyar, N.: Workflow Control-flow Patterns A revised view. BPM Center Report 2006 (2006)

[27] Cordella, L.P., Foggia, P., Sansone, C., Vento, M.: A (Sub)Graph Isomorphism Algorithm for Matching Large Graphs. IEEE Transactions on Pattern Analysis and Machine Intelligence 26(10) (2004)

[28] Edwards, J.D.: Oracle Berkeley DB Java Edition (2006)

[29] Ognyanov, D., Kiryakov, A.: DIP D2.3: Ontology Representation and Data Integration (ORDI) Framework. DIP Integrated Project (2006)

[30] Dijkman, R., Dumas, M., van Dongen, B., Käärik, R., Mendling, J.: Similarity of business process models: Metrics and evaluation. Working Paper 269, BETA Research School, Eindhoven, The Netherlands (2009)

[31] Grigori, D., Corrales, J.C., Bouzeghoub, M., Gater, A.: Ranking BPEL Processes for Service Discovery. IEEE Transactions on Services Computing (February 17, 2010)

[32] Jung, J., Choi, I., Song, M.: An integration architecture for knowledge management systems and business process management systems. Comput. Ind. 58(1), 21–34 (2007)

Object-Sensitive Action Patterns in Process Model Repositories

Sergey Smirnov[1], Matthias Weidlich[1], Jan Mendling[2], and Mathias Weske[1]

[1] Hasso Plattner Institute, Potsdam, Germany
{sergey.smirnov,matthias.weidlich,mathias.weske}@hpi.uni-potsdam.de
[2] Humboldt-Universität zu Berlin, Germany
jan.mendling@wiwi.hu-berlin.de

Abstract. Organizations maintain large repositories of business process models. While maintenance and management of these repositories are challenging, they also offer opportunities when used as a knowledge base systematically. For instance, repositories can be leveraged to provide modeling support and, therefore, help to assure the consistency of newly created models with the existing ones. In the previous work we have introduced action patterns as reusable blocks of process models that can be derived from a model repository. In this paper we advance the initial results interpreting the action concept as a composition of a verb and a business object. The subsequently identified action pattern types allow for fine-grained modeling support. We evaluate the novel concepts and compare them to the established action patterns using as a benchmark the SAP Reference Model, the real world process model collection.

1 Introduction

Enterprises perceive business process management as a vehicle to achieve competitive advantage. As most process management methodologies assume availability of models formally capturing business processes, large enterprises maintain process model collections with hundreds or even thousands of process models. Maintenance of such collections brings up new challenges, among them process variants management and synchronization of several models capturing one business case. At the same time, a model collection is a valuable knowledge resource. The models describe a business domain, capturing relations between activities, events, and data objects. We believe that a thorough analysis of a model collection helps to address challenges in the context of model creation and maintenance. This approach is well-known in engineering and usually referred to as the *reuse* principle.

Various approaches that leverage reuse principles to increase process modeling efficiency have been proposed. For instance, reference modeling accumulates the domain knowledge in a reference model, which is further customized in different application projects [1]. On the opposite, several types of patterns for process models describe recurring situations in a domain independent way [2,3]. Whilst

M. zur Muehlen and J. Su (Eds.): BPM 2010 Workshops, LNBIP 66, pp. 251–263, 2011.

such patterns are well-suited for model verification and generic modeling support, the existing reference models are tightly coupled with their partial domain and can hardly be used in other settings. Recently, several approaches emerged that aim at addressing this inherent trade-off between semantic richness of patterns and their applicability in a broad context [4,5]. In [5], we have introduced an *action pattern* concept and described a method for action pattern mining. The term *action* essentially refers to the verb that describes the work content of an activity. *Action patterns* capture relations between actions. In contrast to workflow patterns [2], action patterns are related to the process model business semantics, yet, unlike reference models, action patterns are abstract enough to be reused in various domains. Thereby, action patterns, for example, can support the modeler during a process model design. Notice that such an interpretation of an action ignores information about the objects to which the action is applied. Actions capturing both a verb and an object provide more information about the model semantics. Hence, the use of object-sensitive actions makes the difference in the context of modeling support: more precise recommendations can be delivered to the modeler.

In this paper we elaborate on the action concept in more detail. In particular, the relations of actions and their subjects, business objects on which the actions are performed, are studied. Once business objects are taken into account, we identify different classes of actions. Hence, different classes of action patterns are derived. Our contribution is the description and formalization of object-sensitive action patterns along with methods for their mining based on association rule learning.

The remainder of the paper is structured as follows. Section 2 describes the background of our work in terms of modeling support based on action patterns. Section 3 introduces the novel concept of object-sensitive action patterns. Section 4 reports on findings on the application of our approach to a collection of industry process models, i.e., the SAP Reference Model [6]. Section 5 discusses related work, before Section 6 concludes the paper.

2   Background

The increasing amount of casual modelers imposes serious challenges for mechanisms that assure process model quality. Among numerous types of support that aim at increasing model quality we study one: a method providing recommendations on the missing activities given an incomplete model. Such recommendations are of particular value in the context of large collaborative modeling initiatives. In this setting, the risk of inconsistent process models is high due to several modelers working on similar processes. Here, domain knowledge manifested in existing process models can be leveraged to assure completeness and consistency of newly created process models. To enable the suggestions we consider the business semantics of model activities. Further, we focus on the activity perspective, as activities are the first class citizens in common process modeling languages, e.g., the Business Process Modeling Notation (BPMN) and Event-driven Process Chains (EPCs).

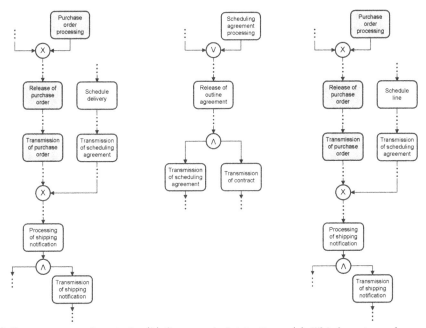

(a) Procurement of materi- (b) Source administration (c) Third-party order pro-
als and external services   cessing

Fig. 1. Fragments of three processes from the SAP Reference Model

Action Patterns. In order to address the need for semantic rich modeling support, we have introduced the notions of *actions* and *action patterns* in [5]. An action corresponds to the verb that describes the work content of an activity. For instance, in activity *Purchase order processing* the action is *process*. This example also illustrates the challenge of action mining: *purchase* can be interpreted as action as well. However, promising results on action mining have been presented for labels of process model activities [7]. Hence, we assume the existence of a mechanism that extracts actions from activity labels. Action patterns organize domain specific knowledge in terms of actions and their relations. The goal of action patterns is to define which actions often occur together in processes and which ordering constraints exist between these actions.

Let us consider a motivating example that appears in the SAP Reference Model [6]. Fig. 1 depicts the fragments of three EPCs from this model collection. All the models describe business processes from the procurement domain. A rough inspection of the models reveals that while model fragments in Fig. 1(a) and Fig. 1(c) are extremely similar, the fragment in Fig. 1(b) is different. Indeed, fragments in Fig. 1(a) and Fig. 1(c) contain almost identical sets of activities, and, hence, actions: *process, release,* and *transmit*. Although the fragment in Fig. 1(b) contains other activities, the set of actions is the same. Thereby, the three discussed fragments are close in terms of observed actions.

Types of Action Patterns. We distinguish two types of action patterns. *Co-occurrence action patterns* capture sets of actions, which often occur together in business processes. Given a set of actions, a co-occurrence pattern specifies which actions are expected to appear as well. An example derived from the process models depicted in Fig. 1 is {*process, release*} ⇒ {*transmit*}. This pattern suggests that once actions *process* and *release* appear in the business process, action *transmit* should also be observed. Co-occurrence action patterns may facilitate model design by suggesting actions missing in the model. In other words, these patterns propose actions to be added to the process.

Co-occurrence action patterns do not reflect the ordering relations between actions. *Behavioral action patterns* address this issue, pointing to actions and the ordering constraints between them. For a given set of actions and relations between a subset of these actions, a behavioral pattern specifies the missing behavioral relations. To this end, we use behavioral profiles [8] as a behavioral abstraction. Such a profile describes behavioral relations on the level of activity pairs. A behavioral profile consists of three relations that partition the Cartesian product of all model activities, such that two activities are either in strict order, exclusive to each other, or in interleaving order. For the model in Fig. 1(a), activities *Release of purchase order* and *Transmission of purchase order* are in strict order, as the former is executed before the latter in any case. Activities *Transmission of scheduling agreement* and *Transmission of contract*, in turn, are in interleaving order as the former might be executed before the latter and vice versa. An example of a behavioral action pattern is the statement that if actions *process, release,* and *transmit* appear together and *release* is executed after *process*, then *transmit* is executed after *process* and after *release*. From a user perspective behavioral action patterns complement co-occurrence patterns: while a co-occurrence pattern hints on which actions are missing, a behavioral pattern suggests how to introduce these actions in the model.

Action Pattern Mining. [5] shows how association rule learning techniques can be applied to derive action patterns given a collection of process models. Association rule learning was introduced by Agrawal et al. in [9]. We shortly recall the basic principles. Let $\mathcal{I}$ be a set of items and C a collection of transactions, where each transaction T is a set of items, i.e., $T \subseteq \mathcal{I}$. Given a set of items $X \subseteq \mathcal{I}$, we say that transaction T satisfies X, if $X \subseteq T$. An association rule in a collection C is an implication of the form $X \Rightarrow Y$, where $X \cap Y = \emptyset$ and $X, Y \subset \mathcal{I}$. Based thereon, two elementary notions can be defined, i.e., *support* and *confidence*. A set $X \subseteq \mathcal{I}$ has support n in a collection C, denoted by $supp(X)$, if n transactions satisfy set X. Support can be related to statistical significance. We are interested in sets with high support and refer to a set as being *large*, if $supp(X) \geq supp_{min}$ for a given threshold $supp_{min}$. An association rule $X \Rightarrow Y$ holds in transaction collection C with confidence $c = \frac{supp(X \cup Y)}{supp(X)}$, if at least c share of transactions satisfying X, satisfies Y as well. The confidence for a rule $X \Rightarrow Y$ is denoted by $conf(X \Rightarrow Y)$. A rule's confidence reflects its strength. Again, we are interested in rules with high confidence, i.e., those that show a confidence that is higher than a threshold $conf_{min}$.

Association rule learning enables identification of action patterns as follows. For co-occurrence action patterns, we interpret actions as items and process models as transactions. Hence, a model collection is a collection of transactions. A process model satisfies an action set, if the model comprises activities that relate to all of the actions. A co-occurrence action pattern is defined as an association rule on the domain of actions associated with values for minimal support and confidence. For the case of behavioral action patterns, we first lift the relation of the behavioral profile from the level of activities to actions. Based thereon, behavioral relations of actions are interpreted as items. Thus, a behavioral action pattern is an association rule on the domain of action pairs along with their behavioral relation, which is associated with values for minimal support and confidence.

3 Object-Sensitive Action Patterns

This section introduces object-sensitive action patterns. First, Section 3.1 elaborates on the limitations of interpreting an action as being a verb only. Subsequently, Section 3.2 and Section 3.3 introduce two novel notions of action sets that underlie object-sensitive action patterns.

3.1 Action Notion Revisited

Action patterns introduced in [5] are independent of the objects on which the actions are performed. We refer to such action patterns as *object-neutral action patterns*. Arguably, two actions such as *accept* and *reject* often occur together and are executed exclusively. However, for other action combinations, patterns might solely be observed, if the notion of an action is refined by taking the respective objects into account.

For instance, in the example in Fig. 1, we observe that all models contain the actions *process* and *release*. However, the actions relate to different objects even within one model, i.e., a *purchase order*, a *shipping notification*, and a *scheduling agreement*. While this does not impact on the co-occurrence of these actions at least in our example, we observe that the three models show different behavioral relations between these actions. In Fig. 1(a) and Fig. 1(c) the action *release* (of a purchase order) can be preceded and followed by the action *process* (of a purchase order, or of a shipping notification). In contrast, the model in Fig. 1(b) shows a strict order of actions: *process* is followed by *release*.

We see that the existing notion of object-neutral action patterns aims at deriving patterns at a coarse-grained level. While object-neutral action patterns are useful for modeling support, certain patterns might solely be observed once a more fine-grained approach is taken. Such fine-grained patterns should consider the combination of a verb and the respective object as the underlying notion of an action. We refer to these patterns as *object-sensitive action patterns*.

The definition of object-sensitive action patterns leads to a different domain for an action pattern, but does not impact on the action pattern types (i.e., co-occurrence and behavioral action patterns) and the way they are mined using the approach summarized in Section 2. Therefore, we focus on the definition of the domain for object-sensitive action patterns and refer the reader to [5] for a formal description of the pattern mining method.

First, we postulate Γ—an alphabet of activity labels in a process model collection. Further, we assume means to extract verbs and business objects from activity labels.

Definition 1 (Verb and Business Object Function). For a given alphabet of activity labels Γ, the *verb function* $v : \Gamma \mapsto \mathcal{V}$ derives a verb from an activity label. The *business object function* $b : \Gamma \mapsto \mathcal{B}$ derives a business object from an activity label. As a shorthand notation, we use $V_\Gamma = \bigcup_{\gamma \in \Gamma}\{v(\gamma)\}$ and $B_\Gamma = \bigcup_{\gamma \in \Gamma}\{b(\gamma)\}$ to refer to the verbs and business objects of all activity labels.

For instance, if an activity is labeled *Schedule delivery*, *v(Schedule delivery)* = *schedule* and *b(Schedule delivery)* = *delivery*.

Apparently, object-neutral action patterns are build solely from the set V_Γ. That is, verbs are the domain for these patterns and represent the items in the sense of association rule learning, cf., Section 2.

3.2   Multi-object Action Patterns

The first kind of object-sensitive action patterns builds on the notion of actions in the sense of an operation expressed by a verb and applied to a business object. Actions become tuples of verbs and business objects, and every such tuple—an item in the sense of association rule learning.

Definition 2 (Multi-Object Action Set). Let Γ be a set of activity labels. The *multi-object action set* $\mathcal{A}_O \subseteq V_\Gamma \times B_\Gamma$ contains all pairs of verbs and objects (x, y), such that $v(\gamma) = x$ and $b(\gamma) = y$ for some activity label $\gamma \in \Gamma$.

We speak of multi-object action sets, as the actions can relate to different business objects. For instance, *(process, purchase order)*, *(release, purchase order)*, and *(transmit, scheduling agreement)* would be actions derived from the exemplary process models in Fig. 1 that can be part of a multi-object action pattern. An example for a co-occurrence action pattern is $\{$*(process, purchase order)*, *(release, purchase order)*$\} \Rightarrow \{$*(transmit, scheduling agreement)*$\}$, i.e., the observation of the actions *(process, purchase order)* and *(release, purchase order)* suggests that the action *(transmit, scheduling agreement)* should be observed as well. Similarly, behavioral action patterns can be specified, e.g., if actions *(process, purchase order)* and *(release, purchase order)* are observed in a strict order, action *(transmit, scheduling agreement)* should be observed exclusively to both.

Multi-object action patterns are more fine-grained than object-neutral action patterns. We assume that multi-object actions allow for unveiling patterns that cannot be detected when considering solely the verbs of model element labels. On the other hand, identification of object-neutral action patterns should be prioritized as several multi-object action patterns together might represent an object-neutral action pattern.

3.3 Single-Object Action Patterns

Single-object action patterns are composed of actions where verbs are applied to a *single* business object. Again, tuples of verbs and business objects are the items in the sense of association rule learning. However, in contrast to multi-object action patterns discussed in the previous section, all actions of a pattern relate to one dedicated business object. Therefore, we need the following definition of an action.

Definition 3 (Single-Object Action Set). Let Γ be a set of activity labels. For each object $o \in B_\Gamma$, the *single-object action set* $\mathcal{A}_O^o \subseteq V_\Gamma \times B_\Gamma$ contains all pairs (x, o), such that $v(\gamma) = x$ for some activity label $\gamma \in \{\omega \in \Gamma \mid b(\omega) = o\}$.

Regarding the models in Fig. 1, again, the actions *(process, purchase order)* and *(transmit, scheduling agreement)* are derived. However, these actions refer to different business objects and, therefore, cannot occur together in a single-object action pattern. Still, we see that the models in Fig. 1 contain various actions that refer to a business object, the *purchase order* object. All these actions might be used as building blocks for single-object action patterns.

4 Evaluation Based on the SAP Reference Model

This section empirically evaluates the impact of object-sensitive actions on the action patterns. The section presents the results of action patterns mining in a large process model collection. We analyze the mining results comparing the patterns discovered for object-neutral and object-sensitive actions. The analysis considers both co-occurrence and behavioral action patterns.

In the evaluation, we use the SAP Reference Model [6]—a process model collection used as a benchmark for object-neutral action patterns evaluation in [5]. The SAP Reference Model includes 604 EPCs, describing business processes supported by the SAP R/3 software. The collection is organized in 29 functional branches of an enterprise, e.g., sales and accounting. The experiment evaluating co-occurrence action patterns makes use of all 604 models. The evaluation of behavioral action patterns exploits 421 models. The decrease in the model number is due to the exclusion of models with ambiguous instantiation semantics, see [10], or behavioral anomalies, see [11]. In the experiment we have used a manual mapping of activity labels to verbs and business objects. However, as discussed before, [7] shows the potential for an automation of this step.

In the first part of the experiment, we compare co-occurrence action patterns describing object-neutral and object-sensitive actions. Table 1 presents the number of action patterns for object-neutral actions. The number of patterns dramatically decreases with the growth of support and confidence values (horizontal and vertical directions in the table, respectively). Table 2 describes the observed results for co-occurrence action patterns capturing object-sensitive actions. Table 2(a) captures the results for multi-object action sets, while Table 2(b)—for single-object action sets. The number of patterns for multi-object action sets is the highest among the three compared tables. This can be explained

Table 1. Dependency of co-occurrence pattern number for object-neutral actions in the SAP Reference Model on $conf_{min}$ and $supp_{min}$

$conf_{min}$ \ $supp_{min}$	3	4	5	6	7	8	9	10
0.50	7395	2353	680	563	41	29	17	11
0.60	6123	2089	610	504	33	22	12	8
0.70	5569	1535	563	469	20	12	6	6
0.80	4684	1238	501	417	15	10	5	5
0.90	4603	1157	420	377	7	3	2	2

Table 2. Dependency of co-occurrence pattern number for object-sensitive actions in the SAP Reference Model on $conf_{min}$ and $supp_{min}$

(a) Multi-object actions

$conf_{min}$ \ $supp_{min}$	3	4	5	6	7	8	9	10
0.50	32072	21019	6171	6010	20	15	7	1
0.60	30127	20373	6154	6007	20	15	7	1
0.70	23884	14130	6013	5870	19	14	6	1
0.80	20601	13731	6009	5867	17	14	6	1
0.90	20300	13430	5708	5588	9	6	4	0

(b) Single-object actions

$conf_{min}$ \ $supp_{min}$	3	4	5	6	7	8	9	10
0.50	408	119	67	53	10	5	5	1
0.60	382	105	60	50	10	5	5	1
0.70	364	87	56	46	9	4	4	1
0.80	326	73	52	43	7	4	4	1
0.90	310	57	36	28	5	2	2	0

by the fact that in the SAP Reference Model one action pattern consisting of object-neutral actions is "split" into several patterns capturing object-sensitive actions. Consider an example object-neutral action set {*transmit, process, release*}. In the case of object-sensitive actions this set is split into 22 action sets, including:

Example 1 {*transmit order, process order, release order*}
Example 2 {*transmit agreement, process notification, release order*}
Example 3 {*transmit order, transmit notification, process order, release order*}

These examples cover different types of object-sensitive actions. Example 1 illustrates a set of single-object actions. Example 2—a set of multi-object actions performed on objects *order* and *agreement*. Finally, Example 3 shows that there are multi-object action sets, where one verb is performed on more than one object, e.g., *transmit agreement* and *transmit notification*. Due to this "split" of actions, the number of patterns describing object-sensitive actions can be greater than the number of patterns for object-neutral actions. Meanwhile, the support value of each individual pattern capturing object-sensitive actions is lower than the support for a pattern for object-neutral actions: the support of one generic pattern is distributed among several more specific patterns. Among the three considered action types, the number of patterns for single-object actions is the lowest. Tables 1 and 2 show that the more specific are the patterns, the bigger is the share of patterns with high confidence.

Table 3. Dependency of behavioral action pattern number for object-neutral actions *transmit*, *process*, and *release* in the SAP Reference Model on $conf_{min}$ and $supp_{min}$

$conf_{min}$ \ $supp_{min}$	2	3	4	5	6	7
0.50	1559	1024	602	310	50	0
0.60	1267	813	602	310	50	0
0.70	959	748	537	310	50	0
0.80	797	586	375	310	50	0
0.90	667	456	245	180	50	0

Table 4. Dependency of behavioral pattern number for a particular object-sensitive action set in the SAP Reference Model on $conf_{min}$ and $supp_{min}$

(a) {*transmit agreement, process order, release order*}

$conf_{min}$ \ $supp_{min}$	2	3	...	8	9
0.50	12	12	...	12	0
0.60	12	12	...	12	0
0.70	12	12	...	12	0
0.80	12	12	...	12	0
0.90	12	12	...	12	0

(b) {*transmit order, process order, release order*}

$conf_{min}$ \ $supp_{min}$	2	3	...	5	6
0.50	12	12	...	12	0
0.60	12	12	...	12	0
0.70	12	12	...	12	0
0.80	12	12	...	12	0
0.90	12	12	...	12	0

Behavioral action patterns describe behavioral relations between actions in large action sets. We illustrate the discussion of behavioral action patterns by the example object-neutral action set {*transmit, process, release*}. Table 3 shows the number of behavioral patterns for the set of object-neutral actions. Table 4 presents the number of object-sensitive action patterns: Table 4(a) illustrates the number of patterns for multi-object action set {*transmit agreement, process order, release order*}, while Table 4(b)—for single-object action set. Note that we consider the patterns for a particular set of object-sensitive actions. Hence, the largest number of patterns is observed for object-neutral actions. Object-sensitive actions result in a lower number of patterns, but without dropping in confidence.

The results obtained through the analysis of the SAP Reference Model can be applied as follows. Consider that a modeler designs a model for a procurement process. The current state of the model is captured in Fig. 2 by the elements colored in black. Given the action patterns captured in Tables 2 and 4, we suggest the user to insert an action *transmit* to be performed on object *agreement* into the model. This suggestion is visualized in Fig. 2 with elements colored in gray. Notice that behavioral action patterns enable us to suggest the user *how* to introduce the new activity in the model.

According to the presented evaluation results, we conclude that in the SAP Reference Model action patterns based on single-object action sets provide the most precise information, have low support, but deliver high confidence.

Fig. 2. A suggestion based on action patterns in Table 4

Object-neutral action patterns are on the opposite side: they provide very generic information, but with high statistical significance. Multi-object patterns are the compromise between these two classes, balancing between the significance and the pattern strength.

5   Related Work

First and foremost, our work relates to various *patterns* proposed for business processes. On the technical level, the workflow pattern initiative has identified patterns for several model aspects, among them the control flow [2] and the data flow [12]. On the conceptual level, Lonchamp proposed a set of collaboration patterns defining abstract building blocks for recurrent situations [13]. Tran et al. introduces a meta-model for process patterns and shows their application in the UML context [14]. Most closely related to our work is the research by Thom et al. [4]. In their work, the authors identify *workflow activity patterns* (WAP) that specify seven different types of micro workflows, e.g., approval or decision. Our action pattern approach builds on the same observation that certain activities often occur jointly to achieve an over-arching goal. In contrast to [4], we do not assume a priori knowledge on which patterns might occur in a process. Instead, object-sensitive action patterns are mined in a collection of process models. Although [15] also advocates the application of association rule learning techniques for WAP, their focus is on mining co-occurrences of these predefined patterns instead of the patterns themselves.

Recently, *intelligent support and recommendations* for process modeling has received much attention. To this end, similar models in a process model repository might be proposed as extensions to the currently modeled process using search techniques [16]. While this approach also builds on a match of actions, business objects, and textual content, we believe that action patterns are more flexible, as they do not require the knowledge about an exact continuation of a process. Consistency between object life cycles and process models is discussed in [17] along with corresponding modeling support. Moreover, modeling support might also be driven by modelers in a collaborative modeling effort [18]. In contrast to our work, this approach builds on suggestions by other modelers. Control flow correctness issues are addressed in [19] where the authors offer continuous verification of process models during modeling. In [20] the authors study how cooperative modeling is supported by fragment-driven modeling approach. However, the derivation of fragments (or action patterns) is not detailed. In order to accelerate business process modeling, structural control flow patterns can be used as suggested in [3]. Still, these suggestions do not consider the business semantics of process models. The change patterns introduced in [21] can also be seen as patterns that allow for intelligent modeling support.

Finally, research on activity labels relates to our work. Textual labels are used for matching and comparing process models [16,22]. Recent works by Becker et al. reuse parsing techniques from computer linguistics to identify the various parts of an activity label [23]. For the experiment of this paper, we have derived the actions manually. Still, the techniques proposed in [7,23] have the potential to automate this step.

6   Conclusion

In this paper, we proposed object-sensitive action patterns as a means for domain-specific modeling support. These patterns are derived from a collection of process models using association rule learning techniques and can be leveraged in order to provide suggestions in the course of modeling. Co-occurrence action patterns hint at missing activities, whereas behavioral action patterns provide information on how an activity should be added to an incomplete model. Taking the relation between verbs and business objects into account, we extended the existing notion of action patterns by multi-object and single-object action patterns. Besides their formal definition, we provide an experimental evaluation of these object-sensitive patterns based on the SAP reference model. It reveals that object-sensitive patterns can be assumed to provide fine-grained modeling support.

As now action patterns have different levels of granularity, the use of synonyms in the activity labels "blurs" the patterns. In the future work, we plan to address the linguistic relations between verbs and business objects, e.g., synonymy and hyponymy. To this end, the application of thesauri like WordNet[1] might prove useful. As single-object action patterns implicitly capture the life cycle of a business object, mining of business object life cycles using action patterns in another direction of the future work. Finally, the mined action patterns call for validation proving their usefulness.

References

1. Rosemann, M., van der Aalst, W.M.P.: A Configurable Reference Modelling Language. IS 32(1), 1–23 (2007)
2. van der Aalst, W.M.P., ter Hofstede, A.H.M., Kiepuszewski, B., Barros, A.P.: Workflow Patterns. DPD 14(1), 5–51 (2003)
3. Gschwind, T., Koehler, J., Wong, J.: Applying Patterns during Business Process Modeling. In: Dumas, M., Reichert, M., Shan, M.-C. (eds.) BPM 2008. LNCS, vol. 5240, pp. 4–19. Springer, Heidelberg (2008)

---

[1] http://wordnet.princeton.edu/

4. Thom, L.H., Reichert, M., Iochpe, C.: Activity Patterns in Process-aware Information Systems: Basic Concepts and Empirical Evidence. IJBPIM 4(2), 93–110 (2009)
5. Smirnov, S., Weidlich, M., Mendling, J., Weske, M.: Action Patterns in Business Process Models. In: Baresi, L., Chi, C.-H., Suzuki, J. (eds.) ICSOC-ServiceWave 2009. LNCS, vol. 5900, pp. 115–129. Springer, Heidelberg (2009)
6. Keller, G., Teufel, T.: SAP(R) R/3 Process Oriented Implementation: Iterative Process Prototyping. Addison-Wesley, Reading (1998)
7. Leopold, H., Smirnov, S., Mendling, J.: Refactoring of Process Model Activity Labels. In: Hopfe, C.J., Rezgui, Y., Métais, E., Preece, A., Li, H. (eds.) NLDB 2010. LNCS, vol. 6177, pp. 268–276. Springer, Heidelberg (2010)
8. Weidlich, M., Mendling, J., Weske, M.: Efficient Consistency Measurement based on Behavioural Profiles of Process Models. IEEE TSE (2010) (to appear)
9. Agrawal, R., Imielinski, T., Swami, A.N.: Mining Association Rules between Sets of Items in Large Databases. In: COMAD 1993, Washington, D.C., pp. 207–216 (1993)
10. Decker, G., Mendling, J.: Instantiation Semantics for Process Models. In: Dumas, M., Reichert, M., Shan, M.-C. (eds.) BPM 2008. LNCS, vol. 5240, pp. 164–179. Springer, Heidelberg (2008)
11. Mendling, J.: Metrics for Process Models: Empirical Foundations of Verification, Error Prediction, and Guidelines for Correctness. LNBIP, vol. 6. Springer, Heidelberg (2008)
12. Russell, N., ter Hofstede, A.H.M., Edmond, D., van der Aalst, W.M.P.: Workflow Data Patterns. Technical Report FIT-TR-2004-01, Queensland University of Technology (2004)
13. Lonchamp, J.: Process Model Patterns for Collaborative Work. In: Telecoop (1998)
14. Tran, H.N., Coulette, B., Dong, B.T.: Broadening the Use of Process Patterns for Modeling Processes. In: SEKE, Knowledge Systems Institute Graduate School, pp. 57–62 (July 2007)
15. Lau, J.M., Iochpe, C., Thom, L., Reichert, M.: Discovery and Analysis of Activity Pattern Cooccurrences in Business Process Models. In: ICEIS 2009, pp. 83–88. Springer, Heidelberg (2009)
16. Hornung, T., Koschmider, A., Lausen, G.: Recommendation Based Process Modeling Support: Method and User Experience. In: Li, Q., Spaccapietra, S., Yu, E., Olivé, A. (eds.) ER 2008. LNCS, vol. 5231, pp. 265–278. Springer, Heidelberg (2008)
17. Küster, J.M., Ryndina, K., Gall, H.: Generation of Business Process Models for Object Life Cycle Compliance. In: Alonso, G., Dadam, P., Rosemann, M. (eds.) BPM 2007. LNCS, vol. 4714, pp. 165–181. Springer, Heidelberg (2007)
18. Koschmider, A., Song, M., Reijers, H.A.: Advanced Social Features in a Recommendation System for Process Modeling. In: Bauer, F.L., Griffiths, M., Hornig, J.J., McKeeman, W.M., Waite, W.M., DeRemer, F.L., Hill, U., Koster, C.H.A., Poole, P.C. (eds.) BIS 2009. LNBIP, vol. 21, pp. 109–120. Springer, Heidelberg (1974)
19. Kühne, S., Kern, H., Gruhn, V., Laue, R.: Business Process Modelling with Continuous Validation. In: MDE4BPM, pp. 37–48 (September 2008)
20. Kim, K.H., Won, J.K., Kim, C.M.: A Fragment-Driven Process Modeling Methodology. In: Gervasi, O., Gavrilova, M.L., Kumar, V., Laganá, A., Lee, H.P., Mun, Y., Taniar, D., Tan, C.J.K. (eds.) ICCSA 2005. LNCS, vol. 3482, pp. 817–826. Springer, Heidelberg (2005)

21. Weber, B., Reichert, M., Rinderle-Ma, S.: Change Patterns and Change Support Features - Enhancing Flexibility in Process-aware Information Systems. DKE 66(3), 438–466 (2008)
22. van Dongen, B., Dijkman, R., Mendling, J.: Measuring Similarity between Business Process Models. In: Bellahsène, Z., Léonard, M. (eds.) CAiSE 2008. LNCS, vol. 5074, pp. 450–464. Springer, Heidelberg (2008)
23. Becker, J., Delfmann, P., Herwig, S., Lis, L., Stein, A.: Towards Increased Comparability of Conceptual Models - Enforcing Naming Conventions through Domain Thesauri and Linguistic Grammars. In: ECIS 2009 (June 2009)

On Reusing Data Mining in Business Processes - A Pattern-Based Approach

Dennis Wegener and Stefan Rüping

Fraunhofer IAIS, Schloss Birlinghoven,
53754 Sankt Augustin, Germany
{dennis.wegener,stefan.rueping}@iais.fraunhofer.de

Abstract. Today's business applications demand high flexibility in processing information and extracting knowledge from data. Thus, data mining becomes more and more an integral part of operating a business.
However, the integration of data mining into business processes still requires a lot of coordination and manual adjustment. This paper aims at
reducing this effort by reusing successful data mining solutions. We describe a novel approach on facilitating the integration based on process
patterns for data mining and demonstrate that these patterns allow for
easy reuse and can significantly speed up the process of integration. We
empirically evaluate our approach in a case study of fraud detection in
the health care domain.

Keywords: Data Mining Patterns, Business Processes, Reuse and Integration, BPM, CRISP.

1 Introduction

Businesses need to be more and more flexible in order to be competitive in today's economy. Two big forces that drive flexibility are data mining, which helps
enterprises to understand their customers, processes, and themselves better, and
service oriented architectures (SOA), which help to be faster in implementing
new business strategies and products. As data mining becomes more and more
an integral part of executing a business, data mining functionality needs to be
integrated into SOA in the context of existing applications [1].

In previous work [2] we presented an initial discussion on how to integrate
data mining into business processes. Here, we focus on how to enable the reuse
of existing solutions that have been proven to be successful. Currently, there
are two approaches of achieving this: Passing through a new CRISP process [3]
while being inspired by existing solutions (e.g. by personal experience or reading
respective documentation and scientific papers), and reuse at implementation
level (e.g. by copy-and-paste of existing code and workflows). In this paper we
argue that there is a need for an approach in between.

The first approach for reuse by following the CRISP process, which describes
the general procedure of performing data mining projects, does not suffice, as this
approach is often too general. E.g. it has been identified that CRISP-DM lacks

M. zur Muehlen and J. Su (Eds.): BPM 2010 Workshops, LNBIP 66, pp. 264–276, 2011.

in the deployment phase [4], in guidance towards implementing particular tasks of data mining methodologies [5], and in the definition of phases important for engineering projects [6]. In addition, we detected that many redundancies and inefficiencies exists when following the CRISP standard data mining process model in parallel to standard BPM approaches [2].

The second approach is to utilize reuse at implementation level. Modern SOA-based Business Process Management (BPM) environments, e.g. based on standards like BPEL [7] and BPMN [8], provide flexible and user friendly environments and tools for designing, deploying and managing business applications. Data mining solutions can be reused in such environments by making use of available data mining workflows and services. However, this approach is often too specific for being reusable efficiently. For example in an analysis of a large set of real-world data mining workflows [9] we found out that the changes of a workflow during the lifetime of a data mining project are made to the same extend at the preprocessing and at the modeling part, which implies that understanding and representing the semantics of the data is a very important step. The changes for the preprocessing part consisted to 50% and for the modelling part to 75% of manual parameter optimizations. The challenge is to reuse such kinds of manual fine-tuning. Also, there are requirements specific to data mining. For instance, the choice of data mining algorithm has impact on the data understanding and the business understanding phase. Thus, data mining is a complex process that requires a lot of manual optimizations and is not always transferable due to the dependency to the data. A copy-and-paste approach, by taking over the data mining part from another business process, will only work if the business process into which the data mining is integrated has exactly the same properties as the original one. What is needed is a way to specify the correct level of abstraction and generalization for enabling reuse.

In this work, we aim at a formal representation of data mining processes to facilitate their reuse in business processes. As visualized in Fig. 1, the approach should support the description of the process at different levels of abstraction between the CRISP model as most general representation and executable workflows and code as most concrete representation. This requires to:

1. support the modeling of the data mining process as a whole, including its unique requirements, according to the CRISP tasks and phases
2. allow for the modeling and specification of tasks at implementation level in order to make use of existing code and services
3. simplify the integration into business processes in the context of modern BPM systems, which requires compatibility to relevant standards and tools.

This work contributes a new process model for the reuse and integration of existing data mining solutions in business processes in the context of modern BPM environments. This includes, based on CRISP, the definition of data mining process patterns, which encode reusable data mining solutions at the appropriate level of generality. They will be defined specific to the data mining problems to

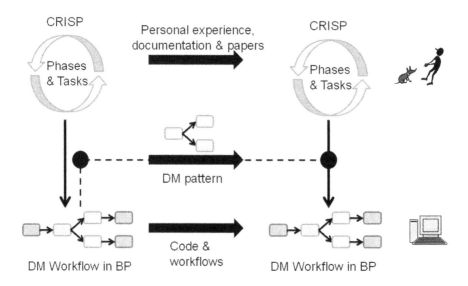

Fig. 1. Different strategies of reusing data mining

be addressed and will be based on a set of underlying data mining services. We will also define a process for applying these data mining patterns to business processes.

The remainder of the paper is as follows: Sec. 2 introduces the field of BPM and data mining and gives an overview over the state-of-the-art and related work. In Sec. 3 we introduce our approach for a new process model for the reuse and integration of data mining into business processes. In Sec. 4 we give a case study on the integration including an example of a data mining process pattern and it's integration. Sec. 5 concludes.

2   State-of-the-Art and Related Work

A business process is a series of steps designed to produce a product or a service which includes all the activities that deliver particular results for a given customer [10]. Business process management (BPM) is a discipline combining software capabilities and business expertise to accelerate business process improvement and to facilitate business innovation. In the context of BPM there exists a variety of standards for process modeling, visualization and execution as well as tools supporting features like pre-deployment validation of processes and the automation of process deployment, hiding the complexity of the distribution middleware. BPEL [7] and BPMN [8] turned out to be one of the de-facto standards for the executable language for specifying interactions with web services resp. the graphical representation of processes. In the following, we will use the BPMN notation for the definition and visualization of process models.

Data mining, often also called knowledge discovery in databases (KDD), is the process of extracting (unknown) patterns from data [11]. There exists a variety of different data mining methods and algorithms [12], which commonly involve the following classes of tasks: Inferring rudimentary rules, statistical modeling, constructing decision trees, constructing rules, mining association rules, linear models, instance-based learning, and clustering. CRISP-DM [3] is a standard process model for data mining that describes the life cycle of data mining projects as iterative process. The CRISP model consists of the following 6 phases:

- Business Understanding - understanding the project objectives and requirements from a business perspective and defining the data mining problem
- Data Understanding - getting to know the data and its quality
- Data Preparation - construct the final dataset from the initial raw data as input for the modeling
- Modeling - various modeling techniques are selected and applied, including the calibration of their specific settings
- Evaluation - assess how well the built model achieves the project objectives
- Deployment - the results of the data mining are delivered to the user.

Typically, the phases from Data Understanding to Evaluation are mainly performed only by the data miner, while the phases Business Understanding and Deployment involve both the data miner and the business user. The latter phases need a lot of knowledge transfer, coordination and manual adjustment.

In our work we refer to data mining as part of the application that is represented by a business process. Data Mining on event log data in order to construct processes (Process Mining) and data mining on business processes in order to improve the business processes as part of the field Business Intelligence are not in the scope of this paper. The question that we want to answer is how can we best reuse data mining as part of a bigger business processes.

In [13] a set of workflow patterns describing the control-flow perspective of workflow systems is defined. Such process patterns have plenty of advantages [14]: BPM processes serve as both the specification and the source code. The modeled processes become the solutions deployed and provide a simple communication tool between end-users, business analysts, developers and the management. Process patterns provide a proven and simple technique to shorten the learning curve and improve productivity and quality of the processes designed as they are simple to understand, learn and apply immediately. Thus, we propose to provide a similar approach for the integration and reuse of data mining - process patterns that represent templates for different data mining problems.

Java Data Mining (JDM) is a standard for developing data mining solutions [1]. JDM provides a web service interface which can be used to set up, integrate and manage data mining processes in the context of BPMN and BPEL based environments. BPEL processes are designed which include calls to the JDM web services. These services interface with the JDM API on top of a Data Mining Engine. However, they do not specify a general concept on how to redesign the business processes in detail and which requirements exist for the modeling of the business process when including data mining.

In [15] a dynamic data mining process system is introduced. The idea is to set up each data mining activity as web service, to model and execute the data mining process in a BPEL environment and to get a PMML compliant model as result. The authors only present a single application as example and do not give a concept on how to model the data mining processes in general.

In [4] a methodology for the implementation of data mining into operational business processes is proposed, consisting of the phases Exploratory Data Mining, Deployment of IT into the Business Process, and Operational Data Mining. However, the authors do not specify detailed concepts for the modeling of the data mining process as part of the business process. In our work, we focus on how to perform the process (re-)design from the modeling point of view and aim at removing complexity for modeling and integration.

In [16] the authors propose a framework for the reuse of scientific workflows, which are also based on reusable patterns that include abstract tasks. However, their work focuses rather on grid-related tasks like copying, job execution and monitoring than on data mining specific tasks.

3   Process Patterns for Integration and Reuse

We aim at reusing existing data mining processes that have proven to be successful, and hence want to develop a formal and concrete definition of the steps that are involved in the data mining process and of the steps that are necessary to reuse it in new business processes. Thus, we focus on the reuse rather than on the data mining problem itself and consider a solution for the data mining problem to be available. In the area of data mining there exist a lot of situations and scenarios where existing solutions are reusable, especially when no research on new algorithms is necessary. These solutions can have different levels of generality. Lots of examples and ready-to-use algorithms are available in toolboxes, which only have to be integrated. However, due to a lack of formal support in practice a reuse and integration of existing solutions is not often or only informally done, which leads to a lot of unnecessary repetitive work. By our approach we want to facilitate the integration and reuse of these data mining solutions.

In the following, we will describe our approach in 3 steps. First, we will show how to modify the CRISP model to focus on the special case of reuse of existing solutions. Second, we will define the concept of data mining patterns. These patterns are created after the initial data mining process ended and include the definition, description and requirements of the data mining process, but are independent of the application scenario. The goal of these data mining patterns is to provide a flexible representation for different levels of generality. Third, we will describe how these patterns are applied for reuse by a meta process. This process will be started if a new application scenario is available and describes the tasks that can only be performed with knowledge on the application scenario.

3.1   Reuse and the CRISP Model

In the following, we will present how the CRISP phases and tasks from [3] differ in the case of executing CRISP from scratch and reusing existing solutions. Fig. 2 visualizes our approach.

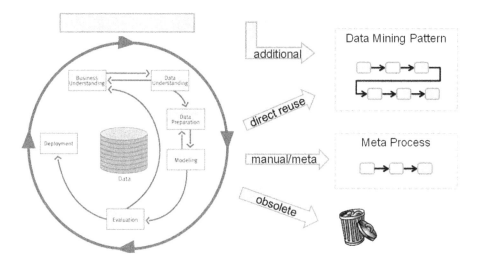

Fig. 2. Mapping CRISP tasks to data mining patterns and a meta-process for reuse

Business understanding phase. The task *Determine Business Objectives* is a general task that is independent of the data mining. We arrange this task at the start of the meta-process, as it provides the information needed for the choice of the pattern. The task *Assess Situation* involves the setup of an inventory of resources, a collection of requirements, assumptions etc. In our scenario, this task does not apply as the important information is already available through the business process. In addition, the data mining goal is already specified by the data mining pattern. Thus, we transform the *Determine Data Mining Goals* task into a task that checks if the data mining goal is still matching and arrange it at the beginning of the data mining pattern. In the deployed executable process, this task will be obsolete. From here, the data mining specific tasks start. In our scenario the *Produce Project Plan* task is outside of the scope, as the project plan consists of following the proposed approach for the integration.

Data understanding phase. The tasks *Collect Initial Data*, *Describe Data* and *Explore Data* are obsolete as we assume the data to be available through the modeled business process. The verification of the data quality is arranged as second task *Verify Data Quality* in the pattern. In the deployed executable process, this task will be obsolete as well.

Data Preparation phase. The *Select Data* task is a preprocessing task of the pattern. E.g., a *Collect Data* task and a *Collect Label* task (in case of supervised learning methods) or a *Data Available* gateway could be part of the BPMN pool that contains the tasks that have to be connected to the tasks of the business process. The further tasks *Clean Data, Construct Data, Integrate Data* and *Format Data* are also preprocessing task of the pattern.

Modeling phase. The tasks *Select Modeling Technique* and *Generate Test Design* do not apply, as this information is already contained in the pattern. The

Build Model task represents the training of the data mining model and specifies the modeling technique and is part of the pattern. The *Assess Model* task is split into the task *Testing* and the gateway *Model Finalized* inside the pattern. They specify the test design and the decision on when to deploy a model.

Evaluation phase. The task *Evaluate Results* involves a matching with the business objectives. Thus, we arrange this task at the meta-process. With this task, the data mining specific part ends. In contrast to CRISP, the evaluation takes place after the deployment of the process. The task *Review Process* is implicit contained in loops of the meta-process (changing the specification of tasks of a data mining pattern or choosing another pattern). The task *Determine Next Steps* does not apply as the next steps are defined by the meta-process.

Deployment phase. The planning of the deployment by the task *Plan Deployment* does not apply, as the way how to deploy the model and the process as a whole are defined by the pattern approach. The deployment itself is two-fold. On the one hand, there is the deployment of the data mining pattern into the business process. This task is arranged in the meta-process. On the other hand, there is the deployment of the data mining model, which is part of the data mining pattern. The task *Plan Monitoring and Maintenance* does not apply as well, as monitoring and maintenance is a general part of the BPM context. The tasks *Produce Final Report* and *Review Project* are outside of the scope, as we are not interested in such a kind of deployment and as a review of the steps of the overall process are considered to be already part of the BPM solution.

Additional Tasks. In addition to the tasks of the CRISP phases there are additional tasks necessary for the deployment, management and usage of the data mining model. Typically, business processes are not designed for ad-hoc but for long term usage. Thus, the data mining has to be able to adapt to changes in the data during time, e.g. by re-building and deploying the data mining model periodically. For re-building a model, a *Re-build model* gateway activity is arranged before the tasks for preprocessing and building the model. The task *DeployModel* is performed after the model evaluation task. In addition, a *Model apply* task for applying the model to new datasets and related additional preprocessing task are part of the data mining pattern.

3.2   Data Mining Patterns

In the following, we will present our approach for the specification of data mining patterns at different levels of generality. The CRISP-DM methodology includes a four-level breakdown, which describes the instantiation of the CRISP process model in order to get a CRISP process. The 6 CRISP **phases** consist of several **generic tasks** which cover all possible data mining applications. Out of these tasks **specialized tasks** are described which specify specific actions for a certain situation. Finally, the **process instances** represent a record of actions and decisions of an actual data mining engagement. This top-down approach is a manual process which is not automated. In our approach, the CRISP breakdown is partially pre-defined by the process patterns, where some of the tasks are already defined on a detailed level.

The data mining tasks, including requirements and preconditions, can be modeled in a uniform way in the context of BPM by representing each task as a task in the business process. However, we need to take into account that reuse may in some cases only be possible at a general or conceptual level. Our approach needs to include the description of the general CRISP model, of executable workflows, and of abstractions in-between. Thus, we model the tasks different levels of granularity, resulting in the following hierarchy of tasks: **conceptual** (manual tasks, only a textual description is available), **configurable** (semi-automatic tasks, code is available but parameters need to be specified), and **executable** (automatic tasks, code and parameters are specified).

Process patterns are only valid for process execution if they are specified to the executable level. Some general CRISP tasks, e.g. *Determine Business Objectives*, cannot be specified as technical step. Thus, the executable specification for such tasks would be a check task or empty/obsolete task. In a meta-process, which describes how to apply a given pattern to a business process, these tasks are specified (with different choices) according to the levels of the hierarchy. E.g., a *Clean Data* task could be specified as human task, as code that deletes records with missing values or as separate DM process for the prediction of missing values. Details on the meta-process will be given later in Section 3.3.

Definition. We consider the phases and tasks of the modified CRISP process from 3.1, including additional tasks and information that are necessary for an execution of such a process, as the most general data mining pattern. Every concretion of this process for an application according to the presented hierarchy is also a data mining pattern.

The idea is to be able to describe all data mining processes, while the description is as detailed as adequate for the given scenario. A data mining pattern only contains tasks that can be specified without having to know the business process in order to keep the feature of reusability. Obviously, the practical relevance of a pattern depends on its generality. An example of a data mining pattern will be given later in Sec. 4.

3.3   The Meta-process

The process of applying a pattern for the integration of data mining into a given business process can be modeled as process in the BPM context. In our approach, this meta-process describes the steps needed to use a pattern for a given business process. Fig. 3 visualizes the meta-process and its steps. The first task is to define the business objectives of the application. After that, a data mining pattern is selected that matches with these business objectives. Then, the tasks of the selected pattern are specified to the executable level according to the hierarchy of our approach proposed or a given specification is chosen. If it is observed that the pattern cannot be specified as executable, the meta-process

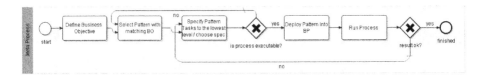

Fig. 3. The meta-process for applying a process pattern to a given business process

steps back to the task of choosing a new pattern. If the pattern is executable, it is deployed into the business process. After that, the integrated process is executed. If the result is satisfying, the meta-process is finished. If it is not satisfying, the meta-process steps back to the task of finding a new specification.

4   Case Study

In [17] a solution for fraud detection based on similarity learning [18] is presented. We choose this scenario as case study, as it already includes well specified business processes as well as a data mining solution that that allows for reuse. The approach for fraud detection from [18] is based on learning similarity measures for data records and is transferable for a generic class of fraud opportunities. The application scenario is based on detecting procurement fraud, e.g. an employee of a company placing an order to another company which is owned by himself. This is done by computing a similarity between employees and company owners based on several features such as name, address or bank accounts. We do not go into more details of the data mining method, as this is not important for understanding our pattern approach. Basically what is needed to apply this data mining solution to a problem is to first check if the problem is a procurement fraud problem, second to specify which features to be used for the similarity, and third to connect the inputs and outputs of the data mining process. For all other steps ready-to-use code is already available.

Fig. 4 shows an example of a pattern for this approach to procurement fraud detection. In the top pool *Requirements* the pre-requirements for applying this pattern are modeled. This includes checking the data mining goal (procurement fraud detection) and the data format as well as sending data, receiving the result and sending labeled data. The other pools *Data Mining Classification*, *Data Mining Model Building* and *Data Mining* contain the (partially already specified executable) tasks of the data mining process and the respective services. It can be seen that the process is a data mining pattern according to our definition from Sec. 3, which contains tasks of all 3 levels of the task hierarchy. E.g., the task *Check DM goal is supervised Fraud Detection* is a specialized task of *Check DM goal*. It is a conceptual task which describes in textual form that the goal of the integration of the data mining solution has to be supervised fraud detection in order to match with the pattern. During the integration, the user manually inspects this task and specializes it to the empty task. The task *Check if each attribute is based on a known data type* represents the requirement for a specific data format. The data mining solution is based on combining different similarity

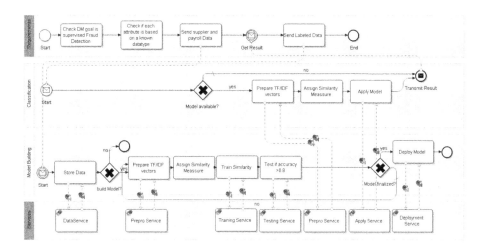

Fig. 4. An example of a data mining pattern

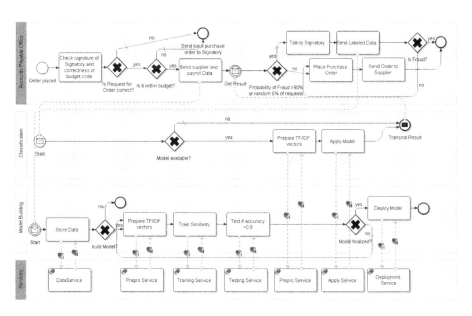

Fig. 5. An example of an integrated process

measures for attributes of different data types. For each of those types, a measure has to exist. The data is sent to the data mining part of the process via the task *Send supplier and payroll data* and the labels via *Send labeled Data*. The assignment of the similarity measures is performed at the task *Assign Similarity Measure*. It is a configurable specialization of the task *Train Model* that can be further specialized by the user, e.g. by a configuration file. All executable tasks, e.g. the task *Train Similarity*, are connected to an underlying service.

In [17] (Section 6) a set of business processes from the health care domain is presented which contains candidates for the integration of the fraud detection solution. We will focus on the business process *Purchase Order Inspection* from the RBH scenario, which consists of a random checking of several rules for a request for an order followed by the decision of placing or not placing this order. Fig. 5 shows how the presented data mining pattern is integrated into the business process. Compared to the pattern, the task *Check DM goal* disappeared because the user took the decision that the data mining goal indeed matched and hence specialized it to an empty task. The tasks for sending data and receiving the results are connected with the tasks of the business process. The tasks *Check if each attribute is based on a known data type* and *Assign Similarity Measure* disappeared as well, as the user manually specified the checking and the assignment of the similarities according to his knowledge of the data (e.g. by a parameter file). During the integration, the pool *Requirements* and its tasks disappeared at all due to the specification and deployment tasks of the meta-process.

By this somewhat simplified example we have shown how to apply a data mining pattern to a business process in order to get an integrated process and how manual steps can be specified to executable tasks.

5   Conclusion and Future Work

This paper is a first step towards support for an automation of a reuse of successful data mining processes. We have presented a new process model for easy reuse and integration of data mining in different business processes. Our approach is based on CRISP and includes the definition of data mining patterns, a definition of a hierarchy of tasks to guide the specialization of abstract patterns to concrete processes, and a meta-process for applying patterns to business processes. These data mining patterns allow for representing the reusable parts of a data mining process at different levels of generalization and provide a simple formal description for the reuse and integration of data mining. We evaluated our approach in a fraud detection case study in the health care domain.

Our approach is focused on reusable cases for data mining problems. Thus, in contrast to the more general CRISP model, the data mining patterns are not applicable in all cases, as several parts of the process are already pre-defined in the pattern. However, by the pre-definition a lot of unnecessary repetitive work is avoided. E.g., if data mining is to be integrated in the context of a very similar problem, the pattern can be just used again instead of applying the full CRISP-DM process twice. CRISP is iterative and does not describe the reuse of existing solutions at all. In our approach, we describe the reusable part by data mining patterns. The iterations are modeled in an outside meta-process.

Details on the definition, architecture and implementation of the underlying services remain to future work. Furthermore, we aim at a formalization that allows for tool support for the design and specification of high-level requirements as well as for the parameterization. In addition, the following questions need to be addressed in the future: How to model the data within the process? Key challenges are to define the data-related interfaces between the business processes and the data mining patterns as well as to specify how to get the data out of the business process. Is the hierarchy adequate or is a more detailed level needed? E.g., more structure could be provided by the use of an ontology [19]. What is a good pattern, how can the quality of a pattern be determined and how to select a pattern from a pattern database?

References

1. Hornick, M.F., Marcadé, E., Venkayala, S.: Java Data Mining: Strategy, Standard, and Practice. Morgan Kaufmann, San Francisco (2006)
2. Wegener, D., Rüping, S.: On Integrating Data Mining into Business Processes. In: Abramowicz, W., Tolksdorf, R. (eds.) BIS 2010. LNBIP, vol. 47, pp. 183–194. Springer, Heidelberg (2010)
3. Shearer, C.: The CRISP-DM model: the new blueprint for data mining. Journal of Data Warehousing 5(4), 13–22 (2000)
4. Rupnik, R., Jaklič, J.: The Deployment of Data Mining into Operational Business Processes. In: Ponce, J., Karahoca, A. (eds.) Data Mining and Knowledge Discovery in Real Life Applications, I-Tech, Vienna, Austria (2009)
5. Sharma, S., Osei-Bryson, K.: Framework for formal implementation of the business understanding phase of data mining projects. Expert Systems with Applications 36(2) (2009)
6. Marbán, O., Segovia, J., Menasalvas, E., Fernández-Baizán, C.: Toward data mining engineering: A software engineering approach. Information Systems 34(1) (2009)
7. Jordan, D., Evdemon, J.: Web Services Business Process Execution Language Version 2.0. Technical report, OASIS Standard (2007)
8. White, S.A., Miers, D.: BPMN Modeling and Reference Guide Understanding and Using BPMN. Future Strategies Inc., Lighthouse Pt (2008)
9. Bremer, P.: Erstellung einer Datenbasis von Workflowreihen aus realen Anwendungen, Diploma Thesis, University of Bonn (2010) (in german)
10. White, S.: Process Modeling Notations and Workflow Patterns. In: Fischer, L. (ed.) The Workflow Handbook 2004. Future Strategies Inc., Lighthouse Point (2004)
11. Fayyad, U., Piatetsky-Shapiro, G., Smyth, P.: From Data Mining to Knowledge Discovery in Databases. AI Magazine 17, 37–54 (1996)
12. Witten, I.H., Frank, E.: Data Mining: Practical machine learning tools and techniques, 2nd edn. Morgan Kaufmann, San Francisco (2005)
13. Russell, N., ter Hofstede, A.H.M., van der Aalst, A.H.M., Mulyar, N.: Workflow Control-Flow Patterns: A Revised View. BPM Center Report BPM-06-22, BPM-center.org (2006)
14. Atwood, D.: BPM Process Patterns: Repeatable Design for BPM Process Models. BPTrends (May 2006)
15. Tsai, C., Tsai, M.: A Dynamic Web Service based Data Mining Process System. In: Proc. of the Fifth International Conference on Computer and Information Technology CIT, pp. 1033–1039. IEEE Computer Society, Washington (2005)
16. Altintas, I., Birnbaum, A., Baldridge, K., Sudholt, W., Miller, M.A., Amoreira, C., Potier, Y., Ludscher, B.: A Framework for the Design and Reuse of Grid Workflows. In: Herrero, P., S. Pérez, M., Robles, V. (eds.) SAG 2004. LNCS, vol. 3458, pp. 120–133. Springer, Heidelberg (2005)

17. iWebCare Project Deliverable D01 – Business process model of e-gov fraud detection processes in the health care domain (2006), `http://iwebcare.iisa-innov.com/documents/D1-BusinessProcessModelingv4.3.zip`
18. Rüping, S., Punko, N., Günter, B., Grosskreutz, H.: Procurement Fraud Discovery using Similarity Measure Learning. Transactions on Case-based Reasoning 1(1), 37–46 (2008)
19. Hilario, M., Kalousis, A., Nguyen, P., Woznica, A.: A Data Mining Ontology for Algorithm Selection and Meta-Learning. In: Proc. of the ECML/PKDD 2009 Workshop on Third Generation Data Mining: Towards Service-oriented Knowledge Discovery (SoKD 2009), Bled, Slovenia, pp. 76–87 (2009)

Configuration of Multi-perspectives Variants

Stephanie Meerkamm

Chair for Applied Computer Science, University of Bayreuth,
Universitätsstr. 30, 95447 Bayreuth, Germany
stephanie.meerkamm@uni-bayreuth.de

Abstract. In order to compete in effectively nowadays an organization has to offer a variety of process to fulfill the individual requirements of the different customers. The management of the process variability is an important aspect not only during execution, but already during modeling. One common way to deal with this is configuration. This paper presents a generic concept of process configuration which does not solely focus on the functional aspect, but also considers others such as, for example, the organizational, operational and data oriented aspects. Furthermore, different levels of abstraction are introduced to further structure the configuration process. At modeling time it is differentiated between process families (a set of variants) and individual variants themselves; concerned with modeling and execution time between variants and alternatives.

Keywords: alternatives, process variants, process family, process configuration, multi perspectives.

1 Motivation

"You can have any colour of car that you want as long as it is black". Henry Ford's statement in 1914 is no longer applicable. Today, there are countless variations to be seen on the streets. But not only the products itself vary; the underlying development and production processes also vary [1-4]. This, however, seems to be a domain independent issue. Process variants do not only exist in the engineering domain [4-6]. According to the experience of our chair they are also to be found in the medical and administrative domains.

Variants are defined as artifacts with a similar form or function and which have a large part in common with similar items or groups [7]. They differ significantly from the basic artifact in order to suit specific requirements [1-3]. Transferring this to the context of process means that there are variations in the process steps or in the actor of the process. Variants are defined without regard to the time i.e. they exist in parallel.

From the foregoing it follows that a user can easily be overwhelmed with the variety and the attending complexity of a process [8]. This holds good not only for the execution of a process, e.g. due to the different demands of a company's individual customers, it likewise holds true for modeling where the entire process and all of its variants are defined and documented. Fig. 1 illustrates a process model including four process steps (PID0 - PID3), one decider, documents (data), roles. Four decision

M. zur Muehlen and J. Su (Eds.): BPM 2010 Workshops, LNBIP 66, pp. 277–288, 2011.
© Springer-Verlag Berlin Heidelberg 2011

points are modeled affecting the organizational (❶,❹), functional (❷) and data oriented aspects (❸ a and b). Dependencies between the decisions are not shown. How many single process variants could be extracted from this?

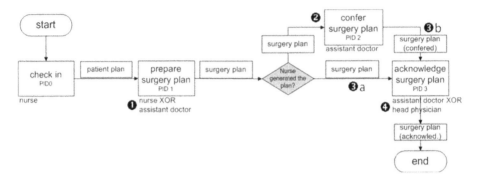

Fig. 1. Integrated process model with possible decision points

It can be seen that already a small process can have several decision points affecting the different perspectives that characterize a process in a particular domain. An example which variant can be extracted from our initial example above can be seen in Fig. 2. Since (integrated) process models are complex and because the stakeholders cannot be modeling experts themselves the process must be made to give them access to the information that they require [9-11], which is, in this case, an individual process variant.

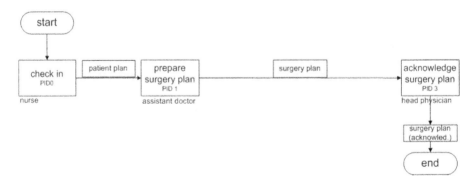

Fig. 2. Process variant derived from Fig 1

One common way to deal with variability management is configuration [1, 3, 8, 12-14]. Configuration is a special type of design activity. It aims at designing an artifact (here the processes) assembled from a set of predefined components (here the different aspects) that can only be connected together in a certain way [15].

As basic paradigm a configurable and generic process model is useful, or rather necessary. It is an integrated representation of multiple variants in one model in a given domain. According to the requirements of the customer each variant of the configurable process model is specified as an individual combination of the pre-designed components. With this, the configurable process model provides a basis for enabling the reuse of process models or separate elements [3, 16-18]. Such a model based approach is compatible with the requirement to structure the configurable objects, viz. processes, for the purpose of reuse and/ or configuration [8].

The benefit derived from configuration and the associated reuse can be seen in time and cost reduction. The efforts involved in the creation of new process elements or processes themselves can be reduced as can the complexity of the work. The quality of the final output increases because a reused part is a part which has already been tried and tested in a manner compliant with best practice [16, 19, 20].

This paper seeks to give an overview of our concept of a process configurator for modeling time. To achieve this we developed a generic and configurable process model (data model) based on a tree structure. In order to configure the model we fabricated a configuration process. The advantages of our approach are two-fold: Firstly, we not only focus on the functional aspect, but also others such as, for example, the organizational, operational and data oriented aspects - only then can the output of the configuration be a comprehensive process model [21-23]. Secondly, we differentiate between different levels of abstraction. At modeling time we differentiate between process families (a set of variants) and variants themselves; with regard to modeling and execution time we differentiate between variation points (at modeling time) and alternatives (at execution time). The idea is to involve different types of domain experts in the configuration process and finally to reduce the number of decision the user has to make during modeling and/ or execution.

The paper is structured as follows: Section 2 gives an overview about existing variability management approaches in the context of process management. In Section 3 first the requirements are analyzed followed by the presentation of the concept of the process configurator. Section 4 goes into detail regarding the data model, while Section 5 explains the configuration process. Section 6 concludes the paper.

2 Process Variant Management

Process variant management has a high relevance in theory and in practice and has been widely studied in different research projects. In this Section we want to give a short overview (we make no claim to be complete) about existing (single model) approaches, including a critical assessment from our own point of view.

By means of configurable event process chains (*C-EPCs*) [3, 24, 25] a single model specifying a whole processes family can be generated. The resulting model, called reference model, can be customized to meet specific needs. For this EPC functions and decision nodes are annotated to indicate whether they are mandatory or optional; the definition of constraints is also possible. The approach also includes other perspectives (data, resources etc.). As C-EPCs are rather difficult to understand, especially for the end-user with a non-technical background, the configuration can be done through questionnaires guiding the user. Although hierarchical decomposition of the processes is not possible and variability regarding roles and objects, which are associated with the tasks, are captured only at the meta model level, it is a very comprehensive approach.

Reijers et al. [11] present an approach by means of which multiple processes or process models (e.g. process variants) are aggregate into a single process model using *aggregated EPC* (aEPC). By means of an algorithm a particular process model can be extracted from the aggregated process model. For this purpose functions and events are annotated with labels, which are used to identify those process elements relevant for extracting the particular process model. This approach focuses only on the functional aspect of the processes. In addition, during configuration there is no interaction with the user of the final process model; the pre-defined algorithm, which comprises the relevant alternatives, is simply applied to the model deciding all alternatives in "one step".

The *Provop* approach [26, 27] is likewise based on a single model collecting all process variants. It applies well-defined change operations (modify, delete, insert) at so called "adjustment points" which are explicitly identified in the basic process model. As a result of configurable attributes which comprise non-functional aspects, it constitutes a very comprehensive approach. It is possible to move and add process elements during configuration, though it is limited to non-composite processes. Nevertheless, the change operations are defined as separate objects in relation to the process model. The objects have to be connected to the model by additional modeling constructs (the "adjustment points"). In doing so the variability is made explicit but outside of the model, which enhance the complexity of the approach.

Each of these approaches optimizes the single model approach on one or more special aspects. None of these approaches, unlike our own, suggest methods which satisfy our main requirements: The support of multi- perspectives and the different abstraction levels. In the following Sections we shall attempt to identify the requirements for the process configurator and report the developed concept.

3   Concept of the Process Configurator

In order to apply the concept of configuration to the process domain, the requirements must be analyzed. We identified the following requirements and classified them according to *basic principal*, *functionality*, *architecture* and *user interaction*.

Basic principal:
- As the intended use already implies the configurator has to be *process oriented*. The characteristics of the process have to be considered, which is strongly related to the subsequent requirement
- In order to comprehensively manage the process variability not only the functional aspect must be considered, but all the other relevant aspect, e.g. data, roles or systems (*multi aspect-oriented*)
- The configuration has to be *domain independent*; nevertheless it has to be flexible for the adaption of domain specific issues

Functionality:
- It should be an *interactive* configuration process involving different types of domain experts

- The configuration process should be *structured*, viz. classified into different abstraction levels in terms of the definition of variants
- The *validation* of the configuration is necessary to guarantee the correctness and completeness of the configuration

Architecture:

- In order to be able to adapt the configurator to meet special requirements or to integrate applications a *modular architecture* is useful
- A knowledge base (*data model*), which captures the variants, is necessary
- A *configuration component* is necessary
- For interaction a *visualization component* is necessary

User interaction

- The *variation points* have to be displayed
- The *aspect-oriented process elements* have to be displayed
- The user must have the *possibility to select* the presented process elements
- The *consequences* of a decision and the *final result* have to be displayed

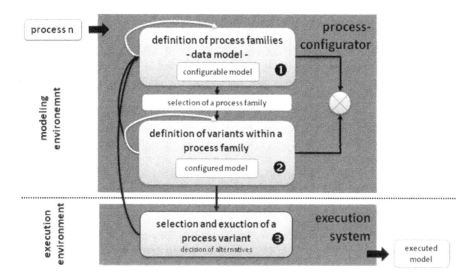

Fig. 3. Concept of the process configurator

Fig. 1 gives an overview of the resulting concept of the process configurator including an intersection to the execution environment: It starts from the top with the specification of a data model which defines the process families (❶). In ❷ a process family is configured resulting in the definition of process variants. Next a process variant is selected and executed in the appropriate system❸. While the execution time is not the focus of this paper, the specification of the data model and the configuration process, the most important components of the configuration at modeling time, are explained in detail. The focus of this work is the implementation of the multi-perspectives of the process and the differentiation between variants (modeling time) and alternatives (execution time).

4   Data Model – The Process Family Model

The data model is the knowledge base of the process configurator. In this Section we analyze the requirements in 4.1 and present the resulting data model in 4.2.

4.1   Requirements Concerning the Data Model

For our approach the initial data model should incorporate all possible process variants that can be selected during configuration. Such a so called *single model* [11, 25, 27] is in line with the notion of reference models which is interpreted as a repository of recommended practices for a certain domain [11, 25, 28].

The model has to describe the functionality and structure of the configurable object (here the process) since a *data structure* is essential for design reuse and configuration [16, 19, 25]. Data without structure remains a mass of vague elements whose significance and relationships are difficult to define, understand and to process. Besides, it offers a high degree of transparency.

One of our main requirements is the implementation of the *different aspects* by which a process can be described (e.g. functional, organizational, operational...). Only if all of the relevant aspects are considered a comprehensive process model can be generated. Nevertheless, it is not enough to list all possible process elements. *Dependencies* between the alternatives have to be presentable.

Further requirements on which the data model is based are *configurability, comprehensiveness, compactness* and *usability* or rather *simplicity*.

The model should capture the potential configuration alternatives in a *language-independent* manner. The aim is that every process model regardless of whether modeled with (e.g. BPMN, EPC) should be transferable into this data model.

The requirements dictate the necessity of a visual approach for the data model consisting of a graphical notation of a part-whole-relationship, and a *tree* based on generalization hierarchies. Trees are extremely expressive means of representing configurable objects. For a logical representation of a structure including the presentation of a high number of variants trees are commonly used because of the high level of abstraction, compactness and clarity that they provide. Our approach is inspired by works such as [6], [29] or [30] in which trees are used to describe configurable products and/or services. Our goal is to transfer the concept to the domain of process configuration.

4.2   Data model Content and Structure

As the generation of a process model which integrates all of the processes of an organization would result in complication and complexity, the initial model should "only" comprise one process family. A process family is defined as a set of process variants of the defined domain [16, 31], e.g., in the medical domain, all non conservative procedures or the process model in Fig. 1. It captures the places of the possible decision

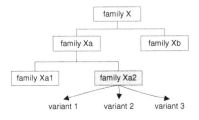

Fig. 4. Data model structure

together with the related possible choices and consequences. With this the model serves the concept of variability which empowers constructive reuse and facilitates the derivation of model variants [20]. A family can be decomposed into a hierarchical structure (see Fig. 4). From the lowest level of the resulting tree process variants as it can be seen in Fig. 2, are derived. This is explained in the next Section of this paper.

4.3 Data Model Elements

The basic modeling elements of the process tree are nodes and leaves with a perspective oriented related semantic. We use the process example from Section 1 in Fig. 1 to illustrate our idea.

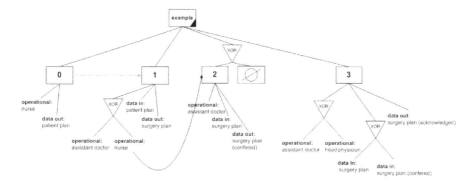

Fig. 5. Example of a data model based on the example in Fig. 1

Processes are symbolized as nodes. In the case of *elementary processes* they are not further decomposable process elements (see Fig. 5, 0-3). *Composite processes* demonstrate that several processes are composed into a higher level. This composition can be done repeatedly resulting in several hierarchical levels of the tree. The root of the tree always has to be a composite process, as it can be seen in Fig. 5. We further define a control flow between the processes. By default the reading direction is from the left to the right side. For complex processes an explicit control flow is introduced, which is demonstrated by the grey dashed arrow between process step 0 and 1.

Disjunctions (OR) and *exclusive disjunctions (XOR)*, modeled as node, aggregate several process elements. They represent decision points concerning the functional aspect of the process model. In order to distinguish between optional and mandatory disjunctions an *Empty Element* is introduced, illustrated by the crossed circle within a process. *Conjunctions (AND)* symbolize the parallel execution of the processes.

This concept leads to the functional, or rather process oriented, structure of our configuration concept - which is a common method to handle the complexity of a configurable object [8, 15, 25].

In order to map further aspects into the data model, the elementary processes are connected with *aspect oriented nodes*. The most common *aspects* are the organizational, operational and data oriented aspects [14, 21, 32]. These are exemplified in Fig. 5. For each aspect the relevant types are defined, e.g. nurse as operational aspect for step 0. They are attached in form of leaves. AND, OR and XOR illustrated logical conjunctions and disjunctions in terms of the types. The disjunctions represent decision points concerning the different aspects. Besides, in- and output data are distinguished; an explicit data flow could be defined illustrated by an arrow from the output data element of the producing process step to the input data element of the subsequent one.

In order to restrict the domain of possible variants and to ensure that the configured process finally realizes its function *implications* are introduced. They specify dependencies between and within the different process elements and capture the consequences of an alternative. E.g. process step 1 implicates the execution of process step 2 in case the nurse is executing process step 1.

This data model is quite well able fulfill the requirements from 4.1. It captures the configurable aspects (decision points) of the processes together with related choices and consequences which empowers re-use and the derivation of variants. All this is possible in a (modeling) language independent manner using a graphical notation of graphs. The model, however, is not without limitations. Existing process models have to be transferred to the tree. This can be done by an information system expert with modeling expertise. It is, however, recommended that the transformation is automated, as a manual execution of this task is both time-consuming and error-prone; then the validation of the correctness of the transformation program would be sufficient, which his much more efficient. The validation of the initially modeled tree itself is, of course, necessary as well. In the following we would like to present the configuration process, which is based on the data model presented in Fig. 4.

5   Definition of Process Variants – Configuration

The main task of configuration is to resolve open alternatives. This Section gives an overview of the configuration process in general in 5.1, and goes into detail in 5.2.

5.1   Overview about the Configuration Process

In the following we present the different steps of the configuration process, which was already introduced, in brief, in Fig. 1.

Definition of process families❶: The specification of the data model in form of a process family is the starting point of the configuration process. The output of this step is a tree as described in Section 4 (an example of a family can be seen in Fig. 1). It contains decision points with regard to the different aspects a process is characterized by. The step is repeated several times, until all families are defined.

Definition of a concrete process variant❷: A concrete variant, based on a process family, has to be configured for the final execution. The decision points which are constitutive for a variant are selected as, so called, *variation points*; these *vXOR*s and *vOR*s respectively clearly have to be separated from a normal XOR and OR as presented in 4.3. XOR and OR is part of the behavioral aspect of the process model. Therefore, after the configuration, the process model still contains decision points, called alternatives, as they cannot be decided until execution. A set of *variation points* is responsible for the definition of a variant and has to be decided before execution. Thus, we can differentiate between variation points (at modeling time) and alternatives (at execution time). This step is done until all required, or rather possible, variants are defined.

Execution of a process variant❸: At this point, a selected variant is transferred into the execution environment. The *alternatives* are dissolved according to the actual circumstances. However, this is beyond the scope of this paper.

We further extend the whole procedure with loops back to the initial data model or the precedent step, as it captures knowledge in the form of current best practice and completes our process by guaranteeing quality based on continuous improvement.

5.2 Detailed Configuration Process

We now want to go into greater detail regarding the configuration task❷. It follows the following procedure: *selection* of the variation points (vXOR, vOR) from the configurable model, *configuration and validation* and the final *extraction* of the configured model. We illustrate our concept using the example from Fig. 5.

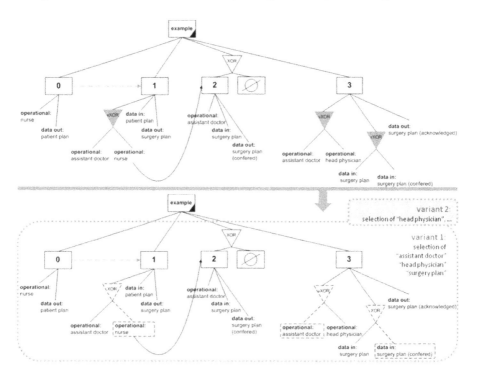

Fig. 6. Configuration process with the definition and configuration of *variation points*

Selection

(1) Starting with the initial family process model (see Fig. 5), first the *variation points* have to be selected. In the example (Fig. 6) three exclusive disjunctions are tagged as (colored) *variation points vXOR*. The unselected disjunctions and non configurable process elements are taken over into the resulting process model per default.

(2) (Optional) In a case where more than one variation point is defined, the sequence in which the variation points have to be dealt in the following can also be defined. For the time being, however, the tree is processed according to the control flow in the following.

Configuration and validation

(3) In this step the *variation points* have to be decided to derive the appropriate variant. In our example this is "assistant doctor" and "head physician" for the operational aspect, "surgery plan" for the data aspect.

(4) The decisions have to be validated according to the configurable model and its constraints. It has to be pointed out that correctness of the configuration depends on the correctness and completeness of the initial configuration model [17]. In case of a positive result the procedure continues with the extraction; otherwise the data model has to be revised.

Extraction

(5) The procedure prunes nodes and leaves, which are no longer part of the model. They are highlighted as dashed lines in Fig.6

(6) It is necessary to check that the actual connector has only one incoming and one outgoing arc. In this case it is no longer part of the model.

(7) The predecessor and successor nodes from the said connector are directly connected, the connector itself is removed. As it would be time-consuming and error prone to manually remove the irrelevant elements of the tree, restore the logic flows between them and regenerating a tree, an automatic solution is preferable.

At the time when all variation points are processed (see resulting tree corresponds to the process model in Fig. 2) the configured model is transferred into the execution system. Following this procedure the end-user has to decide only a limited number of decision points viz. alternatives (in this example only one). Decisions, which are irrelevant during execution, or which the end-user is not able to decide, are already solved by defining and configuring the variants points at modeling time. This facilitates the management of the processes and reduces the complexity.

6 Conclusion

This paper introduces the concept of a process configurator which focuses *not only the functional aspect but likewise other process relevant aspects*. This is facilitated by use of a tree as data model which has a perspectives oriented structure. As a configurable process model this tree provides a basis for enabling the reuse of process models and/ or the elements. The second contribution of this paper is the differentiation between variants and alternatives. *Alternatives* are choices which are relevant at execution time; *variation points* are relevant at modeling time and cause the generation of separate process models, one for each variant. This differentiation facilitates the management of all the decisions which have to be made until the process is finally executed.

Further research involves the comparison of variants in order to give the user more guidance regarding the selection of the appropriate variant. We just started with an implementation of the approach, but this not yet presentable; same as the results of the empirical evaluation with our industrial partners.

References

1. Gottschalk, F., Aalst, W.M.P., Jansen-Vuller, M.H., LaRosa, M.: Configurable Workflow Models. International Journal of Cooperative Information Systems (2007)
2. Hallerbach, A., Bauer, T., Reichert, M.: Issues in Modeling Process Variants with Provop. In: 4th International Workshop on Business Process Design (BPD 2008), Milan, Italy (2008)
3. LaRosa, M.: Managing variability in process-aware information systems. In: Faculty of Science and Technology. Queensland University of Technology, Brisbane (2008)
4. VDA: Recommendation 4965 T1. Engineering Change Management (ECM) - Part 1: Engineering Change Request (ECR) Version 1.1 (2005)
5. Kipp, T., Krause, D.: Design for variety - efficient support for design engineers. In: 10th International Design Conference - Design 2008, Dubrovnik, pp. 425–432 (2008)
6. Rosemann, B., Meerkamm, H., Trautner, S., Feldmann, K.: Design for Recycling, Recycling Data Management and Optimal End-of-Life Planning based on Recycling Graphs. In: International Conference on Engineering Design, ICED 1999, Munich (1999)
7. DIN: Begriffe für Stücklisten und das Stücklistenwesen (DIN 199-2) (2002)
8. Riitahuhta, A.: Views and Experiences of Configuration Management. In: Riitahuhta, A., Pulkinen, A. (eds.) Design for Configuration. Springer, Berlin (2001)
9. Hammer, M., Champy, J.: Reengineering the Cooperation: A Manifesto for Business Revolution. Nicholas Brealy Publishing, London (1993)
10. Becker, J., Rosemann, M., von Uthmann, C.: Guidelines of business process modeling. In: van der Aalst, W.M.P., Desel, J., Oberweis, A. (eds.) BPM 2000. LNCS, vol. 1806, pp. 30–49. Springer, Heidelberg (2000)
11. Reijers, H.A., Mans, R.S., Toorn, R.A.: Improved model management with aggregated business models. Data & Knowledge Engineering 68, 221–243 (2009)
12. Hallerbach, A., Bauer, T., Reichert, M.: Managing Process Variants in the Process Life Cycle - Technical Report. University of Twente, Enschede, The Netherlands (2007)
13. Tryggeseth, E., Gulla, B., Conradi, R.: Modelling Systems with Variability using the PROTEUS Configuration Language. In: Estublier, J. (ed.) ICSE-WS 1993/1995 and SCM 1993/1995. LNCS, vol. 1005, pp. 216–240. Springer, Heidelberg (1995)
14. Blecker, T., Abdelkafi, N., Kreuter, G., Friedrich, G.: Product Configuration Systems: State-of-theArt, Conceptualization and Extensions. In: Hamdou, A.B., Gargouri, F., Jmaiel, M. (eds.) Génie logiciel & Intelligence artificielle. Eight Magrehbian Conference on Software Engineering and Artifical Intelligence (MCSEAI 2004), Sousse, Tunesia, pp. 25–36 (2004)
15. Mittal, S., Fraymann, F.: Towards a Generic Framework of Configuration Task. In: Kaufmann, M. (ed.) 11th International Conference Artifical Intelligence, San Francisco, pp. 1395–1401 (1989)
16. Sabin, D., Weigel, R.: Product Configuration Frameworks-A Survey. IEEE Intelligent Systems 13, 42–49 (1997)

17. Tiihonen, J., Soininen, T.: Product Configurators - Information System Support for Configurable Products. Increasing Sales Productivity through the Use of Information Technology during the Sales Visit. A Survey of the European Market. Hewson Consulting Group (1997)
18. Becker, J., Delfmann, P., Dreiling, A., Knackstedt, R., Kuropka, D.: Configurative Process Modeling – Outlining an Approach to increased Business Process Model Usability. In: 15th IRMA International Conference. Gabler, New Orleans (2004)
19. Smith, H.S., Duffy, A.H.B.: Product Structuring for Design Re-use. In: Riitahuhta, A., Pulkinen, A. (eds.) Design for Configuration. Springer, Heidelberg (2001)
20. Recker, J., Mendling, J., van der Aalst, W.M.P., Rosemann, M.: Model-Driven Enterprise Systems Configuration. In: Martinez, F.H., Pohl, K. (eds.) CAiSE 2006. LNCS, vol. 4001, pp. 369–383. Springer, Heidelberg (2006)
21. Curtis, B., Kellner, M.I., Over, J.: Process Modeling. Communications of the ACM 35 (1992)
22. Davenport, T.H.: The Coming Commoditization of Processes. Havard Business Review 83, 100–108 (2005)
23. Bobrik, R., Reichert, M., Bauer, T.: Requirements for visualization of system-spanning business process. In: DEXA, pp. 948–954 (2005)
24. LaRosa, M., Lux, M., Seidel, S., Dumas, M., Hofstede ter, A.: A Questionnaire driven Configuration of References Models. In: Krogstie, J., Opdahl, A.L., Sindre, G. (eds.) CAiSE 2007. Springer, Berlin (2007)
25. Rosemann, M., van der Aalst, W.M.P.: A Configurable Reference Modeling Language. Information Systems 32, 1–23 (2007)
26. Hallerbach, A., Bauer, T., Reichert, M.: Managing Process Variants in the Process Life Cycle. In: 10th Int'l Conf. on Enterprise Information Systems (ICEIS 2008), Barcelona, Spain (2008)
27. Hallerbach, A., Bauer, T., Reichert, M.: Capturing Variability in Business Process Models: The Provop Approach. Software Process: Improvement and Practice (2009) (accepted for publication)
28. Fettke, P., Loose, P.: Classification of reference models: a methodology and its application. Information Systems and e-Business Management 1, 35–53 (2003)
29. Hümmer, W., Meiler, C., Müller, S., Dietrich, A.: Data Model and Personalized Configuration Systems for Mass Customization - A Two Step Approach for Integrating Technical and Organizational Issues. In: International Conference on Economic, Technical and Organizational aspects of Product Configuration Systems, Kopenhagen, pp. 35–44 (2004)
30. Gairola, A.: Montagegerechtes Konstruieren - Ein Beitrag zur Konstruktionsmethodik. Fachbereich Nachrichtentechnik, Doctoral thesis. Technische Hochschule Darmstadt, Darmstadt (1981)
31. Czarnecki, K., Helsen, S., Eisenecker, U.: Staged Configuration Through Specialization and Multi-Level Configuration of Feature Models. Software Process: Improvement and Practice 10 (2005)
32. Scheer, A.-W.: ARIS - Business Process Modeling. Springer, Berlin (2000)

On Maintaining Consistency of Process Model Variants

Emilian Pascalau[1], Ahmed Awad[1], Sherif Sakr[2], and Mathias Weske[1]

[1] Hasso-Plattner-Institute
University of Potsdam, Germany
{emilian.pascalau,ahmed.awad,mathias.weske}@hpi.uni-potsdam.de
[2] National ICT Australia (NICTA)
University of New South Wales, Australia
ssakr@cse.unsw.edu.au

Abstract. Today's enterprises are dynamic where many variances of business process models can exist due to several reasons such as: the need to target different customer types, rely on particular IT systems or comply with specific country regulations. Automated maintenance of the consistency between process variants is an important goal that saves the time and efforts of process modelers. In this paper, we present a query-based approach to maintain consistency among process variants. We maintain the link between the variant process models by means of defining process model views. These views are defined using, BPMN-Q, a visual query language for business process models. Therefore, dynamic evaluation for the defined queries of the process views guarantee that the process modeler is able to get up-to-date and consistent status of the process model. In addition, our view-based approach allows the building of a holistic view of related variants of the same process model.

Keywords: Business process design, Reuse, Querying business processes, Process variants.

1 Introduction

Business Process Management (BPM) [1] aims at the automated support and coordination of business in an integrated manner by capturing, modeling, implementing and controlling all activities taking place in an environment that defines the enterprise. Business processes enable a better understanding of the business by facilitating communication between business analysts and IT experts.

Business processes, like many information systems, do not exist only under a single version which covers all the issues or the whole market. Instead, many variants of a process exist which are specialized for particular customer types, or for particular IT systems, or some country-specific regulations. However, business process customization and management is done mainly in a manual way which is error prone and time consuming.

Multinational companies have to keep variants of business processes in order to be compliant with local regulations or domain specific settings. We can establish an analogy between process variants on the one hand and object oriented inheritance on the other hand. A process variant is like a child class, where a process variant (child) extends or overrides the behavior of the parent process. Usually, these variants are maintained manually. A direct result of this manual maintenance is the risk of inconsistency.

M. zur Muehlen and J. Su (Eds.): BPM 2010 Workshops, LNBIP 66, pp. 289–300, 2011.

Inconsistency appears when a parent process's behavior is updated without updating the child's behavior accordingly.

In this paper we present a query-based approach to maintain consistency among process variants. We define our approach in the context of a real life context (eBay) that has a set of innovative and special characteristics. Rather than the manual *save-as* style of processes to create variants, we keep the link between child and parent processes by means of defining views in child processes on the behavior of parent processes. These views are created by means of queries. Thus, a process variant combines concrete activities that are meant to provide the behavior specific to the new variation and queries that inherit behavior from parent processes. We call this models partial process models. For the concrete part of the variant, ordinary process modeling constructs are used, e.g., BPMN constructs. For the view part, we rely on BPMN-Q notations, a visual language for querying business processes models [2,3]. In particular, each time a child process is invoked for editing or execution, the view is evaluated against the parent processes and an up-to-date result is returned to the modeler. This view based approach has a two fold meaning: (1) To maintain consistency between variants of process models and (2) To extract variants from holistic process models and partially address the creation of holistic process models from variants.

The remainder of this paper is organized as follows: We discuss some background knowledge about business process models and BPMN-Q in Section 2. To illustrate the problem, we introduce a real-world use case scenario in Section 3. Section 4 describes the details of our approach regarding the maintenance of variants consistency through the definition of process model views. An architectural framework that realizes the implementation of our approach is presented in Section 5. The related work is discussed in Section 6 before we conclude the paper in Section 7.

2   Preliminaries

This section formally introduces process modeling and querying, which forms the groundwork for our approach.

2.1   Business Process Modeling

Currently, there is a number of graph-based business process modeling languages, e.g. BPMN [4], EPC [5], YAWL [6], and UML Activity Diagram [7]. Despite their variance in expressiveness and modeling notation, they all share the common concepts of tasks, events, gateways (or routing nodes), artifacts, and resources, as well as relations between them, such as control flow. Without loss of generality, we can abstract from particular node types as their execution semantics are not vital to structural query matching, which is rather based on the concept of a process graph.

Definition 1 (Process Model). *A process model P is a connected graph (N, E), where N is a non-empty set of control flow nodes and $E \subseteq N \times N$ a nonempty set of directed* control flow edges *where $\bullet n$ ($n \bullet$) stands for the set of immediate predecessor (successor) nodes of $n \in N$.*

A process model has exactly one start event $n_{start} \in N$ with no incoming and at least one outgoing control flow edge, i.e., $|\bullet n_{start}| = 0 \wedge |n_{start} \bullet| \geq 1$, and exactly one end event $n_{end} \in N$ with at least one incoming and no outgoing control flow edge, i.e., $|\bullet n_{end}| \geq 1 \wedge |n_{end} \bullet| = 0$. Each other control flow node $n \in N \setminus \{n_{start}, n_{end}\}$ is on a path from n_{start} to n_{end}.

A connected sub-graph of a process model is a *process model fragment*. We refer to a specific type of process model fragments that have a *single entry* node and a *single exit* node [8] as *process model components*.

Definition 2 (Process Model Component). *A connected subgraph (N', E') of a process model (N, E), where $N' \in N, E' \in E$, is a process model component PC iff it has exactly one incoming boundary node $n_{in} \in N'$, i.e., $\bullet n_{in} \subseteq N \setminus N'$ and one outgoing boundary node $n_{out} \in N'$, i.e., $n_{out} \bullet \subseteq N \setminus N'$.*

2.2 Business Process Model Querying

Based on the definition of process models and process model components, we introduce the concept of process model queries, as a means to obtain business process components from a collection of business processes by structurally matching a query to each of them. BPMN-Q is a visual process model query language designed to help business process designers access repositories of business process models [2]. The language supports querying all the control and artifact concepts of business process models. Moreover, it introduces a set of new *abstraction* concepts that are useful for different querying scenarios.

Definition 3 (BPMN-Q Query). A BPMN-Q query is a tuple
$Q = (QC, QCF, QP)$ *where:*
- *QC is a finite set of* control flow nodes *in a query,*
- *$QCF \subseteq QC \times QC$ is the* control flow relation *between control nodes in a query,*
- *$QP \subseteq QC \times QC$ is the* path *relation between control nodes in a query,*

BPMN-Q Constructs. A BPMN-Q model is called a query. A query declaratively describes a structural connectivity that must be satisfied by a matching process model. In addition to the core business process modeling concepts, BPMN-Q introduces a new concept of **Path edges**. A path edge connecting two control flow nodes represents an abstraction over an arbitrary set of control flow nodes that could exist in between the matching process model.

Matching Queries to Processes. A BPMN-Q query is matched to a candidate process model via a set of refinements to the query. With each refinement node (edge) in a query is replaced with the corresponding node (edge) of the matching process model. If one node can have more than one possible replacement within the process model, a new refined copy of the query is created for each possible replacement. We call the replacement a resolution of an element of the query. Figure 1(a) illustrates a sample process model definition using the BPMN notations, Figure 1(b) illustrates a sample definition of a process model view using the BPMN-Q notations and that nodes and edges highlighted in grey in Figure 1(a) illustrate the matching part of the process model.

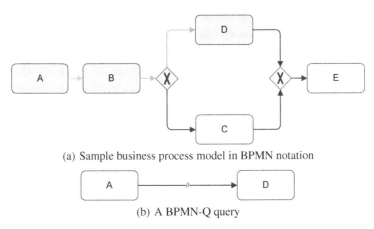

(a) Sample business process model in BPMN notation

(b) A BPMN-Q query

Fig. 1. An example of process model and query

3   Scenario

With more than 90 million active users globally, eBay is the world's largest online marketplace. eBay connects individual buyers and sellers, as well as small businesses in 38 markets using 16 languages[1].

eBay has huge repositories of business processes. Though, many of these processes are variants of other processes. We can argue that variability is imposed on a vertical axis (represented by different departments within the organization) and on a horizontal axis (emphasized by different business elements and/or business aspects, i.e., regulations, IT infrastructure, for example different Customer Relationship Management systems, customer types, countries, payment methods).

The number of possible process variations is determined by the degree of freedom the system has, i.e., the number of possible arrangements of different business contexts. A business process that is influenced by 6 business context elements $\{b_1..b_6\}$, e.g., country, region, etc, that respectively have the following number of subtypes $\{8, 2, 5, 5, 3, 7\}$, will end up having more than 8000 variants.

The required management to ensure the consistency of the process models in such a context is a very difficult and complex undertaking. Current approaches, based on reference process models [9,10], start with a holistic model that gets specialized through a configuration process. As already argued in [11] the management of such huge models is extremely difficult. The modeler is required to know the process beforehand and only predefined configuration (defined beforehand by means of specific configurable nodes, or nodes annotated with labels) can be extracted.

To illustrate the case of inconsistency, we are going to use the two processes from Figure 2. These processes are two real life variants of an eBay process model in the context of customer support. As the labels in figure state one of the models is called a Parent process and the second one is called a Child process. A child process can reuse either parts or an entire parent process. The terminology of child and parent

---

[1] http://www.ebayinc.com/who; June 6th 2010.

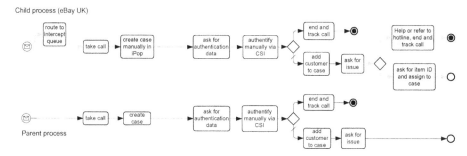

Fig. 2. Parent process vs. Child process

is related to the inheritance concept, as the child (sub) process reuses behavior from the parent (super) process, similarly to how subclasses reuse (inherit) functionality from the superclasses. Any arbitrary process can be used as a parent process. Currently, a child process is derived by making a copy of the parent process and editing that copy, e.g., adding new activities or arbitrary control flow elements. At this point, there is no connectivity between the parent and the child processes. That is, a parent process could be edited by another modeler who might add new functionality without it being reflected on the child process, thus causing inconsistency between the child and parent processes. Moreover, the overriding of the behavior of the parent process is also not tracked.

The second perspective that we want to address concerns that of holistic models. Normally, modelers start with holistic models that contain the configurable nodes [9] where variants correspond to specific configurations. In this case, the management of process variants by means of holistic models that can be configured requires basically two major things: (i) The existence of the holistic model and (ii) The beforehand knowledge about which elements can be configured and what will be the outcome of the configuration. However, in the eBay situation this is not the case. Due to the complexity of the context, it is hard to have a holistic model that comprises more than 8000 variants. Manual creation and configuration of such a holistic model would be almost impossible. In this context, it is rather easier to create variants one by one. Nevertheless, we still need to deal with the problem of managing such a large number of variants. An elegant solution would automatically update a holistic model each time a new variant is created. This solution would address the first point above, the existence of a holistic model. However, the point of configuration is still open.

Figure 3 depicts two variants out of which a holistic model needs to be created. There are at least two possibilities to create holistic models from the variants of processes. One is to purely merge the variants, by simply "overlapping processes" and keeping only one copy of the elements that are the same (type, label and position in the control flow) in all processes, and adding all other different elements. The holistic model obtained by such an approach would not guarantee the maintenance of the initial behavior from the variants.

Figure 4 depicts the holistic model of the two variants from Figure 3, created by simple merge. The holistic model itself created using this approach does not maintain

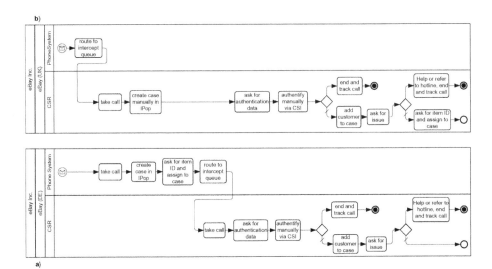

Fig. 3. Variants example

Fig. 4. Holistic model by simple merge of variants from Figure 3

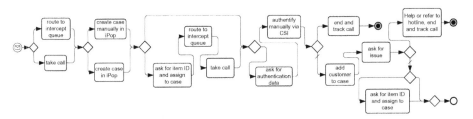

Fig. 5. Holistic model that maintains also initial behavior of variants from Figure 3

the initial behavior specified in the two separate variants but with the use of queries the variants can still be extracted.

The second approach would be to add control flow elements that would allow the holistic model to maintain also the individual variants behavior. A holistic model of the same variants in is shown Figure 3, that also maintains the initial behavior which is presented in Figure 5. Also in this case queries can easily retrieve the initial variants, without requiring the modeler to know which elements can be configured and which not. In addition the modeler will not be required to go through the complete model for configuration, which in the case of a holistic model that comprises more than 8000 variants would be almost impossible.

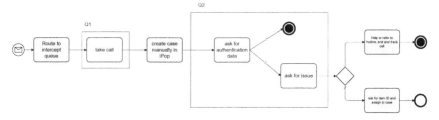

Fig. 6. A partial process model to express inheritance among process variants

4   Process Model Views to Manage Variants

In Section 3, we explained two problems that stem from process variants management and configurable processes which are: variants consistency and deriving variants from holistic processes. In this section, we explain our approach to address these two problems by means of defining queries on process models. In this sense, we see process queries as a means to support *reuse*. We use BPMN-Q to create queries on other processes.

To maintain the parent-child process consistency, we introduce the notion of *partial process models*, Definition 4, that describe a desired process model through a combination of process model fragments and process model queries. Thus, to derive a child process, instead of copying the parent process and then editing that copy, the modeler starts with a partial process model. In this partial process model, ordinary process modeling constructs, e.g., activities, events, are used to model the *new* behavior that distinguish the variant, we call these the *concrete elements*. On the other hand, to reuse behavior of the parent process, BPMN-Q queries are embedded within that partial process model. Each query declaratively describes the behavior to be inherited from a specific parent process. Next, queries and concrete parts of the process are connected via control flow edges.

Definition 4 (Partial Process Model). *A partial process model* $\mathfrak{P} = (\mathfrak{F}, \mathfrak{Q}, \mathfrak{E})$ *is a connected graph that consists of disjoint sets of process model fragments* $\mathfrak{F}$ *and process model queries* $\mathfrak{Q}$ *connected through directed edges* $\mathfrak{E} \subseteq (\mathfrak{F} \times \mathfrak{Q}) \cup (\mathfrak{Q} \times \mathfrak{F})$, *where each outgoing boundary control flow node* $n_{out} \in N$ *of a process model fragment* $F \in \mathfrak{F}$ *is connected to at least one incoming boundary control flow node* $n_{in} \in QC$ *of a process model query* $Q \in \mathfrak{Q}$ *and vice versa.*

Figure 6 shows a partial process model that corresponds to the use case illustrated in Section 3. The partial process model is intended to show how the Child process of Figure 2 can be obtained and maintained from the Parent process, depicted in the same figure. In Figure 6, the parts with grey background represent new activities that are introduced on the child process. To keep the relationship with inherited behavior, queries are used. $Q1$ keeps the link with activity "take call" from the parent process model. Also, $Q2$ keeps the relationship with the behavior of the parent process between activity "ask for authentication data" on the one hand and a termination possibility and activity "ask for issue" on the other hand. Thus, if the parent process behavior is changed by means of, e.g., adding extra activities between "ask for authentication data" and the termination event or "ask for authentication data" and "ask for issue", this is updated automatically on the child process by evaluating the queries against the parent process. Once a partial process model is defined, it can be stored in the repository as a separate artifact that can be invoked in future. Indeed, there are two ways to invoke partial models. The first invocation is to view it. In this case, all queries in the partial model are matched to the respective parent processes. Matching parts are merged with concrete parts and the modeler is given an up-to-date view on how the child process looks like. In the view mode, the modeler might make changes to the process. In this case, if the change concerns overriding the behavior from the parent process, the modeler is warned and switched to the editing mode. In this sense, we partially address the problem of overriding behavior. The other invocation is to edit the partial process model. In that case, the modeler is allowed to arbitrarily edit query components or concrete components of the child process.

The problem of deriving variants from holistic process models can also be addressed in the same way. We store the holistic process model and a set of partial process models that define how variants can be obtained. The step of obtaining the holistic model is out of the scope of this paper. Currently, we assume that we are able to obtain a holistic process model from a set of variants. Our approach addresses and supports the concerns of the steps after the process of obtaining the holistic model. That is, we keep only the holistic model and a set of partial process models that define the variants and get rid of the existing original variants.

5   Framework Architecture

In this section, we envision an architecture for the *partial process modeling* of business processes, illustrated in Figure 7, which consists of the following main components.

– **Process Modeling, Querying, and Composition Environment** provides the process designer with a graphical *modeling interface* [12]. Users express their intention by means of a partial process model (see Section 4). The *query interface* extracts the set of process model queries from the partial process model, and passes them on to the query processor. The matches returned by the set of queries will then be *composed* with the model fragments from the partial model through the *model composer*.
– **Process Model Repository** is a central storage of business process models that is accessed in a uniform way [13].
– **Query Processor** The *query processor* evaluates the queries received from the query interface [3] and passes the resultant process views to the model composer.

Some of the components of this framework do already exist. The client, particularly the *model designer*, is the Oryx editor, an extensible process modeling platform for research that has been designed to model and manage process models online [12]. *Query interface* and *query processor* for BPMN-Q [2] have been implemented as client-side and server-side plugins respectively to the Oryx editor[2] and are able to run process model

---

[2] http://bpt.hpi.uni-potsdam.de/Oryx

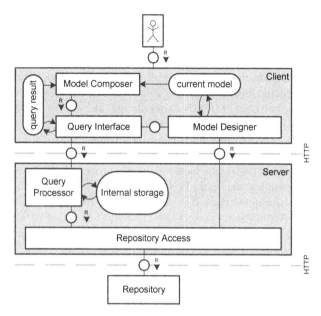

Fig. 7. Framework Architecture

queries against the Oryx process model repository. The model composer component that integrates the results of queries with the concrete parts of the partial process model is available only internally for the time being. Nevertheless, major releases of the Oryx platform will incorporate this one also.

6   Related Work

The management of variants has been addressed in various domains, such as software configuration management [14,15,16] and feature diagrams [17,18,19]. For process models, different approaches have been defined: configurable reference process models, inheritance based and annotations based.

Lu and Sadiq [20] presented a process modeling framework that is conducive to constrained variance by supporting user driven process adaptations. In [21] they described another approach for facilitating the discovery of preferred variants based on the notion of process similarity where multiple aspects of the process variants are compared according to specific query requirements. Compared to our approach, we address the issue of maintaining consistency among variants rather than deciding whether two or more processes are variants of each other.

C-EPCs [9] allows the configuration of process models by distinguishing between choices that can be made at runtime and those that have to be made before, i.e., configuration time. *Configurable nodes* are used as the means to introduce configurability to EPCs. On the other hand aEPC [10] works on the principle of *projection* [11] and only elements that have a particular label are included in the extracted model. Inheritance of behavior in workflows [22,23] is a formal approach for tackling problems that are related to change. Four inheritance rules (*protocol inheritance, projection inheritance, protocol/projection inheritance, life-cycle inheritance*) are defined to tackle dynamic change.

Opposed to the C-EPC or aEPC that deal with reference process models, our approach does not require the existence of an initial holistic model that can be later configured into specific variants, but it is able to create the holistic model on-the-fly from variants, based on a set of BPMN-Q queries that identify the variants. In addition, the query-based approach introduced here brings a new mechanism for consistency between processes. This mechanism is not a fully fledged inheritance mechanism but rather similar to it. Based on the associated queries, if a super process is updated, the updates are projected in a consistent manner on the sub-processes. While other approaches dealt either with workflow nets and EPCs, our approach deals with BPMN models.

Annotations based approaches, e.g., the PESOA (Process Family Engineering in Service-Oriented Applications) project [24,25] defines so-called *variant-rich process models* as process models that are extended with stereotype annotations to accommodate variability. Both UML Activity Diagrams as well as BPMN models can be tackled with this approach. The places of a process where variability can occur are marked with the stereotype `VarPoint`. Several other stereo types , e.g., `Variant`, `Default`, `Abstract`, `Alternative`, `Null`, `Optional`) are used to specify different configuration options. Compared to our approach, we do not predetermine configuration points.

Variants at execution time are addressed in [26]. The notion of process constraints is used to tackle the need for flexibility and dynamic change at execution time. Here a variant of a process is considered as an instance of a process.

La Rosa et al. [27] defined a questionnaire based approach to extract variants from C-EPCs. However, to do so, one needs first the holistic model (the C-EPC), then it needs a questionnaire model and a mapping between the C-EPC and the questionnaire model. Our approach, however, does not require an additional mapping. Queries can be applied directly to the holistic models to derive variants. For us, a holistic or a specific model makes no difference. Because the queries are expressed with constructs similar to those in BPMN, the easiness introduced by the questionnaire approach to extract variants, we argue that it is also maintained here.

7   Conclusion

In this paper, we introduced a new approach to maintain the consistency of process variants. Our approach is defined to address a specific setup, the eBay context. Consistency maintenance is a sort of reuse of process components in other processes. The approach is based on the idea of defining process models views by means of BPMN-Q queries. Thus, the process modeler can define a new process model by specifying concrete parts in addition to queryable process views. Each time the defined model is invoked for viewing, the process views are evaluated, which guarantees returning the up-to-date and consistent model status for the process modeler. In addition, our view-based approach can promise other benefits such as: 1) Extracting variants from holistic process models. Although it is not in our intention to fully address the problem of building holistic models out of related variants of the same process model, we have briefly underlined simple directions on how this could be done in a setup as the one described here. This holistic view reflects virtual global views on the components of the variant process models while keeping them autonomous. 2) Reusing existing business knowledge materialized in existing process models. The reuse is not only on the level of a whole process model, but rather on a fine grain level which is in the form of process model components.

With this approach, we partially addressed the problem of process variants management. What remains open is the support of overriding inherited behavior from a parent process. One other direction for future work is the development of algorithms that generate holistic process models out of a set of variants.

Acknowledgements

We would like to thank Clemens Rath from eBay's European Center of Excellence, for his support.

References

1. Weske, M.: Business Process Management: Concepts, Languages, Architectures. Springer, Heidelberg (2007)
2. Awad, A.: BPMN-Q: A Language to Query Business Processes. In: Proceedings of the 2nd International Workshop on Enterprise Modelling and Information Systems Architecture (EMISA 2007). LNI, vol. P-119, pp. 115–128. GI (2007)
3. Sakr, S., Awad, A.: A framework for querying graph-based business process models. In: Proceedings of the 19th International World Wide Web Conference (WWW 2010), pp. 1297–1300. ACM, New York (2010)
4. OMG: Business Process Modeling Notation 1.2 (BPMN 1.2) Specification, Final Adopted Specification. Technical report, OMG (2009)
5. Keller, G., Nüttgens, M., Scheer, A.: Semantische Prozessmodellierung auf der Grundlage Ereignisgesteuerter Prozessketten (EPK). Technical Report 89, Institut für Wirtschaftsinformatik, Saarbrücken (1992)
6. van der Aalst, W.M.P., ter Hofstede, A.H.M.: YAWL: yet another workflow language. Information Systems 30(4), 245–275 (2005)
7. OMG: UML 2.0 Superstructure Specification (August 2005), http://www.omg.org/spec/UML/2.0/Superstructure/PDF/
8. Vanhatalo, J., Völzer, H., Koehler, J.: The refined process structure tree. In: Dumas, M., Reichert, M., Shan, M.-C. (eds.) BPM 2008. LNCS, vol. 5240, pp. 100–115. Springer, Heidelberg (2008)
9. Rosemann, M., van der Aalst, W.M.P.: A Configurable Reference Modelling Language. Information Systems 32(1), 1–23 (2007)
10. Reijers, H.A., Mans, R.S., van der Toorn, R.A.: Improved Model Management with Aggregated Business Process Models. Data Knowledge Engineering 68(2), 221–243 (2009)
11. Baier, T., Pascalau, E., Mendling, J.: On the suitability of aggregated and configurable business process models. In: Bider, I., Halpin, T., Krogstie, J., Nurcan, S., Proper, E., Schmidt, R., Ukor, R. (eds.) BPMDS 2010 and EMMSAD 2010. LNBIP, vol. 50, pp. 108–119. Springer, Heidelberg (2010)
12. Decker, G., Overdick, H., Weske, M.: Oryx – Sharing Conceptual Models on the Web. In: Li, Q., Spaccapietra, S., Yu, E., Olivé, A. (eds.) ER 2008. LNCS, vol. 5231, pp. 536–537. Springer, Heidelberg (2008)

13. Rosa, M.L., Reijers, H., Aalst, W., Dijkman, R., Mendling, J., Dumas, M., Garcia-Banuelos, L.: Apromore: An advanced process model repository (2009), http://eprints.qut.edu.au/27448/
14. Estublier, J., Casallas, R.: The Adele Software Configuration Manager. Configuration Management. Trends in Software (1994)
15. Tryggeseth, E., Gulla, B., Conradi, R.: Modelling Systems with Variability using the PROTEUS Configuration Language. In: Estublier, J. (ed.) ICSE-WS 1993/1995 and SCM 1993/1995. LNCS, vol. 1005, pp. 216–240. Springer, Heidelberg (1995)
16. Turkay, E., Gokhale, A.S., Natarajan, B.: Addressing the middleware configuration challenges using model-based techniques. In: ACM Southeast Regional Conference, pp. 166–170. ACM, New York (2004)
17. Batory, D.S., Geraci, B.J.: Composition Validation and Subjectivity in GenVoca Generators. IEEE Trans. Software Engineering 23(2), 67–84 (1997)
18. Czarnecki, K., Helsen, S., Eisenecker, U.: Formalizing Cardinality-Based Feature Models and Their Specialization. Software Process: Improvement and Practice 10(1), 7–29 (2005)
19. Schobbens, P.Y., Heymans, P., Trigaux, J.C.: Feature Diagrams: A Survey and a Formal Semantics. In: Proceedings of the 14th IEEE International Requirements Engineering Conference (RE 2006), pp. 138–148 (2006), http://doi.ieeecomputersociety.org/10.1109/RE.2006.23
20. Lu, R., Sadiq, S.W.: Managing Process Variants as an Information Resource. In: Dustdar, S., Fiadeiro, J.L., Sheth, A.P. (eds.) BPM 2006. LNCS, vol. 4102, pp. 426–431. Springer, Heidelberg (2006)
21. Lu, R., Sadiq, S.W.: On the Discovery of Preferred Work Practice Through Business Process Variants. In: Parent, C., Schewe, K.-D., Storey, V.C., Thalheim, B. (eds.) ER 2007. LNCS, vol. 4801, pp. 165–180. Springer, Heidelberg (2007)
22. van der Aalst, W., Basten, T.: Inheritance of Workflows: An approach to tackling problems related to change. Computing Science Report 99(06) (1999), http://is.tm.tue.nl/staff/wvdaalst/publications/p85.pdf
23. Basten, T., van der Aalst, W.: Inheritance of Behavior. Computing Science Report 99(17) (1999), http://is.tm.tue.nl/staff/wvdaalst/publications/p93.pdf
24. Puhlmann, F., Schnieders, A., Weiland, J., Weske, M.: Variability mechanisms for process models. Technical Report 17/2005, Hasso-Plattner-Institut (June 2005)
25. Schnieders, A., Puhlmann, F.: Variability mechanisms in e-business process families. In: Proceedings of the International Conference on Business Information Systems (BIS 2006). LNI, vol. 85, pp. 583–601. GI (2006)
26. Lu, R., Sadiq, S.W., Governatori, G., Yang, X.: Defining Adaptation Constraints for Business Process Variants. In: Abramowicz, W. (ed.) BIS 2009. LNBIP, vol. 21, pp. 145–156. Springer, Heidelberg (2009)
27. Rosa, M.L., Lux, J., Seidel, S., Dumas, M., ter Hofstede, A.H.M.: Questionnaire-driven Configuration of Reference Process Models. In: Krogstie, J., Opdahl, A.L., Sindre, G. (eds.) CAiSE 2007 and WES 2007. LNCS, vol. 4495, pp. 424–438. Springer, Heidelberg (2007)

Reuse-Oriented Business Process Modelling Based on a Hierarchical Structure*

Wassim Derguech and Sami Bhiri

DERI, Digital Enterprise Research Institute,
National University of Ireland, Galway
firstname.lastname@deri.org
http://www.deri.ie

Abstract. Managing variability in business processes has attracted a lot of research interest. Some of the current works try to manage variability at runtime and others at design time. We are interested in the latter where it consists of managing different process variants in order to enable their reuse. Even though there exist different proposals dealing with variability at design time most of them suffer from the major shortcoming of decision support in choosing the suitable alternatives. In this context, we propose a framework that allows for reusing business process models by means of a hierarchical structure. In this paper, we present our ongoing research in defining this framework: its data structure as well as first thoughts about maintaining it.

Keywords: Business process modelling, configurable business process, hierarchical structure, reuse, merging business process models.

1 Introduction

Process Aware Information Systems (PAISs) [1] are used to manage and execute operational processes involving people, applications and data sources on the basis of business process models. The discipline that is concerned by this process-centric trend is known as Business Process Management (BPM) [2].

In Business Process Management the objective of the Business Process modeling phase is to capture the behavioural aspects of a certain business goal into a business process model [3]. There are several modeling approaches that can be split in two categories. The first one consists of designing business process models from scratch, which is an error prone and time consuming task [4]. The second category relies on reusing existing business process models.

The advent of Reuse-Oriented Development (ROD) in BPM brings a number frameworks used to support the design of business process models exploiting proven practices. One of these frameworks is the configurable process model.

Configurable process models are constructed via the aggregation of several *variants* of a process model [5]. In fact, under different requirements, different

---

* This work is funded by the Lion II project supported by Science Foundation Ireland under grant number 08/CE/I1380.

M. zur Muehlen and J. Su (Eds.): BPM 2010 Workshops, LNBIP 66, pp. 301–313, 2011.
© Springer-Verlag Berlin Heidelberg 2011

business processes could achieve the same business goal. We call these business processes business process *variants*. Since they model in essence the same business goal, these variants share many commonalities. Therefore, managing these variants can be made easier by handling the common parts just once and not for each variant separately.

A key aspect of variability handling in process modeling is the explicit representation of *variation points*. A variation point is a special placeholder in the configurable process model in which variants are defined. During the business process modeling phase, the configurable process model is configured by setting up the variation points according to a user's specific requirements. These variation points capture different requirements that discriminate between the distinct parts of business process variants through *configuration parameters*.

To manage a configurable process model, we propose a hierarchical structure that captures variability of business process models. The rationale we opt for a hierarchical structure, which explicitly captures variation points, is to provide a user-friendly experience during the modeling phase while not overwhelming the modeler with cumbersome details from start.

The remainder of the paper is structured as follows. Section 2 introduces a use case scenario to motivate the use of configurable process models in business process management. The example describes 10 process variants of a business process. The hierarchical structure is presented in Section 3, where we formally define it and present how the motivating example can be modeled using it. Section 4 discusses some related work while Section 5 concludes the paper.

2   Motivating Example

In this section we are presenting a fictitious use case example. We have tried to imagine scenarios where different variants of the same business process may appear while satisfying the same business goal.

We have identified 10 possible variants for a business process related to customer enrollment in an insurance contract with Blue Company (fictitious insurance company).

For presentation simplicity, we have used numbers (i.e., 1 to 13) to represent tasks involved in these business process variants. These tasks are:

1. Outdoor sales: When a registration is initiated for example by a third party partner or during an exhibition.
2. Office registration: When a customer moves to the company's office for initiating a registration operation.
3. Internet registration: When a customers initiates a registration operation via the Internet.
4. Membership upgrade: When a customer is already registered but he wants to upgrade his insurance type.
5. Registration for a staff member: The customer is working within Blue Company.
6. Customer Information: Entering or updating customer information.

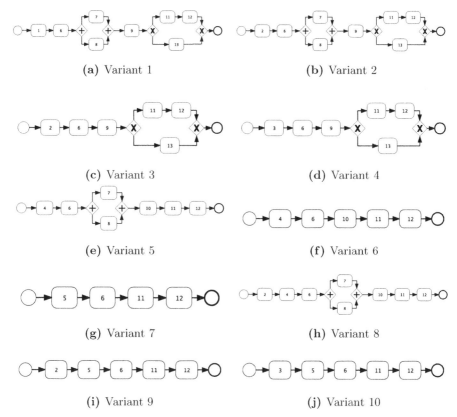

Fig. 1. 10 business process variants for customer enrollment in an insurance contract

7. Credit checking: Checking the customer's credits.
8. Account Checking: Checking the customer's account.
9. Qualification decision: Deciding whether Blue Company is willing to consider the customer.
10. Automatic Acceptance: Automatic acceptance for example in case the customer is a staff member or he was previously insured and no troubles were noticed from him.
11. Customer notification: Sending acceptance notification to the customer.
12. Contract notification: Sending the contract to the customer in order to be signed.
13. Rejection notification: Sending rejection notification to the customer.

Fig. 1 presents possible variants related to different execution scenarios. As example, the variant 2 (see Fig. 1b) describes a scenario where a customer comes to Blue Company's office for registering (Task 2). Then, the agent collects the client's information (Task 6). After checking the customer credits and account (Task 7 and 8) a decision is made for choosing to consider the client or not

(Task 9). In case of acceptance, the customer is notified (Task 11) and he is asked to sign the contract (Task 12). In case of rejection, the customer is notified as well (Task 13).

One of the possible ways to deal with such variability at design time is to incorporate all the alternative execution paths within a single process model. A possible result of merging these variants is depicted in Fig. 2. We used the colored gateway to differentiate between normal BPMN gateways and variation points. A variation point is a special node in the graph that explicitly mentions that these are decisions that need to be taken at design time for generating the desired alternative. This colored gateway is just a design choice and every modeller can use his own notation for presenting the variation points.

With only 10 variants that tasks do not exceed 13, it is still being possible to generate and manage such a model (i.e., Fig. 2). Thinking of more complex business processes, such a model will be *spaghetti* model where it lacks visibility. Additionally, if this model is generated manually, it will be time consuming and error-prone.

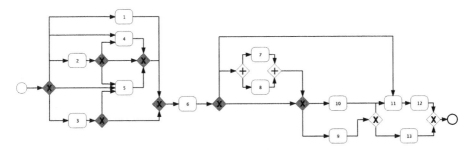

Fig. 2. BPMN model after merging the 10 business process variants for customer enrollment in an insurance contract

In our proposed approach, we consider merging all these process variants into a single model as well. However, we adopt a hierarchical representation of tasks organized in several layers ranging from the coarse-grained to the fine-grained layer. Each layer (of level n) is hiding the complexity of the next layer (of level $n+1$) and allows for refining its tasks by choosing one of the possible alternatives. Fig. 3 presents a final hierarchical structure containing all proposed variants. In this figure, dotted lines represent possible alternatives for achieving a task (e.g., *Collect Information* can be achieved by task *6* or by a sequence between task *6* and *Check*). To build this hierarchy, we introduced the notion of abstract tasks, which represent particular nodes of the hierarchy. Such nodes are for example *Customer Enrollment* or *Notification1*; and for simplicity purposes, some of them are labeled with an asterisk such as *2**.

This divide-and-conquer strategy of presenting a process model helps for overcoming the complexity of process definitions. Apart from that, defining different tasks at different granularity levels of the process definition has the advantages of:

- *enabling the reuse of previously defined tasks*: each task can be integrated in various process models (e.g., task *Notification1* of the Fig. 3),
- *enabling the modelling of multiple process variants*: two business process variants may differ only in the definition of a task at a certain layer. Providing two possible alternatives of that same task implies the modelling of two process variants.
- *easily add a new process variant*: to add a new variant to the process model, we have just to introduce another alternative to one of the tasks of the hierarchy.
- *considering other possible variants*: A hierarchical representation could help for the appearance of new variants that the business expert is not aware of.

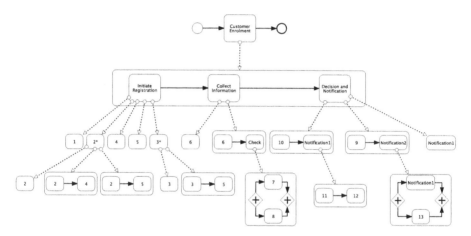

Fig. 3. Hierarchical structure merging the 10 business process variants for customer enrollment in an insurance contract

In the rest of the paper, we will introduce our formal representation of this hierarchical structure and how do we build it.

3   A Framework for Managing Process Variants

This section describes the framework we propose to enable the reuse of business process models. It describes a formal representation of a hierarchical structure (in 3.1) and a first algorithm for maintaining it (in 3.2). But first of all, we would introduce some keywords that are used in the rest of the paper:

- *Business unit*: We use this term to refer either to simple or composite tasks.
- *Hierarchical structure*: In our work, we define a data structure that captures process variants in a hierarchical representation, i.e., we use it as a configurable process model. It is a tree structure as defined in the graph theory. It contains nodes which represent different business units and relations

between them. Each node has zero or more child nodes. A node that does not have any child is called terminal node. An internal node is a node having at least one child (called also non-terminal node).

- *Business unit's definition*: Each non-terminal node in the hierarchy is a business unit that has at least one definition. A definition of a business unit determines what are its possible children.
- *Variation point*: A node (i.e., business unit) that has more than one child is called a variation point.
- *Global*: We use this term as a label for a specific node that represents the root of the hierarchical structure.

3.1 Data Structure Definition

Our framework defines a data structure as a tuple $\{\Sigma, \Gamma, \Delta\}$ where:

- Σ represents the set of business units involved in the whole configurable business process model,
- Γ represents the set of abstract business units and
- Δ represents the definitions of each abstract business unit. Entries of Δ are presented as follows: *BusinessUnit = Pattern(Elements)* such that:
  - *Pattern* defines the orchestration pattern between *Elements* (e.g., Sequence, MulChoice, ExChoice, etc.)
  - *Elements* is a set of business units from $\Sigma \cup \Gamma$

The framework should respect a set of constraints/principles to assure that the data structure will remain valid and well-formed after an update operation.

1. *Minimality*: Each element of Δ has to be defined only once and should not be derived from other elements of Δ.
2. *Coverage*: By necessity and nature, the framework must cover all defined variants.

3.2 Adding a New Variant to the Configurable Process Model

Here, we present our algorithm for adding a new variant to a configurable process model. The inputs of this algorithm are: the configurable process model and the new variant, both expressed as $\{\Sigma, \Gamma, \Delta\}$. The output is the updated configurable process model. This algorithm defines 5 steps which are detailed next.

As part of our future work, we plan to provide complete algorithms to convert BPMN into our framework notation and vice-versa. The idea is to adapt one of the existing algorithm presented by [6,7].

For the moment we present here what we expect to have after converting process variants from Fig. 1 into our framework. For simplicity, we will consider the result of presenting variant 9 (i.e., Fig. 1i) and 10 (i.e., Fig. 1j) **and** show how do we operate for merging them into a configurable process model.

Variant $9 = \{\Sigma_{V9}, \Gamma_{V9}, \Delta_{V9}\}$

- Σ_{V9}={2, 5, 6, 11, 12}
- Γ_{V9}={Global, Initiate_Registration, Collect_Information, Decision_Notification}
- Δ_{V9}={
  Global=Sequence(Initiate_Registration, Collect_Information, Decision_Notification),
  Initiate_Registration = Sequence(2,5),
  Collect_Information = 6,
  Decision_Notification = Sequence(11,12)}

Variant 10 = $\{\Sigma_{V10}, \Gamma_{V10}, \Delta_{V10}\}$

- Σ_{V10}={3, 5, 6, 11, 12}
- Γ_{V10}={Global, Initiate_Registration, Collect_Information, Decision_Notification}
- Δ_{V10}={
  Global=Sequence(Initiate_Registration, Collect_Information, Decision_Notification),
  Initiate_Registration = Sequence(3,5),
  Collect_Information = 6,
  Decision_Notification = Sequence(11,12)}

To merge these two process variants, we go through 5 steps that we will define next. We will consider the variant 9 as the initial configurable process model and we will update it by adding the variant 10.

Substitution. This first step prepares the new variant (i.e., variant 10) by checking its abstract business units (i.e., Γ). It ensures that all its elements' labels are not previously used in the configurable process model. Otherwise, we need to replace their labels by new unused ones.

In variant 10, "*Global*", "*Initiate_Registration*", "*Collect_Information*" and "*Decision_Notification*" are already used in the configurable process model (i.e., variant 9). They need to be substituted by any other unused labels. We choose "Global1", "*Initiate_Registration1*", "*Collect_Information1*" and "*Decision_Notification1*" as respective substitute labels.

After this step, Variant 10 = $\{\Sigma_{V10}, \Gamma_{V10}, \Delta_{V10}\}$

- Σ_{V10}={3, 5, 6, 11, 12}
- Γ_{V10}={Global1, Initiate_Registration1, Collect_Information1, Decision_Notification1}
- Δ_{V10}={
  Global1=Sequence(Initiate_Registration1, Collect_Information1, Decision_Notification1),
  Initiate_Registration1 = Sequence(3,5),
  Collect_Information1 = 6,
  Decision_Notification1 = Sequence(11,12)}

Fusion. Once the abstract business units' labels have been substituted by new labels, we proceed to the second step of the algorithm. This step consists of merging structures of the configurable process model and the new variant.

The fusion of these structures follows these rules[1]:

- $\Sigma_{CPM} = \Sigma_{CPM} \cup (\Sigma_{PV} - (\Sigma_{CPM} \cap \Sigma_{PV}))$: Σ_{CPM} contains all business units involved in both structures without redundancy.
- $\Gamma_{CPM} = \Gamma_{CPM} \cup \Gamma_{PV}$: Γ_{CPM} contains all abstract business units involved in both structures without redundancy.
- $\Delta_{CPM} = \Delta_{CPM} \cup \Delta_{PV}$: Δ_{CPM} contains all definitions of orchestrations between involved business units.

As we consider variant 9 as the configurable process model, here how it becomes after the fusion step, Variant 9 = $\{\Sigma_{V9}, \Gamma_{V9}, \Delta_{V9}\}$

- Σ_{V9}={2, 3, 5, 6, 11, 12}
- Γ_{V9}={Global, Initiate_Registration, Collect_Information, Decision_Notification, Global1, Initiate_Registration1, Collect_Information1, Decision_Notification1}
- Δ_{V9}={
  Global=Sequence(Initiate_Registration,Collect_Information, Decision_Notification),
  Initiate_Registration = Sequence(2,5),
  Collect_Information = 6,
  Decision_Notification = Sequence(11,12),
  Global1=Sequence(Initiate_Registration1,Collect_Information1, Decision_Notification1),
  Initiate_Registration1 = Sequence(3,5),
  Collect_Information1 = 6,
  Decision_Notification1 = Sequence(11,12) }

Unification. The third step of the algorithm concerns Δ. It ensures that elements of Δ are not redundant. In our example, (*Collect_Information* and *Collect_Information1*) and (Decision_Notification and Decision_Notification1) share the same business unit definitions. For this, Collect_Information1 is replaced by Collect_Information and Decision_Notification1 by Decision_Notification and their definitions are removed from Δ_{V9}.

After the Unification, Variant 9 = $\{\Sigma_{V9}, \Gamma_{V9}, \Delta_{V9}\}$

- Σ_{V9}={2, 3, 5, 6, 11, 12}
- Γ_{V9}={Global, Initiate_Registration, Collect_Information, Decision_Notification, Global1, Initiate_Registration1}
- Δ_{V9}={
  Global=Sequence(Initiate_Registration,Collect_Information, Decision_Notification),
  Initiate_Registration = Sequence(2,5),

---

[1] CPM stands for Configurable Process Model and PV stands for Process Variant.

Collect_Information = 6,
Decision_Notification = Sequence(11,12),
Global1=Sequence(Initiate_Registration1,Collect_Information,
Decision_Notification),
Initiate_Registration1 = Sequence(3,5) }

Variants Detection. At this level of the algorithm, we are sure that all element of Δ are not redundant, but we are not sure that our structure is minimal. Ensuring minimality helps for having an optimal structure. A structure is minimal if we cannot find in Δ any element that can be derived from another one.

To detect variants, we examine each element of $\Gamma \cup \Delta$ and check if there are any functional relations between business units.

In the near future, we plan to define the conceptual foundation of a configurable business process model. We plan to provide a formally defined conceptual model for describing: (i)functional, (ii) non-functional and (iii)structural aspects of different concepts involved in a configurable process model. The conceptual model will define clearly the function of each business unit and consequently determine the variation points.

For the moment, we assume that we found that "Initiate_Registration" has the same function as "Initiate_Registration1". Then we assign the definition of "Initiate_Registration1 = Sequence(2,5)" to Initiate_Registration and remove Initiate_Registration1. The result of this step is then, Variant 9 = $\{\Sigma_{V9}, \Gamma_{V9}, \Delta_{V9}\}$

- Σ_{V9}={2, 3, 5, 6, 11, 12}
- Γ_{V9}={Global, Initiate_Registration, Collect_Information,
  Decision_Notification, Global1}
- Δ_{V9}={
  Global=Sequence(Initiate_Registration,Collect_Information,
  Decision_Notification),
  Initiate_Registration = Sequence(3,5),
  Initiate_Registration = Sequence(2,5),
  Collect_Information = 6,
  Decision_Notification = Sequence(11,12),
  Global1=Sequence(Initiate_Registration,Collect_Information,
  Decision_Notification)}

Global Unification. The fifth step is the last step of this algorithm. It consists of detecting where the global business unit of the new variant fits in the configurable process model.

This step is similar to the unification (Step 3). It consist of computing the function of "Global1" and determine where does it fit in the structure.

In our example we suppose that "Global" and "Global1" share the same business function. In this case we just remove the "Global1" expression for Δ_{CPM}. The final configurable process model is then Variant 9 = $\{\Sigma_{V9}, \Gamma_{V9}, \Delta_{V9}\}$

- Σ_{V9}={2, 3, 5, 6, 11, 12}
- Γ_{V9}={Global, Initiate_Registration, Collect_Information, Decision_Notification}
- Δ_{V9}={Global=Sequence(Initiate_Registration,Collect_Information, Decision_Notification),
  Initiate_Registration = Sequence(3,5),
  Initiate_Registration = Sequence(2,5),
  Collect_Information = 6,
  Decision_Notification = Sequence(11,12) }

3.3   Summary and Discussion

This section presented the current level of advancement in our research work. It starts by defining our adopted terminology and then presented our formal description of a data structure for representing configurable process models. We have presented in Section 3.2 a first algorithm for updating the data structure when adding a new variant. This algorithm still need improvements especially for variants detection. This is mainly related to the definition of a complete conceptual model for presenting configurable process models which is part of our future work.

4   Related Work

Several approaches have been proposed for defining and managing business process variants. In this section we state four current approaches dealing with process variability.

The first approach is the most intuitive solution to variability management. It consists of managing a repository of process variants. Each process model is stored as an individual entity in the repository. Users have to formulate a query according to their requirements and the system should provide the most suitable model. This approach has been explored by [8,9,10] where it reveals that it needs a rich formal model for describing business process. In our work, we do not use individual models because the main problems of this solution are resource allocation and inconsistency. Indeed, (i) storing each variant individually leads to duplicated data storage for common parts of the process models and (ii) in case of new regulations enforcement, all process variants have to be updated which is resource consuming and error prone task. In addition, variation points are not explicitly handled and in [8], configuration-based modeling relies on querying the process models repository based on structural aspects of the to-be process. Therefore the business user has to know what are the possible process structures he is allowed to ask for.

The second approach as it is presented in [11,12], overcomes the problems of resource allocation and inconsistency. This solution considers a "basic process model" that represents common parts of all process models and variability is handled as a global property containing a set of operations (e.g., add, delete, modify, move operation). In fact, each variant is then generated via applying these operations on the basic model. However, the business user's control becomes limited to a set of operations generating rules which fire when they comply with all the business requirements. These rules capture only non functional aspects (i.e., quality aspects like cost and performance) leaving out details about structural and functional aspects of the variants.

The third approach consists of generating a global flat process model containing all variations and each individual model is generated by eliminating some branches of the global model. [13,14] model process variability as explicit variation points within the control structure of a flat configurable model. However this solution poses visualization problems because, in a real world setting with a lot of process variants, the configurable process tends to get very large. Therefore the configuration model becomes difficult to comprehend and costly to maintain. But [15,5] reduced these problems by presenting a questionnaire-based configuration which is much more user-friendly than previous solutions.

In [15,5], the user specifies his business requirements by answering a set of domain-related questions. The authors distinguish between domain variability (i.e., it is based on domain facts which are features that can be enabled or disabled) and process variability (i.e., it is based on possible alternatives at a certain variation point). Both are related through a set of mappings such that the result of the domain-specific questions are reflected in the chosen alternative for a variation point. It is a very good option to make configuration user centric but IT experts are still highly needed to define both domain and model variability and their mapping which is manually performed and this makes the approach liable to subjectivity.

In addition, this approach is not flexible enough to manage modularity. Indeed, if the user wants to configure a particular business function that is embedded in the global configurable model, he has to go through this model until reaching the intended business function to be configured. In our solution this problem cannot occur because we consider individual entities that can range from simple activities to complete process models.

The fourth approach studied in [16], is similar to ours as it exploits a hierarchical representation of the process into sub processes. The top level sub process encompasses the core activities and their associated variability, which is annotated by specific stereotypes, while the lower level sub processes express all details related to higher level activities and variabilities residing in them. However, the concept of hierarchical representation is supported more for hiding complexity than for managing variability.

5   Conclusion and Future Work

Reusing process models is an important concept for Business Process Management because it can decrease the modelling time and reduce the business user's work and risk to make errors.

Despite there exist different proposals for capturing variability in business process models, most of them suffer from three major shortcomings: lack of automation support in (i) maintaining the configurable process model, (ii) modelling sub-processes as stand alone entities and (iii) user-centricity and decision support in choosing the suitable alternatives.

We have previously [17] defined a framework for managing configurable process models and in this paper we presented an updated version of it. It defines a data structure that captures process model variability as a hierarchical representation. We presented how it is maintained when adding a new variant.

Our work is still in an early stage and continuous improvements are planned as a future work:

- In the near future, we plan to define the conceptual foundation of a configurable business process model. We plan to provide a formally defined conceptual model for describing: (i)functional, (ii) non-functional and (iii)structural aspects of different concepts involved in a configurable process model.
- We intend to investigate and extend this framework with other maintaining operations such as the deletion of a variant and considering different block patterns.
- The modelling phase, in the context of configuration-based modelling, includes a configuration phase where business analysts have to adapt the configurable process model in order to derive their intended process model. This issue has not been addressed in this paper, it will be part of our future work.

References

1. Dumas, M., van der Aalst, W.M., ter Hofstede, A.H. (eds.): Process-Aware Information Systems: Bridging People and Software through Process Technology. Wiley-Interscience, Hoboken (2005)
2. Weske, M.: Business Process Management: Concepts, Languages, Architectures. Springer, Heidelberg (2007)
3. van der Aalst, W.M.P.: Business process management. In: Liu, L., Özsu, M.T. (eds.) Encyclopedia of Database Systems. Springer, US (2009)
4. Indulska, M., Green, P., Recker, J., Rosemann, M.: Business Process Modeling: Perceived Benefits. In: Laender, A.H.F., Castano, S., Dayal, U., Casati, F., de Oliveira, J.P.M. (eds.) ER 2009. LNCS, vol. 5829, pp. 458–471. Springer, Heidelberg (2009)
5. Rosemann, M., van der Aalst, W.M.P.: A configurable reference modelling language. Inf. Syst. 32(1) (2007)
6. Vanhatalo, J., Völzer, H., Koehler, J.: The refined process structure tree. Data Knowl. Eng. 68(9) (2009)
7. González-Ferrer, A., Fdez-Olivares, J., Castillo, L., Morales, L.: Towards the Use of XPDL as Planning and Scheduling Modeling Tool: The Workflow Patterns Approach. In: Geffner, H., Prada, R., Machado Alexandre, I., David, N. (eds.) IBERAMIA 2008. LNCS (LNAI), vol. 5290, pp. 52–61. Springer, Heidelberg (2008)
8. Lu, R., Sadiq, S.K.: On the Discovery of Preferred Work Practice Through Business Process Variants. In: Parent, C., Schewe, K.-D., Storey, V.C., Thalheim, B. (eds.) ER 2007. LNCS, vol. 4801, pp. 165–180. Springer, Heidelberg (2007)

9. Markovic, I., Pereira, A.C.: Towards a Formal Framework for Reuse in Business Process Modeling. In: ter Hofstede, A.H.M., Benatallah, B., Paik, H.-Y. (eds.) BPM Workshops 2007. LNCS, vol. 4928, pp. 484–495. Springer, Heidelberg (2008)
10. Vulcu, G., Derguech, W., Bhiri, S.: Business Process Model Discovery using Semantics. In: BPM 2010 Workshops, LNBIP. Springer, Heidelberg (2010)
11. Hallerbach, A., Bauer, T., Reichert, M.: Managing Process Variants in the Process Life Cycle. In: Cordeiro, J., Filipe, J. (eds.) ICEIS, vol. (3-2) (2008)
12. Hallerbach, A., Bauer, T., Reichert, M.: Context-based Configuration of Process Variants. In: Proceedings of the 3rd International Workshop on Technologies for Context-Aware Business Process Management, TCoB (2008)
13. Dreiling, A., Rosemann, M., van der Aalst, W.M.P., Sadiq, W., Khan, S.: Model-driven process configuration of enterprise systems. In: Wirtschaftsinformatik. Physica-Verlag, Heidelberg (2005)
14. Lapouchnian, A., Yu, Y., Mylopoulos, J.: Requirements-Driven Design and Configuration Management of Business Processes. In: Alonso, G., Dadam, P., Rosemann, M. (eds.) BPM 2007. LNCS, vol. 4714, pp. 246–261. Springer, Heidelberg (2007)
15. La Rosa, M., Lux, J., Seidel, S., Dumas, M., ter Hofstede, A.H.M.: Questionnaire-driven Configuration of Reference Process Models. In: Krogstie, J., Opdahl, A.L., Sindre, G. (eds.) CAiSE 2007 and WES 2007. LNCS, vol. 4495, pp. 424–438. Springer, Heidelberg (2007)
16. Razavian, M., Khosravi, R.: Modeling Variability in Business Process Models Using UML. In: ITNG. IEEE Computer Society, Los Alamitos (2008)
17. Derguech, W., Vulcu, G., Bhiri, S.: An Indexing Structure for Maintaining Configurable Process Models. In: Bider, I., Halpin, T., Krogstie, J., Nurcan, S., Proper, E., Schmidt, R., Ukor, R. (eds.) BPMDS 2010 and EMMSAD 2010. LNBIP, vol. 50, pp. 157–168. Springer, Heidelberg (2010)

Business Process Families Using Model-Driven Techniques

Vinay Kulkarni and Souvik Barat

Tata Consultancy Services, 54-B, Industrial Estate
Hadapsar, Pune, India
{vinay.vkulkani,souvik.barat}@tcs.com

Abstract. Traditionally, businesses have used IT systems as mechanical advantage for automating static a-priori-defined repetitive tasks. Increased business dynamics has placed greater demands of adaptation and agility on to IT systems. Service oriented architecture is a step in this direction through separation of business process concerns from application functionality. There have been multiple attempts at improving adaptability of application services with varying degrees of success. But current business process modeling languages and execution platforms can at best support optimal point solutions that are not amenable for agile adaptation. Application services have benefited to some extent, from product-line architectures related to adaptation to a-priori known situations. We can apply the same idea to business processes. An extension of essential BPMN meta model supporting business process families, and a set of adaptation operators are presented in this paper. We describe their realization using model-driven techniques.

Keywords: Adaptive business process, business process family, configurable business process.

1 Introduction

Business enterprises use IT systems as a mechanical advantage through automation of a-priori well-defined repetitive operational tasks. With dynamics of business in the past being low, primary objective of business applications was to deliver results with certainty in a fixed operating environment. Increased dynamics has put new demands on businesses and introduced new opportunities that need to be addressed with cost effectiveness in ever-shrinking time window. Demands for agility and adaptiveness seem to be gaining preference over stability and robustness. Imparting these critical properties calls for a new perspective for implementing IT systems.

One of the principal concerns of enterprise IT is to design and develop flexible IT solutions that can rapidly adapt to changing operating environments. Separation of concerns is critical to enable flexibility. Separation of business process concern from application services is a critical requirement for a given set of application services to be orchestrated as per a flow definition. It is observed that application services typically tend to vary along four dimensions, namely, Business logic(L), Design strategies(D), Architecture(A), and Technology platform(T). Current development

M. zur Muehlen and J. Su (Eds.): BPM 2010 Workshops, LNBIP 66, pp. 314–325, 2011.

practice is to make a set of purpose-specific choices along these dimensions, and encode them in a scattered and tangled manner [18]. This scattering and tangling is the principal obstacle in adapting an existing implementation for the desired change. Large size of an enterprise application further exacerbates this problem. Model-driven development enables developers to focus on specifying L-dimension in terms of models and high level languages while addressing concerns along A, D and T dimensions through model-based code generation [17]. Specification-based generation of model-based generators further improves flexibility of IT systems along A, D and T dimensions [19]. Service oriented architecture splits L-dimension by separating business process concerns from application functionality. Application services have benefited, to some extent, from product-line architectures vis-a-vis adaptation to a-priori known situations. However, prevalent business process specification languages [2, 3, 4] are only capable of defining static processes i.e. it is possible to orchestrate the same set of application services as per a given flow definition. No support exists for i) orchestrating subset of a given set of services as per multiple flow definitions and, ii) orchestrating multiple sets of services as per multiple flow definitions. We argue the adequacy of the support of this nature to lend the desired flexibility to IT systems. Also, business processes catering to similar business intent in a domain are likely to be similar. Being ignorant of these similarities would mean redundancies in specification leading to maintenance and evolution problems later. Ability to specify commonality while highlighting the variability can reduce redundancy and improve adaptability of business processes significantly. We present how the product line concept [6, 7] can be used to specify business processes that can be adapted quickly for a changing operating environment.

Rest of the paper is organized as follows. Section 2 presents intuition guiding the proposed solution. Section 3 describes abstractions and formalism supporting the proposed solution. Section 4 describes the meta model for specifying the proposed abstractions. Section 5 illustrates adaptive business process concept with help of an example. Section 6 discusses the proposed approach in the light of related work.

2   Intuition

An enterprise can be viewed as a set of possibly interacting business processes. Business process is a control flow over a set of tasks or activities that may exchange data with each other. Also, business processes catering to similar business intent in a domain are likely to be similar in structure. Thus, a business process can be viewed as an instantiated *template* with *placeholder*s where control flow identifies the template and tasks identify the *part*s that can be suitably plugged at placeholders. A part can be a sub-process as well. Thus emerges a composition structure for business processes whereby a business process can be composed from its parts guided by a template serving as a blueprint. Composition is an inside-out view of business process. Looking outside-in, a business process can be viewed as exposing a set of [own] tasks and placeholders wherefrom interactions with tasks exposed by other business processes are possible. Thus emerges an integration / interaction structure for business processes. We argue that composition structure and integration structure lead to more agile business processes, and hence more agile enterprises, as described below.

One way of improving agility would be to enable choice over a set of equivalent parts to be plugged in at a placeholder – both in composition and integration context. While enabling choice, care needs to be taken to ensure the resultant business process is well formed – structurally as well as semantically. The choice can be made available at design time or run time leading to static and dynamic composition respectively. The same holds true for integration. In essence, the idea is to support the *family* concept [14, 15] for business processes wherein non-varying aspects (i.e. template), places where variations occur (i.e. placeholders), and variants pluggable at a placeholder (i.e. part) are modeled explicitly. We advocate use of feature modeling techniques [8] to derive structurally well-formed configurations of parts. For now, we leave the onus of ensuring semantic well-formed-ness of configurations to modelers.

3   Proposed Solution

Here we present abstractions for describing *template*, *part*, *placeholder*, *composition structure* and *integration structure*. We also present operators for deriving a larger part, selecting a part from the list of available options, and modifying a part so as to meet the context-specific requirements. Though these ideas are discussed here in the context of business processes only, they are found equally applicable to the other behavioural aspects of an enterprise application e.g. application services [16].

3.1   Business Process

Business process is a control flow over a set of activities and events. An activity is either atomic or composite. As composite activity can be decomposed into a set of fine-grained activities, it can be visualized as control flow over its constituent activities i.e. just like a business process. Atomic activity is an atomic unit of work realized either manually or automated through an application service.
We define a business process (P) as a tuple < E, A, s, D >, where

- E is the set of events raised or consumed by the process
- A is the set of activities of the process
- s is a process specification describing the control flow over A and E
- D is a set of data elements defining the process state
    o Each data element is identified by data type.
    o Each event carries data elements
    o Each activity consumes and produces data elements as input and output.

An activity is defined as a tuple <Name, In, Out, Kind >, where

Name: Name of the activity
In: Set of data objects that an activity consumes as input parameters
Out: Set of data objects that an activity produces as output parameters
Kind: Composite or Atomic or Communicating

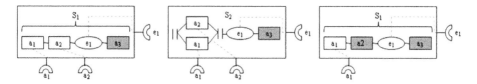

Fig. 1. Business Process Family

Composite Activity: An activity that can be broken down into finer activities and can be specified as a flow over other activities. Thus, each composite activity is essentially a process definition (P).

Atomic Activity: An atomic unit of work either automated through an application service (i.e. Service Task) or carried out manually (i.e. Manual Task)

Communicating Activity: Describes the interaction behaviour with other business processes. It is further classified into three categories: Invoke, Receive and Reply. The semantic of these categories are similar to BPEL/BPMN Invoke, Receive, and Reply semantics.

Business process specification languages [2, 3, 4] that industry practice uses are capable of supporting this abstraction.

3.2 Business Process Family

Business process family (PF) denotes a set of related business processes having well-defined commonality and a-priori known variability.

We define PF as a tuple $< E, A, S', D, TKV >$, where

- E, A, D are same as business process definition P.
- S' is a set of *templates*, essentially each template is process specification s of business process definition P.
- TKV is set of activity types. We define two types of activities: abstract and concrete. Each element $tkv \in$ TKV is tuple $<P, C>$ where P is a set of abstract activities, i.e. placeholders, and C is set of concrete activities.

Figure 1 gives a pictorial description of a process family comprising of three members. First two members expose activities a_1 and a_2, and event e_1 as *placeholders* with different process definition *templates* S_1 and S_2. Third member exposes activity a_1 and event e_1 as *placeholders* with process definition template S_1.

A process family is well-formed if types of all activities are defined, i.e.

$$\forall\ tkv \in TKV, tkv.P \cup tkv.C = A$$

3.3 Configurable Business Process

Configurable business process (P_{cfg}) is a member of a process family having placeholder(s), i.e. a process specification (template) containing atleast one abstract activity. Formally configurable business process (P_{cfg}) of a process family $PF = < E, A, S', D, TKV >$ is defined as:

$P_{cfg} = < E, A, s, D, tkv, >$ where $tkv \in TKV$ and $tkv.P \neq \phi, s \in S'$.

For instance, $< e_1, \{a_1, a_2\}, s_1, D, \{ tkv1 = \{\{a1, a2\} \{\}\}\}>$ of fig. 1. is a configurable business process with s_1 as its template and e_1, a_1 and a_2 as its placeholders. Since P_{cfg} contains placeholders and a placeholder is candidate for fitment by multiple parts, P_{cfg} too is a process family. Therefore, P_{cfg} can be configured to service a specific business intent by choosing a specific part for a placeholder and selecting a specification. The choice can be made either at process design time or process run time. The resultant process must be well-formed both structurally and semantically. Configuration structure defines the context for correct configuration.

3.3.1 Configuration Structure

Configuration structure describes the entire configuration context in terms of parts that can be fitted at placeholders. Configuration structure (CS) is a tuple $<P_{cfg}$, PS, Map> where,

-   P_{cfg} is the configurable process with placeholders
-   PS is a set of business processes i.e. candidate parts for the placeholders
-   Map is a set of mappings describing fitment of a part at a placeholder. There are two kinds of maps namely activity map (a_{map}) and event map (e_{map})

Activity map $a_{map} = P_{src}.a_i \rightarrow P_{dst}.a_j$, such that,

-   $P_{src} \in P_{cfg} \cup PS$
-   $P_{dst} \in PS$
-   $P_{src}.a_i$ is abstract activity
-   $P_{src}.a_i$ and $P_{dst}.a_j$ are compatible, i.e. source and destination activities are compatible w.r.t. activity kind, inputs, and outputs.
-   If $P_{dst}.a_j$ is an abstract activity then there exists a valid a_{map} for $P_{dst}.a_j$ in Map

Similarly, Event map $e_{map} = P_{src}.e_i \rightarrow P_{dst}.e_j$,such that,

-   $P_{src} \in P_{cfg} \cup PS$
-   $P_{dst} \in PS$

$P_{src}.e_i$ and $P_{dst}.e_j$ are compatible, i.e. compatible w.r.t. the data elements.

Figure 2 (a) shows the configuration structure wherein S_1 denotes the business process specification template that has a_1 and a_2 as activity placeholders and e_1 as event. P_{dst_a1} is one of the set of candidate processes (parts) for plugging in at a_1. Similarly, P_{dst_a2} for a_2 and P_{dst_e1} for e_1. Configuration structure is complete i.e. parts exist for all placeholders. Configuration structure is well-formed i.e. a candidate part is type compatible with its placeholder. Onus of ensuring semantic well-formed-ness, i.e. fitting parts meet the desired business intent, is solely with the process designer. Configuration structure serves the purpose of composition structure and integration structure (described in section 2) based on activity types and their corresponding mappings.

We define extension as enhancing configuration structure in order to support new situations. Configuration structure is extended in one of the following ways: i) adding new map over existing *parts* and *templates*, ii) adding new *parts* and iii) adding new *templates*. We support extensions to process family at design time only. However, run time extensions in terms of addition of new configurations seem possible.

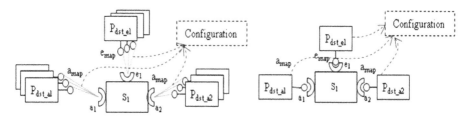

Fig. 2a. Configuration structure for a configurable business process

Fig. 2b. Configure operator for a configurable business process

3.3.2 Configuration

Configuration (cfg) denotes a set of parts that can be plugged in at the placeholders of a configurable process such that the resultant business process is complete and consistent. A configurable business process is complete if all its placeholders are plugged in. A configurable business process is consistent if every part that plugs in at a placeholder is compatible. Thus, configuration is a subset of Map. For instance, Configuration$_1$ of fig. 2 (a). A placeholder can be seen as a variation point and its candidate set of parts as variants. Thus, configuration structure defines a feature model. A configuration, then, is a valid feature configuration over the feature model [8].

Configuration is an act of selecting from many alternatives available. Configure operator of a configurable business process (P_{cfg}) over a configuration structure (CS) for a configuration (cfg) returns a complete and structurally well-formed business process i.e. P_R = Configure (P_{cfg}, CS, cfg). We say P_R is a configuration of P_{cfg} for a specific *situation*. Configuration structure determines all the *situations* that P_{cfg} can be configured for. Fig 2 (b) shows the Configure operator for the configuration structure and configuration of Fig 2 (a). We support configuration to be decided either at process design time or at run time. Deferral of the configuration decision to run time is supported by making the configuration information (i.e. cfg) available in the form of meta data for interpretation by process execution engine.

Composition is an act of deriving a larger unit from parts. Our notion of composition is similar to the concept of service orchestration where the specification of the larger unit decides which part goes in where in order to achieve the larger objective. We support process composition at design time only.

4 Meta Model

Fig 3 shows our meta model for specifying business process families as an extension of essential BPMN meta model that views a business process as a set of *connecting objects* that connect a set of *flow objects* exchanging *data objects*. This essential BPMN meta model captures the fixed behaviour (i.e. process structure) and is sufficient to specify concrete business processes. BPMN specification also enables an *activity* to be specified as *abstract* i.e. a *placeholder* where another process can be made to fit in using orchestration or choreography. However, this does not support i)

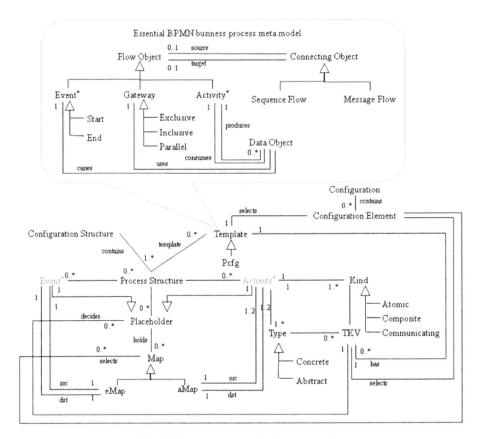

Fig. 3. Business process family meta model

orchestrating a given set of services as per multiple flow definitions, or ii) orchestrating multiple sets of services as per multiple flow definitions. To achieve these objectives, we define a meta model to support the family concept as described below:

- Process structure describes a business process family.
- Process structure is defined by set of activities and events. Fixed set of activities and events participate in many control flow definitions, each termed as template.
- Essentially, each template is specified by BPMN meta model as described in Figure 3.
- Two dimensions of variability, namely *Type* and *Kind*, are introduced for *Activity*. Kind of an activity can either be *Composite* or *Atomic* or *Communicating*. Type of an activity can either be *Concrete* or *Abstract*. *TKV* depicts a specific combination of type and kind for an activity. One can specify multiple TKVs for a process structure.
- A *Placeholder* is introduced to support two kinds of variability w.r.t. composition and integration. Placeholder can either be an *Event* or an *Abstract Activity*, i.e. each placeholder is derived from TKV definition.

- A *Map* defines composition or integration of a process part at a placeholder. It can either be an event map (specifying process integration) or an activity map (specifying process composition or integration as described in Table 1).
- Valid mappings and the corresponding variability are depicted in Table 1.

Table 1. Valid Activity & Event Mappings

→ Destination end of Map	Concrete Activity		Abstract Activity			Event
↓Source end of Map	Atomic	Composite	Atomic	Composite	Communicating	
Abstract Activity — Atomic	X	Composition	X	Variable Composition*	Integration	X
Composite	X	X	X	X	X	
Communicating	X	X	X	X	Integration	
Event	X			X		Integration

- Configuration structure is introduced to describe entire configuration context in terms of parts that can be fitted at placeholders
- Following are the rules for a well-formed model:

    o For activity map defining process composition,

        ▪ *IN* data elements of the source activity is a superset of *IN* data elements of the destination activity
        ▪ *OUT* data elements of the source activity is a subset of *OUT* data elements of the destination activity

    o For activity map defining process integration,

        ▪ *IN* data elements of the source activity is a subset of *OUT* data elements of the destination activity
        ▪ *OUT* data elements of the source activity is a superset of *IN* data elements of the destination activity

    o For event map defining process integration

        ▪ Data elements of the source event is a superset of data elements of the destination activity

Ability to specify multiple placeholders and a set of candidate processes for each placeholder enables modeling of a process family. Mechanisms such as feature models [8] can be used to select candidate parts of a placeholder. The selection can be fixed at process design time or deferred to process run time. We support the latter by making the selection mechanism available as runtime metadata. Defining an internally consistent set of parts – at least one each for a placeholder so that there are no 'holes' – is termed as a Configuration. Defining a new placeholder or adding a new part for an existing placeholder is termed as Extension.

Thus, the meta model in Figure 3 enables modeling of a business process family wherein each member serves the same intent in a specific situation. A new situation can be addressed by configuring available alternatives or, adding new variants and configuring them appropriately. Thus one can adapt to a new situation by switching over to the suitable variants.

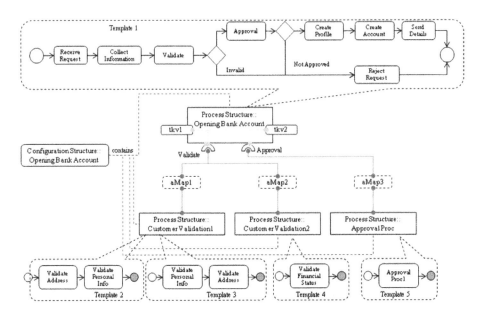

Fig. 4. Process family of opening a bank account

5 Illustrative Example

We use a simplified bank account opening process to illustrate variability, extensibility and configurability. Let us consider that account opening process is a control flow of set of activities A= {Receive Request, Collect Information, Validate, Approve, Create Profile, Create Account, Send Details, Reject Request} as depicted in Fig. 4. In this process definition process step, *validate* is defined as context-specific, i.e. behavior changes with the context. Let's consider that context specific behaviors differ in the following dimensions a) performing same set of activities in different order, let's say one would like to execute verify address and verify personal detail as part of validate process step but in different sequence, b) performing different set of activities, let's say one would like to verify financial details instead of verifying address and personal details. Fig. 4 describes a process family supporting different context specific requirements. In this figure, the account opening process is primarily a configurable business process $P_{AccOpen}$ = <E, A, template1, D, tkv1} of a process family PF = < E, A, {template1}, D, TKV}>, where

> A = {Receive Request, Collect Information, Validate, Approve, Create Profile, Create Account, Send Details, Reject Request},
> E = { },
> template1= instance of essential BPMN meta model, and
> TKV = {tkv1, tkv2} where tkv1 = {P= {validate}, C= {A-{validate}}} and tkv2 = {P={validate, Approval}, C={A-{validate, Approval}}}

The behaviors of configurable business process $P_{AccOpen}$ can differ as different parts can be fitted at defined placeholder, i.e. abstract activity *validate*. Process configuration structure CS=<$P_{AccOpen}$, {Customer Validation1, Customer Validation 2}, {aMap1=validate→Customer Validation1, aMap2=validate→Customer Validation2}> of business configurable process $P_{AccOpen}$ supports different behavioral variances through different configurations as follows:-

a. configuration1=<$P_{AccOpen}$, {Customer Validation1}, {aMap1}> where Customer Validation1 =<{}, {Validate Address, Validate Personal Info}, template2, D, φ}

b. configuration2 =<$P_{AccOpen}$, {Customer Validation1}, {aMap1}> where Customer Validation1 =<{}, {Validate Address, Validate Personal Info}, template3, D, φ}

c. configuration3 =<$P_{AccOpen}$, {Customer Validation2}, {aMap2}> where Customer Validation2 =<{}, {Validate Financial Status}, template4, D, φ}

Configuration1 and Configuration2 support validating address and personal information as part of validate process step. Configuration3 supports validating financial status as part of validate.

As described in the Fig. 4, the process family can be extended in multiple dimensions: i) any process step can be refined by defining some of the activities as abstract, providing refined process steps and corresponding map. For example, approval process step of the account opening process can be refined by defining it as abstract activity using tkv2, providing refined process steps using template5 and corresponding map aMap3, ii) behavioral variability in existing placeholders can be added by adding process steps and corresponding map, and iii) control flow of an existing process structure can be changed by adding new template in existing process structure. Though the illustrating example is limited to the extensibility and configurability of activity type and composition for adaptable activity, on similar lines, extensibility and configurability is possible for service mapping between concrete activity (of service type) to service; and between activity to activity mapping for process to process integration. This enables the extensions of a business process open ended along multiple dimensions, i.e. activity type, composition, integration and service binding.

6 Related Work

Though support for business process families to addresses dynamic business adaptation is highly desirable for enterprises, we came across only a few practical approaches in the literature. Recent literatures on *reference process modeling* [5] address this requirement using variant management techniques. A reference process represents a family of process models which can be customized in different ways to meet situation specific needs. For example, [11] and [13] provide support for both the specification and the customization of reference process models through EPC functions and decision nodes. Approach addresses configurability using annotated mandatory-ness indicator of EPC elements and configurable functions such as included (ON), skipped (OFF) or conditionally skipped (OPT). Similar approaches are presented in [9] and [10], wherein the configurability of a reference process model is achieved through configuration operator (such as enable, hide or block a configurable workflow element) and change operations (such as INSERT, DELETE, MOVE and MODIFY) of process fragments respectively. On the other hand, PESOA project [1] provides concepts for variant modeling based on BPMN specification. They address the variability problem using different variability techniques such as inheritance, parameterization, and extension points. Advancements of these techniques addressing different aspects of business process can be found in recent literature. For example, the approach presented in [12] goes beyond control flow and extends business process configuration to task-roles and task-objects.

Our solution is based on open-ended meta modeling techniques whereas the above mentioned approaches are based on fixed underlying models. Relying on meta modeling technique helps to address variability at different dimensions, i.e. business process composition, integration and bindings. It can be further extended for variability in other dimensions, for example roles and responsibility of human tasks, by extending business process adaptation meta model. Moreover, the existing approaches address variability through fixed variation points whereas our solution is capable of changing variation points using situation-specific activity type and kind definitions.

The existing business process management approaches support modeling and management of situation-specific business processes. However, modeling and management of process variants are not adequately supported in industry practice. As a result, situation-specific variants are either specified in the form of separate process models or expressed in terms of conditional branches within the same process model. Apart from being time and effort intensive, both the approaches result in model redundancies which further complicate maintenance and evolution. We presented an approach that enables quick adaptation of business processes in a consistent manner. We used product line concept wherein each member of a business process family comprises of family-wide fixed part and member-specific variant parts. We presented a composition operator that facilitates reuse of a business process in multiple contexts. The adaptiveness presented in this paper subsumes configurability (i.e. selecting one of the many available variants) and extensibility (i.e. addition of a new variant). The former is addressed through a meta model (business process meta model) and a set of design patterns address the latter. Proposed business process meta model is a pure extension of BPMN specification and, is capable of specifying the changes related to activity types, compositions, integration and binding aspects of business process. Also, it can further be extended for addressing other aspects, for example, the variability related to role and responsibility of human tasks. We justified meta model extensions and design patterns through a set of operators with suitable well-formedness criteria. This will help in creating new variants and configuring them in a consistent manner.

References

1. Schnieders, A., Puhlmann, F.: Variability Mechanisms in E-Business Process Families. In: Abramowicz, W., Mayr, H. (eds.) 9th International Conference on Business Information Systems (BIS 2006). LNI, Klagenfurt, Austria, Gesellschaft für Informatik, vol. P-85, pp. 583–601 (2006)
2. BPDM- Business Process Definition Meta model,
   http://www.omg.org/spec/BPDM/

3. BPEL - Business Process Execution Language,
   `http://docs.oasis-open.org/wsbpel/2.0/wsbpel-v2.0.pdf`
4. BPMN - Business Process Modeling Notation, `http://www.bpmn.org/`
5. Business Process Reference Model,
   `http://wwwcs.upb.de/cs/kindler/events/BPRM05/PDF/`
   `BPRM05_Proceedings.pdf`
6. Clements, P., Northrop, L.: Software Product Lines: Practices and Patterns. Addison-Wesley, Boston (2001)
7. Czarnecki, K., Antkiewicz, M.: Mapping features to models: A template approach based on superimposed variants. In: Glück, R., Lowry, M. (eds.) GPCE 2005. LNCS, vol. 3676, pp. 422–437. Springer, Heidelberg (2005)
8. Czarnecki, K., Helsen, S., Eisenecker, U.: Formalizing cardinality-based feature models and their specialization. Software Process Improvement and Practice 10, 7–29 (2005)
9. Gottschalk, F., van der Aalst, W.M.P., Jansen-Vullers, M.H., la Rosa, M.: Configurable Workflow Models. Int'l J. of Coop Inf. Systems (IJCIS) 17(2), 177–221 (2007)
10. Hallerbach, A., Bauer, T., Reichert, M.: Managing Process Variants in the Process Lifecycle. In: 10th Int'l Conf. on Enterprise Information Systems (ICEIS 2008), Barcelona, Spain, pp. 154–161 (June 2008)
11. La Rosa, M., Lux, J., Seidel, S., Dumas, M., ter Hofstede, A.H.M.: Questionnaire-driven Configuration of Reference Process Models. In: Krogstie, J., Opdahl, A.L., Sindre, G. (eds.) CAiSE 2007 and WES 2007. LNCS, vol. 4495, pp. 424–438. Springer, Heidelberg (2007)
12. La Rosa, M., Dumas, M., ter Hofstede, A.H.M., Mendling, J., Gottschalk, F.: Beyond Control-Flow: Extending Business Process Configuration to Roles and Objects. In: Li, Q., Spaccapietra, S., Yu, E., Olivé, A. (eds.) ER 2008. LNCS, vol. 5231, pp. 199–215. Springer, Heidelberg (2008)
13. Rosemann, M., van der Aalst, W.M.P.: A configurable reference modelling language. Inf. Syst. 32(1), 1–23 (2007)
14. Parnas, D.: Designing software for ease of extension and contraction. In: International Conference on Software Engineering Proceedings of the 3rd International Conference on Software Engineering, Atlanta, Georgia, United States, pp. 264–277 (1978)
15. Parnas, D.: Multi-Dimensional Software Families: Document Defined Partitions of a Set of Products. In: SPLC (2008), Keynote,
    `http://www.lero.ie/download.aspx?f=SPLC08.thumbs.pdf`
16. Barat, S., Kulkarni, V.: Supporting Agile Adaptive Business Services Using Model-based Techniques. In: 3rd International Workshop on Service Oriented Computing, Kochi, India (2009), `http://www.cse.iitb.ac.in/~umesh/WSOC09/program.html`
17. Kulkarni, V., Venkatesh, R., Reddy, S.: Generating Enterprise Applications from Models. In: Bruel, J.-M., Bellahsène, Z. (eds.) OOIS 2002. LNCS, vol. 2426, pp. 270–279. Springer, Heidelberg (2002)
18. Kulkarni, V., Reddy, S.: Separation of Concerns in Model-Driven Development. IEEE Software 20(5), 64–69 (2003)
19. Kulkarni, V., Reddy, S.: An abstraction for reusable MDD components: model-based generation of model-based code generators. In: GPCE, pp. 181–184 (2008)

Business Process Model Discovery Using Semantics*

Gabriela Vulcu, Wassim Derguech, and Sami Bhiri

Digital Enterprise Research Institute (DERI),
National University of Ireland, Galway
`firstname.lastname@deri.org`
`www.deri.org`

Abstract. Business process model discovery represents a pillar technique that enables business process model reuse. In this paper we describe a method for business process model discovery, which uses semantically annotated business processes. We created an RDF vocabulary for business processes that captures functional, non functional and structural properties that is used in the annotations of basic activities. We developed a set of algorithms to automatically generate different representations of the same business process at different granularity levels. We defined a set of rules to extract the RDF meta data in the annotated business process models and to build an RDF knowledge base which then can be interrogated using SPARQL.

Keywords: business process, reuse, discovery, granularity layers, RDF.

1 Introduction

There are two complementary approaches to model a business process (BP). There is modelling from scratch, task that is usually error prone and time consuming, however it is inevitable whenever a totally new business domain needs to be modelled. Then, there is the reusability of existing BP models that can be adapted or used for the auto-completion task. BP reusability helps to comply with best practices because they are already tested and proven to work. A pillar technique that enables BP reusability is BP model discovery.

BP model discovery is currently facing the following problems: First there are several languages used to represent BPs: WS-BPEL, XPDL, EPML etc.. However, current BP model discovery approaches are tailor-made for a specific BP modelling language [1, 2, 3, 4, 5] without taking into consideration the *diversity of BP modelling languages*. Thus, with the same BP discovery approach it is currently hard to discover BPs described with different modelling languages.

Then, current business process models are described at a *syntactic rather than at a semantic level*. It is known what the tasks of a process are, what is their

---

* This work is founded by the Lion II project supported by Science Foundation Ireland under grant number 08/CE/I1380.

M. zur Muehlen and J. Su (Eds.): BPM 2010 Workshops, LNBIP 66, pp. 326–337, 2011.

control flow, but there is no semantic description for them. We do not know what business functions the tasks achieve or under which time or cost. There are few discovery approaches that consider also functional and non functional properties, besides structural ones, although most of them discuss the need for other aspects in order to distinguish between processes with the same structural information.

Moreover, as shown in [6], the information granularity affects the effectiveness of BP model reuse. Without having *different representations of the same BP at different granularity levels*, it is possible that a given query does not match the granularity level of an existing BP and therefore the BP will not be retrieved.

In this paper we propose the use of semantics in order to address these problems. We developed a method for BP model discovery that uses semantically annotated BP models. We have developed an RDFvocabulary for BPs, described in Section 2, that captures functional, non functional as well as structural properties. We assume that the modelling environment supports the RDFa annotations of basic activities following this vocabulary during BP modelling. RDFa is a method for adding RDF meta data in XML files.

We developed a set of algorithms, described in Section 3, to automatically generate different representations of the same BP at different functional granularity levels based on the annotations of basic activities. This is done by identifying both the syntactic and semantic hierarchy of a BP whether it is graph-based, block-based or a hybrid between the two. Based on the result of these algorithms we enhance the annotations in the BP models with granularity-related meta data.

We developed a set of rules, described in Section 4, to extract the meta data from the annotated files and to generate corresponding RDF triples that we store in an RDF knowledge base. The RDF knowledge base can be then interrogated using SPARQL in order to retrieve those BPs that satisfy the business user's requirements. Before concluding (Section 6), we provide a comparative analysis between our method and existing BP model discovery approaches in Section 5.

2   RDF Vocabulary

In this section we describe the developed RDF vocabulary for BPs. As starting point for the creation of this vocabulary we have taken into consideration several projects and initiatives that have previously built ontologies for BP like the ARIS house[7], the OWL-S ontology(focusing on the Service Model part) and the ontologies developed in the SUPER project[1].

We set our model in the context of the enterprise information systems' views as shown in Fig.1. The Organization View describes resources, roles, organization units and relationships between them. The Data View describes the information objects, the concepts in the messages exchanged by process' tasks. The Function View described the functions required to satisfy the objective of the enterprise. The Control View describes the control flow of BPs that carry out the business

---

[1] http://www.ip-super.org/

operations inside the enterprise and it is an integration view between the other views. The Product/Service View describes the result of BP execution. At the current stage, our RDF vocabulary focuses mainly on the Data, Control and Function views, however it can be complemented with the other views.

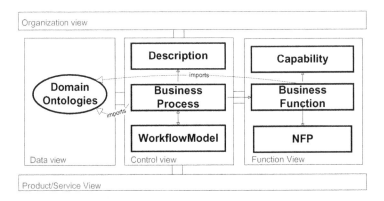

Fig. 1. High level description of the RDF vocabulary for BP

The main concept of the RDF vocabulary is the *BusinessProcess*. A *BusinessProcess* has a *Description* that provides human readable information about the process. It has a *WorkflowModel* that defines the process' structural properties and it achieves a *Business Function*. The *BusinessFunction* concept defines the process' functional properties as a *Capability* and the process' non functional properties through the *NFP* concept. The rest of this section describes the BP properties in more details.

Functional properties
The *Capability* represents a business functionality within an enterprise. It is described in terms of *Input, Output, Precondition, Effect* and *Tags* (Fig. 2). The *Input* and *Output* describe the data concepts (e.g. customer name, book title, delivery confirmation number). The *Precondition* describes the requirements over the input data and the state of the world before the *Capability* can be delivered (e.g. the credit card must be valid). The *Effect* describes the changes over the state of the world upon the execution of the *Capability*(e.g. the credit card will be charged). The *Tags* concept refers to a set of tags from an external ontology or taxonomy of business functionalities.

Non functional properties
The non functional properties represent an important criteria to differentiate between BPs having the same function. The *NFP* concept is refined in policy-related properties like *Cost* and *Availability* and QoS-related properties like *Security and Trust, Execution Time* and *Reliability* (Fig.3).

Structural properties
The structural properties (Fig.4) describe the control flow between the tasks of a BP through the *WorkflowModel* concept. The *WorkflowModel* is refined in

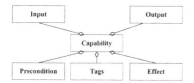

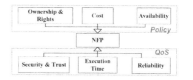

Fig. 2. Functional properties   **Fig. 3.** Non functional properties

GraphModel and *BlockModel*. The rationale for this is to have an RDF vocabulary general enough to describe a BP either from a block-based, graph-based or hybrid perspective.

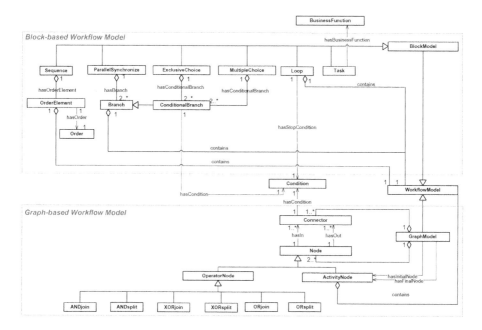

Fig. 4. Structural properties

The *BlockModel* uses workflow patterns to describe a BP as a block structure with one entry and one exit. It is refined in: *Sequence* - a list of *OrderedElements* (OE) that have an *Order* and contain a *WorkflowModel*; *ParallelSynchronize* - a pair of parallel split and synchronizing workflow patterns that consists of a set of *Branches* (Br), a *Branch* contains a *WorkflowModel*; *ExclusiveChoice* - a pair of exclusive choice and exclusive merge workflow patterns that consists of a set of *ConditionalBranches*, a *ConditionalBranch* (CBr) is a *Branch* guarded by a *Condition*(*cond*); *MultipleChoice* - a pair of multi-choice and synchronizing merge workflow patterns that consists of a set of *ConditionalBranches*; *Loop* - a block structure that contains a stop *Condition* and which will execute until *Condition* becomes true; *Task* - a non decomposable unit of work which is described through a *BusinessFunction* attribute.

The *GraphModel* describes a BP as a graph that contains *Nodes* interconnected with *Connectors*. A *Node* can be either an *ActivityNode* or an *OperatorNode*. The *ActivityNode* describes the work that has to be done and it contains a *WorkflowModel*. A special kind of *ActivityNodes* are the initial and the final nodes. The initial node has no input connectors while the final node has no output connectors. The *OperatorNodes*: *ANDjoin*, *ANDsplit*, *XORjoin*, *XORsplit*, *ORjoin*, *ORsplit*, define the control flow within the *GraphModel*.

There are two types of activities in a BP model: basic activities, which are *Tasks*, and structured activities which are *Sequence*, *ParallelSynchronize*, *ExclusiveChoice*, *MultipleChoice*, *Loop* and *ActivityNode*. The structured activities contain other structured activities or *Tasks*. Due to this imbrication, a workflow model can be seen as a tree that has *Tasks* as leaves.

We assume that the modelling environment supports the annotations of basic activities following this vocabulary.

3   Deriving Different BP Representations

In this section we provide a set of algorithms for automatically computing the functional and non functional properties of structured activities based on the annotations of the basic activities. These algorithms are crucial for deriving different representations of the same BP at different functional granularity levels.

There are two steps for deriving these different representation layers of a BP:

- Identify the **syntactic hierarchy** of the BP (Fig. 5.c, without call outs). For the block-based BP (Fig. 5.a), this is inherent to their tree-like structure. For the graph-based BP(Fig.5.b) this hierarchy is not implicit, but there are works like [8, 9] that deal with specifically the issue of finding a decomposition of a workflow graph into a hierarchy of sub-workflows.
- Identify the **semantic hierarchy** of BP (Fig. 5.c, including the call outs). It refers to the functional(i.e. Capability) and non functional(i.e. NFP) properties of each structured activity in the syntactic hierarchy. In the rest of this section we provide algorithms to automatically derive the semantic hierarchy of a BP which determines its different representation layers. We compute the functional and non functional properties of the structured activities in a bottom-up fashion starting from the basic activities and going towards the top of the syntactic hierarchy.

3.1   Block-Based Structured Activities

The algorithms for automatically computing functional and non functional properties of block-based activities are based on a set of **aggregation functions** that are associated to each property:*(aggSeq, aggPS, aggEC, aggMC, aggLoop)*. These aggregation functions define how the properties are computed over different types

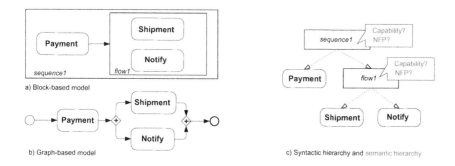

Fig. 5. (a) A block-based BP model; (b) A graph-based BP model (c) Their syntactic and semantic hierarchies

of block-based structures: Sequence, ParallelSynchronize, ExclusiveChoice, MultipleChoice and Loop respectively. The advantage of using aggregation functions is that they can be easily reused for new properties that are added to the conceptual model.

Non functional properties: The aggregation functions for non functional properties depend on their type as shown Table 1. First column stores the name of the non functional property, the second column stores its value type and the remaining columns store its aggregation functions.

Table 1. Aggregation functions for the non functional properties of our model

NFP	Type	aggSeq	aggPS	aggMC	aggEC	aggLoop
Cost	numeric	$sumNum$	$sumNum$	$sumNum$	$maxNum$	$nMultiply$
ExecutionTime	interval	$sumInt$	$maxMaxInt$	$minMaxInt$	$minMaxInt$	$nMultiplyInt$
Availability	percentage	$minNum$	$minNum$	$minNum$	$minNum$	$minNum$
Reliability	percentage	$minNum$	$minNum$	$minNum$	$minNum$	$minNum$
OwnershipAndRights	ds	ds	ds	ds	ds	ds
SecurityAndTrust	ds	ds	ds	ds	ds	ds

For properties with numerical, interval or percentage value types the aggregation functions compute the sum/maximum between numerical values (sumNum, MaxNum), the sum between intervals (sumInt) etc. Interesting functions are *minMaxInt* and *maxMaxInt* for intervals which we describe briefly:
maxMaxInt/minMaxInt applies to a set of interval values and returns the interval from the biggest/smallest minimum and the biggest maximum values. More formally:

$$maxMaxInt([min_1, max_1], ..., [min_n, max_n]) = [\max_{i=1}^{n}(min_i), \max_{i=1}^{n}(max_i)]$$

$$minMaxInt([min_1, max_1], ..., [min_n, max_n]) = [\min_{i=1}^{n}(min_i), \max_{i=1}^{n}(max_i)],$$

where min_i and max_i are the ends of the intervals.

In case of *OwnershipAndRights* and *SecurityAndTrust*, the aggregation functions do not depend on the block-pattern. Instead they might be domain specific complex functions (thus *ds* in the table).

Based on the aggregation functions, Algorithm 1 computes the non functional properties for a block-based structured activity *cnfp(BlockModel bm)*. The input of the algorithm is *bm*, a block-based structured activity. The output is the computed value for the non functional property *nfp*. The algorithm recursively applies the aggregation functions for Sequence (line 6), ParallelSynchronize (line 9), MultipleChoice and ExclusiveChoice (line 12) and for Loop (line 15). The recursion stops when the algorithm is applied to a Task (line 3).

Algorithm 1. Computing non functional properties for block-based structured activities (a.k.a *cnfp(BlockModel bm)*)

Input: BlockModel bm: block-based structured activity.

Output: NFP nfp: computed non functional property of bm.

```
1  begin
2     if bm is Task then
3        |   return bm.getNFP()
4     end
5     if bm is Sequence then
6        |   nfp ← aggSeq(cnfp(OE_1), ..., cnfp(OE_n))
7     end
8     if bm is ParallelSynchronize then
9        |   nfp ← aggPS(cnfp(Br_1), ..., cnfp(Br_n))
10    end
11    if bm is MultipleChoice or ExclusiveChoice then
12       |   nfp ← aggMC/aggEC(cnfp(CBr_1), ..., cnfp(CBr_n))
13    end
14    if bm is Loop then
15       |   nfp ← aggLoop(n, cnfp(bm.CA()))
16    end
17    return nfp;
18 end
```

Functional properties: The aggregation functions for functional properties depend on the semantics of the block-based structured activities with respect to their Capability (more precisely with respect to their input, output, precondition, effect and tags). For a detailed specification of the block-based structured activities we invite the reader to see our previous work [10].

The algorithm for computing the functional properties is similar to Algorithm 1 and computes the precondition, effect and tags for a block-based structured activity. Once these are computed, the algorithm looks for a business function from an existing business functions repository, that satisfies them. This is done using one of the currently existing matchmaking techniques [11, 12].

3.2   Graph-Based Structured Activities

We have adapted the I-propagation algorithm developed in [13] to compute functional and non functional properties of graph-based structured activities. For the rest of the section we adapt the formalizations for *graph model* and *annotated graph model* as described in [13]:

Graph model: is a directed graph $G =< N, C >$, where N is a set of nodes (i.e. ActivityNodes and Operators) and C is a set of connectors. For $n \in N$, IN(n)/OUT(n) denotes the set of incoming/outgoing connectors of n. It is imposed that each split node has exactly one incoming connector; each join node has exactly one outgoing connector, the InitialNode has no incoming connector and one outgoing connector, the FinalNode has one incoming connector and no outgoing connector.

Annotated graph model: is a 4-tuple $G =< N, C, O, \alpha >$, where: $< N, C >$ is a graph model as defined above, O is an ontology used to annotate the graphs nodes and α is an annotation function that associates with each node n a tuple $(prec(n), eff(n), cost(n), time(n))$, where $prec(n)$ (precondition), $eff(n)$(effect) are conjunctions of predicates from the ontology O and $cost(n)$ and $time(n)$ are the Cost and ExecutionTime of node n.

Due to space constraints we describe the algorithms for the Precondition(i.e. $Pre - propagation$) and Effect(i.e. $Ef - propagation$), the other ones being similar adaptations of the I-propagation algorithm.

Let $G =< N, C, O, \alpha >$ be an annotated graph model. We define the functions Pre, Eff with the initial values Pre_0, Ef_0 as $Pre_0(c) = prec(FinalNode)$, if $c = IN(FinalNode)$, $Pre_0(c) = \bot$ otherwise; $Ef_0(c) = eff(InitialNode)$, if $c = OUT(InitialNode)$, $Ef_0(c) = \bot$ otherwise where c is a connector. Given Pre, Ef, we define their propagations Pre' and Ef' with the propagation rules described in Fig.6:

These algorithms compute, for each connector in the graph, the propagated precondition/effect, based on each node's precondition and effect. They start with the function Pre_0/Ef_0 and iteratively, following the propagation rules described in Fig.6 fire subsequent nodes and update the precondition/effect for each connector. The propagation ends when there is no node to fire. Note that in order to compute the precondition of a graph-based structured activity, the propagation algorithm starts from the final node whereas for the effect computation it starts from the initial node.

The precondition/effect assigned by $Pre/Ef - propagation$ to the output/ input connector of graph's initial/final node, after firing all the nodes, represents the computed precondition/effect of the graph model. For more detailed explanations and an illustrative example of how these algorithms work, we invite the reader to have a look at the technical report that is an extension of this paper [14].

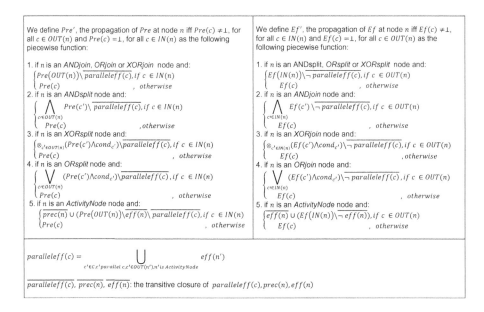

Fig. 6. Computing the precondition and effect of graph-based structured activities

4   Extracting Meta Data from Annotated BP Files

Based on the result of the previous algorithms we enhance the annotations of BP models with granularity-related meta data. In order to extract the meta data from BP annotated files, we developed a set of rules which we describe next.

The result of applying these rules is a set of RDF triples which we store in an RDF knowledge base. The RDF knowledge base can then be interrogated using SPARQL. We extract the functional and non functional properties from the RDFa annotations using an RDFa extractor[2]. We extract the structural properties of the process from the XML structure file. We map the control flow descriptions of BP modelling languages to our RDF vocabulary. So far we developed XSLT transformation rules for WS-BPEL2.0 and XPDL 2.1. However, any XML-based BP language can be used with our approach providing the corresponding rules.

#	WS-BPEL2.0	Our vocabulary
1	\<process\>	Process
2	basic activity	Task
3	\<sequence\>	Sequence
4	\<sequence\> sub element	OrderElement
5	\<if\>	ExclusiveChoice
6	\<else–if\>	ConditionalBranch
7	\<pick\>	ExclusiveChoice
8	\<while\>	Loop
9	\<repeatUntil\>	Loop
10	\<forEach\>	Loop
11	\<flow\>	ParallelSynchronize
12	\<flow\> sub element	Branch
13	\<scope\>	depends on inner activity
14	\<extensionActivity\>	Task

Fig. 7. Rules for WS-BPEL2.0

---

[2] http://kwarc.info/projects/krextor/

As an example, Fig.7 shows some transformation rules for WS-BPEL 2.0.: Rule 2 maps any basic activity element (e.g. $< invoke >$, $< receive >$, $< reply >$ etc.) to a Task concept, rule 3 maps a $< sequence >$ element to a Sequence concept, rule 4 maps every activity subelement of $< sequence >$ to an OrderedElement concept and so on.

Fig.8 shows the result of applying these rules on an annotated WS-BPEL file. We use the following namespaces: *bpel* for the WS-BPEL schema, *bv* for our RDF vocabulary, *ex* for the given WS-BPEL v2.0. process, *bt* for domain specific vocabulary used in the annotations, *rdf* for the RDF schema.

On the left side we have the WS-BPEL2.0 file of the process described in Fig.5.b where the Shipping task has been annotated with the BusinessFunction "bt:BookShipment". On the right side we have the RDF triples generated when applying the XSLT rules and using the RDFa extractor.

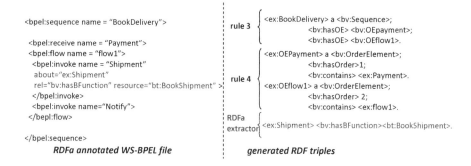

Fig. 8. The result of applying the rules on an annotated WS-BPEL2.0 BP file

5 Related Work

The majority of BP discovery approaches is tailor made for a specific[1, 2, 3, 4, 5] BP modelling language without taking into consideration their diversity. Other approaches [15, 16] propose a more generic solution that treats a process as a graph. However, these solutions are only focusing on retrieving the structural information of a BP without considering its functional and non functional properties.

Our RDF vocabulary for BPs is general enough to describe both graph-based processes, block-based processes and also a hybrid combination between the two. This vocabulary captures functional, non functional and structural properties to describe any structured activity in a BP, including the BP itself.

[15, 2, 3, 4, 5] discuss the need for multi-aspect queries in order to distinguish between several processes with different functional and/or non functional properties (e.g. features like: resources, process relevant data items, textual annotation, business domain, location etc..). However, these properties can be specified only at the global, process level, and not at the individual substructures of the BP.

[6] shows, in an experimental study, the impact of information granularity on the effectiveness of BP model reuse. With this in mind, in our approach we are able to recover different representations of the same BP at different granularity levels. Moreover, except [15], none of the existing works in BP model discovery takes into consideration this important aspect. The authors of [15] address this problem with developing a granularity level analyser that checks whether composition/decomposition operations are necessary when the query and the target graph-based models are at different granularity levels. However their decomposition is tightly coupled to the modelling language used (e.g. for WSCL, a "SendReceive" activity is decomposed into a "Send" and a "Receive" activities). Moreover, judging by the provided demo example, they actually flatten every graph-based model (i.e. query and target) to the finer granularity level without allowing intermediary representations of the BP model.

Table 2 summarizes the related works with respect to the following aspects: (i) the **BP modelling languages** the approach applies to; (ii) the **BP properties** used during BP model discovery (i.e. functional (fp), non functional(nfp) and structural(sp) properties) and (iii) whether they consider different **representations of the same BP at different functional granularity levels**.

Table 2. Related BP model discovery approaches

Approach	BP language	BP Properties	Granularity
BP-QL [1]	BPEL	sp	no
PVR [2]	proprietary language	sp, few nfp	no
SBPR [3, 4]	WSMO/pi-calculus	sp, fp, nfp	no
[5]	OWL/FPN	sp, fp	no
[16]	BPEL	sp	no
BeMatch [15]	BPEL, WSCL	sp, few nfp	yes
our approach	independent	fp, nfp, sp	yes

6   Conclusion

In this paper we presented a method for BP discovery that abstracts from the BP modelling language using semantically annotated BP models. We created an RDF vocabulary that captures BP functional, non functional and structural properties. We assume that the modelling environment supports the RDFa annotations of basic activities using this vocabulary during BP modelling. We developed a set of algorithms to automatically generate the different representations of the same BP at different functional granularity levels based on the annotations of basic activities. The result of these algorithms enhances the annotations in the BP models with granularity-related meta data. We developed a set of rules to extract the meta data from the annotated files and to generate corresponding RDF triples that we store in an RDF knowledge base. The created RDF knowledge base can be then interrogated using SPARQL in order to retrieve those BPs that satisfy the business user's requirements. We are currently in the phase of developing the proposed method as a plug-in of an existing BP modelling environment in order to support the business experts in the BP modelling phase.

References

1. Beeri, C., Eyal, A., Kamenkovich, S., Milo, T.: Querying business processes. In: Proc. of the 32nd International Conference on Very Large Data Bases (2006)
2. Lu, R., Sadiq, S.W.: On the discovery of preferred work practice through business process variants. In: Proc. of the 26th International Conference on Conceptual Modeling (2007)
3. Ma, Z., Wetzstein, B., Anicic, D., Heymans, S., Leymann, F.: Semantic business process repository. In: Proc. of the International Workshop on Semantic Business Process Management (2007)
4. Markovic, I., Costa Pereira, A., de Francisco, D., Muñoz, H.: Querying in business process modeling. In: Di Nitto, E., Ripeanu, M. (eds.) ICSOC 2007. LNCS, vol. 4907, pp. 234–245. Springer, Heidelberg (2009)
5. Men, P., Duan, Z., Yu, B.: Utilizing fuzzy petri net for choreography based semantic web services discovery. In: Proc. of the 28th International Conference on Applications and Theory of Petri Nets and Other Models of Concurrency (2007)
6. Holschke, O., Rake, J., Levina, O.: Granularity as a cognitive factor in the effectiveness of business process model reuse. In: Dayal, U., Eder, J., Koehler, J., Reijers, H.A. (eds.) BPM 2009. LNCS, vol. 5701, pp. 245–260. Springer, Heidelberg (2009)
7. Scheer, A.W.: Aris House of Business Engeneering (1998)
8. Vanhatalo, J., Völzer, H., Koehler, J.: The refined process structure tree. In: Dumas, M., Reichert, M., Shan, M.-C. (eds.) BPM 2008. LNCS, vol. 5240, pp. 100–115. Springer, Heidelberg (2008)
9. Derguech, W., Vulcu, G., Bhiri, S.: An Indexing Structure for Maintaining Configurable Process Models. In: Bider, I., Halpin, T., Krogstie, J., Nurcan, S., Proper, E., Schmidt, R., Ukor, R. (eds.) BPMDS 2010 and EMMSAD 2010. LNBIP, vol. 50, pp. 157–168. Springer, Heidelberg (2010)
10. Vulcu, G., Bhiri, S., Hauswirth, M., Zhou, Z.: A user-centric service composition approach. In: Chung, S., Herrero, P. (eds.) OTM-WS 2008. LNCS, vol. 5333, pp. 160–169. Springer, Heidelberg (2008)
11. Li, L., Horrocks, I.: A software framework for matchmaking based on semantic web. In: Proc. of the 12th International Conference on the WWW (2003)
12. Paolucci, M., Kawamura, T., Payne, T.R., Sycara, K.P.: Semantic matching of web services capabilities. In: Horrocks, I., Hendler, J. (eds.) ISWC 2002. LNCS, vol. 2342, p. 333. Springer, Heidelberg (2002)
13. Hoffmann, J., Weber, I., Governatori, G.: On compliance checking for clausal constraints in annotated process models. Information Systems Frontiers, Special Issue on Governance, Risk, and Compliance (2009)
14. Vulcu, G., Derguech, W., Bhiri, S.: Business process model discovery using semantics. Technical report, DERI, National University of Ireland, Galway (2010)
15. Corrales, J.C., Grigori, D., Bouzeghoub, M., Burbano, J.E.: Bematch: a platform for matchmaking service behavior models. In: Proc. of the 11th International Conference on Extending DataBase Technology (2008)
16. Ma, Z., Lu, W., Leymann, F.: Query structural information of bpel processes. In: Proc. of the 4th International Conference on Internet and Web Applications and Services (2009)

Name-Based View Integration for Enhancing the Reusability in Process-Driven SOAs

Huy Tran, Uwe Zdun, and Schahram Dustdar

Distributed Systems Group
Information System Institute
Vienna University of Technology, Austria
{htran,zdun,dustdar}@infosys.tuwien.ac.at

Abstract. Many companies opt for reusing existing software development artifacts due to the benefits of the reuse such as increasing productivity, shortening time-to-market, and spending less time for testing, debugging, to name but a few. Unfortunately, reusing artifacts in existing process-driven SOA technologies is cumbersome and hard to achieve due to several inhibitors. First, the languages used for business process development are not intentionally designed for reuse. Second, numerous tangled process concerns embraced in a process description significantly hinder the understanding and reusing of its concepts and elements. Third, there is a lack of appropriate methods and techniques for integrating reusable artifacts. In our previous work, we proposed a view-based, model-driven approach for addressing the two former challenges. We present in this paper a named-based view integration approach aiming at solving the third one. Preliminary qualitative and quantitative evaluations of four use cases extracted from industrial processes show that this approach can enhance the flexibility and automation of reusing process development artifacts.

Keywords: reuse, business process, SOAs, view-based, model-driven, name-based, tool support.

1 Introduction

Process-driven, service-oriented architectures (SOAs) advocate the notion of process in order to aggregate various business functionality to accomplish a certain goal, such as fulfilling a purchase order, handling customer complaints, booking a travel itinerary, and so on. A typical business process consists of a number of activities that are orchestrated by a control flow. Each activity is either a communication task (e.g., invoking other services, processes, or an interaction with a human) or a data processing task. Business processes are often designed by business and domain experts using high-level, notational languages, such as Business Process Modeling Notation (BPMN)[1] and UML Activity Diagram[2]. Process designs in the aforementioned languages are mostly non-executable, and therefore, have to be translated into or implemented in low-level,

---

[1] http://www.bpmn.org
[2] http://www.uml.org

M. zur Muehlen and J. Su (Eds.): BPM 2010 Workshops, LNBIP 66, pp. 338–349, 2011.

executable languages such as Business Process Execution Language (BPEL)[3]. After that, process implementations can be deployed in a process engine for executing and monitoring.

The IEEE Glossary of Software Engineering Terminology defines reusability as "*the degree to which a software module or other work product can be used in more than one computer program or software system*" [1]. The significant benefit of reuse is to improve software quality and productivity [2,3]. There are several types of reusable aspects in software projects such as architectures, source code, data, design, documentation, test cases, requirements, etc. [4,5]. The state-of-the-art software reuse practice suffers from several technical and non-technical inhibitors [6,7]. Reuse in business process development is not an exception. We identify the most important factors that hinder the reuse of artifacts during the process development life cycle as:

- Most of the languages used for modeling and developing processes, such as BPMN, UML Activity Diagram, EPC, WS-BPEL, etc., are not intentionally designed for reuse. As a result, none of the plethora of existing tools for business process design and development offers adequate support for reusing development artifacts.
- A process description based on the aforementioned languages is often suffering from various tangled concerns such as the control flow, collaborations, data handling, transaction, and so on. As the number of services or processes involved in a business process grows, the complexity of the process increases along with the number of invocations, data exchanges, and therefore, multiplies the difficulty of analyzing, understanding, and reusing any artifacts.
- The lack of adequate method support for flexibly integrating and composing reusable artifacts also contributes to the difficulty of reusing process artifacts.

In our previous work we proposed a novel approach for addressing the complexity of business process development [8,9,10,11,12]. Our approach explored the notion of views and the model-driven stack in order to separate process representations (e.g. process designs or implementations) into different (semi-)formalized view models. This way, stakeholders can be provided with tailored perspectives by view integration mechanisms [10,8] according to their particular expertise and interests. View models are also organized into appropriate levels of abstraction: high-level, abstract views are suitable for business experts while low-level, technology-specific views are mostly used by technical specialists. In this paper we focus on providing a solution for the third issue mentioned above, i.e., supporting methods for reusing and integrating process artifacts in a flexible manner. In particular, we introduce a name-based matching approach for view model integration and show that this approach can enhance the flexibility and automation of process artifacts (i.e., process views and view elements) reuse via industrial case studies.

This paper is organized as follows. In Section 2 we briefly introduce the View-based Modeling Framework [8,10,9] that realizes the view-based, model-driven approach. Next, Section 3 presents a name-based view integration approach which is simple, efficient, and flexible for improving the reusability. Processes extracted from four case

---

[3] http://docs.oasis-open.org/wsbpel/2.0/OS/wsbpel-v2.0-OS.pdf

studies are exemplified to illustrate our approach in Section 4 along with a quantitative study to evaluate this approach in industrial context. Then Section 5 discusses the related work. Finally, Section 6 summarizes our main contributions.

2 View-Based Modeling Framework

In this section, we briefly introduce the View-based Modeling Framework (VbMF), which is an implementation of our view-based, model-driven approach [8]. VbMF exploits the notion of process views to separate tangled process concerns in order to reduce the complexity and enhance the flexibility and extensibility in process-driven SOA development. Each process concern, i.e., a particular perspective of business processes, is (semi-)formally described by a view model that comprises a number of elements and their relationships. VbMF view models are organized into abstract and technology-specific layers. As such, business experts, who mostly work with the high level view models, can better formulate domain- and business-oriented concepts and knowledge because the technical details have been abstracted away. For particular process-driven technologies, such as BPEL, VbMF provides extension models that add details to the abstract models that are required to depict the specifics of these technologies [8]. These extension views belong to the technology-specific layer shown in Figure 1.

VbMF initially provides stakeholders with basic (semi-)formalizations, which are the FlowView, CollaborationView and InformationView models, for describing a business process. The FlowView model specifies the orchestration of process activities, the CollaborationView model represents the interactions with other processes or services, and the InformationView model elicits data representations and processing. Nonetheless, VbMF is not bound to these view models but can be extended for capturing many other concerns, for instance, human interaction [9], data access and integration [13], and traceability [12]. View models of VbMF are derived from fundamental concepts and elements of the Core model. Thus, the concepts of the Core model are the extension points and integration points of VbMF [8].

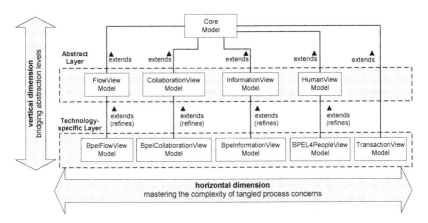

Fig. 1. Overview of the View-based Modeling Framework ([8,9])

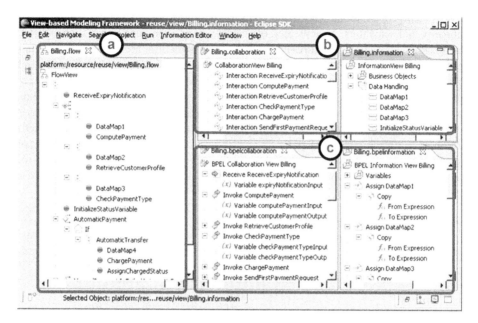

Fig. 2. Billing Renewal process development using VbMF

We implemented VbMF as Eclipse plugins based on the Eclipse Modeling Framework[4]. To illustrate how VbMF works in reality, we exemplify parts of the billing and provisioning system of a domain registrar and hosting provider [14]. The billing system comprises a wide variety of services including: credit bureau services (cash clearing, card validation and payment, etc.), domain services (whois, domain registration and transfer, etc.), hosting services (Web and email hosting, provisioning, etc.), and retail services (customer service and support, etc.). The company has developed a business process, namely, Billing Renewal process, in order to integrate and orchestrate core functionality and the services. We present the VbMF views of the Billing Renewal process that are the FlowView (Figure 2(a)), the high-level CollaborationView and InformationView (Figure 2(b)), and the low-level BpelCollaborationView and BpelInformationView (Figure 2(c)). For further details of VbMF, we would like to refer the readers to [8,10,11,12,9].

3   Name-Based View Integration Approach

In our view-based, model-driven approach, the FlowView – as the most important concern in process-driven SOA – is often used as the central view. Views can be integrated via integration points to produce a richer view or a thorough view of the business process. We propose a name-based matching algorithm for realizing the view integration mechanism (see Algorithm 1). This algorithm is simple, but effectively used at the view level (or model level) because from a modeler's point of view in reality it makes sense, and

---

[4] http://www.eclipse.org/emf

is reasonable, to assign the same name to the modeling entities that pose the same functionality and semantics. Nonetheless, other view integration approaches such as those using class hierarchical structures or ontology-based structures are applicable in our approach with reasonable effort as well. Exploring other view integration mechanisms and comparing them with the name-based matching approach is beyond the scope of this paper. Therefore, we merely focus on the name-based view integration and illustrate its promising advantages contributing to improve the reusability of process artifacts.

Before discussing in detail the name-based view integration, we introduce the definition of conformity of model elements and integration points. Let m be an element of a certain view model, the symbol $\hat{m}$ denotes the hierarchical tree of inheritance of m, i.e., all elements which are ancestors of m, and $m.x$ denotes the value of the attribute x of the element m.

Definition 1 (Conformity). *Let M_1, M_2 be two view models and $m_1 \in M1$ and $m_2 \in M2$. Two elements m_1 and m_2 are **conformable** if and only if m_1 and m_2 have at least one common parent type in their tree of inheritance or m_1 is of type m_2, or vice versa.*

Using $m_1 \uparrow m_2$ to denote m_1 and m_2 are **conformable**, Definition 1 is given as:

$$m_1 \uparrow m_2 \iff (\hat{m}_1 \cap \hat{m}_2 \neq \varnothing) \vee (m_1 \in \hat{m}_2) \vee (m_2 \in \hat{m}_1)$$

Definition 2 (Integration point). *Let M_1, M_2 be two view models and two views V_1, V_2 be instances of M_1 and M_2, respectively. A couple of elements e_1 and e_2, where $e_1 \in V_1$ and $e_2 \in V_2$, e_1 is an instance of m_1, and e_2 is an instance of m_2, is an **integration point** between V_1 and V_2 if and only if m_1 and m_2 are **conformable** and e_1 and e_2 have the same value of the attribute "**name**".*

Using $I(e_1, e_2)$ to denote the integration point between two views V_1 and V_2 at the elements e_1 and e_2, and $x \succ y$ to denote x is an instance of y, Definition 2 can be written as:

$$I(e_1, e_2) \iff (m_1 \uparrow m_2) \wedge (e_1.name = e_2.name)$$

where

$$e_1 \in V_1, e_2 \in V_2, e_1 \succ m_1, e_2 \succ m_2, V_1 \succ M_1, V_2 \succ M_2$$

The main idea of the name-based matching for view integration is to find all integration points $I(e_1, e_2)$ between two views V_1 and V_2 and merge these two views at those integration points. The merging at a certain integration point $I(e_1, e_2)$ is done by creating a new element which aggregates the attributes and references of both e_1 and e_2 (see Algorithm 1). The complexity of the name-based matching algorithm is approximately $O(k + l + k \times l)$, where $k = |V_1|$ and $l = |V_2|$. This complexity can be significantly reduced by generating and maintaining a configuration file containing the integration points of every pair of views with tool support. The integration points can be automatically derived from the relationships between two views. Later on, the view integration algorithm only loads the configuration file and performs view merging straightforwardly. This way, the complexity of the view integration algorithm can be reduced to approximately $O(P)$, where P is the number of integration points between V_1 and V_2. We note that $P \leq k \times l$. In reality, the numbers of elements which are used for view integration are often much less the total number of elements of the containing

---

Algorithm 1. View integration by name-based matching

Input: View V_1 and view V_2
Output: Integrated view V_{12}
begin
    V_{12}.initialize();
    $E_1 \leftarrow V_1$.getAllElements();
    $E_2 \leftarrow V_2$.getAllElements();
    V_{12}.addElements(E_1);
    V_{12}.addElements(E_2);
    foreach $e_1 \in E_1$ **do**
        $found \leftarrow$ **false**;
        while *not* $found$ **do**
            $e_2 \leftarrow E_2$.next();
            if *(e_1.name = e_2.name) $\wedge$ (e_1.superType $\uparrow$ e_2.superType)* **then**
                $found \leftarrow$ **true**;
                $e_{new} \leftarrow$ createNewElement();
                e_{new}.attribute $\leftarrow$ merge(e_1.attribute, e_2.attribute);
                e_{new}.reference $\leftarrow$ merge(e_1.reference, e_2.reference);
                V_{12}.addElements(e_{new});
                V_{12}.removeElements(e_1,e_2);
    return V_{12};
end

---

view, and therefore, $P \ll k \times l$). Nonetheless, this approach requires additional support, especially tool support, for deriving and maintaining the integration points, which is one of our ongoing endeavors to complete the framework.

4 Case Study

In this section, a typical process development scenario is used to demonstrate how the name-based view integration in VbMF can support a flexible reuse of process artifacts. After that, we present a preliminary quantitative evaluation of our approach based on four use cases extracted from industrial business processes.

4.1 Process Artifacts Reuse Scenario

As shown in Section 2, the Billing Renewal process has been developed using VbMF. Now the company starts develop an Order Handling process such that Internet customers can order the company's products via the Web site. Figure 3 shows the core functionality of the Order Handling process in terms of a BPMN diagram. The company opts to reuse existing artifacts as much as possible to develop the Order Handling process rather than starting from scratch. After analyzing the business requirements, the developers identify a number of fragments of process models and services with similar functionality existing across the enterprise. For instance, the Order Handling process requires a task that charges customer payment by invoking the services provided by the credit bureau partner. This task is similar to the *ChargePayment* task of the Billing Renewal process developed before. Therefore, this task should be reused in the Order Handling process rather than being re-developed.

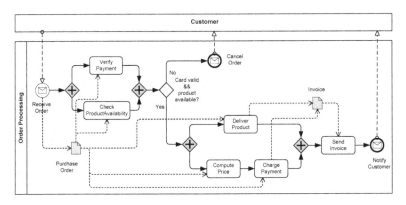

Fig. 3. Overview of the Order Handling process

Figure 4 illustrates how the developers reuse the existing *ChargePayment* activity for modeling the Order Handling process. The scenario is presented in terms of UML object diagrams. On the right-hand side, we show the CollaborationView and BpelCollaborationView of the Billing Renewal process where the *ChargePayment* activity is defined at high-level and low-level of abstract, respectively. In the Billing Renewal CollaborationView, *ChargePayment:Interaction* – an instance of the *Interaction* class – has relationships with three other objects: *CreditBureau:Partner*, *CreditBureau:Interface*, and *charge:Operation*. The *ChargePayment:Interaction* object is refined in the Billing Renewal BpelCollaborationView by the *ChargePayment:Invoke* object – an instance of the *Invoke* class. The *ChargePayment:Invoke* object has two more associations with the *chargePaymentInput:VariableReference* and *chargePaymentOutput:VariableReference* objects.

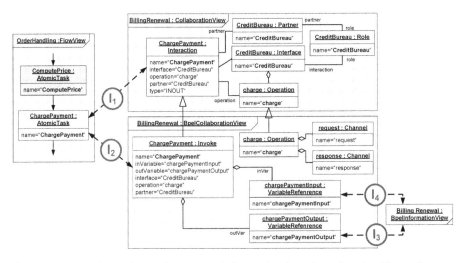

Fig. 4. Name-based view integration approach for reusing by referencing the *Charge Payment* element of the Billing Renewal Process in the Order Handling process

In order to properly reuse the *ChargePayment* activity of the Billing Renewal process, the developers perform two steps:

1. Create a corresponding *ChargePayment:AtomicTask* in the Order Handling FlowView as shown in the right-hand side of Figure 4.
2. Perform one of the following tasks (note that these tasks can be supported by the framework in a (semi-)automatic manner):
   (a) Explicitly define either an integration point I_1 between the *ChargePayment: AtomicTask* and the *ChargePayment:Interaction* or I_2 between the *Charge Payment:AtomicTask* and the *ChargePayment:Invoke*.
   (b) Explicitly specify the CollaborationView and BpelCollaborationView of the Billing Renewal process are input views of the Order Handling process. As VbMF supports view integration by name-based matching (cf. Section 3), the aforementioned integration points can be implicitly resolved by VbMF tooling, for instance, the code generators.

A question might be risen at this point: "*How's about the relationships between the reused elements and other views or elements?*". For instance, the *ChargePayment:Invoke* has associations with *chargePaymentInput:VariableReference* and *chargePaymentOutput:VariableReference* objects which are instances of the *VariableReference* class. In the Billing Renewal process, the actual definitions of these objects belong to the BpelInformationView. Therefore, these objects are part of the integration points I_3 and I_4, respectively, between the BpelCollaborationView and BpelInformationView of the Billing Renewal process. In this situation, the stakeholders can take any one of two possible approaches which can be (semi-)automatically supported by our modeling framework:

1. Reuse the existing integration points between the BpelCollaborationView and BpelInformationView of the Billing Renewal process: The stakeholders can gain more benefit of reusability but they have to analyze the subsequent dependencies of the reused objects in the BpelInformationView. In addition, these subsequent dependencies also require extra effort to maintain view synchronization when making any change in the reused views. This task is supported by our traceability approach [12].
2. Create new objects in the Order Handling BpelInformationView bearing corresponding names, then I_3 and I_4 can be automatically derived. Although no benefit of reusability gained, there is also no binding to the Billing Renewal BpelInformationView. That is, no extra effort for understanding the subsequent dependencies or maintaining view synchronization is required.

4.2   Quantitative Evaluation

So far we presented a development scenario to illustrate how our view-based, model-driven powered by the name-based matching can improve the flexibility and automation of reuse process development artifacts. To explore the application and pragmatic usage of our approach, adequate experiments to quantitatively evaluating it in industrial business process development environment are definitely necessary. As the use cases examined in our work are mostly in the preliminary development phase. Thus, the reuse rate is an adequate factor for the initial assessment of the value of the reuse method [15,5]. We present in this section our quantitative evaluations of the reuse rate according to the model proposed by Gaffney and Cruickshank (which is called *the proportion of reuse*) [15] as well as by Frakes and Terry (which is called *reuse percent*) [5]. Essentially, the reuse rate R_R of each view reflects how much of that view can be attributed to reuse and be computed by the formula $R_R = \frac{E_R}{E} \times 100$, where E_R is the number of reusable/reused elements and E is the total number of model elements of the corresponding view [15,5].

We have conducted the quantitative evaluation in four processes extracted from industrial use cases. Two of them are the Billing Renewal and the Order Handling processes mentioned in the previous sections. Two other processes are the CRM Fulfillment process [14] and the Travel Booking process [16]. The CRM Fulfillment process is part of the customer relationship management (CRM), billing, and provisioning systems of an Austrian Internet Service Provider. The Travel Booking process is based upon the procedure of making itinerary arrangements. It comprises typical steps for accomplishing a travel reservation: Internet customers submit data about the travel itineraries and receive a confirmation number when the travel itineraries have been booked successfully. These processes are mostly in the modeling and implementation phases. In Table 1, we present the reuse rate R_R of VbMF views, such as CollaborationView (CV), InformationView (IV), BpelCollaborationView (BCV), and BpelInformationView (BIV), of each case study.

Table 1. The reuse rate of process view models in four use cases

Process	CV			IV			BCV			BIV		
	E_R	E	R_R (%)	E_R	E	R_R (%)	E_R	E	R_R (%)	E_R	E	R_R (%)
Billing Renewal	49	63	*77.78*	59	85	*69.41*	63	132	*47.73*	407	494	*82.39*
CRM Fulfillment	60	74	*81.08*	63	78	*80.77*	74	131	*56.49*	448	537	*83.43*
Order Handling	29	36	*80.56*	36	44	*81.82*	36	65	*55.38*	238	286	*83.22*
Travel Booking	27	33	*81.82*	33	43	*76.74*	33	56	*58.93*	219	260	*84.23*
Average			**80.31**			**77.19**			**54.63**			**83.32**

As illustrated in the previous development and reuse scenario, each element of VbMF process views is potentially reusable artifact. A FlowView purely contains a control flow that defines the business logic, i.e., the execution order of process activities in order to achieve a particular business goal. Note that detailed specification of process activities, for instance, invoking a service, transforming data objects, are not embraced in the FlowView but others such as (Bpel)CollaborationView and (Bpel)InformationView. Therefore, reusing an existing FlowView to develop a new process is still possible but inefficient. Nonetheless, a FlowView can be reused as the documentation of an "*as-is*" process that can be referenced, or even used as a skeleton, for developing new processes. For this reason, we omit the reuse rate of the FlowView in Table 1.

The ratio of reuse also reflects the tendency of integration of VbMF views. That is, *AtomicTasks* of the FlowView are often integrated with the corresponding elements of the CollaborationView and InformationView such as *Interaction*

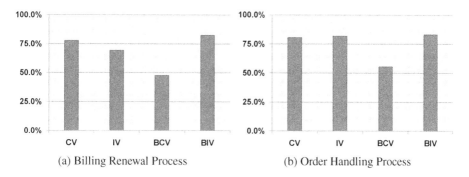

(a) Billing Renewal Process   (b) Order Handling Process

Fig. 5. The reuse rate of view models in the Billing Renewal and Order Handling processes

and *Data Handling*, or elements of the BpelCollaborationView and BpelInformationView, such as *Receive, Reply, Invoke,* and *Assign*. In addition, a number of elements of the (Bpel)CollaborationView have references to corresponding elements of
(Bpel)InformationView whilst none of the (Bpel)InformationView's element depends
on other views' elements. As a result, the ratio of reuse of the (Bpel)InformationView
is much higher than that of the (Bpel)CollaborationView. The ratios of reuse of high-
level views are higher than that of low-level ones because the abstract concepts are more
reusable than the technology-specific counterparts. The average degrees of reuse over
four use cases are very promising: **80.31%** for the CollaborationView (CV), **77.19%**
for the InformationView (IV), **54.63%** for the BpelCollaborationView (BCV), and
83.32% for the BpelInformationView (BIV). Because the reuse rates of view models
of each use case is almost identical to those of the others, we only show the visualiza-
tions of the evaluation results of the Billing Renewal and Order Handling processes (see
Figure 5).

5   Related Work

Software reuse has been an active field of study in software engineering since last three
decades that leads many promising results for reusing existing software or software
knowledge to build new software [7,4,6]. Several work in this field has contributed success stories in various aspects such as reuse libraries, domain engineering methods and
tools, reuse design, design patterns, domain specific software architecture, components,
generators, and so on [6]. Yet there has been very few investigation of reuse in in the
area of business process management, in particular, business process development.

As we mentioned above, most of popular languages used for modeling and developing business processes such as BPMN, UML Activity Diagram, EPC, BPEL, etc., are
not intentionally designed for reuse. As a consequence, developers find it hard to reuse
a certain excerpt of a process represented in any of these languages. Reuse merely exists
in form of *"copy-and-paste"* if the same language is used to model and develop business processes. Otherwise, necessary interpretation and translation must be performed
in order to reuse existing processes. All these are however cumbersome and error-prone
tasks.

To the best of our knowledge, most of researches on software reuse in the domain of business process management focus on the control flow of the business process. Van der Aalst et al. [17] proposed several so-called workflow patterns, which are reusable control flow structures representing frequently occurring knowledge for constructing workflows. Each pattern has a sound semantic and example usage in various workflow products. These patterns can be applied for specifying, analyzing, understanding the control flow of business processes. Similarly, Schumm et al. [18] present an approach based on the notion of process fragment that enables a flexible method for describing and integrating existing artifacts into business processes. From our point of view, the aforementioned approaches and our work in this paper are nicely complementary. We believe that further exploring and integrating can fully benefit the reuse of the control flow. The distinctive point is that our approach does not solely focus on the reuse of the control flow per se. Facilitating VbMF's extension mechanisms [8], we aim at supporting the flexible reuse of business processes from different aspects such as collaborations, data handling, etc., considering the control flow as the central notion.

Markovic and Pereira present a preliminary approach based on π-calculus and ontologies to provide richer representations of business process aspects such as function, information, organization, etc., [19]. This approach aims at using ontologies to explicitly specify business knowledge for better manipulating and reusing. However, the authors have not further mentioned or investigated the reuse of these knowledge in the business process life cycle.

6   Conclusion

In the domain of process-driven SOAs, reusing existing development artifacts is hindered by various factors. First, the languages used for modeling and developing processes are not intentionally designed for reuse. Second, business process representations in these languages are often complex and tangled by various concerns such that it is hard for the stakeholders to analyze, understand, and reuse them. Last but not least, there is still a lack of methods for flexibly integrating reusable artifacts.

In our previous work, we presented a novel solution for addressing the two former challenges. In this paper we focused on a name-based view integration approach aiming at solving the last challenge. Through a qualitative scenario-driven and a quantitative evaluation, we show that promising results on reusing process development artifacts can be achieved using our approach. Nonetheless, further endeavors such as industrial experiments and surveys over several software projects are definitely necessary in order to confirm the application and pragmatic usage of this approach in reality. In addition, exploring other view integration methods, such as those based on concept hierarchies or ontologies, can help fully exploiting the benefit of reuse and enhancing the automation in reusing process development artifacts.

Acknowledgement

This work was supported by the European Union FP7 project COMPAS, grant no. 215175.

References

1. IEEE: Standard Glossary of Software Eng. Terminology (December 1990)
2. Gaffney, J., Durek, T.A.: Software reuse: key to enhanced productivity: some quantitative models. Information and Software Technology 31(5), 258–267 (1989)
3. Fichman, R., Kemerer, C.F.: Incentive compatibility and systematic software reuse. J. Systems and Software 57(1), 45–60 (2001)
4. Krueger, C.W.: Software reuse. ACM Comp. Surv. 24(2), 131–183 (1992)
5. Frakes, W., Terry, C.: Software reuse: metrics and models. ACM Comp. Surv. 28(2), 415–435 (1996)
6. Frakes, W., Kang, K.: Software reuse research: status and future. IEEE Trans. Software Eng. 31(7), 529–536 (2005)
7. Morisio, M., Ezran, M., Tully, C.: Success and failure factors in software reuse. IEEE Trans. Software Eng. 28(4), 340–357 (2002)
8. Tran, H., Zdun, U., Dustdar, S.: View-based and Model-driven Approach for Reducing the Development Complexity in Process-Driven SOA. In: Int'l Conf. Business Process and Services Computing (BPSC). LNI, vol. 116, pp. 105–124. GI (2007)
9. Holmes, T., Tran, H., Zdun, U., Dustdar, S.: Modeling Human Aspects of Business Processes – A View-Based, Model-Driven Approach. In: Schieferdecker, I., Hartman, A. (eds.) ECMDA-FA 2008. LNCS, vol. 5095, pp. 246–261. Springer, Heidelberg (2008)
10. Tran, H., Zdun, U., Dustdar, S.: View-based Integration of Process-driven SOA Models At Various Abstraction Levels. In: 1st Int'l Workshop on Model-Based Software and Data Integration, pp. 55–66. Springer, Heidelberg (2008)
11. Tran, H., Zdun, U., Dustdar, S.: View-Based Reverse Engineering Approach for Enhancing Model Interoperability and Reusability in Process-Driven SOAs. In: Mei, H. (ed.) ICSR 2008. LNCS, vol. 5030, pp. 233–244. Springer, Heidelberg (2008)
12. Tran, H., Zdun, U., Dustdar, S.: VbTrace: Using View-based and Model-driven Development to Support Traceability in Process-driven SOAs. J. Softw. Syst. Model. (2009), http://dx.doi.org/10.1007/s10270-009-0137-0
13. Mayr, C., Zdun, U., Dustdar, S.: Model-Driven Integration and Management of Data Access Objects in Process-Driven SOAs. In: Mähönen, P., Pohl, K., Priol, T. (eds.) ServiceWave 2008. LNCS, vol. 5377, pp. 62–73. Springer, Heidelberg (2008)
14. Evenson, M., Schreder, B.: SemBiz Project: D4.1 Use Case Definition and Functional Requirements Analysis (August 2007), http://sembiz.org/attach/D4.1.pdf
15. Gaffney, J.E., Cruickshank, R.D.: A general economics model of software reuse. In: 14th Int'l Conf. Software Eng. (ICSE), pp. 327–337. ACM Press, New York (1992)
16. IBM: Business process use cases (2006), http://publib.boulder.ibm.com/bpcsamp (accessed 01/05/2008)
17. van der Aalst, W., ter Hofstede, A.H.M., Kiepuszewski, B., Barros, A.P.: Workflow Patterns. Distributed and Parallel Databases 14(1), 5–51 (2003)
18. Schumm, D., Leymann, F., Ma, Z., Scheibler, T., Strauch, S.: Integrating Compliance into Business Processes Process Fragments as Reusable Compliance Controls. In: Multikonferenz Wirtschaftsinformatik (MKWI), pp. 2125–2137. Universitätsverlag, Göttingen (2010)
19. Markovic, I., Pereira, A.C.: Towards a Formal Framework for Reuse in Business Process Modeling. In: BPM Workshops Advances in Semantics for Web services 2007 (semantics4ws 2007), pp. 484–495. Springer, Heidelberg (2008)

3rd International Workshop on Business Process Management and Social Software (BPMS² 2010)

3rd International Workshop on
Business Process Management
and Social Software
(BPMS² 2010)

Workshop Organization

Workshop Organizers

SelminNurcan
University Paris 1 - Panthéon Sorbonne
Centre de Recherche en Informatique
90, rue de Tolbiac
75634 Paris cedex 13
France

Rainer Schmidt
HTW-Aalen
University of Applied Sciences
Anton-Huber-Straße 25
73430 Aalen
Germany

Program Committee

Ilia Bider - IbisSoft, Sweden
Nadine Blinn - University of Hamburg, Germany
Jan Bosch - Intuit, Mountain View, California, USA
DraganGasevic - Athabasca University, Canada
Werner Geyer - IBM T.J. Watson Research Labs, USA
Tad Hogg - HP Information Dynamics Laboratory, USA
Ralf Klamma - RWTH Aachen, Germany
Sai Peck Lee - University of Malaya, Malaysia
Gustaf Neumann - Vienna University of Economics and Business Administration, Austria
SelminNurcan - University Paris 1 Pantheon Sorbonne, France
Gil Regev - EcolePolytechniqueFédérale de Lausanne, Switzerland
Michael Rosemann - Queensland University of Technology, Australia
Nick Russell - Eindhoven University of Technology, The Netherlands
Rainer Schmidt - University of Applied Sciences, Aalen, Germany
Miguel-Ángel Sicilia, University of Alcalá, Spain
PninaSoffer - University of Haifa, Israel
Markus Strohmaier - Graz University of Technology, Austria
KarstenWendland - University of Applied Sciences, Aalen, Germany

Introduction

Selmin Nurcan[1] and Rainer Schmidt[2]

[1] University Paris 1 Panthéon Sorbonne, France
[2] HTW-Aalen, 73430 Aalen, Germany

Social software [1] is a new paradigm that is spreading quickly in society, organizations and economics. Social software has created a multitude of success stories such as wikipedia.org and the development of the Linux operating system. Therefore, more and more enterprises regard social software as a means for further improvement of their business processes and business models. For example, they integrate their customers into product development by using blogs to capture ideas for new products and features. Thus, business processes have to be adapted to new communication patterns between customers and the enterprise: for example, the communication with the customer is increasingly a bi-directional communication with the customer and among the customers. Social software also offers new possibilities to enhance business processes by improving the exchange of knowledge and information, to speed up decisions, etc. Social software is based on four principles: weak ties, social production, egalitarianism and mutual service provisioning.

- Weak ties

Weak-ties [2] are spontaneously established contacts between individuals that create new views and allow combining competencies. Social software supports the creation of weak ties by supporting to create contacts in impulse between non-predetermined individuals.

- Social Production

Social Production [3] is the creation of artefacts, by combining the input from independent contributors without predetermining the way to do this. By this means it is possible to integrate new and innovative contributions not identified or planned in advance. Social mechanisms such as reputation assure quality in social production in an a posteriori approach by enabling a collective evaluation by all participants.

- Egalitarianism

Egalitarianism is the attitude of handling individuals equally. Social software highly relies on egalitarianism and therefore strives for giving all participants the same rights to contribute. This is done with the intention to encourage a maximum of contributors and to get the best solution fusioning a high number of contributions, thus enabling

M. zur Muehlen and J. Su (Eds.): BPM 2010 Workshops, LNBIP 66, pp. 355–358, 2011.

the wisdom of the crowds [4]. Social software realizes egalitarianism by abolishing hierarchical structures, merging the roles of contributors and consumers and introducing a culture of trust.

- Mutual Service Provisioning

Social software abolishes the separation of service provider and consumer by introducing the idea, that service provisioning is a mutual process of service exchange. Thus both service provider and consumer (or better prosumer) provide services to one another in order co-create value [5]. This mutual service provisioning contrasts to the idea of industrial service provisioning, where services are produced in separation from the customer to achieve scaling effects.

Up to now, the interaction of social software and its underlying paradigms with business processes have not been investigated in depth. Therefore, the objective of the workshop has been to explore how social software interacts with business process management, how business process management has to change to comply with weak ties, social production, egalitarianism and mutual service, and how business processes may profit from these principles.

The workshop had three topics:

1. **New opportunities provided by social software for BPM**

2. **Engineering next generation of business processes: BPM 2.0 ?**

3. **Business process implementation support by social software**

The workshop started with an introduction given by Selmin Nurcan and Rainer Schmidt. Then Rainer Schmidt gave a presentation about combining social software and business process management raising the question, whether this paves the way to a BPM 2.0.

Ben Jennings framed the problem of socially generated information in the context of Open Source software development processes and of improved execution of tasks in that domain. His paper introduces a novel two stage mechanism to answer such a problem. First a dynamic domain specific lexicon is created to improve term weighting relevance. Then this weighting is enhanced by analyzing implicit proximity between participants of the socially generated production.

In the following presentation David Martinho and António Rito-Silva proposed ECHO as an evolutive vocabulary system that focuses on the formalization of informal entities. It supports both strategies of top-down and bottom-up.

The paper from Irina Rychkova and Selmin Nurcan formulates 5 challenges of case management encountered while modeling an example process using a traditional, activity-oriented modeling formalism, i.e. BPMN. They proposed the use of declarative specifications, variability modeling, and FOL-based semantics for modeling descriptive processes and, in particular, case management processes. Finally they assembled these theoretical concepts in the form of DeCo process specifications that extend the BPMN notation.

Martin Böhringer proposed case management as a possible solution to include unstructured ad-hoc processes into business process management. In addition to existing top-down approaches, his paper suggests a bottom-up view on Case Management that leverages emergent user-driven case handling. He theoretically derived characteristics of such a system and demonstrated the approach based on a toolset of current Social Software techniques including microblogging, activity streams and tagging.

The paper from Ilia Bider, Paul Johannesson and Erik Perjons develops a system that provides business process support enhanced with properties of social software. Furthermore it shows how the requirements set on the structure and usage of the shared spaces can be implemented in practice. The paper demonstrates how typical features such as blogs/forums found in social software can be naturally introduced into a business process support system.

In the paper from António Rito-Silva, Michael Rosemann and Samia Mazhar: Towards Processpedia – An Ecological Environment for BPM Stakeholders Collaboration, the Processpedia approach is introduced to foster effective collaboration among stakeholders without enforcing egalitarianism. It intends to be an ecological collaboration environment for knowledge production by capitalizing on stakeholders' distinctive characteristics.

The paper "Empowering Business Users to Model and Execute Business Processes" from Florian Schnabel, Jesus Gorronogoitia and Freddy Lecue proposes a novel Lightweight Process Modelling seeking to lower the entrance barrier for modelling executable processes. It provides a specification of a Lightweight Process Modelling process and the Language for Lightweight Process Modelling (LLPM).

We wish to thank all authors for having shared their work with us, as well as the members of the BPMS2'10 Program committee and the workshop organizers of BPM'10 for their help with the organization of the workshop.

Workshop Program Committee

Ilia Bider - IbisSoft, Sweden
Nadine Blinn - University of Hamburg, Germany
Jan Bosch - Intuit, Mountain View, California, USA
Ralf Klamma -Informatik 5, RWTH Aachen, Germany
Sai Peck Lee - University of Malaya, Kuala Lumpur, Malaysia
Dragan Gasevic - School of Computing and Information Systems, Athabasca University, Canada
Werner Geyer - IBM T.J. Watson Research, Collaborative User Experience Group, Cambridge, USA

Gustaf Neumann - Vienna University of Economics and Business Administration, Vienna, Austria
Selmin Nurcan - University Paris 1 Pantheon Sorbonne, France
Gil Regev - EPFL & Itecor, Switzerland
Michael Rosemann - Faculty of Information Technology Queensland University of Technology, Australia
Nick Russell - Eindhoven University of Technology, The Netherlands
Rainer Schmidt - University of Aalen, Germany
Miguel Ángel Sicilia - University of Alcalá, Madrid, Spain
Pnina Soffer - Department of Management Information Systems, University of Haifa, Israel
Markus Strohmaier - Graz University of Technology, Austria
Karsten Wendland - University of Aalen

References

1. Schmidt, R., Nurcan, S.: BPM and Social Software. In: Dumas, M., Reichert, M., Shan, M.-C. (eds.) BPM 2008. LNCS, vol. 5240. Springer, Heidelberg (2008)
2. Granovetter, M.S.: The Strength of Weak Ties. American Journal of Sociology 78, 1360 (1973)
3. Benkler, Y.: The Wealth of Networks: How Social Production Transforms Markets and Freedom. Yale University Press, New Haven (2006)
4. Surowiecki, J.: The Wisdom of Crowds. Anchor, New York (2005)
5. Vargo, S., Maglio, P., Akaka, M.: On value and value co-creation: A service systems and service logic perspective. European Management Journal 26, 145–152 (2008)

Implicit Social Production:
Utilising Socially Generated Data By-Products

Ben Jennings and Anthony Finkelstein

University College London
London, UK
{b.jennings,a.finkelstein}@cs.ucl.ac.uk

Abstract. Enhancing business processes by the integration of social software is an area of active research. Once such integration has occurred, a new problem is presented - that of using social data in an effective manner. With large amounts of user generated data created, finding relevance in both data and in the people who created it as part of a business process becomes problematic. This paper frames the problem of socially generated information in the context of Open Source software development processes and of improved execution of tasks in that domain. Such social processes highlight the research area of facilitating the automatic selection of relevant data as part of a larger process. The paper introduces a novel two stage mechanism to answer such a problem. The approach is built on the concept of using the implicit social connections available from socially generated data artefacts to create a weighting model. This methodology is inherently egalitarian in nature as it uses a folksonomical strategy to construct the model. A dynamic domain specific lexicon is created to improve term weighting relevance. This weighting is then enhanced by analysing implicit proximity between participants of the socially generated production. By combining these two methods within a software framework, finding relevancy within a large corpus of socially generated data is improved. The prototype software framework built on these two approaches is constructed to provide dynamic programatic access to social data which can be incorporated as part of a larger business process to speed up the decision making process.

Keywords: Workflow, Identity, Ad Hoc, Social Production.

1 Introduction

Interest in utilising social software in business processes has been gaining momentum due to successful crowd sourced projects such as Wikipedia. When a business harnesses successfully social production in any numerically significant manner, a new problem presents itself, that of information overload. Such overload presents a new issue. With the abundance of information available from which to make an informed decision there is an inability for an individual to process such data. The term data artefact is used to refer to any interactions by individuals or information generated within a given domain.

Decision scaling, or lack of ability to process, presents a problem for the successful usage of such data within a business process. An exemplar of such a problem domain would be that found in Open Source software development, where in order to complete a task, significant work must be executed to find relevant support documents. Merely

M. zur Muehlen and J. Su (Eds.): BPM 2010 Workshops, LNBIP 66, pp. 359–371, 2011.

gathering such data artefacts is of less value if informed actions may not be informed by the artefacts. There has been much research in the information retrieval and machine learning area on large scale information data sets. Such approaches are, in the main, seeking general purpose solutions and focus on normal language usage.

This paper introduces two approaches used together which are fundamentally built upon social interactions and the concept of weak ties [11]. Both approaches are built on social data by-products. Such a by-product may be considered as an indirect analysis of socially generated data from which implicit information may be realised. This form of analysis is inherently based on a flat structure, as no a priori hierarchical structures are being placed in relation to the relative merit of data artefacts. Domain Specific Nomenclature (DSN) seeks to address the construction of a specific dynamic lexicon to enable more relevant term weighting on socially constructed data sets. Implicit Social Proximity (ISP) is used in conjunction with the first approach and looks at clustered data and historic interactions between people adding to the business process to provide additional weighting metrics. This novel approach focuses on what is being said and to whom, rather than other forms of analysis such as method call traces [15] and commit frequency [17]. The two approaches are shown as part of a software framework. The framework presented is intended for use in the context of a business process and as such is ad hoc and lightweight in nature. The framework is able to re-adjust dynamically over time in relation to new data artefacts added to the business domain. Such a framework will speed up the decision making processes within the execution of a workflow instance and may be executed as part of the business model.

The rest of this paper is structured in four main sections. In the first section, the paper will detail how information overload is a consequence of an active social production [2] environment. The second section of the paper will look at current approaches in information analysis. Sections three will identify two specific implicit data by-products from socially generated content. The paper will then show how these data by-products can be used in tandem to improve the ability to find related data. The concluding section provides a final framing of the dual approach of using socially generated implicit data to assist in decision making within a business process.

2   Ramifications of Successful Social Production

The application of social practices to business processes has been the subject of new research [8] and social production best practices. Typically such production may be in the form of integration into business processes via a socially enabled platform such as wikis, blogs, mailing lists and ticket repositories. Such use of social techniques can, when properly managed [4], provide significant value to a business process. There is however a ramification to successful social interaction and production. This section will introduce this problem and provide a context with subsequent analysis with which to frame this paper.

When human agents interact with a business process in a successful social manner, such agents will generate significant data artefacts. Human agent is a broad general term used in this work for a person within a bounded environment, i.e. a software developer, or contributor. This human agent role will have a varying skill level, from novice to core expert developer. Such an agent will be capable of adding input to the project, via such mechanisms as email, filing a bug ticket or adding software code. The data artefacts generated by such human agents as part of a business process, when taken in aggregate, can be substantive.

Business processes, in the main, represent a restricted problem space for socially generated information artefacts. When analysing such data, rather than a web scale problem, such as Google which deals with a potentially infinite range of quantitative kinds of data, this paper considers a much narrower domain boundary. In this paper, the domain boundary under consideration, or bounded domain, looks at all socially generated content by human agents which contribute to a business process. Restricting the problem domain to focus on bounded domains allows for differing approaches to information overload.

2.1 Information Overload

To contextualise the problem of information overload, this subsection will introduce an experimental analysis using data from Open Source software developments. This domain was chosen as such projects are inherently social since they are dependant on people interacting and adding data artefacts. These data artefacts are both communication and product driven. The communication, via email lists and ticket repositories, may be viewed as socially orientated process co-ordination. To demonstrate that excessive socially generated information has a causal relationship with a growing social population, the instantiation period of an Open Source software development project was chosen.

SourceForge was selected as the common source code repository which would be used as the basis for analysis. SourceForge was started in November 1999, has two million registered users and twenty three thousand projects. For this analysis, five projects from the top popular and active projects were selected. From SourceForge's documentation, popular is defined as top downloads for all time and active as largest number of interactions of all time. This selection was limited by some of the top projects starting before SourceForge existed and so the mailing list archive was incomplete.

This Open Source Analysis is concerned with the initial period of a project as such work gains adoption of developers and users. In order to measure this, two metrics were considered; email frequency and distinct authors. Both metrics were examined over a period of at least two years to study the trending patterns in a time series analysis. In order to normalise fluctuations in the set, the slices of time used were six month periods. A variety of differing software development project genres were used to see whether any common patterns could be observed.

Figure 1 shows such an initial period from one of the projects analysed. This figure is typical of all of the projects analysed. The X axis in the graph shown in figure 1 represents periods of six months, i.e. p0 represents a six month period as does p1. The project in figure 1 is shown with two graphs, Email and Authors. The two graphs represent the two key metrics with which this analysis is concerned. The Y axis in the case of the Email graphs shows absolute volume of emails within each project for each discrete month. In the Author graphs, the Y axis shows the absolute distinct authors for any given six month period.

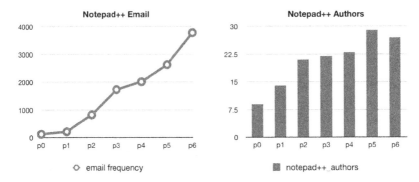

Fig. 1. Open Source Project: NotePad++

The key empirical observation which may be drawn from the information presented in the figure above follows that of the intuitive response when considering a software development project gaining popularity. The intuition would be that, over time, as a project grows more developers and users would be attracted to the development process which would, as a consequence, lead to a significant increase in volume of communications.

As can be seen clearly in the graphs in figure 1, the growth of email frequency and number of human agents grow together. This analysis was repeated over numerous Open Source software development projects, both client and server side technologies, and similar patterns may be observed across their initial phases. A time series analysis is critical to this examination in order to gain perspective on the nature of information density in these projects. If such an analysis were only to observe the end result or a discrete period in time, the correlation between a higher number of human agents directly leading to an increase in multiple agent communication would be missed.

When business processes are successfully integrating social mechanisms, acceleration of information density has the consequence of a decreasing ability to process generated data artefacts. Optimal usage of social practices within such processes requires a lightweight mechanism to respond adaptively to such social data. It is imperative to make good use of such social data, otherwise human agents within the bounds of the domain will lose motivation to participate. The next section of this paper will provide an outline of some of the current work in dealing with extracting meaning from large bodies of data

3   Information Analysis

Social information overload having now been established as a significant problem when dealing with an active group population, this section will look at current approaches to filtering such information. The section will first look at collaborative filtering techniques and secondly at other information retrieval processes. Both of these sections demonstrate an explicit act on the part of the human agents generating such data. This overview will provide a contrast basis for the two passive, or by-product, techniques described in the subsequent section.

3.1 Collaborative Filtering

Collaborative filtering is a well established research area [12]. Such a procedure looks to take the aggregate of data to find patterns of behaviour. Typically this form of analysis will use a large data set. The Movielens [10] research project is one whereby users will create an account and add ratings of movies. This collection of user data may be seen in commercial businesses such as netflix.com or lovefilm.com. The user can also indicate other users of the service as friends which the recommendation mechanism can use to build a social graph. The software then aggregates these ratings and friend data to look for the average response as to what would probably be a well received unseen movie.

Another application area of collaborative filtering is that of content filtering. The PHAOKS [21] UseNet recommendation engine uses this approach. In this system a subset of UseNet content is analysed for recommendation of web-sites from individual human agents of the system. These are then aggregated to look for the most popular recommendations. Akismet [19] takes the inverse of this same approach. Rather than using the population of the group to determine positive input, Akismet uses the same collaborative approach to determine blog spam.

Another application of the collaborative filtering mechanism is that of recommendation being applied to revision change management. Wikipedia is large Open Source project generating a significant amount of readily available revision data. By analysing their revision changes to documents [27], the aggregate response can be found in order to collaboratively filter the best edits. The subjective use of best is broadly defined as most accurate in such an application.

3.2 Information Retrieval

The second domain to be addressed in this section is that of information retrieval. Such a topic is too large to cover in this paper in depth [16], so a few examples which provide context to the subsequent work will be given in overview. These examples look at keyphrase identification in two approaches: assignment, where a phrase is selected from a controlled vocabulary or extraction where a keyphrase is automatically generated.

A machine learning approach has been used in the KEA ([25] and [9]) method. This uses Naive Bayes to try and build relevant key phrases and use those as a weighting metric to improve TF_IDF. For this approach to work, the training corpus must have key phrases identified a priori by an expert. Candidate words cannot be proper names and the work discusses the problem with explicit key phrase in relation to author submission.

GenEx [22] looks at a similar problem but using academic journal papers as the source for the corpus. In this approach, they treat the problem as one of supervised learning. The corpus in this work has a manually created set of keyphrase generated in an a priori manner by experts. This work does not look at synonyms and is considered a potential problem in the work.

Building on the GenEx work, [14] provides an extension to the supervised learning techniques by adding statistical and syntactical information from the document corpus as input to the machine learning algorithm. Such an approach also uses predetermined keywords. One final approach using an a priori keyphrase list is KIP [26]. This algorithm uses those keywords to improve precision and recall by assigning an automatic weighting based on that knowledge.

This section has provided a brief overview on some current approaches to utilising human agent generated data in a more meaningful manner. These approaches tend to use more explicit models and focus on english language based domains. As is appropriate in such domains, stemming is used in many approaches. These approaches all focus on a priori static analysis of a fixed corpus. The next section will introduce two implicit social forms of data, which when used together, can provide a more lightweight, egalitarian mechanism for deriving social significance.

4   Socially Generated Implicit Data

The previous section of this paper outlined some of the previous work focused on working with large amounts of user generated data. This section will present two differing approaches fundamentally predicated on using the social nature of the data set. First a specific data set will be introduced. This will be the foundation for the two subsequent subsections of the paper. These subsections will show how implicit data may be used from socially generated production as part of a business process. Implicit connections between human agents within the business process may be viewed as weak ties and as such give a richer view on data interactions. At the end of the section some preliminary results will show how these approaches, when used in combination as part of a programmatic software framework, work to solve the problem of information overload discussed in section 2.1.

4.1   Data Acquisition

Before presenting the two specific social ad hoc applications, the experimental data set will be described. Both approaches use the same data set. Providing sufficient data from which to examine the two fold social production outlined in the previous section will enable a substantive view upon socially generated information.

A specific Open Source software development project was chosen for this analysis, Dojo Toolkit. Open Source data was chosen due to the large amount of available data and specifically of software project as this form of data has many business style workflows, such as project planning, milestone targets and product delivery. The group was selected as it had been in existence for multiple years and had reasonable adoption and diverse application usage.

In order to examine this project, a software framework was constructed to extract automatically multiple data silos. The phrase data silo is used to represent a collection of human agent generated data with no specific links to any other source of data. The three data silos in typical use within Open Source software development are an email mailing list, a commit database and a ticket (or bug tracking) system. In order to successfully complete any task within such a business process, research of such socially generated data is necessary. Access to such data would typically be presented by collated archived data and subscription to new inbound data. A two year period of data was targeted. From this time period some 22218 emails, 5941 commit messages and 23237 support tickets were extracted. Removing extraneous data from such extracted source material is an important step (as identified by [3]). Data cleaning forms part of the software framework. The extracted data is then used as the basis for the corpus of the analysis. Of this data, there were 1,505,585 term instances and 54510 distinct tokens were identified. The population of this group, after the reduction of multiple identities via the software framework, was 2792 human agents.

The system framework utilises standard textual analysis techniques to tokenise language elements within the data silos, uses stop words and creates an index. Stemming was not used in this work. As Stemming looks to take terms back to a root form, such processing would remove features in which this work is specially interested. This process is based on the "bag-of-words" assumptions. With this extraction process complete, the software framework can now be used to establish programmatically the social product of all human agents to the project across multiple data silos and different pseudonyms. Such programatic access via a software api within the framework provides a flexible mechanism to view the results of the process. This api could be integrated into existing or new workflows.

Now the specific experimental domain has been established, the next two subsections will present how specific socially produced data by-product can be used to find implicit weak ties. Those weak ties will then be used together to facilitate a higher degree of confidence in the ability to use such social data.

4.2   Folksonomies within a Bounded Domain

The first of two social data by-product presented in this paper uses a posteriori method to establish high value features within the bounded domain. Ontological analysis, with respect to the addition of social practices, form an important part of this viewpoint. This evolution of perspective will be outlined to provide the framework for the technique presented.

Standard ontological techniques for feature analysis would take a formal approach to constructing a defined vocabulary which could be used to provide term weighting to proscribed features. A variant of such an approach was mentioned in section 3.2. By relying on a priori knowledge of features, an inherent formal hierarchy is placed on any such feature weighting. Such a hierarchy does not leverage the social benefits of crowd aggregation.

Prescribed taxonomies have limitations of a restricted perspective, that of the architects of the namespace, and significant upfront construction work. Applying social concepts to this problem space has led to the explosion in usage of folksonomies [23] in such applications as Flickr and Del.icio.us. Tagging is the widely used metaphor in the so called flat namespace [18]. By having no predetermined taxonomy, users of the systems are encouraged to tag a data artefact with multiple keywords, or features, which they think are indicative of the nature of the item. Such tagging can be either freeform or guided. In a guided taxonomy, as seen now in Del.icio.us, an autocomplete menu is presented to the user as they generate new tags based upon currently popular tags within their system. Such a guided taxonomy is intended to provide consensus on terminology and plurals.

Due to their nature, folksomonies are explicit in nature. The users of the system are specifically asked to define the nature of the data artefact. A further classification may be performed in a social domain by utilising the intelligence of the community, moving beyond the traditional ontological hierarchical approach and explicit tagging. Using socially implicit organically generated term features, emergent properties may be observed. By performing an analysis of all data artefacts socially generated, frequently used terms will emerge as being of significance to the group. Such an approach will only be of use in a bounded domain as the focus of production will be toward common goals.

4.3   Domain Specific Nomenclature

Linguistics has significant research into language evolution [5] and into that of slang [7] and technical jargon [6]. Domain Specific Nomenclature (DSN) refers to an aspect of language usage which is specific to a group. These terms are normally of a technical nature. DSN seeks to exploit such a facet of a bounded set of data to enable a new technique for extracting potentially high value language features.

Using the sample data as described above, all extracted terms were programmatically compared with a dictionary, using an English dictionary from the GNU iSpell project. All non-dictionary words were compiled and a subsequent frequency analysis was performed within the custom software framework.

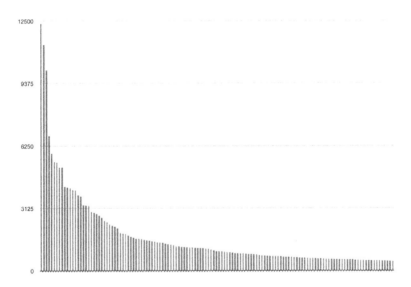

Fig. 2. Domain Specific Nomenclature Word Frequency

Figure 2 shows the result of the non-dictionary automated frequency analysis as part of the software framework. In the graph shown in figure 2, the x axis show discrete word features and the y axis show frequency of those words. The y axis data has been truncated to allow for a clearer representation. This analysis shows a clear power law curve from the Domain Specific Nomenclature terms. As standard English language terms are excluded via the dictionary reduction, all remaining terms will be specific technical terms and real names. By grouping these results by frequency it is possible to build a dynamic lexicon specific to the bounded group. This lexicon can then be used to improve term matching as these features are of specific interest to the population of the group.

As the results form a power curve distribution, not all of the derived terms will be of value. Neither the top, nor long tail [1] of the distribution are of descriptive use. For example, the most popular term, dojo, was referenced 99075 times. As this term is so frequently used, it cannot be considered a distinguishing characteristic. The long tail of the distribution is also of low value as low frequency term usage signifies little usage within the group. Therefore this approach targets the so called *"fat middle"*, looking at the eighty percent middle of the distribution. This DSN lexicon is now used in combination with the results from Term Frequency-Inverse Document Frequency (TF_IDF) to add term weightings.

There is an important restriction to this approach that is inherent within that of the *"Wisdom of Crowds"* [20]. In his work, Surowiecki states that the collection of independently-deciding individuals must be of both significant enough size and diversity. Domain Specific Nomenclature requires a significant data set with a diverse population in order to form an effective ad hoc lexicon. Synonyms are not considered a problem in this approach. Previous work 3.2 identified this as a problem to be solved but the DSN approach specifically targets unique technical terms, or jargon. As such terms will have been created by the group, duplicate derived words are unlikely to occur. If such a fork in term usage does occur, the DSN approach will observe such a change and identify trending usage.

From this subsection, it is possible to see the progression from hierarchical (formal), to the explicit addition of social (folksomony) and then to the passive social (implicit). Such implicit data can be used in the bounds of a restricted domain to produce automatically and adaptively a Domain Specific Nomenclature lexicon. The next subsection will describe the second social production by-product, implicit social proximity and how such data will be used in conjunction with DSN to provide the ability to utilise social data more effectively.

4.4   Implicit Social Proximity

The previous subsection demonstrated how implicit social production can be used to build a lexicon of high value Domain Specific Nomenclature which can be used as the basis for term weighting. The second social by-product looks at social connections [24] between human agents within a bounded domain and how these approaches can be used with each other.

Implicit Social Proximity (ISP) looks to find connected groups within the context of grouped data in a dynamic manner, rather than for posteriori analysis [13]. Using the experimental data as described above 4.1, an initial data analysis was performed on email mailing list threads and ticket system threads. In other business processes such interactions could occur in multiple areas such as in a wiki editing revision system, or blog comment thread. When two or more human agents interact in the same thread, or common socially produced artefact, it is possible to look for previous interactions with that agent subset. A subset, in this instance, is viewed as a partial set of the complete human agent user base. An analysis tool, as part of the software framework, was constructed to look at social proximity between human agents.

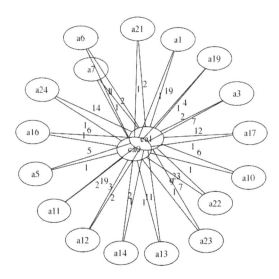

Fig. 3. Social Intersection From Weak Ties

Figure 3 shows an automatic dynamically generated intersection of two human agents within a common email thread. The nodes are representative of a discrete human agent. Nodes *ca0* and *ca1* are the two human agents under consideration of a specific email thread in which they both participate. The software framework then looks for all possible common interactions between human agents and the original two human agents. Nodes *a1* through *a24* are in the general population of the domain but which have previously interacted with both of the original human agents. The edge weighting show the frequency of interactions with the same human agents.

This automatically generated data can be used in a set of socially generated data artefacts to find human agents whose social connections can act as votes of confidence. The process of creating these proximity maps dynamically alter as new socially generated artefacts are added to the framework. Such additions happen in near real time, using social data dynamically to provide a fresher opinion predicated upon the special social zeitgeist of the social business process.

These two approaches are then used in conjunction with TF_IDF to perform within the bounded business process. Domain Specific Nomenclature uses a current in memory model based on the freshest lexicon to provide relevant feature weighting. Implicit social proximity is then used as a further weighting to push increased discoverability of highly linked human agent generated content. As such, this dual process is entirely egalitarian in nature as there is no predetermined hierarchy and uses weak ties to improve the quality of related data. With an understanding of these two approaches in place, the next subsection will show some initial early findings.

Preliminary Usage. An initial small scale evaluation was performed. This evaluation was to determine the effectiveness of the described process, not to detail a deployment within a business context. The participants in this study were programmers with at least two years javascript development experience. This choice is of significance, as the Open Source project under examination is a javascript framework.

For the test procedure, an automated web based testing framework was created. There were no direct interactions in the testing procedure with the subjects apart from an initial instruction page within the testing software. In the evaluation, the five participants were shown three discrete documents, in this instance emails from the test data. These documents were outside of the test corpus so as to not base any predictions on already known data. They were then shown three different potentially related documents per method, positioned randomly, and asked if they thought there were useful correlation. The documents for evaluation were either: selected randomly, using the Numpy random number generator, a standard TF_IDF implementation or TF_IDF enhanced by both the automatically generated social lexicon and the implicit social proximity. Table 1 shows the results of the experts' acceptance of the potentially related documents.

Table 1. Comparative Usage Table

Document	Random	TF_IDF	Social
A	7%	40%	73%
B	13%	47%	60%
C	7%	53%	87%

As expected, the random selection had very low acceptance. TF_IDF performed well in most cases but with the addition of the two social processes described above, the experienced developers noted an improvement. These results are too small in scope to provide a high level of confidence in the general application of this approach but suggests a further more in-depth study would be of value.

Domain Specific Nomenclature and Implicit Social Proximity use socially produced data artefacts to generate a mechanism to improve the ability for a business process to leverage human agent generated content. Such a mechanism would have less value if it only worked in an a priori manner as the corpus of the content will change quickly. The proposed approach processes new data artefacts in near real time. As the framework is lightweight it can respond to ad hoc changes in social usage and behaviour within the business process. The framework presents access to the data via an api and, as such, may be integrated into existing business applications without requiring retooling. This ease of integration is likely to encourage adoption.

5   Conclusions and Future Work

Bringing social applications to business processes can provide valuable input and generate work of significance. Without a mechanism to filter this content, when any substantive scale as been achieved, information overload becomes a problem which should be addressed.

This paper introduced two socially orientated approaches: Domain Specific Nomenclature and Implicit Social Proximity as part of a software framework. Both approaches use existing socially generated data artefacts to derive information. Focusing on terms specific to a domain enables ad hoc lexicons to be dynamically created based upon the most up to date information generated by the group. Such data enables weighting of terms in a dynamic folksonomic manner. The further use of social data generated by human agent interactions facilitates the promotion of content based on popular subset intersections. Both of these approaches require no alteration in human agent behaviour or adjustment to any existing workflows. From this basis, business applications which have already integrated social interactions could utilise such an approach from existing data sets via the programatic interface.

In the future, the first step is to conduct a wider study with a larger range of test documents and more domain experts to provide a higher degree of confidence in the approach. Further applications of DSN could be used, dependant on the business process. In the experimental domain considered in this paper, the whole body of terms were considered, independent of when they were created. In another, time critical news based domain, freshness of term evolution could be of a greater weighting value. Another area under consideration is to expand the silo concept to take in additional information, such as wiki revision changes and blog comment threading. By utilising implicit data by-products, it is possible to improve the ability to use the output of social production in an inherently egalitarian manner. Such enhancements will support ad hoc business processes and enable lightweight interactions.

References

1. Anderson, C.: The Long Tail: Why the Future of Business Is Selling Less of More. Hyperion (July 2006)
2. Benkler, Y.: The Wealth of Networks: How Social Production Transforms Markets and Freedom. Yale University Press, New Haven (2007)
3. Bettenburg, N., Shihab, E., Hassan, A.E.: An empirical study on the risks of using off-the-shelf techniques for processing mailing list data. In: ICSM 2009: Proceedings of the 25th IEEE International Conference on Software Maintenance, pp. 539–542 (2009)
4. Bosman, J.: Chevy tries a write-your-own-ad approach, and the potshots fly. The New York Times (January 2006)
5. Christiansen, M., Kirby, S.: Language evolution: Consensus and controversies. Trends in Cognitive Sciences 7(7), 300–307 (2003)
6. Coombs, R., Chopra, S., Schenk, D., Yutan, E.: Medical slang and its functions. Social Science & Medicine (January 1993)
7. Dumas, B., Lighter, J.: Is slang a word for linguists? American Speech (January 1978)
8. Erol, S., Granitzer, M., Happ, S., Jantunen, S., Jennings, B., Koschmider, A., Nurcan, S., Rossi, D., Schmidt, R.: Combining bpm and social software: Contradiction or chance? Software Process Improvement and Practice Journal Special Issue on BPM 2008 Selected Workshop papers 2009, 9999 (Special Issue on BPM 2008) (2009)
9. Frank, E., Paynter, G.W., Witten, I.H., Gutwin, C., Nevill-Manning, C.G.: Domain-specific keyphrase extraction. In: Proceedings of the 16th International Joint Conference on Artificial Intelligence (IJCAI 1999), pp. 668–673 (1999)
10. Good, N., Schafer, J., Konstan, J., Borchers, A.: Combining collaborative filtering with personal agents for better recommendations. In: Proceedings of AAAI (January 1999)
11. Granovetter, M.: The strength of weak ties. ajs 78(6), 1360 (1973)

12. Herlocker, J.L., Konstan, J.A., Terveen, L.G., Riedl, J.T.: Evaluating collaborative filtering recommender systems. ACM Trans. Inf. Syst. 22(1), 5–53 (2004)
13. Hossain, L., Zhu, D.: Social networks and coordination performance of distributed software development teams. The Journal of High Technology Management Research (January 2009)
14. Hulth, A.: Improved automatic keyword extraction given more linguistic knowledge. In: Proceedings of the 2003 Conference on Empirical Methods in Natural Language Processing, vol. 10, pp. 216–223 (2003)
15. Kagdi, H., Poshyvanyk, D.: Who can help me with this change request? In: Proceedings of 17th IEEE International Conference on Program Comprehension, vol. 9, pp. 273–277 (May 2010)
16. Kosala, R., Blockeel, H.: Web mining research: A survey. ACM SIGKDD Explorations Newsletter (January 2000)
17. Ma, D., Schuler, D., Zimmermann, T., Sillito, J.: Expert recommendation with usage expertise. In: Proceedings of the 25th IEEE International Conference on Software Maintenance (September 2009)
18. Mathes, A.: Folksonomies-cooperative classification and communication through shared metadata. Computer Mediated Communication (January 2004)
19. Mullenweg, M.: Akismet (2007), http://akismet.com/faq/
20. Surowiecki, J.: The Wisdom of Crowds. Anchor (August 2005)
21. Terveen, L., Hill, W., Amento, B., Mcdonald, D., Creter, J.: Phoaks: A system for sharing recommendations. Communications of the ACM 40(3), 59–62 (1997)
22. Turney, P.: Learning algorithms for keyphrase extraction. Information Retrieval (January 2000)
23. Vanderwal, T.: Folksonomy (2007),
    http://www.vanderwal.net/folksonomy.html
24. Wasserman, S., Faust, K.: Social Network Analysis: Methods and Applications (Structural Analysis in the Social Sciences). Cambridge University Press, Cambridge (1995)
25. Witten, I.H., Paynter, G.W., Frank, E., Gutwin, C., Craig: Kea: Practical automatic keyphrase extraction. In: ACM DL, pp. 254–255 (1999)
26. Wu, Y.-F.B., Li, Q., Bot, R.S., Chen, X.: Domain-specific keyphrase extraction. In: CIKM 2005: Proceedings of the 14th ACM International Conference on Information and Knowledge Management, pp. 283–284. ACM Press, New York (2005)
27. Zeng, H., Alhossaini, M., Ding, L., Fikes, R., McGuinness, D., et al.: Computing trust from revision history. In: Intl. Conf. on Privacy, Security and Trust (2006)

A Strategy for Merging Social Software with Business Process Support

Ilia Bider[1,2], Paul Johannesson[1], and Erik Perjons[1]

[1] DSV, Stockholm University, Stockholm, Forum 100, SE-16440 Kista, Sweden
[2] IbisSoft AB, Stockholm, Box 19567, SE-10432 Stockholm, Sweden
ilia@ibissoft.se, {pajo,perjons}@dsv.su.se

Abstract. Contemporary social software and business process support systems utilize different architectural principals. While social software employs the idea of shared spaces for communication/collaboration, most of the contemporary business process support systems employ a workflow engine to coordinate the work of people engaged in the given business process. There are two alternatives when developing a system that provides business process support enhanced with properties of social software. One alternative is to create a mixed shared spaces/workflow architecture. The other alternative is to find a way of both type of systems using the same architectural principle, either shared spaces, or workflow, before trying to merge the two types of systems into one. The paper explores the second alternative, namely, first, moving business process support to the shared spaces architecture, and then adding features typical for social software. The paper discusses the role of shared spaces in business process support systems, sets requirements on their structure and usage, and outlines potential benefits of using shared spaces from the business point of view. Then, the paper shows how the requirements set on the structure and usage of the shared spaces can be implemented in practice, and how typical features such as blogs/forums found in social software can be naturally introduced into a business process support system.

Keywords: business process, social software, groupware, communication, shared space.

1 Introduction

One of today's trends is the growing usage of social software, e.g. Facebook, in private life. A new generation is growing up who are accustomed to communicate with each other through social software. Through this generation, the new way of communication is quickly spreading to the business life. Business-oriented sites, such as LinkedIn, are widely used for informal business networks, personal marketing and sales. The ideas built into social software has started affecting the design of business-oriented software systems, including Business Process Support (BPS) systems, which is reflected in the appearance of new directions in contemporary IS research, and new scientific events such as the international workshop on Business Process Management and Social Software [1].

M. zur Muehlen and J. Su (Eds.): BPM 2010 Workshops, LNBIP 66, pp. 372–383, 2011.
© Springer-Verlag Berlin Heidelberg 2011

Summarizing the above, merging social software with business process support became an important issue for both BPM practice and theory. To complete such a merge, a number of theoretical and practical problems should be overcome. Social software is aimed to support weak ties, social production, egalitarianism, and mutual service provision [1]. A business process support system is aimed to support specialization and standardization, which more or less contradicts the goals of social software. This contradiction is reflected in the different kinds of system architecture employed by those systems, see solid boxes and lines on Fig. 1. While social software employs the idea of shared spaces for communication/collaboration, most of the contemporary business process support systems employ a workflow engine to coordinate the work of people engaged in the given business process.

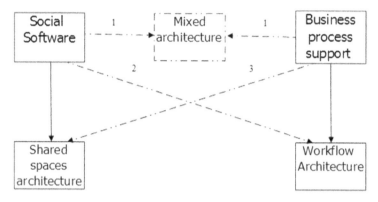

Fig. 1. Architectural alternatives for merging social software with business process support

There are two alternatives when developing a system that provides business process support enhanced with properties of social software for stimulating creative work. One alternative is to create a mixed shared spaces/workflow architecture in a style of Microsoft SharePoint, see dashed lines marked with number *one* in Fig. 1.The other alternative is to find a way of both type of systems using the same architectural principle, either shared spaces, or workflow, before trying to merge the two types of systems into one. These alternatives are represented as dashed lines marked with numbers *two* and *three* in Fig. 1.

We do not know whether social software can be built upon the workflow architecture, and whether it will gain anything from it. However, we believe that building business process support based on the "pure" shared spaces architecture might be beneficial both for business process support systems as such, and for the task of merging social software with business process support. This paper is devoted to exploiting the alternative marked by number *three* in Fig. 1.

While usage of shared spaces is more or less a must in social software, the same cannot be said about business process support. Therefore, first goal of the paper is to show that employment of shared spaces can benefit to the main objective of business process support – stimulating group efficiency in repetitive work. In addition, we show a number of other potential business benefits that could be attained by exploiting shared spaces architecture for business process support. The second goal is to present a practical example of using the shared spaces architecture for building BPS systems to show that it is possible to build a BPS system based on shared spaces without employing a workflow engine. Lastly, the third goal of this paper is to show how a BPS system based on the shared spaces architecture can be enhanced with the features typical for social software, e.g., blogs/forums.

The paper is written according to the following structure. In section 2, we briefly summarize the basic ideas of using shared spaces in BPS systems and set some requirements on the structure and usage of shared spaces in BPS. In section 3, we analyze the environment in which a modern enterprise/organization functions, and show how a BPS system with shared spaces can help the enterprise/organization to survive and grow in this environment. In section 4, we present an example of the BPS system architecture based on shared spaces proven to be working in practice. In this section, we also suggest a natural enhancement of this architecture to introduce some features typical for social software into business process support. Section 5 contains concluding remarks, and plans for future research.

2   Shared Spaces in BPS Systems

The concept of shared spaces is well known in the area of Groupware, and CSCW (Computer supported Cooperative Work), see for example [2]. It became widely used in the Internet era in connection with advances of social software. A blog, personal journal, and even a photo album are all examples of shared spaces, as all these things are aimed to be shared with others and be commented by them.

As the usage of shared spaces in BPS system is not yet widely spread, we summarize the main ideas of using shared spaces in BPS systems. To start with, we clarify our understanding of the concept of business process support systems. Under a BPS system, we mean a system that helps the process participants to run their process instances/cases according to a process (type) definition. A BPS system does not need to automate all operations/tasks. If a system supports information exchange, communication/collaboration in a frame of a process case/instance, it is enough to call such a system a BPS. With such a definition, both workflow-based systems, and so-called case-based systems [3] belong to the BPS class.

The main feature that differentiates the BPS with shared spaces from other kind of BPS systems, is that the former employs a so-called "construction site" information logistics [4]. Such a system has no explicit data/information flow. A shared information space is created for each process instance/case to hold all information that is relevant to the process instance, e.g., documents received and sent, information on tasks planned and completed, reports on results achieved when completing these tasks, etc. All this information is easily available each time a process participant is invited to visit this space and complete some task related to it. A shared space is similar to a construction site where different kinds of workers are invited to complete their own task and leave the rest to the others.

The functioning of a BPS system based on shared spaces can be described in the following way:

- When a new process instance/case starts, a new shared space is created. It gets a unique name, an owner (responsible for the case), and possibly, a case team.

- When the process instance reaches its operational goal, the shared space is closed (sealed), but remains accessible for reading (a case goes to the archive).
- A person who is assigned a task in the frame of the process case "goes" to this case's shared space to get information he/she needs for completing the task and reports the results achieved in the same space.

For the shared space technique to work efficiently in a BPS system two conditions should be fulfilled:

- Shared spaces should be properly structured. In a normal business environment, a person participates in many process instances, and, often, in parallel. For the shared space technique to work efficiently, he/she needs to understand the situation in a shared space he/she is visiting at a glance, and quickly find all information related to the task at hands.
- An invitation technique gives to the process participants a clear understanding why he is invited and what he is expected to do in each particular shared space

3 Potential Benefits of Using Shared Spaces in BPS Systems

To move business process support from workflow to shared spaces architecture just to be able to easier introduce some social software features would not be wise. The move should be justified by getting potential benefits even when no social software features are introduced. To discuss potential benefits of using shared spaces in BPS systems, we start with discussing the environment in which a modern enterprise/organization functions. The main characteristic of this environment is hardening global competition for all resources that the enterprise/organization needs for its normal functioning, more exactly competition for (see Fig. 2):

- Customers
- Labor (manpower, working force, competence)
- Capital (investors)

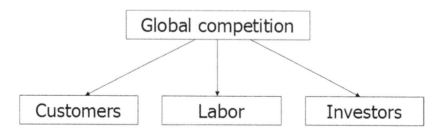

Fig. 2. Environment in which a modern enterprise functions

One thing that helps in this competition is to become more productive/efficient, which allows producing goods/services that cost less with less manpower, and less capital. However, just being efficient/productive is not enough. For example, acquiring and retaining customers requires establishing and maintaining customers trust; just having lower prices may not be sufficient. Acquiring and retaining competent people requires an inspiring working environment as much as high salaries. Attracting investors also requires creating trust in the enterprise's ability to survive and grow in the age of global competition.

In the subsections below we discuss how a BPS system with shared spaces architecture can help an enterprise/organization to function in the age of global competition.

3.1 Efficiency/Productivity

A typical workflow-based BPS system helps to increase efficiency/productivity via:

1. Full or partial *automation* of some operations (activities/tasks).
2. *Standardization* of handling of process instances. The workers do not need to device an unique plan to handle each process instance. A BPS system leads the workers through the predefined sequence of operations (activities/tasks) when they handle a process instance.
3. Optimization of human resource usage through *specialization*. While leading through the sequence of operations (activities/tasks), the BPS also assigns execution of these operations to the right people. Such assignment is meant to ensure that people who complete these operations have right competence. For example, experienced workers complete complex operations, while less experienced complete simple ones. Such a scheme can ensure high quality of process-handling with optimal use of human resources.

A workflow-based BPS system creates a kind of a conveyor belt for handling process instances. In production, the conveyor belt represents the best solution when producing the same kind of goods, e.g. cars of the same model. It is questionable that the conveyor belt can be of much use when there is a need to produce different vehicles, like a personal car, a bus, a lorry, etc. at random. In the same way a workflow-based BPS system supports well a process for which deviations between the process instances are small and/or rare. If a considerable number of process instances cannot be handled according to the predefined scheme, the efficiency of the workflow business process support degrades:

– A plan for handling a deviated process instance should be devised and executed outside the BPS system with the help of some conventional means.
– A mechanism for engaging different competences does not work any more. As a result, some operations are likely to be completed by workers who do not have enough competence, and some by the workers who are overqualified for these operations.

Shared space for each process instance helps to solve problems that arise due to deviations from the standard pattern of handling process instances. This is done by having a special subspace of a shared space to handle deviations. It can be loosely structured, for example, as a journal where process participants leave their comments on how they handle or want to handle a deviation. Having such a subspace allows the process participants to continue using the system even in case of serious deviations. It also helps to continue using special competences through manually inviting various kind of specialists to visit a "deviation" subspace and help in handling it. The instance shared space, including the deviation subspace, contains full information about the process instance, which should encourage seeking help from a specialist who has not been previously engaged in the particular process instance. You don't need to retell the whole story of the instance to him, as it is already there in the shared space.

3.2   Strengthening Trust with the Customers

Having shared spaces in a BPS system makes it easier to invite a customer to visit the process instances that concern this particular customer. To do this, a special view on the instances shared spaces should be created. This view should not include all technical details of the process handling, but show the general progress achieved in the process so far, what is expected to be done in the nearest future, and who will be doing it.

The customer can also be encouraged to leave his/her comments, suggestions, or complaints in the same shared space. Providing that the customer reactions are answered in the process instance sheared space, the customer will have more incentives to visit this space and thus become a participant of the process instance. This may lead to the abolishment of the separation between the provider and consumer [5], especially in the service sector, by realizing the idea, that service provisioning is a mutual process of service exchange. Thus both service provider and consumer provide services to one another in order co-create value [6].

We believe that making a customer to a full-fledged participant of the process can help in both, attracting new customers, and retaining the existing ones. The former because it gives a customer a feeling of control over the delivery. The latter because it creates closer, personal, ties between the customer and vendor. These ties are normally much more difficult to break than the formal relationships on the level of sales/purchase departments.

3.3   Attracting and Retaining Employees

An organization cannot function without people. Thus constant efforts are needed for attracting new employees and retaining the existing ones. Both experienced workers, and the younger, less experienced, ones are needed to create a proper blend that can function as a highly qualified team at a reasonable costs. A successful enterprise, while providing competitive salaries, needs also provide an attractive environment for both categories of employees. Here, a BPS system with shared spaces can be of help.

An obvious attraction for a highly competent, experienced person is an environment where he/she can focus on the expert job, leaving less complex operations to the others. Shared spaces structure of a BPS system provides such a possibility. An experienced worker can ask a less experienced colleague to help via inviting him/her to a process instance shared space to do some task. Such invitations can be issued on the fly without being in details regulated by the BPS system through the process model. As the instance shared space includes all information about the process instance, handing over some job to another person becomes easier. The person that asks for help does not need to retell the whole history of the process instance, the information is easily available to any participant of the process through the instance shared space. Note that using the experts only for doing expert job raises their efficiency and thus provide a possibility to offer them higher salaries.

There are two obvious (interrelated) attractions for a novice:

1. become an expert (and get a higher salary as a result) as soon as possible,
2. could do the job on the limits of his/her capability, but not be left alone in the situations where more knowledge/experience is required.

Both can be arranged when a BPS system with shared spaces architecture is employed:

1. As all details of the history of each process instance is recorded in the instance shared spaces, a novice can learn how the experts handled various cases, and solved the problems that had arose.
2. In the same way as it is easy for en expert to pass a less qualified job to a less experienced colleague, it is easy for a novice to turn to an expert for help. It is done by invitation to a shared space which already contains all information about the current situation.

Note that a novice can learn from an expert that has handled a (difficult) case even when the latter has already left the enterprise/organization. A BPS with shared spaces helps to retain organizational knowledge making it a property of the organization, (and not only of the individuals). More on that see [7].

3.4 Strengthening Ties with Investors

In the same way as a BPS with shared spaces can help in strengthening ties with the customers, it can help in strengthening ties with the investors (e.g. shareholders of an enterprise). This, certainly, cannot be done by inviting the investors to visit customer related process instances, as the latter will give too much of detailed information that is impossible for the investor to interpret. However, having a BPS system with shared spaces employed for support of strategic decision-making, e.g. budget planning, enterprise board meetings, etc. will provide an opportunity for creating tighter connections between the enterprise and its investors.

4 Realizing the Strategy in Practice

4.1 Moving Business Process Support to the Shared Spaces Architecture

As was mentioned in section 3, shared spaces in a BPS system should be properly structured. Below we show an example of such structuring based on our experience of developing BPS systems with shared spaces. Our latest experience has been "materialized" in a web-based tool (service), called iPB, that assists in designing BPS systems [4, 8]. iPB is built based on the state-oriented view on business processes [9] extended in a way described in [4]. (On difference between the state-oriented view and the traditional workflow view, see [10].)

Several BPS systems have been developed with the help of iPB. The biggest one (about 300 end-users) is employed in the social office of one of the Swedish municipalities, where it helps to conduct investigation on suspected child abuses.

In a system designed with iPB, shared spaces are structured according to the process map designed for a particular process type. A process map in iPB is a drawing that consists of boxes placed in some order, see Fig. 3. Each box represents a step inside the process, the name of the step appearing inside the box (no lines or connecters between the boxes). A textual description is attached to each step that explains the work to be done in this step.

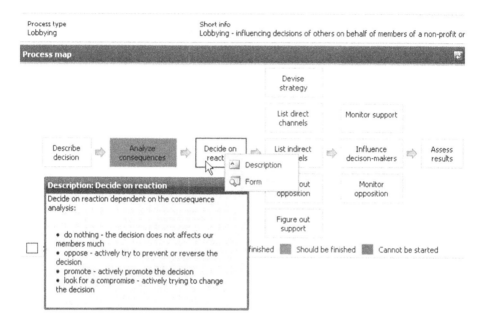

Fig. 3. A process map in iPB

A step in an iPB map represents a work-package (a phase) to be completed in the frame of the process. A step does not correspond to a standalone task/activity, and normally it is not completed at one go. Completing the step, usually, requires performing several tasks at different times. In between, tasks from other steps of the same process can be completed. This makes the map relatively simple and easy to understand for all participant of the process, even for those that work only with one, or few steps. This is important because the map is used directly in the operational practice, not just for process analysis, or staff training. The details of each step are represented differently, namely as an electronic form (see below).

Each process instance gets its own copy of the map that serves as a table of contents for its shared space. The map is used for multiple purposes: as an overview of the case, guidelines for handling the case, and a menu for navigating inside the shared space, see Fig. 4 (do not pay attention to the box in the upper left corner, it will be explained later). The user navigates through the shared space by clicking on the boxes of the steps with which he/she wants to work. Not all boxes are clickable at the beginning, those that are grayed require that one or several previous steps are dealt with first, see Fig. 4.

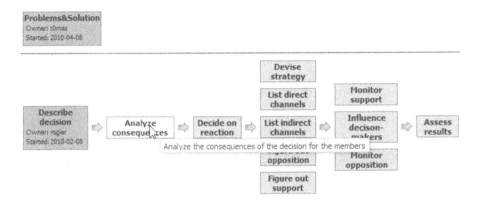

Fig. 4. The map used for structuring an instance shared space

A click on a step box redirects the end-user to a web-form that assists him in completing the step, see Fig.5. The form contains text fields, option menus and radio-buttons to make choices, check-boxes, as well as more complex fields. The form may also include "static" texts that explain what should be done before one can fill some fields. Besides being a guideline for completing the step, the form serves also as a reporting tool, through filling the fields the participants report completion of certain activities. It also serve as a tool of communication between the people engaged in completing the same step.

From the shared space architecture point of view, the iPB solution can be interpreted as follows. The total process instance shared space is divided into a number of subspaces called process steps. The steps are graphically represented to the end-users as boxes. Subspaces may or may not intersect. The structure of a step subspace is represented to the end-users as a form to fill, see for example Fig. 5. Intersecting subspaces means that web forms attached to different steps may contain the same field(s). Usually, in this case, the intersecting fields can be changed only in one form; they are made read-only in the second one.

The progress in filling the step forms is reflected in the map attached to the shared space via steps coloring. A gray box means that the step form has not been filled and cannot be filled for the moment. A white box means that the step form is empty but can be filled. A step with a half-filled form gets the green color, and additional information about when the work on it has been started, and who started it. A step with a fully filled form gets the blue color, and additional information about the finish date.

The main way of inviting a person to visit a particular shared space in iPB is by assigning him/her to become an owner/co-owner of some step. Such an assignment results in an email message delivered to this person, and the process to appear in his/her list of "My processes". When visiting a process shared space, a person can see directly on the map what step(s) are assigned to him. Such an invitation presumes that a person invited to a step subspace knows what is expected from him there.

To add a possibility for ad hoc invitations a special subspace called Notes&Tasks was added to a process instance shared space to allow collaborative planning as

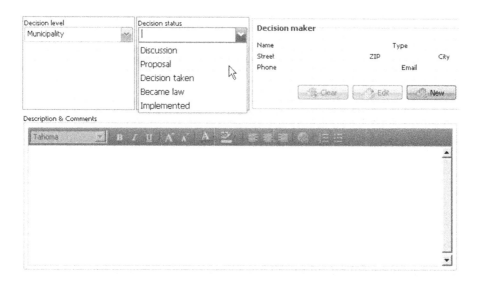

Fig. 5. A step form for the first step from Fig. 3

described in [4, 9]. For an ad hoc invitation a task is planned and assigned to a person to be invited. An email message is dispatched to this person in this case asking him/her to visit the process instance for which the task has been planned. All tasks planned for a particular person appears under "My tasks" lists in his/her user interface screen.

4.2 Adding Social Software Features

We start with explaining the upper area of the map in Fig. 4. The part of the map above the line, not represented in Fig. 3 due to the lack of space, is reserved for so-called general "steps". A general step has no place in the flow sequence, and can be started and finished at any time. As any other step in an iPB-based application, a general step has a form connected to it. Such a step can, for example, be used for reporting and solving problems arising when completing some step in the flow below the "general" line, as shown in Fig. 4. A form attached to this step, in the simplest case, can just have one field – a journal, as shown in Fig. 6. As iPB allows to attach multiple instances of the form to one step, a new form can be activated for each problem encountered when running a particular process instance. By assigning more co-owners to the Problems & Solutions step, a person encountering a problem can get their attention and help in resolving the problem.

A process map of any process can be extended by any (reasonable) number of general steps. For example, we can add such steps as "Suggestions for improvement", "Process blog", "Photo/video gallery", that are typical for social software. The only thing that is needed for adding them to an iPB application is devising field types that can represent photos, blog/forums, etc. As this is a purely technical matter solved in many social software systems, we cannot see any principal problems in adding these types of fields to the iPB tool (except finding human resources, i.e. time for doing it).

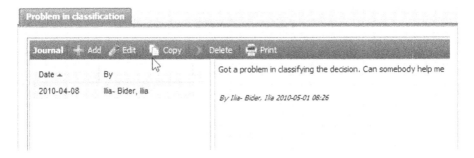

Fig. 6. A form attached to the General step "Problems&Solutions"

Another direction that needs improvement to make an iPB application feel more like a real social software system is to add a more elaborated scheme of issuing invitations. This can be connected to the introduction of new types of fields as suggested above. Once more, the methods of issuing invitation in social software are well-known, adding them to iPB in connection to adding new type of fields is a purely technical matter.

5   Conclusion

In the first part of this paper we formulated a hypothesis that one approach of merging social software with business process support lies through accepting the shared spaces architecture for BPS systems. We summarized the main ideas behind using shared spaces in BPS systems and set requirements on their implementation. Furthermore, we discussed potential benefits of using the shared spaces architecture in a BPS system regardless of the goal of implementing social software features.

In the second part, we demonstrated feasibility of development of BPS support based on the "pure" shared spaces architecture. We also described potential enhancements to the system used for demonstration. These enhancements, when implemented, would give a BPS system real look and feel of social software. We showed that these enhancements extended the system architecture in a natural way, and that they required only proper technical solutions, which are quite attainable given the state of the art in the area of WEB technologies.

We believe that business arguments and practical experience presented in the defense of our hypothesis are strong enough to continue exploiting the ideas presented in this paper. Our plans for the future consist, in the first place, in continuing implementation of the proposed approach in practice. The research question here is to investigate user perception of this kind of systems, as well as evaluate how much of the social software capability will actually be used in practice.

Acknowledgment. This paper would have never been written without considerable efforts of the team of developers who have designed and implemented iPB. We are especially thankful to Tomas Andersson, Alexey Striy and Rogier Svensson.

References

[1] Nurcan, S., Schmidt, R.: Introduction to the First International Workshop on Business Process Management and Social Software (BPMS2 2008). In: Business Process Management Workshops, pp. 647–648 (2009)

[2] Takemura, H., Kishino, F.: Cooperative work environment using virtual workspace. In: Proceedings of the 1992 ACM Conference on Computer-supported Cooperative Work, pp. 226–232. ACM, New York (1992)

[3] Van der Aalst, W.M.P., Weske, M., Grünbauer, D.: Case handling: a new paradigm for business process support. Data & Knowledge Engineering 53, 129–162 (2005)

[4] Bider, I., Johannesson, P., Perjons, E.: In Search of the Holy Grail: Integrating social software with BPM. In: Proceedings of BMPDS 2010. Springer, Heidelberg (2010)

[5] Schmidt, R., Nurcan, S.: Augmenting BPM with Social Software. In: Proceedings of the 2nd International Workshop on Business Process Management and Social Software, Ulm (2009)

[6] Vargo, S.L., Lusch, R.F.: From goods to service (s): Divergences and convergences of logics. Industrial Marketing Management (2008)

[7] Andersson, B., Bider, I., Perjons, E.: Business Process Support as a Basis for Computerized Knowledge Management. In: Althoff, K.-D., Dengel, A.R., Bergmann, R., Nick, M., Roth-Berghofer, T.R. (eds.) WM 2005. LNCS (LNAI), vol. 3782, pp. 542–553. Springer, Heidelberg (2005)

[8] iPB Reference Manual (on-line documentation), IbisSoft (2009),
`http://docs.ibissoft.se/node/3`

[9] Khomyakov, M., Bider, I.: Achieving Workflow Flexibility through Taming the Chaos. In: OOIS 2000 - 6th International Conference on Object Oriented Information Systems, pp. 85–92. Springer, Heidelberg (2000)

[10] Bider, I., Perjons, E.: Evaluating Adequacy of Business Process Modeling Approaches. In: Handbook of Research on Complex Dynamic Process Management: Techniques for Adaptability in Turbulent Environments, IGI 2009, pp. 79–102 (2009)

Emergent Case Management for Ad-hoc Processes: A Solution Based on Microblogging and Activity Streams

Martin Böhringer

Chemnitz University of Technology
Thüringer Weg 7, 09126 Chemnitz, Germany
martin.boehringer@wirtschaft.tu-chemnitz.de

Abstract. Recent research has shown the need to include unstructured ad-hoc processes into business process management. A possible solution for this purpose is Case Management, where information related to a certain process instance is bundled into a case file. In addition to existing top-down approaches, this paper suggests a bottom-up view on Case Management that leverages emergent user-driven case handling. We theoretically derive characteristics of such a system and demonstrate the approach based on a toolset of current Social Software techniques including microblogging, activity streams and tagging.

Keywords: Ad-hoc processes, Social Software, Microblogging, Activity Streams, Tagging, Case Management, Process-enhanced groupware, People-intensive processes.

1 Introduction

Many business processes are difficult to model [19]. That is especially true for knowledge-intensive tasks such as those found in incident management, consulting or sales. The reason for the impossibility of modeling can often be found in the ad-hoc characteristics of these processes. Owing to different contexts and fast-changing environments, they cannot be determined at an appropriate level of granularity before a process begins. However, to achieve the holistic management of all business processes, business process management (BPM) cannot only focus on well-structured, easy-to-model processes but has to integrate ad-hoc processes too. Accordingly, Dustdar et al. [8] compared BPM's classical focus by emphasizing "low hanging fruits," whereas most processes would not fit that pattern and might need different support.

Case Management represents a promising approach to support ad-hoc processes, because it accepts that these activities cannot be modeled in advance and, therefore, provides the minimum amount of documentation and standardization compared with widely used tools such as email and phone. Owing to the increasing importance of ad-hoc processes, this concept has seen a revival in current vendor products and practitioner discussions (see, for example, [7,17,22]). Although existing approaches for Case Management provide more degrees of freedom for process executers and support unstructured processes, they still have a top-down nature and create additional work for their users. Therefore, user adoption can be questioned. This paper suggests

M. zur Muehlen and J. Su (Eds.): BPM 2010 Workshops, LNBIP 66, pp. 384–395, 2011.
© Springer-Verlag Berlin Heidelberg 2011

a bottom-up view of Case Management which enables emergent case creation and structuring. It argues that such an approach has to focus on process actions (e.g. activities in information systems such as ERP) and artifacts (e.g. information snippets) and, therefore, would have to take into account software tools that are already being used by process executers. Based on a conceptual prototype we argue that current developments in Social Software (i.e. tagging, microblogging and activity streams) especially show a perfect fit to build Emergent Case Management systems that seamlessly integrate into everyday work routines.

After theoretically explaining this approach and discussing the existing literature, we develop a framework for Emergent Case Management in Chapter 3. We theoretically derive requirements towards such a system and argue that these requirements can be found in the Social Software principles discussed in Chapter 4. Finally, we demonstrate a prototype based on microblogging, activity streams and tagging in Chapter 5 before discussing our results. A conclusion ends the paper.

2 Ad-hoc Processes

Traditionally, the research and practice of business information systems focuses on well-structured business processes. We have a rich tradition and broad body of knowledge to model these processes and build information systems based on them. However, there are an increasing number of publications both from academia and practitioners arguing that this focus might be too narrow (see [3,12,19,31]). In fact, many activities are started and conducted in an ad-hoc way rather than being planned in advance [31]. This is especially the case for knowledge-intensive or project-based activities [14], which often represent the core competencies of an organization [19].

Bernstein [3] identified the two poles of "highly unspecified" and "highly specified" processes (Figure 1). Although the latter is the classic target of process-based information systems, the first is mostly discussed in disciplines such as computer-supported cooperative work or, more recently, Social Software. Processes belonging to this area including much of the space between the two extremes have been discussed as "ad-hoc processes." They represent a significant part of enterprise activities and, therefore, are an important topic of interest. Surprisingly, compared with its importance, this area has been covered little in previous research.

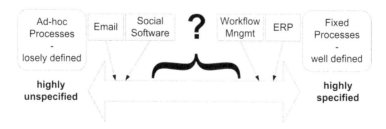

Fig. 1. Degree of process specification (modified from [3])

Ad-hoc processes are sets of business activities and corresponding artifacts (e.g. information, decisions and products) that can only be standardized at a high level of aggregation. The actual kinds of activities and their ordering are different from case to case. Chung et al. stated that "while certain characteristics and activities can be predicted, much of the process cannot be fully specified at the start, since it requires information that only becomes available some way into the project" [6]. If we assume that in the context of ad-hoc processes the next step is never determined, they can only be defined entirely in the form of their instantiations *after* they have been finished. This means that "ad-hoc processes [...] have no underlying process definition" [8]. Therefore, ad-hoc processes by definition cannot be standardized and as such their execution cannot be controlled by classical process-based information systems. This means that human beings and, in most cases, knowledge workers are in control of the process. Jennings and Finkelstein argued that where the interaction of human agents is required, a top-down approach is not suitable because of the lack of *a priori* knowledge [14]. Besides the fact that it seems impossible to think of all possibilities by design time, such a process model would become complex and unmanageable [34].

3 Emergent Case Management

Case Management (also referred to as Case Handling or Case Processes) is an approach to handle business activities that cannot be supported by classical BPM tools. It focuses on process instances and is a collaborative and communicative task [7]. Its origin is situated in domains such as healthcare and governance [17] and, therefore, can be considered to support especially knowledge-intensive processes [34]. Forrester analysts Le Clair and Moore [17] suggested the increasing importance of the concept and OMG (Object Management Group, http://omg.org/) is working on an according standard [22]. However, the exact meaning of Case Management in terms of its actual implementations is still vague and depends on context and use. Therefore, it can be seen as a general approach of handling unstructured business processes rather than being a mature tool category. Accordingly, our general understanding of Case Management in terms of a working definition is as follows: *Case Management is an approach to handling ad-hoc processes. It supports process instances (cases) in providing a collaborative space to store and negotiate case-related activities and artifacts (e.g. information, decisions, workflows) without the need for the* ex ante *modeling of the whole process.*

Existing Case Management approaches nonetheless are oriented towards top-down organization and pre-configuration. Van der Aalst et al. [34], for example, proposed a system that supports the user with information about what activities can be performed based on the current status of the case. This suggests that the Case Management system has to be trained and possible case statuses have to be modeled in advance. Although useful in contexts that are at least semi-structured, this might be a too rigid approach for ad-hoc processes. If we take into account that ad-hoc processes cannot be modeled in advance, a top-down pre-configuration of possible case states might also be incomplete if not impossible. Le Clair and Moore [17] explained Case Management in the context of "people-driven processes." If users are drivers of ad-hoc processes and are crucial to their successful execution, it might be worthwhile thinking about a paradigm shift towards bottom-up solutions. Hagel and Brown [11] suggested that shifting from a push-based approach in BPM and information systems in general to a pull-based, user-driven model is a logical consequence of rising complexity and knowledge-intensity. Applied to Case Management this leads us to the proposal of Emergent Case Management.

Emergent Case Management is an approach for the bottom-up managing of ad-hoc processes. Although existing concepts including "classical" Case Management try to leverage the benefits of structured BPM for unstructured cases and, therefore, modify its methods to achieve greater flexibility, we suggest starting at concepts for unstructured processes (e.g. email and Social Software, Figure 1) and aiming towards enabling users to organize this content in a process-based view. Therefore, people are at the center of such an information system; they are in charge of the process. They have to be able to adopt the tool for their process-related needs. Since the goal is to integrate as many case-related users at possible (executers, stakeholders, knowledge carriers), such an approach has to be as simple as possible and should not burden them with restrictions [26].

Figure 2 visualizes the underlying framework and understanding of Emergent Case Management. Users are at the centre of the solution and the driving force of all actions. In working on an ad-hoc process, they execute activities and act on artifacts such as information, decisions and documents (e.g. by creating, executing and working on them). These artifacts are represented in information systems (including non-technical systems such as face-to-face conversations). The goal of Emergent Case Management is to enable users to assign activities and artifacts independent of their representation to a certain case, which can be dynamically defined by users.

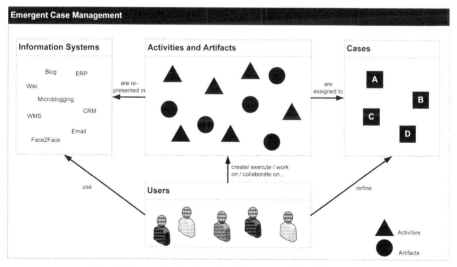

Fig. 2. Conceptual schemata of Emergent Case Management

4 Emergent Case Management and Social Software

There is an ongoing discussion about how BPM and Social Software fit together. Approaches include a wide range of use cases, such as supporting process documentation using wikis, collaborative process modeling and the deployment of processes [9]. Traditional BPM and Social Software leverage different approaches to support users. Johannesson et al. [15] highlighted the points "external authority vs. voluntary participation," "definite endpoint vs. open-endedness," "major efforts vs. quick contributions" and "access control vs. transparency." Owing to these characteristics, several authors have argued that ad-hoc processes show many parallels to Social Software characteristics and have suggested that these tools support unstructured processes (see, for example, [3,15,20]).

A distinct principle of most Social Software tools is their design as a platform [23] that enables but does not force social interaction: "sociality cannot be designed; it can only be designed for" (Wenger [37] paraphrased in [13]). Although classical IT applications are designed for a special purpose and with a special use or business process in mind, platforms go one step back and acknowledge that only the users and process owners in their special (ad-hoc) situations can specify these use cases. Instead of trying to support an ideal process, platforms support users with basic functionalities and a high degree of freedom. The goal of these systems is that users can leverage them to create ad-hoc suitable IT support for their tasks [15].

Based on the framework (Figure 2) and the previous discussion, our assumption here is that the focus of ad-hoc process executers is on getting things done. They are involved in several parallel cases, and this includes a massive amount of multitasking. Since ad-hoc processes are seldom repeated, for workers in ad-hoc processes it is important that the goal can be reached rather than *how* this has to be done [31]. Therefore, the flow of activities is especially crucial for their work. This is why Social Software tools supporting a flow-based representation of their work are central to the concept of Emergent Case Management. A typical platform for this task is microblogging (e.g. Twitter), where users can publish small pieces of information and enhance it with structure (e.g. hashtags "#bpm2010", re-tweets, @-mentions). Combined with automatically generated activity data this leads to so-called activity streams, which can be part of a separate application (e.g. Facebook's "News Feed") or included in microblogging (described, for example, in the concept of "ubiquitous microblogging" [4]).

In a case study on the long-term usage of a microblogging-like enterprise software system called Arinia, Barnes et al. found that Arinia is used to support nearly all customer-related processes [1]. In this case, these processes are project-driven and, therefore, highly unstructured. The company is certified for ISO 9001 and Arinia is seen as a key concept for supporting their processes. Following this initial insight, we suggest that it is blogging, especially microblogging, that is of great interest to BPM, as it follows an activity-driven, time-based approach of interaction management. Rosemann argued that its potential for BPM is still "under-utilized" [28]. Other researchers and practitioners support the idea of microblogging-based process execution (see, for example, [16,35]) and the first vendors are starting to integrate similar features into their products [32]. Furthermore, the approach of focusing on activities is in line with previous research on activity-centric collaboration [10].

5 A Prototype of Emergent Case Management

5.1 Conceptual Description

A basic assumption of the concept of Emergent Case Management is that modeling is not applicable for ad-hoc processes. We argue that ad-hoc processes cannot be modeled by definition and that modeling a single process instance during execution would only create additional work but no benefits. Therefore, we aim to provide bottom-up process support by enabling users to assign artifacts and activities to a case (that is, a process instance). We suggest using activity streams of automatically, semi-automatically and manually created activity logs (microblogging postings), where artifacts are represented a) by activities executed on them (e.g. "Max created the document 'Requirements Engineering'") or b) in postings directly referring to them (e.g. via linking). Table 2 contains examples of these information sources.

Table 1. Sources of activity logs

Source	Description and examples
Manual creation	Since people are in charge of ad-hoc processes, manually created activity logs using microblogging are the focus of our concept. Previous research has suggested that in leveraging microblogging, half of intraorganizational communication can shift from emails to this open communication medium [1], which should be a major goal because email and face-to-face communication cannot be included in the activity stream.
Semi-automated creation	Lots of web applications include a "Tweet this" button, which allows users to edit and tweet a pre-generated text. After finishing rescheduling in the production planning system, user Max could use this functionality to generate the text, add the appropriate hashtags and maybe a certain user who waits for this input to proceed and finally send the posting to the activity stream: Example: Max: "@Paul I created 'Production Planning Rescheduled' at http://bit.ly/2nkmNd #repabc #finished".
Automated creation	Activity logs are automatically created from existing information systems such as CRM, ERP or wikis when actions are conducted. Where possible, such structured tools should be used for parts of the ad-hoc process and, therefore, be integrated into the activity stream [26]. Assignment to a case can be achieved in two ways: a) the source information system 'knows' the case hashtag and includes it in the post (requires a certain level of standardization) or b) users re-tweet such activity logs if they are important for the case and add appropriate hashtags. Example: SAP: "Paul approved order O123." → Max: "RT @SAP Paul approved order O123. #repabc"

Furthermore, Figure 3 presents an overview of the framework. Based on the central understanding of Emergent Case Management, the goal is to include as much information into the activity stream as possible. Therefore, such a system should not ignore existing systems. Where possible, specialized information systems such as ERP or CRM should be used during process execution. The so-created activities and artifacts are posted into the activity stream where they can be assigned to a certain case. As is known from microblogging, the stream is ordered chronologically with the newest entries on top. We propose using hashtags for assigning activity entries to cases. The principle is well known from Twitter and provides high degrees of freedom for users. We will discuss the pros and cons of this decision in Chapter 6.

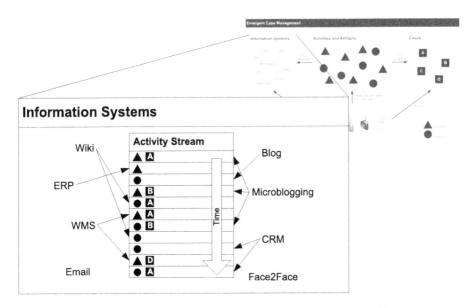

Fig. 3. The prototype's concept of activity stream-based Emergent Case Management

In applying microblogging/activity streams combined with tagging, we are able to support all components of our Emergent Case Management framework. Table 2 summarizes the representation of the different concepts.

Table 2. Concepts of Emergent Case Management and their representation in the prototype

Concept	Representation of the concept
Users	Participants in microblogging, using microblogging for communication
Activities	Microblogging postings and activity stream entries
Artifacts	Links in microblogging postings/activity stream entries
Legacy IS	Own microblogs or postings to the user's activity stream
Cases	Hashtags (e.g. "#emergency_test")
Assignment to cases	Using hashtags in a posting (e.g. "Reminder: the #emergency_test is scheduled for tomorrow.")

5.2 Front-End

To visualize the concept of Social Software-based Emergent Case Management, we will use a short example based on a real world case to demonstrate our prototype (for a comprehensive discussion of the case, see [5]). Our demo company is in the textile business and produces high quality test series. Projects are unique and there are little possibilities for standardization. Customers might require short-run changes to existing or sometimes even already shipped orders. These time-critical ad-hoc processes are called "reparations." Our example refers to such a set of activities for customer "ABC." That is why the sales representative started the process instance with the hashtag "#repabc".

To visualize the prototype we use a Twitter-like interface. Process-related stake-holders as well as existing information systems are represented via their own micro-blogs, which are aggregated in a joint activity stream. For the manual creation of activity entries, people have a simple text box restricted to 140 characters. In our example, a search for the hashtag "#repabc" shows the complete ad-hoc process do-cumentation including human and non-human activity, artifacts (e.g. the bill) and parts of the workflow (using @-referencing), as shown in Figure 4. The Twitter-inspired search screen also shows additional possibilities for analytical support (e.g. trending topics at the right side). Combined with text mining techniques such as opi-nion mining, such scenarios can enable constant process monitoring and process intel-ligence (see, for example, the feature "Social Business Intelligence" of enterprise microblogging vendor socialcast.com).

Realtime results for **#repabc**

Trending topics

#repccc

katrinmueller RT @SAP_Receipts bill no. #R23992383 has been paid by customer #ABC #repabc
about 6 minutes ago from web

quote

#repabc

customer

thorstenmann Quality checked, order shipped to customer #repabc
2 days ago from web

#annualreport

#fail

ottomuster #repabc forwarded to @thorstenmann for quality check.
2 days ago from web

#canoetrip

thomu Meeting with @ottomuster on #repabc
3 days ago from web

thomu RT @ext_klein (Ms Klein, #ABC): Timely delivery is of highest priority for us! #repabc
4 days ago from web

thomu On my way to ##Dresden visiting @ext_klein of #ABC #repabc
4 days ago from mobile client

ottomuster RT @Machine1839 Error Code #F2328. Actuator broken. //@thomu #repabc will be delayed minimum 1 day!
4 days ago from web

ottomuster @thomu we will take care of it, probably will be finished tomorrow appr. 2pm. #repabc
5 days ago from web

thomu @ottomuster Customer #ABC requests repairing the current delivery: the color fidelity is insufficient (cf. colour sample ABC12) #repabc
5 days ago from web

Fig. 4. Monitoring of ad-hoc processes via hashtag filtering

5.3 Technological Foundation

As the scope of this paper is to present the general concept of using microblog-ging/activity streaming for supporting ad-hoc processes, we will only briefly discuss the technological foundation of an appropriate solution. We have evaluated the approach in different laboratory experiments with several existing microblogging applications such as Twitter and StatusNet. Although they show good support for manually created microblogging postings, for automated and semi-automated activity reporting a more sophisticated solution is needed. Big Internet vendors such as Facebook, MySpace and Opera are currently cooperating on a standard format for activity exchange (activitystrea.ms) based on the Atom feed protocol. We suggest building adapters for existing information systems such as CRM and ERP, which publish activity information from these sources in an activity streams format. Our back-end system, therefore, consists of a) a communication and extraction layer to retrieve this information, b) a storage layer and c) a representation layer providing the information feeds to d) the front-end (where users can subscribe/unsubscribe and publish information). Until we have implemented such a system, Twitter, with its millions of users, might be a good proof for the scalability of the concept.

6 Discussion

Our approach of using hashtags as case identifiers provides several possibilities for enhancing structure and standardization. As it can be seen with Twitter, hashtags at first are emergent terms that can be freely defined by users. As observed especially for events such as conferences, different hashtags often evolve for the same event (e.g. "bpm", "bpm10" and "bpm2010"), which leads to fragmented information. A way of handling such problems could be to provide predefined tags or the predefined structuring of tags. However, this is top-down thinking and might decrease people's motivation to use the system. From previous research we already have some knowledge about emergence and shared vocabulary building in folksonomy systems. Muller reported on four tag-based systems in an enterprise and found that tagging use is only consistent inside one system [21]. Interestingly, people used different tags in different systems, which provides evidence for users' possibilities of adapting certain rules in special contexts. Other researchers found similar patterns and described folksonomy building as a "negotiated process of users" [24] and a "self-organizing system towards a shared vocabulary building" [18], which develops towards a group consensus. Therefore, a suitable bottom-up mechanism for governance would not be to restrict tag usage but to enable documentation (e.g. via hashtag wikis similar to hashtags.org or hashdictionary.com) or ways of defining synonymous tags.

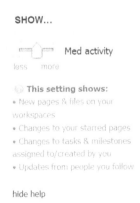

Fig. 5. Activity slider at pbworks.com

Another critical point of the proposed concept is dealing with information overflow. In particular, their context is important to support a flexible process [27]. Therefore, all available information should be provided for process stakeholders. However, this might lead to a plethora of fine-granular activity entries. If we think of the typical knowledge worker as being involved in a high number of parallel ad-hoc processes, there is a need for suitable mechanisms to avoid information overload. A possible solution is to leverage rich user interfaces. Figure 5 shows the activity slider of the Social Software suite PBworks. The user intuitively can filter the incoming information flow by its importance (with human messages being most important and automated activity logs being least important).

Owing to its platform characteristics, the presented solution for Emergent Case Management is expected to be strong in enabling creativity, which can be seen as a key element in ad-hoc processes [30], and facilitating related effects such as serendipity [36]. However, further work has to focus on the possibilities for process evolution. Well-structured business processes can evolve from ad-hoc activities [2]. If a certain process stabilizes or a case has to be repeated, techniques such as process mining [33] could be applied to the activity log to distillate the process structure. Therefore, a strong technological foundation in terms of semantics and open standards is necessary. Besides current initiatives such as the standardization of activity exchange there are already a number of works on reliable decentralized and semantically enriched microblogging solutions (see, for example, [25,29]) that could be applied to the presented scenario.

7 Conclusions

The paper's contributions are as follows: a) it presented a bottom-up solution for supporting and managing ad-hoc processes called Emergent Case Management; b) it suggested using Social Software, in particular a combination of cutting edge technologies such as tagging, microblogging and activity streams, for Emergent Case Management; and c) it presented a conceptual prototype related to a real world example that showed the applicability of the approach. The focus of the discussed approach is on its integration into everyday work and on it being as lightweight as possible. The management part, therefore, is reduced to creating organizational foundations (e.g. simple rules for hashtag creation), gardening the folksonomy and supporting evolving process structures. This represents a paradigm shift in BPM: instead of supporting central planners and analysts, our focus for supporting ad-hoc processes is primarily on the process executers themselves. Hence, factors such as the joy of usage and simplicity become important.

Current vendor developments point towards Emergent Case Management. Salesforce has announced Salesforce Chatter, an activity streaming module for its enterprise software suite. Microsoft Sharepoint will feature activity streaming in its 2010 version. Big Internet vendors such as Facebook, MySpace and Opera are cooperating to build a standard format for activity exchange (activitystrea.ms). In conclusion, the infrastructure for the proposed solution for ad-hoc process support is growing, and further works on the topic are needed to uncover this development's potential for BPM. Accordingly, our roadmap includes running an Emergent Case Management system and evaluating it in real world cases.

References

1. Barnes, S.J., Böhringer, M., Kurze, C., Stietzel, J.: Towards an understanding of Social Software: the case of Arinia. In: Proceedings of the 43rd Hawaii International Conference on System Sciences (HICSS-43). IEEE Computer Society, Los Alamitos (2010)
2. Bernstein, A., Schucan, C.: Document and process transformation during the product life cycle. In: Wakayame, T., Kannapan, S., Khoong, C.M., Navathe, S., Yates, J. (eds.) Information and Process Integration in Enterprises - Rethinking Documents, pp. 277–284. Kluwer Academic Publishers, Dordrecht (1998)
3. Bernstein, A.: How can cooperative work tools support dynamic group process? Bridging the specificity frontier. In: Proceedings of the 2000 ACM Conference on Computer Supported Cooperative Work - CSCW 2000, pp. 279–288. ACM Press, New York (2000)
4. Böhringer, M., Gluchowski, P.: The Beauty of Simplicity: Ubiquitous Microblogging in the Enterprise. In: Proceedings of the 12th International Conference on Enterprise Information Systems (2010)
5. Böhringer, M., Jentsch, D.: Lightweight IT support for ad-hoc-processes in production and logistics. In: Proceedings of the 43rd CIRP International Conference on Manufacturing Systems (2010)
6. Chung, P., Cheung, L., Stader, J., Jarvis, P., Moore, J., Macintosh, A.: Knowledge-based process management – an approach to handling adaptive workflow. Knowledge-Based Systems 16(3), 149–160 (2003)
7. De Man, H.: Case Management: A Review of Modeling Approaches. BPTrends (2009)
8. Dustdar, S., Hoffmann, T., Van der Aalst, W.: Mining of ad-hoc Business Processes with TeamLog. Data and Knowledge Engineering 55(2), 129–158 (2005)
9. Erol, S., Granitzer, M., Happ, S., Jantunen, S., Jennings, B., Koschmider, A., Nurcan, S., Rossi, D., Schmidt, R.: Combining BPM and Social Software: Contradiction or Chance? Software Process: Improvement and Practice Journal, Special Issue on BPM 2008 Selected Workshop Papers (2009)
10. Geyer, W., Muller, M., Moore, M., Wilcox, E., Cheng, L., Brownholtz, B., Hill, C.R., Millen, D.R.: Activity Explorer: Activity-centric collaboration from research to product. IBM Systems Journal 45(4), 713–738 (2006)
11. Hagel, J., Brown, J.: From push to pull – emerging models for mobilizing resources. Journal of Service Science, Third Quarter (2008)
12. Hall, J.M., Johnson, M.E.: When Should a Process Be Art, Not Science. Harvard Business Review 87(3), 58–65 (2009)
13. Hoogenboom, T., Schoondorp, M.: The Realm of Sociality: Notes on the Design of Social Software. Working Papers on Information Systems 8(1) (2008)
14. Jennings, B., Finkelstein, A.: Micro Work Gestural Analysis: Representation in Social Business Processes. In: Proceedings of the 2nd Workshop on Business Process Management and Social Software (2009)
15. Johannesson, P., Andersson, B., Wohed, P.: Business Process Management with Social Software Systems – A New Paradigm for Work Organisation. In: Proceedings of the 1st Workshop on Business Process Management and Social Software (2008)
16. Kemsley, S.: BPM, Collaboration and Social Networking #brf, Column 2 (2009), http://www.column2.com/2009/11/bpm-collaboration-and-social-networking-brf/
17. Le Clair, C., Moore, C.: Dynamic Case Management — An Old Idea Catches New Fire. Forrester (2009)

18. Maass, W., Kowatsch, T., Münster, T.: Vocabulary Patterns in Free-for-all Collaborative Indexing Systems. In: International Workshop on Emergent Semantics and Ontology Evolution, pp. 45–57 (2007)
19. Marjanovic, O.: Towards IS supported coordination in emergent business processes. Business Process Management Journal 11(5), 476–487 (2005)
20. Marjanovic, O.: Inside Agile Processes: A Practitioners Perspective. In: Proceedings of the 42nd Hawaii International Conference on System Sciences (HICSS-42). IEEE Computer Society, Los Alamitos (2009)
21. Muller, M.J.: Comparing tagging vocabularies among four enterprise tag-based services. In: Proceedings of the 2007 International ACM conference on Conference on Supporting Group Work - GROUP 2007 (2007)
22. OMG: Case Management Process Modeling (CMPM) - Request For Proposal (2009), http://www.omg.org/cgi-bin/doc?bmi/09-09-23
23. O'Reilly, T.: What Is Web 2.0 (2005), http://www.oreilly.de/artikel/web20.html
24. Paolillo, J., Penumarthy, S.: The Social Structure of Tagging Internet Video on del.icio.us. In: Proceedings of the 40th Hawaii International Conference on System Sciences (HICSS-40). IEEE Computer Society, Los Alamitos (2007)
25. Passant, A., Hastrup, T., Bojars, U., Breslin, J.: Microblogging: A Semantic and Distributed Approach. In: Proceedings of the 4th Workshop on Scripting for the Semantic Web (2008)
26. Rettig, C.: The trouble with enterprise software. MIT Sloan Management Review 49(1) (2007)
27. Rosemann, M., Recker, J., Flender, C.: Contextualisation of business processes. International Journal of Business Process Integration and Management 3(1), 47–60 (2008)
28. Rosemann, M.: Where BPM and Twitter could meet. ARIS Community (2009), http://www.ariscommunity.com/users/mrosemann/2009-08-07-where-bpm-and-twitter-could-meet
29. Sandler, D.R., Wallach, D.S.: Birds of a FETHR: Open, Decentralized Micropublishing. In: 8th International Workshop on Peer-to-Peer Systems, IPTPS 2009 (2009)
30. Seidel, S., Rosemann, M., Becker, J.: How does Creativity Impact Business Processes? In: Proceedings of the 16th European Conference on Information Systems (2008)
31. Tochtermann, K., Reisinger, D., Granitzer, M., Lindstaedt, S.: Integrating ad hoc processes and standard processes in public administrations. In: Proceedings of the OCG eGovernment Conference (2006)
32. Ultimus, Inc.: Ultimus Enhances BPM Suite with Twitter Updates for Your Business Process (2009), http://www.ultimus.com/Blog/bid/33745/Ultimus-Enhances-BPM-Suite-with-Twitter-Updates-for-Your-Business-Process
33. Van der Aalst, W., Nikolov, A.: Mining E-Mail Messages: Uncovering Interaction Patterns and Processes using E-mail Logs. International Journal of Intelligent Information Technologies 4(3), 27–45 (2008)
34. Van der Aalst, W., Weske, M., Grünbauer, D.: Case handling: a new paradigm for business process support. Data & Knowledge Engineering 53(2), 129–162 (2005)
35. Venkat, J.: BPM and Twitter – Tweeting to BPM (2009), http://www.bouncingthoughts.com/2009/08/bpm-and-twitter-tweeting-to-bpm/
36. Vinoski, S.: Serendipitous reuse. IEEE Internet Computing 12(1), 84–87 (2008)
37. Wenger, E.: Communities of practice: Learning, meaning and identity. Cambridge University Press, Cambridge (1998)

Social Software for Coordination of Collaborative Process Activities

Frank Dengler[1], Agnes Koschmider[1,2], Andreas Oberweis[1], and Huayu Zhang[1]

[1] Institute AIFB, Karlsruhe Institute of Technology (KIT), Karlsruhe, Germany
{frank.dengler,andreas.oberweis,huayu.zhang}@kit.edu
[2] Department of Computer Science, University of Pretoria, Pretoria, South Africa
akoschmider@cs.up.ac.za

Abstract. Recently, a trend toward collaborative, on-line business process modeling can be observed that is also emphasized by several initiatives. Social software has the potential satisfying such a collaborative modeling. It provides tools to collaboratively exchange and share information resources among peers. Despite of the potential that social software has, it is insufficiently used as work resource (e.g., for help requests or partner search) due to a low integration of social software into the workflow management system. The aim of this paper is to exploit Wikis and social networks for the coordination of collaborative process activities. Wikis are suggested in order to reduce the model design phase. A technique will be introduced that allows visualizing a process model from Wiki pages. The connection of process activities with social networks supports browsing for suitable process collaborators. A coordination model will be introduced that governs the collaboration.

1 Introduction

Social software is still gaining high popularity and has attracted a significant amount of users. Social software has been differently exploited and identified as suitable, e.g. for knowledge management [1] and recommender systems [2].

Activities that may highly benefit of further exploitation of social software are business process modeling and process coordination. In particular, a Wiki can accelerate the model design phase. A Wiki stores how-tos and best practices (activities of users for a special task). Consequently, the evaluation of the as-is state (and finally the process model creation) can be facilitated when analyzing Wiki pages. Social networks might help to find appropriate partners and collaborators, respectively. Process activities (e.g., booking, notifying) requiring at least two peers can be performed when browsing user profiles (skills, experiences) in social networks and getting in contact with the appropriate persons.

However, the usage of social software within business process activities also requires coordination mechanisms. Wiki pages that serve as input for the visualization of process models need to be consistently updated (in case of insertion of new process activities). Cooperatively performed activities (with the support of social networks) need to be supervised and managed. In case of missing coordination support, it is left to the user to perform the corresponding tasks.

M. zur Muehlen and J. Su (Eds.): BPM 2010 Workshops, LNBIP 66, pp. 396–407, 2011.
© Springer-Verlag Berlin Heidelberg 2011

In this paper we exploit a Wiki and social networks for the coordination of cooperatively performed activities. The information stored in Wikis and social networks is used to find appropriate collaborators (from internal and external organizations). Changes made in the process model (e.g., insertion of an activity) will be communicated to the Wiki implicating an update of corresponding pages. The approach presented in this paper has the following advantages:

- available best practices are reused facilitating process model creation,
- synchronization between Wikis and the process model facilitates modifications and reduces redundancies,
- parallel existence of textual (Wiki) and graphical (process model) content representation enables users to select the favored style. Validation techniques (for process models) can be used to investigate the reachability of activities,
- controlled coordination of collaborative process activities.

Given this background the remainder of the paper is structured as follows. The following section illustrates our approach and summarizes background we will work upon. In particular the generation of process models from Wiki pages is explained and a model for coordinating process activities based on social networks. Section 3 describes the continuous modeling and coordination of collaborative processes based on social networks and case-based reasoning and the synchronization of the process model with the Wiki. Our approach is applied to a use case in Section 4. Section 5 discusses related work. Eventually, Section 6 concludes the paper and gives an outlook on future research.

2   Coordination of Processes Using Social Software

The next subsection presents a scenario for our approach and motivates the need for coordination mechanism. Subsection 2.2 sketches the foundations of our approach.

2.1   Scenario

Assume somebody has an innovative idea for a third-party founded project and intends to write a project proposal to get fundings (e.g., from the EU). Since he has never written a project proposal before, he has to get familiar with the existing processes and regulations in his department concerning project proposals. Research departments widely use Wiki pages to describe the corresponding processes and best practice approaches. Initially, the researcher invokes the proposal writing page and also remembers colleagues talking about EU projects and project partners. On the Wiki page he finds a set of hints for writing project proposals but no information how to initiate a collaboration. The researcher has specific research departments and companies in mind working in different areas that are relevant for his proposal idea. He looks in his contact lists and finds the address of a person working for one of the companies he has in mind. He contacts her and both agree on writing a proposal. She works for a company, which has their own regulations about collaboration, which means that a non-disclosure agreement (NDA) has to be signed. The process of signing an

NDA is new to the researcher and he has not found any note about this on the Wiki pages. Thus, he decides to make a note about this. After the proposal has been accepted for the hearings, the researcher has to organize the trip to attend the hearings. This process is explained on a Wiki page again. The researcher has to contact the travel agency in order to book train and flight tickets. Finally, he has to book a hotel room. If he is aware of other future project partners that will attend the hearing, he might arrange the hotel booking with additional persons.

This use case requires coordination effort. Wiki pages need to be updated, third-party organizations need to be contacted, collaboration needs to be arranged and managed. In case of no integrated coordination tool support, it is left to the researcher to perform the corresponding tasks and to solely coordinate the activities.

2.2   Background

The approach presented in this paper builds on Semantic MediaWiki (SMW) providing process modeling and visualization functionalities [3]. Additionally, our approach uses a model for the coordination of collaborative process activities.

The SMW allows users to express their knowledge with their natural language combined with formal annotations allowing machines to process and export this knowledge using RDF. Users can connect Wiki pages by using semantic annotations and thus defining associations between pages. In the process visualization a Wiki page is represented by an activity. The flow between activities is built based on semantic annotations and using special predefined process properties[1]. The advantages of using SMW for process development are:

- *Collaboration*: All users have access to the corporate Wiki and thus everybody can contribute in process development and browse existing processes.
- *Versioning*: SMW provides the history of all edits. Old versions can be viewed and compared as well as changes can be undone.
- *Reuse of Process Knowledge*: SMW can be used as a process knowledge repository. The stored knowledge can be reused in other Wiki pages using queries or by other applications using RDF export.

Figure 1 visualizes our scenario and shows where SMW is used in the scenario. SMW describes best practices of an organization (how to write a proposal, how to get in contact) and serves as input for visualization of the process as-is state. In our approach we take the formalized processes in RDF, transform them into simple Petri Nets and use them in a process execution engine. Users can modify either Wiki pages or the process model. The coordination of updates will be explained in Section 3.2.

After the generation of a process model based on SMW, coordination mechanisms are needed to ensure the execution of separate activities, which may be performed by different users in different collaboration contexts. Koschmider et al. [4] have suggested a model called *Community Process* for the coordination of

---

[1] For further information we refer to [3].

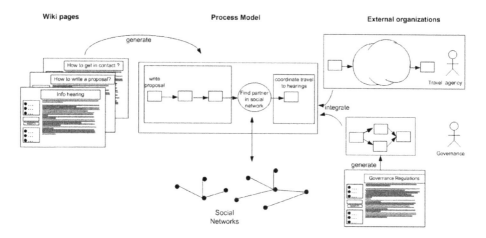

Fig. 1. Proposed approach

collaborations in social networks. The Community Process is a set of related activities of network members that are executed to achieve a collaboration output. The concept of Community Process considers different development stages of social networks (*finding partners, building relationships, executing collaboration*) and uses results of the analysis of interpersonal relationships, so that the activities and human resources can be more easily and purposefully applied for the initiation and execution of a collaboration. It is a user-driven approach and provides flexibility and extensibility in collaborative modeling due to the adoption of lazy and late modeling [5]. The modeling notation of Community Processes is derived from Petri Nets. Figure 2 shows an example of a simple Community Process model related to the scenario in Section 2 that involves two collaborators (Name1 and Name2).

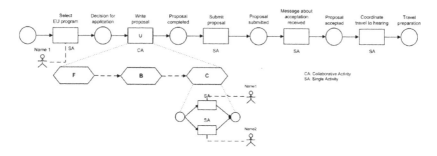

Fig. 2. An example of a simple Community Process - Writing an EU proposal

The special feature of a Community Process model is the labeling of activities with "U". Such a labeling represents collaborative behavior that is performed by a sequence of abstract sub-processes *Finding Partners (F), Building Relationship (B)* and *Collaboration Execution (C)*. The first two sub-processes (F and B) focus on the preparation of a collaboration, while the third sub-process (C) refers to the actual execution of assigned tasks. A Community Process is associated with a set of Community Process Objects that include e.g., Community Users (which describe network members through their user profiles) and Community Contents (that are data objects transferred from one activity to another). Based on user relationships (e.g. obtained through analyzing outgoing Emails or Chats [6]), that are stored and continuously updated in Community Users, social network structure can be created. Upon this structure, analysis methods can be applied to recommend collaborators in one's personal network while executing the sub-process F, or to suggest how to contact potential collaborators in sub-process B. Referring to our scenario, label "U" can be put on the transition *write proposal* in Figure 1, which triggers the Community Process.

3   Coordination of Business Processes

Although the Community Process approach supports an effective utilization of personal resources in social networks, it remains unsolved how resources such as processes or services of conventional business information systems can be integrated into Community Processes. For this reason an extension based on case-based reasoning (CBR) [7] will be suggested and described in the next section. Some ideas how to use CBR in process management can be found in [8,9]. The goal of the integration is to ease an uninterrupted execution of activities in and outside social networks, for example, tickets booking by travel agency and signing an NDA in a company. On the opposite side, a Community Process can also be integrated into business processes to enable self-organized collaborations using social networks, which will be elaborated in a separate paper.

3.1   Integration of Business Processes into Community Process Using CBR

In this section, we describe a CBR-solution for integration of business processes (internal and external) into Community Processes in detail. This rises some challenges. Firstly, it is difficult to identify and select the most appropriate process or service from several providers whose functional and non-functional properties match users' requirements. Secondly, the Community Process may change in case that it is performed each time with different external resources. Thus, a flexible and not fixed connection between a Community Process and a business process or service is desirable.

The goal of using CBR is reuse (sharing) of user experiences obtained during the interaction with business processes of external organizations. Without deep modeling or technical knowledge users will be guided by a reasoning system to easily choose a support provider (just at the moment when they request one). After the execution of a Community Process, including the integrated business processes, the user experiences will be stored as a new or in an existing case. The process owner can finally decide whether the case details should be reconverted to Wiki pages or not, which would be seen as a best practice by other users.

In our approach we treat a business process as a case that will be completely executed to fulfill a support request without revealing process details such as process logic. Each instance of the case has an owner who acts as support responder (provider). A solution to a case (business process) consists of the following three components: (I) description of the support provider. (II) communication details (e.g., contact methods) with the support provider and (III) interface for using the case, such as input and output parameters. Case solutions will be integrated into Community Processes to specify and implement *Collaborative Activities*. In other words, a collaboration behavior between a peer and a business support provider, which also requires the integration of process data, will be recognized and handled in the Community Process.

In this paper we focus on business processes of external organizations (e.g., see Figure 1), which may deliver services to individual peers, so that firstly the subject domains of the cases are restricted. Knowledge of these domains can then be collected and stored in the case database to enable better understanding of the cases. A possible decomposition of business process cases based on the approach of [10] is shown in Figure 3. There are five main subject domains, which relate to different business areas from the tertiary industrial sector and three main subject sub-domains that relate to different function areas.

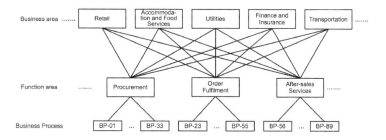

Fig. 3. Subject domains of cases

Within a domain a case can further be refined using, for example, a dynamic memory model [11] or category and exemplar model [12]. For case retrieval, we introduce here our own method, which considers existing information of social relationships of users (e.g., stored in Community Users) in social software systems (Wikis and social networks). We call this method *Network-based Two-way Case Retrieval*. It is two-way in the sense that it supports retrieval both in the network-of-person (i.e. social network structure) and network-of-data (as shown in Figure 3). The method works as follows: Firstly, we define a *personal similarity (PS)* as a concept whereby each node in a network-of-person is assigned a degree as a positive integer based on the number of nodes between the user and his relationships. A *data similarity (DS)* is either a syntactical or a semantic similarity in the network-of-data that is mentioned in [7]. To select the right way for case retrieval, the following decision models can be used.

1. *Match(DS)*: Cases will be returned whose data similarity compared to a new case indicates a significant threshold.
2. *Match(PS)*: Cases used by users in a social network will be listed for selection whose personal similarity to the owner of Community Process have a specific threshold and then matched with the new case by using the first model Match(DS).

The main advantage of this two-way method is that the accuracy of system reasoning can be increased because personal similarity is considered in the case of low data similarity.

Case reuse means in our context that a Collaborative Activity will be refined including the sub-processes *Finding Partners (F)*, *Building Relationship (B)* and *Collaboration Execution (C)*, which will be automatically constructed based on a case solution. The output of the F-sub-process is generated according to Component (I); The B- and C-sub-processes can be built according to Component (II) and (III), respectively.

Case revision will be applied during runtime of a Community Process. If errors occur (e.g., an external service is no more available) a repair process will be triggered that provides necessary general and case-specific knowledge for compensation purpose, such as modifying process details, suggesting other cases and adjusting conditions and constrains on the Collaborative Activity that are given by other process activities.

After the completion of a Community Process, according to the modified process details either a new solution will be generated or existing solutions will be updated in case database. These new solutions can consequently be reused and integrated into other Community Processes.

3.2   Wiki Update Methods

In addition to the reuse of process execution data we also propose to update the process information in the Wiki, because the acceptance of a Wiki depends on the degree to which a person can truly benefit personally from it. Therefore it is important that a certain quantity and quality of content is available in the Wiki [13] and we want to guarantee this by updating the Wiki with executed process information. Updating and storing each case in the Wiki will result in an information overload and make it hard for the users to find the information relevant for their case. Therefore smart update mechanisms have to be applied that only the common relevant information is updated in the Wiki. In a Wiki update process different commands can be executed: New pages can be created, if new process activities are required, information on existing pages can be inserted or deleted and pages can be deleted, if the process activity is no longer required. The Wiki can be updated in different ways. On the one hand a *semi-automated update* can be performed by giving the user a list of the process activities from the process execution engine and let him choose what should be written into the Wiki. On the other hand an *automated* update can be performed by writing information directly into the Wiki applying the following update rules.

- *Counting repetitions*: A simple filter for updating process information is counting the same instances executed by the users. When a specific threshold is achieved, the process has reached a mature level and will be updated in the Wiki.
- *Abstracting similar cases*: Similar cases can be derived and abstracted. Therefore approaches to process mining like producing a taxonomy of workflow models [14] providing an abstraction method and taxonomy of patterns [15] can be used. Then the abstracted patterns can be updated in the Wiki.
- *Skill level*: Users have different levels of skills. If a user with a high skill level has executed the process, the Wiki will be updated with this new process instance.

4   Use Case

In this section our approach is applied to the scenario described in Section 2. A *Proposal Writing* process can be displayed in a Wiki as illustrated in Figure 4. This approach of collaborative process development using SMW including import and export of process activities into/from SMW has been validated and used within the ACTIVE project[2]. One of the findings was that people more likely reuse and refine processes instead of model them from scratch in the Wiki.

Fig. 4. EU Proposal Writing process in SMW

The process skeleton from the Wiki is exported to the process execution engine by transforming RDF format into Petri Nets (as explained in Section 2.2) and is further refined during runtime. During runtime, the users will be guided to fulfill a collaboration starting with the activation of a Collaborative Activity (through labeling with "U"). Subsequently, the abstract sub-processes *Finding Partners*, *Building Relationship* and *Collaboration Execution* will be created and concretized. In the sub-process *Finding Partners*, search criteria muss be defined, such as place of work, working area, interests, skills and experience. Additional search criteria, such as available time in calendar, total number of publications related to a certain topic, may also be included. The defined search criteria will be sent to one or more social networks in order to retrieve a list of suitable collaborators. A keyword retrieval based on user profiles (stored in Community

---

[2] This work has been funded as part of the IST-2007-215040 EU project ACTIVE (http://active-project.eu/).

Users) that also considers social relationships (by calculating the centrality[3], indegree/outdegree[4] and transitivity[5] of the network members [16] according to a logged set of their related actions, such as write, tag and comment, in social networks) may provide a more precise rating. Because of the different data structures in the process and social networks, adapters have to be implemented to mediate the data transfers.

If contact persons or collaborators have been selected from the result list at the end of the sub-process *Finding Partners*, the process continues to highlight the owner of the process and allows him to communicate with these persons in the social networks. A formal collaboration agreement will be prepared by system or the process owner himself, which will be again sent to the selected persons who are able to view and modify the agreement in social networks. While communicating with each other, the communication details among the collaborators, such as communication duration, frequency and media will be collected and then analyzed using Social Network Analysis [16]. According to the analysis results, suggestions can be made to foster the communication or reduce the communication overhead.

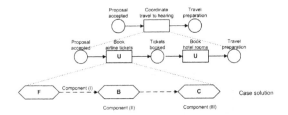

Fig. 5. Process of travel coordination

The communication cycles end as soon as the collaboration agreement is accepted by all participants, implying the end of the sub-process *Building Relationship*. The process continues allowing a coordinated collaboration execution in the sub-process *Collaboration Execution*. Tasks will be assigned to the network members according to the agreement and each member can refine/coordinate his own activities/processes in private. In the case of integration of a business process of external organizations, such as booking airline tickets at a travel agency or signing an NDA, the CBR methods, as described in Section 3.1, will be used. Figure 5 shows for example the refinement of the *Coordinate travel to hearing* activity in Figure 2 and the components related to the solution of a retrieved case. A case revision would possibly take place if the users want to additionally book train tickets besides airline tickets at the same travel agency. From this use case we can see, that our approach takes advantages of a structured process for coordination of collaboration. Consequently, an unstructured communication is improved using social networks.

---

[3] A network member has a lot of relationships to other network members.

[4] Number of incoming/outgoing connections in the role of requester and responder.

[5] Two network members A and C who are both connected to network member B can be considered as directly connected in a transitive network.

The update rules presented in Subsection 3.2 are applied to the changes made during runtime. Activities such as *booking airline tickets at a travel agency* having a high repetition are added to the Wiki.

5   Related Work

The work presented in this paper is related to the following streams (1) collaborative processes, (2) business process coordination and (3) social software for BPM. The idea of coordination support for organizational work is not new and has been early covered by action workflows [17]. The integration of social networks and Wiki with business processes allows reusing best cases and social relationships that are frequently updated. Our coordination mechanism is used only for selected information and is more flexible than works about action workflows.

Coordination can be performed with human interaction [18] or automatically. Workflow Management systems are suitable for an automatic controlled execution and coordination of tasks [19,20,21]. Prior to coordination the preferred work practice needs to be selected. The selection can be implemented based on process models [22] and using expert recommendations [23]. The consideration of knowledge and experiences makes our approach more flexible.

Collaborative works have been early tackled by cross-platforms such as BSCW [24] or groupware [25]. The collaboration can be modeled using several process modeling languages such as BPMN, BPEL and Petri Nets for which concrete implementations for collaborative work exist [26,27]. The advantage of a model is its verification supporting to diagnose incompatibilities in cooperation [28]. Activities in a collaboration are not fully intended for public, therefore privacy preserving coordination was proposed [29]. Aside this, collaboration needs to tackle adequate version control [30] and access control [31]. Our approach combines advantages of conceptual models (e.g., verification) and collaborative working (tackled by BSCW).

Social software has addressed BPM to a different extend. Most approaches discuss the appropriateness of social software in BPM systems for the design and execution phase [32,33,34,35]. Vendors of BPM tools have also identified the trend of social software and offer social software features in their tool suite (http://www.arisalign.com/, http://www.horus.biz/). Our approach additionally shows updates of social software resulting from process model modifications.

6   Conclusion

In this paper we presented an approach to create process models and to coordinate collaborative process activities. We described how to develop process models stored in a semantic Wiki and transform them into simple Petri Nets that can be used in a process execution engine. During runtime this process activities can be coordinated and refined by using social networks and CBR. Changes made in the process model are communicated to the Wiki. One advantage of our approach is that process knowledge is acquired collaboratively in the Wiki or during runtime and made explicit. By using the presented approach available information is reused and synchronized between Wikis and the process model. Less experienced users are more effective in executing the process. The parallel existence of textual (Wiki) and graphical (process model) content representation enables users to select the favored style. In the future we plan to develop a prototype supporting our approach and evaluate it in different case studies.

References

1. Avram, G.: At the crossroads of knowledge management with social software. In: 6th European Conf. on Knowledge Management, pp. 49–58. Academic Conferences Limited, Reading (2005)
2. Kautz, H., Selman, B., Shah, M.: Referral web: combining social networks and collaborative filtering. Commun. ACM 40(3), 63–65 (1997)
3. Dengler, F., Lamparter, S., Hefke, M., Abecker, A.: Collaborative Process Development using Semantic MediaWiki. In: Proc. of 5th Conf. of Prof. Knowl. Management (2009)
4. Koschmider, A., Oberweis, A., Zhang, H.: Process-oriented coordination of collaborations in social networks. In: 6th Int. Conf. on Web Information Systems and Technologies. INSTICC Press, Valencia (2010)
5. Elst, L.V., Aschoff, F.R., Bernardi, A., Maus, H., Schwarz, S.: Weakly-structured workflows for knowledge-intensive tasks: An experimental evaluation. In: WETICE 2003: Proc. of the Twelfth Int. Workshop on Enabling Technologies, p. 340. IEEE Computer Society, Washington, DC (2003)
6. Ehrlich, K., Lin, C.Y., Griffiths-Fisher, V.: Searching for experts in the enterprise: Combining text and social network analysis. In: GROUP (2007)
7. Aamodt, A., Plaza, E.: Case-based reasoning: foundational issues, methodological variations, and system approaches. AI Commun. 7(1), 39–59 (1994)
8. Madhusudan, T., Zhao, J.L., Marshall, B.: A case-based reasoning framework for workflow model management. Data Knowl. Eng. 50(1), 87–115 (2004)
9. Riss, U., Rickayzen, A., Maus, H., van der Aalst, W.: Challenges for business process and task management. J. of Universal Knowl. Management 0(2) (2005)
10. Diaz, A.A., Lorenzo, O., Solis, L.E.: A taxonomy of business processes. Working Papers Economia wp04-24, Instituto de Empresa, Area of Economic Environment (September 2004)
11. Schank, R.C.: Dynamic Memory: A Theory of Reminding and Learning in Computers and People. Cambridge University Press, New York (1983)
12. Bareiss, R.: Exemplar based knowledge acquisition: a unified approach to concept representation, classification, and learning. Academic Press Professional, Inc., San Diego (1989)
13. Ebersbach, A., Glaser, M., Heigl, R., Warta, A. (eds.): Wiki: Web Collaboration, 2nd edn. Springer, Heidelberg (2008)
14. Greco, G., Guzzo, A., Pontieri, L.: Mining taxonomies of process models. Data Knowl. Eng. 67(1), 74–102 (2008)
15. Jagadeesh Chandra Bose, R.P., van der Aalst, W.M.P.: Abstractions in Process Mining: A Taxonomy of Patterns. In: Dayal, U., Eder, J., Koehler, J., Reijers, H.A. (eds.) BPM 2009. LNCS, vol. 5701, pp. 159–175. Springer, Heidelberg (2009)
16. Wasserman, S., Faust, K., Iacobucci, D., Granovetter, M.: Social Network Analysis: Methods and Applications. Cambridge University Press, Cambridge (1994)
17. Medina-Mora, R., Winograd, T., Flores, R., Flores, F.: The action workflow approach to workflow management technology. In: Proc. of the 1992 ACM Conf. on Computer-supported Cooperative Work, pp. 281–288. ACM, New York (1992)

18. Schall, D., Truong, H.L., Dustdar, S.: Unifying human and software services in web-scale collaborations. IEEE Internet Computing 12(3), 62–68 (2008)
19. Jablonski, S., Bussler., C.: Workflow Management: Modeling, Concepts, Architecture, and Implementation. Int. Thomson Computer Press (1996)
20. Kappel, G., Rausch-Schott, S., Retschitzegger, W.: Coordination in workflow management systems - a rule-based approach. In: Coordination Technology for Collaborative Applications - Organizations, Processes, and Agents, pp. 99–120. Springer, Heidelberg (1998)
21. Halliday, J., Shrivastava, S., Wheater, S.: Implementing support for work activity coordination within a distributed workflow system. In: Proc. of the 3rd Int. Conf. on Enterprise Distributed Object Computing, pp. 116–123 (1999)
22. Lu, R., Sadiq, S.W.: On the discovery of preferred work practice through business process variants. In: Parent, C., Schewe, K.-D., Storey, V.C., Thalheim, B. (eds.) ER 2007. LNCS, vol. 4801, pp. 165–180. Springer, Heidelberg (2007)
23. Hu, D., Zhao, J.L.: Expert recommendation via semantic social networks. In: Int. Conf. on Information Systems (2008)
24. Bentley, R., Appelt, W., Busbach, U., Hinrichs, E., Kerr, D., Sikkel, K., Trevor, J., Woetzel, G.: Basic support for cooperative work on the world wide web. Int. J. Hum.-Comput. Stud. 46(6), 827–846 (1997)
25. Nurcan, S.: Analysis and design of co-operative work processes: a framework. Information and Software Technology 40(3) (1998)
26. Oh, J.Y., Jung, J.Y., Cho, N.W., Kim, H., Kang, S.H.: Integrated process modeling for dynamic b2b collaboration. In: Khosla, R., Howlett, R.J., Jain, L.C. (eds.) KES 2005. LNCS (LNAI), vol. 3683, pp. 602–608. Springer, Heidelberg (2005)
27. Wang, X., Zhang, Y., Shi, H.: Scenario-based petri net approach for collaborative business process modelling. In: The 2nd IEEE Asia-Pacific Conf. on Services Computing, pp. 18–25 (2007)
28. De Backer, M., Snoeck, M., Monsieur, G., Lemahieu, W., Dedene, G.: A scenario-based verification technique to assess the compatibility of collaborative business processes. Data Knowl. Eng. 68(6), 531–551 (2009)
29. Chakraborty, S., Pal, A.K.: Privacy preserving collaborative business process management. In: ter Hofstede, A.H.M., Benatallah, B., Paik, H.-Y. (eds.) BPM Workshops 2007. LNCS, vol. 4928, pp. 306–315. Springer, Heidelberg (2008)
30. Bartelt, C., Molter, G., Schumann, T.: A model repository for collaborative modeling with the jazz development platform. In: Hawaii Int. Conf. on System Sciences, pp. 1–10 (2008)
31. Tolone, W., Ahn, G.J., Pai, T., Hong, S.P.: Access control in collaborative systems. ACM Comput. Surv. 37(1), 29–41 (2005)
32. Hussain, T., Balakrishnan, R., Viswanathan, A.: Semantic wiki aided business process specification. In: Proc. of the 18th Int. Conf. on World Wide Web, pp. 1135–1136. ACM, New York (2009)
33. Koschmider, A., Song, M., Reijers, H.A.: Advanced social features in a recommendation system for process modeling. In: Abramowicz, W. (ed.) Business Information Systems. LNBIP, vol. 21, pp. 109–120. Springer, Heidelberg (2009)
34. Dollmann, T., Fettke, P., Loos, P., Vanderhaeghen, D.: Web 2.0 enhanced automation of collaborative business process model management in cooperation environments. In: Proc. 20th Australasian Conf. on Information Systems, ACIS-2009, Melbourne, Australia, pp. 653–663 (2009)
35. Koschmider, A., Song, M., Reijers, H.A.: Social Software for Business Process Modeling. Journal of Information Technology (25), 308–322 (2010)

ECHO
An Evolutive Vocabulary for Collaborative BPM Discussions

David Martinho[1,2] and António Rito-Silva[1,2,3]

[1] Center for Organizational Design and Engineering - INOV,
Rua Alves Redol 9, Lisbon, Portugal
[2] IST/Technical Institute of Lisbon, Av. Rovisco Pais,
1049-001, Lisbon, Portugal
[3] INESC-ID, Rua Alves Redol 9, Lisbon, Portugal
{david.martinho,rito.silva}@inov.pt

Abstract. Nowadays, Business Process Management (BPM) is considering new approaches that use collaborative environments to involve all types of business process stakeholders in the improvement of the organization's business functions. Nevertheless, when evolving different types of stakeholders, the language gap existing between them is disregarded. Also, these new approaches are only focusing on the top-down strategy since they only allow for such collaboration to occur at business process modeling environments. In this paper, we propose ECHO as an evolutive vocabulary system that focus on the formalization of informal entities supporting both strategies of top-down and bottom-up. ECHO's main objective is to support the evolutive process of formalization of the new business process entities that emerge within the stakeholders' discussions. The main function of those informal entities called concepts is to provide a common language that acts as a "bridge" over the gap existing between the business process stakeholder's individual languages.

Keywords: Business Process Management, Social Software, Tagging, Vocabulary, Discussions, Bottom-Up, Collaboration, Formalization.

1 Introduction

Business processes are known to involve different people, from different organizational units, with different responsibilities and distinct concerns, to collaboratively execute the organization's business functions. Although, the design process of such business functions usually disregards the empiric knowledge owned by those who really operate the business on a daily basis: the business process users. Hence, to achieve a proper management of business processes, we must acknowledge their cross-cutting concern nature: most of the business process concerns cannot be cleanly decomposed into different organizational roles. Business process users own important know-how that business process modelers fail to acquire and manage during the interviews within business process discovery

M. zur Muehlen and J. Su (Eds.): BPM 2010 Workshops, LNBIP 66, pp. 408–419, 2011.
© Springer-Verlag Berlin Heidelberg 2011

or documentation efforts. Similarly, business process users also fail to create and understand models using formal notations that help describing and managing the complexity behind a sound business process orchestration and automation.

Aware of such problematic, new emergent BPM tools are focusing on the involvement of all business process stakeholders. Generally speaking, new collaborative BPM environments such as SAP's Gravity [3], Lombardi's BluePrint [2] and the most recent ArisAlign [1], focus on the management of business processes at the modeling level by providing means to collaboratively involve all different types of business process stakeholders: users, modelers, architects, analysts, developers, managers, or any other type of business process stakeholder. This involvement of all business process stakeholders is also due to the acknowledgment of the benefits of adopting philosophies such as crowd-sourcing, also known as the Wisdom of the Crowds [13], which made the Wikipedia project so successful as we know it today.

In order to provide a realistic example of the benefits of involving all business process stakeholders, we will study the BPM collaboration on emergent changes within a patient's management business process. Normally, when a patient arrives at the hospital reception desk, the receptionist opens a new medical record where his symptoms are registered for triage. After the triage is done, the patient's medical record gets updated and the treatment process begins accordingly to the information captured during the triage. However, about a year ago, a new strain of influenza, the H1N1, has contributed to some emergent changes within that patient management business process. Whenever a patient arrived at a hospital, specific procedures needed to be taken instead of following the standard procedure described before. The first action to be done was to ask the patient if he was feeling any H1N1 influenza symptoms lately. Depending on the answer, the patient would either follow the normal patient management process, or would be given a surgical mask, registered as an influenza patient and forwarded to isolation instead of the common shared waiting room. All these changes in the execution flow of the patient management process emerged from the medical staff and not from business process experts or analysts, reflecting the benefits of involving the business process users directly in the organization's BPM efforts.

Let us now consider that this patient management process was fully supported by a Business Process Management System. If the medical staff was enabled to contribute to the management of that business process, it could create a discussion to explain to the business experts, architects and developers these emergent changes so that they could be properly and formally implemented in the workflow system. Nevertheless, some problems exist within those collaborative BPM discussion environments.

This paper proposes a solution to tackle the problems that emerge within collaborative BPM discussions between the business process stakeholders. Before we propose that solution, we will identify three main problems that emerge from such collaborative BPM discussions. Only after these problems are properly depicted and explained, we will propose a solution that focus on their mitigation: an evolutive vocabulary system. Further, we will present some work related with the solution proposed. Finally, we will conclude by taking some insights about the system presented in this paper, and revealing some paths of future work that we intend to follow.

2   Problems

New collaborative BPM approaches [1; 2; 3] are recognizing the benefits of following social software principles such as egalitarianism[1], which focus on the involvement of all types of business process stakeholders to collaborate in the improvement of the organization's business processes. A common form that supports this collaboration appears as textual discussions between the business process stakeholders. Although this textual discussion collaboration has its advantages and benefits to a more fruitful BPM, it can also arises some problematic issues that we must account for:

Ambiguity
As people communicate via conversations[2], they express themselves on those discussion environments in a unstructured textual way. Those discussions are commonly expressed on a natural language, thus, they represent a potential risk for ambiguity issues. For example, referring to *"the process executed to handle patients"* may, or may not, be the same as referring to *"the process executed whenever a patient arrives at the reception desk"*. In addition to the ambiguity issues that this style of reference may cause, also its extensive length nature makes hard to quickly identify the business process entities being discussed.

Language Gap
Since new collaborative BPM approaches are involving all business process stakeholders, modelers, developers, managers, executors, analysts, and so many other, to participate in the improvement of the organization's business functions, different languages will coexist within their discussions. Business process modelers are more likely to make reference to business process models described with formal notations such as BPMN, while business process users will have more tendency to create references to business process execution entities like data forms and enabled tasks, or business process developers to source-code and more technical issues. All these languages are necessary as they focus on different yet complementing concerns, however, they are likely to create misunderstandings and barriers to mutual-understanding of the business processes when mixed up within the same environment.

Dynamic Vocabulary
Due to the dynamic nature of the organization's business functions, which results in the unpredictable emergence of new business entities, new and different

---

[1] Relating to, or believing in the principle that all people are equal and deserve equal rights and opportunities.

[2] By conversation is meant the use of a natural language between two or more participants.

concepts constantly appear within the business process stakeholders' vocabulary. Nevertheless, the business process management system may not allow business process users to create ad-hoc entities and associate them to formal business processes in order to fulfill deviation needs. This limitation creates barriers to organized suggestions of new business process entities that could improve the business processes of the organization.

3 Solution Proposal

In order to achieve a more fruitful management of business processes within the context of collaborative BPM discussions, we need to mitigate the set of problems identified in the previous section. Hence, to enhance the business process stakeholder's collaborative productivity within such discussion environments, we propose an evolutive vocabulary system called ECHO[3].

ECHO embraces social production [5; 14], a social software principle that has been recognized to deliver important contributions to BPM approaches [11], enabling business process stakeholders to create and organize information and knowledge about the organization's business functions. To do so, ECHO allows business process stakeholders to create, manage and use semi-structured entities to empower their textual suggestions about the organization's business processes. In ECHO, such semi-structured entities that can be referenced in the business process stakeholders textual discussions are called *concepts*.

Each *concept* acts as a symbolic representation of a business process construct because it can be used to refer either to an entity that already exists and it is formally defined within its respective business process model, or to a completely new entity that has informally emerged from a business process stakeholder's suggestion within a discussion. To allow business process stakeholders to create and refer to concepts that do not formally exist within the BPMS helps in mitigating the dynamic vocabulary issue depicted on the section before. Also, concepts may represent any business process construct at any level of granularity, meaning that a concept can either represent business processes, sub-processes, activities, tasks, data objects, or any other constructs considered in the Business Process Management System (BPMS) domain.

Each *concept* is defined by a *label* that is semantically described and classified by a set of *tags*. ECHO holds such tagging system component to allow the semantic evolution of the concepts that business process stakeholders simultaneously produce and consume within their textual discussions.

This labeled concepts idea mitigates the ambiguity problem depicted in the previous section as it fosters business process stakeholders to use such entities to unambiguously refer to the business process entities in matter. Also, the set of concepts managed by the ECHO system attempts to be the "bridge that crosses"

---

[3] In reference to the name of the greek mythology nymph who could only repeat the voice of another as a punishment from deceiving Hera from Zeus love affairs with the other nymphs.

the language gap between all different types of business process stakeholders within the same discussion environment. Tagging does not requires any extra knowledge about any other than the natural language.

Typically, the architecture of a tagging system involves defining the rules and relationships between three main entities: users, resources and tags [12].

In our case, the *users* of the tagging system inherent to the ECHO system are all the business process stakeholders; the *resources* are the semi-structured structures "prosumed"[4] by the business process stakeholders that we called concepts; and finally, similarly to concepts, users can also create *tags* or re-use the existing ones to associate to any existing concept with the objective of describing it.

Within the BPM domain, as the nomenclature is uncertain or is constantly evolving due to its dynamic nature, folksonomies appear to be valuable as they provide some structure [12] to the emergent vocabulary of business process entities.

Considering the example given in the introduction section, which is depicted in Figure 1, at least four concepts[5] should be defined within the ECHO system with the following labels: *PatientManagement*, *RegisterPatient*, *Triage* and *UpdatePatientMedicalRecord*. Associating a *label* to a concept is fundamental to understand the semantic direction[6] of its associated tags. At anytime, the ECHO system allows the association of new labels to a given concept so that its semantic direction can be aligned as needed.

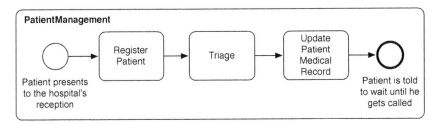

Fig. 1. The patient management business process depicted in this figure is modeled in the Business Process Modeling Notation (BPMN). The business function behind this simple business process allows the initial management of the patient's medical treatment in a hospital. The *PatientManagement* process is composed by three activities: one to register the patient and create his new respective medical process (*Register-Patient*), other to triage the patient in order to obtain a more accurate status of his medical condition (*Triage*), and after these two are executed, another activity that updates the patient's medical record before he gets called to begin the correspondent treatment (*UpdatePatientMedicalRecord*).

---

[4] Prosumed is a portmanteau that represents the simultaneous action of producing and consuming.

[5] We are omitting the start and ending events for simplicity purposes, however, an analogous approach could be used to define the respective event representative concepts.

[6] A pointer to the meaning the tags are trying to describe.

Now that we have exemplified the *label* construct of a concept and its rationale, we will elaborate on the ECHO's strong folsonomic component mentioned before.

Along with the Web 2.0, a new collaborative approach to help classifying and retrieving content emerged: *folksonomies*. Folksonomies are built within a user-centered approach, where users input keywords and associate them to resources. Such associated keywords describe the content and classify it, so that, in the future, users may easily browse or retrieve the content through those associated tags. We use the `concept` as the entity which wraps both a `label` (e.g. *RegisterPatient*) and the set of `tags` that classify or describe that label (e.g. *register, patient, activity*). However, to provide a more structured classification and description tagging mechanism, the ECHO system supports the idea of having different families of tags.

Tag Families

The ECHO system supports the idea of tag families to provide some organizing structure to the set of tags that it holds. A tag family is a category that identifies a particular type of tag and allows one to quickly identify a particular property of a concept by knowing which tags of that particular family tag are in fact associated to the concept in matter. The setup and configuration of these tag families is highly customizable and flexible, depending entirely on the requirements and needs of the ECHO system administrators. However, we can identify two different types of tag families: categorizing tag families and descriptive tag families.

Categorizing tag families are mutually-exclusive sets of tags that make possible to override previously associated tags of that same family. The classification of the concept accordingly to a particular category, i.e. a particular tag family, is known by looking at which tag of that categorizing tag family is currently associated. On the other hand, we have the descriptive tag families which are non mutually-exclusive sets of tags that focus on describing the concept within the category that tag family represents. Both types of family tags are allowed to evolve as new tags are created and associated to the family tags configured within the ECHO system.

Nevertheless, to better explain this family tags feature and its motivation, we will identify four different families of tags: the first three, *class*, *abstraction* and *formality* tags, are motivated by categorization, while the *descriptive* tags family focus on description instead.

Class Tags

As a categorizing family, *class tags* are mutually-exclusive tags[7] that define the concept's class according to the used business process notation. Class tags allow business process stakeholders, for example, to differentiate either the concept they are referring to is a business process or a business activity. The flexibility in creating this family of tags fosters the ECHO system's independence from the used business process notation.

---

[7] By mutually-exclusive tags we mean that only one tag of that particular family of tags is valid at a particular point in time.

Based on the simplified business process example depicted in Figure 1, the respective class tags associated with the business process notation would be: *process* and *activity*. Business process stakeholders may create and classify new concepts as belonging to one of those classes, or when needed, create new tags belonging to this family (e.g. data-object) and associate them to any concept.

Abstraction Tags
Abstraction tags are also defined as mutually-exclusive tags, however, they focus on classifying the abstraction level of the concept. Business process stakeholders can distinguish a concept which exists at the execution level, tagged by the `instance` tag, from those which are placed on the modeling higher level of abstraction, tagged by the `type` tag. Abstraction tags help on mitigating the problems inherent from the differences of abstraction levels, by making an explicit distinction between types and their respective instances. Business process stakeholders may explicitly want to refer to particular occurrence where its context of execution is fundamental to a clear comprehension of his suggestion.

Formality Tags
The last set of mutually-exclusive tags are the formality tags, which focus on the degree of formality of a concept. For instance, when a concept is created by a business process stakeholder, the business process entity it refers to is not formally defined yet, hence, it is associated to the `draft` tag. On the other hand, business process entities that are formalized by business process experts and imbued into the business logic of the application are classified as being formal by associating the respective concept to the `formal` tag instead. This family of tags is very important to differ the concepts which are really implemented and formally deployed within the Business Process Management System from those new concepts which are created during the business process stakeholder's suggestions.

Descriptive Tags
Those tags which give semantic value to the concept itself, not regarding any notation-dependency, abstraction or formality concerns, are known as descriptive tags. Descriptive tags allow business process stakeholders to enrich the concept's semantic value through their association to the concept. Examples of descriptive tags are: `patient`, `influenza`, `H1N1`, `check-up` or any other word which is directly related to the concept in matter.

Although the first three tag families were defined as mutually-exclusive, different tags of the same family may be associated to the same concept, however, only the most recently associated tag of each family is considered to be valid on classification-oriented tag families. This grants flexibility to the concept's semantic value, allowing it to evolve and to transform as necessary.

Another important idea to keep in mind is that the ECHO system does not aim to relate or create semantic value between tags. The ECHO system focus on the social production of concept objects and on their semantic value evolution, which results from the collaborative combination and association of the tags described above. The family tags structure is a feature that allows the administrators of the system to easily identify particular folksonomies that emerge from the free user-tagging mechanism.

Now that we have explained all the ECHO constructs (concept, label and tags), we will use the *PatientManagement* process example, depicted in Figure 1, to illustrate the use of the ECHO system a business process stakeholder's suggestion. Let us imagine that a business process user, a doctor for example, creates a new discussion where he states the following:

> *"The **PatientManagement** process should now consider a new activity %**CheckForFlu**% to be first executed in order to decide if the patient should be treated normally by executing the **RegisterPatient** activity or as a special case, needing to execute a %**GivePatientSurgicalMask**% activity as soon as possible, and then registering him for a specific H1N1 triage so that he can be sent to quarantine."*

In the exemplified suggestion, the business process user recommends two new informal (differentiated as being a draft by the use of the "%" delimiter) activities: *CheckForFlu* and *GivePatientSurgicalMask*. Such concepts were created during that suggestion, and textually related to other formal existing concepts such as the *PatientManagement* process and the *RegisterPatient* activity. The concepts' textual representations are bold and underlined to illustrate the existence of additional information, such as their respective set of associated tags. Nevertheless, this paper does not focus on how that additional information is displayed or digested, and we have only distinguished the draft concept from the remaining formal concepts to depict the emergence of new concepts within textual discussions. The discussion around this suggestion will allow other business process stakeholders to understand it, question it, comment it, and evolve the new concept's semantic value by either associating new tags or new labels. This evolutive aspect of the ECHO system is possible because all the relationships between concept and tag or label objects are defined with temporal awareness. An example of a possible evolution of the *CheckForFlu* concept is illustrated in Figure 2.

This temporal awareness also allows to maintain the evolution history of a concept, meaning that information about previously associated tags or labels is not lost, even when new mutually-exclusive tags are associated. Take the timeline depicted in Figure 2 as an example: both instants c and d override the concept's label and formality tag, nonetheless, such information is not deleted and is possible to be recreated. This allows to rebuild, as shown in Figure 3, snapshots of the originally labeled *CheckForFlu* concept. Generating a snapshot of a given concept at its time of reference will help the reader of the suggestion to better understand its context and relevance.

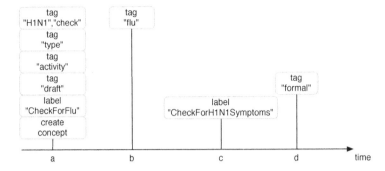

Fig. 2. This figure illustrates a possible evolution of the *CheckForFlu* concept along its lifetime. First, in instant **a**, the *CheckForFlu* concept is created accordingly to the suggestion example. During the concept creation, the business process stakeholder assigns the label "CheckForFlu", tags it as an *activity*, as a *type* and as a new created concept: a *draft*. Also, two descriptive tags are associated in its creation: "H1N1" and "check". Later on instant **b**, another business process stakeholder associates another descriptive tag "flu". Further on instance **c**, another business process stakeholders changes its label to "CheckPatientForH1N1Symptoms". Finally, the instant **d** represents the formalization of the concept, terminating the evolution path between the informal and the formal state of the entity.

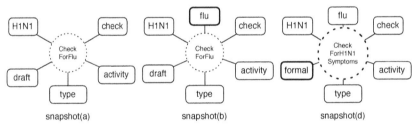

Fig. 3. An important feature of ECHO is that its evolutive aspect allows one to obtain a snapshot of the concept on a given instant in time. Based on the same example depicted in Figure 2, three of the four evolving instants are used to demonstrate this snapshot feature of ECHO.

To conclude, from the ECHO system emerges a weakly-tied[8] type system that business process experts may study, together with the textual suggestions, to better understand the idea behind the business process stakeholders recommendations. Business process experts may look at concepts tagged with the draft tag and understand their semantic value by looking at the concept's evolution and the discussions in which it is referenced. If the discussion and evolution of the patient management business process used in the example had continued, the final business process would have evolved to something like the business process model depicted in Figure 4.

---

[8] Weakly-tied because there is not a strong conformance between the type-system of the BPMS and the concepts managed by the ECHO system.

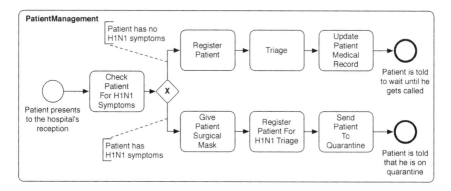

Fig. 4. This figure shows a final version of the *PatientManagement* process after the emergent changes caused by appearance of the H1N1 influenza. According to the concept evolution depicted in Figure 2, a *CheckForH1N1Symptoms* is implemented within the business process, and it becomes the first activity enabled for execution. Depending on the output of that activity, that is, the patient having symptoms of the H1N1 influenza strain or not, the previous flow is taken if there are no symptoms, or in the case there are, a new set of activities will be enabled for execution. Such new activities also appeared in the form of new informal concepts: the *GivePatientSurgeryMask*, *RegisterPatientForH1N1Triage* and *SendPatientToQuarantine* activities.

4   Related Work

In [10], in order to provide some empirical insights and recommendations about activity labeling in process modeling, J. Mendling et al. perceived the usefulness of such labels by analyzing their ambiguity. Also, the existing language gap between business process stakeholders is acknowledged in works like [6] where Cabot et al. proposed a first transformation to bridge the gap from UML/OCL to SBVR specifications.

The family tags were motivated by the work contained in [9] and [7], where two main types of user motivations for tagging are identified: *categorizers* and *describers*. Also, in [8], Jacob identifies the main differences between those two goals when using tagging-systems.

However, there is a main problem with this unrestrictive tagging approach: the semantic of the tags is not explicit as there is no hierarchy and no relationship between the created tags. A method to mitigate this lack of semantics problem is proposed in [15], where users can tag other tags to define the category which they belong to. In the ECHO system, we have used a similar approach, however, instead of tagging other tags, a special "tagable-tag" is used: the concept. Also the family tags serve the purpose to quickly analyze the inherent folksonomies existing within the set of tags associated to a particular concept.

Some interesting metrics are proposed in [4] to identify the type of user motivation. Also, the results shown in [4] reflect that describers are most useful for the emergence of semantics through tagging.

5   Conclusions and Future Work

Business Process Management already considers a large set of approaches and systems that aim for fruitful business process improvements. The use of collaborative environments within those new Business Process Management approaches are a promising attempt to better evolve and improve the business processes of an organization. Focusing on the problems that emerge within the textual discussions between business process stakeholders, this paper proposed a solution based on an evolutive vocabulary system which aims to give support to the formalization process of the informal information that is gathered from those discussions. Based on a strong folsonomic component, the ECHO system allows business process stakeholders to manipulate semi-structured concepts that they may refer to when they want to mention existing business process entities or when they are suggesting new ones. The concepts are allowed to evolve due to the temporal-awareness of the concept's relationships with both label and tag entities. Business process experts may better understand the suggestions made by the business process stakeholders, by analyzing the respective discussions along with the weakly-tied type system that emerges from the set of concepts that the ECHO system holds.

5.1   Future Work

Our future work will focus on the study of another aspects to enhance the ECHO system proposed in this paper.

As ECHO is defined as an independent system to be embedded in a BPM discussion environment, we will study how to provide an Application Programming Interface (API) that will ease the integration of the ECHO system with any Business Process Management System (BPMS).

Another interesting path to investigate is the inference of informal relationships between concepts through the digestion of suggestions. Concepts are related with each other on a unstructured textual form, however, it would be interesting to build a commentary system, on top of the ECHO system, that would concern with those informal relationships between concepts, improving the semantic value of the emergent weakly-tied type system.

Although we are thinking on a well defined API, business process stakeholders are expected to interact with the ECHO system through the means of a Graphical User Interface (GUI). Developers have the freedom to build their own customized GUIs to interact with the ECHO's API, nonetheless, we will study and provide some usability guidelines to improve the User eXperience (UX) of the business business process stakeholders using collaborative Business Process Management Systems (BPMS) that are embedding ECHO.

Finally, when the ECHO system has reached a decent level of maturity, we aim to deploy it on different real Business Process Management Systems to obtain some pragmatic feedback. From such real case studies, we will extract results that will allow us to tweak, tune and improve the system proposed theoretically here in this paper.

References

[1] Arisalign, http://www.arisalign.com/
[2] Lombardi software, http://www.lombardisoftware.com/
[3] Sap gravity, http://www.sdn.sap.com/irj/scn/weblogs?blog=/pub/wlg/15618
[4] Stop Thinking, Start Tagging: Tag Semantics Emerge from Collaborative Verbosity (2010)
[5] Benkler, Y.: The wealth of networks: How social production transforms markets and freedom. Yale University Press, New Haven (2006)
[6] Cabot, J., Pau, R., Raventós, R.: From uml/ocl to sbvr specifications: A challenging transformation. Inf. Syst. 35(4), 417–440 (2010)
[7] Heckner, M., Heilemann, M., Wolff, C.: Personal information management vs. resource sharing: Towards a model of information behaviour in social tagging systems. In: Int'l AAAI Conference on Weblogs and Social Media, ICWSM (2009)
[8] Jacob, E.K.: Classification and categorization: A difference that makes a difference. Library Trends 52 (2004)
[9] Marlow, C., Naaman, M., Boyd, D., Davis, M.: Ht06, tagging paper, taxonomy, flickr, academic article, to read. In: HYPERTEXT 2006: Proceedings of the Seventeenth Conference on Hypertext and Hypermedia (2006)
[10] Mendling, J., Reijers, H.A., Recker, J.: Activity labeling in process modeling: Empirical insights and recommendations. Special Issue on Vocabularies, Ontologies and Rules for Enterprise and Business Process Modeling and Management 4, 467–482 (2010)
[11] Schmidt, R., Nurcan, S.: Augmenting bpm with social software. In: BPM 2009 Workshops, pp. 201–206 (2010)
[12] Smith, G.: Tagging: People-powered metadata for the social web, New Riders, Berkeley, Calif. (2008)
[13] Surowiecki, J.: The Wisdom of Crowds. Anchor (2005)
[14] Tapscott, D., Williams, A.D.: Wikinomies: How mass collaboration changes everything. Portfolio (2006)
[15] Yoo, D., Suh, Y.: User-categorized tags to build a structured folksonomy. In: International Conference on Communication Software and Networks, pp. 160–164 (2010)

The Old Therapy for the New Problem: Declarative Configurable Process Specifications for the Adaptive Case Management Support

Irina Rychkova[1] and Selmin Nurcan[1,2]

[1] CRI, Université Paris 1, Pantheon-Sorbonne,
90, rue Tolbiac, 75013, Paris, France
[2] IAE de Paris Sorbonne Graduate Business School;
21, rue Broca 75005 Paris, France
{Irina.Rychkova,Selmin.Nurcan}@univ-paris1.fr

Abstract. The Case Management Process Modeling RFP released by OMG in 2009 expresses the particular demand of practitioners in the case management solutions. The case is defined as "a situation, set of circumstances or initiative that requires a set of actions to achieve an acceptable outcome or objective." In this paper we consider an example of the case management process - the mortgage approval process. We formulate 5 challenges encountered while modeling this process using a traditional, activity-oriented modeling formalism, i.e. BPMN. We argue that the research methodologies developed during the past decades can be successfully applied to case management modeling. We propose the use of declarative specifications, variability modeling, and FOL-based semantics for modeling descriptive processes and, in particular, case management processes. We assemble these theoretical concepts in the form of DeCo process specifications that extend the BPMN notation.

Keywords: Adaptive Case Management, Declarative process specifications, Configurable processes, First Order Logic.

1 Introduction

The Case Management or Adaptive Case Management is an emerging topic that has been extensively discussed during the last months by the BPM community. In a legislative system or health care, the notion of case has been known for many years: here by a case we understand the set of circumstances or facts related to a criminal act or a patient condition that requires a decision making and a treatment with respect to some norms or regulations. Whereas the norms are well defined, the case-related conditions can vary widely and evolve with time, preventing the agent responsible for the case treatment from applying a standard predefined template or model. The similar notion of the case has been recognized in business process management.

The Case Management Process Modeling (CMPM) Request for Proposal (RFP) released by OMG on September 2009 expresses the particular demand of practitioners in the case management solutions [1]. OMG defines case management as *"coordinative*

M. zur Muehlen and J. Su (Eds.): BPM 2010 Workshops, LNBIP 66, pp. 420–432, 2011.

and goal-oriented discipline, to handle cases from opening to closure, interactively between persons involved with the subject of the case and a case manager or case team." Systematic improvement of this process based on the user experience is one of the main objectives of adaptive case management approaches. This objective can be achieved by following *the social production* principle defined by the social software [26]: ``*Social production is the creation of artifacts, by combining the input from independent contributors without predetermining the way to do this."* Case management is an example of knowledge-intensive process that cannot be fully determined at design-time. Mechanisms of the process evolution and actors contributing in this evolution cannot be specified in advance either: for example, a manager is not any longer a passive process user, it is by aggregation, analysis, and mining [2] of case stories and associated user/designer/manager/customer experience the case management process can be improved. Therefore a mechanism to integrate the *"innovative contributions not identified or planned in advance"* should be provided.

In order to benefit from the social software principles in business process management and case management in particular, the possibility to communicate, negotiate, and change a process definition based on the aggregated knowledge should be provided at all levels of the process lifecycle starting from the design. Thus, an appropriate formalism for business process modeling has to be selected.

We argue that declarative specification languages are the most appropriate ones (compared to imperative languages) (i) to provide means and to facilitate business process evolution; (ii) to coproduce and to share the process knowledge among involved stakeholders; (iii) to "rightsize" the landscape of knowledge in order to be shared when needed. For the traditional formalisms accepted in the industry, such as BPMN or EPC, this represents a real challenge. Being almost systematically imperative and activity-driven, these formalisms encourage the early specification of the explicit order in which the activities of the process will be executed. On the other hand, these formalisms are often implicit in specifying data that is circulating throughout the process. Therefore, these formalisms fail in specifying knowledge-intensive processes and case management processes in particular. Does that mean that to address the Adaptive Case Management a brand-new formalism is needed?

We argue that the research methodologies and techniques developed during the past decades can be successfully tuned and then applied for the case management modeling. In this paper we discuss the use of Declarative specifications [3], Variability modeling [4], and FOL-based Formal semantics for modeling descriptive processes [5] and, in particular, case management processes. We assemble these theoretical concepts in the form of a modeling approach that we call DeCo – for Declarative Configurable process specifications. DeCo process specifications extend the BPMN notation (a de-facto standard for process modeling) providing a mechanism for descriptive process modeling, formal analysis, and step-wise evolution.

The reminder of this paper is organized as follows. In Section 2 we provide the business process models taxonomy, position the case management in this taxonomy and discuss the existing business process modeling formalisms. In Section 3 we consider a mortgage approval process and attempt to model this process in BPMN-BizAgi (www.bizagi.com). Based on the encountered challenges, we formulate 5 issues that have to be addressed by a case management process modeling technique. In Section 4 we introduce DeCo process specification and illustrate how the aforementioned issues are handled in DeCo. Section 5 presents our conclusions.

2 From Business Process to Case Management

2.1 Process Model Taxonomy

Business processes models can be roughly divided into two categories by criterion of requirements representation: *prescriptive and descriptive*. Whereas prescriptive process models specify how things must/should be done, a descriptive process model aims at recording and providing a trace of what happens during the business process [6], [25].

In practice, *prescriptive models* are used to specify processes with predictable sequences of tasks and well defined coordination rules (e.g. repetitive, highly automated production processes). Such processes can be fully specified at design-time.

Knowledge-intensive processes are based on the actor collaboration and information exchange. These processes are characterized by a weak predictability of task sequences and partially defined coordination rules; they can be only "sketched" at design-time by *descriptive models*. Fig. 1 shows the examples of processes that can be specified using one or another (or both) modeling styles.

We distinguish another two categories of business processes models: *context-specific and configurable*. Highly specialized processes, defined for a given execution environment (e.g. a research experiment in chemistry or physics) can be captured by a *context-specific model*. Such processes are hardly reusable and for each new environment a new process (and its corresponding model) has to be defined. Today, organizations are interested to consolidate their processes while keeping them customizable in order to reflect the context-specific parameters [7]. Processes requiring a customization (such as role/task assignment, task ordering, and rule selection) upon their deployment can be specified using *configurable process models*.

Case management. The glossary of RFP for CMPM defines *case* as *"a situation, set of circumstances or initiative that requires a set of actions to achieve an acceptable outcome or objective. ..."* In [1], the case management process is addressed as a knowledge-driven process, where activities do not occur in a predefined order. In addition, case management processes supposed to anticipate the change of a business context at deployment, and also has to react in the consistent and organized manner on all the emerging case-related knowledge at run-time. Thus, we claim that case management processes shall be specified using *descriptive, configurable models* (top-right quadrant of our diagram in Fig. 1).

2.2 Modeling Formalisms

Literature provides various process modeling formalisms that we classify into four categories: activity-, product-, decision- and conversation-oriented models [8].

The Business Process modeling formalisms defined by Unified Modeling Language, Event-Driven Process Chain (EPC), and Business Process Modeling Notation (BPMN) gain the wide recognition among practitioners today. All these formalisms are based on the activity-oriented and/or product-oriented paradigm for business process modeling.

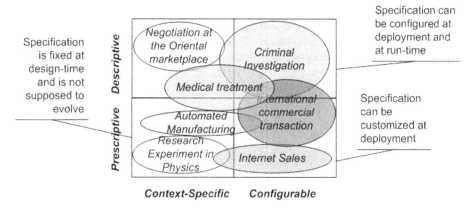

Fig. 1. Business process taxonomy. Case management can be considered as a descriptive, configurable process.

The most recent type of process models [9], [10], [11], [12] is based on the *decision-oriented paradigm* according to which the successive transformations of the product are looked upon as consequences of decisions. Conversation models are based on the speech act theory and on the principle that each sentence expressed by someone represents an intention, a commitment.

BPMN 2.0 beta specification [13] published in August 2009 by OMG supports the increasing demand to the modeling collaborations, communication, and human actor's involvement. Though, it incorporates the elements of the decision-oriented and conversational paradigms.

A possibility to customize a business process taking into account a deployment environment of this process is a part of the more general problem of flexibility. This problem was identified in [14] and [15] in general and in the context of WfMS respectively: Knoll and Jarvenpaa [14] introduce the term of flexibility as a form of alignment between organizations and their IT systems in turbulent environments. The authors recognize three types of flexibility in the context of IT: flexibility in functionality, in use and in modification. Heinl et al. [15] illustrate the necessity of flexibility in workflow management applications and identify two classes of flexibilities: by selection and by adaptation.

Another steam of research presented in [16][17] favors what we refer to as declarative business process modeling. In [16] the representation of a business process as a trajectory in a state space is introduced. The authors attempt to declaratively describe the dynamics of a business process by defining a notion of a valid state. Van der Aalst in [17] presents a case handling paradigm to cope with business process flexibility. In contrast to workflow management, case handling aims to describe what *can* be done to achieve a business goal but not what *should* be done and *how*.

3   Example: The Mortgage Approval Process

Mortgage approval process is a typical example of a case management process. In this section, we provide a generic mortgage approval process description as defined by different financial institutions in the USA. The information provided below results from our study of multiple information sources (e.g. http://www.homebuyinginstitute.com/, http://www.mortgage-resource-center.com/, http://homebuyereducation.bankofamerica. com/, http://www.homeloancenter.com/ etc.) It represents a compilation of guidelines, recommendations, and descriptions of mortgage approval process, provided by different loan consulting firms, financial advisors, and banks and available on the web.

3.1 The Process Description

A mortgage is a loan for buying a house. The terms and length of the mortgages are negotiable and can be adapted for the applicant's situation.The mortgage approval process can be divided into the following steps: Pre-qualification; Formal application; Document review; Pre-approval; Property appraisal; Final approval; Closing.

The goal of the pre-qualification step is to determine the potential mortgage amount that the applicant is eligible for. The purpose of the formal application is to provide the lender with documents characterizing in details the current financial situation of the applicant as well as his/her employment and credit history. Document review follows the formal application and may include the pre-approval step. The pre-approval letter issued as a result of this step indicates that the applicant is pre-approved by a lender for a specific loan amount. When the property is selected by the applicant, the mortgage lender initiates the property appraisal. The appraisal step defines the amount of the mortgage and a corresponding down payment. The lender makes "approve", "not approve", or "approve with conditions" final decisions based on the document review and the appraisal results. If the loan is approved, a commitment letter is issued for the applicant, and a closing date is set up. Closing (also called settlement) is a final step. During the mortgage closing, the mortgage lenders will need to purchase the house and hold the title as the applicant makes payments to them.

3.2 Specification of the Mortgage Case Management Process Using BPMN

Considering the complexity of the complete process, in this paper we will focus on the Formal Application process step. The text below describes this step in details.

Mortgage Approval: Formal Application
0   The applicant can request the application package by e-mail or by post. Alternatively, all the forms can be accessed on the Web.
1   Mortgage application can be submitted electronically or during a personal meeting with the mortgage lender.
2   The exact set of documents may vary depending of the financial institution and the particular situation of an applicant. These documents may include: The Social Security card; Record for past two years for residence address; Employer name, address; W-2 tax forms; federal income tax returns; Most recent pay-stubs, etc.
3-5 During the application, the lender provides the applicant with a Good Faith Estimate (GFE) of costs of loan closing; the applicant can be asked to make a final decision on the type of mortgage loan; also an interest rate for the loan can be locked in this phase.

6   Some lenders will give to the applicant an access to their website where the applicant can check on the approval status of his/her package.
7   Usually an application fee and the appraisal fee will have to be paid by the applicant during the mortgage application submission.

The main purpose of this description is to illustrate the diversity of activities, actors, and information involved and to stress the unpredictable nature and variability of this process – the characteristics that make it's modeling a challenging task. Figure 2 presents the model of the Mortgage approval process specified using BizAgi modeling tool.

3.3   Discussion

Modeling the mortgage approval process in BPMN, we have encountered the following challenges:

Optional tasks. Modeling optional tasks represents one of the major challenges. For example, <Send the forms> task is not needed if an applicant has already downloaded forms from the Web or if he/she fills in the application on-line.

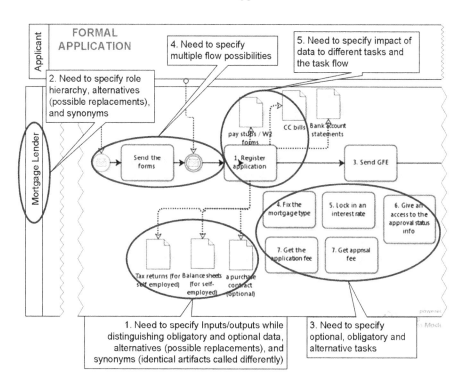

Fig. 2. BMPN specification of the Formal Application in the Mortgage Approval process

Task Ordering. Many tasks, being obligatory for the process, cannot be preordered at design time. Based on the norms and policies of the concrete place/institution, their order may be specified at deployment (e.g. <Get an access to the approval status info>, <Get application fee>). However, some actions (e.g. <Lock in an interest rate>, <Get appraisal fee>) can be ordered only at run-time as they will be executed based on the data availability.

Within the traditional BMPN formalism, task ordering can be expressed using a gateway mechanism; however, considering the large number of such ordering options, this mechanism is not efficient. An explicit specification of conditions under which one or another ordering should be applied is also challenging. In our BPMN diagram, the appropriate solution found was to leave the tasks that could not be explicitly ordered at design time outside of the process flow.

Optional/alternative data objects and synonyms. The mortgage approval process consumes and produces a vast amount of data artifacts. Some of these artifacts may be *obligatory*, whereas the others can emerge (or be requested) in specific situations only. For example, the mortgage loan applicant can be asked to provide the mortgage lender with one or multiple different tax forms. The form W-2 (Wage and Tax Statement) is typically requested from all the applicants in USA (obligatory); the form 2555 (entitled Foreign Earned Income) should be provided by taxpayers who have earned income from sources outside the United States. In order to adapt to different applicant's situations, *the alternative data artifacts* should also bespecified. For example, the form 1040 is a commonly accepted tax return form, whereas the form 1040EZ is a simplified version of this form: for single and joint filers with no dependents the form 1040EZ can replace the form 1040 [source: wikipedia]. Some artifacts also can be called differently from one organization (or country) to another: the tax forms (or IRS forms) defined for USA corresponds to another tax forms in UK. For a mortgage lender working in both countries, having these *synonyms* explicit can be beneficial.

Explicit modeling of data impact on decision making/task ordering. Data artifacts impact the task ordering and decision making at run-time. For example, if the purchase contract is provided during the application, the mortgage lender may want to immediately initiate the appraisal process. We have used BPMN artifacts to specify the relations between data and tasks where these data is required. The way the data is used in general can be indicated using annotations. However, neither one nor another mechanism is formalized in BPMN. Implicit impact of data on the decision making stays out of the process modeling scope within the existing formalism.

Role assignment. Whereas abstract process participants – Mortgage lender and Applicant – are easily recognizable, concrete role assignment may depend on the financial institution: small banks have only several (2-4) roles associated with the process, whereas in the big agencies the application processing and decision making is more likely to be assigned to a number of different roles with different responsibilities. These roles can be assigned only upon deployment. As our study shows, the same task can also be performed by several roles – this postpones the role assignment until the run-time.

In this section, we have listed only several challenges related to the case management process modeling. The modeling of negotiation and communication, internal decision making, modeling data/actor/task ranges are the problems that will be addressed in the future. To conclude our discussion, we formulate five requirements to a descriptive process modeling approach that the traditional formalisms can hardly meet and that we are going to address in further sections:

1. Need to specify inputs/outputs while distinguishing obligatory and optional data, alternatives (possible replacements), and synonyms (identical artifacts called differently).

2. Need to specify role hierarchy, alternative roles, and synonyms.

3. Need to specify optional, obligatory and alternative task.

4. Need to specify multiple flow possibilities.

5. Need to specify impact of data to different tasks and the task flow.

4 Declarative Configurable Process Modeling Notation (DeCo)

In this work, we present the process modeling approach based on Declarative Configurable (DeCo) process specifications that extend the BPMN notation (a widely adopted standard for process modeling with more than 60 current implementations).

4.1 Theoretical Foundations

The theoretical foundations of DeCo are grounded on Declarative modeling [3], Variability modeling [4], Refinement theory, and formal methods - the paradigms, proven in the research community. This work is largely based on the authors' research reported in [5], [18], [19], [12] and is inspired by the results presented in [20], [21].

The declarative specifications for modeling business processes have been presented in [19]: this approach is based on the systematic modeling of process-related data. This allows us to introduce the notion of *state*. Each process task then can be associated with a set of *pre-states* - the states where this task can (but not necessary will!) be executed - and a set of *post-states* – the states resulting from the task execution respectively. Consequently, the process specification represents a set of activities (tasks to be done) with no predefined execution scenario.

The declarative modeling principles allow one to postpone the decision making about the process control flow until its deployment or even execution. As soon as declarative process specification evolves - the mechanism to validate and to control this evolution is required. In the work presented in [19] the evolution from the declarative, nondeterministic process specification at design time towards precise (imperative) process specification at deployment is represented as a set of refinement steps. The notion of refinement for graphical specifications, adopted from software engineering [3], is presented in [5]. In this work, the formal semantics for graphical specifications is defined based on first order logic and set theory. These semantics allows us to reduce the problem of refinement verification to the validation of the first-order logic formula and provides the means for automated process analysis and control using the tools for automated analysis of program specifications defined in software engineering.

The technique presented in [19] allows one to demonstrate that different control flow configurations of the process are valid with respect to a high-level declarative design specification. However, to deal with descriptive processes (and the case management in particular) the process configurability should not be limited by a control flow.

In the literature, several major perspectives of the process models are specified [23]:*the control flow perspective* that captures the temporal ordering of process tasks, events, and decision points; *the data perspective* that captures the lifecycle of data objects (creation, usage, modification, deletion) within the process; *the resource perspective* that describes how the process is carried out within the organization and deals with roles and resource assignments; *the operational perspective* that addresses the technical aspects of process execution and specifies the elementary process tasks and their assignment to concrete applications or application components of the organizations; *the context perspective* that describes the attributes related to the process execution context; *the performance perspective*, addressing the process cost effectiveness.

In [5], [20], [21], [22] the concept of configurable process has been presented and the modeling formalism to deal with process configurability at multiple perspectives is defined. Namely the authors present the Configurable Integrated EPC (C-iEPC) modeling notation that extends the well known Event Process Chain (EPC) notation and addresses the process configurability along the control-flow, data, and resource perspectives. According to this approach, "Given a configurable process model, analysts are able to define a configuration of this model by assigning values to its variation points based on a set of requirements. Once a configuration is defined, the model can be individualized automatically.." Individualization process can be considered as automated synchronization of the process model perspectives in respond to each configuration decision. This guarantees the correctness of individualized process models by construction. To introduce the notion of correctness and to reason about individualized and configurable models, authors define formal semantics for C-iEPC based on FOL[20].

4.2 Multi-perspective Configurability

Inspired by the approach presented in [20]-[22], we propose to address the 3 out of 5 requirements defined in the previous section using the multi-perspective configurability as follows:

1. Need to specify inputs/outputs while distinguishing obligatory and optional data, alternatives (possible replacements), and synonyms (identical artifacts called differently). - This requirement can be addressed by providing configurability along the data perspective.

2. Need to specify role hierarchy, alternatives (possible replacements), and synonyms. - This requirement can be addressed by providing configurability along the resource perspective.

3. Need to specify optional, obligatory and alternative tasks. This requirement can be addressed by providing configurability along the operational perspective.

Due to space limitations, we consider in more details only the DeCo implementation of the data configurability. Figure 3 illustrates the data object hierarchy models for Tax forms and Tax return forms required for formal mortgage application in USA. Vast amount of data artifacts consumed and produced by a process represents a challenge for modeling. The hierarchy model of data objects describes:

- generalization-specialization relations between data objects;
- alternatives – data objects that can replace the data object originally required by the task; For example, the Form 1040EZ can be considered as an alternative of the obligatory 1040 form. The rule 3.2 specifies the condition where this alternative is applicable. Such rule can be described as a text or formalized in FOL.
- synonyms – different terms referred to the same data object. For example, in USA, both tax forms and tax return forms can be called Internal Revenue Service (IRS) forms [source: wikipedia]

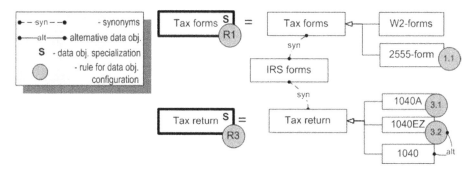

Fig. 3. The data object hierarchy model for the Formal Application

4.3 Declarative Specification of Tasks

The last two requirements:

4. Need to specify multiple flow possibilities
5. Need to specify impact of data to different tasks and the task flow

can be addressed applying the declarative modeling principles as explained in [19], [5]. Formal semantics permits to express the action contracts in terms of pre-condition, post-condition and invariants.We define a formal semantics for DeCo specifications based on first-order logic (FOL). Similarly to results presented in [5], it can be used for the mapping of a DeCo specification to the Alloy specification language [24] for further validation.

At run-time, at any moment a process enactment is characterized by its **state** (a case state). We define a case state in DeCo as a vector $\overline{X} = (p_1, p_2,.., p_n)$. The components $p_1, p_2,.., p_n$ are values of data objects related to this case at a given moment of time. A state space Σ is a set of all possible states of a case.

For every process task A we define a precondition and a postcondition. Postcondition A_{post} is a condition that a case meets after the task termination. Precondition A_{pre} specifies a condition that must hold upon the task invocation: If A is started in a state satisfying A_{pre}, it is guaranteed to terminate in a state satisfying A_{post}.

Precondition and postcondition are modeled as predicates over state space Σ :

$A_{pre} : \Sigma \rightarrow \{true, false\}$,

$A_{post} : \Sigma \times \Sigma \rightarrow \{true, false\}$

In addition to pre- and postcondition, invariants for process tasks can be specified.
Invariant A_{inv} is a condition that holds <u>before and after</u> the task execution.

Task A defines a transition of the case from state $\overline{X}$ to state $\overline{X}'$ (pre- and post-states respectively). We define a task in DeCo as a binary FOL-formula $A : \Sigma \times \Sigma \rightarrow \{true, false\}$. We specify the task using logical implication between precondition and postcondition:

$$A(\overline{X}, \overline{X}') \overset{def}{=} A_{pre}(\overline{X}) \rightarrow A_{post}(\overline{X}, \overline{X}')$$

If at a given state $\overline{X}$ the precondition A_{pre} ,of the task A holds, then the case will be transited to a state $\overline{X}'$, for which the postcondition of A - A_{post} - holds.

Preconditions, postconditions and invariants explicitly relate tasks with data objects within a case.

Example:
To specify the contract for the <Send the Forms> task from Fig. 2, we define 2 supplementory predicates:

isReceived(d: DataType, a:Applicant) { $\exists$ m:ReceivedMessage | m.content = d $\wedge$ m.src = a }
isSent(d: DataType, a:Applicant) { $\exists$ m:SentMessage | m.content = d $\wedge$ m.dst = a }

The former predicate evaluates to True if in the process there exists a message *m* received from an applicant *a* that contains a data object *d*. Along those lines, the second predicate evaluates to True when the message *m* with a content *d* is sent to an applicant *a*. We define the precondition and the postcondition for the <Send the Forms> task as follows:*Pre: isReceived(FormRequest, applicant); Post: isSent(AppForms, applicant)*

There are no invariants specified for this task. The task itself can be denoted as follows:

$\forall$ *apl:Applicant | isReceived(FormRequest, apl)* $\rightarrow$ *isSent(AppForms, apl)* :

Whenever the process receives a form request from an applicant apl, then the execution of this tasks will move the process in the state where the application forms are sent to this applicant.

5 Conclusion and Future Work

OMG RFP demonstrates the increasing interest and the particular needs of the practitioners in the methodologies and tool support for case management process [1]. According to OMG RFP, the objectives of the Case Management methodologies or tools are (i) to accommodate and structure the knowledge of participants about the current case, (ii) to provide the information of the previous similar cases and help the practitioners to learn from best practices, and (iii) to progressively improve case management processes to make them *"evolve toward prescribed processes."*

DeCo defines the concepts for systematic gathering, and structuring the information about the data (consumed or produced), the roles, and the tasks of a process. Namely, based on the configurability modeling along multiple process perspectives, we specify generalization/specialization, synonym, and alternative relations.

Compared to traditional business process modeling formalisms, DeCo provides the means to support the prescriptive nature of the case management process: the declarative modeling principles allow the designer to specify the set of activities that could (but not necessary will) be executed during a process invocation together with the conditions under which this execution can be possible: {pre, post, inv}. Though extending it, DeCo is based on the BPMN graphical notation. Our main objective with DeCo is not to provide yet another set of concepts and shapes representing them, but to reuse as much as possible the notation that (a) has already been known and used by practitioners for years and (b) has a significant developers' support. This can help us to get a useful feedback from the BPM practitioners' community while conceptualizing DeCo.

Social software is software that supports the interaction of human beings. Thus, being largely dependent on such interactions, case management process can benefit from supporting tools based on the social software principles. The following three important missions can be successfully fulfilled by social software: (i) collection of process requirements for their further incorporation into the process design model; (ii) collection of the information related to the process context for the further process model customization at deployment; (iii) collection of the content (case subject) – related information at the process run-time for the further process model analysis and evolution (e.g. implementing process mining [2]).

References

1. Object Management Group, Case Management Process Modeling (CMPM) Request For Proposal OMG Document: Bmi/2009-09-23 (2009)
2. van der Aalst, W.M.P.: Challenges in Business Process Mining. BPM Center Report BPM-10-01, BPMcenter.org (2010)
3. Wirth, N.: Program development by stepwise refinement. Communications of the ACM 14, 221–227 (1971)
4. Rosemann, M., van der Aalst, W.M.P.: A Configurable Reference ModellingLanguage. Information Systems (2007)
5. Rychkova, I.: Formal semantics for refinement verification of entreprise models. PhD Thesis EPFL, no 4210 (2008), http://library.epfl.ch/theses/?nr=4210
6. Van der Aalst, W.M.P., Stoffele, M., Wamelink, J.W.F.: Case Handling in Construction. Automation in Construction 12(3), 303–320 (2003)
7. Regev, G., Wegmann, A.: Regulation Based Linking of Strategic Goals and Business Processes. In: Proceedings of the 3rd BPMDS Workshop on Goal-Oriented Business Process Modeling, GBPM 2002, London (2002)

8. Nurcan, S.: A Survey on the Flexibility Requirements Related to Business Processes and Modeling Artifacts. In: Proceedings of the 41st Annual Hawaii International Conference on System Sciences, Big Island, Hawaii, USA (2008)
9. Dellen, B., Maurer, F., Pews, G.: Knowledge Based Techniques to Increase the Flexibility of Workflow Management. Data and Knowledge Engineering 23(3) (1997)
10. Faustmann, G.: Enforcement vs. Freedom of Action-An Integrated Approach to Flexible Workflow Enactment. In: Workshop on Adaptive Workflow Systems. Conference (1998)
11. Nurcan, S., Etien, A., Kaabi, A., Zoukar, I., Rolland, C.: A Strategy Driven Business Process Modelling Approach. Special issue of the Business ProcessManagement Journal on Goal-oriented business process modeling, Emerald (2005)
12. Nurcan, S.: Business Process Modeling for developing Process Oriented IT Systems. In: The Business Process Management Tools and Technologies Track of the International IRMA Conference (2004)
13. Object Management Group, Business Process Model and Notation (BPMN) FTF Beta 1 for Version 2.0 OMG (2009)
14. Knoll, K., Jarvenpaa, S.L.: Information technology alignment or "fit" in highly turbulent environments:the concept of flexibility. In: Proceedings of the Computer Personnel Research Conference on Reinventing IS (1994)
15. Heinl, P., Horn, S., Jablonski, S., Neeb, J., Stein, K., Teschke, M.: A Comprehensive Approach to Flexibility in Workflow Management Systems. In: Proceedings of the International Joint Conference on Work Activities Coordination and Collaboration (1999)
16. Khomyakov, M., Bider, I.: Achieving Workflow Flexibility through Taming the Chaos. In: OOIS 2000 - 6th International Conference on Object Oriented Information Systems, pp. 85–92. Springer, Heidelberg (2000); Reprinted in the Journal of Conceptual Modeling (2001)
17. van der Aalst, W.M.P., Weske, M., Grünbauer, D.: Case Handling: A New Paradigm for Business Process Support. Data Knowl. Eng. 53(2), 129–162 (2005)
18. Rychkova, I., Regev, G., Wegmann, A.: Declarative Specification and Alignment Verification of Services in ITIL. In: First International Workshop on Dynamic and Declarative Business Processes (DDBP 2008), Munich, Germany (2008)
19. Rychkova, I., Regev, G., Wegmann, A.: Using Declarative Specifications. In: Business Process Design. International Journal of Computer Science & Applications (2008)
20. La Rosa, M., Dumas, M., ter Hofstede, A.H.M., Mendling, J.: Configurable multi-perspective business process models. Preprint submitted to Information Systems (2009), Available at QUT Digital Repository: http://eprints.qut.edu.au/
21. La Rosa, M., Dumas, M., ter Hofstede, A.H.M., Mendling, J., Gottschalk, F.: Beyond Control-Flow: Extending Business Process Configuration to Roles and Objects. In: Li, Q., Spaccapietra, S., Yu, E., Olivé, A. (eds.) ER 2008. LNCS, vol. 5231, pp. 199–215. Springer, Heidelberg (2008)
22. Mendling, J., La Rosa, M., ter Hofstede, A.H.M.: Correctness of Business Process Models with Roles and Objects. Elsevier, Amsterdam (2008)
23. Jablonski, S., Bussler, C.: Workflow Management: Modeling Concepts, Architecture, and Implementation. International Thomson Computer Press (1996)
24. Jackson, D.: Software Abstractions: Logic, Language, and Analysis. MIT Press, Cambridge (2006)
25. Rolland, C., Nurcan, S., Grosz, G.: Enterprise Knowledge Development: the process view. Information and Management Journal 36(3), 165–184 (1999)
26. Nurcan, S., Schmidt, R.: Service-oriented Enterprise Architecture for Enterprise Engineering: Introduction. In: Proceedings of EDOC 2009 IEEE Workshops and Short papers (2009)

Empowering Business Users to Model and Execute Business Processes

F. Schnabel[1], Y. Gorronogoitia[2], M. Radzimski[2], F. Lecue[3],
N. Mehandjiev[3], G. Ripa[4], S. Abels[5], S. Blood[5], A. Mos[6],
M. Junghans[7], S. Agarwal[7], and J. Vogel[8]

[1] SAP Research CEC St. Gallen, Switzerland
stephan.florian.schnabel@sap.com
[2] ATOS Research, Madrid, Spain
[3] University of Manchester, Manchester, England
[4] CEFRIEL, Milan, Italy
[5] TIE, Amsterdam, Netherlands
[6] INRIA, Grenoble, France
[7] KSRI, KIT, Karlsruhe, Germany
[8] SAP Research CEC St. Gallen, Switzerland

Abstract. Existing process modelling languages and especially executable process modelling languages are not designed for business
users without programming knowledge. We therefore propose a novel
Lightweight Process Modelling seeking to lower the entrance barrier for
modelling executable processes. In this sense lightweight applies to the
user interaction and means easy to understand in the context of the modelling language and easy to deploy, implement, and execute processes in
a tooling context. Hence business users get advanced guidance during
their modelling activities. This paper will provide a specification of a
Lightweight Process Modelling process and the Language for Lightweight
Process Modelling (LLPM). The LLPM formal semantic core is fairly
rich, but it is designed to be rendered in a simple graphical form without undue loss of semantics. To achieve this we followed three design
principles of lightweight modelling when supporting a business user: abstracting from executable process details, using semantic annotations,
and reusing process parts through patterns and templates. In order to realize these design principles we have created new elements for the LLPM
that are not yet implemented in existing process modelling languages.
Selected concepts of existing process modelling languages like BPMN
and BPEL complement the LLPM. In this paper we present a coherent specification of the elements, properties, and relationships. Further
a design process is defined revealing the steps of enhancing the abstract
graphical process models with execution details.

1 Introduction

Purposes of Business Process Modelling (BPM) [53] is to document, communicate, analyse, and support collaboration in pursuit of business needs, furthermore

M. zur Muehlen and J. Su (Eds.): BPM 2010 Workshops, LNBIP 66, pp. 433–448, 2011.
© Springer-Verlag Berlin Heidelberg 2011

to automate processes within an existing infrastructure. In order to abstract process logic from application logic Business Process Management Systems (BPMS) [5] allow for the definition and execution of processes by invoking underlying applications or services. Currently, using a BPMS and modelling executable processes requires a high level of expertise in business and IT rendering existing process modelling languages unsuitable for the business user. By business user we refer to users that are 'not casual, novice, or naive' [30] but have got strong domain-specific business skills. Concerning IT they have computational needs but limited IT knowledge and no interest in getting an IT professional [30][37]. Due to the lack of IT-knowledge reuse of existing executable process models is low. There is no common understanding of business process models and the terminology used [2][27]. In addition, users have difficulties in delivering process models at an IT-oriented quality level and commit typical modelling errors [19]. The trend of business user enablement seeks to overcome these issues. A simple way for users to understand business processes is a key success factor to encourage for taking ownership of the process and making process changes [43]. This will speed up process management and lower costs since experts are only needed in few cases. Hence there's a need for a business process modelling solution that the business user can use in a lightweight way, so required for knowledge expression in general in [22]. In this sense the term lightweight concerns the user interaction and means easy to understand in the context of the modelling language and easy to deploy, implement, and execute processes in a tooling context. However in order to realize a lightweight user access sophisticated backend solutions are needed. In this paper we will introduce Lightweight Process Modelling (LPM) seeking to lower the entrance barrier for modelling executable processes. We will investigate how business users can be enabled to express activity requirements rather than to specify services and kept free from execution details. Therefore we are going to specify LPM design principles to be applied by according artifacts such as a process modelling language or supporting tools. Further we will define a process modelling language and tools realizing the vision of LPM and hence implementing these design principles. We will hereby focus on the language, the so-called Language for Lightweight Process Modelling (LLPM). The LLPM itself is complex, however strongly supports principles of business-user empowerment. It comprises new process modelling concepts such as semantic annotations, patterns and templates, goals, and data flow elements that reflect the user support principle and are not yet implemented in existing process modelling languages. Selected concepts of existing process modelling languages like the Business Process Modelling Notation (BPMN) (see www.bpmn.org) and the Web Service Business Process Execution Language (WS-BPEL) (see www.oasis.org) complement the LLPM. We have selected the design science as described in [15][24] as research methodology. With respect to the design science phases described in [35], this paper is organised as follows. Section 2 will give an overview of related work. The design principles for lightweight modelling, representing the design according to Peffers et al., are covered by Section 3. In Section 4 the LLPM itself is described in detail and how it realizes the design principles covering the development phase in the design science. How the LLPM is enhanced by execution details is subject to the design process in Section 5 demonstrating the applicability in terms of the design science. Section 6 reports the evaluation we have undertaken in relation to LLPM. This is in line with the evaluation phase of the design science. Finally a conclusion is given in Section 7.

2   Related Work

The goal of our research work is to empower business users to model executable processes. The used process modelling language should be simple and usable. Any element of a process modelling language should be easily understandable. The process models should further abstract from execution details such as service composition and binding. Reuse of process models and parts of it should be fostered by providing information in a language the business user can understand. In the paper at hand we follow an approach making use of semantic annotations of processes and its elements. These annotations are provided by the user and appropriate tools and are then used to enhance the process models by execution information. A related approach to support the user in process modelling has been described by [16]. The authors have created a recommendation system proposing the use of existing processes or parts of it, based on a tag matching. Furthermore the PICTURE project[1] provides a basic process modelling tool supporting the business user in exchanging documents. Several process modelling languages exist, an overview of current standards can be found in [18]. The most common languages that are related to process automation are the Yet Another Workflow Language (YAWL) [49] and the BPMN. YAWL is an executable business process modelling language founded on workflow patterns presented in [48][47]. The main purpose of BPMN models is to facilitate the communication between domain analysts and the strategic decision-making [40][1]. BPMN models are also used as a basis for specifying software system requirements and providing input to software development projects. BPMN itself is not executable and has hence to be transformed into an executable language that - according to [46] - is often vendor-proprietary. Specifying process models in YAWL and BPMN requires high expertise in IT and formalisms. However, we don't suppose our target users to have that kind of knowledge. Especially YAWL misses acceptance and application by a broad user base [39]. YAWL is oriented towards support of workflow patterns rather than providing a simple language for business users [14]. Furthermore BPMN is mostly used for documentation purposes by users that don't think of implementation details [46]. An analysis of BPMN models revealed that only 20% of its vocabulary is regularly used [55], respectively 36% of respondents use a core BPMN set to develop their process models and 37% use an extended core set [41][38]. Further [41][38] state that formal education is required for using BPMN and events are often not understood by users. Althoug having only three shapes on the surface various subtypes of each shape make BPMN complex [46]. In order to keep a language understandable for

---

[1] http://www.picture-eu.org/

business users we will focus on a minimal set of required elements. A commonly used executable process modelling language for service orchestration is the WS-BPEL and according extensions for other services than Web Services [34][33] such as goals defined in the Web Service Modelling Ontology (WSMO) (see www.wsmo.org) and to interfaces described in OWL/S [25]. The services are integrated into the process model by referencing their WSDL service descriptions. WS-BPEL combines the features of a block structure language with those for directed graphs. A BPEL process works fine within a closed environment where services are harmonized. However, in the heterogeneous, open Web the configuration and composition of services requires more sophisticated mechanisms for discovery, data mapping, and flexible service instantiation. In our research work we envisage to allow for selecting, binding, and replacing services at various stages. Some of the aforementioned aspects have been partially addressed in [6] where SCENE, a BPEL engine supporting dynamic binding and self-adaptation disciplined through rules is described. Finally, similar to YAWL and BPMN, the execution details in BPEL are hard to understand for non-IT-experts. The same applies to SCENE that requires high effort spent by system integrators in defining adaptation rules. An approach to bridge the gap between business specification and execution details and to support the provisioning of execution-related information for services is to attach semantic descriptions to process elements. These descriptions will provide information about discovery, composition, and execution of services. Furthermore, semantic activity descriptions will allow for the definition of requirements rather than specifying concrete services. [42] describe an approach describing services on an intentional level through intentions, pre- and postconditions, and an indication whether a services is atomic or composite. An early approach to automatically compose web services by extending Golog is described in [26]. In our research work we follow this approach of using semantic annotations and apply it to process modelling and execution. Besides WSMO two ontologies for WSDL-based services, WSMO-Lite [50], and for REST services [8], MicroWSMO [20], exist. The WSMO-based Business Process Modelling Ontology (BPMO) [7] provides a framework for describing processes by ontologies. We will use parts of the full-fledged BPMO framework in order to attach semantic concepts to the LLPM, mainly to activities and the process as a whole. To summarize there exists no process modelling language that is simple and usable enough to be understood by the business user, that abstracts from execution details, and that fosters reuse. In our approach we are first going to select a minimal subset of existing process modelling language elements that are easily understandable by the business user. This minimal set of process elements is afterwards enhanced by elements needed for the abstraction through the use of semantic annotations. This new set of elements constitutes the LLPM. An application of this set to existing languages could be performed in terms of profiling as well.

3   Lightweight Modelling Principles

In lighweight process modelling we will support the user in perceiving activities not as operations bound to concrete services but as a set of requirements.

The requirements express desired functionalities and characteristics and are described according to a shared conceptualization such as an ontology. This will ensure a common understanding of the descriptions. The set of semantically described requirements can also follow a goal specification that could be used both at design and runtime to dynamically bind services. Lighweight modelling also exploits preexisting knowledge in terms of patterns and templates acquired during previous modelling and execution activities. The patterns and templates can be published in a repository and made available through search mechanisms or recommendation systems. In order to support the data flow modelling we further present a list of operators enabled by the LLPM.

Graphical Abstraction: Quite some studies exist about whether graphical or textual programming languages are better understandable by users. While [28][10][36] claim benefits of visual programming, [12] argue that graphical representations are only better understandable if the users know well the structure and the symbols. In our research we claim that a graphical process representation is more likely to be understood by the business user. However, for IT experts we provide a textual representation as well. The LLPM mainly comprises two abstraction layers (see Figure 1). The graphical abstraction layer is the modelling interface for the non-experienced user, is kept simple, frees the user from execution aspects, and is represented by the upper layer in Figure 1. A specific process editor designed for the LLPM has been implemented. Wizards in the Process Editor support the user in difficult modelling tasks, such as the specification of gateways. The lower layer in Figure 1 contains the canonical, executable representation of the process model that is semi-automatically created from the abstract model. Further the canonical model is used by tools, such as components for discovery, composition, and execution, in order to complete the abstract model with execution details. The user will only see the abstract graphical model and get guided through wizards in order to formulate the

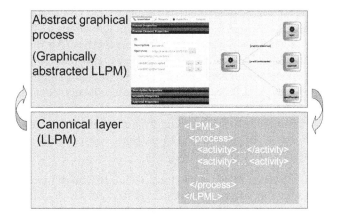

Fig. 1. Graphical abstraction and canonical layer of the LLPM

activity requirements and extend the models. The user however will only get in touch with them indirectly through the process editor in case additional information is needed.

Semantic Annotations and Contextualisation: The LLPM encourages enriching process models with semantic annotations that provide semantic meanings and descriptions and refer to knowledge representation models, such as ontologies. They make hence process models machine-readable and better understandable for human users. The purpose of such annotations is to support a sort of automation during both modelling and execution of processes. Annotations can also be used to check the fulfilment of requirements and constraints. The LLPM annotations are ontology-agnostic and can reference concepts described by different ontologies like WSMO, WSMO-Lite, Micro-WSMO, or the different flavours of OWL-S as well. Reasoners will properly interpret those annotations e.g. to instantiate goals by services. Business users or context-reasoners can use annotations describing the entire process and activities with the following aspects. Requirements and Constraints can be used to specify a domain-specific scope or limitations for the process and other global requirements. For activities, requirements describe the functional classification of desired services. Non-functional Properties and Metadata may specialize the process and activity behaviour according to factors such as dependability, reliability, performance and ability for transactions as well as additional information such as author, creation date, versions, and revisions. Functionality-based annotations can reference preconditions and effects and inputs and outputs. Related to gateways and flows the annotations can refer to conditions.

Patterns and Templates: It is widely agreed that patterns can accelerate the designing of process models, reduce their modelling time and improve the modelling quality by simply being instantiated or customized [48] [45] [13]. Patterns enable community members to communicate more effectively, with greater conciseness and less ambiguity. An approach for reusing processes and parts based on case-based reasoning is described in [17] and [23]. As a starting point we use a part of well-known workflow patterns from [48] as our process patterns in order to support modelling the control flow perspective. We further introduce workflow templates that are more coarse-grained, can combine workflow patterns, and cover a certain business functionality. Workflow templates can cover almost complete processes, however the templates do not contain a start and an end element. The processes composed by one or more workflow patterns or templates are guaranteed to be functionally and syntactically sound. Even for unstructured processes the application of patterns according to predefined rules guarantees soundness of processes [13].

Goals: Process activities are traditionally concrete and bound to services or other means of implementation at design time. In contrast the LLPM introduces goals as unbound activities that are bound to a particular service either later at design time or at runtime by composition tools. This will keep the process models more flexible and agile. Goals will support users in modelling the control flow perspective and refer to process activities. In contrast, related literature mostly defines goals for the entire process [21][31]. The LLPM Goal is based on WSMO-Lite and has optional properties such as functional classification, non-functional property, precondition, and effect. A LLPM Goal can be understood as an abstract classifier for fitting semantic web services. An instance of the goal class represents a concrete goal providing concrete instance references to some of its optional properties. They can be provided by the modeller, but they could also be derived from domain specific contextual information and tools. In particular, business users will benefit from the goal approach. They can browse and inspect available goals stored within a goal registry. The goals are more intuitively understandable than mere service descriptions. An example of a goal is given in section 4.3. A goal for payment handling is integrated in the process. Later on the payment handling goal is instantiated by a credit card service. For binding services to goals and hence to activities we will make use of the semantic service annotation indicating a description of its functionality. A discovery engine matches functionality descriptions of the available web services to the desired functionality of a search query. Goals must be able to express the desired functionality of a web service that is bound at runtime. Goals may be resolved to process templates as well.

Data Connectors: Besides purely control flow oriented constructs, the LLPM provides some data flow oriented constructs for supporting mashup-based service composition. To this end, we present a list of operators enabled by the LLPM. Such operators are required to model data manipulation through the LLPM. By doing so this approach differentiates from existing approaches that handle mediation by dynamically defining mediators [32]. Such an approach would require deep knowledge in ontologies that the typical users of the LLPM won't have. The operators have to consider both semantic and syntactic mapping in the LLPM. Furthermore the operators will allow for the specification of the kind of connection between the services.

4   The Language for Lightweight Process Modelling

The aim of the LLPM is to simplify the work of a process designer by hiding programming aspects, performing automatic compositions, allowing for the late binding to concrete services, and substituting services at runtime. The LLPM is devised taking into account both the LLPM usability in the tool that will be provided to the user and the underlying design process. In this section, we will give an insight into the LLPM and how the design principles of lightweight modelling are reflected. The LLPM metamodel describes the elements, their properties, the relationships between each element and the constraints applicable in their usage. Some elements of the LLPM are not provided directly by the process designer but can be derived automatically by tools exploiting predefined semantic descriptions and ontologies of services and goals. In order to make the specification easily understandable we will first present those elements the user will see in his view. In further steps these process models and their elements are semi-automatically enhanced by information needed for execution purposes. However, these enhancements are not visualized in the process model view. Activities have to be instantiated by goals and services. Further the tools have to define conditions for gateways and those flows connected to a gateway based on the semantic descriptions given by the user. In the following we will cover those aspects of the LLPM that implement the design principles such as semantic annotations, patterns and templates, and goals. The patterns, templates, and goals will support the user in modelling the control-flow of its processes. The data flow aspect highlights the process model from another perspective than the control flow. Semantic annotations can be applied to both the control and data flow perspective.

The User-oriented LLPM Metamodel View: In order to be easily understandable for the non-expert user the LLPM needs to be simple, abstract, and hide programming aspects. Hence, on the abstract LLPM level there are only a number of LLPM elements visible. The abstract LLPM level is represented by the upper layer in Figure 1. The user graphically creates his **Process** by adding exactly one start and one end element and a couple of **Activity** elements and by connecting these elements through a source and destination association characterized by **Flow**. The start element is thereby invoked by external callers and triggers the whole process. The process can be encapsulated and published as a service. For activities the user sets names and provides general information about requirements and constraints, often in natural language. **ProcessElement** is a general construct for the abstraction of flows, gateways, and activities. Flow can represent both control and data flow. **Gateway** is a ProcessElement that represents a process split or merge according to a specific condition. Activity specifies the execution of some unit of work and will be instantiated by an optional goal and a service. However the user's point of view abstracts from the instantiation.

Elements for Semantic Annotations, Contextualisation, Patterns, and Templates: In order to create semantic annotations we use the information provided by the requirements and constraints in the element descriptions. These element descriptions are translated into ontology-based semantic service and goal annotations, e.g. WSMO annotations for goals, WSMO-Lite annotations for Web Services, or MicroWSMO annotations for REST services. The translation is semi-automatically performed by a software component. **SemanticAnnotation** contains the reference to the annotation file in case of an existing ontological annotation, in case the annotation is newly created it is represented by the attribute expression. Any annotation is of a certain type **AnnotationType** enumerating the potential annotation types. It is limited to annotations for functional classification, non-functional properties, preconditions, effects, metadata, requirements, constraints, selection criteria, and replacement conditions. Workflow templates and patterns are similar to processes as their descriptions are stored in a common repository and can be referenced by a URI. Patterns and templates can be instantiated by the user or by a composition tool based on the matching of semantic annotations. In order to distinguish between processes, workflow templates, and patterns two annotations are added to the process element. The flag *isTemplate* is set to true, if a workflow template is described. The flag *isPattern* is set to true, if a process pattern is described. In case of a template or a pattern the process does not necessarily contain a start and an end element.

Activity Instantiation by Goals and Services: In the following we describe the elements for the instantiation of an activity in the abstract process model by a goal and by a service. As explained in section 3.4 the goals serve as input to a discovery engine that finds the right service in order to instantiate the goal. The **Conversation** element separates the activity description and its instantiation by goals or services, similar to the separation of activities and their partner link in WS-BPEL. While the **Goal** element references one goal, the **Service** element provides a list of potential services. A concrete service is selected by analysing the semantic annotations, the referenced goal, and the **SelectionCriteria**. While the SelectionCriteria class defines the ranking of services in the service list, the **ReplacementCondition** defines when to replace a selected service. Service selection and replacement at runtime is performed assuming that all implementations of an abstract service have different interfaces or adopt different communication protocols. These mismatches are solved exploiting the semantic annotations of service descriptions as described in [4]. The relation of inputParameter and outputParameter of an activity is specified by the **Parameter** element.

Support for Data Flow: The LLPM provides a list of operators supporting data manipulation. In the following we will consider only input and output based data manipulation. We will provide a SPARQL[2]-based mechanism to manipulate both RDF[3] data types and values required (as inputs) and provided (as outputs) by services. To this end, the **Connector** element is responsible for the data mapping between services, such as **Merge**, **Split**, **Count**, **Sort**, **Filter**, **Reduction**, **Loop**, **Sub-Description**, or **Aggregation**. Each connection (operator, service) has the optional attributes rounding-up, rounding-down, and truncating in case the data provided and consumed are not of the same type. All described operators are considered as semantic and syntactic mapping elements in the LLPM. The data they manipulate are propagated through the end-user and the tools for enhancing the abstract process model. From an end-user perspective, the aforementioned list of operators will be available through a toolbox provided in the process editor (a la Yahoo!Pipes[4]) and can be used through drag-and-drop. Besides simply drawing connections from outputs of services to inputs of other service the end-user can optionally specify the kind of connection between the services, actually like other Mashup editors. All these connections are stored through the LLPM description of the composition. Alternatively, in case the user requires more specific or advanced data manipulation within his process, the process editor provides functionality for dragging and dropping the

---

[2] http://www.w3.org/TR/rdf-sparql-query/
[3] http://www.w3.org/RDF/
[4] http://pipes.yahoo.com/pipes/

appropriate external built-in service in order to achieve the required specific data manipulation. The built-in services are included as Activities. A semantic data mapping component checks the semantic consistency of data connections through reasoning based on a data type ontology. Since the semantic mapping leaves the issue of syntactic mapping open a component for the syntactic mapping is used in addition. The execution engine will perform this mapping, e.g. through the copy/assign mechanism in WS-BPEL. If the automatic mapping is not possible the process editor will provide a tool for manual mapping.

5   Design Process for Creating Executable Process Models

In this section we introduce the design process for lightweight process modelling and execution. We therefore describe the various enhancement steps to generate executable process models differentiating actions performed by the user and automatically performed by tools. [9] proposes an approach comprising three steps to create executable workflows out of templates. After defining data- and execution-independent workflow templates, still execution-independent workflow instances are created specifying the data needed on activity level and the data flow. In the final step the executable workflows are created by assigning resources that exist in the execution environment. In the paper at hand a similar approach is followed. The business user defines a series of functional activities and the control-flow between them. We will present in the following the further steps needed in order to semi-automatically instantiate the activities and flows and hence make the processes executable. The procedure is performed in four steps that is as well depicted in Figure 2. The first step is performed by the user. He specifies with graphical elements in a Process Editor an abstract process model. Wizards will guide the user to specify process splits and joins as well as producing sound process models. The user's metamodel view (Step 1 in Figure 2) covers the information that is provided by the user's process model in the process editor. The user will specify abstract semantic descriptions for activities, e.g. in natural language (Step 2). These semantic descriptions comprise information like requirements, constraints, non-functional properties, or metadata. The first two steps represent the design time tasks. Ideally the tools will then automatically enhance and execute the process model - both at runtime - without any more user interaction. Semantic annotations similar to service and goal annotations are created out of these informal, unstructured, or semi-structured descriptions. A language processing tool supports enhancing the process model by annotations for the functional classification, non-functional properties, preconditions, and effects. In case this step can not be performed automatically the user will be requested to provide missing information through a wizard. Now the composer and a discovery engine are called (see step 3). They interact to automatically search for an existing goal or services based on a mapping of the semantic annotations in order to find out the goal resp. services that fit best. The found services fitting the goal or the semantic annotations are ordered in

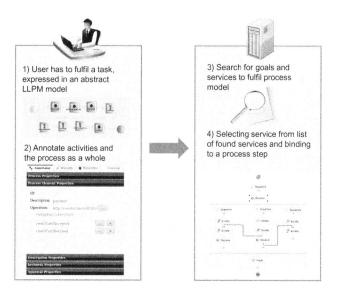

Fig. 2. Design Process

a list. For each service in the list the Service element is instantiated that contains the reference of the service URI. The final step(step 4 in Figure 2) is now performed by the interaction of the composer and the execution engine. These two components select at runtime the best-fitting service out of the list. The execution engine can now execute it adapting the process, in reaction to various kinds of changes, applying the SelectionCriteria and the ReplacementCondition defined at design time.

6   Language Evaluation

In this section we evaluate the LLPM in terms of ontological completeness and coverage as well as simplicity and usability. In this type of evaluation, the constructs provided in the language are compared against a benchmark set of concepts within the perspective of the target usage. Further a user survey has been conducted in order to evaluate the language usability. Besides these evaluation criteria, economic criteria, such as modelling time, training effort, or the degree of reuse contribute as well to the evaluation. However, due to the tools under development, this kind of evaluation will be performed at a later stage.

Completeness and Expressiveness of the LLPM: The process of evaluation has involved three steps. In the first step, a reference set of concepts and constructs was prepared using three widely accepted frameworks: the representational model of the Bunge-Wand-Weber (BWW) framework [51][3], the benchmark set of 20 control flow patterns found in workflow systems [48], and a set of six communication patterns found in Enterprise Application Integration (EAI) systems [44]. In the second step, the reference set of concepts and constructs was mapped to LLPM constructs. In the third step, the mapping tables thus prepared were reviewed by case study owners of a research project, which were asked to identify if the indirect mapping and gaps were significant in the context of target usage of LLPM as signified by their use cases. In the future it is envisaged to evaluate the LLPM against other frameworks as well, such as the suitability for change support as described in [52].

In a study, Green et al. [11] have mapped the BWW representation model onto the constructs of BPEL, in [41] it has been applied to BPMN. We have adapted this analysis for LLPM as a starting point of our ontological completeness evaluation. At the end of the second step of our three-step evaluation process, we identified that 14 out of 30 core BWW concepts do not have direct mappings to LLPM constructs. The most notable of these is the lack of representation for 'thing'. This is common amongst many process specification or service composition languages, including BPEL [11]. Also missing are representations of 'state law' and the related 'lawful state space', 'lawful event space', and 'System environment'. *Transformation* is a core BWW construct, and this has been mapped to a number of LLPM elements, divided into two groups: Control Flow group and Data Flow. To ground these findings in the target usage for LLPM, in the third step we highlighted the shortcomings to the three responsibles for each of our three target case studies. The feedback suggested that the lack of mapping to these 14 elements is not crucial for the models to be created in each case study. Indeed, some of these have been omitted with the aim of simplifying LLPM, for example states can be modelled by preconditions and effects including environment variables. Also notable is use of a single LLPM element *activity* to implement the *Event*, *Transformation* and *Wait* BWW constructs.

Pattern-based Analysis of the LLPM: The previous section revealed that one specific BWW concept *transformation* maps to a number of LLPM constructs to express different patterns of control and communication flow. This provides a focus for the analysis in the current section, which also follows the three-step evaluation process. In the first step, we prepared a benchmark set of 20 control flow patterns found in workflow systems [48] and a set of six communication patterns found in Enterprise Application Integration systems [44]. In the second step, we analysed the coverage provided by LLPM against this benchmark set, using as a starting point a similar analysis of BPEL [54]. The results from the control flow patterns analysis showed that only arbitrary cycles and implicit termination is not supported. Other patterns are appropriately reflected through gateways and semantic annotations. The support of multi-instances will be investigated for the next LLPM release. A similar analysis of the communication patterns was also conducted, and in the third step of the evaluation process, the summary results for both the control flow and communication patterns were evaluated in the context of the three case studies. From the missing elements, only *arbitrary cycles* was considered desirable yet not vital for the case studies, and this has been scheduled for the next release of LLPM. Further three patterns were felt to be covered by the pre-conditions (2 control flow patterns) and data flow split (communication flow patterns). Overall, the coverage provided by LLPM was felt to be adequate for the target usage represented by the case studies.

Usability evaluation: To evaluate the simplicity and usability of the LLPM and the tools we report on a study that aimed to identify the balance between user expectations about costs and benefits [29]. This study serves as guideline for the usability evaluation of the LLPM. While 80% of the users showed an interest in service composition there had been significant fears about the possibility of creating errors in process modelling. Furthermore composition problems of business users could be clearly revealed. The surveyed users agreed on frequent frustration in the context of service complexity, compatibility, and composition. A clear need for simple and guided service composition came out. The LLPM addresses these issues. However, due to the lack of a tooling environment the modelling evaluation will be performed at a later stage of our research work.

7   Conclusion and Future Work

This paper gave an insight into design principles for Lightweight Process Modelling, the Language for Lightweight Process Modelling (LLPM), and the user's modelling procedure. The ability to be transformed into existing standard process modelling languages, such as BPMN or BPEL, is key to the LLPM. It is designed to be flexible enough in order to be easily transformed into various, existing process modelling languages. Currently the tools (process editor, components for composition and discovery) are under development implementing the user support. We have evaluated the LLPM approach using the concepts of ontological completeness and coverage as well as simplicity and usability. The next step in evaluating the LLPM is to further test the usability of the user-facing representation of the language and of the support tool. We will set up experiments where we ask target types of end-users to model their processes using LLPM representations and prototype tools. Any feedback given by these end-users will provide some ideas to further improve the language. The application of ontologies in process modeling languages has to be further evaluated in the future. In the LLPM we have chosen a pragmatic approach, where ontologies are only applied for specifying activities. At the moment this approach seems to be most appropriate in order to achieve a working solution. However, as semantic descriptions will evolve and be attached to more and more artifacts, other full-fledged ontological approaches like BPMO can be applicable as well. In order to provide full benefit of the user support through patterns, templates, and goals a critical mass of existing artefacts has to be provided. In particular, domain-specific patterns, templates and goals will provide an added value to the user.

Acknowledgments

The authors wish to gratefully acknowledge the support for this work provided by the European Commission (EC). This work was partially funded by the EC within the FP7 project SOA4All[5].

References

1. Becker, J., Kugeler, M., Rosemann, M.: Process management: a guide for the design of business processes. Springer, Heidelberg (2003)
2. Blechar, M.: Magic Quadrant for Business Process Analysis Tools, 2H07-1H08. Gartner Research (2007)
3. Bunge, M.: Treatise on Basic Philosophy, Ontology I: The furniture of the world (1977)
4. Cavallaro, L., Ripa, G., Zuccalà, M.: Adapting service requests to actual service interfaces through semantic annotations. In: PESOS, co-located with ICSE, Vancouver, Canada. IEEE Computer Society Press, Los Alamitos (2009)
5. Chang, J.F.: Business Process Management Systems: Strategy and Implementation, 1st edn. Auerbach Publications (September 2005)
6. Colombo, M., Di Nitto, E., Mauri, M.: SCENE: A Service Composition Execution Environment Supporting Dynamic Changes Disciplined Through Rules. In: Dan, A., Lamersdorf, W. (eds.) ICSOC 2006. LNCS, vol. 4294, pp. 191–202. Springer, Heidelberg (2006)
7. Dimitrov, M., Simov, A., Stein, S., Konstantinov, M.: A BPMO Based Semantic Business Process Modelling Environment. In: SBPM (2007)
8. Fielding, R.T.: Architectural Styles and the Design of Network-based Software Architectures. PhD thesis, University of California, Irvine (2000)
9. Gil, Y.: Workflow composition. In: Gannon, D., Deelman, E., Shields, M., Taylor, I. (eds.) Workflows for e-Science. Springer, Heidelberg (2006)
10. Glinert, E.P.: Nontextual programming environments, pp. 144–230 (1990)
11. Green, P., Rosemann, M., Indulska, M., Manning, C.: Candidate interoperability standards: An ontological overlap analysis. Data Knowl. Eng. 62(2), 274–291 (2007)
12. Green, T., Petre, M., Bellamy, R.: Comprehensibility of visual and textual programs: A test of superlativism against the 'match-mismatch' conjecture (1991)
13. Gschwind, T., Koehler, J., Wong, J.: Applying patterns during business process modeling. In: Dumas, M., Reichert, M., Shan, M.-C. (eds.) BPM 2008. LNCS, vol. 5240, pp. 4–19. Springer, Heidelberg (2008)
14. Havey, M.: Essential Business Process Modeling. O'Reilly Media, Inc., Sebastopol (2005)
15. Hevner, A.R., March, S.T., Park, J., Ram, S.: Design science in information systems research. MIS Quarterly 28(1), 75–105 (2004)
16. Hornung, T., Koschmider, A., Lausen, G.: Recommendation based process modeling support: Method and user experience. In: Li, Q., Spaccapietra, S., Yu, E., Olivé, A. (eds.) ER 2008. LNCS, vol. 5231, pp. 265–278. Springer, Heidelberg (2008)
17. Kim, J., Suh, W., Lee, H.: Document-based workflow modeling: a case-based reasoning approach. Expert Systems with Applications 23(2), 77–93 (2002)

[5] http://www.soa4all.eu/

18. Ko, R.K., Lee, S.S., Lee, E.W.: Business process management (bpm) standards: A survey. Business Process Management Journal 15(5) (2009)
19. Koehler, J., Vanhatalo, J.: Process anti-patterns: How to avoid the common traps of business process modelling. IBM WebSphere Developer Technical Journal (2007)
20. Kopecky, J., Vitvar, T., Fensel, D., Gomadam, K.: hRests & MicroWSMO. Technical report (March 2009)
21. Kueng, P., Kueng, P., Kawalek, P., Kawalek, P.: Goal-based business process models: Creation and evaluation. Business Process Management Journal 3, 17–38 (1997)
22. Lillehagen, F., Krogstie, J.: Active Knowledge Modeling of Enterprises. Springer Publishing Company, Heidelberg (2008) (incorporated)
23. Madhusudan, T., Zhao, J.L., Marshall, B.: A case-based reasoning framework for workflow model management. Data Knowl. Eng. 50(1), 87–115 (2004)
24. March, S.T., Smith, G.F.: Design and natural science research on information technology. Decis. Support Syst. 15(4), 251–266 (1995)
25. Martin, D., Burstein, M., Hobbs, E., Lassila, O., Mcdermott, D., Mcilraith, S., Narayanan, S., Parsia, B., Payne, T., Sirin, E., Srinivasan, N., Sycara, K.: OWL-S: Semantic Markup for Web Services. Technical report (November 2004)
26. McIlraith, S., Son, T.: Adapting Golog for Composition of Semantic Web Services. In: Proceedings of the Eighth International Conference on Knowledge Representation and Reasoning, KR 2002 (2002)
27. Mendling, J., Recker, J.: Towards Systematic Usage of Labels and Icons in Business Process Models. In: CAiSE 2008 Workshop Proceedings - Twelfth International Workshop on Exploring Modeling Methods in Systems Analysis and Design, EMMSAD 2008 (2008)
28. Myers, B.: Taxonomies of visual programming and program visualization. Journal of Visual languages and Computing 1, 97–123 (1990)
29. Namoune, A., Wajid, U., Mehandjiev, N.: Composition of interactive service-based applications by end-users. In: UGS 2009 - 1st International Workshop on User-generated Services (2009)
30. Nardi, B.A.: A small matter of programming: perspectives on end user computing. MIT Press, Cambridge (1993)
31. Neiger, D., Churilov, L.: Goal-oriented business process engineering revisited: a unifying perspective. In: Computer Supported Acitivity Coordination, pp. 149–163 (2004)
32. Nitzsche, J., Norton, B.: Ontology-Based Data Mediation in BPEL (For Semantic Web Services). In: Ardagna, D., Mecella, M., Yang, J. (eds.) Business Process Management Workshops. LNBIP, vol. 17, pp. 523–534. Springer, Heidelberg (2008)
33. Nitzsche, J., van Lessen, T., Karastoyanova, D., Leymann, F.: BPEL for Semantic Web Services (BPEL4SWS). In: OTM Workshops (1), pp. 179–188 (2007)
34. Nitzsche, J., van Lessen, T., Karastoyanova, D., Leymann, F.: BPEL-Light. In: Alonso, G., Dadam, P., Rosemann, M. (eds.) BPM 2007. LNCS, vol. 4714, pp. 214–229. Springer, Heidelberg (2007)
35. Peffers, K., Tuunanen, T., Rothenberger, M., Chatterjee, S.: A design science research methodology for information systems research. J. Manage. Inf. Syst. 24(3), 45–77 (2008)
36. Petre, M., Green, T.R.G.: Requirements of graphical notations for professional users: Electronics cad systems as a case study. Le Travail Humain (55), 47–70 (1992)
37. Quinn, K.: Not everyone who drives a car fixes it themselves - Strategic Information Infrastructure (2005), `http://www.dmreview.com/news/1041222-1.html`

38. Recker, J.: BPMN Modeling – Who, Where, How and Why. BPTrends 5(3) (2008)
39. Recker, J., Dreiling, A.: Does it matter which process modelling language we teach or use? An experimental study on understanding process modelling languages without formal education. In: Proceedings 18th Australasian Conference on Information Systems, Toowoomba, Australia (2007)
40. Recker, J., Indulska, M., Rosemann, M., Green, P.: Do Process Modelling Techniques Get Better? A Comparative Ontological Analysis of BPMN. In: Campbell, B., Underwood, J., Bunker, D. (eds.) Proceedings 16th Australasian Conference on Information Systems, Sydney, Australia (2005)
41. Recker, J., Indulska, M., Rosemann, M., Green, P.: An Exploratory Study of Process Modelling Practice with BPMN. BPM Center Report (2008)
42. Rolland, C., Kaabi, R.S., Kraiem, N.: On isoa: intentional services oriented architecture. In: Krogstie, J., Opdahl, A.L., Sindre, G. (eds.) CAISE 2007 and WES 2007. LNCS, vol. 4495, pp. 158–172. Springer, Heidelberg (2007)
43. Rosser, B.: Taking Advantage of User-Friendly Business Process Modeling. Gartner Research, G00156919 (2008)
44. Ruh, W.A., Brown, W.J., Maginnis, F.X.: Enterprise Application Integration: A Wiley Tech Brief. John Wiley & Sons, Inc., New York (2000)
45. Russell, N., Arthur, van der Aalst, W.M.P., Mulyar, N.: Workflow Control-Flow Patterns: A Revised View. Technical report, BPMcenter.org (2006)
46. Silver, B.: BPMN Method and Style. Cody-Cassidy Pre (2009)
47. van der Aalst, W., Aldred, L., Dumas, M., Hofstede, A.H.M.T.: Design and implementation of the YAWL system (2004)
48. van der Aalst, W., ter Hofstede, A., Kiepuszewski, B., Barros, A.: Workflow Patterns. Distributed and Parallel Databases 14(3), 5–51 (2003)
49. van der Aalst, W.M.P., ter Hofstede, A.H.M.: YAWL: Yet Another Workflow Language, vol. 30 (2005)
50. Vitvar, T., Kopeck, J., Zaremba, M., Fensel, D.: WSMO-Lite: Lightweight Semantic Descriptions for Services on the Web. In: ECOWS, pp. 77–86. IEEE Computer Society, Los Alamitos (2007)
51. Wand, Y., Weber, R.: An Ontological Evaluation of Systems Analysis and Design Methods. In: Falkenberg, E., Lindgreen, P. (eds.) Information System Concepts: An In-Depth Analysis, pp. 79–107 (1989)
52. Weber, B., Reichert, M., Rinderle-Ma, S.: Change patterns and change support features - enhancing flexibility in process-aware information systems. Data Knowl. Eng. 66(3), 438–466 (2008)
53. Williams, S.: Business Process Modeling improves Administrative Control, pp. 44–50 (1967)
54. Wohed, P., van der Aalst, W.M.P., Dumas, M., ter Hofstede, A.H.M.: Analysis of Web Services Composition Languages: The Case of BPEL4WS. In: Song, I.-Y., Liddle, S.W., Ling, T.-W., Scheuermann, P. (eds.) ER 2003. LNCS, vol. 2813, pp. 200–215. Springer, Heidelberg (2003)
55. zur Muehlen, M., Recker, J.: How Much Language Is Enough? Theoretical and Practical Use of the Business Process Modeling Notation. In: Bellahsène, Z., Léonard, M. (eds.) CAiSE 2008. LNCS, vol. 5074, pp. 465–479. Springer, Heidelberg (2008)

Towards Processpedia – An Ecological Environment for BPM Stakeholders Collaboration

António Rito Silva[1,2,3], Michael Rosemann[1], and Samia Mazhar[1]

[1] BPM Group/QUT, Level 5 - 126 Margaret Street,
4000 Brisbane, Australia
[2] SAP Research, Building A4, Level 7 - 52 Merivale Street,
4101 Brisbane, Australia
[3] IST/Technical Institute of Lisbon, Av. Rovisco Pais,
1049-001 Lisbon, Portugal
{Michael.Rosemann,Samia.Mazhar}@qut.edu.au
Rito.Silva@ist.utl.pt

Abstract. Current approaches to support stakeholders' collaboration in the modelling of business processes envision an egalitarian environment where stakeholders interact in the same context, using the same languages and sharing the same perspectives on the business process. However, these approaches ignore that Business Process Management (BPM) includes diverse stakeholders groups, such as end users that operate the business, business experts that understand the overall impact of business processes and process experts that master process design and analysis techniques. Therefore, such stakeholders have to collaborate in the context of process modelling using a language that some of them do not master, and integrate their various perspectives. In this paper we propose the *Processpedia* approach to foster effective collaboration among stakeholders without enforcing egalitarianism. *Processpedia* intends to be an ecological collaboration environment for knowledge production by capitalising on stakeholders' distinctive characteristics.

Keywords: *Processpedia*, Business Process Management, Social Software Features, Collaborative Modelling.

1 Introduction

Nowadays dynamic and highly adaptable organisations have been blurring the distinction between strategic decision and operation. In these organisations, it is expected that employees understand the organisation's strategy and goals. They have to react to change according to business goals, even though they may not be explicitly embodied in formal procedures, organisational rules or automated tools. This is particularly relevant when business changes are not foreseen in advance, i.e. the correct answers are not in place. In these exceptional, but not infrequent, situations employees' reactions are driven by the tacit knowledge they possess about the business, which is part of the organisation's culture.

M. zur Muehlen and J. Su (Eds.): BPM 2010 Workshops, LNBIP 66, pp. 449–460, 2011.

Current methodological approaches [Kueng & Kawalek, 1997; Soffer & Wand, 2005; Lapouchnian *et al.*, 2007] for Business Process Management (BPM) tend to follow a top-down decomposition strategy from business goals to business processes and activities [Kaplan & Norton, 1992]. These approaches envisage the alignment of business processes with the organisation's strategy, which is operationalised by a set of key performance indicators (KPI). They consider that all the relevant knowledge is gathered, and that process design and implementation can be sufficiently guided by the defined strategies, goals and KPIs. However, whenever unexpected changes occur in the environment, the formalised knowledge contained in the designed business processes is not sufficient to precisely guide the actions of the managers and employees in charge. Thus, top-down BPM approaches do not consider the potential of end users' tacit knowledge whilst they react to unexpected situations. They rather enforce a knowledge creation model centred on top-down formalisation of knowledge in business process models.

To capture end users tacit knowledge and articulate and integrate it with explicit knowledge contained in business process models, a new set of tools has recently emerged including solutions such as Blueprint [Lombardi, 2009]. These tools are driven by the paradigms of decentralised knowledge gathering and egalitarianism and intend to actively foster end users' collaboration in business process modelling. This way, business process design is driven by both, the organisational strategic goals and end users' tacit knowledge. However, end user participation in the modelling of business processes occurs in the context of business process languages, mainly BPMN [OMG, 2009], which were designed to be readily usable by process and business experts to model efficient implementations of business processes. Furthermore, it is known that end users tacit knowledge is created in the context of their everyday work that is accomplished in a local and bottom up fashion and talking into account the current situation [Suchman, 1987]. Therefore, in approaches like Blueprint [Lombardi, 2009], end users have to map their local and contextual knowledge of business process, circumscribed by the their organisational context and made of concrete situations, into a BMPN like description which crosses several organisational contexts and abstracts concrete situations.

The articulation and integration of tacit and explicit knowledge is proposed in the SECI model [Nonaka & Takeuchi, 1995], depicted in Figure 1. This model provides an integrated perspective to the bottom-up emergence of tacit knowledge and its top-down formalisation. The SECI model comprises four phases: Socialisation, where tacit knowledge is created from tacit knowledge through peoples interactions and shared experience; Externalisation, where explicit knowledge is created from tacit knowledge by creating external and sharable representations of the knowledge; Combination, where explicit knowledge is created by combining explicit knowledge using more complex and abstract forms of knowledge representation; and Internalisation, where tacit knowledge is created from explicit knowledge by behaving accordingly to what is specified in explicit knowledge.

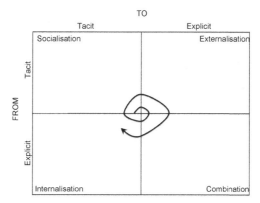

Fig. 1. The SECI Model

In this paper we use the SECI model to highlight existing limitations on the gathering of tacit knowledge by top-down BPM methodological approaches and BPM collaboration tools (Section 2). Then we apply the SECI model to wikipedia to identify how tacit knowledge is captured (Section 3). By integrating the SECI models for top-down BPM approaches, BPM collaboration tools, and wikipedia a new SECI model is defined for a new approach to BPM, *Processpedia* (Section 4). Finally, related work (Section 5) and conclusions (Section 6) are presented.

2   Top-Down BPM in an Evolving Business Environment

In traditional methodological approaches to BPM, business process modelling is driven by a set of key performance indicators. Business processes are traditionally decomposed top-down, from strategy to operation, and focus on optimisation as defined by centrally defined performance targets. However, it is often the case that these organisations are not able to acknowledge environment changes and perish when their KPIs become obsolete, since their optimised operation inhibits both, the perception of changes and the emergence of tacit knowledge.

The above problem stems from the crystallisation of the organisation's strategies in a set of formal procedures that intend to completely describe the organisational behaviours. These formal procedures intend to prescribe an optimised achievement of the strategy. As a consequence, the organisation's knowledge has to be explicitly specified. In this paradigm, tacit knowledge is an untapped resource that is not considered in the pathway towards organisational performance. Hence, these organisations address change by planning, which mean that they try to foresee environmental changes and plan internal reactions before the environment evolves: they have to be ready for change.

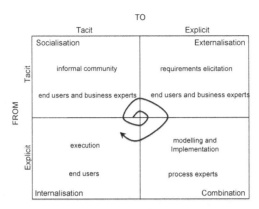

Fig. 2. The SECI Model Applied to Top-down BPM

When applying the SECI model to analyse BPM top-down decomposition approaches, Figure 2, we identify an emphasis on Combination and Internalisation phases. Process experts model and implement business processes while end users execute business processes according to the definition.

BPM top-down approaches obviously do not consider the production of tacit knowledge during the Socialisation phase and requirements engineering techniques are used in the Externalisation phase to capture tacit knowledge and make it explicit. However, requirements engineering techniques are frequently exogenous in the sense that they are not applied in the same context where tacit knowledge creation occurred, i.e., when end users perform their work. Besides, it is the responsibility of the requirements engineer to interpret end users' tacit knowledge and make it explicit.

To cope with top-down methodologies limitations on the gathering of tacit knowledge specific requirements engineering techniques have been applied to reduce this gap, by engaging end users in the requirements gathering process, e.g. scenario-based requirements engineering [Sutcliffe *et al.*, 1998], but yet this occurs outside end users' working environment, or it occurs in the working environment but the requirements are gathered by a third party element [Beyer & Holtzblatt, 1997]. On the other hand, collaborative BPMN editors such as Blueprint [Lombardi, 2009], which aim to provide an egalitarian approach, involve end users in the modelling process but oblige them to express tacit knowledge in a context external to everyday business operation. These tools provide web-based collaborative modelling editors enhanced with social software features [Crumlish & Malone, 2009; Bell, 2009], such as comments and ratings, where end users and experts can work together in the modelling of business processes.

Figure 3 shows the SECI model applied to collaborative modelling BPM tools. Computer-based communities are supported, Socialisation phase, which foster communication among stakeholders. Moreover, these communities mediate end users, business experts and process experts collaboration during modelling

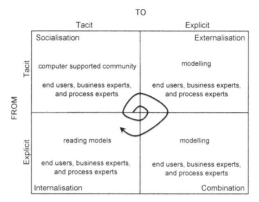

Fig. 3. The SECI Model Applied to Collaborative BPM Modelling Tools

activities. Remarkably, due to the focus on modelling the requirements elicitation phase is biased by modelling: requirements elicitation is done by modelling. Moreover, end users participation occurs at the process experts level of abstraction and not in the context where they execute business processes. They have to proficient in a BPM modelling language.

3   Wikipedia as a Collaborative Bottom-Up Environment

In contrast to the dominating top-down approaches that can be found in most BPM initiatives, the Web 2.0 community can be seen as a successful deployment of the bottom-up paradigm. The most successful and well-known Web 2.0-based knowledge management environment is Wikipedia. Wikipedia is a globally available and free encyclopaedia where knowledge is gathered in a bottom-up manner by blurring the differences between consumers and producers of knowledge ('prosumers'). Anyone is entitled to contribute to the encyclopaedia, at his/her level of knowledge.

There are numerous studies on Wikipedia, e.g. [Spek *et al.*, 2006; Riehle, 2006; Kriplean *et al.*, 2008]. These studies cover both technical and social aspects, ranging from the features provided by the Wikipedia software platform, Wikimedia [Foundation, 2010], to the governance mechanisms used by Wikipedia community.

The following three aspects are relevant:

– Egalitarianism – Wikipedia's knowledge model blurs the differences between producers and consumers of knowledge. Smoothing these differences is a central aspect of the Wikipedia strategy since it fosters a global participation, egalitarianism, in the production of knowledge. This way, it is easier to engage consumers to become producers when they are involved in the consumption of knowledge.

- Governance – Even though the governance is very loose and any person can contribute to Wikipedia, a certain organisational structure exists. This structure follows the principles of meritocracy where the most relevant positions are assigned in recognition for contributions to Wikipedia. Once in place this organisation is responsible for defining Wikipedia rules and to decide accordingly. Additionally, there are sub-organisations, groups, which specialise in a particular area of knowledge and coordinate their contributions.
- Platform – The Wikimedia platform features are essential to the success of Wikipedia. It provides seamless reading, writing and editing features to foster contributions. It also traces all changes, preserving the individual contributions and facilitating reverting to previous versions. Finally, it contains several functionalities for community support. These functionalities are based on social software features, like comments, discussions listing and rating. Overall, these functionalities foster the existence of several communities where discussions about the specific knowledge areas as well as about the Wikipedia management take place.

An aspect that becomes evident when applying the SECI model to Wikipedia, Figure 4, is that Wikipedia's goal is to gather knowledge instead of creating it. However, Wikipedia's community follows a set of rules and templates that emerge from practice. Therefore, knowledge is created about how to capture and foster the gathering of information and how information is structured inside the wiki.

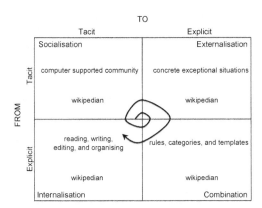

Fig. 4. The SECI Model Applied to Wikipedia

Figure 4 places the reading, writing, editing, and organising of knowledge in the internalisation phase because when users consume and produce information they are doing it according to the Wikipedia templates and are certainly following Wikipedia rules. The creation of new tacit knowledge occurs inside the community and is strongly supported by software for communities and social networking. This software is rich in the so-called social software features. These features support discussion and debate about all emerging situations, concrete cases, where the application of Wikipedia templates and rules is not straightforward and raise doubts and disagreement among the community members. These situations trigger for the emergence of new rules and classifications and, consequently, production of knowledge. Afterwards, during externalisation phase, the results of discussion are applied to the concrete cases and the combination phase occurs when the concrete cases exceptions are generalised into new global rules and/or categories and/or templates.

4 Processpedia

In this section we propose a new approach for BPM called *Processpedia*. We do so by proposing a new knowledge creation model for BPM which integrates the SECI models for top-down BPM, Wikipedia and collaborative BPM tools. Top-down BPM and bottom-up Wikipedia are not mutually exclusive paradigms, but can be regarded as being complementary. Top-down BPM stresses the formalisation during the Combination phase and behavioural compliance at the Internalisation phase, while Wikipedia stresses the creation and capture of tacit knowledge at the Socialisation and Externalisation phases. On the other hand, while both foster egalitarianism, BPM collaborative modelling tools and Wikipedia implement different approaches on how abstractions are defined. BPM collaborative tools focus on modelling by creating abstract models while in Wikipedia abstract representations are created by generalising from the solutions found for concrete exceptional cases. Moreover, Wikipedia fosters the capture of knowledge while users are consuming information but BPM collaborative modelling tools require end users to use an unfamiliar environment, a BPM modelling tool, to make explicit their tacit knowledge.

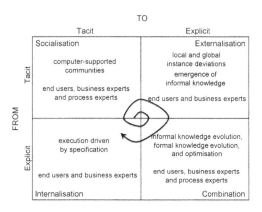

Fig. 5. A SECI Model for Processpedia

Figure 5 shows the *Processpedia* SECI model that integrates the SECI models for top-down BPM, collaborative BMP and Wikipedia. The model incorporates in the socialisation phase the Wikipedia computer-support of communities to foster collaboration and capture of tacit knowledge. Additionally, it also incorporates the Wikipedia bottom-up strategy, during the externalisation phase, to capture tacit knowledge by making it explicit in the context of concrete cases. Therefore, conversely to BPM collaborative tools, where externalisation occurs by modelling using the high level abstract language, it permits the capture of those business process instances which execution deviates from their specification. The deviations represent concrete exceptional situations of business process and social software features can be used to justify deviations' rational and become a source of informal knowledge for the combination phase. During the combination phase, knowledge evolves based on the knowledge made explicit in the externalisation phase. End users and business experts can evolve the informal knowledge by reuse and synthesis, e.g. they create a folksonomy, while business experts and process experts participate in the evolution of the business process abstract models.

Contrary to Wikipedia, the model do not follow a pure egalitarian approach since it aims to integrate the capture of tacit knowledge by end users and business experts during externalisation phase with the formalisation of knowledge by business and process experts during the combination phase. End users are not empowered to create business process models but when performing their work they can deviate the business process execution from the specification and add a rational using social software features.

The following aspects characterise *Processpedia* both from the methodology and platform perspectives:

- Egalitarianism - *Processedia* fosters the collaboration of the different stakeholders in the execution and modelling of business processes but respecting their level of knowledge and competences. It considers three kinds of stakeholders' roles: end-user, business expert and process expert. End users participate in the actual business operation executing business activities. Business experts have a complete vision of the business and can provide a rationale for why and how the business processes operate. Process experts have the process modelling expertise, master the workflow patterns, e.g. workflow data patterns [Russell *et al.*, 2005], and know how to define optimised business process.

- Governance - Business experts' contribution to business process definition evolution is based on their knowledge of the organisational and functional goals of business processes. Therefore they are responsible to ensure that the final definition still accomplishes the organisational and functional goals. Process experts are responsible for ensuring that business processes optimisation goals are achieved according to the defined KPIs. Note that even though each one to the stakeholders has his responsibilities they have to collaborate to create a process definition that accomplishes all the different goals.

- Model - *Processpedia* business process models are broad in the sense that they consider both, the formal process specifications as well as their set of concrete instances. Considering that a model should contain the explicit knowledge about a real entity, the set of process instances that deviated from the business process specification are particularly relevant since they contain information about the real entities that is not represented in the specification. Furthermore, the model specification evolution is triggered by the set of deviations considered worth being formally represented to become the norm of the organisational functioning and which operation needs to be optimised: from concrete knowledge to abstract knowledge.

- Platform - The *Processpedia* integrates modelling and execution of business processes. Business process instances execute according the explicit knowledge contained in the process specification. However, a *Processpedia* platform should support the ad-hoc execution of business processes instances by end users and business experts, allowing deviations from the process model specification to capture the tacit knowledge behind deviations. Thus, end users can make explicit their tacit knowledge while performing their work, avoiding a temporal gap between application of tacit knowledge and its representation, which is a reason for the model-reality divide problem: the interplay of tacit and explicit knowledge.

- Social Software Features - The concrete knowledge captured by the deviation can be enriched with informal information containing the rationale for the deviation. Therefore, social software features should be used, for instance, tagging can be used to give (informal) semantic meaning to deviations and comments can be used to justify and contextualise the deviation. Moreover, the informal semantics should be integrated with the formal semantics in the sense that the type system should be part of the tag system.

5 Related Work

In this section we discuss related work and how it can contribute to the *Processpedia* platform and method. We detail, and suggest extensions, to some concrete tools and techniques that may be integrated in an overall *Processpedia* approach.

Processpedia method is driven by the wiki design principles [Cunningham, 2006] which were successfully applied in the context of Wikipedia [Garud *et al.*, 2008]. Current approaches to BPM follow a top-down strategy and even the collaborative "bottom-up" approaches like Blueprint [Lombardi, 2009] are actually top-down: The end user participation in the modelling of business processes using the experts language is actually a requirements gathering technique associated with a top-down approach. Several top-down BPM methods are driven by measurement criteria [Kueng & Kawalek, 1997; Lapouchnian *et al.*, 2007; Chao *et al.*, 2009]. The goal-based business process modelling approach in Kueng & Kawalek [1997] uses non-functional goals to drive the top-down decomposition of functional goals. The application of artefact-centric at IBM Global Financing [Chao *et al.*, 2009] also follows a top-down approach driven by key performance indicators and the requirements engineering approach presented in Lapouchnian *et al.* [2007] uses soft goals to identify variation points of the business process definition. None of these approaches considers a bottom-up approach, neither they address how can social software features be used. An open research issue is how to effectively integrate a process expert top-down perspective based on systemic qualities with end users bottom-up perspective based on tacit knowledge.

In *Processpedia* business processes modelling and execution activities are intertwined and should be seamlessly supported by a common modelling and execution environment. In most existing approaches end users execution should always follow the business process definition. These approaches confine end users to the execution of a set of activities, according to a predefined sequence, avoiding the capture of tacit knowledge. Some tools, as ADEPT2 [Dadam *et al.*, 2007], already integrate execution and modelling of business processes by allowing end users to deviate the execution of a particular business process instance from its business process definition. However, end users deviate by defining a new business process definition for the instance since the main emphasis of these approaches is to maintain consistency. Therefore, deviations have a global scope, since the end users needs to understand the complete process, and they occur at the process expert level of abstraction, since a new consistent business process definition needs to be modelled. New business process languages need to be defined to represent local organisational contexts, allow the encapsulation of local deviations, allow definition-less or/and definition-incomplete instances, and provide a consistency mapping between deviated instances and the former business process definition. It seems to be promising to follow goal-based approaches. Indeed Kueng & Kawalek [1997] claims that a goal-based approach is better suited to digest organisational changes. Additionally, these languages should incorporate the informal and subjective knowledge provided by social software features. In particular the emergent folksonomies should be integrated with the business process type system to support a smooth evolution of business processes. The current use of social software features associated with business processes management is mainly as recommendations [Koschmider *et al.*, 2009; Sarini *et al.*, 2009] and do not explore how informal and subjective knowledge can be integrated with formal knowledge in a overall knowledge management process for BPM.

Silva *et al.* [2010] presents a set of functionalities and qualities that characterise an agile BPM approach. In this paper we provide a knowledge management perspective that justifies the need for agile BPM approaches and, in addition, integrates them in a hybrid, both top-down and bottom-up, BPM approach.

6   Conclusions

In this paper we propose a new approach to BPM, *Processpedia*, which integrates bottom-up and top-down BPM in order to foster the collaboration of BPM stakeholders while preserving their contextual perspective. Thus, *Processpedia* is a hybrid method to business process design that integrates traditional top-down approaches with a Wikipedia-like bottom-up approach. The SECI model is used throughout this paper to show how *Processpedia* addresses the knowledge gathering and dissemination process of BPM and to compare *Processpedia* with other approaches.

The design of *Processpedia* was driven by an analysis of the top-down BPM, collaborative BPM tools, and wikipedia SECI models. The resulting SECI model was used to characterise *Processpedia* using different perspectives: egalitarianism, governance, model, platform, and social software features.

Processpedia overarches top-down and bottom-up design of business processes by integrating several forms of knowledge: informal and formal, concrete and abstract, and tacit and explicit. The use of social software features is central for the integration. It is used to facilitate collaboration and emergence of tacit knowledge, and provides intermediate semantics between deviated instances and specifications. The knowledge captured using social software features constitute informal and subjective meta-information of business process definitions and instances. Then, process experts use this rich set of information to redefine business processes.

Acknowledgement

The first author was partially supported by the Portuguese Foundation for Science and Technology, FCT-MCTES, under grant SFRH/BSAB/923/2009.

References

Bell, G.: Building Social Web Applications. O'Reilly, Sebastopol (2009)

Beyer, H., Holtzblatt, K.: Contextual Design: Defining Customer-Centered Systems (Interactive Technologies), 1st edn. Morgan Kaufmann, San Francisco (1997)

Chao, T., Cohn, D., Flatgard, A., Hahn, S., Linehan, M., Nandi, P., Nigam, A., Pinel, F., Vergo, J., Wu, F.y.: Artifact-Based Transformation of IBM Global Financing. In: Dayal, U., Eder, J., Koehler, J., Reijers, H.A. (eds.) BPM 2009. LNCS, vol. 5701, pp. 261–277. Springer, Heidelberg (2009)

Crumlish, C., Malone, E.: Designing Social Interfaces. O'Reilly, Sebastopol (2009)

Cunningham, W.: Design principles of wiki: how can so little do so much? In: WikiSym 2006: Proceedings of the 2006 International Symposium on Wikis, pp. 13–14. ACM, New York (2006)

Dadam, P., Reichert, M., Rinderle, S., Jurisch, M., Acker, H., Göser, K., Kreher, U., Lauer, M.: ADEPT2 - Next Generation Process Management Technology. Heidelberger Innovationsforum, Heidelberg (2007)

Foundation, Wikimedia (2010), Wikimedia, http://www.wikimedia.org

Garud, R., Jain, S., Tuertscher, P.: Incomplete by Design and Designing for Incompleteness. Organization Studies 29(03), 351–371 (2008)

Kaplan, R.S., Norton, D.P.: The balanced scorecard–measures that drive performance. Harv. Bus. Rev. 70(1), 71–79 (1992)

Koschmider, A., Song, M., Reijers, H.A.: Social Software for Business Process Modeling. Journal of Information Technology (2009) (to appear)

Kriplean, T., Beschastnikh, I., McDonald, D.W.: Articulations of wikiwork: uncovering valued work in wikipedia through barnstars. In: CSCW 2008: Proceedings of the ACM 2008 Conference on Computer Supported Cooperative Work, pp. 47–56. ACM, New York (2008)

Kueng, P., Kawalek, P.: Goal-based business process models: creation and evaluation. Business Process Management Journal 3(1), 17–38 (1997)

Lapouchnian, A., Yu, Y., Mylopoulos, J.: Requirements-Driven Design and Configuration Management of Business Processes. In: Alonso, G., Dadam, P., Rosemann, M. (eds.) BPM 2007. LNCS, vol. 4714, pp. 246–261. Springer, Heidelberg (2007)

Lombardi, Lombardi Blueprint (2009),
`http://www.lombardisoftware.com/bpm-blueprint-product.php`

Nonaka, I., Takeuchi, H.: The Knowledge Creating Company. Oxford University Press, New York (1995)

OMG. Business Process Modelling Notation (October 2009), `http://www.bpmn.org/`

Riehle, D.: How and Why Wikipedia Works: An Interview. In: Beesley, A., Bauer, E., Naoko, K. (eds.) Proceedings of the 2006 International Symposium on Wikis (WikiSym 2006), pp. 3–8. ACM Press, New York (2006)

Russell, N., ter Hofstede, A.H.M., Edmond, D., van der Aalst, W.M.P.: Workflow data patterns: Identification, representation and tool support. In: Delcambre, L.M.L., Kop, C., Mayr, H.C., Mylopoulos, J., Pastor, Ó. (eds.) ER 2005. LNCS, vol. 3716, pp. 353–368. Springer, Heidelberg (2005)

Sarini, M., Durante, F., Gabbiadini, A.: Workflow Management Social Systems: a new socio-psychological perspective on process management. In: Nurcan, S., Schmidt, R. (eds.) The Second Workshop on Business Process Management and Social Software (September 2009)

Silva, A.R., Meziani, R., Magalhaes, R., Martinho, D., Aguiar, A., Flores, N.: AGILIPO: Embedding Social Software Features into Business Process Tools. In: BPM 2009 Workshops. LNBIP, vol. 43, pp. 219–230. Springer, Heidelberg (2010)

Soffer, P., Wand, Y.: On the notion of soft-goals in business process modeling. Business Process Management Journal 11(6), 663–679 (2005)

Spek, S., Postma, E.O., van den Herik, H.J.: Wikipedia: organisation from a bottom-up approach. CoRR (2006)

Suchman, L.: Plans and situated actions: the problem of human-machine communication. Cambridge University Press, Cambridge (1987)

Sutcliffe, A.G., Maiden, N.A.M., Minocha, S., Manuel, D.: Supporting Scenario-Based Requirements Engineering. IEEE Transactions on Software Engineering 24(12), 1072–1088 (1998)

1st International Workshop on Sustainability and Business Process Management (SusBPM 2010)

Workshop Organization

Workshop Organizers

Jan vomBrocke
Universität Liechtenstein
Fürst-Franz-Josef-Strasse
9490 Vaduz
Liechtenstein

Stefan Seidel
Universität Liechtenstein
Fürst-Franz-Josef-Strasse
9490 Vaduz
Liechtenstein

Program Committee

SalehuAnteneh (Addis Ababa University, Ethiopia)
Marie-Claude (Maric) Boudreau (University of Georgia, USA)
Marco de Marco (UniversitàCattolica del SacroCuore, Italy)
Peter Droege (University of Liechtenstein, Liechtenstein)
Peter Fettke (Saarland University, Germany)
Jan Recker (Queensland University of Technology, Australia)
Michael Rosemann (Queensland University of Technology, Australia)
NarcyzRoztocki, State University of New York, USA
Daniel Schmid (SAP AG, Germany)
ReimaSuomi (Turku School of Economics, Finland)
Cathy Urquhart (Manchester Metropolitan University Business School, UK)
Richard (Rick) Watson (University of Georgia, USA)
Stanislaw Wrycza (University of Gdańsk, Poland)
ZhenxiangZeng (Jessie) (Hebei University of Technology, China)

Preface

The aim of this workshop was to further the discussion of the role of BPM for the sustainable development of organizations. Our intention was to provide thought leaders with a forum where they can contribute to defining and shaping this emergent, and arguably highly relevant, research domain. The workshop attracted 11 submissions of which 6 papers were selected for presentation after a highly competitive review process. Two out of the six papers tackle sustainability from a BPM perspective at a rather general level: Constantin Houy, Markus Reiter, Peter Fettke, and Peter Loos focus on the ecological dimension and discuss how BPM approaches can be leveraged to support sustainability and resource efficiency of IT supported business activities. Getachew Hailemariam and Jan vom Brocke conceptualize the sustainability of BPM initiatives per se, thus focusing on the economic dimension. The other four papers that were accepted pertain to sustainability measurement. Anne Cleven, Robert Winter, and Felix Wortmann propose an approach to process performance management with particular consideration of social, ecological, and economic dimensions. Nicole Zeise, Marco Link, and Erich Ortner also consider all three dimensions when they discuss how dynamic indicators can be used in order to control all levels of enterprise architectures. Jan Recker, Michael Rosemann, and Ehsan Roohi Gohar focus on the ecologic dimension and propose an approach to measure the carbon footprint caused during the execution of a business process. Finally, Wube Alemayehu and Jan vom Brocke discuss the role of ecological and social aspects in the performance measurement of an Ethiopian airline.

The event was opened by Richard (Rick) Watson, who gave a keynote on the role of information systems in creating a sustainable society. Rick is the J. Rex Fuqua Distinguished Chair for Internet Strategy in the Terry College of Business at the University of Georgia. He has published nearly 150 journal articles, written books on electronic commerce and data management, and given invited presentations in more than 30 countries. His most recent research focuses on Energy Informatics and IS leadership.

We are very grateful for the constructive and timely reviews of the members of our program committee. We are confident that program reviewers, presenters and attendees could benefit from the workshop. It will be truly fascinating to see how the field of BPM, and the information systems discipline in general, will be able to contribute to creating more sustainable organizations and a more sustainable society in the future.

Vaduz,   Jan vom Brocke
August 2010   Stefan Seidel

Sustainability Performance Measurement –
The Case of Ethiopian Airlines

Wube Alemayehu[1] and Jan vom Brocke[2]

[1] Ababa University, EthiopiaAddis Ababa, Ethiopia
wub_ale@yahoo.com
[2] University of Liechtenstein,
Martin Hilti Chair of Business Process Management,
Institute of Information Systems, Principality of Liechtenstein
jan.vom.brocke@uni.li

Abstract. This paper presents the findings of an investigation of sustainable performance measurement practices at Ethiopian Airlines. Evidence was gathered through structured interviews conducted with key informants of the airline and document reviews. Reports were assessed with respect to sustainable performance measurement system. The paper demonstrates that, despite the availability of economic performance indicators, there are no measurements concerning the social and environmental performance. However there is some operational practice related to social and environmental responsibility of the airline. The research contributes values to two areas: First, it shares some experience in measuring sustainable performance of the airline or their practical involvement in social and environmental responsibility. Second, it tries to help decision makers – based on the example of Ethiopian Airline –to better understand the level of maturity of their sustainable performance measurement and, thus, to improve decision making through a "sustainability lens".

1 Introduction

Sustainability performance management is an emerging term which addresses the social, environmental and economic performance aspects of corporate management (Schaltegger & Wagner, 2006). Sustainability has been defined as economic development that meets today's generation needs without compromising the opportunity and ability for future generations (Brundtland, 1985). According to the Dow Jones Sustainability Indexes "Corporate sustainability is a business approach that creates long-term shareholder value by embracing opportunities and managing risks deriving from economic, environmental and social developments."

The Introduction of the concept of sustainability into the business organizations' thinking has implications for how it considers its strategy which, on the other hand, affects how it measures its performance.

Contemporary organizations generally tend more to extend the basis of their performance measures: a short-term financial focus expanded by long-term (vom Brocke, Sonnenberg & Simons, 2009) social, environmental and economic impacts

M. zur Muehlen and J. Su (Eds.): BPM 2010 Workshops, LNBIP 66, pp. 467–478, 2011.
© Springer-Verlag Berlin Heidelberg 2011

and value adding (Hardjono & van Marrewijk, 2001). Businesses can gain a competitive advantage, increase their market share and boost shareholder value by adopting and implementing sustainable practices. This can be done by companies "adopting business strategies and activities that meet the needs of the enterprise and its stakeholders today, while protecting, sustaining and enhancing the human and natural resources that will be needed in the future" (IISD, 2003).

Making sustainability a vital part of a company's business strategy is important in order to reach into consistent levels of economic growth or economic sustainability for the organization (Bansal, 2002). But, this requires a drastic shift of the organizations' performance measures to a economic, social and environmental bottom lines perspective (Elkington, 1998), and paying more and more attention to their values and responsibility (Enquist, Johnsson and Skålén, 2006). Sustainability also requires the transformation of mindset and commitment of the leadership and organizational performance to include key stakeholders (Laszlo, 2003; Waddock & Bodwell, 2007; Seidel, Recker, Pimmer and vom Brocke, 2010).

One of the main challenges environmentally and socially responsible companies are facing is the management of sustainability performance that requires a sound management framework. This framework firstly links environmental and social management to the business and competitive strategy and management (Johnson 2007; Schaltegger & Wagner, 2006; Epstein & Roy, 2003) and secondly translates sustainability strategy into coherent action and daily decision-making, and forces it into every level of the business's organization. These challenges arise because implementing sustainability is fundamentally different than implementing other strategies in organizations.

As challenging the management of sustainability is, as demanding is finding an appropriate measuring index. Despite its challenge, a lot of scholars try to identify different indexes to measure the performance. Epstein (2008) indicates how management can identify, manage and measure the drivers, to improve sustainability and the systems, and structures that can be created to enhance performance measurements. Well-designed sustainable performance measures (SPM) can help organizations to improve their sustainable performance each time and to achieve sustainable development.

Research Rationale

The aim of this research paper is, first, to explore different performance measures used by the Ethiopian Airlines to assure corporate sustainability. Second, to help decision makers to understand the level of maturity fo their sustainable performance measures – based on the example of Ethiopian Airlines. Finally, the aim is to discuss performance indicators that would make it possible to increase effectiveness of decision making through a sustainability lens.

Research Motivation

The airline industry has gone through plenty of turbulences over the last few years. Following a period of crisis caused by an economic slowdown in the United States and amplified by the attacks of 9/11, the SARS epidemic and the war in Iraq, air traffic began growing again in 2004. The economic recession, which started in 2008 in the US and spread into the rest of the world, as well as the fuel price hit in 2007 and the swain flue (H1N1) epidemic, which started in 2009 in China, have serious impacts to the airline industry.

However, the airline sector remains fragile and a jump in oil prices, new terrorist attacks or economic recession could set things back again (Montreal Economic Institute, 2006). Airlines are operating in an extremely dynamic, and often highly volatile, commercial environment. Both opportunities and risks are part of everyday business for the company. As with any company, Airlines have sustainability risks (social, environmental, operational, threat, strategic and financial) they have to deal with. Airline managers are responsible for the optimal decision-making about corporate sustainability risks in their daily business.

Despite all these hassles, the past financial indicators of the Ethiopian Airlines have shown a better financial performance. It recorded positive results in many of its economic performance parameters during the fiscal year of 2007/08. According to the released financial reports, Ethiopian Airlines generated 9.2 billion Birr (978 million USD) in operating revenue during the budget year, a 34% increase over that of the previous year.

For the reviewed period a net profit of 508 million Birr (54 million USD) was reached. During the same period, Ethiopian Airlines also transported 2.5 million passengers, an increase of 20% compared to the preceding year (Ethiopian airlines report, 2007/08). According to the US Air Transport Association (the airline industry trade association) the loss from 2001 through 2005 was about $35 billion. Such an economic performance by Ethiopian Airlines while a significant number of US airlines were making a loss during the past few years is a subject for research. The research motivation, therefore, is to disclose the secrets of success of the airline and to find whether the performance is sustainable.

Organization of the Research
The paper is organized into five main sections and begins with a theoretical framework that describes different theories and models. In section two the research method will be explained. Section three describes the case of Ethiopian Airlines and presents the findings of our research. These findings will be discussed in section four. The overall conclusion is given in the last section.

2 Theoretical Framework

The most straightforward and popular tool for sustainability performance evaluation is the use of performance indicators. In principle, indicators enable systematic performance evaluation and present information in a suitable form for decision-making purposes. Pressure from stakeholders to publish sustainability performance information is often perceived as a main driver for sustainability performance evaluation in industrial enterprises. According to the stakeholder view of the firm (Cyert & March, 1963; Donaldson & Preston, 1995; Clarkson, 1995) a company can last over time if it is able to build and maintain sustainable and durable relationships with all members of its stakeholder network. Adopting this stakeholder view means rethinking nature and purposes of firms and the managerial tools, adopted by companies themselves. In this relational view of the firm the success of managerial efforts cannot be measured according to a shareholder perspective, but only by adopting a more holistic and comprehensive stakeholder framework. Thus, the sustainability of a firm depends on the sustainability of its stakeholder relationships: a company relationship with shareholders, employees, clients, suppliers, public authorities, local communities, financial partners, civil society in general etc (Hailemariam & vom Brocke, 2010).

However, modern enterprises use sustainability performance evaluation for both external and internal reasons, because the use of performance indicators can improve effectiveness of the enterprise management. Performance indicators can help to identify the opportunities for operation optimizations, to reveal the inefficiencies that could be removed by preventive measures and to improve internal and external communication. The new evaluation and reporting systems also help extending, integrating and improving the traditional financial/economic approaches to the corporate performance measurement, taking social and environmental requirements into account. However, these benefits will be achieved when performance indicators are properly selected (Perrini & Tencati, 2006). Several sustainable performance measurement frameworks or models are available, like the Sustainable Balanced Scorecard (SBSC), the Performance Prism, Triple Bottom Line (TBL), the Global Reporting Initiative (GRI) guide line, eco-efficiency assessment, ISO 14031, the Dow Jones Sustainability World Index (DJSI World) etc. They offer various approaches for measuring different aspects of business sustainable performance.

Research Method
The research uses a structured interview and a document review methodology to find the different sustainability performance measures used by Ethiopian Airlines. An interview was conducted with a key informant of the airline. Oral interview provides an interactive environment where issues can be clarified and good insights and follow-ups obtained. Relevant documents like annual reports and balanced scorecard were reviewed to find out how, the company measures performance.

The Case of Ethiopian Airlines
The Ethiopian Airlines was found on December 29, 1945 as Ethiopian Air Lines Inc. by Emperor Haile Selassie as a joint venture with American airline and TWA (Trans World Airlines). Initially, they purchased five US Government Surplus C-47 aircrafts (Selamta, the In-Flight Magazine of Ethiopian Airlines, 1996).

The inaugural flight of the Ethiopian Airlines took off from the Addis Ababa Old Airport on Monday April 08, 1946 to Cairo with stopover at Asmara airport for refueling. In 1961, a new east-west service was started across Africa to Monrovia (Liberia) with stopover in Khartoum and Accra (Ghana). Since then EAL (Ethiopian Airlines) has continued its effort to approach more destinations in Africa with its motto "Bringing Africa Together" (Selamta, the In-Flight Magazine of Ethiopian Airlines, 2001).

At present, the airline heads to 58 international destinations and 25 domestic stations. The international destinations are spread across 5 continents from which 37 are in Africa, 6 in Europe, 14 in Middle East and Asia, and 1 in the USA. Currently there are 35 airplanes operated by the airline that include 10 Boeing 767-300,

8 Boeing 757-200, 2 Boeing 757-260 F, 2 Boeing 747F, 2 MD-11F, 5 Boeing 737-700NG, 2 B737-800W, 2 Q400 and 5 Fokker 50 (Annual Report of 2007/08 of Ethiopian Airline, 2010).

The different airline services are passenger transportation, cargo, maintenance, training, personnel secondment and catering services to other airlines. By using the flight simulator the airline trains customers from other airlines and hence generates revenue. The flight simulator is one of the few in Africa and is an invaluable tool in assisting with a high level of flight safety. Only from July 2007 to June 2008, there was an income of 122 million ETB (12.5 Million US dollars) by training customers. For the same period, the airline had income from third party work of a total of 143 million ETB (14.7 million US dollars) from aircraft-, engine- and component maintenance as well as other technical handling for customers. It also provides management and technical assistance to other airlines on secondment basis by using trained and skilled manpower in different areas relative to the airline industry (Annual Report of 2007/08 of Ethiopian Airline, 2010).

One of the main strengths of Ethiopian Airlines in this highly competitive industrial environment is its self-sufficiency in skilled manpower. All the necessary aviation manpower is trained through its aviation academy, which consists of different schools: pilot training school with B757/B767 and B737 NG simulator, aircraft technicians training school, cabin crew (service trainee) and marketing & sales as well as management and finance school.

In order to determine key sustainable performance indicator (KSPI) used by the airline a structured interview was conducted with key personnel of the company. From the interview held with Ato Getachew Tesfa (Public Relation Officer), the review of the 2007/08 report and the balanced scorecard it was found out that the company uses economic performance reporting systems. However, from what the company is doing it seems that there is better awareness of the top management with regard to social and environmental responsibility of the airline.

A. Environmental Performance Indicator

Although always important in the airline industry, the profile of environmental issues at Ethiopian Airlines is on its initial stage as there is no environmental policy and authorized body, except involvement in some environment protection activity. The activities the airline is involved in can be categorized into five issues:

- Noise
- Emissions and fuel efficiency
- Waste, water and materials
- Congestion
- Fly Greener

Noise has historically been considered the most significant environmental impact of aviation. Even though the airline does not take any measurement concerning sound effect to the environment, the airline starts to invest in modern aircrafts which leads to greatly reduced noise levels. The number of people living around Bole affected by the noise is estimated to drop. Nonetheless, noise remains a problem.

The airline has an engine test cell that is made up of sound proof wall in its maintenance workshop. The engine test cell can protect up to 100,000 lb thrust sound.

Emissions
The airline is buying new aircrafts like Boeing 787 Dream liner jets and Airbus A350 XWB which are fuel efficient and reduce the total carbon emissions.

Waste
The airline has got a waste treatment plant in its maintenance premises to avoid and protect the environment from toxic chemicals.

Congestion
In environmental terms, congestion leads to the unnecessary consumption of resources, which results in the increase of emissions and waste contributing to local and global problems. Ethiopian Airlines uses different methods including avoiding various airports that have longer arrival holding delay.

Fly Greener
Ethiopian Airlines acknowledges the environmental impact created by the industry and deforestation. Hence, they launched a fly green program that enables the planting of 7.5 million seedlings of multipurpose and indigenous trees

B. Social Performance Indicator

Although social responsibility is not given to the airline, consideration of social topics started with the establishment of the airline. Even though there is no social performance indicator in the annual report of the company, the airline is involved in various social responsibility activities.

Sports and Social Gathering
Ethiopian Airlines sponsors many sport events. One of them is the Ethiopian GREAT RUN – an annual sporting event with mass jubilation of global participation. The airline pays necessary fees to around 500 staff members to join the rally. At the end of the race Ethiopian Airlines awards premium class tickets for both women and men categories winners. While national teams of different sports are traveling to different countries the airline covers their transportation cost.

The airline is also organized in different social events and sponsors different social gatherings by paying fees to hall or area and lunch. It provides free tickets for those who fly to beauty contest competition.

Health and Medication
Ethiopian Airlines actively participates in the life-saving activities by providing free transportation for patients seeking urgent medical care overseas, for example children with heart problems.

Research and Education
The Ethiopian Airlines sponsors many research seminars, educational symposium and art exhibitions. Free tickets will be given to students who received a scholarship.

Training and Development
Ethiopian Airlines is committed to provide high-quality training to support the safe operation of the business, and specifically, the cultural and personal development of airline employees and the public in general. The training includes leadership development programs to various levels of management and recruitment of students from the general public to its aviation academy in order to enroll them into the different schools. With respect to its employees, the airline introduced comprehensive training programs to empower its employees and create core competencies based on a 'bottom–up' approach.

Charitable Donations
The airline participates in different charitable activities. Some of the donations include money for the construction of hospitals for the children's heart fund of Ethiopia.

C. Economic Performance Indicator

The Ethiopian Airlines uses intensive indicators to measure its economic performance. The indicators are classified into consolidated financial statements, operating statistic measures and safety measures.

Consolidated Financial Statements
The consolidated financial statements consist of total revenue, total expenditure, operating profit and net profit.

Operating Statistic Measure
The operating statistical measure includes performance indicators, fleet (no. of aircraft), production, traffic, employee and safety.
  The performance measurement indicator includes yield (Cents per RTK) that shows cents collected per revenue ton kilometers (RTK). Overall yield per RTK of 2007/08 grew by 10.9% to 595.62 ET Cents from 537.31 ET cents of 2006/2007. Unit Cost (Cents per ATK) measure cents incurred for each available ton per kilometers (ATK). Unit cost per RTK raised by 8.3% to 579.59 ET Cents as compared to the preceding year which was 314.07 ET cents. The increase in overall yield is driven by the increase in passenger yield per revenue passenger kilometers. The breakeven load factor has increased by 6.4 pts due to the fact that the increase in yield is more than the increase in unit costs.
  The Fleet of the airline was enhanced by 6% from 33 in 2006/2007 to 35 in 20007/2008. Destinations also increased by 6.12% from 49 in 2006/2007 to 52 in 20007/2008. Overall capacity including available ton Kms (ATK) raised by 14% from 2,079,917 in 2006/2007 to 2,375,639 in 20007/2008 while available seat kilometers (ASK) increased by 11% to 12,342,519 in 20007/2008. Aircraft departures were incremented by 6.54% from 37,544 in 2006/2007 to 40,002 in 20007/2008. Traffic measured in passengers carried increased by 19.54% to 2,504,646 and passenger seat kilometers grew by 19.86% to 8,681,920. Cargo tones 2007/08 were higher than the preceding year by 11% to 72,758. Employee indicator also tries to show the ratio analysis between performances of the airline against number of employee.

Safety Measures

The airline meets every two years the safety requirements of the IATA operation safety audit. It also correlates with the safety requirements of civil aviation of different destination countries and the USA Federal Aviation Agency (FAA). The aviation academy has got license from Ethiopian Civil Aviation and FAA to operate. The pilot and the ground technicians renew their license accordingly.

D. Communication

The airline communicates its economic performance measures by issuing annual reports to stack holders. However the report is not prepared based on the GRI or ISO 14031 measurement report framework standards as it does not include environmental and social measures.

3 Discussion

Aviation is one of the world's fastest growing industries with demand doubling over the last seven to eight years and predicted to double again in the next ten to twelve years (International Air Transport Association, 2000). Unfortunately, as a sector with major infrastructure requirements and fundamentally reliant on fossil fuel, this growth has resulted in significant environmental impacts. Particular areas of concern include noise, gaseous emissions, water quality and waste.

Some airlines started in the 1990's to measure those environmental and social impacts For example, in 1990 only British Airways and Swissair had produced Corporate Environmental Reports (CERs), whereas by the mid-1990s seven airlines had produced environmental reports of some description. By mid-2001 this number had risen to 17 of which at least 10 companies have started with a continuous program of regular reporting (Dobbie & Hooper, 2000).

Although Ethiopian Airlines has launched significant activities toward sustainability, we can observe that their performance measurement system primarily consists of economic measures. The airline performance report includes financial performance, safety record and statistical operations performances at their best level. However on-time performance which is one of the most important Key Performance Indicators (KPIs) is not included in the economic indicators of the report. The on-time performance stood the test of time for the airline industry. What is so special about this KPI is that it affects all perspectives of the Balanced Scorecard, having financial, customer satisfaction and learning consequences. Both British Airways (BA) and other airlines not only use this KPI, but also make the results public (British Airways, 2000). Most explicitly BA addresses the introduction to the concept of sustainability in the "Social and environmental report 2000" which dedicates a separate section to social indicators of corporate performance. Other airlines are beginning to acknowledge the importance of the "triple bottom line" of environmental, social and economic returns in their report structures, including Air France, Cathay Pacific, Delta, KLM, Lufthansa and SAS; although the degree to which the issues are addressed systematically varies (Dobbie & Hooper, 2000).

Since the 21st century the application of generic guidelines for reporting environmental, social and economic performance within CERs (Corporate Performance Reports) is increasing for the sake of publishing standalone corporate environmental reports. For example, British Airways (BA) was a pilot company in the development of the GRI Sustainability Reporting Guidelines (GRI, 2000) and states that when they prepared their 2000 Report they adhered to these principles. KLM also indicates that they used GRI reporting principles to inform the production of their CER.

Dobbie and Hooper (2001) considered to review the environmental performance indicators (EPIs) from the Corporate Performance Reports (CERs) produced by the airline sector. The review identified the operational areas into namely flight, cabin and ground operations. More than 120 EPIs were used by the airlines to record resource use and consequent waste streams. These EPIs included examples of the types of indicator categorized by the International Standards Organization in ISO 14031 (ISO, 2000), namely:

- Absolute indicators – data representing total quantities of resource use and waste emissions, e.g. fuel use expressed in tones.
- Relative indicators – resource use/emission related to some measure of business service provision (also known as ratio indicators), e.g. liters of fuel per revenue tone kilometer.
- Indexed indicators – link the data to a chosen standard or baseline, e.g. per cent change in carbon dioxide against performance in a base year.
- Aggregated indicators – combine data of the same type from different sources, e.g. carbon dioxide emissions from all transport activities.
- Weighted indicators – attempt to sum different output indicators through the use of conversion factors e.g. SAS's use of a universal environmental impact index.

In general the first step in sustainable performance measurement is the evidence of top management support for environmental improvement and more specifically the 'triple bottom line' agenda. At Ethiopian Airlines it is found that the executives are committed to environmental and social responsibility. However, the airline hesitates to measure sustainability performance and to publish them. As a result the airline lacks to determine a standard performance indicator to measure the social and environmental performance of the company. It is recommendable that the airline is better off to use the GRI sustainable performance measuring and reporting framework in order to bring sustainable development in the airline.

4   Conclusion

This case study research paper tries to find the different sustainability performance measures which are being used by the Ethiopian Airlines. It employs interview and document review research method. Finally it is found that the airline measures and reports only economic performance. However the airline shows in its operation some concerns about social and environmental responsibility as a corporate citizen.

The contribution of this research to sustainable performance management is multilateral. First it shares some experiences of measuring sustainable performance of the airline or their practical involvement in social and environmental responsibility. Second, it tries to help the top management of the airline to understand the level of maturity of their sustainable performance measurement with respect to the rest of the airline or the industry. And finally it recommends acceptable performance indicators.

Acknowledgement

First of all, we would like to express our deepest gratitude to Ethiopian Airlines officials including Ato Getachew Tesfa and others who helped us a lot in providing important information by volunteer for an interview, sacrificing their valuable time. We also wish to thank the organizers of the AAU IS PhD program, who brought us together in course of one unique week of BPM teaching and learning in Addis in February 2010.

References

1. Adams, C., Neely, A.: Using the Performance Prism to Boost the Success of Mergers & Acquisitions, Accenture, New York (2006),
   `http://www.accenture.com/Global/Reserarch_and_Insights/Outlook/By_Alphabet/` Using the Performance Prism to Boost the Success of Mergers & Acquisitions (retrieved April 2010)
2. Air Transport Association of America, Inc. Economics: Annual Revenue and Earnings, selected years (2010), `http://www.airlines.org` (retrieved April 19, 2010)
3. Bansal, P.: The corporate challenges of sustainable development. Academy of Management Executive 16, 2 (2002)
4. British Airways: British Airways Social and Environmental Report 2000, BA, London (2000)
5. Brundtland: Our Common Future, WCED. Oxford University Press, Oxford (1987)
6. Clarkson, M.: A Stakeholder Framework for Analyzing and Evaluating Corporate Social Performance. Academy of Management Review 20(1), 17–92 (1995)
7. Dow Jones Sustainability Indexes (DJSI)-Annual Review (2004),
   `http://www.sustainability-indexes.com/htmle/assessment/review2003.html`
8. Dow Jones Sustainability World Indexes: Corporate sustainability sector overview, 2003 and 2004 (2004)
9. Cyert, R.M., March, J.G.: A Behavioral Theory of the Firm. Prentice-Hall, Englewood Cliffs (1963)
10. Dobbie, L., Hooper, P.D.: Airline Environmental Reporting 2001 Survey, International Air Transport Association, Geneva (2001)
11. Donaldson, T., Preston, L.E.: The Stakeholder Theory of the Corporation: Concept, Evidence, and Implications. The Academy of Management Review 20(1), 65–91 (1995)
12. Elkington, J.: Towards the sustainable corporation: Win-win-win business strategies for Sustainable Corporation: Win-Win-Win Business Strategies for Sustainable Development. California Management Review 36(2) (1994)

13. Elkington, J.: Cannibals with Forks: The Triple Bottom Line of 21st Century Business, Capstone, London (1997)
14. Elkington, J.: Enter the triple bottom line. In: Henriques, A., Richardson, J. (eds.) The Triple Bottom Line – Does It All Add Up?, Earthscan, London, pp. 1–16 (2004)
15. Enquist, B., Johnsson, M., Skålén, P.: Adoption of Corporate Social Responsibility - Incorporating a Stakeholder Perspective Qualitative Research in Accounting & Management 3(3), pp. 188–207 (2006)
16. Environmental and Social Performance, GRI, Boston, USA (2010), http://www.globalreporting.org
17. Epstein, M.J., Roy, M.-J.: Improving sustainability performance: specifying, implementing and measuring key principles. Journal of General Management 29(1), 15–31 (2003)
18. Epstein, M.J.: Making Sustainability Work: Best practices in managing and measuring social and environmental impacts, Greenleaf, Sheffield (2008)
19. Figge, F., Hahn, T., Schaltegger, S., Wagner, M.: The Sustainability Balanced Scorecard – A Tool for Value-Oriented Sustainability Management in Strategy-Focused Organizations. In: Conference Proceedings of the 2001 Eco-Management and Auditing Conference, pp. 83–90. ERP Environment, Shipley (2001)
20. GRI – Global Reporting Initiative: Sustainability Reporting Guidelines, RG 3.0 (2006)
21. GRI – Global Reporting Initiative: Sustainability Reporting Guidelines on Economic, UNEP/SustainAbility (2000) the Global Reporters, SustainAbility Ltd., London (2000)
22. Hailemariam, G., vom Brocke, J.: What is Sustainability in Business Process Management? A Theoretical Framework and its Application in the Public Sector of Ethiopia. In: Proceedings of the First International Workshop on Business Process Management and Sustainability at the 8th Business Process Management Confernece, Hoboken (2010)
23. Hardjono, T.W., van Marrewijk, M.: The Social Dimensions of Business Excellence. Corporate Environmental Strategy 8(3), 223–233 (2001)
24. International Air Transport Association: Environmental Review, IATA, Montreal and Geneva (October 2000)
25. International Standards Organization ISO 14031: 2000 Environmental Management – Environmental Performance Evaluation, European Committee for Standardization, Brussels (2000)
26. ISO (International Organization for Standardization) ISO 14031: Environmental Performance Evaluation - Guideline and general principles, Geneva (1999)
27. Johnson, M.: Stakeholder dialogue for sustainable service, Doctoral dissertation, Karlstad, Karlstad University Studies (2007)
28. Kaplan, R., Norton, D.: Balanced Scorecard: Strategien erfolgreich umsetzen. Schäffer-Poeschel, Stuttgart (1997)
29. Kolk, A.: The Economics of Environmental Management. Prentice Hall, London (2000)
30. Laszlo, C.: The Sustainable Company: How to create lasting value through social and environmental performance. Island Press, Washington DC (2003)
31. Montreal Economic Institute: How to Make the Canadian Airline Industry More Competitive, Economic Note (2006), http://www.iedm.org/uploaded/pdf/nov06_en.pdf (retrieved April 2010)
32. Neely, A., Adams, C.: Perspectives on Performance: the performance prism. In: Handbook of Performance Measurement, Bouine, London (2000)
33. Perrini, F., Tencati, A.: Sustainability and stakeholder management: the need for new corporate performance evaluation and reporting systems. Business Strategy & the Environment 15(5), 296–308 (2006)

34. Schaltegger, S., Burritt, R.: Contemporary environmental accounting: issues, concepts and practice. Greenleaf, Sheffield (2000)
35. Schaltegger, S., Wagner, M.: Integrative management of sustainability performance, measurement and reporting. Int. J. Accounting, Auditing and Performance Evaluation 3(1), 1–19 (2006)
36. Seidel, S., Recker, J., Pimmer, C., vom Brocke, J.: Enablers and Barriers to the Organizational Adoption of Sustainable Business Practices. Paper presented at the 16th Americas Conference on Information Systems (2010)
37. Selamta, the In-Flight Magazine of Ethiopian Airlines, vol. 14(1) (1996)
38. Selamta, the In-Flight Magazine of Ethiopian Airlines, vol. 18(2) (2001)
39. Selamta, the In-Flight Magazine of Ethiopian Airlines, vol. 21(2) (2004)
40. Sauvante, M.: The triple bottom line: A boardroom guide. Director's Monthly 25(11), 1–6 (2002)
41. vom Brocke, J., Sonnenberg, C., Simons, A.: Value-oriented Information Systems Design: The Concept of Potentials Modeling and its Application to Service-oriented Architectures. Business & Information Systems Engineering 1(3), 223–233 (2009)
42. Waddock, S., Bodwell, C.: Total Responsibility Management: The Manual. Greenleaf Publishing, Sheffield (2007)

Process Performance Management as a Basic Concept for Sustainable Business Process Management – Empirical Investigation and Research Agenda

Anne Cleven, Robert Winter, and Felix Wortmann

Institute of Information Management, University of St. Gallen
Müller-Friedbergstrasse 8, CH-9000 St. Gallen
{anne.cleven,robert.winter,felix.wortmann}@unisg.ch

Abstract. *Sustainable development*, the *sustainable organization* and *sustainability strategies* are all terms that are being intensely discussed in the business community just now. Nonetheless, the concept of sustainability still remains vague. Especially its meaning and implications for the field of Business Process Management (BPM) are as of yet by and large unclear. In this paper we set out to advance the understanding of economic sustainability in the context of BPM. We argue that Process Performance Management (PPM) represents a basic approach for establishing and maintaining economic sustainability in BPM. Although the economic dimension of sustainability is commonly believed to have the highest maturity an empirical investigation reveals that organizations are experiencing major difficulties with its implementation—in particular on a process level. Based on the findings, we propose a research agenda for future research efforts in this field.

Keywords: Sustainability, Business Process Management, Performance Management, Research Agenda, Empirical Research.

1 Introduction

Many companies—in particular multinationals with a significant impact on both employment and the economy in general—periodically report their internal and external sustainability results in order to testify their sustainability performance [3, 24, 39]. This reporting habit is achieving growing approval and is adopted by an increasing number of organizations. It is, however, difficult to avoid the impression that a considerable number of companies is only vaguely convinced about their main focus in sustainability concerns [3]. Even after a meanwhile well over 30-year discussion on the concept, the business community does not seem to have agreed upon reasonable and practical approaches for an efficient implementation of sustainability issues [21]. As a consequence companies feel left in suspense and are fishing in murky waters.

Out of the different aspects of sustainability the economic or financial dimension, often termed the baseline of corporate sustainability [39], represents the most widely discussed. Aiming at sustainable profits, high productivity and organizational innovation—in

M. zur Muehlen and J. Su (Eds.): BPM 2010 Workshops, LNBIP 66, pp. 479–488, 2011.

short—at remaining viable in the future, it just now takes on greater significance given the worldwide economic meltdown. Providing an organization with the metrics and measures to survive in a fiercely competitive environment has a long tradition in the field of corporate performance management [8, 28]. Various research efforts from practitioners and researchers alike find expression in a plethora of different approaches, the most famous being the Balanced Scorecard [17]. Only lately, however, have performance measurement and management aspects entered the field of BPM in order to foster corporate sustainability. It is thus not a surprise that a number of surveys and research articles report on severe difficulties companies experience with a successful implementation [26, 37]. Both, measurement and a continuous improvement of business processes appear to be extremely challenging. In a 2009 international survey Wolf et al. revealed that only 29% of the companies polled have always or at least in the majority of cases defined performance measures in place for evaluating the success of their major processes [40]. With 16% the share of organizations always or at least in the majority of cases using performance data to effectively manage their processes is even smaller [40].

We are now in a position to lay out the plan of the article: With this paper we aim at contributing to a better understanding of the concept of economic sustainability in the field of BPM. We argue that—although still young—the concept of PPM provides a valuable backbone for establishing and maintaining sustainable business processes. Based on an empirical study we investigate the maturity of PPM and identify current issues and major challenges. The findings of our study are then translated into a research agenda for potential future efforts in the field.

The remainder of this paper is structured as follows. In the subsequent section, we provide the conceptual background for our research by introducing the concepts of sustainability, BPM, and PPM. We then synthesize the three concepts and propose that PPM may serve as a fundamental approach for achieving sustainability in BPM (section 2). The following section covers the empirical study of PPM (section 3). Section 4 is then devoted to the development of a research agenda for the field of sustainable BPM. The paper concludes with a discussion of limitations and contributions of this research (section 5).

2   Understanding Economic Sustainability in Business Process Management

2.1   Sustainability – Definitional Issues and Scope

The term *sustainability* gained a great popularity with the definition provided by the Brundtland report 'Our Common Future' in 1987. The report defines sustainable development as "development that meets the needs of the present without compromising the ability of future generations to meet their own needs" [7, p. 43]. Based on this definition the term *triple bottom line* was coined, which refers to the three fundamental pillars of corporate sustainability [29]:

- the economic bottom line,
- the social bottom line, and
- the environmental bottom line.

Sustainable organizations search for the "sweet spot" of sustainability, in which injurious social and environmental impacts are minimized, while an adequate rate of return is preserved [23]. Establishing and maintaining this balance, however, represents a major challenge for organizations [11]. Fig. 1 provides an overview of the components of and influences on corporate sustainability.

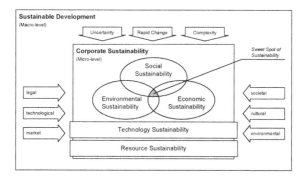

Fig. 1. The Concept of Sustainability [based on 3, 11, 23]

The sustainable development or macro-level of sustainability defines the context in which organizations follow the "process of creating, testing, and maintaining opportunity" [12, p. 390]. Uncontrollable factors like uncertainty, rapid changes in the surroundings, and a high degree of complexity [11] affect an organizations ability to foster its adaptive capabilities and create opportunities just as much as other external influences like legal or societal requirements [3]. For successfully conceptualizing and realizing corporate sustainability it is thus crucial for a company to derive a "consensus on what to sustain" [39, p. 100], analyze external and internal influences, and finally decide on which measures to take and for how long. For the economic perspective in particular, this means translating and making operational "the general concept of sustainability at the level of strategy formulation, process improvement and performance measurement" [14, p. 28]. In the study we discuss later in this paper we investigate the challenges that arise from this claim for the business process context. In order to provide the required background the following section briefly outlines the concept of BPM and research thereof.

2.2 Business Process Management

Analyzing and improving organizational processes has been recognized as key to achieving organizational performance for a considerable time in the business community [2, 22, 32]. BPM as a holistic management concept, however, is rather young and has only emerged around two decades ago. Following Hammer BPM has two "intellectual antecedents" [10, p. 3], the quality management approach Six Sigma and the revolutionary Business Process Reengineering (BPR). While BPR means radical change and is more of a one-time endeavor, BPM takes up the evolutionary character of Total Quality Management and is incremental and continuous in nature [13, 18].

At this point the notion of a (business) process needs some clarification. Within the BPM community a process is commonly described as series of tasks that, executed under certain conditions in a defined temporal and spatial succession, leads to an aspired outcome [5, 35]. Processes are an organization's strategic assets—fundamentally so [31]. They directly contribute to corporate performance by driving operational performance and business process agility [13]. As a consequence, both researchers and practitioners have contributed a huge body of knowledge on how to collaboratively understand, define, model, execute, improve, innovate, and manage business processes and thereby enable an organization to meet its strategic objectives [22, 36]. Across the several approaches that have been developed up to now most agree in that BPM represents an iterative, phased set of activities, often called the BPM lifecycle.

Over recent years, research in the field of BPM has addressed a broad variety of topics like process modeling grammars [25], process-aware information systems, creativity in business processes [30], aspects of strategic alignment as well as issues of people and culture [27]. Despite the high practitioner interest in BPM and its essential meaning for companies' operational and organizational effectiveness, however, there is only little research on performance management aspects in the context of BPM up to now. As reported by a number of studies organizations are in need of a holistic concept for the continuous measurement and improvement of their business processes [20, 37, 40]. The next section briefly introduces the current state in PPM.

2.3 Process Performance Management

Very much like the earlier excitement about the BPM approach [31] the current hype around the management of business process performance is fuelled by an enormous practitioner interest. It is thus not a surprise that the most elaborate conceptions of the notion 'PPM' have so far been provided by practitioners. The *Association of Business Process Management Professionals* (ABPMP), one of the premier non-for-profit practitioner organizations in the field of BPM, defines the measurement of process performance as "the formal, planned monitoring of process execution and the tracing of results to determine the effectiveness and efficiency of the process" [1, p. 22]. The information gained in the measurement process is then "used to make decisions for improving or retiring existing processes and/or introducing new processes in order to meet the strategic objectives of the organization" [1, p. 22]. It becomes obvious from this definition that PPM consists of two major building blocks: The measurement and the improvement of business process performance. Concepts that have been identified as contributing to either of the two components include defining performance metrics, monitoring, controlling, and simulating processes, aligning process and enterprise performance, and a number of other concepts [19].

The subsequent section illuminates how PPM and sustainability are related, and in which way PPM may support in particular the economic perspective of sustainability.

2.4   On the Use of PPM for Sustainable BPM

For sustainability holds true what is valid for any other business initiative: "If you can't measure it, you can't manage it" [23, p. 10]. Traditional performance management approaches, however, tend to overemphasize the measurement of process outcomes and focus primarily on financial metrics such as profitability, liquidity, and solvency ratios. The same applies for sustainability efforts: Pojasek states that it is still a very common belief among organizations that measuring sustainability results provides "a strong indication of […] sustainability performance" [24, p. 78]. In order to measure performance in an immediate and direct way, however, reflecting what, where, and how work is actually accomplished, measurement must not be limited to *process results*, but should also and in particular focus on the effectiveness, efficiency and quality of *process execution* itself.

If we now recall a) the definition of corporate economic sustainability as the pursuit of remaining viable in the future and b) the common perception of business processes as the core asset for value creation it appears palpable to reach for PPM as a suitable means to leverage business processes for corporate sustainability. As has been pointed out earlier in this paper, however, companies are struggling with the implementation of effective PPM approaches. The subsequently described study aims at identifying major challenges in order to both achieve a deeper understanding of the problem situation and reveal opportunities for future research.

3   Empirical Investigation

3.1   Study Objectives and Data Collection

The study was driven by the following research questions (RQ):

RQ 1   *What are the essential requirements for PPM?*
RQ 2   *Are there groups of organizations that reside in similar stages of PPM maturity and how are these stages characterized?*

In order to address these questions we designed a questionnaire-based survey. The questionnaire was distributed at a practitioner event on Business Intelligence (BI) and Business Analytics held in October 2009. The participants were specialists and executives working on both the IT and the business side, thus having the required knowledge and information to answer the questions without any difficulty [4]. The questionnaire was designed to assess the current state of PPM in the participating organizations. Respondents were asked to indicate the degree of realization for each item using a five-tiered Likert scale. The questionnaire was pretested, both on an individual item level in early phases and as a whole before finally being distributed [4].

A total of 49 questionnaires were returned. If a data set was incomplete, i.e. if one or more than one of the 21 items was missing, the questionnaire was disregarded. On the basis of this criterion, 45 questionnaires were selected for further analysis. The interviewed organizations are primarily large and medium-sized companies from the

German-speaking countries. 60% have more than 1000 employees and another 22% have more than 100 employees. The sectors mainly represented were professional services (40%), banking, finance and insurance (29%), high tech (11%) manufacturing and consumer goods (7%), media and telecommunication (5%), and others (8%).

3.2 Data Analysis

The data analysis starts with an exploratory factor analysis (EFA) which serves the purpose of developing a deeper understanding of the current problem situation. In general, EFA serves the identification of a number of important and mutually independent factors from a multiplicity of contingent variables [6]. Subsequently, the question of whether there are common situations which feature the same characteristics can be tackled using cluster analysis. A cluster analysis serves the purpose of partitioning a set of observations into subsets that are homogeneous within and heterogeneous amongst them [16].

The EFA was performed on a data set of 21 items. The measure of sampling adequacy (MSA, "Kaiser-Meyer-Olkin criterion") for the data set is 0.777. MSA represents an indicator for the extent to which the input variables belong together and provides information on whether a factor analysis can reasonably be performed or not. Kaiser and Rice appraise a value of 0.7 or more as "reasonable", i.e. the data set is considered to be appropriate for applying EFA [16, 33]. Five factors that jointly explain about 75.6% of the total variance were extracted by means of principal component analysis. Both the Kaiser criterion and the scree plot point to this solution. The resulting component matrix was rotated using the Varimax method with Kaiser normalization in order to improve the interpretability of the items' assignment to the factors [15]. The rotated component matrix is depicted in Table 1.

Table 1. Factor Loadings

Questionnaire Items	Factors				
	1	2	3	4	5
Adherence to schedules is measured for processes.	.834	.304	.059	.165	.102
Capacity utilization is measured for processes.	.787	.345	.332	.202	.083
Quality is measured for processes.	.758	.209	.228	.202	.190
Process resource utilisation is measured.	.735	.395	.069	.060	.059
Process costs are measured.	.728	.362	.305	.067	-.030
Process cycle times are measured.	.723	.221	.324	.331	.190
The plan-do-check-act (PDCA) cycle is applied for PPM.	.543	.168	.214	.415	.308
Process flows are consistent and transparent beyond functional borders.	.239	.796	.284	.045	.063
Processes have defined process officers.	.203	.765	.057	.105	.044
Processes are consistently documented and/or modelled.	.321	.758	-.062	.180	.216
Process flows are consistent and transparent beyond system borders.	.404	.718	.358	-.047	.167
Process orientation is a central paradigm.	.289	.660	-.110	.220	.046
PPM also covers non-financial measures.	.034	-.047	.843	.280	-.121
PPM is deployed for purchasing processes.	.282	.156	.797	.158	.003
PPM is deployed for production processes.	.260	-.064	.714	.272	.249
PPM is deployed for sales processes.	.268	.394	.702	.008	.137
Defined BI governance responsibilities and processes are in place.	.033	.270	.134	.775	.094
PPM is part of the enterprise-wide Balanced Score Card (BSC).	.392	-.031	.387	.750	-.020
PPM is part of the Corporate Performance Management (CPM).	.297	.153	.469	.613	.102
A central integrated data base is in place (e.g., an Enterprise DWH).	.009	.125	.018	.107	.907
Data quality is consistently high.	.279	.128	.075	.023	.814

In order to identify organizations with similar PPM maturity stages, cluster analysis is used. The cluster analysis is based on factor scores being calculated using the regression method [34]. The Ward fusion algorithm and the squared Euclidean distance are applied for clustering, as this combination finds very good partitions resulting in an appropriate number of clusters and similar number of observations in each cluster [9, 38]. On the basis of the dendrogram, i.e. the graphical representation of the fusion process and the cluster sizes the final number of clusters was defined [9]. Table 2 contains the arithmetic means of the factor scores for each of the four clusters.

Table 2. Arithmetic Means of Factors per Cluster

Cluster	n	F1	F2	F3	F4	F5
Cluster 1	11	-0.264	-0.2140	.206-0	.559	-1.159
Cluster 2	16	-0.2340	.301-0	.069-0	.6050	.702
Cluster 3	11	0.743	-0.626	-0.5990	.5800	.056
Cluster 4	7	-0.2200	.6320	.7751	.3510	.127

3.3 Findings and Interpretation

The results from the EFA allow the conclusion that essential factors for PPM implementations require both a well-established BPM culture and sufficient analytical capabilities for an appropriate performance measurement and improvement.

The following table shows an interpretation of fundamental factors by means of five distinct constructs established by the factor analysis:

Table 3. Factor Interpretation

Factor 1 Broad, PDCA-based use of PPM measures	Factor 2 BPM maturity	Factor 3 PPM process diffusion	Factor 4 BI-enabled, integrated PPM	Factor 5 High quality information base
Seven variables were found to have significant impact on the first factor. All of the items are metric-related and address two questions: a) what is measured in the context of PPM (which key performance indicators (KPIs) are used), and b) how is the measurement accomplished. The plan-do-check-act (PDCA) cycle is applied for the KPI manage-ment.	All five directly BPM-related items were found to have significant impact on the second factor, accounting for the degree of BPM maturity. Organizations having a high BPM maturity, advocate process orientation as a central organizational paradigm, foster process modelling and clear process responsibilities thereby assuring consistent process flows across both organizations and systems.	Another four items load high on the third factor, representing PPM process diffusion. This factor expresses the degree of KPI usage in core business processes (covering procurement, production and sales Activities). Furthermore this factor strengthens the importance of non-financial measures.	Three items load on the fourth factor. The factor indicates well-defined, well-coor-dinated processes and management approaches in performance management as well as in BI. In these companies PPM is part of an integrated and comprehensive management approach i.e. BSC or CPM. To enable concepts like BSC or CPM defined BI governance responsibilities and processes are in place.	Two variables are loading on the fifth factor, which we named high quality information base. According to our analysis, companies having a high quality information base build upon a central integrated data store (e.g., an Enterprise DWH) thereby assuring consistently high (analytical) data quality across the organization.

The cluster analysis yielded four discrete clusters that can be interpreted as follows:

Table 4. Cluster Interpretation

Cluster 1 PPM beginner	Cluster 2 Information Quality- driven BPM traditionalist	Cluster 3 KPI enthusiasts	Cluster 4 PPM expert
The first cluster shows a poor performance regarding four of the five factors. Only PPM process diffusion, i.e. the degree of KPI usage in core business processes is at an above average level. Organizations in this cluster show a significant lack of performance with respect to aggregated high quality information. Neither from a BI nor from a BPM perspective, are concepts in place that could be leveraged as a basis for PPM.	The second cluster shows positive performance in regards to BPM and information quality. BPM as well as a good information quality form a solid basis for PPM. Nevertheless, all three PPM related factors show low performance. Compa-nies of this cluster specifically lack well-defined, well-coordin-ated processes and management approaches in performance management and BI.	The third cluster is characterized by high BI and low BPM performance. The extend to which KPIs are employed can be described as very ambiguous. Organizations in this cluster on the one hand have a huge number of different measures in place. On the other side only a very small number of business processes are actually being measured.	Companies of the fourth cluster show a high performance across four of the five factors. The only low performing factor is factor one: In contrast to the KPI enthusiasts, PPM experts apply PPM to a significant number of their business processes building based upon a consistent set of limited metrics.

4 Research Agenda

Neither of the three fields that have been introduced and discussed in the course of this paper—BPM, sustainability, and PPM—is actually new and untouched or heavily under-researched. Nonetheless, especially the appropriate interplay of these concepts and an efficient implementation still appears highly challenging. Drawing from our knowledge of the fields and the findings from the study we propose the following research questions as intriguing for future research efforts and hope to encourage further researchers to investigate this area.

RQ 1 *How do successful organizations use the outcome of process performance measurement for improvement and change initiatives?*

RQ 2 *How can the worth of disseminating the PPM approach from the core processes to all of an organization's processes be assessed?*

RQ 3 *How are PPM approaches aligned with other strategic performance management and sustainability initiatives?*

RQ 4 *How does PPM influence the motivation of the workforce?*

RQ 5 *How can social and ecological metrics be integrated into PPM?*

5 Conclusion

Our paper was motivated by the pursuit to better understand the concept of sustainability in the context of BPM. It is our strong belief that PPM adds value to the field of BPM in that it aims at maintaining the worth of processes as an organization's essential assets. We are convinced that this area contains highly interesting research opportunities for both information systems and organizational researchers some of which have been outlined herein.

References

1. ABPMP: Guide to the Business Process Management Common Body of Knowledge (2009), http://www.abpmp.org
2. Armistead, C., Pritchard, J.-P., Machin, S.: Strategic Business Process Management for Organizational Effectiveness. Long Range Plan. 32(1), 96–106 (1999)
3. Baumgartner, R.J., Ebner, D.: Corporate Sustainability Strategies: Sustainability Profiles and Maturity Levels. Sustain. Dev. 18(2), 76–89 (2010)
4. Czaja, R., Blair, J.: Designing Surveys - A Guide to Decisions and Procedures. Pine Forge Press, Thousand Oaks (1996)
5. Davenport, T.H.: Process Innovation. In: Reengineering Work Through Information Technology. Harvard Business School Press, USA (1993)
6. de Winter, J.C.F., Dodou, D., Wieringa, P.A.: Exploratory Factor Analysis With Small Sample Sizes. Multivar. Behav. Res. 44, 147–181 (2009)
7. Development, W.C.o.E.a.: Our Common Future. Oxford University Press, Oxford (1991)
8. Folan, P., Browne, J.: A Review of Performance Measurement: Towards Performance Management. Comp. in Ind. 56, 663–680 (2005)
9. Hair, J.F.J., Black, W.C., Babin, B.J., Anderson, R.E., Tatham, R.L.: Multivariate Data Analysis. Pearson Prentice Hall, Upper Saddle River (2006)
10. Hammer, M.: What Is Business Process Management? In: Rosemann, M., vom Brocke, J. (eds.) Business Process Management Handbook, pp. 3–16. Springer, Heidelberg (2010)
11. Hessami, A.G., Hus, F., Jahankhani, H.: A Systems Framework for Sustainability. In: Hessami, A.G., Hus, F., Jahankhani, H. (eds.) Communications in Computer and Information Science. Global Security, Safety, and Sustainability, pp. 76–94. Springer, Heidelberg (2009)
12. Holling, C.S.: Understanding the Complexity of Economic, Ecological, and Social Systems. Ecosyst. 4(5), 390–405 (2001)
13. Hung, R.Y.-Y.: Business Process Management as Competitive Advantage: A Review and Empirical Study. Total Qual. Manag. & Bus. Excell. 17(1), 21–40 (2006)
14. Jones, N.: Building Economic Sustainability - Leading the Pack. Chart. Account. J. 88(2), 28–29 (2009)
15. Kaiser, H.F.: The Varimax Criterion for Analytic Rotation in Factor Analysis. Psychometrika 23(3), 187–200 (1958)
16. Kaiser, H.F., Rice, J.: Little Jiffy, Mark IV. Educ. Psychol. Meas. 34(1), 111–117 (1974)
17. Kaplan, R.S., Norton, D.R.: The Balanced Scorecard: Measures That Drive Performance. Harvard Bus. Rev. 83(7/8), 172–180 (2005)
18. Ko, R.K.L., Lee, S.S.G., Lee, E.W.: Business Process Management (BPM) Standards: A Survey. Bus. Process Manag. J. 15(5), 744–791 (2009)
19. Kueng, P.: Process Performance Measurement System: A Tool to Support Process-Based Organizations. Total Qual. Manag. 11(1), 67–85 (2000)
20. Kueng, P., Krahn, A.: Building a Process Performance Measurement System - Some Early Experiences. Journal of Scientific and Industrial Research 58(3/4), 149–159 (1999)
21. Labuschagne, C., Brent, A.C., van Erck, R.P.G.: Assessing the Sustainability Performances of Industries. J. Clean. Prod. 13(4), 373–385 (2005)
22. Lee, R.G., Dale, B.G.: Business Process Management – A Review and Evaluation. Bus. Process Manag. J. 4(3), 214–225 (1998)
23. Nguyen, D.K., Slater, S.F.: Hitting the Sustainability Sweet Spot: Having It All. J. Bus. Strateg. 31(3), 5–11 (2010)

24. Pojasek, R.B.: Using leading indicators to drive sustainability performance. Environ. Qual. Manag. 18(4), 87–93 (2009)
25. Recker, J.: Understanding Process Modelling Grammar Continuance: A Study of the Consequences of Representational Capabilities. Springer, Heidelberg (2008)
26. Robson, I.: From Process Measurement to Performance Improvement. Bus. Process Manag. J. 10(5), 510–521 (2004)
27. Rosemann, M., De Bruin, T., Power, B.: BPM Maturity. In: Jeston, J., Nelis, J. (eds.) Business Process Management: Practical Guidelines to Successful Implementations, pp. 299–315. Elsevier, Oxford (2006)
28. Saltmarshe, D., Ireland, J.M., McGregor, A.: The Performance Framework: A Systems Approach to Understanding Performance Management. Public Admin. and Dev. 23(5), 445–456 (2003)
29. Savitz, A., Weber, K.: The Triple Bottom Line: How Today's Best-Run Companies Are Achieving Economic, Social and Environmental Success – and How You Can Too. John Wiley & Sons, San Francisco (2006)
30. Seidel, S., Müller-Wienbergen, F., Karow, M., Rosemann, M.: Toward the Concept of Pockets of Creativity in Business Processes. In: 17th European Conference on Information Systems (ECIS 2009), Verona, Italy (2009)
31. Smart, P.A., Maddern, H., Maull, R.S.: Understanding Business Process Management: Implications for Theory and Practice. Br. J. Manag. 20(4), 491–507 (2009)
32. Smith, H., Fingar, P.: Business Process Management – The Third Wave. Meghan-Kiffer Press, Tampa (2003)
33. Stewart, D.W.: The Application and Misapplication of Factor Analysis in Marketing Research. J. Mark. Res. 18(1), 51–62 (1981)
34. Thompson, B.: Exploratory and Confirmatory Factor Analysis: Understanding Concepts and Applications. American Psychological Association, Washington, DC (2004)
35. van der Aalst, W., van Hee, K.: Workflow Management: Models, Methods, and Systems. The MIT Press, USA (2002)
36. van der Aalst, W.M.P., ter Hofstede, A.H.M., Weske, W.: Business Process Management: A Survey. In: van der Aalst, W.M.P., ter Hofstede, A.H.M., Weske, W. (eds.) BPM 2003. LNCS, vol. 2678, pp. 1611–3349. Springer, Heidelberg (2003)
37. Vergidis, K., Turner, C.J., Tiwari, A.: Business Process Perspectives: Theoretical Developments vs. Real-world Practice. Int. J. Prod. Econ. 114(1), 91–104 (2008)
38. Ward Jr, J.H.: Hierarchical Grouping to Optimize an Objective Function. J. Am. Stat. Assoc. 58(301), 236–244 (1963)
39. Wikström, P.-A.: Sustainability and organizational activities - three approaches. Sustain. Dev. 18(2), 99–107 (2010)
40. Wolf, C., Harmon, P.: The State of Business Process Management 2010. BP Trends, pp. 1–52 (February 2010)

What Is Sustainability in Business Process Management? A Theoretical Framework and Its Application in the Public Sector of Ethiopia

Getachew Hailemariam[1] and Jan vom Brocke[2]

[1] Ababa University, Ethiopia
getachew.mengesha@gmail.com
[2] University of Liechtenstein,
Martin Hilti Chair of Business Process Management,
Institute of Information Systems, Principality of Liechtenstein
jan.vom.brocke@uni.li

Abstract. Modern Business Process Management (BPM) is a comprehensive approach for improving business performance by managing end-to-end business processes. It tends to embrace both, radical redesign and continual improvement of business processes. While a plethora of methods for BPM exist, single BPM initiatives still often struggle to prove successful in practice. Hence, with this study we set out to examine the concept of BPM success. We draw from a stakeholder theory and argue that BPM initiatives need to take the perspective of multiple stakeholders (e. g. managers, shareholders, employees) into account in order to prove successful. We evaluate our model within the case of a large scale BPM project in the Ethiopian public sector. Ethiopia is one of the countries that have recognized the need for change in the public sector and have tried to adopt BPM models as a viable radical change instrument. The implementation did show improvement, yet, it remains doubtful how far the initiative can be successfully evaluated. First we present results from applying our BPM sustainability framework and subsequently outline opportunities for future research.

Keywords: BPM, BPR, CSRP, SDI, sustainability, stakeholder theory, public sector.

1 Introduction

Business Process Management (BPM) can be perceived as a comprehensive approach for improving business performance by managing end-to-end business processes. According to Hammer (2010) two former approaches can be identified: (a) statistical process control which leads to modern quality movement and (b) Business Process Reengineering (BPR) (Hammer, 1993). While the quality movement focuses on continuous improvement of process execution, business process reengineering particularly looks at performance improvement arising from radical changes of the structure of business processes (Hammer, 2010). Over the last decade, however, these

M. zur Muehlen and J. Su (Eds.): BPM 2010 Workshops, LNBIP 66, pp. 489–500, 2011.

two approaches of process performance improvement have gradually merged, resulting in modern business process management – an integrated system for managing business performance by managing end-to-end business processes.

BPM is a highly contested tool when it comes to the improvement of organizational performance (Buchanan & Huczynski, 2004). It is expected to cover a wide range of other performance improvement initiatives, including contemporary challenges such as globalization, compliance or continuity. However, BPM is a complex management practice that many organizations find difficult to implement and to progress to a higher stage of maturity (Rosemann & vom Brocke, 2010). A recent study among CIO's conduced by Gartner (2009) confirmed the significance of BPM with identifying the top issue (for the fifth year in a row) as improving business processes. For BPM practitioners', therefore, one concern is that the complexity of BPM may result in the inability of organizations to achieve the desired benefits. Hence, also Hammer (2010) stated that "despite its elegance and power, many organizations have experienced difficulties implementing processes and process management".

The situation outlined can particularly be observed in Ethiopia. It is one of the countries that have recognized the need for change in the public sector and tried to adopt BPR as a viable radical change instrument. Since the current Ethiopian People Democratic Revolutionary Front (EPDRF) government has seized power the public sector has been going through a series of reform processes (Mengesha & Common 2007). According to Clapham (1995, as cited by Mengesha & Common, 2007) when the current (EPDRF) government has seized and consolidated power it acknowledged deep institutional constraints on basic functions such as policy making, service delivery and regulations.

In recognition of these constraints, the government initiated in 1996 a comprehensive Civil Service Reform Program (CSRP), marking the second phase of the reform (Mengesha & Common 2007). Considering BPR as a key instrument in the CSRP package pilot process reengineering studies were conducted in selected government agencies. Starting from 2005 also prototype implementations have been realized. Successful results and positive changes have been reported from the implementation of BPR in government offices such as the Ministry of Trade and Industry or the Immigration and Consular Authority. Later likewise positive outcomes could be reported from a large scale implementation of BPR at the Ministry of Inland Revenue (Mengesha & Common, 2007; Walta, 2009).

According to Walta (2009) public organizations are found to be at different stages regarding the initiation and implementation of BPR. Some institutions have already implemented BPR in its full scale, while others only have finalized studies yet and are heading towards the implementation. Others have finished a situational analysis (first level study) and are moving towards the next stages, while some are still starting with preliminary investigations. Virtually all organizations at federal and regional government level are trying these days to implement BPR. The interview held with the senior BPR expert from the Federal Ministry of Capacity Building on April 22, 2010 revealed that all federal government institutions are required to complete their BPR implementation by August 2010 and are supposed to start the balanced score card implementation by September 2010.

During the implementation of BPR in Ethiopians public institutions various opinions and critiques had been observed (Clapham, 1995). According to a newsletter from Ethiopia-BPR (2009) BPR is resulting in massive layoffs among federal and regional institutions which are likely to result in a catastrophic crisis, especially in increasing unemployment rates and chronic inflation. Regardless of the reported positive effects as well as the downsides of BPR, the ongoing change initiatives can be considered as the first rigorous and systematic attempt to improve the performance of public institutions since their establishment 100 years ago. While some encouraging performance improvements of public organizations have been reported, many researchers are yet skeptical about the sustainability of these achieved positive changes (Chanie, 2001; Mengesha & Common, 2007).

Hence, with our research we commence investigating the construct of "sustainability" in business process improvement projects. For this purpose, we draw from stakeholder theory (e. g. Rappaport, 1986) to develop a framework and then use the case of the Ethiopian public sector as a case study to evaluate our results. That being said, we need to consider potential differences of the meaning when referring to the terms BPR and BPM. Admittedly, we recognize the BPR initiative as a good example for our BPM-related study mainly for two reasons: (a) to follow the approach of Hammer that BPR is actually a part of BPM; and (b) since the Ethiopian government may have followed a different terminology they do not explicitly exclude measures of continuous process improvements from their initiatives.

This study tries to address two essential questions:

(1) How can sustainability of a BPM initiative be conceptualized in general?
(2) How specific can the BPR initiative of the Ethiopian public sector be assessed according to this conceptualization?

According to our research approach the remainder of this paper is structured as follows: First we analyze stakeholder-theory as the potential foundation for conceptualizing sustainability in BPM. Subsequently we present a BPM sustainability framework that puts emphasis on balancing the viewpoints of diverse stakeholders within a BPM initiative. On the basis of interview results, conducted with officials of the project, we then use our model to assess the sustainability of the BPR initiative in the Ethiopian public sector. Considering our research to be preliminary, we then outline future research following up on our findings. We conclude with a discussion and a short summary of our work.

2   Theoretical Framework – A Stakeholder-Oriented View to Sustainability

There are different approaches to the concept of sustainability (Watson, Boudreau and Chen, 2010; Seidel, Recker, Pimmer and vom Brocke, 2010). In this study, we develop an approach that is based on a stakeholder theory. Hence, we recognize a BPM initiative sustainable if it succeeds in obtaining long termed support of all involved stakeholders. This approach is informed by the concept of value-orientation in information systems (vom Brocke, Sonnenberg & Simons, 2009) and business process management (vom Brocke, Recker & Mendling, 2010) and will be further elaborated in the following section:

The concept of stakeholder-oriented thinking can be compared to the shareholder-oriented thinking. Initially, value-based management only aimed at creating value for investors and shareholders of a firm (e.g. Rappaport, 1986). However, focusing only on shareholder interests disregards other stakeholders, who also have a vested interest in the wellbeing of an organization. Freeman (1984) argues that a sustainable increase of a firm's value will not be possible unless the interests of all relevant (primary) stakeholders are addressed. This perception led to the development of more holistic, multi-dimensional performance measurement systems (cf. Gary, 2002, p. 4) such as the balanced score card proposed by Kaplan and Norton (1991). In particular, a holistic value-based management allows for value pluralism, what we perceive as vital for reaching sustainable performance improvements.

Stakeholder thinking is based on the coalition theory of Cyert & March (1963). Cyert and March (1963) considered the firm as a coalition of individuals or groups of individuals such as management, employees, customers, owners and government. They all pursue individual goals but are at the same time willing to contribute to the firm as long as their contribution yields appropriate returns for each of them. Thereby each partner of the coalition is giving a certain contribution while expecting a certain benefit for acting as an incentive for the partner to engage in the coalition. A conceptual framework related to this theory is shown in fig. 1.

Fig. 1. Elements of a BPM sustainability framework

The coalition theory also reflects on the preservation of the coalition. Two elements are thereby important: (a) the coalition can only survive given that all stakeholders pay in; and (b) stakeholders only continue with the coalition as long as they expect the medium-term payback to be greater than their contribution. As a matter of fact, the management of companies needs to regard the intention of all stakeholders in order to sustain. Consequently, we conclude that for a process improvement initiative to be sustainable, the perspectives of all stakeholders need to be taken into account.

When applying the BPM sustainability framework we have to consider the specific organizational context. Accordingly, the stakeholders and incentives displayed in fig. 1 may serve well as a starting point but need to be adapted according to specific context factors of a BPM initiative. Therefore, in order to make sure that a measure is sustainable, we can conclude to (a) identify all stakeholders affected by this measure and then (b) make sure each of them supports the initiative in a medium to long-term thinking. To demonstrate and evaluate this approach, we studied the case of the Ethiopian public sector according to our model.

3 Applying the Framework – The Case of the Ethiopian Public Sector BPR-Initiative

3.1 Adopting the Framework

Using our model as a sensitizing device, an attempt has been made to collect preliminary primary and secondary data for further validation. First on April 22, 2010 an interview was conducted with the civil service reform expert of the Ministry of Capacity Building, an organization in charge of leading the Business Process Reengineering process throughout Ethiopia. Second, relevant information has been extracted from the study conducted by Mengesha and Common (2007). Third, a reform status report produced by the Revenue and Custom Authority discussing BPR implementation, lessons learnt and the way forward, from February 2010 has been used as a good source of data. (Ethiopia 2010) As a result, a first version of a BPM sustainability framework for Ethiopia has been designed. The model is displayed in fig. 2.

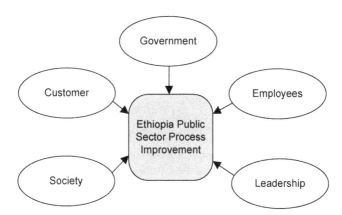

Fig. 2. BPM sustainability framework for the BPR initiative in the Ethiopia public sector

The model has been used to further assess the potential sustainability of the BPR initiative in Ethiopia. That way two objectives could be followed, namely (a) evaluating our model and (b) learning about the specific situation in Ethiopia. In the following, we first briefly outline the BPR approach and then apply our model to assess potential sustainability.

3.2 The BPR Approach in Ethiopia

The information obtained through the interview and from the BPR implementation progress report showed that the BPR processes of all public institution in Ethiopia followed the steps suggested by Hammer and Champy (1993) and Davenport and Short (1990). Some institutions started the reform by first addressing macro issues. For instance the reform carried out at the Ministry of Industry and Trade and at Revenue and Custom Authority was kind of a policy reform. Before the BPR implementation, Revenue and Custom Authority used to be two autonomous organizations, performing duplicate tasks. Realizing the similarity of goals and purposes of these two agencies the decision was made to merge them. The move was legitimized by the House of Representatives in July 15, 2008 and enacted by proclamation no 587/2000. In agreement with the priority given by the government, the Revenue and Customs Authority is one of the 15 organizations selected as a candidate for process change. Following this decision, the reform was planned and moved forward with an initial situational analysis. The analysis report provided baseline information for the subsequent stages.

Immediately after the situational analysis was finalized, orientation and training sessions have been conducted. Initial trainings were scheduled for employees working at various management levels. At a later date the employees of the lower level were trained and integrated. Subsequent needed based trainings were held for change management work teams. Moreover, experience sharing programs and visits were carried out extensively. This process appears to have prepared the environment for change. Figure 3 shows the Business Process Reengineering Model used by Revenue and Custom Authority.

Virtually all public organizations have followed similar business process models. In addition to the core steps cited in figure 3, the following activities have been carried out as well:

- Consideration of best practices of other institutions,
- Development of process working manual,
- Development of service delivery charts,
- Development of work team charts,
- Job and structure development and
- Compensation and benefit schemes development.

Currently, the Revenue and Custom Authority is heading towards introducing the Balanced Score Card (BSC) system. Apart from performance measurement, also an appropriate process infrastructure is known as a major enabler of process change (1). The report produced by Revenue and Custom Authority, which is mentioned as an exemplary institution in implementing change, revealed slow progress of installing proper information and communication technology (ICT) to augment and sustain the process change.

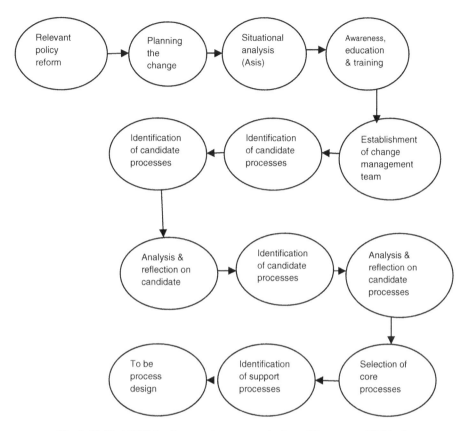

Fig. 3. Unified BPR implementation process in the public sector of Ethiopia

3.3   Assessment of the Expected Sustainability of the Approach

Against the background of this description, we now further analyze the expected sustainability of the Ethiopian approach on BPR. We refer to each identified stakeholder:

(a) Government
The interview results revealed that BPR implementation is a decision on a high level, and is an initiative of the government. Starting from 1994 five civil service reform programs have been initiated including: expenditure management and control, human resource management, service delivery improvement, ethics and top management development programs. From the recited programs, service delivery improvement (SDI) was given a priority. At the initial stage of the SDI implementation Quick WINS (quick ways of implementing new systems) was used as a tool to offer a fast response to the improvement program. This initiative has brought some improvements to many institutions, however it was not substantial. The government believed that public sectors in countries like Ethiopia require radical change. Therefore, BPR was taken as a tool with the prime motive of making the breakthrough of changes in time,

quality, speed and cost. Economic sectors like Ministry of Agriculture, Ministry of Revenue and Ministry of Finance and Economic Development were major focus areas and these institutions took the initiative to implement BPR.

The government decided that all of the 101 institutions should complete their BPR implementation by the end of 2002 Ethiopian Calendar (End of August 2010 G.C) and should start with the Balanced Score Card (BSC) by the year 2003 E.C (September 2010 G.C.). For monitoring and evaluation purposes the government entrusted the responsibility of overseeing the progress of BPR across the board to the Ministry of Capacity Building. Each government institution is supposed to start with the BSC after the assurance of the BPR implementation quality by the team. Since BPR has become the core agenda and directive of the government, leaders of public institutions are highly involved. It appears that the government does not tolerate any failure, therefore, all institutions are expected to implement BPR successfully.

Once the BPR implementations are finalized across all public institutions, the government is planning to focus on: ensuring continuous improvement, implementing an integrated strategic planning, implementing measurement and compensation mechanism – BSC, complementing BPR with TQM and ISO and ensuring organizational transformation.

Apparently BPR has a strong support and commitment of the current government. As long as the current government remains in power the business process reform program is expected to sustain. Ethiopia is a nation heading towards building a culture of democracy. There are some political parties competing for power. The election campaign held in May 2005 has shown that strong oppositional political parties are being created. In May 2010 the fourth national election will be held. Although it appears rather unlikely that one of the opposition parties win the election, the change process will certainly be discontinued if the current government is replaced.

(b) Leadership
As already stated, BPR is a top down initiative which requires high level involvement and top management commitment of public institutions. The survey conducted by Mengesha and Common (2007) revealed that the active involvement of managers at all level was one of the reasons for the successful initiation and implementation of BPR at the Ministry of Industry and Trade. All public institution leaders are considering BPR as their core activity. Still the personal commitment and convictions of the leaders across all levels is highly required. During the interviews held with experts of the Ministry of Capacity Building we learned that change in institutional leadership including promotion or transfer affects the change processes for various reasons. The experts added that due to change in leadership the reform achieved in some institution may be seen as falling behind.

(c) Employees
The study conducted by Mengesha and Common (2007) showed that at least at a micro-level the success of BPR implementation, reported by the Ministry of Industry and Trade, was partly driven by a desire for change of concerned stakeholders (management, clients, staff and political executives). Employees, one of the stakeholder categories, were convinced of and believed in the change and have actively been involved in the change process. The survey from Mengesha and

Common (2007) about MOTI (Ministry of Industry and Trade) revealed that about 67% of employees responded that the implemented reform at their respective work place brought positive change into their duty. Moreover, the same study reported that employees could have improved further if the management had put in place appropriate benefits and incentive schemes. The reform carried out at the Revenue and Customs Authority has shown improvement regarding the motivation of employee by introducing appropriate compensation and benefit scheme in accordance with the performed process changes. A survey is required to see whether all public organization, capable of implementing process change, have made new compensation plans.

Further study is required to determine employee's behavioral readiness towards customer's orientation, employees understanding of end to end process management and its goals, employee's ability to work in teams, employees' capacity to manage their task and cultural changes at the work place, needed to ensure the sustainability of process change.

(d) Customers

Service users' reaction to change and their level of satisfaction and support is considered to be valuable for the sustainability of process change. Process users may be either internal or external. Periodic surveys' and sound complaint gathering and handling techniques provide valid information regarding customer's reaction. The study conducted at the Ministry of Trade and Industry revealed that 68% of customers who used services of the evaluated organization for more than one year have observed positive changes and improvements after the implementation of process change (Mengesha & Common, 2007). Moreover, the report written by the Revenue and Customs Authority showed similar result.

(e) Society

Community's perception and good understanding of the intent of process change contributes to the sustainability of the process. Opinion surveys of the general public will provide indicators regarding the support of the community. Private and foreign mass media have been seen reporting the negative consequences of the business process reform. They try to present some evidence concerning the layoffs caused by the BPR initiative and underscore that the reform is politically motivated. Sound information dissemination mechanisms create a good public impression and eventually contribute to the sustainability of the process change.

The preliminary information obtained regarding the involvement, concern and role of some of the key stakeholders show a mixed result. Rigors study is required to reach a valid conclusion. Apparently, the reform will either backslid or interrupted unless key stakeholders recognize and support it.

3.4 Discussion of Results

The sustainability framework aims at a better understanding of sustainability in BPM. In extension of other approaches (Seidel et al. 2010), we particularly tried to understand the concept of sustainability from a value perspective (vom Brocke, Sonnenberg & Simons, 2009) in this study. From a managerial view point, the framework helped to derive first guidelines on how to support sustainability in BPM initiatives, namely by (a) identifying all stakeholders relevant, and then by (b) making sure to balance out the objectives of each of them in the BPM approach following a mid- to long-termed thinking.

Hence, although research is still at an early stage, we can identify certain obstacles to sustainability in the Ethiopian approach. In particular, we were able to identify a comparably strong role of the government and leadership. While strong leadership support is known to be a major success factor, also the commitment of the employees and the appreciation of the environment are vital to achieve sustainable process improvements. Here, also the concept of trust may play an essential role for people to enduringly engage in improvements. Additionally, from our first results we identify the relation between command and incentives to be of interest for further investigations in order to sustainable involve employees.

With our research, we have not looked into specific measures of change. For example, according to Hammer (2010) there are five critical enablers for a high-performance process; without them, a process will be unable to operate on a sustained basis: Process design, Process metrics, Process performers, Process infrastructure and Process owner. These enablers are expected to be important for sustainable process performance. Other factors like determination, skills (needed to succeed) and leadership are also found to be important. Knowledgeable and passionate senior executive leadership, culture (sharing power) and governance expertise are labeled as organizational capabilities for process (Rosemann & de Bruin 2005). While these studies build the core of a BPM methodology, our work rather observed the objectives a BPM methodology should lead to. In particular, we argue that the measures undertaken for the sake of BPM should bear in mind to meet the perspectives of multiple stakeholders in order to lead to sustainable success.

4   Conclusion and Future Research

In this study we analyzed the concept of sustainability in BPM. We presented an approach based on coalition theory and defined BPM sustainability from a stakeholder-perspective. In order to support the assessment of the sustainability of a BPM initiative we developed a generic BPM sustainability framework to be adapted to specific organizational context factors. In order to evaluate the approach, we investigated a large scale BPR project in the public sector of Ethiopia against the background of our model. We were able to draw first conclusions but, indeed, have to consider our work to be preliminary research.

In future studies, primary and secondary data will be used to continue this study. Secondary data will be extracted and used from the survey conducted by Mengesha and Common (2007). Interviews will be used to gather facts from key officials working at the Ministry of Capacity Building, the Federal Civil Service Agency and at the selected institutions for survey. Measures and questions to be used for the survey are derived from sources cited in this paper (Hammer, 2010) and (Donaldson, & Preston, 1995). The survey will be conducted on those organizations labeled as successful in implementing BPR, the Ministry of Trade and Industry, the Immigration and Consular Authority, the Ministry of Inland Revenue (Mengesha & Common,

2007; Walta, 2009). To deal with time and resource constraints from the three cited organizations the survey will focus only on the two, namely the Ministry of Trade and Industry and the Ministry of Inland Revenue. Moreover, officers at the Ministry of Capacity Building responsible to oversee the Business Process Reengineering process at a national level will be reached and interviewed.

According to preliminary information obtained from the personnel office there are about 350 employees at the Ministry of Trade and Industry and about 600 employees at the Ministry of Inland Revenue and Custom. Considering the suggestion given by Gay (1981), 20% (190) of the subjects will be considered as a sample for the questionnaire survey. A pre-test of the survey instrument will be carried out prior to the actual study. Both quantitative and qualitative data analyses will be carried out and the results will be presented using tables and graphs. An SPSS package will be used for quantitative data analysis and the Miles and Huberman framework will be used for analyzing qualitative data.

Considering the results and future research opportunities, we very much hope that our work may contribute to the future discussion on sustainability in BPM. We firmly believe that this is an important field of research which calls for fundamental investigation of various disciplines in order to overcome short-termed thinking and contribute to a rather balanced and long-termed thinking and management practice.

Acknowledgement

We wish to thank the organizers of the AAU IS PhD program, who brought us together in course of one unique week of BPM teaching and learning in Addis in February 2010.

References

1. Al-Marshi, M., Zairi, M.: Information and Business Process Equality: The case of SAP R/3 implementation. EJISDC 2(4), 1–15 (2000)
2. Buchanan, D., Huczynski, A.: Organizational Behaviour, 5th edn. FT Prentice Hall Berihu Assefa, Harlow (2009)
3. Business Process Re-engineering in Ethiopia: Unpublished report, Addis Ababa, Ethiopia (2004)
4. Chanie, P.: The Challenges of the Civil Service Reform in Ethiopia: Initial Observations. Merit: A Quarterly Bulletin of the Ethiopian Civil Service Commission 3, 26–29 (2001)
5. Clapham, C.: Ethiopia and Eritrea: The Politics of Post-insurgency. In: Wiseman, J. (ed.) Democracy and Political Change in Sub-Saharan Africa. Routledge, London (1995)
6. Collins, E.: Unpublished report. The Risks in Relying on Stakeholder Engagement for the Achievement of Sustainability (2009)
7. Cyert, R.M., March, J.G.: A Behavioral Theory of the Firm. Prentice-Hall, Englewood Cliffs (1963)
8. Davenport, T., Short, J.: The New Industrial Engineering: Information Technology and Business Process Redesign. Sloan Management Review, 11–27 (1990)
9. Donaldson, T., Preston, L.: The stakeholder theory of the modern corporation: Concepts, evidence and implications. Academy of Management Review 20, 65–91 (1995)

10. Ethiopia: Ethiopian Revenue and Custom Authority: BPR implementation, lessons learnt and the way forward, Addis Ababa, Ethiopia (2010)
11. Ethiopia-BPR: Layoffs cause pension rethink (2009), http://www.ethioplanet.com/news/2009/04/29/ethiopia-bpr-lay-offs-cause-pension-rethink
12. Freeman, R.E.: Strategic Management: A Stakeholder Approach. Pitman Publishing (1984)
13. Gartner: Meeting the Challenge: The 2009 CIO Agenda (2009)
14. Gary, L.: How to think about performance measures now. Harvard Management Update, pp. 3–6 (2002)
15. Gay, L.: Educational Research Competencies for Analysis and Application, 2nd edn. Charles E Merrill, New York (1981)
16. Hammer, M.: What is Business Process Management? In: vom Brocke, J., Rosemann, M. (eds.) Handbook on Business Process Management: Introduction, Methods and Information Systems (International Handbooks on Information Systems), vol. 1. Springer, Berlin (2010)
17. Hammer, M., Champy, J.: Reengineering the Corporation: A Manifesto for Business Revolution (1993)
18. Kaplan, R.S., Norton, D.P.: The balanced scorecard - measures that drive performance. Harvard Business Review, pp. 71–79 (January-February 1991)
19. Mengesha, G.H., Common, R.: Public Sector Capacity Reform in Ethiopia: A tale of success in two Ministry. Public Administration and Development 27, 367–380 (2007)
20. Rappaport, A.: Creating Shareholder Value: The New Standard for Business Performance. Free Press, New York (1986)
21. Rosemann, M., de Bruin, T.: Towards a Business Process Management Maturity Model. In: Proceedings of the 13th European Conference on Information Systems, Regensburg, Germany (2005)
22. Rosemann, M.: vom Brocke, J.: The Six Core Elements of Business Process Management. In: vom Brocke, J., Rosemann, M. (eds.) Handbook on Business Process Management: Introduction, Methods and Information Systems (International Handbooks on Information Systems), vol. 1. Springer, Berlin (2010)
23. Seidel, S., Recker, J., Pimmer, C., vom Brocke, J.: Enablers and Barriers to the Organizational Adoption of Sustainable Business Practices. Paper presented at the 16th Americas Conference on Information Systems (2010)
24. Stubbs, M., Cocklin, C.: Conceptualizing a Sustainability Business Model. Organization & Environment 21(2) (2008)
25. vom Brocke, J., Recker, J., Mendling, J.: Value-oriented Process Modeling: Integrating Financial Perspectives into Business Process Re-design. Business Process Management Journal (BPMJ) 16(2), 333–356 (2010)
26. vom Brocke, J., Sonnenberg, C., Simons, A.: Value-oriented Information Systems Design: The Concept of Potentials Modeling and its Application to Service-oriented Architectures. Business & Information Systems Engineering 1(3), 223–233 (2009)
27. Walta News. Business Process Reengineering: key for sustainable development (2009), http://www.waltainfo.com/index.php?option=com_content&task=view&id=10015&Itemid=82 (retrieved May 4, 2009)
28. Watson, R.T., Boudreau, M.-C., Chen, A.J.: Information Systems and Environmentally Sustainable Development: Energy Informatics and New Directions for the IS Community. MIS Quarterly 34(1), 23–38 (2010)

Towards Green BPM – Sustainability and Resource Efficiency through Business Process Management

Constantin Houy, Markus Reiter, Peter Fettke, and Peter Loos

Institute for Information Systems (IWi)
at the German Research Center for Artificial Intelligence (DFKI) and
Saarland University, Stuhlsatzenhausweg 3, Geb. D3$_2$
66123 Saarbrücken, Germany
{Constantin.Houy,Markus.Reiter,
Peter.Fettke,Peter.Loos}@iwi.dfki.de

Abstract. The sustainability of organizations' business activities is gaining increasing importance. Taking the debate on global warming seriously into account, organizations put more effort in improving their sustainability. One central aspect in the debate on global warming is the energy efficiency of information technology (IT) infrastructures. As the energy consumption based on IT has dramatically increased with the development of the Internet in recent years, IT is considered as a part of the problem. IT can however be part of the solution. In order to improve the efficiency and sustainability of information processing, the concept of Green IT offers a set of possible approaches. In our contribution we argue that applying approaches from the field of Business Process Management (BPM) can support Green IT initiatives and thus the sustainability and resource efficiency of IT-supported business activities in general. The application of BPM approaches in the Green IT context requires new methods and techniques which are named Green BPM in this paper. However, the discussion on sustainability through Green BPM is still in its early stages and only rudimentary techniques exist so far. Our contribution aims at illuminating and discussing opportunities and challenges of Green BPM based on conceptual considerations.

Keywords: Business Process Management, BPM, Sustainability, Green BPM.

1 Introduction

The sustainability of business activities is an intensely discussed topic these days. Against the background of the debate on global warming, the matter gains increasing importance and the renewed interest in the environment drives organizations to put more effort into improving their resource efficiency as well as the sustainability of their business activities. As the topic is fervently discussed in many different parts of society and based on its significance for economy, it is also of high importance in the domain of politics. For instance, the 7th framework programme of the European Commission provides for a comprehensive funding for research projects concerning

M. zur Muehlen and J. Su (Eds.): BPM 2010 Workshops, LNBIP 66, pp. 501–510, 2011.
© Springer-Verlag Berlin Heidelberg 2011

sustainability of energy systems ("FP7-ENERGY"). Furthermore the German Federal Ministry of Education and Research (BMBF) has initiated a framework programme for sustainability-related research and development ("Forschung für nachhaltige Entwicklung") with a funding of more than 2 Billion Euros (approx. 2.5 Billion US$) until the year 2015 (http://www.fona.de).

One central topic in the sustainability debate is concerned with the energy efficiency of information technology infrastructures. In recent years based on the worldwide growth of the Internet, the use of computers and information technology in general as well as computer-related energy consumption has dramatically increased [1]. In 2005 the total server infrastructure of the U.S. including auxiliary facilities, such as cooling etc. required a power production of about 5,000 megawatts (MW). Worldwide infrastructure required about 14,000 MW resulting in electricity costs of 7.2 Billion US$ per year [2]. Moreover these significant levels of electric power also result in increased consumption of fossil fuels as well as increased production of green house gases [3]. Based on the actual development a further increase of energy consumption can be expected [4].

Such development has evoked several different initiatives for the improvement of energy efficiency and sustainability in information processing. The so called field of Green IT or Green Computing is an actual trend towards designing, building and operating energy efficient computer systems and IT infrastructures based on sustainable organizational concepts in order to reduce costs as well as to reduce global climate change [3]. Green IT initiatives include investments for the reduction of power consumption, e.g. like server virtualization, organizational methods, like IT outsourcing, personnel training etc. but also the reduction of IT related waste.

In the following we argue that in this context Business Process Management (BPM) can fundamentally support Green IT initiatives and thus improve the sustainability and resource efficiency of business activities in general. BPM has gained remarkable importance in recent years and is increasingly established in enterprises and administrations all over the world [5]. It provides adequate techniques for the design, execution, control as well as the analysis of business processes in order to improve the effectiveness and efficiency of value creation in organizations [6].

In order to support Green IT initiatives the techniques and tools of BPM have to be adapted to the requirements of Green IT. The resulting techniques and tools are summarized under the term "Green BPM"; however, the discussions on techniques for Green BPM are still in the early stages and so far only rudimentary approaches exist. Against this background our contribution aims at illuminating the potentials and challenges of Green BPM for the improvement of resource efficiency and the sustainability of business activities based on conceptual considerations.

The article is structured as follows: In Section 2 the underlying concepts of Green BPM are introduced. Section 3 describes Green BPM as an approach based on the interplay of BPM and Green IT. Section 4 presents example potentials of Green BPM in two application scenarios from different organizational contexts. Section 5 then derives general potentials and challenges of Green BPM before Section 6 summarizes and concludes the paper.

2   Underlying Concepts and Terminology

2.1   Business Process Management

Business Process Management represents an approach which supports organizations in sustaining their competitive advantage [7]. It comprises methods, techniques and tools for the handling of business processes as a sequence of executions in a business context based on the purpose of creating goods and services [8]. BPM supports the management of business processes throughout their whole life cycle which comprises several phases. BPM aims at improving business processes in an evolutionary way based on a continuous transformation process [9]. After the development of a business process strategy, processes are modelled and implemented. Their execution provides the basis for the monitoring and controlling as well as further model improvement [10]. Figure 1 visualizes the BPM life cycle as a reference framework for the description of potentials and challenges of Green BPM.

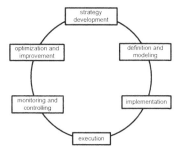

Fig. 1. BPM life cycle for continuous process improvement according to [10]

2.2   Sustainability and Resource Efficiency

Sustainability has become a buzzword which is far from clearly defined in literature [11]. On a general level the sustainability of an entity represents the entity's persistence in time [12]. In a business context sustainability can be understood as an organization's ability to realize profits, as well as sustaining the environment at the same time [13] in order to consider the needs of future generations [14]. The European Commission defines sustainable development as "progress that integrates immediate and longer-term objectives, local and global action, and regards social, economic and environmental issues as inseparable and interdependent components of human progress" [15]. In our contribution sustainability is understood according to this definition. A better sustainability can be supported by higher efficiency of resource consumption in business processes, e.g. a higher energy efficiency of IT infrastructures, a lower level of fuel consumption of a transport medium etc. Furthermore the sustainability of business activities can be improved by a reduction of waste materials and green house gases produced by a business activity.

3   Green BPM as the Interplay of Green IT and BPM

Green IT initiatives focus on designing, building and operating resource efficient computer systems and IT infrastructures in order to improve the sustainability of information processing. BPM can contribute to Green IT initiatives by enabling and supporting sustainable and – derived from that – resource-efficient processes in the context of information processing and business processes in general. It provides adequate techniques for the design, execution, controlling as well as the analysis of processes for the coordination of Green IT initiatives. BPM can for example support the sustainability of IT service management, e.g. by simplifying service processes or by automating activities in order to improve resource efficiency; this can be supported by common techniques and tools of BPM.

However, most BPM techniques and tools are designed in order to support efficiency of business processes focussing on costs and time. In contrast to that, the application of BPM in the Green IT context poses new requirements for BPM. In order to support the sustainability and resource efficiency of business processes by Green BPM, common methods and techniques have to be adapted and extended. This interplay of Green IT and BPM resulting in the concept of Green BPM is visualized in figure 2.

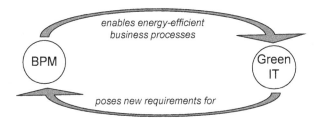

Fig. 2. Green BPM as interplay of Green IT and Business Process Management

The discussions on Green BPM techniques for modeling, implementing, executing and monitoring sustainable business processes are still in their early stages and so far only rudimentary approaches exist. In the scientific literature Ghose et al. [16] have developed an approach for modeling and controlling the carbon dioxide (CO_2) emission in business processes in order to measure a carbon footprint of business activities based on business processes. However, our contribution prefers a wider understanding of Green BPM because business processes are not only producers of CO_2 but also of waste materials and at the same time consumers of other, partly limited resources like water or fossil fuels.

In Green BPM every business activity in a process model can be annotated with an adequate ratio representing the consumption of resources and the production of waste materials. By accumulating these values, the total consumption of needed resources or the total production of waste materials in a process can be measured and controlled. This method facilitates an optimized combination of activities in a process and the controlling of the ecological impact of its execution based on resource consumption and waste production.

4   Application Scenarios for Green BPM

In order to delineate the opportunities of Green BPM for the improvement of process sustainability, two application scenarios are presented. The first scenario is concerned with the management of processes for providing typical IT services, e.g. such as storage, software applications etc. The second scenario broadens the perspective and focuses on business processes in general.

4.1   Management of IT Service Processes

IT services are produced mainly in data centers. Data centers can be regarded as the hot spots of IT-related energy consumption. In order to produce IT services like web hosting or SAP services in a professional way, the application of management practices and standards is obligatory. To some degree, IT Service Management (ITSM) standards refer to the principles of Business Process Management. Several steps and procedures applied in ITSM are based on defined process models. For instance, there exist distinct processes for the realization of the overall service strategy. Moreover ITSM standards include descriptions of the service offering portfolio, guidelines for the successful operation of services and the definition of service qualities, typically described as service level agreements which need to be monitored and reported.

A common best practice supporting these services is the comprehensive IT infrastructure library (ITIL) framework, which is widely accepted and applied in professional IT services organizations. ITIL describes several standardized processes in the context of Service Delivery, e.g Service Level Management or Capacity Management, as well as processes for Service Support, Incident Management or Change Management. However, the ITIL framework has no special focus on the sustainability of ITSM processes. In this context Green BPM can provide an approach for closing this gap in the ITIL framework.

Sustainable IT service management, as a use case of Green BPM, does not only consider adequate service delivery and quality of services; it furthermore focuses on the sustainability of service delivery as the new element. In this context new types of service quality can concentrate on energy efficiency (e.g. "service may not consume more than 10 kWh per 10.000 transactions"). Based on that, the incident management could be extended in a way, in which not only events are considered which are relevant for cost efficiency or availability, but also sustainability incidents, e.g. an exceeding of defined thresholds. If a data processing system consumes more energy than expected, an incident can be triggered, leading to an energy-aware reconfiguration.

Another example can be taken from the context of capacity management which considers the planning of physical capacities necessary for service delivery. Based on sales forecasts (e.g. "100.000 online shop users next year"), the process of capacity management defines the required physical hardware, as well as the required space and energy-related facilities in the data center. Considering input from the business side, over-sizing IT infrastructure can be avoided and energy efficiency can be improved.

Besides that, the implementation quality of IT service management processes may have different levels depending on the company implementing them. In some cases, an individual company may have implemented ITSM processes in a very resource-intensive way, using physical meetings with high travel efforts or printing all process-relevant documents on paper. Although this is a general fault in process design, a careful examination of IT service process implementations with regard to such common mistakes should be considered. Thus the resource efficiency and sustainability of ITSM processes can easily be improved resulting in quick financial returns.

4.2 Management of Business Processes

Not only can the sustainability of an ITSM process be improved by using appropriate ratios but also the sustainability of every business process in an organization. For every activity in a business process, relevant values concerning the consumption of resources or the production of waste materials can be considered. Figure 3 shows a typical sales process represented by an Event-driven Process Chain (EPC) [17]. In the process model different activities are annotated with exemplary values of resource consumption. The sustainability of this process can be optimized by planning and improving it in a way that these values are reduced.

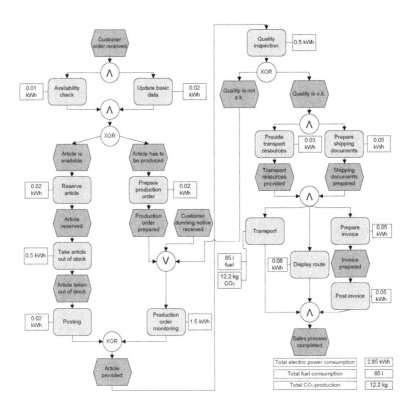

Fig. 3. Sales process annotated with relevant sustainability ratios

As is commonly known, IT infrastructure provides the basis for business operations. As already mentioned, the sustainability of internal ITSM processes can be supported by appropriate planning and forecast figures from the business context, e.g. especially in the context of capacity management. A similar effect can be expected when Green BPM is applied in order to improve the sustainability of business processes of an organization which is embedded in inter-organizational business processes, e.g. supply chain management scenarios. Applying Green BPM methods can also improve the sustainability of inter-organizational business processes. On the one hand an improvement of resource efficiency of global supply chain processes promises to have a positive ecological effect [18]. On the other hand the individual situation of every partner in the supply chain has to be considered and the coordination of the different individual interests of each partner in the supply chain appears to be problematic.

Based on the BPM life cycle the cooperating business partners can appoint a corporate sustainable process strategy as a basis for their Green BPM initiative. This strategy should address sustainability topics like business ethics in general, supplier ethics and practices as well as the sourcing of energy, e.g. the commitment to use green electricity. If every partner in the supply chain is interested in improving the sustainability of the process, sustainability ratios can be appointed as target values which should be achieved by the execution of the whole process. Based on that, the business processes can be modeled using adequate ratios for the consumption of resources and the production of waste materials of each process step. The accumulation of these values represents the total effects of a whole process. The partners could for instance stipulate that the execution of a certain transport process should not consume more than 1,000 liters of fuel in total. The modeled processes are then executed and controlled comparing the planned ratios with the actual values provided by an adequate monitoring system. In the improvement phase of the BPM life cycle the process models could then be enhanced considering the monitoring values. Thus the process sustainability can be optimized.

Based on these considerations, Green BPM could contribute to a more sustainable supply chain management enhancing environmental performance by minimizing waste. Not only has this an effect on the corporate image, but it also improves the competitive advantages based on cost savings [19]. However, appropriate techniques, tools as well as organizational concepts are needed in order to coordinate Green BPM initiatives in an inter-organizational context.

5   Potentials and Challenges of Green BPM

The two application scenarios have presented a set of potentials and challenges of Green BPM for ITSM processes as well as for internal and inter-organizational business processes. These potentials are systematized according to the BPM life cycle in figure 4.

Strategy development: In the phase of strategy development, a single organization or cooperating partners appoint a sustainable corporate business process strategy. The objectives which should be achieved can be documented in a corporate Sustainability Balanced Scorecard (SBSC) with different sustainability ratios [4].

Definition and modeling: In the phase of business process modeling, process models are developed considering the actual production of waste materials and the consumption of resources in order to create awareness for the problem. The individual sub-processes of the participating departments can then be defined in a more sustainable and resource efficient way in order to meet the appointed ratios.

Implementation: During the implementation phase the several sub-processes have to be adequately configured in order to achieve an improvement of the resource efficiency [16]. In the context of configuring the sub-processes the partners in cooperative scenarios should be supported by IT-based communication, e.g. Web 2.0 applications, video conferencing etc. which is normally more efficient than travelling.

Execution: A more ecologically aware execution of business processes can be facilitated by inter-organizational workflow management systems (WfMS) driving the defined sustainable processes. In this context electronic documents are often used in order to support the reduction of paper consumption.

Monitoring and controlling: In this phase the actual ratios of the process execution are measured for controlling purposes and can then be compared to the appointed sustainability ratios.

Optimization and improvement: Based on this comparison in the monitoring and controlling phase, weaker points and sustainability problems of process execution can be identified. Based on this, an improvement of the process models can be furthered.

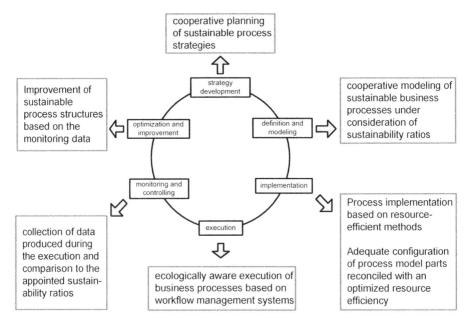

Fig. 4. Potentials of Green BPM

Nevertheless, there are also important challenges which have to be faced in order to tap the full potential of Green BPM. In the first place adequate and measurable sustainability ratios have to be identified and developed as these ratios provide the basis for process implementation, controlling and improvement. In some cases the actual consumption of resources can only be estimated and is not exactly measurable.

Sustainability has become an important factor for many organizations. Nevertheless, cost efficiency usually is the more important factor. In many cases resource efficiency and an environmentally friendly economic activity go along with reduced costs, e.g. an optimized route for a travelling sales man. In other cases cost-conscious business activities on globalized markets accompany high ecological costs, e.g. in the case when simple goods are transported far away to different countries in order to save personnel costs for further processing. Moreover, sometimes business processes have to be executed within a certain time limit producing higher ecological costs.

In such a scenario adequate Green BPM tools are needed to support an adaption of business process models for single process instances in order to facilitate a flexible BPM which can fit the needs of emerging situations. Under exceptional circumstances an optimization of time efficiency can be more important than resource efficiency in order to achieve a business goal [16]. Green BPM research has to examine whether existing tools can be adapted or new ones have to be developed.

In addition, further experience with the application of sustainability ratios in Green BPM is needed. Based on this experience adequate green reference process models can be developed in order to document best practices for improving process sustainability in different business domains.

6   Conclusion and Outlook

Green BPM is of relevance for both research and practice and offers significant opportunities for the improvement of enterprises' sustainability. Our contribution illuminated and discussed the potentials and challenges of Green BPM focussing process-oriented management of enterprise resources. At first the topic was motivated by the actual debate on global warming and the need for better sustainability of business activities. Then our understanding of Green BPM was explained and exemplified in two application scenarios. The potentials and challenges of Green BPM were then presented based on the BPM life cycle and followed by a short discussion.

The presented considerations and the two application scenarios show that Green BPM can contribute to more sustainable business operations. Future research should develop concepts in the form of green reference process models or procedure models for the implementation of green processes as well as adequate techniques and tools for the realization of Green BPM potentials in inter-organizational scenarios.

Acknowledgements. The research described in this paper was supported by a grant from the German Federal Ministry of Education and Research (BMBF), project name: "Process-oriented Web-2.0-based Integrated Telecommunication Service" (PROWIT), support code FKZ 01BS0833. The authors would also like to thank the anonymous reviewers for the valuable comments which helped to improve the presented paper.

References

1. Kurp, P.: Green Computing. Communications of the ACM 51, 11–13 (2008)
2. Koomey, J.G.: Estimating Total Power Consumption by Servers in the U.S. and the World. Lawrence Berkeley National Laboratory, Stanford University, Stanford, California (2007)
3. Binder, W., Suri, N.: Green Computing: Energy Consumption Optimized Service Hosting. In: Nielsen, M., Kučera, A., Miltersen, P.B., Palamidessi, C., Tůma, P., Valencia, F. (eds.) SOFSEM 2009. LNCS, vol. 5404, pp. 117–128. Springer, Heidelberg (2009)
4. Schmidt, N.-H., Erek, K., Kolbe, L.M., Zarnekow, R.: Towards a Procedural Model for Sustainable Information Systems Management. In: Sprague, R.H. (ed.) Proceedings of the 42nd Hawaii International Conference on System Sciences 2009 (HICSS-42). IEEE Computer Society, Los Alamitos (2009)
5. Fettke, P.: How Conceptual Modeling Is Used. Communications of the AIS 25, 571–592 (2009)
6. van der Aalst, W.M.P., ter Hofstede, A.H.M., Weske, M.: Business Process Management: A Survey. In: van der Aalst, W.M.P., ter Hofstede, A.H.M., Weske, M. (eds.) BPM 2003. LNCS, vol. 2678, pp. 1–12. Springer, Heidelberg (2003)
7. Hung, R.Y.: Business Process Management as Competitive Advantage: a Review and Empirical Study. Total Quality Management 17, 21–40 (2006)
8. Scheer, A.-W.: ARIS - Business Process Frameworks. Springer, Berlin (1999)
9. Weske, M.: Business Process Management: Concepts, Languages, Architectures. Springer, Berlin (2007)
10. Houy, C., Fettke, P., Loos, P.: Empirical research in business process management - analysis of an emerging field of research. Business Process Management Journal 16, 619–661 (2010)
11. Pearce, D., Markandya, A., Barbier, E.B.: Blueprint for a Green Economy. Earthscan, London (1989)
12. Garrido, P.: Business sustainability and collective intelligence. The Learning Organization 16, 208–222 (2009)
13. Wikström, P.-A.: Sustainability and Organizational Activities - Three Approaches. Sustainable Development 18, 99–107 (2010)
14. World Commission on Environment and Development: Our Common Future. Oxford University Press, Oxford (1987)
15. European Commission: Sustainable development (2007), http://ec.europa.eu/environment/eussd/ (accessed at: December 16, 2010)
16. Ghose, A., Hoesch-Klohe, K., Hinsche, L., Le, L.-S.: Green Business Process Management: A Research Agenda. Australasian Journal of Information Systems 16, 103–117 (2009)
17. Scheer, A.-W.: Business Process Engineering - Reference Models for Industrial Companies. Springer, Berlin (1994)
18. Piotrowicz, W., Cuthbertson, R.: Sustainability - a new dimension in information systems evaluation. Journal of Enterprise Information Management 22, 492–503 (2009)
19. Rao, P., Holt, D.: Do green supply chains lead to competitiveness and economic performance? International Journal of Operations & Production Management 25, 898–916 (2005)

Measuring the Carbon Footprint of Business Processes

Jan Recker, Michael Rosemann, and Ehsan Roohi Gohar

Information Systems Discipline, Queensland University of Technology
126 Margaret Street, Brisbane QLD 4000, Australia
{j.recker,m.rosemann,ehsan.roohigohar}@qut.edu.au

Abstract. While many corporations and individuals realize that environmental sustainability is an urgent problem to address, the academic community has been slow to acknowledge the problem and take action. We contribute to the emerging academic discussion by proposing a new approach for engaging in the analysis of environmentally sustainable business processes. Specifically, we propose an approach for measuring the carbon dioxide emissions produced during the execution of a business process, and apply this approach in a real-life case of a Direct Invoicing process at a Corporate Services provider. We show how this information can be leveraged in the re-design of "green" business processes.

Keywords: sustainability, process analysis, carbon footprint.

1 Introduction

The increasing awareness for the necessity of sustainability in living and working has put "green" or "sustainable" practices on the radar screen of organizations. Environmental constraints are increasingly imposed on organizations, and demand new levels of operational compliance.

In this context, colloquial terms such as Green IT [1] have emerged to acknowledge information systems and the surrounding business processes as contributors to environmental problems as well as potential enablers of green, sustainable solutions. Yet, while organizations around the globe increasingly realize the demand and potential of the transformative power of information systems [2], to date, few examples of such approaches have been reported in studies.

In this paper, we contribute to the emerging body of research on sustainability by discussing an analysis approach for measuring the carbon footprint of business processes. Our approach extends activity-based costing approaches [e.g., 3] towards the consideration of greenhouse gas emissions alongside the activities of a business processes. Thereby, it facilitates the consideration of environmental sustainability consideration in the improvement or re-design of business processes.

Following this introduction, we review existing research on sustainability. Then, we briefly discuss existing approaches to measuring carbon footprints in organizations. Next, we suggest an approach for measuring the carbon footprints of business processes. We apply our approach to the case of a Direct Invoicing process at an Australian Corporate Services provider. We then conclude this paper with a review of contributions and implications.

M. zur Muehlen and J. Su (Eds.): BPM 2010 Workshops, LNBIP 66, pp. 511–520, 2011.
© Springer-Verlag Berlin Heidelberg 2011

2 Background

With our research we seek to contribute to the development and improvement of sustainable business practices. Sustainability is "development that meets the needs of the present without compromising the ability of future generations to meet their own needs" [4]. Our interest specifically is on environmental aspects of sustainability. The most important environmental sustainability challenge is known as the problem of *global warming*, the increase in the average temperature of Earth's near-surface air and oceans. Global warming is primarily caused by greenhouse gas (GHG) emissions, in particular through Carbon Dioxide produced collaterally through human-triggered actions, such as business travels, paper production, manufacturing and others. We believe that these actions manifest especially in the execution of organizational business processes.

Of course, we are not the first to examine environmental issues and organizational performance. Contributions on environmental quality, lean production, regulatory mechanisms, environmentally benevolent activities and sustainable initiatives have been made in operations research [5] or econometrics [6], to name just two. Yet, few contributions exist that examine the contribution of an organization's business processes to environmental sustainability.

We believe that Business Process Management can assist in the endeavor to extend our perspective on processes and the wider organizational performance. This is because Business Process Management tools and techniques assist organizations in their efforts to (re-) design the organizational processes in light of compliance regulations, operational agility, or other business imperatives such as time, quality or costs [7]. The dedication of BPM approaches to eliminate waste under the "paperless office" paradigm indicates its potential for making processes more environmentally sustainable. We believe that it is possible to extend and adopt Business Process Management tools such that they also allow organizations to manage and improve the organizational processes in light of environmental considerations.

This work is an important move forward because, nowadays, global warming has raised attention about so-called eco-friendly business activities, defined as those processes that produce less carbon dioxide as a main cause of global warming. In this context, it is often referred to the *carbon footprint of business processes* as a measure for the carbon dioxide production alongside organizational operations such as paper-intensive processes (e.g., a bank's mortgage process), fuel consuming processes (e.g., business travels) or a process that produces waste materials and unnecessary power sources (e.g., defect processes, quality rectification processes).

Carbon footprint is commonly understood as the amount of carbon dioxide (CO_2) emitted through the combustion of fossil fuels during daily activities – in the case of a business organization, the amount of carbon dioxide emitted either directly or indirectly as a result of its everyday process operations. It is expressed as grams of CO_2 equivalent per kilowatt hour of generation (gCO_2eq/kWh), which accounts for the different global warming effects of other greenhouse gases.

To facilitate the improvement of the carbon footprint of business processes, it is firstly required to facilitate the documentation and measurement of the carbon dioxide emissions alongside a business process. We discuss some relevant approaches in the following.

3 Carbon Footprint Calculation Approaches

Carbon footprint measurement has become a topic of interest to many business organizations, and has led to the development of several measurement approaches to calculate the footprint of a business as an organizational entity (see, for instance, http://www.carbonfootprint.com/).

Calculating the carbon footprint of an organization can be done via three approaches [8]: bottom-up, based on Process Analysis (PA) or top-down, based on an Environmental Input-Output (EIO) analysis, or through a combination of both. We briefly review the three approaches in the following.

3.1 Process Analysis

Process analysis (PA) is a bottom-up method, which has been developed to understand the environmental impacts of individual products over its lifecycle from cradle to grave [9]. In a process-based Life Cycle Assessment (LCA), one itemizes the inputs (materials and energy resources) and the outputs (emissions and wastes to the environment) for a given step in producing a product.

The bottom-up nature of process-based LCA means that they suffer from a system boundary problem – typically, only on-site and first-order, sometimes second-order impacts are considered. If PA-LCA is used for deriving carbon footprint estimates, a strong emphasis therefore needs to be given to the identification of appropriate system boundaries, which minimize this truncation error. A PA-based LCA runs into further difficulties once carbon footprints for larger entities such as government, households or particular industrial sectors have to be established. Even though estimates can be derived by extrapolating information contained in life-cycle databases, results will get increasingly patchy as these procedures usually require the assumption that a subset of individual products are representative for a larger product grouping and the use of information from different databases, which are usually not consistent.

3.2 Environmental Input-Output Analysis

Environmental Input-Output (EIO) analysis [10] provides an alternative top-down approach suitable to carbon foot printing. Input-output tables are economic accounts providing a picture of all economic activities at the meso (sector) level. In combination with consistent environmental account data they can be used to establish carbon footprint estimates in a comprehensive and robust way taking into account all higher order impacts and setting the whole economic system as boundary. However, the suitability of environmental input-output analysis to assess micro systems such as products or processes is limited, as it assumes homogeneity of prices, outputs and their carbon emissions at the sector level. Although sectors can be disaggregated for further analysis, bringing it closer to a micro system, this possibility is limited, at least on a larger scale. A big advantage of input-output based approaches, however, is a much smaller requirement of time and manpower once the model is in place.

3.3 Hybrid-EIO-LCA

The combination of the above methods in a hybrid approach [11] allows preserving the detail and accuracy of bottom-up approaches in lower order stages, while higher-order requirements are covered by the input-output part of the model. Such a Hybrid-EIO-LCA method, embedding process systems inside input-output tables, is the current state-of-the art in ecological economic modeling [11]. Still, this approach is focused on understanding input-output relations on a broader institutional or economical level. We argue that an understanding of carbon emissions on a business process level would create further opportunities on a meso and micro level to make quick and effective adjustments to an organization with a direct impact on its environmental image. Our argument rests on a tight linkage between carbon emission measurement and the facilitation and implementation of principles associated with Business Process Management.

4   Activity-Based Emission Analysis

Through Business Process Management [12], an organization can create competent processes, which function cost efficiently, with greater precision, reduced errors, and improved flexibility. This is because by using Business Process Management, an organization can enhance its processes in each of the lifecycle stages planning, development and implementation of processes, by identifying errors, bottlenecks and, indeed, waste, before it affects other processes and overall revenue [13]. While typically, process management has focused on the documentation, analysis and improvement of performance objectives such as cost, time, quality or flexibility [7], we will in the following extend a typical process management tool, Activity-Based Costing [3], towards the inclusion of environmental measures in an approach we call *Activity-based Emission (ABE) Analysis*.

4.1 Approach

Activity-Based Costing (ABC) is a collection of financial and operational performance information dealing with significant activities of the business [3]. Key to this approach is the consideration of actual usage of equipment and resources (e.g. machinery, human resources) in the activities that constitute a business process. This approach takes a stance, therefore, on the operational level of a business process, which, through multi-level process architectures, thereby allowing for composition of the measures to a meso- or macro-organizational level.

Based on ABC Analysis, we argue that Activity-Based Emission (ABE) Analysis can be conducted for a process to determine the emission of CO_2 for each activity as well as the overall process. ABE allows the calculation of CO_2 emission more accurate than LCA or EIO approaches by focusing on every step of a business process, by identifying the so-called *emission drivers* and by considering the impact of alternative resources that facilitate the process execution. In fact, by estimating and measuring the CO_2 outturn of each activity, the CO_2 emission of all services and products across all business processes of an organization can be calculated. In turn, ABE analysis can provide a more precise and specific insight into the actual processes, activities and resources within, that directly contribution, positively or negatively, to the carbon emission of an organization. This is because ABE helps to distinguish operations and resources based on their CO2 emissions, and thus allows embedding an environmental view in the decision-making related to process (re-) design.

Further benefits from an ABE approach include that it can also be used within other business analysis tools such as Pareto analyses, to further examine the relation between cost, time and emission of CO2 for a business. We foresee the combination of ABE with other analysis tools as a key step in defining organizational areas which require an improvement in light of sustainability considerations.

4.2 Stage Model

Similarly to a regular ABC analysis, an ABE can be conducted within five main steps:

1. **Identify the product or service to be considered.** This step is typically supported through business or service modeling activities at a strategic level.
2. **Determine all the resources and processes that are required to create the product or deliver the service, and their respective CO2 emission.** To that end, typically, semi-formal graphical models of the business process are considered as documentations of the tasks that have to be performed, the actors and other resources that are involved in the execution of these tasks, relevant data and sources (papers, forms, systems and technology) of the data, and the business rule logic that describes the logical and temporal order in which tasks are to be performed [14]. To measure the CO2 emissions, data will have to be collected, at least, about three important CO2 emission factors, *consumed electricity, consumed paper,* and *consumed fuel.* Arguably, there could be other emission factors that could also be taken into consideration.
3. **Determine the "emission drivers" for each resource.** To that end, in late 1997, the World Resources Institute and the World Business Council, developed the Greenhouse Gas Protocol (GHG Protocol) for Sustainable Development (www.ghgprotocol.org). The GHG Protocol is providing series of accounting tools to understand measure and manage green house gas emissions. In this protocol, three scope levels are defined to define organizational boundaries to enable differentiating between GHG emitting activities that are owned by organizations, and those that are not. These scope boundaries categories owned emitting activities in to three different scopes which is distinguishes between direct and in direct GHG emitting activities:

- *Scope1: direct GHG emissions* – emissions that occur from sources that are owned or controlled by the company. Examples include emissions from boilers, vehicles, electric generators and so forth.
- *Scope2: electricity indirect emissions* – emissions that originate from consuming electricity, heat or steam purchased by the company.
- *Scope3: other indirect GHG emissions* – emissions that are the results of the activities of the company but arise from sources not owned or controlled by

the company. These include emissions from product materials produced by suppliers (newsprint/paper, ink, etc.), contractor delivery vehicles, employee commuting to/from work and business air travel.

4. **Calculate CO2 emission for each activity by gathering Activity Data for each process and resource and define the emission factor for each Activity Data.** The GHG Protocol enables the calculation of the CO2 emission for each defined source in step 3 through GHG Protocol calculation tools. Examples for the three selected emission drivers include the following:

- *Fuel (scope3):* For calculating the CO2 emission of scope3 activities (e.g., business travel between two offices), the GHG protocol provides the formula: *Distance travelled × emissions factor incorporating default fuel efficiency value = CO2 emission*
- *Paper (scope3):* For calculating the CO2 emission of scope3 activities (e.g., transporting paper forms between two offices), the GHG protocol provides the formula: *Weight of paper × emissions factor for manufacture of paper = CO2 equivalent emissions*
- *Electricity (scope2):* CO2 emission of purchased electricity can be calculated by using the GHG Protocol calculation tool for purchased electricity, which is based on the formula: *KWh of electricity used by organization × emission factor = CO2 emissions*

5. **Use the data to calculate the overall CO2 emission of the process.** This is achieved by summing up all CO2 emissions across all activities and scope levels. This analysis will then enable a sixth step (out of scope for this paper) - the actual act of making eco-aware process re-design decisions, and selecting those process and resource variants that help to reduce the carbon footprint during run-time execution.

5   A Case Study: The Direct Invoicing Process

5.1   Case Description

We applied our approach in a case study with Seamless Service Provision (SSP), an Australia-based organization that offers financial and human resource services to organizations in the private and public sector. One of these services is the payment of so-called direct invoices for its clients. A direct invoice is an invoice without a corresponding purchase order.

SSP receives between 15,000-25,000 paper-based invoices per month. The invoices arrive in the incoming mail centre in the city centre (Office 1). Invoices are screened, entered into a system and then forwarded to Data Entry Officers at Office 2 in the north of the city (10 km distance from Office 1). Incomplete or incompliant invoices (10% of all invoices) are sent back to the client via postal mail with the request to complete the invoice.

The data entry officers Attach vendor master records to the invoices. The internal mail collects these forms and takes them to the master data entry department. The master data entry department creates SAP master data (takes 1-5 days) and then the invoice is ready to be entered in the SAP system by Data Entry Officers.

Validation Officers sort the invoices and print a 10-page report per 100 invoices (60 minutes for a batch of 100 invoices). Invoices are now ready for payment. The Payment Office runs a payment process every week. This is a highly automated process, at the end of which a report is generated. This report will be sent via mail to the individual clients to inform them about the successful payment of the invoice. Also, it will be sent to SSP's Accounts Receivable Department at Office 3 located 3km away from Office 2. This department generates monthly invoices for SSP's clients. Third, the payment report will be sent to the Registry (same building). The employee in the Registry selects the paper-based invoices that have been paid and archives the invoices. Sometimes, vendors or clients have an issue with the payment and in these cases it is required to track down the original paper-based invoice together with all information on the invoice entry form. Such requests occur approx. 5-10 times per month.

5.2 ABE Analysis

To calculate the carbon footprint of the direct invoicing process, we firstly created a process model of the process, modelled in BPMN [14]. The model details the process in terms of 43 individual activities, 10 involved departments within SSP, plus required data, paper, forms and other inputs to, and outputs from, the process. We omit the detailed BPMN model from this paper but note that we developed dedicated BPMN notation extensions to capture and illustrate the flow of CO_2 along the processes. The model is available upon request.

In a second step, we selected three CO_2 emission drivers of the process, viz., **fuel** (for delivering invoices between different offices), **paper** (Invoice, Invoice entry form, etc.) and **electricity** (regular office use). We note that our approach can also be used for other emission drivers. In step three, we then identified the sources for each of these three emission drivers (again, other sources are imaginable):

- Fuel: Depends on travelled distance to deliver the invoices between different offices.
- Paper: Depends on number of invoices.
- Electricity: Depends on the overall process cycle time.

In step four, we then calculated the CO_2 emissions alongside the process, the three identified resources, using the three scope levels of the GHG protocol (www.ghgprotocol.org). Due to space restrictions we cannot provide full details about the analysis and results (this information is available from the contact author upon request). Instead, we discuss some exemplary analyses in the following.

For instance, to be able to calculate CO_2 emission from purchased electricity, we firstly gathered data about office electricity consumptions per month (viz., office 1: 5,000 kwh per month, office 2: 2,500 kwh per month, office 3: 10,000 kwh per month). We then used a calculation tool provided in the GHG protocol to estimate the total electricity consumption (see Table 1). Then, by dividing CO_2 emission for each office in a relative fraction per seconds, the emission per seconds for each office can be calculated (Office 1: 4,603,000kg / 748,800 second = 6.15 kg per second; Office 2: 2,301,000kg / 748,800 second = 3.08 kg per second; Office 3: 9,205,000kg / 748,800 second = 12.3 kg per second).

Table 1. Calculation of SSP purchased electricity

To calculate the paper consumption, we assumed that all the consumed papers in company are in same size and weight, and estimated the weight of each paper as 0.03 kg. The emission factor for 1 kg of paper in the SSP company is 10 kg, therefore, each invoice or consumed sheet of paper in the Direct Invoicing process produces 300 gram of CO_2.

Last, we used a calculation tool provided in the GHG protocol to estimate the fuel consumption for delivering invoices and paperwork between offices, assuming company-owned cars with one driver only (see Table 2). The GHG Protocol calculation tool for mobile combustion fuel consumption shows that for each 100 km travelling with a car 24 kg CO_2 (0.024 kg per 1 km) are produced by SSP.

Table 2. Calculation of SSP fuel consumption

Based on these results, in a last step, we calculated the overall CO_2 emission of the Direct Invoicing Process, as described in Table 3. As can be seen, the current paper-based process, considering both direct and indirect emissions, produces over one billion kg of emissions due to its paper-intensive mode, which in turn presents a strong plea for the importance of the "paperless office" paradigm.

Table 3. ABE Analysis of SSP Direct Invoicing Process

Process/process variants		Description	Number of process instances per month	CO2 emission per process instance (kg)	CO2 emission per month (kg)
Complete invoices		95% of received invoices are complete.	19,000	**5233.81**	99,442,390
Incomplete invoices		5% of received invoices are incomplete.	1,000	**861.6**	861,600
Non-compliant invoices (10% of received invoices are non-compliant)	clarified by experienced SSP staff	50% of non-compliant invoices are clarified by experienced SSP staff.	1,000	738	738,000
	completed by calling the customers	25% of non-compliant invoices are completed by calling the customers.	500	738	369,000
	sent back to the customers for completion	25% of non-compliant invoices are sent back to the customers for completion.	500	**1,077.15**	538,575
Invoices for which vendors numbers are not in the SAP system		5% of all invoices do not have a SAP vendor number.	1,000	**863.9**	863,900
Invoices with payment issues that are tracked down		5-10 invoices require the track down of the invoice together with the invoice entry form.	2	7,380	14,760
Total emission per month(kg)					**1,028,282,225**

6   Conclusion

Our work denotes an important step forward towards the eco-friendly management of business processes. By being able to measure the environmental impact of a business process, analysts and managers are empowered to account for environmental information in their decisions to execute or change business processes. Our measurement approach works for as-is as well as for to-be scenarios and can therefore be used to make informed decisions about "green" processes and the improvement of the processes towards environmental as well as classical business objectives.

Our research has some limitations. Notably, we reported on a first exploratory case, and more empirical study is required. We focused on selected emission drivers and emission sources and acknowledge that a different focus could yield different results. Last, we note that the office energy consumption calculation does not take into account the use of office space for multiple processes. Therefore, a split of energy consumption would deliver improved results.

Our research as well as the related studies in this area [15] demand complementary future studies in a number of areas. For instance, we are working towards a process documentation notation that captures carbon footprint drivers, emissions and consequences. Similarly, our research calls for increased attention for approaches that facilitate truly paperless processes, through appropriate digitized information and artifact flow alongside a process. Typical process improvement strategies (e.g., TRIZ, reference modeling, Six Sigma, to name just a few) should be reviewed, to investigate how these techniques allow for an inclusion of environmental data, and how potential goal-conflicts (e.g., costs versus environmental impact) can be resolved.

References

1. Poniatowski, M.: Foundation of Green IT: Consolidation, Virtualization, Efficiency, and ROI in the Data Center. Prentice Hall, Boston (2009)
2. Watson, R.T., Boudreau, M.-C., Chen, A.J.: Information Systems and Environmentally Sustainable Development: Energy Informatics and New Directions for the IS Community. MIS Quarterly 34, 23–38 (2010)
3. Bromwich, M., Hong, C.: Activity-based Costing Systems and Incremental Costs. Management Accounting Research 10, 39–60 (1999)
4. World Commission on Environment nd Development: Our Common Future. Oxford University Press, Oxford (1987)
5. Corbett, C.J., Kirsch, D.A.: International Diffusion of ISO 14000 Certification. Production and Operations Management 10, 327–342 (2001)
6. Lyon, T.P., John, M.: Environmental Public Voluntary Programs Reconsidered. Policy Studies Journal 35, 723–750 (2007)
7. Reijers, H.A., Mansar, S.L.: Best Practices in Business Process Redesign: An Overview and Qualitative Evaluation of Successful Redesign Heuristics. Omega 33, 283–306 (2005)
8. Hendrickson, C., Horvath, A., Joshi, S., Lave, L.: Economic Input-Output Models for Environmental Life-Cycle Assessment. Environmental Science and Technology 32, 184–191 (1998)
9. Smith Cooper, J., Fava, J.A.: Life-Cycle Assessment Practitioner Survey: Summary of Results. Journal of Industrial Ecology 10, 12–14 (2006)
10. Pan, X., Kraines, S.: Environmental Input-Output Models for Life-Cycle Analysis. Environmental and Resource Economics 20, 61–72 (2001)
11. Heijungs, R., Suh, S.: Reformulation of Matrix-Based LCI: From Product Balance to Process Balance. Journal of Cleaner Production 14, 47–51 (2006)
12. vom Brocke, J., Rosemann, M. (eds.): Handbook on Business Process Management 1: Introduction, Methods and Information Systems. Springer, Berlin (2010)
13. Hammer, M.: The Process Audit. Harvard Business Review 85, 111–123 (2007)
14. Recker, J., Rosemann, M., Indulska, M., Green, P.: Business Process Modeling: A Comparative Analysis. Journal of the Association for Information Systems 10, 333–363 (2009)
15. Seidel, S., Recker, J., Pimmer, C., Vom Brocke, J.: Enablers and Barriers to the Organizational Adoption of Sustainable Business Practices. In: Leidner, D.E., Elam, J.J. (eds.) Proceedings of the 16th Americas Conference on Information Systems. Association for Information Systems, Lima (2010)

Controlling of Dynamic Enterprises by Indicators – A Foundational Approach

Nicole Zeise, Marco Link, and Erich Ortner

University of Technology Darmstadt, Hochschulstr. 1,
64289 Darmstadt, Germany
{zeise,link,ortner}@winf.tu-darmstadt.de

Abstract. Controlling of enterprises is an important step to realize dynamic re-actions. Therefore adequate indicator-systems have to be established. Modeling of these indicator-systems in the sense of sustainability offers a basis to use the term "sustainability" not just as a marketing buzz-word. The specific indicator- or attribute-system should be implemented in a way which ensures the control of all levels of enterprise architectures. The goal of the paper is to show on the one hand a language based approach to develop indicator-systems as well as its possible effects to the modeled process-system on the other hand.

Keywords: indicator, indicator-system, measurement, workflow management, dynamic enterprise, quantity aspect, modeling.

1 Introduction

This paper shows an approach to model and structure the top level of dynamic enter-prise architectures, the Enterprise-Management-System characterized by an indicator or attributes system. Therefore we describe first our idea of a dynamic enterprise controlled by indicators (section 1.1 and 1.2). In section 2 we discuss the concepts "indicator" and "indicator-system" to reach clarification about intension and exten-sion of these concepts. Thereby we want to establish a basis for developing a charac-ter model of an enterprise-management-system which enables controlling of all levels of a dynamic enterprise. As far as this model should be based on indicators, indicators are the focus of our attention. Furthermore section 3 details intension and extension of indicators by discussing influences of indicator-systems to internal process systems. Section 4 summarizes the paper and gives an outlook to our further work.

1.1 The Concept "Dynamic"

From a system theoretical point of view enterprises or organizations are characterized as exceeding complex open systems, which are created artificially by human beings [1]. They consist of interconnected elements (humans, tangible means and technique which can be consolidated in subsystems). The relations between the elements (within the system itself or between the system and its environment) are energetic, material or informational [2]. Additionally, organizations are goal-directed, whereas these goals can be differentiated between operational and strategic goals [1]. To reach these

M. zur Muehlen and J. Su (Eds.): BPM 2010 Workshops, LNBIP 66, pp. 521–530, 2011.
© Springer-Verlag Berlin Heidelberg 2011

goals, individual systems, characterized by a functional and a process oriented point of view (which interact and are interdependent), have to be created. In relation to the interaction with the environment (consuming and exporting resources) organizations are open systems which act dynamic.

In the context of this paper the concept "dynamic" is characterized as the force of self adaption to new requirements. For example, water which is influenced by the temperature of the environment: In case of falling temperatures the water changes its aggregate state from liquid to solid. This is possible because of the characteristics of the molecules and their compounds. The appending model would depend on the knowledge of the modeler. If a modeler would act on the assumption of constant environmental conditions or the nescience of the temperature-dependence of water, he would model the system of water molecules and their compounds as a fixed system. However, if he would take changing environmental conditions and the knowledge of the temperature dependence of water into account, he could model two or maybe three aggregate states (aerially, liquid, solid). These simple examples show, that with regard to the modeling of dynamic systems it is important to know: the characterization of the elements of the system, the characterization of the relations between the elements and the influencing variables of the environment.

An example for dynamic reaction of companies is, if new innovative technologies or products which replace older ones are developed by one company of a special market. Other companies of this market have to change their technologies or their range of products too, to secure their further existence at this market. By this companies should early know the influences of markets and as a next step the characterizations of elements and relations of their own system to manage the adaption to new requirements quickly.

1.2 Architecture of Dynamic Enterprises and Sustainability

Due to the ubiquitous use of IT systems, computer-scientists are living in an era characterized by holistic, sustainable and multidisciplinary ideals. "Holistic" contains the context of a system or its environment. "Multidisciplinarity" explores the elements connecting the different disciplines and their objects. The term "sustainability" in a broader sense refers to the protection of resources of our environment. Resources include any physical or intrinsic means (e.g. values, concepts, etc.) which are necessary to preserve actual and prospective (meaning evolutionary) human health, peace and a moderate prosperity.

The idea of sustainability has to be subdivided into further categories such as economical sustainability (industry), social sustainability (individuals as well as communities) and ecological sustainability (nature and environment). In general the term "sustainability" is often used for marketing purposes. In our view the first step to become sustainable is establishing a broad goal and indicator basis within the architecture of organizations.

Our idea of a dynamic enterprise is based on a four-level language based architecture (shown in Figure 1), assuming a process centric enterprise organization including e.g. instruments, processes and environmental influences.

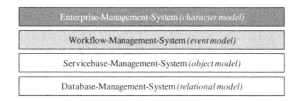

Fig. 1. Four-level architecture of a "dynamic enterprise"

The top level of this architecture, the enterprise organization level, consists of an indicator- or attribute-system to realize the regulation of the enterprise supported by a workflow-management-system (WfMS) on the second level.

With regard to the WfMS, the enterprise-management-system should contain an aligned goal system, which enables the enterprise to initiate actions for goal attainment. By designing a goal system in the subdivisions of sustainability (economical, ecological and social), enterprise value, not only periodical earnings, could be increased with long term view.

2   A Constructive Language Based Approach for Modeling Indicators and Indicator-Systems

To develop indicator-systems for controlling of enterprises in a constructive way we act in two steps. In the first step we develop a conceptual language for indicators, enabling us to use them logically, circle free and explicitly. Therefore we have to establish clarity to the concept "indicator" as foundation to develop a conceptual language. In the second step, we develop a modeling language for the internal design of indicators and the dynamic combination of indicators to a system. As basis to clear the concept "indicator" we use the model of "object classification in constructive computer science" [3] and the "conceptual model for objects in constructive computer science" [4] shown by Figure 2 and Figure 3.

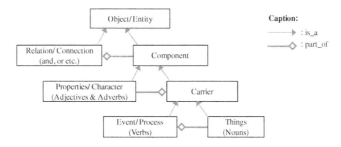

Fig. 2. Object classification in constructive computer science [3]

The object classification of Figure 2 gives us the possibility to model indicators based on their object relation with regard to the properties of elements, processes, and relations they measure. Additionally the conceptual model (shown in Figure 3) supports the detailed modeling of any object classification.

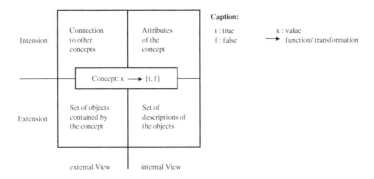

Fig. 3. Conceptual model for objects in constructive computer science [4]

The conceptual model offers the possibility to divide the concept "indicator" with regard to intension and extension. Intension is equivalent to "schema" and the extension to "instance". In relation to the system of an enterprise as an object, the following chapters focus on the intentional - internal and external view of the concept "indicator". The extension of the concept indicator has to be determined by existing indicators e.g. of a selected company.

2.1 Intension of the Concepts "Indicator and Indicator-System" – Internal View

Indicators represent information of measureable facts in a concentrated form. They can be divided according their calculation schema into absolute numbers, relative ratios or index ratios (cf. [5]). The calculations conform to defined formulas, which connect single values by mathematical operators.

Relating to the object classification (cf. Figure 2) every indicator has a set of properties, such as a unit (defined or non-dimensional), a certain acquisition interval (monthly, weekly, daily etc.), a certain acquisition point of time (specific date, weekday, last Friday a month etc.) and a data source (databases, etc.). All these properties are important with regard to extensions and to evaluate the quality of the measurement. The modeling process has to ensure that the relevant data for calculation of indicator values is available. In case of calculation data is missed, the modeler has to establish further processes to gather relevant data. In addition indicators can be monitored through means that facilitate comprehensiveness and analysis using, for example, different types of diagrams, tables or graphs.

By using indicators to support the regulation of systems, it becomes necessary to define actions for regulating processes (whereas these regulations are the external view of the intension). Therefore indicators have target values. They enable companies to identify gaps between goal achievement and reality as well as to initiate actions to reach the target value. In this way, indicators provide an information-base to support decision-making-processes to control entire systems.

2.2 Intension of the Concepts "Indicator and Indicator-System" – External View

Indicator-systems are used to measure, control and regulate company goals as well as process and the behavior elements (resources, employees, financial resources, products etc.). To control dynamic behavior of organizations they have to sum up all relevant information about connections between elements and the system elements themselves in a quantitative and qualitative way. In the form of mathematical calculations, they support transparency, visualization and presentation of information about elements, connections, processes or markets. Additionally they show interactions between the elements of the system as an input-output relation enabling us to draw conclusions about the transformation processes of a system.

Classifying the enterprise model in input, transformation and output and extending the model by supplier, customer, relevant markets and a specific process control unit (e.g. workflow-management-system) leads to a holistic enterprise view. Summarized our idea of an enterprise model is explained above in Figure 4. Additionally the figure shows several measuring points, which have either a direct process regard (as relations between the elements) or a direct element regard (inputs, resources, outputs). Indicators of different measuring points can be influenced directly by the company (indicators of the supply chain) or are non-influence able (indicators of the markets).

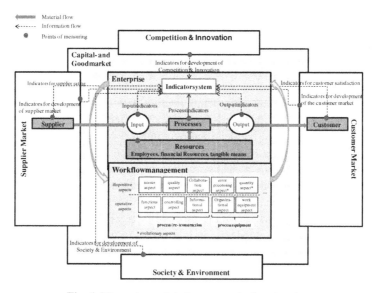

Fig. 4. Measuring points in an organizational system

Indicators which couldn`t be influenced by the company (e.g. development of a market) can be used to estimate the influences and disturbance variables and ultimately, to define goals or target values. Indicators which can be influenced directly by actions of an enterprise (e.g. supplier evaluation and customer satisfaction), measure the behavior and characterization of: resources (e.g. employees, tangible means, technologies or financial resources), supply chain partners (suppliers and customers) and processes. By that they can be used to control processes in time or to control processes by past review. To act sustainable all these indicators have to be considered with regard to the interaction of economic, social and ecological performance at all measurement points. Figure 5 gives some examples for influence able and non-influence able indicators in the sense of sustainability.

		Non-influence able indicators		Influence able Indicators
		Market of competitors	Society and Environment	Processes
Sustainability	Eco-nomical	competitors' prices and performance	development of market of employment and education (e.g. courses of study or training facilities)	supplier evaluation and customer satisfaction,
	Ecological	Innovations - new patents for innovative ecological production processes or products	environmental compatibility of the products (e.g. lifecycle and lifetime of the products, costs of waste disposal)	pollution (e.g. CO2 emission, hazardous waste)
	Social	development of competitors e.g. with regard to organization structure, regions, fair trade	development of social and environmental structures e.g. age distribution, social situation, landscape of the region, quality of recreation areas	social manners within the company or management style

Fig. 5. Examples for indicators in the sense of sustainability

These example are showing, that there do exist a lot of possible indicators. An organization has to choose indicators which correlate with their strategy and measure their goals. If goals and indicators are developed in the three perspectives of sustainability, a holistic indicator system would be constructed.

Indicators of different measuring-points interact with each other. This interaction implies that indicators can show possible causes or effects of development of other indicators. Interactions could be identified by empirical cause and effect chains (e.g. by the balanced scorecard) or by mathematical formulas (e.g. by the ROI model).

According to cause and effect chains common economic literature separates indicators into key performance indicators and key result indicators [6]. They are also called outcome measures and measures which drive future performance [7]. The focus of both concepts is the same: Measuring results and facts which lead to these results. In terms of system theory this classification is realized by the concepts of feed-forward loops and feedback loops [8] which are useful to explain forms of control. To enable dynamic reactions, both forms of indicators and forms of control are important. Result–indicators to help to learn about past performance (feedback loops) and performance-indicators are useful to feed-forward loops. Referring to our language approach, performance indicators as far as result indicators belong to the properties of indicators in the external view (also the differentiation of financial and non financial measures, subjective and objective measures, etc.).

3   Indicator-Effects to the Internal Process System

As a functional control unit for process execution within a "dynamic enterprise", a WfMS is assumed in our approach (level two in Figure 1). The control behavior is based on process descriptions with specific requirements concerning form and content (cf. [9]). Their models act as input parameter for the WfMS. These "model artifacts" are called operative description elements in the present analysis of the aspect-oriented modeling approach (cf. [10],[11]), since they are directly related to the extensional execution. As introduced in [12] and in [11], a dispositive level of description was identified in addition to the modeling of operative aspects. Elements which are modeled within the dispositive aspects, affect the operative modeling artifacts. The influence on the real execution will therefore take place only indirectly. Before possible impacts of indicators in the current approach will be discussed in detail, especially, concerning the quantitative aspect, the various aspects of Figure 6 will be mentioned briefly.

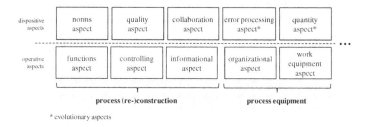

Fig. 6. Aspect-oriented modeling approach on two layers [11]

Operative Aspects:
The functions aspect describes and structures the required process steps (activities) and the involved conditions (rules) within an overall process (cf. [10]). In the controlling aspect causal and temporal dependencies between elements of the functions aspect - mainly the control flows - are defined (cf. [10]). Data and data flows needed in the process are described in the information aspect (cf. [13]). Within the organizational aspect the affected organizational structure and roles together with their allocation to the functional aspect are specified. The work equipment aspect describes available non-human resources and working appliances (IT-services, etc.) which are relevant in the connection to the current process model (allocation to the function aspect).

Dispositive Aspects:
The norms aspect records the necessary internal and external rules, regulations and policies for the present process. Within the quality aspect, the factors of influence with regard to required standards of qualities are specified. The collaboration aspect describes and defines the various points of collaboration and their actors. The error processing aspect complements the operational aspects with every new, on schema level, handled error (cf. [14]). The quantity aspect unites all quantifiable parameters and indicators with an impact on aspects of the operative level.

3.1 The Quantity Aspect as Element Representing the Influence of Processes through Indicators

The quantity aspect combines all quantitative values, which have an influence on the design of the operative aspects. This includes fixed variables (e.g. price information), measurable quantities (e.g. hours of operation) or calculable quantities (e.g. average processing time of an activity in a given period with regard to historical data). Just the latter category is understood by the term "indicator".

According to the model of indicators (see section 2), indicator instances (extensions) are the basis for changes of the general system. These influences are dividable into intensional and extensional effects concerning the operative aspect level.

Intensional effect
Based on the analysis of indicator extensions and their resulting impact on the operative layer, the superior management level (see Figure 1) can –in the case of an intensional effect- initiate a re-run of the life cycle (cf. Figure 7) with adjustments in the design phase. An example could be the identification and elimination of bottlenecks by changing the control flow (controlling aspect) or changes in allocation of resources (organizational or work equipment aspect). So this is a kind of schema modification, which explains the evolutionary nature of this aspect. These adjustments normally happen in context of a manual process and fall into the category of non-functional controlling of business (level 1 in Figure 1) by indicators. Depending on the indicator extension and process objectives appropriate actions may be carried out, as already explained.

Within the next instantiation of the current process, the modified scheme in the preparation and execution phase is used.

Extensional effect
This area refers to an impact which appears within a process instance (extension). It is therefore a functional control of the process instance which depends among others on indicator extensions. If, for example, the branching of the control flow (gateway) is modeled depending on a certain indicator, the process execution of the corresponding extension is influenced. This effect concerns only the execution phase of the life cycle model (see Figure 7).

3.2   Use and Utilization of Indicators in Various Stages of the Life Cycle Model

The life-cycle model [11] provides a good basis for a temporal classification of phases. As shown in Figure 7 the analysis, design, preparation, execution and monitoring phases are distinguished. Due to the main topic of modeling, the focus in this paper is located at the phases design (schema creation and evolution) and preparation. The preparation phase is often implied. In Figure 7 it is made explicit within two phases in the process lifecycle. During build-time, decisions as "make or buy" are already taken into account and enter the model schema. Also the non-specific equipment or role assignments at schema level can be counted into the preparation phase (cf. [15]). Within the run time stage of the preparation phase, the allocations on schema level must be made concrete on the instance level. For example, the modeled role "clerk", is concreted by "Mrs. Gordon". All necessary resources and appliances are allocated and provided concretely and prepared to run. These specific allocations should also conform to the model artifacts of the dispositive aspect layer.

Based on this classification, in analogy to the effects mentioned ahead, two basic variants for the use of indicators can be distinguished. Indicators are either hard-wired parts of the process (anchored at design phase) according to the extensional effect or

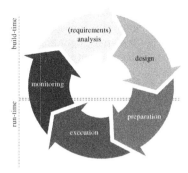

Fig. 7. Process lifecycle with preparation phase [11]

available as an equipment resource (as schematized and utilizable). In the last mentioned variant the indicators are not connected firmly with the process, they can be used if required (at preparation phase).

4 Conclusion and Outlook

The concept "indicator" was analyzed by the conceptual model for objects. As result the intension of indicators in an internal view is characterized for example by formulas, units, single values and time dependence. The external view is characterized by the relations to the elements of the enterprise-system (e.g. the influences to the entire workflow-management) and the relations between the indicators. The next step is to survey the extensions of indicators as proof of the results of the intension. After the complete clearing of the concept "indicator" we can develop a language (like predicate logic) to describe the indicators and their relations. Whereas from a present-day perspective a constructive construction of indicators by concepts for things like [N ε P] (with: N as nominator (like Peter), ε as the term "is a" and P as a predicate (like customer or employee)) is not expedient. Why not? That would be explained by analyzing the extensions of indicators which have no proper names (like if the EBT is 6.5% of sales at the 30.6.2010). Therefore it becomes necessary to use instead of predicate logic, the characterization theory and language, formal defined by Russell (1872 – 1970) [16]. This approach allows the explicit description of objects which do not have nominators.

As considered in the paper, indicators have manifold relations to other indicators of different measuring points and mathematical relations to the single values. To model and to proof the cause and effect chains, these relations can be modeled in a specific language where VDC-L [17] offers an approach. The detailed utilization of this language will be analyzed in following steps, whereby especially the empirical relations offer a broader field of research. Also the specific modeling methods for the mentioned dispositive aspects have to be specified in detail to connect the internal system, according to the approach (cf. [11]), with indicator-systems.

There are approaches (e.g. [18]) to develop languages for the modeling of indicators, even in the sense of sustainability (e.g. [19]). According to these and other publications in combination with our specific view on enterprises, we expect, by our approach the ability to establish a holistic indicator based enterprise controlling which acts dynamic. With view to sustainability this indicator-system should allow open systems (e.g. enterprises) to react dynamic regarding a changing environment (facts measured by indicators) and to achieve potential goals in an efficient way (supported by the underlying infrastructure).

References

1. Daft, R.L.: Organization Theory and Design. Thomson South-Western, Mason (2006)
2. Fuchs, H.: Systemtheorie und Organisation. Die Theorie offener Systeme als Grundlage zur Erforschung und Gestaltung betrieblicher Systeme Gabler, Wiesbaden (1973)
3. Ortner, E.: Methodenneutraler Fachentwurf. Zu den Grundlagen einer anwendungsorientierten Informatik Teubner, Stuttgart, Leipzig (1997)
4. Ortner, E.: Sprachbasierte Informatik. Wie man mit Wörtern die Cyber-Welt bewegt Ed. am Gutenbergplatz, Leipzig (2005)
5. Zeise, N.: Modellierung von Kennzahlen mit BPMN. In: Engels, G., Luckey, M., Schäfer, W. (eds.) Proceedings - Software Engineering 2010, Bonn, pp. 63–74 (2010)
6. Parmenter, D.: Key performance indicators. In: Developing, Implementing, and Using Winning. KPIs Wiley, Hoboken, NJ (2007)
7. Kaplan, R.S., Norton, D.P.: The balanced scorecard. In: Translating Strategy into Action. Harvard Business School Press, Boston (2009)
8. Skyttner, L.: General systems theory. In: Ideas & Applications. World Scientific, Singapore (2001)
9. Link, M., Ortner, E.: Service-oriented Application System Architecture. Business process management meets workflow management. In: AMCIS Proceedings (2009)
10. Jablonski, S.: Prozessdesign und -modellierung für ein holistisches Prozessmanagement. In: Heinemann, E., Ortner, E. (eds.) Anwendungsinformatik. Die Zukunft der Enterprise Engineering, pp. 83–104. Nomos-Verl.-Ges., Baden-Baden (2008)
11. Link, M., Ortner, E.: Dynamic Enterprise (as a composite Service System). In: International Conference on Service Sciences, pp. 66–70. IEEE CS, Los Alamitos CA (2010)
12. Link, M.: Zweistufiger Modellierungsansatz zur nachhaltigen Prozessbeschreibung (2010) (in press)
13. Lehmann, F.R.: Fachlicher Entwurf von Workflow-Management-Anwendungen. Teubner, Stuttgart (1999)
14. Reuter, A.: Fehlerbehandlung in Datenbanksystemen. Datenbank-Recovery Hanser, München (1981)
15. Wiendahl, H.-P.: Betriebsorganisation für Ingenieure Hanser, München, Wien (2008)
16. Linsky, B., Imaguire, G., Russell, B.: On denoting. 1905 - 2005 Philosophia, München (2005)
17. Grollius, T.: Interaktive Konfigurierung dynamischer Anwendungssysteme aus Komponenten. In: Engels, G., Luckey, M., Schäfer, W. (eds.) Proceedings - Software Engineering 2010, Bonn, pp. 75–85 (2010)
18. Frank, U., Heise, D., Kattenstroth, H.: Use of a Domain Specific Modeling Language for Realizing Versatile Dashboards. In: Tolvanen, J.-P., Rossi, M., Gray, J., Sprinkle, J. (eds.) Proceedings of the 9th OOPSLA Workshop on Domain-specific Modeling (DSM), Helsinki (2009)
19. Tolón-Becerra, A., Bienvenido, F.: Conceptual Modeling in a Meta-model of Sustainability Indicators. Knowledge-Based Intelligent Information and Engineering Systems, 716–723 (2010)

1st International Workshop on Process in the Large (IW-PL 2010)

Workshop Organization

Workshop Organizers

HajoReijers
TechnischeUniversiteit Eindhoven
Postbus 513
5600 MB Eindhoven
The Netherlands

Marcello La Rosa
Faculty of Science & Technology
Queensland University of Technology
GPO Box 2434
Brisbane QLD 4001
Australia

RemcoDijkman
TechnischeUniversiteit Eindhoven
Postbus 513
5600 MB Eindhoven
The Netherlands

Program Committee

Wil van der Aalst (Eindhoven University of Technology, The Netherlands)
Marlon Dumas (University of Tartu, Estonia)
Jon Gulla (Norwegian University of Science and Technology, Norway)
Paul Johannesson (Royal Institute of Technology, Sweden)
Agnes Koschmider (University of Karlsruhe, Germany)
Akhil Kumar (Penn State University, USA)
JochenKüster (IBM Research, Switzerland)
Jintae Lee (University of Colorado at Boulder, USA)
Markus Nüttgens (University of Hamburg, Germany)
Manfred Reichert (University of Ulm, Germany)
Michael Rosemann (Queensland University of Technology, Australia)
ShaziaSadiq (University of Queensland, Australia)
Minseok Song (Ulsan National Institute of Science and Technology, South Korea)
Hagen Völzer (IBM Research, Switzerland)
Barbara Weber (University of Innsbruck, Austria)
Mathias Weske (HassoPlattnerInstitut, Germany)
PetiaWohed (Stockholm University, Sweden)
George Wyner (Boston University, USA)

Metric Trees for Efficient Similarity Search in Large Process Model Repositories

Matthias Kunze and Mathias Weske

Hasso Plattner Institute at the University of Potsdam
Prof.-Dr.-Helmert-Strae 2-3, 14482 Potsdam
{matthias.kunze,mathias.weske}@hpi.uni-potsdam.de

Summary. Due to the increasing adoption of business process management and the key role of process models, companies are setting up and maintaining large process model repositories. Repositories containing hundreds or thousands of process models are not uncommon, whereas only simplistic search functionality, such as text based search or folder navigation, is provided, today.

On the other hand, advanced methods have recently been proposed in the literature to ascertain the similarity of process models. However, due to performance reasons, an exhaustive similarity search by pairwise comparison is not feasible in large process model repositories.

This paper presents an indexing approach based on metric trees, a hierarchical search structure that saves comparison operations during search with nothing but a distance function at hand. A detailed investigation of this approach is provided along with a quantitative evaluation thereof, showing its suitability and scalability in large process model repositories.

1 Introduction

Nowadays, one can find large process model collections in almost every company, since the value of business processes has been recognized and acknowledged as an essential asset to drive an organization [26, 28]. Effective reuse, extraction of knowledge, and generation of insights among these model collections require capabilities to efficiently search and navigate within them.

Process models generally expose a high degree of heterogeneity [1] and thus, exact-match searching is neither feasible nor meaningful. Instead, the concept of similarity has been discovered to be a valuable means to compare and search process models and many similarity measures have been proposed [1, 7, 14, 16, 17, 18, 24]. These include semantic approaches to identifying corresponding nodes, structural, and behavioral aspects of process model similarity. Several of the authors mention that their algorithms are in particular expensive with regards to time complexity. Yan et al. [29] comprehensively studied process model repositories currently available for industry and academia. Their survey discloses that efficient implementation of search for similar process models has been widely neglected.

However, applications for fast and efficient similarity search in large process model repositories are manifold, due to the increasing adoption of business

M. zur Muehlen and J. Su (Eds.): BPM 2010 Workshops, LNBIP 66, pp. 535–546, 2011.

process modeling. Aligning large process model collections to changing market opportunities can be achieved through continuous process model refactoring, which, however, bears the risk of introducing inconsistencies [26]. Searching for similar model artifacts yields the set of relevant models and provides a means to track and propagate adoption of process models [23]. Efficient search in process model repositories can also help to discover redundancies when models are added to a collection [17], e.g., when process models of two organizations that engage in a merger need to be consolidated. Furthermore, similarity search among process models offers the chance to obtain reference models, or fragments thereof, as means to semi-automatic modeling assistance [13], or to find normative process models, which are most similar to process models that have been discovered through process mining [1].

In this paper, we do not address optimization of the similarity algorithms' efficiency, but rather try to reduce the number of comparisons required to find models in a repository. We achieve this goal by indexing, i.e., building efficient data structures to guide searching. Metric trees [20, 21] offer a means to increase the efficiency of similarity search by a notion of distance, or dissimilarity. A metric tree is an index that partitions the metric space, i.e., the collection of process models. During search, certain partitions can be safely pruned under some circumstances, reducing the number of comparison operations. We applied similarity search in metric spaces to the field of business process management to evaluate its usefulness and scalability to search within large process model repositories.

The remainder of this work is structured as follows. In Section 2 we give an overview of similarity search that puts metric trees into the context of similarity search and discuss previous work on process model similarity. Subsequently, we introduce our approach to build and search within an index of process models with the help of the M-Tree [6] index structure and an implementation of the graph edit distance for process models, in Section 3. Since we aim at reducing the number of comparison operations when searching for similar process models, in Section 4, we evaluate the implementation of our approach toward this aspect with varying parameters. Finally, we conclude our work and give an outlook on research directions and objectives that we will address in the future, in Section 5.

2   Preliminaries

This section discusses related work with regards to process model similarity and similarity search, which lay the groundwork for our approach, described in Section 3.

Similarity search has received increasing interest in a variety of domains, including multimedia, computational biology, data mining, and pattern recognition, cf. [4, 31]. The idea behind is based on a definition of proximity that can be defined by characteristic features extracted from the actual objects. In the context of process models, such characteristic features can be structure, i.e., the model graph, or behavior, derived by means of the state space [1, 27].

2.1   Process Model Similarity

Many existing approaches to compare process models, such as various notions of bisimulation [25], trace equivalence [11], and workflow inheritance [22], only tell whether two process models are the same in a certain context, but not how similar they are. More meaningful measures that quantify the similarity of process models have been demanded and proposed [1, 7, 17, 24], since. The approaches, which can be generally divided into behavioral and structural ones, ground on the same concept: (1) Identify corresponding process model elements, e.g., activities, gateways, control flow edges, and (2) compare the relations between them.

The behavior of a process is characterized by the set of possible execution sequences of the process model elements. The behavioral similarity of two process models addresses relationships regarding causality, concurrency, and exclusion of corresponding elements [17, 27] and is indicated by a—usually weighted—fraction of common behavior; whereas particular fragments of a process model may be considered more relevant than others [1].

In structural approaches, the relation between process model elements essentially refers to the graph structure of the process model, i.e., which nodes are predecessors and successors of other nodes, connected through edges with each other. Similarity is often based on the fraction of common structural components, such as control flow arcs [1] or activity nodes [13]. Another approach to (dis-) similarity is to calculate the cost of converting one process model into another one with the *graph edit distance* [8, 14, 16, 18]. The graph edit distance is defined by the least expensive sequence of operations to transform one graph into another, where each operation type, including inserting, removing, and substituting elements of the graph, has a cost-weight assigned [9].

Key to identifying corresponding process model elements is labeling. Although correspondences can be found manually through reviews from process model experts [8], researchers addressed this issue applying structural models, e.g., the Levenshtein distance [15], and linguistic models, such as synonyms taken from WordNet[1], [13, 24].

2.2   Indexing in Metric Spaces

In exact-match search, objects of the result set are exact equals among a set of structured data that can be ordered by simple means. In contrast, similarity search does not assume an intrinsic ordering of objects: The result set comprises objects, which are within certain proximity of the query object.

In *coordinate spaces*, objects are treated as vectors in a multidimensional space by mapping each feature to a value of a particular dimension [12]. The concept of vectors in a multidimensional space offers means to calculate distances of two objects by computing the distance of the corresponding feature-vectors, e.g., using the Minkowski distances [31]. Search structures for vector spaces, so-called spatial access methods (SAM), effectively exploit the ordering of feature-values of a dimension to find similar objects. The R-Tree [10] is a well known

---

[1] cf. http://wordnet.princeton.edu/

approach to search within coordinate spaces. However, the notion of distance in a multidimensional space may be of little meaning, due to correlation of features, so-called cross-talk [31], which does not map into vector based similarity.

Generally, one cannot assume feature vectors to be available in certain domains. For example, a representation of graph structure or process behavior in a coordinate space is not feasible or has only limited meaning, and therefore, SAMs cannot be applied. A more general approach has been raised that addresses the similarity searching problem, called *metric spaces* [20, 21], of which coordinate spaces are a special type. In metric spaces, nothing but the distance of two objects can be computed. Yet, the abstract notion of distance offers the opportunity to construct particular means to express proximity of objects, with regards to the desired use case and accounting for cross-talk between the objects' features. Informally, searching in a metric space means to obtain a ranked set of objects that are in proximity to a query object, or whose feature values fall within a given range from those of a query object.

There is a large body of research in similarity searching, cf. [4, 12, 31], and many index structures for metric spaces, which will be referred to as *metric trees* hereafter, have been proposed, including, but not limited to, the GNAT [3], VP-Tree [5], and M-Tree [6]. The common goal of these approaches is to avoid exhaustive examination of the search space and to reduce the number of comparisons required for query processing. This is because cost for query execution is not only constrained by I/O-operations but is also CPU-bound, due to expensive computation of the distance between two objects. This is achieved by preprocessing the data, i.e., building an equivalence relation, so that at search time some classes are discarded and the others are exhaustively searched [4]. The equivalence relation in metric spaces is defined in terms of the distance between two elements. Equivalence classes are generally built using reference objects, *pivots*, that partition the search space, such that all objects within a certain distance to a pivot are within its equivalence class. Recursive partitioning of a class leads to a hierarchical structure of equivalence classes: the index tree. Some indexing approaches use only one pivot per node in the index tree, e.g., the VP-Tree [5], and partition the space by means of spheres of different radii centered at the pivot [30]. Other indexing approaches take two or more pivots into account, i.e., objects are partitioned among several pivots based on their distance to them and fair distribution between them [3, 6].

3   Efficient Search with Metric Trees

This section elucidates how a metric tree can reduce the number of comparison operations to obtain a set of process models similar to a given query q. Search in metric spaces can be coarsely classified into range searches, i.e., given a query model q, find all models that fall within a certain distance range $r(q)$, and into nearest neighbor searches, i.e., find the k models with least distance to q, or a combination of both. Nearest neighbor queries are quite similar to range queries, in that the range iteratively decreases while k candidates are being collected until no models more similar to q can be found.

Metric trees partition metric spaces by means of relative distances between objects instead of their absolute position in a vector space. The only requirement of such indexing is that the notion of distance is a metric [31].

Definition 1 (Distance Metric). *A metric space is a pair $\mathcal{S} = (\mathcal{D}, d)$ where $\mathcal{D}$ is the domain of objects and $d : \mathcal{D} \times \mathcal{D} \to \mathbb{R}$ is a metric, i.e., a distance function with the following properties:*
  - *symmetry:* $\forall o_i, o_j \in \mathcal{D} : d(o_i, o_j) = d(o_j, o_i)$
  - *nonnegativity:* $\forall o_i, o_j \in \mathcal{D}, o_i \neq o_j : d(o_i, o_j) > 0 \bigwedge \forall o_i \in \mathcal{D} : d(o_i, o_i) = 0$
  - *triangle inequality:* $\forall o_i, o_j, o_k \in \mathcal{D} : d(o_i, o_k) \leq d(o_i, o_j) + d(o_j, o_k)$

3.1   A Sample Similarity Measure for Process Models

The concept of metric trees is agnostic of the actual distance notion as long as it is a metric. Most of the similarity notions mentioned earlier satisfy the first two requirements, i.e., symmetry and nonnegativity, while the triangle inequality is the essential property that allows search to prune subtrees in metric trees. To calculate the dissimilarity of process models, we exemplarily chose the graph edit distance, which satisfies the triangle inequality. Since we apply the graph edit distance to process models, they will be introduced first.

Definition 2 (Process Model). *Let $\mathcal{L}$ be a set of labels and $\mathcal{T}$ a set of node types. A process model P is a connected graph (N, E, λ, τ) where*
  - *N is a finite set of nodes,*
  - *$E \subseteq N \times N$ is a set of edges,*
  - *$\tau : N \to \mathcal{T}$ assigns a type to each node, and*
  - *$\lambda : N \to \mathcal{L}$ assigns a label to each node*

Definition 3 (Graph Edit Distance). *A process model $P_1 = (N_1, E_1, \lambda, \tau)$ can be transformed into another process model $P_2 = (N_2, E_2, \lambda, \tau)$ through a finite sequence $\mathcal{O} = \sigma_1, \sigma_2, ..., \sigma_n$ of edit operations σ_i, such that $P_2 = \sigma_n(...(\sigma_2(\sigma_1(P_1)))...)$.*
    Let $\mathcal{M} : N_1^* \to N_2^*; N_1^* \subseteq N_1, N_2^* \subseteq N_2$ be a bijective mapping that indicates that some nodes in P_1 have corresponding nodes in P_2, i.e., $\forall_{n \in N_1^*} \mathcal{M}(n) \in N_2^*$, which are substitutable. Edges established by two succeeding nodes in P_1, i.e., $E_1 \ni e = (n_i, n_j)$ can be substituted, iff the corresponding nodes induced by the mapping $\mathcal{M}$ are connected by an edge $E_2 \ni e' = (\mathcal{M}(n_i), \mathcal{M}(n_j))$ in P_2.
    To quantify the dissimilarity of P_1 and P_2 specific costs are assigned to the edit operations: $w : \sigma_i \to \mathbb{R}$. The edit operations and their specific costs[2] w are classified as follows:

  - *σ_{in} inserts a node to N_1 that has a counterpart in N_2; $w(\sigma_{in}) = 1$*
  - *σ_{rn} removes a node from N_1 that has no counterpart in N_2; $w(\sigma_{rn}) = 1$*
  - *σ_{ie} inserts an edge to E_1 that has a counterpart in E_2; $w(\sigma_{ie}) = 1$*
  - *σ_{re} removes an edge from E_1 that has no counterpart in E_2; $w(\sigma_{re}) = 1$*

---

[2] We used the given costs for our evaluation, cf. Section 4. These can be varied to shift the similarity notion, but costs for insert/remove must be equal to preserve the symmetry property of the metric.

- σ_{sn} *substitutes a node* $n \in N_1$ *with its counterpart* $\mathcal{M}(n) \in N_2$ *induced by the mapping* $\mathcal{M}$; $w(\sigma_{sn}) = 2 \cdot ldn(\lambda(n), \lambda(\mathcal{M}(n)))$

  To calculate the cost of substituted nodes we apply the Levenshtein distance [15] ld *of their labels* $s_1 = \lambda(n)$, $s_2 = \lambda(\mathcal{M}(n))$ *normalized by the longer label, i.e.,* $ldn(s_1, s_2) = \frac{ld(s_1,s_2)}{max(|s_1|,|s_2|)}$, $ldn(\bot, \bot) = 0$
- σ_{se} *substitutes an edge* $e \in E_1$ *with its counterpart* $e' \in E_2$ *induced by the mapping* $\mathcal{M}$, *as explained above;* $w(\sigma_{se}) = 0$

The Graph Edit Distance *is denoted by the least cost of* n *possible sequences of edit operations* $\mathcal{O}_1, ..., \mathcal{O}_n$ *that transform* P_1 *into* P_2:

$$ged(P_1, P_2) = min\left(\left\{\sum_{\sigma_i \in \mathcal{O}_l} w(\sigma_i); l = 1...n\right\}\right)$$

We adapted the greedy algorithm proposed by Dijkman et al. [8] to find a mapping $\mathcal{M}$ and to calculate the graph edit distance iteratively. The Levenshtein distance [15] is used to obtain a set of candidate pairs of process model nodes for the mapping. In our implementation for Event-driven Process Chains (EPC), cf. Section 4, the algorithm further only considers pairs of nodes of the same type $\tau \in \mathcal{T}$.

In contrast to other applications that use the graph edit distance, e.g., obtaining a ranked set of similar models in a repository, we do not normalize the graph edit distance by the size of either process model, because, in order to find models similar to a given query, we are interested in the number of operations to transform the query into a model from the repository.

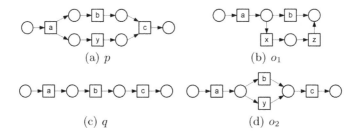

(a) p   (b) o_1

(c) q   (d) o_2

Fig. 1. Sample Petri Net Process Models

To illustrate our approach we use the four process models of Figure 1. For simplicity purposes, these models have been labeled with single characters, resulting in a normalized Levenshtein distance of their labels of either 0 (for equal labels) or 1. Given, for example, models p and o_2 from Figure 1, the difference between both models is the path containing transition y that is a concurrent path in p while being a conflict path in o_2. The least-cost sequence of edit operations to transform p to o_2 consists of removing both places before and after y in p and connected edges, and reconnecting y with the places connected to a and b as well as b and c, respectively. Remaining places and transitions (a, b, and c) as well as the according edges can be substituted at zero cost, which results in a graph edit distance $ged(p, o_2) = 8$. Likewise, the graph edit distance of p and o_1 is 18.

In the next section, we explain how this distance metric is used to build and search efficiently within a process model repository. We will refer to the generic metric d when explaining the concepts of the index; for concrete examples we employ the graph edit distance ged as a representative metric.

3.2   Metric Trees for Process Model Repositories

From the many alternative approaches on metric trees, cf. [4, 12, 31], we chose the M-Tree [6], which, in contrast to other approaches, has been designed to combine a balanced and dynamic index. The latter means that the index does not need to be rebuilt after adding process models to the repository, which is certainly a desirable feature in large, actively used process model repositories.

Nodes of an M-Tree comprise a set of pivots, of which each points to a subtree—a node on the next lower level. This is illustrated in Figure 2: The pivot p in the root node n_{root} references leaf node n_3, which contains three pivots, o_0, o_1, o_2, of which each references a process model. In M-Trees, all indexed objects are referenced in leaf nodes, and feature values of pivots are chosen from the set of indexed objects, rather than being constructed artificially. Thus, the feature value of an object may be referenced several times, once in a leaf node, and in one or more nonleaf nodes. This is why, in Figure 2, p and o_0 have the same feature value, i.e., $ged(o_0, p) = 0$.

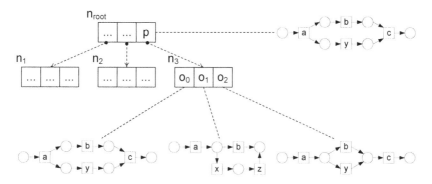

Fig. 2. Example Metric Tree including Process Models of Figure 1. Pivots store their radius and their distance to parent pivot, i.e., $r(p) = 18$, since $ged(p, o_0) = 0$, $ged(p, o_1) = 18$, and $ged(p, o_2) = 8$.

The subtree rooted in pivot p is called a *covering tree*, denoted $T(p)$, and each child element $o \in T(p)$ stores its distance $d(p, o)$ to the pivot, unless o is a pivot in the root node n_{root}. Each pivot maintains its covering radius $r(p)$, such that, $\forall o \in T(p) : d(p, o) \leq r(p)$, cf. Figure 3(a).

Building Metric Trees. These values, i.e., $r(p)$ and $d(o, p), o \in T(p)$, are calculated in a bottom up approach when a new process model, or feature value thereof, o_n is added to the index, which renders the M-Tree both balanced and dynamic. First, o_n is treated like a query to identify the most similar leaf node to add the object to and thus, moves down the tree. Each time o_n passes a pivot vertically, this pivot's covering radius $r(p)$ will be updated by the distance $d(p, o_n)$ if it exceeds $r(p)$. This strategy keeps the covering radii of pivots compact. Finally, a new pivot o_n'—the feature value of o_n along with its distance to its parent pivot—will be added to a leaf node. If adding pivot o_n' to a node $T(p')$ exceeds the maximum size of this node, it will be split. New pivots p_1', p_2' will be chosen from $T(p')$ and its pivots $p_i \in T(p')$ will be distributed among two newly created nodes $T(p_1'), T(p_2')$. The new pivots p_1', p_2' will be added to the parent node of $T(p')$, whereas the old pivot p' will be removed from it. This procedure may require splitting the parent node, if it grows too large, and so on, which may move up to the root node of the tree recursively. Since pivots are distributed evenly among nodes in case of a split, the tree remains balanced, which equalizes search costs.

Search for Similar Process Models and Pruning of Subtrees. Search in metric spaces takes a query process model q and a query radius $r(q)$, which describes the acceptable distance of a matched process model compared with q. The triangle inequality of the metric d is the particular property that makes similarity searching in metric spaces efficient. It allows pruning subtrees of the metric tree without calculating the distance between q and the pivots of these subtrees. Search starts in the root node, and for each pivot $p \in n_{root}$ the distance $d(p, q)$ is calculated. If the covering radius of a pivot and the query radius intersect, i.e., $d(p, q) \leq r(p) + r(q)$, there may exist referenced models in $T(p)$ or in its subtrees that satisfy q with regards to $r(q)$, depicted in Figure 3(b). Let $r(q) = 6$ and take the example metric tree from above, then $ged(p, q) = 7$ and $r(p) + r(q) = 18 + 6 = 24$. This requires comparing each pivot in $T(p)$ with q.

If the distance was greater than the sum of both covering radii, i.e., $d(p, q) > r(p) + r(q)$ then $T(p)$ could not contain any objects that are close enough to q due to the triangle inequality, illustrated in Figure 3(c). Thus, $T(p)$ could be safely pruned from the search.

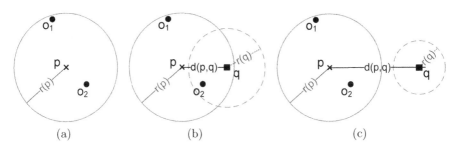

(a)   (b)   (c)

Fig. 3. Space partition with a single pivot (a). Include covering tree $T(p)$ in further (exhaustive) search, if radii $r(p)$ and $r(q)$ intersect (b). Exclude $T(p)$ from search if it is too distant from q (c).

Since the covering radius of p and its distance to all objects $o \in T(p)$, where $T(p)$ is a leaf node, are a priori known, it is also possible to prune them without calculating $d(o, q)$. Recall, if $d(o, q) > r(q) + r(o)$ then o can be safely excluded from the search. Since o references only one object, its covering radius is 0 and can therefore be ignored. From the triangle inequality it follows that $d(o, q) \geq |d(o, p) - d(p, q)|$ and thus, if $|d(o, p) - d(p, q)| > r(q)$ then o can be pruned. Given from the examples above, $ged(o_1, p) = 18$, $ged(p, q) = 7$, $r(q) = 6$, and thus $ged(o_1, q) \geq 11 > 6$, it can be concluded that o_1 is too far away from p with regards to $r(q)$ and can be dismissed from the search result without calculating $ged(o_1, q)$. Searching with q and $r(q) = 6$ among given models would only return o_2, since its distance $ged(o_2, q) = 3$ is within the acceptable range of the query $r(q)$. The distance $ged(o_0, q) = 7$ had already been calculated while visiting pivot p. This particular setting from the examples is depicted in Figure 3(b).

N.B.: Given the distance notion complies with the definition of a metric, cf. Definition 1, pruning subtrees and objects during search does not influence the quality of the result, i.e., provides the same results as exhaustive search.

4   Evaluation

We evaluated the approach described in the previous section with regards to its scalability to process model repositories and present the results within the following paragraphs. As metric trees' efficiency relies on the effective pruning of partitions of the search space, and thus reducing the number of comparison operations, we chose this measure for our evaluation.

To test our approach of indexing business process models using the M-Tree as index structure and the graph edit distance as (dis-) similarity metric, we took the SAP reference model, a set of approximately 600 EPC process models. These models consist of 21 nodes in average, with up to 130 nodes per model. Less than 8 percent of the models comprise 50 or more nodes. Figure 4(a) illustrates the distribution of graph edit distances among the pairs within our dataset. We chose models from the indexed dataset as queries and calculated the average number of comparison operations to find the 10 most similar process models for the given query, i.e., performed a 10-nearest-neighbor search. The baseline for our comparison is sequential search (SEQ), i.e., exhaustive, pair-wise comparison of the query with each stored model.

In a first phase, we compared different methods to choose a pivot when splitting a node, cf. Section 3.2, namely the RANDOM method that randomly chooses two pivots from all available ones, and the MAX_DIST method that chooses pivots with maximal distance to partition the space most effectively [6]. Figure 4(b) shows that RANDOM already saves about 42% of comparison operations compared to SEQ. While MAX_DIST requires more comparison operations to build the index, that is, for finding the most distant pivots, it provides further search improvements over RANDOM, saving up to 85,8% of comparison operations compared to SEQ. Increasing the sample size improves this ratio and indicates that search within the index has logarithmic costs for comparison operations. Due to the

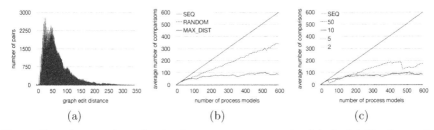

Fig. 4. Distribution of graph edit distance among samples (a). Scalability by method to choose pivot (b) and maximum node size (c).

search algorithm, pruning of subtrees is based on the chosen pivots, and thus search performance varies, observable by the fluctuation of the curves, and can only be measured empirically.

In a second evaluation phase, we compared the impact of different maximum node sizes, using `MAX_DIST`. As Figure 4(c) indicates, this has no significant influence on the efficiency of searching at large dataset sizes if the node size is small. However, large node sizes perform less efficiently, indicated by the dashed curve, representing a node size of 50 pivots. This suggests that moderate node sizes, e.g., 10 pivots per node, are most suitable and scalable.

5   Conclusion and Future Work

Searching in process model repositories needs to be both, meaningful and efficient, to be useful under practical conditions. Much effort has been spent investigating meaningful similarity notions to compare process models considering process behavior and graph structures. However, they lack efficiency in terms of computation time and resources, mainly due to the nature of process models, which, in consequence, requires a detailed comparison to identify corresponding elements within process models and map their semantics. Thus, costs with regards to the number of comparison operations need to be minimized to make search more efficient.

In this paper, we applied an approach known from the database community to business process model repositories, namely metric trees. This index structure leverages nothing but the distance between characteristic feature values of objects to partition the search space and saves comparison operations by safely excluding partitions from exhaustive search. We used the graph edit distance for business process models as distance metric and a greedy algorithm to identify corresponding process model elements. The scalability of this approach has been proved in experiments that show significant savings of comparison operations, using the SAP reference model.

This paper focuses primarily on the suitability and scalability of the metric tree approach to process model repositories, thus using the rather simple graph edit distance as a metric. However, the approach is not limited to process model similarity, such as the graph edit distance. Any method that can be applied to compare a given query model with a model from the repository is applicable if it yields a metric, cf. Definition 1. Other aspects of process model search, cf. Section 2.1, shall be examined in future work, as well as extending this approach to more expressive queries, e.g., BPMN-Q [2]. Using more abstract process model definitions, as, e.g., proposed by La Rosa et al. [19], would make the index applicable to heterogeneous process model repositories regarding different process modeling languages.

References

1. van der Aalst, W.M.P., de Medeiros, A.K.A., Weijters, A.J.M.M.T.: Process equivalence: Comparing two process models based on observed behavior. In: Dustdar, S., Fiadeiro, J.L., Sheth, A.P. (eds.) BPM 2006. LNCS, vol. 4102, pp. 129–144. Springer, Heidelberg (2006)
2. Awad, A.: Bpmn-q: A language to query business processes. In: EMISA, pp. 115–128 (2007)
3. Brin, S.: Near neighbor search in large metric spaces. In: VLDB 1995: Proceedings of the 21th International Conference on Very Large Data Bases, pp. 574–584. Morgan Kaufmann Publishers Inc., San Francisco (1995)
4. Chávez, E., Navarro, G., Baeza-Yates, R., Marroquín, J.L.: Searching in Metric Spaces. ACM Comput. Surv. 33(3), 273–321 (2001)
5. Chiueh, T.-C.: Content-based image indexing. In: VLDB 1994: Proceedings of the 20th International Conference on Very Large Data Bases, pp. 582–593. Morgan Kaufmann Publishers Inc., San Francisco (1994)
6. Ciaccia, P., Patella, M., Zezula, P.: M-tree: An efficient access method for similarity search in metric spaces. In: VLDB 1997: Proceedings of the 23rd International Conference on Very Large Data Bases, pp. 426–435. Morgan Kaufmann Publishers Inc., San Francisco (1997)
7. Dijkman, R.: Diagnosing differences between business process models. In: Dumas, M., Reichert, M., Shan, M.-C. (eds.) BPM 2008. LNCS, vol. 5240, pp. 261–277. Springer, Heidelberg (2008)
8. Dijkman, R.M., Dumas, M., García-Bañuelos, L.: Graph matching algorithms for business process model similarity search. In: Dayal, U., Eder, J., Koehler, J., Reijers, H.A. (eds.) BPM 2009. LNCS, vol. 5701, pp. 48–63. Springer, Heidelberg (2009)
9. Gao, X., Xiao, B., Tao, D., Li, X.: A Survey of Graph Edit Distance. Pattern Analysis & Applications 13(1), 113–129 (2010)
10. Guttman, A.: R-trees: a dynamic index structure for spatial searching. SIGMOD Rec. 14(2), 47–57 (1984)
11. Hidders, J., Dumas, M., van der Aalst, W.M.P., ter Hofstede, A.H.M., Verelst, J.: When are two workflows the same? In: CATS 2005: Proceedings of the 2005 Australasian Symposium on Theory of Computing, pp. 3–11. Australian Computer Society, Inc., Darlinghurst (2005)
12. Hjaltason, G.R., Samet, H.: Index-driven similarity search in metric spaces (survey article). ACM Trans. Database Syst. 28(4), 517–580 (2003)
13. Koschmider, A.: Ähnlichkeitsbasierte Modellierungsunterstützung für Geschäftsprozesse. PhD thesis, Universität Karlsruhe (TH), Fakultät für Wirtschaftswissenschaften (2007)
14. Küster, J.M., Gerth, C., Förster, A., Engels, G.: Detecting and resolving process model differences in the absence of a change log. In: Dumas, M., Reichert, M., Shan, M.-C. (eds.) BPM 2008. LNCS, vol. 5240, pp. 244–260. Springer, Heidelberg (2008)

15. Levenshtein, V.I.: Binary Codes Capable of Correcting Deletions, Insertions and Reversals. Soviet Physics Doklady 10, 707 (1966)
16. Li, C., Reichert, M., Wombacher, A.: On measuring process model similarity based on high-level change operations. In: Li, Q., Spaccapietra, S., Yu, E., Olivé, A. (eds.) ER 2008. LNCS, vol. 5231, pp. 248–264. Springer, Heidelberg (2008)
17. Mendling, J., van Dongen, B.F., van der Aalst, W.M.P.: On the Degree of Behavioral Similarity between Business Process Models. In: Nüttgens, M., Rump, F.J., Gadatsch, A. (eds.) EPK. CEUR Workshop Proceedings, vol. 303, pp. 39–58. CEUR-WS.org (2007)
18. Minor, M., Tartakovski, A., Bergmann, R.: Representation and structure-based similarity assessment for agile workflows. In: Weber, R.O., Richter, M.M. (eds.) ICCBR 2007. LNCS (LNAI), vol. 4626, pp. 224–238. Springer, Heidelberg (2007)
19. Rosa, M.L., Reijers, H.A., van der Aalst, W.M.P., Dijkman, R.M., Mendling, J., Dumas, M., Garcia-Banuelos, L.: Apromore: An advanced process model repository (2009), http://eprints.qut.edu.au/27448/
20. Uhlmann, J.K.: Metric Trees. Applied Mathematics Letters 4, 61–62 (1991)
21. Uhlmann, J.K.: Satisfying general proximity/similarity queries with metric trees. Information Processing Letters 40(4), 175–179 (1991)
22. van der Aalst, W.M.P., Basten, T.: Inheritance of Workflows: An Approach to Tackling Problems Related to Change. Theor. Comput. Sci. 270(1-2), 125–203 (2002)
23. van der Aalst, W.M.P.: Inheritance of business processes: A journey visiting four notorious problems. In: Ehrig, H., Reisig, W., Rozenberg, G., Weber, H. (eds.) Petri Net Technology for Communication-Based Systems. LNCS, vol. 2472, pp. 383–408. Springer, Heidelberg (2003)
24. van Dongen, B., Dijkman, R., Mendling, J.: Measuring Similarity between Business Process Models. In: Bellahsène, Z., Léonard, M. (eds.) CAISE 2008. LNCS, vol. 5074, pp. 450–464. Springer, Heidelberg (2008)
25. van Glabbeek, R.J., Weijland, W.P.: Branching Time and Abstraction in Bisimulation Semantics. J. ACM 43(3), 555–600 (1996)
26. Weber, B., Reichert, M.: Refactoring process models in large process repositories. In: Bellahsène, Z., Léonard, M. (eds.) CAiSE 2008. LNCS, vol. 5074, pp. 124–139. Springer, Heidelberg (2008)
27. Weidlich, M., Weske, M.: Structural and Behavioural Commonalities of Process Variants. In: Gierds, C., Sürmeli, J. (eds.) Proceedings of the 2nd Central-European Workshop on Services and their Composition, ZEUS 2010, Berlin, Germany, February 25-26. CEUR Workshop Proceedings, vol. 563, pp. 41–48. CEUR-WS.org (2010)
28. Weske, M.: Business Process Management – Concepts, Languages, Architectures. Springer-Verlag New York, Inc., Secaucus (2007)
29. Yan, Z., Dijkman, R., Grefen, P.: Business process model repositories - framework and survey (2009), http://cms.ieis.tue.nl/Beta/Files/WorkingPapers/Beta_wp292.pdf
30. Yianilos, P.N.: Data structures and algorithms for nearest neighbor search in general metric spaces. In: SODA 1993: Proceedings of the Fourth Annual ACM-SIAM Symposium on Discrete Algorithms, pp. 311–321. Society for Industrial and Applied Mathematics, Philadelphia (1993)
31. Zezula, P., Amato, G., Dohnal, V., Batko, M.: Similarity Search: The Metric Space Approach. Springer-Verlag New York, Inc., Secaucus (2005)

Process Model Analysis
Using Related Cluster Pairs

Michael Niemann, Melanie Siebenhaar, Julian Eckert, and Ralf Steinmetz

KOM – Multimedia Communications Lab,
Department of Computer Science,
Technische Universität Darmstadt, Germany

Abstract. Due to changing market conditions and resulting flexibility requirements, the reference-conform implementation of processes in companies increasingly gains importance. The internal assessment of the realisation of reference processes (process conformance) is a resource-intensive task in terms of time and cost. The paper at hand presents a process model analysis method to address this issue using a combined structural and semantic comparison and analysis approach. The method provides decision support for process analysts concerning the adjustment of processes to reference processes in IT Governance contexts.

Keywords: static process analysis, structural process analysis, semantic process matching. **Paper category:** Research in progress.

1   Introduction

In Business Process Management, reference models provide predefined solutions to a specific class of problems, e.g., the acceleration of business process implementation, or the harmonisation of internal processes. Process reference models, in particular, describe domain specific processes and generally provide an established and solid foundation for the analysis and improvement of internal processes. By describing dynamic aspects of an enterprise, e.g., activity sequences, organisational activities required to satisfy customer needs, control flow between activities, particular dependency constraints, etc., they help decreasing risk and provide beneficial clues for detection and improvement of weaknesses. [1][2]

IT Governance defines guidelines and reference processes in order to standardise processes in a company and IT departments, aiming at assuring conformance and simplification of control. Reference models in the field of IT Governance (also called best practice frameworks) are voluminous and have a large application scope (cp. [3], [4]). They consist of recommended general procedures, roles, responsibilities, and guidelines, combined with explicit process reference models [5]. Established frameworks, such as the IT Infrastructure Library (ITIL)[6], specify best practices as process or workflow models. As governance targets management processes rather than operative processes, processes and activities defined by IT Governance frameworks generally reside on a relatively high abstraction level.

M. zur Muehlen and J. Su (Eds.): BPM 2010 Workshops, LNBIP 66, pp. 547–558, 2011.
© Springer-Verlag Berlin Heidelberg 2011

Once introduced in companies, the adherence to reference models is diminished over time, e.g., by undocumented changes such as merging with new processes or process fragments, or natural human workflow evolution. In these cases, differences must be identified in retrospect, which mostly is a costly and time consuming procedure.

Reference models for governance purposes rather are *to-do-* or *check-lists* than control flow-oriented models and can be considered abstract models [4][3][6]. Comparing abstract processes is different: it is important to investigate *whether* (activity similarity), and *in what order* (activity permutation) composite, general activities are performed rather than *in what exact way*, e.g., the behaviour. When assessing processes with respect to such abstract process models, it is important for the process engineer to find general correspondences between process model parts. Even if possible, precise matchings are mostly not mandatory. Atomic activities as well as process behaviour are not of central importance in governance reference models – correspondence determination between process models and structure analysis become more important in this respect.

Commonly, process comparisons are performed by considering adequate notions of equivalence, e.g., bisimulation, trace or similar equivalences based on string-based, structural, and behavioural similarity metrics (cp. [7], [8]). For large models, those computations quickly become very complex. In particular, behavioural comparison approaches anticipate the comparability of process models, i.e., the existence of exact pairwise candidate assignments. Existing approaches for reference process analyses are often limited by the high computational complexity of the graph matching problem. Performing process comparison and analysis of process models deployed for governance purposes, i.e., the control and steering of IT systems, raises additional challenges that we address within this paper.

The paper at hand presents an analysis technique for process models identifying related activity groups in terms of structure and content (related cluster pairs). A *related cluster pair*, intuitively, consists of two groups of activities having one correspondent in the other process model, respectively. Generally, clusters abstract from the behaviour of the comprised activities (in terms of activity permutation and gateway conditions).

Using this technique, we are able to provide similarity values not only for entire processes, but also *cluster level* similarities. Additionally, by merging clusters, the technique allows the indication of the position of supplementary or missing activities (*location of differences*) and the indication of *activity order differences* (permutation). The currently realised approach computes similarities between activities of event-driven process chains (EPC) models (events and functions).

The remainder of this paper is structured as follows. In section 2, we introduce fundamental concepts used, in section 3 we explain the analysis approach in detail. After a comparison with related work in section 4, section 5 concludes the paper.

2 Basics

In this section, we introduce basic concepts and definitions such as event-driven process chains, similarity measures, and SESE regions.

2.1 Event-Driven Process Chains

Event-driven process chains (EPC) are a method for the modelling of business processes, introduced within the scope of the Architecture of Integrated Information Systems (ARIS) [9]. The method of EPCs is widespread and its concepts can be easily transferred to other modeling approaches. An basic EPC can be defined as follows:

Definition 1 (Event-driven process chain). *An event-driven process chain represents a directed, connected graph $G = (V,E)$. The set of vertices V consists of three disjoint sets of functions F, events E, and connectors C. The vertices are connected by arcs representing the control flow. Functions and events appear in an alternating sequence.*

Let $I(v)$ and $O(v)$ be the set of incoming and outgoing arcs for a given node $v \in V$, respectively. Then, $\exists e_S \in E$ with $|I(e_S)| = 0$ and $|O(e_S)| = 1$ denoted as start event e_S and $\exists e_E \in E$ with $|I(e_E)| = 1$ and $|O(e_E)| = 0$ denoted as end event e_E. $\forall f \in F$ and $e \in E \setminus \{e_S, e_E\}$: $|I(f)| = |I(e)| = |O(f)| = |O(e)| = 1$.

A connector $c \in C$ of type $t \in \{AND, OR, XOR\}$ represents a logical connection between functions and events. $\forall c_S \in C$ with $|I(c_S)| = 1$ and $|O(c_S)| \geq 1$, c_S is denoted as split connector and $\forall c_J \in C$ with $|I(c_J)| \geq 1$ and $|O(c_J)| = 1$, c_J is denoted as join connector. If one or more functions directly follow an event, the respective connector in between must be an AND connector. Finally, each $f \in F$ and each $e \in E$ is assigned a label.

2.2 Similarity Measures

In order to determine similar function or event pairs, we apply two generally different similarity metrics: string-based and semantic similarity measures. Generally, three major classes of *string-based metrics* can be distinguished: edit-distance-based, token-based, and hybrid metrics [10]. *Edit-distance-based metrics* determine the minimal cost in terms of edit operations to transform a string S into a string T where edit operations are insertions, deletions, and substitutions of characters. *Token-based metrics* compare multi-word strings on token (i.e., word) level (instead of character level) and *hybrid metrics* combine character- and token-based methods. As representatives of token-based and hybrid metrics, the Jaccard (sim_{jac}) and the Monge Elkan metric (sim_{moe}), respectively, are defined as follows for the token sets A and B [10][11]:

$$sim_{jac}(A, B) = \frac{|A \cap B|}{|A \cup B|}; \qquad sim_{moe}(A, B) = \frac{1}{|A|} \sum_{i=1}^{|A|} \max_{j=1}^{|B|} sim(A_i, B_j)$$

The Monge Elkan metric maximises the similarity between the tokens of set A and all tokens of set B. The overall similarity equals the mean average of these maximum scores. As a *semantic similarity metric* distributional similarity is considered in our approach, allowing for the fact that different process designers may use different terms for the same activity. Two kinds of distributional similarity can be distinguished: *first order* and *second order* similarity. The former refers to words occurring in the same context, while the latter concerns words which occur in similar contexts. The corpus is tokenised and stopwords (frequent function words) are eliminated. The metric applies a context window size of ± 3 words. Moving the window over the corpus results in a set of dependency triples for a given word. A dependency triple is of the form (w, r, w'), where w represents the given word whose context is examined, w' is a word occurring in the context of w, and r refers to the relationship between w and w' (e.g., the relative position of w' with respect to w). To obtain the distributional first order similarity of two given words w_1 and w_2, a comparison of their dependency triples is performed using the following information theoretic measure suggested by Lin [12]:

$$sim_{Lin} = \frac{\sum_{(r,w')}(w_1, *_r, *_{w'}) + (w_2, *_r, *_{w'})}{\sum_{(r,w')}(w_1, *, *) + \sum_{(r,w')}(w_2, *, *)}$$

The measure is based on the assumption that the similarity between two words can be expressed as the amount of information contained within the dependency triples which are common to both words, divided by the amount of information contained in all the dependency triples of w_1 and w_2 that match the pattern $(w_1, *, *)$ and $(w_2, *, *)$, where $*$ is a wildcard for r and w', respectively.

2.3   SESE Regions

A Single-Entry Single-Exit (SESE) region, intuitively, represents an area within a graph that has a distinct entry edge and a distinct exit edge [13]. Inside nodes can only be reached from those outside by passing the entry edge and nodes outside can only be reached from inside by passing the exit edge.

Definition 2 (Canonical SESE Region). *For a given edge e, a canonical SESE region R (if it exists) is the smallest SESE region of which e is either the entry or the exit edge. Canonical SESE regions are either node disjoint or nested. [13]*

This definition emphasises that each edge e of a graph G does not necessarily have to be part of an enclosing edge pair of a SESE region. This is especially the case, if e resides inside a canonical region. Furthermore, canonical SESE regions represent a unique and node disjunctive decomposition of a graph-based process model. Additionally, SESE regions meet the condition of transitivity [13]. Given two SESE regions $S_1 = (a, b)$ and $S_2 = (b, c)$, their union also represents a SESE region S_3: $(a, b) \cup (b, c) = (a, c) = S_3$.

3   Related Cluster Analysis

The analysis technique presented in the following consists of two steps: *correspondences and cluster determination*, and *conditioned cluster merging*. Due to

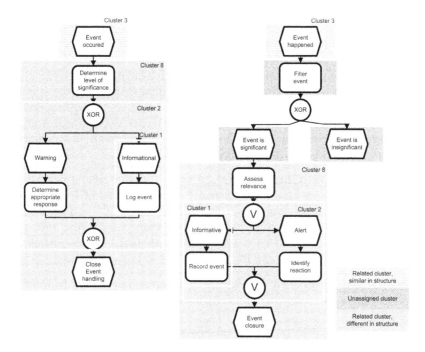

Fig. 1. Simplified Example from ITIL [6]

space limitations, we show a simplified example from ITIL [6] in Figure 1. The EPC model to the right shows a simplified excerpt from the reference process "Event Management Process" defined in the "Service Operation" book of ITIL. An *event*, in this context, "can be defined as any detectable or discernible occurence that has significance for the management of the IT Infrastructure or the delivery of IT services" [6]. The left model shows a simplified potential realisation of this process in an IT department.

3.1   Correspondences and Cluster Determination

Correspondences of process nodes, i.e., functions or events, are identified using a combined string-based and semantic similarity measure. For the nodes k_i of model 1 and m_j of model 2, the node similarity sim_{node} is computed as follows:

$$sim_{node}(k_i, m_j) = w_1 \cdot sim_{fos}(k_i, m_j) + w_2 \cdot sim_{moe}(k_i, m_j) + w_3 \cdot sim_{jac}(k_i, m_j)$$

We compute a similarity value per node pair, that consists of the weighted combination of two string-based metrics (sim_{moe} and sim_{jac}) and a semantic first order similarity measure (sim_{fos}, cf. Section 2.2). The weight for the syntactical metric part is 25% ($w_2 = w_3 = 0.125$), while we weight the semantic part with 75% (w_1). In the result shown in Figure 1, we see that, e.g., "filter event" and "log event" have not been assigned to each other, although they have a high syntactic similarity value (0.50). As well, "determine level of significance" and "assess relevance" have correctly been matched, although only 2 out of 6 words are synonyms. The utilised semantic metric identifies word similarities based on a Wikipedia corpus exceeding synonym relationship. The result is a list of relevant correspondences per node. For the exclusive identification of $1 : 1$ - relationships, we solve the resulting assignment problem with one of the standard procedures [14][15].

In a further step, clusters and related cluster pairs are determined. A cluster C is defined as $C = (F, E)$, by the sets of functions F and events E it comprises. Intuitively, it is a SESE region with additional characteristics.

Definition 3 (Related Cluster Pair). *A related cluster pair is defined as a six-tuple* $(C^A, C^B, M^F, M^E, \text{sim}^R, t)$ *where* $C^A = (F^A, E^A)$ *and* $C^B = (F^B, E^B)$ *are clusters with function sets* F^A *and* F^B, *and event sets* E^A *and* E^B.

$M^F : F^A \to F^B$ and $M^E : E^A \to E^B$ are isomorphisms such that $\forall f \in F^A : \text{sim}^R(f, M^F(f)) \geq t$ and $\forall e \in E^A : \text{sim}^R(e, M^E(e)) \geq t$ where sim^R is a symmetric similarity function and $t \in \mathbb{R}$ with $0 \leq t \leq 1$ is a threshold.

Note, that the set of vertices V of clusters in this case only refers to functions and events. Gateways as well as the ordering of activities are (explicitly) not considered here.

Each related node pair turns into a smallest possible related cluster pair (e.g., cluster 1). All unassigned nodes form unassigned clusters (e.g., node "filter event", cp. Fig. 1). For all nodes of the left model, corresponding nodes have been assigned. In the right model, for the nodes "filter event", "event is significant" and "event is insignificant" no correspondences were found.

3.2   Conditioned Cluster Merging

In the second step, adjacent clusters are merged in both models simultaneously – related cluster pairs as well as unassigned clusters. While the latter are just merged per model, the merging of the first ones is model-spanning and adheres to conditions. The first condition is to demand from an adjacent node B of node A in model 1, that its corresponding node B' in model 2 is adjacent to A', which is the correspondent to A. The second condition is, that the resulting node group must in turn be a cluster. This way, we aggregate sets of nodes to form larger related clusters.

This bottom up-process first merges nested SESE regions to form related clusters and then merges sequences of clusters, and is interrupted by stop conditions such as adjacent unassigned nodes. This way, the process models are transformed into sequences of largest possible related clusters.

During this computation, *cluster types* are determined and assigned to the related cluster pairs. In particular, we distinguish BasicSEQ (sequence), XOR-SJ, OR-SJ, AND-SJ (split-join, respectively), and ITER (loops). In Figure 1, the related cluster pair cluster 8 has the type SEQ, the inner cluster to the left is an XOR-SJ, while on the right, an OR-SJ has been identified.

We determine further cluster characteristics: PERM designates differences in node sequence in the cluster pair, CHILDSTRUCTDIFF and PARENTSTRUCTDIFF mark structural differences of related clusters referring to the resulting parent cluster or the child clusters, NONBASIC tags a related cluster pair that contains more complex than the above simple cluster types. In the example, characteristics of cluster 8 are CHILDSTRUCDIFF and BasicSEQ.

Related clusters are marked according to whether they are internally similar in structure or not (*cluster similarity level*). Generally, we distinguish two different cluster similarity levels: *content-related* cluster pairs contain corresponding elements with differing structure, while *structure-related* cluster pairs consist of clusters that are similar concerning their elements in terms of structure *and* content. In the example, the activities were aggregated to form the shown clusters, however, as outlined, the cluster types cluster 8 refers to are not similar. Those cluster pairs are marked as "content-related", and *not* "structure-related". In these cases, the final decision on whether the modeled activities actually *mean* the same must be left to human experts. Alternatively, formal behaviour investigations can be performed on clusters in order to identify further differences, or to compute change operations to map them.

The *related cluster pair similarity* refers to the similarity of two related clusters and represents the mean average of the similarity value of the node pairs contained in the respective clusters.

3.3 Discussion

Our approach identifies largest-possible related clusters and computes cluster types, structural internal cluster characteristics, as well as similarity levels (*content-related* vs. *structure-related*). Based on these pieces of information, a detailed report on the similarity of process models can be automatically generated, which are used for governance purposes, e.g., supporting process conformance checks. Generally, in our approach, we are able to consider two process models (parts) as similar, even if other similarity notions do not indicate a sufficient relation. Concerning process part similarity and process model similarity, the notion of related cluster pair similarity is different from existing similarity notions.

The computational complexity of solving the assignment problem is $O(n^3)$ [14]. This determines the complexity of the approach presented. The actual calculation of the correspondences matrix is cheaper: $O(nm)$, considering events and functions as input parameter of the first (n) and the second model (m).

In our approach, we combine label and semantic similarity. We weight the latter with 75% with respect to different labels actually describing the same activity. For semantic similarity we use a Wikipedia corpus-based approach. This way, we can identify word relations that exceed synonym-centred investigation. We are able to find, e.g., the mapping of the word pair "hotel" and "accomodation", not representing a synonym relationship.

So far, related work does not address the large-scope investigation of similar process regions. This approach represents an inexact investigation, marking regions similar, even if they differ in structure (e.g., gateways, conditions).

However, this allows for a fast, yet effective investigation of large and complex processes, as it is often needed in application areas in IT Governance. Based on this analysis, detailed reports on process conformance can be computed, and change operations can be formulated, if required. Considering state-of-the-art governance reference processes as counterparts, detailed reports gain special importance, referring to expert conformance check reports.

4   Related Work

In this section, we discuss related work from the field of process analysis, comparable to the IT Governance context of the work at hand (cf. Tab. 1).

Andrews et al. present both a technique and prototype tool for visual graph comparison, which analyses similarities of given graphs and suggests a merged graph [16]. The resulting graph can be manually edited by the process engineer (e.g., replacing labels, changing node positions). The approach assumes the external provision of node similarities. Clearly, the emphasis lies on graphical graph layouting and presentation to the process engineer for final visual assessment.

Dijkman presents a technique to identify the differences between EPC process models. Besides the type of a difference, also the exact position of the differences can be determined [17]. For this, the difference typology presented in [18] is formalised. For the actual computation, the author makes use of formal semantics. Since the approach has exponential complexity, it requires repeated scoping of the process models. The approach processes EPCs with a small number of start events.

A further approach by Dijkman et al. [8] proposes the application of graph matching algorithms to the problem of ranking business process models in a given repository with respect to their similarity to a given process model. The four heuristics presented are based on the graph-edit-distance algorithm, which is NP-complete. To determine the similarity of the graph nodes, the node labels and their types are compared using string-edit-distance measures. The approach does not consider semantic similarity and does not indicate to the process engineer, where similarities and differences are located within the process models. In [19], the authors present several general basic approaches for process comparison, partly used in their later contributions.

Küster et al. introduce an approach for comparing different versions of one process model in the absence of a change log [20]. For the determination of differences, the authors make use of externally provided node correspondances, and SESE fragments. Differences and derived change operations are then grouped by associating them to the affected SESE fragments. Based on this, a hierarchical change log is composed, exploiting the nesting relationship of the SESE fragments and their associated change operations. The change log can be used to resolve all or parts of the differences and to obtain a consolidated model. In general, this approach primarily considers different versions of the same process and does not account for models designed by different parties. Explicitly, a node correspondences matrix is required. Application across tool boundaries, i.e., an

Table 1. Overview of related work

Publication	D	C	M	V	SB	IS	ES	BS	SR	SG	MR
Andrews et al. [16]	×	–	×	×	–	–	–	–	–	–	×
Dijkman [17][18]	×	–	–	–	–	–	–	–	–	×	×
Dijkman et al. [8]	×	–	–	–	×	×	–	–	–	×	–
Küster et al. [20]	×	×	×	×	×	–	–	–	×	–	×
Melnik et al. [21]	–	–	–	–	×	–	–	–	–	–	–
Ehrig et al. [22][23]	–	–	–	–	×	×	×	–	–	–	–
Dijkman et al. [19]	×	–	–	–	×	×	–	×	–	×	–
Li et al. [24][25]	×	×	–	×	–	–	–	×	–	–	×
This approach	×	–	–	×	×	×	–	–	×	–	–

Abbrev.	Meaning	Abbrev.	Meaning
		SB	string-based similarity (labels)
D	differences determination	IS	implicit semantics (for label match.)
C	change suggestions	ES	explicit semantics (for label match.)
V	visualization	SR	structural similarity (SESE regions)
M	(semi-) autom. merging	SG	structural similarity (Graph-Edit Distance)
MR	manual assignment required	BS	behavioural similarity

application area other than version comparison is not intended. In contrast, the approach at hand explicitly targets the analysis of general governance processes, modelled by different parties using different tools. It focuses on the identification of process regions of conformance and non-conformance, as well as on decision support for those regions where process conformance is initially unclear. In a governance context, the computation of change operations is not useful in every case – process conformance might be given, although the structure or the ordering of some activities might not be similar, respectively.

The graph matching algorithm presented by Melnik et al. in [21] performs a mapping between the corresponding nodes of two given graphs and can be applied to different scenarios with diverse data structures (e.g., matching of two data schemas in data warehousing applications). As pre-processing step, the two data structures to be compared are converted into directed labelled graphs. A similarity matrix constitutes the input for the next step, the so-called *similarity flooding*. This step represents an iterative fixpoint computation to determine the set of similar nodes. It is based on the assumption, that if two nodes are similar, their adjacent nodes are more likely to be similar, and thus, their similarity increases. For the determination of node similarities a simple string-based comparison is used. The computation results in a mapping between corresponding nodes. No differences are considered.

Ehrig et al. introduce a (semi-)automatic approach for the detection of similar process elements in business process models based on semantic information using ontologies [22]. To automatically compute similarities, the authors make use of a description of Petri net elements based on OWL-DL, the Pr/T net ontology, introduced in [23]. For their comparison, the authors apply text-based, implicit and explicit semantic similarity measures resulting in a combined similarity measure between concept instances. The similarity values of the concept instances are aggregated to an overall similarity of the two process models. Node similarities and process differences are not indicated.

Li et al. [24] develop an approach ("mining process variants") for identification of a generic process reference model for a given set of variants for integration into Process-Aware Information Systems (PAIS). They identify activities to be clustered as blocks based on an aggregated order matrix. The algorithm has a complexity of $O(n^3)$ and is validated using simulation on 7000 process models [25]. Referring to the blocks, they investigate the behaviour (ordering) of activities. As an activity assignment matrix is required as input, the central intention is different from the approach at hand.

5   Conclusion

In this paper, we presented an analysis technique for process models, computing similarities between activities as well as identifying related activity groups in terms of structure and content (related clusters pairs). A *related cluster* consists of a group of activities, all having one correspondent in the other process model, respectively. Generally, clusters abstract from the behaviour of the comprised activities. Using this technique, we are able to provide similarity values not only for entire processes, but also *cluster level similarities.* Additionally, by merging clusters, the technique determines the position of supplementary or missing activities (*location of differences*) and indicates *activity order differences.* During the computation, we identify largest-possible related clusters and compute cluster *types*, structural characteristics, such as identification of alternating sequences and complex cluster types, as well as cluster similarity levels (*content-related* vs. *structure-related*). Based on these information, detailed reports on the similarity of process models are generated. These are useful for governance purposes, e.g., supporting process conformance checks. The approach supports automated investigation of process models concerning the conformance to governance reference models.

The overall goal is to provide decision support for process owners on how to adjust processes in order to map reference processes in the fastest and cheapest possible way. The approach processes EPC models modeled by different parties using different tools (using the same data format) in $O(n^3)$ time. We realised our approach as a proof-of-concept prototype (ProMatch.KOM [26]). We are currently performing evaluations using 50 EPC models from the reference model "Handels-H" [27], currently showing 85% average accuracy and an F1-Measure of 92%. ProMatch.KOM has been implemented as plug-in for the process mining framework ProM[1].

As part of future work, we currently develop an IT Governance ontology for process annotation. This way, a more precise description and matching of processes and activities is possible, improving analysis quality. Further, we will address the analysis of complex EPCs by defining and computing a third level of cluster similarity, the "partly related cluster pair". Clusters of this type combine nodes having correspondences with a minority of unassigned ones. In order

---

[1] http://prom.win.tue.nl/tools/prom/

to make our approach comparable in terms of evaluation results, we will also perform process model search on established test data sets.

Disclaimer

The project was funded by means of the German Federal Ministry of Economy and Technology under the promotional reference 01MQ07012. The authors take the responsibility for the contents.

This work is supported in part by the E-Finance Lab e.V., Frankfurt am Main, Germany (http://www.efinancelab.com).

References

1. Becker, J., Rosemann, M., Kugeler, M.: Process Management. Springer-Verlag New York, Inc., Secaucus (2003)
2. Fettke, P., Loos, P., Zwicker, J.: Business Process Reference Models: Survey and Classification. In: Bussler, C.J., Haller, A. (eds.) BPM 2005. LNCS, vol. 3812, pp. 469–483. Springer, Heidelberg (2006)
3. IT Governance Institute (ITGI), CObIT 4.1: Control Objectives for Information and Related Technology. Rolling Meadows, IL: IT Governance Institute, ITGI (2007), http://www.itgi.org/cobit
4. Brand, K., Boonen, H.: IT Governance based on CObIT 4.1, 3rd edn. Van Haren Publishing, Zaltbommel (2007)
5. Weill, P., Ross, J.W.: IT Governance - How Top Performers Manage IT Decision Rights for Superiour Results. Harvard Business School Press, Cambridge (2004)
6. Office of Governance Commerce (OGC), ITIL v3: Information Technology Infrastructure Library Version 3, vol. 1-5 (2007), http://www.itil.org
7. Alves de Medeiros, A.K., van der Aalst, W.M.P., Weijters, A.J.M.M.: Quantifying process equivalence based on observed behavior. Data Knowledge Engineering 64(1), 55–74 (2008)
8. Dijkman, R., Dumas, M., García-Bañuelos, L.: Graph matching algorithms for business process model similarity search. In: Dayal, U., Eder, J., Koehler, J., Reijers, H.A. (eds.) BPM 2009. LNCS, vol. 5701, pp. 48–63. Springer, Heidelberg (2009)
9. Scheer, A.-W., Schneider, K.: ARIS - Architecture of Integrated Information Systems. In: Bernus, P., Mertins, K., Schmidt, G. (eds.) Handbook on Architectures of Information Systems, pp. 605–624. Springer, Heidelberg (2006)
10. Cohen, W.W., Ravikumar, P., Fienberg, S.E.: A Comparison of String Distance Metrics for Name-Matching Tasks. In: Proceedings of IJCAI 2003 Workshop on Information Integration, pp. 73–78 (August 2003)
11. Monge, A., Elkan, C.: The Field Matching Problem: Algorithms and Applications. In: Proceedings of the Second International Conference on Knowledge Discovery and Data Mining, pp. 267–270 (1996)
12. Lin, D.: Automatic Retrieval and Clustering of Similar Words. In: Proceedings of the 17th International Conference on Computational Linguistics, pp. 768–774. Association for Computational Linguistics, Morristown (1998)
13. Johnson, R., Pearson, D., Pingali, K.: The Program Structure Tree: Computing Control Regions in Linear Time. In: PLDI 1994: Proceedings of the ACM SIGPLAN 1994 Conference on Programming Language Design and Implementation, pp. 171–185. ACM, New York (1994)

14. Alevras, D.: Assignment and matching. In: Encyclopedia of Optimization, pp. 106–108. Springer, Heidelberg (2009)
15. Mills-Tettey, G.A., Stentz, A.T., Dias, M.B.: The Dynamic Hungarian Algorithm for the Assignment Problem with Changing Costs. Tech. Rep. CMU-RI-TR-07-27, Robotics Institute, Pittsburgh, PA (July 2007)
16. Andrews, K., Wohlfahrt, M., Wurzinger, G.: Visual Graph Comparison. In: IV 2009: Proceedings of the 2009 13th International Conference Information Visualisation, pp. 62–67. IEEE Computer Society, Washington, DC (2009)
17. Dijkman, R.: Diagnosing Differences Between Business Process Models. In: Dumas, M., Reichert, M., Shan, M.-C. (eds.) BPM 2008. LNCS, vol. 5240, pp. 261–277. Springer, Heidelberg (2008)
18. Dijkman, R.: A Classification of Differences between Similar Business Processes. In: IEEE International Enterprise Distributed Object Computing Conference (2007)
19. Dijkman, R.M., Dumas, M., van Dongen, B.F., Käärik, R., Mendling, J.: Similarity of Business Process Models: Metrics and Evaluation. tech. rep., BETA Research School, Eindhoven, The Netherlands (2009)
20. Küster, J.M., Gerth, C., Förster, A., Engels, G.: Detecting and Resolving Process Model Differences in the Absence of a Change Log. In: Dumas, M., Reichert, M., Shan, M.-C. (eds.) BPM 2008. LNCS, vol. 5240, pp. 244–260. Springer, Heidelberg (2008)
21. Melnik, S., Garcia-Molina, H., Rahm, E.: Similarity Flooding: A Versatile Graph Matching Algorithm and its Application to Schema Matching. In: ICDE 2002: Proceedings of the 18th International Conference on Data Engineering. IEEE Computer Society, Washington, DC (2002)
22. Ehrig, M., Koschmider, A., Oberweis, A.: Measuring Similarity Between Semantic Business Process Models. In: Roddick, J.F., Hinze, A. (eds.) Proceedings of the Fourth APCCM 2007, vol. 67, pp. 71–80. Australian Computer Science Communications (January 2007)
23. Koschmider, A., Oberweis, A.: Ontology Based Business Process Description. In: Teniente, J.C.E. (ed.) Proceedings of the CAiSE 2005 WORKSHOPS, Porto/Portugal, vol. 2, pp. 321–333 (June 2005)
24. Li, C., Reichert, M., Wombacher, A.: Discovering Reference Process Models By Mining Process Variants. In: ICWS 2008: Proceedings of the 2008 IEEE International Conference on Web Services, pp. 45–53. IEEE Computer Society, Washington, DC (2008)
25. Li, C., Reichert, M., Wombacher, A.: Discovering Reference Models by Mining Process Variants Using a Heuristic Approach. In: Dayal, U., Eder, J., Koehler, J., Reijers, H.A. (eds.) BPM 2009. LNCS, vol. 5701, pp. 344–362. Springer, Heidelberg (2009)
26. Siebenhaar, M., Niemann, M., Eckert, J., Steinmetz, R.: ProMatch.KOM: Tool Support for Process Model Analysis and Improvement. In: Demonstration Track of the 8th International Conference on Business Process Management (BPM 2010), Hoboken, New Jersey, USA (September 2010) (to appear)
27. Cubetto Toolset HTML Export - Referenzmodell Handel, http://www.semture.de/downloads/cubetto/handels-h/index.html (last accessed on: 2009-11-24)

A Framework for Business Process Model Repositories

Zhiqiang Yan and Paul Grefen

Eindhoven University of Technology, The Netherlands
{z.yan,p.w.p.j.grefen}@tue.nl

Abstract. Large organizations often run hundreds or even thousands of
business processes. Managing such large collections of business processes
is a challenging task. Intelligent software can assist in that task by providing common repository functions such as storage, search and version
management. They can also provide advanced functions that are specific
for managing collections of process models, such as managing the consistency of public and private processes and extracting knowledge from existing processes to better design new processes. This paper, by analyzing
existing business process model repositories, proposes a framework for
repositories that assist in managing large collections of business process
models. The framework consists of a management model and a reference
architecture. The management model lists the functionality that can be
provided by business process model repositories. The reference architecture presents the components that provide this functionality and their
interconnections. The framework provides a reference model for analysis
and extension of existing repositories and design of new repositories.

1 Introduction

As it becomes more common for organizations to describe their operations in
terms of business processes, collections of business process models grow to contain hundreds or even thousands of business process models. For example, the
SAP reference model contains over 600 business process models [15] and a collection of business process models for Dutch local government contains a similar
number of business process models [7]. Managing such complex process landscapes is a difficult task. Typical issues arise, e.g., being able to find a particular
process in a collection, managing different versions of processes and maintaining
consistency when multiple people are editing the same process at the same time.
In addition to that, the availability of a large collection of processes opens up
new possibilities, e.g., extracting knowledge about the operations of the organization from the collection or re-using (best-practice) process fragments from the
collection to design new processes.

As a consequence, software tools have been developed to help perform such
tasks. These tools have been built as extensions of general database and repository systems. However, they have been specialized for storing business process
models by using conceptual models, for example database schemas, that are process specific and by defining process specific interfaces. The interface could, for

M. zur Muehlen and J. Su (Eds.): BPM 2010 Workshops, LNBIP 66, pp. 559–570, 2011.
© Springer-Verlag Berlin Heidelberg 2011

example, take the form of a Web service interface or an API that has operations like 'addProcess' and 'searchTask' and by which process models can be imported or exported in process specific interchange formats like EPML or PNML [13]. We refer to such repositories as BP Model Repositories, which we define as repositories that are structured according to a process-specific conceptual model and/or that have a process-specific interface. In addition to exploiting the functionality that is commonly provided by repository and database management systems [4,14], BP Model Repositories provide functionality that is specific for repositories that contain business process models. Examples of process-specific functionality include: functionality to assist with lifecycle management of business processes, functionality to help maintain consistency between the private view on business processes (which is the view that organizations have internally on their business processes) and the public view on business processes (which is the view on those parts of business processes that companies want to make visible publicly), and functionality to assist with configuration management of business processes as they are composed of (certain versions of) sub-processes and tasks.

To provide an overview of the functionality that should be provided by BP Model Repositories, this paper analyzes and extends existing related works and provides a framework for BP Model Repositories. The contribution of this paper is as follows: it presents a framework for BP Model repositories, which consists of a management model and a reference architecture. The management model lists the functionality that can be provided by BP Model Repositories, while distinguishing between functionality that is provided by general repositories and database management systems [4,14] and functionality that is specific for repositories that contain business process models. The reference architecture presents the components that provide this functionality and their interconnections. The framework serves as a guide for the development of BP Model Repositories.

The remainder of the paper is organized as follows. Section 2 introduces existing BP Model Repositories. Section 3 presents the general BP Model Repository management model, which lists the functionality that can be provided by BP Model Repositories. Section 4 presents a reference architecture for BP Model Repositories. Section 5 concludes the paper.

2   An Overview of Existing BP Model Repositories

This section provides a brief overview of existing BP Model Repositories. Comparisons of existing BP Model Repositories based on the framework are given in our internal report [19]. There are two basic approaches to built BP Model Repositories, i.e., knowledge-based and service-based.

Knowledge-based BP Model Repositories are repositories storing knowledge related to processes. The knowledge can be from different perspectives, e.g., reference models, resources, ontologies, and execution traces. The MIT process handbook [12] and the process reuse architecture [8] take reference models as knowledge, which provide text-based descriptions for processes of different areas.

To manage business processes throughout their lifecycle, the repository for integrated process management (IPM) [5] stores different types of knowledge, e.g., resources and business rules. The semantic business process repository [11] considers ontologies as its knowledge and the ontologies include sBPMN, sEPC and sBPEL. The process variant repository (PVR) [10] provides a mechanism to monitor the executions of processes, and stores the execution traces as knowledge to improve processes.

Service-based BP Model Repositories are repositories storing processes that are defined in the context of services. The two main advantages of service-based BP Model Repositories are distribution and collaboration. For example, OSIRIS (Open Service Infrastructure for Reliable and Integrated process Support) [16], combining the ideas of web services and hyperdatabases, to support peer-to-peer process execution by invoking services from distributed repositories. The BPMN repository architecture [17] provides a virtual service platform, which makes it easy to support collaborative scenarios between different organizations.

BP Model Repositories can be both knowledge-based and service-based at the same time. For example, Both the BPEL repository [18] and BP-Mon [3] store process models based on the web services technology; the BPEL repository stores associated metadata as knowledge, while BP-Mon stores execution traces as knowledge.

3   BP Model Repository Management Model

Although, by definition, BP Model Repositories have in common that they have a process-specific conceptual model or interface, they vary with respect to the form of that structure or interaction facility. Also, BP Model Repositories vary with respect to the functions that they provide. This section defines the possible forms of a BP Model Repository structure or interaction facility and the functions that a BP Model Repository can provide.

We consider a BP Model Repository as a specialized repository. According to Bernstein and Dayal [4], a repository is "a shared database of information about engineered artifacts produced or used by an enterprise". Consequently, it should provide common database management services for data model creation and adaption, data retrieval, enabling data views, integrity management, access management and state management. It should also provide services that are specific for managing objects as opposed to data in general: object checkout/checkin, version management, configuration management, notification management, context management and workflow management. The functionality for general repositories, as it is summarized by Bernstein and Dayal [4] and by Sagawa [14], can be specialized and extended to develop repositories that are specific for storing and managing business process models. We developed such an extension by taking the work of Bernstein and Dayal [4] and Sagawa [14] as a starting point and specializing and extending it, based on functionality that can be observed in existing BP Model Repositories, as described in Section 2.

The resulting BP Model Repository management model is shown in table 1. It consists of three parts: the process data model, the process function model and the process management model.

3.1   Process Data Model

The process data model prescribes what kinds of business process models and related data can be stored in the BP Model Repository. It consists of the meta-model, the storage model and the index model.

The *meta-model* prescribes what information can be and must be stored in the BP Model Repository by defining the concepts that are used in the repository and the relations between those concepts. Each BP Model Repository potentially supports a large number of concepts. We classify those concepts by identifying the *process aspects* and the *process types* that are supported by a BP Model Repository. We distinguish the following process aspects.

- The activity aspect (A) contains concepts to describe the activities that are performed in the context of a process, e.g., [12].
- The control-flow aspect (CF) contains concepts to describe the control-flow relations between activities, e.g., [3,5].
- The data aspect (D) contains concepts to describe the information that is used and changed during the execution of a process, e.g., [3,5].
- The resource aspect (R) contains concepts to describe physical resources that are required to execute (activities in) a process, including human resources, e.g., [3,5].
- The authorization aspect (Au) contains concepts to describe who is authorized to perform which part of a process, e.g., [3,5].
- The organization aspect (O) contains concepts to describe the organizational structure, as it consists of people and organizational units, related to a collection of processes, e.g., [3,5].
- The strategic goals aspect (G) contains concepts to describe the hierarchy of strategic goals and to describe the relations of those goals to the processes that are meant to achieve them, e.g., [8].
- The monitoring aspect (M) contains concepts to define how the performance of a process should be monitored, e.g., [3,5].
- The management control (MC) aspect contains concepts to define the management controls that are implemented by (parts of) processes, e.g., [17].

We distinguish the following process types.

- A company specific process (C) is a process that is designed by a specific company to describe its own operations, e.g., [3,5].
- A reference process (Re) is an abstract and standard process that can be reused and adapted to develop company specific processes. If a reference process contains pre-defined configuration options, it is also called a configurable reference process, e.g., [12,8].
- A process pattern (P) is a partial process that describes a best practice summarized from former experience, e.g., [8].

- A process instance (I), or case, is an execution of a process for a customer, e.g., [3,10].
- Historical information (H) consists of logs that contain information about executions of the process instances, e.g., [3,10].

Table 1. BP Model Repository Management Model

Process data model	Process meta model	Process aspect Process type Process notation
	Process storage model	External process data model Internal process data model Process related data model
	Process index model	Process classifications Other process indices
Process function model	Storage functions	Create Delete Update Import Export
	Retrieval functions	Navigate Search Query
	Integration functions	[Depend on external tools]
Process management model	Process-specific management	Version management Configuration management Lifecycle management Process view management
	General repository management	Access management Integrity management Transaction management Checkin/out management Dispatch management Notification management Context management

The meta-model also prescribes how information that is stored in a BP Model Repository is presented to the end-user, by associating a notation with its concepts. For example, a BP Model Repository can store the information for activities and control-flow relations between those activities, but that information can be presented to the user in (structured) natural language, in a standardized graphical notation like EPC or BPMN, or in a proprietary graphical notation. It is also common for a BP Model Repository not to prescribe a notation, but focus solely on defining its conceptual model and/or interchange format, e.g., the MIT process handbook [12].

The *storage model* prescribes how the original information about the process must be technically provided to the BP Model Repository (*external data model*) and how it must be internally stored by the BP Model Repository (*internal data model*). The external and the internal model can be the same, for example each process can be stored as an XML file that is also used to exchange the process between the BP Model Repository and related tools, or they can differ, for example processes can be exchanged using XML but stored in a relational database. Other than that process related data, which is data that is used by, but not part of, the processes can be stored in the repository. Process related data includes: descriptors of web services that are used by the processes and ontologies that are used to relate terms from different processes. For example, the IBM BPEL repository [18] also stores WSDL web-service descriptors.

The *index model* prescribes the indices that are kept for process models, to allow both the user and the repository manager itself to quickly browse or search the collection of processes. An index that is commonly used is a *classification* of process models in terms of the business functions for which they are available. For example, we can classify processes into processes for: sales, procurement, production, finance and support. Subsequently, we can distinguish different classes of procurement processes, like procurement of product related materials and procurement of non-product related materials, etceteras.

3.2   Process Function Model

A BP Model Repository should support a series of basic functions to effectively manipulate the processes that it stores. We identify storage functions, retrieval functions and integration functions.

The *storage functions* are the functions to create, update and delete processes or parts of processes, by creating, updating or deleting instances of the concepts that are defined in the process meta model. In addition to that functions exist to import complete processes into the repository, using the interchange format from the external data model, and to export complete processes from the repository using that interchange format.

The *retrieval functions* can be used to obtain the required process according to some criteria. There are three methods for retrieving processes: navigate, query and search. Navigation is the method of manually scanning processes in a list, or by using a classification or some other index. Search provides the function to get processes that match criteria that are given as keywords. Query provides more advanced functions to specify search criteria using a query language, such as IPM-PQL [5] or BPMN-Q [2]. Queries and query languages can have a focus on one or more process aspects or process types. Awad distinguishes the following foci for process query languages [2]; languages that focus on retrieving (elements of) processes (company specific or reference), languages that focus on retrieving (elements of) process instances and languages that focus on retrieving (elements of) process execution history.

The *integration functions* can be used to integrate a process repository with external tools. Integration varies, depending on the types of tools a repository integrates. In the BP Model Repositories that we have studied, we have observed integrations with the following types of tools.

- Process modeling tools, which can be used to visually create, retrieve, update and delete processes, e.g., OSIRIS [16] provides them.
- Report generators, which can be used to generate reports about (monitoring information of) processes and their properties, e.g., BP-Mon [3] and PVR [10] provides them.
- Process analysis tools, which can be used to analyze correctness, selected properties or performance of processes, e.g., IPM [5] provides them.
- Workflow engines, which can be used to execute business processes by performing activities, or notifying human resources that activities must be performed, according to the order specified by the control-flow relations. When executing a business process a process instance is created and monitoring information is generated, e.g., BP-Mon [3] and PVR [10] provide them.
- Process administration and monitoring tools, which can be use to manage or monitor the (executions of) processes, e.g., BP-Mon [3] provides them.
- Collaboration tools, which can be used to establish business collaborations based on processes in the repository, e.g., the BPMN repository architecture [17] provides them.

Within the set of BP Model Repositories that we studied, there was no strict separation with respect to what is considered internal functionality of the repository and what is considered external functionality that can be integrated with the repository. For example, query tools have been proposed as external tools [2], but at the same time tools for establishing collaborations between organizations, based on their processes, have been proposed as internal parts of the repository [17]. We made the separation between internal and external functionality above, based on what we most frequently observed in the analyzed BP Model Repositories.

3.3   Process Management Model

Advanced management functions can be subdivided into functions that are provided by general repositories and functions that are provided only by BP Model Repositories.

The *process specific management functions* are: version management, configuration management, lifecycle management and view management. Although version management, configuration management and view management are also general repository functions (or even general database functions in the case of view management), these functions have been specialized to meet process specific requirements [1,5,6,9,20]. The version management function enables multiple versions of the same process or activity to be maintained. The configuration management function makes it possible to maintain the relation between (a version of) a process and the (versions of) subprocesses and activities that it consists of. Although version and configuration management are also general repository functions, specialized functionality is added to support requirements in the context of BP Model Repositories. For example, when a process is being executed and a new version of that process or a part of that process is created, a decision must be made as to whether the new version will be put into effect for process instances that are already running or not and, if so, for which process instances. The lifecycle management function maintains the stage in its lifecycle that a process is currently in. For example, a process can be under design, validation and current. Depending on the stage that it is, some operations can be performed on it and others cannot. For example, a new version cannot be created of a version that is under design, nor can a process that is still under validation be executed. The view management function makes it possible to create multiple views on a process. Although view management is a general database function, specialized functionality is added to support requirements in the context of BP Model Repositories. For example, it is common to keep a private view on a process, which represents the process as it is performed inside an organization. At the same time a public view (also called service) can be provided of what the behavior of the process to the outside world will be like, therewith preserving company secrets of how services are internally implemented and not bothering clients with details that do not concern them. To support the generation of the public view from the private view and to keep the two views consistent, BP Model Repository specific functionality is needed.

The *general repository management functions* are: access management, integrity management, transaction management, checkin/out management, dispatch management, notification management and context management. The access management function ensures that people only have access to the objects in the repository that they are authorized to view. The integrity management function ensures that the repository cannot get into an inconsistent state. Transaction management ensures that multiple operations on a repository can be performed in a transactional manner (i.e.: either all at once or not at all). Checkin/out management allows a user to check-out objects from the repository, therewith locking them so others cannot change them, make the desired changes and then check them in again by releasing the lock. Optionally, multiple people can be allowed to check-out an object at the same time, in which case check-in management should ensure that changes that are made to the same object by multiple people are properly merged. Dispatch management makes it possible to associate a work-order with an object, such that it is forwarded to people in the order specified in the work-order along with notes about what these people have to do with the object. (This is usually called 'workflow management' in repositories. We call it dispatch management to avoid the confusion with workflow tools that execute the processes in a BP Model Repository.) Notification management enables notifications to be generated in case an object in the repository is changed. The context management function allows collections of repository objects, called 'contexts', (also called 'projects' or 'workspaces') to be created and manipulated. Contexts can be stored persistently.

4   BP Model Repository Reference Architecture

This section presents a reference architecture for BP Model Repositories. The reference architecture is obtained by analyzing the architectures of existing BP Model Repositories, as described in Section 2, and by integrating the analysis results into a cohesive architecture. Figure 1 shows the reference architecture. It has five layers: the presentation layer, the process repository management layer, the repository management layer, the database management layer and the storage layer.

The presentation layer provides GUIs for users to interact with a BP Model Repository, so the users can easily interact with the functions provided by the repository. Not all concrete BP Model Repositories have a presentation layer.

The process repository management layer provides repository functions that are specific for BP Model Repositories. The functions are described in detail in the previous section. Although general database management systems and repositories implement general functions, such as querying and checkin/checkout, most BP Model Repositories choose to implement these functions themselves, because this allows them to at least provide a facade that applies the functions specifically to processes instead of general repository objects or database tables. The functions may, or may not, use general functionality provided by a general database management system or repository to implement the BP Model Repository-specific functions.

The repository and database management layers provide the functions that are generally provided by repository and database management systems, respectively. Most BP Model Repositories that we studied do not distinguish the repository management layer from the layer with process specific functionality. Instead, they will have a single layer that contains all management functionality. We introduce the distinction between the layers here, to clearly show that there is an architectural choice between implementing these layers in the process repository or obtaining them from general purpose repositories or database management systems.

The storage layer stores the process models, the related data and indices or classifications to enable fast querying, searching and navigation of the BP Model Repository. Process models can be stored both in an internal format, for example as rows in database tables, and in their original external format. In that case the internal format is used for fast and unified processing of process models in spite of their external format and the external format is used to maintain the relation with the original models. In most cases the storage layer is implemented by a general database management system. Relational (e.g., [12,8,3,5]), object-oriented (e.g., [17,18]) and XML databases (e.g., [8,3,5,17,18]) have all been observed in the concrete BP Model Repositories that were studied. Alternative implementations that have been observed are implementations using general repositories, of which one using a distributed repository, and an implementation in which the data is stored as files in a filesystem.

Well-defined interfaces should exist between the different layers. In most BP Model Repositories well-defined interfaces exist between the presentation

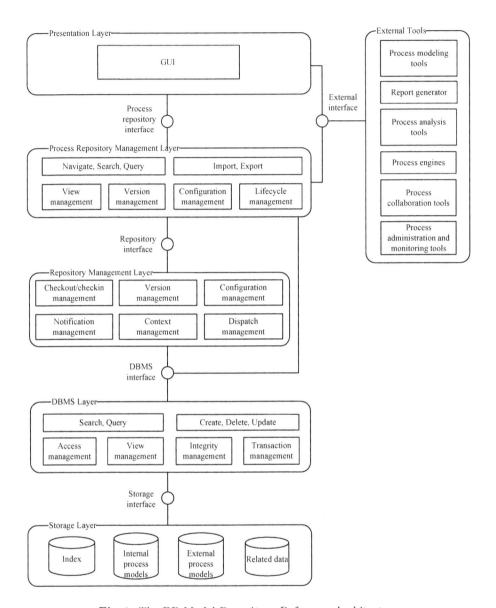

Fig. 1. The BP Model Repository Reference Architecture

layer and the process repository management layer and between the repository management layer and the database management layer. The technology that is used to implement the interfaces varies. The process repository interface can be implemented using a programming language API, but also using remote method invocation or even using web-services. The DBMS interface can be implemented using a (standard) API, but we have also observed concrete BP Model

Repositories that added an additional layer that abstracts from the storage technology that was used, to allow different storage technology to be used without having to implement the repository functions.

In addition to the interfaces between the layers, interfaces can exist between the BP Model Repository and external tools. The presence and implementation of these interfaces varies largely. However they are all defined either to interact with the presentation layer, with the process repository management layer or with both. Interaction with the presentation layer enables the BP Model Repository to open a tool from the GUI of the BP Model Repository. Interaction with the process repository management layer enables an external tool to directly invoke the functions that are provided by the BP Model Repository.

5   Conclusion

This paper defines a Business Process Model Repository (BP Model Repository) as a repository that is structured according to a process-specific conceptual model and/or has a process-specific interface. It presents a framework for BP Model Repositories, which consists of a list of functions that such repositories can provide and a reference architecture that is an abstraction of the architectures that they observe.

By observing existing BP Model Repositories, we conclude that complete repositories, as described in the framework, are not yet available. Therefore, the framework is a basis of future works. We will try to implement a complete BP Model Repository in the future.

Acknowledgement

The research reported in this paper is supported by the China Scholarship Council (CSC).

References

1. van der Aalst, W.M.P., ter Hofstede, A.H.M., Weske, M.: Business Process Management: A Survey. In: van der Aalst, W.M.P., ter Hofstede, A.H.M., Weske, M. (eds.) BPM 2003. LNCS, vol. 2678, pp. 1–12. Springer, Heidelberg (2003)
2. Awad, A.: BPMN-Q: A language to query business processes. In: Proceedings of EMISA 2007, Nanjing, China, pp. 115–128 (2007)
3. Beeri, C., Eyal, A., Milo, T., Pilberg, A.: BP-Mon: Query-based monitoring of BPEL business processes. SIGMOD Record 37(1), 21–24 (2008)
4. Bernstein, P.A., Dayal, U.: An overview of repository technology. In: Proceedings of VLDB 1994, Santiago de Chile, Chile, pp. 707–713 (1994)
5. Choi, I., Kim, K., Jang, M.: An xml-based process repository and process query language for integrated process management. Knowledge and Process Management 14(4), 303–316 (2007)
6. Dijkman, R.M., Quartel, D.A.C., van Sinderen, M.J.: Consistency in Multi-Viewpoint Design of Enterprise Information Systems. Information and Software Technology (IST) 50(7-8), 737–752 (2008)

 7. Documentair structuurplan, `http://www.model-dsp.nl` (retrieved February 20, 2009)
 8. Fiorini, S., Leite, J., Lucena, C.: Process reuse architecture. In: Dittrich, K.R., Geppert, A., Norrie, M.C. (eds.) CAiSE 2001. LNCS, vol. 2068, pp. 284–298. Springer, Heidelberg (2001)
 9. Lapouchnian, A., Yu, Y., Mylopoulos, J.: Requirements-Driven Design and Configuration Management of Business Processes. In: Alonso, G., Dadam, P., Rosemann, M. (eds.) BPM 2007. LNCS, vol. 4714, pp. 246–261. Springer, Heidelberg (2007)
10. Lu, R., Sadiq, S.: Managing process variants as an information resource. In: Dustdar, S., Fiadeiro, J.L., Sheth, A.P. (eds.) BPM 2006. LNCS, vol. 4102, pp. 426–431. Springer, Heidelberg (2006)
11. Ma, Z., Wetzstein, B., Anicic, D., Heymans, S.: Semantic business process repository. In: Proceedings of SBPM 2007, Innsbruck, Austria, pp. 92–100 (2007)
12. Malone, T.W., Crowston, K., Herman, G.A.: Organizing Business Knowledge: The MIT Process Handbook. MIT Press, Cambridge (2003)
13. Mendling, J., Neumann, G., Nüttgens, M.: A Comparison of XML Interchange Formats for Business Process Modelling. In: Proceedings of EMISA 2004, Luxembourg, pp. 129–140 (2004)
14. Sagawa, J.M.: Repository manager technology. IBM Systems Journal 29(2), 209–227 (1990)
15. Curran, T.A., Keller, G.: SAP R/3 Business Blueprint - Business Engineering mit den R/3-Referenzprozessen. Addison-Wesley, Reading (1999)
16. Schuler, C., Weber, R., Schuldt, H., Schek, H.-J.: Peer–to–peer process execution with OSIRIS. In: Orlowska, M.E., Weerawarana, S., Papazoglou, M.P., Yang, J. (eds.) ICSOC 2003. LNCS, vol. 2910, pp. 483–498. Springer, Heidelberg (2003)
17. Theling, T., Zwicker, J., Loos, P., Vanderhaeghen, D.: An architecture for collaborative scenarios applying a common BPMN-repository. In: Kutvonen, L., Alonistioti, N. (eds.) DAIS 2005. LNCS, vol. 3543, pp. 169–180. Springer, Heidelberg (2005)
18. Vanhatalo, J., Koehler, J., Leymann, F.: Repository for business processes and arbitrary associated metadata. In: Proceedings of BPM 2006, Vienna, Austria, pp. 25–31 (2006)
19. Yan, Z., Dijkman, R.M., Grefen, P.W.P.J.: Business Process Model Repositories - Framework and Survey. BETA Working Paper WP-292, Eindhoven University of Technology, Eindhoven, The Netherlands (2009)
20. Zhao, X., Liu, C.: Version Management in the Business Process Change Context. In: Alonso, G., Dadam, P., Rosemann, M. (eds.) BPM 2007. LNCS, vol. 4714, pp. 198–213. Springer, Heidelberg (2007)

1st International Workshop on Cross-Enterprise Collaboration, People and Work (CEC-PAW 2010)

Workshop Organization

Workshop Organizers

Daniel Oppenheim
IBM T. J. Watson Research Center
PO Box 704,
Yorktown Heights, NY 10598
USA

Francisco Curbera
IBM TJ Watson Research Center
PO Box 704,
Yorktown Heights, NY 10598
USA

Frank Leymann
Institute of Architecture of Application
Systems
Universitätsstraße 38
70569 Stuttgart
Germany

DimkaKarastoyanova
Institute of Architecture of Application
Systems
Universitätsstraße 38
D-70569 Stuttgart
Germany

Marcelo Cataldo
Institute for Software Research
Carnegie Mellon University
Wean Hall 8127
5000 Forbes Avenue
Pittsburgh, PA 15213
USA

Alex Norta
University of Helsinki
Department of Computer Science
P.O. Box 68
GustafHaellstroeminkatu 2b
FIN-00014 Helsinki
Finland

Program Committee

Rama K. Akkiraju,IBM Research, USA
VasiliosAndrikopoulos, University of Tilburg, The Netherlands
Marco Comuzzi, Eindhoven University of Technology, The Netherlands
Cleidson de Souza, IBM Brazil
Christoph Dorn, Technical University of Vienna, Austria
RikEshuis, Eindhoven University of Technology, The Netherlands
Marta Indulska, University of Queensland, Australia
Lea Kutvonen, University of Helsinki, Finland
Awais Rashid, Lancaster University, UK
Grace Lewis, Software Engineering Institute, USA
Ralph Mietzner, IAAS, University of Stuttgart, Germany
Florian Rosenberg, Technical University of Vienna, Austria
Daniel Schall, Technical University of Vienna, Austria
Matthias Weidlich, HassoPlattner Institute, Germany
Liang (Leon) Zhang, Fudan University, China

First International Workshop on Cross Enterprise Collaboration, People, and Work (CEC-PAW): Current State of Affairs and Future Research Directions

Daniel Oppenheim[1] and Marcelo Cataldo[2]

[1] IBM T.J. Watson Research, Hawthorne, NY 10532, USA
[2] Carnegie Mellon University, Pittsburgh, PA 15213
music@us.ibm.com, mcataldo@cs.cmu.edu

Introduction

On September 13th, 2010, the 1st International Workshop on *Cross Enterprise Collaboration, People and Work* (SG-PAW) was held as part of the 8th International Conference on Business Process Management (BPM 10) in Hoboken, New Jersey, USA. The workshop focused on the problem of enabling an enterprise to leverage internal and external global services and combine them in new ways that optimize its end-to-end operations. The goal was to combine academics and practitioners to identify together core issues, research challenges, learn from successful attempts or approaches, and propose new formalisms, models, architectures, frameworks, methodologies, or approaches.

A keynote presentation by Professor Schahram Dustdar from the Technical University of Vienna was followed by four paper presentations. This workshop ended in a collaborative discussion that included the organizers and participants; its output is presented in the workshop Manifesto below.

Keynote Presentation

ON DYNAMIC TEAM COMPOSITION AND CROWDSOURCING NOVEL ALGORITHMS AND APPROACHES

Schahram Dustdar, Technical University of Vienna

Abstract. The transformation of how people collaborate and interact on the Web has been poorly leveraged in existing service-oriented architectures (SOA). The paradigm of SOA and Web services is based on loose coupling and dynamic discovery of services. The user should be able to define interaction interfaces (services) following the same principles to avoid the need for parallel systems of software services and Human-Provided Services (HPS). The benefit of this approach is a seamless service-oriented infrastructure of human- and software services. In this talk I will focus on the research challenges in this new field and present some of our current developments.

M. zur Muehlen and J. Su (Eds.): BPM 2010 Workshops, LNBIP 66, pp. 575–578, 2011.
© Springer-Verlag Berlin Heidelberg 2011

Workshop Manifesto

The following list summarizes the key findings and recommendations made by this group.

Findings

1. **Process.** There is a fundamental tension between **routine** and **free-form** that stems from the desire for standardization, consistency and repeatability vs. the need to continuously evolve and adapt. Standardized processes can be executed routinely, yield predictable results, and lend themselves well to machine-automation. Examples of routine processes include using an ATM to withdraw money from a bank, or requesting a loan from a financial institution. But when unpredictable things happen there can be a need for almost free-form agility to respond and adapt. This need to quickly modify how things are done occurs frequently in large projects, such as collaborative development of an airplane or a complex software system. Currently, adaptation is handled primarily through human creativity, expertise, and ability to improvise; the failure rate of such projects is very high. There is a need for a framework that would support both routine and free-form; not only during the process-design, but especially during execution. The need for process flexibility during runtime also blurs the current separation between the activities of *designing* a process and *performing* a task, as both activities become an integral part of *doing* work.

2. **People.** The need for people as a requirement to ensure effective execution of enterprise processes is not sufficiently understood. Current process definitions address people by specifying *roles* that are required to execute a task. This approach considers people merely as resources that could, in theory, be replaced by automation. However, some types of processes *must* rely on people to execute effectively. Humans may be required for a variety of reasons, for example: the complexity of the domain; the need to drive recovery when unexpected things happen; to resolve issues at runtime; or to negotiate and coordinate work across enterprise boundaries. Most BPM frameworks do not address these different roles of people; nor do they adequately support teamwork around tasks or the creation and execution of dynamic service plans. There is no model of the "human system" that identifies the different types of actors, teams, or organizations, and that can be used to bring this together with current BPM practices.

3. **Globalization.** Globalization creates an ever-growing abundance of resources, innovation, and specialization. In order for business to harness those potential benefits, they require flexible frameworks into which they can "plug-and-play" relevant entities such as partners, suppliers, service providers, or resources.

4. **Models.** There is a need for capability-oriented models and languages that can address both the routine and the free-form in a uniform way. Beyond providing a well defined starting point for enterprise-work, they will also provide a formalism that enables ongoing evolution and adaptation in response to new needs or unpredictable events; and do so in a way that can be supported by machines. Such models will have to address many elements of the problems, including business, process, data, IT, people, resources, and organization. Current disciplines tend to focus on a limited subset of these aspects; the challenge is to bring them together. Business Process Management (BPM), for example, does not adequately support teamwork around tasks or the creation and execution of dynamic service plans. Enterprise Architecture (EA) models use a layered approach to bridge between the business and IT that does not adequately consider the role of people, process, or organization. Computer Supported Collaborative Work (CSCW) focuses on people, awareness, and distributed collaboration to enable cooperative work; but does not adequately connect this with process, data, or organization. Services Oriented Computing (SOC) tends to focus on composable bite-size processes that can be executed by machines, but does not provide the flexibility required to scale and support complex cross-organizational work. BPEL4People and similar standards do not address the full scope of cross-enterprise work or the complex needs of humans in their various roles.

Recommended Research Areas

1. Exploring the new capabilities enabled by human flexibility, creativity, and communication patterns and integrating them systematically into BPM, SOA/SOC, EA, and CSCW.

2. A framework that allows us to understand the trade-offs between automated vs. free form approaches, what should be done by machine and what by human, where flexibility and creativity is required vs. where not, and how to set up or re-engineer an enterprise with these tradeoffs in mind.

3. A model or theory of non-functional characteristics of people work, such as trust, reputation, or quality. What they are and how to measure them. This will be analogous to non-functional characteristics of SOA services or hardware components.

4. How to ease the understandability, use, and communication of knowledge-rich processes, operations and services. This relates not only to pre-designed processes but also to dynamically create and/or customized business processes, and should enable non-IT people take advantage of free-form processes.

5. Model of people, teams, and organizations. This will identify the different type of roles people play in cross organizational work. It will also focus on issues specific to people, such as incentives, accountability, authority, trust, collaboration, productivity, or quality of output.

6. Relationship between process design and execution, especially when ongoing adaptation and transformation is required.

7. Models, methods, formalisms, and languages that focus on the role people play in the control and coordination of cross enterprise collaboration in different domains.

8. Dynamic flow engines that can support such models and provide the flexibility required for runtime adaptation and evolution.

9. Adaptation, versioning and evolution of process, work, collaborating organizations and collaboration patterns.

10. Extending SOA formalisms and constructs to facilitate the definition, dispatch, and orchestration of work as services that can be carried out by and for organizations.

11. Context, data, and knowledge management as required for managing and coordinating work across organizations and their interrelationship with the domain data, tools, and processes.

12. IT, middleware, systems, tools, and framework that support cross enterprise collaboration, and their relationship with current enterprise or domain specific tools and IT.

13. Utilization of crowd sourcing and social computing paradigms for the coordination and/or execution of work and business processes that span across organizational boundaries.

Collaboration Aspects of Human Tasks

Tobias Unger and Sebastian Wagner

Institute of Architecture of Application Systems, University of Stuttgart, Germany
Universitätsstraße 38, 70569 Stuttgart, Germany
lastname@iaas.uni-stuttgart.de

Summary. Many of today's development and manufacturing projects are so complex that they cannot be conducted only by one company anymore. Such collaborations are mostly modeled and executed using business processes. Business processes are increasingly controlled automatically by IT-systems, but they still consist of many tasks that have to be performed by people. Collaborations using business process are are widely discussed in the context of choreographies and subprocesses. However, collaborations on human task level are discussed much less. The goal of this work is to lay a foundation of a cross-organizational federated task management infrastructure, which supports collaborations on task level.

1 Introduction

Many of today's development and manufacturing projects are so complex that they cannot be conducted only by one company anymore. For instance when modern high speed trains are developed several companies are involved which form a virtual enterprise during the development project. The coordination of these projects is usually supported by business processes that are modeled in state of the art workflow languages like BPEL [1]. These processes run either distributed at the participating enterprises, i.e. the fragments of the process model are deployed across the infrastructures of the enterprises [2, 3]. However, it is even more likely that each enterprise runs its own private process and only the parts of the process are exposed that have to communicate with the processes of the participating enterprises via a predefined communication model based on WS-Coordination [4].

Especially in the area of cross-enterprise prototype development many tasks have to be performed manually. For this reason the integration of people on task level from multiple enterprises is of great importance. For instance to find an ideal fit between a vehicle concept and its components the employees of the car manufacturer and the suppliers have to collaborate closely [5].

The importance of human tasks is for instance accommodated by the WS-HumanTask specification [6] (WS-HT) which provides the foundation for our work. The specification addresses issues like the assignment of people to tasks, task manipulation (e.g. to control the lifecycle of a task) and the coordination between task and task parent which denotes the initiator of the task

M. zur Muehlen and J. Su (Eds.): BPM 2010 Workshops, LNBIP 66, pp. 579–590, 2011.

(e.g. a process or a human being). Also some software products exist that conform at least partly to the WS-HumanTask specification (in the community this software is referred as "Human Task Manager" or abbreviated HTM). For instance the WebSphere Process Server [7] contains a Human Task Manager. We also provide our own open source implementation of a Human Task Manager named Project Bangkok [1].

In collaboration scenarios where multiple enterprises are involved the task management becomes more sophisticated. If for instance multiple Human Task Managers are involved (e.g. one per company) they have to be coordinated. In this paper we focus on task-based collaboration, i.e. we do not discuss cross-enterprise collaboration from a process perspective. In this work we present the following key contributions: (i) In Section 3 we discuss different task-based cross-collaboration scenarios and identify issues that emerge in these scenarios. (ii) In Section 4 we propose a runtime architecture for the execution of collaboration tasks and the concept of a *federated task*.

We conclude this paper with a brief discussion about how the proposed architecture solves the scenarios presented in Section 3. Moreover, an overview of the related work is given in Section 5.

2   Running Example

In our running example a train manufacturer named "FastRail" wants to develop a new high speed train. FastRail has outsourced the development of wheels to a company called "TrackSystem" that has a strong expertise in this area. As FastRail has very special requirements concerning of the design of the wheels the two enterprises have to collaborate very closely, i.e. they form a virtual enterprise during the development process. In the planing phase, i.e. before the actual development starts, the management of both companies agrees on the different tasks that have to be performed. Some tasks are performed together by FastRail and TrackSystem employees at the FastRail site. This includes for instance the planing of the wheel design which has to be performed jointly in order to tailor the wheels to the technical requirements of the train. The creation of the wheel prototypes on the other hand is triggered by FastRail but completely done on the TrackSystem site, i.e. FastRail delegates this task to TrackSystem.

3   Task-Driven Collaborations

In this Section we discuss the different task management aspects and challenges of task-driven cross-enterprise collaboration scenarios. Thereby we not only focus on single tasks but also on composite tasks (cf. [6]) because they provide a good means to structure work. In contrast to single tasks, which can be regarded as atomic unit of work, a composite task consists of several (usually semantically related) units of work - that are called *subtasks*. Each subtask can be assigned to

---

[1] http://code.google.com/p/projectbangkok

another employee. However, it is also possible that one employee performs more than one subtask of a composite task. In our discussion we act on the assumption that each enterprise hosts its own HTM. The challenges described here partly base on the task collaboration requirements that were described in [8].

As indicated before, this Section only describes issues of task-based cross-enterprise collaboration scenarios. In Section 4 extensions of the WS-HT specification are proposed to accommodate these issues.

We have to provide a clear definition of task-driven collaborations before we can start to describe the challenges that are related to them. This definition along with definitions of the terms parent organization and participating organization lays the foundation for the following discussion.

Definition 1 (Task-driven Collaboration). *A task-driven collaboration describes a collaborative execution of a (human) task of a certain process in whose execution at least two organizations are involved. Besides responsibilities (competences/roles) a task-driven collaboration defines temporal, spatial, and granularity (structural) aspects which are execution relevant. The collaboration is transparent to the process and completely handled on task level.*

Definition 2 (Parent Organization). *A parent organization represents the organization which initially creates a collaborative task and, furthermore, may participate in the execution of the task.*

Definition 3 (Participating Organization). *A participating organization represents an organization participating in the execution of a collaborative task.*

3.1   Place of Performance

In virtual enterprises it is very likely that certain tasks can (or must) only be performed at a dedicated location. These place of performance restrictions might be caused for instance by legal requirements or through the availability of resources at a certain location. If FastTrain wants to perform the task *Test Train Prototype* but only TrackSystem owns a test track FastTrain employees have to perform the testing on the TrackSystem site. The challenge for the involved HTMs is to ensure that the locally restricted tasks can only be started by persons that reside at locations the task is restricted to. The HTM can determine the location of a user by using techniques like GPS or network triangulation (TODO reference?). However, there are further issues that have to be addressed by an HTM when the task performance location matters. For instance how does a HTM has to react when the task performer leaves the location where the task execution is restricted to while she is still performing the task? Is the task processing only suspended until the performer returns to the location or is the processing of the task completely stopped?

3.2   Temporal Dependencies

As mentioned before temporal aspects must also be reflected in task-driven collaborations. These aspects mainly encompass temporal dependencies between two or more tasks that have to be performed in the participating enterprises. A temporal dependency could for instance define that two tasks have to be executed in sequence or simultaneously. Simultaneous executions can become important if people have to collaborate in groups, i.e. they have to work on certain tasks at the same time to achieve a business goal. In our example scenario TrackSystem can for instance not start with the development of a wheel prototype until it has received the technical parameters of the train from FastRail.

Here we distinguish between single and composite tasks that can be either `Temporal Independent` or `Temporal Dependent`. A temporal independent task has obviously no temporal relation to other tasks. Consequently, it can be executed no matter which other tasks are currently running or were already executed in the past.

A temporal dependent task on the other hand has a temporal relation to one or more tasks. The task *Develop Wheel Prototype* in the example provided above can not be executed by TrackSystem until the task *Define Technical Parameters* was completed by FastTrain.

Also between subtasks of the same composite task temporal dependencies can exist. The task *Test Train Prototype* could consists among others of the subtasks *Drive Train* and *Monitor Train*. As the train has to be monitored during the test drive a temporal relation between the two subtasks has to be imposed to ensure that both subtasks are executed simultaneously.

If cross-enterprise processes are deployed in a virtual enterprise, temporal dependencies can be reflected by the control flow. However, if the involved enterprises do not use cross-enterprise processes or if no processes were defined for a given business scenario the modeling temporal dependencies between tasks can become an issue.

Even though WS-HT provides temporal parameters (e.g. *StartBy* or *CompleteBy* that define start and completion deadlines for tasks) temporal dependencies between tasks can not be modeled explicitly. Between subtasks WS-HT supports temporal dependencies to some extent. It can be defined that subtasks have to be performed sequentially and that subtasks are assigned simultaneously to certain persons. However, it can be only defined that people are assigned to tasks simultaneously but this does not ensure that they really execute the subtasks at the same time.

3.3   Staff Assignment

To assign people to tasks staff assignments have to be performed. WS-HT suggests three ways to assign people to tasks - statically, by using expressions or by querying organizational directories (briefly org. directories). When static assignments are used the user identifier of the employees that can execute the task are already defined when the task definition [2] is designed. This approach is very inflexible because organizational structures change often. This can for instance lead to the problem that a task is assigned to an employee that is on

---

[2] The task definition is a template or a model where the tasks are created from.

leave or that is not working for the company anymore. A more flexible approach to assign people to tasks is using expressions that extract the user identifiers from the input data of a task. However, this approach has the disadvantage that user identifiers have to be stored somewhere in in the payload of the input message. The most flexible approach is to evaluate parameterized staff assignments against org. directories at creation time of the task. Thereby a staff assignment returns only a particular subset of people from the org. directory that meet certain conditions to perform a task. An informal example for a staff assignment is "Assign all employees to the task *Drive Train* that are member of the group engine drivers". It was mentioned before that these staff assignments are parameterized. The staff assignment parameters can be utilized to refine the result set (e.g. specifying that only engine drivers with more than 10 years experience are allowed to drive the train). We only discuss the last staff assignment approach here. Firstly because it is the most flexible approach for assigning people to tasks and secondly it is more sophisticated since several org. directories are involved in a virtual enterprise. We have identified three types of staff assignments in the context of enterprise cross-collaboration scenarios: user level, organization level and mixed staff assignments.

User level staff assignments indicate that only employees that are available in the internal org. directory of the task parent enterprise are assigned to a task. Note, that this can be also employees of the participating enterprises when they were added to the task parent org. directory before. In the context of single tasks this means that the staff assignment that is attached to this task is only evaluated against the internal org. directory. For composite tasks the staff assignment for each subtask is evaluated against the internal org. directory.

Organization level staff assignments on the other hand are evaluated against the org. directory of the partner enterprise. This is especially relevant for delegation scenarios where the task parent enterprise delegates work to the participating enterprise. The manufacturing of new wheels would for instance be delegated from FastTrain to TrackSystem employees. However, this is not trivial because the user data that are hosted in organizational directories of an enterprise are very sensitive. That is the reason why it is very likely that an enterprise will not provide access to its org. directory to other enterprises. As stated above, in Section 4 an approach is proposed that describes how this issue can be resolved or at least relaxed.

When composite tasks are instantiated also mixed staff assignments can be performed. A mixed staff assignment consists of staff assignments that are attached to the subtasks where one subset the staff assignments is evaluated against the internal org. directory and another subset is evaluated against the external org. directory of the participating enterprise.

4   Realization Proposal

In section 3 we introduced the concept of *task-driven collaborations*. Based on this we introduce in this section the concept of a *task federation* which enables the execution of *task-driven collaborations*. The concept encompasses an architecture, a modeling concept, the concept of a participant tasks, and a coordination protocol for coordinating human tasks.

4.1 Architecture

In the following section the architecture of our task management federation is presented. Indeed existing WfMS (e.g [9,7]) have integrated task management functionality, but w.r.t. to our requirements they are insufficient; e.g. none of these systems support the federation of tasks across multiple participants. Also existing standards (e.g. BPEL and BPMN) focus on partner-integration based on sub-processes or choreographies (cf. [10,3,1,11]). WS-HT provides a notation for human tasks, a behavioral description, an architecture, an interfaces for interacting with human tasks. Aspects of partner-integration are neglected, too. However, our work is based on WS-HT, as it provides the best foundation as it is designed to be extensible (cf. [6]).

Compared to traditional workflow technology WS-HT removes the tight-coupling between processes and tasks. Human tasks can be instantiated standalone in a service-oriented manner by any application. For this purpose WS-HT introduces a standalone component called *task processor* for managing human tasks. This feature is an important prerequisite for our work, as we can build a dedicated task management infrastructure.

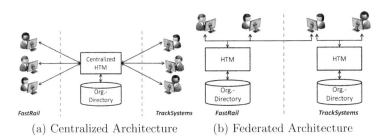

(a) Centralized Architecture   (b) Federated Architecture

Fig. 1. Architecture Variants

The architecture presented in Figure 1a represents basically the architecture proposed by WS-HT. At the center of this architecture the human task manager (HTM) is located. The HTM corresponds with the *task processor* proposed by WS-HT. The *organization directory* stores the organizational structure of an organization and can be used for evaluating staff queries. To allow task-driven collaboration using this architecture, all tasks involving persons employed at different applications must be created within a central HTM. This implies that the HTM must have access to the organizational structure of all involved organizations, i.e. the organizational structure must be stored in a (logically) centralized organization directory. A major drawback of this architecture is that organizations have expose task definitions as well as task runtime data as well as organizational data.

Alternatively, each organization can provide its own task management infrastructure (cf. Figure 1b). Compared to the architecture presented previously in this case the organization don't need to expose data, which is irrelevant for collaborations with partners. As WS-HT allows no federation of tasks across several HTMs, people which are involved in tasks created by different organizations must connect to different task managers. As a result the complete list of tasks a person has to perform is only available at the person's client. A second drawback of this architecture is, that an organization participating in a task on organization level has to expose parts of its organizational structure to the organization creating the task (parent organization), even if the participating organization can decide autonomously which person should perform the task. As the task instance is located only at the parents task manager, the assignment must be done within the parent's task manager. This solution might be reasonable for a set of scenarios, but in scenarios requiring that the real performer of a task is hidden to the parent organization this solution is unusable.

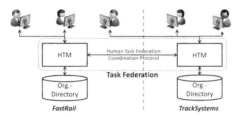

Fig. 2. Optimized Federated Architecture

The drawbacks of the federated architecture presented in Figure 1b can be solved by federating the tasks across the HTMs of the involved organizations (cf. Figure 2). All tasks involving people from other organization than the parent organization, which has created the task, are federated to the HTMs of the corresponding organizations. As a result, a person has only to access the HTM of the organization to which he belongs, even if he is working locally at the parent organization. This architecture supports participation at organization level as well as participation on user level. In case of a user level participation the affected persons of the participating organizations must be known in the parent's org. directory.

4.2   Modeling

As mentioned earlier cooperation contracts build the foundation of task-driven collaborations. Based on the collaboration contract the *task definitions* of the collaboration tasks can be modeled. In the global task definition the involved organizations agree on the parts of the task definition, which must be globally equal. For example *FastRail* and *TrackSystems* agree on the schema of the input data, etc.

Each partner refines the task definition later on by modifying the parts of the task definition, which don't need to be globally equal. For example *Fas-tRail* adds the people assignment. *TrackSystems* also adds a people assignment, as *TrackSystems* participates on organization level at the task and can assign people autonomously. If *TrackSystems* would participate on user level in the collaboration, no staff assignment would be modeled by *TrackSystems*. In this case the staff assignment is done at *FastRail*.

After completion of the modeling the task definitions are deployed to the HTMs. In case of a user level participation the involved persons of the participant must be added to the parents organization directory. In case of an organization level participation a reference to the participating organization must be added to the parent's organization directory. For example a reference to the HTM of *TrackSystems* must be added to the HTM of *FastRail*.

4.3   Task Federation

To allow the federation of tasks across multiple participants requires several adaptations in the task handling compared to traditional WFMS and the task handling described by WS-HT. These systems normally generate a workitem for each user returned by the staff query. Facilities provided by the runtime allow people to organize workitems into worklists. People then use the workitems to control the life-cycle of the task. However, the assumption here is that each person is directly connected to the HTM executing the task.

Our HTM decides whether a task must be federated or not based on the result of the staff assignment. To determine whether a task should be federated to a partner or not, we use the normal staff assignment process in combination with a resource virtualization: each partner, which should participate at organization level is registered as virtual resource in the organizational directory. If a organization participates on user level, the persons suitable for performing the task must be added to the task parent's organization directory. Unlike existing WfMS we don't create a workitem for each person or organization returned by the staff query (cf. [12]). We introduce an abstraction level called *participant* for grouping the returned persons or organizations (cf. Figure 3). Therefore, we also extend the staff query mechanism to return not only a list of resources but also the organization a person belongs to. Basically, we distinguish between three types of participants (cf. Figure 3):

- *Local Participant:* The local participant groups all persons returned by the staff query belonging to the organization owning the task.
- *User Level Participant:* A user level participant groups all persons of one single organization participating in the execution of a task.
- *Organization Level Participant:* A organization level participant is created for an organization participating in a task on organization level. This means that the organization specifies and executes the staff query on its own. Therefore, an organization level participant is not associated with any persons (cf. Figure 3).

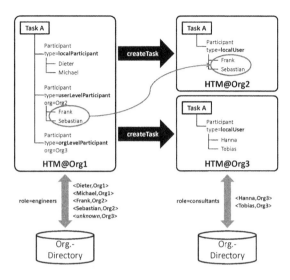

Fig. 3. Federation of Tasks

After executing the staff query and creating the participants, the task is federated by the HTM. We call the task instance initiating the federation the *parent task*. Task instances participating in a federation are called *participant tasks*. E.g. in Figure 3 three participants have been created at the task parent. A local participant, a user level participant for the persons of *Org 2* and a organization level participant for *Org 3*. The task is transferred to a partner using a push mechanism. The HTM executing the parent task creates task instances at the HTM of each participant. In case of a user level participant the selected persons are transfered to the HTM of the participant. This situation is showed in Figure 3. Frank and Sebastian belonging to *Org 2* are selected by the staff query of the parent task and transfered to the HTM of *Org 2* at the creation of the participant task. In case of a organization level participant a participant task is created at the participant's HTM but no persons are transferred. The participant's HTM executes the staff query modeled during the refinement phase. For example *Org 3* modeled that *Task A* should be performed by a *consultant*, if federated from *Org 1*. Now the instance of the federated task is activated, i.e. all participant task instances and the parent task instance are transitioned into the *Ready* state (cf. [6]), so people can perform the task. After activating of the participant task instances, the participants are able to read and write task data of the parent task. However, as potentially many participants are involved, the life-cycle commands must be coordinated across all participants. For example, if *Hanna* claims the task at *Org 3*, *Org 1* and *Org 2* must be informed that the task is already claimed.

Note that composite tasks can also be executed using our architecture. In this case for each user participating at the collaboration a subtask instance can be created (cf. [6]), which can be federated, if necessary.

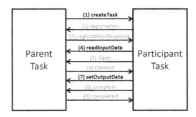

Fig. 4. Example of Federated Task Coordination Protocol

4.4   Task Federation Coordination Protocol

The following section describes the behavior of the parent task instance and the participating task instances w.r.t. to the exchanged protocol messages. The goal of the coordination is that the group of coordinated task instances behave roughly like a single logical task instance, which is called *federation task*. After the task is transferred to the partner organization, instances of the same task exist in every involved HTM. If one partner organization is involved, there are two instances and for every further partner the number of instances increases. Thus the HTMs must exchange coordination messages in order to synchronize the task state. Thereby, the HTM of the task owner acts as coordinator. If a task is claimed at one HTM, the task has to be locked at all other HTMs, in order to avoid redundant work. Furthermore, if a process terminates a task, the task must be terminated at each involved HTMs. To address the issue of coordinating the life-cycle of the participating task instances, we introduce a coordination protocol, namely *Task Federation Coordination Protocol*. The protocol defines the exchange of task life-cycle commands between the task parent and the task participants. The protocol is based on the life-cycle of a human task defined in [6]. The basic principle of the protocol is: a participant requests a state transition by invoking a life-cycle command. Then the coordinator located at the task parent confirms the state transition to the requester and informs all participants about the state change of the task.

Figure 4 shows an example for such an coordination. At some point in time the HTM of the task parent creates task instances at the HTMs participants resulting from the evaluation of the staff query (step (1) in Figure 4). Then the HTMs of the participant tasks register their tasks for coordination at the task parent (step (2) in Figure 4). The coordinator of the task parent confirms the registration by sending a registration response to the participant (step (3) in Figure 4). From that point on a coordination channel is established between the task parent and a task participant to exchange life-commands. Thus, people assigned to the task at the task participant can e.g. claim or complete the task (steps (5, 6) or steps (8, 9) in Figure 4). A participant can request the completion of a task by sending a *completion* message to the coordinator. The coordinator confirms the completion by sending a *completed* message to all participants. Upon receipt of the *completed* message the participants must transition their local task instance into the *completed* state. If the requested state transition cannot be executed the coordinator sends a *invalid state* message to the requesting participant.

5   Related Work

The Workflow Management Coalition proposes a reference architecture for Workflow Management Systems [13]. It allows to connect WfMS from different vendors by standardized interfaces. In contrast to our architecture, the WfMC promotes a monolithic architecture for WfMS. [14] proposes a distributed workflow system for the Internet. By using a generic workflow framework based on well-defined interfaces, components can be distributed cross-boundaries. For assigning tasks to an actor, a component based on the worklist interface can be built that is similar to our HTM. However, resource virtualization is not supported and most of the functional requirements (e.g. delegation, substitution) are not mentioned. [12] presents an algorithm for federating workitems to a remote workflow system. However, resource virtualization is not supported. In [8] requirements and an architecture for cross-enterprise task management are presented, which also requires the federation of tasks.

Furthermore, there is related work addressing the topic staff assignment. As we do not focus on staff assignment, this complements our work. Russel et al. [15] describe various patterns, how staff can be assigned to a task w.r.t. the task's life-cycle. However, collaborations aspects are not picked up.

6   Conclusion and Future Work

In this paper we identified scenarios and issues that can emerge in the area of cross-enterprise task-collaborations. We also proposed a WS-HumanTask based federated architecture to enable the execution of this cross-enterprise task-collaborations.

The architectural approach solves the problem of location dependency, i.e. no matter in which enterprise an employee is currently working she always has access to all tasks that were assigned to her. However, we do not consider location dependency in the sense that tasks can only be executed at a predefined location (e.g. due to the availability of resources at a certain location). The architecture solves also the issue described in 3.3 that employees from the participating enterprise have be assigned to a task that was created at the task parent enterprise. Because of the distribution of tasks across several HTMs, we introduced a coordination protocol to build a logical federated task, which behaves roughly like a task that is executed in a centralized manner.

As already indicated in section 3.2 WS-HumanTask also covers temporal dependencies. However, it does not solves issues like parallel task execution, i.e. it can not be ensured that two or more tasks are performed simultaneously. We will also address this issue in future work.

Another aspect that has to be discussed in future work are dynamic collaborations. In these collaborations participating enterprises are not determined before a collaboration starts but automatically during the runtime of a collaboration (similiar to automatic service discovery). In this case the parent enterprise might not know the participating enterprises beforehand, thus trust plays an important role.

Acknowledgments. This research was supported by EU FP7 research grants 213339 (ALLOW) and 216917 (MASTER).

References

1. OASIS: Web Services Business Process Execution Language Version 2.0 – OASIS Standard (2007)
2. Khalaf, R., Leymann, F.: Role-based Decomposition of Business Processes using BPEL. In: ICWS (2006)
3. Decker, G., Kopp, O., Leymann, F., Weske, M.: BPEL4Chor: Extending BPEL for Modeling Choreographies. In: Proceedings of the IEEE 2007 International Conference on Web Services. IEEE, Los Alamitos (2007)
4. OASIS: Web Services Coordination (WS-Coordination) 1.2 (2009)
5. Takeishi, A.: Bridging Inter- and Intra-Firm Boundaries: Management of Supplier Involvement in Automobile Product Development. Strategic Management Journal 22(5), 403–433 (2001)
6. OASIS: Web Services Human Task Specification Version 1.1, Committee Draft 06 (2009)
7. IBM: WebSphere Process Server V7.0,
   `http://www.ibm.com/software/integration/wps/`
8. Unger, T., Bauer, T.: Towards a Standardized Task Management. In: Multikonferenz Wirtschaftsinformatik (2008)
9. IBM: MQ Series Workflow 3.6
10. Object Management Group (OMG): Business Process Model and Notation (BPMN) Specification 2.0 Beta 1 (August 2009)
11. IBM, SAP: WS-BPEL Extension for Sub-processes – BPEL-SPE (2005)
12. Leymann, F., Roller, D.: Production Workflow: Concepts and Techniques. Prentice Hall PTR, Englewood Cliffs (2000)
13. Hollingsworth, D.: The Workflow Reference Model. Technical report, Workflow Management Coalition (1995)
14. Paul, S., Park, E., Chaar, J.K.: RainMan: A Workflow System for the Internet. In: USENIX Symposium on Internet Technologies and Systems (1997)
15. Russell, N., van der Aalst, W.M.P., ter Hofstede, A.H.M., Edmond, D.: Workflow Resource Patterns: Identification, Representation and Tool Support. In: Pastor, Ó., Falcão e Cunha, J. (eds.) CAiSE 2005. LNCS, vol. 3520, pp. 216–232. Springer, Heidelberg (2005)

Value-Sensitive Design for Cross-Enterprise Regulation

Sietse Overbeek, Virginia Dignum, and Yao-Hua Tan

Faculty of Technology, Policy and Management, Delft University of Technology,
Jaffalaan 5, 2600 GA Delft, The Netherlands
{S.J.Overbeek,M.V.Dignum,Y.Tan}@tudelft.nl

Abstract. The pressure to increase organizational transparency, the rise of proper IT support for regulative activities and the increasing cost of regulation are a few notable drivers that stress the significance of cross-enterprise regulation. Compliance to regulations fuels the added-value that business processes represent and prevents judiciary pursuits. Norm enforcement mechanisms are used to determine whether organizations have complied with the regulations or norms, which can be divided into mechanisms that are oriented towards direct control and mechanisms that are oriented towards self regulation. When designing a system to support agents in norm fulfillment and enforcement, the relation between norm enforcement mechanisms and the abstract values that are behind them should be explicitly incorporated in the development of the system. In this paper, a first step in the development of such a value-sensitive system is taken by formalizing the values of direct control and self regulation. The paper also outlines the following steps that are necessary to complete the development of the proposed value-sensitive system process towards a full system implementation.

Keywords: Agent systems, Cross-enterprise regulation, Norms, Self regulation, Value Sensitive Design.

1 Introduction

Over the past several years, the business community has devoted considerable attention to corporate responsibility, in order to address significant social and environmental questions with value for business and society. Organizational activities are expected to be transparent to governments, investors, and other stakeholders. Organizations are increasingly aware that not only their business processes must be efficient, they are also subject to regulations. Failure to comply to regulations diminishes the added-value that business processes represent for the organization, e.g. through non-optimal alignment with (i) quality standards, (ii) business partner service agreements or (iii) non-identified security flaws [1]. Non-compliance to regulations can also be the cause of judiciary pursuits as many financial scandals in recent years demonstrate. Examples of these are the cases of Enron, WorldCom, Roche, Siemens, and Volkswagen. Enterprises, governmental institutions, and the public in general benefit from well-defined and well-enforced laws and legal guidelines, in order to protect companies and their stakeholders from manipulations of financial reporting data. Traditionally, control and enforcement were government tasks, however, the advent of sound IT support and the increasing cost and

M. zur Muehlen and J. Su (Eds.): BPM 2010 Workshops, LNBIP 66, pp. 591–602, 2011.

complexity of regulatory activities are leading towards collaborative regulatory processes between enterprises and governments.

In this paper, we present a model to design cross-enterprise regulation as a collaborative process that takes into account the basic values behind the different stakeholders. Specifically, we take a Value Sensitive Design (VSD) perspective that allows to formalize and operationalize abstract values and norms.

The paper is organized as follows. In the next section, we provide some background on normative systems. The notion of Value Sensitive Design is described in section 3. Section 4 provides a formalization of values based on predicate logic and section 5 shows how formal values can be implemented in operational systems. Finally, in section 6 we present our conclusions and directions for future work.

2   Normative Systems

Globalization, specialization, and innovation are changing many aspects of how businesses operate. The nature of interaction between regulating institutions or governments and the actors or companies being regulated is changing from monolithic control by governments to distributed environments where companies are free to regulate their affairs within boundaries set by governing instances. A special case in which centralized models of operation is increasingly hard to sustain is that of regulation or norm enforcement. Regulation of organizational processes is based on the norms that organizations have to comply with [2]. A *norm* can be defined as standard behavior that is acceptable for the regulating institutions, indicating desirable behaviors that should be carried out as well as undesirable behaviors that should be avoided [3].

Norm enforcement mechanisms are used to determine if organizations have complied to the *norms* that they should satisfy [4]. If norms are to be enforced, then the institution should specify and handle sanctions for every possible violation of the norms. This means that enforcement mechanisms often require the introduction of special 'regulator actors' that actively monitor the behavior of the other agents [4]. Such agents are assigned to monitor the behavior of organizations and sanction them in case of norm violations. Implementing self-regulation as a control mechanism thus results in a redistribution or delegation of control tasks among the actors.

Which enforcement mechanisms are effective and how sanctions are likely to be followed is directly related to the values of an organization. Moral values are the standards of good and evil that guide an individual's behavior and choices [5]. Individuals, groups, and societies develop own value systems used for the purpose of ethical integrity. The value notion and the two mentioned different types of norm enforcement mechanisms can be combined to design a *value-sensitive system* that supports agents in *norm fulfillment* and *norm enforcement*.

3   Value Sensitive Design

Value Sensitive Design (VSD) is a methodological design approach that aims at making moral values part of technological design, research, and development [6]. Values are typically high-level abstract concepts that are difficult to incorporate in software design.

In order to design systems that are able to deal with moral values, norms must be oper-ationalized while maintaining traceability of its originating values. The VSD process, which is depicted in figure 1, traces the influence of values in the design and engineering of systems. The values of direct control and self regulation values are in fact the result

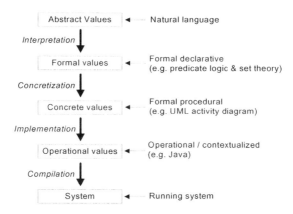

Fig. 1. Value-sensitive system development process, based on [7]

of applying the *value interpretation* phase of a Value-sensitive System Development (VSD) process [6,7]. In this paper, we argue that this change calls for architectures that satisfy the following principles: (1) coordination policies need to be described at a high level of abstraction; (2) the enforcement needs to be negotiated between governments and enterprises; (3) coordination policies need to be formulated explicitly rather than being implicit in the interactions; and (4) it should be possible to deploy and enforce a policy incrementally.

In particular, value descriptions do not provide enough formality to be usable at the system specification level. Therefore, the first step in VSD is to provide a formal repre-sentation of values, that 'translates' a natural language description into formal values in a formal language, as further elaborated in section 4. The translation to formal values will provide the basis for the remainder of the VSD process, eventually leading to a system that supports agents in direct control and self regulative contexts. This is shown in section 4. However, the relation between abstracts values and formal norms is more complex than mere formal interpretation. Institutions provide structured interpretations of the concepts in which norms are stated. In particular, institutions do not only consist of norms, but also describe the ontology of the to-be-regulated domain. For instance, whether something within a given institution counts as personal data and should be treated as such depends on how that institution interprets the term 'personal data' [8].

Steps towards the completion of the remaining phases of the VSD process, namely the design and engineering of a system to support agents, are outlined in section 5. As is shown in figure 1, the formal values can be further concretized by translating them in a formal procedural language. For example, the Unified Modeling Language (UML) includes an activity diagramming technique [9] that can be used to concretize formal values. More specifically, a UML activity diagram is used in section 5.1 to describe the operational step-by-step workflows of the direct control and self regulation mechanisms. The final step of the VSD process consists of translating the concrete values to operational values by implementing the concrete values by means of a programming language.

4   Formalization of Values

An increasingly important value in organizations is that of *ethical and transparent business practices*. The development of codes and standards for ethical and transparent business practices can help limit corruption, ensure fair and open competition, and encourage a better business environment. All these practices are essential to economic growth and improved standards of living. For the last decade, organizations have been faced with an increase in regulation changes demanding transparency in an organization's books and its operational management. Examples of such changes are: the Sarbanes-Oxley (SOx) Act[1] intended for American organizations quoted on the stock exchange, the Dutch counterpart 'Tabaksblat'[2], the Basel II Accords[3] for banks, and the 'Markets in Financial Instruments Directive' (MiFID)[4] for the European stock exchange.

A formalism for values must be able to describe and reason about social structures and interactions, facilitating analysis and verification through logical reasoning. Moreover, in open systems where agents are assumed to be autonomous and rational, agents can, involuntarily or by deliberate choice, violate social norms and regulations and therefore one must be able to deal with and reason about such violations. Much existing work on business rules concentrates on the development of standards for contracts. However, many such standards mostly provide a purely syntactic formalization of contracts. In multi-agent systems, norms have been identified as crucial tools to formally express the expected behaviour of agents in open environments. Current norm formalisms focus on the declarative nature of norms but, in order to be implemented, norms should be translated into operational representations.

In normative systems, interactions between actors are regulated by normative templates that describe desired behavior in terms of deontic concepts (obligations, prohibitions and permissions), deadlines, violations and sanctions [10]. Deontic logic provides mechanisms to reason about violability of norms, that is, about how to proceed when norms are violated. In previous work [11,12], we have focused on the formal definition of norms by means of some variations of deontic logic that include conditional and temporal aspects, and we provided formal semantics and verification mechanisms. In this section, we provide a set-theoretic overview of normative systems in which norms are seen as elements of sets representing a state of affairs.

---

[1] See e.g. http://en.wikipedia.org/wiki/Sarbanes-Oxley_Act
[2] See e.g. http://www.commissiecorporategovernance.nl/ Information in English
[3] See e.g. http://www.bis.org/publ/bcbsca.htm
[4] See e.g. http://en.wikipedia.org/wiki/Markets_in_Financial_ Instruments_Directive

4.1   Set-Theoretic Representation of Values

In the case of enterprise regulation, we assume a set of *agents* denoted as $\mathcal{AS}$, a set *roles* denoted as $\mathcal{RO}$ and a set of tasks $\mathcal{T}$. Specifically, the set contains the roles of *actor* and *regulator*:

$$\mathcal{RO} = \{\texttt{actor}, \texttt{regulator}\} \tag{1}$$

The predicate $\mathsf{rea}(a, r)$, where $a \in \mathcal{AS}$ and $r \in \mathcal{RO}$ defines role enacting agents. The set of all agents enacting a certain role is defined as a subset of $\mathcal{AS}$:

$$\mathcal{AS}_r = \{a \in \mathcal{AS} | \mathsf{rea}(a, r)\} \tag{2}$$

As an illustration, consider a tax officer denoted as a to be an agent that can play the two mentioned roles. Suppose that a tax officer working at the national Tax Administration inspects the completed tax returns for a citizen. In such a situation, the tax officer enacts the role of regulator, that is $\mathsf{rea}(a, \texttt{regulator})$, because he checks whether the tax returns are excluded from any tax violations. In a different evaluative situation, for example a job performance evaluation, the manager of the tax officer may inspect whether the officer is functioning properly. In that case, the tax officer enacts the role of *actor* who is being regulated, that is $\mathsf{rea}(a, \texttt{actor})$.

The set of tasks being fulfilled at a given moment by an agent a is defined as $\mathcal{TI}_a \subseteq \mathcal{T}$. The fulfillment relation between agent and task is then defined as:

$$\mathsf{fulfill}(a, t) \; \textit{iff} \; t \in \mathcal{TI}_a \tag{3}$$

Task fulfillment can be illustrated by the tax officer who inspects the tax returns. In this case, the inspection of the tax returns is a task instance that is fulfilled by the tax officer. Such a task instance can then be classified as a task of the type 'tax return inspection' for example.

The set of norms is denoted as $\mathcal{NS}$. A $\texttt{regulator}$ agent uses a *norm framework* $\mathcal{NF}$ to regulate an $\texttt{actor}$ agent. Formally, a *norm framework* $\mathcal{NF}_x$ is a subset of norms $\mathcal{NF}_x \subseteq \mathcal{NS}$ enforced by a regulator x. Similarly, we define the set of norms applicable to a task $\mathcal{NT}_t$ as a subset of norms $\mathcal{NT}_t \subseteq \mathcal{NS}$ applicable to a task $t \in \mathcal{T}$.

$$\mathsf{enforce}(x, n) \; \textit{iff} \; n \in \mathcal{NF}_x \; \textit{and} \; \mathsf{rea}(x, \texttt{regulator}) \tag{4}$$

$$\mathsf{apply}(n, t) \; \textit{iff} \; n \in \mathcal{NT}_t \; \textit{and} \; t \in \mathcal{T} \tag{5}$$

For a specific agent x, given $\mathcal{TI}_x$ (the set of tasks of x) and $\mathcal{NT}_t$ (the set of norms applicable to a task, we can define the *containment* set $\mathcal{NC}_x$ of the norms applicable to the agent as a subset of norms $\mathcal{NC}_x \subseteq \mathcal{NS}$ applicable to an actor x.

$$\mathsf{contain}(x, n) \; \textit{iff} \; n \in \mathcal{NT}_t \; \textit{and} \; t \in \mathcal{TI}_x \; \textit{and} \; \mathsf{rea}(x, \texttt{actor}) \tag{6}$$

Being autonomous, an actor can decide whether to comply or not with the norms in its containment set $\mathcal{NC}_x$. We define the compliance set $\mathcal{NH}_x \subseteq \mathcal{NC}_x$ as the set of norms the actor is complying to, such that:

$$\mathsf{comply}(x, n) \; \textit{iff} \; n \in \mathcal{NH}_x \tag{7}$$

An actor agent can violate, consciously or unconsciously, norms in its containment set by pursuing an illegal goal or by performing an illegitimate action, i.e. when an actor agent doesn't comply to the containment set. A violation is then defined as:

$$\text{violation}(x,t,n) \text{ iff } \text{fulfill}(x,t) \wedge \text{apply}(n,t) \wedge \neg\text{comply}(x,n) \tag{8}$$

4.2   Applying Formal Values

In this section, we demonstrate the formalization of the value *ethical and transparent business practice* as an example of the application of the formalism proposed above.

The norm enforcement mechanisms of direct control and self regulation have been elaborated in natural language in [4], which is used to interpret the abstract values. In direct control the regulator directly controls the tasks that are fulfilled by actors in an organization. In the model of self regulation, actors control their own behavior. A self-regulating actor is sanctioned if a regulator determines that an actor fails to comply to the norm framework, despite its self-regulative activities. The formal values are then based on these interpretations. Given the formalization of values above, we can now formally distinguish these two models of regulation.

In direct control, it is assumed that there is a separation of concerns between `actor` and `regulator`, that is

$$\text{rea}(x,\texttt{actor}) \wedge \text{rea}(y,\texttt{regulator}) \rightarrow x \neq y \tag{9}$$

In self regulation, the separation of roles is not assumed and an actor will try to prevent sanctions itself. Regulative activities that are performed by regulator agents are special kind of tasks. It is assumed that a regulator agent uses the norm framework to derive a set of norms tailored to an actor's specific situation. For example, if a tax officer detects that a tax return doesn't comply with one or more norms the officer can sanction the responsible agent by imposing a fine. An example of a norm that must be fulfilled when completing a tax return is the norm 'provide an overview of all collected earnings'. The actor agent will risk a fine if this norm is not complied with and if the tax officer detects the failure to comply with this norm. Formally, control is defined as:

$$\text{control}(x,y,t,n) \text{ iff } \text{enforce}(y,n) \wedge \text{fulfill}(x,t) \wedge \text{apply}(n,t) \tag{10}$$

This means that when actor x fulfills task t to which norm n is applicable, the activity of x is controlled by the regulator agent y that enforces norm n. Finally, a sanction s is a special type of norm, to which an actor has to comply in case of a violation:

$$\text{sanction}(x,y,s) \text{ iff } \text{control}(x,y,t,n) \wedge \text{violation}(x,t,n) \tag{11}$$

Figure 2 shows the set-theoretic representation of these predicates. Note that the dark-grey shaded area indicates the violation set of x, whereas the black area indicates the violations which are effectively controlled by y and over which sanctions will be applied. The tax return example can be used to further explain the difference between direct control and self regulation. Assume that a tax officer x regulates a citizen y by inspecting a citizen's completed tax form and that no flaws are detected. This means

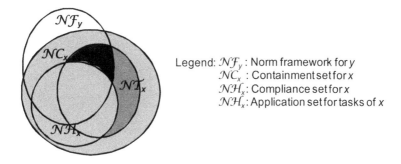

Legend: $\mathcal{NF}_y$: Norm framework for y
$\mathcal{NC}_x$: Containment set for x
$\mathcal{NH}_x$: Compliance set for x
$\mathcal{NH}_x$: Application set for tasks of x

Fig. 2. Enforcement, containment, compliance, and violation

that the norms n that are contained in some norm framework equate to the norms that actor y complies with during the fulfillment of a task i in which a citizen y completes a tax form. One or more sanctions S are issued by the tax officer in case the norms n that are contained in some norm framework don't equate to the norms that actor y should've complied with. A sanction can be a fine or the reclaim of unlawfully obtained tax money. In the formal model of direct control, a regulating agent directly controls the actions of an actor agent. In the formal model of self regulation, which is discussed next, the actor agent regulates itself.

5   From Formal Values to a Running System

The formal values that have been introduced are expressive enough to enable a discussion with stakeholders of a value-sensitive system that has to be developed, but do not provide enough information on how to build a system that complies with those values. *Concrete value* descriptions, which are the result of further concretizing the formal value descriptions, specify the behavior of the system, define constraints, and indicate how to react in case of unwanted behavior. As discussed in previous sections, regulatory systems must consider both the perspective of the regulating institutions as that of the actors. That is, in order to implement norms it is not enough to include a model-checking module by, e.g., implementing a theorem prover that, using the norms semantics, checks whether a given interaction protocol complies with the norms. This means that implementation of norms must consider (a) how the agents behavior is affected by norms, and (b) how the institution should ensure the compliance with norms [8].

In the latter case, developing concrete value descriptions corresponds to general analysis and design steps in system development. Examples of system design artifacts reflecting concrete values are Unified Modeling Language (UML) diagrams such as an activity diagram, a sequence diagram, and a collaboration diagram. Other examples include a Business Process Modeling Notation (BPMN) model, a Petri net, and a Data Flow Diagram (DFD). In the former case, it is necessary to provide means to analyse the impact of norms in the agents reasoning cycle. As part of the outline of the remaining development phases of a value-sensitive system, the formal values of direct control and self regulation are concretized by designing two activity diagrams.

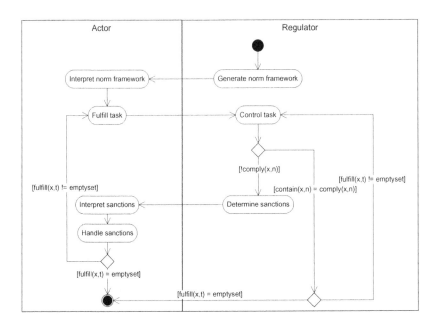

Fig. 3. Activity diagram reflecting the concrete value of direct control

5.1 Concrete Values

The formal value of direct control expressed by means of the equations in section 4.2 can be concretized as a UML activity diagram shown in figure 3. Activity diagrams can be divided into object swimlanes that determine which object is responsible for which activity [9]. The direct control activity diagram shows the swimlanes for an actor and a regulator. Arrows indicate transitions coming out of each activity, connecting it to the next activity. A transition may branch into two or more mutually exclusive transitions. Guard expressions shown inside brackets label the transitions coming out of a branch. A branch appears in the diagram as a hollow diamond. The activities that are performed after the 'control task' activity which is carried out by a regulator are dependent of the outcome of an actor's norm fulfillment performance. Sanctions will follow in case the regulator finds out that an actor doesn't comply to one or more norms. After dealing with those sanctions, an actor can finish working if there are no tasks left or he can continue with another task. A regulator can finish controlling if an actor has ceased working or he can continue to control if an actor is going to fulfill remaining tasks.

The formal value of self regulation expressed by means of the equations in section 4.2 can be concretized as a UML activity diagram shown in figure 4. When comparing both activity diagrams it is clear that the 'control actor' activity is not a regulator's responsibility in the case of self regulation. The only two activities that are left for a regulator are the tailoring of a norm framework to an actor and the issuing of sanctions when norms aren't fulfilled. Figure 1 shows that the final step of the VSD process consists of the implementation of concrete values to get operational values. Operational values are the codification of functions in a system level language that contributes to

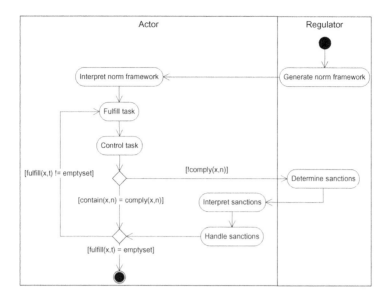

Fig. 4. Activity diagram reflecting the concrete value of self regulation

the value implementation. It would go beyond the scope of this paper to completely operationalize the concrete values, but the 'interpret norm framework' activity of the actor is further operationalized in the next section to outline the value-sensitive system.

5.2 Operational Values

The activity 'interpret norm framework' can be found in both activity diagrams and is performed by an actor. An attribute-value pair is a fundamental data representation, in which all or part of the data model may be expressed as a collection of tuples <attribute, value>, see e.g. [13]. Table 1 shows four example attribute-value pairs that are part of the tax return example. These pairs are included in the 'normframework.txt' text file

Table 1. Example attribute-value pairs and parsed output

Norm type	Norm instance
Venture capital	The maximum amount for deductible venture capital $< €46.984$
Income	The tax free income is $€20.661$
Deduction	Senior deduction is granted if age > 64 and collective income $< €34.282$
Deduction	Bonus for work continuation is granted if birthdate < 1948 or if work income $> €8.859$
...	...

that is parsed to generate norms that apply for citizens who complete tax forms. In other words, the text file represents a norm framework that is tailored to citizens who complete tax forms. Table 1 shows norms of a certain type (the attributes) with their corresponding instances (the values of the attributes). The norm types that are shown are related to venture capital, income, and deduction and should be taken into account when completing tax returns. Specific instances of these types are shown in the right column of the table. Once the norm framework is parsed, it can be interpreted by an actor to understand which norms have to be complied when fulfilling tasks. Subsequently, the next activity shown in the activity diagrams can be performed. Finally, an overview of the current static structure of the value-sensitive system to support agents in norm fulfillment and enforcement is provided.

5.3   Static Structure Diagram

Figure 5 shows a UML class diagram that shows all classes and their relationships of the outlined value-sensitive system to map out the system's structure. The equations

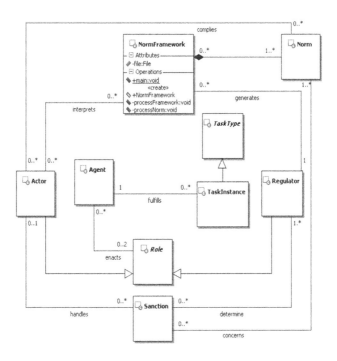

Fig. 5. Class diagram reflecting the static structure of the system

that have been introduced in section 4 and the activities as part of the activity diagrams have been used to design the class diagram. The *sets* that are part of the formal values are the *classes* in the class diagram. The relationships between the classes can be identified by studying the equations that constitute the formal values and the activities in the activity diagrams. The *composition* relationship between the norm framework class and the norm class shows that every norm framework is composed of at least one or more norms. Furthermore, three generalization relationships are shown. Two of the generalization relationships show that the actor class and the regulator class are subtypes of the *abstract* role class. The role class is abstract to indicate that the class itself can't be instantiated, but its child classes 'actor' and 'regulator' can be instantiated instead. The third generalization relationship shows that the *abstract* task type class is a supertype of the task instance class. The generalization shows that a task instance is of a certain type, e.g. all task instances that are related to tax return inspections can be classified as tasks of the type 'tax return inspection'. The task type class is abstract, because agents fulfill a task *instance* instead of a *type*. The class diagram provides a leg up to future research in which attributes and operations can be added to the classes. Furthermore, this exercise will then pave the road for a full system implementation.

6   Conclusions and Future Research

The results of the presented research provide the basis for a value-sensitive system to support actor agents in norm fulfillment and regulating agents in norm enforcement. This foundation has been laid by applying a value-sensitive system development process and by incorporating the principles of the norm enforcement mechanisms of direct control and self regulation in the system design. By following this specific system development process, the value that is created for the agents that apply the norm enforcement mechanisms of direct control and self regulation is explicitly incorporated in the development of the system. The process consists of three phases: value interpretation, value concretization, and implementation of the values into the development of the system. The interpretation phase has been fully described by means of formalisms that express the values of direct control and self regulation in an exact and precise manner. The remaining phases have been outlined by providing two UML activity diagrams that describe the workflows of the direct control and self regulation mechanisms and by implementing one of system classes. Finally, the static structure of the current system design has been mapped out in a UML class diagram. Our current work, as described in this paper, is geared towards the specification of regulatory collaboration. However, the approach taken is generic enough to be applied to other types of cross-enterprise collaboration. The current formalization of norms is based on predicate logic. In order to provide a richer semantics to this formal model, we are working on a deontic logic representation.

Moreover, we are extending this research towards the realization of a full system implementation by fulfilling the VSD process. In concrete, this means that the outline that has been provided of the concretization and implementation phases needs to be completed. Finally, case studies and experiments can be conducted to evaluate and test the system in operation and to evaluate and test its supportive possibilities for agents.

Acknowledgement. This work was supported by the ABC project (acronym for Agent-mediated Business Coordination). ABC is funded by the Netherlands Organisation for Scientific Research (NWO) under grant number 612.066.515.

References

1. El Kharbili, M., Stein, S., Markovic, I., Pulvermüller, E.: Towards policy-powered semantic enterprise compliance management. In: Hepp, M.e.a. (ed.) Proc. 3rd International Workshop on Semantic Business Process Management (SBPM 2008), Spain, pp. 16–21 (2008)
2. Boella, G., Lesmo, L., Damiano, R.: On the ontological status of plans and norms. Artificial Intelligence and Law 12(4), 317–357 (2004)

3. Meneguzzi, F., Luck, M.: Norm-based behaviour modification in bdi agents. In: Sierra, C.e.a. (ed.) Proc. 8th International Joint Conference on Autonomous Agents and Multiagent Systems (AAMAS 2009), Hungary, vol. 1, pp. 177–184 (2009)

4. Burgemeestre, B., Hulsteijn, J., Tan, Y.H.: Towards an architecture for self-regulating agents: a case study in international trade. In: Proc. 2nd Multi-Agent Logics, Languages, and Organisations Federated Workshops, Italy. CEUR Workshop Proceedings, vol. 494 (2009)

5. Scott, E.: Organizational moral values. Business Ethics Quarterly 12(1), 33–55 (2002)

6. van den Hoven, M.: Design for values and values for design. Information Age +, Journal of the Australian Computer Society 7(2), 4–7 (2005)

7. Aldewereld, H.: Autonomy vs. Conformity: an Institutional Perspective on Norms and Protocols. PhD thesis, Utrecht University, The Netherlands (2007)

8. Vázquez-Salceda, J., Aldewereld, H., Grossi, D., Dignum, F.: From human regulations to regulated software agents' behavior. Artificial Intelligence and Law 16(1), 73–87 (2008)

9. Rumbaugh, J., Jacobson, I., Booch, G.: The Unified Modeling Language Reference Manual, 2nd edn., Boston, MA. The Addison-Wesley Object Technology Series (2004)

10. Jones, A., Sergot, M.: A formal characterisation of institutionalised power. Journal of the IGPL 4(3), 429–445 (1996)

11. Dignum, V., Meyer, J., Dignum, F., Weigand, H.: Formal Specification of Interaction in Agent Societies. In: Hinchey, M.G., Rash, J.L., Truszkowski, W.F., Rouff, C.A., Gordon-Spears, D.F. (eds.) FAABS 2002. LNCS (LNAI), vol. 2699, pp. 37–52. Springer, Heidelberg (2003)

12. Dignum, V.: A Model for Organizational Interaction: based on Agents, founded in Logic. PhD thesis, Utrecht University, The Netherlands (2004)

13. Magnani, M., Montesi, D.: A unified approach to structured and XML data modeling and manipulation. Data & Knowledge Engineering 59(1), 25–62 (2006)

Business Process-Based Testing of Web Applications

Andreas Heinecke[1], Tobias Griebe[2], Volker Gruhn[2], and Holger Flemig[3]

[1] Applied Telematics and e-Business Group, University of Leipzig, Department of
Computer Science, Klostergasse 3, 04109 Leipzig, Germany
{heinecke,griebe}@ebus.informatik.uni-leipzig.de
[2] Software Engineering Group, University of Duisburg-Essen, paluno - The Ruhr
Institute of Software Technology, Gerlingstraße 16, 45127 Essen, Germany
[3] itCampus GmbH (a Software AG Company), Nonnenstraße 42, 04229 Leipzig,
Germany

Abstract. Software testing claims a big amount of software development costs as a rule. Particularly, manually operated software tests are
on the critical path during realising a software product since the execution of these tests is very time-consuming. Furthermore, it is cumbersome
for domain experts to participate in the development process since they
have a low level of software engineering knowledge. However, their participation is important and a crucial factor to success since they have
the domain expertise.

In this paper we propose an approach that enables domain experts to
generate test cases alongside business processes. Our contribution targets a holistic approach that supports the modelling of the graphical
user interface (GUI) for web-based information systems, the generation
of test cases from modelled business processes, the automated execution
of the generated test cases, and the reporting of test results, which includes a backtracking of the results to the respective elements within the
workflows of the business process.

1 Introduction

Software testing claims a big amount of software development costs as a rule.
Depending on the defined quality requirements the software test claims between
40% or 60% of the whole development costs. Manually operated software tests
are a straight approach as they do not need to be exhaustively engineered in
terms of preparation of test scripts prior to testing. They can be conducted intuitively and yield instant results. Yet, manually operated software tests are on
the critical path during the realisation of a software product since their execution
is very time-consuming. In particular in the context of a highly iterative development process, regression testing causes a huge dissemination effect. Hence, the
automation of software tests provides a big potential for optimisation. Contrary
to low-level module tests high-level system tests are difficult to automate since
they provide an abstract view onto the system and therefore hide important
details.

M. zur Muehlen and J. Su (Eds.): BPM 2010 Workshops, LNBIP 66, pp. 603–614, 2011.

Besides the general problems of the software test, it is cumbersome for domain experts to participate in the development process since they have a low level of software engineering knowledge. However, their participation is a crucial factor to success since they have the domain expertise and the most authoritative idea of the software system under development. The domain experts are the stakeholders of the software system. Hence, the software specification is defined on the basis of their requirements and the intended purpose. To decide whether a system behaves as specified and expected meaningful test cases have to be designed. The most suitable solution would be to have the domain experts to develop these test cases, which often leads to dissatisfactory results due to the lack of software engineering knowledge. Requiring the software engineers to design the test cases often leads to improper test cases due to the low level of domain expertise.

In this paper we propose an automatable approach that enables domain experts to participate in the software development process by generating test cases alongside business processes. We spotlight business processes since the main interest of domain experts is the support of the business processes by software. In the context of software development, the modelled business process is a communication medium between domain experts and software engineers. Our approach involves the use of a structured procedure for the test case generation as well as the test execution, and therefore simplified regression testing, the ability to measure the test coverage and a strong focus on automation. The increased level of automation aims at reduced testing costs, increased the test adequacy and is the key factor to integrate the domain expert into the software development process since typical tasks that require software engineering knowledge are performed by a tool. In the context of a highly iterative development process that involves frequent software revisions, manually operated software tests are inadequate since their time-consuming execution opposes the nature of quick iteration steps. Hence, the quality of the software revision cannot be tested thoroughly. Our contribution targets a holistic approach that supports the modelling of the graphical user interface (GUI) for web-based information systems, the generation of test cases from business processes, the automated execution of the generated test cases, and the reporting of test results, which includes a backtracking of the reported issues to their origin within the workflows of the business process. The modelling of the GUI for the web-based information system is based on a ruler-based layout and generation method that enables the declarative description of the GUI, which enables the integration with the business process model. The test case generation method is based on several model transformations that derive test cases from modelled business processes. The execution of the generated test cases and the evaluation of the results is based on a capture/replay test framework. The integration of these techniques results in a completely integrated approach that provides domain experts with a tool-supported method for deriving automatic executable test cases from rather abstract models.

The proposed approach is currently work in progress within the scope of a research project called "ProBaTe-Web" which aims at providing a tool supported test automation approach for web-based information systems. The project intends to provide domain experts with a tool that enables them to design a GUI, adjust GUI models and business process models, generate test cases, execute the generated test cases and report the test results. The project's contribution is partitioned into three parts: the design of GUIs for web information systems and the alignment of the GUI models with the business process, the test case generation, and the test case execution.

2   Related Work

In recent years a lot of research focusing on the testing of web applications has been conducted. To put the present paper into context, a selection of related work is discussed in this section.

In [1] Reza et al. study model-based testing techniques for web applications using state charts. Their work is focused on testing the front-end functionality of web applications by verifying that links, forms and images conform to the specification documents in terms of functionality and appearance. An algorithm is introduced that models a web site as state chart using its HTML code. The state chart is then used for further analysis by inspecting states and transitions. Once a complete state chart has been generated, the web application is tested by visiting the individual nodes of the state chart. Errors can be found if the underlying state machine does not reach the desired state after a given set of transitions. Detection of errors within the HTML code allows the indirect detection of errors in the web application. In contrast to our work, the proposed algorithm does not work on design documents but derives a model of the web application based on the HTML output created by a web server. Thus, a web site tested using this method may seem to contain no errors while still being non-compliant to specification. Furthermore, the proposed approach primarily targets to test the correctness of links, forms and images, while our approach aims to test the correct implementation of the business process.

Raffelt et al. [2] propose an technique for web application testing where no design time model is available. Their method is a black-box approach based on gathering information about the system under test by means of capture/replay and automata learning techniques for on the fly generation of models conforming to the web application under test. Their tool *Webtest* is designed to test web applications that implement services using (X)HTML and client side scripts. *Webtest* enables the dynamic recording and execution of web applications and can be employed for automatic and efficient regression testing by implementing a set of typical actions that can be executed on a web site such as providing input or calling a hypertext link. The recording of test cases can be done either in modelling mode or in harvesting mode. In modelling mode, the test engineer manually selects and configures actions from a web application and appends them to an executable graph forming the test case. In harvesting mode the test engineer freely browses the web application under test using a special browser while actions are captured. Both modes yield a test script that can be executed within a test execution environment providing extensive reporting functionality. The obtained test script serves as input alphabet for a learning algorithm that is used for further automatic exploration of a web site and executing test cases. This approach uses basic automation techniques, but still requires extensive manual interaction. Opposed to our approach it does not use design-time models but relies on a model derived from an existing application.

Ricca et al. [3] propose a semi-automatic testing technique that exploits a generated model of the system under test. The contribution of the paper is the definition of an UML-based analysis model and the proposition of several verification and analysis techniques exploiting this model. Furthermore, the approach is supported by two tools *ReWeb* and *TestWeb* and supports both static analysis and dynamic validation. Static analysis checks for faults like dead links or unreachable pages. The dynamic validation employs a white-box testing technique that requests certain pages from the web server and stores the resulting page. The white-box method enables the application of different coverage criteria like page testing and hyperlink testing among others to select a test suite. The test case generation employs algebraic path expression based on the work of Beizer [4]. Although this approach provides basic automation of the extraction of the UML model and test case generation there are many issues that have to be done manually. For instance, the test data has to be entered manually for each generated test case, the extracted analysis model has to be refined manually by entering variables and defining conditions for edges, and the test result has to be determined manually by evaluating the resulting web page. Our approach provides a higher level of automation as the test case generation and execution is completely automated.

Andrews et al. [5] contribute an approach for testing web applications by modelling them with Finite State Machines (FSMs). The generation of tests is based on FSMs that are hierarchically modelled. The authors argue that the employment of constraints to reduce the set of inputs handles the problem of state explosion, which is inherent to FSMs. Furthermore, the authors employ a hybrid approach that separates the choice of input parameters and the generation of test sequences to cope with the state explosion problem. Their approach is able to test three aspects: single functions on a web page, navigation between pages, and state-dependent behaviour. Although the authors propose a research prototype implementation that generates *WinRunner* scripts, which is a capture/replay test tool, the exact level of automation is not revealed. In addition to that, our approach does not only provide a consistently automated method but also a modelling language that is, contrary to FSMs, well suited to be used by domain experts.

3   Approach

The testing of web applications is a time consuming and cumbersome, yet inevitable task. Its versatile and efficient automation requires a structured procedure for the generation of test cases as well as efficient means of test execution.

The technology of web applications has advanced significantly from static HTML to highly dynamic web content, that not only is created dynamically by the back-end upon user interaction, but is also represented in a dynamic fashion (e.g. by AJAX technology). These aspects pose increasing challenges to test automation for web applications. Furthermore, there is currently less or no support for domain experts to test if the system behaves as expected.

In this paper an approach to automatically generate and execute test cases for web applications is proposed. The primary objective of our method is to enable the domain expert to plan and execute test cases without software engineering knowledge. We further aim at reducing testing costs and increasing test adequacy at the same time. Our current research is conducted within the scope of a research project called "ProBaTe-Web" (an acronym for Process Based Testing of Web Applications). The project aims at providing tool supported test automation for web-based information systems. The contribution of the research project mainly consists of automatically generating test cases from design time system models and the automatic execution of the test cases. The test case generation process is based on the method proposed by Heinecke et al. in [6] while the execution of test cases is based on the capture/replay tool *web2test* [7,8] by itCampus Software-und Systemhaus GmbH (a Software AG Company). In the test case generation process high-level system test cases are created from modelled business processes. The generated test cases serve as input to the framework for automatic test case execution. To generate executable test cases from the business process model, a number of model transformations is required to adapt the initial model to the requirements of the next process step.

3.1 Graphical User Interface Modelling

As web applications become more complex, the creation of the user interface (UI) becomes a labour-intensive task as the dialog flow needs to be aligned with the business process. Especially the maintenance of the UI as the web application is adapted to new or changed business processes or in the context of a software revision is time-consuming and error prone.

In [9,10,11] Book et al. propose a method to declaratively model the UI of a web application. As the complexity of data intensive business processes is typically reflected in user interfaces, the structure of both the business process and the user interface are usually closely aligned. Using their ruler-based approach the UI is designed with a graphical tool using predefined elements such as textfields, labels and buttons which are aligned on a flexible grid with a close focus on the business process workflow. If the application is adapted to new requirements, it can easily be extended by adding new user interface elements bound to newly introduced variables representing business data. While preserving the original data records a new version of the web application can be generated and deployed on a web server.

We use this web UI modelling method as it enables not only an easy way to design and generate a graphical user interface for web-based information systems but also a declarative model of the GUI, which is one of the cornerstones to enable our automatic test case generation and execution approach based on business processes.

3.2   Test Case Generation

We assume the business processes to be modelled in a suitable modelling language like Event-Driven Process Chains (EPC), Business Process Modelling Notation (BPMN), or UML Activity Diagrams (ACD). Our current research prototype implementation handles UML Activity Diagrams only. The test case generation from UML Activity Diagrams is accomplished using our method from [6] which consist of a number of model transformations. Each transformation removes information from the model which is considered irrelevant.

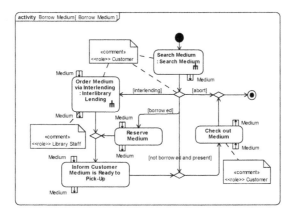

Fig. 1. UML ACD representing the process of borrowing an item from a library

To explain the test case generation process, a library system is introduced as example business process. Figure 1 shows an UML ACD representing the business process of borrowing a medium from a library. It has two user roles associated with five actions, two of which are composite actions depicted in separate figures. Actions that are associated with a particular user role (e.g. "Customer") are executed by according actors. Our approach respects the role model of the business process and maps it to the test cases. The mapping of the role model is important as it puts every action of the generated test cases in the fitting context of execution. Our approach [6] differentiates between actions that are executed by a user (like "Enter Search Phrase" from activity "Search Medium") and actions that are executed by the system (like "Show Error Message" from activity "Search Medium"). Actions performed by the system without involving the user are filtered during the model transformation.

In a first step the input model is transformed into an Interaction Flow Diagram (IFD) using model transformation. The IFD model consists of a reduced set of elements that are used to outline the business process workflow (for a

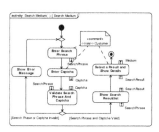

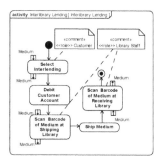

Fig. 2. UML ACD representing the process of searching a medium in a library

Fig. 3. UML ACD representing the process of borrowing an item via interlending from a library

detailed description of the Interaction Flow Diagram see [6]). The result of the transformation applied to the example introduced in figure 1 is shown in figure 4. The IFD represents the same workflow of the business process as the ACD in figure 1 with all actions executed automatically by the system omitted. The actions "Enter Search Phrase" (C1), "Enter Captcha" (C2), "Select a Result and Show Details" (M1), "Select Interlending" (M2) and "Check out Medium" (M5) have been integrated with the user role "Customer" and the corresponding input/output objects in IFD syntax.

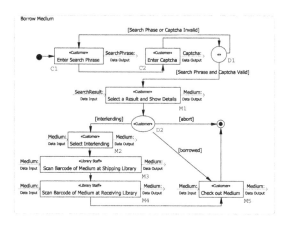

Fig. 4. IFD representing the process of borrowing an item from a library

The second step is to transform the IFD into an Interaction Flow Graph (IFG). The content of the IFG depends on the applied coverage criterion. The IFG is a directed acyclic graph. As cycles in the workflow yield the risk of creating a state explosion problem, the transformation algorithm ensures that each cycle is traversed only once. The obtained IFG shown in figure 5 represents the base for test case selection according to criteria defined by the test engineer.

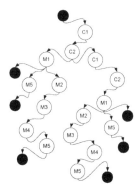

Fig. 5. IFG representing all paths through the process of borrowing an item from a library

In the last step the IFG is compiled into a set of test cases that can either be represented in a human-readable fashion for direct use by a test engineer or domain expert or to be used as input for automated testing using a test script execution engine as proposed in this paper.

3.3   Compiling the Test Suite

The test suite represents the set of test cases that are selected to be executed and evaluated. Simple models, which comprise only a few nodes with some alternate paths, already provide a multitude of execution possibilities. Especially, if they contain nested loops. A test case generation algorithm that derives test cases from complex business processes typically results in a huge set of test cases. Even if executed automatically, the execution of each test case consumes time. Since time is a critical resource within the development process, the size of the test suite has to be limited without a significant reduction of the test adequacy, which is challenging. To compile the test suite and limit the set of test cases to be executed we employ several test coverage criteria:

All Paths Coverage / Transition Coverage Requires to cover all possible execution paths of the IFD. That implies that each possibility to execute a workflow from start to end point is mapped to the IFG. The all paths coverage criterion is analogue to the transition coverage criterion,

State Coverage Requires that each state of a data object that is involved in a workflow is reached. This implies that each node that alters the state of a data object is visited and mapped into the IFG.

Decision Coverage Requires to generate as much test cases as needed so that each decision is evaluated to true in one test case and false in another test case.

Condition Coverage Requires that each boolean sub-expression of a decision evaluates to both true and false. If there is at least one condition that comprises several sub-conditions, this coverage criterion generates more test cases than decision coverage. Otherwise both coverage criteria are congruent.

Generally, test data needs to be supplied for the automated test execution. In case that there already is a test database, possibly derived from a live system, that complies to the data model of the system under test, it is used by the test framework to supply data to the test case execution. If there is no initial test database available, the generated data model is used to automatically generate valid test data into the test database. The process of automated test data generation is quite challenging as the test data needs to meet a number of requirements such as correctness of data types, correctness of value range and finally it needs to be meaningful and close to reality in the context of the domain. The generation of test data is a quite complex area of research and is beyond the scope of this paper. However, once the test data has been generated it is supplied to the test environment in the same way as data from an existing test database.

To integrate the test data with the test cases, eventually forming the test suite, three problems have to be solved: first, data objects that are part of the nodes within the IFG have to be linked to a corresponding data record. Second, since the data objects within the IFG take several states, the data records must be provided with the state information. Third, the data records need to be mapped to the input elements of the web page. The links between data objects of the IFD and their respective data records are established via the data model that defines the persistence of each data object. The data records are tagged with the state information as depicted in Table 1. The mapping of data records to their corresponding input elements of the web page is accomplished via the data model that preserves the unique identifier of each input element of the web page.

Table 1. Simple Test Data Record Example

State	SearchPhraseStr	Captcha
created	Gustav Mahler	
valid	Gustav Mahler	n34fh7
invalid	Gustav Mahler	h56d

Table 1 shows a example of a test data record. This data record is used in our example by the nodes "C1" and "C2" (cf. IFD and IFG). The IFG depicted in Fig. 5 shows that there are six test scenarios for the workflow of borrowing a medium from a library. Each test scenario starts either with the sequence (C1, C2, M1, . . .) or (C1, C2, C1, C2, M1, . . .), depending on the first decision node depicted in Fig. 4. The decision either requires the return to the interaction step that requires to the enter the search phrase in case of a invalid captcha / search phrase combination, or leads to the next node. Hence, our test database must reflect this by providing both a valid and an invalid combination of search phrase and captcha.

3.4 Test Case Execution

The test case execution framework is based on the capture/replay testing tool *web2test* that has been designed with special attention to the testing of web applications at a functional level. In order to state input data to the application or interact with UI widgets, the tool identifies the component within the website and feeds the input data (or events) into the component. To identify components, the generation tool stores information about a component for look-up in the web sites DOM tree. We chose *web2test* as foundation for our test execution framework because it features a flexible design, an XML-based test script language and modularised test cases. The tool already provides the technical basis to trigger actions, check the availability of elements within the web site, and a sophisticated flow control.

The input to the test execution framework are the generated test cases and the test database. Prior to test case execution the test cases are transformed into web2test's XML-based test script format. Since our test case generation respects the sequence of workflows within the business process, the generated test cases are ordered compliant to the IFG model. The test cases are executed sequentially. One test case is based on all previous test cases as they set up the preconditions. If a test case fails, subsequent test case cannot pass. If a subsequent test case does not fail, it can be regarded as an indicator for an errorneous software implementation. Hence the test case execution is continued through the complete test script despite failing test cases.

Using the example depicted in 4 the first action of the test execution framework is to access the web page that implements the search for a medium to borrow. The next step is the execution of the node that requires to enter a search phrase. The test case contains the information to create a "SearchPhrase" data object that has to be in state "created" and enter the string to the corresponding input field. The data object is described by the data model that preserves the link to the test database that contains the corresponding test data record. The test execution framework utilises the link to the test database to retrieve the data record and provides the corresponding input element with this data. The identification of the input element within the web page is accomplished via the data model that preserves the identification characteristics of that element. Once all data is supplied, the web page is submitted.

At each step in the execution process that is not a control flow the results are recorded immediately for evaluation after the testing process is done. This is motivated by the fact that the evaluation is time-consuming and web applications may define a short timeout period. The evaluation computes the test verdict. Therefore, we employ the well-established test verdicts: "pass", "fail", which are the possible results of each test case execution. The verdict "warning" is issued when a component could not be found with the web site.

4   Discussion

With the variety of web browsers for each operating system, testing web applications is difficult as the application may behave different when executed on different systems. Different versions of browsers impose a major challenge on automated testing, as they may behave different. Hence, an automated test environment needs to be provided with different versions of each browser running on different systems. Capture/replay testing methods are currently regarded state of the art when testing GUIs. This test method is based on recording test scripts by capturing a user's workflow through the application. As of todays web applications using HTML/AJAX technologies providing dynamic UI layout, capture/replay testing tools have proven to be inconvenient. Also, a software revision which affects the GUI of the system under test (SUT) requires a new capturing of the interaction flow. Our approach derives this information from the GUI model and the business process model. Since it features consistent automation, the adaption changes must only be applied to the model. Thus, our approach yields a significant time advantage compared to traditional GUI-based testing methods. In addition, it goes far beyond GUI testing as it verifies the support of the business process by the SUT.

In this paper we proposed an approach to business process based testing of web applications on a high level of abstraction by utilising the web application's UI which is designed declaratively by using a graphical modelling tool. Subsequently, the application is generated using the declarative UI description ready for deploy to a web server. Using our method from [6], test cases are derived for testing the web application implementing the business process. This method derives test cases automatically from business processes using a selected coverage criterion and uses a test execution engine to run the test cases. The method enables the creation and execution of the test cases by domain experts and therefore a better integration into the software engineering process.

The main contribution of this work is an approach with a strong focus on automation that is capable to derive executable test cases from business processes models. This tool supported approach moves the test case creation from a technical to a functional level of business processes and thus enables the domain expert to participate in the test case development significantly. The proposed approach reflects the status quo of our research project "ProBaTe-Web". The project and therefore the approach is still work in progress. An number of issues have been identified as fields for further investigation in our future research.

Currently, our research prototype is only capable to apply the all-paths coverage criterion. The integration of other coverage criteria is a topic for further research. Here, especially boundary-value tests are considered important in which critical values (e.g. supplying input values exactly at or very close to threshold values) for input fields are tested. Another important prospect for future work is the automatic generation of test data to be supplied to the testing process. Due to legal restrictions the use of live data from a business system might be prohibited. Here the manual creation of a small dataset and its automated transformation to a large set of test data is an option. Furthermore, the use of invalid data might be required as some paths can only be covered when invalid input is supplied. Hence, the creation of invalid test data is required to ensure a full path coverage when executing test cases.

Acknowledgements

The Applied Telematics/e-Business Group is endowed by Deutsche Telekom AG. ProBaTe-Web is a joint research and development project of the University of Leipzig and itCampus Software- und Systemhaus GmbH (a Software AG Company) in Leipzig, supported by a technology support grant from the European Regional Development Fund (ERDF) 2007–2013 and funds of the Free State of Saxony.

References

1. Reza, H., Ogaard, K., Malge, A.: A model based testing technique to test web applications using statecharts. In: ITNG 2008: Proceedings of the Fifth International Conference on Information Technology: New Generations, pp. 183–188. IEEE Computer Society, Washington, DC (2008)
2. Raffelt, H., Margaria, T., Steffen, B., Merten, M.: Hybrid test of web applications with webtest. In: TAV-WEB 2008: Proceedings of the 2008 Workshop on Testing, Analysis, and Verification of Web Services and Applications, pp. 1–7. ACM, New York (2008)
3. Ricca, F., Tonella, P.: Analysis and testing of web applications. In: International Conference on Software Engineering, vol. 23, pp. 25–36 (2001)
4. Beizer, B.: Software testing techniques, 2nd edn. Van Nostrand Reinhold Co., New York (1990)
5. Andrews, A., Offutt, J., Alexander, R.: Testing web applications. Software and Systems Modeling (January 2004)
6. Heinecke, A., Brueckmann, T., Griebe, T., Gruhn, V.: Generating test plans for acceptance tests from uml activity diagrams. In: Proceedings of the 17th International Conference on Engineering Computer-Based Systems. IEEE, Los Alamitos (2010)
7. itCampus: web2test - web application test tool
8. Franke, B.: Die hohe Kunst der GUI-bezogenen Testautomatisierung. Javaspektrum (2) (2009)
9. Book, M., Brückmann, T., Gruhn, V., Hülder, M.: A conceptual framework for user input evaluation in rich internet applications. In: Gaedke, M., Grossniklaus, M., Díaz, O. (eds.) ICWE 2009. LNCS, vol. 5648, pp. 275–282. Springer, Heidelberg (2009)
10. Batsukh, N., Book, M., Brückmann, T., Geier, J., Gruhn, V., Klebeck, A., Schäfer, C.: Automatic generation of ruler-based user interfaces of web applications. In: Proceedings of the 2008 Third International Conference on Internet and Web Applications and Services, pp. 103–108 (2008)
11. Book, M., Brückmann, T., Gruhn, V., Hülder, M.: Specification and control of interface responses to user input in rich internet applications. In: 24th IEEE/ACM International Conference on Automated Software Engineering, ASE 2009 (January 2009)

Taming Unbounded Variability in Service Engineering

Pauline Anthonysamy[1], Awais Rashid[1], and Andreas Rummler[2]

[1] Computing Department, InfoLab 21, Lancaster University,
Lancaster LA1 4WA, UK
{anthonys,awais}@comp.lancs.ac.uk
[2] SAP Research
andreas.rummler@sap.com

Abstract. Service Engineering has appeared as a paradigm where businesses can easily collaborate and take advantage of services provided by other organizations or third-party entities for efficient delivery of software-solutions. Although the open-ended landscape of service engineering provides high degrees of flexibility, it also leads to extreme diversity in terms of service development environments, service configuration mechanisms, etc. The number of service variants that arise from such diversity can increase tremendously and potentially can be unbounded. In this paper, we highlight the challenges arising from unbounded variability and present a vision of how it may be tamed without compromising the flexibility afforded by the open-ended nature of service engineering.

Keywords: Unbounded Variability, Service Engineering, Software Product Lines.

1 Introduction

We are at the cusp of a paradigm shift in the way enterprises perform their businesses. Businesses are moving from rigid silo-ed application development approaches to more flexible business-focused solutions. Collaboration is vital as these organizations continuously strive for shorter time to market and try to lower their costs. *Service Engineering* has appeared as a paradigm where software functionalities can be provisioned and flexibly composed to implement business processes [1]. The open-ended paradigm provided by the notion of a services ecosystem enables organizations to take advantage of services provided by other organizations or third-party entities for efficient delivery of software-solutions. Although this open-endedness provides a wide range of flexibility, challenges such as extreme diversity in service development environments (i.e. target device, operating systems, etc.), service variations (in terms of configuration and infrastructure) and stringent non-functional requirements can all hamper the development and deployment of software services. Managing these high divergences is a core issue especially in this large open landscape.

M. zur Muehlen and J. Su (Eds.): BPM 2010 Workshops, LNBIP 66, pp. 615–619, 2011.

This heterogeneity leads to the need to support service variations that are multi-faceted and may occur in different layers of the services stack i.e. business process, service, component and operational layers. Cross-organizational collaboration provides a further dimension of diversity and, hence, complexity in this context, leading to service providers having to support variations that are potentially *unbounded* in number. We define unbounded variability as follows: *"Unbounded variability within a service is the potentially limitless number of variations or alternatives in its realization and use."* Naturally, not all services are faced with unbounded variability, however if cross-organizational collaborations become sufficiently complex then the number of potential variations of a service needed can become infinitely large.

In this paper, we highlight the problem of unbounded variability arising from both management of services within a single organization and across organizational boundaries. Section 2 highlights these problems. Section 3 provides insights into a taxonomy of service variability we are developing to analyze the complexity arising from unbounded variability in a service ecosystem. Finally, Section 4 outlines our future vision.

2   Complexity Arising from Unbounded Variability

Service-orientation offers an open-ended development model that builds on composability, reuse and integration. Fig. 1 illustrates a typical example of the service solution stack adopted by enterprise organizations. At the top level, business processes define the orchestration and choreography of services exposed in the service layer. The service layer consists of all the services, which includes atomic services and composite services that are aligned with specific business functionalities. The component layer, includes software components and an operational layer that includes packaged application assets and data models. Each layer contributes to the implementation for realization of a service. The variabilities in the service ecosystem arise in two dimensions:

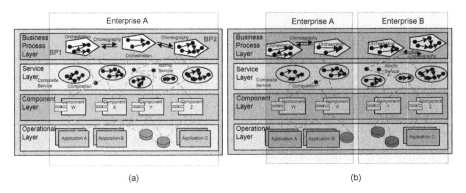

(a)   (b)

Fig. 1. Variabilities that occur (a) within an enterprise organization providing services (b) when enterprises collaborate

Variations within an enterprise (or service provider): Considering the variations in the business process layer as an example (cf. Fig. 1(a)), enterprise solution providers usually cater for certain business scenarios for different organizations. Variations in these business scenarios arise due to diverse business processes and practices among these organizations. For instance, an enterprise organization provides an order-to-cash application, which essentially includes activities such as ordering, invoicing, delivery and payment. However, variations would occur when these business processes are implemented in organizations that are fundamentally different. For example, an order-to-cash process for a warehouse supplying chemicals (BP1) is different from the one implemented in a machinery industry (BP2). While the machinery industry buys discrete materials (e.g. lights, batteries) from suppliers, chemical industry uses materials (e.g. water, oxygen) that are delivered and processed in amounts measured in units like kilograms or liters. Besides the fact that calculations done in the business application must be executed in different units, the software components supporting the whole process must deal with the different handling of these materials. For this reason, simple variations of the order-to-cash process are not possible. Instead, they need to be extended or redeveloped and replaced. These kinds of variations can occur within different layers of the solution stack as illustrated in Fig. 1(a).

Variations among enterprises: A range of variations can exist among organizations. For example, different organizations often use different service standards (e.g. service level agreements, quality attributes, etc.), service composition technologies (e.g. BPEL, WSCI), development platforms and data models (e.g. J2EE Platform, OSGi, ORACLE), communication protocols (e.g. SOAP, HTTP GET), middleware platforms and policy frameworks. There are also varying levels of service paradigm maturity across these organizations i.e. from full service paradigm deployment to non-service-oriented systems as well as hybrid systems that incorporate service and non-service elements. These various dimensions of variability are non-orthogonal and interact in a complex way across organizations. Referring to Fig. 1(b), when enterprises A and B collaborate, variabilities between them are essentially multiplied i.e. variability within enterprises A and B in addition to compounded variability of both organizations. The complexity is magnified when there are more organizations and if they have overlapping functionalities, as the number of service variants can potentially increase exponentially. Additionally, this situation is further amplified by the fact that the collaborating organizations demand effective integration between the different layers, which in turn, requires better integration of these variations across layers or the kinds of devices within a layer.

Given the number of variations in these two dimensions, the variability in a service ecosystem can potentially be unbounded and therefore, leads to arising complexity.

3   Managing Unbounded Variability

The potentially unbounded variability in the service landscape needs to be tamed and controlled without compromising its flexibility. This is essential as it would enable systematic reuse of services, control service evolution and provide a systematic means to deal with the dynamicity of service engineering. A service variability taxonomy that covers the different dimensions (as in Section 2) will serve as a guideline which will aid enterprises to have a clear understanding of the variabilities that may potentially occur. Fig. 2 illustrates some parts of the taxonomy that we are currently constructing. The taxonomy is according to the service engineering analysis and design process in [1] . It starts at an abstract level (i.e. analysis and design), but it is refined within each category. For ease of discussion, we focus only on the business process and workflow parts of the taxonomy. These levels are further refined in our detailed taxonomy.

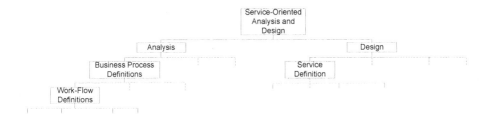

Fig. 2. Snippet of the service taxonomy

The taxonomy can offer a means to analyze variability in a services context and offer a steppingstone towards taming the potential unbounded nature of these variations. Consider an example of a solution provider who delivers Production Control and Monitoring services for chemical and machinery industries. Although, Production Control and Monitoring is catered for these industries, it requires non-trivial variation of software services underpinning such processes. For instance, an interruption of the production process in the machinery industry (e.g. automotive industries), although not being desirable, is manageable (i.e. the production process simply stops in such a case). However, this is often not possible for a chemical plant. Running out of appropriate supplies for production may lead to serious damages in the production facilities. Consequently, enterprise services for process control need to be capable of handling waiting lines in the latter case, while such mechanisms are simply not needed in the former.

Here the fundamental variation arises in the business processes and workflows (i.e. in terms of workflow input, tasks, turn-around time, legal requirements etc.) for handling these situations. Variations may also occur at the service level (i.e. during design) in terms of service definitions e.g. exposed interfaces, integration with legacy applications, etc. The complexity is further increased by operational level variabilities where these industries may require that the applications be developed in different platforms. All the pertinent variabilities presented here are covered by our detailed taxonomy, which in turn eases the mapping between requirements and variabilities. Enterprises will have a solid infrastructure i.e. knowledge on the types of variations and where they can potentially occur, that can be utilized in the management of these variabilities. Additionally, the taxonomy would facilitate enterprises in identification of the set of services that can be used in multiple contexts and help us understand and future-proof the complex nature of the service ecosystem.

4 Vision

We envision *Service Product Lines* as a means to address the range of technical and business needs of enterprise organizations concerning two key challenges of managing variabilities in services, and service variation across organizational boundaries. *Software product line engineering techniques (SPLE)* [2] have been shown to be highly effective in managing large sets of variants in conventional software products and rapidly responding to market needs. SPLE techniques enable the systematic identification, representation and composition of variations that occur within software products across a product family. However, the tools and techniques are designed for a *bounded* set of variabilities in a specific product domain [2,3] and not for the open-ended development model advocated by service engineering. While there are potential to adapt some SPLE techniques to service engineering [4], a number of fundamental research questions must be answered:

- Can SPLE techniques be evolved and expanded to support the potential emergence of unbounded variability in a services context?
- How will the fundamental concepts of domain analysis and application engineering from SPLE change when mapped onto the open-ended nature of services?
- Given the dynamic nature of services and service compositions, how runtime variability can be anticipated early on and managed in a service engineering setting?

Acknowledgments. This research is being funded by a Lancaster University 40th Anniversary Research Studentship.

References

1. Erl, T.: Service-Oriented Architecture: Concepts, Technology & Design. Prentice Hall PTR, Upper Saddle River (2005)
2. AMPLE Project: Survey of the state-of-the-art in Requirements Engineering for SPL and Model-Driven Requirements Engineering. Del. 1.1 IST - 33710 (2007)
3. Kang, K., Cohen, S., et al.: Feature-Oriented Domain Analysis (FODA) Feasibility Study. SEI, Technical Report, CMU/SEI-90-TR-021 (1990)
4. Schnieders, A., Puhlmann, F.: Variability Mechanisms in E-business Process Families. In: Proceedings of 9th International Conference on BIS, Austria (2006)

1st International Workshop on Traceability and Compliance of Semi-structured Processes (TC4SP 2010)

Workshop Organization

Workshop Organizers

Juliana Freire
University of Utah
Salt Lake City, UT
USA

Francisco Curbera
IBM TJ Watson Research Center
PO Box 704,
Yorktown Heights, NY 10598
USA

Frank Leymann
IAAS
University of Stuttgart
Universitätsstraße 38
70569 Stuttgart
Germany

Beth Plale
Indiana University
Bloomington, IN
USA

AmitSheth
Wright State University
Dayton, OH
USA

Program Committee

Fabio Casati, University of Trento, Italy
Marcelo Cataldo,Carnegy Mellon University, USA
SchahramDustdar, TU Wien, Austria
DimkaKarastoyanova, University of Stuttgart, Germany
Jude Fernandez,SETLabs, Infosys, India
Geetika T. Lakshmanan, IBM Research, USA
Axel Martens, IBM Research, USA
Paolo Missier, University of Manchester, UK
Luc Moreau, University of Southampton, UK
Hamid Motahari, HP Labs, USA
Sudha Ram, University of Arizona, USA
Florian Rosenberg, CSIRO, Australia
SatyaSahoo, Wright University, USA
HeikoSchuldt, University of Basel, Switzerland
Mathias Weske, University of Potsdam, Germany

Enabling Cross-Application Traceability of Semi-structured Business Processes

Andreas Emrich, Frieder Ganz, Dirk Werth, and Peter Loos

German Research Center for Artificial Intelligence (DFKI)
Stuhlsatzenhausweg 3, Campus D3.2
66123 Saarbrücken
{andreas.emrich,frieder.ganz,dirk.werth,peter.loos}@dfki.de

Abstract. A big number of concepts have been developed in the past to address the traceability of business data throughout business processes. Business process monitoring and controlling, business activity monitoring, provenance analysis, etc., describe techniques how to capture event-driven data in business processes. Nevertheless, current workflow systems only achieve a technical integration with some applications and services in the enterprise context, but not all of them. Moreover, a common semantic concept in terms of a context model is crucial to assess event-driven changes in a model-specific manner. The presented work develops an extensible semantic context model for business process management and proposes an architecture for integrating event-driven changes from various data sources and augmenting these events, in order to derive appropriate courses of action.

Keywords: traceability, business process management, cross-application.

1 Introduction

Nowadays business environment is dynamic and ever-changing. Trends such as globalization, mergers and acquisition, outsourcing, industry collaborations and cooperation all foster a paradigm shift away from a view on IT architectures that is focused on a single enterprise towards service-oriented architectures.

For traditional scenarios of business process management, a number of solutions have been developed to monitor data in business processes and to control the system by administrating these data. Although service-oriented architectures are capable of integrating with various external services and applications in a simple manner (e.g. via web services), common concepts for tracing and managing such data artifacts across enterprise borders and applications are missing. Traditionally, only structured business processes are considered by workflow engines. Whenever semi-structured or ad-hoc processes are concerned, it is hard to trace the data within the workflow engine. Approaches that address this problem, such as BPEL4People [1] are already integrated with many BPM suites. Nevertheless, many proprietary applications, such as personal information management systems, groupware, etc., offer no or only limited support for tracing data in processes, that are handled by such systems.

M. zur Muehlen and J. Su (Eds.): BPM 2010 Workshops, LNBIP 66, pp. 625–633, 2011.
© Springer-Verlag Berlin Heidelberg 2011

In order to leverage insights gained from traceability, changes should be assessed according to their impact on business processes and related data. Not only business processes themselves, but also associated resources, organizational units, data, etc., can be affected by such changes. According to that, any change on workflow artifacts such as activities, but also changes on organizational units (e.g. staff decisions) or resources (e.g. machine upgrades) should be traced. This enables real-time analysis of the impact of such changes. In order to achieve that, a context model for BPM is needed, that is capable of describing these relationships.

This paper will propose a new architecture for integrating BPM solutions with external applications and services and will provide a first draft of a semantic context model for BPM that takes into account organizational, data and resource aspects. Furthermore, we present preliminary results from current research, that demonstrate, how external applications can be integrated with workflow engines, and how events can be evaluated using the previously defined semantic context model. The paper concludes with a summary and an outlook on future research in this area.

2 Related Work

In current research one can find many works which are located in the field of traceability of processes. The ambiguous field is prevalently coined in many terms. The concept of business process intelligence has been accomplished in latest research work. It is defined as execution, and tracking of business processes, which is realized by business process management systems (BPMS)[3].

Modern BPM approaches can be seen as an extension to classical workflow management systems (WFM) [2] where WFMs are rather used to track the usage of process instances and their logged audit trail [4], BPI tries to find correlations in many process instances and automatically predict business metrics. Process and data mining are common techniques to discover such relationships.

A problem which arises is that the source of the data, strictly speaking, the data representation of the processes and instances just contains the information defined by process and workflow managers. Several papers show that in practical use cases processes are defined in a non-formalized way. They are neither explicitly defined by an manager nor by the user himself. Thus, attempts to formalize such processes often fail, as they do not fully consider process variations and process complexity. Therefore, semi-structured and ad-hoc process definitions offer a larger degree of freedom for such use cases [5]. As model-based approaches have less information for these process types, a context-aware architecture has to be developed that takes into account the business process and its context.

The term of data provenance appears in several research work as an approach to analyse where and when data are used and produced throughout a business process. Then the data which is already defined in the workflow system but in the end is not used through unforseen events which are not covered by any platform. Artifacts as an product of a users work in an ad-hoc process have to be considered. They can be created through usual determined workflows but also during not well defined steps in the process. A general context model which includes all possible artifacts in an business environment has to be exploited [6].

Semantic models enable the tracking of data related to a process through the fact that an activity can have several relationships. This can be used to infer in the model even artifacts which are only slightly affected by process change events. To find possible changes in inferred artifacts information entered by the user has to be considered to find possible sources of changes.

The semantic event-driven process chain [7] extends the classical event-driven process chain (EPC) [8] by semantic relations. This enables an cross-process based view on business scenarios. The SUPER IP Project [9] formalised the semantic EPC in the WSML (Web Service Modeling Language) format and introduced a more sophisticated definition of artifacts. As the classic EPC, it features not only process flow related elements, but also exposes the interrelations with other artifacts, such as organizational units, resources, documents, IT systems, etc.

There exist platforms,which try to track each step made by the user . This includes that every application (personal information management systems, browsers, data repositiories, enterprise resource planning systems, etc.) is monitored by the platform. In the approach from Plale, B. et. al [10] service wrappers are utilized to keep track of each used application. The wrapper catches events and extracts the information by the user and forwards the found context information to a workflow system which has to decide if the data is relevant to a process executed by the user.

As the following table indicates, none of these approaches allows for an integrated management of the processes, a full traceability of all process-related artifacts and a consideration of impact analysis and event-driven, context aware recommendations:

Table 1. Comparison of related approaches

System / Trace Information	BPM	WFM	BPI	Data Provenance	sEPC / SUPER IP
Process Data	•	•			•
Workflow Management	•	•			
Cross-Process View			•	•	•
Related Artifacts			•		•
De-centralised Information Gathering				•	
Context-Aware Recommendation			•		
Impact Analysis			•		•

3 Towards a Semantic Context Model for BPM

Leveraging semantic modeling languages to represent business processes has been a topic of research for years. A common problem in semantic research is that there exists a large number of different ontologies. With the hereby described approach we do not want to introduce another taxonomy but try to build a wrapper ontology where other ones could be easily attached. As an initial point we will use the semantic event-driven process chain, and extend it with workflow elements from the SUPER IP project and describe how process relevant data from several sources could be detected and exploited.

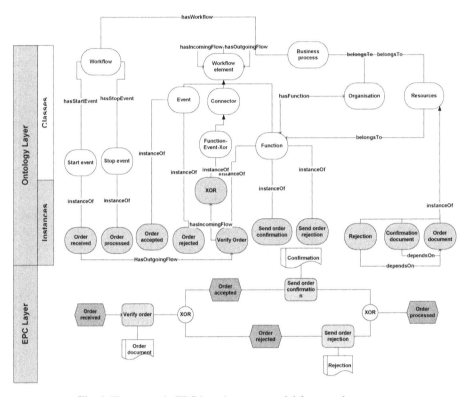

Fig. 1. The semantic EPC-based context model for an order process

The model represents EPCs on the instance layer. Furthermore, EPCs and associated functions can be connected to other business processes and workflow elements on instance and class layer. This enables a linked view on all related processes and artifacts. In the case of an incoming event the interlinked artifacts could be easily found through reasoning in the context model. To get more conceptual information the model should be extended by other business relevant ontologies.

E.g., rejections have to be re-formulated, as the old versions caused several law suits against the company. The semantic context model can be used to determine the affected processes (e.g. the above shown order process). Thus, all processes can be determined and employees can be proactively informed to use the new templates for the rejection letters. Another example could be organization units that are attached to certain functions. If the person that is a process owner has changed, the impact of that change can be automatically evaluated in real-time, when statistics are collected according to the semantic context model.

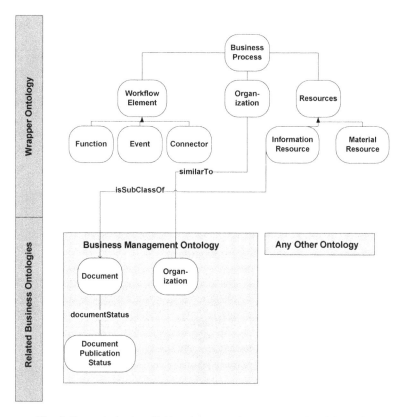

Fig. 2. Example for interlinking the semantic context model with BMO

We can easily attach existing ontologies by using the pre-defined hierarchical relations from the Web Ontology Language (OWL)[11] to specify subclass relations to our existing top-level ontology. In this example we attach the Open Source Business Management Ontology (BMO) [12] by declaring that *Document* is a sub class element of Information Resource. Another possibility is to define new properties like the *similarTo* relation which describes the relation between similar classes. In this example we connect *Organization* from the top-level ontology to organization from the BMO. A new *Document* instance can have a *DocumentPublicationStatus* Information. Later while trying to trace back information to that specific instance the relation *documentStatus* is automatically considered. Rule patterns can be automatically applied to that property or any other defined property from different ontologies. Rules like "Show related artifacts with a distance of one" would show a status artifact, if defined.

Adding several ontologies also helps the user to add information to business artifacts. While the user is creating a new artifact, the system could recommend related artifacts such as *DocumentPublicationStatus* or *DocumentAuthor* from the ontology to gain more information about the artifact context.

4   Architecture Proposal for Cross-Application Traceability in BPM

As stated before, enterprise IT landscapes have a vast number of applications and data sources that need to be integrated. Especially well-structured processes are well-supported by contemporary BPM suites. However, although approaches for human-centric workflows exist [1], they do not provide means to semantically link data semantically that are mapped between IT systems.

The following figure shows a sketch of an architecture proposal, that incorporates the semantic context model as designed in the previous section, and associates it with different applications in the enterprise's IT landscape.

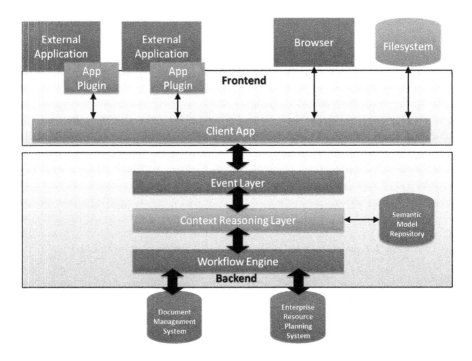

Fig. 3. Architecture proposal for traceability in business processes

Basically, any kind of transaction is being forwarded to the event layer in the backend, which has access to the semantic context model. For that purpose, events can be either thrown from the backend (workflow engine) and applications or other interactions in the frontend. Each of the frontend interactions is wrapped by a client application that forwards this event information to the backend.

The backend provides the client application with necessary information about extraction mechanisms and monitoring rules for the respective application or filesystem. The client application itself or respective application plug-ins for certain applications monitor the changes on artifacts in a business process and forward the information to the event layer. A specific context API defines which information can be submitted about an occurring artifact change. This information includes:

- *Change ID*: The unique ID of the given change action
- *Artifact ID*: The ID of the artifact, that is being changed[1]
- *Artifact type ID*: The ID of the artifact type, that is being changed[2]
- *Artifact revision*: The current revision of the artifact after the change
- *Origin*: The application / user that is triggering the given change
- *Modification date*: Timestamp, that indicates the time of change

The backend interprets these event information in the context reasoning layer, facilitating the information of the semantic context model. Relations of the observed artifact are analyzed to find related information through the properties connecting them. Defined rules trigger new events, which could lead to notification of users, start/stop processes in the workflow engine or deploy new process derived from the new circumstance to the workflow engine. All following changes caused by the event or related artifacts, are saved in a database and can therefore be traced back to their initial version. This also enables tracebility in the model layer, as classes and properties are artifacts as well. The information, which changes happened at a certain point of time can be displayed. Moreover, it can be shown, which artifact has been involved in the change including its version at the time of change. Changes might be conflicting or need approval, moreover dependencies can be discovered, in order to determine subsequent changes or other actions (e.g. if a payment process changes). Depending on the discovered implications, several types of content can be sent to the frontend. Additional information to help users advance with this process step can be presented, such as information about automatically propagated changes (e.g. that have been executed within the workflow engine) or possible, uncertain pending changes that need user approval (i.e. such cases that cannot be determined on a model level). [13] gives a more thorough explanation, what kind of assistance can be provided by the semantic context model infrastructure.

Backend applications such as enterprise resource planning systems, document management systems, etc., can either be orchestrated by means of the workflow engine (for structured processes) or by respective client applications in the frontend (for semi-structured and ad-hoc processes) as described above. In this aspect, the presented approach differs from wrapper and plugin approaches, as it does not only encapsulate functionalities of underlying systems, but also enables context-driven propagation of work-relevant events. By that means, the traceability features also deliver some kind of decision support by providing the application user with information, that are not transparent from a single application's perspective. E.g., if an event occurs, that demands human intervention; this step is recognized in the semantic context layer. Then the context layer identifies the respective user, and forwards the relevant information to his email application.

As the approach covers a single backend application and several client applications, it supports a distributed environment in a single organization. In general, the approach can be applied to collaborative scenarios for several organizations. In that case, either a common semantic context model should exist, or ontology matching mechanisms [14]

---

[1] Please note, that an artifact can also be an artifact type. E.g. a change in a specific order process could occur, or even a change to the process model itself.
[2] This parameter is optional and only needed, when the type of an artifact changes.

can be used to determine incoming, semantically annotated events and identify their representations in the organization's own semantic context model.

5   Conclusion and Outlook

This paper has presented an approach for a semantic context model of BPM, that is extensible and that can be reasoned throughout runtime. Moreover, an architecture draft has been developed, that allows traceability support for both structured and semi-structured business processes. The semantic context model is following a multi-dimensional approach for describing business processes and their context using event-driven process chains. Although ad-hoc processes do not expose a modeled structure for the process flow itself, they include model relationships for work artifacts, such as documents, data, events, etc. that are linked to a specific ad-hoc process. By that means, the traceability approach shown in this paper even goes beyond pure process flow related issues and can also take into account structural dependencies in the data models or resource models.

For future work, the limitations of EPCs such as error handling, concurrency, etc. should be considered to refine the existing design for the context model. Moreover, mechanisms should be developed, that enable the (semi-)automatic creation of a semantic context model from legacy data sources and applications. Although the concepts have been prototypically been implemented, they need to be evaluated and validated in real-life business scenarios.

Overall, model-based traceability for all artifacts in the semantic context of business processes can enable better transparency for data in business processes across applications, help to identify helpful, related materials in real-time and can determine the impacts of changes when they occur.

References

[1] WS-BPEL Extension for People (BPEL4People), Version 1.0. Active Endpoints Inc., Adobe Systems Inc., BEA Systems Inc., International Business Machines Corporation, Oracle Inc., and SAP AG (2007)

[2] Grigori, D., Casati, F., Castellanos, M., Dayal, U., Sayal, M., Shan, M.: Business process intelligence. Comput. Ind. 53(3), 321–343 (2004), http://dx.doi.org/10.1016/j.compind.2003.10.007

[3] van der Aalst, W.M.P., ter Hofstede, A.H.M., Weske, M.: Business Process Management: A Survey. In: van der Aalst, W.M.P., ter Hofstede, A.H.M., Weske, M. (eds.) BPM 2003. LNCS, vol. 2678, pp. 1–12. Springer, Heidelberg (2003)

[4] zur Muehlen, M., Rosemann, M.: Workflow-Based Process Monitoring and Controlling: Technical and Organizational Issues. In: 33rd Hawaii International Conference on System Sciences, vol. 6, p. 6032 (2000)

[5] Curtis, B., Kellner, M.I., Over, J.: Process Modeling. Communications of the ACM 35(9) (1992)

[6] Bhattacharya, K., Gerede, C.E., Hull, R., Liu, R., Su, J.: Towards Formal Analysis of Artifact-Centric Business Process Models. In: Alonso, G., Dadam, P., Rosemann, M. (eds.) BPM 2007. LNCS, vol. 4714, pp. 288–304. Springer, Heidelberg (2007)

[7] Thomas, O., Fellmann, M.: Semantic event-driven process chains. In: Workshop SBPM at the ESWC (2006)

[8] Keller, G., Nüttgens, M., Scheer, A.-W.: Semantische Prozeßmodellierung auf der Grundlage Ereignisgesteuerter Prozeßketten (EPK). In: Scheer, A.-W. (ed.) Veröffentlichungen des Instituts für Wirtschaftsinformatik, Saarbrücken, vol. 89 (1992)

[9] SUPER IP, http://www.ip-super.org/content/view/129/136/

[10] Plale, B.B., Cao, C., Sun, Y.: Data Provenance for Preservation of Digital Geoscience Data, Societal Challenges and Geoinformatics. Geological Society of America (GSA) Memoir Volume (2010)

[11] OWL Web Ontology Language Overview,
     http://www.w3.org/TR/owl-features/

[12] Jenz, D.E.: Ontologies in Business Process Automation. Jenz & Partner (2003),
     http://www.bpiresearch.com/Resources/RE_SWPr/
     A_OntologiesInBPA.pdf

[13] Emrich, A., Weber, S., Ras, E.: Towards Proactive and Intelligent Assistance in Experience Management. In: Springer (ed.) Workshop on Learning Software Organizations (LSO 2009) at the 10th Conference on Product-focused Software Processes, PROFES 2009 (2009)

[14] Shvaiko, P., Euzenat, J.: Ten Challenges for Ontology Matching. In: Proceedings of the OTM 2008 Confederated International Conferences, CoopIS, DOA, GADA, IS, and ODBASE 2008. Part II on On the Move to Meaningful Internet Systems, Monterrey, Mexico, pp. 1164–1182 (2008)

Rationale in Semi-structured Processes

Udo Kannengiesser and Liming Zhu

NICTA, Australia, and
School of Computer Science and Engineering, University of New South Wales,
Sydney, Australia
{udo.kannengiesser,liming.zhu}@nicta.com.au

Abstract. This paper argues that an explicit account of rationale is essential for the effective management and evolution of semi-structured processes. Our approach is based on a view of semi-structured process models as unfinished products whose design is implicitly completed through their execution by process model users. The resulting refinements and modifications of the process models are instances of user-driven design innovation. Our framework shows how rationale can explain a user's individual execution decisions, as a basis for process modelers to improve the original process specifications. We propose and illustrate the ontological foundations of a modeling approach.

Keywords: Semi-structured processes; rationale; function-behavior-structure.

1 Introduction

In semi-structured processes, not all process information is fixed or known at design time [1]. Traditional approaches to business process management (BPM) are poorly suited for this class of processes, because of their underlying assumption that all tasks, roles and artifacts in a process are fixed and well defined prior to execution. Their applicability is often restricted to specifying high-level process models, and supplying organizational and IT infrastructures that allow for fast response to changing process environments. The expertise required for "filling in the blanks" and adapting the process to the situation at hand resides in the human users of the process models. Explicitly capturing the assumptions that underpin the users' execution choices may be a basis for a more effective management of these processes.

This paper explores this issue by adopting a design stance. An inherent characteristic of designing is that it generates the structure of "things" based on knowledge about their usefulness and applicability in specific environments. Representations of this knowledge as goals and assumptions that explain individual design decisions are referred to as design rationale [2]. Rationale may relate to any kind of design, including the design of process models and process executions. For example, the rationale associated with the decision to use a standard spreadsheet application for data analysis may include the goals of transparency and reproducibility (because, unlike traditional, non-programmable calculators, spreadsheets enforce the capture of all mathematical operations), and cost considerations (as standard applications are usually cheaper to

M. zur Muehlen and J. Su (Eds.): BPM 2010 Workshops, LNBIP 66, pp. 634–639, 2011.

acquire than most specialized applications). This paper presents the role of rationale in managing semi-structured processes and proposes the ontological foundations of a modeling approach.

2 Process Model Use as Process Design

Semi-structured processes can be viewed as unfinished products, whose design is implicitly completed by their users as they execute them. There are a number of examples in other domains where the use of designed objects includes design activities. For example, mass-customized products defer some design or configuration decisions to their users [3]. Most physical materials are designed for being used in the design of other objects. For example, certain fibers may be used in the design of certain textiles, which in turn may be used in the design of certain pieces of clothing, and so on [4]. The same applies to virtual materials such as software libraries, which are designed so that programmers can use them for their own software designs. In case of open-source software, the intended use includes activities of re-designing the software itself. Software is particularly well suited for being used for re-designing, as modifications are generally less costly than for physical objects [5].

Many processes in the domains of business and science can be seen as virtual objects, similar to software. Models of these processes are used for designing actions resulting in a "real" (or executed) process. This idea follows Simon's [6] broad claim that "everyone designs who devises a course of action aimed at changing existing situations into preferred ones". When the course of actions (i.e., the executed process) is represented through a process model (e.g., using process mining), that model may or may not be consistent with the original process model. In case of the latter, one may interpret the model of the executed process as a re-designed process.

The extent to which a process model constrains the (design) actions of its users varies with the level of detail provided by the process model and with the enforcement mechanisms prevailing in the social or organizational context. Models of semi-structured processes are intended to allow a certain amount of "design freedom" [7] through their coarse-grained description of process elements and the expectation that some *ad-hoc* refinements and changes will be tolerated. Recent work on modeling goals and context of processes and process fragments [8, 9, 10] can be used to enhance user guidance and compliance by constraining possible design actions.

Providing process model users with constraints and then monitoring the resulting process execution can be used for achieving sufficiently controlled process flexibility. On the other hand, this approach cannot support reasoning about the relative benefits and drawbacks of alternative process structures beyond the pre-specified goals and constraints. This is because the user is viewed as a "black box", and the rationale for the user's decisions must be inferred from the executed process due to the lack of explicit representation of that rationale. As a result, this approach may be suitable for controlling compliance but is not appropriate for swiftly improving process structures in response to problems, opportunities, or new knowledge gained from previous process executions. There is a need for continuous interaction between designers and users of semi-structured process models that includes their rationale.

3   Rationale of User-Driven Process Innovation

Using semi-structured process models can be viewed as an instance of user-driven innovation. An existing framework of design innovation [11] includes this notion by explicitly representing bi-directional interactions between producers (i.e., designers) and adopters (i.e., users) of designed objects. Figure 1 shows a specialization of this framework for semi-structured processes as the objects of design innovation. Producers and adopters can interact directly, and indirectly via a use environment that includes modeled and executed processes. Processes are assumed to comprise any combination of control-flow, data-flow and organizational aspects [12, 1].

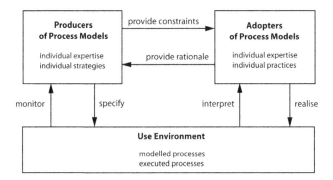

Fig. 1. Producers and adopters of process models, and their interactions

Producers specify process models, provide process constraints, and monitor the execution of the resulting processes. Adopters interpret the specified process models, realize (i.e., execute) them, and provide process rationale to producers. Both producers and adopters interact based on their individual expertise and strategies that change over time as they learn from their interactions. This, in turn, affects the kinds of information represented in the process models, the constraints and the rationale.

Rationale provides a basis for analyzing an adopter's assumptions and reasoning that can explain any refinements or changes of the original process model. It addresses an important aspect of provenance that is often neglected in the process domain, *viz.* the "why" of particular execution choices [13]. The insights gained from rationale can be used in two ways. First, producers can identify misinterpretations and eliminate them through clarified or more complete models of the process structure and constraints. Second, producers can recognize potential process improvements or pitfalls, and respond to them by changing the original process models and constraints.

If BPM tools are to be made more effective for semi-structured processes, they should support the capture and exchange of rationale between adopters and producers.

4   Modeling Rationale

The function-behavior-structure (FBS) ontology [14, 15] represents design objects irrespectively of the particular domain of designing.

Function (F) is defined as an object's teleology ("what the object is for"). It is the usefulness ascribed to the object. Typical functions of processes include process goals (e.g., "to generate purchase orders") and quality goals (e.g., "efficiency").

Behavior (B) is defined as the attributes that can be derived from the object's structure and its interactions with the environment. Behavior provides measurable criteria for evaluating and selecting different structures based on their applicability in different contexts. Process behaviors often relate to accuracy, speed and cost.

Structure (S) is defined as an object's components and their relationships. The structure of processes comprises their interconnected inputs, transformations (including resources and sub-processes) and outputs.

The FBS ontology supports all the interactions shown in Figure 1. The notion of structure captures the various elements of modeled and executed processes (e.g., tasks, resources and data), and the notions of function and behavior capture the producer's constraints as well as the adopter's rationale for decisions on structure [2, 16]. Such a uniform representation of all interactions makes explicit the relationships between the modeled and the executed process structure, and between the producer's constraints and the adopter's rationale. Adopters can use these relationships to choose those parts of their rationale that are of most interest to a producer. With respect to a given set of constraints, rationale can represent (1) *subsumptions* (i.e., same or similar behavior values), (2) *improvements* (i.e., significantly "better" behavior values), or (3) *expansions* (i.e., additional classes of behavior or function). Those parts of a rationale that are subsumptions of (i.e., that are subsumed by) constraints are usually of little value, unless suspected misinterpretations need to be addressed. Improvements and expansions, however, are most relevant and should be made available to producers so that they can adapt their specifications for more effective or efficient process executions in the future.

Typical examples of semi-structured processes are software development models, as they can be pre-defined only on a high level. Figure 2 shows the structure of such a process, specified by a producer in BPMN. Constraints are included via an annotation that specifies overall functions and behaviors required of the process.

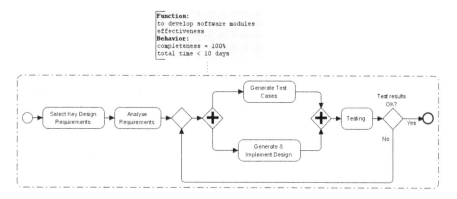

Fig. 2. A process model with annotated constraints, specified by a producer

Figure 3 shows a model of an executed process structure and the rationale associated (via annotations) with those process parts that the adopter has modified. The rationale includes a significant behavior improvement ("total time" from 10 days to 7 days), achieved by tightly coupling the generate-and-test activities rather than executing them in sequence. The executed process also introduces a "firefighting" activity ("Deploy Additional Developers") that aims to prevent development delays. It expands the original constraints by introducing a new behavior ("on-schedule rate") and a new function ("reliability").

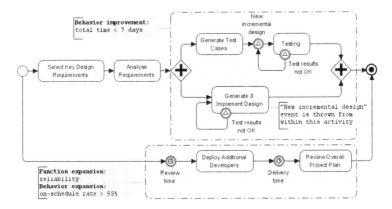

Fig. 3. A model of an executed process with annotated rationale, described by an adopter

The producer is now in a position to analyze the reasoning that led to the adopter's process changes, and to consider whether to modify the original process specifications either to formally integrate these changes or to prevent them from being introduced by future process executions. In both cases, the producer's decision can take account of assumptions of usefulness and applicability, both of which are included in the adopter's rationale.

5   Conclusion

Semi-structured processes differ from fully-structured ones in that they tolerate and encourage flexible execution decisions that may refine or deviate from the specified process model. This relaxes the burden of having to specify a detailed and complete process structure. However, it also creates a stronger need for explicitly representing process function and behavior to more effectively manage process execution. These notions capture the usefulness and applicability of different process structures. They can be used for specifying constraints with which the executed process needs to comply. Their use as rationale allows associating individual execution decisions with underlying assumptions. The uniform ontological representation of both constraints and rationale allows directly relating different assumptions about the process. This is essential for adapting interactions between producers and adopters, and thus for evolving the process structure according to changes in the environment.

The nature of our approach is conceptual. While we have illustrated it using BPMN models with annotations that are structured according to the FBS ontology, we do not intend to limit its use to any specific notation. Its "adoption" in practice will require well-defined annotation schemas and domain vocabulary to unambiguously represent, capture and exchange rationale between process stakeholders. Methods need to be developed for eliciting the rationale that is most relevant and appropriate in specific contexts (e.g., considering privacy concerns), and for automated analysis and comparison of rationale and constraints.

Acknowledgments. NICTA is funded by the Australian Government as represented by the Department of Broadband, Communications and the Digital Economy and the Australian Research Council through the ICT Centre of Excellence program.

References

1. Loeffeler, T., Striemer, R., Deiters, W.: A Framework for Identification, Classification and IT Support of Semi-Structured Business Processes. Knowledge and Process Management 5, 51–57 (1998)
2. Lee, J.: Design Rationale Systems: Understanding the Issues. IEEE Expert 12, 78–85 (1997)
3. von Hippel, E., Katz, R.: Shifting Innovation to Users via Toolkits. Management Science 48, 821–833 (2002)
4. Redström, J.: RE: Definitions of Use. Design Studies 29, 410–423 (2008)
5. Kruchten, P.: Casting Software Design in the Function-Behavior-Structure Framework. IEEE Software 22, 52–58 (2005)
6. Simon, H.A.: The Sciences of the Artificial. MIT Press, Cambridge (1996)
7. van Aken, J.E.: Design Science and Organization Development Interventions: Aligning Business and Humanistic Values. Journal of Applied Behavioral Science 43, 67–88 (2007)
8. Soffer, P., Regev, G.: On the Notion of Soft-Goals in Business Process Modeling. Business Process Management Journal 11, 663–679 (2005)
9. Rosemann, M., Recker, J., Flender, C.: Contextualisation of Business Processes. International Journal of Business Process Integration and Management 3, 47–60 (2008)
10. Kannengiesser, U.: Process Flexibility: A Design View and Specification Schema. In: Mendling, J., Rinderle-Ma, S., Esswein, W. (eds.) Enterprise Modelling and Information Systems Architectures 2009, pp. 111–124. University of Ulm, Germany (2009)
11. Gero, J.S., Kannengiesser, U.: Understanding Innovation as Change of Value Systems. In: Tan, R., Cao, G., León, N. (eds.) Growth and Development of Computer-Aided Innovation, pp. 249–257. Springer, Boston (2009)
12. Curtis, B., Kellner, M.I., Over, J.: Process Modeling. Communications of the ACM 35, 75–90 (1992)
13. Ram, S., Liu, J.: Understanding the Semantics of Data Provenance to Support Active Conceptual Modeling. In: Chen, P.P., Wong, L.Y. (eds.) ACM-L 2006. LNCS, vol. 4512, pp. 17–29. Springer, Heidelberg (2007)
14. Gero, J.S.: Design Prototypes: A Knowledge Representation Schema for Design. AI Magazine 11, 26–36 (1990)
15. Gero, J.S., Kannengiesser, U.: The Situated Function-Behaviour-Structure Framework. Design Studies 25, 373–391 (2004)
16. Chandrasekaran, B., Goel, A.K., Iwasaki, Y.: Functional Representation as Design Rationale. Computer 26, 48–56 (1993)

Predictive Analytics for Semi-structured Case Oriented Business Processes

Geetika T. Lakshmanan, Songyun Duan, Paul T. Keyser,
Francisco Curbera, and Rania Khalaf

IBM T.J. Watson Research Center, USA
{gtlakshm,sduan,pkeyser,curbera,rkhalaf}@us.ibm.com

Abstract. The goal of our work is to examine the utility of predictive analytics for case-oriented semi-structured business processes. As a first step towards this goal, this paper describes an approach to leverage case history to predict outcomes at decision points in case-oriented semi-structured processes, and examine how the contents of documents at these decision points influence their outcomes. We apply an ant-colony optimization (ACO) based algorithm to create a probabilistic activity graph from traces, and use it to identify key decision points in a given process. For each activity node that represents a decision point in the mined probabilistic graph, the likelihood of different outcomes from the node can be correlated with the contents of documents accessed by the activity node. This is achieved by using a standard decision tree learning algorithm. We validate our approach on correlated case instance traces generated by a simulator that we constructed to implement non-deterministic executions of an automobile insurance claims scenario. In practice we find that our approach can lead to useful predictions at different stages of execution in a semi-structured case oriented process.

Keywords: Semi-structured business processes, case-oriented, decision tree, Ant Colony Optimization, predictions.

1 Introduction

Semi-structured processes are emerging at a rapid pace in industries such as government, insurance, banking and healthcare. These business or scientific processes depart from the traditional kind of structured and sequential predefined processes. Their lifecycle is not fully driven by a formal process model. While an informal description of the process may be available in the form of a process graph, flow chart or an abstract state diagram, the execution of a semi-structured process is not completely controlled by a central entity (such as a workflow engine). Case oriented processes are an example of semi-structured business processes. Newly emerging markets as well as increased access to electronic case files have helped to drive market interest in commercially available content management solutions to manage case oriented processes [14,17].

Traditional business process management system (BPMS) products do not support case handling well and lack the requisite capabilities to coordinate this

M. zur Muehlen and J. Su (Eds.): BPM 2010 Workshops, LNBIP 66, pp. 640–651, 2011.

more complex use case [6]. Business process management systems typically include restrictions such as rigid control flow and context tunneling. Context tunneling refers to the phenomena in workflow management systems where only data needed to execute a particular activity is visible to respective actors but not other workflow data. These restrictions allow BPMS to make processes transparent and reproducible and provide the means for intricate mining of activities and process related information. Case handling systems aim for greater flexibility by avoiding such restrictions. Usually case handling systems present all data about a case at any time to a user who has relevant access privileges to that data. Furthermore, case management workflows are non-deterministic, meaning that they have one or more points where different continuations are possible. They are driven more by human decision making and content status than by other factors.

Given the document-driven nature of case executions, it would be particularly useful to provide business users with some insight into how the contents of the documents (E.g. case files containing customer order details) they currently have access to in a case management system affect the outcome (E.g. future activities) of the activity they are currently involved in. This paper describes an algorithm to make predictions to case workers and managers of case-oriented semi-structured processes. We leverage case history to understand the likelihood of different outcomes at specific points in a cases execution, and how the contents of documents influence the decisions made at these points. The emphasis of our work is on applying probabilistic and learning techniques to develop an algorithm for conducting analytics on case history data. This has given us some preliminary understanding of the utility of this approach. We assume that a provenance-based system [8] collects case history from diverse sources and provides us with integrated, correlated traces where each trace represents the end-to-end execution of a single case including contents of documents accessed or modified or written by each activity in the trace. Our work includes the following main contributions:

1. **ACO-based probabilistic graph.** Since the lifecycle of semi-structured processes is not fully driven by a formal process model, we mine a probabilistic graph from case execution data rather than settling on mining a formal process model. By applying Ant-colony optimization (ACO) techniques we construct a probabilistic graph from traces that represent correlated case history data. In Section 3 we describe the details of how we construct this graph and its advantages and limitations.

2. **Document content and activity correlation for prediction.** By applying a decision tree learning algorithm we can compute the correlation between the content of documents accessed by an activity and the execution of one of its subsequent (or downstream) activities in a semi-structured case oriented process, and use this to predict the outcome of an activity instance based on the contents of the documents it has access to. In Section 4 we describe the details of this algorithm. We use the probabilistic graph generated in step 1 to automatically determine the decision points (i.e. activities

where decisions are made) in a case management scenario, and use the decision tree algorithm described in step 2 to learn the circumstances under which document contents accessed by a particular decision point would lead to different outcomes. We validate our approach on correlated case instance traces generated by a simulator (Section 5) that we constructed to implement non-deterministic executions of an automobile insurance claims scenario. The scenario is derived from typical insurance industry practices [13]. In section 6 we discuss how the application of our proposed algorithms on automobile insurance case traces generated by the simulator can lead to meaningful predictions for a business user.

2   Related Work

Although formal business process modeling and mining are heavily researched areas [2], the analysis of semi-structured business processes, particularly case management, has received limited attention thus far. Van der Aalst et al. propose case handling as a new paradigm for supporting flexible, knowledge-intensive semi-structured business processes [3]. Using a case perspective they also examine the application of process mining for an industrial application, namely invoices sent by subcontractors for the Dutch national public works department [1]. Most relevant to our work is how they examined possible correlations between the practical processing of a case and properties directly linked to a case. They specifically tried to answer the question of whether there is a relationship between the time that an invoice is being paid, and the amount of money involved in the invoice. Using the SPSS Answer Tree tool (that conducts classification of large amounts of data) they found that multiple executions of specific activities contributed to the late processing of invoices. Our work is distinct from this work because we attempt to automate the task of determining the decision points in a semi-structured process, and we focus on a general approach to determine the impact of document contents on the outcomes of an activity rather than answering specific predetermined questions. There has been extensive research activity on using machine learning techniques for process mining. Herbst presents a machine learning approach for sequential workflow induction and concurrent workflows [11,12]. Cook and Wolf use the concept of Markov models to find the most probable event sequence productions, and algorithmically convert these probabilities into states and state transitions [7]. Nakatumba et al. explore the impact of workload on service times using historic data and regression analysis [16]. Serebrenik et al. use logs to derive information about ongoing processes such as statistical models expressing (pairwise) correlations between services (or activities) [21]. Silva et al. describe a learning algorithm to learn an acyclic workflow model from execution logs [20]. Beginning from a process model, Rozinat et al. explore how data attributes influence the choices made in a process based on past process executions [19]. They explore in detail many of the broadly scoped ideas presented by Grigori et al. [10] who develop a set of process analysis tools for managing process execution quality. While

we use the same decision tree learning algorithm in our work as Rozinat et al., there are some important differences between our contributions. While Rozinat et al. assume that a process model is available, we focus on a probabilistic graph mined from case execution trace data and use it to determine which decision points to explore for the purposes of learning a decision tree. Rozinat et al. focus on how to effectively achieve decision point analysis in the presence of duplicate and invisible activities in the process model whereas this is not the focus of our paper. Furthermore, in case oriented semi-structured process scenarios, conducting decision tree analysis on a mined process model may not be optimal if case executions are non-deterministic and data-driven, and consequently highly disparate. In such situations no single process model may correctly capture the behavior of the semi-structured process, and it may be inefficient to keep re-computing a process model to correctly represent the mined data. Finally, the goal of our work is to automatically conduct decision tree analysis in order to provide predictive recommendations to a business user that are easy to understand. Eventually we would like to feed the predictions generated by our algorithm to case workers and managers in a manner similar to the way in which the self-adjusting recommender system created by Dorn et al. [9] provides context sensitive process recommendations. As a consequence our experimental analysis is targeted towards this goal, and we deliberately choose an industry derived scenario to validate our work. On the other hand Rozinat et al. allow the user to orchestrate the decision tree analysis by hand selecting decision points, making the assumption that the user has sufficient technical knowledge to accomplish this.

3   Probabilistic Graph Obtained by Application of Ant Colony Optimization Algorithm on Trace Data

ACO-based algorithms have been applied to stochastic time varying problems such as routing in telecommunications networks [5] and distributed operator placement for stream processing systems [15]. These algorithms are well known for their dynamic, incremental and adaptive qualities. Since case executions are not usually driven by a formal process model, and are non-deterministic, driven by humans, and document contents, we choose to apply ACO to obtain a probabilistic graph that can provide decision points rather than continually mining a formal process model from case oriented process data in order to achieve the same goal. By periodically decaying probabilities, ACO ensures that transitions that did not execute recently in the case scenario have a lower probability in the mined probabilistic graph. Furthermore ACO updates an existing probabilistic model, whereas process mining algorithms do not have a way to dynamically and automatically update an existing process model. Some recent process mining algorithms require explicit change logs [4] to compute changes to a process model.

We can model each process definition using a directed graph, $G(V, E)$, in which the nodes, V, of the graph are activities in a semi-structured case oriented process and edges, E, indicate control flow dependencies between activities. Each vertex in the graph has a set of neighbors, $N(V)$. Vertex v maintains a transition vector that maps each neighbor vertex k into a probability ϕ_v^k of choosing neighbor k as the next hop to visit from v. Since these are probabilities, $\sum_{k \in N(v)} \phi_v^k = 1$. ϕ_v represents the transition vector at vertex v, which contains the transition probabilities from v to all of v's neighbors in $N(v)$. We use pheromone update rules from Ant Colony Optimization [5,16] to update the transition vector probabilities. Each time an edge $e_{v,k}$ is detected in a process trace file, we update ϕ_v^k which represents the probability of arriving at k as the next hop from vertex v. The transition vector at vertex v is updated by incrementing the probability associated with neighbor node k, and decreasing (by normalization) the probabilities ϕ_v^s associated with other neighbor nodes s, such that $s \neq k$. The update procedure modifies the probabilities of the various paths using a reinforcement signal r, where $r \in [0, 1]$. The transition vector value at time t is increased by the reinforcement value at time $t + 1$ as follows:

$$\Phi_v^k(t + 1) = \Phi_v^k(t) + r.(1 - \Phi_v^k(t)) \tag{1}$$

Thus the probability is increased by a value proportional to the reinforcement received, and to the previous value of the node probability. Given the same reinforcement, small probability values are increased proportionally more than big probability values. The probability ϕ_v^q is decayed for all neighbor nodes where $q \in N(v)$, and $q \neq v$. The decay function helps to eliminate edges (and consequently nodes) in G that cease to be present in the process execution traces and are thus indicative of changes in the process model. These $|N(v)| - 1$ nodes receive a negative reinforcement by normalization. Normalization is necessary to ensure that the sum of probabilities for a given pheromone vector is 1.

$$\Phi_v^q(t + 1) = \Phi_v^q(t).(1 - r), q \neq k \ . \tag{2}$$

While a probabilistic graph representation of the underlying process is useful for our purposes, it also has some limitations. Firstly we find that a probabilistic graph may generate a case execution sequence that is not reflected in any of the traces parsed to generate the graph. Secondly a probabilistic graph does not retain information about parallelism detected in execution traces. Any probabilistic graph mined from process data assumes that all points where control flow splits in the data are exclusive ORs, because constructing that kind of graph does not retain information about parallelism. (Modeling only exclusive OR type decisions in our auto insurance scenario suffices for the purpose of this paper since the goal of this paper is to explore the circumstances under which control flow is guided by document contents.) We intend to develop heuristics to address these limitations in future work.

4   Learning Decision Trees for Choices Obtained by ACO

A decision point corresponds to a place in an execution sequence where the process splits into alternative branches. Having automatically identified decision points through ACO, we want to investigate how document contents impact this decision and whether this can help to predict different types of outcomes in the case. The idea is to convert every decision point into a classification problem. As training examples we can use the case instances in the log. The attributes to be analyzed are case attributes contained in the log such as numerical values in documents accessible at an activity (E.g. car value, damage estimate). A training example for a decision point, d, contains data from n traces, where n in our case is on the order of thousands of traces. For each trace, a training example for decision point d contains the attribute values available at the decision point, as well as the outcome of the decision point. For further details on formulating a decision tree problem from process execution history we refer the reader to [18,19,22].

5   Implementation

In order to investigate our proposed algorithm we have designed an automobile insurance claims scenario and implemented it in a simulator. Our scenario is in accordance with typical insurance industry practices [13]. The scenario has been simplified for the sake of achieving clarity in our experiments and results. This scenario factors the process into actions taken by a customer-service representative (CSR), a claim-handler (CH), an adjustor (ADJ), an automobile-repair shop (ARS), and the police department (PD). The roles of the CSR and PD are restricted to a single action each. Fig. 1 shows a Visio diagram of the auto-insurance claims scenario that we implemented. Notice that the diagram presented is not a process model but rather something similar to what case workers may sketch as their conception of how cases may be handled by their organization. Since we are targeting semi-structured case oriented processes, we deliberately did not begin with a formal process model.

In order to simulate a realistic semi-structured case oriented process, we introduced the following stochastic variations in the simulator:

1. **Document content driven decision making**. Alternate paths, such as "Repair the car" or not, are taken depending on the values of one or more document contents, such as the "car value," "damage estimate amount," "age of car," etc.
2. **Human decision making.** Actors in the simulator have properties modeled as probabilities, such as the Claim Handlers probability of overestimating the car value.
3. **Invalid deviations.** Activity outcomes may deviate from expected behavior. For instance the notify state activity is typically executed when the dollar amount in the payment document is greater than a threshold (in accordance with typical state laws). However, due to deviations that we introduce in the simulator, the state may sometimes not be notified, even when the payment document dollar amount exceeds the threshold.

The automobile insurance claims scenario is modeled as a semi-structured case oriented process and implemented in Java. At each step of the scenario, XML

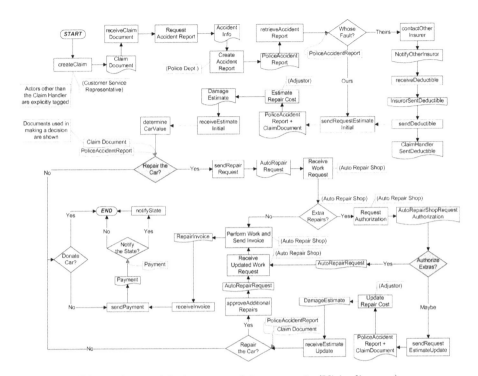

Fig. 1. Automobile insurance claims scenario (Visio diagram)

strings are output, so that at the completion of each end-to-end case instance, a complete valid XML document is produced. These XML documents are parsed and analyzed by our analytics tool that implements our ACO-based algorithm. The simulator is written in Eclipse as an RCP application, and provides a complete small development environment in which one can configure and run simulations of the automobile insurance scenario and view individual traces. We examine the "completed" status logged by activities in a trace to determine their control flow dependency. We can generate 2000 simulator traces in a few seconds. We implemented the ACO algorithm in Java and used a constant reinforcement parameter in all experiments. The time complexity to build a probabilistic graph using ACO is $O(ma^2)$, where m is the number of traces, and a is the number of activities. In practice it typically takes 6.56 seconds to read and parse 2000 traces on an IBM T60 machine with 2 GB RAM, and processor T2600 @ 2.16 GHz, and it takes typically 0.53 seconds to build a probabilistic model using ACO from these traces where $a < 20$. We use the implementation of the decision tree algorithm J48 provided by the Weka software library [22] which is an implementation of the C4.5 decision tree learning algorithm [18]. The time complexity of the C4.5 learning algorithm is $O(mn^2)$, where m is the number of traces, and n is the number of attributes in the documents in each trace. In our experiments, the number of attributes is typically small ($n < 10$), and m is roughly 2000. In practice the learning time is quite small (< 2 seconds).

Fig. 2 shows the result of applying ACO on 2000 traces of the simulator for one of many sets of parameter-values we used. We conducted an experiment in which we compared the results of applying ACO to three sets of 2000 traces where each set involves the simulator being configured with different settings. We found that the three resulting ACO graphs had very different sets of mined activities, and while the sets overlapped they were not identical. This validates our intention of making the simulator model a non-deterministic case oriented process. It should be noted that the probabilistic graph in Fig. 2 includes paths not reachable in the flow of the process in Fig. 1, and in general is not guaranteed to exclude all unreachable paths. This is a limitation of our current work, and due to space limitations we defer a detailed discussion to future work.

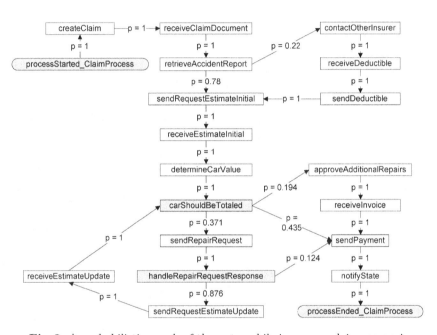

Fig. 2. A probabilistic graph of the automobile insurance claims scenario

6   Results

The goal of our experimental analysis is to evaluate the effectiveness of learning decision trees for a decision point provided by the probabilistic graph. In particular we examine the effectiveness of the decision tree in predicting different outcomes based on document contents.

Predicting immediate one hop outcomes. The ACO-based probabilistic graph in Fig. 2 indicates that the case has three main decision points. We examined the *carShouldBeTotaled* decision point because it has three immediate potential outcomes. In particular we examined how we could use the document contents accessed by *carShouldBeTotaled* to predict under what circumstances

(i.e. document content values) a case leads to *sendRepairRequest* and under what
circumstances (i.e. document content values) a case leads to *approveAdditional-
Repairs*. In order to formulate the decision problem we examine the values of the
document content variables (six attributes in this scenario) that are accessible to
carShouldBeTotaled. Fig. 3 shows the decision tree (obtained with 80% prediction accuracy) learned by the C4.5 algorithm for predicting *sendRepairRequest*
where we restricted the parameter *minNumObj* of the Weka library to 100. *min-
NumObj* refers to the minimum number of traces classified by a given leaf node
of the decision tree. A large value of *minNumObj* corresponds to the aggregation
of more cases per leaf node, and thus a simpler decision tree. The actual calculation in the simulator code for *sendRepairRequest* is "if the total estimated
damage is less than the current computed value of the car, go to *sendRepair-
Request*." However, since (A) the current computed value of the car depends on
the make/model (and varies a great deal in a way that would look random) and
also on the age of the car (in a way that would work well with a classifier system), and (B) the total-estimated-damage increases with the damage-area-size,
it makes sense that the decision tree depends on *CarInfo.getAge()* and the *Po-
liceAccidentReport.getDamageAreaSize()*. We found the decision tree learned for
predicting *approveAdditionalRepairs* based on the document contents accessed
at *carShouldBeTotaled* to be similarly meaningful. We did not find it necessary
to compute a decision tree for *sendPayment* from *carShouldBeTotaled* because
the probabilistic graph indicates that *sendPayment* always executes after *approveAdditionalRepairs* and because we have already learned the decision trees
from *carShouldBeTotaled* for all other immediate outcomes.

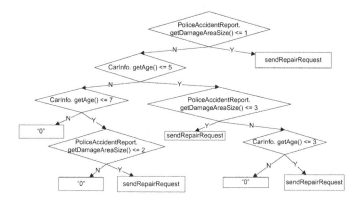

Fig. 3. A binary decision tree learned to predict whether *sendRepairRequest* would
execute given the document contents accessible at *carShouldBeTotaled*

Predicting intermediate outcomes. A case worker may find it extremely
useful to know whether a case will lead to *sendRepairRequest* at the
point where he or she is still retrieving the accident report at *retrieveAccidentReport*. In order to answer this question we attempted to learn a decision tree
for predicting whether *sendRepairRequest* would execute based on the document

contents accessed at *retrieveAccidentReport*. The corresponding decision tree has an 80% accuracy and is displayed in Fig. 4. This result is somewhat surprising (and promising) because the tree and prediction accuracy indicates that we could make a meaningful prediction about the likelihood of a repair request being sent at the point where a case has reached the *retrieveAccidentReport* stage in its execution, even though all the data necessary to make the decision about whether the repair request should be sent is not known at the stage of *retrieveAccidentReport*. In particular, the variable, *CarInfo.getValue()* which plays a role in the decision for *sendRepairRequest* is not initialized at *retrieveAccidentReport*. Given these results, the system could make a recommendation to a case worker to begin gathering documents to send the repair request if the current document contents meet the decision trees prediction of *sendRepairRequest*. It is important to note that 80% accuracy is applicable to the specific test runs that we ran. For 80% of the test runs, our prediction is correct. Further detailed experimentation is required to determine whether this is applicable beyond these test runs.

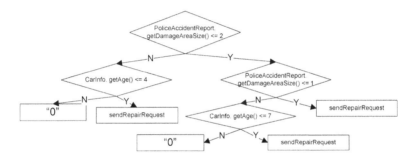

Fig. 4. A binary decision tree learned to predict whether *sendRepairRequest* would execute given the document contents accessible at *retrieveAccidentReport*

Predicting final outcomes. It may be valuable to predict the final outcome of a case when a case worker is involved in an activity somewhere in the middle of the cases execution. In order to explore this question we first introduced a second final outcome in the simulator called *sendFraudAlert* that executes after *handleRepairRequestResponse* and indicates that the auto shop detected that a false repair claim was sent, and cancels any work on the case. Using the simulator we obtain a decision tree for predicting whether *sendFraudAlert* would execute based on the document contents accessed at *carShouldBeTotaled*. Fig. 5 shows the corresponding decision tree which predicts this situation with 96% accuracy. This could be extremely useful for a case worker because he or she could cancel the case or send the case to an auditor rather than having to process a fraudulent case unnecessarily. Our system could make such a recommendation to the case worker by evaluating the document contents against the decision tree.

Recall that increasing the value of the Weka library parameter, *minNumObj* leads to a simpler decision tree. On average we found that over all of our experiments, when we adjusted the value of *minNumObj* to 100 from its default

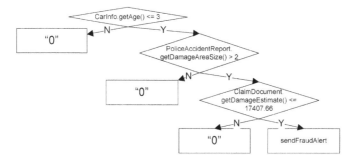

Fig. 5. A binary decision tree learned to predict whether *sendFraudAlert* would execute given the document contents accessible at *carShouldBeTotaled*

value of 2, the prediction accuracy of Wekas C4.5 algorithm decreased by at most 2%. We also find that we need traces in the order of thousands to achieve an acceptable level of prediction accuracy.

7 Conclusion and Future Work

In this paper we demonstrated the utility of leveraging case history to predict outcomes at decision points in case-oriented semi-structured processes, and how the contents of documents influence the outcomes of the decisions. Experimental results on an automobile insurance industry claims scenario indicate that our approach can be useful for predicting (1) outcomes that immediately follow a given decision point, (2)final outcomes, and (3) intermediate outcomes that occur between immediate and final outcomes. Furthermore our experiments indicate that our approach can be useful for predicting outcomes of decisions in situations where *not all* the data values necessary to make a decision are available. Finally, our approach also demonstrates a way to identify decision points in a semi-structured process using a probabilistic graph without necessarily mining a process model to represent the process. In future work we would like to further develop our algorithm towards making consumable recommendations for case workers and managers as part of a self-adjusting recommender system. We also intend to improve the accuracy of our probabilistic graph algorithm in terms of its ability to represent mined trace data of a case oriented semi-structured processes, and develop heuristics to allow the probabilistic graph to show parallel flows in cases where parallelism is detected.

References

1. van der Aalst, W.M.P., Reijers, H.A., Weijters, A.J.M.M., van Dongen, B.F., Alves de Medeiros, A.K., Song, M., Verbeek, H.M.W.: Business process mining: An industrial application. Inf. Syst. 32(5), 713–732 (2007)
2. van der Aalst, W.M.P., van Dongen, B.F., Herbst, J., Maruster, L., Schimm, G., Weijters, A.J.M.M.: Workflow Mining: A Survey of Issues and Approaches. Data and Knowledge Engineering 47(2), 237–267 (2003)

3. van der Aalst, W.M.P., Weske, M., Grnbauer, D.: Case handling: a new paradigm for business process support. KDE 53(2), 129–162 (2005)
4. van der Aalst, W.M.P., Gunther, C.W., Recker, M.J., Reichert, M.: Using Process Mining to Analyze and Improve Process Flexibility (Position Paper). In: CAiSE 2006 Workshops -7th Intl Workshop on Business Process Modeling, Development (2006)
5. Di Caro, G., Dorigo, M.: AntNet: Distributed Stigmergetic Control for Communucation Networks. Journal of Artificial Intelligence, 317–365 (1998)
6. Critical Capabilities for Composite Content Management Applications. Gartner Report (2010)
7. Cook, J.E., Wolf, A.L.: Discovering Models of Software Processes from Event-Based Data. ACM Trans. Softw. Eng. Methodol. 7(3), 215–249 (1998)
8. Curbera, F., Doganata, Y., Martens, A., Mukhi, N., Slominski, A.: Business Provenance - A Technology to Increase Traceability of End-to-End Operations. In: OTM Conferences, pp. 100–119
9. Dorn, C., Burkhart, T., Werth, D., Dustdar, S.: Self-adjusting recommendations for people-driven ad-hoc processes. In: Hull, R., Mendling, J., Tai, S. (eds.) BPM 2010. LNCS, vol. 6336, pp. 327–342. Springer, Heidelberg (2010)
10. Grigori, D., Casati, F., Castellanos, M., Dayal, U., Sayal, M., Shan, M.: Business process intelligence. Comput. Ind. 53(3), 321–343 (2004)
11. Herbst, J.: A Machine Learning Approach to Workflow Management. In: Lopez de Mantaras, R., Plaza, E. (eds.) ECML 2000. LNCS (LNAI), vol. 1810, pp. 183–194. Springer, Heidelberg (2000)
12. Herbst, J., Karagiannis, D.: Integrating Machine Learning and Workflow Management to Support Acquisition and Adaption of Workflow Models. In: DEXA Workshop 1998, pp. 745–752 (1998)
13. IBM Insurance Application Architecture, http://www-03.ibm.com/industries/insurance/us/detail/solution/P669447B27619A15.html?tab=3
14. IBM Advanced Case Management, http://www-01.ibm.com/software/data/advanced-case-management/technologies.html
15. Lakshmanan, G.T., Strom, R.: Biologically-Inspired Distributed Middleware Management for Stream Processing Systems. ACM Middleware, 223–242 (2008)
16. Nakatumba, J., van der Aalst, W.M.P.: Analyzing Resource Behavior Using Process Mining. In: Business Process Management Workshops, pp. 69–80 (2009)
17. Oracle JD Edwards EnterpriseOne Case Management, http://www.oracle.com/applications/peoplesoft/crm/ent_one/module/case_management.html
18. Quinlan, J.R.: C4.5: Programs for Machine Learning. Morgan Kaufmann, San Francisco (1993)
19. Rozinat, A., van der Aalst, W.M.P.: Decision mining in proM. In: Dustdar, S., Fiadeiro, J.L., Sheth, A.P. (eds.) BPM 2006. LNCS, vol. 4102, pp. 420–425. Springer, Heidelberg (2006)
20. Silva, R., Zhang, J., Shanahan, J.G.: Probabilistic workflow mining. Knowledge Discovery in Data Mining, 275–284 (2005)
21. Serebrenik, A., Sidorova, N.: Predicting service request rates for adaptive resource allocation in SOA. In: Proceedings 5th International Workshop on Enterprise and Organizational Modeling & Simulation (EOMAS 2009), pp. 1–14 (2009)
22. Witten, I.H., Frank, E.: Data Mining: Practical machine learning tools and techniques, 2nd edn. Morgan Kaufmann, San Francisco (2005)

Business Control Management – A Discipline to Ensure Regulatory Compliance of SOA Applications

Axel Martens, Francisco Curbera, Nirmal K. Mukhi, and Aleksander Slominski

IBM T J Watson Research Center, 19 Skyline Drive, Hawthorne NY 10532
{amarten,curbera,nmukhi,aslom}@us.ibm.com

Abstract. The success of today's business operations depends largely on the ability to react to changing factors of influence. With the increasing distribution and heterogeneity of enterprise applications, the challenge is to gain and sustain oversight and to manage the different aspects of business operations systematically. Many disciplines and best practices have been established: On the infrastructure level, Service oriented architectures provide a common base to compose distributed applications. On the operational level, business process management provides high level visibility of end-to-end transactions. On the information level, master data management aggregates and consolidates data throughout the organization. There is, however, an aspect that is becoming more and more relevant but still lacks a proper discipline: Regulatory compliance of business operations. The pressure to prove compliance with legal obligations and industry wide requirements has risen tremendously in recent years – and in light of the ongoing economic crises it is likely to rise further. To address this gap, this paper presents a systematic development method to define, deploy and monitor business controls across a distributed enterprise application. First, we establish a repository of obligations that keeps track of the dependencies between processes, data, applications, and regulations. Second, we define and deploy operational controls as a set of services to gather, classify and correlate information. Finally, we provide end-to-end visibility of the business transactions for monitoring and reporting.

Keywords: Regulatory compliance, CMS, Continuous assurance, Provenance.

1 Introduction

The way companies organize and conduct their business operations is influenced by many factors, for instance by the desire to maximize profits. Also among those factors is the obvious requirement to act in strict conformance with relevant laws and regulations – called *regulatory compliance*. While the pressure on enforcing regulatory compliance has risen tremendously in recent years – mainly because of large scale corporate scandals and the near collapse of the entire financial system – achieving regulatory compliance is a complex challenge. One reason is the growing diversity of regulations on a variety of levels – state, federal, and international – which may overlap each other. Secondly, regulations typically cut across the process and organizational structure. On the other hand, failure to comply with those regulations may

M. zur Muehlen and J. Su (Eds.): BPM 2010 Workshops, LNBIP 66, pp. 652–666, 2011.

result in severe fines and penalties, and might ruin the company's reputation. Hence, there is a need to address regulatory compliance in a systematic and transparent manner. This paper presents a first approach to establish an engineering discipline for regulatory compliance.

1.1 Compliance of SOA Applications

To achieve regulatory compliance it is necessary to break down the abstract and high-level obligations of the relevant laws and regulations into specific requirements for the company's line-of-business processes. For each process, this happens typically in two steps: First, situations are identified that hold potential risks of violation, e.g. a particular behavioral pattern. Second, appropriate controls are established, e.g. the thorough investigation and if necessary reporting of the situation. Obviously, this requires transparency and oversight of the end-to-end business operations. While full-fledged business process management might provide a practical starting point, most business operations are not thoroughly implemented by formal process models. In reality, business applications mostly consist of distributed, heterogeneous systems and services and a combination of structured and unstructured processes and data. In such a scenario, it is difficult to follow the methodology described above, because the data to detect and investigate situations is not homogeneously accessible. We have seen in customer engagements that a large percentage of audit failures were caused by missing, inaccessible or uncorrelated data. Hence, the goal of our research is to support the management of compliance regulations, control points and auditable evidence especially in the case of semi-structured, SOA based enterprise applications.

1.2 Business Control Management

With ever changing legal obligations, ensuring regulatory compliance is not a one-off activity. Instead companies need to keep track of relevant regulations and adapt the depending controls constantly. They have to provide evidence of compliant behavior at audit time and it is incumbent upon them to improve compliance rates continuously

Fig. 1. Phases of Business Control Management

by investigating the root cause of detected violations. In many cases, companies even have to document their processes of putting effective controls into place. To meet these requirements, we propose Business Control Management – as a new systematic development method in four phases as shown in Figure 1 – that is based on content management and business provenance [1], and that provides a build-time as well as runtime environment for compliance solutions. Here a short overview:

Phase 1 – Define Business: Legal obligations will often affect multiple line-of-business processes. Additionally, processes might have multiple implementations in different business units and geographies. The goal of the first phase is to list the relevant obligations, the affected processes and the involved systems and to describe the dependencies between those artifacts. Based on content management, a repository of obligations is established that holds various kinds of documents describing the artifacts together within an interlinked structure to enable browsing, dependency analysis and change management.

Phase 2 – Model Controls: Having established the high-level relation between obligations and processes, the goal of the second phase is to define control points within each affected process to monitor and assure compliance, respectively. A control point model consists of two parts. The descriptive part explains in English the potential compliance risk and resulting objective of the control point. Additionally, it lists the ownership and responsibilities of the control. The second, operational part models the testing of the control point. It therefore lists the controlled artifacts (evidence) and the required compliance condition. While many approaches on governance, risk and compliance apply a similar structure to model control points, our approach goes beyond the description alone. Based on the system context of a control point as provided in phase 1, we provide a systematic, top-down approach to transform the high-level compliance condition into operational rules on the level of observable system events and enable the capability of continuous compliance monitoring.

Phase 3 – Monitor Operations: The control point model is the central artifact of our proposed business control management approach. It connects the high-level obligations with the system-level observable behavior. To do so, it uses concepts (these are akin to data types) that have certain properties and hold references to other concepts. Low-level concepts (e.g. an email) are gathered from the runtime environment (e.g. adapter to Domino server). High-level concepts (e.g. an approval) are derived from low-level concepts by our rule engine (e.g. email sent by certain person with particular subject). Our prototype infrastructure comes with a set of runtime adaptors while the rules for aggregation are derived automatically from the control point model.

Phase 4 – Report Compliance: Once adaptors and rules are deployed, the compliance runtime gathers and correlates information. The information is stored in two different places. Relevant business data like documents, emails, etc. are stored in the evidence repository to be available for audit and root cause analysis. Meta-data providing an index structure for the evidence, documenting the lineage of compliance findings, and enabling the end-to-end visibility of business transactions are stored in the provenance store [1]. The provenance store provides a powerful API to query and navigate the individual instance data, to aggregate and forward compliance data to standard reporting portals, and to raise alerts or escalate processes in certain situations, respectively. The provenance store is the essential middleware infrastructure for our proposed compliance solutions. With it's capability to address and retrieve evidence from different sources it is not necessary to add a separate evidence repository to the IT infrastructure if the company already uses content management to maintain audit relevant information.

While the development process of compliance solutions is broken into four major phases, it does not have to follow a linear order. Instead many feedback loops exist between the phases to allow rapid prototyping as well as quality and change management. After a review of related research areas, the remainder of the paper is organized according to the development method and will explain each phase in greater detail applied to a customer inspired scenario.

1.3 Related Research

Regulatory compliance, especially with respect to financial reporting, has been targeted by many different frameworks and software solutions. The most widely used framework is COSO ERM [2]. Business control management adapts this framework by mapping the components of risk management into four phases of the development cycle similar to the approach taken in [3]. Most software products on the market address the information and communication element of the COSO framework, but rely on manual implementation of control activities and monitoring requirements. For instance, IBM's Workplace for Business Controls and Microsoft's Solution Accelerator for Sarbanes-Oxley provide central content repositories with controlled access to company financial data. But process owners within the company must manually verify whether each control has been implemented and has been effective. Our goal is to adopt the best practices within a system that enables transparent development of automated controls for continuous compliance monitoring.

There are two major topics in scientific literature dealing with regulatory compliance: Formal representations of regulations, e.g. with logic (e.g. [4], [5], [7]) and integration of compliance requirements into the business process management (e.g. [5], [6], [8]). Both areas often overlap since either the formal representation is used to drive the business process modeling process (compliance by design) or the process model is analyzed with respect to the regulations (compliance verification). While our work has been greatly inspired by the structured approach presented in [4], we do not assume full-fledged business process management. Our focus lies on compliance management for applications that are heterogeneous, distributed and difficult to change or replace. In this scenario, the models and formalization have to bridge the gap between high-level requirements and observable system level operations (cf. [9]). Thus we used a lightweight, UML like type system to characterize the significant artifacts and PROLOG like rules to define correlations and compliance constraints which can be evaluated using the provenance store rule engine [1].

2 Define Business

The presented approach and infrastructure has been successfully applied to different compliance projects. To illustrate the phases of business control management, we use a customer inspired scenario from the pharmaceutical domain. While the chosen scenario hides confidential information from our real engagement, it combines typical components and recurring challenges from our real engagements.

2.1 Register Obligation

Companies that distribute controlled substances have to comply with federal regulations on monitoring the order fulfillment process to identify and further investigate suspicious orders of unusual size, frequency or order pattern (*Title 21 CFR 1301.74(b)*). The goal is to detect, investigate and prevent the diversion of controlled substances while ensuring an adequate and uninterrupted supply for legitimate purposes.

As often, the legal regulation describes the compliance goal on a high level of abstraction. It is the task of the company's Chief Compliance Officers (CCO) to determine the direct implications to the company's operations:

- Compare all orders with customer classification, profile and history
- Investigate all unusual orders thoroughly and document findings
- Block all dubious orders and report to authorities

In addition, it is required, as often, to provide evidence for the company's actions to put effective controls into place. Using a linked repository of obligations, it is not only easier to formulate the relations between the external requirement and the CCO's directives, it also fulfills the additional transparency requirement.

2.2 Define High-Level Process

In our scenario there hasn't been a suitable order monitoring process in place. Thus it is part of the business control management to define the process up to a level of precision that allows the definition of control points. This does not require a BPM system.

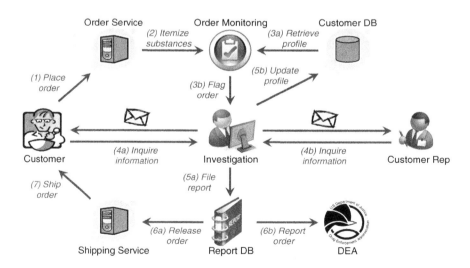

Fig. 2. Order Monitoring Process

The process might as well be described in an MS Office document or Visio diagram. Also as mentioned before, our BCM approach is not strictly linear. If in later stages adjustments or refinements to the process description are required, the link between the registered artifacts allows an easy identification and modification of the process document. Figure 2 shows the high-level order monitoring process.

Each incoming order (1) is broken down into classes of controlled substances (2) and individually compared to the customer's profile and previous ordering pattern (3a). If flagged as unusual order (3b), a thorough investigation of the order follows that might include a correspondence with the customer (4a) to inquire the reason for higher demand of a specific substance and/or a background check by the local customer representative (4b). The investigation itself has to be recorded (5a) and might yield to an update of the customer profile (5b). Depending on the investigation results, the order will be finally released (6a) or blocked and reported (6b) to the authorities.

2.3 Define System Mapping

While the high level order monitoring process looks straightforward, its implementation is far more complex due to the underlying IT architecture: There are different order channels and systems for different product and customer groups. Thus there is no central database containing all orders and profiles for one customer and the order monitoring service has to be hooked into each of the different silos. Additionally, the communication between customer, investigator and customer representative is email based and manually triggered. To gather the case information and control evidence end-to-end, the actual IT infrastructure has to be taken into account. The first BCM phase lays the foundation for that by enabling the definition of relations between systems or services on the one hand and process or tasks on the other hand. These relations are stored in the repository besides the actual artifacts and provide a rich context for the succeeding control point definition. Depending on the level of formalization, the endpoints of a relation might be defined precisely using the object IDs (server endpoint URL or BPM process task ID) or more fuzzy characterizations (name of a task mentioned in PDF document describing the process). The extensible data model of the repository of obligation therefore accommodates a wide spectrum of data precision and is able to utilize the available information to provide a transparent view on the dependencies from compliance goals down to system level.

3 Model Controls

As mentioned before, a compliance obligation might affect multiple line-of-business processes. Conversely, each such process might be affected by multiple compliance obligations. Given one process and one obligation, the process owner identifies potential compliance risks in cooperation with the compliance officer and establishes control points to detect and/or prevent compliance violations. Typically, a control point is attached to an activity within the process by adding requirements to the controlled action, for example maintaining certain documentation. At execution time, each instance of the controlled activity is supposed to fulfill the additional requirement and provide evidence, for example the maintained documentation. The control point can be tested by investigating the evidence. This is done mostly for a few sampled instances at a later time (i.e. auditing). Our proposed BCM approach allows additionally the control point testing for each instance shortly after the execution (i.e. continuous monitoring) as shown in Figure 3.

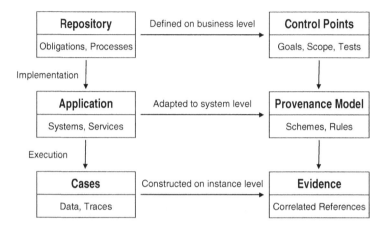

Fig. 3. System Engineering and Control Engineering

The selection of process and obligation as defined in phase one provides the context for the control point model. Thus it is possible to reuse already defined vocabulary and concepts, and to link back to higher lever artifacts. Taking into account the information on systems and services, the control point description is systematically transformed into the provenance model – a set of operational rules that gather and correlate evidence based on observable concepts. Thus at the runtime level, evidence for each control point instance is available for near-real-time testing or batch auditing. With the generic provenance infrastructure in place the crucial task is to map the control point description into the provenance model.

3.1 Control Point Description

The control point description itself is stored as a document within the repository of obligations. Besides information on author and ownership, version and activation status, each control point description contains an English description of the control objective. Here are a few examples:

- KCR 1: Each unusual order has to be flagged and forwarded to investigation
- KCR 2: For each flagged order there has to be an investigation report
- KCR 3: Each release of an unusual order requires supporting evidence
- KCR 4: Each update of customer profile requires supporting evidence
- KCR 5: Each dubious order has to be blocked and reported to the authorities
- KCO 1: Each order has to be released in 24 h or the customer has to be notified

As established best practice the control point description contains tags in addition to the objective that allow a grouping with respect to severity, test strategy, and impact on the process. Our control point data model supports an extensible set of tags including the *class*: key control of reporting (KCR) or operations (KCO); the *type*: preventive or detective; and the *execution mode*: manual or automatic. KCR 1 for example is executed automatically and descriptive while KCR 5 is manual but preventive. The set of tags and the control point objective are the basis on which to define the precise compliance condition and test procedure using the provenance model.

3.2   Provenance Model Definition

The provenance model formalizes the artifacts of the control point description as well as the visible artifacts at system level in a simple, hierarchical, and extensible model. It is used to derive the runtime configuration that gathers and correlates provenance data. Basically the provenance model consists of concepts, properties, references and definitions. Figure 4 shows the provenance model for control point KCR 3.

Concept: A concept represents a set of semantic objects like instances of control points at the business level or database records on the system level. Similar to a data type, a concept has properties and references to other concepts including inheritance.

Property: A property is a name value pair whereby the value can be of simple or structured type. A concept might define default and fixed values for its properties.

Reference: A reference is a named link to another concept. References are the core correlation mechanism for building end-to-end visibility of business operations.

Definition: The evidence repository is an instantiation of the provenance model (PM), i.e. each meta-data artifact is an instance of a PM concept and each correlation between meta-data artifacts is an instance of a PM reference. A definition describes how to create an instance of a concept, how to establish a reference between instances, or how to set the value of a property. To do so, a definition either builds on observable system events or on other concepts, properties, and references.

With the provenance model at hand, it is now possible to map the control point objective into operational rules. Following a top down approach, the control point

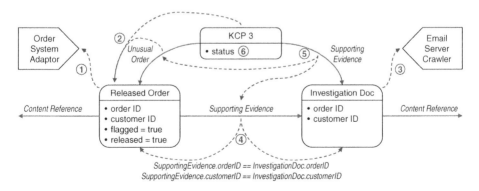

Fig. 4. Data for Auditing and Reporting

becomes a concept as well as the artifacts mentioned in the objective. Then, references between the concepts are established to enable the definition of the control point status. Since most likely the now present concepts are not directly observable, they need to be defined hierarchically using other concepts and references. Figure 4 illustrates this process for control point KCR 3.

We start modeling by adding a concept for the control point KCP 3 itself, along with a property called *status*. As mentioned in the control point objective, KCP 3 requires a relation between a released order and its supporting evidence. To express this fact we add references to the unusual order and to supporting evidence (solid lines). Then, we go on defining the properties for the new concepts according to the correlation requirements and with regard to the underlying data structure. To put the provenance model into operation we finally have to provide definitions (dashed lines) for all concepts, properties and references. This goes as follows: (1) The instances of released orders are defined by the order system adaptor selecting those records which are flagged and released. (2) An instance of *KCP 3* together with the reference is created for each released order. (3) Instances of investigation documents are created by the email crawler which uses text analytics to extract the properties. (4) The properties of each pair of created instances of order and document are compared, and if they match a reference is established between those instances. (5) The *KCP 3* reference to the supporting evidence is defined as transitive reference via the order instance. (6) Using the established references, the value of the *KCP 3*'s *status* property is updated.

4   Monitor Operations

With the definition of a control point model or provenance model, respectively, the foundation for continuous compliance monitoring of business operations has be laid. We are proposing a runtime environment that consists of flexible SOA components

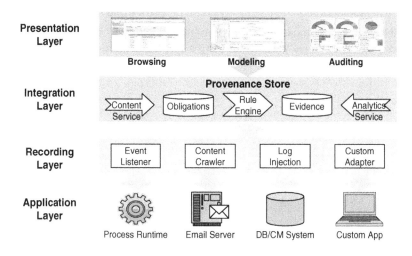

Fig. 5. Architecture Framework for Business Control Management

which are configured automatically to gather, correlate, and visualize compliance information using the provenance model. Figure 5 shows the architecture framework.

4.1 Recording Layer

The task of the recording layer is to fill the evidence repository by gathering relevant system information as the business operations unfold. To achieve this goal, three steps have to be taken: First, access to the system data has to be established. Second, the relevant system data has to be selected. Finally, the system data has to be transformed and stored.

Access System Data: We have developed a set of adaptors to widely used applications which can be deployed close to the applications due to the service oriented architecture of our compliance runtime. Modern enterprise applications like business process runtimes typically emit easy accessible monitoring events. Our prototypical runtime includes a default listener to IBM's Common Base Event (CBE) specification. To access unstructured data like emails and file systems, we are building on top of crawler systems like IBM's content collector. To support legacy systems which do not provide an easy real-time access, we added the capability to inject log data in batch mode using preferably XSL transformations. If none of the options above is feasible, the chosen architecture enables the simple development of a custom adaptor.

Filtering data: Having accessed runtime data from the application, it is now the challenge to select the relevant information. As mentioned before, each concept in the provenance model has to have at least one definition based on other concepts or on observable information at system level. It is easy to run a dependency analysis to find all definitions that refer to a particular application, and to use the attached concept as filter specification. For example in the case of KCP 3 (Figure 4), only orders with the conditions *flagged = true* and *released = true* will be selected.

Transforming data: As the provenance model uses concepts and references to provide an abstract and company-wide unified way to represent business transactions, it is often necessary to transform the incoming data. Ideally, this transformation is specified as part of the concept definition and pushed down to the recording layer. The control point modeling environment therefore allows to import schemata of observable information or to synthesize schemata out of sample data. Thus it is possible to have source (schema) and target (concept) side by side to define the transformation graphically. We are currently working on polishing this capability in the presentation layer.

4.2 Integration Layer

In essence, business control management is about management of data: Model level data on obligations, processes, controls and their dependencies on the one hand and instance level data on business operations and compliance tests on the other hand. In both sets of data we find strongly correlated meta-data records that typically point to a real-world artifact like a document or a person. That's why the provenance store has proven to be a fitting container to maintain relationships between both sets of data. Basically, the provenance store holds directed graphs: Each node represents the meta-data of one artifact. Being an extensible XML data type, each node can hold as much information as needed. Each edge represents a relation or reference between two artifacts. Besides holding model and instance level information in separated but connected domains (cf. Figure 5: Obligations and Evidence), the provenance store provides a powerful rule engine as well as interfaces to retrieve the content or run external analytics.

Rule Engine: The recording layer fills the evidence repository with isolated meta-data records representing observable system level data. To correlate those records and thus to build business cases and higher level information, provenance rules are executed. A provenance rules is triggered by the arrival of new records, might depend on the existence of other records, is guarded by a conditions based on the properties of the new and required records, and can create, update and connect records. While they operate on the evidence repository, the definitions for provenance rules are derived automatically from the control point definition. Referring to the example of Figure 4, one rule is triggered by the arrival of a new investigation document, and if a released order exists with matching properties, a reference (i.e. edge) between the order and the document is established.

Content Service: The provenance store only holds the correlated meta-data. The actual content of the real-world artifacts is stored externally in a content management system (CMS) because of multiple reasons. On the one hand, CMS provide the capability of storing all kinds of content safely, including aspects like versioning, accessibility and retention policies. On the other hand, many companies have already systems in place to store the relevant business artifacts. Thus it makes sense to externalize the content and access it through the content service.

Analytics Service: The rule engine operates on the meta-data records and supports a rich set of expressions and functions for comparing and manipulating the properties. In some cases, however, classifications could only be achieved and correlations only be established be analyzing the content thoroughly. To do so it is possible to register analytics services that will be called by special rules. An analytics service will be provided visibility to the meta-data as well as the context and is expected to return information to be used within the action part of the calling rule. In the example scenario we have used an unstructured information analytics pipeline based on the UIMA [11] architecture successfully to extract the order and customer ID from the crawled emails (cf. Figure 4).

4.3 Presentation Layer

The presentation layer enables the browsing, discovery, and visualization of the repository of obligations as well as the evidence repository. Additionally, it provides the development environment for business control management. Besides the connection to commercial reporting and portal systems (e.g. IBM Cognos Now! Monitor), our prototypical implementation provides a web based front-end which can be adjusted to the needs of different user groups.

The **Chief Compliance Officer**'s focuses on the obligations, line-of-business processes, and organizational structure. Thus he uses the interface to browse the repository of obligations, to manipulate the content and relations of the respective documents as well as to investigate the dependencies between those artifacts. Due to our integrated approach he will also be able to inspect the deployment process of business controls and to view the aggregated compliance status for entire obligations, business units or line-of-business processes.

The **Process Owner** is responsible for establishing and maintaining control points. Thus primary focus lies on creating / editing the control point description. The ability to browse higher level documents and process to system mappings supports his tasks significantly. To investigate the effectiveness of control points, the process owner uses the aggregated compliance dashboard. Additionally, he has also access to individual instances the evidence repository and can investigate the root cause of occurred violations as well as suspicious behavioral patterns.

The **IT Architect** takes over from the process owner to define the operational provenance model for each control point description. Basically, his task is bridge the gap between business level concepts and observable system level data. Hence he requires a modeling environment that lets him import or synthesize schemata from the affected systems as input, and which allows simulate the rule execution on sample data to test the control point model and to document the testing. Because this is a crucial part of business control management, our current research efforts focus on the functional extension of the existing prototype.

The **Auditor** primary consumes data. He uses an interface that has been configured automatically by the provenance model to navigate the evidence, to sample control points, and to investigate the end-to-end business operations. Additionally, he has the ability to annotate data with his findings and to inspect the business control development process.

5   Report Compliance

The final phase in our business control management approach is the compliance reporting. The provenance store query layer builds the foundation for reporting, regardless whether aggregated compliance data is visualized in a dashboard or individual control point reports are generate. As shown in figure 6, the provenance store holds persisted system events that have been correlated to form higher level concepts and that are liked to the original content if needed via the content service.

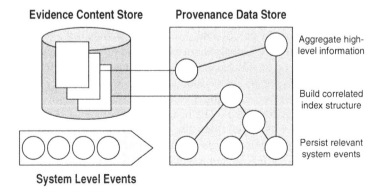

Fig. 6. Data for Auditing and Reporting

5.1 Query Layer

The task of the query layer is to provide a method by which compliance applications can interrogate the provenance store about existing linkages, recover evidence relating to a particular control violation from the evidence store and finally gain access to actual content repositories where relevant artifacts are stored.

The query layer, as in the case of the recording layer, provides a web service-based API for this purpose. Queries are similar in expressive power to SQL queries, but have a few crucial differences as far as syntax and semantics are concerned. The queries into the provenance store essentially describe a template for a pattern in the provenance graph, i.e. they describe nodes and relations between nodes, with constraints on the characteristics of the nodes and relationships. They are thus closely tied to the provenance data model and idea of concepts linked via references. For example, to query KCP 3 control instances that where found defective, the compliance application would issue a query looking for concepts of type KCP 3, where the *status* was false. To then look up the evidence for a particular case, the application would issue a query to look for concepts of type Order Document and Email connected to that particular control point instance in the graph via references. The provenance graph also transparently uses the Content Service described earlier to provide access to the actual artifacts when requested.

5.2 Compliance Dashboard

The provenance store, which keeps track of the compliance status of the control points in near real time, reports this status to a compliance dashboard. This dashboard is one of many possible compliance applications, but is the most useful one, since it is a useful tool to provide the requisite oversight that is currently lacking in many LOB processes. From the compliance status, through the linkages maintained in the provenance store, it is possible to navigate to the evidence that backs up the reported status, and go from the evidence repository to the actual data repositories themselves. This dashboard provides different views for different user roles: a process-oriented view for process owners, a summary view for compliance officers etc. Since people involved in the processes are also linked within the provenance graph, it is possible to navigate in a resource-centric manner as well, enabling, for example, auditors to investigate actions of a particular employee as relates to the process. Going back to our earlier example, it would be possible through the provenance store to establish that a particular customer is repeatedly involved in suspicious order activity. Besides allowing for the discovery of this pattern, the provenance provides the evidence to detect the build a legal case against the customer if necessary.

We have also adapted process mining algorithms to execute on provenance traces as opposed to business process traces. The resulting mined process is a useful way to provide process owners with a view into the actual statistical process executed, as opposed to the one that is modeled. Large deviations from *normal* patterns can also be detected and highlighted for investigation. Other applications, such as leveraging the control information stored in the provenance store for mining in a business intelligence tool are also possible.

6 Summary and Outlook

The Business Control Management approach outlined in this paper is the outcome of an obvious need for enterprises which have complex line of business processes subject to regulatory control, as well as the experience of the authors' actual client engagements. Building on an established but simplistic notion of business controls that exist today, we have described a methodology to extend this definition so that we can reach into the underlying process implementations and IT systems to enable continuous compliance monitoring. A cornerstone of our solution is the use of a provenance store. This is employed to link static artifacts (such as obligations and process descriptions) and dynamic artifacts (such as data produced during the execution of the process), as well as to use rules and other analytics to surface higher-level concepts from low-level system events, on the basis of which controls can be defined and tested. We have successfully used the described methodology and system internally within IBM and are in the process of doing so with other customers.

There are a number of research challenges that will need further investigation as we continue this effort: The first concerns scalability. We described in section 4.2 that the provenance store maintains only correlated metadata, and uses a *Content Service* to link to an external repository where the actual artifacts reside. Even given this separation, scalability issues may arise when dealing with processes that run extremely frequently and produce large amounts of data. We have not encountered such problems so far since most of the processes we have tackled have at least a few manual procedures and are thus more tractable, but this is certainly a concern. The manner in which provenance data is added by the recording layer, the representation of that data and query mechanism have all been designed to deal with scalability, but we lack sufficient real-world tests of the limits.

The second challenge concerns how we deal with imperfect data. Correlation of data to a particular instance or with other data may certainly be imperfect, especially when dealing with unstructured data sources. Currently we design and test analytical components that classify and correlate such unstructured data well, but we do not have any mechanisms in place to deal with conflicting information or uncertain conclusions about compliance status.

Thirdly, our solution provides security at various layers: the recording layer accesses required data and stores only relevant information in a particular provenance store. Rules execute within a controlled environment within the provenance system. Applications such as compliance dashboards use their own security mechanisms to restrict user access to the dashboard; furthermore access to the evidence repository by the dashboard can also be restricted. However our security is based on a simple role-based access control mechanism. Given the sensitive nature of the information accessible, we would need to provide not only more fine grained security but also strong privacy guarantees. Some of these are mandated by regulations. We fall short of addressing them at this point but plan to do so in the future.

Finally, we aim to have a system useable by compliance officers and process owners, as well as one where SOA IT architects can map control point concepts to IT artifacts produced by applications. The need for user-friendly tools is always important, but magnified for Business Control Management since the user community is so diverse. In the process of developing our solution, we have used a combination of off-the-shelf components like dashboards along with custom development environments to describe and map controls. We are currently working with user groups to determine our future efforts in this direction.

References

1. Curbera, F., Doganata, Y., Martens, A., Mukhi, N., Slominski, A.: Business Provenance - A Technology to Increase Traceability of End-to-End Operations. In: Proceedings of Coopis 2008. LNCS, vol. 5331. Springer, Heidelberg (2008)
2. Committee of Sponsoring Organizations of the Treadway Commission:Enterprise Risk Management – Integrated Framework (2004), http://www.coso.org
3. Agrawal, R., Johnson, C., Kiernan, J., Leymann, F.: Taming Compliance with Sarbanes-Oxley Internal Controls Using Database Technology. In: Proceedings of the 22nd Conference on Data Engineering, ICDE. IEEE Computer Society, Washington, DC (2006)
4. Christopher, G., Müller, S., Pfitzmann, B.: From Regulatory Policies to Event Monitoring Rules: Towards Model-Driven Compliance Automation. IBM Research Report RZ 3662, IBM Zurich Research Laboratory (2006)
5. Lu, R., Sadiq, S., Governatori, G.: Compliance Aware Business Process Design. In: ter Hofstede, A.H.M., Benatallah, B., Paik, H.-Y. (eds.) BPM Workshops 2007. LNCS, vol. 4928, pp. 120–131. Springer, Heidelberg (2008)
6. Goedertier, S., Vanthienen, J.: Designing Compliant Business Processes with Obligations and Permissions. In: Eder, J., Dustdar, S. (eds.) BPM Workshops 2006. LNCS, vol. 4103, pp. 5–14. Springer, Heidelberg (2006)
7. Governatori, G., Milosevic, Z., Sadiq, S.: Compliance checking between business processes and business contracts. In: Proceedings of the 10th IEEE Conference on Enterprise Distributed Object Computing, EDOC. IEEE Computer Society, Washington, DC (2006)
8. Namiri, K., Stojanovic, N.: A Formal Approach for Internal Controls Compliance in Business Processes. In: Proceedings of 8th Workshop on Business Process Modeling, Development, and Support (BPMDS 2007), Trondheim, Norway (2007)
9. Verver, J.: Building and Implementing a Continuous Controls Monitoring and Auditing Framework, ACL Services Ltd. (2005)
10. Brown, R.L.: The SOA road to sustainable risk and control management. IBM White Paper (January 2007), ftp://ftp.software.ibm.com/software/lotus/lotusweb/sox/TheSOARoadtoSustainableRiskandControlManagementJan2007.pdf
11. Ferrucci, D., Lally, A.: Building an example application with the Unstructured Information Management Architecture. IBM Systems Journal 43(3), 455–475 (2004)

Workshop Organization

Workshop Organizers

Rainer von Ammon
Centrum fürInformations-Technologie
Transfer GmbH
Konrad-Adenauer-Allee 30
93051 Regensburg
Germany

NenadStojanovic
FZI ForschungszentrumInformatik
Haid-und-Neu-Str. 10-14
76131 Karlsruhe
Germany

OpherEtzion
IBM R&D Labs in Israel
Haifa University Campus
Mount Carmel
Haifa, 31905
Israel

Adrian Paschke
Free University Berlin
Königin-Luise-Straße 24/26
14195 Berlin
Germany

Program Committee

Rama Akkiraju
AlexandreAlves
Pedro Bizarro
SchahramDustdar
DimkaKarastoyanova
Agnes Koschmider
Jim Laredo
Mack Mackenzie
Prabir Nandi
Marco Seiriö
Guy Sharon
Jan Vanthienen

Online Monitoring and Control of Enterprise Processes in Manufacturing Based on an Event-Driven Architecture

Manfred Grauer, Sachin Karadgi, Daniel Metz, and Walter Schäfer

University of Siegen, Information Systems Institute, Hoelderlinstr. 3,
57068 Siegen, Germany
{grauer,karadgi,metz,jonas}@fb5.uni-siegen.de

Abstract. Manufacturing enterprises strive for improvements in their monitoring and control of enterprise processes (i.e., business and manufacturing processes) with intention to sustain competitive advantages, and achieve higher degree of flexibility and adaptability of enterprise processes. Hence in the current contribution, a framework based on event driven architecture is elaborated which can be employed to realize enterprise integration, and enhance online monitoring and control of enterprise processes. A process model is been presented that assists the introduction, configuration and implementation of the envisaged framework. The framework is composed of following components: data collection engine, data aggregation engine, process database, complex event processing engine, and process visualization clients. Finally, the framework has been validated in an industrial scenario.

Keywords: event-driven architecture, enterprise integration, online monitoring and control, complex event processing.

1 Introduction

In recent years, the pressure on enterprise to manufacture products with high quality reduced lead times and low cost has been intensified. Also, an enterprise's environment has become complex, volatile and mainly driven by uncertainties. Hence, aforementioned challenges are further compounded with events occurring during execution of enterprise processes (i.e., business and manufacturing processes) like cancellation of an order, resource breakdown, and non-adherence to part specifications. As a consequence, online monitoring and control of enterprise processes has gained significant attention [1]. Online (re)actions to events of an enterprise are essential to remain competitive, and enhance flexibility and adaptability of enterprise processes [2].

The vertical integration of business and manufacturing processes located at different enterprise levels can be seen as a prerequisite for establishment of online monitoring and control of enterprise processes [3] and the vision of a real-time enterprise (RTE) [4]. According to VDI 5600 standard [5], an enterprise can be classified into different manufacturing execution system (MES) levels as depicted in Fig. 1: (i) enterprise control level, (ii) manufacturing control level, and (iii) manufacturing level.

M. zur Muehlen and J. Su (Eds.): BPM 2010 Workshops, LNBIP 66, pp. 671–682, 2011.
© Springer-Verlag Berlin Heidelberg 2011

At enterprise control level, business processes are performed to achieve the enterprise's long term strategies. Thus, business processes can be designed, configured, enacted, and analyzed applying four steps of a business process management (BPM) life cycle [6], [7]: (i) business process design, (ii) business process configuration, (iii) business process enactment, and (iv) business process diagnosis. Process-aware information systems (PAIS) like workflow management systems (WMS) are in charge to invoke business applications (e.g., ERP systems) and (web) services along the workflow execution (i.e., automation of a business process) to fulfill certain business strategic objectives [6], [7]. During business process execution, planned performance values (i.e., TO-BE values) are generated offline i.e., in month or weeks and these values are transactional [8].

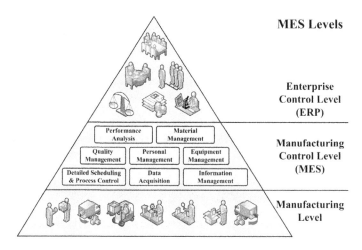

Fig. 1. Enterprise levels as defined in MES (according to VDI 5600 [5])

Automation systems and operators are employed to accomplish the aforesaid enterprise's strategic objectives at manufacturing level. Enormous amount of data (e.g., sensor data) is generated in seconds or even milliseconds by automation systems during execution of manufacturing processes. Also, operators provide necessary data related to automation systems after resource breakdown, order details during start of order execution, and so forth. Overall, these data (i.e., AS-IS values) indicate the actual performance of the manufacturing processes.

Consequently, online monitoring and control of enterprise processes has to be based on a comprehensive view of an enterprise, which can be revealed by the actual situation at each of the enterprise levels (i.e., MES levels). Unfortunately, different characteristics of the previously elaborated enterprise levels result in a vertical integration gap [9]. Hence, attempts are being made to integrate enterprise levels based on ISO 15704 [10]. Several software vendors have developed MES solutions to bridge the gap between different enterprise levels (e.g., [9]). Nevertheless, major problems remain open with respect to the interfaces between the enterprise control level and manufacturing level [9], [11]. Today, enterprise integration (EI) is still an elusive goal and in most enterprises, it is not addressed or inadequately achieved [12].

Besides the aforesaid challenges of EI, events are simultaneously triggered during execution of enterprise processes at different enterprise levels. These events denote insufficient resource capacity, and breakdown of resources, among others. In addition, events can be related (e.g., logical, temporal and causal), and hence, complex events can be created [13]. The information related to the events can be stored in process database for offline analysis. Unfortunately, these events are not considered for online monitoring and control of enterprise processes. Overall due to the lack of an integrated enterprise and unhandled events, online monitoring and control of enterprise processes is perceived as a complex task.

In the current contribution, a framework based on an event-driven architecture (EDA) is envisaged to integrate aforementioned enterprise levels, and to enable the online monitoring and control of enterprise processes. This framework incorporates various industrial standards, employs publish-subscribe and request-reply mechanisms for integrating heterogeneous data, and capitalizes on an available state-of-the-art complex event processing (CEP) engine for processing simple and complex events. The remainder of the contribution is organized as follows. Section 2 presents related work regarding EI, EDA and CEP. The envisaged framework is elaborated in Section 3. Validation of the framework is presented in Section 4 using an industrial case study. Finally, conclusions and future work are discussed in Section 5.

2   Related Work

EI comprises reference architectures and models, engineering methodologies, enterprise modeling languages, and tools [10]. Enterprise reference architecture provides different abstract views of an enterprise, specifies modeling approaches and defines life cycle phases of enterprise activities [14], [15]. Therefore, several enterprise reference architectures have been developed to close the vertical integration gap conceptually, and provide guidance for design and implementation of an integrated enterprise. However, they do not mention on how to realize the integration in terms of technologies. Numerous architectures have been reviewed from business [16], [17] and engineering perspective [18]. Apart from enterprise reference architectures, several software vendors have developed MES solutions to bridge the vertical integration gap between enterprise levels [19]. But also with MES, the exchange of data between enterprise levels is done manually or at most semi-automatically due to inflexible and proprietary interfaces [9], [11].

An agent-based production monitoring and control (PMC) system named Provis.Agent has been presented [20]. This system is based on JADE framework [21] and integrates various IT-systems and automation systems. Data from manufacturing level can be visualized in visualization clients. Similarly, IT-framework for EI and control of manufacturing processes has been proposed [1]. This IT-framework capitalizes various protocols (e.g., Modbus, OPC) to integrate heterogeneous automation systems and business applications. Online control of manufacturing processes is performed using a rule-based system (RBS) that is employed on traceable objects [2]. Traceable objects are control-relevant entities of an enterprise process like orders, parts or resources. In addition, traceable objects comprise AS-IS and TO-BE values, and are instantiated simultaneously with a workflow instance conducted in a

WMS. On every change of traceable objects' status, the RBS analyses these objects and dispatches control data to influence the manufacturing processes.

In recent years, web service technology as a mean for implementing service-oriented architectures (SOA) has become a de facto standard for enterprise application integration (EAI) [22]. Subsequently, web services have been used for horizontal integration of an enterprise [22]. (Web) Services can be loosely coupled and orchestrated to complex workflows using WMS. Also, an enterprise service bus (ESB) can be employed to realize an integrated enterprise based on an SOA [23]. IT-architectures built on web service technology tend to be flexible and adaptable. Due to these benefits, European-funded projects SIRENA [24] and SOCRADES [25] aim to exploit aforementioned SOA paradigm to seamlessly integrate heterogeneous resources located at manufacturing level with business applications at enterprise control level. In this regard, a prototype for vertical integration of SOA-ready devices with SAP MII has been presented [26].

Apart from request-reply communication pattern of SOA, numerous events are raised during enterprise process execution and hence, necessitate the implementation of publish-subscribe mechanisms for online monitoring and control of enterprise processes. None of the aforementioned frameworks uses CEP for online monitoring and control of enterprise processes. Also, the usage of RBS like Drools Expert [27] implicates the lack of taking temporal and causal relations between events into account. In addition, it is remarkable that only a few WMS support the collection and interpretation of real-time data [6], [7]. Current BPM approaches to add dynamics and flexibility to enterprise processes still contain lack of transparency with respect to actual process execution on functional level [28]. Apart from the aforementioned SOA paradigm, an EDA is "an architectural style in which some of the components are event driven and communicate by means of events" [29]. However, EDA doesn't make SOA obsolete as SOA and event processing are complementary concepts for achieving modularity, loose-coupling, and flexibility [30]. In addition, business activity monitoring (BAM) has been introduced as a concept to establish real-time access to key performance indicators (KPIs) for improving of business processes [31].

To overcome the aforementioned drawbacks, an open source framework for online monitoring and analysis of manufacturing processes has been presented [32]. This framework includes data delivery, data collection, and data analysis. Data delivery from different automation systems is achieved through a data bus called MTConnect. The acquired data is stored in databases using functionality of data collection. Data analysis can be done online utilizing RBS Drools Fusion [33] or EsperTech CEP engine [34]. In addition, offline data analysis is performed to calculate various (performance) metrics like KPIs.

To deal with primitive and complex events for monitoring and control of manufacturing processes, unified event management architecture has been conceptualized [13]. This architecture is located at manufacturing control level and integrates real-time data from manufacturing level but does not consider transactional data from enterprise control level. Finally, architecture for an extensible event driven manufacturing system has been elaborated and built on an MES platform [35]. It realizes a tight integration between enterprise control level and manufacturing level, and utilizes a CEP engine to manage events triggered at manufacturing level.

3 Enterprise Integration, and Online Monitoring and Control of Enterprise Processes

A framework based on EDA for realizing EI, and subsequently enhancing online monitoring and control of enterprise processes is been elaborated in following sub-sections. A process model is been presented in Section 3.1 that assists the introduction, configuration and implementation of the envisaged framework. The presentation of the framework in Section 3.2 comprises the description of several components required for enabling EI, and enhancing online monitoring and control of enterprise processes: data collection engine, data aggregation engine, process database, complex event processing engine, and process visualization clients.

3.1 Process Model towards Online Monitoring and Control of Enterprise Processes

An overview of the process model towards the realization of online monitoring and control of enterprise processes has been depicted in Fig. 2, according to [36]. Prior to the implementation of the framework for EI, and online monitoring and control of enterprise processes, it is essential to analyze and (re-)design the processes as it is in the case of BPM life cycle [6], [7] (s. Step I in Fig. 2). An enterprise data model based on industrial standards like IEC 62264 [37] is in charge of relating AS-IS and TO-BE values from different enterprise levels (s. Step II in Fig. 2). Also, data flow diagrams (DFDs) can be created to reveal the interdependencies of automation systems and their events at various enterprise levels.

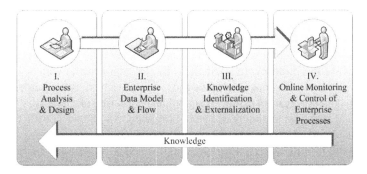

Fig. 2. Process model towards the realization of EI, and online monitoring and control of enterprise processes (according to [36])

Knowledge for online control of enterprise processes is embedded in process data (e.g., pressure, temperature) generated before and during execution of these processes i.e., TO-BE and AS-IS values [36]. This process data is mapped onto the aforementioned enterprise data model and stored in a process database. Subsequently, offline knowledge discovery in databases (KDD) can be employed on data stored in the process database to externalize knowledge (s. Step III in Fig. 2). Applying repeated and time-consuming database queries executed on the integrated database are not useful for online control of enterprise processes [38]. Instead, event streams created during process execution need to be analyzed and processed online using a CEP engine (s Step IV in Fig. 2). Here, the externalized knowledge can be codified as event processing statements, and used for analyzing event streams during online control of enterprise processes.

The presented process model is a prerequisite for the implementation of the envisaged framework which will be elaborated in the subsequent subsection. The presentation of the framework puts emphasis on EI and CEP for online monitoring and control of enterprise processes.

3.2 Framework Based on Event Driven Architecture for Online Monitoring and Control of Enterprise Processes

An overview on the framework based on EDA for EI, and online monitoring and control of enterprise processes is depicted in Fig. 3. At the bottom, representations of enterprise process instances are shown (see Logical Process Layer in Fig. 3). At a certain time, different enterprise processes would have been instantiated to achieve enterprise's strategic objectives set at enterprise control level. The instances of enterprise processes are composed of process steps which utilize automation systems and operators to fulfill assigned tasks (e.g., molding, melting material, pouring of molten material). If required, enterprise processes can be (re-)designed and configured using methods and techniques from BPM (s. Step I in Fig. 2). In addition, the enterprise processes can be coordinated by a WMS and linked with graphical user interfaces to incorporate human interactions.

The framework comprises several components required for enabling EI, and enhancing online monitoring and control of enterprise processes: data collection engine, data aggregation engine, process database, complex event processing engine, and process visualization clients. The data collection engine has been designed to acquire data from different automation systems in real-time. As a consequence, it incorporates various protocols (e.g., Siemens S7) to communicate with heterogeneous automation systems. The acquired data (i.e., AS-IS values) is forwarded as event streams to a data aggregation engine using publish-subscribe mechanism.

The data aggregation engine is in charge of relating AS-IS and TO-BE values from different enterprise levels. Besides processing AS-IS values, it encompasses interfaces to business applications (e.g., ERP system) located at enterprise control level to access TO-BE values. The interfaces to business applications can be implemented as a set of (wrapper) services which encapsulate certain business functionalities. The AS-IS and TO-BE values are stored in a process database for genealogy and product tracking, and offline KDD process, among others. It is crucial that configuration of data aggregation engine and process database has to be done in accordance with the enterprise data model. Further, it has to respect the revealed interdependencies between automation systems (s. Step II in Fig. 2).

Event streams composed of AS-IS and TO-BE values can be compared at manufacturing control level for online monitoring and control of enterprise processes. This can be achieved using CEP engine which constantly analyzes event streams, and subsequently dispatches control data to achieve the enterprise's strategic objectives concerning production, maintenance, quality and inventory [37]. CEP can be defined as "computing that performs operations on complex events, including reading, creating, transforming or abstracting them" [29], [39].

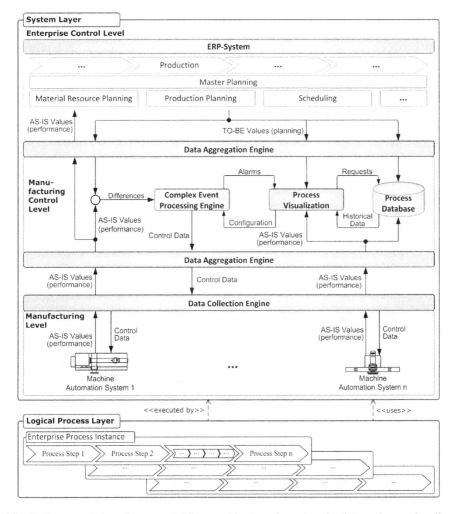

Fig. 3. Framework based on event-driven architecture for enterprise integration, and online monitoring and control of enterprise processes

Events can be classified as simple or composite events based upon the level of abstraction. Usually, a simple event does not provide sufficient information for online monitoring and control of enterprise processes [13]. In contrary, a composite event with high abstraction can be described with an event pattern based on simple events. Further, higher abstraction events can be derived from composite events. In summary, a composite event can be defined as a "complex event that is created by combining base events using a specific set of event constructors such as disjunction, conjunction, sequence, etc" [29]. Using publish-subscribe mechanism implemented in the data aggregation engine, events are forwarded immediately to the CEP engine after their occurrence for processing using event processing statements.

Event processing statements expressed by an event processing language (EPL) are used within the CEP engine to analyze logical, temporal, or causal event patterns. These event processing statements define how the CEP engine reacts to the occurrence of a certain event pattern. Identified externalized knowledge as depicted in Step III in Fig. 2 can be modeled as event processing statements. An example of an EPL statement using logical and temporal event patterns is depicted in Fig. 4. There are two implementations on how the CEP engine controls the actual enterprise processes. First, the CEP engine uses interfaces and services provided by the data aggregation engine to automatically dispatch control commands to the automation systems. Second, before manipulating enterprise processes, CEP engine exposes envisaged decision as a suggestion via process visualization client to operators (e.g., worker, manager), who in turn accept or decline the proposition. Obviously, the latter is used in cases where operators should take liability.

```
insert into AlarmEvent
select ProductionRessourceName, ProductionProcessDataName,
ProductionProcessData, 'Pressure is too high' as AlarmMessage from
ProcessDataEvent(ProductionRessourceName='MOLDING_1' and
ProductionProcessDataName='Pressure').win:length(2) having
avg(cast(ProductionProcessData, double)) > cast(22.5, double)
```

Fig. 4. Event pattern codified as an EPL statement in EsperTech CEP engine

Process visualization clients are employed to visualize alarms derived by the CEP engine. In addition, the AS-IS and TO-BE values delivered by the data aggregation engine using publish-subscribe mechanism can be visualized online using visual elements like charts and gauges. Process visualization clients also provide interfaces to domain experts to configure the behavior of the CEP engine by defining and modifying EPL statements. Finally, historical data can be requested from the process database for genealogy and product tracking, among others.

4   Industrial Case Study

The envisaged framework based on EDA for enabling EI, and online monitoring and control of enterprise processes elaborated in Section 3 can be put into practice in different types of manufacturing, especially in batch manufacturing (e.g., casting processes) and discrete manufacturing (e.g., sheet metal forming processes). Here, an attempt is made to realize the framework for casting processes. The enterprise in consideration has special purpose machines with a high production rate (e.g., molding machine can produce approximately 250 molds per hour). To efficiently utilize capital intensive resources, online monitoring and control of enterprise processes is mandatory.

The process model described in Section 3.1 assists in realizing online monitoring and control of enterprise processes. Therefore, enterprise processes have been analyzed and modeled using ARIS (utilizing Event-driven Process Chains (EPCs) and Entity Relationship Models) [40]. IEC 62264-2 [37] and DIN 61512-2 [41] have been adapted to create an enterprise data model. In addition, DFDs are created to reveal interdependencies, and dynamic behavior between various automation and business systems.

The envisaged framework has been implemented using Microsoft™ Visual Studio IDE and .NET framework 3.5. Different screenshots of the implemented event driven software, stacked one over other, are displayed in Fig. 5. The data collection engine implements various standard and proprietary protocols, collects process data (i.e., AS-IS values) from different sources (e.g., INAT OPC server [42], raw TCP sockets, flat files) and forwards these process data to the subscribed data aggregation engine. Therefore, the data collection engine provides a windows communication foundation (WCF) interface for subscribing to process data. At the data aggregation engine, delivered process data is managed in numerous ways.

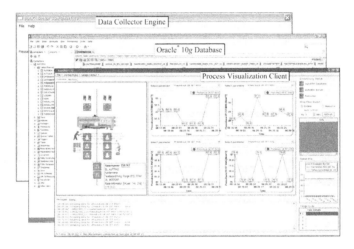

Fig. 5. Screenshots of the implemented event-driven software for enterprise integration, and online monitoring and control of enterprise processes

First, the process data (i.e., event stream) is forwarded immediately to be processed in EsperTech CEP engine [34] for online control of enterprise processes, especially with the objective to enhance productivity and reduce wastage of raw material due to rejects (e.g., sand, molten material). For instance, an event can be defined for control of manufacturing required quantity of molds. An alarm can be raised if the quantity of accepted molds is less than the required quantity of molds, leading to an action not to start the execution of next scheduled order. The created alarm is displayed online in a process visualization client.

Second, process data along with corresponding TO-BE values from an ERP system are mapped onto the enterprise data model and stored in an Oracle® 10g database for offline process analysis. The process visualization clients provide an interface to configure the CEP engine and supervise alarms. Also, a process visualization client provides interfaces to track parts, orders and resources using request-reply mechanism (i.e., accessing historical process data). Finally, process data is delivered to all subscribed process visualization clients for online monitoring of enterprise processes and subscription to process data is provided through WCF interface. Delivered process data is displayed online by the process visualization client using different types of visual elements like charts and gauges.

5 Conclusions and Future Work

Today's enterprise environment is complex, volatile and driven by uncertainties, forcing enterprises to become more flexible and adaptable. Consequently, enterprises endeavor to overcome the aforesaid challenges by enhancing the online monitoring and control of their enterprise processes. In the current contribution, a framework based on an EDA is presented to enhance online monitoring and control of enterprise processes.

A process model has been described which assists in realizing online monitoring and control of enterprise processes. Before implementation, enterprise processes need to be analyzed and modeled and if necessary, the processes need to be (re-)designed. Various available standards (e.g., IEC 62264-2 [37]) should be considered to build enterprise data model which guides in mapping data from different enterprise levels. In addition, DFDs can be created to reveal interdependencies, and dynamic behavior between various automation and business systems.

The objective of the envisaged framework is two-fold. First, integration of various enterprise levels which is a prerequisite for online monitoring and control of enterprise processes. Second, the establishment of online monitoring and control of enterprise processes based on the integrated enterprise. Different standard and proprietary protocols for acquiring process data from various automation systems, located at manufacturing level, have been implemented in a data collection engine. The acquired process data is delivered to a data aggregation engine at manufacturing control level. This engine preprocesses the process data and stores it along with business data from enterprise control level in a process database for offline KDD process, and product tracking and genealogy, among others. Simultaneously, process data (i.e., event streams) are made available to a CEP engine for online control of enterprise processes. Finally, process visualization clients subscribe to process data from data aggregation engine and visualize these values online employing visual elements like charts and gauges. Also, the process visualization clients provide access to historical process data for offline process analysis, and interfaces to configure the CEP engine.

At the moment, the framework has been introduced in an enterprise for online monitoring and control of batch manufacturing (i.e., casting processes). Future implementation is planned for discrete manufacturing processes i.e., for an automotive sheet metal component supplier.

Acknowledgments

We are thankful to our industrial partner Ohm & Häner Metallwerk GmbH & Co. KG, Germany for the opportunity to implement the elaborated methodology and framework in a casting enterprise. Especially, we would like to acknowledge Dr.-Ing. Ludger Ohm and Dr.-Ing. Georg Dieckhues for their valuable comments and support.

References

1. Grauer, M., Metz, D., Karadgi, S.S., Schäfer, W., Reichwald, J.W.: Towards an IT-Framework for Digital Enterprise Integration. In: Huang, G.Q., Mak, K.L., Maropoulos, P.G. (eds.) Proc. of the 6th Int. Conf. on Digital Enterprise Technology. AISC, vol. 66, pp. 1467–1482. Springer, Berlin (2009)
2. Grauer, M., Karadgi, S., Metz, D., Schäfer, W.: An Approach for Real-Time Control of Enterprise Processes in Manufacturing using a Rule-Based System. In: Proc. of Multikonferenz Wirtschaftsinformatik, pp. 1511–1522 (2010)
3. Lee, J., Siau, K., Hong, S.: Enterprise Integration with ERP and EAI. Communications of the ACM 46(2), 54–60 (2003)
4. Drobik, A., Raskino, M., Flint, D., Austin, T., MacDonald, N., McGee, K.: The Gartner Definition of Real-Time Enterprise, Tech Report, Gartner Inc. (2002)
5. VDI 5600: Manufacturing Execution System (MES) - VDI 5600 Part 1 (2007)
6. van der Aalst, W.M.P., ter Hofstede, A.H.M., Weske, M.: Business Process Management: A Survey. In: van der Aalst, W.M.P., ter Hofstede, A.H.M., Weske, M. (eds.) BPM 2003. LNCS, vol. 2678, pp. 1–12. Springer, Heidelberg (2003)
7. Weske, M., van der Aalst, W.M.P., Verbeek, H.M.W.: Advances in business process management. Data & Knowledge Engineering 50, 1–8 (2004)
8. Kjaer, A.: The Integration of Business and Production Processes. IEEE Control Systems Magazine 23(6), 50–58 (2003)
9. Karnouskos, S., Baecker, O., de Souza, L., Spiess, P.: Integration of SOA-ready Networked Embedded Devices in Enterprise Systems via a Cross-layered Web Service Infrastructure. In: Proc. of 12th IEEE Int. Conf. on Emerging Technology and Factory Automation, pp. 293–300 (2007)
10. ISO 15704: Requirements for Enterprise Reference Architecture and Methodologies, ISO 15704:2000/Amd 1:2005 (2005)
11. Panetto, H., Molina, A.: Enterprise Integration and Interoperability in Manufacturing Systems: Trends and Issues. Computers in Industry 59(7), 641–646 (2008)
12. Lasi, H., Koch, M., Kemper, H.G.: Process transparency as a critical success factor in the industry (in German). Productivity Management (1), 29–31 (2010)
13. Walzer, K., Rode, J., Wünsch, D., Groch, M.: Event-Driven Manufacturing: Unified Management of Primitive and Complex Events for Manufacturing and Control. In: Workshop on Factory Communication Systems (2008)
14. Neaga, E.I., Harding, J.A.: An Enterprise Modelling and Integration Framework Based on Knowledge Discovery and Data Mining. Int. Journal of Production Research 43(6), 1089–1108 (2005)
15. Giachetti, R.E.: A Framework to Review the Information Integration at the Enterprise. Int. Journal of Production Research 42(6), 1147–1166 (2004)
16. Aier, S., Riege, C., Winter, R.: Unternehmensarchitektur - Literaturüberblick und Stand der Praxis (in German). Wirtschaftsinformatik 50(4), 292–304 (2008)
17. Schönherr, M.: Enterprise Architecture Frameworks (in German). In: Aier, S., Schönherr, M. (eds.) Enterprise Application Integration - Serviceorientierung und nachhaltige Architekturen, Gito, Berlin. Enterprise Architecture, vol. 2, pp. 3–48 (2004)
18. Chen, A., Vernadat, F.: Standards on Enterprise Integration and Engineering - State of the Art. Int. Journal of Computer Integrated Manufacturing 17(3), 235–253 (2004)
19. Kletti, J. (ed.): Manufacturing Execution System – MES. Springer, Berlin (2007)
20. Sauer, O., Sutschet, G.: Agent-Based Control. Computing & Control Engineering Journal 17(3), 32–37 (2006)

21. Java Agent Development Framework, http://jade.tilab.com/
22. Linthicum, D.S.: Next Generation Application Integration: from Simple Information to Web Services. Addison-Wesley Professional, Amsterdam (2003)
23. Chappell, D.: Enterprise Service Bus. O'Reilly, CA (2005)
24. Bohn, H., Bobek, A., Golatowski, F.: SIRENA - Service Infrastructure for Real-Time Embedded Networked Devices: A Service Oriented Framework for Different Domains. In: Int. Conf. on Mobile Communication and Learning Technology (2006)
25. de Souza, L.M.S., Spiess, P., Guinard, D., Köhler, M., Karnouskos, S., Savio, D.: SOCRADES: A Web Service Based Shop Floor Integration Infrastructure. In: Floerkemeier, C., Langheinrich, M., Fleisch, E., Mattern, F., Sarma, S. (eds.) Internet of Things. Springer, Berlin (2008)
26. Karnouskos, S., Guinard, D., Savio, D., Spiess, P., Baecker, O., Trifa, V., de Souza, L.: Towards the Real-Time Enterprise: Service-Based Integration of Heterogeneous SOA-Ready Industrial Devices with Enterprise Applications. In: Proc. of the 13th IFAC Symposium on Information Control Problems in Manufacturing (INCOM 2009), pp. 2127–2132 (2009)
27. Drools Expert, http://www.jboss.org/drools/
28. Schmidt, B., Schief, M.: Towards Agile Business Processes Based on the Internet of Things. In: Dangelmaier, W., Blecken, A., Delius, R., Klöpfer, S. (eds.) IHNS 2010. LNBIP, vol. 46, pp. 257–262. Springer, Heidelberg (2010)
29. Luckham, D., Schulte, R. (eds.): Event Processing Glossary - Version 1.1, Event Processing Technical Society (2008)
30. Yuan, S.T., Lu, M.R.: A Value-Centric Event Driven Model and Architecture: A Case Study of Adaptive Complement of SOA for Distributed Care Service Delivery. Expert Systems with Applications 36(2), 3671–3694 (2009)
31. McCoy, D., Schulte, R., Buytendijk, F., Rayner, N., Tiedrich, A.: Business Activity Monitoring: The Promise and Reality. Gartner, Gartner's Marketing Knowledge and Technology Commentary COM-13-9992 (2001)
32. Vijayaraghavan, A.: MTConnect for Realtime Monitoring and Analysis of Manufacturing Enterprises (2009), http://www.systeminsights.com/
33. Drools Fusion, http://www.jboss.org/drools/
34. EsperTech, http://www.espertech.com/
35. Zhang, Y.H., Dai, Q.Y., Zhong, R.Y.: An Extensible Event-Driven Manufacturing Management with Complex Event Processing Approach. Int. Journal of Control and Automation 2(3), 13–24 (2009)
36. Grauer, M., Metz, D., Karadgi, S.S., Schäfer, W.: Identification and Assimilation of Knowledge for Real-Time Control of Enterprise Processes in Manufacturing. In: Second Int. Conf. on Information, Process, and Knowledge Management (eKNOW 2010), pp. 2213–2216 (2010)
37. IEC 62264. Enterprise-Control System Integration. All Parts
38. Cammert, M., Heinz, C., Krämer, J., Riemenschneider, T., Schwarzkopf, M., Seeger, B., Zeiss, A.: Stream processing in production-to-business software. In: Proc. of the IEEE Int. Conf. on Data Engineering, pp. 168–169 (2006)
39. Walzer, K., Schill, A., Löser, A.: Temporal Constraints for Rule-Based Event Processing. In: Proc. of the ACM first Ph.D. Workshop in CIKM, pp. 93–99 (2007)
40. Scheer, A.: Business Process Engineering. In: Reference Model for Industrial Enterprise. Springer, Berlin (1994)
41. DIN EN 61512-2. Batch Control - Part 2: Data Structures and Guidelines for Languages. Ref. Nr. DIN EN 61512-2:2003-10 (2003)
42. INAT GmbH, http://www.inat.de/

Object-Centered Process Modeling: Principles to Model Data-Intensive Systems

Rui Henriques and António Rito Silva

Center for Organization and Engineering (CODE) – INESC-ID
Instituto Superior Técnico (IST-UTL), Lisboa, Portugal
rui.henriques@inov.pt, rito.silva@inov.pt

Abstract. New modeling approaches appeared in the last decade based on the premise that process structures in data-intensive landscapes are pushed by data-driven events. However, since emergent approaches as *artifact-centered*, *data-driven*, *product-based* and *document-based* modeling cover reduced subsets of all data-related needs, they have a limited practical impact [13]. This work structures the set of requirements to model responsive data-intensive systems, studies the emergent object-centered approaches to retrieve a set of principles and, finally, defines a solution direction, centered in expressive object models and in model transformations, for the support of the introduced principles.

Keywords: process modeling, data-intensive system, object-orientation.

Topics: Concepts: data- and event-driven BPM; Design-time CEP: modeling notations and methods for event-driven BPM. LongPaper category.

1 Introduction

The increasingly uncertain, dynamic and data-intensive landscape where some systems operate triggers challenges to process models *evolution*, either when processes need to be modeled from scratch or, as this work focuses, to organically adapt through local improvements. Since *data-intensive* systems highly depend on their passive participants – system entities subjected to transformation – to prescribe its elements, their evolution is pushed by changes at the data level. Exemplifying, a health-care system that relies on the state and mediation of patients, exams, reports and historicals to deliver a diagnosis, *evolves* by changing the way these passive participants are constrained through process models in order to abstract and prescribe the new desired operation [29].

In traditional approaches, the modelind of processes is independent from the system data, historically hidden behind applications [23], disabling synergies between informational and functional views required for data-intensive scenarios.

Process models can create an environment for the evolution of data-intensive systems if they foster: *integration* by prescribing the relationships among system elements while bridging functional, informational, organizational, technological and contextual views [33], and *adaptability* and *agility* by promoting flexible and data-centered models with changes performed in a timely manner [19].

M. zur Muehlen and J. Su (Eds.): BPM 2010 Workshops, LNBIP 66, pp. 683–694, 2011.

Motivation. Barriers for the evolution of data-intensive process models are pointed in [19][13] and their resolution is particularly important for scientific workflow systems [1], manufacturing systems [22][18], government systems [7] or insurance systems [31]. Common *problems* of traditional approaches include the context-isolated enactment of activities causing data-access challenges and a loss of the process global view, the absence of criteria for the activities granularity and the rigidity required to specify networks of activities when loosely-coupled, dynamic and data-based constraints foster models flexibility and expressivity.

Results from research [6][18] support the fact that a system modeling integrating the data and process perspectives reveals opportunities that disrupt traditional modeling discipline. The natural outcome orientation of many administrative and operational processes [32] turns the progress of single process instances not directly dependent on the execution of activities but reactive on data changes [13]. Contrasting to traditional approaches that force the system modeling into monolithic processes, objects seem promising to model data-based processes as they capture the system operation as a collection of intertwined loosely-coupled life-cycles running at different speeds [29], coping with different levels of granularity [13] and providing a natural basis to derive key performance indicators [6], to become the ground of process users vocabulary [6], to define access levels [9] and to model systems' constraints in usable ways [15].

Since data-intensive processes rely on the premise that relations between the passive participants' components implicitly define sub-process dependencies [13], new ways of dynamically support processes' evolution can be exploited.

Contribution. This work proposes an analysis of the potentialities of emergent object-centered approaches to develop a solution basis of an approach where retrieved lessons coexist to foster the evolution of data-intensive systems.

Although research exist in the scope of process modeling centered on objects [13] and on process evolution [24], since existing approaches were developed to face small and specific sets of concerns [13], their practical applicability coverage and impact is limited [13]. This seems unaccountable in the contemporary era where, for instance, AI systems, several enterprises and many of their subsystems are truly data-intensive systems. This observation fosters the need to re-look to them from scratch in order to understand how potentialities can be combined.

This work systematizes the object-centered universe and it serves as a meta-guider for principles integration on tacit and data-intensive process modeling.

Structure. This work is divided into four logical sections. First, *Conceptual Foundations*, provides a structured context for the universe of discourse. Second, *Related Work*, identifies a specific set of requirements based on the limitations of traditional modeling approaches, and studies how emergent approaches answer them. Third, *Solution Basis*, presents a set of principles that restrict the solution space, derives an initial skeleton for their coexistence and presents some of the taken concretion and implementation directions. Finally, *Concluding Remarks*, presents the resultant theorems and lines of thought for future research.

2   Conceptual Foundation

The Systemic Context. Inserted in the context of increasing data-intensive landscapes, this work adopts the process perspective to introduce new postulates on the modeling of system elements coordination that fosters evolution. Concepts are introduced below to structure the object-centered modeling.

Def.1 A **system** is a tuple $<R, C, E, G>$, where R is the structure, set of relationships among a composition of system elements C and external elements E, that satisfies a purpose G grounded on exchanges with its environment [8].

The system composition, C, is a set of *subsystems* or, from an elementary perspective, a set of participants P. *Participants* can either be *passive* ($P_P \subset P$) if subjected to transformation by a set of system actions, or *active* or agents ($P_A \subset P$) if performing actions aimed at changing passive participants [5].

Def.2 **System evolution** is the process of increasing the system responsiveness to its environment by continually optimizing the efficiency to pursue its purpose under changing conditions. It depends on its ability to behave as an integrated, adaptable and agile system, to timely improve its structure ($R \rightarrow R'$) when internal, external or purposeful changes occur ($\{C, E, G\} \rightarrow \{C, E, G\}'$).

Functional decomposition of a system defines hierarchies of abstractions needed for the modeling of systems operation [33]. *Activities*, units of work, are its nodes. In open ($E \neq \emptyset$) and dynamic or multi-state systems, a system act or an *event* (implying a system action) produces a change to the system state. System activities coherently and consistently relate system acts.

Def.3 A system **process**, $<A_\wp, P_\wp, G_\wp, R_\wp>$, structures a set of system activities ($A_\wp \subseteq A$) performed in a constrained manner ($R_\wp \subseteq R$) based on the coordination of a set of system participants ($P_\wp \subseteq P$) to realize a set of system goals ($G_\wp \subseteq G$). A **process model** is a model for system processes, an abstraction $m(A_\wp, P_\wp, G_\wp, R_\wp)$, which *describes* and *prescribes* the operation of an object system by its interacting systems based on its functional composition.

The Role of Data. Different data taxonomies for process modeling can be found in [34][25]. Weske [33] depicts the role of data within processes according to data visibility, interaction, transfer and support to routing logic. Aalst [30] distinguishes two main types of data: case and non-case. *Case data* is the data used by system applications to support activities. The non-case data can be divided into *support data*, if it affects the process routing logic, and *management data*, if it is produced by the process execution environment (e.g. audit trails). Muehlen [34] does the same distinction under a different analysis.

In fact, this work simplifies this taxonomy into data generated and consumed by processes [34]. The reason behind this simplification – the increasingly blurry boundary between data exposed for process routing decisions and pure application data – lead us, finally, to the notion of data-intensive system.

In data-intensive systems, the data consumed and generated by some of system elements is related with the production of other system elements [34].

Def.4 A **data-intensive system** is a system with a structure R that relates its elements C based on data mediation and transformation. Thus, its operation is constrained by the passive participants state and relations or, more broadly, by the way the system productions to the environment realize the system goals.

For instance, automotive industrial systems rely on the entanglement of data components, the passive participants, to deliver a physical production. Claim-processing systems use claimer's information, regulatory and financial reviews and claim state to audit and deliver a decision.

Def.5 A process within a data-intensive landscape is referred as **data-intensive process**. Scientific research has been focusing on two main types of data-intensive processes: *i)* processes driven by the state of passive participants [6][31] and *ii)* collaborative and tacit processes that use passive participants as record objects to capture the system operation [26].

Research on data-intensive vertents has been adopting different terms as *documents*, *products* and *artifacts*, here all generalized and captured as objects, either simple or compound (encapsulating a set of related objects). Objects, either representing logical or physical elements, can be seen as building blocks that bridge the functional and informational perspectives [6].

Def.6 A system **object** represents any relevant state-based system element, either a simple participant or a composition of system participants. Its state is defined by the object content and it is modified during its life-cycle as the result of an invocation of a set of activities that act upon its data-attributes.

Informational decomposition of a system defines hierarchies of object models.

Modeling Orientation. Process modeling approaches can be divided according to their main focus of modeling: activity-flow, agent-coordination or data-needs focus lead, respectively, to *activity-centered*, *agent-centered* or *object-centered* languages. For instance, agent-centered modeling is the natural choice for processes with strict distribution of responsibilities owned by specialized agents, since activities precedences are implicitly derived from agent-interaction constraints [17]. This work also distinguishes *multi-paradigm* approaches where process models have not a clear orientation [5], and *hybrid* approaches where different approaches co-exist exposing different views for different users.

Since objects are generically used to model simple and compound structures of system participants, the dependencies among activities in object-centered approaches is derived from constraints on these participants state and relations.

Def.7-1 An **object-centered process model** is a process model that uses the knowledge of the participants composition $P_\wp$ to derive the system structure under modeling $R_\wp$. Modeling of participants must be expressive, so changes at the system data models dynamically affect the system process models.

If we recover the system definition, we detect four main perspectives: functional, informational, instrumental and contextual, or, respectively, the activity-based, object-based, agent-based and goal-based views. All these models are integrated by a process model, the governance model, that constrains their interaction to capture and prescribe the operation of a target system.

Fig.1 and Fig.2 depict, respectively, an abstract data-intensive system and the different system modeling views structure.

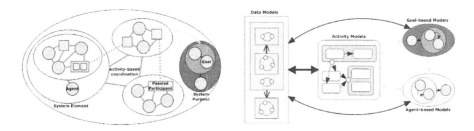

Fig. 1. Abstract data-intensive system   **Fig. 2.** Abstract process model

3   Related Work

In this section research problem is reduced to *five* requirements and emergent approaches are evaluated according to their ability to answer them.

Research Problem. The pushing of passive participants to the processes background as a result of an historical hidden of data behind service and application layers is explained in [33][34]. Seven reasons are pointed in [23]. Nevertheless, our work aims to develop an environment for the integrated management of system data and system activities since their independence in data-intensive landscapes blocks benefits obtained from their coupled evolution.

IBM's *Global Financing* case, a system specialized in financing assets is partially depicted in Fig.3. The process modeling layer was based on a typical activity-centered approach.

A synthesized description of the traditional approaches limitations in supporting the evolution of data-intensive process models is presented in Table 1.

This study led this analysis to a point where the initial problem was breakdown into five pieces. Table 2 structures the five requirements triggered by the limitations of traditional approaches when modeling data-intensive processes.

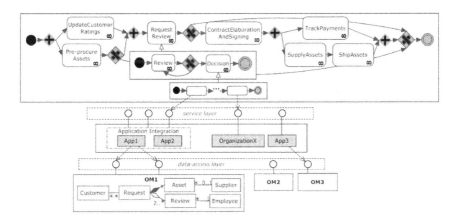

Fig. 3. Traditional Process Modeling Landscape

Table 1. Problems of Traditional Modeling Approaches in Data-Intensive Landscapes

Area of Concern	Problems	*GF* Challenges (Fig.3 upgrades)
Data Access	Process data redundantly created with application data poses consistency problems. Isolated execution of activities cause a loss of process contextual view. Data-access needs to be explicitly specified for every activity, leading to non-usable models. There is no support for an integrated access to old or non-related process data;	Reviews or contract negotiations become: affected by the state of assets procurement (if running in parallel) or other request's reviews, their progress depends on customer's past and similar requests' information, and their contextual data continues accessible without the need to specify all attributes as input parameters for each activity;
Data-state Reaction	Activities have to be related in a net of ordering dependencies, turning difficult a spontaneously repetition of process instances, their stoppage and caught up at a later point in time and a dynamic reaction on data conditions;	Contract negotiation becomes reactively available on a condition satisfaction over reviews' data, independently from executing reviews' progress. Assets and reviews are dynamically instantiated based, respectively, on request and customer's data;
Data-based Synchro.	Process instances (from the same or different process types) are executed in isolation to each other, hampering the support for expressive communication patterns among processes;	Decoupling of process segments in a modular way (e.g. Reviews and Assets). Aggregation of related segments: collective reviewal, collective asset supplying and shipping;
Data-based Granularity	Service layers turn impossible the definition of criteria for the processes granularity since client application activities may reside at different granular levels;	Activities for accessing and changing customer or request attributes (e.g. customer address) must be available, and their composition must follow concrete criteria;
Data Modeling	Since data-centered and activity-centered models are separated by an application layer, modeling of data objects is roughly done at the process modeling level.	A request becomes handled by multiple customers (the process modeling environment detects the change of an association multiplicity on an underlying data model).

Introductory remarks for the understanding of data-awareness requirements can be found in [13][14][20]. Table 2 reviews and structures them under a taxonomy oriented to incremental steps for process models' evolution.

Def.8 An **object-centered system** is, thus, a data-intensive system with a structure R that satisfies the introduced requirements, i.e., a system where its passive participants are visible to every system agent, dynamically affect activities progress and composition, and are adequately accessed and expressively captured at the process modeling level.

State-of-the-Art Analysis. Six mature object-centered approaches were evaluated according to their ability to answer to the introduced *five* requirements. Their selection was based on the practical maturity, data-orientation and novelty of aspects. Table 3 groups these approaches and clarifies their focus.

Results were collapsed in Table 4. We say that an approach *answers* a requirement when satisfies almost of its clauses, *partially answers* a requirement when satisfies at least one of its clauses, and *not answers* a requirement if does not approach it. A brief analysis done in Table 5 supports the presented results.

Data-based multiple instantiation [12], batch-orientation [3], objects and activities connection through procedural links [10], data-based clustering for objects definition [16] or the attachment of operational semantics within objects [6] are some other interesting directions on this field of knowledge.

Discussion reveals that each approach answers in different ways to the introduced requirements. Neither approach satisfies all of them, which may justify

Table 2. Data-related Requirements for Object-centered Approaches

Data Access	Process and application data must be coherently and consistently integrated, meaning that system's activity and data models must be bridged and evolve in a coupled way according to a well-defined set of relations. Process models must avoid data-context tunneling (causing the loss of a broader view on the process) when executing isolated or groups of activities, and additionally must expressively hold data-access contexts from single to multiple activities [31]. Data-scope specification must additionally be usable, seizing benefits of using data models expressivity (e.g. accessing compound or sets of data-objects). Authorized users must access data at any time regardless of the process status [31][14];
Data-state Reaction	Processes must dynamically react on data constraints, turning optional the definition of precedence networks. Since activities are related to objects, they must adapt their behavior (e.g. availability) based on objects' state (horizontal dynamic granularity) [13] and provide a natural method to deduce omission path localization, minimizing sequentiality and, thus, fostering process flexibility;
Data-based Coordination	Processes must use data models constructors to express advanced patterns of synchronization, including: i) the aggregation of multiple related instances to reduce execution effort (e.g. grouping related requests – vertical aggregation) [3], ii) the definition of asynchronous points of coordination to minimize processes coupling (e.g. synchronize the progress of a set of instances responsible for the assets procurement with their related request) [13], and iii) the definition of expressive transition's rule-sets;
Data-based Granularity	Atomicity and composition of activities must be based on the underlying process data [13] to, respectively, safeguard the availability of fine-grained activities and of a criterion to infer compound processes using multiple levels of modeling abstractions;
Data Modeling	There must be possible to model and adapt expressive data models at the process modeling level [13]. Evolution of processes is, thus, fostered by the previous requirements, which assure that execution constraints are dynamically derived from the dependencies of object models in a usable manner, with this one, which enables modeling flexibility.

Table 3. Chosen Object-centered Approaches

Approach		Process constraints driven from...	Belief
Document-based Modeling	[21][2]	documents dependencies (either internal and external)	documents shape and track all the operations of data-intensive systems
Artifact-centric Modeling	[11][4][6]	artifacts' state and life-cycle synchronization (restricting activity models invocation)	artifacts' information models and synchronized states fosters data acess and processes modularity
Product-based Modeling	[22][32]	production components dependencies and quality criteria affecting activity ordering	models for the systems production contain the needed information to affect the process flow
Case Handling	[31][28][33]	data-objects labeled associations and activities precedences	activities of data-intensive cases can be captured and grouped as form-based operations over simple data-objects
Data-driven Coordination	[19][18]	object models' internal transitions and relationship types	dependencies among passive components completely prescribe and support evolution of complex processes
Proclets	[27][29]	interaction of loosely-coupled non-data-container objects' life-cycles	modeling centered on processes communication, instead of ordering emphasis, fosters modeling expressivity

Table 4. Approaches Evaluation [subtitles: + answers; +/- partially answers; - not answers]

Approach	Data Access	Data-state Reaction	Data-based Synchronization	Data-based Granularity	Data Modeling
Document-based Modeling	+/-	+	+/-	–	+/-
Artifact-centric Modeling	–	+	+/-	+/-	+/-
Product-based Modeling	–	–	–	+/-	+/-
Data-driven Coordination	–	–	+	+/-	+/-
Case Handling	+	+	–	–	+/-
Proclets	–	–	+	–	–

Table 5. Brief Review of the Emergent Approaches' Relevant Aspects

Document-based Modeling	It fosters simplicity by modeling constraints recurring to data-dependencies, guides enactement, can support authorized data-access using knowledge-bases and can capture ad-hoc forms of collaboration. However, it limits data modeling to plain structures, it does not support advanced relations among documents, and instances are defined statically;
Artifact-centric Modeling	It is oriented to business needs and execution constraints are automatically driven from artifacts modeling. However, activity data-access is limited to the related artifact, life-cycles synchronization does still not support advanced patterns and, finally, composition of artifacts is not possible;
Product-based Modeling	It is good for process models that periodically require a clean-sheet, uses quality attributes for dynamic path choice. However, data-access is restricted to operations' input components, there must exist an explicit precedence network of operations, and applicability relies on the ability to specify a produc using composition relationships and is limited to productions that can be assembled into a single product;
Data-driven Coordination	It is indicated for large and numerous concurrently executing processes. It adds advanced communication patterns, as the definition of synchronization points among instances (belonging to the same or different process types), based on objects relationship types, and allows for complex structures specification that can guide functional decomposition. However it disregards simplicity, data content (leading to data-reaction and data-access problems) and atomicity of activities;
Case Handling	It is unique in providing a global view of the process to its users, data-access is expressive and users can surpass the activities by accessing any data element for which they have access levels. It allows for horizontal dynamic aggregation and, since it is fully state-based, it is easy to conceptualize. However, processes hierarchies and data object-oriented patterns for synchronization purposes are poorly exploited;
Proclets	It promotes a shift from control to communication emphasis, where processes interact according to an agreed level of reliability, security, closure and formality. It supports multiple messages-exchange patterns and batch-oriented tasks, thus, enabling vertical dynamic aggregation of proclets instances. Although proclets are decoupled process fragments, each fragment can still be considered an activity-centered model, thus, suffering from same data-access and data-state reaction limitations.

their limited real-case applications coverage and impact. However, lessons can be used to retrieve principles to derive a more mature modeling approach.

4 Solution Basis

This section uses the understanding of how emergent approaches answer data requirements to retrieve principles and to define a structure for their coexistence.

Event-orientation. A process is here captured as a set of state-based and synchronized entities objects, activities, goals and time. Exemplifying, a transition between states of an entity A can trigger an event for another transition occurrence in an entity B if B has some sort of dependency with A.

Two *axioms* must be introduced. *First*, process state is a function of time and of its activity, object, and goal models. *Second*, synchronization among entities is defined through event-driven state transitions recurring to rule-set models.

Object models and *activity models* in the modeling landscape of data-intensive systems are integrated by a *process model* (the governance model) that establishes relationships and constrains their interaction through *rule-set models*.

Note that the notion of system applications that frequently intertwined data and process models are in data-intensive landscapes pushed back and here seen as work ow systems' additions to implement non-trivial system rules.

Def.7-2 An **object-centered process model**, $<OM, AM, GM, RM>$, is a model derived from a set state-based object or participant models OM, activity models AM and goal models GM. All of them synchronized through rule-set models RM that constraint the availability to invoke activities based on restrictions or concessions specified for each governed model. Generically can be defined as a pair $<N, E>$, where $N = N_{OM} \cup N_{AM} \cup N_{GM} \cup N_{RM}$, and $E \subseteq NxN$.

Principles. The solution space constraints that support the satisfaction of the introduced requirements are synthesized in Table 6. Note that since, execution constraints for data-intensive processes mainly derive from objects' state and relations, object models adaptation becomes the great source to evolve processes.

Table 6. Principles for the FIVE Requirements

Data Access	*First*, all system data is captured (by modeling either tacit or non-tacit applications and using their trace to feed their objects), standardized (by using a widely-accepted data modeling notation) and accessible (by not hiding data behind applications). *Second*, activity models prescribe objects' data access by specifying labeled associations, both imperative and declarative, at any granular level of activities and of objects. *Third*, related running activities are presented using forms. Forms fields change dynamically since aggregated activity-related attributes can be alternately submitted and may turn new attributes available (soundness criteria must answer form's deadlocks). *Fourth*, there is a default criteria for the automatic definition of the activities' data scope based on the object models. An activity has not only access to its related object or attribute but may access related/internal/super objects and attributes if these associations declare *public* visibility. *Fifth*, authorization is separated from distribution using an object-based structure to manage agents' privilege access levels. Vertical (instance-based) and state-based authorization also define access levels.
Data-state Reaction	*First*, the object-centered models' interplay assures that activities react on objects state in a traceable manner. Even activity's completion, failure or cancellation behaviour is, by omission (although editable), retrieved from related object specification. *Second*, it is possible to specify dependencies of different types (e.g. start-to-start, finish-to-start, start-to-finish, finish-to-finish) among data-attributes or any granular level of objects, which generates expressive dependencies on the functional level and fosters an usable parallelization of attributed-based activities and the ability of process models to evolve through object models adaptation.
Data-based Coord.	*First*, object state transitions may depend and affect other object instances' markings. Communication among objects, always mediated by a third object, is derived from object models to process models and it enables the definition of asynchronous points of synchronization between processes. *Second*, the skeleton for the rule-set models is automatically generated on the basis of their input and output states and of expressive constructors. *Third*, rule-set models placed in objects' state transitions can comprise advanced formulas based on aggregation constructors, data-scope settings, time conditions and executable code additions.
Data-based Granularity	*First*, each compound activity is a composition of fine-grained activities and for each data-field there is an activity that triggers system acts to access and modify its content. *Second*, object model's relations of encapsulation constitute a criterion to derive the processes' composition, enabling zoom operations through different operational levels either by hiding internal life-cycles or by collapsing them into compound states.
Data Modeling	Definition and continuously adaptation of data-intensive system is possible through dynamical creation, edition and removal of objects at the process modeling level by assuring that the derivation of processes from data-structures is performed on-the-fly. Soundness is verified before each modeling change and a coherent migration of the affected object-centered instances applied when changes are sound.

The *process* of modeling data-intensive processes. The modeling of the target process models begins with the objects' specification by enriching the system data models with synchronized life-cycles and data dependencies. Rule-set models are used to specify advanced behaviour. Activity models, partially derived from object models, contain editable functional aspects and data-scope. Process models are dynamically derived from the previously defined models.

Object-centered modeling steps are synthesized by the following algorithm:

1. (Manual) Definition of a data model for the target system using UML;
2. (Automatic) Generation of the object models skeleton;
3. (Manual) Edition of object models to capture the system semantics;
4. (Automatic) Test of object models' soundness. Generation of activity models;
5. (Manual) Definition of additional constraints for activity models;
6. (Automatic) Test of activity models' soundness. Derivation of the object-centered process models net. Generation of default rule-set models;

foreach *true* **do**

    7. (Manual) Adaptation of one of the system object-centered models;
    8. (Automatic) Test of models' soundness. Change of the affected models;

end

Object-centered meta-models, language's constructors, soundness criteria and other relevant aspects will be presented in future publications.

Implementation Aspects. Algorithms were developed for the generation and completion of object and activity models, and to derive simple and compound process models. Object-centered models were formalized and their soundness criteria defined. To assure the execution, advanced verification, instances migration and interoperability of the target models, a mapping to YAWL was defined. As the set of object-centered models can be considered a high-level domain-specific language to lower-level constructs provided by YAWL, syntax specification and model-to-model transformations were defined using ASF+SDF.

Contribution Reviewed. A recently enriched data-centric direction [20] supports most of these principles, although still neglects composition and advanced synchronization patterns. [13] stream of research retrieves a relevant subset of the introduced principles, although does not provide an approach for their support.

Object-centered investigation besides presenting a basis for all principles integration, is unique in presenting a direction for an approach that: *i)* fully derives and adapts process models from enriched data models ([20] still requires the manual definition of activities for the manipulation of system participants), *ii)* defines advanced behavior based on formal rules, *iii)* uses objects data-visibility to formulate new soundness criteria, and *iv)* exploits object-oriented inheritance and encapsulation patterns for an expressive derivation of processes.

5   Conclusions

Activity-centered approaches are limited in modeling data-intensive processes. Such limitations can be translated into a set of requirements that foster the ability to process models evolve in data-intensive landscapes. Emergent object-centered approaches do not successfully satisfy all requirements, which may be correlated with their limited practical applicability and impact. Such approaches provide important principles to satisfy the introduced requirements. More mature object-centered models can benefit from their mutual support.

These principles are not mutually exclusive in an event-driven solution basis centered on expressive object models. The alignment between object and activity models, although preserving the models independence, fosters an evolution of process models centered on object models adaptation. Model-to-model transformations were used to implement the target approach.

Possible lines of though for future research comprise the development of an usable graphical layer on top of the textual models, the continuously systematization and enrichment of rule-set models expressivity, the conception of an hybrid approach for heterogeneous systems where object-centered modeling plays its part, and the attachment of semantics to objects so their composition and constraints can be dynamically derived to satisfy sets of system goals.

Future publications will work on the hypothesis that expressive, sound and executable process models can be derived from object-centered models.

References

1. Abiteboul, S., Segoufin, L., Vianu, V.: Modeling and verifying active xml artifacts. IEEE Data Eng. Bull. 32(3), 10–15 (2009)
2. Abrahams, A., Eyers, D.: Using annotated policy documents as a user interface for process management. In: ICAS 2007. IEEE CS, DC, USA (2007)
3. Barthelmess, P., Wainer, J.: Workflow systems: a few definitions and a few suggestions. In: COCS 1995, pp. 138–147. ACM, New York (1995)
4. Bhattacharya, K., Gerede, C.E., Hull, R., Liu, R., Su, J.: Towards formal analysis of artifact-centric business process models. In: Alonso, G., Dadam, P., Rosemann, M. (eds.) BPM 2007. LNCS, vol. 4714, pp. 288–304. Springer, Heidelberg (2007)
5. Bider, I.: Choosing approach to business process modeling - practical perspective. Journal of Conceptual Modeling (January 2005)
6. Cohn, D., Hull, R.: Business artifacts: A data-centric approach to modeling business operations and processes. IEEE Data Eng. Bull. 32(3), 3–9 (2009)
7. Corradini, F., Polzonetti, A., Pruno, R., Forastieri, L.: Document exchange methodology for collaborative work in e-government. In: DEXA 2006, pp. 283–287. IEEE Computer Society, Washington, DC, USA (2006)
8. Dietz, J.L.G.: Architecture - Building strategy into design. Academic Service, The Hague (2008)
9. Domingos, D., Rito Silva, A., Veiga, P.: Workflow access control from a business perspective. In: ICEIS (3), pp. 18–25 (2004)
10. Dori, D.: Object-process methodology as a bp modelling tool. In: ECIS 2000 (2000)
11. Fritz, C., Hull, R., Su, J.: Automatic construction of simple artifact-based business processes. In: ICDT 2009, pp. 225–238. ACM, New York (2009)
12. Guabtni, A., Charoy, F.: Multiple instantiation in a dynamic workflow environment. In: Advanced Information Systems Engineering, pp. 175–188 (2004)
13. Künzle, V., Reichert, M.: Towards object-aware process management systems: Issues, challenges, benefits. In: Enterprise, BP and IS Modeling. LNBIP, vol. 29, pp. 197–210. Springer, Heidelberg (2008)
14. Künzle, V., Reichert, M.: Integrating users in object-aware process management systems: Issues and challenges. In: Rinderle-Ma, Sadiq, Leymann (eds.) BPM Workshops. Lecture Notes in BIP, vol. 43, pp. 29–41. Springer, Heidelberg (2009)

15. Linehan, M.H.: Ontologies and rules in business models. In: EDOCW 2007, pp. 149–156. IEEE Computer Society, Washington, DC, USA (2007)
16. Liu, R., Bhattacharya, K., Wu, F.Y.: Modeling business contexture and behavior using business artifacts. In: Krogstie, J., Opdahl, A.L., Sindre, G. (eds.) CAiSE 2007 and WES 2007. LNCS, vol. 4495, pp. 324–339. Springer, Heidelberg (2007)
17. Merz, M., Liberman, B., Lamersdorf, W.: Using mobile agents to support interorganizational workflow-management. Int. Journal on Applied AI 11(6) (1997)
18. Müller, D., Reichert, M., Herbst, J.: Data-driven modeling and coordination of large process structures. In: OTM Conferences (1), pp. 131–149 (2007)
19. Müller, D., Reichert, M., Herbst, J.: A new paradigm for the enactment and dynamic adaptation of data-driven process structures. In: Bellahsène, Z., Léonard, M. (eds.) CAiSE 2008. LNCS, vol. 5074, pp. 48–63. Springer, Heidelberg (2008)
20. Nandi, P., König, D., Moser, S., Hull, R., Klicnik, V., Claussen, S., Kloppmann, M., Vergo, J.: Introducing business entities and the business entity definition language. Technical report, IBM (2010)
21. Rahaman, M., Roudier, Y., Schaad, A.: Document-based dynamic workflows: Towards flexible and stateful services. IEEE Congress on Services, 87–94 (2009)
22. Reijers, H.A., Limam, S., van der Aalst, W.M.P.: Product-based workflow design. J. Manage. Inf. Syst. 20(1), 229–262 (2003)
23. Sadiq, W., Schulz, K., Orlowska, M.E., Sadiq, S.: When workflows will not deliver: The case of contradicting work practice. In: Abramowicz, W. (ed.) BIS 2005, pp. 69–84. Wydawnictwo Akademii Ekonomicznej w Poznaniu (2005)
24. Schonenberg, H., Mans, R., Russell, N., Mulyar, N., van der Aalst, W.M.P.: Process flexibility: A survey of contemporary approaches. In: Dietz, J., Albani, A., Barjis, J. (eds.) CIAO! EOMAS. LNBIP, vol. 10, pp. 16–30. Springer, Heidelberg (2008)
25. Truong, H.L., Dustdar, S.: Integrating data for business process management. IEEE Data Eng. Bull. 32(3), 48–53 (2009)
26. van Bussel, G., Ector, F., van der Pijl, G., Ribbers, P.: Building the record keeping system: Process improvement triggered by management of archival documents. In: HICSS 2001, vol. 8, p. 8060. IEEE CSociety, Washington, DC, USA (2001)
27. van der Aalst, W.M.P., Barthelmess, P., Ellis, C., Wainer, J.: Workflow modeling using proclets. In: CoopIS 2002, pp. 198–209. Springer, London (2002)
28. van der Aalst, W.M.P., Berens, P.: Beyond workflow management: product-driven case handling. In: GROUP 2001, pp. 42–51. ACM, NY (2001)
29. van der Aalst, W.M.P., Mans, R.S., Russell, N.C.: Workflow support using proclets: Divide, interact, and conquer. IEEE Data Eng. Bull. 32(3), 16–22 (2009)
30. van der Aalst, W.M.P., van Hee, K.: Workflow Management: Models, Methods, and Systems. MIT Press, Cambridge (2002)
31. van der Aalst, W.M.P., Weske, M., Grünbauer, D.: Case handling: A new paradigm for business process support. Data and Knowledge Eng. 53 (2005)
32. Vanderfeesten, I.T.P., Reijers, H.A., van der Aalst, W.M.P.: Product based workflow support: Dynamic workflow execution. In: Bellahsène, Z., Léonard, M. (eds.) CAiSE 2008. LNCS, vol. 5074, pp. 571–574. Springer, Heidelberg (2008)
33. Weske, M.: Business Process Management: Concepts, Languages, Architectures. Springer-Verlag New York, Inc., Secaucus (2007)
34. Muehlen, M.z.: Volume versus variance: Implications of data-intensive workflows. IEEE Data Eng. Bull. 32(3), 42–47 (2009)

Decentralized Event-Based Orchestration

Pieter Hens[1], Monique Snoeck[1], Manu De Backer[1,2,3,4], and Geert Poels[2]

[1] K.U. Leuven, Dept. of Decision Sciences and Information Management,
Naamsestraat 69, 3000 Leuven, Belgium
[2] Universiteit Gent, Dept. of Management Information and Operations Management,
Tweekerkenstraat 2, 9000 Gent, Belgium
[3] Universiteit Antwerpen, Dept. of Management Information Systems,
Prinsstraat 13, 2000 Antwerpen, Belgium
[4] Hogeschool Gent, Dept. of Management and Informatics,
Kortrijksesteenweg 14, 9000 Gent, Belgium

Summary. Today, in the state of the art process engine solutions, process models are executed by a central orchestrator (i.e. one per process). There are however a lot of drawbacks in using a central coordinator, including a single point of failure and performance degradation. Decentralization algorithms that distribute the workload of the central orchestrator exist, but they still suffer from a tight coupling and therefore decreased scalability. In this paper, we aim to investigate the benefits of using an event driven architecture to support the communication in a decentralized orchestration. This accomplishes space and time decoupling of the process coordinators and hereby creates autonomous fine grained self-serving process engines. Benefits include an increased scalability and availability of the global process flow.

Keywords: Dynamic workflows, Orchestration, Decentralization.

1 Introduction

In the last couple of years, process modeling got a lot of attention from researchers and practitioners. Especially with the arrival of service oriented computing, process modeling became even more important. Starting from atomic services, new aggregate services can be build by combining the atomic services and describing an execution flow between the different entities. This way composite services are created, which can again be used in other compositions. When these compositions are described with a specific executable language (e.g. BPEL4WS [1]), automated enactment using a process engine can be accomplished. The description of the process flow can be interpreted by a process engine, which coordinates and triggers the described work.

In the current situation, the execution of one process or one composite service is typically coordinated by one central entity (Fig. 1a, coordinator C0). This central coordinator gets a request from a client and starts the execution of the workflow described in the composite service (Fig. 1a, tasks T1, T2 and T3). The coordinator chooses between paths in the workflow that need to be followed, does

M. zur Muehlen and J. Su (Eds.): BPM 2010 Workshops, LNBIP 66, pp. 695–706, 2011.

data manipulation and invokes the necessary (atomic or composite) services. The central coordinator contains all the logic necessary to execute a complex service or process. Note that the coordinator only *routes work*, it doesn't perform any actual work itself. The actual work is executed by the triggered services (Fig. 1a, services S1, S2 and S3). This is called CENTRALIZED ORCHESTRATION [2].

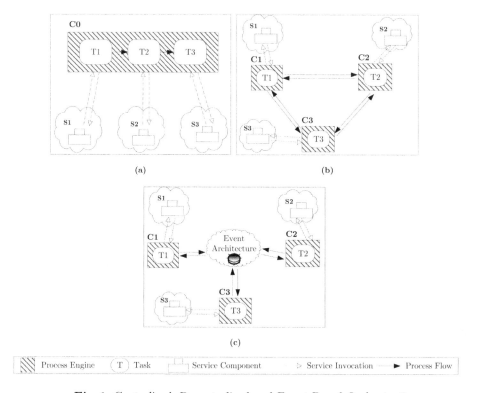

Fig. 1. Centralized, Decentralized and Event-Based Orchestration

The use of a central coordinator per process struggles with a few problems in today's highly decentralized world, and contradicts some of the key aspects of service oriented computing. The use of service oriented computing promises loose coupling (separation of interface and functionality) [3], which increases distributable functionality and reusability [4]. Using a central execution engine or coordinator for a composite service creates a bottleneck and single point of failure. The services (work items) are distributed and decentralized, but the decision logic and coordination is still located at one point. A central coordinator also decreases scalability. For a simple change in the process flow, the entire process description needs to be renewed. Another drawback of a central coordinator is the unnecessary network traffic and performance degradation it creates [5]. This problem of centralized process coordination is also recognized by other researchers [6,7,8].

To overcome this bottleneck, solutions are given to decentralize the coordination work. For example, Nanda et al. [9] define an algorithm to transform a single BPEL process into multiple (smaller) processes using program dependency graphs. This results in separated process engines, which remove the need for a central coordinator and decentralizes the workflow logic (Fig. 1b, process engines C1, C2 and C3). Advantages of this approach include a significant decrease in network traffic, improved concurrency and availability [5]. This decentralization of the workflow of one composite service is termed DECENTRALIZED ORCHES-TRATION.

There are however still a few problems left unsolved in the afore mentioned decentralized orchestration. The execution engines are still mutually tightly coupled, which decreases scalability of the process flow. Each process engine has a direct link to the other process engines that make up the entire composite service. The start of one execution engine in the composite service relies on its invocation by another execution engine. The engines by itself are not autonomous and have to rely on decisions made by others as the logic of the next step in the process is located with the caller, and not with the callee.

In this paper we propose the use of an event based architecture within the decentralized orchestration of a composite service, which we'll term DECENTRAL-IZED EVENT-BASED ORCHESTRATION (see Fig. 1c). This will create autonomous process engines, capable of assessing their environment and deciding on their own when to invoke their respective service(s) (which is a useful property in process management [10]). An event based communication paradigm also creates a highly loose coupled infrastructure, which makes changes to the process flow relatively easy ('plug and play' of process engines).

The use of an event-driven architecture (EDA) in combination with the service oriented architecture is already thoroughly discussed in research and practice [11,12,13,14]. The difference with these proposals and our work, is the place where the event based communication paradigm is used. In current literature about SOA and EDA, event communication is used for the invocation of services (work items) by the central coordinator (dashed, open arrowhead arrows in Fig. 1). In our approach, we look at the use of an event based architecture *within* the decentralized orchestration of *one* composite service. These are the calls from coordinator to coordinator (full arrowhead arrows in Fig. 1). They correspond with the *control flow* described in one workflow model (sequence, choice, loop).

In the next section we clarify our viewpoint on orchestration and process based composition, and give some definitions of terms used in this paper. In the following two sections we answer the most viable questions for our research: why do we need to decentralize the process flow execution (Sect. 3 and 4) and why is an event based communication a feasible strategy to do so (Sect. 5). In the remaining sections we describe how this can work in practice (Sect. 6) and set a few key points for further research (Sect. 7).

2   Viewpoint

In order to explain the ideas in this paper, we give an overview of our viewpoint on service oriented computing and its link to process composition.

Our goal is to split up one process from one organization in order to distribute the execution load of that process. We look at coordination from a one-process point of view. This enables the abstraction of the interplay between different processes from different entities (organizations, departments, customer-supplier, ...). We are only interested in the control flow (sequence, choice, loop) within one process execution. We also assume that a global process view is at hand. The process modelers have defined a process model that is to be deployed in the company. Decentralization of the model takes place in the deployment stage.

A second viewpoint we take is a strict separation between coordination or process logic and functionality. With coordination logic we mean the *description* of the work that needs to be done. This description can be interpreted by a process engine, which makes sure that all the work that is written down in the description is carried out. The process engine is thus a coordinator, it doesn't perform any work itself. The actual work is executed by services that are triggered by the coordinator. These services contain the functionality or actual work packets of the process description (see Fig. 2). Note that the service that is triggered by the coordinator can be a composite service, which itself contains a process description and thus is a coordinator. Because we look at the problem from a one process point of view, calls to atomic or composite services are treated the same way. They both belong to the functionality side and get triggered by the coordinator. How the actual work is eventually handled isn't of interest to the coordinator of this one process (it just wants the work done). Like it is said in the introduction, we look at the decentralization of the process logic (top part of Fig. 2), not at the invocations of services or other process compositions (bottom part of Fig. 2).

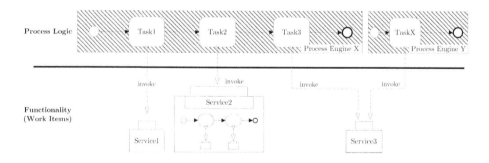

Fig. 2. Separation of the process logic and functionality

This separation of process logic and actual work packets creates a loose coupling between the two. Because the logic on when something has to happen and the work packet itself is separated, the work packets become highly reusable. Other process flows can also trigger the same functions to create new composite services (see Fig. 2, process engine Y). With the help of standard interfaces like WSDL [15] and interaction protocols like SOAP [16], the services and the process logic are not location bound. The services can position themselves anywhere in the IT infrastructure, the same goes for the process engine(s). This creates a highly distributable process architecture. One thing that is still left as a single monolithic entity is the process description. This paper further investigates the possibilities to distribute this process logic.

2.1 Terminology

To exclude ambiguity, we define some terminology used in this paper.

EVENT ARCHITECTURE. An event architecture is an architecture that supports the event communication paradigm by implementing a publish/subscribe interaction scheme [17,18]. Events are instantaneous happenings. When an event happens, a notification of its (past) occurrence is routed to interested parties. This routing is done by an event service that also keeps track of which entity is interested in which event and which entity is able to publish which event.

LOCUS OF CONTROL. The locus of control is the place that holds the decision logic of the next step in the process. In a centralized orchestration, there is only one locus of control and it lies with the coordinator. The coordinator knows what and when something has to happen. When decentralizing the process logic, there isn't a single locus of control, but multiple loci of control. At anytime in the process flow the decision logic of the next step in the process can be located at one of the distributed process engines. There can be as much loci of control as there are process engines for a given process.

ORCHESTRATION. We adopt the interpretation of orchestration as described by Barros et al. [2]. Orchestration is the execution of the internal actions of one composite service. The execution engine reads and interprets the predefined process flow and invokes the services that have to perform some kind of work.

3 Limitations of Centralized Orchestration

When using a centralized orchestration, two groups of limitations can be identified. First there are technical limitations, like a performance bottleneck and unnecessary data traffic. Second, there could be managerial reasons to not use a centralized orchestration. Technical limitations of a centralized process execution are:

SINGLE POINT OF FAILURE. If the central coordinator fails (either by hardware or software), all process instances will fail. The services capable of performing the work items described in the process flow may still be available (they are distributed), but because of the failure of the coordinator, these services aren't triggered, and therefore aren't executed anymore (see Fig. 3a). Even though there is a high decentralization and distribution of the services described in the process flow, the availability of the entire composite service is still dependent on one single entity: the central coordinator.

UNNECESSARY NETWORK TRAFFIC. All (data) traffic runs through the central coordinator. For example, when data generated by one service is important for another service, this data will be routed through the central coordinator (from the first service to the second service), even if this data is of no importance to the coordinator. This creates a lot of unnecessary network traffic from and to the central coordinator (see Fig. 3b).

PERFORMANCE BOTTLENECK. Real life processes can build up in scale and complexity and for one process description, multiple process instances can be created (see Fig. 3c). In process intensive organizations, these process instances can run up very quickly. When all the instances are coordinated at one point in the IT infrastructure, performance throughput decreases significantly.

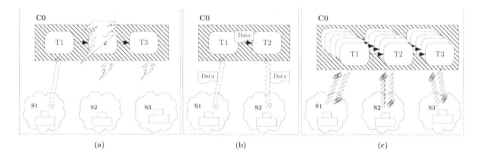

(a)   (b)   (c)

Fig. 3. Limitations of a centralized orchestration: Single point of failure, Unnecessary network traffic and a Performance bottleneck

There are also managerial reasons for not having a central process coordinator. These include security, privacy, visibility, etc. In extended enterprises it is viable that no single organization has control over the entire process (enforced through policies), or that no central entity is allowed to view the entire process, which makes encapsulation necessary.

4   Decentralized Orchestration

The drawbacks of a centralized orchestration have already been recognized by many researchers and practitioners [5,7,8,9,19,20]. To overcome these problems, proposals have been made to decentralize the process execution. These proposals are algorithms which take as input a global process description and give as result a divided process flow. Differences in the algorithms are the way in which the algorithm works, depending on the eventual goal of the division. Nanda et al. [9] use program dependency graphs, a tool borrowed from compiler optimization, to split up the process flow. Their goal is to reduce the network traffic involved. For the same reasons, Fdhila et al. [20] decentralize the process flow using dependency tables and Muth et al. [7] perform decentralization using state and activity charts. Chen et al. [19] use a different division metric, namely business policies, which accomplishes encapsulation of parts of the process flow.

The eventual result is however always the same. After dividing the original process flow, the outcome is a set of control flows, each of which can be interpreted by a different process engine (see Fig. 4). The coupling between these flows is always tight. The locus of control of one process engine is located at another engine. The start of a process flow is dependent on the invocation done by another process flow. Each process engine thus knows what the next step in the global process flow should be ("I am done, now I'll request the start of engine x"). This is the source of the tight coupled communication.

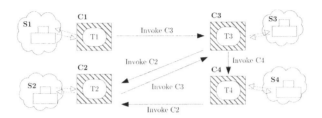

Fig. 4. Decentralized Orchestration

This decentralization thus solves the problems associated with centralized orchestration, but not to a full extend. Because of tight coupling, scalability is still a problem. The availability of the global process flow can also still be optimized. This is why we look at the use of an event based communication paradigm.

5   Event-Based Orchestration

We propose to take the decentralization one step further and extend the decentralization of the coordination work with an event-based communication paradigm. This will create highly loose coupled, autonomous process engines. The use of an event-based architecture to accomplish loose coupling has already been thoroughly studied in process modeling and other domains [12,17,18]. The novelty of this proposal is to use the event-based architecture to decouple the internal process flow. Starting from a global process flow, it is the next step in the decentralization algorithms (from central to decentralized to event based process execution).

Using an event architecture as communication scheme between the decentralized process engines is shown in Fig. 5. Each decentralized coordinator listens to its environment and reacts accordingly. A single process engine doesn't invoke the next step in the process flow anymore, it just publishes a notification of the event that just happened ("job x is done"). This leaves the decision on what the next step in the global process is, completely in the hands of the next step itself.

The advantage of using an event architecture is decoupling between the sender and receiver of a message. We validate the usefulness of using an event architecture in decentralized orchestration by looking at this decoupling. Decoupling in event architectures is defined by Eugster et al. [17], who give three meanings to decoupling accomplished by using an event architecture: space decoupling, time decoupling and synchronization decoupling.

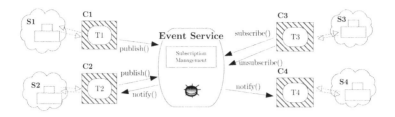

Fig. 5. Decentralized Event-Based Orchestration

SPACE DECOUPLING. Space decoupling refers to the unawareness of interaction partners. Publishers publish events without knowing who receives them and subscribers consume these events, without knowing who sent them. When using an event-based architecture, space decoupling is the biggest contribution to decentralized orchestration. The locus of control shifts from the sender to the receiver of a message (or event notification). This creates autonomous process engines. The engines themselves decide when they start the execution of the process flow, they don't rely on a decision made by another process engine. Space decoupling also shields the different process engines from each other, which increases scalability. Because a process engine doesn't rely on others, but rather on its own decision on when to start the process, a plug and play architecture becomes feasible. Even when using automated transformations from a global process flow to a decentralized one, a plug and play ability to change the deployed process flow is a definite plus. With a tight coupled decentralization, even small changes in the process flow result in big changes to all the different process engines (which can become cumbersome when they are all physically distributed in far away locations). Because of space decoupling, changing the process flow influences only those process engines which are actually involved in that specific change.

TIME DECOUPLING. Interacting parties do not need to be active at the same moment in time. This allows a process engine to be offline, while others continue their regular course of action. Time decoupling, together with a distributed location of the process engines, increases the protection of the global process against a single point of failure. A process flow, implemented with an event communication scheme, doesn't get interrupted when one (or more) process engines in the process flow fail. The still active entities keep working and when the failed engine comes back online, all published events of interest that happened during the failure, will still be delivered. Time decoupling thus guarantees availability of the global process flow.

SYNCHRONIZATION DECOUPLING. Synchronization decoupling refers to the asynchronous send and receive of messages. The sender, nor the receiver gets blocked while sending or receiving events. Asynchronous invocations are already present in current orchestration decentralizations. In terms of synchronization decoupling, an event architecture doesn't add a surplus value versus classical decentralized orchestration.

Space and time decoupling are an added value of using an event-based communication paradigm in a decentralized orchestration. They will increase the scalability and availability of the process flow.

High decoupling of sender and receiver in decentralized orchestration is however not a silver bullet. A few disadvantages of using an event communication paradigm between the partial process flows can be identified:

LOSS OF A GLOBAL PROCESS OVERVIEW. A disadvantage of using an event architecture is that, at runtime, the global overview of the process flow gets lost. Every process engine works autonomously, without the knowledge of any other part of the process flow. The execution of the process flow thus becomes stateless. Although the overview of the process flow gets lost at runtime, there still exists a process model. Decentralization happens at deployment, where one starts with a global process overview. This overview will thus still be available. In service oriented computing it is also advised to design services in a stateless way [4,21]. Using stateless process engines thus fits in this ideal. Inspection of the process state at runtime can still be done by monitoring the events at runtime and relating them with the global process model.

LOSS OF COUPLING PROCESS INSTANCE AND ACTION. Related to the loss of the global process view, is the difficulty of relating events to process instances. If a decentralized process engine subscribes to two events, e.g. `OrderCreated` and `PaymentComplete`, and defines in its process flow that the order should be shipped when it gets notified of these two events, it is imperative that these two events belong to the same process instance (order) before it ships the goods. A way to insure instance-event coupling is to add instance ids to each event (similar to *correlation sets* in BPEL). For every new request from the client, the published events, and any following, get the same instance id. This can be accomplished by the event architecture itself. This way a process engine shall always perform the necessary actions for the correct process instance.

REDUCED COORDINATION. Because of space decoupling, an event communication paradigm strongly reduces coordination between interacting partners, which creates a particular challenge for transactions. To accomplish a transaction, knowledge of participating partners is required, which conflicts with the space decoupling. This problem can be overcome by intelligent modularization of the process flow, i.e. keeping tasks in a transaction in the same partial process engine.

6   In Practice - Case Study

When starting from a global process description, any process decentralization algorithm presented in Sect. 4 can be used to first create decentralized process engines. These engines then have to be modified to use the event communication paradigm. To accomplish the resulting publishing and catching of events in a service oriented environment, event architectures like WS-Notification [14], EVE [22] or the more recently proposed BPEL and WSDL extensions for an event driven architecture [23] can be used.

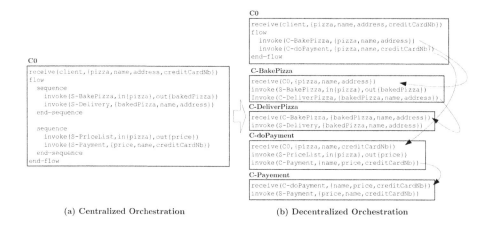

(a) Centralized Orchestration   (b) Decentralized Orchestration

Fig. 6. From centralized process execution to decentralized execution

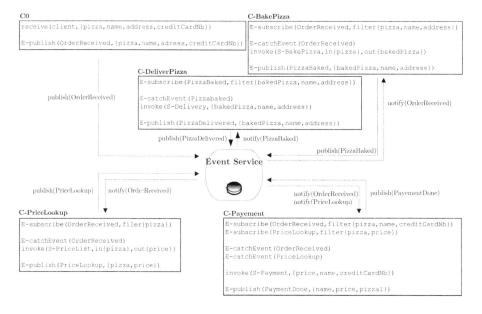

Fig. 7. Decentralized event based execution

We give a simple example to demonstrate the two steps involved in trans-forming a global process flow to a decentralized event based one, hereby showing the feasibility of this approach. A pizza delivery company accepts orders from clients. If an order is received, the payment of the order and the baking + delivery of the pizza are executed in parallel. Delivery is only started after the baking is complete, and payment is only started after price calculation. This process is shown in Fig. 6a. We used a pseudo-BPEL code, as introduced by [9] to describe the process flow. The first step is to decentralize this process. We did this using the decentralization algorithm described in [9]. Each resulting process engine calls the next one by means of `invoke` and `receive` operations (see Fig. 6b). The second step is to change this to event communication. For every coordinator to coordinator communication, each `invoke` operation is changed to a publish of the recent happenings: `E-publish(eventName,payload)`, and every `receive` operation is changed to accept notifications: `E-catchEvent(eventName)`. This also means adding a subscription to this notification in the beginning of the process flow: `E-subscribe(eventName,filter)`. Note that invocations from the decentralized process engines to their respective services (functionality) remain unchanged.

Figure 7 shows the resulting pseudo BPEL for the different coordinators. A big difference we see with Fig. 6b is the non-occurrence of references to the other coordinators. In Fig. 6b each coordinator still has a hard-coded link to another one (see the arrows). This is removed when an event driven architecture is used. The global process flow is now executed by loosely coupled, autonomous coordinators.

7 Conclusion and Future Research

In this paper, we promoted and examined the idea of using an event driven architecture to further extend decentralized orchestration. An added value of the use of an event driven communication paradigm is space and time decoupling between the decentralized orchestration engines. This increases the scalability and availability of the global process flow and creates autonomous process engines, which can be deployed at runtime (plug and play) and can be distributed in the global IT infrastructure. With an example we showed the feasibility of this transformation to an event based orchestration.

Further research involves the formalization of these transformation rules from a global process model to a decentralized event based orchestration. We intend to prove the correctness of these transformation rules with process algebra and formally validate the added value (see Sect. 5), by testing on availability (stress testing) and scalability of the decentralized event-based process flow.

References

1. Oasis: Web service business process execution language version 2.0. Oasis Standard
2. Barros, A., Dumas, M., Oaks, P.: Standards for web service choreography and orchestration: Status and perspectives. In: BPM Workshops, pp. 61–74
3. Papazoglou, M.: Extending the service-oriented architecture. Business Integration Journal 7(1), 18–21 (2005)
4. Erl, T.: SOA: Principles of service design. Prentice Hall Press, NJ (2007)
5. Chafle, G., Chandra, S., Mann, V., Nanda, M.: Decentralized orchestration of composite web services. In: Proceedings of the 13th International World Wide Web Conference on Alternate Track Papers & Posters, pp. 134–143 (2004)
6. Benatallah, B., Dumas, M., Sheng, Q.: Facilitating the rapid development and scalable orchestration of composite web services. Distributed and Parallel Databases 17(1), 5–37 (2005)

7. Muth, P., Wodtke, D., Weissenfels, J., Dittrich, A., Weikum, G.: From centralized workflow specification to distributed workflow execution. Journal of Intelligent Information Systems 10(2), 159–184 (1998)
8. Yu, W.: Decentralized Orchestration of BPEL Processes with Execution Consistency. In: Advances in Data and Web Management, pp. 665–670
9. Nanda, M., Chandra, S., Sarkar, V.: Decentralizing execution of composite web services. ACM SIGPLAN Notices 39(10), 170–187 (2004)
10. Jennings, N., Norman, T., Faratin, P., OBrien, P., Odgers, B.: Autonomous agents for business process management. Applied Artificial Intelligence 14(2) (2000)
11. Michelson, B.: Event-driven architecture overview. OMG report (2006)
12. Pedrinaci, C., Moran, M., Norton, B.: Towards a Semantic Event-Based Service-Oriented Architecture. In: Workshop: 2nd International Workshop on Semantic Web Enabled Software Engineering, SWESE 2006 (2006)
13. Sriraman, B., Architect, L., Radhakrishnan, R., Architect, E.: Event Driven Architecture Augmenting Service Oriented Architectures. Sun Microsystems (2005)
14. Niblett, P., Graham, S.: Events and service-oriented architecture: the OASIS web services notification specifications. IBM Systems Journal 44(4), 869–886 (2005)
15. Chinnici, R., Gudgin, M., Moreau, J., Weerawarana, S.: Web services description language (WSDL) version 1.2 part 1. W3C Working Draft 11 (2003)
16. Gudgin, M., Hadley, M., Mendelsohn, N., Moreau, J., Nielsen, H., Karmarkar, A., Lafon, Y.: SOAP Version 1.2. W3C Working Draft 9 (2001)
17. Eugster, P., Felber, P., Guerraoui, R., Kermarrec, A.: The many faces of publish/subscribe. ACM Computing Surveys (CSUR) 35(2), 131 (2003)
18. Mühl, G., Fiege, L., Pietzuch, P.: Distributed Event-Based Systems. Springer-Verlag New York, Inc., Secaucus (2006)
19. Chen, Q., Hsu, M.: Inter-enterprise collaborative business process management. In: International Conference on Data Engineering, p. 0253 (2001)
20. Fdhila, W., Yildiz, U., Godart, C.: A flexible approach for automatic process decentralization using dependency tables. In: ICWS 2009: Proceedings of the 2009 IEEE International Conference on Web Services, pp. 847–855. IEEE Computer Society, Washington, DC, USA (2009)
21. Krafzig, D., Banke, K., Slama, D.: Enterprise SOA: Service-Oriented Architecture Best Practices (The Coad Series). Prentice Hall PTR, NJ (2004)
22. Geppert, A., Tombros, D.: Event-based distributed workflow execution with EVE. In: Proc. of the IFIP Int. Conf. on Distributed Systems Platforms and Open Distributed Processing, pp. 427–442 (1998)
23. Juric, M.B.: Wsdl and bpel extensions for event driven architecture. Information and Software Technology (2010) (in press, accepted manuscript)

Event-Based Business Process Editor and Simulator

Vatcharaphun Rajsiri, Nicholas Fleury, Graham Crosmarie, and Jean-Pierre Lorré

EBM WebSourcing, 4 rue Amélie, 31000 Toulouse, France
{netty.rajsiri,nicholas.fleury,graham.grosmarie,
jean-pierre.lorre}@petalslink.com

Abstract. The growing of business market dictates new requirements of agility to the business process environment. An event-driven approach can deal with this issue since an event can be defined as a significant change in the state of a system or an environment. This paper is focused on the combination of the event-driven approach and the business process modeling one by developing a cloud-enabled event-based business process editor and simulator. BPMN2.0 is the relevant business process formalism used since it can represent graphically various kind of operating activities and events.

Keywords: BPMN, business process modeling, simulation, EDA, SOA.

1 Introduction

This paper aims at presenting the value of the event-based business process modeling approach illustrated thanks to software components which are part of a complete event based open-source platform.

The paper starts by discussing the importance of business process modeling and event-driven approaches and synergies with the Service-Oriented Architecture (SOA) principles. Then, it presents the goals of EBM WebSourcing in terms of open-source cloud enable platform based on such approaches. Finally, the software components designed to support these perspectives are described.

1.1 Event and Business Process Management (BPM)

Enterprises are now operating in a complex economical environment where markets are more competitive and dynamic. They require the agility to be able to operate under such pressures and thus ensure their survival. The way for an enterprise to do business is captured in its business process which is seen today as the most valuable corporate asset. A business process according to [18] is an artifact made of a set of activities executed in order to achieve at least one objective. The agility of enterprise business processes to change in a timely manner and rapidly adapt themselves to new conditions is though very important.

SOA promises to provide a decentralized and loosely coupled environment that enables flexible, reliable and coordinated integration of dynamic applications belonging to different organizations. More and more enterprises start organizing their business processes by means of service aggregation. We assume that business process

M. zur Muehlen and J. Su (Eds.): BPM 2010 Workshops, LNBIP 66, pp. 707–718, 2011.
© Springer-Verlag Berlin Heidelberg 2011

is based on the SOA principles, with both aiming to empower the organization to more quickly respond to changing business requirements that result from events [3]. This is where an event-driven approach comes into play.

The fundamental concept of the event-driven approach is, obviously, an event. An event is a notable thing that happens inside or outside the enterprise [11]. It can be defined as a significant change in the state of a system or an environment [10]. The event-driven approach concerns the production, detection, consumption of, and reaction to events. This event-driven approach may be applied to the design and implementation of applications and systems which transmit events among loosely coupled software components and services.

Business process and event-driven approach complement service-oriented architecture because services (within business process) can be started by triggering events which can influence the execution of a process or a service.

Moreover, nowadays the modern enterprise operates in a cloud of business events emanating from sources all over the world. Events can be monitored, managed and processed by a complex event processing (CEP) engine using event patterns [17]. CEP allows real-time respond and better control of business processes.

[2] confirms the requirements for handling events in process models and discusses the notion of events for triggering process instantiation or steps within a process instance. Events provide content for analyzing and acting during the business process. They are a way to loosely interconnect different process instances: Events produced in one process instance are consumed by one or several other process instances. Furthermore, composite events, i.e. the combination of different interrelated events, must also be handled in process models thanks to Complex Event Processing (CEP).

Besides of describing the architecture and tools, [4] outlines a methodology by which each participant can define, detect, and respond to events. It proposes an Event-driven Architecture (EDA) which aims to address the engineering challenge of incorporating events in a web process in a reusable manner - that is, without hard coding events into a process model. From [17], an EDA provides a way of organizing systems that sense, analyze, and respond to events. For business processes, sensing involves receiving events from multiple sources (sensors, software applications, and such), analyzing involves deciding a response (perhaps by aggregating such events), and responding involves updating expectations and modifying executions.

According to [7], the trend of BPM is shifting from the design of business process towards improving and analyzing business processes. Therefore, we have devoted our interests to a platform allowing collaborative design and verification of event driven business processes through the development of an editor and a simulator. The editor is dedicated to the process design, whereas the simulator is focused on the process verification.

1.2 Technologies Positioning

An event-driven business process modeling approach is the basis of the development of the Business process editor and simulator which aim to offer users the ability to collaboratively create, modify, and simulate processes made of events and services.

The positioning of the editor and simulator in the existing open-source SOA products portfolio of EBM WebSourcing is shown in Fig.1 below:

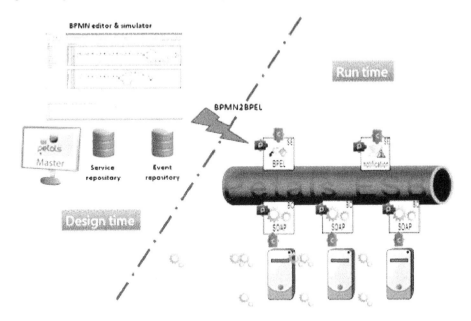

Fig. 1. Positioning of the Business Process Editor and Simulator

The editor and simulator are used during design time to build Event Driven Applications deployed into the service cloud managed by the Petals ESB (Enterprise Service Bus) event enabled service infrastructure. Users define processes using available event types and services from the event and service repositories. The service repository is the Petals Master open-source registry. Event repository contains an event taxonomy that describes event types.

The process designed with the editor is then translated to be executed by the BPEL [9] (Business Process Execution Language) engine provided by the Petals ESB open-source JBI[1] compliant ESB. This ESB may be distributed either physically or logically on many nodes that manage their own services and events according to an OASIS/WS-Notification[2] compliant engine. Communication between service providers and consumers use the event paradigm as explain below:

An event can happen at any moment produced by any kind of services: a new observation, a file created or deleted, a change on a meta-data, etc. Once events have been produced, consumers have to be notified. However, in order to ensure loose coupling between services, event producers should not know event consumers, neither the means to send them notifications. The classical way to deal with such a schema is to route the notifications via a broker who will be in charge of maintaining a list of

---

[1] Java Business Integration: http://jcp.org/en/jsr/detail?id=208

[2] http://www.oasis-open.org/committees/tc_home.php?wg_abbrev=wsn

consumers with their specific protocol of exchange, as well as their subjects of interest (also known as topics of publish/subscribe design pattern). Such kind of communication is covered by the OASIS WS-Notification standard.

The BPMN2BPEL translator converts BPMN 2.0 compliant business processes to a set of executable artifacts: BPEL code, WSDL service interfaces, JBI configuration files, XSD data models (service parameters and events). The BPEL engine orchestrates services in order to implement the specified process. It takes in charge service invocation triggered by events thanks to features provided by the underlying bus infrastructure and notification engine.

The business process editor and simulator are detailed in Sections 2 and 3 respectively.

2 Business Process Editor

The Business Process Editor aims at providing an environment for users to be able to model their business processes through a Web client interface. It provides a set of features allowing the creation of standard elements of BPMN 2.0 (Business Process Modeling Notation).

In this section, we will survey the main reasons behind the choice of the BPMN syntax, the functionalities of the editor that have already been implemented in the current version, and finally detail the collaborative feature.

2.1 Business Process Modeling Notation (BPMN)

The Business Process Editor has been developed to support the process representation based on the BPMN 2.0 specification [15]. BPMN 2.0 introduces additional constructs and a standardized serialization format to the previous one (BPMN 1.2).

BPMN is a semi-formal language for graphically representing processes defined initially by the BPMI[3] (Business Process management Initiative). BPMI has been established in order to promote and develop the use of Business Process Management (BPM) through the use of standards for process design, deployment, execution, maintenance, and optimization of processes. It merged with OMG (Object Management Group) in 2005.

BPMN is compatible with XML-based workflow languages like BPEL. The version 2.0 provides a complete mapping between BPMN models to BPEL. This facilitates the transformation of a BPMN model into an executable process one.

According to [13], BPMN can cover mainly the functional view and partially the organizational, informational, and resource views of enterprise modeling through pools, lanes, activities, flows, and data notations. BPMN integrates the event notation which is the fundamental concept of the event-driven approach.

In the first section, we discussed about the necessary of taking the event-driven approach into account when modeling a business process. An event gives the dynamic behavior to business process because it can deal with changes that happen in any moment of times and affect the sequence of activities of a process.

---

[3] www.bpmi.org

BPMN takes into account event by specifying three types of events: start, intermediate, and end events. A BPMN process is triggered by an event to start. Events can also appear anywhere within the process (as intermediate events) and it is always placed at the end of process (as end events), for instance, the process is stopped immediately when an error occurs within the process.

Thus, BPMN language is the relevant formalism for us since it allows combining BPM and event approaches.

2.2 Technologies

The main target user group of the Business Process Editor and Simulator are business users, not technical ones; consequently tools should be easy to install, update, and use. Moreover business processes instances will run into the cloud, meaning services and events managed by the bus are available through Internet. Such requirements imply to develop our software as lightweight Web applications.

Rich Internet Application (RIA) [6] aims to build lightweight applications that can be accessible from anywhere and they are upgraded instantly while providing the same rich full features as the classical software. The HTML standard and Javascript language are commonly used to develop RIA as they are supported on many devices and are quiet easy to manipulate. However, over time, it becomes difficult to maintain applications developed with such technologies. On one hand, the supports on which they are based are evolving rapidly and are also quiet numerous. The problem is that all these technologies have no common standards, thus requiring specific development for the application to develop. On the other hand, developing rich applications involve the integration of many features that require a development language that can lead to a robust application. A language such as Javascript does not allow this because it is weakly typed making the developed application hard to maintain.

We selected Google Web Toolkit (GWT) [5] since it is a framework that aims to develop RIAs using Java as a language of development which, unlike JavaScript, is a strongly typed language and whose maintenance can be easier. Moreover GWT offers the advantage of not having to worry about the supports on which the application will run, because once the application has been developed, it is compiled to be compatible with a maximum of support. GWT also allows developing libraries that can easily be integrated within other applications, helping by the way the reuse of components.

Besides, Scalable Vector Graphic (SVG) [15] is used to deal with the graphical representation of the main BPMN widgets. It allows rendering graphical elements within an HTML page. SVG is an XML-based file format for describing two dimensional vector graphics. The advantage of SVG, in addition of being easily manipulated, is that it is readable by many applications as this is a well established standard.

2.3 Features

The aim of the Business Process Editor is to be a design tool for business process in BPMN representation. The Fig. 2 shows the user interface of the editor:

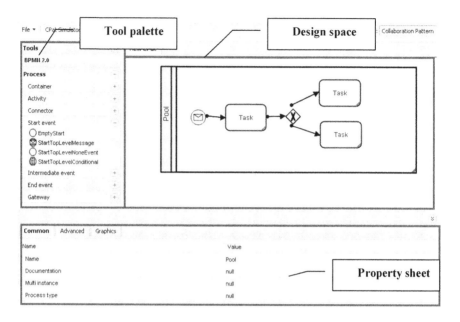

Fig. 2. User interface of the Business Process Editor

The editor provides a tool palette, a design space, and a property sheet. The tool palette contains the widgets for creating a BPMN diagram. Here below are the BPMN elements that are already implemented:

- • Containers: pool, and lane
- • Activity: task
- • Start event: empty, message, and conditional events
- • Intermediate event: message event
- • End event: empty, and message events
- • Gateway: exclusive, inclusive, and parallel gateways
- • Connector: sequence, and message flows

The design space is an empty space for drawing a BPMN process by drag and drop from the palette. The graphics displayed on this space is compliant with the BPMN 2.0 specifications. The property sheet is a set of attributes that correspond to the selected BPMN element.

The above functionalities concern the client side of the editor. The server side of the editor hosts the database that stores BPMN processes for reusability. The processes stored can then be used by the simulator (Section 3) or by the editor itself to modify it and save as a new process.

The editor can generate two kinds of artifacts:

- • An XML file compliant with the BPMN 2.0 metamodel. This is the primary objective of the version 2.0 that allows enabling the exchange of business process models and their diagram layout among process modeling tools to preserve semantic integrity.

– • An XPDL (XML Process Definition Language) file compliant to the XPDL 2.1 specification [19] exchange format. It allows representing process description and graphical information (e.g. coordinates, width, and height) of process's objects.

There is already a rich set of available tools allowing to design BPMN compliant business processes, however none of them combine the following benefits: to be based on open-standards, to be cloud ready and to be provided as a component of a complete open-source SOA stack. Moreover our tools provide a very advance collaborative feature that allows a group of business process designers to collaborate in real-time on processes definition.

Most of the market tools are provided as client / server applications. Some are proprietary (ARIS Express, Tibco Business studio, Intalio, BizAgi), some are open-source (jBPM, Bonitasoft). Among the cloud based solutions (Lombardi Blueprint, Appian Anywhere, Cordys Process Boardroom, IBM Blueworks, etc.) only Oryx Editor is provided under open-source license, however it is written in Javascript and doesn't provide any collaborative features.

2.4 Collaborative Edition

The BPMN editor allows an unlimited number of users to collaborate in real-time on the definition of business processes. The central concept is the collaboration session where members of a group of work collaborate on the same process by alternatively bringing their own contributions on the designed process.

The collaboration session is instantiated by a member of a virtual organization; this member is therefore considered as the founder of the concerned collaboration. The founder can then invite other members (of the same group of work or not) to join the session, but external members can also ask to join the session as they can see all the ongoing sessions (of the same group of work to which they belongs) on the main dashboard.

When a new member arrives in an ongoing session he is notified of all the previous transactions that were made and can start to contribute to the actual process. The other members are also automatically notified of the arrival of a new participant as a transactional history system allows seeing all the participants of the collaboration and their respective contributions since the beginning of the session. This system also allows to roll-back on the contributions that are not accepted by the majority of the participants. The collaborative process can be exported to BPMN standard format or saved at any time to be completed later on.

The main difficulty in collaborative tools is to deal with distributed transactions. In a tool such as the BPMN editor multiple clients interact on the same process that is stored on the same server.

In a web environment the classical paradigm is the client pull where a client request is responded to by a server whenever there is a full/effective response or not. Using such an approach for a collaborative tool can lead to a loss of efficiency as all clients would have to constantly check for new updates even if there is none and therefore increasing the server calls.

Rather than using this classical approach the collaborative editor has adopted the Comet [14] approach along with an event-based communication where each client subscribe and publishes events notified through a server push mechanism. Thus, all clients are notified of any update only when there is an effective one.

The collaborative BPMN editor uses the GWTEventService[4] open-source library to achieve this goal as it perfectly integrates the Comet approach within the GWT framework.

3 Event-Driven Simulator

The main aim of the simulator is to let users to testing processes behavior at design time from the event point of view. Processes may be very complex by involving a combination of sub-processes triggered by many kinds of events. Due to such events combinatory the global behavior of such a system is hard to address for the end user. Moreover some process representation languages, like BPMN, include many elements, some are simple to understand and others require a little more expertise before they can be mastered. Thus, being able to simulate a process allows the designers to compare their expectations with the actual outcome, eliminating by this way any doubt about the process behavior.

According to [8], simulation is mentioned as one of the techniques suitable for the support of redesign of business process. The simulation of business processes helps in understanding, analyzing, and designing processes. With the use of simulation the (re)designed processes can be evaluated and compared.

The simulation is mostly useful if a report summarizes, for a specific scenario, the process flow that is produced. The result of a process is determined by the semantic of all of the involved elements (activities, events, flows etc.). Our focus is to study how gateways and events may affect the flow of a process, while activities represent the work performed within a Business Process.

Simulating a maximum of scenarios can reduce the risks and contingencies that may arise in a real environment. It can also be interesting to see the effects of introducing new processes within an organization as the new process can affect the old ones. As mentioned in [12], simulation is largely used to assess the impact that changes to business processes may have on the organization and to explore different business process scenarios.

3.1 Simulation Concepts – An Event-Based Approach

According to [15], research on discrete event-simulation mostly dates back to the eighties of the last century and no major progress has been made lately. However, the current emergence of event-driven architectures for business applications continues these efforts.

[16] summarizes different approaches of simulation found in the literatures: the event-scheduling approach uses an ordered set of timed (so-called determined events), on the other hand, it includes condition checks for other (so-called contingent events). As discussed in [1], a simulated system can be described in terms of objects (entities),

---

[4] http://code.google.com/p/gwteventservice/

attributes defining these objects, events causing changes in object states, activities that transform an object's state over time and processes that are a sequence of activities or events ordered by time.

Our simulator works on the basis of an event-driven business process approach. It can be considered as discrete event simulation because the operation of the system is represented as a sequence of events and activities. BPMN is used as the business process representation language in our simulator. BPMN is a formalism that uses event as a first order element to describe process. A BPMN process is always started and ended with an event, and deals with intermediate events during the course of the process, the simulation takes into account all these events during the execution.

The basic principle is that a triggering event of the process will create a token and instantiate the process. These triggering events are most of the time starting events. A token is a "theoretical" object used to create a descriptive simulation of the behavior of BPMN elements (it is not currently a formal part of the BPMN specification). When an item receives a token it can then go through several states. Thus, some items may be put on hold while others continue to be executed. As long as an activity does not have all the needed resources it cannot be performed. Once the element is considered as complete, the token may "pass through" the next element by the connecting sequence flow.

The specific behavior of each BPMN elements is also taken into account because it influences the process flow. The gateways are useful to control how the process diverges or converges; they represent points of control for the paths within the process. Gateways can either split or merge the flow of a process through sequence flow. Events can start, delay, interrupt or end the flow of the process.

3.2 Functional Description

The primary intention of the simulator is to provide users the possibility to verify their business processes. It is also aimed at providing the ability to interact with the BPMN process, so that users can play with the process elements and their behaviors. The users can make any changes on the process scenario during execution in order to observe the consequences of changes.

The Simulator integrates an engine which manages the token(s) within a process through all the various elements while "executing" their behavior and considering the scenario that the designer specified for each element. Once all the tokens have been consumed, the process can be considered as complete and a report on the simulation of the process is generated.

The Fig. 3 shows the graphical interactive web interface of the simulator:

The graphical simulation allows the user to see the progress of the simulation by the presence of markers (in the blue and yellow colors) for distinguishing the state of each elements of the process. The maker represents the token of the simulation engine. The blue marker stresses on the already executed elements, while the yellow one shows elements in waiting status for receiving a message.

The simulation tool is an interactive window shown during the simulation. It describes the current status of the process and asks the user for inputs when necessary, for example, when the simulator arrives at a gateway that requires

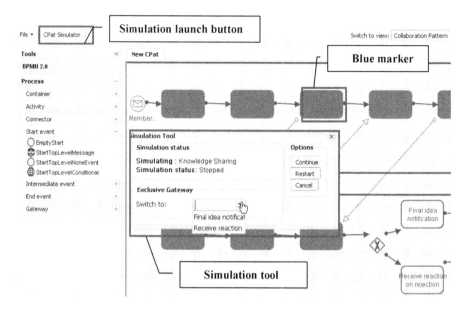

Fig. 3. Graphical interactive interface of the Simulator

selecting an appropriate route to continue, or an intermediate event where user must attach a document. The simulation tool can also be used to pause, restart or cancel the simulation.

Once a simulation is completed or if the user decides to cancel the simulation, a result window is automatically shown. This result window summarizes the choices that were made during the simulation (ex. gateways), messages exchanged between the activities, and the activities that have been executed. The Fig. 4 shows the result window:

Simulation Result

Activities	Messages	Gateways		
Activity	Collaboration Pattern	▼ Participant	Role	
⊟ Triggering Event: Trigering event (11 Items)				
Fill in idea entry template	Knowledge Sharing	VO Member (idea creator)	VO Member (idea creator)	
Store in VO's KB	Knowledge Sharing	VO Member (idea creator)	VO Member (idea creator)	
Send Template	Knowledge Sharing	VO Member (idea creator)	VO Member (idea creator)	
Receive	Knowledge Sharing	VO MemberS	VO Member (idea creator)	
Send comments	Knowledge Sharing	VO MemberS	VO Member (idea creator)	
Receive comments	Knowledge Sharing	VO Member (idea creator)	VO Member (idea creator)	
Send decision	Knowledge Sharing	VO Member (idea creator)	VO Member (idea creator)	
Receive Decision	Knowledge Sharing	VO MemberS	VO Member (idea creator)	
Decide on rejection	Knowledge Sharing	VO Member (idea creator)	VO Member (idea creator)	
Decide on rejection	Knowledge Sharing	VO Member (idea creator)	VO Member (idea creator)	
Final idea notification	Knowledge Sharing	VO MemberS	VO Member (idea creator)	

Fig. 4. Three-panels simulation result window

4   Conclusions and Future Works

The objective of this paper is to present the Business Process Editor and Simulator developed on the basis of an event-driven business process modelling approach. Our motivations to develop such tools originally come from the interests in providing cloud enabled event infrastructure that fully support the collaborative business process management from the design to the execution phases. The business process management is nowadays an important element of every organization, according to the SOA principles. It is required to support the real time changes of events in the current business environment. The integration of an event-driven approach into a business process modelling can empower the organization to more quickly respond to changing business requirements (business agility).

Future work deals mainly, for the design part, with the implementation of the new features provided by BPMN 2.0 to support choreographies and for the runtime part to address large scale distributed event driven architectures.

Integration of the event run-time infrastructure with a Complex Event Processing (CEP) engine is foreseen in order to handle complex events. This requires interfacing the Petals notification engine and the CEP in order to be able to detect event patterns.

The first open-source version of the Business Process Editor and the Simulator will be released under the GNU Affero General Public Licence. They support the BPMN 2.0 specification and provide as outputs a BPMN XML file compliant with BPMN 2.0 meta-model and a XPDL 2.1 file, as well as the necessary artefacts to deploy applications into a private or public cloud supported by the Petals ESB with notification and BPEL engines.

Acknowledgments. This work has been partially funded by the European Commission in the frame of the STREP research project SYNERGY (Supporting highlY-adaptive Network Enterprise collaboration thRouGh semanticallY-enabled knowledge services), ICT No 63637. The authors would like to thank the project partners for their advices and comments regarding this work.

References

1. Balci, O.: The implementation of four conceptual frameworks for simulation modeling in high-level languages. In: Proceedings of the 20th Conference on Winter Simulation, SanDiego, CA, pp. 287–295 (1988)
2. Barros, A., Decker, G., Grosskopf, A.: Complex Events in Business Processes. LNCS (2007)
3. Carter, S.: Management in SOA. Information Management Magazine (May 2007)
4. Chakravarty, P., Singh, M.P.: Incorporating Events into Cross-Organizational Business Processes. IEEE Internet Computing, 46–53 (2008)
5. Dwyer, J.: Pro Web 2.0 Application Development with GWT. Apress, USA (2008) ISBN 978-1590599853
6. Jaber, S.: Programmation GWT 2: Développer des applications RIA et Ajax avec Google Web Toolkit. Eyrolles, France (2010) ISBN 978-2-212-12569-6
7. Jansen-Vullers, M., Netjes, M.: Business Process simulation – a tool survey. Paper presented at 7th Workshop and Tutorial on the Practical Use of Coloured Petri Nets and the CPN Tools (CPN 2006), Denmark (2006)

8. Kettinger, W.J., Teng, J.T.C., Guha, S.: Business Process Change: A Study of Methodologies, Techniques, and Tools. MIS Quarterly 21(1), 55–80 (1997)
9. Lorré, J.P., Verginadis, Y., Papageorgiou, N., Salatge, N.: Ad-hoc execution of collaboration patterns using dynamic orchestration. In: Proceedings of the I-ESA Conference, Coventry UK (2010)
10. Mani Chandy, K.: Event-Driven Applications: Costs, Benefits and Design Approaches, California Institute of Technology, Gartner Application Integration and Web Services (2006)
11. Michelson, B.M.: Event-Driven Architecture Overview, Patricia Seybold Group (2006)
12. Paul, R.J., Serrano, A.: Collaborative Information Systems and Business Process Design Using Simulation. In: Proceedings of the 37th Annual Hawaii International Conference on System Sciences (HICSS 2004) - Track 1, January 05-08, p. 10009.1 (2004)
13. Rajsiri, V.: Knowledge-based system for collaborative process definition, Ph.D Thesis, Institute Nationale Polytechnique de Toulouse (2009)
14. Russell, A.: Comet: Low Latency Data for the Browser. Alex Russell's blog (2006)
15. Scalable Vector Graphics (SVG). W3C (2010),
   `http://www.w3.org/Graphics/SVG/`
16. Schiefer, J., Roth, H., Suntinger, M., Schatten, A.: Simulating business process scenarios for event-based systems. In: Vortrag: 15th European Conference on Information Systems (ECIS 2007), Proceedings of the 15th European Conference on Information Systems (ECIS), University of St. Gallen (2007)
17. SYNERGY project. Deliverable D4.1 Collaboration patterns model and ontology (2008)
18. Vernadat, F.: Techniques de modelisation en entreprise: Applications aux processus Operationnels, economica (1999)
19. White, S., Miers, D.: BPMN Modeling and Reference Guide. Future Strategies Inc., Florida (2008) ISBN 978-0-9777527-2-0
20. Workflow standard process definition interface – XML Process Definition Language, version 2.1a, Workflow Management Coalition, WFMC-TC-1025 (October 2008)

Real-Time Monitoring of Web-Based Processes: A Use Case for the Event-Driven Advertisement

Liljana Stojanovic and Roland Stuehmer

FZI-Research Center for Information Technology at the University of Karlsruhe, Germany
{Ljiljana.Stojanovic,Roland.Stuehmer}@fzi.de

Abstract. The modern advertisement theory is based on the "contextual priming effects": the product attributes primed by the ad context may result in the formation or change of beliefs about the advertised brand, thereby affecting consumers' evaluations of the brand. Therefore, a web ad should be tailored as much as possible to the user's current context (interests) in order to affect the user' attention appropriately. In this paper we present an approach for the semantic-based personalized advertising on the web.

Keywords: Personalized advertisement, complex event processing, semantics.

1 Introduction

A contextual web advertising system scans the text of a website for keywords and returns advertisements to the webpage based on what the user is viewing. Contextual advertising has made a major impact on earnings of many websites. Because the advertisements are more targeted, they are more likely to be clicked, thus generating revenue for the owner of the website (and the server of the advertisement). However, despite being targeted, current approaches for contextual web advertising are not personalized, i.e. they are not taking into account the user, but only the characteristics of the web site. On the other hand, the modern advertisement theory is based on the "contextual priming effects": the product attributes primed by the ad context may result in the formation or change of beliefs about the advertised brand, thereby affecting consumers' evaluations of the brand. Therefore, an ad should be tailored as much as possible to the user's interests in order to affect the user appropriately. Consequently, this implies a need for real-time tracking a web user's behavior in order to detect her/his current interests, by assuming that her/his current interest will correlate to the visited elements in a web page. Moreover, due to the different contexts that can be found in a web page, such personalized ads should be dynamically changed, according to the changes in the user's interests. However, due to the request/response style of web communication, the user's behavior cannot be captured in the real-time (on the client side) easily and is therefore omitted from the traditional web advertisement process.

Modern web technologies are enabling more client-side control of the user's behavior and there is already work done in developing technologies for gathering a web user's behavior while browsing AJAX-based web pages [1].

M. zur Muehlen and J. Su (Eds.): BPM 2010 Workshops, LNBIP 66, pp. 719–729, 2011.

In this paper we leverage on that work in developing an approach for the dynamic and personalized web advertisement. In the nutshell of the approach is the real-time and complex processing of the user's behavior in a web page.

In fact, the user's interaction with a web page is interpreted as a set of events, which are combined in order to discover the "very current" interest of the user. Events, simple or complex, are models for things that happen e.g., when a user interacts with a Web page. Events are consumed in some meaningful way e.g., for monitoring reasons or to trigger actions such as responses. Semantics is used for a better interpretation of the user's behavior by taking into account the meta information assigned to parts of the web page, which the user has visited. The user's interest/profile generated in this way is used for the very personalized ad generation.

Additionally we define a model for updating ads once the current user's interest has been changed such that displayed ads are not any more the most relevant one. In that way our approach supports dynamic adaptation of ads ensuring their high relevance for the user.

In this paper we present the whole approach for the personalized and dynamic web advertisement, including the technical architecture for detecting and composing (semantic) events in Web clients, that is, as explained above, the basic mechanism for discovering and updating real-time profile of a web user (i.e. her/his interests). Additionally we demonstrate the validity of the approach in two evaluation studies.

The paper is structured as follows: In Section 2 we describe methods for tracking a user's behavior in a web page (as a set of semantically enriched events), whereas in Section 3 the methods for complex processing of these events are given as an approach for discovering the current interest of the web user. Section 4 presents the architecture for generating personalized and dynamic web ads based on detecting "unusual" user's behavior, whereas Section 5 contains some implementation details and in Section 6 we present some evaluation results. We will discuss related work and conclude the paper in the last remaining sections.

2 Tracking a Web User's Behaviour

The main issue in enabling personalization of the web usage is to enable capturing of actions or changes in Web documents. These can be treated as events, which an event-driven system will react to. For our use case of advertising we will focus on events created from a user's interaction with Web documents. After having extracted events from a Web document, they must be processed in order to interpret them semantically, to be able to react on them appropriately. The following two subsections describe our approach for these two issues: generation and processing of Web events.

2.1 Simple Event Generation

A simple event in Web clients is characterized by two dimensions; the type of event (e.g. click, mouseover) and the part of the Web page, where the event occurred (e.g. a node of the Document Object Model of the Web document). This node is, however, just a syntactical artifact of the document as it is presented in a Web browser. Adding this node or parts of it to the event body will not significantly add meaning to the event and not ease the understanding of the event for the recipient of the event.

```
 1  <div xmlns:rdf = "http://www.w3.org/1999/02/22-rdf-syntax-ns#"
 2      xmlns:dc = "http://purl.org/dc/elements/1.1/"
 3      xmlns:vCard = "http://www.w3.org/2001/vcard-rdf/3.0#"
 4      xmlns:iCal = "http://www.w3.org/2002/12/cal/ical#">
 5     <ul about="events/Mary_Poppins_Show">
 6       <li typeof="cal:Vevent">
 7         <a property="ical:categories">Classic, Comedy, Kid Friendly, Musical<
                /a>
 8         <a property="cal:dtstart" content="20081008T180000Z">October 8th at
                18am</a>
 9         <a property="cal:duration" content="PT2H">2 hour</a>
10         <vCard:TEL rdf:parseType="Resource">
11          <rdf:value>(212) 307-4100</rdf:value>
12          <rdf:type rdf:resource="http://www.w3.org/2001/vcard-rdf/3.0#work"/>
13         </vCard:TEL>
14         <vCard:ADR rdf:parseType="Resource">
15          <vCard:Street>   214 West 42nd Street </vCard:Street>
16          <vCard:Locality> New York City </vCard:Locality>
17          <vCard:Pcode>    NY 10036 </vCard:Pcode>
18          <vCard:Country> USA </vCard:Country>
19         </vCard:ADR>
20         <a property="cal:description">Mary Poppins takes up residence at
                magnificent New Amsterdam Theater.
21         </a>
22       </li>
23     </ul>
24  </div>
```

Fig. 1. An example for a musical listed in a Semantic Web Widget

We therefore propose to add semantic information to the event which pertains to the actual domain knowledge that the Web page is about. In order to enable this, the first step is to represent the content of a Web page in a form that can be used for generating meaningful events. To do so without having to manually annotate every Web document, we envision a mechanism, which ensures the relevance of the annotations. This can be done in many (semi-) automatic ways, e.g. by providing Web forms (page templates), which for a given user's input, automatically adds the proper semantic relationships between the form fields. In this way all user generated content will be annotated. The Web forms are created based on supported vocabularies for a particular Web site. Our particular focus is on widely spread vocabularies such as Dublin Core, Creative Commons, FOAF, GeoRSS and OpenCalais. Regarding the format of structured data, RDFa [2], eRDF and Microformats are all good candidates for this purpose. They support semantics embedded within actual Web page data and allow reusable semantic markup inside of Web pages. In our implementation we use RDFa, since in comparison to eRDF it is a more encouraged candidate by the W3C. Comparing it further to Microformats, RDFa is more flexible in mixing different existing vocabularies.

In the remaining part of this section we give an example demonstrating the generation of events in the context of a Semantic Advertising scenario. The ad space is a part of the Web page which can be dynamically filled by an ad provider as a response to an event the client sends. In our approach ad content is created based on a current user's attention. In order to accomplish this we need as much (meta-) information as possible about the content of the Web page. Therefore, we assume semantically enriched Web content such that context extraction is easier and more precise. Additionally, every page is split up in a number of Semantic Web Widgets (SWW).

We introduce Semantic Web Widgets as self-contained components annotated with semantic data and displayed in a Web page. Semantic Web Widgets give a high-level description of the content, and provide the basic context of data contained in the widgets. For instance on a news portal incorporating semantic advertising one widget could be used for listing all news belonging to one subcategory, e.g., politics, another one for arts, etc. In Figure 1 we show an RDFa example of the semantic description for an arts event listed in a widget related to musicals. The code snippet presents an event named "Mary Poppins Show" described using RDF Schemata for Dublin Core, vCard and iCal vocabularies. Information such as categories, start and duration of the musical are provided together with contact information, location and so on.

2.2 Event Enrichment

In this subsection we focus on enriching simple events with semantics from the context of the Web page in which the event occurred.

A simple event in Web clients is characterized by two dimensions; the type of event (e.g. click, mouseover) and the part of the Web page, where the event occurred (e.g. a node in the Document Object Model of the Web document). Subscribing to simple events of these types therefore requires the specification of type and the specification of the node or nodes where the events may originate. Both dimensions are retained in an event instance by using the attributes jsEventType and cssSelector (see Figure 2 for more explanations).

In order to better understand these events and make sense of what happened we must enrich the content of events when they are produced. The jsEventType tells us what a user has done and the cssSelector tells us where on the Web page the user did it. However, the latter is a purely presentation-dependent measure. There is no semantics which has any meaning beyond the context of a specific Web page structure. We propose to extract presentation-independent semantic information from the Web page if present. Instead of creating events from interaction with purely syntactic items of a Web document, we create events about interaction with semantic concepts which the document stands for. As an example, an event should not represent e.g., a click on a certain headline element of a Web document but rather a user's interaction with an article talking about politics and certain persons mentioned within.

To annotate a Web page with semantic data such as the topics of an article, we use RDFa. Defined in [2] RDFa is a means of adding RDF data to existing Web pages by using inline XHTML attributes.

After detecting an event which happened in the context of a certain DOM node of a Web document, we collect all semantic information in the Web page about the thing that is reported in that given DOM node. We currently achieve this by employing the client-side RDFa library ubiquity (http://ubiquity-rdfa.googlecode.com/). The lifting of context is achieved in a two-phase process. In the first phase we collect the list of RDF subjects of possible triples. This is done close to where the event happened in the document to provide accurate context. In the second phase we collect every triple with these subjects from the overall document in order to provide a very rich context. To find valid subjects the first phase traverses the node where the event happened and its complete subtree. If the given main node does not contain a subject, the immediate dominator node containing a subject is added to the list. This serves two purposes, guaranteeing a single root subject for orphan properties and objects in the subtree and guaranteeing a non-empty result set.

In the second phase all triples with the given subjects are collected from the entire document tree. The gathered triples are then reified and appended as a bag to the event payload. Even if the event itself becomes part of more complex events during the process of correlating and aggregating events, this basic data is retained as part of the simple event.

```
 1  {
 2    "meta": {
 3      "rule": "Politics->Science=>2%"
 4    },
 5    "event": {
 6      "type": "SEQ",
 7      "children": [
 8        {
 9          "type": "DOM",
10          "selector": "div[property=dc:keywords][content~=politica]",
11          "event": "click"
12        },
13        {
14          "type": "DOM",
15          "selector": "div[property=dc:keywords][content~=science]",
16          "event": "click"
17        }
18      ]
19    },
20    "action": [
21      {
22        "type": "EVENT",
23        "trigger": "unusual",
24        "parameters": {"probability": 0.02}
25      }
26    ]
27  }
```

Fig. 2. Example of a single Rule

3   Understanding the User's Interest – Complex Event Processing

Simple events extracted from Web documents must be combined in order to detect complex situations which might be interpreted as a user's interest. This is the task of Complex Event Processing. Detecting the behavior of Web users according to our proposal is divided into design time and run time. The design time consists of (i) semantically enhancing the Web page and then (ii) recording average viewing statistics of the annotated elements, e.g. from log files. From the statistical data we generate client-side rules. Once these rules are created they are pulled by the next client request and loaded into the rule engine for the run time.

For the run time we have developed a client-side event-condition-action (ECA) rule engine. It uses a lightweight rule language which supports ECA rules described in more detail in [3].

Very briefly, we JSON-Rules, our client-side rule language that resembles a lightweight reaction rule language tailored to the needs of Rich Internet Applications, specifically applications that profit from or require Complex Event Processing, condition evaluation on a working memory, and running rule actions written in JavaScript. As a representation for our rules we use JSON, because it is natively usable within JavaScript. JSON can specify objects, arrays and primitives. Rule objects in our JSON-Rules language contain the three attributes event, condition and action. The event part consists of patterns in the event pattern language Snoop [4]. Snoop contains a fairly comprehensive list of Boolean and temporal operators. They are modeled in our ontology. What is missing in Snoop are operators which inspect the contents of input events such as attributes other than timestamps and type. Therefore, we added a FilterEvent as an example of what is needed to filter events by their content.

The condition part consists of conjunctive predicates over variables from a working memory. The action part in turn contains one or more JavaScript code blocks to gain a maximum degree of versatility for the rule author. Alternatively for rule actions we offer to trigger certain desired events as well as manipulations of the working memory. The latter types of action offer greater declarativity while formulating rules. This increase is, however, bought at the price of some flexibility. Thus, we still offer all three kinds of rule actions which can be freely mixed.

The rules on the client serve to detect users exhibiting interesting behavior as learned from the average usage patterns. The user causes events to occur by interacting with the Web page, detected by the event processor and rule engine. Rules are triggered which create intermediate events in a hierarchy of event abstraction. These events are subsequently accumulated until sufficient interest according to the ad provider is recorded (threshold achieved) and actions can be taken by further rules.

The distinction between run time and design time in this section is not a strict temporal distinction as the names would suggest. Rather, because new users will inevitably alter our knowledge of what is interesting there is a loop in the process, feeding back from the run time into the design time to evolve new rules for future users.

Figure 2 shows an example rule. It can be automatically created from analyzing histories of interesting behavior. The only requirement is knowledge, that e.g. states that only two percent of users look at a politics item followed by a science item. The actual rule consists of an event part starting at line 5 and an action part starting at line 20. The rule resembles an event-condition-action rule where the condition is left blank, i.e. is always true.

4   Generating the Personalized Ads Dynamically

Figure 3 shows a rough architecture of our approach: Part b) on the right hand side of the figure depicts the components of our client-side rule engine. Multiple event sources provide input for the event detection, creating complex events. Also, a working memory submits its changes to a Rete network, evaluating rule conditions. The logic for both the event detection and condition evaluation is supplied by rules from a repository, generated from past user activities. Part a) on the left hand side places the client-side components above the protocol boundary dividing client and server. Below on the server or several distributed servers hold the Web content as well as the advertising content. The Web content is annotated, providing semantic relations to the advertisements. Short-term user models provide a temporal model of how a user interacts with the Web content. The ad provider analyses user models to provide up-to-date and personalized advertisements.

On the other hand we anticipate annotations to be mostly used on elements at, or not far below the level of single widgets or paragraphs. Reasons for this are of practical nature, in keeping the number of events manageable. Handling too much detail might have further adverse effects at this point, creating a large number of event types which are almost never used (created or consumed). There might, for example, be no measurable interaction of the user with a certain word in a Web page, whereas the surrounding paragraph might encounter detectable mouse clicks or mouse hovering/movement.

As mentioned in the introduction, web ads should be continuously updated to the web user's interests, which implies a need for the automatic triggering of a new ad, once that user's interests has been dramatically changed. In this work we use the notion of unusual behavior as the criteria for generating a new ad. In the following we describe that principle shortly.

In order to form complex event expressions, the RFDa annotations are combined with a temporal model. Such expressions group the user's atomic actions into temporal contexts like e.g. sequences of clicks. Determining sequences of interest is based on analyzing historical (log) data statistically. By using data mining algorithms for click streams such as [5], historical data is transformed into knowledge about unusual sequences of interaction such as clicks. Subsequently, the corresponding complex event expressions can be created.

This process can be done automatically. A simple sequence along with its confidence might be "politics" followed by "flowers" with a low confidence of 2%. This means that from previous users only a fraction of 2% have looked at a politics widget followed by looking at a flowers widget.

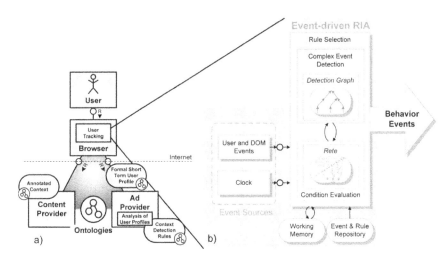

Fig. 3. Architeture: a) Logical Architecture b) Client-side User Behaviour Analysis

This pattern in the users behavior can be treated as unusual, i.e. his/her interests for "politics" and "flowers" are distinguished from the interest of others, so that this can be used for developing a very personalized ad. In fact, we argue that more information content (for generating ads) is stored in the exceptional behavior, than in the usual/expected one. A simple explanation is that expected behavior is too general to detect what is specific in the behavior of the customers (cf. example from the brick and mortar environment from Introduction). Once when enough "unusual behavior" is accounted for a user a new ad should be issued.

Such an ad will very likely attract the attention of the user, since it directly corresponds to his short-term profile. Further processing of e.g. the time interval within the two participating events could be envisioned.

Each complex event expression is embedded in an event-condition-action rule with the probability as the consequence. The consequence forms another event which is processed further by higher-level rules.

In order to enable such a processing, we extended the set of traditional event processing operators with two additional ones *Filter*(E1; condition) and Thres(E1; threshold) as follows:

Filter is modeled like event masks. The Filter enforces a condition on each occurrence of event E1. This allows e.g. for fine-grained content-based filtering/masking of events.

Thres is another content-based operator which we need to extend the Snoop algebra with. Thres(E1; threshold) accumulates the events of type E1 until the boolean function "threshold" returns true, releasing all accumulated events as a complex event and starting accumulation anew.

5 Implementation: Client-Side Event-Enabled Rule Engine

For our implementation we chose JavaScript from the available Web programming languages, for reasons of widespread availability. The data structures and program logic we implemented are roughly divided into the following areas: adapters for the rule language and remote event sources, the working memory, condition representation and evaluation as well as complex event detection.

For Complex Event Processing we are using a graph based approach as proposed in [4]. Initially the graph is a tree with nested complex events being parents of their less deeply nested sub-events, down to the leaves being simple events. However, common subtrees may be shared by more than one parent. This saves space and time compared to detecting the same sub-events multiple times, and renders the former tree a directed acyclic graph.

When using the term event, the distinction must be drawn between event occurrences (i.e. instances) and event types, usually done implicitly. In the detection graph the nodes are event types, they exist before there are any instances. Event instances exist after simple instances arrive and are fed into the graph at the leaves. Complex instances are then formed at the parent nodes, which in turn propagate their results upwards. Every complex event occurrence carries pointers to the set of its constituent event occurrences, so that the events and their parameters can be accessed later. Once an occurrence is computed at a node which is attached to a rule, the state of the associated Rete node is started and actions are triggered.

6 Evaluation

To evaluate the return of targeted advertisements we created a demo Web page with some news articles. Each news article is contained in a separate part of the page, termed Semantic Web Widget (cf. Section 2.1). Each widget is annotated using RDFa using basic keywords and concepts pertaining to the article. For a user entering our demo, each widget is at first partially concealed. This is done to solicit an action from the user when "unfolding" the widget. Thereby the user expresses interest. This creates explicit events which can then be processed by our engine. Our initial evaluation of the ad quality was performed as follows:

1. We selected three different news domains (politics, culture, sports) in order to prove the domain-independence of the approach and pull into the demo Web page, as separate evaluation sessions.
2. We selected five users (PhD students from the Institute) with different cultural backgrounds.
3. The users should browse the demo Web page and judge about the relevance of generated ad-keywords in the case of a) the keywords generated statistically from the Web page (Google approach) and b) keywords generated by using the event-driven approach described in this paper. In order to ensure a fair comparison, the users did not know which list of ad-keywords was produced by which method.

We ask the users to rate the gathered keywords in terms of relevance to what they had been doing in the news portal and to compare this with a static list of keywords extracted from the overall page. The results are very encouraging: in the average 85% of keywords generated in our approach were described as "very relevant" and 98% as "relevant" (very similar results across all three domains).

The traditional approach achieved 65% success for "very relevant" and 85% success for "relevant" ad-keywords. This result demonstrates the advantages of our approach for generating very relevant ads.

In comparison, Web Usage Mining (e.g., [5]) is used on log files which are analyzed on the server side at certain intervals or possibly in a continuous fashion. It is important, however, to stress that our approach detected all events on the client. Events occurred purely by folding and unfolding widgets as parts of the page. No communication with the server took place and hence no artifacts are visible in server log files. Thus, our approach extends clickstream analysis to regions which were previously invisible to server-based mining techniques.

Moreover, our approach is a truly event-driven application, meaning that we detect events in real-time, as soon as they happen. In contrast, traditional mining techniques function in a query-driven manner where results are only created at intervals, such as daily analyses of the log files.

7 Related Work

In Web advertising there are essentially two main approaches, contextual advertising and behavioral advertising. Contextual advertising [6] is driven by the user's context, represented usually in the form of keywords that are extracted from the Web page content, are related to the user's geographical location, time and other contextual factors. An ad provider (ad serving service) utilizes these meta data to deliver relevant ads. Similarly, a users' search words can also be used to deliver related advertisement in search engine results page, Google's second pillar in online advertising. However, contextual advertising, although exploited today by major advertising players (e.g., GoogleAdsense, Yahoo! Publisher Network, Microsoft adCenter, Ad-in-Motion etc.), shows serious weaknesses. Very often the automatically detected context is wrong, and hence ads delivered within that context are irrelevant. For instance, a banner ad offering a travel deal to Florida can possibly be seen side-by-side to a story of a tornado tearing through Florida. This is happening because the context was determined using purely keywords such as "Florida, "shore" etc (i.e., without taking keyword semantics into account). While there are improvements in contextual advertising (e.g., language-independent proximity pattern matching algorithm [7]), this approach still often leads companies to investments that are wasting their advertising budgets, brand promotion and sentiment. In contrast, our approach utilizes semantics to cure major drawbacks of today's contextual advertising. Semantic Web technologies can be used to improve analysis of the meaning of a Web page, and accordingly to ensure that the Web page contains the most appropriate advertising.

The second approach to Web advertising is based on the user's behavior, collected through the user's Web browsing history (i.e., behavioral targeted advertising). The behavior model for each user is established by a persistent cookie. For example, Web sites for online shopping utilize cookies to record the user's past activities and thereby gain knowledge about the user or a cluster of users. There are several reasons why behavioral targeted advertisement via cookies is not a definitive answer to all advertisement problems. First, if a user, after browsing the information about an item purchases that item, he or she will not be interested in that particular good afterwards. Therefore, all ads and "special deals" offered to the user later while browsing that Web site are useless. Also, the short-term user interest should be detected more quickly (i.e., during the current user session). Displayed ads need to reflect current moods or transient user interest. For example, a user looking hastily to buy a gift of flowers is not interested in ads related to his/her long-term profile, created during previous purchases unrelated good or services. Further on, there are problems with cookies. Computers are sometimes shared and users get to see ads governed by other user's cookies. Finally, given the European Union's Directive and US legislation concerned with restricted use of cookies, behavioral targeted advertisement based on cookies is not a promising direction for Web advertising.

We believe that short-term profiling (in contrast to long-term profiles created by cookies) is a valid and possibly augmenting approach in terms of personalization and identification of the user's interest. We realize a short-term profiling using client-side Complex Event Processing techniques (cf. Section 2.2), and background semantics (cf. Section 2). Such profiles are automatically detected, are always up-to-date and fully personalized.

The work from [8] describes event processing for Web clients. Events are observed on the client; however, complex events are not detected in the client. All simple events are propagated to the server for detection of patterns. This incurs latency and reduced locality for the processing of events, so the advantages of client-side event processing are lost.

8 Conclusion

In this paper we present a novel approach for the personalized and dynamic ad delivery on the web. The approach is based on the complex processing of the semantically enriched events generated out of the user's interaction with web content. Additionally, the approach introduce the notion of "unusual behavior" as a criteria for determining the dynamics of the new ads delivery for a particular user. This work goes beyond the web advertisement use case – in fact it opens possibilities to build event-driven applications for the (Semantic) Web. We envision the future of the (Semantic) Web as a huge, decentralized event repository (the so-called Event Cloud in Event processing terminology), which will contain information about the real-time activities of different Web users. Such an event repository will enable different kinds of processing of the real-time information, making the Semantic Web really active, i.e. the environment can react and adapt itself on the signals sensed from the environment, connecting the Internet of Things with the Internet of Services, two basic elements of the Future Internet.

References

1. Schmidt, K.-U., Stojanovic, L., Stojanovic, N., Thomas, S.: On enriching ajax with semantics: The web personalization use case. In: Franconi, E., Kifer, M., May, W. (eds.) ESWC 2007. LNCS, vol. 4519, pp. 686–700. Springer, Heidelberg (2007)
2. Adida, B., Birbeck, M., McCarron, S., Pemberton, S.: Rdfa in xhtml: Syntax and processing (October 2008) Online Resource, http://www.w3.org/TR/rdfa-syntax/
3. Schmidt, K.U., Stühmer, R., Stojanovic, L.: From business rules to application rules in rich internet applications. Scalable Computing: Practice and Experience 9(4), 329–340 (2008)
4. Chakravarthy, S., Krishnaprasad, V., Anwar, E., Kim, S.K.: Composite events for active databases: Semantics, contexts and detection. In: Bocca, J.B., Jarke, M., Zaniolo, C. (eds.) 20th International Conference on Very Large Data Bases, Santiago, Chile proceedings, Los Altos, CA 94022, USA, September 12-15, pp. 606–617. Morgan Kaufmann Publishers, San Francisco (1994)
5. Liu, B.: Web Data Mining. In: Data-Centric Systems and Applications. Springer, Heidelberg (2007)
6. Kenny, D., Marshall, J.: Contextual marketing–the real business of the Internet. Harvard Business Review 78(6), 119–125 (2000)
7. Schonfeld, E.: Proximic signs deals with yahoo and ebay to turn product listings into contextual ads; taking on adsense. Online Article (January 2008),
   http://www.techcrunch.com/2008/01/15/proximic-signs-deals-with-yahoo-andebay-to-turn-product-listings-into-contextual-ads-taking-on-adsense/ (Last visited: August 2009)
8. Carughi, G.T., Comai, S., Bozzon, A., Fraternali, P.: Modeling Distributed Events in Data-Intensive Rich Internet Applications. In: Benatallah, B., Casati, F., Georgakopoulos, D., Bartolini, C., Sadiq, W., Godart, C. (eds.) WISE 2007. LNCS, vol. 4831, pp. 593–602. Springer, Heidelberg (2007)

Unified Patterns to Transform Business Rules into an Event Coordination Mechanism

Willem De Roover and Jan Vanthienen

Department of Decision Sciences & Information Management,
Katholieke Universiteit Leuven, Belgium
{willem.deroover,jan.vanthienen}@econ.kuleuven.be

Summary. Business rules define and constrain various aspects of the business, such as vocabulary, behavior and organizational issues. Enforcing the rules of the business in information systems is however not straightforward, because different mechanisms exist for the (semi-) automatic transformation of various business constraints and rules. In this paper, we examine if and how business rules, not only data rules, but also process rules, timing rules, authorization rules, etc., can be expressed in SBVR and translated using patterns into a more uniform event mechanism, such that the event handling could provide an integrated enforcement of business rules of many kinds.

Keywords: business rules, event coordination, business processes, SBVR, declarative process modeling.

1 Introduction

Enforcing the various rules of the business in information systems is not straightforward, because different mechanisms exist for the transformation of business constraints, process rules, timing rules, access control rules, or other rules into model driven implementations, leading to partial solutions for process management, data constraints, audit constraints, etc.

In this paper, we examine if and how business rules can be translated into a more uniform event mechanism, such that the event handling could provide an integrated enforcement of business rules of many kinds. To this end, we provide a pattern mechanism to transform SBVR (Semantics of Business Vocabulary and Business Rules) [1] integrity constraints and derivation rules into event-driven enforcement rules. We also use an extension of SBVR to declaratively model business processes [2] and use similar patterns to transform the process rules into event driven process enactments. The result is a set of event rules, enabling an integrated enforcement of business rules of many kinds.

The paper is structured as follows. In section 2 we describe the use of SBVR for vocabulary constraints and process constraints. The different types of business rules are identified in section 3. In section 4 we examine some example transformation patterns. Finally, in section 5 we relate the approach to the relevant literature.

M. zur Muehlen and J. Su (Eds.): BPM 2010 Workshops, LNBIP 66, pp. 730–742, 2011.
© Springer-Verlag Berlin Heidelberg 2011

2   The Need for a Unified Framework

Business rules should be on the one hand comprehensible so that they can be understood by business people and on the other hand formal so that they can be enforced by information systems. The Semantics of Business Vocabulary and Business Rules (SBVR) is a language for business modeling that has such property [1], as long as it is extended with a vocabulary for expressing process-related concepts.

2.1   SBVR for Vocabulary Constraints

The Semantics of Business Vocabulary and Business Rules (SBVR) is a new standard for business modeling within the Object Management Group (OMG). SBVR provides a vocabulary called the 'Logical Formulation of Semantics Vocabulary' to describe the structure and the meaning of vocabulary and business rules in terms of formalized statements about the meaning. In addition to fundamental vocabularies, the SBVR provides a discussion of its semantics in terms of existing, well-established formal logics such as First-Order logic, Deontic Logic and Higher-Order logic. The SBVR specification defines a structured, English vocabulary for describing vocabularies and verbalizing rules, called SBVR Structured English [1]. One of the techniques used by SBVR structured English are font styles to designate statements with formal meaning. In particular,

- the term font (green) is used to designate a noun concept.
- the name font (green) designates an individual concept.
- the *verb* font (blue) is used for designation for a verb concept.
- the keyword font (red) is used for linguistic particles that are used to construct statements.

The definitions and examples in the remainder of the text use these SBVR Structured English font styles.

2.2   Procedural versus Declarative Process Modeling

A business process model is called **procedural** when it contains explicit information about how processes should proceed, but only implicitly keeps track of why these design choices have been made, the underlying business rules. Procedural process models are modeled with **procedural languages** such as the Business Process Modeling Notation (BPMN) and UML Activity Diagrams. These languages predominantly focus on the control-flow perspective of business processes. In such process languages it might be possible to **enforce business rules** using a control-flow-based modeling construct. For instance, the enforcement of a derivation or integrity constraint can be directly modeled as a calculation or input validation step, but the disadvantage of procedural process modeling is that business rules cannot be formulated independently from the process models in which they are to be enforced.

The counterpart of a procedural process model is a declarative one. Process modeling is said to have a **declarative** nature, when it explicitly takes into account the business concerns that govern business processes and leaves as much freedom as is permissible at execution time for determining a valid and suitable execution scenario. Examples of declarative languages are: the case handling paradigm [3], the constraint specification framework of Sadiq et al. [4], the Con-Dec language [5] and the PENELOPE language [6]. An overview is given in [7]. Declarative process modeling separates business rule modeling from business rule enforcement. In particular, it does not make use of control flow to indicate when and how business rules are to be enforced [8]. Instead, it is left to the execution semantics of the declarative process models to define an execution model in which different business rule types are automatically enforced.

Procedural process models depict communication logic in a procedural manner, because they specify how and when business events are communicated and information is transmitted. Declarative process models are only concerned with the ability of business agents to perceive business events and business concepts. When an agent can perceive a particular event, the event becomes non-repudiable to the agent, irrespective of how the agent is notified of the event. The execution semantics of a declarative process model determines how events are communicated. In particular, events can be communicated as messages that are sent by the producer (push model), retrieved by the consumer (pull model) or via a publish-subscribe mechanism. This declarative modeling style enhances design-time flexibility, as it allows to model business processes irrespective of the used communication channels.

2.3   SBVR for Process Constraints

SBVR is a suitable base language for defining process-aware rules, but it does not contain a vocabulary with process related concepts such as agents, activities, process states and events. In [2,9] we defined an SBVR vocabulary for expressing process-related concepts, called the EM-BrA^{2}CE Vocabulary. EM-BrA^{2}CE stands for 'Enterprise Modeling using Business Rules, Agents, Activities, Concepts and Events'. The vocabulary thinks of a business process instance as a *trajectory* in a *state space* that consists of the possible sub-activities, events and business concepts. Activities are performed by agents and have a particular duration whereas events occur instantaneously and represent a state change in the world. Changes to the life cycle of an activity are reflected by means of activity events. Each activity in a process instance can undergo a number of distinct state transitions. Business rules determine whether or not a particular state transition can occur.

The following state transitions are e.g. considered: create, assign, updatefact, complete. In [2] a total of twelve generic state transitions have been identified and a generic execution model has been defined in terms of Colored Petri Nets. Figure 1 illustrates a number of state transitions that occur to a given place order activity a1. Notice that each state transition results in a new set of concepts and ground facts, and thus a new state, that are partially represented in the columns of the figure.

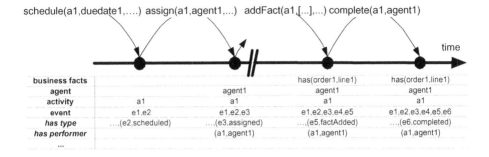

schedule(a1,duedate1,....) assign(a1,agent1,...) addFact(a1,[...],...) complete(a1,agent1)

business facts			has(order1,line1)	has(order1,line1)
agent		agent1	agent1	agent1
activity	a1	a1	a1	a1
event	e1,e2	e1,e2,e3	e1,e2,e3,e4,e5	e1,e2,e3,e4,e5,e6
has type	...(e2,scheduled)	...(e3,assigned)	...(e5,factAdded)	...(e6,completed)
has performer		(a1,agent1)	(a1,agent1)	(a1,agent1)
...				

Fig. 1. An illustration of the state transitions for a place order activity a1

In the vocabulary, the state of an activity (or service instance) includes the history of events related to the activity or its sub-activities. Unlike many ontologies for business modeling, such as for instance the UFO [10], a distinction is made between activities and events. Activities are performed by agents and have a particular duration whereas events occur instantaneously and represent a state change in the world. Changes to the life cycle of an activity are reflected by means of activity events. Activity events allow process modelers to distinguish between the activity state transitions that occur when, among others, creating, scheduling, assigning, starting and completing an activity.

3   Business Rule Types

Given the SBVR vocabulary for process-related concepts, each business process can be modeled by describing its state space and the set of business rules that constrain the possible transitions in this state space. For instance, the state space of an order-to-cash process is described by the following concepts:

- **composite activity types**: coordinate sales order
- **atomic activity types**: place order, accept order, reject order, pay, ship
- **activity event types**: created, assigned, started, completed
- **business concepts**: order, order line
- **business fact types**: order *has* order line, order *is critical*,...

Business rules come in different forms (structural/definitional rules, derivation rules, behavioral rules, permissions and obligations), and refer to different aspects (data, behavior, organization). In [2] a total of sixteen business rule types are identified that can constrain specific activity state transitions, as indicated in Table 1. They refer to one of the three aspects of business process modeling that are generally considered [11]: control-flow, data and organizational aspects. For reasons of brevity, only a number of these business rule types are included in this text.

Table 1. Business rule types

aspect	business rule type	related work
control flow	Temporal deontic rule	[12],[6]
	Activity precondition	[13]
	Activity postcondition	[13],[3]
	Dynamic integrity	[14]
	Activity cardinality	[5]
	Serial activity constraint	[4]
	Activity order	[4],[5]
	Activity exclusion	[4],[5]
	Activity inclusion	[4],[5]
	Reaction rule	[12]
data	Static integrity	[14]
	Derivation rule	[14]
organization	Activity authorization	[15]
	Activity allocation rule	
	Visibility constraint	[15]
	Event subscription	[15]

Control-flow Aspects. Business policy and regulations contain a lot of constraints (partial order, timing, exists, activity pre- and postconditions). In a trade community, for instance, different business protocols lay down the obligations of business partners and can be expressed in the form of temporal deontic rules [6].

Data aspects. The performer of an activity can perform particular manipulations (addition, removal or update) of business facts. These state transitions can be constrained by integrity constraints and derivation rules.

Organizational aspects. Organizational aspects relate to the visibility of business concepts and events and the authorization to perform particular activities.

4   Example Patterns for Transforming Business Rules into Event Rules

We examine how various business rules can be translated into more uniform event rules, such that the event handling could provide an integrated enforcement of business rules of many kinds, not only process rules, but also data rules, timing rules, authorization rules and others. To this end, we provide a pattern mechanism to transform SBVR (Semantics of Business Vocabulary and Business Rules) integrity constraints, derivation rules and process rules into event-driven enforcement rules and notifications.

4.1   Data Constraints and Derivations

Example patters for integrity constraints and derivations are shown in figures 2, 3 and 4.

Vocabulary Rule: Integrity constraint

Business Rule Template:

- General integrity constraint:
     <u>\<Concept1\></u> must be {less/larger/earlier/...} than <u>\<Concept2\></u>

The general integrity constraint can be specialized into several integrity constraints:

- A possible specialized integrity constraint:
     <u>\<Concept1\></u> must be less than <u>\<Concept2\></u>

Business Rule Example:

   #1: The <u>Totalprice</u> *specified by* each <u>Order</u> *of a* <u>Customer</u> must be less than the <u>Creditlimit</u> *specified by* the <u>Customer</u>.

Translation to Event Rules:

- On IsCreated (<u>\<Concept1/2\></u>) :
     if <u>\<Concept1\></u> is no less than <u>\<Concept2\></u> then *notify* (Rule #)
- On IsModified (<u>\<Concept1/2\></u>) :
     if <u>\<Concept1\></u> is no less than <u>\<Concept2\></u> then *notify* (Rule #)

notify signals the systems that a violation of a Business rule is about to occur. It is the responsibility of the systems to refuse the action that caused the violation or if decided otherwise to handle it in a specific way.

Translation to Event Rules Example:

- On IsCreated (<u>Totalprice</u>) : if <u>Totalprice</u> is no less than <u>Creditlimit</u> then *notify* (#1)
- On IsCreated (<u>Creditlimit</u>) : if <u>Totalprice</u> is no less than <u>Creditlimit</u> then *notify* (#1)
- On IsModified (<u>Totalprice</u>) : if <u>Totalprice</u> is no less than <u>Creditlimit</u> then *notify* (#1)
- On IsModified (<u>Creditlimit</u>) : if <u>Totalprice</u> is no less than <u>Creditlimit</u> then *notify* (#1)

Fig. 2. Integrity Constraint

For each type of business rule we have defined a general template. The use of templates limits the ways in which rules can be formulated, but in this way it will be easy to extract the necessary information from a business rule. This information includes the type of the business rule and the concepts used in the rule. We use this information in event based rules and notifications. For each type of business rule we have defined corresponding Event-Condition-Action (ECA) rules. The extracted concepts from the business rule are filled in into the corresponding ECA rule. The sets of ECA rules are equivalent to the business rules that they express. However ECA rules have the advantage that they make clear when they have to be checked. The condition of a ECA rule checks whether the business rule is violated and in case of a violation the system will be notified of this violation.

Some business rules will also generate events. This is the case when a business rule changes the value of some concept. Derivation rules e.g. calculate the value of a concept based on other concepts. These rules will generate an event that signals that the value of the calculated concept has changed.

Vocabulary Rule: Derivation rule

Business Rule Template:

- A specialized derivation rule:
  <Concept1> must be computed as <Concept2> {plus /minus/ times /divided by}
  <Concept3>

Business Rule Example:

#2: The LinePrice specified by each Orderline must be computed as the
ProductPrice specified by the Product of the Orderline times the Amount
specified by the Orderline

Translation to Event Rules:

- Create the following rules:
  - On IsCreated (<Concept1>) : compute (<Concept1>)
  - On IsModified (<Concept2>) : compute (<Concept1>)
  - On IsModified (<Concept3>) : compute (<Concept1>)
- Signal the following event:
  - On compute (<Concept1>) : signal IsModified (<Concept1>)

**Translation to Event Rules
Example:**

- Create the following rules:
  - On IsCreated (LinePrice) : compute (LinePrice)
  - On IsModified (ProductPrice) : compute (LinePrice)
  - On IsModified (Amount) : compute (LinePrice)
- Signal the following event:
  - On compute (LinePrice) : signal IsModified (LinePrice)

Fig. 3. Derivation Rule

4.2   An Example

The following rule stated in [16] explains our case: *The total value of a customers
unpaid orders must not exceed his credit limit.* This rule will have to be checked
at several points in the execution of some processes as indicated in [16]:

- When a customer submits an new order
- When a customer changes an existing order (adds items,changes quantities,
  substitutes products)
- When a customers credit limit is changed
- When product prices are changed (unless prices are frozen at order time)
- and for any other relevant events the system recognizes.

In figure 5 three business rules are presented with their corresponding event rules
and notifications. As the three rules are closely related to each other, changes
that occur due to one rule can be propagated to other rules. For example, if
the LinePrice of an OrderLine is recalculated due to changes in ProductPrice or
Amount then this results in an event that signals that the LinePrice has changed.

Vocabulary Rule: Derivation rule (dynamic)

Business Rule Template:

- *General derivation rule:*
  <Concept1> must be computed as <calculation>

The general derivation rule can be specialized into several derivation rules.

- *A specialized derivation rule:*
  <Concept1> must be computed as the sum of <Concept2> contained in the <Concept3>

Business Rule Example:

#3: The TotalPrice specified by each Order must be computed as the sum of the LinePrices specified by each OrderLine contained in the Order

Translation to Event Rules:

- *Create the following rules:*
  - On IsCreated (<Concept1>) : compute (<Concept1>)
  - On IsModified (<Concept2>) : compute (<Concept1>)
  - On IsAdded (<Concept2>) : compute (<Concept1>)
  - On IsRemoved (<Concept2>) : compute (<Concept1>)
- *Signal the following event:*
  - On compute (<Concept1>) : signal IsModified (<Concept1>)

Translation to Event Rules Example:

- *Create the following rules:*
  - On IsCreated (TotalPrice) : compute (TotalPrice)
  - On IsModified (LinePrice) : compute (TotalPrice)
  - On IsAdded (OrderLine) : compute (TotalPrice)
  - On IsRemoved (OrderLine) : compute (TotalPrice)
- *Signal the following event:*
  - On compute (TotalPrice) : signal IsModified (TotalPrice)

Fig. 4. Derivation Rule (dynamic)

This event is handled by an ECA-rule generated from rule #b and leads to the recalculation of the TotalPrice. The change of TotalPrice will be signaled to the system by means of a new event. This will trigger all event rules that act on changes to TotalPrice including an ECA rule generated from rule #a. This rule will check if the new TotalPrice is no less than the specified CreditLimit. If this is the case, the system will notify this violation.

4.3 Control Flow

The approach is not limited to data rules. It is possible to develop patterns for control flow and organization rules, as already indicated in [17,18,19,20]. As

---

The CrediLimit example

#a: The Totalprice *specified by* each Order *of* a Customer must be less than the Creditlimit *specified by* the Customer.

#b: The TotalPrice *specified by* each Order must be computed as the sum of the LinePrices *specified by* each OrderLine *contained in* the Order

#c: The LinePrice *specified by* each Orderline must be computed as the ProductPrice *specified by* the Product *of* the Orderline times the Amount *specified by* the Orderline

- Create the following rules for #a :
  - o   On IsCreated (Totalprice): if Totalprice is no less than Creditlimit then *notify (#a)*
  - o   On IsCreated (Creditlimit): if Totalprice is no less than Creditlimit then *notify (#a)*
  - o   On IsModified (Totalprice): if Totalprice is no less than Creditlimit then *notify (#a)*
  - o   On IsModified (Creditlimit): if Totalprice is no less than Creditlimit then *notify (#a)*

- Create the following rules for #b :
  - o   On IsCreated (TotalPrice) : *compute* (TotalPrice)
  - o   On IsModified (LinePrice) : *compute* (TotalPrice)
  - o   On IsAdded (OrderLine) : *compute* (TotalPrice)
  - o   On IsRemoved (OrderLine) : *compute* (TotalPrice)
- Signal the following event for #b:
  - o   On *compute (*TotalPrice) : signal IsModified (TotalPrice)

- Create the following rules for #c:
  - o   On IsCreated (LinePrice) : *compute* (LinePrice)
  - o   On IsModified (ProductPrice) : *compute* (LinePrice)
  - o   On IsModified (Amount) : *compute* (LinePrice)
- Signal the following event for #c:
  - o   On *compute* (LinePrice) : signal IsModified (LinePrice)

Fig. 5. Credit Limit example

SBVR does not provide process related concepts, we used the concepts provided by the EM-BA^{2}CE framework. For the sake of simplicity we present these concepts as simple SBVR fact types in our patterns. Figures 6 and 7 present two patterns for transforming control flow and organizational rules into event-driven enforcement rules and notifications.

5   Evaluation

Languages for declarative process modeling often do not cover the many real-life business concerns that exist in reality. Some only allow to express business rules about sequence and timing constraints, i.e. the control-flow perspective, others include the organizational and data model aspects, but do not provide a temporal logic to express temporal relationships between concepts such as activities or events. Moreover, these languages make use of very different knowledge representation paradigms. These heterogeneous knowledge representation paradigms raise the question how to reason about such heterogeneously expressed knowledge.

Moreover, not all these languages have an explicit execution model or they have an execution model that explicitly assumes either human or machine-mediated service enactment. The EM-BrA^{2}CE framework with its formal execution model [2] makes abstraction of the differences between humans and

Behavior Rule: *Timed precedence of activities*

Business Rule Template:

<Activity2> *may ... only* <time constraint> *after* <Activity1>

Business Rule Example:

- *Activities:*
  - o *Activity1:* Trainee *applies for* license
  - o *Activity2:* Trainee *takes* practical car examination
- *Business Rule:*
  - #5: A trainee *may take a* practical car examination *only within 1 year after that* trainee *has applied for a* license

Remarks:

Activity2 can only be performed (a limited time) after Activity1 has been performed. However performing Activity1 does not imply that Activity2 will be performed.

Visual Representation:

The representation makes clear that this rule only puts a constraint on the execution of Activity2.

Translation to Event Rules:

- *On start (<Activity2>) : if not ended(<Activity1>) or (<Activity2> expired) then notify (Rule #)*
- Add the following events to the event list:
  - o on <time constraint> : signal that <Activity2> is expired.
  - o on <time constraint * [notice factor]> : signal that <Activity2> will expire.

  The event list keeps track of events that will have to happen in the future. Every event in the event list will have a timer. If the timer expires that event will be triggered.

Translation to Event Rules Example:

- On start (trainee *takes a* practical car examination) : if not end(trainee *applies for* license) then notify (#5)
- Add the following events to the event list:
  - o On 1 year : signal that trainee *takes* practical car examination is expired.
  - o On 0.9 year : signal that trainee *takes* practical car examination will expire.

Fig. 6. Control flow: timed precedence

Management Rule: Authorization

Business Rule Template:

> <Concept1> *that* <verb phrase><Concept2> *must be different from* <Concept3> *that* <verb phrase><Concept4>

Business Rule Example:

> #6: *The* Person1 *that applies for a* Loan *must be different from the* Person2 *that approves the* Loan

---

Translation to Event Rules:

- On IsCreated (<Concept1> <verb phrase> <Concept2>):
  if <Concept1> is equal to <Concept3> then *notify* (Rule #)
- On IsCreated (<Concept3><verb phrase> <Concept4>) :
  if <Concept1> is equal to <Concept3> then *notify* (Rule #)
- On IsModified (<Concept1>) :
  if <Concept1> is equal to <Concept3> then *notify* (Rule #)
- On IsModified (<Concept3>) :
  if <Concept1> is equal to <Concept3> then *notify* ((Rule #)

Translation to Event Rules Example:

- On IsCreated (Person2 *approves* Loan) :
  if Person1 is equal to Person2 then *notify* (#6)

Remarks:

- There is no need to check any other event rules in the example.
  - Applying for a loan always happens before the loan is approved, this can be enforced by a behavioural rule, therefore it is not necessary to check the rule when a person applies for a loan.
  - Approving a loan happens at one point in time. In this example we only keep track of the actual approver, not any planned approver. Therefore it is not necessary to keep track of the changes before the actual approval.

Fig. 7. Authorization rule

machines. Coordination work such as creating, scheduling, assigning, skipping, aborting or redoing an activity can then be performed by humans, machines or both.

6   Conclusion

In this paper, we have examined if and how business rules in SBVR, not only data rules, but also process rules, timing rules, authorization rules, etc., can be translated using patterns into a more uniform event mechanism, such that the event handling could provide an integrated enforcement of business rules of many kinds. Future work consists of developing a tool that uses these templates to transform SBVR rules into ECA rules and creates an execution model that is compliant with these rules.

References

1. Object Management Group: Semantics of Business Vocabulary and Business Rules (SBVR) – Interim Specification. OMG Document – dtc/06-03-02 (2006)
2. Goedertier, S., Haesen, R., Vanthienen, J.: EM-BrA^{2}CE v0.1: A vocabulary and execution model for declarative business process modeling. FETEW Research Report KBI_0728, K.U.Leuven (2007)
3. van der Aalst, W.M.P., Weske, M., Grünbauer, D.: Case handling: a new paradigm for business process support. Data & Knowledge Engineering 53(2), 129–162 (2005)
4. Sadiq, S.W., Orlowska, M.E., Sadiq, W.: Specification and validation of process constraints for flexible workflows. Information Systems 30(5), 349–378 (2005)
5. Pesic, M., van der Aalst, W.M.P.: A declarative approach for flexible business processes management. In: Business Process Management Workshops, pp. 169–180 (2006)
6. Goedertier, S., Vanthienen, J.: Designing Compliant Business Processes with Obligations and Permissions. In: Eder, J., Dustdar, S. (eds.) BPM Workshops 2006. LNCS, vol. 4103, pp. 5–14. Springer, Heidelberg (2006)
7. Goedertier, S., Vanthienen, J.: An overview of declarative process modeling principles and languages. Communications of SWIN 6, 51–58 (2009)
8. Morgan, T.: Business Rules and Information Systems: Aligning IT with Business Goals. Addison-Wesley Professional, Reading (2002)
9. Goedertier, S., Mues, C., Vanthienen, J.: Specifying process-aware access control rules in SBVR ((Best Paper Award)). In: Paschke, A., Biletskiy, Y. (eds.) RuleML 2007. LNCS, vol. 4824, pp. 39–52. Springer, Heidelberg (2007)
10. Guizzardi, G., Wagner, G.: in: Ontologies and Business Systems Analysis. In: Rosemann, M., Green, P. (eds.) Some Applications of a Unified Foundational Ontology in Business Modeling, pp. 345–367. IDEA Publisher, USA (2005)
11. Jablonski, S., Bussler, C.: Workflow Management. In: Modeling Concepts, Architecture and Implementation. International Thomson Computer Press, London (1996)
12. Paschke, A., Bichler, M., Dietrich, J.B.: ContractLog: An approach to rule based monitoring and execution of service level agreements. In: Adi, A., Stoutenburg, S., Tabet, S. (eds.) RuleML 2005. LNCS, vol. 3791, pp. 209–217. Springer, Heidelberg (2005)
13. Roman, D., Keller, U., Lausen, H., de Bruijn, J., Lara, R., Stollberg, M., Polleres, A., Feier, C., Bussler, C., Fensel, D.: Web service modeling ontology. Applied Ontology 1(1), 77–106 (2005)
14. Wagner, G.: The agent-object-relationship metamodel: towards a unified view of state and behavior. Information Systems 28(5), 475–504 (2003)
15. Strembeck, M., Neumann, G.: An integrated approach to engineer and enforce context constraints in RBAC environments. ACM Transactions on Information System Security 7(3), 392–427 (2004)
16. Ross, R.: Business Rule Concepts, 3rd edn. Business Rule Solutions, LLC (2009)
17. Pesic, M.: Constraint-based workflow management systems: Shifting control to users. PhD thesis, Eindhoven University of Technology (2008)

18. van der Aalst, W.M.P., Pesic, M.: Decserflow: Towards a truly declarative service flow language. In: Leymann, F., Reisig, W., Thatte, S.R., van der Aalst, W.M.P. (eds.) The Role of Business Processes in Service Oriented Architectures. Dagstuhl Seminar Proceedings, vol. 06291, Internationales Begegnungs- und Forschungszentrum fuer Informatik (IBFI), Schloss Dagstuhl, Germany (2006)
19. Wang, M., Wang, H.: From process logic to business logic–A cognitive approach to business process management. Information & Management 43(2), 179–193 (2006)
20. Ceponiene, L., Nemuraite, L., Vedrickas, G.: Separation of event and constraint rules in uml & ocl models of service oriented information systems. Information Technology and Control 38(1), 29–37 (2009)

Optimising Complex Event Queries over Business Processes Using Behavioural Profiles

Matthias Weidlich[1], Holger Ziekow[2], and Jan Mendling[2]

[1] Hasso Plattner Institute, Potsdam, Germany
matthias.weidlich@hpi.uni-potsdam.de
[2] Humboldt-Universität zu Berlin, Germany
{holger.ziekow,jan.mendling}@wiwi.hu-berlin.de

Abstract. Complex event processing emerged as a technology that promises tight integration of business process management with the flow of products in a supply chain. As part of that, complex event querying is used to monitor and analyse streams of events. The amount of data that needs to be processed along with the distribution of the event-emitting sources impose serious challenges for efficient event querying mechanisms. In this paper, we assume that the business process to which the events relate is defined in terms of a normative process model. Based thereon, we show how this knowledge can be leveraged to optimise complex event queries and their processing. To this end, we use the formal concept of behavioural profiles as a behavioural abstraction of the process model.

Keywords: Complex Event Processing, Query Optimization.

1 Introduction

Traditional business process management has put a strong emphasis on business process design based on both conceptual and executable models. The latter are used in workflow management systems for process automation, mostly in a rather narrow organizational setting. Recent technological innovations including information systems standards for RFID applications offer the chance of a much tighter coupling of a business process management system with the physical flow of goods in a supply chain, and event-based systems play an important role in tying informational process and object flow closer together.

In order to monitor and analyse the event streams produced by event-based systems, mechanisms to query complex events are of particular importance. In this paper, we consider an information system environment in which events are recorded at different distributed locations. This is a scenario that we frequently encountered in prior case studies in the manufacturing sector. The challenge in such scenarios is to find a strategy to handle querying in an efficient manner. Here, most research centres around the advantages and drawbacks of push and pull strategies in minimizing event propagation traffic.

Our approach for optimisation of complex event querying builds on the assumption that a normative process model is available. Such a process model

M. zur Muehlen and J. Su (Eds.): BPM 2010 Workshops, LNBIP 66, pp. 743–754, 2011.

captures external knowledge about the potential sequence of events, which can be utilized for optimisation. The contribution of this paper is an approach that leverages such external knowledge based on the formal concept of behavioural profiles. Such a behavioural profile can be efficiently calculated from a process model. It covers constraints about the execution sequence, mutual exclusion, and potential concurrency of activities specified in a business process model. Our approach uses this knowledge to optimise query processing. Therefore, we rely on the accuracy of this knowledge and focus on expected events of the process.

The remainder of the paper is structured accordingly. Section 2 introduces basic terminology and concepts of complex event processing. Section 3 discusses the process knowledge that is leveraged in our approach. Based thereon, Section 4 introduces rules for optimisation based on behavioural profiles of processes. Section 5 discusses related work. Finally, Section 6 concludes the paper.

2   Complex Event Processing

In this section, we present the background of our work in terms of complex event processing. We introduce some basic terminology and concepts, including an event model and a syntax for a pseudo query language and execution plans that we use throughout this paper.

Complex Event Processing. Event processing refers to continuous real-time processing of data items (events) as they enter an IT system [7]. This is in contrast to traditional data bases where queries run on an ad-hoc basis over stored data. Event processing systems store event queries and continuously evaluate them as new events arrive. Application examples are manifold and include monitoring financial stocks, supply chain activities, or production processes [8,15]. The term *complex event* refers to events that are defined trough more than one input event. For instance, one may define the complex event of a correctly finished process by a sequence of events about corresponding process activities. Complex event processing (CEP) is the process of detecting complex events.

Event Model. Most event models define an event as a tuple containing a unique ID, a type, a timestamp, and a set of attributes. In the context of business processes, events typically reflect the execution of an activity in a certain process instance. For the discussion in this paper, we build on this simple model and assume that the type denotes the process activity which caused the event. We further assume that each event holds an attribute $Case_{ID}$ that has the same value for all events generated in the same process instance. This basic model is in line with existing models for monitoring business processes, such as the EPCglobal standard for RFID events [6]. Further on, we use capital letters to denote events of a certain type and '.' to denote the attribute of an event (e.g.: A.ID for the ID of an event of type A).

Complex Event Queries. Several approaches to phrasing and executing complex event queries exist. Dedicated query languages for complex event processing provide means to correlate, filter, and transform events from several sources. These languages typically use an SQL like syntax, follow a Pattern Condition Action (PCA) structure, or provide support for both. Without loss of generality, we use a simplified PCA based language in this paper.

The patterns in PCA based queries define relations between events that together cause an event of interest. The sequence operator SEQ and the logical operators AND, OR, and NOT are common operators for defining event patterns. $SEQ(A, B)$ matches if event A is followed by event B, $AND(A, B)$ if A and B occur in any order, $OR(A, B)$ if A or B occur, and $NOT(A)$ if A does not occur. Note that events A and B can be events or event patterns. This enables nested constructs such as $SEQ(A, OR(B, C))$ that matches sequences AB or AC as well as queries for long event sequences.

The constraint part in PCA based queries defines conditions on event attribute values that must hold in matching event sequences. These constraints resemble the *where* clause of SQL queries and compare attribute values of different events or attribute values against constants. To monitor events of a certain process instance one must query event sequences with the same value for $Case_{ID}$. In this paper, we assume this condition to always be in place without explicit mentioning. That is, the query $SEQ(A, B)$ matches only event sequences AB where $A.Case_{ID} = B.Case_{ID}$ holds true.

The action part in PCA based queries defines which action the system should trigger if the defined event queries matches. This is often issuing of a notification or triggering of some actuator. We focus on optimisations for detecting complex events and, therefore, do not discuss the action part in more detail, which is not affected by our contribution.

Execution Model. In this paper, we consider execution of complex event queries based on state machines. We choose this model for the sake of an intuitive illustration and because state machines (or variations of state machines) are widely used in complex event processing [4,11,17]. However, our approach to query optimisation may also be applied to other execution models.

The pattern part of PCA based complex event queries intuitively translates to transitions in state machines. The event types in a query define the input alphabet of the machine. A query for a single event A is realized by a transition on A from the start state to the final state. Queries for complex event sequences are built by concatenating state machines for detecting single events.

Our solution builds upon two important extensions of the simple state machine based model. One extensions is constraint evaluation along state transitions as proposed in [17]. In particular we assume that the state machine performs equivalence checks on the $Case_{ID}$ along transitions. That is, in a query $SEQ(A, B)$ the machine transitions on any event A but only transitions further if an event B with $A.Case_{ID} = B.Case_{ID}$ occurs. This optimisation avoids extracting irrelevant events sequences that do not belong to the same processes case (those sequences would have to be filtered out later on).

The other extension that we build upon concerns the employed communication paradigm. Event processing typically builds on push-based communication, often realized with a publish/subscribe mechanism [10]. Thus, events must be processed when they occur. While this scheme is appropriate in many applications of CEP, it is unnecessarily restrictive for monitoring business processes. Many business applications keep records of event data in transaction logs. This allows pulling (some) events from logs and processing them later. Akdere et al. exploit this by proposing plan based execution of complex event queries [2]. The plan based approach combines push-based and pull-based communication.

For illustration consider the query $SEQ(A, B)$. With push based communication the processing machine subscribes for events A and subsequently waits for corresponding events B. In a hybrid model, the processing machine can subscribe to events B and then pulls corresponding events A from the transaction log (with $A.timestamp < B.timesamp$ and $A.Case_{ID} = B.Case_{ID}$). The latter plan saves network traffic if events B occur with a much lower frequency than events A.

In our approach, we use process models to derive optimised hybrid execution plans. Throughout this paper, $A \rightarrow B$ denotes the processing order of events in an execution plan. We assume push based communication unless denoted by the keyword *pull*. Thus, '$A \rightarrow B$' and '$B \rightarrow pull\ A$' are both execution plans for the query $SEQ(A, B)$. The first plan passively waits for events A and subsequently for corresponding events B. The second plan waits for events B and subsequently actively pulls corresponding events A that happened before B.

3   Process Knowledge

This section introduces the process knowledge that we use for query optimisation. It combines event querying with behavioural profiles, a technique for deriving behavioural constraints from a process model (see Fig. 1). We start our discussion from the perspective of the process model, which we will use to derive a behavioural profile and its relations. Information about relations between events can directly be derived from process models [16]. Most of our optimisation rules solely build upon these relations. However, some rules need information about the absolute or relative frequencies of events.

Process Models. Process models are extensively used in companies for describing business operations and technical workflows. In many cases, they are directly used as a template for execution by a process engine. Then, the process model plays a normative role and is explicitly enforced by the engine. If, for instance, the process model depicted in Fig. 2 is used by a process engine, it is only possible to execute A and B, potentially repeatedly, followed either by C and E, or D and E, or none of the two before F is executed towards completion of the process.

Behavioural Profiles. In our event query optimisation, we will exploit the fact that behavioural constraints can be defined in a normative process model. In particular, we use the notion of a behavioural profile [16]. Such a profile describes

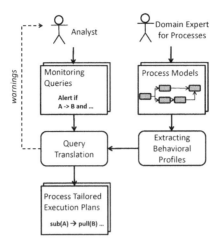

Fig. 1. Automatic tailoring of queries to processes

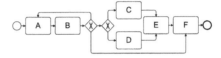

Fig. 2. Example of a process model in BPMN notation

behavioural relations on the level of activity pairs. A behavioural profile consists of three relations that partition the Cartesian product of all activities, such that two activities are either in strict order, exclusive to each other, or in interleaving order. Behavioural profiles can be efficiently calculated for process models as the one shown in Fig. 2. Semantics of the relations of the behavioural profile are defined on the possible execution sequences, alias traces, of the process model.

- The *strict order* relation, denoted by $\rightsquigarrow$, holds between two activities x and y, if x might happen before y, but not vice versa. In other words, x will be before y in all traces that contain both activities.
- The *exclusiveness* relation, denoted by $+$, holds for two activities, if they never occur together in any process trace.
- The *interleaving order* relation, denoted by $\|$, holds for two activities x and y, if x might happen before y and y might also happen before x. Thus, interleaving order might be interpreted as the absence of any specific order between two activities.

Further on, the causal behavioural profile defines an additional *co-occurrence* relation, denoted by $\gg$, between activities. Two activities are co-occurring, if any trace (from the initial to the final state of the process) that contains the first activity contains also the second activity. For the process model in Fig. 2, for instance, the behavioural profile states that B is always preceding E, both activities are in strict order, and that C is exclusive to D. The co-occurrence relation states that every trace containing C also contains B, but not vice versa.

Event Frequencies. As stated above, some optimisation rules require knowledge about event frequencies. Such information could be provided by domain experts or derived through analysis of event logs. In the remainder of this paper, knowledge of the frequency of an event A will be referred to by λ_A. Still, information on the relative order between frequencies of different events is sufficient for our purposes.

4   Process Tailored Query Optimisation

Process tailored query optimisation follows the idea of using process knowledge to enhance the execution of complex event queries regarding an optimisation goal. This approach complements existing query optimisation techniques. A feature of our solution is that it allows abstracting from details of process instances during query formulation but considers these details in query execution (see Fig. 1).

We provide a set of rules that consider different information about processes and serve different optimisation goals. (1) One goal is reducing the number of required event messages for query processing. This is relevant in scenarios where the network is a bottleneck or communication uses scarce resources. For instance, battery powered sensor devices aim to reduce energy intensive communication in order to maximize battery lifetime. (2) Another optimisation goal is reducing required memory for intermediate query results. This is relevant if resource constrained devices run the query and/or if intermediate results grow large. The latter is the case if queries cover a large time span or events occur at high frequencies. (3) Furthermore, reducing delay between event occurrence and event detection can be a goal for optimisation. This is relevant whenever systems have real-time constraints, i.e., an immediate response to the event is required. These constraints can be found in automated production processes where events trigger production tasks.

We consider optimisation at three stages. First, we provide transformation rules that target complex event queries on the language level (see Section 4.1). Such rules change the semantics of the original query without changing the result set. Second, we provide rules that address the generation of query execution plans (see Section 4.2). A complier can generate several candidate execution plans for the same query. Our rules help selecting the most efficient plan. Third, we provide rules that transform execution plans (see Section 4.3). Transformed plans use events that are outside the scope of the original query but provide information that allow for more efficient query execution.

We use the notation '$A \Rightarrow B$, if X' for describing rules. Here, This denote that A translates to B if condition X applies. A and B can be parts of query expressions in a high level language or parts of query execution plans. X is a logical expression that involves processes knowledge. For each rule we discuss the effect on optimisation goals and provide some intuitive discussion how the optimisation is achieved. In addition, we also depict small process model fragments that illustrate the applicability of certain rules.

4.1   Query Transformation

Rules for query transformation operate on a high level language level. They change the semantics of the query but - given the considered processes - they do not change the result set of detected events. Below, we list such optimisation rules.

Rule 1: $and(A, B) \Rightarrow seq(A, B)$
if $A \rightsquigarrow B$

Effect of the rule: The rule reduces memory consumption and event messages.
Intuition behind the rule: Any B that matches in a query has a preceding A, while B cannot be observed before A. The rule avoids receiving and storing events B that will have no matching A.
Required knowledge: $\rightsquigarrow$

Fig. 3. Process where rule 1 applies

Rule 2: $and(...and(E_1, E_2), ...), E_i) \Rightarrow false$
if $\exists\, E_x, E_y \in \{E_1, ..., E_i\} : (E_x, E_y) \in +$

Effect of the rule: The rule reduces memory consumption and event messages.
Intuition behind the rule: The rule avoids querying for event combinations that cannot occur because involved events are mutually exclusive.
Required knowledge: $+$

Fig. 4. Process where rule 2 and 3 apply

Rule 3: $seq(...seq(E_1, E_2), ...), E_i) \Rightarrow false$
if $\exists\, E_x, E_y \in \{E_1, ..., E_i\} : (E_x, E_y) \in +$

Effect of the rule: The rule reduces memory consumption and event messages.
Intuition behind the rule: Similar to rule 2, this rule avoids querying for event combinations that cannot occur because involved events are mutually exclusive.
Required knowledge: $+$

Rule 4: $seq(...seq(E_1, E_2), ...), E_i) \Rightarrow false$
if $\exists\, E_x, E_y \in \{E_1, ..., E_i\} : y > x \land E_y \rightsquigarrow E_x$

Effect of the rule: The rule reduces memory consumption and event messages.
Intuition behind the rule: The rule avoids querying for combinations that cannot
occur because events cannot happen in the queried order.
Required knowledge: ⤳

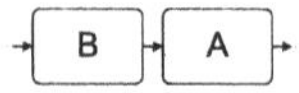

Fig. 5. Process where rule 4 applies

Rule 5: $and(...and(E_1, E_2), ...), E_i) \Rightarrow false$
if $\exists \; false \in \{E_1, ..., E_i\}$

Effect of the rule: The rule reduces memory consumption and event messages.
Intuition behind the rule: The rule propagates rules 2, 3, and 4 through query
hierarchies in complex events. If the query includes a complex event E_i that was
falsified by any of these rules the queried combination cannot occur.
Required knowledge: + and/or ⤳

Rule 6: $seq(...seq(E_1, E_2), ...), E_i)) \Rightarrow false$
if $\exists \; false \in \{E_1, ..., E_i\}$

Effect of the rule: The rule reduces memory consumption and event messages.
Intuition behind the rule: Similar to rule 5, this rule propagates rule 2, 3 and 4
thought queries hierarchies. If the query includes a complex event E_i that was
falsified by any of these rules the queried combination cannot occur.
Required knowledge: + and/or ⤳

4.2   Plan Selection

Rules for plan selection apply in the process of query plan generation. The rules
help picking the most efficient execution plan from a set of candidate plans. It is
important to note that these rules allow optimal plan selection without knowledge about event frequencies and solely use information of standard process
models. Below, we list rules that illustrate optimisation based on plan selection:

Rule 7: $seq(A, B) \Rightarrow B \rightarrow pull\; A$
if $A \not\gg B \wedge B \gg A$

Effect of the rule: The rule reduces messages and memory consumption in the
event processor.
Intuition behind the rule: We derive from the behavioural profile that each B
matches an A but not vice versa. Thus, A happens more often than B and pulling
As (instead of pushing) avoids processing irrelevant As.
Required knowledge: ≫

Fig. 6. Process where rule 7 applies

Rule 8: $seq(A, B) \Rightarrow A \rightarrow B$
if $A \gg B \wedge B \not\gg A$

Effect of the rule: The rule reduces messages but (compared to the alternative plan '$B \rightarrow pull\ A$') increases memory consumption in the event processor.
Intuition behind the rule: We derive from the behavioural profile that each A matches a B but not vice versa. Thus, B occurs more often than A. Pushing A allows to efficiently filter out Bs (those with no preceding A). However, the execution plan requires to keep events A in a buffer until corresponding Bs arrive. It is therefore more memory consuming than the alternative plan '$B \rightarrow pull\ A$'.
Required knowledge: $\gg$

Fig. 7. Process where rule 8 applies

4.3 Plan Transformation

Rules for plan transformation apply after generation of an initial execution plan. The rules add additional events to the execution plan to facilitate more efficient execution. Below, we list rules that illustrate this kind of optimisation:

Rule 9: $A \rightarrow B \Rightarrow A \rightarrow \neg C \rightarrow B$
if $A \rightsquigarrow C \wedge (B, C) \in +$

Effect of the rule: The rule reduces memory consumption in the rule engine but increases the number of event messages.
Intuition behind the rule: The occurrence of C indicates that $A \rightarrow B$ will never match. Thus, A can be dropped from the memory on the occurrence of a corresponding C. The rule is applicable if saving memory is more crucial than reducing event messages.
Required knowledge: $+$ and $\rightsquigarrow$

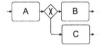

Fig. 8. Process where rule 9 applies

Rule 10: $A \rightarrow B \Rightarrow C \rightarrow$ *pull* $A \rightarrow B$
if $A \not\gg C \wedge C \gg B \wedge C \gg A \wedge A \rightsquigarrow B \wedge \lambda_C \ll \lambda_A \wedge \lambda_C \ll \lambda_B$

Effect of the rule: The rule minimizes memory consumption in the rule engine and reduces event messages.
Intuition behind the rule: The rule is beneficial in processes where activities A and B often occur independently but are rare in combination. If an event C indicates that the combination A and B will occur, we can use this C to trigger the processing of queries for combinations of A and B.
Required knowledge: $\gg, \rightsquigarrow$ and event frequencies λ

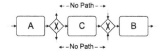

Fig. 9. Process where rule 10 applies

Rule 11: $A \rightarrow B \Rightarrow C \rightarrow$ *pull* $A \rightarrow B$
if $A \gg C \wedge C \gg B \wedge A \rightsquigarrow C \wedge C \rightsquigarrow B$

Effect of the rule: The rule reduces buffer sizes and results in shorter delay than $B \rightarrow$ *pull* A. However, it increases the number of event messages.
Intuition behind the rule: The data for A can already be pulled if C indicates that B is going to happen. This helps to have A available if the matching B occurs and reduces the delay for detecting the combination of A and B.
Required knowledge: $\gg, \rightsquigarrow$, and knowledge about timing between events is useful

Fig. 10. Process where rule 11 applies

5   Related Work

Technologies for complex event processing and event stream processing are receiving continuously growing attention in the research community. Several research projects addressed different aspects of event processing technologies [1,3,5,9]. A significant proportion of research on query optimisation addresses the application domain of wireless sensor networks (e.g. [9,18]). Solutions for this domain mainly aim at reducing network load by pushing query operators close to the event sources. Other work presents general purpose approaches to query optimisation. Srivastava et al. optimise query plans under consideration of differences in the capabilities of available devices [14]. Moreover, network delays can be considered in finding optimal operator placements and corresponding query plans [13]. Query plans can also be rewritten to reuse query operators and minimize resource consumption [12]. Other work optimises the evaluation of query constraints in order to reduce intermediate result sets in query processing [17]. Akdere et al. present an approach that combines push- and pull-based combination to optimise query plans [2].

No approach to our knowledge uses process models to optimise event processing. By extracting behavioural profiles from process models our approach enables optimisations that go beyond general purpose approaches. We foresee potential that solutions presented in existing work can be applied in combination with our work. Still, attention has to be paid to possible interferences between optimization strategies.

6   Conclusion

In this paper, we addressed the challenge of realising complex event processing in an efficient manner. Under the assumption of a normative process model, we showed how the behavioural profile of this process model can be exploited to optimise complex event queries. That is, information of the behavioural profile is used to rewrite queries, select execution plans, or rewrite execution plans. This also enables analysts to abstract from details of process instances during query formulation but still to exploit specifics of process instances in query execution.

While our approach highlights the potential of process model-based query optimisation, we also have to reflect on some limitation. Our approach works solely for expected events representing the accurate behaviour of the process or foreseen exceptional cases, and assumes accurate process models. Therefore, our approach should be applied in a setting where a technical workflow model is directly used for process enactment (e.g. in some manufacturing applications).

In future work, we want to investigate the usage of further information contained in process models for query optimisation. In particular, casual data dependencies between process model activities might be exploited similar to the control flow dependencies that are used in this paper. Moreover, we aim at applying our approach in an industrial case study.

References

1. Abadi, D.J., Ahmad, Y., Balazinska, M., Cetintemel, U., Cherniack, M., Hwang, J.H., Lindner, W., Maskey, A., Rasin, A., Ryvkina, E., Tatbul, N., Xing, Y., Zdonik, S.: The design of the Borealis stream processing engine. In: Intl. Conf. on Innovative Data Systems Research (CIDR), pp. 277–289 (2005)
2. Akdere, M., Çetintemel, U., Tatbul, N.: Plan-based complex event detection across distributed sources. Proc. VLDB Endow. 1(1), 66–77 (2008)
3. Arasu, A., Babcock, B., Babu, S., Cieslewicz, J., Datar, M., Ito, K., Motwani, R., Srivastava, U., Widom, J.: Stream: The stanford data stream management system. Technical report, Stanford University (2004)
4. Brenna, L., Gehrke, J., Hong, M., Johansen, D.: Distributed event stream processing with non-deterministic finite automata. In: DEBS 2009: Proceedings of the Third ACM International Conference on Distributed Event-Based Systems, pp. 1–12. ACM, New York (2009)

5. Chandrasekaran, S., Cooper, O., Deshpande, A., Franklin, M.J., Hellerstein, J.M., Hong, W., Krishnamurthy, S., Madden, S., Raman, V., Reiss, F., Shah, M.A.: Telegraphcq: Continuous dataflow processing for an uncertain world. In: Intl. Conf. on Innovative Data Systems Research, CIDR (2003)

6. EPCglobal. EPC Information Services (EPCIS) Version 1.01 Specification (September 2007)

7. Luckham, D.C.: The Power of Events: An Introduction to Complex Event Processing in Distributed Enterprise Systems. Addison-Wesley, Boston (2001)

8. Luckham, D.C., Frasca, B.: Complex event processing in distributed systems. Technical Report CSL-TR-98-754 (1998)

9. Madden, S.R., Franklin, M.J., Hellerstein, J.M., Hong, W.: TinyDB: An acquisitional query processing system for sensor networks. ACM TODS 30(1), 122–173 (2005)

10. Muehl, G., Fiege, L., Pietzuch, P.R.: Distributed Event-based Systems. Springer, Heidelberg (2006)

11. Pietzuch, P.R., Shand, B., Bacon, J.: Composite event detection as a generic middleware extension. IEEE Network 18(1), 44–55 (2004)

12. Schultz-Møller, N.P., Migliavacca, M., Pietzuch, P.: Distributed complex event processing with query rewriting. In: DEBS 2009: Proceedings of the Third ACM International Conference on Distributed Event-Based Systems, pp. 1–12. ACM, New York (2009)

13. Shneidman, J., Pietzuch, P., Welsh, M., Seltzer, M., Roussopoulos, M.: A cost-space approach to distributed query optimization in stream based overlays. In: ICDEW 2005: Proceedings of the 21st International Conference on Data Engineering Workshops, p. 1182. IEEE CS, Washington, DC (2005)

14. Srivastava, U., Munagala, K., Widom, J.: Operator placement for in-network stream query processing. In: Proc. of the ACM symposium on Principles of Database Systems (PODS). ACM, New York (2005)

15. Wang, F., Liu, S., Liu, P., Bai, Y.: Bridging physical and virtual worlds: Complex event processing for RFID data streams. In: Ioannidis, Y., Scholl, M.H., Schmidt, J.W., Matthes, F., Hatzopoulos, M., Böhm, K., Kemper, A., Grust, T., Böhm, C. (eds.) EDBT 2006. LNCS, vol. 3896, pp. 588–607. Springer, Heidelberg (2006)

16. Weidlich, M., Polyvyanyy, A., Mendling, J., Weske, M.: Efficient computation of causal behavioural profiles using structural decomposition. In: Proceedings of Petri Nets 2010. LNCS. Springer, Heidelberg (2010)

17. Wu, E., Diao, Y., Rizvi, S.: High-performance complex event processing over streams. In: SIGMOD 2006: Proceedings of the International Conference on Management of Data, pp. 407–418. ACM, New York (2006)

18. Yao, Y., Gehrke, J.: The cougar approach to in-network query processing in sensor networks. In: Proc. of the Intl. ACM Conf. on Management of Data, SIGMOD (2002)

Special Track on Education in Business Process Management

Track Chairs

Yvonne Antonucci
School of Business
Widener University
Chester, PA 19013
USA

Catherine Usoff
Bentley University
175 Forest Street
Waltham, Mass 02452
USA

WasanaBandara
Information Systems Discipline
Faculty of Science and Technology
Queensland University of Technology
126 Margaret Street
Brisbane, QLD 4000
Australia

Professionalizing Business Process Management: Towards a Body of Knowledge for BPM

Wasana Bandara[1], Paul Harmon[2], and Michael Rosemann[1]

[1] Queensland University of Technology, 126,
Margaret Street, Brisbane, Australia
{w.bandara,m.rosemann}@qut.edu.au
[2] Business Process Trends, 1819 Polk Street #334,
San Francisco, CA 94109
pharmon@sbcglobal.net

Abstract. Business Process Management (BPM) is rapidly evolving as an established discipline. There are a number of efforts underway to formalize the various aspects of BPM practice; creating a formal Body of Knowledge (BoK) is one such effort. Bodies of knowledge are artifacts that have a proven track record for accelerating the professionalization of various disciplines. In order for this to succeed in BPM, it is vital to involve the broader business process community and derive a BoK that has essential characteristics that addresses the discipline's needs. We argue for the necessity of a comprehensive BoK for the BPM domain, and present a core list of essential features to consider when developing a BoK based on preliminary empirical evidence. The paper identifies and critiques existing Bodies of Knowledge related to BPM, and firmly calls for an effort to develop a more accurate and sustainable BoK for BPM. An approach for this effort is presented with preliminary outcomes.

Keywords: Business process management, body of knowledge, evaluation, content analysis, ontology, interviews.

1 Introduction

Business Process Management (BPM) is rapidly proliferating as an emerging discipline [1, 2]. Despite BPM being ranked as a top priority by organizations, current status of BPM research and reports from practice suggests major gaps in the field: lack of a common consensus of what BPM really entails, lack of appropriate expertise in the field, lack of resources to develop BPM expertise, and a difficulty in communicating across multiple stakeholders of the field are some examples of these major hindrances [3, 4]. As the global uptake of BPM increases, the demand for skilled BPM professionals is growing, encouraging many universities to design BPM course contents. However, BPM is making strides in academia, currently with a large amount of variation on the BPM content that is taught. One root cause is the still limited consensus on Business Process Management. Used broadly, BPM refers to managing, coordinating, prioritizing and monitoring an organization's process change resources and undertakings [5]. To manage and coordinate process efforts throughout

M. zur Muehlen and J. Su (Eds.): BPM 2010 Workshops, LNBIP 66, pp. 759–774, 2011.

an organization, a common vocabulary is necessary, both for the organizations' managers and for its BPM practitioners. At this stage, there is little common understanding of the set of BPM-related roles and the "common body of BPM knowledge" has not yet been confirmed. Olding [6] states that not understanding the specialized skills and knowledge needed for BPM is one of the worst issues in BPM practice. A Body of Knowledge (BoK) for BPM can address many of these limitations, but an empirically validated, accurate and complete BoK for BPM is yet to be developed. The aim of this paper is to address the following research questions:

1. *What Bodies of Knowledge exist in relation to the BPM domain?*
2. *How can a BoK for BPM be evaluated?*
3. *How can a BoK for BPM be derived?*

In this paper, we first present an overview of BPM-related Bodies of Knowledge, and conclude that the BoK derived by the ABPMP [2] is the closest Body of knowledge the BPM discipline has to date. The paper then systematically derives an a-priori model for the BoK evaluation, with 5 dimensions; Completeness, Extendability, Understandability, Application and Utility. The ABPMP's BoK [2] is critically evaluated using this framework, calling for the need for a more rigorous and relevant BoK for BPM. The study proposes a new project design for the derivation of a BoK for BPM. While the overall project design is not presented here (due to scope and space issues), we argue that early core steps when building a BoK are to identify what to include and the structure they will reside in the BoK. We propose an ontological basis for this, and propose an a-priori Ontology based on early empirical evidence for a Body of Knowledge in BPM. The paper ends with conclusions, limitations and an outlook on related future research opportunities.

2 Existing Bodies of Knowledge for Business Process Management

A BoK refers to a peer-developed compendium of what a competent professional in the field must know [7]. It is the sum of knowledge within a profession that includes proven traditional practices which are widely accepted, emerging innovative practices as well as published and unpublished material. It is a living body of information that requires updating and feeding to remain current [8]. There exist many good reasons for defining the nature and extent of knowledge pertaining to a discipline [9]. A BoK provides and promotes a common lexicon for discussing, writing and applying the profession. It defines the knowledge underlying the profession, and describes and points to methods, knowledge and skills [8] or other related elements that a professional must 'know'. The existence of a BoK for a field enables the necessary knowledge to be systematically defined, located, organised and upgraded over time. Missing areas can be identified and added as they are seen to be needed [9]. It promotes the advancement, understanding and recognition of the profession among those who interact with it, and facilitates professional development for practitioners at any stage in their careers as well as people who come to the profession from other backgrounds and disciplines. A BoK also provides the basis for curriculum development and maintenance and supports professional development and any current and future certification schemes. Lastly, it promotes integration and connections with related disciplines [8].

A global environmental scan in relation to the BPM domain conducted in November 2009, resulted in the identification of five BoK/Certification efforts that all defined BPM-related knowledge, some of which lies within a broad definition of Business Process Management. These include: (i) American Society of Quality (ASQ) Black Belt BoK and Lean Six Sigma Certification [10], (ii) IIBA and the Business Analysts BoK (BABOK) [11], (iii) OMG, Business Process Standards, and Certification [12], (iv) ISPI Human Performance Technology BoK [13], and (v) ABPMP and the Core BoK [2]. These five Bodies of Knowledge were examined and analyzed against the BPM domain.

BoK descriptions like those provided by the International Institute of Business Analysis (IIBA) and the Object Management Group (OMG) include much that pertains to BPM, but also include knowledge that is more appropriate for software development or software tool design than for BPM. The International Society for Performance Improvement (ISPI) BoK contains some knowledge of BPM but other knowledge that is properly addressed to those involved in analyzing and designing training materials. The American Society for Quality's (ASQ) Black Belt BoK also includes much that is germane to BPM, but it also includes much that is very specific to statisticians and metrics experts and falls outside of the normal concerns of BPM experts. The one BoK that falls completely within the area that we defined as the BPM space, was defined by the Association of Business Process Management Professionals (ABPMP). The following section briefly introduces this BoK.

2.1 Overview of the ABPMP CBOK

The Association of Business Process Management Professionals released the first Business Process Management Common Body of Knowledge, BPM CBOK, in April 2009. The primary purpose of the guide is to identify and provide an overview of the knowledge areas that are generally recognized and accepted as good practice. It is also the intent to provide a general overview of each knowledge area and provide links and references to other sources of information which are part of the broader BPM Common Body of Knowledge [2].

ABPMP's Guide to the BPM CBOK is organized around 9 knowledge areas and includes a number of appendices, a model BPM curricula, reference disciplines, and information on the BPM community [2]. The nine knowledge areas are: 1) Business Process Management; 2) Process Modeling; 3) Process Analysis; 4) Process Design; 5) Process Transformation; 6) Process Performance Management; 7) Process Organization; 8) Enterprise Process Management, and 9) BPM Technologies [2]. ABPMP [2] argues that core BPM concepts are covered in the Business Process Management Knowledge group, which overlays and sets the stage for all the subsequent knowledge areas. Process modeling, process analysis, process design, process performance management and process transformation represent the core activities and skills sets within BPM initiatives. The Process Management Organization and Enterprise Process Management areas capture BPM environmental issues and how BPM relates to other organizational aspects (i.e. governance, strategic planning etc). Finally, ABPMP argues that the BPM technologies layer captures how BPM practices are supported by technology.

3   Understanding the Essential Elements of a BoK

This section was motivated by the quest to answer "How can a BoK be evaluated?" The overall tasks here occurred in multiple phases and was synthesized to a single a-priori BoK evaluation framework summarized in Table 1. The next section describes the process of deriving this a-priori BoK evaluation framework.

3.1   Deriving an A-priori Model to Evaluate Bodies of Knowledge Related to BPM

First, a detailed review of potential publications on BoK evaluations was conducted. Core databases in Education[1], Business[2], and IT[3], were searched for, to identify papers that provided direct or implied criteria to evaluate a BoK. The search strategy included searching for (i) "Body of knowledge" (and synonyms such as knowledge frameworks, discipline summary, domain expertise building blocks etc) in the title, key word and abstracts, and (ii) 'evaluation' (with other synonyms like assessment, critique, appraisal etc) in the body text. No papers that directly described how to evaluate a BoK were found through this extensive effort. Some provided indirect insights to possible evaluation criteria, when they presented the outcomes and processes of their BoK efforts. These were collated and synthesized in deriving the a-priori BoK evaluation framework.

A BoK is essentially a meta-level abstract account of a chosen discipline; a 'conceptual model' of all the core elements of the chosen discipline. Due to dearth of literature on BoK evaluation as mentioned before, and justified by this analogy that a BoK is essentially a form of a conceptual model, in the second phase, we also searched for possible evaluation criteria we can borrow from the conceptual modeling domain as a proxy for BoK core characteristics. Prior studies that had consolidated this literature [14-17] were used as a base. Forward and backward searching based on these papers was also conducted to extract more related literature.

A BoK is a kind of an artifact. Artifacts are broadly defined as constructs (vocabulary and symbols), models (abstractions and representations), methods (algorithms and practices), and instantiations (implemented and prototype systems) [18]. A BoK is an abstract depiction of a discipline through constructs and instantiations structured within some framework. The design and evaluation of artifacts are discussed in detail in Design Science literature. Design Science research has gained momentum in IT and business research [19]. Hence, Design Science literature, in particular papers that discussed how artifacts should be evaluated, were also looked into when deriving the a-priori framework for BoK evaluation.

In search of possible evaluation criteria, insights from the BPM Community were also sought in addition to the above mentioned literature analysis. A series of

---

[1] Examples include but not limited to; ProQuest Education Journals, Professional Development Collection (via EBSCOhost), ERIC (via EBSCOhost), Emerald Management Xtra, A+ Education.

[2] Examples include but not limited to ABI/Inform Global, Business Source Elite (*many relevant papers found here*) and Business, Management and Accounting Subject Corner.

[3] Examples include but not limited to ACM Digital Library Emerald Management, ProQuest, Science direct.

semi-structured interviews were conducted with BPM academics (5) and practitioners (6) to contextualize and validate the details obtained from the literature extraction. These studies were conducted solely as an exploratory exercise and to further support and augment the findings of the literature review effort. The participants were identified and approached based on a judgmental- convenience sample. The five academics were those who have been teaching BPM for at least 1 year in Australian Universities and the six practitioners were active members (for at least the last 3 years) in a well-established national BPM community of Practice[4].

Table 1 presents the amalgamated criteria extracted from this effort, and the following section presents a summary evaluation of the ABPMP CBoK based on this criteria. While this preliminary evaluation is qualitative in nature, qualitative evaluations have proven to be well suited for evaluating artifacts of this nature, where "moves towards increased quantification may be counterproductive" [20, pp. 1].

Table 1. Summary criteria to evaluate a BoK

Evaluation criteria	Description	Supporting evidence
Completeness	Degree to which all the critical components of the BoK (as per the predefined scope) are present.	[7, 15-17, 21-24] and Interview data
Extendability	Ease with which the BoK can adapt and accommodate to changes in the discipline	[9, 16, 24-26] and Interview data
Understandability	Degree to which the purpose, concepts, and structure of the BoK is clear to the users	[16, 17, 24, 27] and Interview data
Application	The degree to which the users apply the Bok	[9, 16, 17, 21, 28-30] and Interview data
Utility	The extent to which a person uses the BoK or intends to use it	[18, 24, 31, 32] and Interview data

3.2   Evaluating the Current ABPMP BoK

This section critically evaluates the ABPMP BoK [2] against the criteria presented above.

Completeness

The most fundamental and crucial aspect for the development of a body of knowledge in any discipline is the agreement on the constitutional elements of the discipline. As mentioned earlier, BPM is in terms of its components, their relationships and its disciplinary boundaries, still not a precisely defined domain. This creates a significant challenge when trying to design and deliver a BoK.

ABPMP [2] defines BPM as "a disciplined approach to identify, design, execute, document, measure, monitor and control both automated and non-automated business processes to achieve a consistent, targeted results aligned with an organisation's strategic goals" ABPMP (p.23) [2]. However, the core knowledge areas proposed by

---

[4] The Australian BPM Community of Practice fosters communication between Australian BPM practitioners. Founded in 2004, the by-invitation-only members meet every quarter and interact via a platform accessible at http://bpm-collaboration.com

the BoK, does not completely cover or relate to the definition provided. For example, while 'identifying', 'monitoring' and 'control' are stated in the definition as core tasks of BPM, there is no core knowledge area in the BoK that supports these.

The validity and reliability of the discipline knowledge within the BoK underpins its ultimate quality and applicability. With the ABPMP CBoK, not only is there no evidence of why and how the proposed categories were selected to form the 'core', they are presented in a very loose manner and rarely consists of the characteristics that discipline knowledge definitions should hold [following 24])

"How do I know that this is the real core of BPM? There is nothing that explains how they were derived" (Academic # 4)

Most BoK efforts have multiple iterations of feedback loops from key stakeholders of the discipline, built into the very early phases of the BoK design process, to identify and validate the core areas to include in the BoK [e.g. 7, 33]. This community engagement is very important for the success of a BoK. The ABPMP CBoK was primarily built by a referent group and the BoK was released to the BPM community for feedback only after its full creation. This disenables the community to contribute to the core content and structure in a meaningful manner.

"As an educator, I am more interested to see skills than knowledge domains. Core skills, is what helps BPM practitioners to learn and evolve in the field"
(Academic # 5)

Generic skills are practical and portable life skills essential for both personal and career success [22] and allow professionals to *"function across different cognitive domains or subject areas and across a variety of social, and in particular employment situations"* [23 p. 45]. Examples of such skills are: problem solving, critical thinking, effective communication, teamwork and ethical thinking. They complement the discipline specific skills and professional knowledge, and are critical when describing the skills and knowledge essential for the field under investigation. ABPMP [2 p. 20] states that *"the practice of BPM is defined by a set of values, beliefs, leadership and culture which form the foundation of the environment in which an organisation operates"*, and recognises the value of generic skills that individuals require to survive and strive. They state that such skills required are "weaved throughout the knowledge areas", but has very little content related to these.

Extendability
Any body of knowledge should be a living-body of information that requires updating and maintenance to remain current [26]. This is especially true for a discipline such as BPM that is evolving very rapidly. Thorn and Sydenham [9] argue that there are three functions that need to be provided when building a BoK:

1- BoK development and maintenance. These functions need a well defined methodology for developers to feed in relevant information, and must support:
   a. Rapid determination of the location of a likely topic under consideration for inclusion.
   b. Establishing if a topic is already covered and how.
   c. Setting up logical relationships with other items.

2- Browsing capability by users who use lists to stimulate thinking about a topic.

3- Specific topic(s) retrieval (this is the most likely need of users).

A BoK can be in both paper and electronic form. Electronic projects such as Wikipedia allow an on-line body of knowledge to be expanded and moderated in a controlled fashion by the community which uses it [9] – Thorn and Sydenham [9] describes more details of online Bodies of Knowledge]. When a BoK aims at also accumulating actual knowledge items (i.e. various resources) that populates the knowledge categories, then, its implementation needs to be able to accommodate the many types and formats of the methods used to store knowledge (i.e. text, tables, figures, sound, animations, presentations, other digital media) [9]. There is no evidence of ABPMP[2] having considered these in their BPM CBoK development.

"Key concepts, definitions, methodologies, and other material placed in a nearly random manner in the different knowledge areas." (Academic # 3)

"No provision is made for elements that might be used in more than one knowledge area. This makes the document almost impossible to edit in any systematic manner." (Practitioner # 6)

Understandability
A Body of Knowledge should be easily understandable; if they are not easily understood they are not likely to be adopted [16]. While a BoK can be a very complex phenomena to communicate, understandability can increase by providing supporting documentation, educating the users, and using simple and consistent language within the BoK documentation [17]. Clarity is critical in abstract accounts of information [27]. While the ABPMP [2] have attempted to address these (i.e through the documentation of the introduction and supporting appendixes), there are many parts that are quite confusing to a user. For example, while the ABPMP Guide says that its BoK "is organized in nine areas.", this is hard to understand.

"We frankly do not understand this diagram. Normally, when one shows a box inside another box, it suggests that the contained box is a subset or part of the larger box. This diagram seems to show that Business Process Management is contained within Enterprise Process Management, which is, in turn, contained within Business Process Management Technologies. Then again, there is the light box without a boarder for Process Management Organization that seems to fall within Business Process Management." (Practitioner # 6)

"Sometimes definitions in one section are incompatible with definitions offered elsewhere." (Practitioner # 3)

"The ABPMP CBOK first says it doesn't concern itself with methodologies – but then proceeds to define a lifecycle approach... That's confusing, how does the life-cycles relate to the knowledge areas." (Academic # 1)

Application
If the BoK is aimed at reflecting the fundamental knowledge required of a BPM professional and developing certification programs for the discipline, then the developers of a BoK should identify (at least) the most common roles of the discipline and also describe the inter-relationship between the various dimensions and how they

relate to the various roles and responsibilities [21]. Different roles and their entailing responsibilities may require different skills sets and different degrees of expertise.

> "... no, I didn't consider to use it when designing the BPM curricula, it doesn't show any guidelines for this anyway." (Academic # 4)

Many of the available Bodies of Knowledge deliver guides on the knowledge needed for new recruits (i.e. graduates) and thus are aimed at academic/ professional course development. They do not offer the detailed knowledge [9] instead depict the high level knowledge required for each target area. Some on the other hand, are more than a guide to the topics of the discipline; it contains knowledge prepared by subject experts to fit a well-researched scope and contents [9]. While, ABPMP[2] attempts this (see Appendix C of [2]), it is yet at a very abstract level.

Furthermore, it is useful to make distinctions between capabilities which have an organizational focus (i.e. Management, Business Acumen, Teamwork, Information Literacy) and those which have a personal, individual focus (i.e. Self Management, Lifelong Learning, Ethics and Social Responsibility, Problem Solving, Critical Thinking) [21]. Different trainings and certifications can be catered for these specific foci, if clearly specified in the BoK. Boughton [25, 28] and [29] provides an example of how a BoK has been used to design a series of certification courses for various roles and levels of a discipline that covers the different knowledge categories of the BoK. Boyle [30] also depicts how a domain specific course structure for tertiary courses of a discipline, can be designed using a BoK as the founding basis.

Utility

A BoK should be judged "based on value or utility to a community of users" [following 32]. Regardless of whether the BoK improves the status of the discipline, unless it is used in practice, its benefits cannot be realized [18, 31]. When asked about the use of the ABPMP BoK from the interview participants, 4 out of 5 academics and all practitioners interviewed knew about it, but none had used it in a meaningful way, mainly due to limitations in completeness, understandability and usability (as discussed above).

Relationships to other disciplines; the principles that determine how a discipline is related to other disciplines, is another element that increases utility of a BoK [24]. This is especially true with BPM, being a multidisciplinary domain. However, no attempts to describe potential relationships to other fields is provided in the ABPMP [2] BoK.

Summary Analysis

In summary, the current ABPMP BoK, while still in its early phases and is evolutionary; it consists of a number of core limitations that is worth-while to be addressed now without any further delay. First, the process of deriving and maintaining the BoK should be more systematic and transparent. This will assist the perceived validity and adoption of it. Secondly, the content that forms the BoK needs to be defined and scoped, and most of all, checked for completeness, correctness and relevance to the field. Also, consensus definition of the content of a BoK is needed for it to be accepted as industry standard. Thirdly, the structure of the BoK should be carefully thought about and documented; this will assist in the correct interpretation of the BoK by its adapters and will also support sustainability and growth of the BoK.

We acknowledge that there will not be a "one size fits all" solution with BPM knowledge specifications. But, what is needed and what can be achieved, is a meta-level model of the knowledge types. This is an evolutionary process that will take a number of iterations. Even with its current limitations, the ABPMP CBOK is a good 'starting point'. The question is *what can we do to further develop it and address these limitations?*

4   Proposed Project Design

During the analysis that was described earlier in section 3.1, information about the process of deriving a BoK were also captured and analyzed, to recognize best practices in developing bodies of knowledge, which can then, in return, be applied in the development approach for the proposed Bok for BPM.

Although there are many Bodies of Knowledge developed and under development, there appears to be many different strategies for deciding their scope and contents. Generally BoK development groups have used their experience to decide the draft content with consensus being developed by inviting membership to provide further comment. A more defendable and rational approach to the development of the scope and content of a BoK is needed [9]. Not many BoK development processes are documented and shared. Most use multi-method approaches and commence with an initial phase of content analysis of different forms of literature that define the field. These include reviewing scholarly papers published in higher education, human resources management, and the relevant domain areas and also an internationally scoped critical examination of courses and curriculum offered under the discipline by higher education institutions (e.g. [21]). Some also examine the common 'roles' of varying-level professionals of the target discipline and analyse emerging trends [30]. Most of these content analysis approaches are complimented in a later stage with input from members of a task force, in depth telephone interviews with target professionals and/ or focus groups with multiple stakeholders such as professionals, educators and students (e.g. [7]). Some use various surveying techniques to empirically derive at a solid BoK [34]. Overall, the methods applied are varied and rarely transparent in the published outcomes.

4.1   Proposed Approach and Methodology

This section proposes a methodology to build an empirically validated Body of Knowledge for the BPM domain. Ownership of the BoK (and continuous control and updates), the overall project management of the BoK derivation effort, certification processes that might arise from the BoK, potential to standardise the BoK for varying applications across the industry, means to disseminate the BoK and its updates, implication to education (both higher education and professional education) are some aspects that will have a large influence over the BoK derivation process and its overall governance. These aspects will be addressed in concurrence with the broader BPM community and will be discussed in detail in a subsequent paper. The focus of *this* paper is how the *content* of a BoK for BPM will be derived.

Essentially, the overall initiative consists of two main phases. Phase 1 is targeted at determining *what to include* in the proposed BoK for BPM. Phase 2, targets *how to populate* each of the components of the BoK. The scope of this discussion is limited to Phase 1. The aim is to provide a justified conceptualisation on what to include in a BoK for BPM. For this, we propose an ontology-based approach to form the founding structure for the BoK [35]. The entire BoK derivation and maintenance efforts will be done through an established consortium, consisting of BPM practitioners, BPM educators, BPM thought leaders and representation from other established associations that have related BoKs (e.g. IIBA).

One of the main barriers to effective knowledge sharing is the inadequate documentation of existing knowledge bases. Conceptual analysis and knowledge representation often requires to develop an ontological support [36]. An Ontology is an appropriate solution when (due to different needs and background contexts) there can be widely varying viewpoints and assumptions regarding what is essentially the same subject matter [37, 38]. While such a lack of common consensus can lead to many issues in the domain [39], an Ontology resolves this by providing a *unifying framework* [37 p, 2].

With input from general literature, analysis of related bodies of knowledge and input from BPM academics and practitioners (as described in section 3.1), we have derived a basic Ontology for this effort which is presented in detail in the next section.

4.2 Presenting the Ontology Proposed for a BoK for BPM

Ontology is the term used to refer to the shared understanding of some domain of interest which may be used as a unifying framework to create a common consensus about the domain [37, 38]. The process consists of the emergence of some interpretable schema, according to which it makes sense to organise and define things in that way [36]. It embodies some sort of 'world view' with respect to the given domain. This world view is often conceived as a set of concepts (e.g. entities, attributes, and processes), their definitions and their interrelationships. Essentially an ontology consists of agreements about shared conceptualisations of a domain. [37, 40] presents the many uses of ontologies; in summary they are used for communication (i.e. to share common understanding of the structure of information among the stakeholders of a domain and to make domain knowledge assumptions specific), interoperability and systems (can be soft or hard) specifications, reliability and reusability (i.e. to enable reuse of domain knowledge).

The development of an open and comprehensive BoK for BPM requires a systematic approach that is built on clear categories. Similarly, the elements need to be independent of each other to assure that a wide variety of people can edit the document, each focusing on different elements [following 26].

We have borrowed key constructs from the Bodies of Knowledge observed, and used learnings extracted from the research conducted, as presented in section 3.1. The IIBA's [11] basic approach to the structure of the BoK has been adopted as a basis here.

The IIBA BABOK [11] was prepared using a very systematic approach. They begin by defining knowledge areas. Each knowledge area contains tasks. The tasks are processes, with inputs, transformations and outputs. Each knowledge area can contain any number of tasks and the same task can be used in more than one knowledge area. Tasks contain techniques, which describe how to accomplish a specific goal. A task can contain any number of techniques and a single technique can be used in any number of tasks. By keeping the basic elements of the BoK independent of each other IIBA assure that it is easy to systematically develop and edit the BoK [11]. IIBA does not cover as much BPM knowledge as ABPMP's BoK, but what it does cover, is systematic and consistent. That said, one thing that is missing is the current IIBA BoK is some way of grouping techniques to allow the reader to see all of the techniques available to deal with a specific type of problem. Thus, the BoK has information about BPMN[5], but not IDEF[6] or SIPOC[7]. If there was a category for generic techniques, like Process Flow Modeling, which could group specific Process Flow Modeling techniques, like BPMN, IDEF, SIPOC, users would be able to see at a glance what specific types of flow modeling techniques were covered in the BoK.

Following this observation, we adopt the three basic elements from the IIBA BABOK; Knowledge Areas, Tasks, and Techniques. And have proposed to add groupings of techniques creating 'Technique groups'. Skills and skills groups were also added. As Partridge and Hallam [41] argue, the 'DNA of a professional' should consist of two intertwined and complementary strands; the discipline knowledge and generic capabilities. These *together* make up the genome of the successful professional. Hence, a BoK that is designed to describe the core characteristics of a professional (of any field) should integrate generic skills for a more complete illustration. Figure 1 depicts the ontology proposed for a Body of Knowledge for BPM.

Knowledge Areas: A domain, like Business Process Management is divided into a number of Knowledge Areas. If appropriate, a given Knowledge Area may be subdivided into Subsidiary Knowledge Areas. We propose to start with a small number of knowledge areas and then invite, first a board of experts, and then the entire BPM community to edit and propose changes. Our goal will be to keep a small group of basic knowledge areas while identifying labels that a majority of the community can accept as appropriate and descriptive.

Tasks: A task is a process or an activity. It describes how a set of inputs are transformed into outputs of increased value. Each knowledge area is comprised of tasks which are defined by their inputs and outputs. Tasks can also be defined by the rules that constrain the use of the task and by the resources required to undertake the task. Task may further be defined by concepts appropriate to the task. (In this sense, concepts include any models that define the vocabulary and discriminations appropriate to understanding and performing the specific task). Tasks use techniques to accomplish their transformations. A single task can use many different techniques. The same task can occur in more than one knowledge area. Thus we can analyze BPM tasks independently of the knowledge areas that use the tasks.

---

[5] BPMN (Business Process Modelling Notation) is a graphical representation for specifying business processes.

[6] IDEF is also a modeling technique, designed to capture the processes and structure of information in an organization.

[7] SIPOC stands for suppliers, inputs, process, outputs, customers. SIPOC is a tool used early in process analysis work to analyze the scope and purpose of a process.

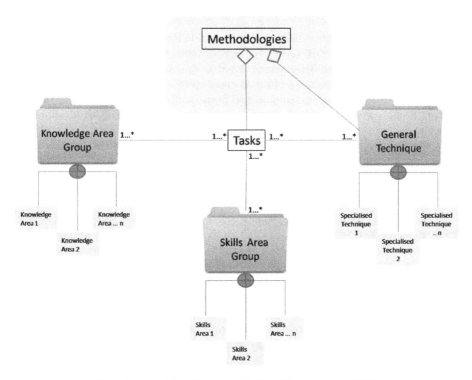

Fig. 1. Proposed Ontology for a Body of Knowledge for BPM

Techniques: Techniques describe how something is accomplished. A technique describes a procedure, formula, steps, models, diagrams or other resources that a user will need to accomplish the something. We maintain a catalog of all the techniques that BPM practitioners might use.

Techniques can be divided into two categories; Generic Techniques that describe an overall goal, and Specific Techniques that define specific procedures, models, etc. Our catalog of techniques will be divided into sections. In effect each section represents a generic technique and each section can contain one or more specific techniques. As a strong generalization, we specify general techniques for tasks, and allow practitioners to decide which specific techniques they might want to use to accomplish a specific instance of the task. We expect that the ultimate catalog of BPM techniques will run to several hundred entries. We will start by eliciting specific techniques to be included, then group them, and then ask practitioners to suggest additions and alternatives.

Skills: Skills describe an acquired or learned capacity to do something well. Most tasks will also require skills in addition to knowledge, and techniques. These may be *Basic skills (like* foundation skills in using information and communication technology), *Intellectual abilities (like* critical and creative thinking, and planning and organization) and *Personal attributes (like* attitudes and abilities of self-management, on-going learning, and collaboration) [42]. Skills can often be divided into domain-general and domain-specific skills. The proposed BoK will capture the different skills that are specifically associated with any BPM task. We will elicit these at a general level and later group them to categories such as Basic skills, Intellectual abilities and Personal attributes.

Methodologies: Methodologies are procedures designed to achieve a specific end. Methodologies make up a different dimension. They use but are independent of the task and technique elements described above. In effect, a methodology is an ordered set of tasks that are undertaken in a particular sequence or according to an established set of rules. In this first round, we propose to ignore methodologies, leaving their definition to those who use them. We will define the tasks and techniques in a sufficiently modular manner, enabling methodologists to define their steps and then indicate which tasks and techniques are used in their specific methodology.

As an example, let's assume that we agree that **Redesign Process** as a Knowledge Area and decide that it contains several tasks, including one called **Analysis of As-Is Process**. We might also conclude that the generic technique **Model Process Flow** is used in the **Analysis of As-Is Process** task. This generic technique, **Model Process Flow**, might include a number of specific techniques including:

Generic Technique: Model Process Flow
     Specific Techniques:
          SIPOC <Six Sigma>
          BPMN   <OMG Standard>
          IDEF <US Commerce Dept Standard>
          UML Activity Diagrams <OMG Standard>
          Rummler-Brache   <de facto standard defined in *Improving Performance*>
          LOVEM <IBM notation>
          EPC (Event-Driven Process Chains) <ARIS notation>

The **Analysis of As-Is Process** task will also require certain skills. For example, it will require one to understand the basics of processes and process models (example of Basic skill), critical and creative thinking about the processes (example of Intellectual ability) and collaboration to get the right insights and on-going learning about the processes (example of Personal attributes).

5 Conclusions

There is currently a lot of interest in defining the knowledge that business process practitioners and managers use to analyze, redesign, monitor and manage business processes in their organizations. Several groups have started working on Bodies of Knowledge that seek to define the domain and the knowledge used by business process practitioners and managers. This paper first re-established the need for a comprehensive and systematic BoK for BPM, and presented a number of Bodies of Knowledge that were related to BPM, identified after an environmental scan. The paper then derived and presented and an a-priori criteria list for evaluating a BoK based on a series of analogous literature domains and interviews (with academics and practitioners), and critiqued the ABPMP's [2] BoK, which is the only BoK, thus far that is dedicated solely to the BPM domain. A number of limitations of the current ABPMP's [2] BoK was identified through this analysis. This established a critical gap in the field and a call for action; the BPM field is yet to derive a rigorous and relevant BoK, founded with empirical evidence.

To further this interest, we propose an open, community-wide effort to define and document the core knowledge used by BPM practitioners. We propose to undertake this effort as a public service and to make the results available to the various specific professional groups that are seeking to define the BPM space. We acknowledge that this is a large undertaking with many layers of effort, and that a variety of aspects (such as, governance, project management, education impacts and dissemination) needs to be taken into account in the overall project design. Two major phases will reside within these contextual aspects; the i) derivation of what to include in the BoK, and ii) populating of each area decided upon. Both phases will be conducted with the open involvement of the BPM community. This paper, proposes an Ontological approach based in empirical evidence as the basis to deciding what to include in the BoK. It presented an a-priori ontology for a BoK for BPM, based on early empirical evidence. We invite the BPM community to critically review our propositions and join forces to build a BoK for BPM that will fulfil our professional and educational needs.

References

1. Gartner: Leading in Times of Transition: The 2010 CIO Agenda. Gartner Executive Programs (2010)
2. ABPMP (ed.): Guide to the Business Process Management Common Body of Knowledge, BPM COK (2009)
3. Gartner: Improving Business Processes. Gartner Executive Programs, pp. 1–7 (2009)
4. Harmon, P. (ed.): Business Process Change. A Guide for Business Managers and BPM and Six Sigma Professionals. Morgan Kaufman Publishers, Amsterdam (2007)
5. Harmon, P. (ed.): Business process change: A Manager's Guide to Improving, Redesigning, and Automating Processes. Morgan Kaufmann, San Francisco (2003)
6. Olding, E.: Three Examples of BPM Worst Practices and How to Avoid Them. Gartner Research. Gartner (2007)
7. Becker, R.E., Montgomery, L.E.: A profession defined: Association management's body of knowledge. Association Management 47, 221 (1995)
8. Fanning, F., Camplin, J.C.: Body of Knowledge. Professional Safety 53, 54–54 (2008)
9. Thorn, R., Sydenham, P.H.: Developing a measuring systems body of knowledge. Measurement 41, 744–754 (2008)
10. American Society of Quality (ASQ): Six Sigma Black Belt Certification (2009)
11. International Institute of Business Analysis: Guide to the Business Analysis Body of Knowledge, BABOK (2009)
12. Object Management Group - OMG: OMG Certified Expert in BPM^{TM} Overview (2009)
13. International Society for Performance Improvement - ISPI: ISPI Human Performance Technology BoK Certified Performance Technologists, CPT (2009)
14. Moody, D.: Theoretical and practical issues in evaluating the quality of conceptualmodels: current state and future directions. Data & Knowledge Engineering 55 (2005)

15. Lindland, O.I., Sindre, G., Solvberg, A.: Understanding quality in conceptual modeling. IEEE Software 11 (1994)
16. Matook, S., Indulska, M.: Improving the quality of process reference models: A quality function deployment-based approach. Decision Support Systems 47, 60–71 (2009)
17. Taylor, C., Sedera, W.: Defining the quality of business process reference models. In: 14th Australasian Conference on Information Systems (2003)
18. Hevner, A.R., March, S.T., Park, J., Ram, S.: Design Science in Information Systems Research. MIS Quarterly 28, 75, 31 pages (2004)
19. Gregor, S., Jones, D.: The Anatomy of a Design Theory. Journal of the Association for Information Systems 8, 312–335 (2007)
20. Moody, D.L.: Measuring the Quality of Data Models: An Empirical Evaluation of the Use of Quality Metrics in Practice. In: European Conference of Information Systems (2003)
21. Partridge, H., Hallam, G.: The double helix: a personal account of the discovery of the structrue of the information professional's DNA. In: Challenging ideas. . Australian Library and Information Association (ALIA) Biennial Conference, Gold Coast, Australia (2004)
22. George Brown Coll, T.: The Generic Skills Subcommittee Final Report to the Academic Plan Steering Committee. General Education Task Force (1994)
23. Bridges, D.: Transferable skills: a philosophical perspective. Studies in Higher Education 18, 8 (1993)
24. Dressel, P.L., Marcus, D. (eds.): On teaching and learning in college. Jossey-Bass, San Francisco (1982)
25. Cameron, N.S., Braiden, P.M.: Using business process re-engineering for the development of production efficiency in companies making engineered to order products. International Journal of Production Economics 89, 261–273 (2004)
26. American Society of Safety Engineers: ASSE Body of Knowledge, BoK (2010)
27. Schuette, R., Rotthowe, T.: The guidelines of modeling - an approach to enhance the quality in information models. In: Ling, T.-W., Ram, S., Li Lee, M. (eds.) ER 1998. LNCS, vol. 1507, pp. 240–254. Springer, Heidelberg (1998)
28. Boughton, C.: Begining to define a body of Knowledge for safety practitioners. In: Lindsay, P. (ed.) 7th Australian Workshop on Safety Critical Systems and software, Australian Computer Society, Adelaide (2002)
29. Muller, F.L., O'Reilly, I.R., Rutherfurd, G.G., Sharpe, W.F., S. Jr, F.H., H. III, W.V., Zeikel, A., Bayston, D.M., Bowman, T.A.: CFA Body of Knowledge. Financial Analysts Journal 47, 16–19 (1991)
30. Boyle, T.A.: Technical-Oriented Enterprise Resource Planning (ERP) Body of Knowledge for Information Systems Programs: Content and Implementation. Journal of Education for Business 82, 267–275 (2007)
31. Moody, D.L.: The Method Evaluation Model: A Theoretical Model for Validating Information Systems Design Methods. In: European Conference of Information Systems (2003)
32. March, S.T., Smith, G.F.: Design and natural science research on information technology. Decision Support Systems 15, 251–266 (1995)
33. Association for Computing Machinery: Computing Curricula 2005: The Overview Report. In: The Joint Task Force for Computing Curricula (ed.): Computing Curricula Series (2006)
34. Juristo, N., Moreno, A.M., Vegas, S.: Towards building a solid empirical Body of Knowledge in testing techniques. In: WERST Proceedings/ACM SIGSOFT SEN 29 (2004)

35. Benjamins, V.R., Fensel, D., Perez, A.G.: Knowledge management through ontologies. In: Reimer, U. (ed.) 2nd International Conference on Practical Aspects of Knowledge Management (PAKM 1998), Basel, Switzerland, pp. 5/1–5/12 (1998)
36. Cristani, M., Cuel, R.: A comprehensive guideline for building a domain ontology from scratch. In: International Conference on Knowledge Management (I-KNOW 2004), Graz, Austria, pp. 205–212 (2004)
37. Uschold, M., Gruninger, M.: Ontologies: principles, methods and applications. The Knowledge Engineering Review 11, 93–136 (1996)
38. Chandrasekaran, B., Josephson, J.R., Benjamins, V.R.: What are ontologies, and why do we need them? IEEE Intelligent Systems and their Applications 14, 20–26 (1999)
39. Bandara, W., Indulska, M., Sadiq, S., Chong, S.: Major Issues in Business Process Management: An Expert Perspective. In: Österle, H., Schelp, J., Winter, R. (eds.) 15th European Conference on Information Systems, pp. 1240–1251. University of St. Gallen, St. Gallen (2007)
40. Noy, N.F., McGuiness, D.L.: Ontology development 101: a guide to creating your first ontology. Stanford KSL Technical Report KSL (2009)
41. Partridge, H., Hallam, D.G.: The Double Helix: A Personal Account of the Discovery of the Structure of [the Information Professional's] DNA1. In: Challenging ideas: Australian Library and Information Association (ALIA) Biennial Conference, Gold Coast, Australia (2004)
42. Australian Government: Skilling Australia for the Future. SkillsInfo. Australian Government

The Current State of BPM Education in Australia: Teaching and Research Challenges

Olivera Marjanovic[1] and Wasana Bandara[2]

[1] Business Information Systems Discipline, Faculty of Economics and Business,
University of Sydney, Australia
olivera.marjanovic@sydney.edu.au
[2] Information Systems Discipline, Queensland University of Technology,
126, Margaret street, Brisbane, Australia
w.bandara@qut.edu.au

Abstract. As business processes, services and relationships, are now recognized as key organizational assets, the demand for the so-called boundary-spanning roles and process-aware professionals is continuing to grow. The world-wide demand for these roles will continue to increase, fueled by the unprecedented interest in Business Process Management (BPM) and the other emerging cross-functional disciplines. This, in turn, creates new opportunities, as well as some unforeseeable challenges for BPM education, both in university and industry. This paper reports on an analysis of the current BPM offerings of Australian universities. It presents a critical review of what is taught and how it is taught, and identifies a series of gaps and concerns. Explanations and recommendations are proposed and a call made for BPM educators worldwide, for urgent action.

Keywords: Business Process Management, Education, Content mapping, Educators, curricula design.

1 Introduction

BPM has evolved and organizations are becoming more business process oriented, the need for BPM expertise and experience has increased [1, 2]. People skills are considered a key factor of BPM; as evidenced by the many BPM critical success factor studies [e.g. 3, 4, 5] that specifically state the role of people for the success and failure of BPM. BPM guidelines for success often provide advice such as: 'Establish a robust governance framework that identifies process ownership', 'Appoint a business process analyst to work on each major business process', 'Create a BPM center of excellence', 'Select an experienced person to head the BPM center of excellence' [e.g. 6, 7]. There is a significant need for BPM skilled people to fill these roles and the demand is rapidly increasing [8-10]. However, a number of years after identifying this need, lack of appropriate BPM education is still a topic that is raised as a perennial issue.

Organizations are now recognizing their critical assets: processes, services and relationships, all requiring cross-functional integration, collaboration and a multidisciplinary

M. zur Muehlen and J. Su (Eds.): BPM 2010 Workshops, LNBIP 66, pp. 775–789, 2011.
© Springer-Verlag Berlin Heidelberg 2011

approach. "Boundary-spanning roles become pivotal towards the expression and capture of business value" [11]. Clearly, functional areas alone cannot prepare (business) students for the boundary spanning roles. Cross-functional integration, especially from the business rather than technical side, is at the core of BPM education. Many of the world's best business organizations such as CISCO, Dell and Amazon have embraced 'process-centered thinking' or 'process view' and changed their organizational structures, strategies, and models in response to this cross-functional, process-centered movements [12].

BPM Experts state *"the university ought to jump into ..., teach it and research it"* [13]. In Australia, employer representatives and professional associations (i.e. such as Business Council of Australia, Australian Chamber of Commerce, Australian Computer Society, Australian Management Institute etc.), have advocated incorporating 'employability' skills which include business process orientation and related generic graduate attributes (such as communication, leadership, and group work into the curricula) [14]. The Federal government and other government bodies are also encouraging the development of a higher education strategy to embed such employability skills in universities [12]. The latest IS curriculum [15] includes, for the very first time, the BPM course, recognizing its importance for the future business practitioners. Following the publication of this very influential document, it is expected that the number of IS or IS-related disciplines will start to offer more BPM courses.

The multidisciplinary talent required for BPM can be hard to find [16]. The dynamic, complex and interdependent nature of the business process environment means that business process roles require a breadth of various expertise (ranging for example from the strategic alignment of a BPM initiative to the configuration of process-aware information) across different levels of an organization (i.e. top executives to management and operational staff) [17]. BPM professionals also have to have additional skills such as ability to learn and creativity [1]. We need to teach them how to develop these skills. This points to the need to critically look at *what* we teach and *how* we teach the chosen content. Motivated by this need, this paper tries to address the following questions looking at the Australian BPM education context:

- What BPM content do we teach; to what extent do we follow the holistic approach to BPM?
- What teaching methods do we use?

The paper first presents the research approach, then discusses the main findings. Explanations and related recommendations are presented and a call for action for BPM educators is made as the paper concludes.

2   Research Method

This study aims to investigate the current status of Business Process Management (BPM) education offered at Australian universities. Our analysis has been informed by two different sources of data; i) Content analysis of BPM offerings found from a web search, and ii) interviews conducted with BPM educators delivering these offerings.

2.1 Content Analysis of BPM Offerings Found from a Web Search

The first part of our study was designed to identify the BPM offerings in Australia, more precisely who is teaching BPM, and what they offer under the BPM banner. The data collected in this phase, has enabled us to identify the interview-candidates – the BPM educators currently involved in the design and delivery of BPM courses.

The authors conducted the search in the following manner, in order to systematically identify and extract details. First, the search commenced by identifying a total list of Australian Universities.[1] Then, a search using related key terms[2] were conducted within the web sites of each listed university. Since most BPM offerings sit within Business and/ or IT faculties, the web pages of these faculties (or equivalents to them- of each listed universities) were also screened in search of potential BPM offerings. Course and unit outlines related to BPM were sought for from this effort. When such details were not readily available or up-to-date on the web, the research team contacted the relevant department, and requested the details.

2.2 Interviews Conducted with BPM Educators of Australia

The purpose of the interviews was to gather further details from Australian BPM educators about their offerings. Current Unit coordinators[3] and Course coordinators[4] of the BPM offerings identified from the search described above were targeted participants of the interviews. A total of 6 interviews were conducted (within a 4 week period in November 2009), each lasting for 60-75 minutes.

This study used a semi-structured interview approach, with the anticipation that the interviews would help gain deeper understanding into the current status of BPM education in Australia. Both researchers took part in the data collection process where a protocol on the overall interview conduct was followed. The interviews were audio recorded and transcribed. The interviewers were equipped with a 'field kit', which consisted of a standard introduction to the project, the core interview questions and a summary notes template to take down effective notes to support the probing process throughout the interview.

2.3 Data Analysis

NVIVO 8.0 was used as a qualitative data management and analysis tool; to systematically code and analyse the data within one single repository. In preparation

---

[1] The list provided at http://www.australian-universities.com/list/ was used for this (last accessed, November 3rd 2009).

[2] The key terms used here included (but not limited to) "Business Process", "Process Management".

[3] 'Unit coordinators', here refer to those who teach and coordinate the activities within on subject.

[4] 'Course Coordinators', here refer to those who coordinate the activities across an entire degree program. Only one university offered a BPM course, and the course coordinator here was also a unit coordinator.

for the coding, 'tree-level nodes'[5] were created within NVIVO for each main topic area of interest. The results from the web search and Interview transcripts were entered and saved within NVIVO, as two Sets of data. A detailed coding-protocol was devised by the researchers, to confirm the coding plan and scheme. Both researchers were involved in the coding process, and the devised coding protocol was strictly followed. The overall research findings and the analytical activities that supported these findings are presented in detail in the next section.

3 Findings

This section presents the results of the data analysis guided by the research questions, as stated earlier in the paper. First we aim to provide a brief description of the context of BPM education in Australia, necessary for a proper interpretation of the main findings and recommendations. Then for each identified question, we provide a descriptive overview of the data gathered, along with the indentified themes and issues discovered during data analysis. This is then followed by our recommendations for the individual educators as well as the BPM community, grounded in the relevant educational literature.

3.1 The Context of BPM Education in Australia

Only 6 universities (out of 39 nation-wide) provided evidence of teaching some form of BPM in Australia. Amongst this, the offerings were quite diverse, in terms of their focus, approaches and departments/schools where the BPM courses reside in. Table 1 depicts a high-level summary of our current offerings. Participating University Identities are made anonymous for confidentiality in the ethical clearance process of this study.

Some differences could be explained by the programs offering the BPM courses (e.g. Major in BPM, Major in Commerce, Major in IT), as well as the overall learning objectives for the course that are inevitably influenced by the program.

Additionally, the BPM courses are offered as core or elective, within specialist BPM programs with a major in BPM as well as the business and IT programs specializing in related or unrelated disciplines (e.g. Major in Commerce, Software Engineering etc). Due to a very large number of possible majors, this information was not included in Table 1.

3.2 What BPM Content Do We Teach?

In order to systematically examine the content that we teach, we used and cross-referenced well known and emerging frameworks that described the field of BPM from several different perspectives. This was very important, given the fact that the Body of Knowledge is still emerging and therefore, there is not a single, complete and authoritative guide setting up the boundaries of the BPM field and determining the content.

---

[5] A tree-level node is a physical location within the tool, where you store the groups of ideas that would be coded.

Table 1. Summary overview of BPM offerings in Australia

University	Type of offering(s)	Degree level	Department	Core/ elective
University A	Part of a unit	Undergraduate	IT	Core
University B	Unit	Undergraduate	Business and IT	Elective Core
University C	Unit	Post graduate	Business	Core
University D	Part of a unit Unit	Undergraduate Postgraduate	Business Information Systems	Elective Core
University E	Part of a unit Unit	Undergraduate Post graduate	IT	Elective Core
University F	Part of a unit Unit Course	Undergraduate Post graduate	IT	Elective Core

Therefore, the identified frameworks were used to help us to assess the currency and completeness of what we teach, in terms of the latest industry approaches as well as the most relevant BPM topics, as identified by the business and academic communities world-wide. Some guidance is offered by the recently published IS curriculum [13, 15, 18]. It is intended to provide a guidance to the IS or IS-related programs. However, it does not provide a big picture explaining how these topics are interrelated and where the main emphasis should be placed in different versions of the BPM courses, offered, for example, in the specialists programs or the other business majors.

To reflect the holistic nature of the BPM discipline, and interconnectedness of different aspects of this field, we decided to adopt one of the most prominent holistic models of BPM – the one proposed by Harmon (2007) [19]. This model reflects the current developments in the BPM field that extend well beyond technology and even process redesign and implementation projects. Most importantly, this model emphasizes the importance of the often missing link between organizational strategy, business processes and technology.

This link between strategy and IT, enabled by the business processes, is important not only for organizations aiming to bridge the gap between business and IT, but to also justify the business value of their BPM initiatives. Without any doubt, this is equally important for students both in IT and business, who may be in charge of BPM initiatives but also be on their receiving end. Not having a holistic view of BPM blocks the ability to link these core elements together, this is a critical issue for the progression of BPM [20, 21], especially in terms of value-creation.

The importance of this link has also been confirmed by the latest world-wide survey of BPM practitioners conducted by BPTrends [22]. The survey confirmed that not being able to define the relationship between Strategy and Processes, continues to be one of the key BPM-related problems. In fact, a significant number of respondents (40%) confirmed that if they could hire external BPM consultants, this would be the area to focus on [22].

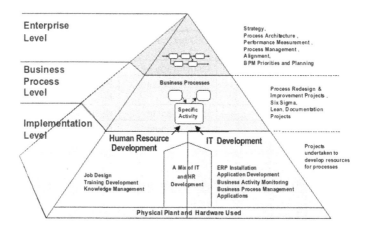

Fig. 1. A Holistic view approaches to BPM *Source: Harmon, P. (2007)*

In terms of our research, Harmon's model has enabled us to position BPM in our programs and use the same reference point.

Figure 1 depicts the holistic framework, proposed by Harmon (2007) [19]. The strategy component includes the enterprise-level process architecture, issues related to process-related performance measurement and the overall BPM governance. The Business Process component includes methodologies for process design and ongoing improvement. The people component includes BPM related knowledge management, training and issues related to BPM-related job design. This is highly relevant for the emerging boundary-crossing roles such as a business process owner. Finally, its technology component includes issues and practices relevant for the IT development, including the BPM systems.

To assess what we currently teach in Australia and to what extent we cover all components of the holistic model, we extracted relevant information from the unit outlines and mapped them to the core areas of the Harmon's model. Figure 2 depicts a summary of the mapping in a visual form [following qualitative data summary techniques presented by 23]. To make sure that our interpretation of the identified concepts was correct, further confirmation was sought during the interviews.

3.3 BPM Content: Current Trends

Our analysis of the BPM curricula offered by Australian universities reveals the following trends:

3.3.1 Our BPM Courses Predominantly Focus on Modeling

Our analysis confirms that we are yet to fully adopt a 'holistic BPM' approach. When put in the context of the Harmon's model, it is possible to confirm that majority of the Australian BPM offerings focus on the modeling and the technical components. The strategy and people-related components are not always included, and when they are, they are covered by a week or two, if at all.

While the technical/modeling focus is naturally more appropriate for the BPM courses offered by the IT/CS school, business schools also place very strong emphasis on modeling. Yet evidence show that all components are equally important, with the non-technical components being more challenging [19, 24].

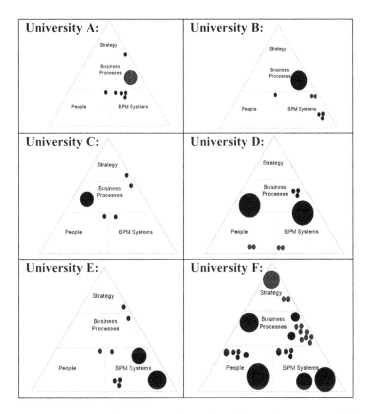

Fig. 2. Analysis of the Australian BPM offerings, in relation to the Harmon (2007) model

While a holistic understanding of BPM continue to play a very important role in professional practice [19], our research confirms that teaching BPM in a holistic manner is rare and is due to a range of contextual and disciplinary aspects and challenges. Below we present further explanations, extracted from the interviews and augmented with literature.

- **Perceived need to present the students with tangible skills sets**

BPM modeling is still perceived to be one of the core BPM skills and for a very long time, the very core of this field [1]. This is still reflected by the job advertisements in this area and therefore, giving students a widely available reference point of what employees want. Therefore, modeling provides students with a tangible skills-set to offer to their future employees, provided that they will work as BPM specialists and more at the entry level where modeling is required.

Looking from the educational perspective, a set of tangible skills acquired through well structured learning - as facilitated by modeling- is also important, especially with novice students, with very little previous experience in BPM and business in general. This type of learning experience helps them to "anchor" the new concepts in a structured way and construct new mental models to accommodate their previous experience, as modeling could focus on any domain they have previous experience with. This particular approach follows the so-called constructivist model of learning that has been used for decades and, when implemented properly, proven to be very effective [25].

- **Ease of teaching**

Modeling is much easier to learn and teach, especially for the educators without a sufficient previous BPM experience, as techniques and concepts are more structured and easier to grasp from the available textbooks and do not require prior experiential knowledge (which is different to the other topic areas of BPM like strategy for instance) nor substantial teaching experience (as model answers and guidelines are easily and often available). Especially, when the less experienced BPM educators "are simply told to teach this new BPM course", as an interviwee pointed out!

- **Availability of educational resources related to modeling**

Compared to the other components of the holistic model, the modeling component is well catered for, in terms of the educational resources. The learning and teaching resources, required for the modeling components of our BPM courses are also widely available and therefore almost "ready-made" to be used. For example, process modeling is the core component of any process-related textbook with "the-end-of-the-chapter" exercises, questions and answers as well as problem solving activities made available to students. This is quite often supplemented by teaching resources including solutions to modeling exercises and questions. This is certainly not the case with the people and strategy components where activities need to be designed – a much more challenging task for the non-expert BPM educators.

3.3.2   The Content Is Determined by the Educator in Charge of the BPM Course and Is Significantly Influenced by His/Her Current Experience and Understanding of This Field

This is the second significant theme related to the BPM content, discovered in our research. It is that educator's prior experience, or even lack of it, influence what has been taught. This is very likely to be a reflection of the emerging nature of this discipline and the absence of the authoritative, widely available reference curriculum.

Our research has discovered the following two issues, both problematic in their own ways:

- **Misunderstanding of the BPM discipline**

One of the important consequences of the limited, up-to-date expertise is a demonstrated misunderstanding of the BPM discipline by some interviewees. Even though the BPM experts could not always agree on all aspects of this field, some areas are clearly out of the scope such as for example data mining. Even though data mining was not thought as one of the topics, the educators misunderstanding is likely to come through practical examples used in the class and translated into possible misunderstanding of their students.

- **Research driven content**

Having very little or no experience in this area is certainly a problem, for both educators and their students. However, we also discovered another problem, somewhat opposite to the first one, but equally challenging. We discovered an instance of the BPM content being heavily driven by the educator's BPM-related research, focusing on the topics that are yet to enter the mainstream BPM practice and are therefore, largely unknown to the employers. At the same time, this could easily create an impression of the content being irrelevant, especially among the students with the current BPM experience, as much as teaching the dated content. While this is not an issue unique to BPM only, it is a critical element to address in order to best align curricula to industry needs and trends, rather than to the educator's research passion and background.

3.3.3   Recommendations for the BPM Content

The above analysis and observation leads to a few recommendations about the content we teach for the individual BPM educators as well as the wider community.

- *Recommendations for the individual BPM educators*

a)   All BPM teachings should be positioned in relation to a holistic BPM view

We argue that all BPM teachings should be positioned in relation to a holistic BPM view, even when one chooses to focus teaching on specific aspects. This will help students to understand the value proposition of the BPM initiatives in their workplace, regardless of the roles they would take.

For example, even though one may be focused solely on the modeling component, it is important not just to teach the mechanics of the modeling process, but to also show how modeling plays a role in a holistic BPM environment, when and where models are used and should not be used at all. In order to help prepare students for the real world experience, they need to understand where and how these models are best used or should not be used at all. The world of BPM practice has certainly evolved from business process modeling to business process management practice and that should be reflected by our courses.

b)   Consider the learning objectives for the program/course/discipline, when deciding the elements to focus teaching on

The extent to which individual components of the holistic model should be covered would vary among different courses, based on a number of factors, including; the overall program within which the BPM course reside, the faculty and discipline, the student majors as well as the intended learning objectives for the course.

When considering the elements to focus teaching on, it is also important to take into account the learning objectives for the overall program as well as the individual BPM offerings. While we cannot accurately predict the educational backgrounds of our BPM students, nor their intended professional destination, the learning objectives describe the intended learning outcomes that need to be achieved at the end of the course. The learning objective designed for the BPM course, need to be fully aligned with the learning objectives for the program or the whole discipline, to help students to place their learning into the overall context and better appreciate its significance.

For example, Business students coming from different majors need to understand the principles of modeling, but more importantly how these models could be used in the context of cross-functional integration to enable knowledge sharing and collaborative process improvement involving multidisciplinary teams of functional specialists. Students need to develop this awareness, rather than spend the majority of their learning experience on the syntax of the chosen modeling language.

c) *The content should reflect the reality of BPM practice and industry needs*
Blue sky predictions and leading-edge research, as much as they are interesting to the BPM educators who are also active researchers in this field, and therefore passionate about their research, might not be of an immediate use to our graduates for many years or sometimes not at all. At the same time, this could easily create an impression of the content being irrelevant as teaching dated content.

- *Recommendations for the BPM community*

d) *Cross-university community of practice, both local and international should be involved in the co-design and ongoing review of BPM curricula*
Rather than leaving for the individual educators to design their own classes and look for the reputable sources to confirm that what they are doing is relevant and up-to-date, it is the collective responsibility of the BPM community to provide the authoritative guide. Only the BPM community has the specialist knowledge to provide more details than what is currently the case, but also cater for differences in relation to different disciplinary majors (e.g. major in BPM, major in business-related discipline or major in a technical discipline). This would largely prevent some of the above listed problems with less experienced staff having to teach the course (but hopefully not design it) or BPM researchers teaching their research topics. At the same time, this would open new opportunities related to cross-university collaboration, and where possible, exchange of staff and students.

3.4 Teaching Methods Used

Teaching methods refer to the ways the content is delivered to students. Each topic could be delivered in many ways, using very different learning/teaching activities, suitable for different types of students and aiming to achieve different learning objectives. This information is very contextual and therefore, impossible to accurately determine without attending classes and experiencing them first-hand. However, different components of the course outline, especially the delivery method and the assignments used, reflect the targeted students' learning experience and provide some insight into the teaching methods used. Table 2 describes how the Australian BPM courses are currently delivered, while Table 3 describes the assessment methods we use to assess student learning.

Table 2. Delivery methods used by BPM educators in Australia

Delivery method	University					
	A	**B**	**C**	**D**	**E**	**F**
Lectures	X	X	X	X	X	X
Tutorials	X	X	X	X	X	X
Labs (practical)	X	X	X	X	X	X
Extra Workshops *(for special topics like generic skills)*						X
Work integrated learning *(or similar)*					X	X
Guest speakers				X	X	X
Case study method	X		X	X	X	X

Table 3. Assessment types used by BPM educators in Australia

Assessment Type	University					
	A	**B**	**C**	**D**	**E**	**F**
Mid-semester Examination		X				
Final Examination	X	X	X	X	X	X
BPM Group Assignment(s)	X		X	X	X	X
Individual Assignment(s)	X	X			X	X
BPM Reflective Journal			X			
Modelling skills test				X		
Seminar/Tutorial/ Workshop Exercises		X	X		X	

Our research has resulted in the following observations, all giving very important clues related to the teaching methods the BPM educators use to structure and deliver students' learning experience:

a) *BPM courses are still delivered in lectures*

Majority of the analyzed case universities still structure student learning experiences, around lectures combined with tutorials and in some cases laboratories.

While it is not possible to accurately assess how the content gets delivered in the lecture components of the BPM courses, without attending the actual lectures, based on the interviews conducted, it is possible to conclude that these are indeed traditional lectures, structured around presentation of the weekly topics. In education literature this mode of delivery is widely known as the 'transmissive teaching paradigm', which is centered around teachers, and his/her ability to present the content (Dillenbourg et. al, 1996). This mode of learning has been researched for decades, in terms of its effectiveness for student learning and retention of the acquired knowledge [26]. The results confirm that the content-driven transmissive model of teaching promote passive learning and does not help students to develop the advanced learning skills including critical thinking, problem solving and reflective skills [27]. Given the problem-solving nature of this discipline, we argue that all these skills are vital for the future BPM professionals. As Biggs [27] pointed out: *"It is helpful to remember that what the student does is actually more important in determining what is learned than what the teacher does"* (pg. 229). The so called student-centered learning requires student active engagement that is known to lead to much better learning outcomes. In essence, in order to learn, students need to be actively engaged [26]. However, design of the learning activities, appropriate for developing students' higher level cognitive skills, remains a major challenge in university education today, as most educators are not formally trained to do so [28], and we often don't have the appropriate support systems and infrastructure to sustain and maintain it.

b) Case studies are widely used in the BPM courses
More active, student-centered learning is currently incorporated into tutorials and workshops. It is also possible to observe that the case studies appear to be the most popular method to promote student engagement and bring the real-life experience to students. It is important to point out that case studies could be used in many different ways to structure student learning experiences and encourage learning at very different levels. However, not all of them are suitable for problem-based learning and, therefore, require experienced teachers [29].

c) Group assignments and group activities are used in most courses
The educational literature also confirms that students' approaches to learning are very much influenced and guided by the types of assessments we use to assess their learning [26]. As Table 3 depicts, most universities (5 out of 6) included in this analysis, incorporate an assessment item in the form of practical group project that requires students to further develop their problem-solving skills. Some case universities also use interactive games, helping students to further develop their skills related to team work, especially their negotiation skills.

The BPM educators use group assignments or even workshop activities which are typically organized as group projects, requiring students to work in teams, just like in the real environment. However, as Michaelson et al [28] pointed out, many educators are not trained to implement the effective group work activities in their classes, assuming that groups will turn into teams. Team building is a separate process, and require a very careful scaffolding and guidance, especially with the so-called dependent learners.

3.4.1   Recommendations for the BPM Teaching Methods

- For the individual BPM educators

a) *Use group assignments and activities as an opportunity to help students to acquire the BPM skills at the meta-level.*
Group assignments could and should be used to help students to learn very important concepts such as leadership and proactive team management. This applies to any teaching discipline, regardless of the domain. At the same time, it is also important to point out that group work in BPM, offers unique opportunities for learning and reflection at the meta level, teaching students valuable lessons related to cross-functional integration and different perspectives that need to be negotiated and

consolidated and the leadership role they will be expected to take during their future BPM projects. Making students recognize this aspect of their group work is very important in BPM teaching.

Given the importance of this type of reflection, this should be incorporated in their assessment. For example, students could be asked to reflect back on their group project and explained how it relates to the team-based nature of BPM, summarizing the main lessons learned. In this way they will be learning about BPM in order to reflect back on their own group experience and vice versa.

b) *Replace the transmissive model of teaching with more student centered learning, even in the large lectures*.
While large lecture teaching is always a more challenging aspect of teaching, regardless of the domain, the applied disciplines such as BPM are even less suitable for this mode of teaching than descriptive disciplines. While lectures are inevitable for many universities, professional development course as well as a wealth of resources are available to the educators to turn their lectures into more interactive experiences.

c) *It is necessary to offer a very different type of professional development courses to BPM educators*
In addition to keeping up with the disciplinary knowledge, the BPM educators require to keep up to date with advanced learning methods and new developments in the field of education. We argue that they require a very different type of professional development. This is another domain where the wider BPM community, needs to take an active role and through teaching-related research define the set of skills that the educators need to have in order to help their students to develop into high quality professionals. As Ericsson et al. [30] pointed out, to become experts, professionals need expert teachers, not only in terms of their professional knowledge but also their expertise in the most effective teaching methods for the particular domain.

- *Recommendation for the BPM community*

d) *Given the challenges of this profession, world-wide collaboration of the BPM educators becomes a necessity.*
At the present time, collaboration of the BPM educators is very much left to the individuals, we argue that the BPM community should provide structured opportunities for teaching and teaching-related research collaboration, very much similar to what we already have in the research world. In this respect we could certainly learn from the other more established and highly successful teaching communities, currently operating in the other related disciplines such as for example, Teradata University Community in BI/DW discipline [31] with industry practitioners actively involved in teaching-related research.

4   Conclusion

The main objective of this paper was to report on the current state of the BPM education in Australia, identify the main teaching and teaching-related research challenges and propose possible ways of how these challenges could be addressed by the individual educators as well as the wider BPM community, both at the national and international levels. While this study reports on an Australian scope, this can be extended later to a larger geographical coverage.

Apart from offering a practical guidance to the current and future BPM educators, their students and the employers of their students, this research aims to discover and analyze our current BPM-related challenges. Many of the BPM education studies completed to date are very early in its maturity. Some are very limited in their scope and address very specific institutional issues. The ones with a broader scope are mostly at a stage of identifying issues and challenges rather than providing resolutions Thus, none of the key issues or areas of consideration have yet been addressed. We anticipate that the identified challenges will offer further opportunities for community engagement, collaborative problem solving, as well as sharing of good teaching practices in this emerging field.

References

1. Bandara, W., Rosemann, M., Davies, I., Tan, C.: A Structured Approach to Determining Appropriate Content for Emerging Information systems Subjects: An Example from BPM Curricula Design. In: Australasian Conference on Information Systems, Toowoomba, Australia (2007)
2. Gartner: Meeting the Challenge: The, CIO Agenda. Gartner Executive Programs, pp. 1–7 (2009)
3. Amoroso, D.L.: Developing a model to understand reengineering project success. IEEE, Los Alamitos (1998)
4. Grover, V., Teng, J., Segars, A.H., Fiedler, K.: The influence of information technology diffusion and business process change on perceived productivity: The IS executive's perspective. Information & Management 34, 141–159 (1998)
5. Raymond, E.M., Coleman Jr., H.J., Creed, W.E.D.: Key to success in cooperate redesign. California Management Review (1995)
6. Hill, J.B., Sinur, J., Flint, D., Melenovsky, M.J.: Gartner's Position on Business Process Management. Gartner Research reports. Gartner (2006)
7. Olding, E., Rosser, B.: Getting Started With BPM, Part 3: Understanding Critical Success Factors. In: Reports, G.R. (ed.) Gartner (2007)
8. Hung, R.Y.Y.: Business Process Management as Competitive Advantage: a Review and Empirical Study. Total Quality Management 17, 21–40 (2006)
9. Henry, P.: Process-centricity and the Business Analyst's NEW Role. BPTrends (2010)
10. Gartner: Who's Who in Business Process Management Consulting and System Integration. In: Cantara, M. (ed.) Gartner Research (2009)
11. Gartner: Creating enterprise leverage: the 2007 CIO agenda. EXPPremier Report (2007)
12. Seethamraju, R.: Process Orientation to Business Students – Enabling Role of Enterprise Systems in Curriculum. In: Australasian Conference on Information Systems, Toowoomba, Australia (2007)
13. Bandara, W., Indulska, M., Chong, S., Sadiq, S.: Major Issues in Business Process Management: An Expert Perspective. In: European Conference on Information Systems, ECIS 2007 (2007)
14. Curtis, D., McKenzie, P.: Employability Skills for Australian Industry: Report to Business Council of Australia and Australian Chamber of Commerce and Industry. Australian Council for Educational Research, Camberwell (2001)

15. Topi, H., Valacich, J.S., Kaiser, K., Nunamaker Jr., J.F., Sipior, J.C., Vreede, G.d., Wright, R.T. (eds.): Association for Information Systems: Curriculum Guidelines for Undergraduate Degree Programs in Information Systems. Association for Computing Machinery, New York (2009)
16. Olding, E.: Case Study: 'Try Before You Buy' Pays Off When Hiring BPM Talent. Gartner Research. Gartner (2008)
17. Jeston, J., Nelis, J.: Business Process Management: Practical Guidelines to Successful Implementations. Butterworth-Heinemann, Butterworth (2006)
18. Sadiq, S., Indulska, M., Bandara, W., Chong, S.: Major Issues in Business Process Management: A Vendor Perspective. In: Pacific Asian Conference on Information Systems (PACIS 2007), Auckland, New Zealand (2007)
19. Harmon, P. (ed.): Business Process Change. A Guide for Business Managers and BPM and Six Sigma Professionals. Morgan Kaufman Publishers, Amsterdam (2007)
20. Bruin, T.D.: Business Process Management: A Formative Maturity Model and Theory on Progression. PhD Thesis. Queensland University of Technology, Brisbane (2009)
21. Bandara, W., Indulska, M., Sadiq, S., Chong, S.: Major Issues in Business Process Management: An Expert Perspective. In: Österle, H., Schelp, J., Winter, R. (eds.) 15th European Conference on Information Systems, pp. 1240–1251. University of St. Gallen, St. Gallen (2007)
22. Harmon, P., Wolf, C.: The State of Business Process Management. In: BPTrends (ed.): BPTrends (2010)
23. Miles, M., Huberman, M. (eds.): Qualitative Data Analysis - An expanded Sourcebook. Sage Publications, Thousand Oaks (1994)
24. Gartner: New Roles and New Competencies: Blurring Boundaries. Gartner Repor. Gartner Research (2006)
25. Bostok, S.J. (ed.): Designing Web-based Instructions for Active learning. Educational Technology Publications, New Jersey (1997)
26. Ramsden, P.: Learning to Teach in Higher Education. Taylor and Francis Group, Abington (2003)
27. Biggs, J.: Teaching for Quality Learning at University. Open University Press, Buckingham (1999)
28. Michaelson, L.K., Knight, A.B., Fink, L.D. (eds.): Team-Based Learning. Stylus Publishing, Sterling (2004)
29. Wassermann, S. (ed.): Getting down to cases: learning to teach with case studies. Teachers College Press, New York (1993)
30. Ericsson, K.A., Prietula, M.J., Cokely, E. (eds.): The Making of an Expert (2007)
31. TUN: Teradata University Network,
http://www.teradatauniversitynetwork.com

Service Learning and Teaching Foundry: A Virtual SOA/BPM Learning and Teaching Community

Hye-Young Paik[1], Fethi A. Rabhi[1],
Boualem Benatallah[1], and Joseph Davis[2]

[1] School of Computer Science and Engineering,
University of New South Wales, Australia
{hpaik,fethir,boualem}@cse.unsw.edu.au
[2] School of Information Technologies,
University of Sydney, Australia
joseph.davis@sydney.edu.au

Abstract. With the growing presence of BPM and SOA in the IT industry, their impact on the IT education will be profound. Many institutions
are becoming aware of the acute need of developing learning and teaching
resource frameworks for the BPM and SOA. In this paper, we present
part of such an effort from a team at the University of New South Wales,
currently developing Service Learning and Teaching Foundry as a dedicated virtual teaching and learning space for BPM/SOA. We present the
motivation, design and current implementation of the foundry, as well as
a curriculum design of a Service Technologies module which is used to
pilot the foundry system.

1 Introduction

BPM (Business Process Management) and SOA (Service Oriented Architecture)
are fast becoming an integral part of the way modern business organisations understand their business architecture, and manage their business processes. BPM
offers a methodology and tools for organisations to model, analyse and integrate
business processes that involve IT systems and human interaction. SOA provides
the principles of developing reusable business service and applications that collectively fulfil an organisation's business processes and goals [1–3]. The tools and
methodologies from both paradigms have equipped the enterprises with cross-
platform compatibility, agility and cost-efficiency for continual improvements in
their core operations [4].

With the growing popularity of BPM and SOA in the IT industry, their impact
on the IT education will be profound. Many already anticipate that one of the
most important skills for an IT graduate today is to be able to understand the
role of BPM and SOA in different contexts and to articulate the motivation
behind service-based technologies and their practical implications in terms of
engineering complex software systems and automating business processes [5–7].

M. zur Muehlen and J. Su (Eds.): BPM 2010 Workshops, LNBIP 66, pp. 790–805, 2011.

In 2008, a consortium of leading universities in Australia was awarded an Australian Learning and Teaching Council (ALTC) grant to investigate the development of industry relevant curriculum modules and other educational resources. The context of the investigation is inline with the *SSME (Service Science Management and Engineering)* movement [8, 9] which is gathering support from leading IT companies and higher education sectors worldwide[1], especially the institutions associated with SOA and BPM are active participants of the movement[2].

As part of the investigation, the University of New South Wales team are proposing two modules: Engineering Service Systems and Service Technologies, under which the core theoretical concepts and practical tools and skills of SOA and BPM are discussed. An innovative part of the proposed modules is Service Learning and Teaching foundry which is a dedicated virtual teaching and learning space for SOA/BPM. The foundry provides an open and collaborative environment for teaching resources to be created, shared and re-used, all in the context of educating SOA/BPM.

In this paper, we present the detail of one of the two modules: Service Technologies, and the foundry. In particular, we explain how the foundry underpins the design and delivery of the module.

2   The SSME Curriculum Renewal Project

One of the first-stage outcomes the SSME project is an interim report from focus group discussions [10]. This section gives an overview of the focus group discussions and the key themes identified as a result.

2.1   SSME Focus Group Discussions

The focus groups consisted of various stakeholders in industry, recent graduates and academic staff members. The report frames the information gathered from the discussions to give in-depth description about key knowledge and skill sets required in the workplace and the challenges faced by the industry due to the recent development in technologies (e.g., Services, Web 2.0, Cloud Computing).

As an industry trends report suggests[3], business process modelling and middleware/SOA were named number one and three skills that are in demand. The SSME project interim report also confirms such trends in Australia, where companies are looking into offering their traditional software package products as services (Software as a Service), dealing with the challenges of carrying the old technology environment, which was never designed to be open and shared, into the new environment.

The traditional role of an IT person is changing, in the sense that the person should have understanding of the 'end-to-end' business, client perspectives and

---

[1] IBM SSME Portal, http://www.ibm.com/developerworks/spaces/ssme

[2] https://www.ibm.com/developerworks/wikis/display/ssme/Universities

[3] http://www.networkworld.com/news/2009/040609-10-tech-skills.html

the complete life cycle of services. This requires a clear overview of how various technologies fit into different areas in the business and how they are reused when necessary [11, 12].

The focus group discussion also highlighted that the real challenge is to equip graduates, not only with technical competency, but also with an appreciation of the global, collaborative nature of modern software development. In this aspect, two important aspects of software development skill sets are identified: the ability to work in a virtual (distributed) team and competency in using online collaboration tools.

2.2   SSME Key Modules Overview

We identified the following major themes from the focus groups discussions. Figure 1 depicts the key modules planned for the SSME project, some of which

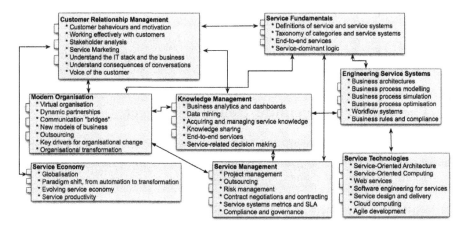

Fig. 1. SSME modules and their relationships

are already being designed and delivered on a trial basis, others are in initial discussion stage. The outcomes will collectively make up the SSME modules and would form the basis for the renewal of IT curriculum for participating institutions and also inform the wider education community [13].

The diagram shows the diverse nature of the disciplines involved. With regards to the SOA and BPM topics, the implicitly expressed view here is that the two areas are intrinsically linked. As [3, 7] point out, the industries are leading the consolidation of SOA and BPM. The evolution of standards, such as WSDL (Web Service Description Language), BPEL (Business Process Execution Language), BPMN (Business Process Modelling Notation), allow the smooth integration of compatible SOA-based tools and business processes across heterogeneous deployment environments.

It is noted that the "Engineering Service Systems" and "Service Technologies" modules focus on systems and technologies aspect of SOA and BPM, i.e., Web services and Service-Oriented Architectures (SOAs) are discussed as underlying technical operating systems for BPMS (Business Process Management Systems), especially in the context of enterprise application integration architectures.

3   Motivations

In this section, we present the motivations which inform our vision and approach for SOA/BPM education.

3.1   Student Feedback

The authors have been involved in the design and delivery of courses in the area of Service-Oriented Architectures and Business Process Modelling and Engineering for a number of years. Initially started as 'WS-*' services and Web application engineering course in 2005, in the last couple of years, the syllabus of the course gradually changed. We included related subject matters that are emerging and becoming increasingly important to IT students [6, 14, 15]: understanding of service-orientation, enterprise systems and application integration, business process modelling, automation, and alternate ways to model and implement services such as REST (Representational State Transfer) based architecture.

To accommodate the need for opportunities to practice the technical skills, we increased the number of activities in labs and assignments in the course. We also streamlined the design of the activities with the weekly lecture topics (as shown in Table 1).

The direction was chosen based on the feedback from students (both formal and informal) and received positive responses such as "Very useful for graduates' future", "the course teaches emerging and new technologies", "the course introduces various and useful tools for real world problems"[4], etc.

3.2   Building the Community of SOA/BPM Learning and Teaching

Another strong influence is our aspiration for working towards building a community of learners and teachers who share common interests and passion for SOA/BPM education. There are many online teaching resource sharing Web sites and portals (e.g., Blackboard, Moodle). However, most portals are mainly designed for limited types of users (e.g., students and teachers from the same faculty/institution) and coordinating cross-institutional collaboration, or cross-student-groups (e.g., year 3 students and year 2 students) is not straightforward.

We have not yet seen a complete teaching environment designed with *a long term vision* of underpinning a virtual community of learners and teachers of this topic, especially in terms of crossing physical, time, and discipline boundaries.

Figure 2 presents an online portal environment in which open, but well-organised teaching materials are created, shared and reused by multiple institutions. The vision is to create a meaningful repository of community knowledge

---

[4] Direct quotes from student evaluation forms, 2008, UNSW.

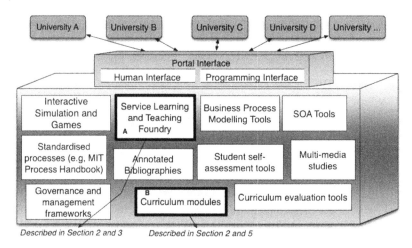

Fig. 2. Service Learning and Teaching Online Portal Environment

for educating the students and instructors in the area. The portal will provide, not only a repository of document-based resources (e.g., reference processes, annotated bibliographies), but also a hosting environment for many SOA and BPM related tools (e.g., BPMN modeller, WSDL inspector, Apache Axis runtime).

We strongly believe that the teaching and research discipline we are in gives us an opportunity to create an innovative and interesting learning and teaching community that uniquely represents what we do.

For example, take the concept of consuming a service designed by someone else in SOA. One group of students can develop a service in a class that is *consumed* by another group of students from a different class as learning resources. The same service can be *reused* in different learning contexts depending on the learning objective (e.g., exposing WSDL view or BPEL view). The same service can be *re-engineered* by one class and its design process can be debated in a different class as a case study. The process of developing and administering an assignment itself can provide an experience of business processes - a concept students could easily relate to. Of course, the experiences can be shared amongst multiple institutions to create interesting BPM case studies. In our opinion, the possibility of applying our own discipline principles to the portal vision is endless.

Based on the vision depicted in Figure 2, our work starts with implementing and contributing to realising the concrete building blocks of the portal. In particular, the rest of the paper focuses on the development of a Service Learning and Teaching Foundry

3.3   Service Learning and Teaching Foundry

Service Learning and Teaching Foundry, or *the foundry* for short, is the first concrete step towards realising the type of unique learning and teaching community we mentioned earlier in Section 3.2. We believe it could potentially enable us, IT educators, to re-think the way the core business of IT, systems design, implementation and re-engineering, are taught.

The foundry aims to provide an open, collaborative, continuously evolving and growing virtual space for students to learn the concepts of SOA/BPM, and practice their skills using real-world examples. The collaborative nature of the foundry means that it enables the students to interact with groups of students at many different levels: across classes in the same institution, across institutions or across different disciplines (e.g., Computer Science students interacting with Business Administration students). The continuously growing side of the foundry means that it will become a rich repository of services and processes designed and built over time by students. It will be an important resource for training the very concept SOA/BPM preaches on services and business processes: identify, define, capture, store, reuse and optimize [1].

Also, we see that the foundry, once matured, will become an effective teaching and experimentation tool for learning the lifecycle management aspects of SOA/BPM. That is, the foundry can provide a real-world example of case studies on studying an impact of retiring a service, updating a service or analysing the dependencies between the services in the repository and process implementation.

4   The Foundry Design and Implementation

In this section, we explain in more detail the design, architecture and current implementation of the foundry.

4.1   Domain of the Foundry

Central to the foundry design is the belief that it should contain a sufficient number of properly designed and well-documented services that interoperate with each other. For this reason, the foundry services are built around the requirements of a small number of application domains. The current domain of the foundry is in finance trading.

The field of financial trading has seen an unprecedented increase in the number of participants and the volumes of trades conducted via electronic markets, high frequency data has become increasingly available for historical analysis by researchers in fields like econometrics, finance and accounting. The foundry includes basic material that describes basic concepts of finance, market structures and microeconomics. It includes information on the trading lifecycle, the different types of computer systems involved and how trading data is captured from exchanges and distributed by third party providers. It also explains the different types of analysis that can be performed on the data.

4.2   Design of the Foundry

The main purpose of the foundry is to act as a repository of Web services to enable the development of practical assignments and projects which are part of some of the Curriculum Modules. For example, a technically-oriented module could require students to contribute services to the foundry whereas a more business-oriented module could involve students developing their own mash-ups of services to satisfy a business objective.

Figure 3 depicts the overall architecture of the foundry. The figure shows that the Foundry Core contains information specific to the target application domain. Besides background documentation and material, it includes a data model that concretely represents business entities in this domain and a data repository that contains instances of the data model (e.g. sample files and databases). In addition, the core contains tools and services for manipulating (i.e. accessing, creating and modifying) instances of the data model together with their API documentation.

The Foundry Core is one of the salient features of the foundry design. It is the source of the common data model, services, ample test data and documentation. Because of the core, all learning activities of the students can be designed around a single application domain.

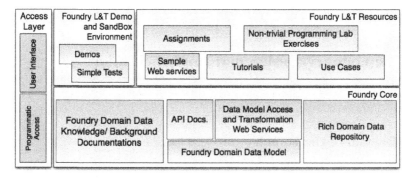

Fig. 3. The Architecture of the Foundry

There are five types of *Foundry L&T Resources* built on top of the core:

- Use Cases describe in detail user requirements around the application domain(s) of interest. They should be written in a way that students can see links with the underlying data model and the sample Web services provided.
- Sample Web services (complete with their code) are provided to underpin the material contained in the tutorials, assignments and projects.
- Tutorials introduce a particular topic (e.g. securing Web services).
- Assignments are "hands-on" tasks given to students with a particular learning objective (e.g. developing a simple WSDL interface). Such assignments will be set according to the learning objectives of particular modules but it is expected that some assignments will be shared by several modules.
- Non-trivial programming exercises will require students to undertake project work at different levels of difficulty (e.g. extend the SOA with new services).

Resources on the foundry can be accessed in two ways: direct user interface (i.e., Web-based GUI) and APIs (i.e. programmable interfaces)[5]. Therefore, access to these resources is possible for students with different levels of technical skills. It also expected that the foundry will include a separate area for demonstrations and testing.

4.3 Current Implementation

The implementation of the foundry described in this paper revolves around the area of financial market data analysis. This application domain was selected for three reasons:

- it is a non-trivial domain in which most IT students have no prior knowledge. This encourages them to undertake a significant effort in acquiring such knowledge
- our team was granted access to vast amounts of Reuters financial market data by SIRCA[6]. This provides second-to-none opportunities for the students to explore and experience with real world data.
- there are many analysis scenarios which involve generic techniques (e.g. regression analysis). Therefore, the scope of defining services and business processes is very large. This provides many opportunities for collaborative projects with industry as well as reusing such knowledge in other application domains (e.g. business intelligence).

The current foundry is at `http://soc.cse.unsw.edu.au/teachingfoundry/`. It is not yet open for general public contributions. We will soon officially launch the foundry with collaboration features. In the rest of this section, we explain the main elements of our implementation in more detail.

Data Model. The data model allows uniform representation of financial market data. It is based on the following essential entities:

- *Event source*: This is the primary source of high frequency data. Sources can be log files, databases, web services, information portals, etc. The main event source in this implementation is SIRCA's TRTH system [16].
- *Event*: An event is the base entity from which other types of event entities are derived. The most important attributes in an event are the timestamp and the financial product concerned by the event. In our case study, the three types of events are *Trade* (representing the occurrence of a trade), *Quote* (representing the broadcast of a quote) or *Measure* (representing a snapshot of one of the market measures like volume-weighted average price (VWAP)).
- *Product*: A product (tradable or non-tradable) is uniquely identified through some identification code. In this implementation, products are named using the Reuters Identification Code (RIC).

---

[5] The API to the foundry itself is not yet available.
[6] `www.sirca.org.au`

The proposed event-based data model makes it possible for several services to process data in a consistent way by sharing a common data reference model. Additional details of the model can be found in [17].

Data Repository. This implementation is based on the Thomson Reuters Tick History (TRTH) system [16]. TRTH allows access to intra-day trade and quote information for over 244 exchanges and Over The Counter (OTC) markets around the world. Datasets are stored in a format suitable for viewing as a spreadsheet. A row corresponds to a time-stamped piece of information such as the occurrence of a trade, a variation in an instrument's quoted price or an index, the publication of a news story or a market announcement etc. The sample repository consists of files from different types of markets (e.g. equities and options) as well as geographic areas (e.g. USA, Europe and Australia). A number of tools are also available for converting files from their native format into data model compliant instances.

Use Cases. There is a wide range of possible analysis business processes that can be defined around financial market data. Most of them start by aggregating data in some way to build *financial time series*. Such timeseries can be visualised or compared with each other using a number of techniques (e.g. statistics, machine learning). In this implementation, the main use case defined involves detecting price jumps in the time series data (e.g. identifying abnormal returns for a particular stock).

Sample Web services. The Web services provided in this implementation are designed to interoperate with each other using the producer-consumer model of interactions. The basic unit being transmitted between services are *event streams*. There are three types of services:

- Event Sources: produce event streams from some kind of data set of an on-line source of information.
- Event Transformers: transform one or more streams of events into one or more streams of events
- Event Sinks: consume events to produce some kind of results

The sample services provided in this implementation (Figure 4) are intended to implement the main use case. They can be briefly described as follows:

- TRTH Import Service: builds an event dataset from market data files. These files will be preloaded from TRTH system into the data repository.
- Timeseries Building Service: will aggregate events according to regular time intervals. This is a prerequisite to most time-series analysis
- Merge Service: will merge different streams of data into one, for example it can be used to relate trade prices with index prices.
- Price Jump Service: will detect "price jumps" in the timeseries data according to some reference timeseries (e.g. index data).

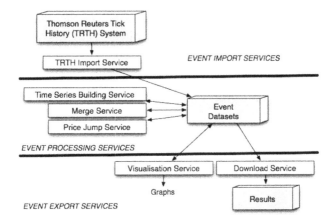

Fig. 4. Sample Web services in the *Foundry L&T Resources*

- Download Service: will allow events to be downloaded into a format suitable for viewing or further processing by the user (only CSV is supported in the sample implementation).
- Visualisation Service: will allow events to be visualised in the form graphs.

These services were initially developed as part of the ADAGE Project [17, 18]. The idea is that each service illustrates a particular *building block* and can be used in several use cases. Assignments and projects can be defined by using, modifying, composing or extending these sample services. A sample of assignments specific to the learning outcomes of the Services Technologies module will be illustrated in the next section.

5   Syllabus of Service Technologies

This year, the early prototype of the foundry implementation is being used in delivering the course in *Service Technologies*. The course syllabus[7] has been revised to utilise the services provided by the foundry. This revision is also part of the *Curriculum Modules* design and development effort which is underway in the SSME project (cf. Figure 2).

In this section, we present the overview of the course outline and its relationship with the foundry.

5.1   Background/Assumed Knowledge

The course is offered to advanced undergraduate and postgraduate students and attracts around 40-50 students every semester. As the course is technical in nature, students will need to have completed at least one programming language

---

[7] The concrete name at our university is *COMP9322: Service Oriented Architectures*.

course, database course and a Web application development course. For BPM topics, students will also need to have some basic understanding of XML languages and UML (Unified Modelling Language).

5.2   Learning Outcomes

The expected learning outcomes of the course are at two levels: broad outcomes and specific knowledge/skills.

Broad outcomes:

- Describe architectural design styles in enterprise application integration,
- Apply the concept of business processes in a concrete setting and be competent in developing solutions using SOA and related technologies,
- Learn to work as a team and be efficient in managing collaboration. Be competent in choosing and utilising online collaboration tools.

Specific knowledge/skills outcomes:

- Identify the communication and integration patterns in enterprise systems,
- Discuss the role of various XML technologies in Web Services,
- Be competent users of Web services and BPM (both traditional and emerging) technology such as WS-* standards, BPEL, BPMN and process modelling methods, Data access services and RESTful services.

5.3   Assessment

The assessment consists of the following components. Besides the formal and practical parts of the assessment, we also emphasise teamwork management and use of various collaboration tools (such as Google Sites or open-source project/issue management software). This helps the students keep track of their collaboration trails and have hands-on experience with using collaborative software in a project setting.

- 40% formal written exam: this component is going to assess the various facts-and-knowledge level learning outcomes. The exam is a mixture of multiple choice questions and written answer questions.
- 50% on laboratory work: this component assesses the practical-skills-and-tools level learning outcomes. The assessment activities include five programming assignments. Each assignment is designed for students to explore a important technology. Labs are released every two weeks to encourage students to progressively develop their skills.
- 10% on the management of teamwork: this component assesses the level of coordination and management of group work. It evaluates how effectively the students use a (online) collaboration tool and peer-assessment of team members in a team on the level of collaboration and participation in the group work.

5.4   Key Learning Resources/Materials

Overview. The key learning resources consist of three components: (i) lecture
and lecture notes, (ii) lab exercises and assignments and (iii) the service learning
and teaching foundry. Figure 5 illustrates how they are organised.

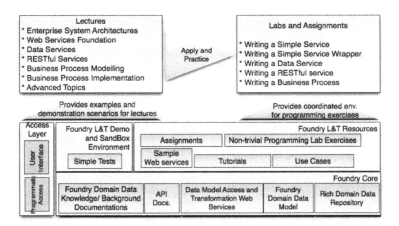

Fig. 5. Overview of the Module Components

The lectures introduce the theory and concepts in course. For each lecture
topic, we associate a simple lab exercise to familiarise students with the topic. To
let them investigate further and develop deeper understanding about the topic,
at the end of lab exercise, we give not-so-trivial design and implementation tasks
as assignments. More details about the practical exercises and the role of foundry
are presented Section 5.5.

Weekly Activity Schedule. Table 1 shows the weekly student activities. They
are streamlined according to lectures and assessment tasks.

5.5   Foundry Support for Labs and Assignments

As illustrated in Figure 5, we design the lab exercises and assignment tasks
around the data and sample services available in the foundry. Clearly, as the
foundry matures and its links with other modules in the portal consolidate, the
number, variety and technical levels of exercises and assignments will increase.
The following lists the plan for this semester only.

- *Environment setup*: students are first introduced to the background documentations and event data model in the foundry. The exercise will ask them
  to read the background materials and install software (e.g., Tomcat and Web
  services libraries).

Table 1. Weekly Activity Schedule

W.	Lecture Topic	Lab/Assignment	Expected Activities
1	Enterprise Application Integration Architectures	Lab Zero: Setup Exercise Environment and Necessary Tools	Students install and test all necessary development tools used in the course and familiarise themselves with the structure and concept of the foundry.
2	Service-Oriented Architecture Foundations (I): SOA concepts and Web Services Standards (WSDL, SOAP, UDDI)	Lab/Assignment I: on Writing a Simple Service	Students can start to describe the basic concepts of SOA and the main Web service standards. Students are engaged in conceptual design of a simple service and a client, using the data and sample services at the foundry.
3	Service-Oriented Computing Foundations (II) SOA concepts and Web Services Standards (WSDL, SOAP, UDDI)	Lab/Assignment I due	Students can fully describe the concepts of SOA and the Web service standards. Based on the conceptual design, students are able to implement a simple WSDL-based service and a client program.
4	Data as Services (I): XML data access and transformation technologies	Lab/Assignment II: on Writing a Simple Service Wrapper	Students can identify XML technologies for data access and manipulation for Web services. Using the existing domain applications available in the foundry, students design a way to expose the functionality for a client as a service.
5	Data as Services (II): XML data access and transformation technologies	Lab/Assignment II due	Students can fully describe how XML technologies are used for data access and transformation in Web services. Using the foundry's existing domain-specific applications, students are able to expose the functionality as a fully-fledged Web service by writing a wrapper.
6	RESTful Services (I): REST architecture and REST-based services	Lab/Assignment III: on Writing a Data Service	Students can describe REST architecture as an alternative Web service development technology. Based on the foundry's sample services, students design a data access and transformation service for a client using XML technology.
7	RESTful Services (II): REST architecture and REST-based services	Lab/Assignment III due	Students understand the steps and knowledge involved in developing a REST-based service. Using the foundry's sample services, students fully implement the data access and transformation service.
8	Business Process Management	Lab/Assignment IV: on REST-based service development	Students learn the important concepts in business processes and their relationships to Web services. Based on the foundry's sample services, students design a REST-based service. for a client.
9	Business Process Execution: BPEL and Web service composition	Lab/Assignment IV due	Students learn the important concepts in business processes automation and service composition techniques. Based on the foundry's sample services and the design, students fully implement the REST-based service.
10	Advanced Topics in Web service composition	Lab/Assignment V: on Business Processes and BPEL	Students learn more advanced concepts and open issues in service composition techniques. Based on the foundry's sample services, applications and previously built services from the assignments, students design a business process to be automated.
11	Open Topic	Lab/Assignment V due	An industry guest speaker or researcher in the area of Web services may be invited to give talks about emerging issues and visions in SOA. Based on the design from the previous week, students fully implement the automated business process and its client using BPEL.
12	Revision	No lab activity	The final week is used to revise and reflect on the topics taught over the weeks.

- *Lab/Assignment 1*: the exercise leads students to learn top-down and bottom-up approaches to Web service design and implementation. A sample Web service (TRTH data import and download) skeleton code and accompanying WSDL are provided from the foundry. In the assignment, students are asked to fully implement the TRTH data import and download service. The foundry provides test files directly derived from the TRTH repository.
- *Lab/Assignment 2*: the second lab and assignment are focused on the concept of designing and implementing a service which exposes some existing functionality in a system. The foundry provides a fully working implementation of a data transformation program (written in Haskell). The students are asked to design appropriate interfaces and provide implementation with a view to be, later, integrated with the TRTH download/import service.
- *Lab/Assignment 3*: the third lab and assignment are about understanding data services. We provide two different scenarios in business processes that either requires extracting data from the foundry and generate RSS-feed service, or requires transformation of output message formats to the correct input message formats expected by another service in the foundry.
- *Lab/Assignment 4*: the lab shows the basics steps in building a simple REST-based service. The assignment asks the students to provide an alternative implementation of the services introduced in assignment 1 and 2.
- *Lab/Assignment 5*: the final lab and assignment are about modelling and implementing business processes. The foundry provides the fully working sample Web services on the TRTH dataset (cf. Figure 4) for this exercise, so that the students can focus on building a process model on top of the services. In the assignment, students use 3-4 services in the foundry to implement an end-end process of history data analysis.

6 Module and Foundry Evaluation Plan

The evaluation of this module will require a long-term approach where continuous feedback and response cycles are applied. The experience gained through the evaluation and revision cycle will inform the direction of the foundry and the portal development overtime.

The university conducts a formal course evaluation at the end of every semester. However, the design of the evaluation process is such that only a small number of students and academic staff members participate and the results of the survey are often released to the lecturer-in-charge only. That is, it is difficult to consult wider audience and stakeholders.

Since it is important for us to collect meaningful and insightful feedback throughout the module and portal development process, we are proposing to host a dedicated Wiki/Blog-style Web site for soliciting comments, suggestions and self-reflective remarks about the learning activities from the students, tutors and colleagues. At the end of each semester, a moderator will summarise the feedback and post an official follow-up response so that it is visible to the relevant audience how the module and portal development are progressing. This semester, we expect to receive feedback from 54 students and 3 tutors.

Ultimately, our experience gained through the evaluation process will contribute to the development of the *Curriculum Evaluation Tools* in the roadmap (cf. Figure 2). After initial trials, we hope to report the findings in the next appropriate forum.

7   Conclusion and Future Work

In this paper, we described outcomes and on-going work of the SSME project. Particularly, we presented the UNSW team's roadmap for building a community of SOA/BPM education as a foundation for a collaborative learning and teaching environment. We have taken concrete steps to design and implement the Service Teaching and Learning Foundry using financial data analysis as a target application domain. We have revised our offering of "Service Oriented Architectures" course (i) to reflect the student feedback over the years and industry focus group discussions and (ii) to utilise the foundry structure and materials.

The results from the pilot course from this semester will be a valuable source of information for designing the next version of the course, but also designing the other courses in the SSME project curriculum as planned in Figure 1. Our interests are in extending the foundry L&T resources so that the foundry applies to the modules beyond technical topics intended for computer science students. We will collaborate with other university team members in the SSME project to communicate the requirements and applications of the foundry during the other module developments.

There are a number of teaching and learning related tools being developed at UNSW through student-led projects (e.g., online Q/A (Question/Answer) system that automatically suggests an answer based on the past Q/A data and collaborative lecture slides authoring tool), some of which may be contributed to the portal through our foundry framework in the future. Also, we plan to investigate and design a generic repository framework for hosting other innovative tools (e.g., Business process modelling tools, Multi-media education games).

Acknowledgements

This paper has been supported by Australian Learning and Teaching Council Ltd, an initiative of the Australian Government Department of Education, Employment and Workplace Relations. The views expressed in this paper do not necessarily reflect the views of the Australian Learning and Teaching Council. We thank Lawrence Yao for his effort in the implementation, SIRCA for giving the data and use cases and DEST for funding the ADAGE project. We thank the other university participants and industry supporters of the SSME project.

References

1. Goos, G., Hartmanis, J., van Leeuwen, J. (eds.): Business Process Management: Models, Techniques and Empirical Studies. LNCS, vol. 1806. Springer, Heidelberg (2000)
2. Alonso, G., Casati, F., Kuno, H., Machiraju, V.: Web Services: Concepts, Architecture and Applications. Springer, Heidelberg (2003)
3. Behara, G.K.: BPM and SOA: A Strategic Alliance. BPTrends Columns (May 2006), www.bptrends.com
4. Rosen, M.: Designing Service Oriented Solutions (Part I and II). BPTrends Columns (May 2009), www.bptrends.com
5. Lopez, N., Casallas, R., Villalobos, J.: Challenges in Creating Environments for SOA Learning. In: SDSOA 2007: Proc. of the International Workshop on Systems Development in SOA Environments, IEEE CS, Washington, DC (2007)
6. Maurizio, A., Sager, J., Jones, P., Corbitt, G., Girolami, L.: Service Oriented Architecture: Challenges for Business and Academia. In: The 41st Annual Hawaii International Conference on System Sciences (HICSS), Hawaii, pp. 315–323 (2008)
7. Kamoun, F.: A Roadmap Towards the Convergence of Business Process Management and Service Oriented Architecture. Ubiquity, 1–8 (June 2007)
8. Spohrer, J., Maglio, P.P., Bailey, J., Gruhl, D.: Steps toward a science of service systems. Computer 40, 71–77 (2007)
9. Communications of the ACM: Service Science, Special Issue. ACM, New York, NY, USA, 49(7) (July 2006)
10. The University of Sydney: SSME Project - Interim report of the Focus Group discussions on knowledge and skill requirements of successful service professionals (2009) Australian Learning and Teaching Council (ALTC) Project (2009)
11. Fingar, P.: Extreme Competition: The MBA is Dead, Long Live the MBI. BPTrends Columns (December 2006), www.bptrends.com
12. Cantara, M.: Eleven Steps to Take Before Staffing Business Process Management Projects With Internal or External Resources. Gartner Reports (August 2008), http://www.webwire.com/ViewPressRel.asp?aId=76215
13. U. of Sydney, UNSW, U. of QLD and U. of Melbourne: Curriculum Renewal in Postgraduate Information Technology Education: a Response to Growing Service Sector Dominance (2008-2010) Australian Learning and Teaching Council Grant
14. van Vliet, H.: Some Myths of Software Engineering Education. In: ICSE 2005: Proceedings of the 27th International Conference on Software Engineering, pp. 621–622. ACM, New York (2005)
15. Recker, J., Rosemann, M.: Teaching Business Process Modelling: Experiences and Recommendations. Communications of the Association for Information Systems 25(32), 379–394 (2009)
16. Reuters, T.: Thomson Reuters Tick History (TRTH). available from the Securities Industry Research Centre of Asia-Pacific (SIRCA)
17. Rabhi, F., Guabtni, A., Yao, L.: A Data Model for Processing Financial Market and News Data. International Journal of Electronic Finance 3(4), 387–403 (2009)
18. Guabtni, A., Kundisch, D., Rabhi, F.: A User-Driven SOA for Financial Market Data Analysis. Enterprise Modelling and Information Systems Architectures (2010) (to appear)

Author Index